SAS USER'S GUIDE:
Basics
1982 Edition

SAS INSTITUTE INC.
BOX 8000
CARY, NORTH CAROLINA 27511

Alice Allen edited the *SAS User's Guide: Basics, 1982 Edition*. **Kathryn A. Council** and **John P. Sall** were contributing editors. Editorial staff: **Marian Saffer** and **Brenda C. Kalt**, associate editors; **Stephenie P. Joyner** and **Judith K. Whatley**, copy editors. Support staff: **Andrea U. Littleton**.

Composition and production were provided by **Stephen K. Douglas**, **Elisabeth C. Smith**, and **June L. Woodward** under the direction of **W. Wayne Lindsey**.

Program authorship includes design, programming, debugging, support, and preliminary documentation. The SAS staff member listed first currently has primary responsibility for the procedure; others give specific assistance.

Procedures:

APPEND R.D. Langston
BMDP R.D. Langston, J.P. Sall
BROWSE R.D. Langston
CALENDAR G.K. Howell
CHART J.H. Goodnight
CONTENTS W.H. Blair
CONVERT R.D. Langston
COPY D.D. Ingold
CORR J.P. Sall, D.M. Delong
DATASETS J.S. Wallace
DELETE W.H. Blair
EDITOR R.D. Langston
FORMAT R.D. Langston, J.P. Sall
FORMS J.P. Sall
FREQ J.P. Sall, W.M. Stanish
MEANS J.H. Goodnight

OPTIONS P.W. Malpass
PDS P.W. Malpass
PDSCOPY W.H. Blair
PLOT J.H. Goodnight
PRINT R.D. Langston
PRINTTO W.H. Blair
RELEASE P.W. Malpass
SORT W.H. Blair
SOURCE W.H. Blair
SUMMARY J.H. Goodnight
TABULATE A.R. Eaton, G.K. Howell
TAPECOPY W.H. Blair
TAPELABEL W.H. Blair
TRANSPOSE W.S. Sarle
UNIVARIATE D.M. Delong

Systems:

SAS under CMS C.P. Whitman, W.F. Miller, P.L. Jobusch, J.C. Weathers
SAS under OS C.H. Dunham, R.M. Oatsvall, S.E. Webb
SAS under TSO R.L. Cross
SAS under VSE O.T. Bradley
SAS Data Library Access Method W.H. Blair
Macro Facility D.D. Cockrell
SAS Supervisor Data Step Compiler R.L. Cross
SAS Parsing Mechanism D.D. Ingold
SAS Full Screen Interface S.F. Kuekes

(If you have questions or encounter problems, call the Institute and ask for technical support rather than an individual staff member.)

The correct bibliographic citation for this manual is: SAS Institute Inc. *SAS User's Guide: Basics, 1982 Edition*. Cary, NC: SAS Institute Inc., 1982. 923pp.

SAS User's Guide: Basics, 1982 Edition

Acknowledgments

SAS Institute Inc. is unusually fortunate to have had many people make significant and continuing contributions to its development.

First among them are the chairpersons and other active members of the SAS Users Group International (SUGI). Julian Horwich, now of American Hospital Supply Corporation, set up the first regional meetings at Abbott Laboratories in North Chicago in 1975, and organized and chaired the first international SUGI meeting in Lake Buena Vista, Florida, in 1976. Dr. Ronald W. Helms of the University of North Carolina at Chapel Hill chaired the second annual conference, held in New Orleans in 1977; Kenneth Offord of the Mayo Clinic was program chairman.

The 1978 SUGI conference in Las Vegas was co-chaired by Dr. Rodney Strand and Dr. Michael Farrell of Oak Ridge National Laboratories. Dr. Ramon C. Littell of the University of Florida and Dr. William Wilson of the University of North Florida co-chaired the 1979 SUGI meeting in Clearwater, Florida. The 1980 SUGI conference in San Antonio, Texas, was chaired by Rudolf J. Freund of Texas A&M University. Kenneth L. Koonce of Louisiana State University chaired the 1981 SUGI conference held in Lake Buena Vista, Florida. The 1982 conference held in San Francisco, California, was chaired by Helene Cavior of the Bureau of Prisons.

The University Statisticians of the Southern Experiment Stations have made numerous contributions over the years. We are especially indebted to:

Wilbert P. Byrd, Clemson University
Richard Cooper, USDA
R.J. Freund of Texas A & M University
Charles Gates of Texas A & M University
Don Henderson, ORI
David Hurst, University of Alabama at Birmingham
Kenneth Koonce, Louisiana State University
Clyde Y. Kramer (deceased), Virginia Polytechnic Institute
University of Kentucky, and Upjohn Laboratories
Robert D. Morrison, Oklahoma State University
Richard M. Patterson, Auburn University
William L. Sanders, University of Tennessee
Glenn Ware, University of Georgia
T.J. Whatley, University of Tennessee.

We are deeply grateful to our good neighbor, the Department of Statistics at North Carolina State University, and especially to these staff members:

David D. Mason, Chairman (retired)
Jolayne Service (now at the University of California, Irvine)
Sandra Donaghy
Carroll Perkins (now with Westinghouse)
Francis J. Verlinden
Evelyn Wilson.

We also wish to express our sincere gratitude to the following people who have contributed in many different ways to the success of SAS. Others who made contributions to the statistical procedures are recognized in *SAS User's Guide: Statistics, 1982 Edition*:

Dick Blocker, Washington University
George Chao, Arnar-Stone Laboratories
Daniel Chilko, University of West Virginia
Ray Danner, National Institutes of Health
Paul Fingerman, Boeing Computer Services
Terry Flynn, Tymshare
Michael Foxworth, University of South Carolina
Harold Gugel, General Motors Corporation
Donald Guthrie, University of California at Los Angeles
James Guthrie, Ameritrust
Frank Harrell, Duke University
Loren Harrell, Business Information Technology Inc.
Jim Harrington, Monsanto Research
Walter Harvey, Ohio State University
Ronald Helms, University of North Carolina at Chapel Hill
Harold Huddleston, Data Collection & Analysis, Inc.
  Falls Church, Virginia
Emilio A. Icaza, Louisiana State University
Ruth Ingram, Proctor & Gamble
William Kennedy, Iowa State University
Melvin Klassen, University of Victoria
John Klinkner, American Republic Insurance Company
H.W. (Barry) Merrill, Suntech, Inc.
J. Philip Miller, Washington University
Mario Morino, Morino Associates Inc.
Curt Mosso, University of California at Santa Barbara
Richard Nelson, Clemson University
Robert Parks, Washington University
Virginia Patterson, University of Tennessee
Pete Rikard, Virginia Commonwealth University
John Ruth, University of Toronto
Robert Schechter, Scott Paper Company
Roger Smith, USDA
Robert Teichman, ICI Americas Inc.
Jim Walker, Morino Associates Inc.

Two of the founders of SAS Institute Inc. deserve special mention.

The present SAS documentation can be traced to the work of Jane T. Helwig, now at Seasoned Systems Inc., Chapel Hill, N.C., who gathered and wrote much of the material on which this manual is based.

Finally, SAS Institute and all SAS users owe a debt of gratitude to Anthony J. Barr, Barr Systems, Raleigh, N.C. His work on the SAS supervisor and compiler, as well as the procedures that he wrote, help make SAS the useful tool it is today.

The final responsibility for SAS lies with SAS Institute alone. We hope that you will always let us know your feelings about the system and its documentation. It is through such communications that the progress of SAS has been accomplished.

THE STAFF OF SAS INSTITUTE

Preface

This manual, *SAS User's Guide: Basics, 1982 Edition*, contains the fundamentals of the SAS® system: an introduction to DATA and PROC steps; the syntax and use of SAS statements; macros; system options; and procedures for descriptive statistics, report writing, and utilities. *SAS User's Guide: Basics* is the first of two volumes that are the primary documentation for the 1982 release of the SAS system (SAS82). The other volume is *SAS User's Guide: Statistics, 1982 Edition*, which contains advanced statistical procedures in the areas of regression, analysis of variance, categorical data analysis, multivariate analysis, discriminant analysis, clustering, scoring, and the MATRIX language.

Many SAS users need only the data processing, summarizing, and reporting features of the system without further statistical analysis. This two-volume format provides a choice of one or both manuals depending on whether you are using SAS primarily for data processing or for statistics.

What is SAS?

SAS is a computer software system for data analysis. Since its beginnings in 1966, the goal of SAS has been to provide data analysts one system to meet all their computing needs. When your computing needs are met, you are free to concentrate on results rather than on the mechanics of getting them. Instead of learning programming languages, several statistical packages, and utility programs, you only need to learn SAS.

The letters SAS are an acronym for Statistical Analysis System, and SAS was originally developed for statistical needs. It grew into an all-purpose data analysis system in response to the changing needs of its user community. To the basic SAS system, users can add tools for graphics, forecasting, data entry, and interfaces to other data bases to provide one total system. (SAS runs on IBM 370/30xx/43xx and compatible machines in batch and interactively under OS, OS/VS, VM/CMS, DOS/VSE, SSX, and TSO.)

The basic SAS system provides tools for:

- information storage and retrieval
- data modification and programming
- report writing
- statistical analysis
- file handling.

Information storage and retrieval SAS reads data values in virtually any form from cards, disk, or tape and then organizes the values into a SAS data set. The data set can be combined with other SAS data sets using the file-handling operations described below; it may be analyzed statistically; and reports on its contents may be produced. SAS data sets are automatically self-documenting, since they contain both the data values and their descriptions. The special structure of a SAS data library minimizes maintenance.

Data modification and programming A complete set of SAS statements and functions is available for modifying data. Some program statements perform standard operations such as creating new variables, accumulating totals, and checking for errors; others are powerful programming tools such as DO/END and IF-THEN/ELSE statements. The data-handling features of the SAS System are so valuable that SAS software is used by many as a data base management system.

Report writing Just as SAS software reads data in almost any form, it can write data in almost any form. In addition to the preformatted reports that SAS procedures produce, SAS users can design and produce printed reports in any form, as well as punched cards and output files.

Statistical analysis The statistical analysis procedures in the SAS System are among the finest available. They range from simple descriptive statistics to complex multivariate techniques. Their designs are based on our belief that you should never need to tell the SAS System anything it can figure out by itself. Statistical integrity is thus accompanied by ease of use. Two especially noteworthy statistical features are the linear model procedures, of which GLM (General Linear Models) is the flagship, and the MATRIX procedure, which gives users the ability to handle any problem that can be expressed in traditional matrix notation.

File handling Combining values and observations from several data sets is often necessary for data analysis. SAS software has tools for editing, subsetting, concatenating, merging, and updating data sets. Multiple input files can be processed simultaneously, and several reports can be produced in one pass of the data.

Computer work usually involves related chores: data sets must be copied, tape contents investigated, program libraries moved. To help users cope with these needs, the SAS System includes a group of utility procedures.

Other SAS Institute Program Products

With the basic SAS system, you can integrate SAS Institute Program Products for graphics, forecasting, data entry, and interfaces to other data bases to provide one total system:

- SAS/GRAPH™—device-intelligent color graphics for business and research applications
- SAS/ETS™—expanded tools for business analysis, forecasting, and financial reporting
- SAS/FSP™—interactive, menu-driven facilities for data entry, editing, retrieval of SAS files, and letter writing on IBM 327x-series terminals
- SAS/IMS-DL/I™—interface for reading, updating, and writing DL/I data bases through IMS/VS DB, IMS/VS DD/DC, CICS/OS/VS, CICS/DOS/VS, DL/I DOS/VS
- SAS/OR™—procedures for business planning and scheduling using operations research tools.

SAS Documentation

Using SAS software Because the SAS System was designed as an all-purpose data analysis tool, many SAS features are needed only for complex problems. You don't need to know everything in the SAS manuals in order to use SAS software. In fact, 90% of SAS jobs use only 10% of the information.

The *SAS Introductory Guide* contains this first 10% and gets you started quickly using the SAS System. Another helpful manual is the *SAS Applications Guide*, which deals with common data-handling applications.

Organization

Using this manual   To serve both as a reference for experienced SAS users and as a learning tool for new users, this manual is organized to reflect the structure of the SAS language. All SAS programs are composed of single DATA or PROC steps, or combinations of DATA and PROC steps. Similarly, the information in this manual is arranged according to where it can be used in a SAS program—in a DATA step, in a PROC step, or anywhere.

Introductory chapters   The book begins with an overview of the SAS language that describes the basics of the SAS System and defines the terms used throughout SAS literature.

The next section describes the DATA step and includes an introduction, statements used in the DATA step (in alphabetical order), SAS expressions, SAS functions, and a chapter on DATA step applications.

The PROC step is described in the next section with an introductory chapter, the statements used in the PROC step (in alphabetical order), and some procedure step applications.

The next major section gives an introduction to the SAS System and includes the statements used anywhere in a SAS job (in alphabetical order), and chapters describing SAS data sets, SAS informats and formats, missing values, the SAS macro language, and SAS log and procedure output.

Procedure descriptions   The procedures in this volume are divided into the following major sections:

- Descriptive Statistics
- Reporting
- SAS Utilities
- System-Dependent Utilities.

The introductory chapter in each major section briefly describes the procedures available for that category and what they do. Each procedure description is self-contained; you need to be familiar with only the most basic features of the SAS System and SAS terminology to use most procedures. The statements and syntax necessary to run each procedure are presented in a uniform format throughout the manual. You can duplicate the examples by using the same statements and data to run a SAS job. The examples are also useful as models for writing your own programs.

Each procedure description is divided into the following major parts:

ABSTRACT: a short paragraph describing what the procedure does.

INTRODUCTION: introductory and background material, including definitions and occasional introductory examples.

SPECIFICATIONS: reference section for the syntax of the control language for the procedure.

DETAILS: expanded descriptions of features, internal operations, output, treatment of missing values, computational methods, required computational resources, and usage notes.

EXAMPLES: examples using the procedure, including data, SAS statements, and printed outputs. You can reproduce these examples by copying the statements and data and running the job.

REFERENCES: a selected bibliography.

If you have any problem with this SAS manual, please take time to complete the review page at the end of this book and send it to SAS Institute Inc. We will consider your suggestions for future editions. In the meantime, ask your installation's SAS expert for help.

New SAS Features

The 1982 version of the SAS System includes many new features. Below is a list of changes and additions, including new procedures, enhancements to existing procedures, and new system features. Each of these changes is described in detail elsewhere in this manual.

The most basic change to the SAS System since the *SAS User's Guide, 1979 Edition* is that SAS software now runs under several operating systems including OS, OS/VS, VM/CMS, and DOS/VSE.

New procedures New procedures documented in this manual are:

APPEND	adds observations to the end of a SAS data set
CALENDAR	produces summary and schedule calendars
FORMS	prints labels and forms (supplemental procedure added to the SAS library)
TABULATE	produces descriptive statistics in tabular form
TRANSPOSE	transposes a SAS data set.

Changes to existing procedures Changes to existing procedures in this manual are:

FORMAT	includes picture formats
PRINT	prints subtotals and can use labels in headings
EDITOR	provides additional operators and commands.

New system features A major enhancement to the SAS language is the addition of a macro processor, which has its own language and syntax. Using the new macro facility, you can:

- define macros that accept parameters
- retain macro variables across SAS steps
- conditionally create entire SAS statements.

Other important changes include the ability to read VSAM files and random access to observations in SAS data sets. Several new system options have been added.

New SAS statements include DO WHILE and DO UNTIL statements; the %INCLUDE statement and CMS GETSAS command for specifying a secondary source of SAS input text; the TSO and CMS statements and functions, which allow you to execute TSO and CMS commands within a SAS session, and the HELP statement, for obtaining additional information about SAS features and syntax, and the status of SAS Institute Program Products at your installation.

A number of functions are new in SAS82, including several character-handling functions, state and ZIP code functions, and mathematical and probability functions. New date, time, and datetime formats and functions have also been added.

Documentation   Some procedures, familiar from SAS79, are now documented elsewhere.

These procedures are documented in *SAS User's Guide: Statistics, 1982 Edition*: ANOVA, CANCORR, CANDISC, CLUSTER, DISCRIM, FACTOR, FASTCLUS, FUNCAT, GLM, MATRIX, NEIGHBOR, NESTED, NLIN, NPAR1WAY, PLAN, PRINCOMP, PROBIT, RANK, REG, RSQUARE, RSREG, SCORE, STANDARD, STEPDISC, STEPWISE, TREE, TTEST, VARCLUS, and VARCOMP.

The AUTOREG, SPECTRA, and SYSREG procedures are now documented in the *SAS/ETS User's Guide, 1982 Edition*, since they concern econometric and time series features. SYSREG features for ordinary least squares are found in the REG procedure.

The GUTTMAN and DUNCAN procedures have been moved to the *SUGI Supplemental Library User's Guide*, where they will be supported as contributed works.

Documents now obsolete   This volume and the *SAS User's Guide: Statistics, 1982 Edition* include or supersede these earlier documents:

SAS User's Guide, 1979 Edition
SAS Technical Report P-111 (for the SAS79.3 and SAS79.4 releases), April 1980
SAS Technical Report P-115 (for the SAS79.5 release), February 1981

SAS82 release?   To find out which release of SAS software you are using, run any SAS job and look at the first line on the log printout. The release number should start with the digits 82. If you have a later release, you should get new documentation. If you have an earlier release (for example, SAS79.5 or SAS79.6) your data center has not installed the latest version and you should use older documentation until they do.

Other SAS manuals   Below is a list of other SAS manuals that can be obtained by contacting the SAS Institute Book Order Department:

SAS User's Guide: Basics, 1982 Edition
SAS User's Guide: Statistics, 1982 Edition
SAS Introductory Guide
Guía Introductoria al SAS
Eine Einfuehrung in das SAS
Guide d'Introduction à SAS
SAS Applications Guide
SUGI Supplemental Library User's Guide, 1983 Edition
SAS Programmer's Guide, 1981 Edition
SAS Views: SAS Basics, 1983 Edition
SAS Views: SAS Color Graphics, 1983 Edition
SAS Companion for the VM/CMS Operating System, 1983 Edition
SAS Companion for the VSE Operating System, 1983 Edition
SAS/GRAPH User's Guide, 1981 Edition
SAS/ETS User's Guide, 1982 Edition
SAS/IMS-DL/I User's Guide, 1981 Edition
SAS/FSP User's Guide, 1982 Edition
SAS Video Training: Basics 100-Series Workbook, 1981 Edition
SAS Color Graphics 100-Series Video Training Course Workbook, 1983 Edition
SAS Color Graphics 100-Series Video Training Course Instructional Guide, 1983 Edition

1981 SUGI Proceedings
1982 SUGI Proceedings
1983 SUGI Proceedings
SAS for Linear Models: A Guide to the ANOVA and GLM Procedures
Merrill's Guide to CPE

Technical reports   The SAS Technical Report Series documents work-in-progress, describes new supplemental procedures, and covers a variety of application areas. Some of the features described in these reports are still in experimental form and are not yet available as SAS procedures.

Write to the Institute for the current list of reports in the Technical Report Series and their costs.

Services to SAS Users

Technical support   The Institute supports users through the Technical Support Group. If you have a problem running a SAS job, you should contact the individual at your site who is responsible for maintaining and supporting SAS software. If the problem cannot be resolved locally, you or your local support personnel should call the Institute's Technical Support Group at (919) 467-8000 on weekdays between 9:00 AM and 5:00 PM Eastern Standard Time. A brochure describing the services provided by the Technical Support Group is available from the Institute.

SAS training   The Institute sponsors a comprehensive training program, including programs of study for novice data processors, statisticians, applications programmers, systems programmers, and local support personnel. *SAS/Course*, a semi-annual training publication, describes the total training program and each course currently being offered by SAS Institute.

News magazine   *SAS Communications* is the quarterly news magazine of SAS Institute Inc. Each issue contains ideas for more effective use of SAS software, preliminary documentation of new features, information about research and development underway at SAS Institute, the current training schedule, and news of the SAS Users Group International (SUGI).

To receive a copy of *SAS Communications*, send your name and complete address to:

SASCOM
SAS Institute Inc.
Box 8000
Cary, NC 27511-8000

Supplemental library   You can write your own SAS procedure in PL/I or FORTRAN taking advantage of the SAS supervisor for data input, manipulation, and output formatting. The *SAS Programmer's Guide*, available from SAS Institute, gives directions for writing SAS procedures.

We encourage you to contribute SAS procedures you have written to the Institute for inclusion in the SUGI Supplemental Library. The *SUGI Supplemental Library User's Guide* includes descriptions of all the procedures contributed by users.

Note: all user-contributed procedures are tested by the Institute with their accompanying sample jobs. However, the Institute cannot guarantee that user-contributed procedures perform as described.

Sample library One of the SAS data sets included on the SAS installation tape is called SAS.SAMPLE under OS in unloaded PDS form, SAMPBASE MACLIB under CMS, and SASXMPL under VSE. This data set contains sample SAS applications to illustrate features of SAS procedures and creative SAS programming techniques that can help you gain an in-depth knowledge of SAS capabilites.

Here are just a few examples of programs included:

ANOVA	analyzing a Latin-square split-plot design
CENSUS	reading hierarchical files of the U.S. Census Bureau Public Use Sample tapes
HARRIS	reading Harris Poll tapes coded in column-binary format
TEACH	teaching arithmetic to your child.

The library is on the installation tape in unloaded-PDS form under OS and in macro library form under CMS. Check with the person who installed SAS software to find out how to access the library, since it may have been put on disk.

SUGI The SAS Users Group International (SUGI) is a non-profit association of professionals who are interested in how others are using the SAS System. Although the Institute provides administrative support, SUGI is independent from the Institute. Membership is open to all users at SAS sites, and there is no membership fee.

Annual conferences are structured to allow many avenues of discussion. Users present invited and contributed papers on various topics, for example:

- computer performance evaluation and systems software
- econometrics and time series
- graphics
- information systems
- interactive techniques
- statistics
- tutorials in SAS.

Proceedings of the annual conferences are distributed free to SUGI registrants. Extra copies are available from the Institute.

SUGI also sponsors a code-critiquing service to assist SAS users who are unsure about how to approach a problem or who want help in writing programs.

SASware index The SASware Index lists user-contributed SAS procedures and macros, as well as materials about teaching the SAS System. Information on ordering complete documentation is also included. Additions to the SASware Index are listed in *SAS Communications*. The complete index is published annually in the *SUGI Proceedings*.

SASware ballot SAS users provide valuable input toward the direction of future SAS development by ranking their priorities on the annual SASware ballot. The top vote-getters are announced in the spring *SAS Communications*. In this listing, completed projects, projects planned for the coming year, and long-term plans are noted. Complete results of the SASware ballot are also printed in the *SUGI Proceedings*.

Licensing the SAS System

The SAS System is licensed to customers in the Western Hemisphere from the Institute's headquarters in Cary, NC. To better serve the needs of our international customers, the Institute maintains subsidiaries in the United Kingdom, New Zealand, Australia, and Germany. In addition, agents in other countries are licensed distributors for the SAS System. For a complete list of offices, write or call:

SAS Institute Inc.
SAS Circle
Box 8000
Cary, NC 27511-8000
(919) 467-8000

Contents

DESCRIPTIVE STATISTICS

REPORTING

SAS UTILITIES

SYSTEM-DEPENDENT UTILITIES

APPENDICES

THE SAS LANGUAGE

Introduction to the SAS Language

Introduction to the SAS Language

SAS (Statistical Analysis System) is a computer software system for organizing data. People who need SAS have at least two things in common: a collection of data and questions about the data.

Like any language, SAS has its own vocabulary and syntax—words and the rules for putting them together. You define your data and the questions you have about them using the SAS language, and this sequence of SAS statements is called a *SAS program*. A SAS program and some statements in a control language appropriate to the operating system you are using make up a *SAS job* or *session*.

Your computer system   Before you start using SAS, you first need to be familiar with:

- the operating system you are using—OS batch or TSO, CMS, or VSE.
- any special requirements at your installation.

Ask your SAS installation representative for help and see the appendix in this manual that discusses using SAS under your operating system. Then you will be prepared to use the appropriate control language statements and commands to invoke SAS. In most SAS jobs, the SAS program is the same regardless of the operating system you are using; only the control language for each system varies.

SAS STATEMENTS

A *SAS statement* is a string of SAS keywords, SAS names, and special characters and operators ending in a semicolon that requests SAS to perform an operation or gives SAS information.

Here are some examples of SAS statements:

```
PUT X $15.;
DATA ONE;
FORMAT VALUE1 ABCD.;
PROC MEANS DATA=STORE.SUPPLY MAXDEC=3;
INFILE RAWDATA;
DO OVER EACHITEM;
VAR %MACODE;
KEY1: TOTAL+1;
```

SAS Keywords

A SAS statement begins with a keyword that identifies the kind of statement it is (special cases are assignment, sum, and null statements). The SAS statements shown above do not form a SAS program but are single SAS statements referred to by their keywords as a PUT statement, a DATA statement, a FORMAT statement, a PROC statement, an INFILE statement, a DO OVER statement, and a VAR statement. The last statement, preceded by the statement label KEY1, is a sum statement that does not have a keyword.

SAS Names

Among the kinds of names that can appear in SAS statements are the names of variables, SAS data sets, formats, procedures, options, DDnames, arrays, statement labels, and macros.

SAS names can be up to 8 characters long. The first character must be a letter (A, B, C, ..., Z) or underscore (__). Later characters may be letters, numbers (0, 1, ..., 9), or underscores.

Blanks may not appear in SAS names, and special characters (for example, $, @, #), except for the underscore, are not allowed. SAS uses names that both begin and end with underscores for special variables (for example, __N__, __ERROR__, __I__).[1] Exceptions: macro keywords begin with a percent sign (%) and references to macro variables begin with an ampersand (&).

In the sample SAS statements shown earlier:

X, VALUE1, and TOTAL are variable names.
ONE and STORE.SUPPLY are SAS data set names.
The items $15. and ABCD. are format names.
MEANS is a procedure name.
DATA= and MAXDEC= are options in the MEANS statement.
RAWDATA is a DDname.
In the DO OVER statement, EACHITEM is the name of an array.
%MACODE is a macro call.
KEY1 is a statement label.
TOTAL + 1 is an expression, which includes the constant 1.

Special Characters and Operators

Every SAS statement ends with a semicolon (;). Other special characters and operators illustrated in the statements above are the dollar sign ($), period (.), equal sign (=), colon (:), addition operator or plus sign (+), and the percent sign (%).

Statement Descriptions

In this manual the form of a SAS statement is specified with these conventions:

KEYWORD *parameter* ... [*item*|*item*| *item*] *options*;

where

KEYWORD in bold capitals	indicates that you use exactly the same spelling and form as shown
italics	mean that you supply your own information
[*bracketed information*]	is optional
parameters not in brackets	are not optional
three periods (...)	mean that more than one of the parameters preceding ... may be optionally specified

vertical bar (|)   separating keywords and options means to choose
only one of the terms separated by vertical bars (|)

   options   are keyword options specific to a particular SAS statement.

For the syntax of SAS statements, see the SAS Reference Card at the back of this manual.

A SAS PROGRAM

The statements in a SAS program are divided into two kinds of steps: DATA steps and PROC steps, the building blocks of all SAS programs. Usually DATA steps create SAS data sets, and PROC steps analyze SAS data sets, which are the special way that SAS organizes and stores data. A SAS program is made up of either a DATA step or a PROC step, or both DATA and PROC steps. DATA and PROC steps may appear in any order, and any number of DATA or PROC steps may be used.

DATA Steps

The DATA step can include statements asking SAS to create one or more new SAS data sets and programming statements that perform the manipulations necessary to build the data sets. The DATA step begins with a DATA statement and may include any number of program statements. Report writing, file management, and information retrieval are all handled in DATA steps.

PROC Steps

The PROC step (or PROCEDURE step) asks SAS to call a procedure from its library and to execute that procedure, usually with a SAS data set as input. The PROC step begins with a PROC statement. Other statements in the PROC step give the program more information about the results that you want. The statements that are available for your use in each PROC step depend on the specific SAS procedure that is called. Thus, each procedure description gives the statements that may accompany the PROC statement for that procedure.

SAS DATA SETS

A *SAS data set* is a collection of data values arranged in the rectangular form shown in Figure 1. The number of SAS data sets that you can use in a SAS job is limited only by space requirements.

DATA VALUES

The basic unit that SAS works with is the *data value*.

Consider the following example. A researcher collects data from men in an exercise program. Each man's weight, pulse, and waist measurements are recorded, as well as the number of chin-ups, sit-ups, and jumps he can do before tiring.

Each of the measurements—the first man's weight, the second man's pulse, the last man's chin-ups—is a data value.

```
HODGES    191  36  50   5  162   60
KERR      189  37  52   2  110   60
PUTNAM    193  38  58  12  101  101
ROBERTS   162  35  62  12  105   37
BLAKE     189  35  46  13  155   58
ALLEN     182  36  56   4  101   42
HOWARD    211  38  56   8  101   38
VINCENT   167  34  60   6  125   40
STEWART   176  31  74  15  200   40
PERRY     154  33  56  17  251  250
HOWELL    169  34  50  17  120   38
ELLIS     166  33  52  13  210  115
SMITH     154  34  64  14  215  105
CROWE     147  46  50   1   50   50
CARTER    193  36  46   6   70   31
MOORE     202  37  62  12  210  120
LEE       176  37  54   4   60   25
VARNER    157  32  52  11  230   80
STONE     156  33  54  15  225   73
SCOTT     138  33  68   2  110   43
```

Fig. 1

OBSERVATIONS

The data values associated with a single entity—an individual, a record, a year, a geographic region, an experimental animal—make up an *observation*. In Figure 1, each row represents one observation. The first observation represents all the data values associated with the first man whose measurements were recorded. The last observation represents all the data values for the last man.

The only limit to the number of observations that a SAS data set may contain is the space available on disk or tape to store them.

VARIABLES

The set of data values that describe a given attribute makes up a *variable*. Each observation in a SAS data set contains one data value for each variable. In Figure 1 each column of data values is a variable. For example, the first column makes up the variable NAME and contains all the names of the men in the club, the second column makes up the variable WEIGHT and contains their weight measurements, and so on.

The maximum number of variables in a SAS data set is limited only by the maximum size of an individual observation (see Chapter 12, "SAS Data Sets").

Variable Attributes

SAS variables are of two types: numeric and character. In addition to their type, SAS variables have these attributes: length, informat, format, and label. Variable attributes are either explicitly specified or defined from the context at their first occurrence.

Type   Values of a numeric variable can only be numbers. In the fitness example the data values for the measurements recorded are numeric; their values are represented by numbers. Numeric values in the data lines can be preceded by plus or minus signs. Decimal points may be included, but commas may not appear. Numeric values can range in magnitude from approximately 10^{-73} to 10^{73}.

Data values may also be character; letters and special characters as well as numeric digits may make up character data values. In the fitness data, the men's names stored in the NAME variable are character data values. The dollar sign ($) following the name of a variable in some SAS statements used in the DATA step indicates that the data values are character rather than numeric. Character data values in SAS can range from 1 to 200 characters long.

Length   The length attribute of a variable is the number of bytes used to store each of its values in a SAS data set. The default length is 8. (To store a variable in a length different from the default and for a discussion of other length considerations, see the LENGTH statement.)

Informat   A variable's informat is the format that SAS uses to read data values into the variable. The default informat is *w.* for numeric variables, $*w.* for character variables. (To use an informat other than the default, see the INFORMAT statement. The *w.* informat and other SAS informats are described in Chapter 13, "SAS Informats and Formats.")

Format   A variable's format is the format SAS uses to write each value of a variable. The default format is *w.* for numeric variables, $*w.* for character variables. (To use a format other than the default, see the FORMAT statement. The *w.* and $*w.* formats and other SAS formats are described in Chapter 13, "SAS Informats and Formats." To define your own formats, see the FORMAT procedure.)

Label   The label attribute of a variable is a descriptive label of up to 40 characters that may be printed by certain procedures instead of the variable name. The default label is blank. (For information on how to specify a variable label, see the LABEL statement.)

VARIABLE ATTRIBUTE	POSSIBLE VALUES	DEFAULT VALUE*	ATTRIBUTE CAN BE SPECIFIED IN...
Type	numeric character ($)	numeric	LENGTH statement**
Length numeric character	2 to 8 bytes 1 to 200 bytes	8 bytes 8 bytes	LENGTH statement LENGTH statement
Informat numeric character	(see Chapter 13)	*w.* $*w.*	INFORMAT statement INFORMAT statement
Format numeric character	(see Chapter 13)	*w.* $*w.*	FORMAT statement FORMAT statement
Label	up to 40 characters	blank	LABEL statement

*The value used if no other specification is made.
**A variable's type and length are implicitly defined by its first occurrence in any of the following statements: INPUT, PUT, ARRAY, assignment, sum, DO, and RETAIN.

PUTTING TOGETHER DATA AND PROC STEPS

The DATA step that describes to SAS the collection of fitness data looks like this:

```
DATA FITNESS;
  INPUT NAME $ WEIGHT WAIST PULSE CHINS SITUPS JUMPS;
  CARDS;
HODGES  191 36 50 5 162 60
KERR    189 37 52 2 110 60
more data lines
;
```

- The DATA statement tells SAS to create a SAS data set named FITNESS.
- The INPUT statement tells SAS to read the data and gives the order and format of the data values.
- The CARDS statement tells SAS that the lines containing the data values follow immediately.
- The null statement (;) signals the end of the data lines.

The first PROC step asks SAS to sort the observations according to the NAME variable:

```
PROC SORT;
  BY NAME;
```

Since no other data set is specified, SAS uses the most recently created data set, which is the FITNESS data set.

The PROC statement that asks SAS to print a list of the data values looks like this:

```
PROC PRINT;
  TITLE FITNESS DATA;
```

These statements tell SAS to use the PRINT procedure to list the data with the title FITNESS DATA.

The PROC step that asks SAS to find the mean values for the fitness measurements looks like this:

```
PROC MEANS MAXDEC=1;
```

This statement tells SAS to execute the MEANS procedure to get means and other summary statistics for all the numeric variables in the SAS data set. The MAXDEC=1 option specifies that the statistics should be printed with one decimal place.

The final PROC step statements:

```
PROC CORR;
  VAR WEIGHT WAIST PULSE CHINS;
```

ask for the CORR procedure and use a VAR statement to request correlations for the four variables WEIGHT, WAIST, PULSE, and CHINS.

WRITING SAS PROGRAMS

The SAS language allows flexibility in the way SAS statements are written in a program.

Required Spacing

SAS statements may begin in any column of a line, and several statements may appear on the same line. You may begin a statement on one line and continue it to another line. Since column 1 of a line follows column 80 of the previous line immediately, with no blank in between, you may split a word if you end in column 80 and continue in column 1. (If your SAS statements are sequence-numbered in columns 73–80, then column 1 follows column 72 of the previous line.)

You need at least one blank between each separate item in a SAS statement as in the statements above. Some special characters, such as the equal sign after a word, can take the place of a blank, although blanks are always allowed.

For example, in the statement

    TOTAL2=TOTAL+10;

you do not need a blank before or after the equal sign or before or after the plus sign, because the equal sign and the plus sign are special characters, but you can also have any number of extra blanks. The statement

    TOTAL2 = TOTAL + 10 ;

is equivalent to the statement above.

(Although SAS does not have rigid spacing requirements, SAS programs are easier to read if the statements are indented consistently. The examples in this manual illustrate our spacing conventions.)

Comments

Comments of the form /* COMMENTS HERE */ may appear within SAS statements wherever a single blank may appear. For example, the statement

    PROC SORT /* SORT THE DATA SET */;

is a valid SAS statement. Comments within a TITLE statement are replaced with blanks when the title is printed.[2]

Variable Name Abbreviations

In some SAS statements that are used after a variable has been defined, variable names may be shortened to the shortest name that is not ambiguous. For example, in the VAR statement above, the variable WEIGHT can be shortened to WE and WAIST to WA.

Variable Lists

Variables are defined in the order in which they first appear. In the INPUT statement above, NAME is the first variable defined, followed by WEIGHT, WAIST, PULSE, CHINS, SITUPS, and JUMPS. In a DATA step with a SET, MERGE, or UPDATE statement or in a PROC step, the currently defined names are the names of the variables in the data set being processed.

After a complete list of variables has been defined in a SAS program, you can use abbreviated variable lists in many later SAS statements.

The different kinds of abbreviated lists are shown in the following table:

NAMES OF THE FORM...	CAN BE ABBREVIATED...	TO REPRESENT...
Numbered names of the form X1,X2,...,Xn	X1–Xn	all variables from X1 to Xn
Ranges of names of the form X P A*	X--A	all variables from X to A
	X–NUMERIC–A	all numeric variables from X to A
	X–CHARACTER–A	all character variables from X to A
Special SAS names	__NUMERIC__	all numeric variables
	__CHARACTER__	all character variables
	__ALL__	all variables

*Note: in variable ranges of this type, the list of variables in the range is not determined alphabetically but by the order in which they are defined.

For example, the INPUT statement above:

INPUT NAME $ WEIGHT WAIST PULSE CHINS SITUPS JUMPS;

can also be written to include a numbered variable list:

INPUT NAME $ VAR1–VAR6;

Note that the character variable NAME is not included in this abbreviated list. Variables in a numbered list need not be but are usually of the same type, numeric or character.

The VAR statement for the CORR procedure

VAR WEIGHT WAIST PULSE CHINS;

in the example can also be abbreviated as a range:

VAR WEIGHT--CHINS;

Other examples of abbreviated variable lists are shown throughout this manual. (Note: abbreviated variable lists are not allowed in some SAS data set options described in Chapter 12.)

OUTPUT FROM A SAS PROGRAM

Below is the complete SAS program including all the data lines and the output it produces. For a detailed discussion of SAS output features, see Chapter 16, "SAS Log and Procedure Output."

```
DATA FITNESS;
  INPUT NAME $ WEIGHT WAIST PULSE CHINS SITUPS JUMPS;
  CARDS;
HODGES       191 36 50  5 162  60
KERR         189 37 52  2 110  60
PUTNAM       193 38 58 12 101 101
ROBERTS      162 35 62 12 105  37
BLAKE        189 35 46 13 155  58
ALLEN        182 36 56  4 101  42
HOWARD       211 38 56  8 101  38
VINCENT      167 34 60  6 125  40
STEWART      176 31 74 15 200  40
PERRY        154 33 56 17 251 250
HOWELL       169 34 50 17 120  38
ELLIS        166 33 52 13 210 115
SMITH        154 34 64 14 215 105
CROWE        147 46 50  1  50  50
CARTER       193 36 46  6  70  31
MOORE        202 37 62 12 210 120
LEE          176 37 54  4  60  25
VARNER       157 32 52 11 230  80
STONE        156 33 54 15 225  73
SCOTT        138 33 68  2 110  43
;
PROC SORT;
  BY NAME;
PROC PRINT;
  TITLE FITNESS DATA;
PROC MEANS MAXDEC=1;
PROC CORR;
  VAR WEIGHT WAIST PULSE CHINS;
```

```
1        S A S   L O G    SAS/OS 82.0       VS2/MVS JOB FITDATA  STEP SASTEST   PROC

NOTE: THE JOB FITDATA HAS BEEN RUN UNDER RELEASE 82.0 OF SAS AT SAS INSTITUTE INC.

NOTE: CPUID    VERSION = 04  SERIAL = 020091  MODEL = 0158 .
      CPUID    VERSION = 03  SERIAL = 024001  MODEL = 0158 .

NOTE: NO OPTIONS SPECIFIED.

1          DATA FITNESS;
2              INPUT NAME $ WEIGHT WAIST PULSE CHINS SITUPS JUMPS;
3          CARDS;

NOTE: DATA SET WORK.FITNESS HAS 20 OBSERVATIONS AND 7 VARIABLES. 317 OBS/TRK.
NOTE: THE DATA STATEMENT USED 0.67 SECONDS AND 300K.

24         ;
25         PROC SORT;
26             BY NAME;

NOTE: 1 CYLINDER DYNAMICALLY ALLOCATED ON RIO FOR EACH OF 3 SORT WORK DATA SETS.
NOTE: DATA SET WORK.FITNESS HAS 20 OBSERVATIONS AND 7 VARIABLES. 317 OBS/TRK.
NOTE: THE PROCEDURE SORT USED 1.57 SECONDS AND 504K.

27         PROC PRINT;
28             TITLE FITNESS DATA;

NOTE: THE PROCEDURE PRINT USED 0.95 SECONDS AND 260K AND PRINTED PAGE 1.

29         PROC MEANS MAXDEC=1;

NOTE: THE PROCEDURE MEANS USED 0.90 SECONDS AND 260K AND PRINTED PAGE 2.

30         PROC CORR;
31             VAR WEIGHT WAIST PULSE CHINS;

NOTE: THE PROCEDURE CORR USED 0.94 SECONDS AND 260K AND PRINTED PAGE 3.

NOTE: SAS INSTITUTE INC.
      SAS CIRCLE
      PO BOX 8000
      CARY, N.C. 27511-8000
```

```
                                    FITNESS DATA                                              1

           OBS    NAME      WEIGHT    WAIST   PULSE    CHINS    SITUPS    JUMPS

            1    ALLEN       182       36      56       4       101       42
            2    BLAKE       189       35      46      13       155       58
            3    CARTER      193       36      46       6        70       31
            4    CROWE       147       46      50       1        50       50
            5    ELLIS       166       33      52      13       210      115
            6    HODGES      191       36      50       5       162       60
            7    HOWARD      211       38      56       8       101       38
            8    HOWELL      169       34      50      17       120       38
            9    KERR        189       37      52       2       110       60
           10    LEE         176       37      54       4        60       25
           11    MOORE       202       37      62      12       210      120
           12    PERRY       154       33      56      17       251      250
           13    PUTNAM      193       38      58      12       101      101
           14    ROBERTS     162       35      62      12       105       37
           15    SCOTT       138       33      68       2       110       43
           16    SMITH       154       34      64      14       215      105
           17    STEWART     176       31      74      15       200       40
           18    STONE       156       33      54      15       225       73
           19    VARNER      157       32      52      11       230       80
           20    VINCENT     167       34      60       6       125       40
```

```
                                    FITNESS DATA                                              2

VARIABLE    N      MEAN     STANDARD    MINIMUM    MAXIMUM    STD ERROR     SUM     VARIANCE    C.V.
                            DEVIATION    VALUE      VALUE     OF MEAN

WEIGHT     20     173.6       19.7       138.0      211.0        4.4       3472.0    389.6      11.4
WAIST      20      35.4        3.2        31.0       46.0        0.7        708.0     10.3       9.0
PULSE      20      56.1        7.2        46.0       74.0        1.6       1122.0     52.0      12.9
CHINS      20       9.4        5.3         1.0       17.0        1.2        189.0     27.9      55.9
SITUPS     20     145.5       62.6        50.0      251.0       14.0       2911.0   3914.6      43.0
JUMPS      20      70.3       51.3        25.0      250.0       11.5       1406.0   2629.4      72.9
```

```
                                    FITNESS DATA                                              3

VARIABLE    N        MEAN          STD DEV            SUM          MINIMUM          MAXIMUM


WEIGHT     20    173.60000000    19.73882095    3472.00000000    138.00000000    211.00000000

WAIST      20     35.40000000     3.20197308     708.00000000     31.00000000     46.00000000

PULSE      20     56.10000000     7.21037265    1122.00000000     46.00000000     74.00000000

CHINS      20      9.45000000     5.28627817     189.00000000      1.00000000     17.00000000


              CORRELATION COEFFICIENTS / PROB > |R| UNDER HO:RHO=0 /   N = 20

                          WEIGHT     WAIST     PULSE     CHINS


           WEIGHT    1.00000    0.20585   -0.23194   -0.06123
                     0.0000     0.3839     0.3251     0.7976

           WAIST     0.20585    1.00000   -0.35289   -0.55223
                     0.3839     0.0000     0.1270     0.0116

           PULSE    -0.23194   -0.35289    1.00000    0.15065
                     0.3251     0.1270     0.0000     0.5261

           CHINS    -0.06123   -0.55223    0.15065    1.00000
                     0.7976     0.0116     0.5261     0.0000
```

Acknowledgment   The data for the example in this chapter were provided by A.C. Linnerud of North Carolina State University.

[1] Other examples of automatic special variables used by SAS under certain circumstances include: __COL__, __FDBK__, __FREQ__, __IORC__, __LABEL__, __LNDET__, __MODEL__, __NAME__, __PRIOR__, __RBA__, __ROW__, __RRN__, __SIGMA__, __TITLES__, __TYPE__, and __WEIGHT__.

[2] If the /* is in column 1, both SAS and OS treat it as a JCL delimiter indicating the end of your SAS program.

THE DATA STEP

Introduction to the DATA Step

SAS Statements Used in the DATA Step

SAS Expressions

SAS Functions

DATA Step Applications

14

Introduction to the DATA Step

Before you can use SAS to prepare your data for analysis or use a SAS procedure to analyze your data, you must first get them into a SAS data set. Once your data are in a SAS data set, you can combine the data set with other SAS data sets in many different ways and use any of the SAS procedures.

The DATA step includes statements asking SAS to create one or more new data sets and programming statements that perform the manipulations necessary to build the data sets. Report writing, file management, and information retrieval are all handled in DATA steps.

You can use the DATA step for these purposes:

- retrieval—getting your input data into a SAS data set
- editing—checking for errors in your data and correcting them; computing new variables
- printing reports according to your specifications, writing disk and tape files, and punching cards
- producing new SAS data sets from existing ones by subsetting, merging, and updating the old data sets.

What Is a DATA Step?

A DATA step is a group of SAS statements that begins with a DATA statement and usually includes all the statements in one of these three groups:

Data on disk or tape

DATA *statement;*
  INFILE *statement;*
  INPUT *statement;*
  other SAS statements used in the DATA step

Data in job stream

DATA *statement;*
  INPUT *statement;*
  other SAS statements used in the DATA step
  CARDS *statement;*
data lines
;

Data in existing SAS data set

DATA *statement;*
  SET | MERGE | UPDATE *statement;*
  other SAS statements used in the DATA step

In the last DATA step the bar (|) notation indicates that either a SET, MERGE, or UPDATE statement may be used.

A DATA step may also include any of the other statements used in the DATA step described in Chapter 3 and briefly introduced later in this chapter.

Creating SAS Data Sets

The three types of simple DATA steps and a special DATA step for writing reports are shown below.

Data on disk or tape   The form of a DATA step for producing SAS data sets from input data on disk or tape is:

DATA *statement;*
   INFILE *statement;*
   INPUT *statement;*
   other SAS statements used in the DATA step

The statements in the DATA step above have these functions:

- The DATA statement signals the beginning of the DATA step and gives a name to the SAS data set you are creating.
- The INFILE statement gives the DDname of the job control statement describing the file that contains the data. When the INFILE statement is executed, the external file is opened.
- The INPUT statement describes your input data, giving a name to each variable and identifying its location on the disk or tape file. If you are modifying the data, optional program statements give SAS directions for the changes you want.

In-stream data   The form of a DATA step for producing a SAS data set from input data in the job stream with SAS statements is:

DATA *statement;*
   INPUT *statement;*
   other SAS statements used in the DATA step
   CARDS *statement;*
data lines
;

If you enter data from a terminal or if your data are on cards, you still need to describe the data's format to SAS in an INPUT statement. The required statements are identical to those in the example above, except that:

- No INFILE statement is needed.
- A CARDS statement immediately precedes the data lines or cards, signaling the end of the statements and the beginning of the data for the DATA step.

Data from other SAS data sets   The form of a DATA step for producing a SAS data set from one or more existing SAS data sets is:

DATA *statement;*
   SET | MERGE | UPDATE *statement;*
   other SAS statements used in the DATA step

You can create a SAS data set from one or more existing SAS data sets. For example, if you have questionnaire data stored in a SAS data set, you may want to build another data set containing only the responses for males. Rather than read the original raw data again to produce a data set for males only, it is easier to use a SET statement to read the SAS data set, selecting only those observations where the SEX value is M.

- The DATA statement tells SAS to start this DATA step and name the new data set.
- The SET, MERGE, or UPDATE statement identifies the old SAS data sets. (Optionally, a BY statement gives the identifying variables for the SET, MERGE, or UPDATE.)

Writing reports   The form of a DATA step for producing a report is:

DATA __NULL__;
{ INPUT and (CARDS | INFILE) *statement;*
{   or
{ SET | MERGE | UPDATE *statement;*
 FILE *statement;*
 PUT *statement;*
 other SAS statements used in the DATA step

If you want to report your data values in a form different from that produced by SAS reporting procedures, you can do it in a DATA step:

- The DATA __NULL__ statement tells SAS to begin the DATA step; using the special name __NULL__ means that a SAS data set is not produced.
- To provide the input data for the report, you need either INPUT and CARDS or INFILE statements with accompanying data; or SET, MERGE, or UPDATE statements; or program statements to generate data.
- The FILE statement tells SAS where to print the report or write the file. Optionally, you may use program statements to compute some new values.
- One or more PUT statements write the lines of the report or file.

DATA Step Statements

The SAS statements that can appear in a DATA step fall into several categories: file-handling statements, action statements, control statements, and information statements. Each statement is also either executable, positional, or declarative:

- executable statements (denoted by an X in the discussion below) are programming statements that cause some action
- positional statements (P) cause no action at execution, but their position in the DATA step is important
- declarative statements (D) supply additional information to SAS. Their position in the step is not usually important.

Other statements available for use within a DATA step are described in Chapter 11, "SAS Statements Used Anywhere."

File-handling statements   File-handling statements let you work with files used as input to the data set or files to be written by the DATA step. SAS's file-handling statements are:

CARDS	precedes card data or lines entered at a terminal—data that are part of the job stream. (P)
CARDS4	precedes in-stream data lines containing semicolons. (P)
DATA	tells SAS to begin a DATA step and to start building a SAS data set. (P)
FILE	identifies the external file where lines are to be written by the DATA step. (X)
INFILE	identifies the external file containing raw input data to be read in the DATA step. (X)
INPUT	describes the records on the external input file. (X)
MERGE	combines observations from two or more SAS data sets into a new data set. (X)
PUT	describes the format of the lines to be written by SAS. (X)
SET	reads observations from one or more existing SAS data sets. (X)
UPDATE	applies transactions to a master file. Both transaction and master file are SAS data sets. (X)

Action statements   While creating a SAS data set in a DATA step, you may want to modify your data from the way they appear on the input lines, select only certain observations for the data set being created, or look for errors in the input data. Action statements allow you to work with observations as they are being created. SAS action statements are:

ABORT	stops the job. (X)
assignment	creates and modifies variables. (X)
CALL	invokes or calls a routine. (X)
DELETE	excludes observations from the data set being created. (X)
ERROR	writes messages on the SAS log. (X)
LIST	lists input lines. (X)
LOSTCARD	corrects for lost cards when an observation has an incorrect number of data lines. (X)
null	holds a place for a label or signals the end of data lines. (P)
OUTPUT	creates new observations. (X)
STOP	stops creating the current data set. (X)
subsetting IF	selects observations for the data set being created. (X)
sum	accumulates totals. (X)

Control statements   SAS statements in a DATA step are executed one by one for each observation. In some cases, you may wish to skip statements for certain observations or to change the order of the statements encountered. SAS statements that let you transfer control from one part of the program to another are called *control statements*. SAS control statements are:

DO	sets up a group of statements to be executed as one
DO OVER	statement or iteratively; for each element in an array
DO UNTIL	(DO OVER); until some condition is true (DO UNTIL);
DO WHILE	or until some condition is no longer true (DO WHILE). (X)

END	signals the end of a DO group. (P)
GO TO	causes SAS to jump to a labeled statement in the step and continue execution from that point. (X)
IF-THEN/ELSE	conditionally executes a SAS statement. (X)
LINK-RETURN	causes SAS to jump to a labeled statement in the step and execute statements until it encounters a RETURN statement. (X)
RETURN	when not combined with a LINK statement, causes SAS to return to the beginning of the DATA step to begin execution. When combined with a LINK statement, returns to the statement immediately following the most recently executed LINK. (X)

Information statements   In the last category of SAS statements are information statements. These statements give SAS extra information about the data set or sets being created. Information statements are not executable and can appear anywhere in the DATA step with the same effect. The information provided in the statement takes effect either prior to the execution of the step or at the time observations are written to the SAS data set. SAS information statements are:

ARRAY	defines a set of variables to be processed the same way. (D)
BY	specifies that the data set is to be processed in groups defined by the BY variables. (D)
DROP	identifies variables to be excluded from a data set or analysis. (D)
FORMAT	specifies formats for printing variable values. (D)
INFORMAT	specifies informats for storing variable values. (D)
KEEP	identifies variables to be included in a data set or analysis. (D)
LABEL	associates descriptive labels with variable names. (D)
LENGTH	specifies the number of bytes to be used for storing SAS variables. (D)
RENAME	changes the names of variables in a data set. (D)
RETAIN	identifies variables whose values are not to be set to missing each time the DATA step is executed and gives the variables an initial value. (D)

DATA Step Flow

The DATA statement that begins each DATA step always signals the beginning of the step. The remaining statements can be called the "program," because SAS translates them to the computer's machine language and executes them each time it goes through the DATA step—usually, once for each observation of your input data.

In Figure 1 you can see the normal flow of the DATA step for creating a new data set.

SAS compiles the program into machine code. (SAS is a compiler; however, the machine code generated cannot be stored and reused without recompiling the SAS statements.) All the variables mentioned in the DATA step become part of the vector of current values, also called the program data vector. The variables from each source of input data, together with variables created by program statements, are in the program data vector and are available to program statements in the DATA step.

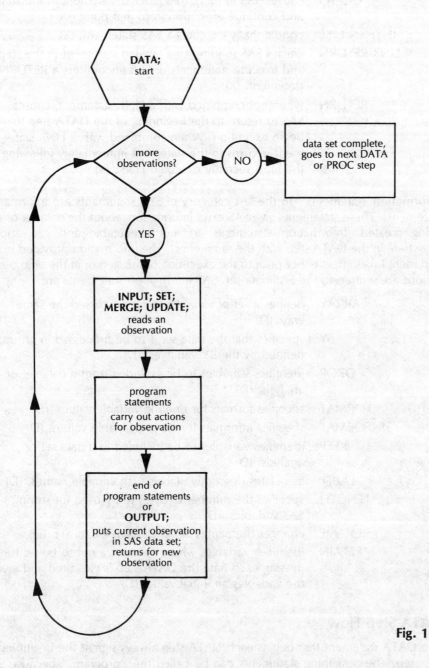

DATA;
start

more
observations?

NO

data set complete,
goes to next DATA
or PROC step

YES

INPUT; SET;
MERGE; UPDATE;
reads an
observation

program
statements
carry out actions
for observation

end of
program statements
or
OUTPUT;
puts current observation
in SAS data set;
returns for new
observation

Fig. 1

The new SAS data set or data sets can contain all of these variables, or you can choose any subset of variables to be output to the data set.

Variables read with an INPUT statement or created in programming statements are set to missing before execution of the DATA step. (Variables read with a SET, MERGE, or UPDATE statement are retained.) SAS executes each statement in the step, building observations for the SAS data set.

When SAS executes the last statement in the DATA step (or a RETURN statement that causes a return to the beginning of the step for a new execution), it normally writes the current values from the program data vector to the SAS data set being created.

SAS returns to the first statement after the DATA statement, initializes non-retained variables in the program data vector to missing, and begins executing statements to build the next observation.

When SAS has read and processed all the data from any of the input files, it goes on to the next DATA or PROC step.

How many times is a DATA step executed?   It is important to remember that SAS goes through the statements in the DATA step for each record that it reads. So although each statement appears only once, SAS carries it out for every observation. A DATA step that does not contain an INPUT, SET, MERGE, or UPDATE statement is executed only once. Otherwise, the step is repeated until SAS runs out of data in one of the input sources, or until a STOP or ABORT statement is executed. Program statements may be included that cause other statements in the DATA step to be executed many times: for example, DO loops, LINK/RETURN, or GO TO statements.

The SAS variable __N__ is automatically generated by SAS for each DATA step. Its value is the number of times SAS has begun executing the DATA step. You can use this variable in program statements in the DATA step. For example, to execute the statements in a DO group the first time through the DATA step, use the statement

IF __N__ = 1 THEN DO;

How SAS executes a DATA step: an example   A typical SAS job includes an INPUT statement that describes data values on cards, disk, or tape. The variables given in this INPUT statement make up the program data vector. If any program statements create new variables, these new variables also become part of the program data vector. For example, consider this DATA step:

```
DATA FITNESS;
   INPUT WEIGHT WAIST JUMPS SITUPS PULSE;
   RATIO = PULSE/JUMPS;
   CARDS;
data lines
```

These statements ask SAS to create a data set named FITNESS, to read five variables for this data set from input data lines, and to create a sixth variable, RATIO. The program data vector for this DATA step contains six variables:

WEIGHT WAIST JUMPS SITUPS PULSE RATIO

SAS executes this DATA step once for each observation.

SAS reads the current record's data values using the directions in the INPUT statement. SAS carries out the program statement, adding to the program data vector the value of RATIO.

After the last program statement, the values in the program data vector (the observation) are automatically added to the data set FITNESS being created. (This automatic outputting is equivalent to what would happen if an OUTPUT statement were present.)

SAS returns for another execution of the DATA step. (This automatic return is equivalent to what would happen if a RETURN statement were present.)

If there were 20 data lines, each containing the five INPUT variables, this DATA step would be executed 20 times; the new data set FITNESS would contain 20 observations. Each observation would contain six variables.

Another example   It is possible for a DATA step to contain several INPUT, SET, MERGE, or UPDATE statements. In such cases, the observations contain variables contributed by each statement. For example, consider this DATA step:

```
DATA FITNESS;
   INPUT WEIGHT WAIST JUMPS SITUPS PULSE;
   SET MORE;
   RATIO = AGE/JUMPS;
   DROP AGE JUMPS HEIGHT;
   CARDS;
data lines
```

The program data vector for this DATA step is like that in the example above, except that it also includes whatever variables the SAS data set MORE contains. If MORE contains the variables AGE and HEIGHT, the program data vector contains the variables shown in Figure 2. Since a DROP statement appears, observations written to the new data set FITNESS contain only these variables:

WEIGHT WAIST SITUPS PULSE RATIO

Note that when a DATA step has more than one source of input data, the step ends when all the data have been read from one of the sources. Thus, the example above is normally used only if there are an equal number of raw data records and observations in data set MORE.

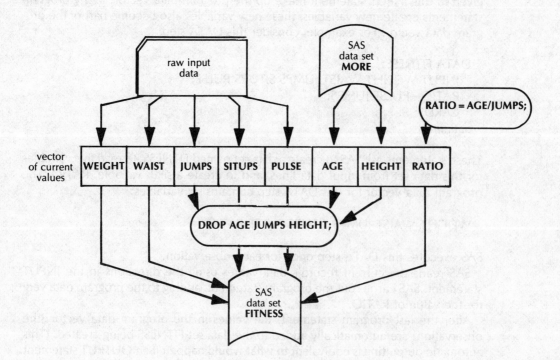

Fig. 2

SAS Statements Used in the DATA Step

The SAS statements that can be used in a DATA step are described alphabetically in this chapter. For a discussion of the four general groups into which these statements fall, see the preceding chapter, "Introduction to the DATA Step,"

ABORT Statement
ARRAY Statement
Assignment Statement
BY Statement
CALL Statement
CARDS and CARDS4 Statement
DATA Statement
DELETE Statement
DO Statement
DROP Statement
END Statement
ERROR Statement
FILE Statement
FORMAT Statement
GO TO Statement
IF Statement
INFILE Statement
INFORMAT Statement
INPUT Statement
KEEP Statement
LABEL Statement
Labels, Statement
LENGTH Statement
LINK Statement
LIST Statement
LOSTCARD Statement
MERGE Statement
MISSING Statement
Null Statement
OUTPUT Statement
PUT Statement
RENAME Statement
RETAIN Statement
RETURN Statement
SET Statement
STOP Statement
Sum Statement
UPDATE Statement

ABORT Statement

You can use the ABORT statement in a DATA step to stop the execution of a SAS job immediately. When the ABORT statement is executed, SAS stops executing statements and prints a message. Unless you are executing SAS interactively or specify the RETURN option, SAS enters syntax check mode by setting the OBS= option to OBS=0 in the input stream and by setting a flag to indicate that permanent SAS data sets are not to be replaced. Use the STOP statement instead of ABORT if you want SAS to stop a DATA step and go on to execute the next steps in the job.

The form of the ABORT statement is:

ABORT[ABEND]|[RETURN][n];

You may specify these options on the ABORT statement:

n   terminates the SAS job and sets the step return or condition code to *n*, an integer. For example, if *n* is 255,

   ABORT 255;

sets the step condition code to 255. (The *n* option is not valid under DOS/VSE.)

ABEND   abnormally terminates the SAS job immediately with a user completion code of U0999. For example,

   ABORT ABEND;

Under DOS/VSE, abnormal termination always produces a dump.

   When both ABEND and *n* are specified, SAS abnormally terminates the job with the user completion code that you specify. For example,

   ABORT ABEND 255;

RETURN   normally terminates the SAS job immediately with the step return or condition code set to 12. SAS does not enter syntax check mode or continue to process statements. When both RETURN and *n* are specified, SAS normally terminates the job with the step return or condition code that you specify. For example,

   ABORT RETURN 16;

Before you perform extensive analysis on your data, you can use the ABORT statement to halt execution if the data are not error-free. For example,

```
DATA CHECK;
   INPUT SSN 1-9 PAYCODE 11-13;
   IF __ERROR__ THEN ABORT;
```

The automatic variable __ERROR__ is set to 1 if errors occur in the data lines. If any errors are found, SAS stops executing statements immediately.

ARRAY Statement

If you need to process many variables the same way, you can use the ARRAY statement to define the set of variables (either all numeric or all character) as elements of an array. When the array name appears in SAS statements later in the DATA step, one of the elements of the array is substituted for the array name in the statement. The value of the array's index variable determines which variable is substituted.

Note: do not confuse array processing in SAS with that in other programming languages. SAS arrays are simply a convenient way of processing several SAS variables the same way.

You define arrays in SAS with the ARRAY statement:

ARRAY *arrayname* [(*indexvariable*)] [**$**] [*length*] *arrayelements*;

You may specify the items below on the ARRAY statement:

arrayname names the array. The array name is a valid SAS name that is not the name of a SAS variable in the same DATA step. When the array name appears in a SAS statement, one of the array elements is substituted for the array name based on the value of the index variable.

(indexvariable) gives the name of a variable whose value defines the current element of the array. All arrays use an index variable even if one is not specified in the ARRAY statement. If no index variable is specified, SAS uses the automatic variable __I__ as the index variable. The value of the index variable may range from 1 to the number of elements in the array.

The index variable you specify is included in the SAS data set unless it is excluded by a DROP or KEEP statement. The automatic index variable __I__ is not included in the data set.

If the index variable's value is not an integer, it is truncated to an integer using the rules of the INT function, described in Chapter 5, "SAS Functions."

Note: the rules for truncating differ for array index variables and the INT function on the order of 10^{-12}.

**$** tells SAS that the array you are defining is composed of character elements. The dollar sign ($) is not necessary if the character variables have been previously defined as character in the step. Do not include a $ if the elements in the array are numeric.

length gives a length value, a numeric constant from 1 to 200, to character array elements. SAS uses the length value for each array element not previously assigned a length. For example, the statements

```
DATA A;
  INPUT X1-X2 $3.;
  ARRAY ITEM(I) $ 12 X1-X10;
  other SAS statements
```

define a character array ITEM. The first two elements X1 and X2 have lengths of 3, defined in the INPUT statement. The other elements of ITEM are given a length of 12 by the length specification in the ARRAY statement. You must use a separate LENGTH statement to specify lengths of numeric variables in an array.

arrayelements   names the variables that make up the array. Array elements may be the names of variables or other arrays and must be either all numeric or all character. A variable may be an element in more than one array. Any valid form of the variable list, as described in Chapter 1, "Introduction to the SAS Language," may appear.

For example, the statement

    ARRAY QUESTION (I) Q1–Q20;

defines an array QUESTION with 20 elements Q1–Q20. Using the name QUESTION in a subsequent SAS statement refers to the ith element of QUESTION, where i is the current value of the index variable I.

The array elements may be listed in any order and the names of array elements do not have to be numbered names as in the example above. This ARRAY statement

    ARRAY QUIZ (NUM) Q10 Q3–Q5 TEST4;

is a valid array definition. Q10 is the first element of the array QUIZ, Q3 is the second, Q4 the third, Q5 the fourth, and TEST4 the fifth. NUM is the index variable. When NUM's value is 1, Q10 is the variable SAS processes when the array name QUIZ appears in a SAS statement.

Referencing arrays   You can use an array name in almost any executable SAS statement where a variable name can appear. Before you use the array name, however, the ARRAY statement defining the array name must appear in the same DATA step. An array definition is only in effect for the duration of the DATA step. If you want to use the same array in several DATA steps, you must redefine the elements of the array in each step. Arrays are used in DATA steps and in several SAS procedures that allow programming (including PROC NLIN, PROC MATRIX, and in SAS/ETS, the COMPUTAB procedure).

To refer to an element of an array, set the index variable to the index of the element you want and then use the array name in a SAS statement. (Note: you cannot reference an element of array Y by coding a subscript like Y(INDEX) as you can in some other languages.)

For example, say that you want to print the value of the eleventh element of the array ALL:

```
DATA ONE;
  ARRAY ALL (I) X1–X10 Y1–Y10;
  INPUT ID X1–X10 Y1–Y10;
  I=11;
  PUT ALL;
  CARDS;
```

The PUT statement writes the value of Y1, the eleventh element of ALL.

Using arrays with DO groups   Combining a DO group with arrays is often useful. For example, the statements below change all missing values in the array ALL to the value zero:

```
DATA TWO;
   ARRAY ALL (I) X1-X10 Y1-Y10;
   INPUT ID X1-X10 Y1-Y10;
   DO OVER ALL;
     IF ALL= . THEN ALL=0;
     END;
   CARDS;
```

If the array subscript is out of range (less than 1 or greater than the number of elements in the array) when the array name appears, the DATA step stops and SAS prints an error message on the log.

Using arrays as elements of other arrays   Since an array may be an element of another array, double and higher-level subscripting is possible. For example, say your data values consist of answers from 3 tests, 20 questions per test. For each student, there are 60 answers. You can use the ARRAY statements in the DATA step below to easily change missing values to zeros in these 60 answers:

```
DATA THREE;
   ARRAY TEST1 (J) T1Q1-T1Q20;
   ARRAY TEST2 (J) T2Q1-T2Q20;
   ARRAY TEST3 (J) T3Q1-T3Q20;
   ARRAY ANSWER (K) TEST1-TEST3;
   INPUT T1Q1-T1Q20 T2Q1-T2Q20 T3Q1-T3Q20;
   DO OVER ANSWER;
     DO J= 1 TO 20;
       IF ANSWER= . THEN ANSWER=0;
       END;
     END;
   CARDS;
```

Each time the array name ANSWER appears in a SAS statement, the current value of K (the index for ANSWER) determines which of the three arrays (TEST1, TEST2, or TEST3) you want to process. The substitution of one of these three array names in the statement then substitutes the appropriate variable from that array based on J's value.

More array examples are given in Chapter 6, "Data Step Applications."

Assignment Statement

Assignment statements evaluate an expression and store the result in a variable. Assignment statements have the form:

   variable = *expression*;

The terms in the assignment have these definitions:

> *variable*   names a new variable or an existing variable. (See Chapter 1, "Introduction to the SAS Language," for a discussion of SAS variables.)
>
> *expression*   is one or more variable names, constants, and function names linked by operators and by parentheses where appropriate. (See Chapter 4, "SAS Expressions," and Chapter 5, "SAS Functions," for more information.)

For example, the statements

```
DATA ONE;
   INPUT A B;
   X=A+B;
   CARDS;
data lines
```

read values of A and B from cards and create a new variable X that is the sum of A and B values in each observation. (Note: if either A or B is missing, X will be missing. See Chapter 14, "Missing Values," for details.) You can modify existing variables by writing assignment statements like this:

```
A=A+B;
```

The sum of A and B replaces the original value of A. Note that the variable A appears on both sides of the statement: the original value of A on the right side is used in evaluating the expression. The result is stored in the variable A.

Variables in assignment statements   If a variable appears for the first time in a DATA step as the result variable in an assignment statement, it has the same type (character or numeric) as the result of the expression. If the variable is character, the length is the length resulting from the first execution of the statement unless a LENGTH statement specifies a length.

If a variable appears for the first time (the variable has not been assigned a value) on the right side of an assignment statement, SAS assumes that its value is missing. A message is printed on the log that the variable is uninitialized.

If a variable has been defined as numeric and then used as a result variable in an assignment statement with a character result, character-to-numeric conversion takes place and the statement is executed. (See Chapter 4, "SAS Expressions," for further discussion.)

More examples of using assignment statements in the DATA step are given in Chapter 6, "DATA Step Applications."

BY Statement

A BY statement is used in a DATA step to control the operation of a SET, MERGE, or UPDATE statement and to set up special grouping variables.

The BY statement has the form:

BY [DESCENDING] *variable* ... **[NOTSORTED];**

where

variable	names each variable by which the data set is sorted. The list of variables defines the data set's BY groups.
DESCENDING	specifies that the data set is sorted in descending order by the variable that follows the word DESCENDING in the BY statement.
NOTSORTED	specifies that observations with the same BY values are grouped together but the BY values are not necessarily sorted in alphabetical or numerical order. The NOTSORTED option may appear anywhere in the BY statement. The option may only be used with a SET statement which reads a single data set.

For example, data set CLASS contains observations with a variable MONTH whose values are the three-character abbreviation for month. If all the observations with the same MONTH value are grouped together in the data set the values are in calendar order rather than alphabetical order. Then the statement

    BY MONTH NOTSORTED;

can be used with a SET statement that reads the CLASS data set.

When a BY statement is used and NOTSORTED is not specified, the data set used as input to the step need not have been previously sorted by the SORT procedure. However, the data set must be in the same order as though the SORT procedure had been used.

BY groups   These statements:

    PROC SORT DATA=DEGREES;
      BY STATE CITY MONTH;

produced the SAS data set below using the SORT procedure. The data set DEGREES is sorted by STATE, CITY within STATE, and MONTH within CITY. The fourth variable in the data set, DEGDAY, represents winter degree days.

STATE	CITY	MONTH	DEGDAY	
NC	CHARLOTTE	1	716	
NC	CHARLOTTE	2	588	
NC	CHARLOTTE	3	461	
				——— CITY break
NC	RALEIGH	1	760	
NC	RALEIGH	2	638	
NC	RALEIGH	3	502	
				——— CITY break–STATE break
VA	NORFOLK	1	760	
VA	NORFOLK	2	661	
VA	NORFOLK	3	532	
				——— CITY break
VA	RICHMOND	1	853	
VA	RICHMOND	2	717	
VA	RICHMOND	3	569	
				——— CITY break–STATE break

The BY groups in the data set, from largest to smallest, are represented by different values for STATE, CITY within STATE, and MONTH within CITY within STATE. In the data set above, NC and VA observations break the data set into two STATE BY groups; CHARLOTTE and RALEIGH observations divide the NC observations into CITY BY groups, NORFOLK and RICHMOND observations divide VA observations into CITY BY groups; and within CITY each observation, with its different value for MONTH, is itself a MONTH BY group.

FIRST. and LAST.byvariables   You can process the data set in BY groups if you include a BY statement after the SET, MERGE, or UPDATE statement in the DATA step.

Then SAS creates two variables, FIRST.*byvariable* and LAST.*byvariable*, for each variable in the BY statement. The FIRST. and LAST.*byvariables* let you know when you are processing the first or last observation in a BY group.

If an observation is the first in a BY group, then FIRST.*byvariable* has the value 1. For all observations in the BY group except the first, FIRST.*byvariable* is 0. If an observation is the last in a BY group, LAST.*byvariable* is 1. For all observations in the BY group except the last, LAST.*byvariable* is 0.

The data set DEGREES is shown with values of the FIRST. and LAST.*byvariables*:

STATE	CITY	MONTH	DEGDAY	FIRST.byvariables STATE	FIRST.byvariables CITY	FIRST.byvariables MONTH	LAST.byvariables STATE	LAST.byvariables CITY	LAST.byvariables MONTH
NC	CHARLOTTE	1	716	1	1	1	0	0	1
NC	CHARLOTTE	2	588	0	0	1	0	0	1
NC	CHARLOTTE	3	461	0	0	1	0	1	1
				——— CITY break					
NC	RALEIGH	1	760	0	1	1	0	0	1
NC	RALEIGH	2	638	0	0	1	0	0	1
NC	RALEIGH	3	502	0	0	1	1	1	1
				——— CITY break–STATE break					
VA	NORFOLK	1	760	1	1	1	0	0	1
VA	NORFOLK	2	661	0	0	1	0	0	1
VA	NORFOLK	3	532	0	0	1	0	1	1
				——— CITY break					
VA	RICHMOND	1	853	0	1	1	0	0	1
VA	RICHMOND	2	717	0	0	1	0	0	1
VA	RICHMOND	3	569	0	0	1	1	1	1

Notice that each MONTH BY group consists of 1 observation. Thus, FIRST.MONTH and LAST.MONTH are both 1 in each observation. Notice also that when the FIRST.byvariable is 1 for a variable in the BY statement, the FIRST.byvariable is also 1 for all variables following it in the BY statement. Thus, when FIRST.STATE is 1 for an observation, FIRST.CITY and FIRST.MONTH are also 1 for that observation. The same is true for LAST.byvariables.

For example, the data set below is sorted by DAY within WEEK. Notice the values of the FIRST. variables:

OBS	WEEK	DAY	FIRST WEEK	FIRST DAY
1	1	MONDAY	1	1
2	1	TUESDAY	0	1
3	1	TUESDAY	0	0
4	2	TUESDAY	1	1
5	2	TUESDAY	0	0
6	2	WEDNESDAY	0	1

Although in observation 4, the DAY value is not the first with the value 'TUESDAY', it is the first value of TUESDAY within WEEK=2. That is, since FIRST.WEEK is 1, FIRST.DAY is 1.

BY statement with MERGE When a BY statement is used in a DATA step with a MERGE statement, the data sets listed in the MERGE statement are joined by matching values of the variables listed in the BY statement. FIRST. and LAST.byvariables are created for each variable listed in the BY statement. See the MERGE statement for more information.

The statements below perform a match-merge, matching on STATE, and CITY within STATE. SAS data sets YR82 and YR83 have been previously sorted by STATE and CITY using the SORT procedure. The last observation in each CITY BY group is output to data set SINGLE:

```
DATA NEW SINGLE;
  MERGE YR82 YR83;
  BY STATE CITY;
  IF LAST.CITY THEN OUTPUT SINGLE;
  OUTPUT NEW;
```

The NOTSORTED option may not be used in a BY statement in a DATA step with MERGE; the DESCENDING option may be used if the observations being MERGED are sorted in descending order of the variable mentioned with the BY statement.

See the MERGE statement description for more information.

BY statement with UPDATE A BY statement must appear in a DATA step with an UPDATE statement to identify the matching variable or variables to be used in the update. See the UPDATE statement later in this chapter for more information. FIRST. and LAST.byvariables are created, and the NOTSORTED option may not be used. Chapter 6, "DATA Step Applications," contains more examples using a BY statement.

See the UPDATE statement description for more information.

BY statement with SET When a BY statement is used in a DATA step that includes a SET statement with one data set name, the data set being read is processed just as though a BY statement were not included. The difference is that the BY statement causes FIRST. and LAST.byvariables to be created and produces an error message if the data set is not sorted.

For example, the DATA step below creates a SAS data set named SUBSET which includes only the first observation in each STATE BY group from data set DEGREES:

    DATA SUBSET;
      SET DEGREES;
      BY STATE;
      IF FIRST.STATE;

Notice that only STATE, the primary BY group, is used in the BY statement, since only the FIRST.STATE variable is needed.

When a BY statement is used in a DATA step with a SET statement, both the NOTSORTED and DESCENDING options may be used.

See the Set statement description for more information.

CALL Statement

The purpose of the CALL statement in the DATA step is to invoke or call a routine. The routine is called each time the CALL statement is executed. You can write your own call routine in assembler or FORTRAN to process observations in a SAS data set and then invoke this routine with a CALL statement.

The form of the CALL statement is:

   CALL *routine(parameters)*;

where

   routine   names the routine you want to call.
   parameters   lists one or more SAS variables, separated by commas.

For example, the SYMPUT function is used to give the value of an ordinary SAS variable to a macro variable. You can use the CALL statement to invoke the SYMPUT function with this statement:

   CALL SYMPUT(*macvar,SASvar*);

where *macvar* is the name of a macro variable; *SASvar* is the name of a SAS variable. The function assigns the value of the SAS variable to that of the macro variable.

For more information about using the CALL statement, see Chapter 5, "Functions," and Chapter 15, "SAS Macro Language." For details on how to write a call routine, see the *SAS Programmer's Guide*.

CARDS and CARDS4 Statements

If you are entering your data in the job stream with your SAS program, the CARDS statement

    CARDS;
   data lines

comes before the data lines to signal to SAS that the data follow. If you use a CARDS statement, it must be the last statement in your DATA step, and it must be followed immediately by data lines.

SAS recognizes the end of the data lines when it sees a semicolon. The first line after the last data line should be either a null statement (a line containing a single semicolon) or another SAS statement ending with a semicolon on the same line:

    CARDS;
   data lines
   ;

If a CARDS statement appears in a DATA step, an INPUT statement must be present. For example,

   DATA ENTRIES;
     INPUT X Y;
     CARDS;
   data lines
   ;

The CARDS statement is for in-stream data; if your input lines are on disk or tape, use instead the INFILE statement described later in this chapter.

You can use both an INFILE statement and a CARDS statement if you want to take advantage of some of the INFILE statement options. For example,

   DATA TEMP;
     INFILE CARDS MISSOVER;
     INPUT X Y Z;
     CARDS;
   data lines
   ;

Only one CARDS statement may be used in a DATA step. If you want to enter two sets of data, either use two DATA steps or two INFILE statements, one for each set of data. (See the INFILE statement for an example.)

Since a semicolon signals to SAS the end of the data lines, if the data lines following the CARDS statement happen to contain semicolons, you must substitute the CARDS4 statement for the CARDS statement. The form of the CARDS4 statement is:

    CARDS4;
   data lines

After the last data line, put a line consisting of four semicolons in columns 1-4 to signal the end of the data. For example:

```
DATA;
  INPUT X Y;
  CARDS4;
```
data lines containing semicolons
`; ; ; ;`
another DATA or PROC statement

DATA Statement

The DATA statement begins a DATA step and provides a name for the SAS data set or data sets being created. (SAS data sets are described in detail in Chapter 12.)
The form of the DATA statement is:

DATA   [[*SASdataset* [(*dsoptions*)]]...]**;**

The terms in the DATA statement are described below:

SASdataset   names one or more SAS data sets being created in the DATA step.

> The data set name given in the DATA statement may be a one-word name (for example, FITNESS), a two-word name (for example, OUT.FITNESS), or one of the special SAS names __NULL__, __DATA__, or __LAST__.
> A DATA statement may name one data set:

> DATA FITNESS;
> DATA OUT.FITNESS;
> DATA __NULL__;

> or more than one:

> DATA YEAR1 YEAR2 YEAR3;
> DATA MALES FEMALES;
> DATA LIBRARY.TOTAL ERRORS;

> You may omit the data set name entirely:

> DATA;

> Then SAS names the data set using the DATA*n* convention (see below). (Chapter 12 gives more information on naming SAS data sets.)

(*dsoptions*)   gives SAS more information about the data set being created. Data set options in parentheses follow the name of the data set in the DATA statement to which they apply.

> For example, LABEL= allows you to specify a label of up to 40 characters for the data set. To give the FITNESS data set the label HEALTH CLUB DATA, use the statement:

> DATA FITNESS (LABEL=HEALTH CLUB DATA);

The use of these options is not confined to the DATA statement. Data set options may be associated with a data set name where it occurs in other SAS statements (except the OUTPUT statement in the DATA step).
Options most commonly used in the DATA statement are summarized below:

DROP=   lists the variables not to be included in the data set.

GEN=   specifies the number of generations of history information that are stored with the data set.

KEEP=	lists the variables to be included in the data set.
LABEL=	provides the data set with a label that is printed along with the name in the output of the CONTENTS procedure.
PROTECT=	specifies a write-only password for the data set. The password should be a valid SAS name.
READ=	specifies a read-and-write password for the data set. The password should be a valid SAS name.
RENAME=	changes variable names.
TYPE=	specifies the data set's type. Use TYPE= only when the data set contains specially structured data such as a covariance matrix.

Refer to Chapter 12, "SAS Data Sets," for a complete description of these and other data set options as well as further discussion of the naming conventions mentioned below.

Choosing a Data Set Name in the DATA Statement

You should name each SAS data set in a SAS program that creates several data sets. While some SAS users omit the data set name for very simple SAS jobs, you can keep track of your data sets more easily if you give each of them a unique name.

You must include a two-word data set name when you are storing your SAS data set on disk or tape for use in a future SAS job. (The only exception is when you specify the USER= option; see Chapter 12 for discussion.)

Default data set name   If you omit a data set name from the DATA statement as shown below:

DATA;

SAS still creates a data set. The data set is named automatically; the first such data set created in a job is called DATA1, the second is called DATA2, and so on through the job. This is called the DATA*n* naming convention and is equivalent to specifying:

DATA __DATA__;

One-word data set name   All SAS data sets have two names: the first part identifies the library where the data set is stored; the second part identifies the particular data set. Unless you plan to store your SAS data set on disk or tape, you may give your data set a one-word name. For example, to begin creating a SAS data set named FITNESS, you use the statement

DATA FITNESS;

When you give a one-word name like FITNESS, SAS uses that name as the second part of the data set name and uses WORK (or the DDname specified by the USER= option) as the first part.

When the first-level name is WORK, the data set is temporary; it is only available during the current job or interactive session.

Two-word data set name   You use a two-word data set name if you want to store your SAS data set on disk or tape. For example,

DATA OUT.FITNESS;

If you have used a two-word data set name in the DATA step to create a data set, you then continue to use the two-word name if you refer to the data set later in your SAS job. For example, if you use OUT.FITNESS as shown above to create a SAS data set on disk or tape, and you want to refer to the data set in a SET statement later in the job, you use the statement

SET OUT.FITNESS;

If you used the statement

SET FITNESS;

the system would look for WORK.FITNESS since it always uses the name WORK as the first part of one-word names.

The first part of a two-word name is not a permanent part of the SAS data set name under OS. It is a reference to the job control for the current job, which points to the file containing the SAS library. If a later job references the same SAS data library with a different DDname, that DDname would be the first part of the two-word data set name. Under CMS the first part of the name is used for the CMS filetype.

Using Special SAS Data Set Names

Data set name __NULL__   You may give the special SAS data set name __NULL__ in the DATA statement whenever you want to execute the statements in a DATA step but do not want to create a SAS data set. For example, if you are using SAS to print a report with PUT statements based on the values contained in a SAS data set, you probably do not want to create another SAS data set containing the same data. Using __NULL__ means that SAS goes through the DATA step just as though it is creating a data set, but it does not write any observations nor does it use the resources necessary to create the entry in the SAS data library.

Data set name __LAST__   __LAST__ refers to the name of the most recently created SAS data set. If a DATA statement includes the name __LAST__, the data set created has the same name as the most recently created data set and replaces the earlier data set.

Using More Than One Data Set Name

Subsets of observations   When you are creating several data sets in one DATA step and want each data set to include a subset of the observations that the DATA step is processing, you can use the OUTPUT statement to add the appropriate observations to each data set. For example, you might use these statements:

```
DATA YEAR79 YEAR80 YEAR81;
   INPUT YEAR X1 – X20;
   IF YEAR = 1979 THEN OUTPUT YEAR79;
   ELSE IF YEAR = 1980 THEN OUTPUT YEAR80;
   ELSE IF YEAR = 1981 THEN OUTPUT YEAR81;
   CARDS;
   data lines
```

The YEAR79 data set contains only those observations where the YEAR value is 1979; the YEAR80 data set contains only those observations where the YEAR value is 1980; the YEAR81 data set contains only those observations with YEAR = 1981. Observations with any other year values are not written to any data set.

Subsets of variables When you want to create several data sets containing different groups of variables, you can use the KEEP= or DROP= data set options after each data set name in the DATA statement.

For example, say that you want the data set YEAR79 to include, in addition to the variable YEAR, variables X1 – X5; data set YEAR80 to include YEAR and X6 – X20; and data set YEAR81 to include YEAR and all of the variables X1 – X20 except X13:

```
DATA YEAR79(KEEP= YEAR X1 – X5)
    YEAR80(KEEP= YEAR X6 – X20)
    YEAR81(DROP= X13);
```

Either KEEP= or DROP= may be used. The advantage of DROP= is that you can write a shorter list when you are dropping fewer variables than you are keeping.

DELETE Statement

A DELETE statement tells SAS to stop processing the current observation. The observation is not automatically written to any data set being created, and SAS returns to the beginning of the DATA step for another execution.

The DELETE statement has the form:

DELETE;

Here is an example:

```
DATA JRHIGH;
   INPUT SSN 1-9 GRADE 10 PRETEST1 14–16 PRETEST2 18–20;
   IF GRADE<6 THEN DELETE;
   TOTAL = PRETEST1 + PRETEST2;
   CARDS;
data lines
;
```

In this example, observations with a GRADE value less than 6 are not added to the SAS data set JRHIGH. The assignment statement is not executed for those observations.

When a DELETE statement is executed, SAS immediately stops executing program statements for the current observation. SAS returns to the statement following the DATA statement and begins executing the statements that follow. The DELETE statement is usually used as the THEN clause in an IF statement or as part of a conditionally executed DO group. If DELETE is executed for every observation, the new data set will have no observations.

In general, use the DELETE statement when it is easier to specify a condition for excluding observations from the data set. Use the subsetting IF statement (discussed later in this chapter) if it is easier to specify a condition for including observations.

DO Statement

The DO statement specifies that the statements following the DO are to be executed as a unit until a matching END statement appears. The statements between the DO and the END statement are called a DO group. Any number of DO groups can be nested. SAS has several forms of the DO statement:

> DO;
> *iterative* DO;
> DO WHILE;
> DO UNTIL;
> DO OVER;

The number of times the DO group is executed depends on the form used.
The form of a simple DO statement is:

> **DO;**
> *more SAS statements*
>   **END;**

DO statements are often used within IF-THEN/ELSE statements where they designate groups of statements to be executed depending on whether the IF-condition is true or false.

For example, the statements

> IF X = Y THEN DO;
>   X = X + 1;
>   PUT X;
>   END;
> OUTPUT;

specify that the statements between DO and END (the DO group) are to be performed only if X = Y. If X is not equal to Y, the statements in the DO group are skipped and the next statement executed is the OUTPUT statement.

Iterative Execution of DO Groups

Iterative execution of a DO group can be specified by using an index variable in the DO statement. When the DO statement has this form, the statements between the DO and the END are executed repetitively:

> **DO** *indexvariable* = *start* [**TO** *stop* [**BY** *increment*]]...;
> *more SAS statements*
>   **END;**

where

indexvariable	names a variable whose value governs execution of the DO group. After the DO loop is executed, the value of the index variable is:

$$start + increment * (INT((stop\text{-}start)/increment) + 1).$$

Unless dropped, the index variable is included in the data set being created.

start
stop
specifies numbers or expressions that yield numbers to control the number of times the statements between DO and END are executed. The iterative DO group is executed first with the *indexvariable* equal to *start* and continues (based on *increment*'s value) until the *indexvariable* is equal to *stop*. Values of *start* and *stop* are evaluated prior to the execution of the first loop.

increment
specifies a number or an expression that yields a number to control incrementing of the value of the index variable between the *start* and *stop* values. The value of *increment* is evaluated prior to the execution of the loop. For example,

        DO COUNT = 2 TO 8 BY 2;

causes the DO group to be executed for COUNT = 2,4,6,8.

If no increment is specified, the index variable is incremented by 1. If *increment* is negative, then *start* is the upper bound and *stop* is the lower bound for the loop.

A number of clauses separated by commas may be included in the statement. For example, the statement

        DO COUNT = 2 TO 8 BY 2,11,13 TO 16;

causes the DO group to be executed for the following values of COUNT: 2,4,6,8,11,13,14,15, and 16.

Here are some other examples of valid DO statements:

```
DO;
DO I = 1 TO N;
DO I = N TO 1 BY -1;
DO I = K + 1 TO N-1;
DO I = 1 TO K-1, K + 1 TO N;
DO I = 2,3,5,7,11,13,17;
DO I = 1 TO 10 BY 1, 20 TO 100 BY 10;
```

The values of *start, stop,* and *increment* are evaluated before the statements in the DO group are executed. Any changes to the upper bound or increment made within the DO group do not affect the number of iterations. For example, consider this DATA step:

```
DATA TWO;
  INPUT X;
  STOP = 10;
  DO I = 0 TO STOP;
    Y = X*NORMAL(0);
    OUTPUT;
    IF Y>25 THEN STOP = I;
    END;
CARDS;
```

Setting STOP to the current value of I does not stop execution of the DO loop. You can, however, change the value of the index variable. Thus, you can stop execution of the loop by setting I to STOP's value. Use a GO TO statement to jump to a statement outside the loop. For example,

```
DATA THREE;
  INPUT X;
  STOP = 10;
  DO I = 0 TO STOP;
    Y = X*NORMAL(0);
    OUTPUT;
    [IF Y>25 THEN GO TO OUT;] or [IF Y>25 THEN I = STOP;]
    END;
  OUT: CARDS;
```

Consider these statements:

```
DATA ONE;
  INPUT X Y Z;
  IF X = . THEN DO K = 1 TO 25;
    X = UNIFORM(0)*100;
    OUTPUT;
    END;
  CARDS;
```

Each time X is missing, 25 observations are output, each with the current values of Y and Z and with randomly generated values of X. Each time the value of X is not missing, no observation is output.

DO OVER Statement

You can execute the statements in a DO group for every element in an array with the DO OVER statement.

The form of the DO OVER statement is:

DO OVER *arrayname***;**

where

> *arrayname*   specifies an array that has been previously defined in an ARRAY statement (see the description of ARRAY earlier in this chapter for details).

The DO OVER statement is equivalent to the statement

DO I = 1 TO K;

where I is the index variable of the array, and K is the number of elements in the array.

For example, consider this DATA step:

```
DATA FOUR;
  ARRAY F F1-F100;
  ARRAY C C1-C100;
  INPUT F1-F100;
  DO OVER F;
    C = (F-32)*5/9;
    END;
```

Each ARRAY statement defines an array with 100 elements. The INPUT statement reads elements for the F array. The function of the DO OVER group is to give the elements in the C array their values. The DO OVER statement here is equivalent to the statement

        DO __I__ = 1 TO 100;

Thus, either array name F or C could appear in the DO OVER statement, since both arrays have the same number of elements and the same index variable.

DO WHILE Statement

You can execute the statements in a DO group repetitively while a condition holds using the DO WHILE statement. The form of the DO WHILE statement is:

        DO WHILE(*expression*)**;**

where

> *expression*   is any numerically valued expression (see Chapter 4, "SAS Expressions" for details). The expression is evaluated at the top of the loop before the statements in the DO group are executed. If the expression is true, the DO group is executed.
>
> These statements repeat the loop as long as N is less than 5:
>
>   N=0;
>   DO WHILE(N LT 5);
>   PUT N=;
>   N+1;
>   END;
>
> See Chapter 6, "Data Step Applications," for additional examples of DO WHILE.

DO UNTIL Statement

The DO UNTIL statement, like the DO WHILE statement, executes the statements in a DO loop conditionally. The DO UNTIL evaluates the condition at the bottom of the loop rather than at the top (as DO WHILE). Thus, the statements between DO and END are always executed at least one time. The form of the DO UNTIL statement is:

        DO UNTIL(*expression*)**;**

where

> *expression*   is any numerically valued expression (see Chapter 4, "SAS Expressions" for details).
>
> The expression is evaluated at the bottom of the loop after the statements in the DO group have been executed. If the expression is true, the DO group is not executed again. The DO group is always executed at least once.

These statements repeat the loop until N is greater than or equal to 5:

```
N=0;
DO UNTIL(N >= 5);
  PUT N=;
  N+1;
END;
```

See Chapter 6, "Data Step Applications," for additional DO UNTIL examples.

DROP Statement

You can use the DROP statement in a DATA step to specify variables that are not to be included in the SAS data set or sets being created. A DROP statement in a DATA step applies to all the SAS data sets being created in the step. To selectively drop variables when multiple data sets are being created, use the DROP= data set option with each data set name. (See Chapter 12, "SAS Data Sets," for more information about data set options.)

Although variables appearing in a DROP statement are not included in any SAS data set being created, these variables can be used in program statements. The DROP statement may appear anywhere in the DATA step with the same effect since it is not an executable statement.

The form of the DROP statement is:

   DROP *variables*;

where

> *variables*   specifies the variables you want omitted from the data set(s) being created. Any form of variable list may be used (see Chapter 1 for details). Do not abbreviate the variable names.

Here is an example:

```
DATA PARTS;
   INPUT NAME $ PARTA PARTB;
   TEST = PARTA + PARTB;
   DROP PARTA PARTB;
   CARDS;
data lines
```

The variable TEST is computed for each observation by adding the values of PARTA and PARTB. The DROP statement tells SAS not to include the variables PARTA and PARTB in the new data set.

The effect of the DROP statement is the reverse of the KEEP statement's effect. To save writing, the DROP statement is preferred if fewer variables are being dropped than kept. Do not use both DROP and KEEP statements in the same DATA step.

When both RENAME and DROP statements are used in a DATA step, the DROP statement is applied first. This means that the old name should be used in the DROP statement.

END Statement

The END statement is the last of the SAS statements that make up a DO group. The form of the END statement is:

END;

An END statement must end every DO group in your SAS job. For example, a simple DO group is shown below:

DO;
  SAS statements
  END;

See the DO statement description earlier in this chapter for examples using END.

ERROR Statement

The ERROR statement prints a message on the SAS log and sets the automatic SAS variable __ERROR__ to 1. The action of the ERROR statement is equivalent to a PUT statement including a quoted string and another statement setting __ERROR__ to 1.

The form of the ERROR statement is like that of the PUT statement:

ERROR *message*;

where

> *message*   can include character literals, variable names, formats, and pointer controls just as those described in the PUT statement description later in this chapter.

When the value of __ERROR__ is 1, SAS writes the data lines corresponding to the current observation on the SAS log.

For example, these statements

```
DATA CHECK;
   INPUT TYPE $ AGE;
   IF TYPE='TEEN' & AGE>19 THEN
      ERROR 'TYPE AND AGE DON''T MATCH ' AGE=;
```

are equivalent to the statements

```
DATA CHECK;
   INPUT TYPE $ AGE;
   IF TYPE='TEEN' & AGE>19 THEN DO;
   PUT 'TYPE AND AGE DON''T MATCH ' AGE=;
   __ERROR__=1;
   END;
```

```
NOTE: THE DATA STATEMENT USED 0.86 SECONDS AND 292K.

6              DATA CHECK;
7                 INPUT TYPE $ AGE;
8                 IF TYPE='TEEN' & AGE>19 THEN
9                    ERROR 'TYPE AND AGE DON''T MATCH ' AGE=;
10                CARDS;

TYPE AND AGE DON'T MATCH AGE=25

RULE:     1234567 101234567 201234567 301234567 401234567 501234567 601234567 701234567 80

12         TEEN    25
TYPE=TEEN AGE=25 _ERROR_=1  _N_=2
NOTE: DATA SET WORK.CHECK HAS 3 OBSERVATIONS AND 2 VARIABLES. 953 OBS/TRK.
NOTE: THE DATA STATEMENT USED 0.88 SECONDS AND 292K.

14       ;
NOTE: SAS USED 292K MEMORY.

NOTE: SAS INSTITUTE INC.
      SAS CIRCLE
      PO BOX 8000
      CARY, N.C. 27511-8000
```

FILE Statement

The function of the FILE statement is to define the current output file. Lines produced by PUT statements executed later in the DATA step are written to this file.

In addition, options in the FILE statement may be used to set up variables where SAS puts the current line and column values of the pointer and the number of lines left on the current page. Other options specify the number of lines per page for printed reports, the number of columns per line, and a set of statements to be executed whenever printing of a new page begins.

More than one FILE statement may appear in a DATA step. PUT statements always write lines to the current output file, defined by the most recently executed FILE statement. The FILE statement is executable and therefore may appear in an IF-THEN statement.

The form of the FILE statement is:

FILE *filename* [*options*]**;**

where

filename	specifies the file to which the PUT statements are directed. The filename specified can be one of several forms:
DDname	gives a DDname defined in the control language. Control languages differ among installations and among operating systems, but a general description of the control language needed to describe files in OS batch and TSO, CMS, and VSE is given in the appendix for each system.
DDname (*membername*)	identifies a member of an OS partitioned data set where output is to be written. You must use a member name in addition to a DDname when the OS data set to which you are writing output is a partitioned data set and the member name into which you wish to write your data was not specified in the control language (DD statement for OS, ALLOCATE command for TSO) or, if one is, it is not the one you want.
	Using a member name on the FILE statement instead of in the control language for the job is useful when more than one member is to be stored on the same partitioned data set in different DATA steps of the SAS job. (Not valid under CMS or VSE.)
PRINT	specifies that the lines produced by PUT statements are to be printed on the standard SAS print file with the pages produced by SAS procedures. When PRINT is the FILE name, SAS uses carriage control characters and writes the lines with characteristics given below in **PRINT files and non-PRINT files.**
PUNCH	punches the lines produced by PUT statements on the standard SAS punch file (which is usually directed to cards).
LOG	prints the lines produced by PUT statements on the SAS log. Since this is the default action of SAS, the FILE LOG statement is only needed if another FILE

statement appears before it and you want to restore the default action, or if you need to specify any additional FILE statement options (see below).

At the beginning of each execution of a DATA step, SAS automatically sets the default FILE name to LOG. Thus, the first PUT statement in this DATA step always writes a line on the SAS log; the second PUT statement writes a line to the PRINT file:

```
DATA __NULL__;
    first PUT statement
    FILE PRINT;
    second PUT statement
    more SAS statements
```

options	specifies one or more file options from the list below:
HEADER=label	specifies a label to link to whenever SAS begins printing a new page. Label is a statement label that identifies the first statement in the group of statements. Put a RETURN statement before the HEADER= statement label and at the end of the statements to be executed. For example, consider this DATA step:

```
DATA __NULL__;
    SET SPRINT;
    BY DEPT;
    FILE PRINT HEADER=NEWPAGE;
    PUT @22 DEPT @34 SALES;
    RETURN;
NEWPAGE:
    PUT @ 20 'SALES FOR 1979' /
    @25 DEPT =;
    RETURN;
```

	The statements after the NEWPAGE label are executed whenever SAS begins printing a new page. Any SAS statements may be used here, and the PUT statements may include constants or variable names, making the HEADER= feature valuable for printing titles based on variable values.
NOTITLES NOTITLE	suppresses printing of the current TITLE lines on the pages of PRINT files—those where the file name is PRINT, or where the PRINT option appears in the FILE statement, or where the corresponding control language includes a SYSOUT= or "print" specification. When NOTITLES is omitted, SAS prints any titles currently defined. See Chapter 11, "SAS Statements Used Anywhere," for a complete description of the TITLE statement.
LINESLEFT=variable LL=variable	sets up a variable whose value is the number of lines left on the current page. For example, consider this DATA step:

```
DATA __NULL__;
   SET INFO;
   FILE PRINT LINESLEFT=L;
   PUT @10 NAME /
      @10 ADDRESS1 / @10 ADDRESS2 /
      @20 PHONE //;
   IF L<7 THEN PUT __PAGE__@;
```

In this example, if there are fewer than seven lines
left on the page, PUT __PAGE__ @; tells SAS to begin
a new page and remain on the first line for printing.

LINE=*variable*   sets up a variable whose value is the current line location of the pointer. SAS automatically assigns the cur-
rent line location of the pointer to this variable.

COLUMN=*variable*   sets up a variable whose value is the current column
location of the pointer. SAS automatically assigns the
current column location to the COLUMN= variable.

MOD   writes the output lines after any existing lines on the
file. If MOD is specified, it overrides the disposition
specified in the control language. (Under VSE, the
MOD option cannot be used. Lines are always written
at the beginning of the file.)

N=PS   gives the number of output lines available to the
N=PAGESIZE   pointer. When the value of N is 1, SAS writes each
N=*value*   line before it begins the next. When N=3, for example, you can move the pointer from line 1 to line 3
and back to line 1; the three lines are available to the
pointer until a PUT __PAGE__ appears or until you
move the pointer to line 4.

For PRINT files, N must equal 1 or the characters
PAGESIZE or PS. The default value of N is 1.

When N=PS is specified, you can format pages
completely before writing them. For example, you can
use the job below to produce a four-column
telephone book listing; each column contains a name
and a phone number.

```
DATA __NULL__;
   FILE PRINT N=PS;
   DO C=1 TO 91 BY 30;
      DO L=1 TO 50;
         SET PHONE;
         PUT #L @C NAME $20. +1 PHONE $8;
      END;
   END;
   PUT __PAGE__ @;
```

The N=PS option in the FILE statement sets up the
page to be formatted. The L and C variables mark the
current line and column of the pointer. The PUT
statement writes the NAME and PHONE values on the
current line (the L value) at the current column (the C
value). L's value is incremented by 1 until fifty names
are printed.

When the inner DO loop is satisfied, the column value is incremented by 30 to move the pointer over to the second column, and fifty more names are printed in that column. When the outer DO loop is satisfied, the report includes four columns of fifty names each.

When the last value in the last column has been written, the PUT __PAGE__ @ ; is executed to write the entire page, and the C and L values begin at 1 again.

OLD writes the output lines at the beginning of the file. Using OLD is only necessary if you used MOD for the file in an earlier SAS DATA step and now want to return to the default, OLD. (Not valid under VSE, where lines are always written at the beginning of the file.)

PAGESIZE=*value* sets the number of lines per page for your reports. SAS
PS=*value* keeps track of the number of lines printed for each page; after the *n*th line is printed, where *n* is the PAGESIZE= value, SAS starts a new page.

The value may range from 20 to 500. If no value is specified, SAS uses the value of the system option PAGESIZE=. See the OPTIONS statement in Chapter 11, "SAS Statements Used Anywhere," for more information.

For files with the PRINT attribute, if any TITLE statements are currently defined, the lines they occupy are included in counting the number of lines for each page.

LINESIZE=*value* sets the number of columns per line for your reports.
LS=*value* The default LINESIZE value is the current value of the system option LINESIZE. The maximum linesize value that can be specified is 255. See the OPTIONS statement in Chapter 11, "SAS Statements Used Anywhere," for more information.

PRINT produces a printed report in which carriage control characters appear in column 1 of the output lines. The PRINT option is only needed when you are using a FILE name other than PRINT and your control language does not include a SYSOUT= or "print" specification; for example, if you are producing a report on tape for microfiche.

NOPRINT suppresses printing of the carriage control characters in column 1 of the output lines for a PRINT file. The most frequent use of the NOPRINT option is in printing a file that already contains these carriage control characters in column 1.

For example, say that you used a text-editing program to produce formatted pages that were written to disk. You could use these statements to print the pages:

```
DATA __NULL__;
  INFILE FORMAT;
  INPUT;
  FILE PRINT NOPRINT;
  PUT __INFILE__;
```

RECFM= *recordformat*

is a JCL-like parameter that gives the record format of the output file. Values allowed are F, FB, V, VB, U, and except under VSE, VBS may be specified. An A or M value may be included in any of these; each may end in T. Under VSE, if RECFM= is not specified in the FILE statement, the default value of FB is used. In other systems, if the RECFM= parameter appears in the control language describing the file, it is not needed in the FILE statement. Should a RECFM= value appear in both the control language and the FILE statement, the value in the FILE statement is used. The default RECFM value for non-PRINT files is FB.

When RECFM=V, VB, or U, each record's length is determined by the highest column written. For example, the statements

```
DATA;
  Z=77;
  FILE OUT RECFM=V;
  PUT @51 '*' @20 Z;
```

write a record of length 55. (Four bytes of length information are automatically added to the beginning of the record.)

LRECL=*lrecl*

is a JCL-like parameter that gives the logical record length of the output file. If LRECL appears in the control language describing the file, it is not needed in the FILE statement. If LRECL values appear in both the control language and the FILE statement, the value in the FILE statement is used. Under VSE, LRECL= cannot be specified in the control language. The default LRECL for non-PRINT files is 80.

BLKSIZE=*blksize*
BLK=*blksize*

is a JCL-like parameter that gives the block size of the output file. If BLKSIZE= appears in the control language describing the file, it is not needed in the FILE statement. If BLKSIZE values appear in both the control language and the FILE statement, the value in the FILE statement is used. Under VSE, BLKSIZE= may not be specified in the control language. The default BLKSIZE for non-PRINT files is the smaller of the value of the SAS system option FILEBLKSIZE(*device*) or the maximum blocksize for the output device, rounded down to a multiple of 80.

DCB=*DDname*

gives the DDname of a file appearing in an earlier FILE or INFILE statement in the same DATA step. SAS uses the file's DCB information for the file described in the FILE statement.

The options below, which are described with the INFILE statement, may also be used in the FILE statement except under VSE:

CLOSE=*volumepositioning*
DEVTYPE=*variable*
DSCB=*variable*
JFCB=*variable*
UCBNAME=*variable*
VOLUME(S)=*variable*

Print files and non-PRINT files   The print file contains ASA carriage control characters in column 1 of each line. These characters direct the line printer to skip 1, 2, or 3 lines; to begin a new page; or to overprint the preceding line. A file that will be printed on a line printer needs these characters, which are automatically inserted by SAS in the first column of PRINT files that it produces.

The ASA characters used by SAS are:

blank	skips one line
0	skips two lines
minus (−)	skips three lines
1	begins a new page
plus (+)	overprints the preceding line.

Non-PRINT files do not contain carriage control characters; column 1 of records in non-PRINT files contains whatever data were written there by the program that produced the records.

SAS automatically produces PRINT files when PRINT is specified as the FILE name, when the PRINT option appears in the FILE statement, when the DD statement for the file includes a SYSOUT= or "print" specification, or, in VSE, when the logical unit specified as part of the DDname is assigned to a virtual or real printer. These PRINT files have the default DCB characteristics RECFM=VBA, LRECL=137, and BLKSIZE=141.

Non-PRINT files have the default characteristics RECFM=FB, LRECL=80, and BLKSIZE= the value of the SAS system option FILEBLKSIZE(*device*) appropriate for the output device on which the file is being written.

FORMAT Statement

You can use the FORMAT statement to associate output formats with variables in a DATA step. Output formats may be either SAS formats or formats you have defined with PROC FORMAT. If you want to give the same output format to several variables or different formats to different variables, you can do it with one FORMAT statement. When SAS prints values of the variables, it uses the associated format to print the values.

You can associate output formats with variables with the statement

> **FORMAT** *variables [format]* ... ;

These terms are included in the FORMAT statement:

variables names the variable or variables you want to associate with an output format.

format gives the output format you want SAS to use for writing values of the variable or variables in the previous variable list. Every format name ends with a period (for example, SEXFMT.) or has a period between the width value and number of decimal places (for example, DOLLAR8.2).

See Chapter 13, "SAS Informats and Formats," for more information on the types of SAS formats that are available. See the FORMAT procedure for information on how to define your own output formats.

If a variable appears in more than one FORMAT statement, the output format given in the last FORMAT statement is used. A FORMAT statement used in a DATA step to associate one format with a variable can be overridden by a FORMAT statement in a later PROC step. The original format name remains stored with the variable in the data set. To disassociate a format from a variable, use the variable's name in a FORMAT statement with no format.

If you have used the FORMAT procedure to define your own formats, you need a FORMAT statement to associate the format with one or more variables:

```
PROC FORMAT;
   VALUE SEXFMT  1 = MALE
                 2 = FEMALE;
DATA ALL;
   INPUT NAME $ SEX@@;
   FORMAT SEX SEXFMT.;
   CARDS;
JANE 2 BILL 1
more data lines
```

The FORMAT procedure defines the SEXFMT. format. The FORMAT statement in the DATA step associates SEXFMT. with the variable SEX. When the values of SEX are printed by any procedure, MALE and FEMALE are printed instead of the numbers 1 and 2.

When a FORMAT statement associating a variable or variables with an output format is used in a DATA step, SAS associates the specified format with the variables in the SAS data sets being created and uses the format for printing values of the variables. The format name is stored with the data set. (Note: for permanantly stored SAS data sets, if you associate a user-defined format with a variable, the format must be accessible when the data set is referenced even if you will not be printing the variable's values. See the FORMAT procedure description for more information.)

When a variable that has been associated with a format in a FORMAT statement later appears in a PUT statement without a format specification, the variable's values are left-aligned in the output field with leading blanks trimmed.

Using FORMAT for Datetime Values

If you read date, time, or datetime values with an INPUT statement, you must assign them a corresponding date, time, or datetime format in a FORMAT statement in order for the values to be printed in an understandable form. For example, consider this DATA step:

```
DATA INVENTRY;
   INPUT DESCRIPT $20. ACQUIRED DATE7.;
   FORMAT ACQUIRED WORDDATE.;
   CARDS;
 data lines
 ;
```

The FORMAT statement associates the format WORDDATE. with the variable ACQUIRED, which contains SAS date values. Without the FORMAT statement, values of ACQUIRED are printed as the number of days between January 1, 1960 and the ACQUIRED date, a large number that is difficult to interpret. See Chapter 13, "SAS Informats and Formats," for more information on date, time, and datetime formats.

GO TO Statement

A GO TO (or GOTO) statement tells SAS to jump immediately to another statement in the same DATA step and begin executing statements from that point. The statement has the form:

GO TO *label*;
GOTO *label*;

The label is specified on the GO TO statement:

label   identifies the GO TO destination, which must be within the same DATA step. See **Labels, Statement** listed alphabetically later in this chapter for more information.

GO TO statements usually appear as the THEN clause in IF-THEN statements. In the example below, SAS jumps over the assignment statement to the OK label when X is between 1 and 5.

```
DATA INFO;
  INPUT X Y;
  IF 1<=X<=5 THEN GO TO OK;
  X=3; COUNT+1;
OK:SUMX+X;
  CARDS;
data lines
;
```

In the example above, the labeled statement is executed for every observation. Sometimes you want a labeled statement to be executed only under certain conditions. For example,

```
DATA RECORD;
  INPUT X Y Z;
  IF 1<=X<=5 THEN GO TO  OK;
  X=3;   COUNT+1;
  RETURN;
OK:SUMX+X;
  CARDS;
data lines
;
```

The statement

```
  SUMX+X;
```

is executed only for observations with X values between one and five. When the RETURN statement is executed, SAS outputs the current observation to data set RECORD and returns to the beginning of the DATA step and a new execution. GO TO statements can often be replaced by DO-END statements. For example, using DO-END in the first example above results in:

```
DATA INFO;
  INPUT X Y;
  IF X<1 OR X>5 THEN DO;
  X=3;
  COUNT+1;
  END;
  SUM+X;
```

The second example above with DO-END and IF-THEN-ELSE is:

```
DATA RECORD;
  INPUT X Y Z;
  IF X<1 OR X>5 THEN DO;
  X=3;
  COUNT+1;
  END;
  ELSE SUMX+X;
```

See the discussion of the RETURN statement later in this chapter and Chapter 6, "Data Step Applications," for other examples using GOTO.

IF Statement

In SAS there are two kinds of IF statements:

- conditional IF statements, written with a THEN clause, are used to conditionally execute a SAS statement. An optional ELSE statement gives an alternative action if the THEN clause is not executed.
- subsetting IF statements, with no THEN clause, are used to subset observations or records.

IF-THEN and IF-THEN/ELSE Statements

Use the IF-THEN statement when you want to execute a SAS statement for some but not all of the observations in the data set being created. SAS evaluates the expression following the IF. When the expression is true for the observation being processed (is nonzero and nonmissing), the statement following THEN is executed. When the expression is false (zero or missing), SAS ignores the statement following THEN and executes the ELSE statement immediately following the IF. If no ELSE statement is present, SAS executes the next program statement.

The form of the IF-THEN statement is:

IF *expression* **THEN** *statement*;

where

    expression   is any valid SAS expression. See Chapter 4, ''SAS Expressions,'' for the way SAS evaluates expressions.

    statement   may be any executable SAS statement or DO group. These statements are executable SAS statements: ABORT, assignment, DELETE, DO, ERROR, FILE, GO TO, IF-THEN, INPUT, INFILE, LINK, LIST, LOSTCARD, MERGE, OUTPUT, PUT, null, sum, RETURN, SET, STOP, and UPDATE.

For example, the statement

  IF YEAR = 1976 THEN COLOR = 'BLUE';

assigns the value 'BLUE' to a variable named COLOR when the value of YEAR is 1976.

The ELSE statement can immediately follow an IF-THEN statement to specify a statement that is to be executed when the condition of the IF is false.

The form of the ELSE statement is:

ELSE *statement*;

where

    statement   is any executable SAS statement or DO group as described above.

These statements:

  IF YEAR = 1976 THEN COLOR = 'BLUE';
    ELSE COLOR = 'RED';

assign 'RED' to the variable COLOR when the value of year is not 1976.

Here are some other examples of IF-THEN/ELSE statements:

```
IF RESPONSE = . THEN DELETE;

IF STATE = 'CA' OR STATE = 'OR'
   THEN REGION = 'PACIFIC COAST
ELSE IF STATE = 'NC' OR STATE = 'VA' OR STATE = 'MD'
   THEN REGION = 'MID ATLANTIC COAST';
```

IF-THEN/ELSE statements may be nested, as in this example:

```
IF X=0 THEN IF Y¬=0 THEN PUT 'X ZERO, Y NONZERO';
ELSE PUT 'X ZERO, Y ZERO';
ELSE PUT 'X NONZERO';
```

To execute more than one statement for a true condition, follow THEN with a DO group:

```
IF ANSWER=9 THEN DO;
  ANSWER = .;
  PUT 'INVALID ANSWER FOR ' ID=;
  END;
ELSE OUTPUT VALID;
```

See the DO statement description earlier in this chapter for more information.

Subsetting IF Statement

A subsetting IF statement is used to subset observations from the file or data set being used as input to a DATA step.

The form of the subsetting IF is:

IF *expression***;**

where

> *expression*   is any valid SAS expression. The expression should conform to the general rules for expressions given in Chapter 4.

If the expression is true (is nonzero and nonmissing), SAS continues executing statements in the DATA step for the observation it is building. If the expression is false (0 or missing), SAS immediately returns to the beginning of the DATA step for another execution without outputting the observation. The remaining program statements in the DATA step are not executed.

For example, the statement

```
IF SEX = 'F';
```

results in a data set containing only observations with a SEX value of 'F'.

Here is an example of using subsetting IF statements to produce new data sets that are subsets of an original data set.

```
DATA POPULACE;
  INPUT NAME $ SEX $ AGE MARITAL $;
  CARDS;
data lines
```

```
DATA SENIORS;
  SET POPULACE;
  IF AGE >=65;
DATA WIVES;
  SET POPULACE;
  IF SEX='F' AND MARITAL='M';
```

Data set SENIORS contains only those observations from POPULACE with an AGE value of 65 or greater. The data set WIVES contains those observations for which the SEX value is 'F' and the MARITAL value is 'M'.

INFILE Statement

An INFILE statement identifies a non-SAS file on disk, tape, cards, or terminal containing input data to be read with an INPUT statement. If your data are stored on disk or tape in a SAS data set, you do not need an INFILE statement; use a SET, MERGE, or UPDATE statement to work further with the data set or go directly to a SAS procedure.

Using INFILE options you can

- define variables whose values reflect the current pointer location, the length of the last line read, or whether the current line is the last in the file
- define what happens when the pointer reaches past the end of the current line
- restrict processing of the file by skipping lines at either the beginning or end of the file or both
- define the number of columns containing data in the input lines—useful for line-numbered files such as those edited under TSO.

Examples You have a file on disk containing raw data that you want SAS to read and put into a SAS data set. You must define the file in the control language of your job with a command similar to one of the following:

OS batch

    //GREEN DD DSN = P.ALGAE,DISP = SHR

TSO

    ALLOC FI(GREEN) DA('P.ALGAE') SHR

CMS

    FILEDEF GREEN DISK P ALGAE A

VSE

    // DLBL GREEN30,'P.ALGAE'
    // EXTENT SYS030,ABC123
    // ASSGN SYS030,DISK,VOL = ABC123,SHR

The SAS statements you need to create your SAS data set from raw data (except in VSE) are

    DATA FARM;
      INFILE GREEN;
      INPUT...;
    other SAS statements

Under VSE, the INFILE statement could be:

    INFILE GREEN30 RECFM = FB LRECL = 100 BLKSIZE = 4000;

The INFILE statement gives the DDname of the file containing the input data. SAS looks for a corresponding name in the control language for the job, and then reads the data from the file described in the DD statement, the ALLOCATE or FILEDEF command, or the VSE DLBL, EXTENT, and ASSGN statements.

Where the INFILE statement goes The INFILE statement must be executed before the INPUT statement that reads the data lines. In the INFILE statement, DDname is the DDname used in the control language for the job to describe the file containing the data lines that you want to read. Control languages differ among installations and among operating systems, but a general description of the control language needed to describe files in OS batch, TSO, CMS, and VSE is given in the appendix for each system.

Types of files SAS can read Under OS or CMS, the DDname given in the INFILE statement can be that of a sequential file (DSORG=PS), a BDAM file (DSORG=DA), a VSAM file (AMP=('AMORG')), a partitioned data set (DSORG=PO) or under OS only, an ISAM file (DSORG=IS). ISAM, BDAM, and VSAM files are read sequentially. Random-access processing of VSAM data sets is also possible and is discussed in a SAS Technical Report.
  Under VSE, the files must be sequential or VSAM files.
  The INFILE statement has this form:

> **INFILE** *DDname* [*(member)*]|**CARDS** [*options*]...;

where

DDname	specifies the DDname of the file to be read. The file must be defined using the same DDname in the control language for the job.
member	specifies the member name in parentheses when the input file is a partitioned data set (not valid in VSE). The member name may be specified after the DDname in the INFILE statement, or in OS, in the DD statement defining the file in the job control language.
CARDS	specifies that the data to be read appear after a CARDS statement in the SAS job. This is only needed when you want to take advantage of the INFILE statement options and your data are on cards or entered at a terminal with your SAS statements. In this case, you must use both an INFILE statement and a CARDS statement: substitute the word CARDS for the DDname in the INFILE statement:

> DATA EXAM;
>   INFILE CARDS;
>   INPUT...;
>   *other SAS statements*
>   CARDS;
> *data lines*
> ;

options	specifies one or more INFILE statement options from the list below:

Options for reading any input record

BLKSIZE=	specifies the block size.
CLOSE=	tells SAS the close disposition to use for the file (not valid under CMS and VSE).

COLUMN=	gives the column location of the input pointer.
DCB=	specifies the DDname of a file whose DCB information you want SAS to use.
END=	tells when you are processing the last record in the input file.
EOF=	tells SAS to jump to a labeled statement when it is processing the last record in the file.
EOV=	tells when you are at the last of a file in a series of concatenated files (not applicable under CMS or VSE).
FIRSTOBS=	specifies which record in the file to begin with.
LENGTH=	gives the length in bytes of the current input line.
LINE=	gives the line location of the input pointer.
LINESIZE=	specifies the number of columns to read for each record.
LRECL=	specifies the logical record length.
MISSOVER	tells SAS to assign missing values to all variables included in the INPUT statement that do not appear on the data line.
N=	specifies the number of data lines available to the pointer.
OBS=	specifies which record in the file to end with.
RECFM=	specifies the record format.
START=	specifies which column of each record to start using with PUT __INFILE__;.
STOPOVER	tells SAS to stop the DATA step if it encounters a record that does not contain all the expected values.
UNBUFFERED	tells SAS not to look ahead to the next record (as it normally does.)

Options for reading the VTOC of an OS disk volume

CCHHR=	returns the cylinder-head-record address of each DSCB read.
CVAF	allows compatible processing of OS/VS indexed VTOCs.
VTOC	reads the VTOC of a direct-access volume.

Options for OS control block information

DEVTYPE=	returns the device type information from the DEVTYPE macro.
DSCB=	returns the DSCB of a non-VSAM disk data set.
JFCB=	returns the job file control block (JFCB) for the DD statement.
UCBNAME=	returns the unit name (device address) field from the unit control block (UCB).
VOLUME(S)=	returns volume serials from the JFCB.

Options for reading a VSAM data set

BACKWARD	tells SAS to read a VSAM data set backwards.
BUFND=	gives the number of data buffers for the VSAM file.
BUFNI=	gives the number of index buffers for the VSAM file.

CONTROLINTERVAL	reads physical VSAM control intervals rather than logical records.
READPW=	gives a read-access password.
RECORDS=	returns the number of logical records in the data component of the VSAM cluster.
VSAM	tells SAS that the file is a VSAM file.

All of the INFILE statement options are described below in alphabetical order.

BACKWARD BKWD	tells SAS to read a VSAM data set backwards. BACKWARD is valid only when the VSAM data set is read sequentially.
BLKSIZE=*blocksize*	specifies the block size for the file if your input lines are on a non-labeled file. You do not need to specify the BLKSIZE in both your control language and in the INFILE statement; if it appears in both places, the value in the INFILE statement is used. Under VSE, except for VSAM files, BLKSIZE **must** be specified in the INFILE statement. If not specified elsewhere, the default BLKSIZE is the maximum permitted blocksize for the device.
BUFND=*integer*	gives the number of data buffers for a VSAM input file. The BUFND= option may also be specified in the control language defining the VSAM data set. If BUFND= is not specified, VSAM provides a default value. For sequential processing, two data buffers are usually sufficient.
BUFNI=*integer*	gives the number of index buffers for a VSAM input file. The BUFNI= option may also be specified in the control language defining the VSAM data set. If BUFNI= is not specified, VSAM provides a default value. For sequential processing, one index buffer is usually sufficient.
CCHHR=*variable*	returns the cylinder-head-record address of each record read from the VTOC data set. (Not a valid option under CMS or VSE.) This option is used only in conjunction with the VTOC option (see below) on OS systems.
CLOSE= *keyword*	indicates the volume positioning to be performed at the end of the DATA step for the data set you are reading. These values may be specified:
keyword	*access mechanism positioning*
REREAD	logical beginning of the data set
LEAVE	logical end of the data set
REWIND	physical beginning of volume
FREE	dynamically deallocate (MVS only)
DISP	as implied by the control language
	(Not a valid option under CMS or VSE.)
COLUMN=*variable* COL=*variable*	keeps track of the pointer's value. You can define a variable whose value will be the column location of the pointer. For example, these statements

```
DATA;
   INFILE A COLUMN=C;
   INPUT @5 X 3.;
   PUT C=;
```

produce the line

```
C=8
```

CONTROLINTERVAL
CTLINTV
CNV
reads physical VSAM control intervals rather than logical records. If CONTROLINTERVAL is specified and the data set is VSAM password-protected, then a control interval access password must be specified by the READPW= option. Control interval access is typically used only for diagnostic applications or for reading a VSAM catalog.

CVAF
reads the volume table of contents (VTOC) of the direct-access volume identified by the DDname given in the INFILE statement. This option causes SAS to attempt to use the Common VTOC Access Facility (CVAF) of the IBM program product Data Facility/Device Support (DF/DS) for indexed VTOCs. On systems without DF/DS and for unindexed VTOCs, the CVAF option is treated as if the VTOC option is specified.

Format five data set control blocks (DSCBs) are constructed from information in the VTOC space map. The CCHHR data for these format five DSCBs and the pointer to the next available format five DSCB (DS5PTRDS) are not valid.

DCB=DDname
specifies the DDname of an input file used earlier in the same DATA step whose DCB attributes you want to use for the current input file. (Not a valid option under VSE.)

DEVTYPE=variable
defines a character variable of length greater than or equal to 24, whose value is the device type information from the DEVTYPE macro. You can use DEVTYPE= to access control block information both initially and at DD statement concatenation boundaries. The EOV= variable described below is set to 1 when a concatenation switch occurs, indicating that new information has been placed in the DEVTYPE= variable. (Not a valid VSE option.)

DSCB=variable
defines a character variable of length greater than or equal to 140 whose value will be the Data Set Control Block (DSCB) information from a non-VSAM disk data set. The DSCB= option lets you access control block information both initially and at DD statement concatenation boundaries. The variable defined with the EOV= option, described below, is set to 1 when a concatenation switch occurs, indicating that the DSCB= variable contains new information. (Not a valid option under VSE.)

END=variable name
defines a variable whose value is set to 1 when the current line is the last in the input file; the value is in-

initially set to 0 for all other lines in the input file. Do not use the END= option for UNBUFFERED files or for files allocated to your terminal.

EOF=*label* specifies a statement label that is the object of an implicit GO TO when the INFILE statement reaches end-of-file. SAS jumps to the labeled statement when it tries to execute the INPUT statement that will fail because there are no more data in the file. EOF= (and not END=) should be used for UNBUFFERED files, and is recommended in DATA steps that contain multiple INPUT statements, INPUT statements that read more than one data line at a time, or INPUT statements that are executed conditionally.

In the statements below, the EOF= option used on the first INFILE statement tells SAS to go to the statement labeled NEXT when there are no more data in INFILE INPUT1; EOF=LAST tells SAS to go to the statement labeled LAST when INFILE INPUT2 has no more data.

```
DATA;
  INFILE INPUT1 EOF=NEXT;
  INPUT ...;
  RETURN;
NEXT: INFILE INPUT2 EOF=LAST;
  INPUT ...;
  RETURN;
LAST: INFILE INPUT3;
  INPUT ...;
```

EOV=*variable* defines a variable whose value is set to 1 at the end of each DD statement in a series of concatenated files. Like END=, EOV= is not automatically reset to 0 after SAS encounters the first boundary; your program must reset EOV=. (EOV= is not a valid option under CMS or VSE.)

FIRSTOBS= begins processing your file with a record other than
line number the first. You can use the FIRSTOBS= option to specify the number of the first line to be read. For example, if you want to begin processing with record 100, this INFILE statement might be used:

INFILE D FIRSTOBS=100;

JFCB=*variable* defines a character variable of length 176 or greater into which job file control block (JFCB) information is placed. The JFCB= option makes it possible to access OS control block information initially and at DD statement concatenation boundaries. The EOV= variable described above is set to 1 when a concatenation switch occurs, indicating that new information has been placed in the JFCB= variable. (Not a valid option under VSE.)

LENGTH= defines a variable name whose value will contain the
variable name length of the current line.

For variable-length records, the 4-byte length descriptor (RDW) is not included in the length value.

For undefined-length records, the length value is the length of the current block.

You can reset the value of the LENGTH= variable in programming statements. This can be useful if you are copying the input file to another file with PUT __INFILE__; you can use the LENGTH= option to truncate the copied records. For example, the statements below truncate the last 20 columns from the input lines before they are copied to the output file:

```
DATA;
   INFILE TAPE LENGTH=L;
   INPUT;
   L=L-20;
   FILE TAPEOUT;
   PUT __INFILE__;
```

LINE=*variable*   keeps track of the pointer's line location by defining a variable whose value will be the line location of the pointer. For example, the statements

```
DATA;
   INFILE B LINE=L;
   INPUT NAME 1-10 #2 ID 3-5;
   PUT L=;
```

produce the line

```
L=2  .
```

LINESIZE=*linesize*   gives the number of columns to be read for each
LS=*linesize*   record if your data include sequence numbers in the last columns of each line, or other information that you do not want the INPUT statement to read.

For example, say that your data lines contain a sequence number in columns 73 through 80. You could use the INFILE statement

```
INFILE C LINESIZE=72;
```

to restrict the INPUT statement to the first 72 columns of the lines.

LRECL=   specifies the logical record length if your input lines
logical record length   are on a non-labeled file. You do not need to specify the LRECL both in the control language and in the INFILE statement; if it appears in both places, the value in the INFILE statement is used. Under VSE, except for VSAM files, LRECL **must** be specified in the INFILE statement. If not specified elsewhere, the default depends upon the values specified (or defaulted) for BLKSIZE= and RECFM=.

MISSOVER   is used to prevent SAS from going to a new input line if it does not find values for all the variables specified in the INPUT statement in the current line. All values of variables not found are set to missing.

For example, say you are reading temperature data. Each input line contains from 1 to 5 temperatures:

```
DATA WEATHER;
  INFILE CARDS MISSOVER;
  INPUT TEMP1-TEMP5;
  CARDS;
97.9 98.1 98.3
98.6 99.2 99.1 98.5 97.5
;
```

SAS reads the three values on the first data line as values of TEMP1, TEMP2, and TEMP3. Then SAS sets the values of TEMP4 and TEMP5 to missing values for that observation, since MISSOVER appears in the INFILE statement and since no more values appear on that data line.

If MISSOVER does not appear, SAS goes to the second data line for the TEMP4 and TEMP5 values, printing the message

NOTE: SAS WENT TO A NEW LINE WHEN INPUT STATEMENT REACHED PAST THE END OF A LINE.

SAS reads data line 3 the next time it executes the INPUT statement.

N=*number of lines*   defines the number of lines available to the pointer.
When the N= option is omitted, the number of lines available to the pointer is the highest value following a # pointer direction in any INPUT statement in the DATA step. If no # directions are used, N's value is 1. The only time that you need to specify the N= option is when you are reading a variable number of lines per observation and you do not use # pointer direction. The N value has no effect on the number of lines read with an INPUT statement; only on the number of lines that the pointer can access at any given time.

OBS=*line number*   specifies the last line to be read from the input file. This option is especially useful when you want to test your SAS program using just a few of the records in your file. For example, say you want to process only the first 100 records in the file:

INFILE INB OBS=100;

You can use the OBS= and the FIRSTOBS= options together when you want to read records from the middle of your file. For example, say that you want to begin processing with record 100 and end with record 200:

INFILE IN2 FIRSTOBS=100 OBS=200;

READPW=*password*   gives a read-access password for the VSAM data set being read. Any level password may be specified. READPW= is required if the VSAM component or cluster and its catalog are both VSAM password-protected.

RECFM=
record format

specifies the record format for a file if your input lines are on a non-labeled file. You do not need to specify the RECFM value in the INFILE statement if it also appears in the control language defining the input file; when it appears in both places, the value in the INFILE statement is used. Under VSE, except for VSAM files, RECFM **must** be specified in the INFILE statement. If not specified elsewhere, the default RECFM is U (for OS and CMS) or F (for VSE).

RECORDS=
variable name

defines a variable whose value will be set by SAS to the number of logical records in the data component of the VSAM cluster being read.

START=
variable name

defines the starting column PUT __INFILE__ by giving that value to the variable name following the START= option.

For example, say that you are making a copy of the file TAPE, but you do not want the first 10 columns of the records copied. These statements copy only columns 11–80:

```
DATA;
   INFILE TAPE START=S;
   INPUT;
   S=11;
   FILE TAPEOUT;
   PUT __INFILE__;
```

STOPOVER

stops processing if SAS encounters an input line that does not contain the expected number of values.

When your INFILE statement includes the word STOPOVER, SAS sets __ERROR__ to 1 if an INPUT statement reaches past the end of a line. SAS then stops building the data set as though a STOP statement had been executed and prints the incomplete data line. Here is an example:

```
DATA;
   INFILE CARDS STOPOVER;
   INPUT X1–X4;
   CARDS;
1 2 3
5 6 7 8
;
```

When SAS reads the first data line, it does not find an X4 value. Since STOPOVER is specified in the INFILE statement, SAS sets __ERROR__ to 1, prints data line 1, and stops building the data set.

If STOPOVER does not appear in the INFILE statement, SAS prints the message

NOTE: SAS WENT TO A NEW LINE WHEN INPUT STATEMENT REACHED PAST THE END OF A LINE

and goes to line 2 and reads 5 as the value of X4. Then, since this INPUT statement reads a new line

each time it is executed, SAS reads line 3 the next
time it executes the INPUT statement.

UCBNAME=*variable*   defines a character variable of length greater than or
equal to 3, whose value is the unit name (device ad-
dress) from the OS unit control block (UCB) or CMS
active device table. You can use UCBNAME= to access control block information both initially and at DD
statement concatenation boundaries. The EOV=
variable described above is set to 1 when a concatenation switch occurs, indicating that new information has
been placed in the UCBNAME= variable. (Not a valid
VSE option.)

UNBUFFERED   tells SAS not to perform a look-ahead read. When
UNBUF   UNBUFFERED appears, the END= variable is never set
to 1. (TSO and CMS terminal data sets are automatically UNBUFFERED.)

VOLUME=*variable*   defines a character variable of length greater than or
VOLUMES=*variable*   equal to 6, whose value is (up to 5) volume serials
from the job file control block (JFCB). You can access
control block information both initially and at DD
statement concatenation boundaries. The EOV=
variable described above is set to 1 when a concatenation switch occurs, indicating that new information has
been placed in the VOLUME= variable. (Not a valid
option under VSE.)

VSAM   tells SAS that the DDname specified on the INFILE
statement defines a VSAM cluster or component. The
VSAM option is normally not necessary. However, you
must specify the VSAM option in four situations:

1. when you are executing SAS in TSO on OS/VS2
Release 1.X (SVS), and the VSAM data set was
dynamically allocated with the ALLOCATE command
rather than defined by a DD statement in your TSO
LOGON cataloged procedure.
2. when you have bypassed the VSAM catalog to
determine the volume location of the VSAM component or cluster. Instead of specifying the VSAM option
in this case, you may code the AMP=('AMORG')
parameter in the control language defining the VSAM
component or cluster.
3. when you are reading a VSAM file under VSE.
4. when you are reading a VSAM file under CMS.

VTOC   reads the volume table of contents (VTOC) for the
direct-access volume identified by the DDname given
in the INFILE statement. If a data set name appears in
the control language, SAS ignores it. (VTOC is not a
valid option under CMS or VSE.) This option may be
restricted by your installation.

INFORMAT Statement

The INFORMAT statement associates informats with variables. It can be used in a DATA step to specify a default informat for variables listed in an INPUT statement and in PROC EDITOR to specify informats for variables. (The INFORMAT statement is also used to create data sets with no observations for the FSEDIT procedure.)

You can associate informats with variables by using the statement

    INFORMAT *variable [informat]* ...;

These terms are included in the INFORMAT statement:

    variable   names the variable or variables you want to associate with an informat.

    informat   gives the informat you want SAS to use for reading values of the variable or variables in the previous variable list. When an informat is specified in an INFORMAT statement, only the informat type (RB, IB, $, and so on) is used. Every informat name ends with a period (for example, $15.) or has a period between the width value and number of decimal places (for example, 8.2). For character variables, this specified width determines the length of the variable; any decimal specification is ignored. All the informats described in Chapter 13, ''SAS Informats and Formats,'' may be used.

When you use an INFORMAT statement to associate an input format with a variable and then use the variable's name without a format in an INPUT statement, SAS reads the value using list input mode (described with the INPUT statement later in this chapter).

For example, these statements

    INFORMAT FRSTNAME LASTNAME $15.;
    INPUT FRSTNAME LASTNAME;

are equivalent to the statement

    INPUT FRSTNAME : $15. LASTNAME : $15.;

The colon format modifier (:) is described with the INPUT statement later in this chapter.

INPUT Statement

The INPUT statement reads values into variables from input data lines. INPUT is a flexible, and at the same time a complex, SAS statement. When the data values are arranged in a simple way, the INPUT statement will also be simple. When the data values are arranged in a complex way, you may need some of the INPUT statement's advanced features.

You can define your input in an INPUT statement in three basic styles: column input, list or free-format input, and formatted input. (One other special input style called named input is available for a special kind of data.)

The simple INPUT statements below use the three input styles to read AGE, a numeric variable, and NAME, a character ($) variable:

Column input

   INPUT NAME $ 1–8 AGE 11–12;

List input

   INPUT NAME $ AGE;

Formatted input

   INPUT NAME $CHAR11. AGE 2.;

You can read one variable with one input style and the other variable with another input style (for example, NAME with column input and AGE with formatted input):

   INPUT NAME $ 1–10 AGE 2.;

You can also point to where you want SAS to read your data values. For example,

   INPUT @1 NAME $ @11 AGE 2.;

tells SAS to go to column 1 and read a NAME value, then to column 11 to read AGE.

Standard display forms for data   All three styles of input support a standard form for (displayable) numeric and character data. Only formatted input supports special (non-displayable) forms of data.

A character value is simply a sequence of characters. The only characters that may cause trouble are semicolon (for CARDS infiles) and blanks (for LIST input). Leading blanks are trimmed from a character value before it is moved to a variable.

A number can be represented in many ways, and still conform to standard displayable form. Decimal points, minus signs, and E-notation are allowed. Blanks may lead or trail the number but no embedded blanks are allowed.

Examples of valid standard numbers:

DATA	RESULT	
2 3	23	right justified
2 3	23	not justified
– 2 3	–23	negative
2 3 . 0	23	decimal
2 3	23	left justified
2 . 3 E 1	23	in E-notation, 2.3x10^1
– 2 E – 2	–.02	in E-notation, –2x10^{-2}
0 0 0 2 3	23	leading zeroes
.	.	missing value

Examples of invalid standard numbers:

DATA	REASON
2 3	embedded blank
– 2 3 0	embedded blank
E 1	not a number
. .	not a number
1 D E C 7 9	dates need special informats
1 A 4 2 7 C	hex needs special informats
2 3 –	sign must be on left
(2 3)	invalid (use COMMA. informat)
1 2 , 3 4 1	commas invalid (use COMMA. informat)

See **SPECIAL TOPICS**, below, for SAS's response to invalid standard numbers.

A decimal specification is available to describe decimal scaling factors. You do not need the decimal specification for standard numeric input if you put decimal points in your data. In fact, the specification is overridden if a decimal point (period) is encountered in the data. Use a decimal specification when you key in data with an implied decimal, for example, if you key in 230 for 23.0.

Suppose a decimal specification parameter of 2 is used in the INPUT statement:

DATA	RESULTS	
2 3 1 4	23.14	
2	.02	
4 0 0	4.00	
– 1 4 0	–1.40	
1 2 . 2 3	12.23	
1 2 . 2	12.2	(overridden by .)
1 E – 2	.01	(overridden by E)

COLUMN INPUT

An INPUT statement that reads data values with column input lists the variable's name and the columns that it occupies on the data lines.

You can consider using column input when your data values are:

- in the same columns on all the data lines
- in standard numeric or character form.

When a data value occupies only one column, give only that column number. For example, if column 10 contains a student's year in college—1, 2, 3, or 4—the INPUT statement reads:

INPUT YEARCOLL 10;

If the numeric variable COUNT occupies columns 7 and 8 on all the data lines, this INPUT statement:

INPUT COUNT 7-8;

tells SAS to read a value of the variable COUNT from columns 7 and 8 of each data line.

The form of the INPUT statement for reading one variable with column input is:

INPUT *variable [$] startcolumn–endcolumn [decimals]*;

where

variable	names the variable you want the INPUT statement to read.
$	indicates that the variable contains character values rather than numeric values. SAS assumes a variable in an INPUT statement is numeric unless it is followed by a dollar sign or has been previously defined in the step as being character. For example, in this statement

INPUT NAME $ 1-10 PULSE 11-13 WAIST 14-15
   AGE 16-18;

the NAME variable has character values.

startcolumn	is the first column of the field containing data values for the variable.
endcolumn	is the last column of the field containing data values for the variable.
	For example,

INPUT NAME $ 1-10 PULSE 11-13 WAIST 14-15
   AGE 16-18;

The variable NAME starts in column 1 and ends in column 10, PULSE starts in column 11 and ends in column 13, and so forth.

decimals	gives the number of digits to the right of the decimal if no decimals are coded in the data lines. For example, the statement

INPUT PRICE 10-15 2;

reads the value of PRICE with two decimal places. See the section, **Standard display forms for data**, above.

Order of variables   You can read variables in any order with column input. For example, the statement:

INPUT FIRST 73-80 SECOND 10-12;

first reads a value of the variable FIRST from columns 73 through 80, and then a value of SECOND from columns 10 through 12.

Rereading columns   With column input you can read the same columns more than once. For example, in these statements:

INPUT ID 10–15 GROUP 13;

columns 10–15 contain an ID value; the third digit of the ID in column 13 is a group number.

Missing values   If you want data read with column input to represent missing values, code the values as either blank fields or periods (.).

Blanks   SAS ignores both leading and trailing blanks within the field when it is reading data with column input. This means that if you use the INPUT statement

INPUT COUNT 7–9;

and COUNT's value appears in columns 7 and 8 with column 9 blank, the value in columns 7 and 8 is used; SAS does not treat trailing blanks as zeros as do some other languages (for example, FORTRAN).

If your numeric values are punched with blanks representing zeros, read your data with formatted input and the BZ. (blanks are zeros) format. If you want to keep these surrounding blanks as part of a character value, you must use the $CHAR. informat with formatted input described below.

LIST INPUT

List input scans across the line looking for values, rather than looking in specific columns. List input is the easiest mode of input to specify, since you simply list the names of the variables in the INPUT statement. You can consider using list input when:

- each value in your data lines is separated from neighboring values by at least one blank
- missing values are represented by periods rather than blanks.

To read a variable with list input, SAS scans a data line until it comes to a nonblank character and takes that as the beginning of the variable's value. This value ends at the first blank or at the end of the data line, whichever comes first.

With unmodified list input, SAS stores both numeric and character values in a length of 8 bytes.

The form of the INPUT statement for reading one variable with list input is:

INPUT *variable* **[$]** ;

where

variable   names the variable you want the INPUT statement to read.

The simplest INPUT statement to read three numeric variables PULSE, WAIST, and AGE in list input mode is:

INPUT PULSE WAIST AGE;

$ a dollar sign indicates that the preceding variable contains character values rather than numeric values. For example,

INPUT NAME $ PULSE WAIST AGE;

This statement tells SAS that each data line contains first a value of the character variable NAME and then values of the numeric variables PULSE, WAIST, and AGE.

Order of variables   If all the variables in an INPUT statement are read with list input, these variables must be listed in the order that they appear on the data lines.

With simple list input, there are no provisions for skipping values on the data lines, so you must list all the variables on the line up to the last one you want. For example, say that each of your data lines contains the five values A, B, C, D, and E. You want only A, B, and D. If you are using simple list input, you cannot skip C, but you can omit E since it appears after the last value you want:

INPUT A B C D;

Missing values   Using list input requires that a missing value be represented in the data lines as a single period (.).

Blanks   Since blanks are used to delimit values, list input cannot be used for data values that contain leading, trailing, or embedded blanks. For data values with leading or trailing blanks, use column or formatted input. To read embedded blanks as part of a character data value, use the ampersand (&) format modifier described later in **Advanced INPUT Statements: Pointer Controls and Format Modifiers**.

FORMATTED INPUT

Formatted input increases the flexibility of the INPUT statement, since informats are available to read data written in virtually any form. An INPUT statement to read data values with formatted input lists the variable's name and a SAS informat for reading the values. The feature that distinguishes formatted input from list input is the SAS informat that is specified.

You can use formatted input when your data lines contain values in a format other than the standard character and numeric forms. See Chapter 13, "SAS Informats and Formats," for a description of the available SAS informats.

Formatted input is often used with the pointer controls discussed in **Advanced INPUT Statements: Pointer Controls and Format Modifiers**, below.

The form of the INPUT statement for reading one variable with formatted input is:

INPUT *variable* **[$]** *informat***;**

where

variable	names the variable you want the INPUT statement to read for the data values.
informat	specifies an informat for SAS to use for reading the data values. An informat name always includes or ends with a period (.), for example, 3.2 and $CHAR.
	When the variable is character, the informat begins with the dollar sign ($).
	Decimal points coded in the data lines override any other decimal specification in an informat.

Order of variables   Simple formatted input (without pointer controls) requires that the variables be listed in the order in which they occur on the data lines. Pointer controls make it possible to read variables in any order.

Missing values   Simple formatted input requires that missing numeric values be coded as a single period or blank and missing character values be coded as blanks.

Blanks   The way blanks are handled with simple formatted input is determined by the format that is specified. For example, the $CHAR. format reads blanks as blanks, while the BZ. format reads blanks as zeros.

Format lists   When values are entered on your data lines in a pattern, it is helpful to use format lists that describe several values at once. A format list consists of first the variable names, enclosed in parentheses, followed by the corresponding formats, which are also enclosed in parentheses. You can use as many format lists as necessary in an INPUT statement. Format lists cannot be nested.

For example, say that values of the 5 variables SCORE1–SCORE5 are entered on your data lines, four columns per value with no blanks between the values. You can use the INPUT statement

    INPUT (SCORE1–SCORE5) (4. 4. 4. 4. 4.);

to read the values. However, when there are more variables than format items, SAS uses the same format list again and again until all the variables have been read. So a simpler way to write the INPUT statement is

    INPUT (SCORE1–SCORE5) (4.);

For another approach to this example, see the n* format modifier described in **Advanced INPUT Statements: Pointer Controls and Format Modifiers.**

ADVANCED INPUT STATEMENTS: POINTER CONTROLS AND FORMAT MODIFIERS

Most of the INPUT statements shown so far are examples of simple column, list, and formatted input modes. Two advanced SAS features—pointer controls and format modifiers—can add flexibility regardless of the input mode you are using.

Pointer Directions

As SAS reads data values from the input lines, it keeps track of its position with a pointer. You can use pointer directions in INPUT statements to move a pointer from column to column, line to line. For example, if you have several data lines for each observation and SAS is reading a value that begins in the tenth column of the second line, the pointer says, "current line is 2, current column is 10."

Column control   With formatted input you move the pointer to the column containing the data value, give the variable name, and then specify a format to read the value. Included in the format is the value's width—how many columns the value occupies. For example, the statement

    INPUT @7 AGE 2.;

first moves the pointer to column 7 and then asks SAS to read a value of the variable AGE using the numeric format 2., specifying that the AGE value occupies 2 columns.

The major advantage of this pointer-and-format approach is the control that you have over how SAS reads your data lines. You tell SAS exactly the column to begin reading the value and exactly the format to use to read it. However, you must know which columns your data values occupy or be able to calculate their location based on information in the data line.

The pointer's location after a value has been read depends on the input mode used to read the value. If the value is read with list input, SAS sets the pointer to the second column after the value. For example, say that the statement

INPUT X Y;

reads a line containing the X value in columns 3 and 4. Since the X value was read with list input, SAS sets the pointer at column 6, the second column after the value, and begins reading the Y value at column 6.

Exception: when a value is read with list input and the ampersand format modifier (discussed later with format modifiers), SAS sets the pointer to the third column after the value, since the ampersand requires two spaces between data values.

When column input or formatted input is used to read a value, the pointer is set to the first column after the end of the field containing the value. For example, consider the statement

INPUT A 3–4 B;

or the statement

INPUT @3 A 2. B;

The field containing the A value ends at column 4 (even if the value itself only occupies column 3), and the pointer is set to column 5 after the A value is read.

Line control The pound sign (#) pointer control is used to control the current input line being read. When data for each observation require more than one data line, a pound sign followed by a line number signals to SAS which data line contains values for the variables that follow in the INPUT statement. For example, the statement

INPUT A 3–4 #2 B 5–6;

tells SAS to find the values for A in columns 3 and 4 of the first data line and to go on to the second data line to find values for B in columns 5 and 6.

You can find out the column and line of the pointer's current location using the COLUMN and LINE options of the INFILE statement.

Reading past the end of a line When @ or + pointer controls are used with a value that sends the pointer past the end of the current line, and a variable name to be read from the current column follows, SAS goes to column 1 of the next line to read the variable. It also prints the message on the SAS log:

NOTE: SAS WENT TO A NEW LINE WHEN INPUT STATEMENT REACHED
   PAST THE END OF A LINE.

If you want SAS to stop building the data set when the pointer reaches past the end of a line, use the STOPOVER option on an INFILE statement. You can also use the MISSOVER option in the INFILE statement to set to missing all the remaining variables in the INPUT statement when the pointer reaches past the end of a line. See the INFILE statement description in this chapter for more information.

Formatted lists with pointer controls   Format lists can save time. For example, say you want SAS to read 20 LOC values and 20 AMOUNT values for each observation. The values are stored on the data lines as a LOC value followed by an AMOUNT value; then the next LOC and AMOUNT values; and so on. Rather than write a lengthy INPUT statement listing all 40 variable names, you can use a format list to first read in all the LOC values in columns 1–2, 4–5, 7–8, and so on; the AMOUNT values are in columns 3, 6, 9, and so on. You can use this INPUT statement to read the values:

    INPUT (LOC1–LOC20) (2. +1) @1 (AMOUNT1–AMOUNT20) (+2 1.);

After the LOC values have been read, the @ pointer control resets the pointer to the beginning of the data line in column 1. You can include any of the pointer directions @, #, /, and + in the list of formats.

Format Modifiers

Format modifiers are signals to SAS that the data values should be read in a special way. Colon, ampersand, and n* format modifiers affect the format that SAS uses to read the data values. The ? and ?? modifiers affect how much information is printed on the log when SAS encounters an error in the data values.

With the addition of pointer controls and format modifiers to the INPUT statement, the form for reading one variable in any input mode becomes:

    INPUT [*pointercontrol...*] *variable[formatmodifier...][$] [startcol–endcol]*
    [*informat pointercontrol...*]**;**

where

pointercontrol	tells SAS where to find a data value. There are several types of pointer controls:
@n	moves the pointer to column *n*.
@pointvariable	moves the pointer to the the column given by the value of *pointvariable*.

To move the pointer to a specific column, use the @ followed by the column number or by a variable name whose value is that column number. For example, the statement

    INPUT @15 SALES;

moves the pointer to column 15. The INPUT statement in this example

    DATA ONE;
      A=15;
      INPUT @A NAME $10.;
    more SAS statements

also moves the pointer to column 15, since A's value is 15.

The pointer can go backward as well as forward. For example, this INPUT statement

INPUT @26 BOOK @1 COMPANY;

first reads BOOK starting at column 26 and then moves back to column 1 on the same line to read COMPANY.

In this example mixing input modes,

INPUT NAME $ 1–10 @15 PULSE 3. @20 WAIST 2.
    AGE;

SAS reads NAME with column input from columns 1 through 10, moves the pointer to column 15 , reads PULSE from 15, 16, and 17 and WAIST from 20 and 21, both with formatted input, and then reads AGE with list input.

+n   moves the pointer n columns

+pointvariable   moves the pointer the number of columns indicated by the value of pointvariable.

The + pointer direction, followed by a number or a variable name, advances the pointer by the number or the variable's value. For example, the statement:

INPUT @23 LENGTH 4. +5 WIDTH;

first moves the pointer to column 23, then reads a value of LENGTH from the next 4 columns (23, 24, 25, and 26), then advances the pointer five columns and begins reading a WIDTH value in column 32.

The number after the + must be a positive integer. To move the pointer back, you can set a variable in the DATA step to the number of columns you want to back up and then use the name of the variable after the + direction. For example, say you want to back up 1 column:

DATA FOUR;
    M=–1;
    INPUT X 1–10 +M Y;

This INPUT statement reads a value of X in columns 1 through 10 and then backs up the pointer by one column to read Y's value from column 10.

#n   moves the pointer to line n.

#pointvariable   moves the pointer to the line number given by the value of pointvariable.

When you write the INPUT statement for a set of data with several lines per observation, you need to let SAS know which variables are on which lines. The symbol # followed by a number tells SAS which line contains the next group of variables.

For example, the statement:

INPUT @12 NAME $10. #2 ID 3–4;

implies a #1 between INPUT and the @12 pointer direction and asks SAS to read a value of NAME beginning in column 12 of the first line of input data. Then SAS reads a value of ID in columns 3 and 4 of the second line of input data. The number of lines per observation that SAS reads is determined by the highest number following the # pointer direction in the INPUT statement.

For example, in this statement

INPUT @31 AGE 3. #2 @6 NAME $20.;

the highest value after the # is 2; thus SAS reads two lines of data each time the INPUT statement is executed.

This means that if you have more than one line of input data, but you are not reading any variables from the last line, you must let SAS know how many lines to read per observation by putting a # and the number of lines per observation at the end of the INPUT statement. For example, if you have four lines per observation but only need to read data values from the first two lines, your INPUT statement might look like this:

INPUT NAME $ 1–10 #2 AGE 13–14 #4;

If your DATA step includes more than one INPUT statement, the same number of lines is read by every INPUT statement in the DATA step. For example, this DATA step includes two INPUT statements:

DATA TWO;
    INPUT NAME $ 1–10 #2 AGE 13–14;
    IF AGE = 15;
    INPUT HEIGHT 20–25 WEIGHT 26–30;

Since the first INPUT statement includes #2, the statement reads two data lines when it is executed. The #2 sets the number of lines per observation for every INPUT statement in this DATA step. Thus, the second INPUT statement also brings in two data lines, although values are read only from the first line.

/ moves SAS to the next line. The slash (/) pointer direction advances the pointer to column 1 of the next input line. For example, the statement

INPUT AGE GRADE / SCORE1–SCORE5;

first reads values of AGE and GRADE from one data line and then skips to the next line to read values of SCORE1–SCORE5.

When you use a / to go to the next line, you cannot move the pointer back to an earlier line unless you have also followed a # with the number of lines per observation in the INPUT statement. When you are reading from multiline input and want to return to an earlier line, you must use a #n on your INPUT statement to give the total number of lines in the input record. The following example would not work without the #2:

INPUT A / B #1 @52 C #2;

SAS reads A from the first line, B from the second, then returns to the first line to read C. Two lines are always available to the pointer and SAS can go back to the first line of the record to read C.

If the number of input lines per observation varies, use the N option on the INFILE statement to denote the maximum number of lines per observation. See the INFILE statement description for more information.

@, trailing "holds" a data line for the next INPUT statement in the step. The next INPUT statement executed for the same observation in the DATA step then accesses the same data line rather than reading in a new one.

The @ is called a trailing at-sign because it trails all other items in the INPUT statement.

Normally, each INPUT statement in a DATA step reads a new data line. When you want to use more than one INPUT statement to read values from the same data line (or set of data lines), you can use an @ as the last item in your INPUT statement to hold the pointer on the current line.

For example, say that your input data contain two kinds of data lines. One type of data line gives information about a particular college course; the other contains information about the students taking that course.

The lines have different variables and different formats, so you will need two INPUT statements to read the two different kinds of lines. Lines containing class information have a C in column 1; lines containing student information have an S in column 1. You need to check each line as it is read to know which INPUT statement to use. You need an INPUT statement that reads only the variable telling whether the line is a student or class record:

DATA SCHEDULE;
  INPUT TYPE $ 1 @;
  IF TYPE='C' THEN INPUT COURSE $ PROF $;
  ELSE IF TYPE='S' THEN INPUT NAME $ ID;

The first INPUT statement reads the TYPE value from column 1 of the line. Since this INPUT statement ends with a trailing @, the next INPUT statement executed in the DATA step reads the same line. The IF statements that follow check whether the line is a class or student line and each gives an INPUT statement to read the rest of the line.

When you use a trailing @ in your INPUT statement to hold a data line for another INPUT statement, you sometimes want to release the held line. You can release the held line with the statement

INPUT;

This statement does not read any data, but it releases the current data line. The next INPUT statement executed will read a new line.

An input line held by a trailing @ is automatically released at the next execution of the DATA step. Thus, a RETURN or DELETE statement releases the line. If you want to read the same data line in more than one execution of the DATA step, use the trailing @@, described below.

@@, trailing   holds a data line for other executions of the DATA step. When each data line contains several observations, you can hold the data line for repeated executions of the INPUT statement by ending the statement with two @ signs.

For example, say that you have entered your data in a stream: each line contains several NAME and AGE values. You want SAS to read first a NAME value, then an AGE value, then output the observation; then read another NAME, another AGE and output; and so on until all the data values on the line has been read and each combination of NAME and AGE values has been output to the SAS data set. Use a double trailing @ in your INPUT statement:

```
DATA THREE;
  INPUT NAME $ AGE @@;
  CARDS;
JOHN 13 MARY 12 SUE 15 TOM 10
```

When you use the trailing @@, SAS releases the line when there are no more data on the line. You can also release the held line with a simple INPUT statement:

INPUT;

or with an INPUT statement that ends with a trailing @:

INPUT @;

This method of entering data is especially convenient in interactive mode.

formatmodifier   signals SAS that special instructions for handling data values follow. The format modifiers are:

:   allows you to combine the scanning feature of list input mode with informats. The colon tells SAS to read a variable's value with list input at the next nonblank column and to continue reading for the number of columns specified by the informat up until a blank column or the end of the data line is reached.

For example, say that the first value on each data line is a last name that may contain as many as 15 characters so you need the informat $15. to read the value. Put a colon (:) after the variable name and follow it with the informat:

INPUT LASTNAME :$15.;

The colon tells SAS to look for the next nonblank column and then to begin reading a LASTNAME value. SAS reads up to 15 columns, ending the value at the first blank column, or at the end of the data line, or at the end of 15 columns, whichever comes first.

Here is an example that uses a format other than the standard numeric *width.decimal (w.d.)* format after a format modifier:

INPUT A : $HEX4.;

The variable A is read in $HEX. format.

&   allows you to use list input mode on character values with single embedded blanks. The ampersand tells SAS that data values are separated by two blank columns and to allow single embedded blanks in the values.

In simple list input mode or with the colon format modifier, SAS stops reading a value when it comes to a blank, so you need a special signal when you want to read character values with embedded blanks. An embedded blank is a blank that appears in the value rather than before or after the value, for example, the blank between the two words in 'JOHN SMITH'. Only single embedded blanks can be handled with list input.

For example, the statement

INPUT LASTNAME $ STATE & $;

tells SAS that each data line contains first a value of the character variable LASTNAME, and then a value of the character variable STATE which may include a blank.

Note: when entering data values, be sure to separate data values that may contain embedded blanks by two blanks so that SAS knows when it has reached the end of the value.

The ampersand also serves the function of the colon. For example:

INPUT LASTNAME & $15.;

You do not need the colon in this case since the ampersand implies the colon's function. SAS begins reading the value of LASTNAME at the first nonblank column and reads up to 15 columns until it reaches two consecutive blanks or the end of the data line.

?   suppresses the invalid data message that SAS prints when an invalid character is encountered. For example:

INPUT X ? 10-12;
INPUT (X1-X10) (? 3.1);

When SAS encounters an invalid character for a variable whose format includes the ? format modifier, SAS sets the variable value to missing, sets the value of __ERROR__ to 1, and prints the listing of the input lines. The warning message is not printed.

To suppress the listing of input lines containing invalid characters, set the value of the automatic variable __ERROR__ back to 0 with this statement

  __ERROR__ = 0;

after your INPUT statement. Invalid X values are still set to missing values.

?? suppresses both the error messages and the listing of the input lines when invalid data values are read. The effects of the ? and ?? format modifiers are the same in suppressing any SAS messages about invalid data for that variable. But ?? prevents __ERROR__ from being set to 1 when invalid data are read. Thus the statement

  INPUT X ?? 10–12;

is equivalent to

  INPUT X ? 10–12;
  __ERROR__ = 0;

Invalid X values are still set to missing values.

*n** specifies in format lists that the next format is to be repeated *n* times. For example, say that you want to read first a value of the variable NAME, followed by the five SCORE values:

  INPUT (NAME SCORE1–SCORE5) ($10. 5*4.);

This INPUT statement first reads a value of the variable NAME from columns 1 through 10; then reads the five SCORE values from the next 20 columns.

A SPECIAL INPUT MODE: NAMED INPUT

Named input allows the values of a variable to be coded on the data lines with the variable name followed by an equal sign preceding the data value. For a numeric variable AGE, the data line would contain AGE = 21 rather than simply the value 21.

An equal sign is added to the INPUT statement for reading one variable with named input:

INPUT [*pointercontrol*] *variable*[=] [**$**] [*formatmodifier*] [*startcol–endcol*]
  [*informat*] [*pointercontrol*] ;

where

  = indicates that the data values include the variable name followed by an equal sign before the variable's value.

The INPUT statement begins reading named input at the current location of the input pointer. Thus, if your data lines include some data values at the beginning of the line that should not be read using named input, these values can be read using another SAS input method. For example, the INPUT statement

INPUT PULSE WAIST AGE=;

reads the data line

80 32 AGE=35   .

The appearance in the INPUT statement of a variable name followed by an equal sign tells SAS to use the named input mode to read the remainder of the input data line. Once SAS enters this mode for reading data, the order of the named variables on the input line is unimportant. For example, this statement,

INPUT ID NAME=$30. SEX=$1. AGE=;

could be used to read the input line

4798 AGE=23 SEX=F NAME=SMITH   .

In this case, SAS reads the variable ID using ordinary list input. Then SAS reads the remaining values on the input line using named input.

All of the variables that appear on the data lines in named input form do not have to be listed on the INPUT statement. Variables that are first mentioned in other statements in the DATA step can also appear on the data line as named input. Conversely, variables that are to appear on the data set but that will not have values in the data lines may appear on the INPUT statement in named input form in order to assign their formats. The variables may get their values from assignment or other SAS statements.

Formats following the equal sign are used to define an output format for the variable. To specify an informat for a variable being read with named input, use an INFORMAT statement.

If there are too many values to fit on the current data line, a / at the end of the data line tells SAS to continue to the next line of data still using the named input mode.

If character data values on the input data lines contain an equal sign, two blanks should precede the data value and two blanks should follow it. For example, the data line

 TITLE= AGE=60 AND UP NAME=JOHN DOE

could be read with the INPUT statement

INPUT TITLE=$30. NAME=$15.;

since two blanks come before and after the value of TITLE, which contains an equal sign.

SPECIAL TOPICS

Error diagnostics   The rules for standard display informats are illustrated at the beginning of this section. When SAS encounters a character in a numeric field that is not one of these, it takes the following actions:

- SAS sets the value of the variable being read to missing.
- SAS prints a message on the SAS log saying in which column of which input line the invalid character was found.
- SAS sets the value of the automatic variable __ERROR__ to 1 for the current observation.
- SAS prints the input lines corresponding to the current observation. If the line contains unprintable characters, it is printed in hexadecimal notation. A rule is printed so that you can tell which column is which.

See Chapter 16, "SAS Log and Procedure Output," for an example.

End-of-file   End-of-file occurs when the INPUT statement reaches the end of the data. When a DATA step runs past the end-of-file, the DATA step stops. You can detect end-of-file using the INFILE options END= and EOF=. (See the INFILE statement for details.)

KEEP Statement

You can use the KEEP statement in a DATA step to specify the variables that are to be included in any SAS data sets being created. The KEEP statement applies to all data sets being created in the step. To selectively keep variables in data sets when more than one data set is being created in the DATA step, use the KEEP= data set option with each data set name. (See Chapter 12, "SAS Data Sets," for more about data set options.)

If a DATA step includes a KEEP statement, only variables appearing in the KEEP statement are included in new data sets. Variables not listed in the KEEP statement remain available for use in program statements. The KEEP statement may appear anywhere among the program statements in the DATA step; it is not an executable statement.

The form of the KEEP statement is:

KEEP *variables*;

where

variables   specifies the variables you want included in the data set or data sets being created. Any form of variable list may be used (see Chapter 1 for details). Do not abbreviate the variable names.

Here is an example:

```
DATA AVERAGE;
   INPUT NAME $ SCORE1–SCORE20;
   AVG = MEAN(OF SCORE1–SCORE20);
   KEEP NAME AVG;
   CARDS;
data lines
```

The effect of the KEEP statement is the reverse of the DROP statement's effect. To save writing, the KEEP statement is preferred if fewer variables are being kept than dropped.

Do not use both KEEP and DROP statements in the same step. When both RENAME and KEEP statements are used in a DATA step, the KEEP statement is applied first. This means that the old name should be used in the KEEP statement.

LABEL Statement

You can use LABEL statements in a DATA step to give labels to variables. The label is stored with the variable name in the SAS data set and printed by many SAS procedures.

The form of the LABEL statement is:

LABEL *variable=label* ...;

where

    variable   names the variable to be labeled.

    label   specifies a label of up to 40 characters including blanks. If the label includes a semicolon or an equal sign, the label must be enclosed in either single or double quotes. (If double quotes are used, the SAS system option DQUOTE must be in effect.) When single quotes are part of the label, they must be written as two single quotes. When two single quotes are used within a label to represent one single quote, they are counted as one character.

Any number of variable names and labels can appear. Here are examples of LABEL statements:

```
LABEL COMPOUND = TYPE OF DRUG;
LABEL SCORE1 = GRADE ON APRIL 1 TEST
   SCORE2 = GRADE ON MAY 1 TEST;
LABEL DATE = 'IF Y = 0 W = DATE OF TEST';
LABEL N = MARK''S EXPERIMENT NUMBER;
```

Labels, Statement

You can use a statement label to identify a statement referred to by a GO TO or LINK statement. A statement label has the form:

> *label*: *statement*;

These terms make up the statement label:

label identifies the destination of a GO TO statement, a LINK statement, the HEADER= option in a FILE statement, or the EOF= option in an INFILE statement. The label may be any valid SAS name followed by a colon (:).

statement is any executable statement in the same DATA step as the statement that is referencing it. No two statements in a DATA step should have the same label. If a statement in a DATA step is labeled, it should be referenced by a statement or option in the step.

For example:

```
DATA INVENTRY ORDER;
   INPUT ITEM $ STOCK @;
   IF STOCK=0 THEN GO TO REORDR;
   OUTPUT INVENTRY;
   RETURN;
REORDR: INPUT SUPPLIER $;
   PUT 'ORDER ITEM #' ITEM 'FROM' SUPPLIER;
   OUTPUT ORDER;
   CARDS;
data lines
```

In the example above, the first INPUT statement reads a record containing an item description (ITEM) and the number in stock (STOCK). If STOCK=0, the GO TO statement causes SAS to jump to the statement labeled REORDR—another INPUT statement. SAS reads the name of the supplier for that item, writes a message on the log, and outputs the record to data set ORDER. When STOCK is not zero, the record is output to data set INVENTRY, and SAS returns to the beginning of the DATA step for a new observation.

LENGTH Statement

You can include a LENGTH statement in a DATA step to specify the number of bytes for storing values of variables in each data set being created.

   LENGTH [*variables* [**$**] *length*...] [**DEFAULT**=*length*]**;**

These terms are included in the LENGTH statement:

variables	names the variable or variables to which you want to assign a length. The variable list can include any variables in the data set; an array name may not appear.
$	indicates that the variable or variables in the list are character variables.
length	is a numeric constant that can range from 2 to 8 for numeric variables and from 1 to 200 for character variables. Note that this length value is not a format; it does not contain a period.
DEFAULT=*n*	optionally, changes the default number of bytes used for storing the values of newly created numeric variables from 8 to the number *n* that you specify. *N* can range from 2 to 8.

For example, the statement

   LENGTH NAME $ 20;

sets the length of the character variable NAME to 20.

Numeric Data

Normally, numeric variables in SAS data sets have a length of 8 bytes. However, many values can be represented exactly in fewer than 8 bytes. When your data set is very large, using fewer than 8 bytes to store values that do not need that much precision can significantly decrease external storage requirements. Before you use the LENGTH statement to change the number of bytes for storing numeric values, however, note carefully the discussion below on truncation problems.

Truncation   Consider the case where numeric values are represented in a base-16 number system. Exact decimal fractions, such as .3, are not necessarily exact fractions in base-16 representations. This situation can create difficulties.

For example, suppose that you use a LENGTH statement to store the values of a variable in 4 bytes:

LENGTH A 4;

Each value of A is initially moved into an 8-byte field during the DATA step. When the value is moved to the SAS data set, the last 4 bytes of the value are dropped. Then, when the value is used for processing in a later DATA or PROC step, its representation is again brought up to 8 bytes by appending nonsignificant zeros.

Unless the part of the representation originally dropped consists of all zeros, something is lost in truncation. The example below illustrates how that loss can affect the behavior of SAS.

```
DATA ONE;
  INPUT A 1-4 B 6;
  LENGTH DEFAULT=4;
  CARDS;
1.4 6
1.1 5
1.1 6
1.3 4
1.3 3
2.0 4
DATA TWO;
  SET ONE;
  IF A=1.3;
```

Data set TWO will have no observations! The constant 1.3 in the subsetting IF statement in the second DATA step has the full 8-byte representation of the 1.3, while the fourth and fifth values of A are identical to it only in the first 4 bytes of their values. Hence A will never be found equal to 1.3.

Although you should be aware of problems like these, using single-precision storage of 4 bytes does give you 7 significant digits, which is sufficient for most applications. Thus, using a default length of 4 to store numeric values when space is an important consideration is usually safe.

Integers   The discussion above applies to data values that are not whole numbers or integers. When a variable's values are all integers, you can safely use the LENGTH statement to save storage space for the data set being created. The table below shows, for each possible length, the minimum number of significant digits that can be represented in that length and the magnitude of the largest integer that can be represented exactly in that length.

LENGTH	SIGNIFICANT DIGITS RETAINED	LARGEST INTEGER REPRESENTED EXACTLY
2	2	255
3	4	65,535
4	7	16,777,215
5	9	4,294,967,295
6	12	1,099,511,627,775
7	14	281,474,946,710,655
8	16	72,057,594,037,927,935

Character Data

The length of a character variable is set the first time that the variable is used in a SAS DATA step. After the length has been specified, you cannot change it except in a later DATA step using a LENGTH statement. (See **Changing Variable Lengths** below.)

Since the INPUT statement can implicitly define a character variable's length by the format associated with the variable, the LENGTH statement should precede the INPUT statement when it is used to define lengths for character variables that are different from the length implied in the INPUT statement.

For example, the statements

```
DATA ONE;
  INPUT NAME $ 1-10;
  CARDS;
data lines
```

implicitly assign the variable NAME a length of 10. If a LENGTH statement appears before the INPUT statement,

```
DATA TWO;
  LENGTH NAME $ 20;
  INPUT NAME $ 1-10;
  CARDS;
data lines
```

NAME's length in the output data set is 20 instead of 10.

When a character variable appears for the first time in a DATA step, its length is determined from the context of its use. For example, consider these statements:

```
DATA TWO;
  INPUT X;
  IF X=1 THEN A='NO';
  ELSE A='YES';
```

A appears for the first time in the assignment A='NO'. Thus A's length is 2 in the data set, the length of the character literal 'NO'. When the value 'YES' is assigned to A, only the first 2 letters are saved; the 'S' is lost. To avoid this problem, use a LENGTH statement to give A the length you want:

```
DATA TWO;
  INPUT X;
  LENGTH A $ 3;
  IF X=1 THEN A='NO';
  ELSE A='YES';
```

or rearrange the statements:

```
DATA TWO;
  INPUT X;
  IF X⌐=1 THEN A='YES';
  ELSE A='NO';
```

A's length in both data sets is 3, and so the complete value 'YES' can be saved. In another example below:

```
DATA TWO;
  LENGTH B $ 15;
  INPUT X B ;
  IF X=1 THEN A=B;
```

B's length is defined as 15 by the LENGTH statement. The first appearance of A in the step is in the assignment A=B. Thus A's length is 15, determined by the length of B.

When you use list input to read a character variable, a length of 8 is assumed. If any of the values are longer than 8, they are truncated to 8 unless a LENGTH statement defines a longer length, as in the previous example.

Also note that when you use a LENGTH statement for a character variable before the INPUT statement, you need not specify the dollar sign ($) in the INPUT statement, since SAS knows that the variable is character by the time it encounters the INPUT statement.

Changing variable lengths   The contents of SAS data set ONE shows the length and type of its two variables B and X: B is character of length 10; X is numeric of length 8.

```
                        ALPHABETIC LIST OF VARIABLES

        #   VARIABLE   TYPE LENGTH POSITION  FORMAT          INFORMAT
                       LABEL

        1   B          CHAR    10       4

        2   X          NUM      8      14


   +------------------------------ SOURCE STATEMENTS ------------------------------
   |DATA ONE;
   | LENGTH B $ 10;
   | INPUT X B;
   | CARDS;
   +------------------------------------------------------------------------------
```

To change the length of B, a character variable, you must create a new data set and precede the SET statement with a LENGTH statement. You may also change X's length in the LENGTH statement.

```
DATA TWO;
  LENGTH B $ 8 X 4;
  SET ONE;
```

The variables have different lengths in data set TWO.

```
                        ALPHABETIC LIST OF VARIABLES

        #   VARIABLE   TYPE LENGTH POSITION  FORMAT          INFORMAT
                       LABEL

        1   B          CHAR     8       4

        2   X          NUM      4      12


   +------------------------------ SOURCE STATEMENTS ------------------------------
   |DATA TWO;
   | LENGTH B $ 8 X 4;
   | SET ONE;
   +------------------------------------------------------------------------------
```

Although a character variable's length must be changed by placing a LENGTH statement **before** the SET, you can change X's length in a LENGTH statement placed anywhere in the step.

```
DATA THREE;
  SET ONE;
  LENGTH X 4;
```

The result

```
                       ALPHABETIC LIST OF VARIABLES

        #   VARIABLE   TYPE LENGTH POSITION  FORMAT        INFORMAT
                       LABEL

        1   B          CHAR    10       4

        2   X          NUM      4      14



   +----------------------------- SOURCE STATEMENTS -----------------------------
   |DATA THREE;
   | SET ONE;
   | LENGTH  X 4;
   +------------------------------------------------------------------------------
```

The same rules apply to changing lengths on any previously existing SAS data set, whether read with a SET, MERGE, or UPDATE statement.

LINK Statement

A LINK statement tells SAS to jump immediately to another statement in the same DATA step and begin executing statements from that point. SAS executes the statement whose label appears in the LINK statement. Execution continues with the statements following the labeled statement and continues until a RETURN statement is executed. RETURN causes SAS to return to the statement immediately following the LINK statement. Execution continues from there.

The statement has the form:

> **LINK** *label*;

The statement label is specified in the LINK statement:

> *label*   identifies the LINK destination, which must be within the same DATA step. (See **Labels, Statement** listed alphabetically earlier in this chapter for more information.)

The difference between the LINK and GO TO statements is in the action of a subsequent RETURN statement. A RETURN after LINK returns SAS to the statements following the LINK; a RETURN statement after a GO TO returns SAS to the top of the DATA step.

When another LINK statement appears with a LINKed routine, this is called *nesting*. Up to ten LINK statements can be nested. When more than one LINK statement has been executed, a RETURN statement tells SAS to return to the statement following the last LINK statement executed.

Here is an example using one LINK statement:

```
DATA PARTIME;
   INPUT SSN 1–9 SEX $ HOURS MIN;
   IF SSN = 238666804 THEN LINK FIXUP;
   HOURS = HOURS + (MIN/60);
   RETURN;
   FIXUP: SEX = 'F';
   PUT SSN = 'WAS CORRECTED';
   RETURN;
   CARDS;
data lines
;
```

When SAS encounters the observation with SSN = 238666804, the statement

LINK FIXUP;

is executed. SAS jumps to the statement labeled FIXUP and executes that statement and the next two. The RETURN statement causes SAS to return to the statement

HOURS = HOURS + (MIN/60);

Note that an earlier RETURN statement appears in the program. This RETURN statement keeps the next three statements from being executed for each observation.

Normally a LINK-RETURN can be replaced in your program by a DO-END. For example, the example above may be written:

```
DATA PARTIME;
  INPUT SSN 1-9 SEX $ HOURS MIN;
  IF SSN = 238666804 THEN DO;
    SEX = 'F';
    PUT SSN = 'WAS CORRECTED';
    END;
  HOURS = HOURS + (MIN/60);
  CARDS;
data lines
;
```

See the DO statement description for more information.

The example below links to a statement that recodes grades of 'E' to 'F' for grades on three tests:

```
DATA CLASS;
  INPUT ID TEST1 $ TEST2 $ TEST3 $;
  TEST = TEST1;   LINK RECODE;   TEST1 = TEST;
  TEST = TEST2;   LINK RECODE;   TEST2 = TEST;
  TEST = TEST3;   LINK RECODE;   TEST3 = TEST;
  RETURN;
RECODE: IF TEST = 'E' THEN TEST = 'F';
  RETURN;
```

To recode each test grade, SAS moves the grade to a variable TEST, links to RECODE and recodes it, and then moves the recoded value to the original variable. This step could be accomplished more easily with an ARRAY statement:

```
DATA CLASS;
  ARRAY TEST $ TEST1–TEST3;
  INPUT ID TEST1 $ TEST2 $ TEST3 $;
  DO OVER TEST;
    IF TEST = 'E' THEN TEST = 'F';
    END;
```

See the ARRAY statement description for more information.

LIST Statement

You can use the LIST statement to list on the SAS log the input data lines for the observation being processed. When the LIST statement is executed, SAS sets a flag that causes the current input lines to be printed at the end of the DATA step.

The form of the LIST statement is:

LIST;

The LIST statement is useful for printing suspicious input lines read by an INPUT statement. Here is an example:

```
DATA EMPLOYEE;
   INPUT SSN 1–9 #3 W2AMT 5–12 2;
   IF W2AMT=. THEN LIST;
   CARDS;
123456789
JAMES SMITH
356.79
345671234
JEFFREY THOMAS
.
;
```

Each time W2AMT is missing, SAS prints the three current input data lines on the SAS log. Below is the log for the DATA step above.

```
6            DATA C;
7              INPUT SSN 1-9 #3 W2AMT 5-12 2;
8              IF W2AMT=. THEN LIST;
9              CARDS;

RULE:      1234567 101234567 201234567 301234567 401234567 501234567 601234567 70

13         345671234
14         JEFFREY THOMAS
15             .
NOTE: DATA SET WORK.C HAS 2 OBSERVATIONS AND 2 VARIABLES. 953 OBS/TRK.
NOTE: THE DATA STATEMENT USED 0.97 SECONDS AND 380K.

16             ;
```

The DATA step below illustrates how SAS prints lines from a LIST statement at the end of the DATA step. The step includes both a LIST statement and a PUT statement. Lines printed by the PUT statement are printed first on the log.

```
DATA D;
   INPUT X Y Z;
   LIST;
   IF X=Y THEN PUT X=;
   CARDS;
1 2 3
2 2 4
1 1 7
```

```
17          DATA D;
18           INPUT X Y Z;
19           LIST;
20           IF X=Y THEN PUT X= ;
21           CARDS;


RULE:       1234567 101234567 201234567 301234567 401234567 501234567 601234567 70

22          1 2 3
X=2
23          2 2 4
X=1
24          1 1 7
NOTE: DATA SET WORK.D HAS 3 OBSERVATIONS AND 3 VARIABLES. 680 OBS/TRK.
NOTE: THE DATA STATEMENT USED 0.94 SECONDS AND 368K.

25          ;
NOTE: SAS USED 380K MEMORY.

NOTE: SAS INSTITUTE INC.
      SAS CIRCLE
      BOX 8000
      CARY, N.C. 27511-8000
```

The current value of the SAS system option C48/C60/C96 determines how characters in the data line are printed. When CHAR48 or CHAR60 is in effect, all characters in the 48- or 60-character set are printed as is. If any unprintable characters are present in the data line, SAS prints the hex representation of the line. When the system option CHAR96 is in effect, lowercase letters are considered printable characters and are printed as they appear rather than with their hex representations. See the OPTIONS statement in Chapter 11 for more information on SAS system options.

LOSTCARD Statement

The LOSTCARD statement is used to resynchronize the input data when SAS encounters a missing record in data with multiple records per observation. When each observation is formed from several input data lines, you need to make sure that no data lines are missing. Since SAS does not discover that a data line is missing until it reaches the end of the data, the values for the remaining observations in the SAS data set being created may be incorrect.

The form of the LOSTCARD statement is:

LOSTCARD;

LOSTCARD is used most effectively when each data line for an observation contains an identification variable with the same value. Here is an example:

```
DATA PRODUCT;
  INPUT ID 1-3 X 6-7 #2 IDCHECK 1-3 Z;
  IF ID¬=IDCHECK THEN DO;
    PUT 'ERROR' ID= IDCHECK=;
    LOSTCARD;
    END;
  CARDS;
301 32
301 61432
302 53
302 83171
400 92845
411 46
411 99551
PROC PRINT;
```

In this example, two input data lines make up each observation. Columns 1-3 of each line contain an identification number. When the ID number in data line 1 does not equal the ID number in data line 2 (IDCHECK), you assume that a line has been misplaced or left out. Note that the first data line for the third observation (IDCHECK=400) is missing. An error message is printed by the PUT statement, and SAS encounters the LOSTCARD statement.

When LOSTCARD is executed, SAS returns to the two lines just read:

```
400 92845
411 46
```

and prints them on the log with a lost card note. Then SAS returns to the beginning of the DATA step. The INPUT statement ignores the first line and reads the second line as the first line of the observation (ID=411). The next input data line becomes the second line of the observation.

```
411 46
411 99551
```

SAS then executes the remaining statements in the step with the new data lines. The PRODUCT data set that is created contains three observations with ID values 301, 302, and 411. There is no observation for ID=400.

You can also use the LOSTCARD statement for observations with more than two lines. In general, when LOSTCARD is executed, formation of the current observation stops. SAS returns to the start of the DATA step. All variables not retained in a RETAIN statement are set to missing (except the automatic variable __N__, which is not incremented). The next INPUT statement ignores the first line previously read, and reads the appropriate number of lines beginning with the second line previously read. These lines are then used for the current observation.

Once a lost card message has been written on the LOG, SAS continues to synchronize the data lines with the program without reissuing the message.

For example, consider the DATA step below, which reads three data lines per observation. The first observation has two missing records; the second has one. SAS does not have a complete observation until the last three data lines are being read.

```
DATA A;
   INPUT ID X #2 ID2 Y #3 ID3 Z;
   IF ID⌐=ID2 OR ID2⌐=ID3 THEN LOSTCARD;
   CARDS;
100 1
101 2
101 3
102 4
102 5
102 6
;
```

Here is the log from the DATA step above:

```
1           DATA A;
2              INPUT ID X #2 ID2 Y #3 ID3 Z;
3              IF ID⌐=ID2 OR ID2⌐=ID3 THEN LOSTCARD;
4              CARDS;

NOTE: LOST CARD.

RULE:    1234567 101234567 201234567 301234567 401234567 501234567 601234567 70

5           100 1
6           101 2
7           101 3
8           102 4
9           102 5
NOTE: DATA SET WORK.A HAS 1 OBSERVATIONS AND 6 VARIABLES. 366 OBS/TRK.
NOTE: THE DATA STATEMENT USED 0.93 SECONDS AND 380K.

11          ;
12             PROC PRINT;

NOTE  THE PROCEDURE PRINT USED 0.99 SECONDS AND 420K
         AND PRINTED PAGE 2.
NOTE: SAS USED 420K MEMORY.

NOTE: SAS INSTITUTE INC.
         SAS CIRCLE
         BOX 8000
         CARY, N.C. 27511-8000
```

The resulting data set A has one observation:

```
                                                              2
         OBS    ID    X    ID2    Y    ID3    Z

          1     102   4    102    5    102    6
```

MERGE Statement

The function of the MERGE statement is to join corresponding observations from two or more SAS data sets into single observations in a new SAS data set. The way SAS joins the observations depends on whether a BY statement accompanies the MERGE statement.

The form of the MERGE statement is:

> **MERGE** *SASdataset*[(*dsoptions* **IN**=*name*)]
> *SASdataset*[(*dsoptions* **IN**=*name*)]...[**END**=*variable*]**;**

These terms and options may appear in the MERGE statement:

SASdataset   names two or more existing SAS data sets from which to read observations each time the MERGE statement is executed.

            A MERGE statement may contain two or more data set names to specify the data sets to merge:

             MERGE MALES FEMALES;
             MERGE IN.FITNESS LIB.VITALSTAT;
             MERGE YEAR1 YEAR2 YEAR3;

            Up to 50 data set names can appear in the MERGE statement. The number depends on the memory available to hold the data. (See Chapter 12, "SAS Data Sets," for more information on using SAS data set names.)

dsoptions   specifies any number of dsoptions (data set options) in parentheses after each SAS data set name. These options include those described in Chapter 12, "SAS Data Sets," as well as the following special data set option unique to the SET, MERGE, and UPDATE statements.

IN=*name*   creates a variable with the name given after the equal sign. An IN= variable can be associated with each data set. The MERGE statement indicates which data sets contributed data to the current observation by setting values of this variable to 1 or 0. Specify IN= in parentheses after the names of the data sets in the MERGE statement as shown below:

            DATA THREE;
             MERGE ONE(IN=INONE)
             TWO(IN=INTWO);

            INONE has the value 1 when information in the current observation comes from ONE; otherwise, it has the value 0. The value of INTWO is determined similarly. Both variables INONE and INTWO are equal to 1 if both data sets contribute information to the new observation. The IN= variables are not added to the data set.

END=*name*   creates a variable with the name given after the equal sign to contain an end-of-file indication. The variable,

which is initialized to zero, is set to 1 when the
MERGE statement is processing the last observation.
This variable is not added to any SAS data set being
created.

In any MERGE operation, when the observations being joined contain variables with the same name, the resulting observation contains one variable of that name. The value of the variable in the new observation is the value taken from the data set appearing latest in the MERGE statement.

Merging Without a BY Statement: One-to-One Merging

When no BY statement is used, the MERGE statement joins the first observation in one data set with the first observation in another, the second observation in the data set with the second observation in another, and so forth. The number of observations in the new data set is the maximum number of observations in any of the data sets listed in the MERGE statement. When a data set being merged runs out of observations, missing values for variables are joined with the remaining observations from the other data sets.

Example   You have two data sets, each with the same number of observations, each with different variables. One contains the name and home town of car owners; the other contains the year and model of their cars.

```
                      DATA SET DRIVER


          OBS    NAME      CITY

           1     CATHY     PORTLAND
           2     NANCY     RALEIGH
           3     SUE       NASHVILLE
```

```
                      DATA SET VEHICLE


          OBS    YEAR     MODEL

           1     1982     SEDAN
           2     1949     JEEP
           3     1977     BUS
```

You want to merge the first observation in the DRIVER data set with the first observation in the VEHICLE data set; the second observation with the second observation, and so on. The new data set contains the same number of observations as each of the input data sets, but the number of variables equals the total of the variables in the two input data sets.

```
DATA MATCH;
  MERGE DRIVER VEHICLE;
```

```
                            DATA MATCH


       OBS    NAME     CITY        YEAR    MODEL

        1     CATHY    PORTLAND    1982    SEDAN
        2     NANCY    RALEIGH     1949    JEEP
        3     SUE      NASHVILLE   1977    BUS
```

Match-Merging

If you want to match observations from two or more SAS data sets based on the values of some variables, then use a BY statement after the MERGE statement. In order to perform match-merging, there must be at least one variable common to each data set, and each data set must be sorted by these variables. The variables used for matching are called BY variables; the BY statement is used to identify the matching variables.

The MERGE operation combines all the data from each data set that has an observation with the current BY values.

Nonmatches   When nonmatching BY values occur, MERGE selects the lower BY value, bringing in data only from the data sets having that BY value in an observation. The IN= variable, described earlier, lets you know if a data set contributed information to the observation being built. Thus, the IN= variable can be used to detect nonmatches.

Multiple observations with the same BY value in a data set   If a data set has more than one observation with the same BY value, MERGE outputs each observation. The first observation of the BY group is combined with the first observation in the BY group from every data set with observations for that BY value; the second observation is combined with the second, and so on. The resulting data set contains as many observations for a BY group as the largest number in that BY group in any of the data sets.

When a data set runs out of observations for a BY value, values from the last observation contributed by the data set are retained for the remaining observations in the BY group. The FIRST. and LAST. variables are used to detect the beginning and end of BY groups, and thus let you control whether to output, delete, or count multiple observations in a BY group. The IN= variable is set to 1 if a data set contributes information to the current observation; once the IN= variable is set to one in a BY group it stays 1 for the remainder of the BY group even if the data set stops contributing information. You can reset the IN= variable to 0 in an assignment statement before the MERGE statement if you want to detect only new information.

Variables with the same name in more than one data set   If a variable other than a BY variable occurs in more than one data set being merged, only one variable of that name occurs in the new, merged data set. When a BY group has only one observation in each of the data sets being joined, the value of the variable in the new observation is the value from the data set mentioned latest in the MERGE statement. When multiple observations occur within a BY group, the value in the new data set is the value from the data set mentioned latest in the MERGE statement that is still contributing information to the BY group.

Example

You have two data sets. Data set ONE contains the variables NAME and SEX; data set TWO contains the variables NAME, CITY, and AGE.

```
                          DATA ONE


            OBS      NAME     SEX

             1       ANN       F
             2       MARY      F
             3       TOM       M
```

```
                          DATA TWO

            OBS     NAME     CITY     AGE

             1      ANN      TAMPA     30
             2      JOSE     ERIE      55
             3      MARY     MIAMI     24
             4      MARY     TAMPA     72
```

You want to merge each observation in data set ONE with the observation in TWO that has a matching value of the common variable NAME.

```
DATA THREE;
  MERGE ONE TWO;
  BY NAME;
```

```
                        DATA THREE

        OBS   NAME    SEX   CITY    AGE

         1    ANN     F     TAMPA    30
         2    JOSE          ERIE     55
         3    MARY    F     MIAMI    24
         4    MARY    F     TAMPA    72
         5    TOM     M              .
```

Note that data set ONE has no observation with the name JOSE, so that in data set THREE the JOSE observation has a missing value for SEX, the variable from data set ONE. Although only one observation in ONE has the name MARY, both observations in THREE use the SEX value 'F' for MARY. TOM has no match in TWO, so his CITY and AGE values are missing in THREE.

Example: table lookup You have one data set that is your table: it contains an identifier variable and corresponding descriptions. You want to merge the descriptions with another data set that contains the identifier variable. For example, say the data set containing the table has two variables, NUMBER and DESCRIPT: NUMBER contains the part number and DESCRIPT contains the part description. The other data set contains the part number and the name of a customer. Both data sets are sorted by NUMBER, the identifier variable.

```
                        PARTDATA

        OBS     NUMBER     DESCRIPT

         1       155       SCREWDRI
         2       244       WRENCH
         3       501       PLIERS
         4       796       HAMMER
```

```
                         ORDERS

        OBS     NUMBER     NAME

         1       155       R.JONES
         2       155       B.SMITH
         3       244       WILSON
         4       244       MCKINLEY
         5       244       LLOYD
         6       796       HERNDON
         7       796       LLOYD
```

```
PROC SORT DATA=PARTDATA;
  BY NUMBER;
PROC SORT DATA=ORDERS;
  BY NUMBER;
DATA COMPLETE;
  MERGE PARTDATA ORDERS;
  BY NUMBER;
```

```
                          COMPLETE


       OBS     NUMBER     DESCRIPT      NAME

        1       155       SCREWDRI      R.JONES
        2       155       SCREWDRI      B.SMITH
        3       244       WRENCH        WILSON
        4       244       WRENCH        MCKINLEY
        5       244       WRENCH        LLOYD
        6       501       PLIERS
        7       796       HAMMER        HERNDON
        8       796       HAMMER        LLOYD
```

Since you combined the data sets in order to have a list of customers with a description of the part they buy, you want to delete observations from the table (PARTDATA) that have no match in ORDERS. Part number 501, PLIERS, has no match in ORDERS. You can use the IN= variable on the ORDERS data set to ensure that all observations in the result are also in the ORDERS data set:

```
DATA COMPLETE;
  MERGE PARTDATA ORDERS(IN=A);
  BY NUMBER;
  IF A;
```

Observations are only output to COMPLETE when the value of IN variable A is 1:

```
                     COMPLETE (WITH IN=)


       OBS     NUMBER     DESCRIPT      NAME

        1       155       SCREWDRI      R.JONES
        2       155       SCREWDRI      B.SMITH
        3       244       WRENCH        WILSON
        4       244       WRENCH        MCKINLEY
        5       244       WRENCH        LLOYD
        6       796       HAMMER        HERNDON
        7       796       HAMMER        LLOYD
```

Details and further examples of MERGE including using more than one BY variable, merging more than two data sets, and merging one observation onto every observation in another data set are given in Chapter 6, "Data Step Applications."

MISSING Statement

You can use a MISSING statement in a DATA step to declare that certain values in your input data represent special missing values for numeric data.

The MISSING statement has this form:

MISSING *values*;

where

> *values*   are the values in your input data that you are using to represent special missing values. These special missing values may be any of the 26 capital letters of the alphabet or the underscore (__). See Chapter 14, "Missing Values," for further discussion of special missing values in SAS.

For example, with survey data, you may want to identify certain kinds of missing data. Suppose an 'A' is coded when the respondent was absent from home at the time of the survey; an 'R' when the respondent refused to answer.

```
DATA SURV;
  MISSING A R;
  INPUT ID ANSWER1;
  CARDS;
1001 2
1002 R
1003 1
1004 A
1005 2
more data lines
;
```

The MISSING statement indicates that values of A and R in the input data lines are to be considered special missing values rather than invalid numeric data values.

Null Statement

The null statement is a single semicolon. The statement does not perform any action but can play the role of a placeholder. Although a null statement may be used anywhere in a SAS program, it is most useful in the DATA step. For example, in some SAS programs that include a CARDS statement you may also need a null statement to signal the end of the data lines.

The form of a null statement is

```
;
```

In the DATA step, a CARDS statement signals to SAS that data lines follow immediately in the job stream. SAS recognizes the end of the data lines when it sees a semicolon on a line. If the first line after the last data line already contains a semicolon, you do not need a null statement. For example,

```
DATA COMM;
  INPUT X Y Z;
  CARDS;
data lines
PROC PRINT;
```

However, if a semicolon does not appear in the line after the last data line, a null statement can signal the end of the data:

```
DATA COMM;
  INPUT X Y Z;
  CARDS;
data lines
;
PROC PRINT
  DATA = COMM(KEEP = X RENAME = (X = VISIT1));
```

When your data contain semicolons and you use the CARDS4; statement, the null statement is indicated by four semicolons. For example,

```
DATA COMM;
  INPUT X Y Z;
  CARDS4;
data lines containing semicolons
;;;;
```

Although no action is performed by the statement, it is considered an executable statement. Thus, a label can precede it. For example,

```
DATA LAB;
  INFILE IN;
  INPUT X Y Z;
  IF X = . THEN GO TO FIND;
  LIST;
FIND: ;
  DROP X;
```

See the section **Labels, Statement** listed alphabetically in this chapter for more information on using statement labels.

OUTPUT Statement

The OUTPUT statement tells SAS to write the current observation to the data set being created.

The form of the OUTPUT statement is:

OUTPUT [*SASdataset*] ...;

where

> *SASdataset*   optionally specifies the data sets to which the current observation should be written. More than one SAS data set name may be given. All names specified must also appear in the DATA statement. When no SAS data set name is given, the current observation is written to all data sets being created in the step.

Simple SAS DATA steps do not need an OUTPUT statement since observations are automatically output before SAS returns to the beginning of the step for another execution. The OUTPUT statement is useful when you need to control the normal output of observations in situations like these:

- you want to create two or more observations from each line of input data
- you are creating more than one SAS data set from one input data file
- you want to combine several input observations into one observation.

When an OUTPUT statement appears among the program statements in the DATA step, SAS adds an observation to the SAS data set(s) only when the OUTPUT statement is executed. No automatic output occurs.

Creating several observations from one input line   Here is an example of creating several observations from one input line. Each line contains a subject identifier and three measurements for that subject. For each input line, you want to produce three observations. Each new observation should contain the subject identifier and one measurement.

```
DATA REPEAT;
  INPUT SUBJECT $ MEASURE1-MEASURE3;
  DROP MEASURE1-MEASURE3;
  MEASURE = MEASURE1;  OUTPUT;
  MEASURE = MEASURE2;  OUTPUT;
  MEASURE = MEASURE3;  OUTPUT;
  CARDS;
A 2 5 4
B 3 6 2
;
```

The new data set contains these observations:

```
                        REPEAT                                1

              OBS    SUBJECT    MEASURE

               1        A          2
               2        A          5
               3        A          4
               4        B          3
               5        B          6
               6        B          2
```

Creating more than one data set in a single DATA step   These statements create two data sets from a single input record:

```
DATA COLLEGE HISCHOOL;
  INPUT NAME $ 1-30 SEX $ YRS__EDUC;
  IF YRS__EDUC<=12
    THEN OUTPUT HISCHOOL;
  ELSE OUTPUT COLLEGE;
  CARDS;
data lines
  ;
```

The data set HISCHOOL contains all observations with a YRS__EDUC value of 12 or less. Data set COLLEGE contains observations with a YRS__EDUC value greater than 12.

Combining information from several records   These statements combine the information from several input records into one observation in the SAS data set.

```
PROC SORT DATA=PAYROLL;  BY SSN;
DATA CHECKS;
  SET PAYROLL;  BY SSN;
  IF FIRST.SSN THEN TOT__PAY=0;
  TOT__PAY+PAY;
  DROP PAY;
  IF LAST.SSN THEN OUTPUT;
```

SAS data set PAYROLL, which has been sorted by SSN, is used as input to the DATA step. PAYROLL contains several observations for each SSN. Since the BY statement appears in the DATA step, the FIRST. and LAST. automatic variables can be used to check for the first and last observations with each SSN value. A sum statement accumulates total pay for each SSN. When an observation is the last with a particular SSN value, SAS writes the observation to the new data set. Thus, the new data set contains one observation for each SSN value in the PAYROLL data set.

Here are the contents of data set PAYROLL after sorting:

```
                  PAYROLL AFTER SORTING                       2

              OBS      SSN         PAY

               1    111442222     100.00
               2    111442222      25.00
               3    333115555     160.00
               4    333115555      80.00
               5    777668888     142.66
```

Here are the contents of data set CHECKS:

```
                          CHECKS                                    3

          OBS        SSN        TOT_PAY

           1      111442222     125.00
           2      333115555     240.00
           3      777668888     142.66
```

PUT Statement

The PUT statement's function is to write output lines. Lines written by PUT statements can be directed to the SAS log, to the output pages that follow the log, to external files on disk or tape, or to punched cards.

The PUT statement and the INPUT statement are near mirror images of each other. The similarity between the PUT and INPUT statements makes it easy to learn about the PUT statement when you know about the INPUT statement.

A PUT statement writes lines to the file described in the most recently executed FILE statement. If no FILE statement appears before a PUT statement in a DATA step, the lines are written on the SAS log. See the FILE statement description earlier in this chapter for more information.

The PUT statement can write variable values or strings of text. Variable values can be labeled with the name of the variable using named output. You can define your output in a PUT statement using three basic styles: column, list or free-form, and formatted style.

The general form of the PUT statement is:

PUT [*specification*]...;

where

specification	tells SAS how to write a variable or character string in the output line, to write the current input line, or to list all the current variables. Each specification can be one of the following forms:
columnstyle	of the form *variable*[=] [$] *startcolumn*[–*endcolumn*][*decimals*]
	See **COLUMN STYLE**, below.
liststyle	of the form *variable*[=] [$]
	See **LIST STYLE**, below.
formattedstyle	of the form *variable*[=] [*format*]
	or
	(*variablelist*) (*formatlist*)
	See **FORMATTED STYLE** and **Grouping variables and formats**, below.
'*characterstring*'	enclosed in single quotes (or double quotes if the SAS system option DQUOTE is in effect), specifies a string of text to be written by the PUT statement. See **Writing character constants**, below.
pointercontrol	tells SAS where to move the output pointer. See **POINTER DIRECTIONS AND FORMAT MODIFIERS**, below.
__INFILE__	specifies that the line read by the most recently executed INPUT statement be written. See **Writing the current input line,** below.
__ALL__	tells SAS to write the values of all variables defined in the DATA step using named output. See **Listing values of the current variables**, below.

Any number of these specifications can appear in a single PUT statement. The PUT statement writes each item in the order it appears. Details for using each specification are given below.

COLUMN STYLE

Column style describes the output lines by giving the variable's name and the columns the variable is to occupy on the output line. The PUT statement writes the values of the variable in the specified columns of the output line.

The form of the PUT statement for writing the value of one variable with column output is:

PUT [*variable*][=] [**$**] *startcolumn*[–*endcolumn*] [*decimals*]**;**

where

variable	names the variable whose value is to be written.
=	specifies that the variable value is to be labeled with the variable name and an equal sign. See **Labeling variable values: named output** for more information.
$	indicates that the variable contains character values rather than numeric values. The $ is necessary only for character variables that have not yet been defined as character in the DATA step, and thus is usually not used.
startcolumn	is the first column of the field where the data value is to be written.
endcolumn	is the last column of the field for the value. If the value is to occupy one column in the output line, omit the *endcolumn* specification.
decimals	gives the number of digits you want printed to the right of the decimal.

Any number of column style specifications can appear in a single PUT statement. This PUT statement tells SAS to write the values of two variables on each output line:

PUT NAME $ 1-8 ADDRESS $ 10-35;

The value of NAME is written in columns 1 through 8, then the value of address in columns 10 through 35.

When more than one specification is listed, the PUT statement writes each item in the order it appears in the PUT statement. For example, the statement

PUT FIRST 73-80 SECOND 10-12;

first writes a value of the variable FIRST in columns 73-80, then a value of SECOND in columns 10 through 12.

If a variable is previously defined as character by a statement earlier in the step, no $ is needed in the PUT statement. For example, in the DATA step:

```
DATA A;
  INPUT NAME $ 1-15;
  FILE OUT;
  PUT NAME 1-15;
```

no $ is necessary in the PUT statement since the variable NAME has been previously defined as character by the INPUT statement.

LIST STYLE

The list style specification lets you simply list the names of the variables you want written. The PUT statement writes the value of the first variable listed in the PUT statement, leaves a blank, and then writes the next value.

The form of the PUT statement for writing one variable with list output is:

   PUT *variable*[=] [**$**] **;**

where

variable	names the variable you want written.
=	specifies that the variable be written using named output. See **Labeling variable values: named output** for more information.
$	specifies that the variable contains character data if the variable has not yet been defined as character.

In the DATA step below, the PUT statement writes values of NAME, SEX and AGE on the SAS log using list output style:

```
DATA CLASS;
  INPUT NAME $ 1-10 SEX $ 12 AGE 14-15;
  PUT NAME SEX AGE;
  CARDS;
HENRY           M    13
JOE             M    14
HENRIETTA       F    11
;
```

The data lines written by the PUT statement are:

```
HENRY M 13
JOE M 14
HENRIETTA F 11
```

One blank separates the data values on the output line.

With list output, missing values for numeric variables are printed as a single period (.). Character values are left-aligned in the field. List style should not be used for data values that contain leading blanks if you want the blanks included in the value that is printed.

You can tell the PUT statement to use the list output form—a variable value followed by a blank—and also specify the format to use for printing the value with the colon (:) format modifier. See **POINTER CONTROLS AND FORMAT MODIFIERS**, below.

FORMATTED STYLE

You can use formatted style to describe the output lines by listing the variable's name and a SAS format for writing the values. With formatted style, the PUT statement writes each variable's value using the specified format. No blanks are automatically added between values. Formatted style combined with pointer controls discussed in **Controlling the output pointer** make it possible to specify the exact line and column location to print each variable.

The form of the PUT statement for writing one variable with formatted output is:

> **PUT** *variable*[=] *format*;

where

variable	names the variable you want written.
=	specifies that the variable value should be written using named output. See **Labeling variable values: named output** for more information.
format	specifies a format for SAS to use for writing the data values. The format specified may be either a SAS format (see Chapter 13, "SAS Informats and Formats,") or a format you define (see the FORMAT procedure description). Every format includes a period.

Several variables can be listed in formatted style using a format list:

> **PUT** (*variablelist*) (*formatlist*);

where

(*variablelist*)	is any valid variable list (described in Chapter 1), appearing in parentheses.
(*formatlist*)	lists the formats to be used to write the preceding list of variables. See the section **Grouping variables and formats** below.

The format should be wide enough to write the value and any commas, dollar signs, or other special characters that the format includes.

Suppose X's value is 100. You want to print the value using the DOLLAR. format and include two decimal places for cents. This PUT statement:

> PUT X DOLLAR7.2;

is needed to print the formatted value, which takes 7 columns:

> $100.00   .

POINTER CONTROLS AND FORMAT MODIFIERS

Most of the PUT statements shown so far are examples of simple column, list, and formatted styles. Two advanced features—pointer controls and format modifiers—can add flexibility regardless of the output style you are using.

You can use pointer directions in PUT statements to move a pointer from column to column, line to line. As SAS writes data values to the output lines, it keeps track of its position on the lines with a pointer. For example, if you have several data lines for each observation and SAS is writing a value that begins in the tenth column of the second line, the pointer value indicates that the current line is 2, current column is 10. The n* format modifier is used in the PUT statement to tell SAS to duplicate the format which follows n times.

The pointer controls and format modifiers are described below:

pointer controls

@*n*	moves the pointer to column *n*.
@*pointvariable*	moves the pointer to the column given by the value of *pointvariable*.

To move the pointer to a specific column, use the @ followed by the column number or by a variable name whose value is that column number. For example, the statement

    PUT @15 SALES;

moves the pointer to column 15.

The PUT statement in this example

    DATA ONE;
      INPUT SPACE X;
      PUT @SPACE X 5.2;

moves the pointer to the column indicated by the value of SPACE.

The pointer can go backward as well as forward. For example, this PUT statement

    PUT @26 BOOK @1 COMPANY;

first writes BOOK's value beginning in column 26 and then returns to column 1 on the same line to write COMPANY's value.

+*n*	moves the pointer forward *n* columns.
+*pointvariable*	moves the pointer forward the number of columns indicated by the value of *pointvariable*. The + pointer direction, followed by a number or a variable name, advances the pointer by the number or the variable's value. For example, the statement

    PUT @23 LENGTH 4. +5 WIDTH;

moves the pointer first to column 23, writes LENGTH's value in the 4 columns starting there (23, 24, 25, and 26) leaving the pointer at column 27, then advances the pointer five columns and begins writing a WIDTH value in column 32.

If a number is specified, it must be a positive number. To move the pointer back, you can set a variable in the DATA step to the number of columns you want to back up and then use the name of the variable after the + direction.

For example, after writing a value with list output,

you may want to back up one column to write over the blank that the PUT statement automatically writes with list output. This DATA step can be used:

```
DATA ONE;
   INPUT X Y Z;
   M=-1;
   PUT X +M Y +M Z;
```

Since the X, Y, and Z values are written using list output, a blank would normally be added after each value is written. The +M pointer control moves the pointer back 1 space to eliminate the blank.

#n   moves the pointer to line *n*.

#pointvariable moves the pointer to the line number indicated by the value of *pointvariable*.

When you want to write several lines of data with one PUT statement, you can use the # to indicate on which line the information is to be written. The symbol # followed by a number (or variable name whose value represents a number) tells SAS which line is to be written on. For example, the statement

```
PUT @12 NAME $10. #2 ID 3-4;
```

asks SAS to write a value of NAME beginning in column 12 of the first output line and then to write a value of ID in columns 3 and 4 of the second line.

/   moves the pointer to the next line. The slash (/) pointer direction advances the pointer to column 1 of the next output line. For example, the statement

```
PUT AGE GRADE / SCORE1-SCORE5;
```

first writes values of AGE and GRADE on one line and then skips to the next line to write values of SCORE1-SCORE5.

@, trailing   ''holds'' a data line for another PUT statement. The @ is called a trailing at-sign, because it must trail all other items in the PUT statement.

Normally, each PUT statement in a DATA step writes a new data line. When you want to use more than one PUT statement to write values on the same output line (or set of output lines), you can use an @ as the last item in your PUT statement at its current location. The next PUT statement executed in that DATA step then accesses the same line rather than writing a new one.

For example,

```
DATA _NULL_;
   INPUT NAME $ WEIGHT;
   PUT NAME @;
   IF WEIGHT¬=. THEN PUT @15 WEIGHT;
```

The trailing @ in the PUT statement above prevents SAS from going to the next output line. If a WEIGHT value is present, it is printed on the same line as the name.

Say you have a SAS data set named DEXT containing two observations for each child in a class. Each observation contains either a right- or left-hand dexterity test score for the child. You want to print the data with the right- and left-hand scores on the same output line:

```
DATA __NULL__;
  SET DEXT;
  BY CHILD;
  IF FIRST.CHILD THEN PUT CHILD @;
  IF TYPE='LEFT' THEN PUT @25 SCORE 4.2 @;
  ELSE IF TYPE='RIGHT' THEN
      PUT @35 SCORE 4.2 @;
  IF LAST.CHILD THEN PUT;
```

Each time SAS reads a record from DEXT, if the observation is the first for a CHILD, the child's name is written. The pointer holds that same line until the left- or right-hand score is written. Still holding the line, the next record is read from DEXT, the score written, and since the record is the last for a child, the line is released by the last PUT statement.

Note: unlike the INPUT statement, the trailing @ in a PUT statement holds the current line for the next execution of a PUT statement even if another execution of the DATA step begins. Thus the double trailing @ pointer control is not needed in PUT statements. Although it may be used, its effect is identical to the @.

__PAGE__   advances to the first line of a new page. SAS automatically begins a new page when a line exceeds the current PAGESIZE value; in this case, you do not need to specify __PAGE__.

The __PAGE__ keyword is not needed in PUT statements executed by a HEADER= option in the FILE statement. Lines produced by those statements are automatically printed on a new page.

For example, suppose you want to end a page when you have printed information in the last observation in a county, as in this example:

```
DATA __NULL__;
  SET STATES;
  BY COUNTY;
  PUT NAME 1-10 @15 POP COMMA9. ;
  IF LAST.COUNTY THEN PUT __PAGE__;
```

PUT __PAGE__ tells the PUT statement to advance to line 1 of the new page when the value of LAST.COUNTY is 1. (A discussion of FIRST. and LAST. variables is given in the BY statement description.)

Note that for the first observation printed on a new page, printing begins on line 2. If you add a trailing @

to the PUT __PAGE__ statement, the pointer advances to line 1 of the next page **and remains there**.

The __PAGE__ option can appear in the same PUT statement with variables, strings of text, and other PUT statement features. For example, suppose you want to print a footer message before exiting from the page:

```
DATA __NULL__;
  SET STATES;
  BY COUNTY;
  PUT NAME 1-10 @15 POP COMMA9. ;
  IF LAST.COUNTY
    THEN PUT // 'THIS IS THE LAST OF '
  COUNTY $10. __PAGE__;
```

When an observation is the last for a county, the PUT statement skips two lines and prints the message 'THIS IS THE LAST OF ' followed by the current value of county before skipping to the next page.

OVERPRINT   overprints the previous line.

When SAS sees the OVERPRINT option, it prints a new line with the overprint carriage control (+) in column 1. The specifications following the keyword OVERPRINT are then written on the output line to be overprinted.

The OVERPRINT option may be used when your PUT statements are directed to a PRINT file and the N= option of the FILE statement is set to a value of 1. For example, to underline a title, this PUT statement can be used:

```
PUT 'TITLE OF PAGE' OVERPRINT '_____';
```

A line written by a PUT statement containing OVERPRINT as the first keyword is written over the line written by the most recent PUT statement in the step. For example, the statements

```
DATA __NULL__;
  SET CLASS;
  PUT NAME 1-10 @15 GRADE 2.;
  IF GRADE>=96
    THEN PUT OVERPRINT @15 '_____';
```

underline grades above 95 on the output line.

The OVERPRINT option may be used just as any other line pointer control. Thus, other line controls can be used in the same PUT statement:

```
PUT @5 NAME $8. OVERPRINT @5 8*'_' /
  @20 ADDRESS;
```

This PUT statement writes a value of NAME, underlines it by overprinting underscores and then goes to the next line to write an ADDRESS value.

Since the OVP system option (see the OPTIONS statement in Chapter 11) must be in effect in order to overprint, the OVERPRINT option on the PUT statement has no effect when you are printing lines at a terminal.

format modifiers

$n*$ specifies in format lists that the next format is to be repeated n times.

colon (:) preceding a format, causes SAS to print a variable's values with that format and to automatically skip one column. The PUT statement writes the value using the format, trimming off leading and trailing blanks, and follows the value with one blank. For example, the statements

```
DATA A;
   X = 12353.2;
   Y = 15;
   PUT X : COMMA10.2 Y : 5.2;
```

produce the line

  12,353.20 15.00   .

SPECIAL TOPICS

When the pointer goes past the end of a line When the @ or + is used with a value that sends the pointer past the end of the current line and a variable name to be written to the current column follows, the PUT statement goes to column 1 of the next line to write the variable.

The pointer's location after writing a data value The pointer's location after a value has been written depends on the output style used in the PUT statement.

If list style was used in the PUT statement, SAS sets the pointer to the second column after the value, since the PUT statement automatically skips a column after writing each value.

If column or formatted style was used, the pointer is set to the first column after the end of the field specified in the PUT statement.

You can find the column and line location of the pointer's current location using the COLUMN and LINE options of the FILE statement. See the FILE statement description for more information.

Grouping variables and formats When you want your values written in a pattern on the output lines, format lists can be used to shorten your coding time. A format list consists of a list of variable names, enclosed in parentheses, followed by a corresponding list of formats, which are also enclosed in parentheses. You can use as many format lists as necessary in a PUT statement. You can include any of the pointer directions @, #, /, +, and OVERPRINT in the list of formats. Format lists cannot be nested.

For example, say you want to write the five variables SCORE1-SCORE5 one after another using four columns to print each value with no blanks between. You can use the PUT statement

  PUT (SCORE1-SCORE5) (4. 4. 4. 4. 4.);

to write the values.

When there are more variables than format items, SAS uses the same format list again and again until all the variables have been written. So a simpler way to write the same PUT statement is

PUT (SCORE1-SCORE5) (4.);

The format list can include pointer controls and format modifiers. For example, say that you want to write first a value of the variable NAME, followed by the five SCORE values:

PUT (NAME SCORE1-SCORE5) ($10. 5*4.);

This PUT statement first writes a value NAME in columns 1 through 10 and then writes the five SCORE values in the next 20 columns.

When the format list includes more formats and pointer controls than are needed, the PUT statement ignores any remaining specifications in the format list after all the variable values have been written. For example, the PUT statement

PUT (X Y Z) (2. +1);

writes the value of X using the format 2., skips the next column, writes Y's value using the 2. format, skips a column, then writes Z's value using the 2. format. The +1 pointer control remaining in the third cycle of the format list is not used. When all the values in the variable list have been written, the PUT statement ignores any directions remaining in the format list.

Here is another example:

PUT (X Y Z) (5*2. +1);

In this case, the values of X, Y, and Z are written consecutively using the 2. format. No column is ever skipped (that is, the +1 pointer direction is never used), since the variable list is exhausted before the 5*2. specification.

Writing character constants   You may include any number of character strings in a PUT statement. Character strings may appear anywhere except between a variable and its column locations or formats. For example, the PUT statement:

PUT NAME $ 1-8 +1 'IS IN THE CLASS';

writes the value of NAME in columns 1-8, skips column 9, then writes the character string 'IS IN THE CLASS' beginning in column 10.

When not enough space remains on the current line to write the entire text of a character string, SAS writes the excess on the next line.

You can repeat a character constant on the output line by preceding it by the format modifier n*. For example, the PUT statement

PUT 132*'–';

prints a line made up of 132 minus signs.

After writing a character constant, the pointer is set to the first column after the constant. Thus, if you are planning to follow a character constant with a value on the output lines, you may want to use a blank as the last character of the constant. For example, say that values for the variables YEAR and TOTAL are 1982 and 1000, respectively. The statement

```
PUT 'THE PROFIT FOR ' YEAR 'IS ' TOTAL;
```

writes the line

```
THE PROFIT FOR 1982 IS 1000
```

The blank in each of the character constants in the PUT statement prevents the values for YEAR and TOTAL from following the constants without an intervening space.

Writing the current input line   When __INFILE__ is specified in a PUT statement, the line read by the most recently executed INPUT statement is written. If the most recent INPUT statement reads more than one record, only the last record is written by the __INFILE__ specification.

For example,

```
DATA ONE;
   INPUT A B;
   PUT __INFILE__;
   CARDS;
data lines
```

Each time this PUT statement is executed, the line just read by the INPUT statement is written to the SAS log.

An entire input line is written, not simply the fields read by the INPUT statement. Thus, the INPUT statement need not contain any variable names for the __INFILE__ feature to work. For example, the DATA step below produces an exact copy of the input file on the file described by DDname OUT:

```
DATA;
   INFILE IN;
   INPUT;
   FILE OUT;
   PUT __INFILE__;
```

The __INFILE__ feature can be combined with column output specifications to change the input file. For example, suppose you want to prepare a copy of a file but suppress the identifying variable:

```
DATA __NULL__;
   INFILE IN;
   INPUT;
   FILE OUT;
   PUT __INFILE__ 'XXXX' 1-4;
```

In this example, the current input line from the file with DDname IN is copied to the file described by DDname OUT, then the character string 'XXXX' is written over the first four columns of the record.

Listing values of the current variables   When __ALL__ is specified in a PUT statement, all the currently defined variables are written using named output. For example, the statement

```
PUT __ALL__;
```

prints labeled values of all currently defined variables. Named output is described below.

Labeling variable values: named output   When the PUT statement writes a variable's value, the value can be labeled with the variable name. This form of writing variable values is called *named output* and can be specified in column, list, or formatted output styles by following the variable name in the PUT statement with an equal sign (=). For example, this statement:

    PUT NAME @10 HEIGHT= WEIGHT=;

writes first the value of NAME, then beginning at column 10, the values of HEIGHT and WEIGHT using named output. Thus, if the current record has a NAME value of ANN, and HEIGHT and WEIGHT have values of 63.3 and 95.1, respectively, then this line is written by the PUT statement above:

    ANN   HEIGHT=63.3 WEIGHT=95.1

Formats following the equal sign are used to define an output format for the variable. For example, the statement

    PUT AMOUNT= DOLLAR8.2;

could be used to tell SAS to write the current value of AMOUNT in named output style with the format DOLLAR8.2.

If there are too many values to fit on the current output line, SAS continues to the next output line to write the values.

RENAME Statement

You can use the RENAME statement in a DATA step to give variables new names in any data sets being created.

The form of the RENAME statement is:

> **RENAME** *oldname = newname ...;*

where

> *oldname*   is the name of the variable you want renamed.
>
> *newname*   specifies the new name for the variable.

More than one set of names can appear.

Here is an example:

```
DATA SUBSET;
  SET MASTER;
  RENAME OLD=NEW X2=X;
```

In this example, the variable OLD, a variable in data set MASTER, is given the name NEW in data set SUBSET; variable X2 from MASTER is given the name X. (See the RENAME= data set option in Chapter 12, "SAS Data Sets," for another way to change variable names.)

When both RENAME and KEEP (or DROP) statements are used in a DATA step, the KEEP (or DROP) statement is applied first. This means that the old name should be used in the KEEP (or DROP) statement.

RETAIN Statement

If you want a variable to retain its value from the previous execution of the DATA step, give its name in a RETAIN statement. Normally SAS sets all variables to missing automatically before each execution of the DATA step. When a variable name appears in a RETAIN statement, the variable keeps its value from the previous execution.

Initial values can be specified in RETAIN statements. If an initial value appears, variables appearing in the list before it are set to that value before the first execution of the program. The RETAIN statement can appear anywhere in the DATA step with the same effect; it is not an executable statement.

The form of the RETAIN statement is:

RETAIN [*variable* ... [*initialvalue*]] ...;

where

variables names the variables whose values you want retained. If no variables are listed, for example,

RETAIN;

SAS retains the values of all variables in the DATA step (see **Cautions** below.)

initialvalue optionally specifies an initial value for the preceding variables. On the first execution of the DATA step, variables preceding it (up to the preceding initial value) in the RETAIN statement are set to this value. If initial values are not specified, numeric variables appearing in a RETAIN statement are initially missing; character variables are initially blank. If an initial value is specified, at least one variable name must precede it.

RETAIN statements are useful for variables that compute totals and counts of other variables in the data set. Here is an example:

RETAIN X1–X5 1 Y1 0 A B C 'ABC';

Variables X1 through X5 are set initially to a value of 1; Y1 starts out at 0; variables A, B, and C are each set to a value of 'ABC'.

Retaining values Normally SAS sets all variables to missing values before each execution of the DATA step. Values of variables are retained when a new execution of the DATA step occurs if:

- the variable is named in a RETAIN statement
- the variable is the accumulator variable in a sum statement
- the variable is read in by a SET, MERGE, or UPDATE statement or is specified as an IN= variable.

See Chapter 6, "DATA Step Applications," for more information about SET, MERGE, and UPDATE statements.

Example   In this example, the data set TIMECARD contains several observations for each SSN value.

```
PROC SORT DATA=TIMECARD;
  BY SSN;
DATA WORKERS;
  SET TIMECARD;
  BY SSN;
  IF FIRST.SSN THEN HIGHEST=.;
  RETAIN HIGHEST;
  HIGHEST=MAX(HIGHEST,GRADE);
  DROP GRADE;
  IF LAST.SSN THEN OUTPUT;
```

Data set WORKERS contains one observation for each SSN value. The variable HIGHEST is created in the DATA step and contains the highest GRADE value found for that SSN value. The RETAIN statement tells SAS not to set the value of HIGHEST to missing each time a new observation is read.

Since you want the highest GRADE value for each different SSN, not the highest value in the entire data set, the statement

```
IF FIRST.SSN THEN HIGHEST=.;
```

sets HIGHEST to a missing value for each new SSN value. Here are the contents of data set TIMECARD after sorting by SSN:

SSN	GRADE
111442222	2
111442222	4
333115555	6
333115555	1

The contents of data set WORKERS:

SSN	HIGHEST
111442222	4
333115555	6

Cautions   When just the keyword RETAIN appears without a variable list, all the variables are retained. Thus, data values may be retained in observations that should have missing values. For example, consider this program:

```
DATA GROUP;
  INPUT X;
  RETAIN;
  IF X=1 THEN SEX='M';
  IF X=2 THEN SEX='F';
  CARDS;
data lines
  ;
```

When the value of X is either 1 or 2, all is well. But if X is 3, neither of the IF-conditions is true, and SEX does not receive a new value. SEX retains its value from the preceding observation, producing an inaccuracy. Removing the RETAIN statement from this program results in SEX having a blank value when the value of X is other than 1 or 2.

RETURN Statement

The RETURN statement tells SAS

- to stop executing statements in a DATA step immediately and return to the beginning of the step for another execution, or
- when a LINK statement has been executed, to return to the statement immediately following the LINK and continue executing.
- in a HEADER= group of statements, to return to the statement immediately following the last statement executed prior to beginning a new page. (See the FILE statement for details.)

When a RETURN statement causes a return to the beginning of the DATA step, SAS first writes the current observation to any new data sets (unless OUTPUT statements are used in the step). Every DATA step has an implied RETURN as its last executable statement.

The form of the RETURN statement is:

RETURN;

Here is an example of a RETURN statement used in an IF-THEN statement:

```
DATA SURVEY;
  INPUT X Y Z;
  IF X=Y THEN RETURN;
  X=Y+Z;
  A=X**2;
  CARDS;
data lines
;
```

When X equals Y, the RETURN statement is executed. SAS adds the observation to the data set and returns to the beginning of the DATA step. The two statements

```
X=Y+Z;
A=X**2;
```

are not executed.

When X is not equal to Y, the RETURN statement is not executed. The two assignment statements are executed before the observation is added to the data set.

The example below has a RETURN and an OUTPUT statement. The RETURN statement causes SAS to return to the beginning of the step without outputting the current record (like the DELETE statement).

```
DATA REPORT;
  INPUT A B C;
  IF A>=0 THEN DO;
    ROOTA=SQRT(A);
    IF ROOTA<10 THEN RETURN;
    ELSE OUTPUT;
    END;
  CARDS;
```

Data set REPORT includes only those observations where A is positive and the square root of A is 10 or more. Note that a DELETE statement could be substituted for the RETURN statement in this example with the same result.

See the GO TO and LINK statements earlier in this chapter for other examples using the RETURN statement.

SET Statement

The SET statement in a DATA step tells SAS to read observations from one or more SAS data sets. Use SET when you want to read, subset, concatenate, or interleave observations from existing SAS data sets into a new data set. The SET statement brings in all variables from the SAS data sets listed unless otherwise directed by DROP or KEEP data set options. For example, the statements below create data set TWO as a copy of data set ONE:

```
DATA ONE;
  INPUT X Y Z;
  CARDS;
data lines
;
DATA TWO;
  SET ONE;
```

The form of the SET statement is:

SET [[*SASdataset*[(*dsoptions*)]...] [*setoptions*]]**;**

These terms and options may appear on the SET statement:

> *SASdataset*   names one or more existing SAS data sets from which to read observations each time the SET statement is executed.
>
> A SET statement may contain one name:
>
> ```
> SET FITNESS;
> SET SAVE.FITNESS;
> ```
>
> or more than one name to bring in observations from more than one data set:
>
> ```
> SET YEAR1 YEAR2 YEAR3;
> SET MALES FEMALES;
> ```
>
> If more than one data set name is listed, SAS reads all observations from the first data set, then all from the second data set, and so on until all observations from all the data sets have been read. (In SAS this operation is called concatenation.) SAS then treats all the data sets listed in the SET statement as one aggregate SAS data set.
> Or you may omit the data set name entirely in the SET statement.
>
> ```
> SET;
> ```
>
> which is equivalent to:
>
> ```
> SET __LAST__;
> ```

__LAST__ is a special SAS word that refers to the most recently created SAS data set in the job stream.

See Chapter 12, ''SAS Data Sets,'' for more information on using SAS data set names.

(*dsoptions*) specifies data set options in parentheses after each SAS data set name. For example,

DATA THREE;
  SET ONE(READ = PASSWORD);

These options include those described in Chapter 12, ''SAS Data Sets,'' as well as the following special data set option unique to the SET statement:

(**IN**=*name*) creates a variable with the name given after the equal sign. A different IN= variable can be associated with each data set. The SET statement indicates which data set contributed data to the current observation by setting the value of this variable to 1 or 0. Specify IN= in parentheses after the name of each data set in the SET statement as shown below:

DATA FOUR;
  SET ONE(IN = INONE READ = PASSWORD)
    TWO(IN = INTWO)
    THREE(IN = INTHREE);

INONE has the value 1 when an observation is read in from ONE; otherwise, it has the value 0. The values of INTWO and INTHREE are determined similarly.

setoptions specifies the SET statement options described below.

POINT=*name* refers SET to a variable for direct (or random) access by observation number. Normally, SAS executes a SET statement by reading sequentially from the data sets listed. However, you can access SAS data sets directly by observation number with POINT=. POINT= cannot be used with a BY statement.

The value of the POINT= variable, which must be a numeric variable, is the number of the observation that is retrieved. The POINT= variable is available anywhere in the DATA step and is not added to any new SAS data set. When you use POINT=, you usually also include a STOP statement to explicitly stop processing the DATA step.

If you execute a random access SET statement with an invalid value of the POINT= variable, SAS sets the automatic variable __ERROR__ to 1. It is a good idea to check for this indication after a random access SET statement since it is more likely that your DATA step will go into an endless loop when this error goes undetected.

For example, the statements below create a subset of ALL that contains only observations 3, 5, 7, and 4. The STOP statement tells SAS to stop building the data set after the DO loop is complete:

```
DATA SUBSET;
  DO N = 3,5,7,4;
    SET ALL POINT = N;
    IF __ERROR__ = 1 THEN ABORT;
    OUTPUT;
    END;
  STOP;
```

See Chapter 6, "DATA Step Applications," for an example where a STOP statement is not needed.

If more than one data set is listed in the SET statement, for example,

```
SET ALL ALL2 POINT = N;
```

the POINT= variable retrieves observations from all the data sets as though they are concatenated. If the POINT= variable assigned is a value greater than the total number of observations, SAS sets the automatic variable __ERROR__ to 1.

NOBS=_name_ creates a variable with the name given after the equal sign to contain a value that is the total number of observations in the data set. If more than one data set is listed in the SET statement, the value of the NOBS= variable is the total number of observations in the data sets listed. Since NOBS= is evaluated at compilation time, the NOBS= variable is available in the DATA step and may appear before the SET statement. The variable is not added to the new data set. You must use NOBS= in conjunction with POINT=.

END=_name_ creates a variable with the name given after the equal sign to contain an end-of-file indication. The variable, which is initialized to zero, is set to 1 when the SET statement reads the last observation of the input data set or concatenated data sets. This variable is not added to any new data set. If more than one data set is listed in the SET statement, the END= variable is set to 1 when SET reads the last observation in the last data set listed.

Copying Data Sets

To make a new copy called B of a SAS data set named A, write

```
DATA B;
  SET A;
```

This SET statement brings all variables and observations into the DATA step to create B.

Subsetting variables   To make a copy subsetting variables, use DROP or KEEP specifications in any of three ways;

```
DATA B;
  SET A(KEEP=X Y);

DATA B;
  SET A;
  KEEP X Y;

DATA B(KEEP=X Y);
  SET A;
```

When DROP or KEEP are used as data set options in the SET statement, the subset is formed before the data are brought into the DATA step. DROP and KEEP statements prevent variables from being output to SAS data sets; these variables still can be used in program statements.

Subsetting observations   To copy a data set subsetting observations, use program statements such as the subsetting IF, DELETE, or OUTPUT to control which observations are output to SAS data sets. For example, the statements

```
DATA MALES;
  SET PEOPLE;
  IF SEX='M';
```

uses a subsetting IF statement to select only the observations where the variable SEX has the value of M to write to the output data set.

Creating new variables   You can also add program statements to create new variables. For example, your original data set, MONTHLY, contains figures for several companies. The sales figures are represented by the variables MONTH1-MONTH12. You want to create a new variable to contain the total sales for the year for each company. You use a SET statement to tell SAS where to find the observations for the new data set and then create the new variable TOTAL with an assignment statement.

These SAS statements create a new data set YEARLY containing the same observations as MONTHLY plus a variable, TOTAL, which is the yearly sales figure.

```
DATA YEARLY;
  SET MONTHLY;
  TOTAL=SUM(OF MONTH1-MONTH12);
```

Maybe you no longer want the values of MONTH1-MONTH12 to be included in the YEARLY data set above once you have created the total sales for the year. You can add a DROP statement to the previous DATA step so that data set YEARLY contains all the observations from data set MONTHLY, but excludes the monthly sales figures:

```
DATA YEARLY;
  SET MONTHLY;
  TOTAL=SUM(OF MONTH1-MONTH12);
  DROP MONTH1-MONTH12;
```

Concatenating Data Sets

To concatenate two or more data sets to create a new one, name them in a SET statement. The new data set contains all the observations in all the input data sets listed.

Same variables   In the simplest case, all the input data sets contain the same set of variables, which also are the variables in the new data set.

For example, say you have two data sets, each containing the same variables. One is made up of data for 1980; the other, data for 1981. You want to combine them into a single data set containing all observations for 1980 and 1981 with these statements:

```
DATA BOTHYEAR;
  SET Y1980 Y1981;
```

The number of observations in the new data set is the sum of the number of observations in the Y1980 data set and the number of observations in the Y1981 data set. The order of the observations in BOTHYEAR is all the observations of Y1980 followed by all the observations of Y1981. The new data set's variables are the same as those in the old data sets.

Different variables   If the data sets in the SET statement contain different sets of variables, observations obtained or retrieved from one data set have missing values for variables that are present or defined only in the other data set or data sets.

Different variable attributes   Data sets listed in the SET statement may share some of the same variables. SAS takes the length of a variable for the new data set as the length of the variable in the first data set in which it occurs in the SET statement. If the variable has a longer length in a data set listed later in SET, its value is truncated to the shorter length from the data set listed earlier. To avoid truncation, give the variable its maximum length in a LENGTH statement preceding the SET statement. See the LENGTH statement elsewhere in this chapter for an example.

Interleaving Data Sets

To interleave two or more data sets (like concatenating but combined in sorted order), use a BY statement as well as a SET statement. Up to 50 SAS data sets may be interleaved. The data sets listed in the SET statement must be sorted on any BY variables. The new data set contains all the observations in the input data sets in sorted order by the variables in the BY statement.

Suppose you have two data sets, one for each department in your company. Each data set must be sorted by the same variable, LASTNAME. You want to combine the two input data sets, interleaving observations from each one, and you want to end up with one data set sorted by the BY variable, LASTNAME. The number of observations in the new data set equals the total of the number of observations in each of the original data sets. These statements perform this interleaving operation:

```
PROC SORT DATA = DEPT1;
   BY LASTNAME;
PROC SORT DATA = DEPT2;
   BY LASTNAME;
DATA ALLEMPL;
   SET DEPT1 DEPT2;
   BY LASTNAME;
```

Note: although the term "merge" is often used to mean "interleave," SAS reserves merge for a matching operation described under the MERGE statement.

For more examples using SET statements, including the use of two SET statements in the same DATA step, see Chapter 6, "DATA Step Applications."

STOP Statement

You can use the STOP statement to stop processing a SAS DATA step. The observation being processed when the STOP statement is encountered is not added to the SAS data set.

The form of a STOP statement is:

STOP;

The STOP statement does not affect the execution of any subsequent DATA or PROC steps. Execution continues from the first DATA or PROC statement found after the STOP statement. (Use the ABORT statement if you want SAS to stop processing the entire SAS job.)

Here is an example:

```
DATA COUNT1;
  INPUT X Y Z;
  IF __N__ = 250 THEN STOP;
  CARDS;
more than 250 data lines
PROC PRINT;
```

In this example, the value of the automatic variable __N__ corresponds to the number of observations processed so far. When the DATA step has been executed 250 times, the STOP statement is executed and SAS stops building the data set. SAS then executes the PROC PRINT step. The data set COUNT1 contains 249 observations. The 250th observation was being processed when the STOP statement was encountered and was not added to the data set.

Sum Statement

Sum statements add the result of an expression to an accumulator variable as observations are being added to the data set.

The form of a sum statement is:

   variable **+** *expression*;

where

variable	specifies the name of the accumulator variable. The variable must be a numeric variable; any valid SAS variable name can be used. The variable is automatically set to 0 before the first observation is read. Its value is retained from one execution to the next, just as if it had appeared in a RETAIN statement. (See the RETAIN statement description for more information.)
expression	is any valid SAS expression. The expression is evaluated and the result added to the accumulator variable. When the evaluation of the expression results in a missing value, it is treated as zero.

Here is an example:

```
DATA ACCUM;
   INPUT X Y Z;
   IF X = 4 THEN N + 1;
   IF N = 250 THEN STOP;
   CARDS;
data lines
;
```

Each time the sum statement

N + 1;

is executed, 1 is added to the value of N. When 250 observations with an X value of 4 have been read, the value of N is 250. The statement

IF N = 250 THEN STOP;

tells SAS to stop building the data set when N equals 250.

Some examples of sum statements:

BALANCE + (− DEBIT);

The first sum statement is used to subtract the DEBIT amount from BALANCE. The plus (+) is required in a sum statement; the statement

BALANCE − DEBIT;

is incorrect.

In the sum statement:

SUMXSQ + X*X;

the result of X*X is added to SUMXSQ each time the sum statement is executed. This statement

NX + X⌐ = .;

shows the use of the comparison operator. When the value of X is not missing, the expression is true (has the value 1). When X is missing, the expression's value is 0. Thus NX contains the number of observations processed with a nonmissing X value. See Chapter 4, ''SAS Expressions,'' for more information about logical expressions.

The sum statement is equivalent to using the SUM function and a RETAIN statement as shown below:

variable = SUM(variable, expression, 0);
RETAIN variable 0;

(If you want to initialize a sum variable to a value other than 0, include it in a RETAIN statement with an initial value.)

UPDATE Statement

The UPDATE statement combines observations from two SAS data sets in a manner similar to the MERGE statement, but UPDATE performs the special function of updating a master file by applying transactions. The UPDATE statement must be accompanied by a BY statement giving the name of an identifying variable by which to match observations in the two data sets. The data set containing the master file and the data set containing the transactions must both be sorted by this identifying variable or variables, and the master data set must not contain observations with duplicate values of the identifying variable. The new data set contains one observation for each observation in the master data set; if any transaction observations were not matched with master observations, these become new observations in the new data set as well.

The form of the UPDATE statement is:

UPDATE *masterdataset* [(*dsoptions* **IN**=*variable1*)] *transactiondataset* [(*dsoptions* **IN**=*variable2*)] [**END**=*variable*]**;**

where

masterdataset	names the SAS data set used as the master file. Only one observation in this data set can have each value of the variable(s) in the BY statement.
transactiondataset	names the SAS data set containing transactions to be applied to the master. This data set must contain the BY variable(s), but multiple observations with the same BY value can occur.
dsoptions	give SAS more information about the data set to which the data set options refer. See Chapter 12, "SAS Data Sets" for the data set options that are available.
IN=*variable*	creates a variable with the name given after the equal sign. A different IN= variable should be associated with each data set. The UPDATE operation indicates which data sets contributed data to the current observation by setting values of this variable to 1 or 0. Specify IN= in parentheses after the names of the data sets in the UPDATE statement as shown below:

DATA THREE;
    UPDATE ONE(IN=INONE) TWO(IN=INTWO);

INONE has the value 1 when information in the current observation comes from the master data set ONE; otherwise, it has the value 0. The value of INTWO is determined similarly. Both variables INONE and INTWO are equal to one if both data sets contribute information.

END=*name*   is used optionally to create a variable with the name given after the equal sign to let you know when the last observation in the UPDATE operation is being processed. The variable, which is initialized to zero, is set to 1 when the UPDATE statement is on the last observation. This variable is not added to any new data set.

Example   You have a SAS data set containing your master file and another SAS data set containing updates—your transaction file. There may be several transactions for each master observation. Usually, both data sets contain the same variables, but the transaction data set need not contain variables that will not be updated and may contain variables to be added to the master data set. If a variable is being updated in some, but not all of the observations, its value is missing in observations where it is not to be changed. Both data sets are sorted by the identifying variable. Below is an example:

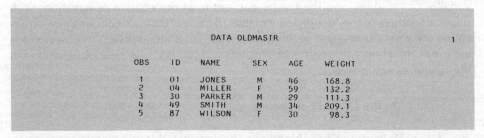

Since both data sets are sorted in order of ID, these statements perform the update:

```
DATA NEW;
  UPDATE OLDMASTR TRANS;
  BY ID;
```

The resulting data set NEW:

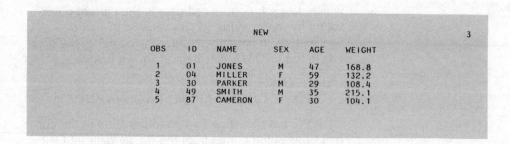

Note that:

- since the variable SEX is not updated, it does not appear in the TRANS data set.
- variables need not appear in the same order in the two data sets.
- only values to be updated are specified in the transaction data set; missing values in TRANS do not change the original values in OLDMASTR.
- multiple transaction records (as with ID 87) are all applied to the master before the record is output to NEW.

• if a record is not to be updated, it need not appear in the transaction data set (see ID 04).

Updating values to missing   To set the value of any variable in the master data set to missing, you must use the special missing value, underscore (__), as the variable's value in the transaction data set. (See the MISSING statement description or Chapter 14, "Missing Values," for more information.)

For example, suppose data set TRANS, described in the previous example, was created with these statements:

```
DATA TRANS;
   MISSING __;
   INPUT ID $ AGE WEIGHT NAME $;
   CARDS;
```

To set the value of AGE in JONES' master record to a missing value, use a special missing value underscore in the transaction data set:

```
            DATA TRANS WITH SPECIAL MISSING VALUE                    4

        OBS    ID     AGE     WEIGHT     NAME

         1     01              30.0
         2     49     35      215.1
         3     87       .                CAMERON
         4     87       .      104.1
```

When you update MASTER with TRANS, JONES' age is updated to a missing value.

```
DATA NEW;
   UPDATE OLDMASTR TRANS;
   BY ID;
```

```
            NEW WITH SPECIAL MISSING VALUE                           5

        OBS    ID    NAME       SEX     AGE     WEIGHT

         1     01    JONES       M       .       30.0
         2     04    MILLER      F      59      132.2
         3     30    PARKER      M      29      111.3
         4     49    SMITH       M      35      215.1
         5     87    CAMERON     F      30      104.1
```

When an underscore is coded as the value of a character variable in the transaction data set, it is considered a special missing value and updates the value in the master data set to missing. No MISSING statement is needed in the DATA step that creates the transaction data set.

Details and additional examples of using UPDATE are given in Chapter 6, "DATA Step Applications."

SAS Expressions

INTRODUCTION

An *expression* is a sequence of operators and operands forming a set of instructions that are performed to produce a result value. The operands are variable names and constants. The operators are special-character operators, functions, and grouping parentheses. (There are over 110 SAS functions that can perform a variety of roles and are especially useful as programming shortcuts. See Chapter 5, "SAS Functions," for a complete discussion.)

Expressions can be *simple* (using only one operator) or *compound* (using more than one operator). The following are examples of expressions:

```
X+1
3
LOG(Y)
PART/ALL*100
1 – EXP(N/(N – 1))
AGE<100
STATE='NC' | STATE='SC'
```

Expressions can be used in DATA step programming statements for transforming variables, creating new variables, conditional processing, calculating new values, assigning new values, and bit testing.

SAS CONSTANTS

A *SAS constant* is a number, or a character string in single quotes (or double quotes if the DQUOTE system option is in effect), or other special notation that indicates a fixed value. Constants are also called *literals*. In the assignment statement:

```
X=7;
```

the number 7 is a numeric constant and X is a variable name.

SAS uses five kinds of constants:

- numeric
- character
- date, time, and datetime numeric
- hexadecimal character
- hexadecimal numeric.

The hexadecimal constants are special constants discussed separately at the end of this chapter in **SPECIAL CONSTANTS AND OPERATORS**.

Constants may be used in assignment statements, sum statements, IF-conditions, RETAIN statements, PUT and ERROR statements, and as values for certain procedure options.

Numeric Constants

A numeric constant is simply a number that appears in a SAS statement. Most numeric constants are written just as numeric data values are. The numeric constant in this expression:

    PART/ALL*100

is 100.

Numeric constants can use a decimal point, a minus sign, and E-notation (scientific notation). For example:

    1
    1.23
    01
    -5
    1.2E23
    0.5E-10

In E-notation, the number before the E is scaled to the power of ten indicated by the number after the E; for example, 2E4 is the same as 2×10^4 or 20000.

A constant representing an ordinary numeric missing value is written as a single decimal point (.). A constant representing a special numeric missing value is written as two characters: a decimal point followed by a letter (for example, .B) or an underscore (.__).

Character Constants

A character constant consists of one to 200 characters enclosed in single quotes (or double quotes if the DQUOTE system option is in effect). For example, in the statement:

    IF NAME='TOM' THEN DO;

'TOM' is a character constant.

If a character constant includes a single quote, write it in a SAS expression as two consecutive single quotes; SAS treats it as one. For example, if you want to specify the character value TOM'S as a constant, you enter:

    NAME='TOM''S'

If DQUOTE is in effect, you can write

    NAME="TOM'S"

A constant representing a missing character value consists of a blank enclosed in quotes (for example, ' ').

Date, Time, and Datetime Constants

To express a date, time, or datetime value as a constant, use the same notation used in the informats and formats: TIME., DATE., and DATETIME. (See Chapter 13, "SAS Formats.") Enclose the formatted value in single quotes, and follow it with a D (date), T (time), or DT (datetime). Here are some examples:

    '1JAN1980'D
    '01JAN80'D
    '9:25'T
    '9:25:19'T
    '18JAN80:9:27:05'DT

A date constant might be used in an expression like this:

    IF BEGIN='01JAN1981'D THEN END='31DEC1981'D;

SAS OPERATORS

SAS operators are symbols that request a comparison, logical operation, or arithmetic calculation. SAS uses two major kinds of operators: prefix operators and infix operators.

A *prefix operator* is an operator that is applied to the variable, constant, function, or parenthesized expression immediately following it, for example, –6. The plus sign (+) and minus sign (–) may be used as prefix operators. The word NOT or the symbol ¬ is also a prefix operator (see **Logical operators**). Some examples of prefix operators used with variables, constants, functions, and parenthesized expressions are shown below:

    +Y
    –25
    –COS(ANGLE1)
    +(X*Y)

Infix operators apply to an operand on each side of an operator, for example, 6<8. There are four general kinds of infix operators: arithmetic; comparison; logical or Boolean; and others (minimum, maximum, and concatenation). Bit-mask testing is a special case of a comparison operation and is described in a separate section, **Bit Testing**, at the end of this chapter.

Number of Operators: Simple and Compound Expressions

When there is only one operator in an expression (for example, A/B), it is a *simple expression*. When there is more than one operator in an expression (for example, 1–EXP(N/N–1)), it is a *compound expression*.

Order of Performing Operations

The rules describing the order of evaluation for compound expressions are:

Rule 1: Expressions within parentheses are evaluated before those outside. 18/3*2 is the same as 6*2 or 12, but 18/(3*2) is equivalent to 18/6 or 3. –(X**2) is equivalent to the mathematical expression $-(X^2)$, but (–X)**2 is the same as the mathematical expression $(-X)^2$.

Rule 2:   Higher priority operations are performed first. The table below shows the priority groups:

Group I	**
	+ prefix only
	– prefix only
	¬ (NOT)
	>< (MINIMUM)
	<> (MAXIMUM)
Group II	*
	/
Group III	+ infix only
	– infix only
Group IV	||
Group V	< <= = ¬= >= > ¬> ¬<
Group VI	& (AND)
Group VII	| (OR)

Note that plus (+) and minus (–) can be either prefix or infix operators. A plus or a minus is a prefix operator only when it appears at the beginning of an expression or when it is immediately preceded by a left parenthesis or another operator.

Rule 3:   For operators with the same priority, the left operation is done first. There are two exceptions to this:

1. For the highest priority group (Group I), the right operation is done first.
2. When two comparison operators surround a quantity, the expression is evaluated as if an AND is present. For example, the expression:

    12<AGE<20

   is evaluated as if it is written:

    12<AGE & AGE<20

Arithmetic Operators

Arithmetic operators indicate that an arithmetic calculation is to be performed. The arithmetic operators are:

**	raise to a power
*	multiplication
/	division
+	addition
–	subtraction

For example, A**3 means raise the value of A to the power 3. The expression 2*Y means multiply 2 by the value of Y.

Note: the asterisk (*) is always necessary to indicate that a multiplication is to be performed; thus 2Y is **not** a valid expression.

If a missing value is an operand for an arithmetic operator, the result is a missing value.

Comparison Operators

Comparison operators propose a relationship between two quantities and ask SAS to determine whether or not that relationship holds. If it does hold (in other words, if it is true), the result of carrying out the operation is the value 1; if it does not hold (in other words, if it is false), the result is the value 0. The comparison operators are:

= or EQ	equal to
¬= or NE	not equal to
> or GT	greater than
¬> or NG	not greater than
< or LT	less than
¬< or NL	not less than
>= or GE	greater than or equal to
<= or LE	less than or equal to

Consider the expression A<=B. If A has the value 4 and B has the value 3, then A<=B has the value 0 (false). If A is 5 and B is 9, then the expression has the value 1 (true). If A and B each have the value 47, then again the relationship holds and the expression assumes the value 1.

Comparison operators appear frequently in IF statements. For example:

```
IF X<Y THEN C=5;
  ELSE C=12;
```

Comparisons are also used in expressions in assignment statements. For example, the above statements could be recoded:

```
C=5*(X<Y)+12*(X>=Y);
```

Since quantities inside parentheses are evaluated before any operations are performed on them, the expressions (X<Y) and (X>=Y) are evaluated first and the result (1 or 0) is substituted for the parenthesized expression. Therefore, if X=6 and Y=8:

```
C=5*(1)+12*(0)
C=5
```

Note: in a comparison operation a missing value of any kind compares smaller than any other numeric value.

Character comparisons   Comparisons are performed on character-valued as well as numeric operands, although the comparison always yields a numeric result (1 or 0). Character operands are compared character-by-character from left to right. Character order is determined by machine-collating sequence, which for the IBM 370 is:

blank ¢.<(+|&!$*);¬-/¦,%__>?` :#@'=''
abcdefghijklmnopqr~stuvwxyz
{ABCDEFGHI}JKLMNOPQR\STUVWXYZ
0123456789

The expression 'GRAY'>'ADAMS' is true, as is the expression 'JONES, C.'<'JONES, CLYDE'.

Two character values of unequal length are compared as if blanks are attached to the end of the shorter value before the comparison is made. So, 'FOX' is equivalent to 'FOX '. (However, 'FOX' is not equivalent to '   FOX', because blanks at the beginning and in the middle of a character value are meaningful to SAS.)

For example, say you want to create a data set that includes a variable called NAME. You only want to include observations for which the NAME value begins with the letters S through Z. The statement:

    IF NAME>='S';

is equivalent to:

    IF NAME>='S   ';

where blanks are extended after the S to the length of the variable NAME. Thus, the data set being created contains all observations with NAME values beginning with S through Z, that is, all values alphabetically greater than 'S   '.

To compare only the first letter of the NAME values to the letter S, you can use a colon : after the comparison operator. SAS then truncates the longer value to the length of the shorter value for the comparison. For example, the SAS statement:

    IF NAME>:'S';

compares the first character of NAME values with S. Any observations having NAME values beginning with T or later in the alphabet are included in the data set being created.

Note that SAS truncates and extends values only during the comparison. The values themselves keep their lengths. Any of the eight comparison operators listed above may be used with the colon in this way.

Logical Operators

Logical operators, also called *Boolean operators*, are usually used in expressions to link sequences of comparisons. The logical operators are:

    &   AND
    | OR
    ¬   NOT

If **both** of the quantities surrounding an AND are 1 (true), then the result of the AND operation produces a 1; otherwise, the result is 0. For example, the expression:

    A<B & C>0

is true (has the value 1) only when **both** A<B is 1 (true) **and** C>0 is 1 (true) that is, when A is less than B **and** C is positive.

If **either** of the quantities surrounding an OR is 1 (true), then the result of the OR operation is 1 (true); otherwise, the OR operation produces a 0. For example, the expression:

    A<B | C>0

is true (has the value 1) when A<B is 1 (true) regardless of the value of C. It is also true when the value of C>0 is 1 (true), regardless of the values of A and B. It is true, then, when either or both of those relationships hold.

Be careful when using the OR operator with IF statements:

    IF X=1 OR 2;

is not the same as:

    IF X=1 OR X=2;

The first IF statement is always true. X=1 is evaluated first and the result may be 1 or 0; however, the 2 is evaluated as 2=2, and since 2=2 is always true, the whole expression is true. The second IF statement is not necessarily true.

The prefix operator NOT is also a logical operator. The result of putting NOT in front of a quantity whose value is 0 (false) is 1 (true). That is, the result of negating a false statement is 1 (true). For example, if X=Y is 0 (false) then NOT(X=Y) is 1 (true). The result of NOT in front of a quantity whose value is missing is also 1 (true). The result of NOT in front of a quantity with a non-zero, nonmissing value is 0 (false); in other words, the result of negating a true statement is 0 (false).

For example:

    ¬(NAME='SMITH')

is equivalent to

    NAME ¬='SMITH' .

By DeMorgan's law, the NOT of an AND is the OR of the NOTs. The NOT of an OR is the AND of the NOTs. That is, ¬(A&B) is equivalent to ¬A|¬B, and ¬(A|B) is equivalent to ¬A&¬B. For example:

    ¬(A=B & C>D)

is equivalent to

    A¬=B | C<=D .

Do not use the keyword NOT as a variable name.

Other Operators

The operators in this category are >< (MIN), <> (MAX), and || (concatenation).

The >< and <> operators are surrounded by two quantities. The result is the quantity that is the minimum if >< is the operator or the maximum if <> is the operator. For example, if A<B, then A><B has the value of A.

The || operator concatenates two character values. For example, if the variable COLOR has a value of BLACK, and the variable NAME has a value of JACK, then:

    LENGTH GAME $ 9;
    GAME=COLOR || NAME;

results in GAME having a value of BLACKJACK.

If ALPHA='TEK' and MODEL='4662' then the statement:

    DEVICE=ALPHA || MODEL;

results in DEVICE='TEK4662' .

You can concatenate several character variables in one expression. If A='ONE' and B='AND' and C='ONLY', then

    D=A || B || C;

results in D='ONEANDONLY'.

You can also concatenate character constants. For example, if OLDNUM='123', then:

    NEWNUM=OLDNUM || '80';

causes NEWNUM to be assigned the value of '12380'.

The concatenation operator does not trim leading or trailing blanks. This expression:

    NAME='JOHN   '||'SMITH'

produces the value:

    'JOHN   SMITH' .

Use the TRIM function (described in Chapter 5, "SAS Functions") if you want SAS to trim trailing blanks from values before concatenating them.

SPECIAL CONSTANTS AND OPERATORS

Hexadecimal Constants

You can also represent hexadecimal character and numeric values as constants.

Hexadecimal Character Constants   A character hex constant is a string of an even number of hex characters enclosed in single quotes, followed immediately by an X. For example:

    'E2C1E2'X

A comma can be used to make the string more readable, but it is not part of, and does not alter, the hex value. If the string contains a comma, the comma must separate an even number of hex characters within the string. For example:

    IF VALUE='F1F2,F3F4'X THEN DO;

Hexadecimal Numeric Constants   Hexadecimal numeric constants can be specified in SAS statements. A numeric hex constant starts with a numeric digit (usually a zero), may be followed by more hexadecimal digits, and ends with the letter X. If the constant does not begin with a numeric digit, SAS may treat it as a variable name. The constant may contain no more than 16 valid hexadecimal digits (0–9, A–F). Here are some examples of numeric hex constants:

```
0C1X   0B37X   322X   0C4X   9X
```

Numeric hex constants may be used in a DATA step like this:

```
DATA;
  INPUT ABEND PIB2.;
  IF ABEND=0C1X OR ABEND=0B0AX THEN DO;
```

Bit Testing

Bit testing is a special comparison operation that tests internal bits in a value's representation. The general form of the operation is:

> expression = bitmask

You use a bit mask to test bits. The bit mask is a string of 0s, 1s, and periods in quotes, immediately followed by a B. 0s test whether the bit is off; 1s test for the bit on; and periods ignore the bit. Commas and blanks can be inserted in the bit mask for readability without affecting its meaning.

Both character and numeric variables may be the subject of bit testing. When testing a character value, SAS aligns the leftmost bit of the mask with the leftmost bit of the string; the test proceeds through the corresponding bits, moving to the right. When SAS tests a numeric value, the value is truncated to an integer and converted to a fixed-point number ($2^{31} - 1$). The rightmost bit of the mask is aligned with the rightmost bit of the number, and the test proceeds through the corresponding bits, moving to the left.

Here is an example of a test of a character variable:

> IF A='..1.0000'B THEN DO;

If the third bit of A (counting from the left) is on, and the fifth through eighth bits are off, then the comparison is TRUE and the expression results in 1. Otherwise the comparison is FALSE and the expression results in 0. Here is another example:

```
DATA;
  INPUT @88 DSORG $CHAR1.;
  IF DSORG='10000000'B THEN DSORGC='IS';
    ELSE IF DSORG='01000000'B THEN DSORGC='PS';
    ELSE IF DSORG='00100000'B THEN DSORGC='DA';
```

Note that bit masks are a special convention that may follow =, ¬=, EQ, and NE comparison operators. They **cannot** be used as bit literals in expressions. For example, the statement:

> X='0101'B;

is not valid.

NOTE: NUMERIC-CHARACTER CONVERSION

SAS automatically converts character variables to numeric variables, and numeric variables to character variables, according to these rules:

- If you use a character variable with an operator that requires numeric operands (for example, the plus sign) SAS converts the character variable to numeric.
- If you use a comparison operator to compare a character variable and a numeric variable, the character variable is converted to numeric.
- If you use a numeric variable with an operator that requires a character value (for example, the concatenation operator), the numeric value is converted to character using the BEST12. format.
- If you use a numeric variable on the left side of an assignment statement, and a character variable on the right, the character variable is converted to numeric. In the opposite situation, where the character variable is on the left and the numeric is on the right, SAS converts the numeric variable to character using the BESTn. format, where n is the length of the variable on the left.

Whenever SAS performs an automatic conversion, it prints a message on the SAS log warning that the conversion took place.

If converting a character variable to numeric produces invalid numeric values, SAS assigns a missing value to the result, prints an error message on the log, and sets the value of the automatic variable __ERROR__ to 1.

SAS Functions

INTRODUCTION

A *SAS function* is a routine that returns a value computed from arguments. Each SAS function has a keyword name. To invoke a function, write its name and then the argument or arguments for which the calculation is to be performed enclosed in parentheses:

FUNCTIONNAME(*argument,argument*)

Arguments can be simply variable names or constants, or they can be expressions, including expressions involving other functions. The arguments of SAS functions are usually numerically-valued expressions, except for the SAS character functions. Some functions require no argument, some only one argument, and some operate on several arguments. (No function allows more than 2000 arguments.) Below are some examples of functions and arguments.

This function yields the absolute value of the variable CASH:

ABS(CASH)

This function produces the absolute value of the quotient obtained when CASH is divided by the value of the variable BILLS:

ABS(CASH/BILLS)

In this example, the result of one function (SUM) is an argument of another function (MIN):

    MIN(SUM(CASH,BONUS),1000)

The MIN function compares the value of the first argument to that of the second argument and produces the smaller of the two values. The first argument is the result of the SUM function, which adds the variables CASH and BONUS, and the second argument is a constant, 1000.

All expression arguments are evaluated before a function is called. For example, 2*LOG(X+Y) is twice the natural logarithm of the sum of the value of X and the value of Y. The addition is performed first, then the logarithm of the sum is calculated, and that result is multiplied by 2.

Normally, when there is more than one argument, they must be separated by commas. However, if the arguments of a function are all variables and are in a sequence (say, X1 through X5, or X, Y, and Z), the function can also be written in one of these two forms:

    FUNCTIONNAME(OF *variable1 – variablen*)
    FUNCTIONNAME(OF *variable variable variable ...*)

For example, any of these forms is correct:

    SUM(OF X1–X100 Y1–Y100)
    SUM(OF X Y Z)
    SUM(X1,X2,X3,X4)

You **cannot** use these forms to list sequential variable arguments of a function:

    FUNCTIONNAME(*variable1 variable2 ...*)
    FUNCTIONNAME(*variable1variable2...*)
    FUNCTIONNAME(*variable1 – variablen*)

Each of these statements produces an error message:

    Y = SUM(X1 X2 X3);
    Y = SUM(XYZ);
    Y = SUM(X1–X3);

SAS functions fall into a number of categories: arithmetic, truncation, mathematical, trigonometric, probability, sample statistics, random number, character, date and time, state and ZIP code, system, and special.

SAS functions are especially useful as programming shortcuts for many numeric calculations and manipulations of character and numeric data. They are also useful for creating new variables from existing data. For example, say that you want to create a variable called LEAST whose value is the smaller of (1) the sum of ten variables (X1, X2, ..., X10) and, (2) a variable called Y. You could create the variable LEAST by writing:

    TOTX = X1 + X2 + X3 + X4 + X5 + X6 + X7 + X8 + X9 + X10;
    IF TOTX < Y THEN LEAST = TOTX;
    ELSE LEAST = Y;

It is faster, however, to write:

    LEAST = MIN(SUM(OF X1–X10),Y);

Some functions require that their arguments have values only in a certain range, for example, the argument of the LOG function must be greater than zero. Most functions (with the exception of those producing sample statistics) do not permit missing values as arguments. If the value of a function's argument is inadmissible (that is, missing or outside a certain range), SAS prints an error message and sets the result to a missing value. If an argument of a function that produces sample statistics is missing, that value is not included in the calculation of the statistic.

The default length of the resulting or target variable for most functions is eight for numeric variables and 200 for character variables. For example, the length of LEAST in the example above is eight. However, for the DIF, INPUT, LAG, PUT, SUBSTR, and TRIM functions, the default length of the target variable is the length of the first argument.

All functions in the SAS function library can be used in DATA step programming statements and in the MATRIX procedure.

FUNCTION CATEGORIES

The SAS functions are listed below by category. The function descriptions appear alphabetically, following the categorical listing.

Arithmetic functions

ABS	returns the absolute value
MAX	returns the largest value (see also **Sample statistic functions**)
MIN	returns the smallest value (see also **Sample statistic functions**)
MOD	calculates the remainder
SIGN	returns the sign of the argument or 0
SQRT	calculates the square root

Truncation functions

CEIL	returns the smallest integer>=argument
FLOOR	returns the largest integer<=argument
FUZZ	returns the integer if the argument is within 1E-12
INT	returns the integer value (truncates)
ROUND	rounds a value to the nearest roundoff unit

Mathematical functions

DIGAMMA	computes the derivative of the log of the GAMMA function
ERF	is the error function
EXP	raises e (2.71828) to a specified power
GAMMA	produces the complete gamma function
LGAMMA	calculates the natural logarithm of the GAMMA function of a value
LOG	produces the natural logarithm (base e)
LOG2	calculates the logarithm to the base 2
LOG10	produces the common logarithm

Trigonometric functions

ARCOS	calculates the arc cosine
ARSIN	calculates the arc sine
ATAN	calculates the arc tangent
COS	calculates the cosine
COSH	calculates the hyperbolic cosine
SIN	calculates the sine
SINH	calculates the hyperbolic sine
TAN	calculates the tangent
TANH	calculates the hyperbolic tangent

Probability functions

BETAINV	inverse beta distribution function
GAMINV	inverse gamma distribution function
POISSON	Poisson probability distribution function
PROBBETA	beta probability distribution function
PROBBNML	binomial probability distribution function
PROBCHI	chi-square probability distribution function
PROBF	F distribution function
PROBGAM	gamma probability distribution function
PROBHYPR	hypergeometric probability distribution function
PROBIT	inverse normal distribution function
PROBNEGB	negative binomial probability distribution function
PROBNORM	standard normal probability distribution function
PROBT	Student's t distribution function

Sample statistic functions

There are 15 functions whose results are sample statistics of the values of the arguments. The functions correspond to the statistics produced by the MEANS procedure and the computing method for each statistic is discussed in "Introduction to Descriptive Statistics." In each case, the statistic is calculated for the nonmissing values of the arguments.

CSS	calculates the corrected sum of squares
CV	calculates the coefficient of variation
KURTOSIS	gives the kurtosis
MAX	returns the largest value
MIN	returns the smallest value
MEAN	computes the arithmetic mean (average)
N	returns the number of nonmissing arguments
NMISS	returns the number of missing values
RANGE	returns the range
SKEWNESS	gives the skewness
STD	calculates the standard deviation
STDERR	calculates the standard error of the mean
SUM	calculates the sum of the arguments

USS	calculates the uncorrected sum of squares
VAR	calculates the variance

Random number functions

You can generate random numbers for various distributions using the random number functions. As explained in the RANUNI function description later in this chapter, the functions use a seed value to initialize a seed stream, which in turn generates a random number stream. You cannot control seed values, and therefore random numbers, after initialization. For cases where you want more control of the number streams, use the CALL subroutine (described in RANUNI) corresponding to the random number function. There are CALL subroutines for all random number functions except NORMAL and UNIFORM.

NORMAL	generates a normally-distributed pseudo-random variate
RANBIN	generates an observation from a binomial distribution
RANCAU	generates a Cauchy deviate
RANEXP	generates an exponential deviate
RANGAM	generates an observation from a gamma distribution with shape parameter *alpha*
RANNOR	generates a normal deviate
RANPOI	generates an observation from a Poisson distribution with a parameter *lambda*
RANTBL	generates deviates from a tabled probability mass function
RANTRI	generates an observation from the triangular distribution with parameter *h*
RANUNI	generates a uniform deviate
UNIFORM	generates a pseudo-random variate uniformly distributed on the interval (0,1)

Character functions

COLLATE	generates a string of characters in collating sequence
COMPRESS	removes characters from a character variable argument
INDEX	searches for a pattern of characters
INDEXC	finds the first occurrence of any one of a set of characters
LEFT	left-aligns a character string
LENGTH	returns the length of a character argument
REPEAT	repeats characters
REVERSE	reverses characters
RIGHT	right-aligns a character string
SCAN	scans for words
SUBSTR	extracts a substring
TRANSLATE	changes characters
TRIM	removes trailing blanks
UPCASE	converts to upper case
VERIFY	validates a character value

Date and time functions

DATE	returns today's date as a SAS date value
DATEJUL	converts a Julian date to a SAS date value
DATEPART	extracts the date part of a SAS datetime value or literal
DATETIME	returns the current date and time of day
DAY	returns the day of the month from a SAS date value
DHMS	returns a SAS datetime value from date, hour, minute, and second
HMS	returns a SAS time value from hour, minute, and second
HOUR	returns the hour from a SAS datetime or time value or literal
INTCK	returns the number of time intervals
INTNX	advances a date, time, or datetime value by a given interval
JULDATE	returns the Julian date from a SAS date value or literal
MDY	returns a SAS date value from month, day, and year
MINUTE	returns the minute from a SAS time or datetime value or literal
MONTH	returns the month from a SAS date value or literal
QTR	returns the quarter from a SAS date value or literal
SECOND	returns the second from a SAS time or datetime value or literal
TIME	returns the current time of day
TIMEPART	extracts the time part of a SAS datetime value or literal
TODAY	returns the current date as a SAS date value
WEEKDAY	returns the day of the week from a SAS date value or literal
YEAR	returns the year from a SAS date value
YYQ	returns a SAS date value from the year and quarter

State and ZIP code functions

FIPNAME	converts FIPS code to state name (all upper case)
FIPNAMEL	converts FIPS code to state name in upper and lower case
FIPSTATE	converts FIPS state codes to two-character postal code
STFIPS	converts state postal codes to FIPS state codes
STNAME	converts state postal codes to state names (all upper case)
STNAMEL	converts state postal codes to state names (upper and lower case)
ZIPFIPS	converts ZIP codes to FIPS state codes
ZIPNAME	converts ZIP codes to state names (all upper case)
ZIPNAMEL	converts ZIP codes to state names (upper and lower case)
ZIPSTATE	converts ZIP codes to two-letter state codes

System functions

CMS   invokes a CMS command and returns the status code
SYSPARM   returns the system parameter string
TSO   invokes a TSO command and returns the status code

Special functions

DIF   calculates the first difference for the nth lag
INPUT   defines an informat for a character value
LAG   lags variable values
PUT   specifies an output format for a value.
SASVER   returns the version of SAS
SYMGET   returns the value of a macro variable

FUNCTION DESCRIPTIONS

ABS: returns the absolute value

ABS(*argument*)

This function returns a positive number of the same magnitude as the value of the argument.

Examples:

ABS(2.4) = 2.4
ABS(–3) = 3   .

ARCOS: calculates the arc cosine

ARCOS(*argument*)

The result of this function is the arc cosine (inverse cosine) of the value of the argument. The result is in radians. The argument must have a value between –1 and +1.

Examples:

ARCOS(1) = 0
ARCOS(0) = 1.57079   .

ARSIN: calculates the arc sine

ARSIN(*argument*)

This function returns the arc sine (inverse sine) of the value of the argument. The result is in radians. The argument must have a value between –1 and +1.

Examples:

ARSIN(0) = 0
ARSIN(1) = 1.57079   .

ATAN: calculates the arc tangent

ATAN(*argument*)

The result of this function is the arc tangent (inverse tangent) of the value of the argument. The result is in radians.

Examples:

    ATAN(1) = .785398
    ATAN(0) = 0 .

BETAINV: computes the inverse of the cumulative beta distribution

    BETAINV(p,a,b)

where $0<=p<=1$, $a>0$, and $b>0$.

BETAINV returns the pth quantile from a beta distribution with density:

$$\Gamma(a+b)x^{a-1} (1-x)^{b-1} / \Gamma(a)\Gamma(b) .$$

For example, BETAINV(.001,2,4) returns a value of .0101. The beta distribution is related to many common statistical distributions including the F distribution (Abramowitz and Stegun, 1964, p.945).

CEIL: returns the smallest integer>=argument

    CEIL($argument$)

This function results in the smallest integer greater than or equal to the value of the argument. If the argument's value is within 10^{-12} of an integer, the function results in that integer.

Examples:

    CEIL(2.1) = 3
    CEIL(3) = 3
    CEIL(-2.4) = -2
    CEIL(-1.6) = -1 .

CMS: invokes a CMS command and returns the status code

    CMS($command$)

The CMS function invokes a single CMS or CP command as SAS statements are executed. The *command* is a character string enclosed in quotes corresponding to a CMS or CP command (CP commands must be preceded by CP.) The function returns the status code set by the execution of the command. For CP commands, the status code is always 0. Any CMS subset command may be invoked with the CMS function.

Example:

    RC = CMS('FILEDEF DAILY DISK DAY DAILY A');

The variable RC contains the status code returned after the CMS FILEDEF command specified by the CMS function is executed.

COLLATE: generates a string of characters in collating sequence

    COLLATE(n,m,l)

COLLATE returns up to 200 characters, beginning with the nth character in the IBM 360/370 collating sequence. You may specify either m, the last character in the sequence to generate, or l, the number of characters to generate. For example, the statements:

    X = COLLATE(240,249);
    X = COLLATE(240,,10);

both give X the value '0123456789'.

If the string requested by *n* and *m* is longer than 200 characters, only the first 200 characters are returned. If the string requested by *n* and *l* includes characters with values greater than 255, the string is truncated with value 255 (hex 'FF').

If both *m* and *l* are omitted, *l* is assumed to be 200. If both *m* and *l* are specified, *l* is ignored.

COMPRESS: removes characters from a character variable argument

> COMPRESS(*variable*)
> COMPRESS(*variable,variable*)

If you specify one character *variable*, COMPRESS returns it with all blanks removed. If you specify two character variables, COMPRESS returns the first value, with any characters in the second value removed.

For example, the statements below remove blanks from a value:

> A = 'AB C D ';
> B = COMPRESS(A);

B's value is 'ABCD'.

The statements below remove the special characters . ; ( ) from the value of X:

> X = 'A.B (C = D);';
> Y = COMPRESS(X,'. ; ( ) ');

Y's value is 'AB C = D'.

COS: calculates the cosine

> COS(*argument*)

The result of this function is the cosine of the value of the argument. The value of the argument is assumed to be in radians.

Examples:

> COS(.5) = .877582
> COS(0) = 1 .

COSH: calculates the hyperbolic cosine

> COSH(*argument*)

The result of this function is the hyperbolic cosine of the value of the argument. It is equivalent to:

> (EXP(*argument*) + EXP(−*argument*))/2 .

Example:

> COSH(0) = 1 .

CSS: calculates the corrected sum of squares

> · CSS(*argument,argument*)

This function results in the corrected sum of squares of the arguments. Abbreviated argument lists preceded by OF can be used.

Example:

> CSS(2,6) = 8 .

See "Introduction to Descriptive Statistics" for a definition of this statistic.

CV: calculates the coefficient of variation

CV(*argument,argument*)

The result of the CV function is the coefficient of variation of the arguments. Abbreviated argument lists preceded by OF can be used.

Example:

CV(2,6) = 70.71   .

See "Introduction to Descriptive Statistics" for a definition of this statistic.

DATE: returns today's date as a SAS date value

DATE( )

The DATE function, which may also be written:

TODAY( )

produces today's date as a SAS date value. For example, if you execute the following statements on March 15, 1982:

CURRENT = DATE( );
PUT CURRENT = ;

CURRENT has the value 8109. To produce a readable date, add a format to the PUT statement. For example:

PUT CURRENT= DATE7.;

produces:

CURRENT = 15MAR82   .

See **USING SAS DATE, TIME, AND DATETIME INFORMATS AND FORMATS** in Chapter 13 for a discussion of date and time values, informats, formats, and literals.

DATEJUL: converts a Julian date to a SAS date value

DATEJUL(*Juliandate*)

The DATEJUL function converts a *Julian date* to a SAS date value. A Julian date has the form YYDDD, where YY is the year 19YY and DDD is the day of the year. For example, the SAS statements:

DATA A;
  JULIAN = 82001;
  NEW = DATEJUL(JULIAN);
  PUT NEW = ;

produce:

NEW = 8036   .

To print the result as a readable date, add a DATE7. format to the PUT statement; for example:

PUT NEW= DATE7.;

produces:

NEW = 1JAN82   .

If the last three digits of the argument's value represent a value less than 1 or greater than 366, the function prints an "invalid argument" message. See **USING SAS DATE, TIME, AND DATETIME INFORMATS AND FORMATS** in Chapter 13 for a discussion of date and time values, informats, formats, and literals.

DATEPART: extracts the date part of a SAS datetime value

> DATEPART(*datetime*)

The DATEPART function converts a SAS *datetime* value or datetime literal into just the date part of the value. For positive dates, the statement:

> DATE = DATEPART(*datetime*);

is equivalent to:

> DATE = INT(*datetime*/(24*60*60));

For example:

> DATA A;
>   DATE = DATEPART(700650061);
>   PUT DATE = ;

produces:

> DATE = 8109   .

To print a readable date, specify the DATE7. format:

> PUT DATE = DATE7.;

produces:

> DATE = 15MAR82   .

See **USING SAS DATE, TIME, AND DATETIME INFORMATS AND FORMATS** in Chapter 13 for a discussion of date and time values, informats, formats, and literals.

DATETIME: returns the current date and time of day

> DATETIME( )

The DATETIME function produces the current time of day and date as a SAS datetime value. For example, executing the following statements at 09:03:25 on March 15, 1982:

> DATA A;
>   RIGHTNOW = DATETIME( );
>   PUT RIGHTNOW = ;

produces the line:

> RIGHTNOW = 700650061   .

To produce a readable datetime value, specify the DATETIME. format:

> PUT RIGHTNOW = DATETIME.;

See **USING SAS DATE, TIME, AND DATETIME INFORMATS AND FORMATS** in Chapter 13 for a discussion of date and time values, informats, formats, and literals.

DAY: returns the day of the month from a SAS date value

> DAY(*date*)

The DAY function produces the day of the month from a SAS date value or date literal. For example, the SAS date value 8109 is 15MAR82. The statements:

```
DATA DAYS;
  X=DAY(8109);
  PUT X=;
```

produce:

```
X=15   .
```

These statements:

```
DATA DAYS;
  X=DAY('15MAR82'D);
  PUT X=;
```

also produce:

```
X=15   .
```

See **USING SAS DATE, TIME, AND DATETIME INFORMATS AND FORMATS** in Chapter 13 for a discussion of date and time values, informats, formats, and literals.

DHMS: returns a SAS datetime value from date, hour, minute, and second

DHMS(*date,hour,minute,second*)

The DHMS function produces a SAS datetime value from *date, hour, minute*, and *second* values. The date value can either be a SAS date value or a SAS date literal. For example, the SAS statements:

```
DATA A;
  INIT=DHMS('20FEB82'D,13,23,19)
  PUT INIT= DATETIME.;
```

produce:

```
INIT=20FEB82:13:23:19   .
```

Note that without the DATETIME. format specification in the PUT statement, the result would be printed as a SAS datetime value (the number of seconds between 00:00 01JAN60 and the specified date and time).

See **USING SAS DATE, TIME, AND DATETIME INFORMATS AND FORMATS** in Chapter 13 for a discussion of date and time values, informats, formats, and literals.

DIF: calculates the first difference for the nth lag

DIF*n*(*argument*)

A family of DIF functions, named DIF1, DIF2, ..., DIF100, is available for numerical arguments only. (DIF1 can also be written DIF.) The result of the DIF*n* function is the current value of *argument* minus the current LAG*n* value of *argument*, that is:

DIF*n*(X) = X − LAG*n*(X).

Consider this DATA step:

```
DATA TWO;
  INPUT X @@;
  Z=LAG(X);
  D=DIF(X);
  CARDS;
1 2 6 4 7
```

Data set TWO looks like this:

```
X   Z   D
1   .   .
2   1   1
6   2   4
4   6  -2
7   4   3
```

Note: the function DIF2(X) is not equivalent to the second difference DIF(DIF(X)). DIFs are only generated when a DIF function is executed; they are not automatically generated for each observation. If the DIF function is used in the THEN clause of an IF statement (that is, if it is executed conditionally), only values from those observations meeting the IF condition are differenced.

If the argument is an array name, each array element is differenced separately.

DIGAMMA: computes the digamma function

DIGAMMA(x)

The DIGAMMA function computes the derivative of the log of the gamma function, that is, $DIGAMMA(x) = \Gamma'(x)/\Gamma(x)$. The value of this function is undefined for non-positive integers.

Example:

Y = DIGAMMA(1)

returns:

Y = − .5772...

which is the negative of Euler's constant.

ERF: error function

ERF(*argument*)

The result of this function is $2/\sqrt{\pi}$ times the definite integral from 0 to *argument* of e^{-x^2}.

The ERF function can be used to find the probability (P) that a normally distributed random variable with mean 0 and standard deviation 1 will take on a value less than X:

P = .5 + ERF(X/√2)/2

This is equivalent to PROBNORM(X).

Examples:

ERF(1) = .842701
ERF(−1) = −.842701 .

EXP: raises e (2.71828) to a specified power

EXP(*argument*)

This function raises e to the power specified by the argument. E, the base of natural logarithms, is approximately 2.71828. The value of the argument must be less than 174.673.

Examples:

```
EXP(1) = 2.71828
EXP(0) = 1 .
```

FIPNAME: converts FIPS code to state name (upper case)

```
FIPNAME(FIPS)
```

The FIPNAME function takes a numeric FIPS code and returns a 20-character state name in upper case. For example, FIPNAME(37) returns NORTH CAROLINA.

FIPNAMEL: converts FIPS code to state name in upper and lower case

```
FIPNAMEL(FIPS)
```

The FIPNAMEL function takes a numeric FIPS code and returns a 20-character state name in upper and lower case. For example, FIPSNAMEL(37) returns North Carolina.

FIPSTATE: converts FIPS code to two-character postal code

```
FIPSTATE(FIPS)
```

The FIPSTATE function takes the numeric FIPS state code and returns the two-character postal code. For example, FIPSTATE(37) returns NC.

FLOOR: returns the largest integer<= argument

```
FLOOR(argument)
```

This function results in the largest integer less than or equal to the value of the argument. If the argument's value is within 10^{-12} of an integer, the function results in that integer.

Examples:

```
FLOOR(2.1) = 2
FLOOR(-2.4) = -3
FLOOR(3) is = 3
FLOOR(-1.6) = -2 .
```

FUZZ: returns the integer if the argument is within 1E-12

```
FUZZ(argument)
```

The FUZZ function returns an integer value if the argument is within 1E-12 of the integer; that is, if the difference between the integer and argument is less than 1E-12. For example, these statements:

```
DATA __NULL__;
  X= 5.9999999999999;
  Y= FUZZ(X);
  PUT Y= 15.13;
```

produce this line:

```
Y= 6.0000000000000   .
```

GAMINV: inverse of the PROBGAM function

```
GAMINV(p,eta)
```

where $0<p<1$, and $eta>0$.

The GAMINV function computes a value of X such that:

$$\int_0^X t^{eta-1}e^{-t}dt/\Gamma(eta)$$

is equal to p.

GAMMA: produces the complete gamma function

GAMMA(x)

The result of this function is the definite integral:

$$\int_0^\infty t^{x-1}e^{-t}dt \quad .$$

The value of x must be a positive number less than 57.5744. If it is an integer, then GAMMA(x) is $(x-1)!$. This function is commonly denoted by $\Gamma(x)$.

Example:

GAMMA(6) = 120 .

HMS: returns a SAS time value from hour, minute, and second

HMS(hour,minute,second)

The HMS function produces a SAS time value from *hour*, *minute*, and *second* values. For example, the SAS statements:

DATA A;
  START = HMS(3,19,24);
  PUT START = TIME8.;

produce the line:

START = 03:19:24 .

Without the TIME8. format specification in the PUT statement, the result is printed as a SAS time value (the number of seconds since 12:00 PM).

See **USING SAS DATE, TIME, AND DATETIME INFORMATS AND FORMATS** in Chapter 13 for a discussion of date and time values, informats, formats, and literals.

HOUR: returns the hour from a SAS datetime or time value or literal

HOUR(time)
HOUR(datetime)

The HOUR function operates on a SAS *time* or *datetime* value, or a SAS time or datetime literal, to produce a numeric value containing the hour. For example, the SAS statements:

DATA CLOCK;
  TIME = HMS('3:19:24'T);
  H = HOUR(TIME);
  PUT H = ;

produce:

H = 3 .

See **USING SAS DATE, TIME, AND DATETIME INFORMATS AND FORMATS** in Chapter 13 for a discussion of date and time values, informats, formats, and literals.

INDEX: searches for a pattern of characters

> INDEX(*charactervariable,string*)

The INDEX function searches the first argument from left to right for the first occurrence of the pattern specified in the second argument, and returns the position of the first character in the pattern. If the pattern is not found, a value of 0 is returned.

Example:

    A = 'ABC.DEF (X = Y)';
    B = 'X = Y';
    X = INDEX(A,B);

The value of X is 10, the starting position in A of the pattern X = Y.

INDEXC: finds the first occurrence of any one of a set of characters

> INDEXC(*charactervariable,string,...,string*)

The INDEXC function searches the first argument from left to right for the first occurrence of any character in any string you specify. The index of the character, its position in the argument, is returned. If no character in any specified string is found, a value of 0 is returned.

For example, to find the first numeric or special character in a string, you could use these statements:

    A = 'ABC.DEP (X2 = Y1)';
    X = INDEXC(A,'0123456789',';( ) = . ');

The value of X is 4, because the period (.) in the second string is the first character INDEXC finds in the A value, and it is the fourth character in A.

INPUT: defines an informat for a value

> INPUT(*argument,informat*)

This function allows you to "read" *argument,* a character value or a numeric value converted to character, using any informat you specify. The informat specified determines whether the result is numeric or character. For example:

    RELEASE = '76.6';
    NRELEASE = INPUT(RELEASE,4.1);

results in NRELEASE having the numeric value 76.6.

INT: returns the integer value (truncates)

> INT(*argument*)

This function results in the integer portion of the value of the argument. If the argument's value is within 10^{-12} of an integer, the function results in that integer. Hence if the value of *argument* is positive, INT(*argument*) has the same result as FLOOR(*argument*). If the value of *argument* is negative, INT(*argument*) has the same result as CEIL(*argument*).

Examples:

    INT(2.1) = 2
    INT(-2.4) = -2
    INT(3) = 3
    INT(-1.6) = -1 .

INTCK: returns the number of time intervals

INTCK(*interval,from,to*)

The INTCK function determines the number of time intervals that occur in a given time span. The result is always an integer value. For example, you could use the INTCK function to find the number of weeks in the time span beginning 27MAR80 and ending 20DEC80:

```
DATA A;
  N = INTCK('WEEK','27MAR80'D,'20DEC80'D);
```

The value of N is 39.

The *interval* must be a character constant or variable whose value is one of those listed below. Use date intervals when *from* and *to* contain date values; use datetime intervals when *from* and *to* contain datetime values; and use values listed under time intervals when *from* and *to* contain time values. The *from* and *to* values can be expressed as SAS date, datetime, or time values; or as SAS date, datetime, or time literals.

date intervals	datetime intervals	time intervals
DAY	DTDAY	HOUR
WEEK	DTWEEK	MINUTE
MONTH	DTMONTH	SECOND
QTR	DTQTR	
YEAR	DTYEAR	

See **USING SAS DATE, TIME, AND DATETIME INFORMATS AND FORMATS** in Chapter 13 for a discussion of date and time values, informats, formats, and literals.

The INTCK function counts intervals from fixed interval beginnings, not in multiples of an interval unit from the *from* value. For example, WEEK intervals are counted by Sundays rather than seven-day multiples from the *from* argument. YEAR intervals are counted from 01JAN, not in 365-day multiples. The result of:

INTCK('YEAR','31DEC81'D,'1JAN82'D)

is 1, even though only one day has elapsed. The result of:

INTCK('YEAR','1JAN81'D,'31DEC81'D)

is 0, even though 364 days have elapsed. In the first example, an 01JAN date is counted between the *from* and *to* values, so a YEAR interval is added. In the second example 01JAN is not counted between the *from* and *to* values, so an interval is not added.

INTNX: advances a date, time, or datetime value by a given interval

INTNX(*interval,from,number*)

The INTNX function generates a SAS date, time, or datetime value that is a given *number* of time intervals from a starting value (*from*). The *interval* must be a character constant or variable whose value is one of those listed under the INTCK description (see above). The *from* argument must be a SAS date, time, or datetime value, or a SAS date, time, or datetime literal; and *number* gives the number of intervals to use.

For example, you could use the INTNX function to determine the first day of the week that is 38 weeks after 27MAR80:

```
DATA A;
  WANTED= INTNX('WEEK','27MAR80'D,38);
  PUT WANTED= DATE7.;
```

The value of WANTED is 14DEC80, the Sunday of the 38th week.

If the *number* argument is 0 the returned value is the first value of the specified *interval* in which the *from* argument falls. For example:

```
X= INTNX('MONTH','05JAN82'D,0);
PUT X= DATE.;
```

produces X= 01JAN82.

Note that you must specify a SAS date, time, or datetime format to print the result as a readable value; otherwise, results are printed as SAS date, time, or datetime values. See **USING SAS DATE, TIME, AND DATETIME INFORMATS AND FORMATS** in Chapter 13 for a discussion of date and time values, informats, formats, and literals.

JULDATE: returns the Julian date from a SAS date value or literal

JULDATE(*date*)

The JULDATE function converts a SAS *date* value or date literal to a numeric value containing the Julian representation of the date. If the date is a 20th century date there are five digits; the first two are the year, and the next three the day of the year. If the date is not a 20th century date, there are seven digits; the first four are the year, and the next three the day of the year. Thus, 1JAN79 is 79001 in Julian representation; 31DEC1878 is 1878365. The SAS statements:

```
DATA A;
  DATE= MDY(1,1,79);
  JULIAN= JULDATE(DATE);
  PUT JULIAN=;
```

produce:

JULIAN= 79001   .

See **USING SAS DATE, TIME, AND DATETIME INFORMATS AND FORMATS** in Chapter 13 for a discussion of date and time values, informats, formats, and literals.

KURTOSIS: calculates the kurtosis, the 4th moment

KURTOSIS(*argument,argument,...*)

The result of this function is the kurtosis statistic of the arguments. Abbreviated argument lists preceded by OF can be used.

Example:

KURTOSIS(0,1,0,1) = -6 .

See "Introduction to Descriptive Statistics" for a definition of this statistic.

LAG: lagged values

LAG*n*(*argument*)

A family of LAG functions, named LAG1, LAG2, ..., LAG100, is available for obtaining up to 100 lags of a variable's value. (LAG1 can also be written as LAG.) The LAG function can have either numeric or character arguments. It "remembers" values of the argument from a previous execution of the function.

Each LAG function in a program has its own "stack" of lag values. The stack for a LAG*n* function is initialized with *n* missing values, where *n* is the number of lags (for example, a LAG2 stack is initialized with two missing values). Each time the function is executed, the value at the top of the stack is returned, and the current value of the argument is placed at the bottom of the stack. This means that missing values are returned for the first *n* executions of a LAG function, after which the lagged values of the argument are returned.

For example, consider this DATA step:

```
DATA ONE;
  INPUT X@@;
  Y = LAG1(X);
  Z = LAG2(X);
  CARDS;
1 2 3 4
```

Data set ONE contains the following values for X, Y, and Z:

```
X   Y   Z
1   .   .
2   1   .
3   2   1
4   3   2
```

The LAG1 function returns one missing value and then the values of X (lagged once); the LAG2 function returns two missing values and then the values of X (lagged twice).

Note: LAGs are only generated when a LAG function is executed; they are not automatically generated for each observation. If the LAG function is used in the THEN clause of an IF statement (that is, if it is executed conditionally), only values from those observations meeting the IF condition are used for lagging. The following example demonstrates this:

```
DATA A;
  INPUT Y@@;
  IF __N__>1 THEN X=Y*2+LAG(X);
    ELSE X=Y*2;
  CARDS;
1 2 3 4
```

The DATA step causes this error message:

MISSING VALUES WERE GENERATED AS A RESULT OF PERFORMING
AN OPERATION ON MISSING VALUES.

Data set A contains these values:

```
OBS   Y   X
 1    1   2
 2    2   .
 3    3   .
 4    4   .
```

X is always missing except in the first observation, because LAG1(X) returns a value from the last time the LAG was executed, not from the previous observation. The first time the DATA step is executed __N__=1, so the conditions of the IF statement are not met. The ELSE statement is executed and X has a value of 2. The first time the LAG function is executed, the lag value is a missing value, which causes X to be missing, and all succeeding X values to be missing.

If the argument to LAG is an array name, each array element is lagged separately.

LEFT: left-aligns a character string

> LEFT(*charactervar*)

The LEFT function returns the argument with beginning blanks moved to the end of the value. The result has the same length as the original value. For example, the statements:

> A = ' HI THERE';
> B = LEFT(A);

give B the value 'HI THERE   '.

LENGTH: length of a character argument

> LENGTH(*argument*)

This function takes a character argument. The result is the position of the right-most non-blank character in the argument. If the argument is missing, a 1 is returned.

Example:

> LENGTH('ABCDEF') = 6   .

LGAMMA: calculates the natural logarithm of the GAMMA function of a value

> LGAMMA(*argument*)

This function results in the natural logarithm of the GAMMA function of the value of *argument* (see GAMMA). The value of *argument* must be positive.

Example:

> LGAMMA(2) = 0 .

LOG: natural logarithm

> LOG(*argument*)

The result of this function is the natural (Naperian) logarithm of the value of *argument*. The argument must have a positive value.
  The base of natural logarithms is e, approximately 2.71828.

Examples:

> LOG(1) = 0
> LOG(10) = 2.30259   .

LOG2: logarithm to the base 2

> LOG2(*argument*)

This function results in the logarithm to the base 2 of the value of *argument*. The argument must have a positive value.

Examples:

> LOG2(2) = 1
> LOG2(.5) = −1 .

LOG10: common logarithm

> LOG10(*argument*)

This function results in the common logarithm (log to the base 10) of the value of the *argument*. The argument must have a positive value.

Examples:

    LOG10(1) = 0
    LOG10(10) = 1
    LOG10(100) = 2 .

MAX: returns the largest value

    MAX(*arguments*)

This function may have two or more arguments. Its result is the largest value among the *arguments*. Abbreviated argument lists preceded by OF can be used.

Examples:

    MAX(2,6) = 6
    MAX(2,-3) = 2
    MAX(3,-3,MISSING) = 3 .

See "Introduction to Descriptive Statistics" for a definition of this statistic.

MDY: returns a SAS date value from month, day, and year

    MDY(*month,day,year*)

The MDY function produces a SAS date value from numeric values that represent *month*, *day*, and *year*. For example, the SAS statements:

    DATA A;
      M=8;
      D=27;
      Y=47;
      BIRTHDAY=MDY(M,D,Y);
      PUT BIRTHDAY= DATE7.;

produce the line:

    BIRTHDAY=27AUG47   .

Note that this result is printed as a SAS date value (number of days from 01JAN60) unless a date format is specified.

See **USING SAS DATE, TIME, AND DATETIME INFORMATS AND FORMATS** in Chapter 13 for a discussion of date and time values, informats, formats, and literals.

MEAN: computes the arithmetic mean (average)

    MEAN(*arguments*)

The MEAN function results in the average of the values of the arguments. Abbreviated argument lists preceded by OF can be used.

Example:

    MEAN(2,6) = 4   .

See "Introduction to Descriptive Statistics" for a definition of this statistic.

MIN: returns the smallest value

    MIN(*arguments*)

This function may have two or more arguments. Its result is the smallest value among the nonmissing values of the *arguments*. Abbreviated argument lists preceded by OF can be used.

Examples:

```
MIN(2,6) = 2
MIN(2, – 3) = – 3
MIN(0,4,MISSING) = 0  .
```

See "Introduction to Descriptive Statistics" for a definition of this statistic.

MINUTE: returns the minute from a SAS time or datetime value or literal

```
MINUTE(time)
MINUTE(datetime)
```

The MINUTE function operates on a SAS *time* or *datetime* value or SAS time or datetime literal to produce a numeric value containing the minute. For example, the statements:

```
DATA A;
   TIME = '3:19:24'T;
   M = MINUTE(TIME);
   PUT M = ;
```

produce the line:

```
M = 19  .
```

See **USING SAS DATE, TIME, AND DATETIME INFORMATS AND FORMATS** in Chapter 13 for a discussion of date and time values, informats, formats, and literals.

MOD: calculates the remainder

```
MOD(argument1,argument2)
```

The result of this function is the remainder when the quotient of *argument1* divided by *argument2* is calculated.

Examples:

```
MOD(6,3) = 0
MOD(10,3) = 1
MOD(11,3.5) = .5
MOD(10, – 3) = 1  .
```

MONTH: returns the month from a SAS date value or literal

```
MONTH(date)
```

The MONTH function operates on a SAS *date* value or date literal to produce a numeric value containing the month. For example, the statements:

```
DATA A;
   DATE = '25DEC79'D;
   M = MONTH(DATE);
   PUT M = ;
```

produce the line:

```
M = 12  .
```

See **USING SAS DATE, TIME, AND DATETIME INFORMATS AND FORMATS** in Chapter 13 for a discussion of date and time values, informats, formats, and literals.

N: reports the number of nonmissing arguments

N(*argument,argument,...*)

This function returns the number of nonmissing arguments. Abbreviated argument lists preceded by OF can be used.

Example:

N(1,0,.) = 2   .

See "Introduction to Descriptive Statistics" for a definition of this statistic.

NMISS: reports the number of missing values

NMISS(*argument,argument,...*)

This function gives the number of missing values in a string of arguments. Abbreviated argument lists preceded by OF can be used.

Example:

NMISS(1,10,3,.) = 1   .

See "Introduction to Descriptive Statistics" for a definition of this statistic.

NORMAL: generates a normally distributed pseudo-random variate

NORMAL(*argument*)

The result of this function is a pseudo-random variate; the variates generated by NORMAL appear to be normally distributed with mean 0 and standard deviation 1.

Argument should be either 0 or a 5-, 6-, or 7-digit odd integer. The *argument* is used only the first time SAS evaluates the function. Each subsequent time the function is evaluated, the result of the last evaluation is used in generating the new variate. If *argument* is 0, SAS uses a reading of the time of day from the computer's clock to generate the first variate. Otherwise, the constant specified is used to generate the first variate. An expression:

M + S*NORMAL(*argument*)

can produce variates with mean M and standard deviation S.

NORMAL uses a central limit theorem approximation:

$$x = (\Sigma u_i - n/2)/\sqrt{n/12}$$

where u_i are from UNIFORM and n is 12. (See the RANNOR function for a better generator.)

POISSON: probability values for the Poisson distribution

POISSON(*lambda,n*)

where $0 <= lambda$ and $0 <= n$.

This function returns the probability that an observation from a Poisson distribution is less than or equal to n. *Lambda* is the value of the mean parameter. A single term of the Poisson distribution may be computed as a difference of two values of the cumulative distribution. If X = POISSON(*lambda,n*) then:

$$X = \Sigma_{j=0}^{n} e^{-\lambda}(\lambda^j/j!)   .$$

Example:

POISSON(1,2) = .9197   .

PROBBETA: probability values from a beta distribution

PROBBETA(x,a,b)

where $0 <= x <= 1$ and $0 < a,b$.

This function returns probability values from a beta distribution. The a and b values are the shape parameters of the beta distribution, and x is the value at which the distribution is to be evaluated. The density is:

$$x^{a-1}(1-x)^{b-1}\Gamma(a + b)/\Gamma(a)\Gamma(b) \quad .$$

The incomplete beta function may be obtained from this function by multiplying the beta probability by values of the complete beta function, which may be computed from the GAMMA function.

This function is related to many of the common distributions of statistics and also has applications in analyzing order statistics (see Michael and Schucany, 1979).

PROBBNML: probability values from a binomial distribution

PROBBNML(p,n,m)

where $0 <= p <= 1$, $1 <= n$, $0 <= m <= n$.

This function returns the probability that an observation from a binomial distribution with parameters p and n is less than or equal to m. The binomial probability parameter is p, and n is the degree of the binomial distribution. A single term in the binomial distribution can be obtained as the difference of two values of the cumulative binomial distribution.

If X = PROBBNML(p,n,m), then:

$$X = \sum_{j=0}^{m}\binom{n}{j}p^{j}(1-p)^{n-j} \quad .$$

Example:

PROBBNML(.5, 10, 4) = .37695 .

PROBCHI: computes probability values for the chi-square distributions

PROBCHI(x,df)

The PROBCHI function computes the probability that a random variable with a central chi-square distribution, with df degrees of freedom, falls below the x value given.

PROBF: the probability for the F distribution

PROBF(x,ndf,ddf)

The PROBF function computes the probability that a random variable with an F distribution, with ndf numerator degrees of freedom and ddf denominator degrees of freedom, falls below the x value given. To find the significance level, use:

$1 - $PROBF(x,ndf,ddf) .

This function accepts noninteger degrees of freedom.

PROBGAM: probability values for the gamma distribution

PROBGAM(x,eta)

The PROBGAM function computes the probability that a random variable with a gamma distribution with shape parameter η falls below the x value given. The GAMINV function is the function inverse of PROBGAM.

The density is:

$$x^{\eta-1}e^{-x}/\Gamma(\eta)$$

where η is the shape parameter.

PROBHYPR: probabilities from a hypergeometric distribution

PROBHYPR(*nn,k,n,x,or*)

where:

$1 <= nn$
$1 <= k <= nn$
$1 <= n <= nn$
$\text{MAX}(0,k+n-nn) <= x <= \text{MIN}(k,n)$.

This function returns the probability that an observation from a hypergeometric distribution with total sample *nn*, margins *n* and *k*, and odds ratio *or* is less than or equal to *x*. The *or* argument can be omitted; if it is, the *or* parameter is assumed to be 1.

Example:

PROBHYPR(10,5,3,2) = .9167
PROBHYPR(10,5,3,2,1.5) = .8541   .

PROBIT: inverse normal distribution function

PROBIT(*argument*)

This function is the inverse of the standard normal cumulative distribution function. The value of *argument* should be between 0 and 1. The result will lie between -5 and $+5$. PROBIT is the function inverse of PROBNORM. If X is a normally distributed random variable with mean 0 and standard deviation 1, then *argument* is the probability that X will take on a value less than PROBIT(*argument*).

Examples:

PROBIT(.25) = $-$ .67449   .

PROBNEGB: probability values for the negative binomial distribution

PROBNEGB(*p,n,m*)

where $0<=p<=1$, $1<=n$, and $0<=m$.

This function returns the probability that an observation from a negative binomial distribution with parameters *p* and *n* is less than or equal to *m*. The binomial probability parameter is *p* and *n* is the degree of the negative binomial distribution. The value of a single term in the negative binomial distribution can be obtained by a difference of two values of the cumulative distribution.

If X = PROBNEGB(*p,n,m*) then:

$$X = \sum_{j=0}^{m}(1-p)^n p^j \binom{n+j-1}{j}$$

Example:

PROBNEGB(.5,2,1) = .5   .

PROBNORM: computes probabilities for normal distributions

PROBNORM(*x*)

The PROBNORM function computes the probability that a random variable with a normal (0,1) distribution falls below the *x* value given. This function is equivalent to:

$$.5 + \text{ERF}(X/\sqrt{2})/2 \quad .$$

The PROBIT function is the function inverse of PROBNORM.

Examples:

    PROBNORM(0) = .5
    PROBNORM(1.96) = .975   .

PROBT: the probability for the *t* distribution function

   PROBT(x,df)

The PROBT function computes the probability that a random variable with a Student's *t* distribution with *df* degrees of freedom falls below the *x* value given. For a two-tailed test, compute the significance level by:

    $(1 - \text{PROBT}(\text{ABS}(x),\text{DF}))*2$.

This function accepts noninteger degrees of freedom.

Example:

    PROBT(.9,5) = 0.795   .

PUT: specifies an output format for a value

   PUT(*argument,format*)

This function allows you to "write" a value using the format you specify. For example, this statement converts the values of a numeric variable CC containing completion codes into the 3-character hex representation of the codes:

    CCHEX = PUT(CC,HEX3.);

CCHEX's value is the same as the characters that would be written with the statement:

    PUT CC HEX3.;

   If the variable argument is a numeric variable the resulting string is right-aligned. If the variable argument is a character variable, the result is left-aligned.

QTR: returns the quarter from a SAS date value or literal

   QTR(*date*)

The QTR function returns a value of 1, 2, 3, or 4 from a SAS *date* value or date literal to indicate the quarter in which a date value falls.

Examples:

    QTR(3005) = 1
    QTR('20JAN82'D) = 1   .

RANBIN: generates an observation from a binomial distribution with arguments *n* and *p*

   RANBIN(*argument,n,p*)

where $n > 0$ integer, and $0 < p < 1$.

   For any numeric argument (see the RANUNI function for a complete discussion of *argument*) the RANBIN function generates an observation of a binomial variate with mean np and variance $np(1-p)$. If $n <= 50$ the inverse transform method is applied to a RANUNI uniform deviate. If $n > 50$, the normal approximation to the binomial distribution is used. In this case, the normal deviate is generated using the Box-Muller transformation of RANUNI uniform deviates.

The CALL RANBIN subroutine is an alternative to the RANBIN function that gives you greater control of the seed and random number streams. See **CALL Subroutines** in the description of the RANUNI function for complete details on the use of CALL RANBIN.

RANCAU: generates a Cauchy deviate

RANCAU(*argument*)

For any numeric *argument* (see the RANUNI function for a complete discussion of *argument*) the RANCAU function generates an observation of a Cauchy random variable with location parameter 0 and scale parameter 1. An acceptance-rejection procedure and RANUNI uniform deviates are used for generation. The technique relies on the fact that if u and v are independent uniform $(-1/2, 1/2)$ variables and $u^2 + v^2 \le 1/4$ then u/v is a Cauchy deviate.

If:

$$X = ALPHA + BETA*RANCAU(SEED)$$

then X is a *Cauchy variate* with location parameter ALPHA and scale parameter BETA.

The CALL RANCAU subroutine is an alternative to the RANCAU function that gives you greater control of the seed and random number streams. See **CALL Subroutines** in the description of the RANUNI function for complete details on the use of CALL RANCAU.

RANEXP: generates an exponential deviate

RANEXP(*argument*)

For any numeric *argument* (see the RANUNI function for a complete discussion of *argument*) the RANEXP function generates an observation of an exponential variate with parameter 1. The inverse transform method applied to a RANUNI uniform deviate is used for generation.

If:

$$X = RANEXP(SEED)/LAMBDA$$

then X is an *exponential variate* with parameter LAMBDA.

If:

$$X = ALPHA - BETA*LOG(RANEXP(SEED))$$

then X is an an *extreme value variate* with location parameter ALPHA and scale parameter BETA.

If:

$$X = FLOOR(-RANEXP(SEED)/LOG(P))$$

then X is a *geometric variate* with parameter P.

The CALL RANEXP subroutine is an alternative to the RANEXP function that gives you greater control of the seed and random number streams. See **CALL Subroutines** in the description of the RANUNI function for complete details on the use of CALL RANEXP.

RANGAM: generates an observation from a gamma distribution with shape parameter *alpha*

RANGAM(*argument,alpha*)

where *alpha*>0.

For any numeric *argument* (see the RANUNI function for a complete discussion of *argument*) the RANGAM function generates an observation from a gamma distribution with density function:

$$f(x) = x^{\alpha-1}e^{-x}/\Gamma(\alpha)$$

where $\alpha>0$, and $x>0$.

A combination of techniques is used in generating an observation. For a noninteger *alpha* two independent gamma variates are generated: one with parameter INT(*alpha*), the integer part of *alpha*, and the other with parameter *alpha*–INT(*alpha*). The sum of the gamma variates has the desired distribution. For integer *alpha* only the first of these need be generated. The inverse transformation of a RANUNI uniform deviate is used to generate the gamma variate with parameter INT(*alpha*) and an acceptance-rejection method is used to generate the other gamma variate (Fishman, 1978). To expedite execution, internal variables used in generation are calculated only on initial calls (that is, with each new *alpha*).

If:

    X = BETA*RANGAM(SEED,ALPHA)

then X is a *gamma variate* with shape parameter ALPHA and scale parameter BETA.

If 2*ALPHA is an integer, and:

    X = 2*RANGAM(SEED,ALPHA)

then X is a *chi-square variate* with 2*ALPHA degrees of freedom.

If:

    X = BETA*RANGAM(SEED,N)

where N is a positive integer, then X is an *Erlang variate*. It has the distribution of the sum of N independent exponential variates whose means are BETA.

If:

    Y1 = RANGAM(SEED,ALPHA);
    Y2 = RANGAM(SEED,BETA);
    X = Y1/(Y1 + Y2);

then X is a *beta variate* with parameters ALPHA and BETA, and density function:

$$f(x) = x^{\alpha-1}(1-x)^{\beta-1}\Gamma(\alpha+\beta)/\Gamma(\alpha)\Gamma(\beta)$$

where $0<= x <= 1$ and $\alpha,\beta>0$.

The CALL RANGAM subroutine is an alternative to the RANGAM function that gives you greater control of the seed and random number streams. See **CALL Subroutines** in the description of the RANUNI function for complete details on the use of CALL RANGAM.

RANGE: reports the range of values

    RANGE(*arguments*)

The result of this function is the range of the values of the arguments. Abbreviated argument lists preceded by OF can be used.

Example:

    RANGE(2,6,3) = 4 .

See "Introduction to Descriptive Statistics" for a definition of this statistic.

RANNOR: generates a normal deviate

RANNOR(*argument*)

For any numeric *argument* (see the RANUNI function for a complete discussion of *argument*) the RANNOR function generates an observation of a normal random variable with mean 0 and variance 1. The Box-Muller transformation of RANUNI uniform deviates is used for generation.

If:

X = MU + SQRT(SIGMASQ)*RANNOR(SEED)

then X is a *normal variate* with mean MU and variance SIGMASQ.

If:

X = EXP(MU + SQRT(SIGMASQ)*RANNOR(SEED))

then X is a *lognormal variate* with mean:

EXP(MU + SIGMASQ/2)

and variance:

EXP(2*MU + SIGMASQ)*(EXP(SIGMASQ)–1) .

The CALL RANNOR subroutine is an alternative to the RANNOR function that gives you greater control of the seed and random number streams. See **CALL Subroutines** in the description of the RANUNI function for complete details on the use of CALL RANNOR.

RANPOI: generates an observation from a Poisson distribution with parameter *lambda*

RANPOI(*argument,lambda*)

where *lambda*>0.

For any numeric *argument* (see the RANUNI function for a complete discussion of *argument*) the RANPOI function generates an observation of a Poisson variate. The inverse transform method applied to a RANUNI uniform deviate is the generating technique. The method for inverting the cumulative distribution function varies with the value of the parameter *lambda*. For a noninteger *lambda* two independent Poisson variates are generated: one with parameter INT(*lambda*), the integer part of *lambda*; the other with parameter *lambda*–INT(*lambda*). The sum of the Poisson variates is returned (Fishman, 1976). To expedite execution, internal variables used in generation are calculated only on initial calls (that is, with each new *lambda*).

The CALL RANPOI subroutine is an alternative to the RANPOI function that gives you greater control of the seed and random number streams. See **CALL Subroutines** in the description of the RANUNI function for complete details on the use of CALL RANPOI.

RANTBL: generates deviates from a tabled probability mass function

RANTBL(*argument*,$p_1,...p_i,...,p_n$)

where $0<=p_i<=1$ for $0<i<=n$.

For any numeric argument (see the RANUNI function for a complete discussion of *argument*) the RANTBL function returns an observation generated from the probability mass function defined by p_1 through p_n. In particular:

RANTBL =   1 with probability p_1
2 with probability p_2
.
.
n with probability p_n .

The inverse transform method applied to a RANUNI uniform deviate is used in generation.

Note: if you execute:

X = RANTBL(SEED,P1,...,Pn);
IF X=1 THEN X = M1;
ELSE IF X=2 THEN X = M2;
.   .
.   .
ELSE IF X=n THEN X=Mn;

then X takes the values M1 through Mn with probabilities P1 through Pn, respectively.

The CALL RANTBL subroutine is an alternative to the RANTBL function that gives you greater control of the seed and random number streams. See **CALL Subroutines** in the description of the RANUNI function for complete details on the use of CALL RANTBL.

RANTRI: generates an observation from the triangular distribution with parameter h

RANTRI(argument,h)

where $0 < h < 1$.

For any numeric *argument* (see the RANUNI function for a complete discussion of *argument*) the RANTRI function returns an observation generated from the triangular distribution with density function:

$$f(x) = 2x/h$$

where $0 <= x <= h$; or

$$f(x) = 2(1-x)/(1-h)$$

where $h < x <= 1$.

The inverse transform method applied to a RANUNI uniform deviate is used for generation.

The CALL RANTRI subroutine is an alternative to the RANTRI function that gives you greater control of the seed and random number streams. See **CALL Subroutines** in the description of the RANUNI function for complete details on the use of CALL RANTRI.

RANUNI: generates a uniform deviate

RANUNI(argument)

For any numeric argument the RANUNI function returns a number generated from the uniform distribution on the interval (0,1) using a prime modulus multiplicative generator with modulus $2^{31}-1$ and multiplier 397204094 (Fishman and Moore, 1982). The argument must be a numeric constant.

The technique requires the initialization of a random number stream with a seed. The *argument* specifies one of three types of initializations. The conventions for *argument*, described below, are identical for all of the random number generators.

argument	action
0	On the first execution of a function, giving 0 for an *argument* initializes the stream with a seed equal to a computer clock observation and returns an observation generated with this seed. On subsequent executions the function returns an observation generated with the current seed.
>0	On the first execution of the function the *argument* is used as the current seed to initialize the stream and return an observation. On subsequent executions an observation generated with the current seed is returned.
<0	When negative values are given for the *argument*, a new clock observation is used as the current seed to generate an observation at **every** execution of the function.

Note: the performance of the generator has not been evaluated when the *argument* is either zero or negative.

Note: although the current seed changes each time the function is executed, the value of *argument* remains unchanged.

CALL Subroutines

SAS provides a series of subroutines that give you more control over the seed stream and the random number stream than is possible with the random number generating functions. These random number generating subroutines are invoked with CALL statements. The general form of a CALL statement is:

   CALL *routinename(seed,variate)*;

where *routinename* is the name of any SAS random number generating subroutine (except NORMAL or UNIFORM), *seed* is the name of a variable to hold the current seed values, and *variate* is the name of a variable to hold the generated variates. The *seed* variable should be initialized prior to the first execution of the CALL statement.

After an execution of the CALL statement, *seed* contains the current seed in the stream (that is, the seed that will generate the next number), and *variate* contains the generated number.

Using the CALL subroutines rather than the random number functions allows you to initialize more than one random number stream in a DATA step. With the random number functions, more than one set of random numbers can be created, but they all come from one stream (only one stream is initialized). The example below illustrates this.

```
DATA A;
  RETAIN SEED1 SEED2 1613218064;
  DO I = 1 TO 5;
    X1 = RANUNI(SEED1);
    X2 = RANUNI(SEED2);
    OUTPUT;
    END;
PROC PRINT;
```

PROC PRINT produces this output:

OBS	SEED1	SEED2	I	X1	X2
1	1613218064	1613218064	1	0.800831	0.770936
2	1613218064	1613218064	2	0.009603	0.498510
3	1613218064	1613218064	3	0.442188	0.646033
4	1613218064	1613218064	4	0.500457	0.731599
5	1613218064	1613218064	5	0.558058	0.500674

Notice that although the initial values of SEED1 and SEED2 are the same (1613218064), the numbers generated and held in X1 and X2 are different. This is because only one stream was initialized; the program ignores the value given for SEED2, and uses the current seed in the stream begun by the first RANUNI statement instead. Thus, the first value of X2 is not the result of a seed value of 1613218064; it is the result of an unknown seed.

Below is an example that shows that more than one stream can be initialized if a CALL subroutine is used.

```
DATA;
  RETAIN SEED4 SEED5 1613218064;
  DO I=1 TO 5;
    CALL RANUNI(SEED4,X4);
    CALL RANUNI(SEED5,X5);
    OUTPUT;
  END;
PROC PRINT;
```

PROC PRINT produces this output:

OBS	SEED4	SEED5	I	X4	X5
1	1719772190	1719772190	1	0.800831	0.800831
2	1655573359	1655573359	2	0.770936	0.770936
3	20623105	20623105	3	0.009603	0.009603
4	1070543076	1070543076	4	0.498510	0.498510
5	949591638	949591638	5	0.442188	0.442188

After the DATA step is completed, the values of X4 and X5 are identical for each observation, because the CALL statement initialized a second seed stream that began with the same value as the first stream. By initializing SEED4 and SEED5 with different seeds, you can obtain observations from independent streams. Notice that with the CALL subroutines it is possible to see what the current seed is at any time; this is not possible with the random number functions.

REPEAT: repeats character strings

REPEAT(*charactervariable,n*)

The REPEAT function returns a character value consisting of the first argument repeated n times. Thus, the first argument appears $n + 1$ times in the result. For example, the statement:

X = REPEAT('ONE',2);

gives the value 'ONEONEONE'.

REVERSE: reverse characters

REVERSE(*argument*)

This function takes a character argument. It returns a character result the same length as *argument*. The order of the characters in the result is the reverse of the order in *argument*.

Example:

REVERSE('abc') = 'cba' .

RIGHT: right-aligns a character string

RIGHT(*charactervariable*)

The RIGHT function returns the argument with trailing blanks moved to the beginning of the value. The result is the same length as the original value. For example, the statements:

A = 'HI THERE   ';
B = RIGHT(A);

give B the value '   HI THERE'.

ROUND: rounds a value to nearest roundoff unit

ROUND(*argument,roundoffunit*)

The ROUND function rounds a value to the nearest roundoff unit.

Examples:

ROUND(223.456,1) = 223
ROUND(223.456,.01) = 223.46
ROUND(223.456,100) = 200
ROUND(223.456) = 223 .

The value of the *roundoff unit* must be greater than zero. If the *roundoff unit* is omitted, a value of 1 is used and *value* is rounded to the nearest integer.
ROUND(X,D) is equivalent to INT(X/D + .5)*D.

SASVER: returns the current version of SAS

SASVER( )

The SASVER function returns the current version of SAS. For example:

SASVER( ) = 82 .

SCAN: scans for words

SCAN(*charactervariable,n,delimiters*)
SCAN(*charactervariable,n*)

SCAN separates the first argument, a character value, into "words," returning the nth word. The characters that separate words are the *delimiters*. If you do not specify *delimiters*, these characters are considered *delimiters*:

blank . < (+ | & ! $ *) ; ¬ – / , % ¦ ¢

The character values must be enclosed in single quotes.
The statements:

ARG = 'ABC.DEF(X = Y)';
WORD = SCAN(ARG,3);

give WORD the value X = Y, the third "word" in the value of ARG.

If two or more delimiters appear together, they are treated as one. If the number of words in the argument is less than *n*, the value of the second argument, a blank is returned.

SECOND: returns the second from a SAS time or datetime value or literal

SECOND(*time*)
SECOND(*datetime*)

The SECOND function operates on a SAS *time* or *datetime* value or a SAS time or datetime literal to produce a numeric value containing the seconds part of the value. For example, the statements:

```
DATA A;
  TIME='3:19:24'DT;
  S=SECOND(TIME);
  PUT S=;
```

produce:

S=24 .

See **USING SAS DATE, TIME, AND DATETIME INFORMATS AND FORMATS** in Chapter 13 for a discussion of date and time values, informats, formats, and literals.

SIGN: returns the sign of a value

SIGN(*x*)

The SIGN function, also known as the signum function, returns a value of –1 if $x < 0$; a value of 0 if $x = 0$; and a value of +1 if $x > 0$. Its action is similar to $x/ABS(x)$.

SIN: trigonometric sine

SIN(*argument*)

This function results in the sine of the value of *argument*. The value of *argument* is assumed to be in radians.

Examples:

SIN(.5)=.479425
SIN(0)=0 .

SINH: hyperbolic sine

SINH(*argument*)

The result of this function is the hyperbolic sine of the value of *argument*. It is equivalent to:

(EXP(*argument*) − EXP(−*argument*))/2 .

Example:

SINH(0) =0 . .

SKEWNESS: gives the skewness

SKEWNESS(*arguments*)

The result of this function is a measure of the skewness of the argument values. Abbreviated argument lists preceded by OF can be used.

Example:

SKEWNESS(0,1,1) = -1.73 .

See "Introduction to Descriptive Statistics" for a definition of this statistic.

SQRT: square root

SQRT(*argument*)

The result of this function is the square root of the value of *argument*. The value of *argument* must be non-negative.

Example:

SQRT(9) = 3 .

STD: calculates the standard deviation

STD(*argument*)

This function gives the standard deviation of the values of the arguments. Abbreviated argument lists preceded by OF can be used.

Example:

STD(2,6) = 2.83 .

See "Introduction to Descriptive Statistics" for a definition of this statistic.

STDERR: calculates the standard error of the mean

STDERR(*argument,argument,...*)

This function results in the standard error of the mean of the values of the arguments. Abbreviated argument lists preceded by OF can be used.

Example:

STDERR(2,6) = 2 .

See "Introduction to Descriptive Statistics" for a definition of this statistic.

STFIPS: converts state postal code to FIPS state code

STFIPS(*postalcode*)

The STFIPS function takes a two-character state postal code (enclosed in quotes) and converts it to the numeric FIPS state code.

Example:

```
ST = 'NC';
FIPS = STFIPS(ST);
PUT FIPS = ;
```

produces:

FIPS = 37 .

STNAME: converts state postal code to state name (all upper case)

STNAME(*postalcode*)

The STNAME function takes a two-character state postal code (enclosed in quotes) and returns a 20-character state name in upper case.

For example:

```
ST = 'NC';
STATE = STNAME(ST);
PUT STATE = ;
```

produces:

```
STATE = NORTH CAROLINA   .
```

STNAMEL: converts state postal code to state name in upper and lower case

STNAMEL(*postalcode*)

The STNAMEL function takes a two-character state postal code (enclosed in quotes) and returns a 20-character state name in upper and lower case. For example:

```
DATA A;
  ST = 'NC';
  STATE = STNAMEL(ST);
  PUT  STATE = ;
```

results in the value:

```
STATE = North Carolina   .
```

SUBSTR: substring and pseudo-variable for character insertion

The SUBSTR function actually serves two roles. They are described below.

substring

SUBSTR(*argument,position,n*)

This function extracts a substring of *argument* beginning at *position* and consisting of *n* characters. If *n* is omitted, the number of characters extracted is the remainder of *argument,* beginning at *position*.

For example, the statements:

```
DATA A;
  DATE = '06MAY78';
  MONTH = SUBSTR(DATE,3,3);
  YEAR = SUBSTR(DATE,6,2);
```

result in the value MAY for MONTH and the value 78 for YEAR.

When the SUBSTR function is used for this purpose you can use an expression for any argument.

pseudo-variable for character insertion

The second role is the SUBSTR pseudo-variable function. You can use SUBSTR on the left side of an equal sign to replace contents of a character value.

SUBSTR(*charvar,position,n*) = *x*;

The value of the variable or constant on the right side of the equal sign is placed into the *charvar* value (the first argument) starting at *position* (given by the second argument), replacing *n* characters (given by the third argument).

For example, the statements:

```
A='KIDNAP';
SUBSTR(A,1,3)='CAT';
```

give A the value CATNAP.

If the *n* value is omitted, characters in the first argument are replaced from *position* to the end of the value. For example, the statements:

```
A='CATNAP';
SUBSTR(A,4)='TY';
```

give A the value CATTY.

SUM: calculates the sum of the arguments

SUM(*arguments*)

The result of the SUM function is the sum of the arguments. Abbreviated argument lists preceded by OF can be used.

Example:

SUM(4,9,3,8)=24 .

See "Introduction to Descriptive Statistics" for a definition of this statistic.

SYMGET: returns the value of a macro variable

SYMGET(*variable*)

The *variable* specified in the SYMGET function is a macro variable, or a variable whose values are names of macro variables. If you want to use a macro variable as the argument, it must be enclosed in single quotes; for example, SYMGET ('MACNAME'). Macro variables are discussed in chapter 15, "SAS Macro Language." The value of a macro variable is a character string, so the SYMGET function returns a character value. If the function is used in an assignment statement, the resulting variable is a character variable.

If the value of the macro variable is longer than the resulting variable, SAS truncates the returned value on the right.

In these statements macro variables SYM1, SYM2, and SYM3 are created, and their values are retrieved with the SYMGET function in a DATA step.

```
%LET SYM1=AAA;
%LET SYM2=BBB;
%LET SYM3=CCC;

DATA NEW;
  INPUT CODE $ @@;
  X=SYMGET(CODE);
  PUT CODE= X=;
  CARDS;
SYM2 SYM3 SYM1 SYM1 SYM3
```

These lines are produced:

```
CODE=SYM2  X=BBB
CODE=SYM3  X=CCC
CODE=SYM1  X=AAA
CODE=SYM1  X=AAA
CODE=SYM3  X=CCC
```

The SYMGET function is especially useful with the CALL SYMPUT statement. Both are described in "SAS Macro Language."

SYSPARM: returns the system parameter string

SYSPARM( )

The SYSPARM function lets you access a character string specified with the SYSPARM= system option in the job control for your job or in an OPTIONS statement.

Example:

```
OPTIONS SYSPARM='YES';
DATA A;
  IF SYSPARM( )='YES' THEN DO;
    .
    .
    .
```

See the **Options Statement** in Chapter 11 for a discussion of the SYSPARM= option.

If the SYSPARM= option is not specified, executing the SYSPARM function returns a null string.

TAN: trigonometric tangent

TAN(*argument*)

This function results in the tangent of the value of the argument. The value of the argument is assumed to be in radians; it may not be an odd multiple of $\pi/2$.

Examples:

```
TAN(.5) = .546302
TAN(0) = 0   .
```

TANH: hyperbolic tangent

TANH(*argument*)

The result of this function is the hyperbolic tangent of the value of the argument. It is equivalent to:

$$\frac{(EXP(argument) - EXP(-argument))}{(EXP(argument) + EXP(-argument))}.$$

Examples:

```
TANH(.5) = .462117
TANH(0) = 0   .
```

TIME: returns the current time of day

TIME( )

The TIME function produces the current time of day as a SAS time value. For example the statements below:

```
DATA A;
  CURRENT = TIME( );
  PUT CURRENT = TIME.;
```

if executed at exactly 2:32 P.M., produce the line:

```
CURRENT = 14:32:00   .
```

Note that unless a TIME. format is specified, the result is printed as a SAS time value (the number of seconds since 12:00 PM). See **USING SAS DATE, TIME, AND DATETIME INFORMATS AND FORMATS** in Chapter 13 for a discussion of date and time values, informats, formats, and literals.

TIMEPART: extracts the time part of a SAS datetime value or literal

TIMEPART(*datetime*)

The TIMEPART function converts a SAS *datetime* value or datetime literal into just the time part. For positive dates, the statement:

TIME = TIMEPART(*datetime*);

is equivalent to:

TIME = MOD(*datetime*,24*60*60);

For example, at 10:40:17 AM, these statements:

DATIM = DATETIME( );
TIME = TIMEPART(DATIM);
PUT TIME = TIME.;

result in this line:

TIME = 10:40:17   .

Note that the result is printed as a SAS time value (number of seconds since 12:00 PM) unless a SAS time format is specified. See **USING SAS DATE, TIME, AND DATETIME INFORMATS AND FORMATS** in Chapter 13 for a discussion of date and time values, informats, formats, and literals.

TODAY: returns the current date as a SAS date value

TODAY( )

The TODAY function, which may also be written:

DATE( )

produces the current date as a SAS date value. For example, executing the statements below on January 20, 1979:

DATA A;
  CURRENT = TODAY();
  PUT CURRENT = DATE7.;

produces the line:

CURRENT = 20JAN79   .

Note that unless you specify a date format, the result is printed as a SAS date value (the number of days since 01JAN60).
See **USING SAS DATE, TIME, AND DATETIME INFORMATS AND FORMATS** in Chapter 13 for a discussion of date and time values, informats, formats, and literals.

TRANSLATE: changes characters in a character variable

TRANSLATE(*charactervariable,to,from,...,to,from*)

The TRANSLATE function allows you to replace any occurrence of a specified character in the first argument with a corresponding character from the second argument. For example, the statement:

X = TRANSLATE('XYZW','AB','VW');

gives X the value XYZB. The character value XYZW is searched for any occurrence of the characters V and W; a W appears in XYZW. In this case, since W is the second character of the value VW, the second character of the value AB replaces W. Thus X's value becomes XYZB.

If the TO value is shorter than FROM, TO is padded with blanks. If the TO value is longer than the FROM value, the TO value is truncated on the right.

You may specify multiple sequences of TO and FROM values. If one or more FROM values are missing, the IBM System 360/370 collating sequence is assumed, in ascending order from '00'X to 'FF'X. Each new sequence starts in the collating sequence where the last missing sequence stops. If the TO value is so long that it causes the collating sequence to exceed the highest possible character, 'FF'X, the TO value is truncated and the next missing sequence starts over at '00'X.

TRIM: removes trailing blanks

TRIM(*charactervariable*)

TRIM returns the argument with trailing blanks removed. For example, the statements:

```
A = 'WXYZ ';
LENGTH B $ 4;
B = TRIM(A);
```

give B the value 'WXYZ'.

Note: you must give the variable on the left side of the equal sign an explicit length; if B's length had not been specified using a LENGTH statement in the example above, it would have been set to A's length, and the trimmed blanks would have been put back to bring B's length up to A's length.

TRIM is useful with other functions, especially since trailing blanks are not automatically trimmed during concatenation. For example, consider these statements:

```
DATA A;
   INPUT FIRST $ 1–10 LAST $ 12–25;
   LENGTH NAME $ 25;
   NAME = TRIM(FIRST)||' '||TRIM(LAST);
   CARDS;
JOHN   SMITH
```

NAME's value is 'JOHN SMITH'. (The single quotes surrounding the blank between the concatenation symbols are used to write a blank between the values of FIRST and LAST.) If the TRIM function had not been used, and the statement:

NAME = FIRST||LAST;

replaced the fourth statement in the example above, NAME's value would have been 'JOHN   SMITH' with ten trailing blanks.

TSO: invokes a TSO command and returns the status code

TSO(*command*)

The TSO function invokes a TSO command that is executed during the SAS job. The *command* is a character string enclosed in quotes corresponding to a TSO command. The function returns the status code after the TSO command has been executed.

Example:

    RC = TSO('ALLOC F(STUDY) DA(MY.LIBRARY)')

The variable RC contains the status code generated after the TSO ALLOC command specified in the TSO function is executed.

UNIFORM: generates a pseudo-random variate uniformly distributed on the interval (0,1)

    UNIFORM(seed)

The result of this function is a pseudo-random variate; the variates generated by UNIFORM appear to be uniformly distributed on the interval (0,1).

Seed must be a constant; either 0 or a 5-, 6-, or 7-digit odd integer. The argument is used only the first time SAS evaluates the function. Each subsequent time the function is evaluated, the result of the last evaluation is used in generating the new variate. If the argument is 0, SAS uses a reading of the time of day from the computer's clock to generate the first variate. Otherwise, the constant specified is used to generate the first variate.

UNIFORM is a multiplicative congruential generator with multiplier 16807, modulus 2^{31}, and a 64-value shuffle table to remove autocorrelation. The method used is documented in Lewis, Goodman, and Miller, 1969, and Kennedy and Gentle, 1980.

(See the RANUNI function for a better generator.)

UPCASE: converts a character string to uppercase

    UPCASE(argument)

The UPCASE function converts a string containing at least one lowercase character to a string of all uppercase letters. For example:

    NAME = UPCASE('John B. Smith');

produces the NAME value JOHN B. SMITH.

The *argument* may be a string enclosed in single quotes or a character variable whose value contains lowercase characters.

USS: calculates the uncorrected sum of squares

    USS(argument,argument,...)

The result of the USS function is the uncorrected sum of squares of the arguments. Abbreviated argument lists preceded by OF can be used.

Example:

    USS(2,6) = 40   .

See "Introduction to Descriptive Statistics" for a definition of this statistic.

VAR: calculates the variance

    VAR(argument,argument...)

The VAR function calculates the variance of the arguments. Abbreviated argument lists preceded by OF can be used.

Example:

    VAR(2,6) = 8   .

See "Introduction to Descriptive Statistics" for a definition of this statistic.

VERIFY: validates a character value

VERIFY(*charactervariable,string,...,string*)

The VERIFY function returns the position of the first character of *charactervariable* that is not present in one of the *string* arguments. If all characters in the first argument are found in at least one of the *string* arguments, a 0 is returned. For example, consider these statements:

```
DATA A;
  CHECK='ABCDE';
  INPUT GRADE $ 1;
  X=VERIFY(GRADE,CHECK);
  IF X NE 0 THEN PUT 'INVALID GRADE VALUE';
```

These statements read a character value from data lines and check that its characters are the letters A through E. If any other characters are found, a message is printed on the log.

WEEKDAY: returns the day of the week from a SAS date value or literal

WEEKDAY(*date*)

The WEEKDAY function converts a SAS *date* value or date literal into a number representing the day of the week, where 1=Sunday, 2=Monday, ..., 7=Saturday.

Example:

WEEKDAY('14MAR82'D)=1 .

See **USING SAS DATE, TIME, AND DATETIME INFORMATS AND FORMATS** in Chapter 13 for a discussion of date and time values, informats, formats, and literals.

YEAR: returns the year from a SAS date value or literal

YEAR(*date*)

The YEAR function operates on a SAS *date* value or date literal to produce a 4-digit numeric value containing the year. For example, the statements:

```
DATA A;
  DATE=MDY(12,25,79);
  Y=YEAR(DATE);
  PUT Y=;
```

produce:

Y=1979 .

See **USING SAS DATE, TIME, AND DATETIME INFORMATS AND FORMATS** in Chapter 13 for a discussion of date and time values, informats, formats, and literals.

YYQ: returns a SAS date value from the year and quarter

YYQ(*year,quarter*)

The YYQ function returns a SAS date value corresponding to the first day of the specified quarter. The *year* value may be either a two- or four-digit year the *quarter* value must be either 1, 2, 3, or 4. If either the year or quarter is missing, or if the quarter value is not 1, 2, 3, or 4, the result is missing. For example, these statements:

```
DATA DATES;
  DV = YYQ(80,3);
  PUT DV = DATE7.;
```

produce this line:

```
DV = 01JUL80  .
```

The result is printed as a SAS date value (number of days since 01JAN60) unless you specify a date format. See **USING SAS DATE, TIME, AND DATETIME INFORMATS AND FORMATS** in Chapter 13 for a discussion of date and time values, informats, formats, and literals.

ZIPFIPS: converts ZIP code to FIPS state code

ZIPFIPS(*ZIP*)

The ZIPFIPS function takes a five-character ZIP code (enclosed in quotes) and returns the numeric FIPS state code. For example, the statements:

```
DATA A;
  ZIP = '27511';
  FIPS = ZIPFIPS(ZIP);
  PUT  FIPS = ;
```

give FIPS the value 37.

ZIPNAME: converts ZIP codes to state names (all upper case)

ZIPNAME(*ZIP*)

The ZIPNAME function takes a five-character ZIP code (enclosed in quotes) and returns a 20-character state name in upper case. For example, the statements:

```
DATA A;
  STATE = ZIPNAME('27511');
  PUT  STATE = ;
```

result in the value:

```
STATE = NORTH CAROLINA
```

for STATE.

ZIPNAMEL: converts ZIP codes to state names in upper and lower case

ZIPNAMEL(*ZIP*)

The ZIPNAMEL function takes a five-character ZIP code (enclosed in quotes) and returns a 20-character state name in upper and lower case. For example, the statements:

```
DATA A;
  STATE = ZIPNAMEL('27511');
  PUT  STATE = ;
```

produce:

```
STATE = North Carolina  .
```

ZIPSTATE: converts ZIP codes to state postal codes

ZIPSTATE(*ZIP*)

The ZIPSTATE function takes a five-character ZIP code (enclosed in quotes) and returns the two-character state postal code. For example, the statements:

```
DATA A;
  ST = ZIPSTATE('27511');
  PUT ST =;
```

produce:

```
ST = NC  .
```

REFERENCES

Abramowitz, M. and Stegun, I. (1964), *Handbook of Mathematical Functions with Formulas, Graphs, and Mathematical Tables*, National Bureau of Standards Applied Mathematics Series #55, Washington, D.C. : U.S. Government Printing Office.

Fishman, G.S. (1976), "Sampling from the Poisson Distribution on a Computer," *Computing*, 17, 147–156.

Fishman, G.S. (1978), *Principles of Discrete Event Simulation*, New York: John Wiley & Sons.

Fishman, G.S. and Moore, L.R. (1982), "A Statistical Evaluation of Multiplicative Congruential Generators with Modulus $(2^{31} - 1)$," *Journal of the American Statistical Association*, 77, 129–136.

Kennedy, W.S. and Gentle, J.E. (1980), *Statistical Computing*, New York: Marcel Dekker, Inc.

Lewis, P.A.W., Goodman, A.S. and Miller, J.M. (1969), "A Pseudo-Random Number Generator for the System/360," *IBM Systems Journal*, 8.

Michael, J. and Schucany, W. (1979), "A New Approach to Testing Goodness of Fit for Censored Data," *Technometrics*, 21, 435–441.

Data Step Applications

This chapter describes some common DATA step applications. In the first section, examples illustrate DO-group processing, arrays, and selected functions. The next part gives details on using the SET, MERGE, and UPDATE statements. The third section describes how to write customized reports.

PROGRAMMING IN THE DATA STEP

This section gives examples of using the DO statement, the ARRAY statement, and selected functions.

DO-Group Processing

Suppose you have a file of prospective clients containing three different kinds of records: name records, address records, and comment records. Each record type is identified by a code in the first two bytes of the record: .n identifies name records, .a identifies address records, and .c, comment records. The number of times each record type occurs varies in each group of name, address, and comment records. The data below are stored in a file described in the job control by DDname IN.

```
.n Ann Lincoln
.a 101 S. Main St.
.a Anytown, USA
.c good prospect
.c called 01MAY81
.c called 04AUG81
.n Mary Scott
.a 1 Castle Street
.a Scotland
.c referred by J. B. King
.c personal visit 01MAY82
.n John B. Doe
.a P.O. Box 3939
.a University of Anystate
.a Local, USA
.n Mary B. Smith
.n Mark E. Smith
.a 123 Home Street
.a Hometown, USA
```

You want to create a SAS data set and a non-SAS file that contain only the name records from the original file. The SAS data set should contain only the variable name; the non-SAS file contains a copy of the name records. The non-SAS file is described in the job control by DDname OUT.

The following three DATA steps each use a statement from the DO/END family of statements.

IF/THEN/DO

```
DATA NEW;
  INFILE IN;
  FILE OUT;
  INPUT CODE $2. @;
  IF CODE='.n' THEN DO;
    PUT __INFILE__;
    INPUT NAME $CHAR25.;
    OUTPUT;
    END;
  KEEP NAME;
```

The DATA step above illustrates these SAS features:

- creating a SAS data set and an external file in the same step
- trailing at sign (@) in an INPUT statement
- PUT __INFILE__ for copying input records
- KEEP statement.

The first INPUT statement brings a record into the input buffer and reads the code value from the first two bytes of the record. The trailing at sign holds the record in the buffer. The DO group is executed only when the value of CODE is '.n'. In that case:

1. the PUT __INFILE__ statement writes the current record from the input buffer to the file described by DDname OUT
2. the second INPUT statement reads the value of NAME from the record in the buffer
3. SAS outputs the new observation to the SAS data set.

The KEEP statement appears at the end of the DATA step. It could appear anywhere in the step and have the same effect of specifying the variable to be output to the SAS data set being created.

The lines written to the external file:

```
                                                                    5
.n Ann Lincoln
.n Mary Scott
.n John B. Doe
.n Mary B. Smith
.n Mark E. Smith
```

The SAS data set NEW:

```
                                                                    4
        OBS      NAME
         1       Ann Lincoln
         2       Mary Scott
         3       John B. Doe
         4       Mary B. Smith
         5       Mark E. Smith
```

Note: if the system option CAPS is set, the job above never finds a CODE value of
'.n' since SAS would change all code in the job to uppercase before executing it.
See the OPTIONS statement in Chapter 11, "SAS Statements Used Anywhere," for
details.

DO WHILE   You can create the same data set and external file with this DATA
step using a DO WHILE statement:

```
DATA NEW;
  KEEP NAME;
  INFILE IN END=EOF;
  FILE OUT;
  INPUT CODE $2. @;
  DO WHILE(CODE='.n');
    PUT __INFILE__;
    INPUT NAME $CHAR25.;
    OUTPUT;
    IF EOF THEN STOP;
    INPUT CODE $2. @;
    END;
```

The first few statements in the step above are identical to those in the previous example except that here the KEEP statement appears first in the DATA step. SAS
evaluates the expression in the DO WHILE statement at the beginning of the loop
before the statements in the DO group are executed. When SAS reads a CODE
value of '.n':

1. PUT __INFILE__ writes the input buffer to file OUT
2. the INPUT statement reads the NAME field from the current record
3. the OUTPUT statement causes the observation to be written to SAS data
   set NEW
4. the next INPUT statement brings in a new record and reads the CODE
   value.

If the CODE value just read is again '.n', SAS repeats the statements just described.
If not, SAS returns to the beginning of the DATA step and a new record.
   Although not required, the STOP statement prevents a lost card message if SAS
reaches end-of-file before all the INPUT statements in the step have been executed.

DO UNTIL   The next DATA step uses a DO UNTIL statement to create the SAS
data set and the output file:

```
DATA NEW(KEEP=NAME);
  INFILE IN END=EOF;
  FILE OUT;
  DO UNTIL(CODE='.n');
    IF EOF THEN STOP;
    INPUT CODE $2. NAME $CHAR25.;
    END;
  PUT __INFILE__;
```

The expression in a DO UNTIL is evaluated at the **bottom** of the loop after the statements in the DO loop are executed. Thus, you can include a variable in the expression that has not yet been given a value. (Note, however, that the first occurrence of the variable in the DATA step determines the variable's attributes.)

The DATA step above reads records from INFILE IN until it finds a CODE value equal to '.n'. In this DATA step the trailing at sign is not used in the INPUT statement, since that would cause SAS to read from the same record, two bytes at a time, looking for the string '.n'. When the CODE value just read is '.n', SAS drops out of the DO loop, executes the PUT __INFILE__ statement, automatically outputs a record to SAS data set NEW, and returns to the beginning of the step for a new execution. If the DATA step included an INPUT statement before the DO UNTIL, the first record in INFILE IN would be lost, since a DO UNTIL is always executed at least one time.

The STOP statement again prevents a lost card message from occurring. A KEEP= data set option giving the variables to appear on the SAS data set is used in the example.

Another DO WHILE and DO UNTIL example   Suppose your file of prospective clients contains codes only for the comment records. The first comment record for an individual or prospective client has a '.c' in the first two bytes of the record; the series of comment records ends with a record containing only a '##' in the first two bytes. The data are shown below:

Ann Lincoln
101 S. Main St.
Anytown, USA
.c good prospect
called 01MAY81
called 04AUG81
##
Mary Scott
1 Castle Street
Scotland
.c referred by J. B. King; called 23APR82;
personal visit 01MAY82
##
John B. Doe
P.O. Box 3939
University of Anystate
Local, USA
Mary B. Smith
Mark E. Smith
123 Home Street
Hometown, USA
.c called 5MAY82
doesn't seem interested now
##

Your goal is to create a file with only the names and addresses from the original file. The DATA steps below create the file without comment records. The new file is described in the job control by DDname OUT.

```
DATA __NULL__;
  INFILE IN;
  FILE OUT;
  INPUT REC $CHAR50.;
  IF REC=:'.c' THEN DO WHILE(REC¬='##');
    INPUT REC $CHAR50.;
    END;
  ELSE PUT REC;
```

The first INPUT statement reads the entire record at once and stores it in the variable REC. If the value of REC begins with the characters '.c', then SAS executes the DO WHILE statement. (See Chapter 4, "SAS Expressions," for more about using the colon (:) in character comparisons.)

Each time the current REC value is not '##', SAS reads another record, replacing the current REC value in the program data vector with a new one. This process continues until the value of REC is '##'. Then SAS exits from the DO WHILE loop and returns to the beginning of the DATA step and a new record.

The lines written by the PUT statements above:

```
                                                               2

Ann Lincoln
101 S. Main St.
Anytown, USA
Mary Scott
.1 Castle Street
Scotland
John B. Doe
P.O. Box 3939
University of Anystate
Local, USA
Mary B. Smith
Mark E. Smith
123 Home Street
Hometown, USA
```

You can replace the DO WHILE statement with a DO UNTIL in the example above, with the same results.

```
DATA __NULL__;
  INFILE IN;
  FILE OUT;
  INPUT REC $CHAR50.;
  IF REC=:'.c' THEN DO UNTIL(REC='##');
    INPUT REC $CHAR50.;
    END;
  ELSE PUT REC;
```

Jumping out of a loop   Once SAS is executing a loop, it is possible to jump out of the loop at any point. You can jump out long enough to execute a series of SAS statements and then return. Or, you can end the loop permanently for that execution of the DATA step.

Below is a list of bank customers along with their initial investments in a savings account. The data are stored in a SAS data set named BANK. (The variable DATE is the date on which the initial investment was deposited. The variable is stored on the SAS data set as a SAS date value and printed using the DATE7. format.)

```
                                                                       2

      OBS    ACCT_NO    AMT      DATE      PERCENT    TYPE

       1      12321    1000    12NOV81     0.0550      A
       2      24242     200    01JAN82     0.0560      M
       3      54321     500    23DEC81     0.0525      A
       4      89921     700    23FEB82     0.0525      M
```

You want to calculate the interest earned for each customer, add it to the initial investment, and obtain a new balance. Interest is paid on the balance in savings accounts of type 'A' on a certain day of the year. Type 'M' savings accounts pay interest every 30 days. In the following program, run on the day of payment to 'A' accounts, the balance in 'M' accounts is calculated in an iterative DO loop; 'A' accounts are handled by the statement following the label CALC.

```
DATA NEW__BAL;
  SET BANK;
  INITIAL = AMT;
  TODAY = TODAY( );
  IF TYPE = 'M' THEN DO;
    MONTH = INT((TODAY-DATE)/30);
    PERCENT = PERCENT/12;
    DO I = 1 TO MONTH;
      LINK CALC;
    END;
  RETURN;
  END;
  CALC: AMT = AMT + AMT*PERCENT;
  RETURN;
```

The DATA step above illustrates several SAS features:

- nested DO loops
- jumping out of a DO loop and returning
- using an expression as the stopping value for a DO-group index variable
- datetime functions.

The resulting data set is NEW__BAL:

```
                                                                                 3

  OBS  ACCT_NO    AMT     DATE     PERCENT   TYPE  INITIAL  TODAY   MONTH    I

   1    12321   1055.00  12NOV81  0.0550000   A     1000    8190      .      .
   2    24242    204.71  01JAN82  0.0046667   M      200    8190   5.13333   6
   3    54321    526.25  23DEC81  0.0525000   A      500    8190      .      .
   4    89921    709.23  23FEB82  0.0043750   M      700    8190   3.36667   4
```

SAS reads observations from SAS data set BANK and stores the initial investment amounts (AMT) in variable INITIAL. TODAY is the SAS date value corresponding to the day the program is run. The number of full (30-day) months (MONTH) is used to determine the number of times the iterative DO loop is executed.

When the TYPE value is 'M', the percent of interest is divided by 12. Then, for each month SAS jumps to the statement labeled CALC and adds the interest to the AMT value.

When the TYPE value is not 'M', SAS skips the outside DO group and executes statements starting with the statement labeled CALC.

Jumping to the end of the DO group   Sometimes you want to end the current execution of a DO loop before all the statements in the loop have been executed, and return to the top of the loop for another execution. You can jump to the END statement for the loop; SAS increments the index for the loop and continues processing.

For example, suppose you want to calculate anticipated monthly sales for each sales representative in a company for determining the annual budget and setting individual goals. The representative's name, length of service with the company, and average monthly sales for the preceding year are stored in a SAS data set named SALES:

NAME	YEARS	AVERAGE
JONES	3	543
SMITH	12	1620
THOMAS	1	210
MARKS	6	895
ADAMS	1	356
DOE	2	250

Each sales representative is expected to increase his or her average monthly sales from the preceding year by five percent in January, five and a half percent in February, six percent in March, six and a half percent in April, and so on for the year. Those employed for more than two years are entitled to a bonus if their total sales for the year reach $10,000. Those eligible for a bonus are output to another SAS data set. The DATA step below creates two SAS data sets: one containing anticipated sales for each sales representative for each month in the coming year, the other containing the names of sales representatives who earned bonuses.

```
DATA YEARLY(KEEP=NAME MONTHTOT) BONUS(KEEP=NAME TOTAL);
  SET SALES;
  TOTAL=0;
  INCREASE=.045;
  DO MONTH='JAN', 'FEB', 'MAR', 'APR', 'MAY', 'JUN', 'JUL',
    'AUG', 'SEP', 'OCT', 'NOV', 'DEC';
    INCREASE=INCREASE+.005;
    MONTHTOT=AVERAGE+AVERAGE*INCREASE;
    OUTPUT YEARLY;
    TOTAL=TOTAL+MONTHTOT;
    IF YEARS<=2 THEN GO TO SKIP;
    IF MONTH='DEC' THEN IF TOTAL>=10000
      THEN OUTPUT BONUS;
  SKIP: END;
```

The DATA step above illustrates:

- creating more than one SAS data set in a single DATA step
- keeping different subsets of variables on data sets created
- using a character variable to index a DO loop
- jumping to the END statement of a DO loop.

SAS first reads an observation from the SALES data set and initializes the variables TOTAL and INCREASE for that representative. Then the DO loop creates new observations for each value of MONTH.

After each observation is output to YEARLY, if the YEARS value is two or less, SAS skips to the END statement. This causes SAS to return to the top of the DO loop, increment the MONTH value, and generate another observation. The resulting data set YEARLY contains twelve observations for each observation from SALES. Each new observation contains a representative's expected sales for that month.

DATA=YEARLY

OBS	NAME	MONTH	MONTHTOT
1	JONES	JAN	570.15
2	JONES	FEB	572.86
3	JONES	MAR	575.58
4	JONES	APR	578.29
5	JONES	MAY	581.01
6	JONES	JUN	583.72
7	JONES	JUL	586.44
8	JONES	AUG	589.15
9	JONES	SEP	591.87
10	JONES	OCT	594.58
11	JONES	NOV	597.30
12	JONES	DEC	600.01
13	SMITH	JAN	1701.00
14	SMITH	FEB	1709.10
15	SMITH	MAR	1717.20
16	SMITH	APR	1725.30
17	SMITH	MAY	1733.40
18	SMITH	JUN	1741.50
19	SMITH	JUL	1749.60
20	SMITH	AUG	1757.70
21	SMITH	SEP	1765.80
22	SMITH	OCT	1773.90
23	SMITH	NOV	1782.00
24	SMITH	DEC	1790.10
25	THOMAS	JAN	220.50
26	THOMAS	FEB	221.55
27	THOMAS	MAR	222.60
28	THOMAS	APR	223.65
29	THOMAS	MAY	224.70
30	THOMAS	JUN	225.75
31	THOMAS	JUL	226.80
32	THOMAS	AUG	227.85
33	THOMAS	SEP	228.90
34	THOMAS	OCT	229.95
35	THOMAS	NOV	231.00
36	THOMAS	DEC	232.05
37	MARKS	JAN	939.75
38	MARKS	FEB	944.22
39	MARKS	MAR	948.70
40	MARKS	APR	953.17
41	MARKS	MAY	957.65
42	MARKS	JUN	962.12
43	MARKS	JUL	966.60
44	MARKS	AUG	971.07
45	MARKS	SEP	975.55
46	MARKS	OCT	980.02
47	MARKS	NOV	984.50
48	MARKS	DEC	988.97
49	ADAMS	JAN	373.80
50	ADAMS	FEB	375.58
51	ADAMS	MAR	377.36
52	ADAMS	APR	379.14
53	ADAMS	MAY	380.92
54	ADAMS	JUN	382.70
55	ADAMS	JUL	384.48

(continued on next page)

```
(continued from previous page)          DATA=YEARLY


                    OBS    NAME     MONTH    MONTHTOT

                    56     ADAMS    AUG      386.26
                    57     ADAMS    SEP      388.04
                    58     ADAMS    OCT      389.82
                    59     ADAMS    NOV      391.60
                    60     ADAMS    DEC      393.38
                    61     DOE      JAN      262.50
                    62     DOE      FEB      263.75
                    63     DOE      MAR      265.00
                    64     DOE      APR      266.25
                    65     DOE      MAY      267.50
                    66     DOE      JUN      268.75
                    67     DOE      JUL      270.00
                    68     DOE      AUG      271.25
                    69     DOE      SEP      272.50
                    70     DOE      OCT      273.75
                    71     DOE      NOV      275.00
                    72     DOE      DEC      276.25
```

When the value of YEARS is more than two, SAS checks to see if the TOTAL sales figure date exceeds \$10,000. Observations whose total sales exceed that amount are output to SAS data set BONUS at the end of the DO loop. (The MONTH='DEC' condition ensures that an observation is output to BONUS only once.)

```
                         DATA=BONUS


               OBS    NAME      TOTAL

                1     SMITH     20946.6
                2     MARKS     11572.3
```

The observations in YEARLY provide the information necessary to determine anticipated sales for the coming year. For example, these statements use the SUMMARY procedure for descriptive statistics to summarize total sales for each month:

```
PROC SUMMARY DATA=YEARLY;
  CLASS MONTH;
  VAR MONTHTOT;
  OUTPUT OUT=SUMMARY SUM=TOTSALES;
```

The DATA step above illustrates what happens when you jump to the END statement of a DO loop. You can create the same YEARLY and BONUS data sets in this simpler DATA step:

```
DATA YEARLY(KEEP=NAME MONTHTOT) BONUS(KEEP=NAME TOTAL);
  SET SALES;
  TOTAL=0;
  INCREASE=.045;
  DO MONTH='JAN', 'FEB', 'MAR', 'APR', 'MAY', 'JUN', 'JUL',
    'AUG', 'SEP', 'OCT', 'NOV', 'DEC';
    INCREASE=INCREASE+.005;
    MONTHTOT=AVERAGE+AVERAGE*(INCREASE);
    OUTPUT YEARLY;
    TOTAL+MONTHTOT;
    IF YEARS>2 THEN IF MONTH='DEC' THEN
      IF TOTAL>=10000 THEN OUTPUT BONUS;
  END;
```

If the statement

PROC PRINT;

had followed the DATA step above, which data set would be printed? When no data set name is specified in a PROC statement, SAS uses the most recently created data set. When more than one data set is created in a step, which is the most recently created?

The answer: when more than one data set is being created in a DATA step, the last data set created is the last one named in the DATA statement. Thus, the data set BONUS would be printed by the PROC PRINT statement above.

Jumping out of a loop permanently   Sometimes you want to jump completely out of a DO loop before the index variable has reached its stopping value. Perhaps you are indexing through the variables in an array and want to stop processing when you find the value for which you are searching.

For example, suppose you have a data set containing monthly gross salaries for each employee in a company. You want to deduct FICA tax from each salary value; tax is paid on every dollar earned up to $32,400.

In the statements below, the array SALARY contains twelve variables corresponding to the months of the year; the value of each variable is monthly gross income. You want to deduct FICA tax from each month's salary and store the adjusted salaries back in the SALARY array.

The SAS data set EMPLOYEE contains the gross salaries of employees.

```
                                    EMPLOYEE                                              2

              M    M    M    M    M    M    M    M    M    M    M    M
              O    O    O    O    O    O    O    O    O    O    O    O
         N    N    N    N    N    N    N    N    N    N    N    N    N
    O    A    T    T    T    T    T    T    T    T    T    T    T    T
    B    M    H    H    H    H    H    H    H    H    H    H    H    H
    S    E    1    2    3    4    5    6    7    8    9    1    1    1
                                                          0    1    2

    1  ADAMS  1950 1950 1950 1950 1950 1950 2000 2000 2000 2000 2000 2000
    2  BROWN  2250 2250 2250 2250 2250 2250 2350 2350 2350 2350 2350 2350
    3  CARTER 3250 3250 3250 3250 3250 3250 3400 3400 3400 3400 3400 3400
    4  DAVIS  2950 2950 2950 2950 2950 2950 3100 3100 3100 3100 3100 3100
    5  EDEN   3450 3450 3450 3450 3450 3450 3656 3656 3656 3656 3656 3656
```

```
DATA TOTAL;
   ARRAY SALARY (I) MONTH1-MONTH12;
   SET EMPLOYEE;
   MAX=0;
   DO OVER SALARY;
     MAX=MAX+SALARY;
     IF MAX>=32400 THEN DO;
       SALARY=SALARY-(SALARY-(MAX-32400))*.067;
       GO TO OUT;
       END;
     ELSE SALARY=SALARY-(SALARY*.067);
     END;
OUT: ; or other SAS statements
```

This example illustrates several SAS features:

- ARRAY statement
- DO OVER statement
- jumping out of a DO loop permanently
- null statement.

The resulting data set is TOTAL:

OBS	I	MONTH1	MONTH2	MONTH3	MONTH4	MONTH5	MONTH6	MONTH7
1	13	1819.35	1819.35	1819.35	1819.35	1819.35	1819.35	1866.00
2	13	2099.25	2099.25	2099.25	2099.25	2099.25	2099.25	2192.55
3	10	3032.25	3032.25	3032.25	3032.25	3032.25	3032.25	3172.20
4	11	2752.35	2752.35	2752.35	2752.35	2752.35	2752.35	2892.30
5	10	3218.85	3218.85	3218.85	3218.85	3218.85	3218.85	3411.05

OBS	MONTH8	MONTH9	MONTH10	MONTH11	MONTH12	NAME	MAX
1	1866.00	1866.00	1866.00	1866.00	1866.00	ADAMS	23700
2	2192.55	2192.55	2192.55	2192.55	2192.55	BROWN	27600
3	3172.20	3172.20	3219.10	3400.00	3400.00	CARTER	33100
4	2892.30	2892.30	2892.30	2945.90	3100.00	DAVIS	33200
5	3411.05	3411.05	3606.96	3656.00	3656.00	EDEN	35324

The DO OVER statement performs an automatic iterative DO over the range of I, the index variable for the array. I ranges from one to twelve, the number of variables in the array. I is included in the new data set. (If you do not specify an index variable, SAS creates an index variable named __I__, which is not included in the data set being created.)

To process each observation from data set EMPLOYEE, SAS:

- totals the unadjusted monthly salaries (MAX).
- deducts the remaining FICA tax when MAX reaches $32,400, then jumps out of the DO loop. Note that at this point no further salaries are added to MAX so its value in data set TOTAL is not the total salary for an employee.
- deducts the FICA tax from monthly salary and replaces the old salary with the adjusted salary when MAX has not reached the maximum.

To discontinue array processing in the example above you jump out of the DO loop to a null statement and the end of the DATA step. Thus a RETURN statement could replace the GO TO statement with the same result. However, you can continue processing observations after jumping out of the loop if other SAS statements appear after the label OUT.

More array examples Suppose you are coding responses to a questionnaire in which customers voted on selected enhancements to a product. They were each given 50 points to divide among 25 possible changes. A respondent could weight a few items more heavily by placing most of the 50 points on those items or could vote on more changes by spreading the 50 points over a larger number of items.

The item number and number of points are coded in sequence for each item voted on along with the respondent's ID. For example, the possible changes are numbered 1 to 25. The customer with ID 903 voted on four items:

- item 5: 10 points
- item 16: 10 points
- item 17: 10 points
- item 24: 20 points,

and has this data line:

903 5 10 16 10 17 10 24 20   .

The responses are stored in a file with DDname USER. This DATA step reads the raw data and creates a SAS data set:

```
DATA RESULTS;
  INFILE USER MISSOVER;
  ARRAY ALL (I) ITEM1-ITEM25;
  INPUT ID 1-3 @;
  DO UNTIL(I=. OR I=25);
    INPUT I @;
    IF I⌐=. THEN INPUT ALL @;
  END;
```

This example illustrates:

- MISSOVER option of INFILE statement
- ARRAY without DO OVER
- complex expression in DO UNTIL
- reading index variable in INPUT statement
- using an array name in an INPUT statement.

The SAS data set RESULTS is:

```
                              DATA RESULTS                              2

                         I  I   I   I  I I   I   I I I I I   I   I   I
        I I     I I    I I I T T   T   T  T T   T   T T T T T   T   T   T
        T T     T T    T T T E E   E   E  E E   E   E E E E E   E   E   E
     O  E E     E E    E E E M M   M   M  M M   M   M M M M M   M   M   M
     B  M M     M M    M M M 1 1   1   1  1 1   1   1 1 2 2   2   2   2   I
     S  1 2     3 4    5 6 7 8 9   0 1 2   3 4 5 6   7 8 9 0 1 2 3 4 5   D

     1    .  25  .  .    .  .  .  .  .  .   .   .  .   .   .  25  .  .  .  .  901
     2    .   .  10 .    .  .  .  .  .  .   . 15  .   .   .   .  .  25  .  .  902
     3    .   .   .  10  .  .  .  .  .  .   .   .  . 10 10  .   .   .  20 .  903
     4  25 2   2  1  .   .  .  .  .  .  .   .   .  .   .   .   .   .  . 45  904
     5    .   .   .  .   .  .  .  .  .  . 50  .   .   .   .   .   .   .  .  .  905
     6    .   .   .  .   .  .  .  . 45  .   .   .   .   .   .   .   .   .  .  906
     7    .   .   .  .   .  .  . 40 5  5   .   .   .   .   .   .   .   .  .  907
```

Since a customer's response is always coded on one record, the MISSOVER option prevents SAS from going past the end of a record to read values. Instead, any values not found in the current record are set to missing in the SAS data set. Thus, when all responses have been read from an individual record, I is either a missing value (because of MISSOVER) or 25 (the last item in the questionnaire).

The INPUT statement inside the DO loop first reads a value for I. If I is not missing, I's value determines which element of the array is to be referenced in the INPUT statement by the array name ALL.

Array of arrays   Suppose the 25 questionnaire items in the example above relate to five different products. Besides the customer's ID, each item voted on is coded with three values: a product code (1 to 5), an item number (1 to 5), and the number of points voted.

The data defined by DDname IN are shown below. The first line represents user 801, who voted 25 points on item #2 under product 1 and 25 points on item #1 of product 5:

```
801 1 2 25 5 1 25
802 1 3 10 3 4 15 5 3 25
803 1 5 10 4 1 10 4 2 10 5 4 20
804 1 1 2 1 2 2 1 3 1 5 5 45
805 3 3 50
```

This DATA step reads the data and creates SAS data set RESULTS2:

```
DATA RESULTS2;
  INFILE IN MISSOVER;
  ARRAY ONE ITEM1–ITEM5;
  ARRAY TWO ITEM6–ITEM10;
  ARRAY THREE ITEM11–ITEM15;
  ARRAY FOUR ITEM16–ITEM20;
  ARRAY FIVE ITEM21–ITEM25;
  ARRAY PRODUCT (J) ONE TWO THREE FOUR FIVE;
  INPUT ID 1–3 @;
  DO UNTIL(J = . OR J*__I__ = 25);
    INPUT J @;
    IF J¬ = . THEN INPUT __I__ PRODUCT @;
  END;
```

This example is similar to the previous example, but illustrates these additional DATA step features:

- arrays as elements of arrays
- several arrays with same index variable.

Six arrays are defined in the DATA step. The first five contain as elements the items from the questionnaire corresponding to the five products. The sixth array contains as elements the arrays defined above it.

The first five arrays use as their index variable the automatic variable __I__. It is possible to use the same index variable for several arrays **as long as the arrays have the same number of elements**. Note that the variables defined for each of these product arrays have names ending with a numeric suffix. This suffix has no relationship to the value of the index variable, which ranges from 1 to 5.

The first INPUT statement in the DO loop reads a value for J. As before, J is missing when there are no more values on the data line. Otherwise, J's value determines to which of the product arrays the next two values refer. The next INPUT statement reads a value for __I__, which references the item number in the appropriate product array. When the array name PRODUCT appears in the same INPUT statement, the current values of J and __I__ determine which variable is given the value.

The resulting SAS data set RESULTS2 is:

```
                              DATA RESULTS2                                          2

                      I I        I  I I  I  I I I I I  I   I I  I
            I I      I I      I I I I I I T T T  T  T T T  T  T T T T T  T  T T  T
            T T      T T      T T T T T E E E  E  E E  E  E E E E E  E  E E  E
          O E E      E E      E E E E E M M M  M  M M  M  M M M M M  M  M M  M
          B M M      M M      M M M M M 1 1 1  1  1 1  1  1 1 1 2 2  2  2 2  2      I
          S 1 2      3 4      5 6 7 8 9 0 1 2  3  4 5  6  7 8 9 0 1  2  3 4  5  J  D

          1 .  25     .  .      .  .  .  .  .  .  .  .   .   .  .   .   .   .  25  .  25  .    .  .    . 801
          2 .   .     10 .      .  .  .  .  .  .  .  .   15  .  .   .   .   .   .  . 25  .    . 802
          3 .   .      .  .     10 .  .  .  .  .  .  .   10 10 .   .   .   .   .  . 20  .   . 803
          4 2  2      1 .      .  .  .  .  .  .  .  .   .   .  .   .   .   .   .  . 45 5 804
          5 .   .      .  .     .  .  .  .  .  50 .  .   .   .  .   .   .   .   .  . 805
```

SAS Functions

The examples below illustrate the use of selected SAS functions.

Recoding using the PUT function   Suppose you have data for a class of students and you want to print a report showing their average grades. Grades on each test range from 0 to 100. For the final grade, you want both a numeric grade and a letter grade (A,B,C,D, or F). Use PROC FORMAT to define letter grades for each range of numeric grades:

```
PROC FORMAT;
  VALUE GRADE 0-69 = F
        70-75 = D
        76-85 = C
        86-92 = B
        93-100= A;
```

You can associate this format with the variable containing the average grade using a PUT or FORMAT statement. However, if you want a new variable on the data set whose values are the letter grades, you can use a PUT function in a DATA step.

The data containing student grades are stored in a file with DDname CLASS:

NAME	TEST1	TEST2	TEST3	EXAM
ANN	84	87	82	92
BILL	E	75	79	79
CAROL	95	97	100	98
TOM	66	74	79	83
MARY	76	88	90	84

The letter E is coded for Bill's TEST1 score since he was excused on the day the test was given. The value is to be treated as a missing value in the calculation of Bill's average grade. The DATA step below reads the data, averages the grades, and creates the two new variables AVERAGE and LETTER:

```
DATA FINAL;
  INFILE CLASS;
  MISSING E;
  INPUT NAME $ TEST1-TEST3 EXAM;
  AVERAGE=MEAN(OF TEST1-TEST3,EXAM);
  LETTER=PUT(AVERAGE,GRADE.);
```

This example illustrates:

- MISSING statement
- special missing values
- MEAN function
- PUT function with user-defined format
- how SAS prints formats that will not fit.

The resulting data set:

```
                                                                           2

     OBS    NAME     TEST1    TEST2    TEST3    EXAM    AVERAGE    LETTER

      1     ANN       84       87       82       92     86.2500      B
      2     BILL      E        75       79       79     77.6667      C
      3     CAROL     95       97      100       98     97.5000      A
      4     TOM       66       74       79       83     75.5000      *
      5     MARY      76       88       90       84     84.5000      C
```

Data set FINAL contains two calculated variables: AVERAGE, a numeric variable containing the mean of the test grades and exam grade, and LETTER, a character variable whose values are the letter grades corresponding to the average grades.

The MISSING statement tells SAS that the letter E, appearing in a numeric field, is not to be considered an invalid value but a special missing value. Since the MEAN function uses only nonmissing values in its calculations, Bill's missing TEST1 value is not used to calculate his average grade.

Note that in the resulting data set FINAL, the LETTER value for Tom is an asterisk (*). This value is returned since Tom's average grade falls out of the range specified in PROC FORMAT. Normally when a value is undefined by PROC FORMAT, SAS uses the original value. In this case, however, the value 75.5 is too large to fit into the one-character length of LETTER, so SAS puts an asterisk instead.

You can get around the problem by including the FUZZ= option in the VALUE statement of PROC FORMAT. The following VALUE statement could replace the earlier one:

```
VALUE GRADE (FUZZ=.5)
   0–69  = F
   70–75 = D
   76–85 = C
   86–92 = B
   93–100= A;
```

The VALUE statement causes the grade of 75.5 for TOM to be rounded to the category with label C.

The result:

```
                                                                           3

     OBS    NAME     TEST1    TEST2    TEST3    EXAM    AVERAGE    LETTER

      1     ANN       84       87       82       92     86.2500      B
      2     BILL      E        75       79       79     77.6667      C
      3     CAROL     95       97      100       98     97.5000      A
      4     TOM       66       74       79       83     75.5000      C
      5     MARY      76       88       90       84     84.5000      C
```

Note that if you are interested only in the variable LETTER, and not in its numeric counterpart AVERAGE, you can combine the last two statements in the DATA step above:

```
DATA FINAL;
  INFILE CLASS;
  MISSING E;
  INPUT NAME $ TEST1–TEST3 EXAM;
  LETTER = PUT(MEAN(OF TEST1–TEST3,EXAM),GRADE.);
```

Character to numeric: the INPUT function Suppose you have a character variable containing product codes for drugstore items. The product codes are 13 characters long; the first three digits are an alphanumeric code describing the department that sells the product, the next three digits identify the product, and the last seven digits contain the date the product was purchased for resale. The variable's name is CODE in a SAS data set named PRODUCT.

Below are some typical CODE values. The first two from the pharmacy department identify products 001 and 201 and were purchased March 10 and April 29, 1982, respectively. The third item is from households; the fourth item is from the book department.

```
PHA00110MAR82
PHA20129APR82
HOU09918JAN81
BOO40402FEB82
```

You want to include the date part of the product code as a SAS date value so that you can determine when a product's shelf life has expired. The DATA step below creates a numeric variable named DATE containing the SAS date value corresponding to the date part of the CODE values:

```
DATA PRODUCT2;
  SET PRODUCT;
  DATE = INPUT(SUBSTR(CODE,7,7),DATE7.);
```

This DATA step illustrates:

- using SAS functions to generate arguments to functions
- SUBSTR function
- INPUT function
- DATE7. format.

The resulting data set PRODUCT2 is:

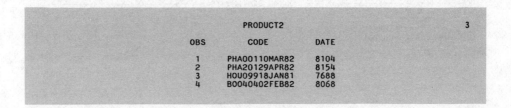

```
                        PRODUCT2                              3

          OBS        CODE          DATE

           1      PHA00110MAR82     8104
           2      PHA20129APR82     8154
           3      HOU09918JAN81     7688
           4      BOO40402FEB82     8068
```

The SUBSTR function causes only the last seven characters of CODE to be read by the INPUT function using the DATE7. format. Note that the value of DATE is stored on the new data set as the number of days between the date read and January 1, 1960.

A FORMAT statement added to the DATA step associates a date format with the SAS date value. For example, if the following FORMAT statement is added to the DATA step above:

FORMAT DATE WORDDATE.;

any SAS procedure would use the associated format WORDDATE. to print values of DATE:

PROC PRINT DATA=PRODUCT2;

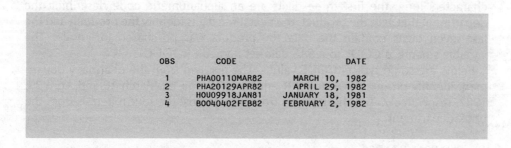

```
OBS        CODE              DATE

  1      PHA00110MAR82     MARCH 10, 1982
  2      PHA20129APR82     APRIL 29, 1982
  3      HOU09918JAN81     JANUARY 18, 1981
  4      B0040402FEB82     FEBRUARY 2, 1982
```

The contents of the data set show that the DATE variable is numeric and has the format WORDDATE. associated with it:

PROC CONTENTS DATA=PRODUCT2;

```
                                SAS

                 CONTENTS OF SAS DATA SET WORK.PRODUCT2

TRACKS USED=2  SUBEXTENTS=1  OBSERVATIONS=4  CREATED BY OS JOB UG7

ON CPUID 01-3083-221547  AT 9:54 WEDNESDAY, JUNE 1, 1983

BY SAS RELEASE 82.3  DSNAME=SYS83152.T095406.RA000.UG7.R0000001  BLKSIZE=19054

LRECL=25  OBSERVATIONS PER TRACK=762  GENERATED BY DATA

                   ALPHABETIC LIST OF VARIABLES

   #  VARIABLE  TYPE LENGTH POSITION  FORMAT            INFORMAT
                                LABEL

   1  CODE      CHAR    13        4

   2  DATE      NUM      8       17   WORDDATE18.


+----------------------------- SOURCE STATEMENTS -----------------------------
|DATA PRODUCT2;
|  SET PRODUCT;
|   DATE=INPUT(SUBSTR(CODE,7,7),DATE7.);
|FORMAT DATE WORDDATE.;
+----------------------------------------------------------------------------
```

WORKING WITH SAS DATA SETS:
SET, MERGE, AND UPDATE

This section of the chapter describes how to work with existing SAS data sets using the SET, MERGE, and UPDATE statements. Additional examples using these statements are given with the statement descriptions and in the *SAS Applications Guide*.

Comparison of Methods: Combining SAS Data Sets

Suppose you have collected sales data for the first two months of the year. Each month's data are stored in a separate SAS data set, and each data set contains the variables REGION, SALESREP, and SALESAMT with corresponding values for the month.

```
                              JAN                            2

          OBS     REGION     SALESREP     SALESAMT

           1      EAST       STAFER          9664
           2      EAST       YOUNG          22969
           3      EAST       STRIDE         27253
           4      WEST       VETTER         38928
           5      WEST       CURCI          21531
           6      WEST       GRECO          18523
           7      WEST       RYAN           32915
           8      WEST       TOMAS          42109
           9      SOUTH      ROCKFELT       38737
          10      SOUTH      MOORE          25718
          11      SOUTH      STELAM         27926
          12      NORTH      FARLOW         32719
          13      NORTH      SMITH, T.      38712
```

```
                              FEB                            3

          OBS     REGION     SALESREP     SALESAMT

           1      EAST       YOUNG          20866
           2      EAST       STRIDE         29100
           3      EAST       ISSAC          21991
           4      WEST       CURCI          18432
           5      WEST       GRECO          21497
           6      WEST       RYAN           33041
           7      WEST       TOMAS          38300
           8      SOUTH      ROCKFELT       34212
           9      SOUTH      MOORE          23312
          10      SOUTH      STELAM         25371
          11      NORTH      FARLOW         29219
          12      NORTH      SMITH, T.      31909
          13      NORTH      RICHARDS       11927
```

These data sets can be combined in several ways: concatenating, interleaving, or merging.

Concatenating You can create a data set with observations for each sales representative for each month by using the concatenation operation. In this case you want to create a new variable containing the current value for the current month:

```
DATA CONCAT;
   SET JAN(IN=J) FEB(IN=F);
   IF J THEN MONTH='JAN';
   ELSE MONTH='FEB';
```

The special IN= variables are used with each data set named in the SET statement to indicate the data set from which SAS read the current observation.

The resulting data set CONCAT contains as many observations as there are in the total of JAN and FEB:

```
                            CONCAT                              4

        OBS   REGION   SALESREP    SALESAMT   MONTH
         1    EAST     STAFER        9664     JAN
         2    EAST     YOUNG        22969     JAN
         3    EAST     STRIDE       27253     JAN
         4    WEST     VETTER       38928     JAN
         5    WEST     CURCI        21531     JAN
         6    WEST     GRECO        18523     JAN
         7    WEST     RYAN         32915     JAN
         8    WEST     TOMAS        42109     JAN
         9    SOUTH    ROCKFELT     38737     JAN
        10    SOUTH    MOORE        25718     JAN
        11    SOUTH    STELAM       27926     JAN
        12    NORTH    FARLOW       32719     JAN
        13    NORTH    SMITH, T.    38712     JAN
        14    EAST     YOUNG        20866     FEB
        15    EAST     STRIDE       29100     FEB
        16    EAST     ISSAC        21991     FEB
        17    WEST     CURCI        18432     FEB
        18    WEST     GRECO        21497     FEB
        19    WEST     RYAN         33041     FEB
        20    WEST     TOMAS        38300     FEB
        21    SOUTH    ROCKFELT     34212     FEB
        22    SOUTH    MOORE        23312     FEB
        23    SOUTH    STELAM       25371     FEB
        24    NORTH    FARLOW       29219     FEB
        25    NORTH    SMITH, T.    31909     FEB
        26    NORTH    RICHARDS     11927     FEB
```

CONCAT observations appear in the order they were read from the two monthly data sets: all observations from JAN followed by all observations from FEB.

The concatenation of SAS data sets is also performed by the SAS procedure APPEND which copies observations from one SAS data set to the end of another. See the APPEND procedure description for more information.

Interleaving   If you want your new data set to include all the observations from the JAN and FEB data sets in order of REGION, you can interleave the two data sets. An interleave operation uses a BY statement in the DATA step; the interleaved data sets must be sorted in the order described by the BY statement.

```
PROC SORT DATA=JAN;   BY REGION;
PROC SORT DATA=FEB;   BY REGION;
DATA INTERLV;
  SET JAN(IN=J) FEB(IN=F);
  BY REGION;
  IF J THEN MONTH='JAN';
  ELSE MONTH='FEB';
```

Observations in SAS data set INTERLV are sorted by REGION. For each region, all observations from JAN are followed by all FEB observations.

```
                            INTERLV                             5

        OBS   REGION   SALESREP    SALESAMT   MONTH
         1    EAST     STAFER        9664     JAN
         2    EAST     YOUNG        22969     JAN
         3    EAST     STRIDE       27253     JAN
         4    EAST     YOUNG        20866     FEB
         5    EAST     STRIDE       29100     FEB
         6    EAST     ISSAC        21991     FEB
         7    NORTH    FARLOW       32719     JAN
         8    NORTH    SMITH, T.    38712     JAN
         9    NORTH    FARLOW       29219     FEB
        10    NORTH    SMITH, T.    31909     FEB
        11    NORTH    RICHARDS     11927     FEB
```

(continued on next page)

(continued from previous page)

```
12    SOUTH    ROCKFELT    38737    JAN
13    SOUTH    MOORE       25718    JAN
14    SOUTH    STELAM      27926    JAN
15    SOUTH    ROCKFELT    34212    FEB
16    SOUTH    MOORE       23312    FEB
17    SOUTH    STELAM      25371    FEB
18    WEST     VETTER      38928    JAN
19    WEST     CURCI       21531    JAN
20    WEST     GRECO       18523    JAN
21    WEST     RYAN        32915    JAN
22    WEST     TOMAS       42109    JAN
23    WEST     CURCI       18432    FEB
24    WEST     GRECO       21497    FEB
25    WEST     RYAN        33041    FEB
26    WEST     TOMAS       38300    FEB
```

If you want your new data set to have observations for each SALESREP appearing together, use these statements:

```
PROC SORT DATA=JAN;   BY REGION SALESREP;
PROC SORT DATA=FEB;   BY REGION SALESREP;
DATA INTERLV2;
  SET JAN(IN=J) FEB(IN=F);
  BY REGION SALESREP;
  IF J THEN MONTH='JAN';
  ELSE MONTH='FEB';
```

The result:

```
                          INTERLV2                                    6

    OBS    REGION    SALESREP     SALESAMT    MONTH
     1     EAST      ISSAC          21991     FEB
     2     EAST      STAFER          9664     JAN
     3     EAST      STRIDE         27253     JAN
     4     EAST      STRIDE         29100     FEB
     5     EAST      YOUNG          22969     JAN
     6     EAST      YOUNG          20866     FEB
     7     NORTH     FARLOW         32719     JAN
     8     NORTH     FARLOW         29219     FEB
     9     NORTH     RICHARDS       11927     FEB
    10     NORTH     SMITH, T.      38712     JAN
    11     NORTH     SMITH, T.      31909     FEB
    12     SOUTH     MOORE          25718     JAN
    13     SOUTH     MOORE          23312     FEB
    14     SOUTH     ROCKFELT       38737     JAN
    15     SOUTH     ROCKFELT       34212     FEB
    16     SOUTH     STELAM         27926     JAN
    17     SOUTH     STELAM         25371     FEB
    18     WEST      CURCI          21531     JAN
    19     WEST      CURCI          18432     FEB
    20     WEST      GRECO          18523     JAN
    21     WEST      GRECO          21497     FEB
    22     WEST      RYAN           32915     JAN
    23     WEST      RYAN           33041     FEB
    24     WEST      TOMAS          42109     JAN
    25     WEST      TOMAS          38300     FEB
    26     WEST      VETTER         38928     JAN
```

Match-merging Suppose that you want your combined data set to include one observation for each sales representative, with each monthly sales total included as a separate variable in that observation. Use the merge operation, matching on SALESREP.

```
PROC SORT DATA=JAN;   BY SALESREP;
PROC SORT DATA=FEB;   BY SALESREP;
DATA MATCH1;
  MERGE JAN(RENAME=(SALESAMT=JANSALES))
   FEB(RENAME=(SALESAMT=FEBSALES));
  BY SALESREP;
```

The MERGE operation, when combining observations, overlays variables with the same name from the data sets being merged. The result in the new data set is one variable of that name; its value is the value from the last data set appearing in the MERGE statement. Thus, in the example above, if the RENAME data set option is not used to change the name of the variable SALES, the January sales amount will be lost.

Data set MATCH1:

```
                           MATCH1                              7

       OBS   REGION   SALESREP   JANSALES   FEBSALES

        1    WEST     CURCI       21531      18432
        2    NORTH    FARLOW      32719      29219
        3    WEST     GRECO       18523      21497
        4    EAST     ISSAC         .        21991
        5    SOUTH    MOORE       25718      23312
        6    NORTH    RICHARDS      .        11927
        7    SOUTH    ROCKFELT    38737      34212
        8    WEST     RYAN        32915      33041
        9    NORTH    SMITH, T.   38712      31909
       10    EAST     STAFER       9664        .
       11    SOUTH    STELAM      27926      25371
       12    EAST     STRIDE      27253      29100
       13    WEST     TOMAS       42109      38300
       14    WEST     VETTER      38928        .
       15    EAST     YOUNG       22969      20866
```

Note that when a sales representative appears in only one of the data sets JAN or FEB, his sales value for the month he was not working is missing on the new data set.

In a match-merge, you want the matching variable to uniquely identify observations in the data sets being merged. Suppose that SALESREP values are not unique, but that you need both REGION and SALESREP to uniquely identify each sales representative. Then you can sort and merge on these two variables. To get a match, both the REGION and then SALESREP values must be the same.

```
PROC SORT DATA=JAN;   BY REGION SALESREP;
PROC SORT DATA=FEB;   BY REGION SALESREP;
DATA MATCH2;
  MERGE JAN(RENAME=(SALESAMT=JANSALES))
   FEB(RENAME=(SALESAMT=FEBSALES));
  BY REGION SALESREP;
```

The resulting data set is in order of REGION and SALESREP:

```
                                 MATCH2                                    8

            OBS     REGION     SALESREP     JANSALES     FEBSALES

             1      EAST       ISSAC             .         21991
             2      EAST       STAFER          9664           .
             3      EAST       STRIDE         27253        29100
             4      EAST       YOUNG          22969        20866
             5      NORTH      FARLOW         32719        29219
             6      NORTH      RICHARDS           .        11927
             7      NORTH      SMITH, T.      38712        31909
             8      SOUTH      MOORE          25718        23312
             9      SOUTH      ROCKFELT       38737        34212
            10      SOUTH      STELAM         27926        25371
            11      WEST       CURCI          21531        18432
            12      WEST       GRECO          18523        21497
            13      WEST       RYAN           32915        33041
            14      WEST       TOMAS          42109        38300
            15      WEST       VETTER         38928           .
```

Updating The UPDATE operation in SAS is similar to MERGE but is specialized to handle the function of updating a master file with transactions. In the example above you do not want to "lose" the January sales amount from the combined data set, so the traditional update is inappropriate for creating a combined data set.

Instead suppose that you have a master data set containing all sales representatives along with some background information about each of them. At the end of the month, you want to update this master with the monthly sales record for each representative.

Below is SAS data set MASTER:

```
                                 DATA MASTER                              10

     OBS   REGION   SALESREP    NAME                   BEGDATE    SALES

      1    EAST     GREEN       GREEN, ROBERT C.       02JAN81    551165
      2    EAST     ISSAC       ISSAC, HOWARD T.       16JAN81    281910
      3    EAST     STAFER      STAFER, MICHAEL C.     30JAN81     15458
      4    EAST     STRIDE      STRIDE, JOHN M.        05APR81    498108
      5    EAST     YOUNG       YOUNG, MARTIN V.       19APR81    354962
      6    NORTH    FARLOW      FARLOW, DOUGLAS C.     08JUL82    447859
      7    NORTH    RICHARDS    RICHARDS, BRENDA K.    22JUL82    169780
      8    NORTH    SMITH, M.   SMITH, MARY A.         11OCT82    508701
      9    NORTH    SMITH, T.   SMITH, THOMAS M.       25OCT82    748036
     10    SOUTH    MOORE       MOORE, PATRICIA P.     30JAN82    480404
     11    SOUTH    ROCKFELT    ROCKFELT, STEPHEN L.   05APR82    160566
     12    SOUTH    STELAM      STELAM, MICHAEL O.     19APR82    644936
     13    WEST     CURCI       CURCI, CYNTHIA L.      08JUL81    869282
     14    WEST     GRECO       GRECO, ANTHONY T.      22JUL81    122341
     15    WEST     HARRELL     HARRELL, DAVID R.      11OCT81    297837
     16    WEST     RYAN        RYAN, HENRY H.         25OCT81    816871
     17    WEST     TOMAS       TOMAS, JAMES M.        02JAN82    162072
     18    WEST     VETTER      VETTER, WILLIAM A.     16JAN82    958498
```

The SALES variable in the MASTER data set contains the total-to-date sales for each representative. Every other month you want to update this total with the monthly sales (SALESAMT) from the previous two months.

This is not an update in the sense that you do not want to replace values in the MASTER with new values. But you can use programming statements to add each month's total to the value of SALES. The resulting data set is a copy of MASTER, but with new total SALES.

Any of the combined data sets created above could be used as the transaction data set and matched with the MASTER data set in the UPDATE operation. The three SAS data sets CONCAT, INTERLV, and INTERLV2 all contain the same observations, but in a different order.

The MASTER data set is sorted by REGION and alphabetically by SALESREP within REGION. Since the data set INTERLV2 is already sorted in that order, use INTERLV2 as a transaction data set with UPDATE.

```
DATA UPDATE; DROP MONTH SALESAMT;
  UPDATE MASTER INTERLV2;
  BY REGION SALESREP;
  SALES+SALESAMT;
```

The resulting data set UPDATE now includes the new total SALES.

```
                                  UPDATE                              11

  OBS    REGION    SALESREP    NAME                  BEGDATE    SALES
    1     EAST      GREEN      GREEN, ROBERT C.       02JAN81    551165
    2     EAST      ISSAC      ISSAC, HOWARD T.       16JAN81    303901
    3     EAST      STAFER     STAFER, MICHAEL C.     30JAN81     25122
    4     EAST      STRIDE     STRIDE, JOHN M.        05APR81    554461
    5     EAST      YOUNG      YOUNG, MARTIN V.       19APR81    398797
    6     NORTH     FARLOW     FARLOW, DOUGLAS C.     08JUL82    509797
    7     NORTH     RICHARDS   RICHARDS, BRENDA K.    22JUL82    181707
    8     NORTH     SMITH, M.  SMITH, MARY A.         11OCT82    508701
    9     NORTH     SMITH, T.  SMITH, THOMAS M.       25OCT82    818657
   10     SOUTH     MOORE      MOORE, PATRICIA P.     30JAN82    529434
   11     SOUTH     ROCKFELT   ROCKFELT, STEPHEN L.   05APR82    233515
   12     SOUTH     STELAM     STELAM, MICHAEL O.     19APR82    698233
   13     WEST      CURCI      CURCI, CYNTHIA L.      08JUL81    909245
   14     WEST      GRECO      GRECO, ANTHONY T.      22JUL81    162361
   15     WEST      HARRELL    HARRELL, DAVID R.      11OCT81    297837
   16     WEST      RYAN       RYAN, HENRY H.         25OCT81    882827
   17     WEST      TOMAS      TOMAS, JAMES M.        02JAN82    242481
   18     WEST      VETTER     VETTER, WILLIAM A.     16JAN82    997426
```

Notice that unlike MERGE, UPDATE outputs an observation only at the end of a BY group—in this case, only once for each unique combination of REGION and SALESREP. Thus, even though many sales representatives occur twice in the INTERLV2 data set (for example, STRIDE in region EAST), the SALESAMT values are added from both INTERLV2 observations before the new observation is output.

Note that in any combining operation, the resulting data set contains all the variables from the data sets being joined unless a DROP or KEEP statement or data set option subsets the variables.

If you always want the current master data set to have the name MASTER and the previous master to have the name UPDATE, use the DATASETS procedure to exchange the two names after performing the update:

```
PROC DATASETS DDNAME=WORK;
EXCHANGE MASTER=UPDATE;
```

Suppose that you want to use the data set MATCH2, which resulted from the second merge example above, as your transaction data set in the update. MATCH2 has only one observation for every REGION/SALESREP combination. To perform the update, these statements are needed:

```
DATA UPDATE2;
  UPDATE MASTER MATCH2;
  BY REGION SALESREP;
  SALES+SUM(JANSALES, FEBSALES);
  DROP JANSALES FEBSALES;
```

The result:

```
                                    UPDATE2

      OBS    REGION    SALESREP      NAME                        BEGDATE    SALES

        1    EAST      GREEN         GREEN, ROBERT C.            02JAN81    551165
        2    EAST      ISSAC         ISSAC, HOWARD T.            16JAN81    303901
        3    EAST      STAFER        STAFER, MICHAEL C.          30JAN81     25122
        4    EAST      STRIDE        STRIDE, JOHN M.             05APR81    554461
        5    EAST      YOUNG         YOUNG, MARTIN V.            19APR81    398797
        6    NORTH     FARLOW        FARLOW, DOUGLAS C.          08JUL82    509797
        7    NORTH     RICHARDS      RICHARDS, BRENDA K.         22JUL82    181707
        8    NORTH     SMITH, M.     SMITH, MARY A.              11OCT82    508701
        9    NORTH     SMITH, T.     SMITH, THOMAS M.            25OCT82    818657
       10    SOUTH     MOORE         MOORE, PATRICIA P.          30JAN82    529434
       11    SOUTH     ROCKFELT      ROCKFELT, STEPHEN L.        05APR82    233515
       12    SOUTH     STELAM        STELAM, MICHAEL O.          19APR82    698233
       13    WEST      CURCI         CURCI, CYNTHIA L.           08JUL81    909245
       14    WEST      GRECO         GRECO, ANTHONY T.           22JUL81    162361
       15    WEST      HARRELL       HARRELL, DAVID R.           11OCT81    297837
       16    WEST      RYAN          RYAN, HENRY H.              25OCT81    882827
       17    WEST      TOMAS         TOMAS, JAMES M.             02JAN82    242481
       18    WEST      VETTER        VETTER, WILLIAM A.          16JAN82    997426
```

Another example of combining SAS data sets in a way similar to MERGE and UPDATE is shown below in the section **Multiple SET Statements: direct access.**

More Than Two SAS Data Sets

The concatenation, interleave, and merge operations discussed above can be applied to as many as 50 SAS data sets in a single step. Suppose that the MERGE operation in the sales example is done quarterly and that you have collected sales data for March in a SAS data set named MAR:

```
                        DATA MAR

      OBS    REGION    SALESREP      SALESAMT

        1    EAST      GREEN         24960
        2    EAST      YOUNG         19866
        3    EAST      STRIDE        24700
        4    EAST      ISSAC         27997
        5    WEST      CURCI         18432
        6    WEST      GRECO         20497
        7    WEST      RYAN          29047
        8    WEST      TOMAS         30300
        9    SOUTH     ROCKFELT      29272
       10    SOUTH     MOORE         28372
       11    NORTH     FARLOW        21279
       12    NORTH     SMITH, T.     30909
       13    NORTH     RICHARDS      17927
```

Concatenating three data sets   For example, to concatenate the three data sets JAN, FEB, and MAR:

```
DATA QUARTER1;
    SET JAN(IN=J) FEB(IN=F) MAR(IN=M);
    IF J THEN MONTH='JAN';
    ELSE IF F THEN MONTH='FEB';
    ELSE MONTH='MAR';
```

And the result:

```
                              QUARTER1                              2

        OBS    REGION    SALESREP      SALESAMT    MONTH

          1    EAST      STAFER           9664     JAN
          2    EAST      YOUNG           22969     JAN
          3    EAST      STRIDE          27253     JAN
          4    WEST      VETTER          38928     JAN
          5    WEST      CURCI           21531     JAN
          6    WEST      GRECO           18523     JAN
          7    WEST      RYAN            32915     JAN
          8    WEST      TOMAS           42109     JAN
          9    SOUTH     ROCKFELT        38737     JAN
         10    SOUTH     MOORE           25718     JAN
         11    SOUTH     STELAM          27926     JAN
         12    NORTH     FARLOW          32719     JAN
         13    NORTH     SMITH, T.       38712     JAN
         14    EAST      YOUNG           20866     FEB
         15    EAST      STRIDE          29100     FEB
         16    EAST      ISSAC           21991     FEB
         17    WEST      CURCI           18432     FEB
         18    WEST      GRECO           21497     FEB
         19    WEST      RYAN            33041     FEB
         20    WEST      TOMAS           38300     FEB
         21    SOUTH     ROCKFELT        34212     FEB
         22    SOUTH     MOORE           23312     FEB
         23    SOUTH     STELAM          25371     FEB
         24    NORTH     FARLOW          29219     FEB
         25    NORTH     SMITH, T.       31909     FEB
         26    NORTH     RICHARDS        11927     FEB
         27    EAST      GREEN           24960     MAR
         28    EAST      YOUNG           19866     MAR
         29    EAST      STRIDE          24700     MAR
         30    EAST      ISSAC           27997     MAR
         31    WEST      CURCI           18432     MAR
         32    WEST      GRECO           20497     MAR
         33    WEST      RYAN            29047     MAR
         34    WEST      TOMAS           30300     MAR
         35    SOUTH     ROCKFELT        29272     MAR
         36    SOUTH     MOORE           28372     MAR
         37    NORTH     FARLOW          21279     MAR
         38    NORTH     SMITH, T.       30909     MAR
         39    NORTH     RICHARDS        17927     MAR
```

As before, SAS reads observations from one data set until the data set contains no more observations, then goes on to the next data set listed in the SET statement, and so on until it has read all the observations in all the data sets listed in the SET statement.

Match-merging: three data sets   The DATA step below merges the three SAS data sets JAN, FEB, and MAR, renaming the SALESAMT variable to correspond to the month to which the sales total refers.

```
PROC SORT DATA=JAN;   BY REGION SALESREP;
PROC SORT DATA=FEB;   BY REGION SALESREP;
PROC SORT DATA=MAR;   BY REGION SALESREP;
DATA MATCH3;
  MERGE JAN(RENAME=(SALESAMT=JANSALES))
     FEB(RENAME=(SALESAMT=FEBSALES))
     MAR(RENAME=(SALESAMT=MARSALES));
  BY REGION SALESREP;
```

The resulting data set MATCH3:

```
                              MATCH3                                5

     OBS    REGION    SALESREP    JANSALES    FEBSALES    MARSALES

       1    EAST      GREEN            .           .        24960
       2    EAST      ISSAC           .        21991       27997
       3    EAST      STAFER        9664          .            .
       4    EAST      STRIDE       27253       29100       24700
```

(continued on next page)

(continued from previous page)

5	EAST	YOUNG	22969	20866	19866
6	NORTH	FARLOW	32719	29219	21279
7	NORTH	RICHARDS	.	11927	17927
8	NORTH	SMITH, T.	38712	31909	30909
9	SOUTH	MOORE	25718	23312	28372
10	SOUTH	ROCKFELT	38737	34212	29272
11	SOUTH	STELAM	27926	25371	.
12	WEST	CURCI	21531	18432	18432
13	WEST	GRECO	18523	21497	20497
14	WEST	RYAN	32915	33041	29047
15	WEST	TOMAS	42109	38300	30300
16	WEST	VETTER	38928	.	.

You can merge up to 50 SAS data sets in a single DATA step. SAS keeps a pointer on the next observation in each data set being merged. It selects the observation with the "lowest" BY value, then brings in information from each data set containing that observation, reading from data sets in the order they appear in the MERGE statement. If a data set does not contain the current "lowest" BY value, variables appearing only in that data set have a missing value in the new, combined observation. Thus, observations like GREEN from the EAST, who appears only in the MAR data set, have missing values in MATCH3 for both the JAN and FEB variables.

Merging a few observations with all observations in a SAS data set: two SET statements You want to include in each observation in MATCH3 the overall average monthly sales for the company. With this value added to each observation, you can then calculate for each sales representative whether his/her sales are above or below the company average.

You can use the MEANS procedure to create an observation containing the average monthly sales to date. (Analyze the data set QUARTER1 created by concatenating the JAN, FEB, and MAR data sets.)

```
PROC MEANS DATA=QUARTER1;
  VAR SALESAMT;
  OUTPUT OUT=MEANOUT MEAN=AVERAGE;
```

The resulting observation, output from the MEANS procedure, is shown below.

```
                          MEANOUT                          4

                      OBS     AVERAGE
                       1      26677.9
```

You can merge this observation containing one variable, AVERAGE, with each observation in data set MATCH3. Use these statements:

```
DATA COMBINE;
  IF __N__=1 THEN SET MEANOUT;
  SET MATCH3;
```

Data set COMBINE contains all the observations from MATCH3. Each observation is combined with the one observation in MEANOUT.

```
                            COMBINE                                    6

 OBS    AVERAGE    REGION    SALESREP    JANSALES    FEBSALES    MARSALES

  1     26677.9    EAST      GREEN           .                     24960
  2     26677.9    EAST      ISSAC                       21991      27997
  3     26677.9    EAST      STAFER          9664          .
  4     26677.9    EAST      STRIDE         27253        29100      24700
  5     26677.9    EAST      YOUNG          22969        20866      19866
  6     26677.9    NORTH     FARLOW         32719        29219      21279
  7     26677.9    NORTH     RICHARDS                    11927      17927
  8     26677.9    NORTH     SMITH, T.      38712        31909      30909
  9     26677.9    SOUTH     MOORE          25718        23312      28372
 10     26677.9    SOUTH     ROCKFELT       38737        34212      29272
 11     26677.9    SOUTH     STELAM         27926        25371
 12     26677.9    WEST      CURCI          21531        18432      18432
 13     26677.9    WEST      GRECO          18523        21497      20497
 14     26677.9    WEST      RYAN           32915        33041      29047
 15     26677.9    WEST      TOMAS          42109        38300      30300
 16     26677.9    WEST      VETTER         38928          .          .
```

Combining subtotals with each detail record   Suppose that you have calculated averages for each REGION and want to combine the regional average sales with observations from that region. You can create observations containing the regional sales average using the MEANS procedure.

```
PROC SORT DATA=QUARTER1; BY REGION;
PROC MEANS DATA=QUARTER1;
   VAR SALESAMT;
   BY REGION;
   OUTPUT OUT=AVERAGE MEAN=AVGSALES;
```

Data set AVERAGE:

```
                    AVERAGE                        8

     OBS    REGION    AVGSALES

      1     EAST      22936.6
      2     NORTH     26825.1
      3     SOUTH     29115.0
      4     WEST      27965.5
```

SAS does not support using a BY statement with more than one SET statement in the same DATA step. You can combine the regional averages with each observation in MATCH3 by merging the two data sets:

```
DATA NEW;
   MERGE MATCH3 AVERAGE;
   BY REGION;
```

```
                        NEW WITH MERGING                              9

 OBS    REGION    SALESREP    JANSALES    FEBSALES    MARSALES    AVGSALES

  1     EAST      GREEN           .                     24960      22936.6
  2     EAST      ISSAC                       21991      27997      22936.6
  3     EAST      STAFER          9664          .                   22936.6
  4     EAST      STRIDE         27253        29100      24700      22936.6
  5     EAST      YOUNG          22969        20866      19866      22936.6
  6     NORTH     FARLOW         32719        29219      21279      26825.1
  7     NORTH     RICHARDS                    11927      17927      26825.1
  8     NORTH     SMITH, T.      38712        31909      30909      26825.1
```

(continued on next page)

(continued from previous page)

9	SOUTH	MOORE	25718	23312	28372	29115.0
10	SOUTH	ROCKFELT	38737	34212	29272	29115.0
11	SOUTH	STELAM	27926	25371	.	29115.0
12	WEST	CURCI	21531	18432	18432	27965.5
13	WEST	GRECO	18523	21497	20497	27965.5
14	WEST	RYAN	32915	33041	29047	27965.5
15	WEST	TOMAS	42109	38300	30300	27965.5
16	WEST	VETTER	38928	.	.	27965.5

More Uses of SET Statements

One-to-one matching   Suppose that you want to read an observation from one data set and then an observation from another data set and combine them into a new observation; then read another one from the first data set, another from the second, and combine them into a second observation, and so on. New observations are formed by combining the observations in the two data sets. The statements:

```
DATA NEW;
   SET A;
   SET B;
```

read an observation from A, followed by an observation from B, then output the combination to data set NEW. It is important to note that:

- SAS stops building the data set NEW when **either** A or B runs out of observations. Thus, the DATA step above differs from the step

```
DATA NEW;
   MERGE A B;
```

  only because MERGE continues to match observations one-by-one from A and B even if one of the data sets contains no more observations. In that case, variables from the empty data set have missing values in the new combined observation.
- Variables with the same name in the two data sets have the values from B (the last data set read in the step) in the new observation.
- When variables with the same name in the two data sets have different attributes (length, label, format), the attributes of the variable in the new data set depend on the order in which the data sets are mentioned in the step. The rule is: the **length** of the variable in the new data set is the length of the variable in the first data set mentioned that contains the variable. The label and format are taken from the first data set that was created with an explicit FORMAT or LABEL statement specification for the variable.

Reading from the same data set more than once   You can read from the same data set more than once in a DATA step by giving the name of the data set in more than one SET statement. Each SET statement treats the data set independently from other SET statements and reads records sequentially from the last time **the same** SET statement was executed. If you want to **continue** reading sequentially from the same data set, you must execute the same SET statement.

For example, suppose you have a SAS data set named A. The two DATA steps below read data set A in different ways:

```
DATA B;
  SET A;
  IF condition THEN SET A;
```

To visualize how this step works, imagine that each SET statement in a DATA step makes available an entire data set from which to read. Each data set has its own pointer. In this case, having two SET statements that reference the same data set A is to SAS the same as having two data sets A: each SET statement is treated independently. The first statement causes SAS to read sequentially from the "first" data set A; when the conditional SET is executed, SAS reads from the "second" data set A.

The DATA step below differs from the previous example.

```
DATA B;
  LINK IT;
  IF condition THEN LINK IT;
  RETURN;
IT: SET A;
  RETURN;
```

Here, a LINK statement causes SAS to jump to the same SET statement so that SAS reads sequentially from data set A each time the statement labeled IT is executed.

An example of using the same data set more than once with the MERGE statement is shown in the section, **Merging a data set with itself**.

Direct access of SAS data sets   You can access SAS data sets directly rather than sequentially by using the POINT= and NOBS= options in the SET statement. For example, suppose that you want to select every fifth sales representative from data set MASTER, described above. If you are uncertain of the total number in data set MASTER, you can use these statements.

```
DATA SUBSET;
  DO NUMBER=1 TO TOTAL BY 5;
    SET MASTER POINT=NUMBER NOBS=TOTAL;
    OUTPUT;
  END;
  STOP;
```

The variable name given by the NOBS= option contains the total number of observations in MASTER. In this case, the SET statement reads the observation from MASTER corresponding to the value of the POINT= variable. Compare the resulting data set SUBSET with the original data set MASTER to verify that it chose observations 1, 6, 11, and so on from MASTER:

```
                                SUBSET                                      2

OBS    REGION    SALESREP    NAME                  BEGDATE    SALES

 1     EAST      GREEN       GREEN, ROBERT C.      02JAN81    551165
 2     NORTH     FARLOW      FARLOW, DOUGLAS C.    08JUL82    447859
 3     SOUTH     ROCKFELT    ROCKFELT, STEPHEN L.  05APR82    160566
 4     WEST      RYAN        RYAN, HENRY H.        25OCT81    816871
```

Multiple SET statements: direct access   Suppose that each of the JAN, FEB, and MAR data sets described earlier contains a variable that identifies the observation number of the sales representative in the MASTER data set. For example, below is the JAN data set. The value of ID is the observation of the corresponding observation in MASTER:

```
                    DATA JAN WITH ID VARIABLE                        3

         OBS    REGION    SALESREP    SALESAMT     ID

          1     EAST      STAFER        9664        3
          2     EAST      STRIDE       27253        4
          3     EAST      YOUNG        22969        5
          4     WEST      CURCI        21531       13
          5     WEST      GRECO        18523       14
          6     WEST      RYAN         32915       16
          7     WEST      TOMAS        42109       17
          8     WEST      VETTER       38928       18
          9     SOUTH     MOORE        25718       10
         10     SOUTH     ROCKFELT     38737       11
         11     SOUTH     STELAM       27926       12
         12     NORTH     FARLOW       32719        6
         13     NORTH     SMITH, T.    38712        9
```

Below is the MASTER data set:

```
                         MASTER DATA SET                             4

   OBS   REGION   SALESREP     NAME                 BEGDATE    SALES

    1    EAST     GREEN        GREEN, ROBERT C.     02JAN81   551165
    2    EAST     ISSAC        ISSAC, HOWARD T.     16JAN81   281910
    3    EAST     STAFER       STAFER, MICHAEL C.   30JAN81    15458
    4    EAST     STRIDE       STRIDE, JOHN M.      05APR81   498108
    5    EAST     YOUNG        YOUNG, MARTIN V.     19APR81   354962
    6    NORTH    FARLOW       FARLOW, DOUGLAS C.   08JUL82   447859
    7    NORTH    RICHARDS     RICHARDS, BRENDA K.  22JUL82   169780
    8    NORTH    SMITH, M.    SMITH, MARY A.       11OCT82   508701
    9    NORTH    SMITH, T.    SMITH, THOMAS M.     25OCT82   748036
   10    SOUTH    MOORE        MOORE, PATRICIA P.   30JAN82   480404
   11    SOUTH    ROCKFELT     ROCKFELT, STEPHEN L. 05APR82   160566
   12    SOUTH    STELAM       STELAM, MICHAEL O.   19APR82   644936
   13    WEST     CURCI        CURCI, CYNTHIA L.    08JUL81   869282
   14    WEST     GRECO        GRECO, ANTHONY T.    22JUL81   122341
   15    WEST     HARRELL      HARRELL, DAVID R.    11OCT81   297837
   16    WEST     RYAN         RYAN, HENRY H.       25OCT81   816871
   17    WEST     TOMAS        TOMAS, JAMES M.      02JAN82   162072
   18    WEST     VETTER       VETTER, WILLIAM A.   16JAN82   958498
```

You want to determine which employee in the JAN data set began work before January 1982. You can read in an observation from JAN, access that observation directly from the MASTER data set using the variable ID, then check the value of BEGDATE. Consider these statements:

```
DATA CHECK;
  SET JAN;
  SET MASTER POINT=ID;
  IF BEGDATE<='01JAN82'D;
  KEEP REGION NAME;
```

The result:

```
                    CHECK                                            5

         OBS    REGION       NAME

          1     EAST      STAFER, MICHAEL C.
          2     EAST      STRIDE, JOHN M.
          3     EAST      YOUNG, MARTIN V.
          4     WEST      CURCI, CYNTHIA L.
          5     WEST      GRECO, ANTHONY T.
          6     WEST      RYAN, HENRY H.
```

When SAS reads from data set JAN, the value of ID in the record is the value used by the POINT= option to retrieve the correct observation from MASTER. If BEGDATE has a SAS date value corresponding to a date before January 1, 1982, the observation is selected.

Note that this step does not need a STOP statement since the DATA step stops when the JAN data set runs out of observations.

Merging a Data Set with Itself

The last example in this chapter merges one SAS data set with itself to create a network of connecting routes. For example, data set TRAVEL contains direct routes from several North Carolina cities to others, showing the direction, highway, and number of miles:

```
                          TRAVEL DATA SET                              2

     OBS    FROM            TO              DRECTN    HIWAY    MILES

       1    RALEIGH         WAKEFIELD        NE         64       18
       2    WAKEFIELD       WILSON           SE        264       24
       3    RALEIGH         CLAYTON          SE         70       13
       4    CLAYTON         WILSON           NE         42       28
       5    CHAPEL HILL     PITTSBORO        S         501       16
       6    PITTSBORO       ASHEBORO         W          64       38
       7    GREENSBORO      SANFORD          SE         87       34
       8    RALEIGH         PITTSBORO        W          64       32
       9    PITTSBORO       SILER CITY       W          64       16
      10    SILER CITY      GREENSBORO       NW        421       35
      11    PITTSBORO       BURLINGTON       NW         87       28
      12    RALEIGH         DURHAM           NW         70       23
      13    DURHAM          GREENSBORO       W          85       54
      14    RALEIGH         LOWES GROVE      NW         40       18
      15    LOWES GROVE     CHAPEL HILL      W          54       11
      16    CHAPEL HILL     BURLINGTON       NW         54       22
```

You want to create a new data set containing routes to additional cities which includes intermediate cities. You can merge data set TRAVEL with itself by matching TO with FROM. Create differently sorted versions of TRAVEL with the SORT procedure:

```
PROC SORT DATA=TRAVEL OUT=START; BY TO;
PROC SORT DATA=TRAVEL OUT=FINISH; BY FROM;
DATA CONNECTN;
   MERGE START(IN=INSTART RENAME=(TO=VIA))
   FINISH(IN=INFINISH RENAME=(FROM=VIA DRECTN=DRECTN2
     HIWAY=HIWAY2 MILES=MILES2));
   BY VIA;
IF INSTART AND INFINISH;
   TOTAL=MILES+MILES2;
```

Data CONNECTN:

```
                          CONNECTN (ONE MERGE)                              3

                                        D              D
                                        R      H   M   R      H   M
                                        E      I   I   E      I   I   T
                             F          C      W   L   C      W   L   O
                     O       R      V   T      A   E   T      A   E   T
                     B       O      I   N      Y   S   N2     Y2  S2  A
                     S       M      A          S       2              L

                     1   LOWES GROVE  CHAPEL HILL  W   54  11  PITTSBORO   S   501  16  27
                     2   LOWES GROVE  CHAPEL HILL  W   54  11  BURLINGTON  NW   54  22  33
                     3   RALEIGH      CLAYTON      SE  70  13  WILSON      NE   42  28  41
                     4   RALEIGH      DURHAM       NW  70  23  GREENSBORO  W    85  54  77
                     5   SILER CITY   GREENSBORO   NW 421  35  SANFORD     SE   87  34  69
                     6   DURHAM       GREENSBORO   W   85  54  SANFORD     SE   87  34  88
                     7   RALEIGH      LOWES GROVE  NW  40  18  CHAPEL HILL W    54  11  29
                     8   CHAPEL HILL  PITTSBORO    S  501  16  ASHEBORO    W    64  38  54
                     9   RALEIGH      PITTSBORO    W   64  32  SILER CITY  W    64  16  48
                    10   RALEIGH      PITTSBORO    W   64  32  BURLINGTON  NW   87  28  60
                    11   PITTSBORO    SILER CITY   W   64  16  GREENSBORO  NW  421  35  51
                    12   RALEIGH      WAKEFIELD    NE  64  18  WILSON      SE  264  24  42
```

The variables TO on data set START and FROM on data set FINISH are renamed to VIA and used as the matching variable for the merge. Other variables with duplicate names are also renamed on data set FINISH so that the information in those variables is not lost in the new data set. TOTAL contains the total mileage between the starting point and the final destination.

You can repeat this process over and over. To get routes between cities with two intermediate cities, merge CONNECTN with FINISH:

```
PROC SORT DATA=CONNECTN; BY TO;
DATA CONNECT2;
  MERGE CONNECTN(IN=INCONN RENAME=(TO=VIA2))
     FINISH(IN=INFINISH RENAME=(FROM=VIA2 DRECTN=DRECTN3
       HIWAY=HIWAY3 MILES=MILES3));
  BY VIA2;
  IF INCONN AND INFINISH;
  TOTAL=MILES+MILES2+MILES3;
```

The result:

```
                          CONNECT2 (TWO MERGES)                            4

     OBS    FROM            VIA          DRECTN   HIWAY   MILES    VIA2

      1    RALEIGH      LOWES GROVE       NW       40      18    CHAPEL HILL
      2    RALEIGH      LOWES GROVE       NW       40      18    CHAPEL HILL
      3    RALEIGH      DURHAM            NW       70      23    GREENSBORO
      4    PITTSBORO    SILER CITY        W        64      16    GREENSBORO
      5    LOWES GROVE  CHAPEL HILL       W        54      11    PITTSBORO
      6    LOWES GROVE  CHAPEL HILL       W        54      11    PITTSBORO
      7    LOWES GROVE  CHAPEL HILL       W        54      11    PITTSBORO
      8    RALEIGH      PITTSBORO         W        64      32    SILER CITY

     OBS   DRECTN2  HIWAY2   MILES2   TO           DRECTN3  HIWAY3   MILES3   TOTAL

      1     W        54        11    PITTSBORO      S        501      16       45
      2     W        54        11    BURLINGTON     NW        54      22       51
      3     W        85        54    SANFORD        SE        87      34      111
      4     NW      421        35    SANFORD        SE        87      34       85
      5     S       501        16    ASHEBORO       W         64      38       65
      6     S       501        16    SILER CITY     W         64      16       43
      7     S       501        16    BURLINGTON     NW        87      28       55
      8     W        64        16    GREENSBORO     NW       421      35       83
```

Data set CONNECT2 shows that you can get from Raleigh to Pittsboro via Lowes Grove and Chapel Hill, a total distance of 45 miles.

REPORT WRITING

You can write reports that meet your specifications by using FILE and PUT statements in a SAS DATA step. If the data to appear in the report exist in one or more SAS data sets, you use a SET, MERGE, or UPDATE statement to read the data. Or the data may be stored in a non-SAS file, in which case you need an INPUT statement and an INFILE or CARDS statement in the report-writing DATA step. In either case, a FILE statement defines the output file where the report is to be written; PUT statements describe the lines in the report.

Since you are using a DATA step to do the report-writing, you have access to all DATA step features. For example,

- options to check for end-of-file can be used to handle final processing for the report.
- special variables set up when a BY statement is used let you check for control breaks in the data.
- statements can be executed conditionally when a new page begins.

For example, suppose you want to print an annual sales report. The data you need are in SAS data set SALES:

```
                              SALES                                    2

        OBS    REGION    MANAGER      SALESREP    SALESAMT

          1    EAST      STAFER          64          9664
          2    EAST      YOUNG           89         22969
          3    EAST      STRIDE          90         27253
          4    EAST      ISSAC           41         21991
          5    EAST      GREEN           29         23804
          6    EAST      MOTTERS         82         20243
          7    EAST      KRAUSE          71         18209
          8    EAST      POST            55         20660
          9    EAST      POWELL          10          6753
         10    WEST      LARSON          57         21547
         11    WEST      ARNOLD          56         35687
         12    WEST      MANSTART        21         15034
         13    WEST      VETTER          95         38928
         14    WEST      CURCI           62         21531
         15    WEST      GRECO           31         18523
         16    WEST      RYAN            61         32915
         17    WEST      TOMAS           84         42109
         18    SOUTH     MORING          18         10343
         19    SOUTH     WOOD            13          9817
         20    SOUTH     GREENE          76         52516
         21    SOUTH     STAYDEN         43         20354
         22    SOUTH     TAYLOR          43         28722
         23    SOUTH     ROCKFELT        81         38737
         24    SOUTH     MOORE           49         25718
         25    SOUTH     STELAM          58         27926
         26    NORTH     FARLOW          49         32719
         27    NORTH     SMITH, T.       52         38712
         28    NORTH     RICHARDS        10         11927
         29    NORTH     SMITH, M.       37         34709
         30    NORTH     MURPHY          17         17266
         31    NORTH     BARREY          62         42166
```

The report is to list each sales manager (variable MANAGER), the number of representatives in his district (SALESREP), and the total sales made by that district in the past year (SALESAMT). The report is to be printed in order of sales region (REGION), with subtotals for sales force and total sales for each region. Overall totals are to be printed at the end of the report. The report in its finished form is shown below.

DATA Step Applications   233

```
                        ANY COMPANY
                   REGIONAL SALES TOTALS
                         1982
                                    TOTAL        TOTAL
                          SALES     SALES        GOODS
                REGION    MANAGER   FORCE        SOLD
                ------    -------   -----        -----

                EAST      STAFER      64          9,664
                          YOUNG       89         22,969
                          STRIDE      90         27,253
                          ISSAC       41         21,991
                          GREEN       29         23,804
                          MOTTERS     82         20,243
                          KRAUSE      71         18,209
                          POST        55         20,660
                          POWELL      10          6,753
                                    ------      ---------
                TOTAL                531        $171,546


                NORTH     FARLOW      49         32,719
                          SMITH,_T    52         38,712
                          RICHARDS    10         11,927
                          SMITH,_M    37         34,709
                          MURPHY      17         17,266
                          BARREY      62         42,166
                                    ------      ---------
                TOTAL                227        $177,499


                SOUTH     MORING      18         10,343
                          WOOD        13          9,817
                          GREENE      76         52,516
                          STAYDEN     43         20,354
                          TAYLOR      43         28,722
                          ROCKFELT    81         38,737
                          MOORE       49         25,718
                          STELAM      58         27,926
                                    ------      ---------
                TOTAL                381        $214,133


                WEST      LARSON      57         21,547
                          ARNOLD      56         35,687
                          MANSTART    21         15,034
                          VETTER      95         38,928
                          CURCI       62         21,531
                          GRECO       31         18,523
                          RYAN        61         32,915
                          TOMAS       84         42,109
                                    ------      ---------
                TOTAL                467        $226,274


                ALL REGIONS         1606        $789,452
```

Printing individual lines   One way to begin writing the SAS program for completing the report is to consider what should be printed for each record read by the DATA step and then to handle exceptions. Observations in data set SALES correspond to district managers, and you want to print a line of information about a manager each time the DATA step is executed. The statements below print the individual manager lines.

```
DATA _NULL_;
  SET SALES;
  FILE PRINT;
  PUT @14 MANAGER $15.
      @35 SALESREP 3. @45 SALESAMT COMMA6.;
```

The DATA statement uses the special data set name _NULL_, since you do not need to create a new data set. (See the DATA statement in Chapter 3, "SAS Statements Used in the DATA Step," for more information about _NULL_.)

The SET statement reads observations from the SAS data set SALES.

The FILE statement uses the special DDname PRINT in which lines printed by the corresponding PUT statements are printed in the procedure output file.

Each time the PUT statement is executed, SAS writes the values of MANAGER, SALESREP, and SALESAMT from the current observation. The PUT statement gives the positions and formats the values should have on the output lines.

Note: outlining the report on a coding form is a good way to determine each variable's position on the report. Do this before you begin writing the SAS program.

Printing titles on the report   To execute a group of statements only when SAS begins printing a new page, use the HEADER= option of the FILE statement to give the label of the group of statements. To cancel the default SAS title or any other titles defined by earlier TITLE statements, use the NOTITLES option of the FILE statement. The boldface additions to the program below add titles and column headings to the listing of individual lines.

```
DATA __NULL__;
  SET SALES;
  FILE PRINT HEADER=H NOTITLES;
  PUT @14 MANAGER $15.
    @35 SALESREP 3. @45 SALESAMT COMMA6.;
  RETURN;
  H: PUT / @19 'ANY COMPANY'
     / @15 'REGIONAL SALES TOTALS'
     / @23 '1982'
     //@34 'TOTAL' @46 'TOTAL'
     / @19 'SALES' @34 'SALES' @46 'GOODS ' / @4 'REGION'
     @18 'MANAGER' @34 'FORCE' @46 'SOLD'/
     @4 6*'-' @18 7*'-' @34 5*'-' @46 5*'-'/;
  RETURN;
```

The RETURN statement before the labeled PUT statement prevents the statements following the label H from being printed for every observation. The RETURN statement after the labeled PUT statement completes the HEADER= statements; in this case, the group contains only the PUT and RETURN statements.

Accumulating totals   As each observation is processed, you want to accumulate totals for regional sales force and regional total sales (TOTREP and TOTSALES) and for overall totals (ALLREP and ALLSALES). The sum statements needed to accumulate these totals appear in bold below:

```
DATA __NULL__;
  SET SALES;
  FILE PRINT HEADER=H NOTITLES;
  PUT @14 MANAGER $15.
    @35 SALESREP 3. @45 SALESAMT COMMA6.;
    TOTSALES + SALESAMT;
    TOTREP + SALESREP;
    ALLSALES + SALESAMT;
    ALLREP + SALESREP;
  RETURN;
```

```
H: PUT / @19 'ANY COMPANY'
     / @15 'REGIONAL SALES TOTALS'
     / @23 '1982'
    //@34 'TOTAL'  @46 'TOTAL'
     / @19 'SALES'  @34 'SALES'  @46 'GOODS' / @4 'REGION'
      @18 'MANAGER'  @34 'FORCE'  @46 'SOLD'/
      @4 6*'–'  @18 7*'–'  @34 5*'–'  @46 5*'–'/;
   RETURN;
```

Beginning a new BY group   Since the report shows managers by region, the input data should be sorted by region. A BY statement then takes advantage of the special FIRST. and LAST. variables, which let you check for changes in region.

When an observation is the first in the data set to have a given value of REGION, you want to reset the variables containing regional subtotals to zero before printing the observation. In addition, on the line with the first observation in the region you want to print the name of the region. The DO group shown below in bold is executed only for the first observation in a department.

```
PROC SORT DATA = SALES;
  BY REGION;
DATA __NULL__;
  SET SALES;
  BY REGION;
  FILE PRINT HEADER = H NOTITLES;
  IF FIRST.REGION THEN DO;
    TOTSALES = 0;   TOTREP = 0;
    PUT @4 REGION $5. @;
    END;
  PUT @14 MANAGER $15.
    @35 SALESREP 3. @45 SALESAMT COMMA6.;
    TOTSALES + SALESAMT;
    TOTREP + SALESREP;
    ALLSALES + SALESAMT;
    ALLREP + SALESREP;
  RETURN;
H: PUT / @19 'ANY COMPANY'
     / @15 'REGIONAL SALES TOTALS'
     / @23 '1982'
    //@34 'TOTAL'  @46 'TOTAL'
     / @19 'SALES'  @34 'SALES'  @46 'GOODS' / @4 'REGION'
      @18 'MANAGER'  @34 'FORCE'  @46 'SOLD'/
      @4 6*'–'  @18 7*'–'  @34 5*'–'  @46 5*'–'/;
   RETURN;
```

When the value of FIRST.REGION is 1, the current observation is the first to have the REGION value, and the statements following the DO group are executed. The PUT statement in this group of statements ends in a trailing at sign (@), so the pointer remains on the line after printing the value of region. The next PUT statement in the DATA step begins printing at that point. Normally, after a PUT statement that does not end in a trailing @ sign is executed, SAS releases the line just written on.

Ending a BY group   When information for the last manager in a region has been printed, you want to print regional subtotals.

```
   PROC SORT DATA = SALES;
     BY REGION;
   DATA __NULL__;
     SET SALES;
     BY REGION;
     FILE PRINT HEADER = H NOTITLES;
     IF FIRST.REGION THEN DO;
       TOTSALES = 0; TOTREP = 0;
       PUT @4 REGION $5. @;
       END;
     PUT @14 MANAGER $15.
       @35 SALESREP 3. @45 SALESAMT COMMA6.;
       TOTSALES + SALESAMT;
       TOTREP + SALESREP;
       ALLSALES + SALESAMT;
       ALLREP + SALESREP;
     IF LAST.REGION THEN
       PUT @33 6*'-' @42 9*'-'
       / @10 'TOTAL'
         @33 TOTREP 5.
         @42 TOTSALES DOLLAR9.//;
   RETURN;
   H: PUT / @19 'ANY COMPANY'
       / @15 'REGIONAL SALES TOTALS'
       / @23 '1982'
       //@34 'TOTAL' @46 'TOTAL'
       / @19 'SALES' @34 'SALES' @46 'GOODS' / @4 'REGION'
         @18 'MANAGER' @34 'FORCE' @46 'SOLD'/
       @4 6*'-' @18 7*'-' @34 5*'-' @46 5*'-'/;
   RETURN;
```

The PUT statement in this new group of statements prints a line containing dashes under the TOTAL SALES FORCE and TOTAL GOODS SOLD columns and then prints the word 'TOTAL' and the TOTREP and TOTSALES values using the DOLLAR. format.

Printing grand totals   After information for all regions is printed, you want to print the total sales force and total sales values for all departments. The END = option in the SET statement lets you define a variable whose value is 1 when the current observation is the last from SALES. When this variable's value is 1, print the overall totals on the report.

```
   PROC SORT DATA = SALES;
     BY REGION;
   DATA __NULL__;
     SET SALES END = EOF;
     BY REGION;
     FILE PRINT HEADER = H NOTITLES;
     IF FIRST.REGION THEN DO;
       TOTSALES = 0; TOTREP = 0;
       PUT @4 REGION $5. @;
       END;
```

```
            PUT @14 MANAGER $15.
              @35 SALESREP 3. @45 SALESAMT COMMA6.;
              TOTSALES + SALESAMT;
              TOTREP + SALESREP;
              ALLSALES + SALESAMT;
              ALLREP + SALESREP;
          IF LAST.REGION THEN
              PUT @33 6*'-' @42 9*'-'
              / @10 'TOTAL'
              @33 TOTREP 5.
              @42 TOTSALES DOLLAR9.//;
          IF EOF THEN PUT / @10 'ALL REGIONS'
              @32 ALLREP 6. @41
              ALLSALES DOLLAR10.;
          RETURN;
      H: PUT / @19 'ANY  COMPANY'
              / @15 'REGIONAL SALES TOTALS'
              / @23 '1982'
              //@34 'TOTAL' @46 'TOTAL'
                / @19 'SALES' @34 'SALES' @46 'GOODS' / @4 'REGION'
                @18 'MANAGER' @34 'FORCE' @46 'SOLD'/
                @4 6*'-' @18 7*'-' @34 5*'-' @46 5*'-'/;
          RETURN;
```

Whole-page access: the N = PS option   Normally when you print a report, you have access to one line at a time. Once you execute a PUT statement that prints on that line, you cannot return to the line for later printing. This poses a problem for printing reports containing multiple columns of information, among others. The N = PAGESIZE or N = PS option of the FILE statement tells SAS to hold an entire page in the output buffer until the page is full or until you tell SAS to release it. This means that for multiple columns, you can print a column at a time; when PUT statements have printed one column, you can return to the top of the next column to continue printing.

Suppose that you want to print a listing of district managers from the data set above. The multicolumn list is to show the rank order of salesmen based on their district's total sales for the previous year.

The SAS program below first sorts the SALES data set in descending order of sales and then prints the two-column report.

```
      OPTIONS LS = 72 NODATE;
      PROC SORT DATA = SALES;
        BY DESCENDING SALESAMT;
      TITLE ANY COMPANY;
      TITLE2 SALES MANAGERS FOR 1982;
      TITLE3 RANKED BY TOTAL SALES;
      DATA __NULL__;
        FILE PRINT N = PS HEADER = COLUMNS;
        DO C = 2,36;
          DO L = 6 TO 25;
          SET SALES;
          PUT #L @C
            MANAGER $10. +1 '(' REGION $5. ')' +5 SALESAMT DOLLAR8.;
          END;
        END;
```

```
PUT __PAGE__;
RETURN;
COLUMNS: PUT / @2 'MANAGER' +4 '(REGION)' @24 '''82 SALES'
    @36 'MANAGER' +4 '(REGION)' @58 '''82 SALES'
    / @2 32*'-' @36 32*'-';
RETURN;
```

The job above uses both TITLE statements and the HEADER= option of the FILE statement to produce table headings. When TITLE statements are used, PUT statements that are part of a header group of statements print in the "window" remaining after all TITLEs are printed.

The two DO loops in the job represent column and line counters. The variable C, which is the index for the outer DO loop, becomes the value of the horizontal print position where each column of information begins. L, the index for the inner loop, determines the line, or vertical print position. Printing of each column begins at line 6, leaving three blank lines after the column heading.

PUT __PAGE__ tells SAS to release the output to the print file specified by the FILE statement when both DO loops have been satisfied. SAS then returns to the top of the DATA step for a new execution and a new page. This process continues until all observations in SALES have been read. PUT __PAGE__ also releases the page when the DATA step is complete.

Notice in the report below that only part of the second column is needed to print the SALES data set in this format:

```
                            ANY COMPANY                          3
                     SALES MANAGERS FOR 1982
                      RANKED BY TOTAL SALES

    MANAGER    (REGION)   '82 SALES   MANAGER    (REGION)   '82 SALES
    --------------------------------   --------------------------------

    GREENE     (SOUTH)    $52,516     MOTTERS    (EAST )    $20,243
    BARREY     (NORTH)    $42,166     GRECO      (WEST )    $18,523
    TOMAS      (WEST )    $42,109     KRAUSE     (EAST )    $18,209
    VETTER     (WEST )    $38,928     MURPHY     (NORTH)    $17,266
    ROCKFELT   (SOUTH)    $38,737     MANSTART   (WEST )    $15,034
    SMITH, T.  (NORTH)    $38,712     RICHARDS   (NORTH)    $11,927
    ARNOLD     (WEST )    $35,687     MORING     (SOUTH)    $10,343
    SMITH, M.  (NORTH)    $34,709     WOOD       (SOUTH)     $9,817
    RYAN       (WEST )    $32,915     STAFER     (EAST )     $9,664
    FARLOW     (NORTH)    $32,719     POWELL     (EAST )     $6,753
    TAYLOR     (SOUTH)    $28,722
    STELAM     (SOUTH)    $27,926
    STRIDE     (EAST )    $27,253
    MOORE      (SOUTH)    $25,718
    GREEN      (EAST )    $23,804
    YOUNG      (EAST )    $22,969
    ISSAC      (EAST )    $21,991
    LARSON     (WEST )    $21,547
    CURCI      (WEST )    $21,531
    POST       (EAST )    $20,660
    STAYDEN    (SOUTH)    $20,354
```

Unequal column sizes   The last example shows another multicolumn report using the SALES data set. Each column in the report corresponds to a different region. Since all regions do not have the same number of district managers, the columns contain different numbers of observations.

```
PROC SORT DATA=SALES;
   BY REGION DESCENDING SALESAMT;
OPTIONS LS=120 NODATE;
TITLE ANY COMPANY;
TITLE2 SALES MANAGERS FOR 1982;
TITLE3 RANKED BY TOTAL SALES WITHIN REGION;
DATA __NULL__;
   FILE PRINT N=PS;
   DO C=2, 29, 56, 84;
      DO L=6 TO 25;
      SET SALES; BY REGION;
      IF FIRST.REGION THEN LINK HEADING;
      PUT #L @C MANAGER $12. +3 SALESAMT DOLLAR8.;
      IF LAST.REGION THEN GO TO NEWCOL;
      END;
   NEWCOL:END;
RETURN;
HEADING: PUT #1 / @C +8 REGION / @C 24*'-'/
   @C +2 'MANAGER' @C +14 '' '82 SALES'/;
   RETURN;
```

The report:

```
                                     ANY COMPANY                                                        4
                               SALES MANAGERS FOR 1982
                           RANKED BY TOTAL SALES WITHIN REGION

         EAST                      NORTH                     SOUTH                      WEST
----------------------     ----------------------     ----------------------     ----------------------
  MANAGER    '82 SALES       MANAGER    '82 SALES       MANAGER    '82 SALES       MANAGER    '82 SALES

STRIDE        $27,253     BARREY        $42,166     GREENE        $52,516     TOMAS         $42,109
GREEN         $23,804     SMITH, T.     $38,712     ROCKFELT      $38,737     VETTER        $38,928
YOUNG         $22,969     SMITH, M.     $34,709     TAYLOR        $28,722     ARNOLD        $35,687
ISSAC         $21,991     FARLOW        $32,719     STELAM        $27,926     RYAN          $32,915
POST          $20,660     MURPHY        $17,266     MOORE         $25,718     LARSON        $21,547
MOTTERS       $20,243     RICHARDS      $11,927     STAYDEN       $20,354     CURCI         $21,531
KRAUSE        $18,209                               MORING        $10,343     GRECO         $18,523
STAFER         $9,664                               WOOD           $9,817     MANSTART      $15,034
POWELL         $6,753
```

This example is similar to the one above except that instead of the HEADER= option in the FILE statement, the job uses TITLE statements for report titles. It links to a labeled statement outside the DO loop each time the REGION value changes. When the last manager for a region has been printed, the program jumps to the END statement for the outer DO loop. This causes SAS to increment the column counter and begin printing a new column.

THE PROC STEP

Introduction to the PROC Step

SAS Statements Used in the PROC Step

PROC Step Applications

Introduction to the PROC Step

Once you have created a SAS data set with a DATA step, you can analyze and process it with SAS procedures. SAS procedures are programs that read a SAS data set, compute statistics, print results, and create other SAS data sets. In a DATA step you can do your own programming using SAS statements to manipulate your data and to describe the SAS data set being created. In a PROC step, you normally call a procedure by its name—the program is already written for you.

What is a PROC Step?

A PROC step is a group of one or more SAS statements that begins with a PROC statement.

In the simplest PROC step,

- you want to process the most recently created SAS data set.
- you want all the variables processed and computations performed on all numeric variables.
- you want the entire data set processed at once rather than in subsets.

Since SAS handles this situation automatically, your PROC step is only a PROC statement to name the procedure you want:

PROC *program*;

For other analyses, you can include options in the PROC statement, or you can add other statements and their options to the PROC step to specify the analysis you want in more detail.

For example, to process a data set other than the most recently created one, you can specify its name in the DATA= option in the PROC statement:

PROC *program* DATA=*SASdataset*;

You can also add other statements to your PROC step to specify that the data should be processed in a special way. If you add a BY statement, for example:

PROC *program*;
  BY *variables*;

the data are processed in BY groups.

PROC Step Statements

The SAS statements that can appear in a PROC step are procedure information statements and variable attribute statements. Other statements also available for use within a PROC step are described in Chapter 11, "SAS Statements Used Anywhere."

The statements that are shared by a number of SAS procedures are introduced here; many other statements are unique to different procedures. All procedure information statements that can be used with each procedure are also explained in detail in the individual procedure descriptions.

Commonly used procedure information statements are:

BY	specifies that the input data set is to be processed in groups defined by the BY variables.
CLASS	identifies any classification variables in the analysis.
FREQ	identifies a variable that represents the frequency of occurrence of the observation.
ID	specifies one or more variables whose values identify observations in the printed output or SAS data set created by the procedure.
MODEL	specifies the variables that represent the dependent variables and independent effects for a model.
OUTPUT	gives information about any output data set created by the procedure.
VAR	identifies the variables to be analyzed by the procedure.
WEIGHT	specifies a variable whose values are relative weights for the observations.

Commonly used variable attribute statements are:

DROP	identifies variables to be excluded from a data set or analysis.
FORMAT	specifies formats for printing variable values.
KEEP	identifies variables to be included in a data set or analysis.
LABEL	associates descriptive labels with variable names.

The variable attribute statements INFORMAT and LENGTH can also be used with a few SAS procedures. The functions of the KEEP and DROP statements can be performed by data set options, which are available in the PROC step wherever data set names are used. See Chapter 12, "SAS Data Sets," for descriptions of these options.

SAS Statements Used in the PROC Step

The SAS statements commonly used in a PROC Step are described alphabetically in this chapter. All procedure information statements that can be used with each procedure are explained in detail with the procedure.

BY Statement
CLASS Statement
DROP Statement
FORMAT Statement
FREQ Statement
ID Statement
KEEP Statement
LABEL Statement
MODEL Statement
OUTPUT Statement
PROC Statement
VAR Statement
WEIGHT Statement

BY Statement

You can use a BY statement in a PROC step when you want SAS to process the data set in groups. A BY statement is always used with the SORT procedure to define the order in which the data set should be sorted. When a BY statement is used with most other procedures that analyze SAS data sets, the procedure processes each BY group separately. See the BY statement description in Chapter 3, "Statements Used in the DATA Step," for a discussion of BY groups.

The BY statement has the form:

BY [DESCENDING] *variable* ... **[NOTSORTED]**;

where

variable	names the variable or variables which define the BY group. The procedure processes the data set by the groups defined in the BY statement.
DESCENDING	specifies that the data set is sorted in descending order by the variable that follows the word DESCENDING in the BY statement.
NOTSORTED	specifies that observations with the same BY values are grouped together but the BY values are not necessarily sorted in alphabetical or numerical order. It may appear anywhere in the BY statement. The NOTSORTED option may not be used with the SORT procedure.

For example, data set CLASS contains observations with a variable MONTH whose values are the three-letter abbreviation for month. The observations with the same MONTH values are grouped together in the data set but the MONTH values are in calendar order and are not sorted alphabetically. This statement

BY MONTH NOTSORTED;

can be used with a PROC statement to process the data set by MONTH.

When a BY statement is used with a procedure to process the BY group, the data set being processed need not have been previously sorted by the SORT procedure. However, the data set must be in the same order as though the SORT procedure had sorted it unless NOTSORTED is specified.

For example, below is a listing of SAS data set DEGREES. The data set is sorted by STATE, CITY within STATE, and MONTH within CITY.

STATE	CITY	MONTH	DEGDAYS
NC	CHARLOTTE	1	716
NC	CHARLOTTE	2	588
NC	CHARLOTTE	3	461
NC	RALEIGH	1	760
NC	RALEIGH	2	638
NC	RALEIGH	3	502
VA	NORFOLK	1	760
VA	NORFOLK	2	661
VA	NORFOLK	3	532
VA	RICHMOND	1	853
VA	RICHMOND	2	717
VA	RICHMOND	3	569

With the data set sorted in this order, these statements

```
PROC PRINT;
  BY STATE;
```

cause SAS to print three listings—a separate listing for each state. (The PRINT procedure has several options that allow enhanced BY-group processing when a BY statement is in effect. See the PRINT procedure description for details.)

These statements:

```
PROC MEANS;
  BY STATE CITY;
  VAR DEGDAYS;
```

produce descriptive statistics in separate reports for each combination of STATE and CITY values.

CLASS Statement

The CLASS (or CLASSES) statement is used by several SAS procedures to identify classification variables by which the analysis is to be performed.

The form of the CLASS statement is:

CLASS *variables*;

or

CLASSES *variables*;

where

variables   specifies the classification variable(s) in the analysis. When more than one classification variable is allowed by the procedure, any form of variable list described in Chapter 1 may be used.

DROP Statement

You can use the DROP statement in a PROC step that processes variables in a SAS data set to specify variables that are not to be included in the analysis. The variables listed are unavailable to the procedure. The DROP statement applies only to the data set being used as input to the procedure. Its effect is not permanent; the input data set is unchanged.

The form of the DROP statement is:

> **DROP** *variables*;

where

> *variables*   specifies the variables you want omitted from the analysis. Any form of variable list may be used (see Chapter 1 for details). Do not abbreviate the variable names.

The DROP statement is ignored if a VAR statement is also present. (Some procedures use a statement other than VAR to list the variables to be analyzed. If such a statement is present, the DROP statement is ignored.) Here is an example:

> PROC PRINT DATA=CLASS;
>   DROP HEIGHT;

Data set CLASS contains five variables: NAME, SEX, AGE, HEIGHT, and WEIGHT. If you want all but the HEIGHT variable printed, the statements above would be equivalent to specifying:

> PROC PRINT DATA=CLASS;
>   VAR NAME SEX AGE WEIGHT;

The effect of the DROP statement is the reverse of the KEEP statement's effect. To save writing, the DROP statement is preferred if fewer variables are being dropped than kept. Do not use both DROP and KEEP statements in the same step.

The DROP= data set option is preferred to using the DROP statement in a procedure step. See Chapter 12, ''SAS Data Sets,'' for more information about data set options.

FORMAT Statement

You can use the FORMAT statement to associate output formats with variables in PROC steps. Output formats may be either SAS formats or formats you have defined with PROC FORMAT. If you want to give the same output format to several variables or different formats to different variables, you can do it with one FORMAT statement. When SAS prints values of the variables, it uses the associated format to print the values.

You can associate output formats with variables with the statement

FORMAT *variables [format] ...;*

These terms are included in the FORMAT statement:

variables	names the variable or variables you want to associate with an output format.
format	gives the output format you want SAS to use for writing values of the variable or variables in the previous variable list. Every format name ends with a period (for example, SEXFMT.) or has a period between the width value and number of decimal places (for example, DOLLAR8.2).
	See Chapter 13, "SAS Informats and Formats," for more information on the types of SAS formats that are available. See the FORMAT procedure for information on how to define your own output formats.

If a variable appears in more than one FORMAT statement, the output format given in the last FORMAT statement is used. A FORMAT statement used in a DATA step to associate one format with a variable can be overridden by a FORMAT statement in a later PROC step. The original format name remains stored with the variable in the data set. To disassociate a format from a variable, use the variable's name in a FORMAT statement with no format.

If you have used the FORMAT procedure to define your own formats, you need a FORMAT statement to associate the format with one or more variables:

```
PROC FORMAT;
   VALUE SEXFMT   1 = MALE
                  2 = FEMALE;
PROC PRINT DATA = ALL;
   FORMAT SEX SEXFMT.;
```

The FORMAT procedure defines the SEXFMT. format. The FORMAT statement in the PROC step associates SEXFMT. with SEX, a variable in data set ALL. When the values of SEX are printed by any procedure, MALE and FEMALE are printed instead of the numbers 1 and 2.

When a FORMAT statement is used in a PROC step, the procedure prints values of all variables using formats associated with them in the FORMAT statement. The format is associated with the variable only for the duration of the procedure.

To use some SAS procedures like FREQ and GLM, you may need to divide observations on continuous variables into distinct groups or categories. You can use the FORMAT procedure to define these categories or ranges of values. If you then use a FORMAT statement to associate the new format defined by PROC FORMAT with the variables, FREQ or GLM will use the formatted values to determine the category or group into which each observation falls. See Chapter 9, "PROC Step Applications," for an example using the FORMAT statement with the FREQ procedure.

Using FORMAT for Datetime Values

When you are using datetime values in procedures, you must assign them a corresponding date, time, or datetime format in order for the values to be printed in an intelligible form. If you want to associate the format with the variable only for the duration of the procedure, use a FORMAT statement in the PROC step. For example:

```
PROC PRINT;
   VAR DATE FARENHT CELSIUS;
   FORMAT DATE DATE7.;
   TITLE HIGH TEMPERATURE FOR DAY;
```

The result of the PRINT procedure is a listing of each date in the data set in the form *ddMMMyy* (DATE7.) with the Fahrenheit and Celsius temperature values. Without the FORMAT statement, values of DATE appear as the number of days between January 1, 1960, and the value of the variable DATE, a large number which is difficult to interpret. See Chapter 13, "SAS Informats and Formats," for more information on date, time, and datetime values.

FREQ Statement

The FREQ statement is used with several procedures to identify a variable which represents the frequency of occurrence for the other values in the observation.
The form of the FREQ statement is:

FREQ *variable*;

where

> *variable*   represents the frequency of occurrence for the observation.

When a FREQ statement appears, the procedure treats the data set as though each observation appears *n* times, where *n* is the value of the FREQ variable for that observation.
If the value of the FREQ variable in an observation is less than one, the observation is not used in the analysis. If the value is not an integer, only the integer portion is used.

ID Statement

The ID statement is used by several SAS procedures to specify one or more variables whose values identify observations in the printed output or SAS data set created by the procedure.

The form of the ID statement is:

ID *variables*;

where

variables   specifies the identifying variables.

For example, when an ID statement is used with the PRINT procedure, the observations are identified by the value of the ID variable; the observation number is not printed.   See the census data example in Chapter 9, ''PROC Step Applications,'' for output showing the effect of an ID variable.

KEEP Statement

You can use the KEEP statement in a PROC step that processes variables in a SAS data set to specify the variables that are to be included in the analysis. The variables not listed in the KEEP statement are unavailable to the procedure. The KEEP statement applies only to the data set being used as input to the procedure. Its effect is not permanent; the input data set is unchanged.

The form of the KEEP statement is:

KEEP variables;

where

variables   specifies the variables you want included in the analysis. Any form of variable list may be used (see Chapter 1 for details). Do not abbreviate the variable names.

The KEEP statement is ignored if a VAR statement is also present. (Some procedures use a statement other than VAR to list the variables to be analyzed. If such a statement is present, the KEEP statement is ignored.)

Here is an example:

```
PROC PRINT DATA=CLASS;
  KEEP NAME;
```

The PRINT procedure prints only the variable NAME from data set CLASS.

The effect of the KEEP statement is the reverse of the DROP statement's effect. To save writing, the KEEP statement is preferred if fewer variables are being kept than dropped. Do not use both KEEP and DROP statements in the same step.

The KEEP= data set option is preferred to using the KEEP statement in a procedure step. See Chapter 12, "SAS Data Sets," for more information about data set options.

LABEL Statement

You can use a LABEL statement in a PROC step to give labels to variables. Most SAS procedures use these variable labels in writing the results of analyses. The LABEL statement is an attribute statement that can occur anywhere among the statements in a PROC step. Although the statement is available to all procedures that read SAS data sets, it is not described in any procedure description. When a LABEL statement is used in a PROC step, the labels are associated with the variables for the duration of the procedure step.

The form of the LABEL statement is:

LABEL *variable = label* ...;

where

<table>
<tr><td>*variable*</td><td>specifies the variable to which you want to assign a label.</td></tr>
<tr><td>*label*</td><td>specifies a label of up to 40 characters, including blanks, for the variable. If the label includes a semicolon or an equal sign, the label must be enclosed in single quotes. Any label can be enclosed in single quotes. When single quotes are part of the label, they must be written as two single quotes. When two single quotes are used within a label to represent one single quote, they are counted as one character.</td></tr>
</table>

Any number of variable names and labels can appear.

Here is an example:

```
PROC PLOT;
  PLOT X*Y;
  LABEL X= RESPONSE TIME
    Y= HOUR OF DAY;
```

In this example, labels rather than variable names are used to label the vertical and horizontal axes of the plot.

MODEL Statement

The MODEL statement is used by several SAS statistical procedures described in the *SAS User's Guide: Statistics, 1982 Edition,* to identify the model to be analyzed.

Although the form of the MODEL statement depends on the procedure used, the general form of the MODEL statement is:

MODEL *dependents=independenteffects* / [*options*]**;**

where

dependent	specifies the dependent variable or variables in the analysis.
independenteffects	specifies the independent variables or regressors in the analysis.
options	specifies one or more MODEL statement options. See the individual procedure descriptions for a list of options available with that procedure.

OUTPUT Statement

The OUTPUT statement is used by several SAS procedures to tell the procedure to create a SAS data set as output.

Although the form of the OUTPUT statement may vary with each procedure, the general form is:

OUTPUT [OUT = *SASdataset*] [*keyword* = *names*] **... ;**

where

SASdataset	specifies the name of the new SAS data set to be created by the procedure.
keyword = *names*	names the output variables on the data set associated with keywords. Keywords vary with each procedure but are usually descriptive of a statistic or other value being output to the new data set.

For example, in the MEANS procedure step below:

```
PROC MEANS;
  VAR X;
  OUTPUT OUT = OUTMEAN MEAN = MEANX;
```

the MEAN = keyword specifies that the mean of X, calculated by the MEANS procedure, should be given the name MEANX in the new data set OUTMEAN.

PROC Statement

The PROC or PROCEDURE statement is used to begin a PROC step and to identify the procedure you want to use.

The form of the PROC statement is:

PROC *program* [*options*]**;**

where

program	names the program you want to use. Normally, the name you specify is the name of a SAS procedure. You can, however, call your own program from SAS in a PROC statement. See below for directions on calling your own procedure from SAS.
options	specifies one or more options for the procedure. See the individual procedure descriptions for options that may be specified in the PROC statement.

Three kinds of options are commonly used:

keyword	single keyword to request a feature of the procedure.
keyword = value	keyword and value, where value is a number or character string.
keyword = SASdataset	specifies an input or output SAS data set.

The options that may be specified with each procedure are described in detail in the individual procedure description.

Using other programs in SAS   Unless disallowed by your installation, you can call any program from SAS by putting its name in a PROC statement. For example, if you want to call a program of yours named RECORDS in a SAS job, you can use the SAS statement

PROC RECORDS;

Your program will then be executed.

When you are using this feature, keep in mind these facts:

- The library containing your program must be available to SAS or defined in the control language for your job.

For example, in an OS batch job, use this JCL:

// EXEC SAS
//SASLIB DD DSN = userid.mypgms.load,DISP = SHR
.
.SAS statements
.

For more information, see "SAS under OS Batch."

Under TSO, use the LOAD operand of the SAS CLIST:

SAS LOAD(mypgms)

For more information, see "SAS Under TSO."

Under CMS, it is usually only necessary to have the disk containing your programs accessed. Note that a CMS module that expects a CMS parameter list should be invoked by the CMS statement. For more information, see ''SAS Under CMS.''

- You can check the return code issued by your program by adding a CC= option, giving the maximum acceptable return code, to your PROC statement:

    PROC RECORDS CC=4;

If the return code issued by your program is greater than the CC value, and you are not executing SAS interactively, SAS sets OPTIONS OBS=0 and enters syntax check mode. (See Chapter 16, ''SAS Log and Procedure Output,'' for more about syntax check mode.)

VAR Statement

The VAR (or VARIABLES) statement is used by several SAS procedures to identify the variables to be analyzed.

The form of the VARIABLES statement is:

VAR *variables*;

or

VARIABLES *variables*;

where

variables   identifies the variables in the data set you want analyzed by the procedure. Any valid form of variable list may be used. (See Chapter 1 for details.)

WEIGHT Statement

The WEIGHT statement is used by several SAS procedures to specify a variable whose values are relative weights for the observations.
The form of the WEIGHT statement is:

WEIGHT *variable*;

where

variable   names the variable whose values contain the relative weights.

The WEIGHT statement is often used in analyses where the variance associated with each observation is different and the values of the weight variable are proportional to the reciprocals of the variances.

The WEIGHT statement should not be confused with the FREQ statement, which identifies a variable that represents frequency of occurrence for the observation. See the FREQ statement description for more information.

PROC Step Applications

Census Data: Example 1

This example applies several SAS procedures for descriptive statistics to U.S. census data. The data are selected characteristics of U.S. cities with populations over 50,000 according to the *County and City Data Book, 1977*. The raw data are read into a SAS data set and then prepared for analysis with a variety of DATA step techniques.

Data set CCDB77 The statements in the first DATA step below read in data from an external file labeled CENSUS into a SAS data set called CCDB77. The data set contains 383 cities as observations with data on a number of variables related to choice of retirement community.

The PUT __INFILE__ statement prints the raw data for the first five observations. The file contains city records for all U.S. cities and some state and national summary records. An IF-THEN statement is used with a DELETE statement to delete the summary records, which have missing values of the PLACE variable. A subsetting IF statement is used to select only cities with populations greater than or equal to 50,000. The LIST statement lists the only one of the first five observations (BIRMINGHAM) that is included in the data set being built.

Using an array named CHECK, SAS checks the variables to be analyzed for missing values (.) and values greater than 100,000,000 (other codes that should not be included in the analysis).

A combination of IF-THEN/ELSE statements divides the cities into three groups based on the size of the population. LABEL statements provide variable labels.

```
DATA CCDB77;
  INFILE CENSUS;
  ARRAY CHECK(I) POP1975 OVER65 INCOME HOUSING
    ELECTRIC CITYGOVT ROBBERY JANTEMP JULYTEMP SUNSHINE;
  DROP I;
  INPUT
          STATE              3-4
          PLACE              8-11
          CITY $             12-60
          POP1975            81-90
          OVER65             191-200    1
          INCOME             711-720
          HOUSING            1101-1110
          ELECTRIC           1281-1290  2
          CITYGOVT           1300
          ROBBERY            1671-1680
          JANTEMP            2978-2980  1
          JULYTEMP           2988-2990  1
          SUNSHINE           3021-3030  ;
```

```
IF __N__<= 5 THEN PUT __INFILE__;
IF PLACE=. THEN DELETE;
IF POP1975>= 50000;
IF __N__<= 5 THEN LIST;

DO OVER CHECK;
  IF CHECK⌐=. AND CHECK<100000000;
END;

IF 50000<POP1975<= 75000 THEN POPGRP= 1;
ELSE IF 75000<POP1975<= 100000 THEN POPGRP= 2;
ELSE IF POP1975>100000 THEN POPGRP= 3;

LABEL POP1975= 1975 POPULATION ESTIMATE;
LABEL OVER65= % PERSONS 65 & OVER (1970);
LABEL INCOME= PER CAPITA MONEY INCOME (1974);
LABEL HOUSING= MEDIAN SINGLE-FAMILY OWNER-OCCUP (1970);
LABEL ELECTRIC= TYPICAL RESID. ELECTRIC BILL/MO. (1976);
LABEL CITYGOVT= FORM OF CITY GOVERNMENT;
LABEL ROBBERY= ROBBERY RATE/100,000 POP (1975);
LABEL JANTEMP= MEAN JANUARY TEMPERATURE (DEGREES F);
LABEL JULYTEMP= MEAN JULY TEMPERATURE (DEGREES F);
LABEL SUNSHINE= POSSIBLE SUNSHINE ANNUAL % (DAYS);
```

```
NOTE: INFILE CENSUS IS:
      DSNAME=CCDB77.CITIES,
      UNIT=TAPE,VOL=SER=S10247,LABEL=3,DISP=OLD,
      DCB=(BLKSIZE=12168,LRECL=3042,RECFM=FB)
4 01      ALABAMA                             00000000003000000000000361590700000007160000000060000000000
0003444354600000000000000005180000000736000000002620-0000000780000000640000000095000000019900000000900000001890000000004
00000000050600000000000000060000000000000000000005460000000000000000058086000000001610000066832000000194000003365800000093000003374 3
00000000009860000000000000000600000000000000600000000006000000000000000006000000000000000000000001490000024449600000000000
00006786790000000013200000017321000000479000006348900001808798000000010700000041300008651060000000325600000000006000000000
00012491956000000000000119331500000002860000000173600000000000000000600000000000000000006000000000000000000000000000003624
00000000089300000000000000007263000004047600000000000008746590000186092000002070000004680000027360000000000000000000000089
00000000230000852111600000000000006000000000006000000006000000000000006000000000000000006000000000000006000000000000000000
60000000000000600000000006000000000006000000000060000000001114845000000017400000082900000296000103411300000066700000000222
0000000154000000010900001257400000070000025020001262500000776000000057000000167000025348400000017104000000702
00000000310000002660000359844600000000000000000000000000060000000000000575700000161330000000000000000000049400000001145
0000000641000001972000000183000000016000005190000051990000001700000001200000009200000002600000000000000176
00000000930000013567000006350000009860000030328600000000000022428000005850760000000000006000000000000000123
6000000000000006000000006000000060000000001254970000142010000111296000003471000000160000000204600000000000000000123
6000000000000000233600000000000000116300000164560000000000000000027000000137000000169100000000000000004984000000327
6000000000000003226000002396800000262200000005193000001730800000506480000035510000625830000112412000000012700000000117
00000004370-000006300000054340000080160000000000753804660000000000005770000558710000422730000032401000000643
0000000626600000000000000658600000273700000148600000384400000451000000206100000013430000023460000009993000000000
0000658361500000010000000005980000009466000000147077360000000153597260000000000008827186000000000000000348554
600000000000004760086000000000003223806000000000000423958600000000000003787356000000000002071020000149241000068274 4
00000203800000000468000000076300000095600000219700000069400000015440000002110000013610001119812000000952000102047 8
600000000000000084600000000000008900000000480000008600000000000019000000000900000058173000312366600000000000
6000000000006000000006000000060000000006000000000600000000060000000006000000000600000000600000000600000006000000000
6000000000006000000006000000060000000006000000000600000000060000000006000000000600000000600000000600000006000000000
60000000000060000000060000000600000000060000000006000000000600000000060000000006000000300000000030000000003000000000
3000000000030000000030000000300000000030000000000
4 01    0060ANNISTON..................       000000001670000000713000030622000000183460000000006000000000
0000031533600000000000000000000053900000006540000000345 0-0000004600000006480000000011100000000149000000090000002972000000000
0-0000029600000000006000000000000-00000063600000000005960000001950000085400000027100000046300000015100000004 36
0000000138600000000600000000000000600000000006000000000006000000000006000000000002000000004096000000000
0000157680000000020000000409000013356000001576800000173580000000094000004250000077820000000424600000000000000000000
00000113136000000000000000107440000027800000018600002096000000000600000000006000000000600000000850000003696
0000000860000000875000000693100000409760000000000081760000023950000022100000453000000291600000000000000000089
00000000330000087726000000006000000000000600000000006000000000600000000060000000006000000006000000006000000000
60000000000600000000060000000060000000001109100000005100000075700000136000010266000005800000029 4
0000000660000010300001154700000067000002191000001290000010000000000000000000000033080000001440000001000
0000000000000004358600000000060000000006000000000001000000001694900000001000000117500000001 2
0000007730000000400000017000000022000006450000013900004350000003000000400000004600000000000000114
0000000420000009100000300000099590000012976000000000000092200004952600000060000000600000006000000001 14
600000000010000000060000000006000000100000001000000010000000010000000100000001000000001 000000000
60000000001000000000100000001000000010000000010000000100000001000000069000000460000067000000567
60000000000830000006140000006900000141000004800000010400000510000001161000021400000005830000537
00000077200000645000007900000089960000001629236000000020000000001116000007788000000535000000710
00000056460000000073000000017000000170000000670000000500000026000000140000000436
0000148382000000023000000623000009706000000237666000000400060000000000002776960000000000005353
600000000007602600000000000084436000000854860000000881760000000000431400003335400016060
00000036900000055800000079100000015000006400000013000000270000005000000180000151720000049800013657
```

```
3
000000036900000005580000007910000000015000000064000000001300000002700000000050000000180000015172000000049800000013657
6000000000000000000080600000000000000000014020000000000000000077600000000002000000000020000000000000001052000003660600000000
6000000000060000000006000000000060000000006000000000060000000006000000000060000000006000000000060000000006000000000060000000
6000000000060000000006000000000060000000006000000000060000000006000000000060000000006000000000060000000006000000000060000000
60000000000600000000060000000006000000000060000000006000000000060000000006000000000060000000004500000007930000000095
000000002000000052190000000056100000000000
4 01     0110AUBURN.....................             00000002640000000904000002506100000009496000000000006000000000
0000002276760000000000000000000480000000082600000001690000000035000000775000000004300000000399000000009000000001702000000000
000000001016000000000600000000000600000004006000000000000002700000000108000000044200000001940000000093000000000370000000101
000000044600000000000000006000000000006000000000060000000000060000000006000000000006000000001000000000556000000000
0000000391000000001000000000550000002195000000391000007389000000070000000741000000338400000003426000000006000000000
0000007962600000000000000000767900000000860000000140000000531600000000600000000600000000600000000600000000872000003564
0000000800000008320000007667000000470760000000000000000447300000008210000001610000003650000000211600000000000000000159
000000003800000041446000000000000600000000006000000006000000000060000000006000000005340000000451000000614300000004480000000167
600000000060000000006000000006000000006000000006490000000064300000005340000000451000000614300000004480000000167
10000000000000000007500000218000000000941000000000000000002390000000615000000420000000343000006345000000020800000000577
000000009600000003270000005785600000060000000060000000006000000001000000000000000016949000000010000000035000000006
000000071900000002000000002480000000220000000344000000370000000110000000710000000147000000560000000000000000236
0000000141000000006600000002890000009560000002436000000001640000002236000000000000000800000001606000000000000000040
60000000006000000000600000000060000000006000000873000000460000008270000003484000000008000000001606000000000000000040
6000000000600000000120600000010220000021556000000000000000124100000000000000000183100000001000000000100000001000000000
10000000001000000000100000001000000000100000001000000000167960000000100000000100000001000000002600000001520000001780000000736
0000000567600000000000000003300000001100000000040000000029000000020000000009000000009000000170000000004000000872
0000039830000000006000000068200000097060000000000009970600000000000000008434600000000002000000006000000000000003412
600000000003836600000000020000000006000000003099600000000000003153600000000002000000000600000000888000000004216
00000011600000003620000008020000000081000000010000000001000000000100000000300000044740000000382000003983
6000000000000000002686000000001000000001000000000100000006000000001000000020000000000003650000013776000000000
600000000060000000006000000006000000000060000000006000000006000000000060000000006000000006000000006000000000
600000000060000000006000000006000000000060000000006000000006000000000060000000006000000006000000006000000000
60000000006000000006000000000060000000006000000006000000000060000000006000000000450000000797000000095
000000002400000056000000000000651000000000000
4 01     0175BESSEMER...................         0000000153000000/0000000315310000002061600000000000006000000000
0000003366360000000000000540000000047600000005180-000008100000000628000000011600000001890000001300000033120000000000
0-00000636000000000060000000000000000186000000000000000077600000024600000010060000029900000004100000013000000000583
000000017360000000000000000006000000000000006000000000006000000000060000000006000000000060000000001686000000000
0000005172000000000100000001680000005328000005172000017718000001390000003330000089030000006306000000060000000000
00000110476000000000000000010368000003040000022900000013960000000000006000000006000000000887000003377
000000107000000008850000006514000000428860000000008214000003741000002510000004340000032660000006000000000064
000000001400000010245600000000006000000006000000006000000006000000006000000006000000006000000006000000000
60000000006000000000000600000000060000000006000000001088600000001120000008600000181000010379000005620000000474
0000001870000001360000010455000000059000002199000000910000010000000000000000001947000001380000000942
00000000000000005800000029296000000000006000000006000000001000000001409000000020000000044000000008
00000036600000029000000003080000000260000004550000004400000011100000025000000314000000000000319
0000000000000000000530000015500000008860000000421600000000003590000001516000000600000000060000006000000000
600000000060000000006000000006000000002209000000374000001835000007006000000034900000050760000000339
6000000000076160000000000001925000003324600000000571000001620000006800000006300000045000000311
6000000000430000003770000000370000007400000029400000058800000082000010620000167200000770-00000104
00000017800000139000004500000084460000005735260000000020000000671000000560500000451000000716
000000053960000000000930000003700000019000000054000000051000000340000023000038000017000000619
00011039790000001600000044000009696000000257956000000199066000000000001876160000000000000003985
600000000651760000000479060000000636160000000050316000000363100000257400000011959
00000026300000044900007830000111000000010000000010000000190000917100000179700000008034
600000000094600000100000010000000006000000001000000001000000147000052800002197600000000
60000000006000000006000000006000000006000000006000000006000000006000000006000000000
60000000006000000006000000006000000006000000006000000006000000006000000004420000007990000000095
000000002000000565400000000581000000000
4 01     0185BIRMINGHAM..................         000000082600000000540000276273000003345600000000006000000000
```

4
00003058936000000000000000005410000000578000000041300-0000006500000674000000011800000000319000000013000000022300000000004
0-0000009760000000006000000000000-00000103600000000000000005348000000194000000730800000002390000003385000000123000000004250
000000013960000000000000000000600000000000006000000000000000000000000006000000000000001500000044956000000000
00001516570000000015000000449500001627000001516570000167678000000087000000441000000722500000000512600000000006000000000
00001205626000000000000011472500000021600000002310000001366000000000006000000000006000000000006000000000000000007520000004023
00000000090000000008230000007735000000518460000000000000076697000000028587000000001740000000034300000002326000000000000000092
000000001800000678326000000006000000000000000006000000000000000000000600000000000006000000000006000000006000000000
600000000060000000000000000006000000000006000000001053140-000000033000000070200000001580000099916000000054000000036200000000027000000097
0000000270000000970000126770000000076000002366000000686000003980000000055000000547000000906700000011670000000338
0000000023000000639000001998660000000000000000600000000000000000006000000000006075000000169490000000030000000948000000000261
00000006840000000445000000021700000003300000029200000099300000002330000000053000000000000600000000000000000000000213
0000000068000002576000000087100000010000000036356000000000003209000007833600000006000000000000060000000000006000000000
600000000006000000000600000000000000600000000000006000000254590000033640000022095000000921500000003220000000641600000000563
6000000000000000005596000000000000000248100000043026000000000000000000121500000001490000000930000000644000000458000000437
600000000000000003540000030100000026200000052300000206000000580700000385000006522000001228000-000000780-00000030
00000002560000006240000008990000007406000000000001902451600000000000581000015284000012866300000026490000000733
000000054160000000000003770000002190000000730000004820000003440000002100000000830000002000000009300000040
000009474860000001440000003440000009796000000000014312660000000000002706666000000000006061770
600000000000000047709600000000000005227260000000000004101560000000707696000000001894700002298700001180154
00000023370000057100000670000000560000015800000008800000181000001800000028000031099400000141600029959I
60000000000000000000526000000000004700000050000000596000002000000000009500001437700008465560000000
600000000000600000000600000000000600000000000006000000000006000000000006000000000000060000000000000600000000
6000000000600000000600000000600000000600000000600000000600000000600000000600000000600000000600000000600000000
6000000000600000000600000000600000000600000000600000000600000000600000000600000004420000007990000000095
00000000020000000532300000000580000000074

RULE: 1234567 101234567 201234567 301234567 401234567 501234567 601234567 701234567 801234567 901234567 00

5   4 01   0185BIRMINGHAM...................   00000008260000000054000002762730000003345
    101   6000000000060000000000000003058936000000000000000000054100000005780000000413000000065000006740000000118
    201   0000000031900000013000000022300000040-000009760000000006000000000000000-0000010360000000000000005348
    301   0000000194000000730800000002390000003385000000123000000042500000013960000000060000000000000000006000000000
    401   6000000000006000000000000000006000000000006000000000000000001500000044956000000000000000015165700000000015
    501   000000044950000016270000015165700001676780000000870000004410000007225000000005126000000000006000000000
    601   00001205626000000000000001147250000000216000000023100000013660000000000000060000000000006000000000
    701   0000000752000000402300000000900000008230000077350000000518460000000000000076697000002858700000001740
    801   0000000343000000023260000000000920000000001800000678326000000006000000000000000006000000000000006000000000
    901   60000000000060000000000000000006000000000006000000000000000000000006000000006000000000006000000000
   1001   6000000000000001053140-000000033000000070200000001580000099916000000054000000036200000000027000000097
   1101   000012677000000076000002366000000686000003980000000055000000547000000906700000011670000000338
   1201   00000002300000063900000199866000000000000060000000000000000000000060750000001694900000003
   1301   0000000094800000026100000006840000004450000002170000000330000002920000009930000002330000000005
   1401   00000000053000000000000000000002130000068000002576000000087100000010000000036356000000000
   1501   0000003209000007833600000006000000000000600000000000000600000000000006000000000000006000000000
   1601   000002545900000033640000022095000000921500000003220000000641600000000000005636000000000000000000559
   1701   6000000000000000000248100000043026000000000000000121500000001490000000930000000644000000458000000437
   1801   600000000000000000003540000030100000026200000052300000206000000580700000385000006522000012280
   1901   0-000000780-00000030000000256000000062400000089900000074060000000000019024516000000000581
   2001   00000152840000128663000000264900000007330000005416000000000377000000021900000000730000000482
   2101   000000034400000002100000000830000002000000093000000040000947486000014400000034400000000979
   2201   6000000000000001431266000000000000002706666000000000000061770600000000000047709
   2301   600000000000000005227260000000000004101560000000707696000000001894700002298700001180154
   2401   000000233700000057100000670000000560000015800000008800000181000001800000028000031099
   2501   0000001416000029959160000000000000000526000000000004700000050000000596000002000000000
   2601   000000000950000014377000084655600000006000000000000060000000000006000000000000060000000000
   2701   600000000006000000000600000000000600000000000006000000000006000000000006000000000
   2801   600000000006000000000600000000600000000600000000600000000600000000600000000
   2901   600000000006000000000600000000600000000600000000600000000600000000600000004420000007990000000095
   3001   00000000020000000532300000000580000000074

Using PROC UNIVARIATE   With the exception of CITYGOVT, the variables to be analyzed are continuous variables. For the tables generated by later SAS statements, the variables need to have only a few discrete values. PROC UNIVARIATE provides descriptive statistics that can help in determining appropriate cutoff points for recoding original continuous values into new categorical values.

```
PROC UNIVARIATE;
   TITLE CENSUS DATA: OUTPUT FROM PROC UNIVARIATE
     TO DETERMINE CUTOFFS;
   ID CITY;
```

```
                    CENSUS DATA: OUTPUT FROM PROC UNIVARIATE TO DETERMINE CUTOFFS                    1

                                            UNIVARIATE

VARIABLE=POP1975        1975 POPULATION ESTIMATE

              MOMENTS                              QUANTILES(DEF=4)                      EXTREMES

N                 383   SUM WGTS        383   100% MAX   7481613   99%    1961582   LOWEST     ID      HIGHEST     ID
MEAN           188173   SUM        72070312    75% Q3     152959   95%     621822   50105(MIDWEST )   1335085(DETROIT.)
STD DEV        463968   VARIANCE  2.153E+11    50% MED     86610   90%     362394   50107(OSHKOSH.)   1815808(PHILADEL)
SKEWNESS      11.5512   KURTOSIS    166.54     25% Q1      65395   10%    56603.6   50264(FAIRFIEL)   2727399(LOS ANGE)
USS        9.579E+13    CSS       8.223E+13     0% MIN     50105    5%    53673.2   50357(GADSDEN.)   3099391(CHICAGO.)
CV           246.564    STD MEAN    23707.6                         1%    50342.1   50425(EAST LAN)   7481613(NEW YORK)
T:MEAN=0      7.93724   PROB>|T|     0.0001   RANGE      7431508
SGN RANK        36768   PROB>|S|     0.0001   Q3-Q1        87564
NUM ~= 0          383                         MODE         50105
```

```
                    CENSUS DATA: OUTPUT FROM PROC UNIVARIATE TO DETERMINE CUTOFFS                    2

                                            UNIVARIATE

VARIABLE=OVER65        % PERSONS 65 & OVER (1970)

              MOMENTS                              QUANTILES(DEF=4)                      EXTREMES

N                 383   SUM WGTS        383   100% MAX      48.8   99%    21.0392   LOWEST     ID      HIGHEST     ID
MEAN          9.80418   SUM            3755    75% Q3       12.1   95%         15       2(ANCHORAG)    18.7(WEST PAL)
STD DEV       4.27427   VARIANCE    18.2694    50% MED       9.9   90%      14.22    2.3(RICHARDS)    19.6(HOLLYWOO)
SKEWNESS       2.4094   KURTOSIS    19.1045    25% Q1        7.2   10%        4.5    2.4(FOUNTAIN)    28.6(CLEARWAT)
USS           43793.6   CSS         6978.89     0% MIN         2    5%       3.52    2.4(SIMI VAL)    30.7(ST PETER)
CV            43.5964   STD MEAN   0.218405                         1%        2.4    2.4(STERLING)    48.8(MIAMI BE)
T:MEAN=0      44.8899   PROB>|T|     0.0001   RANGE         46.8
SGN RANK        36768   PROB>|S|     0.0001   Q3-Q1          4.9
NUM ~= 0          383                         MODE          10.6
```

```
                    CENSUS DATA: OUTPUT FROM PROC UNIVARIATE TO DETERMINE CUTOFFS                    3

                                            UNIVARIATE

VARIABLE=INCOME        PER CAPITA MONEY INCOME (1974)

              MOMENTS                              QUANTILES(DEF=4)                      EXTREMES

N                 383   SUM WGTS        383   100% MAX      8841   99%    7478.56   LOWEST     ID      HIGHEST     ID
MEAN           4795.7   SUM         1836752    75% Q3       5146   95%     6423.8   2196(BROWNSVI)   7258(ALEXANDR)
STD DEV       858.806   VARIANCE    737547     50% MED      4677   90%     5984.8   2279(LAREDO..)   7413(PALO ALT)
SKEWNESS      1.00921   KURTOSIS   2.56859     25% Q1       4233   10%     3936.2   2593(EAST ST )   7823(SKOKIE..)
USS        9090249286   CSS       281742995     0% MIN      2196    5%     3752.4   2839(COMPTON.)   8479(SOUTHFIE)
CV            17.9078   STD MEAN   43.8829                          1%    2799.64   3207(CAMDEN..)   8841(NEWPORT )
T:MEAN=0      109.284   PROB>|T|     0.0001   RANGE         6645
SGN RANK        36768   PROB>|S|     0.0001   Q3-Q1          913
NUM ~= 0          383                         MODE          4527
```

```
                    CENSUS DATA: OUTPUT FROM PROC UNIVARIATE TO DETERMINE CUTOFFS                    4

                                            UNIVARIATE

VARIABLE=HOUSING        MEDIAN SINGLE-FAMILY OWNER-OCCUP (1970)

              MOMENTS                              QUANTILES(DEF=4)                      EXTREMES

N                 383   SUM WGTS        383   100% MAX     48774   99%    42080.9   LOWEST     ID      HIGHEST     ID
MEAN          18825.5   SUM         7210167    75% Q3      22379   95%    30257.4   7718(ALTOONA.)   39155(MIAMI BE)
STD DEV       6291.61   VARIANCE  39584323     50% MED     17264   90%      26694   7822(LAREDO..)   41822(STAMFORD)
SKEWNESS      1.28181   KURTOSIS   2.54638     25% Q1      14456   10%      12136   8268(BROWNSVI)   43441(HONOLULU)
USS         1.509E+11   CSS       1.512E+10     0% MIN      7718    5%      11071   8414(CAMDEN..)   43882(NEW ROCH)
CV            33.4207   STD MEAN   321.486                          1%    8390.64   8546(READING.)   48774(NEWPORT )
T:MEAN=0      58.5577   PROB>|T|     0.0001   RANGE        41056
SGN RANK        36768   PROB>|S|     0.0001   Q3-Q1         7923
NUM ~= 0          383                         MODE         19673
```

CENSUS DATA: OUTPUT FROM PROC UNIVARIATE TO DETERMINE CUTOFFS   5

UNIVARIATE

VARIABLE=ELECTRIC   TYPICAL RESID. ELECTRIC BILL/MO. (1976)

	MOMENTS			QUANTILES(DEF=4)			EXTREMES			
N	383	SUM WGTS	383	100% MAX	36.64	99%	36.17	LOWEST ID		HIGHEST ID
MEAN	18.2115	SUM	6975.02	75% Q3	20.84	95%	25.3319	5.42(SEATTLE.)		26.74(SPRINGFI)
STD DEV	4.26653	VARIANCE	18.2033	50% MED	17.57	90%	22.902	8.05(TACOMA..)		36.17(MOUNT VE)
SKEWNESS	0.680725	KURTOSIS	2.43552	25% Q1	15.26	10%	13.518	8.3(PROVO...)		36.17(NEW ROCH)
USS	133980	CSS	6953.66	0% MIN	5.42	5%	11.54	8.36(SPOKANE.)		36.17(YONKERS.)
CV	23.4276	STD MEAN	0.21801			1%	8.3504	8.66(PALO ALT)		36.64(NEW YORK)
T:MEAN=0	83.5355	PROB>|T|	0.0001	RANGE	31.22					
SGN RANK	36768	PROB>|S|	0.0001	Q3-Q1	5.58					
NUM ¬= 0	383			MODE	14.23					

CENSUS DATA: OUTPUT FROM PROC UNIVARIATE TO DETERMINE CUTOFFS   6

UNIVARIATE

VARIABLE=CITYGOVT   FORM OF CITY GOVERNMENT

	MOMENTS			QUANTILES(DEF=4)			EXTREMES			
N	383	SUM WGTS	383	100% MAX	3	99%	3	LOWEST ID		HIGHEST ID
MEAN	1.83551	SUM	703	75% Q3	3	95%	3	0(HONOLULU)		3(MADISON.)
STD DEV	0.963519	VARIANCE	0.928369	50% MED	1	90%	3	1(OSHKOSH.)		3(MILWAUKE)
SKEWNESS	0.316868	KURTOSIS	-1.82034	25% Q1	1	10%	1	1(HUNTINGT)		3(RACINE..)
USS	1645	CSS	354.637	0% MIN	0	5%	1	1(TACOMA..)		3(WAUWATOS)
CV	52.4933	STD MEAN	0.0492335			1%	1	1(SPOKANE.)		3(WEST ALL)
T:MEAN=0	37.2817	PROB>|T|	0.0001	RANGE	3					
SGN RANK	36576.5	PROB>|S|	0.0001	Q3-Q1	2					
NUM ¬= 0	382			MODE	1					

CENSUS DATA: OUTPUT FROM PROC UNIVARIATE TO DETERMINE CUTOFFS   7

UNIVARIATE

VARIABLE=ROBBERY   ROBBERY RATE/100,000 POP (1975)

	MOMENTS			QUANTILES(DEF=4)			EXTREMES			
N	383	SUM WGTS	383	100% MAX	1799	99%	1285.12	LOWEST ID		HIGHEST ID
MEAN	281.183	SUM	107693	75% Q3	342	95%	855.599	15(BROWNSVI)		1258(NEWARK..)
STD DEV	266.466	VARIANCE	71004.1	50% MED	199	90%	579.799	18(PROVO...)		1284(DISTRICT)
SKEWNESS	2.27074	KURTOSIS	6.42416	25% Q1	111	10%	61	22(APPLETON)		1291(INGLEWOO)
USS	57404971	CSS	27123555	0% MIN	15	5%	46.2	24(GREEN BA)		1597(DETROIT.)
CV	94.7661	STD MEAN	13.6158			1%	23.68	24(RICHARDS)		1799(EAST ST)
T:MEAN=0	20.6513	PROB>|T|	0.0001	RANGE	1784					
SGN RANK	36768	PROB>|S|	0.0001	Q3-Q1	231					
NUM ¬= 0	383			MODE	99					

CENSUS DATA: OUTPUT FROM PROC UNIVARIATE TO DETERMINE CUTOFFS   8

UNIVARIATE

VARIABLE=JANTEMP   MEAN JANUARY TEMPERATURE (DEGREES F)

	MOMENTS			QUANTILES(DEF=4)			EXTREMES			
N	383	SUM WGTS	383	100% MAX	72.3	99%	67.4079	LOWEST ID		HIGHEST ID
MEAN	36.8838	SUM	14126.5	75% Q3	48.6	95%	54.58	5.9(FARGO CI)		66.8(FORT LAU)
STD DEV	12.9238	VARIANCE	167.025	50% MED	32.9	90%	54.5	8.5(DULUTH..)		67.2(MIAMI...)
SKEWNESS	0.272366	KURTOSIS	-0.85799	25% Q1	26.4	10%	22.38	11.8(ANCHORAG)		68.5(HOLLYWOO)
USS	584843	CSS	63803.7	0% MIN	5.9	5%	19.42	11.8(BLOOMING)		68.5(MIAMI BE)
CV	35.0393	STD MEAN	0.660377			1%	11.8	11.8(MINNEAPO)		72.3(HONOLULU)
T:MEAN=0	55.8527	PROB>|T|	0.0001	RANGE	66.4					
SGN RANK	36768	PROB>|S|	0.0001	Q3-Q1	22.2					
NUM ¬= 0	383			MODE	54.5					

```
            CENSUS DATA: OUTPUT FROM PROC UNIVARIATE TO DETERMINE CUTOFFS                    9
                                        UNIVARIATE
VARIABLE=JULYTEMP        MEAN JULY TEMPERATURE (DEGREES F)
            MOMENTS                              QUANTILES(DEF=4)                    EXTREMES
N              383    SUM WGTS       383   100% MAX     91.2    99%    89.8559   LOWEST    ID        HIGHEST    ID
MEAN        74.8838   SUM        28680.5    75% Q3      78.6    95%    84.78      57.9(ANCHORAG)     89.2(MESA....)
STD DEV     5.75067   VARIANCE   33.0703    50% MED       74    90%    82.46      61.6(BERKELEY)     89.6(LAS VEGA)
SKEWNESS   0.207451   KURTOSIS -.00127801   25% Q1      71.4    10%    68.5       61.9(SALINAS.)     91.2(GLENDALE)
USS         2160338   CSS        12632.8     0% MIN     57.9     5%    65.28      62.5(VALLEJO.)     91.2(PHOENIX.)
CV          7.67946   STD MEAN  0.293846                         1%    62.404     62.5(SUNNYVAL)     91.2(SCOTTSDA)
T:MEAN=0    254.841   PROB>|T|    0.0001   RANGE        33.3
SGN RANK      36768   PROB>|S|    0.0001   Q3-Q1         7.2
NUM ¬= 0        383                        MODE         73.3
```

```
            CENSUS DATA: OUTPUT FROM PROC UNIVARIATE TO DETERMINE CUTOFFS                   10
                                        UNIVARIATE
VARIABLE=SUNSHINE       POSSIBLE SUNSHINE ANNUAL % (DAYS)
            MOMENTS                              QUANTILES(DEF=4)                    EXTREMES
N              383    SUM WGTS       383   100% MAX       89    99%    86.1599   LOWEST    ID        HIGHEST    ID
MEAN        61.8433   SUM          23686    75% Q3        70    95%    75         46(ANCHORAG)       85(LAS VEGA)
STD DEV     8.31081   VARIANCE   69.0696    50% MED       60    90%    72         48(PORTLAND)       86(SCOTTSDA)
SKEWNESS   0.457179   KURTOSIS -0.228633    25% Q1        55    10%    50         49(WYOMING.)       87(GLENDALE)
USS         1491206   CSS        26384.6     0% MIN       46     5%    50         49(GRAND RA)       87(TEMPE...)
CV          13.4385   STD MEAN  0.424663                         1%    49         50(HUNTINGT)       89(TUCSON..)
T:MEAN=0    145.629   PROB>|T|    0.0001   RANGE          43
SGN RANK      36768   PROB>|S|    0.0001   Q3-Q1          15
NUM ¬= 0        383                        MODE           60
```

```
            CENSUS DATA: OUTPUT FROM PROC UNIVARIATE TO DETERMINE CUTOFFS                   11
                                        UNIVARIATE
VARIABLE=STATE
            MOMENTS                              QUANTILES(DEF=4)                    EXTREMES
N              383    SUM WGTS       383   100% MAX       55    99%    55        LOWEST    ID        HIGHEST    ID
MEAN        25.4987   SUM           9766    75% Q3        39    95%    51         1(MONTGOME)       55(MILWAUKE)
STD DEV     16.1149   VARIANCE    259.69    50% MED       25    90%    48         1(MOBILE..)       55(OSHKOSH.)
SKEWNESS   0.185519   KURTOSIS  -1.29292    25% Q1         9    10%    6          1(HUNTSVIL)       55(RACINE..)
USS          348222   CSS        99201.7     0% MIN        1     5%    6          1(GADSDEN.)       55(WAUWATOS)
CV           63.199   STD MEAN  0.823434                         1%    1          1(BIRMINGH)       55(WEST ALL)
T:MEAN=0    30.9663   PROB>|T|    0.0001   RANGE          54
SGN RANK      36768   PROB>|S|    0.0001   Q3-Q1          30
NUM ¬= 0        383                        MODE            6
```

```
            CENSUS DATA: OUTPUT FROM PROC UNIVARIATE TO DETERMINE CUTOFFS                   12
                                        UNIVARIATE
VARIABLE=PLACE
            MOMENTS                              QUANTILES(DEF=4)                    EXTREMES
N              383    SUM WGTS       383   100% MAX     8904    99%    7263.42   LOWEST    ID        HIGHEST    ID
MEAN        1747.75   SUM         669390    75% Q3      2505    95%    4401.99     5(DISTRICT)     7180(PHILADEL)
STD DEV     1421.96   VARIANCE   2021977    50% MED     1410    90%    3688       10(ALAMEDA.)     7234(PITTSBUR)
SKEWNESS    1.43522   KURTOSIS   3.18611    25% Q1       700    10%    204        15(ABILENE.)     7418(READING.)
USS      1942324620   CSS      772395189     0% MIN        5     5%    82         15(ALBUQUER)     7698(SCRANTON)
CV          81.3594   STD MEAN   72.6589                         1%    15         25(ALEXANDR)     8904(WILKES-B)
T:MEAN=0    24.0542   PROB>|T|    0.0001   RANGE        8899
SGN RANK      36768   PROB>|S|    0.0001   Q3-Q1        1805
NUM ¬= 0        383                        MODE          760
```

UNIVARIATE

VARIABLE=POPGRP

	MOMENTS				QUANTILES(DEF=4)			EXTREMES			
								LOWEST	ID	HIGHEST	ID
N	383	SUM WGTS	383	100% MAX	3	99%	3		1(WEST ALL)		3(SEATTLE.)
MEAN	2.06527	SUM	791	75% Q3	3	95%	3		1(WAUWATOS)		3(SPOKANE.)
STD DEV	0.882299	VARIANCE	0.778451	50% MED	2	90%	3		1(OSHKOSH.)		3(TACOMA..)
SKEWNESS	-0.127733	KURTOSIS	-1.7068	25% Q1	1	10%	1		1(APPLETON)		3(MADISON.)
USS	1931	CSS	297.368	0% MIN	1	5%	1		1(HUNTINGT)		3(MILWAUKE)
CV	42.7206	STD MEAN	0.0450833			1%	1				
T:MEAN=0	45.8101	PROB>|T|	0.0001	RANGE	2						
SGN RANK	36768	PROB>|S|	0.0001	Q3-Q1	2						
NUM ¬= 0	383			MODE	3						

Data set CITIES   Based on the UNIVARIATE results, the programming statements in this DATA step define the categories. LABEL statements provide labels for the new variables.

Also in this DATA step, two new geographic variables are created to represent the official U.S. REGION and DIVISION for each city. The original data contain a two-digit numeric code representing state along with the name of the city represented as a character variable. The FIPSTATE function used with the STATE variable (the numeric code) obtains the two-digit character abbreviation for each state. Then the INDEX function checks for values of ST (state abbreviation) and SAS assigns states to DIVISION. IF-THEN/ELSE statements code the nine geographical divisions into the four U.S. REGIONS of the country.

The previous analysis with UNIVARIATE revealed for Honolulu County a value of zero for the CITYGOVT variable, which is recoded to a missing value in the last statement of this DATA step.

```
DATA CITIES;
  LENGTH REGION $ 13 ST $ 3;
  SET CCDB77;

  IF OVER65 <=7.0 THEN OVR65GRP=1;
  ELSE IF 7.0 <OVER65<=12.0 THEN OVR65GRP=2;
  ELSE IF OVER65 >12.0 THEN OVR65GRP=3;

  IF INCOME <=4677 THEN INCOMGRP=1;
  ELSE IF INCOME >4677 THEN INCOMGRP=2;

  IF HOUSING <=15000 THEN HOUSGRP=1;
  ELSE IF 15000<HOUSING<=25000 THEN HOUSGRP=2;
  ELSE IF HOUSING >25000 THEN HOUSGRP=3;

  IF ELECTRIC <=15.00 THEN ELECGRP=1;
  ELSE IF 15<ELECTRIC<=20.00 THEN ELECGRP=2;
  ELSE IF ELECTRIC>20 THEN ELECGRP=3;

  IF ROBBERY<=100 THEN ROBGRP=1;
  ELSE IF 100<ROBBERY<=200 THEN ROBGRP=2;
  ELSE IF 200<ROBBERY<=300 THEN ROBGRP=3;
  ELSE IF ROBBERY>300 THEN ROBGRP=4;

  IF JANTEMP <=32.0 THEN JANGRP=1;
  ELSE IF JANTEMP>32 THEN JANGRP=2;
```

```
IF JULYTEMP< = 75.0 THEN JULYGRP=1;
ELSE IF JULYTEMP>75.0 THEN JULYGRP=2;

IF SUNSHINE< = 55 THEN SUNGRP=1;
ELSE IF 55<SUNSHINE< = 70 THEN SUNGRP=2;
ELSE IF SUNSHINE>70 THEN SUNGRP= 3;

LABEL POPGRP= 1975 POPULATION ESTIMATE;
LABEL OVR65GRP= % PERSONS 65 & OVER (1970);
LABEL INCOMGRP= PER CAPITA MONEY INCOME (1974);
LABEL HOUSGRP= MEDIAN SINGLE-FAMILY OWNER-OCCUP (1970);
LABEL ELECGRP= TYPICAL RESID. ELECTRIC BILL/MO. (1976);
LABEL ROBGRP= ROBBERY RATE/100,000 POP (1975);
LABEL JANGRP= MEAN JANUARY TEMPERATURE (DEGREES F);
LABEL JULYGRP= MEAN JULY TEMPERATURE (DEGREES F);
LABEL SUNGRP= POSSIBLE SUNSHINE ANNUAL % (DAYS);

ST = FIPSTATE(STATE);

IF INDEX('MS AL TN KY ',ST)¬=0
  THEN DIVISION='EAST SOUTH CENTRAL';
IF INDEX('FL GA SC NC VA WV MD DE DC ',ST)¬=0
  THEN DIVISION='SOUTH ATLANTIC';
IF INDEX('AR LA OK TX ',ST)¬=0
  THEN DIVISION='WEST SOUTH CENTRAL';
IF INDEX('PA NJ NY ',ST)¬=0
  THEN DIVISION='MIDDLE ATLANTIC';
IF INDEX('VT NH ME MA CT RI ',ST)¬=0
  THEN DIVISION='NEW ENGLAND';
IF INDEX('IL IN OH MI WI ',ST)¬=0
  THEN DIVISION='EAST NORTH CENTRAL';
IF INDEX('MN IA MO KS NE SD ND ',ST)¬=0
  THEN DIVISION='WEST NORTH CENTRAL';
IF INDEX('MT WY CO UT ID NV AZ NM ',ST)¬=0
  THEN DIVISION='MOUNTAIN';
IF INDEX('WA OR CA AK HI ',ST)¬=0
  THEN DIVISION='PACIFIC';

IF DIVISION='EAST SOUTH CENTRAL' OR
  DIVISION='SOUTH ATLANTIC' OR
  DIVISION='WEST SOUTH CENTRAL' THEN
  REGION='SOUTH';
ELSE IF DIVISION='MIDDLE ATLANTIC' OR
  DIVISION='NEW ENGLAND' THEN
  REGION='NORTHEAST';
ELSE IF DIVISION='EAST NORTH CENTRAL' OR
  DIVISION='WEST NORTH CENTRAL' THEN
  REGION='NORTH CENTRAL';
ELSE IF DIVISION='MOUNTAIN' OR
  DIVISION='PACIFIC' THEN
  REGION='WEST';

IF CITYGOVT=0 THEN CITYGOVT=.;
```

Grouping values with PROC FORMAT The new variables in data set CITIES are now categorical, but their numerical values are not very descriptive for the tables that are planned. To obtain more easily understood values, we use PROC FORMAT to define formats for these variables. FORMAT statements in later PROC steps will associate these formats with the appropriate variables.

```
PROC FORMAT;
  VALUE PC  1 = '50,001–75,000'
            2 = '75,001–100,000'
            3 = 'OVER 100,000';

  VALUE OC  1 = UNDER 7%
            2 = '7–12%'
            3 = OVER 12%;

  VALUE IC  1 = UNDER $4677
            2 = $4677 OR MORE;

  VALUE HC  1 = LOW
            2 = MEDIUM
            3 = HIGH;

  VALUE EC  1 = LOW
            2 = MEDIUM
            3 = HIGH;

  VALUE CC  1 = COUNCIL MANAGER
            2 = COMMISSION
            3 = MAYOR COUNCIL
            4–5 = TOWN MEETING;

  VALUE RC  1 = 100 OR LESS
            2 = '101–200'
            3 = '201–300'
            4 = OVER 300;

  VALUE JAN 1 = UNDER 32 DEGREES
            2 = 32 DEGREES OR HIGHER;

  VALUE JUL 1 = UNDER 75 DEGREES
            2 = 75 DEGREES OR HIGHER;

  VALUE SC  1 = UNDER 55%
            2 = '55–70%'
            3 = OVER 70%;
```

Printing the values The PRINT procedure prints the unformatted values of the variables in data set CITIES. (Although the formats could have been used with PRINT, using unformatted values here results in a more concise printout.)

```
PROC PRINT;
  VAR CITY ST REGION DIVISION POP1975 OVER65 INCOME HOUSING
    ELECTRIC CITYGOVT ROBBERY JANTEMP JULYTEMP SUNSHINE
    POPGRP OVR65GRP INCOMGRP HOUSGRP ELECGRP ROBGRP
    JANGRP JULYGRP SUNGRP;
  TITLE CENSUS DATA: OUTPUT FROM PRINT PROCEDURE;
```

CENSUS DATA: OUTPUT FROM PRINT PROCEDURE   14

OBS	CITY	ST	REGION	DIVISION	POP1975	OVER65	INCOME	HOUSING	ELECTRIC	CITYGOVT
1	BIRMINGHAM.....................	AL	SOUTH	EAST SOUTH CENTRAL	276273	11.8	4023	12677	16.94	3
2	GADSDEN........................	AL	SOUTH	EAST SOUTH CENTRAL	50357	10.3	3840	11781	16.94	2
3	HUNTSVILLE.....................	AL	SOUTH	EAST SOUTH CENTRAL	136419	4.3	4927	19164	12.89	3
4	MOBILE.........................	AL	SOUTH	EAST SOUTH CENTRAL	196441	8.7	4195	14257	16.94	2
5	MONTGOMERY.....................	AL	SOUTH	EAST SOUTH CENTRAL	153343	9.3	4253	17106	16.94	2
6	ANCHORAGE, CITY AND BOROUGH OF	AK	WEST	PACIFIC	161018	2.0	6886	33113	16.00	3
7	GLENDALE.......................	AZ	WEST	MOUNTAIN	65671	6.6	4465	16756	22.51	1
8	MESA...........................	AZ	WEST	MOUNTAIN	99043	10.3	4719	17577	22.51	1
9	PHOENIX........................	AZ	WEST	MOUNTAIN	664721	8.7	4942	16569	22.83	1
10	SCOTTSDALE.....................	AZ	WEST	MOUNTAIN	77529	6.4	5838	22820	22.51	1
11	TEMPE..........................	AZ	WEST	MOUNTAIN	84072	3.5	5136	21406	22.51	1
12	TUCSON.........................	AZ	WEST	MOUNTAIN	296457	10.4	4385	15981	21.16	1
13	FORT SMITH.....................	AR	SOUTH	WEST SOUTH CENTRAL	64734	11.1	4456	12229	11.78	1
14	LITTLE ROCK....................	AR	SOUTH	WEST SOUTH CENTRAL	141143	11.2	4687	16042	16.40	1
15	NORTH LITTLE ROCK..............	AR	SOUTH	WEST SOUTH CENTRAL	61768	9.9	4143	14491	12.75	3
16	PINE BLUFF.....................	AR	SOUTH	WEST SOUTH CENTRAL	54631	10.7	3624	11603	16.40	3
17	ALAMEDA........................	CA	WEST	PACIFIC	72017	8.8	5793	26571	17.19	1
18	ALHAMBRA.......................	CA	WEST	PACIFIC	60715	16.4	5612	23669	20.82	1
19	ANAHEIM........................	CA	WEST	PACIFIC	193616	6.1	5191	24839	20.00	1
20	BAKERSFIELD....................	CA	WEST	PACIFIC	77264	9.4	4584	16483	14.86	1
21	BELLFLOWER.....................	CA	WEST	PACIFIC	51145	8.4	5071	22275	20.82	1
22	BERKELEY.......................	CA	WEST	PACIFIC	110465	11.2	5539	26513	14.16	1
23	BUENA PARK.....................	CA	WEST	PACIFIC	61840	3.7	4849	22817	21.23	1
24	BURBANK........................	CA	WEST	PACIFIC	86001	10.4	5915	26501	19.00	1
25	CARSON.........................	CA	WEST	PACIFIC	78671	3.0	4104	25719	21.23	1
26	CHULA VISTA....................	CA	WEST	PACIFIC	75497	7.4	4704	22472	21.60	1

OBS	ROBBERY	JANTEMP	JULYTEMP	SUNSHINE	POPGRP	OVR65GRP	INCOMGRP	HOUSGRP	ELECGRP	ROBGRP	JANGRP	JULYGRP	SUNGRP
1	563	44.2	79.9	58	3	2	1	1	2	4	2	2	2
2	113	42.8	79.2	64	1	2	1	1	2	2	2	2	2
3	108	40.9	79.5	56	3	1	2	2	1	2	2	2	2
4	326	51.2	81.6	63	3	2	1	1	2	4	2	2	2
5	190	47.5	81.0	59	3	2	1	2	2	2	2	2	2
6	137	11.8	57.9	46	3	1	2	3	2	2	1	1	1
7	123	51.2	91.2	87	1	1	1	2	3	2	2	2	3
8	99	50.3	89.2	82	2	2	2	2	3	1	2	2	3
9	292	51.2	91.2	82	3	2	2	2	3	3	2	2	3
10	121	51.2	91.2	86	2	1	2	2	3	2	2	2	3
11	115	50.5	88.9	87	2	1	2	2	3	2	2	2	3
12	238	51.1	86.5	89	3	2	1	2	3	3	2	2	3
13	60	39.0	82.2	64	1	2	1	1	1	1	2	2	2
14	600	39.5	81.4	63	3	2	2	2	2	4	2	2	2
15	199	39.5	81.4	63	1	2	1	1	1	2	2	2	2
16	167	44.2	83.0	62	1	2	1	1	2	2	2	2	2
17	175	48.6	63.1	70	1	2	2	3	2	2	2	1	2
18	239	54.5	68.5	76	1	3	2	2	3	3	2	1	3
19	277	54.5	68.5	75	3	1	2	2	2	3	2	1	3
20	528	47.5	83.9	78	2	2	1	2	1	4	2	2	3
21	278	54.5	68.5	75	1	2	2	2	3	3	2	1	3
22	509	49.3	61.6	75	3	2	2	3	1	4	2	1	3
23	210	54.5	68.5	76	1	1	2	2	3	3	2	1	3
24	149	53.7	74.2	76	2	2	2	3	2	2	2	1	3
25	295	54.5	68.5	75	2	1	1	3	3	2	2	1	3
26	163	52.6	66.6	69	2	2	2	3	3	2	2	1	2

CENSUS DATA: OUTPUT FROM PRINT PROCEDURE   15

OBS	CITY	ST	REGION	DIVISION	POP1975	OVER65	INCOME	HOUSING	ELECTRIC	CITYGOVT	ROBBERY	JANTEMP	JULYTEMP	SUNSHINE	POPGRP	OVR65GRP	INCOMGRP	HOUSGRP	ELECGRP	ROBGRP	JANGRP	JULYGRP	SUNGRP
27	COMPTON......................	CA	WEST	PACIFIC	75143	4.1	2839	17682	20.82	1	985	54.5	68.5	76	2	1	1	2	3	4	2	1	3
28	CONCORD......................	CA	WEST	PACIFIC	95114	4.1	5248	26304	14.86	1	96	54.5	68.5	70	2	1	2	3	1	1	2	1	2
29	COSTA MESA...................	CA	WEST	PACIFIC	76058	7.2	5072	27299	21.23	1	122	54.2	72.2	74	2	2	2	3	3	2	2	1	3
30	DALY CITY....................	CA	WEST	PACIFIC	72741	5.3	5402	27056	14.16	1	227	54.2	74.5	70	1	1	2	3	1	3	2	1	2
31	DOWNEY.......................	CA	WEST	PACIFIC	85812	6.6	6270	25609	21.23	1	158	54.5	68.5	74	2	1	2	3	3	2	2	1	3
32	EL CAJON.....................	CA	WEST	PACIFIC	60404	8.9	4811	21084	21.60	1	151	55.2	69.6	74	1	2	2	2	3	2	2	1	3
33	EL MONTE.....................	CA	WEST	PACIFIC	67698	8.1	3649	19578	21.23	1	344	54.2	73.8	75	1	2	1	2	3	4	2	1	3
34	FAIRFIELD....................	CA	WEST	PACIFIC	50264	2.5	4188	19588	15.26	1	101	45.0	75.7	72	1	1	1	2	2	2	2	2	3
35	FOUNTAIN VALLEY..............	CA	WEST	PACIFIC	52377	2.4	5432	30553	21.64	1	86	54.2	71.7	72	1	1	2	3	3	1	2	1	3
36	FREMONT......................	CA	WEST	PACIFIC	117862	3.6	5157	24560	14.86	1	93	48.6	63.1	71	3	1	2	2	1	1	2	1	3
37	FRESNO.......................	CA	WEST	PACIFIC	176528	10.7	4233	15409	14.86	1	321	45.3	80.6	72	3	2	1	2	1	4	2	2	3
38	FULLERTON....................	CA	WEST	PACIFIC	93692	6.6	6032	26208	21.23	1	156	52.1	76.0	71	2	1	2	3	2	2	2	1	3
39	GARDEN GROVE.................	CA	WEST	PACIFIC	118454	4.8	4762	23891	21.23	1	263	54.2	72.2	71	3	1	2	3	3	2	2	1	3
40	GLENDALE.....................	CA	WEST	PACIFIC	132360	15.6	6316	30306	19.75	1	99	53.7	74.2	72	3	3	2	3	2	2	2	1	3
41	HAWTHORNE....................	CA	WEST	PACIFIC	53953	6.3	5296	24729	20.82	1	549	54.5	68.5	72	1	1	2	3	4	2	1	3	
42	HAYWARD......................	CA	WEST	PACIFIC	92802	5.2	4941	22619	14.86	1	184	48.6	63.1	70	2	1	2	2	1	1	2	1	2
43	HUNTINGTON BEACH.............	CA	WEST	PACIFIC	149706	3.9	5640	28679	21.64	1	76	54.2	72.2	71	3	1	2	3	1	2	1	3	
44	INGLEWOOD....................	CA	WEST	PACIFIC	86610	11.5	4947	24958	20.44	1	1291	54.5	68.5	71	2	2	2	3	4	2	1	3	
45	LAKEWOOD.....................	CA	WEST	PACIFIC	81802	4.2	5306	22379	20.82	1	156	54.5	68.5	71	2	1	2	2	3	2	2	1	3

(continued on next page)

274   Chapter 9

(continued from previous page)

```
46 LONG BEACH.................. CA WEST PACIFIC  335602 14.1 5652 23030 20.44 1   584 54.2 72.2 71 3 3 2 2 3 4 2 1 3
47 LOS ANGELES................ CA WEST PACIFIC 2727399 10.1 5277 26736 20.46 3   535 54.5 68.5 71 3 2 2 3 3 4 2 1 3
48 MODESTO.................... CA WEST PACIFIC   83540  9.9 4833 18148  9.91 1   148 45.1 76.3 72 2 2 2 2 1 2 2 2 3
49 MOUNTAIN VIEW.............. CA WEST PACIFIC   55143  6.1 6631 28589 14.86 1   214 49.5 68.4 71 1 1 2 3 1 3 2 1 3
50 NEWPORT BEACH.............. CA WEST PACIFIC   61853  9.9 8841 48774 20.82 1    61 54.0 66.8 70 1 2 2 3 3 1 2 1 2
51 NORWALK.................... CA WEST PACIFIC   86826  3.7 4000 19063 21.23 1   266 54.5 68.5 71 2 1 1 2 3 3 2 1 3
52 OAKLAND.................... CA WEST PACIFIC  330651 13.3 5034 21401 14.16 1   963 48.6 63.1 70 3 3 2 2 1 4 2 1 2
53 OCEANSIDE.................. CA WEST PACIFIC   56003 10.2 4563 20084 22.09 1   530 51.6 72.6 71 1 2 1 2 3 4 2 1 3
54 ONTARIO.................... CA WEST PACIFIC   63140  8.3 4023 17171 21.64 1   242 54.5 68.5 72 1 2 1 2 3 3 2 1 3
55 ORANGE..................... CA WEST PACIFIC   82157  6.4 5160 28353 21.64 1   150 54.5 68.5 71 2 1 2 3 3 2 2 1 3
56 OXNARD..................... CA WEST PACIFIC   86506  5.3 3982 19116 21.23 1   325 53.8 65.2 72 2 1 1 2 3 4 2 1 3
57 PALO ALTO.................. CA WEST PACIFIC   52277 10.3 7413 33822  8.66 1   186 47.3 66.0 70 1 2 2 3 1 2 2 1 2
58 PASADENA................... CA WEST PACIFIC  108220 17.1 6159 26441 23.00 1   566 54.2 73.8 71 3 3 2 3 3 4 2 1 3
59 PICO RIVERA................ CA WEST PACIFIC   51495  5.2 3821 19654 21.23 1   256 54.5 68.5 71 1 1 1 2 3 3 2 1 3
60 POMONA..................... CA WEST PACIFIC   82275  9.0 3975 17562 21.23 1   602 50.8 74.4 77 2 2 1 2 3 4 2 1 3
61 REDONDO BEACH.............. CA WEST PACIFIC   62400  6.1 5533 24073 20.82 1   264 54.2 72.2 71 1 2 2 3 3 2 2 1 3
62 REDWOOD CITY............... CA WEST PACIFIC   54160  8.8 6134 29312 14.86 1   140 48.4 68.2 70 1 2 2 3 1 2 2 1 2
63 RICHMOND................... CA WEST PACIFIC   69713  7.7 4652 19846 14.86 1   717 48.6 63.1 70 1 2 1 2 1 4 2 1 2
64 RIVERSIDE.................. CA WEST PACIFIC  150612  8.4 4714 19643 19.98 1   236 52.1 76.0 80 3 2 2 2 3 2 2 2 3
65 SACRAMENTO................. CA WEST PACIFIC  260822 11.1 4765 16840 10.27 1   432 45.1 75.2 72 3 2 2 2 1 4 2 2 3
66 SALINAS.................... CA WEST PACIFIC   70438  7.6 4659 19974 15.26 1   145 50.0 61.9 70 1 2 1 2 2 2 2 1 2
67 SAN BERNARDINO............. CA WEST PACIFIC  102076 11.0 4128 15776 21.23 3   572 52.0 78.2 80 3 2 1 2 3 4 2 2 3
68 SAN DIEGO.................. CA WEST PACIFIC  773996  8.8 5016 22548 22.01 1   284 55.2 69.6 69 3 2 2 2 3 3 2 1 2
69 SAN FRANCISCO.............. CA WEST PACIFIC  664520 14.0 5990 28165 14.16 1   857 48.3 62.5 70 3 3 2 3 1 4 2 1 2
70 SAN JOSE................... CA WEST PACIFIC  555707  5.6 4972 25437 14.86 1   160 49.5 68.4 71 3 1 2 3 1 2 2 1 3
71 SAN LEANDRO................ CA WEST PACIFIC   66953 10.1 6042 23943 14.16 1   208 48.6 63.1 70 1 2 2 2 1 3 2 1 2
72 SAN MATEO.................. CA WEST PACIFIC   77878 10.6 6910 31211 14.86 1   172 49.5 65.0 70 2 2 2 3 1 2 2 1 2
73 SANTA ANA.................. CA WEST PACIFIC  177304  7.5 4153 22255 21.23 1   310 54.2 71.7 71 3 2 1 2 3 4 2 1 3
74 SANTA BARBARA.............. CA WEST PACIFIC   72125 18.0 5140 25044 21.23 1   155 53.2 66.6 72 1 3 2 3 3 2 2 1 3
75 SANTA CLARA................ CA WEST PACIFIC   82822  5.5 5409 24124 13.72 1   157 48.6 68.1 70 2 1 2 2 1 2 2 1 2
```

CENSUS DATA: OUTPUT FROM PRINT PROCEDURE   16

OBS	CITY	ST	REGION	DIVISION	POP1975	OVER65	INCOME	HOUSING	ELECTRIC
76	SANTA MONICA.............	CA	WEST	PACIFIC	92115	16.5	6487	35824	20.44
77	SANTA ROSA...............	CA	WEST	PACIFIC	65087	14.9	5295	22504	15.26
78	SIMI VALLEY..............	CA	WEST	PACIFIC	70086	2.4	4184	24420	22.08
79	SOUTH GATE...............	CA	WEST	PACIFIC	56560	12.2	4452	19191	20.44
80	STOCKTON.................	CA	WEST	PACIFIC	117600	11.4	4626	16419	14.86
81	SUNNYVALE................	CA	WEST	PACIFIC	102462	4.5	6081	29366	14.86
82	TORRANCE.................	CA	WEST	PACIFIC	139776	5.1	6285	29567	20.82
83	VALLEJO..................	CA	WEST	PACIFIC	70681	9.3	4733	18281	15.26
84	VENTURA %SAN BUENAVENTURA<....	CA	WEST	PACIFIC	63441	9.9	5421	23182	21.23
85	WEST COVINA..............	CA	WEST	PACIFIC	75783	3.7	5313	23121	21.23
86	WESTMINSTER..............	CA	WEST	PACIFIC	66758	4.1	4844	24284	21.64
87	WHITTIER.................	CA	WEST	PACIFIC	72059	11.2	6089	24221	20.82
88	ARVADA...................	CO	WEST	MOUNTAIN	74254	3.0	5177	21247	17.75
89	AURORA...................	CO	WEST	MOUNTAIN	118060	3.8	5146	19722	17.75
90	BOULDER..................	CO	WEST	MOUNTAIN	78560	6.5	4919	23358	17.75
91	COLORADO SPRINGS.........	CO	WEST	MOUNTAIN	179584	7.6	4336	18553	14.99
92	DENVER...................	CO	WEST	MOUNTAIN	484531	11.5	5585	17081	17.75
93	FORT COLLINS.............	CO	WEST	MOUNTAIN	55984	8.3	4312	18995	10.10
94	LAKEWOOD.................	CO	WEST	MOUNTAIN	120350	4.9	5656	22994	17.75
95	PUEBLO...................	CO	WEST	MOUNTAIN	105312	10.0	4198	12763	14.31
96	BRIDGEPORT...............	CT	NORTHEAST	NEW ENGLAND	142960	12.0	4424	24249	21.17
97	BRISTOL..................	CT	NORTHEAST	NEW ENGLAND	58560	8.1	4731	21256	24.74
98	DANBURY..................	CT	NORTHEAST	NEW ENGLAND	54512	9.6	5131	26619	24.74
99	HARTFORD.................	CT	NORTHEAST	NEW ENGLAND	138152	11.1	3997	20761	21.02
100	MERIDEN..................	CT	NORTHEAST	NEW ENGLAND	57697	10.8	4617	21758	24.74
101	NEW HAVEN................	CT	NORTHEAST	NEW ENGLAND	126845	12.3	4247	22795	21.17

OBS	CITYGOVT	ROBBERY	JANTEMP	JULYTEMP	SUNSHINE	POPGRP	OVR65GRP	INCOMGRP	HOUSGRP	ELECGRP	ROBGRP	JANGRP	JULYGRP	SUNGRP
76	1	358	55.5	66.3	71	2	3	2	3	3	4	2	1	3
77	1	160	46.1	66.8	70	1	3	2	2	2	2	2	1	2
78	1	41	53.8	65.2	72	1	1	1	2	3	1	2	1	3
79	1	352	54.5	68.5	72	1	3	1	2	3	4	2	1	3
80	1	453	44.6	76.7	72	3	2	1	2	1	4	2	2	3
81	1	100	48.3	62.5	72	3	1	2	3	1	1	2	1	3
82	1	170	54.2	68.4	65	3	1	2	3	3	2	2	1	2
83	1	265	48.3	62.5	70	2	2	2	2	2	3	2	1	2
84	1	120	53.8	65.2	71	1	2	2	2	3	2	2	1	3
85	1	158	54.5	68.5	70	2	1	2	2	3	2	2	1	2
86	1	213	54.5	68.5	72	1	1	2	2	3	2	2	1	3
87	1	143	54.5	68.5	71	1	2	2	2	3	2	2	1	2
88	1	54	32.9	74.2	65	1	1	2	2	2	1	2	1	2
89	1	145	32.9	74.2	65	3	1	2	2	2	2	2	1	2
90	1	70	33.0	73.9	62	2	1	2	2	2	1	2	1	2
91	1	246	28.6	70.7	71	3	2	1	2	1	3	1	1	3
92	3	530	32.9	74.2	65	3	2	2	2	2	4	2	1	2
93	1	29	26.8	70.8	63	1	2	1	2	1	1	1	1	2
94	3	133	32.9	74.2	65	3	1	2	2	2	2	2	1	2
95	1	111	30.1	76.4	72	3	2	1	1	1	2	1	2	3
96	3	297	30.2	73.8	60	3	2	1	2	3	3	1	1	2
97	3	24	24.8	72.7	56	1	2	2	2	3	1	1	1	2
98	3	72	24.8	71.1	58	1	2	2	3	3	1	1	1	2
99	1	1134	24.8	72.7	56	3	2	1	2	3	4	1	1	2
100	3	127	24.8	72.7	58	1	2	1	2	3	2	1	1	2
101	3	423	28.9	72.3	60	3	3	1	2	3	4	1	1	2

CENSUS DATA: OUTPUT FROM PRINT PROCEDURE   17

OBS	CITY	ST	REGION	DIVISION	POP1975	OVER65	INCOME	HOUSING	ELECTRIC
102	NORWALK	CT	NORTHEAST	NEW ENGLAND	76688	8.7	5736	33754	24.74
103	STAMFORD	CT	NORTHEAST	NEW ENGLAND	105151	9.4	6629	41822	21.02
104	WATERBURY	CT	NORTHEAST	NEW ENGLAND	107065	12.6	4484	18703	24.74
105	WILMINGTON	DE	SOUTH	SOUTH ATLANTIC	76152	14.0	4235	11244	22.95
106	DISTRICT OF COLUMBIA	DC	SOUTH	SOUTH ATLANTIC	711518	9.4	5659	21400	17.40
107	CLEARWATER	FL	SOUTH	SOUTH ATLANTIC	67069	28.6	5552	17672	21.82
108	FORT LAUDERDALE	FL	SOUTH	SOUTH ATLANTIC	152959	18.6	6843	20335	18.99
109	GAINESVILLE	FL	SOUTH	SOUTH ATLANTIC	72236	5.5	4274	16110	21.59
110	HIALEAH	FL	SOUTH	SOUTH ATLANTIC	117682	7.7	4553	16951	18.99
111	HOLLYWOOD	FL	SOUTH	SOUTH ATLANTIC	119002	19.6	6054	19831	18.99
112	JACKSONVILLE	FL	SOUTH	SOUTH ATLANTIC	562283	7.5	4615	12154	21.25
113	MIAMI BEACH	FL	SOUTH	SOUTH ATLANTIC	94063	48.8	7130	39155	18.99
114	MIAMI	FL	SOUTH	SOUTH ATLANTIC	365082	14.5	4416	16720	18.99
115	ORLANDO	FL	SOUTH	SOUTH ATLANTIC	113179	13.0	4609	15305	20.69
116	PENSACOLA	FL	SOUTH	SOUTH ATLANTIC	64168	9.6	4341	14450	19.47
117	ST PETERSBURG	FL	SOUTH	SOUTH ATLANTIC	234389	30.7	4940	13613	21.82
118	TALLAHASSEE	FL	SOUTH	SOUTH ATLANTIC	83725	5.4	4649	16810	22.23
119	TAMPA	FL	SOUTH	SOUTH ATLANTIC	280340	12.4	4362	11099	22.00
120	WEST PALM BEACH	FL	SOUTH	SOUTH ATLANTIC	61471	18.7	5787	15424	18.99
121	ALBANY	GA	SOUTH	SOUTH ATLANTIC	73373	6.4	3859	15723	19.66
122	ATLANTA	GA	SOUTH	SOUTH ATLANTIC	436057	9.2	4527	17315	16.96
123	AUGUSTA	GA	SOUTH	SOUTH ATLANTIC	54019	12.1	3862	11947	16.96
124	COLUMBUS	GA	SOUTH	SOUTH ATLANTIC	160103	6.0	4212	16187	16.96
125	MACON	GA	SOUTH	SOUTH ATLANTIC	121157	9.2	4125	13963	16.96
126	SAVANNAH	GA	SOUTH	SOUTH ATLANTIC	110348	10.1	3872	11982	18.90
127	HONOLULU COUNTY	HI	WEST	PACIFIC	705381	6.9	5065	43441	23.60

OBS	CITYGOVT	ROBBERY	JANTEMP	JULYTEMP	SUNSHINE	POPGRP	OVR65GRP	INCOMGRP	HOUSGRP	ELECGRP	ROBGRP	JANGRP	JULYGRP	SUNGRP
102	3	103	28.3	72.4	60	2	2	2	3	3	2	1	1	2
103	3	204	30.2	73.8	59	3	2	2	3	3	3	1	1	2
104	3	135	24.8	72.7	56	3	3	1	2	3	2	1	1	2
105	3	563	32.0	75.8	58	2	3	1	1	3	4	1	2	2
106	3	1284	35.6	78.7	57	3	2	2	2	2	4	2	2	2
107	1	182	61.0	82.1	67	1	3	2	2	3	2	2	2	2
108	1	401	66.8	82.2	67	3	3	2	2	2	4	2	2	2
109	1	293	57.0	81.1	64	1	1	1	2	3	3	2	2	2
110	3	187	65.8	81.3	68	3	2	1	2	2	2	2	2	2
111	1	319	68.5	82.5	68	3	3	2	2	2	4	2	2	2
112	3	319	54.6	81.0	63	3	2	1	1	3	4	2	2	2
113	1	196	68.5	82.5	68	2	3	2	3	2	2	2	2	2
114	1	728	67.2	82.3	68	3	3	1	2	2	4	2	2	2
115	3	269	60.4	82.4	64	3	3	1	2	3	3	2	2	2
116	1	268	52.1	81.8	64	1	2	1	1	2	3	2	2	2
117	1	343	62.2	82.6	67	3	3	2	1	3	4	2	2	2
118	1	221	52.6	81.1	66	2	1	1	2	3	3	2	2	2
119	3	497	60.4	81.9	67	3	3	1	1	3	4	2	2	2
120	1	530	65.5	81.9	65	1	3	2	2	2	4	2	2	2
121	1	240	50.7	81.8	65	1	1	1	2	2	3	2	2	2
122	3	891	42.4	78.0	59	3	2	1	2	2	4	2	2	2
123	3	324	45.8	80.4	65	1	3	1	1	2	4	2	2	2
124	1	272	46.9	80.6	64	3	1	1	2	2	3	2	2	2
125	3	162	47.8	81.4	65	3	2	1	1	2	2	2	2	2
126	1	428	49.9	81.1	64	3	2	1	2	2	4	2	2	2
127	.	149	72.3	80.1	65	3	1	2	3	3	2	2	2	2

CENSUS DATA: OUTPUT FROM PRINT PROCEDURE   18

OBS	CITY	ST	REGION	DIVISION	POP1975	OVER65	INCOME	HOUSING	ELECTRIC
128	BOISE CITY	ID	WEST	MOUNTAIN	99771	10.0	4767	15822	11.66
129	ARLINGTON HEIGHTS	IL	NORTH CENTRAL	EAST NORTH CENTRAL	70019	4.5	6874	36256	16.73
130	AURORA	IL	NORTH CENTRAL	EAST NORTH CENTRAL	76955	9.7	5061	18699	15.82
131	CHAMPAIGN	IL	NORTH CENTRAL	EAST NORTH CENTRAL	58398	6.9	4758	19483	17.28
132	CHICAGO	IL	NORTH CENTRAL	EAST NORTH CENTRAL	3099391	10.6	4689	21290	16.44
133	CICERO	IL	NORTH CENTRAL	EAST NORTH CENTRAL	63444	12.2	5273	21029	15.82
134	DECATUR	IL	NORTH CENTRAL	EAST NORTH CENTRAL	89604	11.9	5133	14370	16.76
135	DES PLAINES	IL	NORTH CENTRAL	EAST NORTH CENTRAL	55828	6.2	6115	30063	15.82
136	EAST ST LOUIS	IL	NORTH CENTRAL	EAST NORTH CENTRAL	57929	10.5	2593	8812	17.50
137	ELGIN	IL	NORTH CENTRAL	EAST NORTH CENTRAL	59754	13.4	5099	21270	15.82
138	EVANSTON	IL	NORTH CENTRAL	EAST NORTH CENTRAL	76665	14.1	6771	33481	16.73
139	JOLIET	IL	NORTH CENTRAL	EAST NORTH CENTRAL	74401	11.2	5004	17666	15.82
140	OAK LAWN	IL	NORTH CENTRAL	EAST NORTH CENTRAL	62317	7.5	6089	26570	15.82
141	OAK PARK	IL	NORTH CENTRAL	EAST NORTH CENTRAL	59773	16.3	6590	26472	16.73
142	PEORIA	IL	NORTH CENTRAL	EAST NORTH CENTRAL	125983	11.0	5370	16404	17.30
143	ROCKFORD	IL	NORTH CENTRAL	EAST NORTH CENTRAL	145459	10.6	5029	19312	15.62
144	SKOKIE	IL	NORTH CENTRAL	EAST NORTH CENTRAL	67674	7.6	7823	36416	15.82
145	SPRINGFIELD	IL	NORTH CENTRAL	EAST NORTH CENTRAL	87418	13.4	5143	15891	14.26
146	WAUKEGAN	IL	NORTH CENTRAL	EAST NORTH CENTRAL	65133	8.1	5284	19941	15.82
147	ANDERSON	IN	NORTH CENTRAL	EAST NORTH CENTRAL	69486	9.6	4590	13266	14.89
148	EVANSVILLE	IN	NORTH CENTRAL	EAST NORTH CENTRAL	133566	12.4	4244	11973	16.42
149	FORT WAYNE	IN	NORTH CENTRAL	EAST NORTH CENTRAL	185299	10.3	4661	13626	13.33
150	GARY	IN	NORTH CENTRAL	EAST NORTH CENTRAL	167546	7.6	4038	15051	19.55
151	HAMMOND	IN	NORTH CENTRAL	EAST NORTH CENTRAL	104892	7.8	4872	16513	19.55
152	INDIANAPOLIS	IN	NORTH CENTRAL	EAST NORTH CENTRAL	782139	8.7	4922	14911	13.68
153	KOKOMO	IN	NORTH CENTRAL	EAST NORTH CENTRAL	52022	10.1	4527	12918	20.50

(continued on next page)

(continued from previous page)

OBS	CITYGOVT	ROBBERY	JANTEMP	JULYTEMP	SUNSHINE	POPGRP	OVR65GRP	INCOMGRP	HOUSGRP	ELECGRP	ROBGRP	JANGRP	JULYGRP	SUNGRP
128	3	74	29.0	74.5	62	2	2	2	2	1	1	1	1	2
129	1	37	22.9	71.9	55	1	1	2	3	2	1	1	1	1
130	2	330	22.2	72.9	55	2	2	2	2	2	4	1	1	1
131	1	163	26.9	75.3	60	1	1	2	2	2	2	1	2	2
132	3	715	22.9	71.9	55	3	2	2	2	2	4	1	1	1
133	3	183	31.3	78.6	55	1	3	2	2	2	2	1	2	1
134	1	99	28.3	76.5	61	2	2	2	1	2	1	1	2	2
135	3	56	22.9	71.9	55	1	1	2	3	2	1	1	1	1
136	3	1799	31.3	78.6	63	1	2	1	1	2	4	1	2	2
137	1	124	22.2	72.9	55	1	3	2	2	2	2	1	1	1
138	1	286	22.9	71.9	55	2	3	2	3	2	3	1	1	1
139	1	379	23.9	74.2	56	1	2	2	2	2	4	1	1	2
140	1	43	22.9	71.9	55	1	2	2	3	2	1	1	1	1
141	1	398	22.9	71.9	55	1	3	2	3	2	4	1	1	1
142	1	357	23.8	75.1	60	3	2	2	2	2	4	1	2	2
143	3	282	20.2	72.8	56	2	2	2	2	2	3	1	1	2
144	1	52	22.9	71.9	55	1	2	2	3	2	1	1	1	1
145	2	292	26.7	76.1	61	2	3	2	2	1	3	1	2	2
146	3	513	22.5	71.9	55	1	2	2	2	2	4	1	1	1
147	3	99	28.2	74.3	59	1	2	1	1	1	1	1	1	2
148	3	193	32.6	77.8	63	3	3	1	1	2	2	2	2	2
149	3	220	25.3	73.0	55	3	2	1	1	1	3	1	1	1
150	3	597	24.7	74.0	54	3	2	1	2	2	4	1	1	1
151	3	347	24.7	74.0	54	3	2	2	2	2	4	1	1	1
152	3	457	27.9	75.0	59	3	2	2	1	1	4	1	1	2
153	3	121	27.6	75.5	58	1	2	1	1	3	2	1	2	2

CENSUS DATA: OUTPUT FROM PRINT PROCEDURE   19

OBS	CITY	ST	REGION	DIVISION	POP1975	OVER65	INCOME	HOUSING	ELECTRIC
154	MUNCIE....................	IN	NORTH CENTRAL	EAST NORTH CENTRAL	78329	9.5	4136	11555	15.33
155	SOUTH BEND................	IN	NORTH CENTRAL	EAST NORTH CENTRAL	117478	11.5	4685	12062	15.33
156	TERRE HAUTE...............	IN	NORTH CENTRAL	EAST NORTH CENTRAL	63998	14.0	3933	9191	20.50
157	CEDAR RAPIDS..............	IA	NORTH CENTRAL	WEST NORTH CENTRAL	108998	9.5	4901	18097	19.72
158	COUNCIL BLUFFS............	IA	NORTH CENTRAL	WEST NORTH CENTRAL	58660	10.7	4139	12771	17.72
159	DAVENPORT.................	IA	NORTH CENTRAL	WEST NORTH CENTRAL	99941	10.6	4831	18059	16.53
160	DES MOINES................	IA	NORTH CENTRAL	WEST NORTH CENTRAL	194168	11.4	4975	14800	17.72
161	DUBUQUE...................	IA	NORTH CENTRAL	WEST NORTH CENTRAL	61754	11.2	4479	18039	16.64
162	SIOUX CITY................	IA	NORTH CENTRAL	WEST NORTH CENTRAL	85719	12.5	4495	13694	19.56
163	WATERLOO..................	IA	NORTH CENTRAL	WEST NORTH CENTRAL	77681	10.6	4920	15657	19.18
164	KANSAS CITY...............	KS	NORTH CENTRAL	WEST NORTH CENTRAL	168153	10.4	4220	12044	15.46
165	OVERLAND PARK.............	KS	NORTH CENTRAL	WEST NORTH CENTRAL	81013	3.7	6759	24495	15.05
166	TOPEKA....................	KS	NORTH CENTRAL	WEST NORTH CENTRAL	119203	11.4	4881	14432	14.45
167	WICHITA...................	KS	NORTH CENTRAL	WEST NORTH CENTRAL	264901	8.8	4951	13701	11.85
168	LEXINGTON-FAYETTE.........	KY	SOUTH	EAST SOUTH CENTRAL	186048	7.8	4621	19075	13.95
169	LOUISVILLE................	KY	SOUTH	EAST SOUTH CENTRAL	335954	12.4	4302	13005	13.81
170	OWENSBORO.................	KY	SOUTH	EAST SOUTH CENTRAL	50788	10.0	4123	14253	16.35
171	BATON ROUGE METRO.........	LA	SOUTH	WEST SOUTH CENTRAL	294394	7.6	4187	17795	13.03
172	LAFAYETTE.................	LA	SOUTH	WEST SOUTH CENTRAL	75430	6.0	3760	17037	17.17
173	LAKE CHARLES..............	LA	SOUTH	WEST SOUTH CENTRAL	76087	6.9	3730	13974	13.03
174	MONROE....................	LA	SOUTH	WEST SOUTH CENTRAL	61016	9.9	3244	13880	16.91
175	NEW ORLEANS...............	LA	SOUTH	WEST SOUTH CENTRAL	559770	10.7	4029	21157	10.63
176	SHREVEPORT................	LA	SOUTH	WEST SOUTH CENTRAL	185711	10.3	4086	14140	12.24
177	PORTLAND..................	ME	NORTHEAST	NEW ENGLAND	59857	14.8	3992	16808	17.42
178	BALTIMORE.................	MD	SOUTH	SOUTH ATLANTIC	851698	10.6	4330	9976	23.11
179	BOSTON....................	MA	NORTHEAST	NEW ENGLAND	636725	12.8	4157	19770	23.84

OBS	CITYGOVT	ROBBERY	JANTEMP	JULYTEMP	SUNSHINE	POPGRP	OVR65GRP	INCOMGRP	HOUSGRP	ELECGRP	ROBGRP	JANGRP	JULYGRP	SUNGRP
154	3	230	28.2	74.3	57	2	2	1	1	2	3	1	1	2
155	3	312	24.0	72.3	53	3	2	2	1	2	4	1	1	1
156	3	116	28.7	75.9	61	1	3	1	1	3	2	1	2	2
157	2	100	20.4	73.9	60	3	2	2	2	2	1	1	1	2
158	1	126	22.6	77.2	63	1	2	1	1	2	2	1	2	2
159	3	266	22.9	75.4	60	2	2	2	2	2	3	1	2	2
160	1	287	19.4	75.1	62	3	2	1	2	2	3	1	2	2
161	1	60	17.7	71.7	58	1	2	1	2	2	1	1	2	2
162	1	59	18.0	75.3	62	2	3	1	1	2	1	1	2	2
163	3	161	16.3	72.6	59	2	2	2	2	2	2	1	1	2
164	2	425	28.8	78.8	63	3	2	1	1	2	4	1	2	2
165	1	79	28.8	78.8	63	2	1	2	2	2	1	1	2	2
166	2	154	28.0	78.2	65	3	2	2	1	2	2	1	2	2
167	1	242	31.3	80.7	68	3	2	2	1	1	3	1	2	2
168	3	248	32.9	76.2	55	3	2	1	1	1	3	2	2	1
169	3	466	33.3	76.9	60	3	3	1	1	1	4	2	2	2
170	1	61	34.9	78.2	62	1	2	1	1	2	1	2	2	2
171	3	116	51.0	82.0	61	3	2	1	2	1	2	2	2	2
172	3	134	51.9	81.9	60	2	1	1	2	2	1	2	2	2
173	3	121	52.3	82.4	60	2	1	1	1	2	1	2	2	2
174	2	100	46.7	82.3	63	1	2	1	1	2	1	2	2	2
175	3	642	52.9	81.9	59	3	2	1	2	1	4	2	2	2
176	2	130	47.2	83.2	66	3	2	1	1	2	1	2	2	2
177	1	229	21.5	68.0	60	1	3	1	2	2	3	1	1	2
178	3	1063	33.4	76.6	55	3	2	1	1	3	4	2	2	1
179	3	1222	29.2	73.3	55	3	3	1	2	3	4	1	1	1

CENSUS DATA: OUTPUT FROM PRINT PROCEDURE   20

OBS	CITY	ST	REGION	DIVISION	POP1975	OVER65	INCOME	HOUSING	ELECTRIC
180	BROCKTON...............	MA	NORTHEAST	NEW ENGLAND	95878	11.0	4189	18259	23.80
181	CAMBRIDGE.................	MA	NORTHEAST	NEW ENGLAND	102420	11.8	5278	24738	22.49
182	CHICOPEE................	MA	NORTHEAST	NEW ENGLAND	57771	8.6	4252	17264	17.73
183	FALL RIVER...............	MA	NORTHEAST	NEW ENGLAND	100430	13.8	3685	16056	24.12
184	LAWRENCE.............	MA	NORTHEAST	NEW ENGLAND	67390	14.9	4035	18111	20.84
185	LOWELL...............	MA	NORTHEAST	NEW ENGLAND	91493	12.1	3959	16199	20.84
186	MALDEN..............	MA	NORTHEAST	NEW ENGLAND	55778	13.7	4586	19863	20.84
187	MEDFORD.............	MA	NORTHEAST	NEW ENGLAND	60769	13.1	4680	22660	20.84
188	NEW BEDFORD...........	MA	NORTHEAST	NEW ENGLAND	100133	14.7	3784	16944	24.90
189	NEWTON...............	MA	NORTHEAST	NEW ENGLAND	88559	12.2	7129	33923	23.84
190	PITTSFIELD............	MA	NORTHEAST	NEW ENGLAND	54893	12.0	4759	18174	26.74
191	QUINCY...............	MA	NORTHEAST	NEW ENGLAND	91494	13.6	5057	20260	20.84
192	SOMERVILLE...........	MA	NORTHEAST	NEW ENGLAND	80798	12.2	4278	16815	23.84
193	SPRINGFIELD..........	MA	NORTHEAST	NEW ENGLAND	170790	12.8	4145	15613	26.74
194	WALTHAM..............	MA	NORTHEAST	NEW ENGLAND	56251	10.3	4748	23869	23.84
195	WORCESTER............	MA	NORTHEAST	NEW ENGLAND	171566	14.7	4435	17919	20.84
196	ANN ARBOR............	MI	NORTH CENTRAL	EAST NORTH CENTRAL	103542	5.4	5562	27766	14.23
197	DEARBORN.............	MI	NORTH CENTRAL	EAST NORTH CENTRAL	98986	11.4	6388	22863	14.23
198	DEARBORN HGTS.........	MI	NORTH CENTRAL	EAST NORTH CENTRAL	79239	4.9	5521	22184	14.23
199	DETROIT..............	MI	NORTH CENTRAL	EAST NORTH CENTRAL	1335085	11.5	4463	15603	14.23
200	EAST LANSING..........	MI	NORTH CENTRAL	EAST NORTH CENTRAL	50425	3.3	4594	29339	15.18
201	FLINT................	MI	NORTH CENTRAL	EAST NORTH CENTRAL	174218	8.8	4449	14662	18.55
202	GRAND RAPIDS..........	MI	NORTH CENTRAL	EAST NORTH CENTRAL	187940	12.2	4463	14775	18.55
203	KALAMAZOO............	MI	NORTH CENTRAL	EAST NORTH CENTRAL	79542	9.9	4542	14456	18.55
204	LANSING..............	MI	NORTH CENTRAL	EAST NORTH CENTRAL	126805	8.4	4614	16356	15.18
205	LIVONIA..............	MI	NORTH CENTRAL	EAST NORTH CENTRAL	114881	4.4	5715	27218	14.23

OBS	CITYGOVT	ROBBERY	JANTEMP	JULYTEMP	SUNSHINE	POPGRP	OVR65GRP	INCOMGRP	HOUSGRP	ELECGRP	ROBGRP	JANGRP	JULYGRP	SUNGRP
180	3	189	29.2	73.3	55	2	2	1	2	3	2	1	1	1
181	1	446	29.2	73.3	55	3	2	2	2	3	4	1	1	1
182	3	61	27.1	73.6	50	1	2	1	2	2	1	1	1	1
183	3	165	28.9	72.8	58	3	3	1	2	3	2	1	1	2
184	3	183	25.8	72.6	56	1	3	1	2	3	2	1	1	2
185	1	108	26.4	73.7	56	2	3	1	2	3	2	1	1	2
186	3	102	29.2	73.3	56	1	3	1	2	3	2	1	1	2
187	1	130	29.2	73.3	55	1	3	2	2	3	2	1	1	1
188	3	164	31.4	72.7	58	3	3	1	2	3	2	1	1	2
189	3	53	29.2	73.3	55	2	3	2	3	3	1	1	1	1
190	3	118	22.1	67.6	50	1	2	2	2	3	2	1	1	1
191	3	144	29.2	73.3	55	2	3	2	2	3	2	1	1	1
192	3	222	29.2	73.3	55	2	3	1	2	3	3	1	1	1
193	3	327	27.1	73.6	50	3	3	1	2	3	4	1	1	1
194	3	76	29.2	73.3	55	1	2	2	2	3	1	1	1	1
195	1	413	23.6	70.1	57	3	3	1	2	3	4	1	1	2
196	1	244	25.5	73.3	52	3	1	2	3	1	3	1	1	1
197	3	283	25.5	73.3	53	2	2	2	2	1	3	1	1	1
198	3	202	25.5	73.3	53	2	1	2	2	1	3	1	1	1
199	3	1597	25.5	73.3	53	3	2	1	2	1	4	1	1	1
200	1	46	22.6	70.9	51	1	1	1	3	2	1	1	1	1
201	3	525	22.3	69.7	52	3	2	1	1	2	4	1	1	1
202	1	233	23.2	71.5	49	3	3	1	1	2	3	1	1	1
203	1	395	24.8	72.9	50	2	2	1	1	2	4	1	1	1
204	3	235	22.6	70.9	51	3	2	1	2	2	3	1	1	1
205	3	105	25.5	73.3	53	3	1	2	3	1	2	1	1	1

CENSUS DATA: OUTPUT FROM PRINT PROCEDURE   21

OBS	CITY	ST	REGION	DIVISION	POP1975	OVER65	INCOME	HOUSING	ELECTRIC
206	PONTIAC...............	MI	NORTH CENTRAL	EAST NORTH CENTRAL	76027	8.6	3885	15345	14.23
207	ROSEVILLE.............	MI	NORTH CENTRAL	EAST NORTH CENTRAL	58141	4.2	4678	18862	14.23
208	ROYAL OAK.............	MI	NORTH CENTRAL	EAST NORTH CENTRAL	79191	8.4	6072	21378	14.23
209	SAGINAW...............	MI	NORTH CENTRAL	EAST NORTH CENTRAL	86202	9.8	4216	13833	18.55
210	ST CLAIR SHORES........	MI	NORTH CENTRAL	EAST NORTH CENTRAL	85934	5.9	5427	22572	14.23
211	SOUTHFIELD............	MI	NORTH CENTRAL	EAST NORTH CENTRAL	75978	6.8	8479	36235	14.23
212	STERLING HEIGHTS........	MI	NORTH CENTRAL	EAST NORTH CENTRAL	86932	2.4	5205	28039	14.23
213	TAYLOR................	MI	NORTH CENTRAL	EAST NORTH CENTRAL	76626	3.0	4570	18694	14.23
214	TROY..................	MI	NORTH CENTRAL	EAST NORTH CENTRAL	55169	4.7	6835	29741	14.23
215	WARREN................	MI	NORTH CENTRAL	EAST NORTH CENTRAL	172755	3.8	5140	23469	14.23
216	WESTLAND..............	MI	NORTH CENTRAL	EAST NORTH CENTRAL	92689	4.0	4787	21475	14.23
217	WYOMING...............	MI	NORTH CENTRAL	EAST NORTH CENTRAL	57918	6.4	4482	14382	18.55
218	BLOOMINGTON...........	MN	NORTH CENTRAL	WEST NORTH CENTRAL	79210	2.9	5773	26148	19.30
219	DULUTH................	MN	NORTH CENTRAL	WEST NORTH CENTRAL	93971	13.4	4469	14381	20.54
220	MINNEAPOLIS...........	MN	NORTH CENTRAL	WEST NORTH CENTRAL	378112	15.0	5161	18024	19.88
221	ROCHESTER.............	MN	NORTH CENTRAL	WEST NORTH CENTRAL	56211	9.8	5170	21069	17.50
222	ST PAUL...............	MN	NORTH CENTRAL	WEST NORTH CENTRAL	279535	13.3	4931	18639	20.98
223	JACKSON...............	MS	SOUTH	EAST SOUTH CENTRAL	166512	8.0	4514	13858	19.35
224	COLUMBIA..............	MO	NORTH CENTRAL	WEST NORTH CENTRAL	63227	6.0	4333	21845	18.44
225	FLORISSANT............	MO	NORTH CENTRAL	WEST NORTH CENTRAL	70465	3.1	4391	18154	16.73
226	INDEPENDENCE..........	MO	NORTH CENTRAL	WEST NORTH CENTRAL	111481	8.0	4970	16524	15.12
227	KANSAS CITY...........	MO	NORTH CENTRAL	WEST NORTH CENTRAL	472529	11.9	4736	14114	16.54
228	ST JOSEPH.............	MO	NORTH CENTRAL	WEST NORTH CENTRAL	77679	15.9	4021	11107	16.75
229	ST LOUIS..............	MO	NORTH CENTRAL	WEST NORTH CENTRAL	524964	14.7	4006	13310	17.48
230	SPRINGFIELD...........	MO	NORTH CENTRAL	WEST NORTH CENTRAL	131557	11.8	4169	13911	21.20
231	BILLINGS..............	MT	WEST	MOUNTAIN	68987	8.3	4910	17784	12.71

(continued on next page)

(continued from previous page)

OBS	CITYGOVT	ROBBERY	JANTEMP	JULYTEMP	SUNSHINE	POPGRP	OVR65GRP	INCOMGRP	HOUSGRP	ELECGRP	ROBGRP	JANGRP	JULYGRP	SUNGRP
206	1	712	23.5	71.9	53	2	2	1	2	1	4	1	1	1
207	1	144	25.5	73.3	53	1	1	2	2	1	2	1	1	1
208	1	148	25.5	73.3	53	2	2	2	2	1	2	1	1	1
209	1	836	21.4	70.6	51	2	2	1	1	2	4	1	1	1
210	1	93	25.5	73.3	53	2	1	2	2	1	1	1	1	1
211	1	217	25.5	73.3	53	2	1	2	3	1	3	1	1	1
212	1	56	25.5	73.3	53	2	1	2	3	1	1	1	1	1
213	3	210	25.5	73.3	53	2	1	1	2	1	3	1	1	1
214	1	114	25.5	73.3	53	1	1	2	3	1	2	1	1	1
215	3	171	25.5	73.3	53	3	1	2	2	1	2	1	1	1
216	3	112	25.5	73.3	53	2	1	2	2	1	2	1	1	1
217	1	60	23.2	71.5	49	1	1	1	1	2	1	1	1	1
218	1	48	11.8	71.2	57	2	1	2	3	2	1	1	1	2
219	3	67	8.5	65.6	52	2	3	1	1	3	1	1	1	1
220	3	486	11.8	71.2	57	3	3	2	2	2	4	1	1	2
221	3	85	12.9	70.1	57	1	2	2	2	2	1	1	1	2
222	3	429	11.8	71.2	57	3	3	2	2	3	4	1	1	2
223	2	172	47.1	81.7	63	3	2	1	1	2	2	2	2	2
224	1	85	29.3	77.3	64	1	1	1	2	2	1	1	2	2
225	3	50	31.3	78.6	63	1	1	1	2	2	1	1	2	2
226	1	65	27.8	78.8	63	3	2	2	2	2	1	1	2	2
227	1	652	27.8	78.8	63	3	2	2	1	2	4	1	2	2
228	3	138	26.2	78.2	64	2	3	1	1	2	2	1	2	2
229	3	1198	31.3	78.6	64	3	3	1	1	2	4	1	2	2
230	1	93	32.9	77.8	65	3	2	1	1	3	1	2	2	2
231	3	117	21.9	71.8	62	1	2	2	2	1	2	1	1	2

CENSUS DATA: OUTPUT FROM PRINT PROCEDURE   22

OBS	CITY	ST	REGION	DIVISION	POP1975	OVER65	INCOME	HOUSING	ELECTRIC
232	GREAT FALLS....................	MT	WEST	MOUNTAIN	60868	9.0	4823	16943	12.71
233	LINCOLN.......................	NE	NORTH CENTRAL	WEST NORTH CENTRAL	163112	10.1	4860	16310	16.75
234	OMAHA.........................	NE	NORTH CENTRAL	WEST NORTH CENTRAL	371455	10.1	4887	14561	15.74
235	LAS VEGAS.....................	NV	WEST	MOUNTAIN	146030	5.8	4972	23852	14.69
236	RENO..........................	NV	WEST	MOUNTAIN	78097	9.4	5954	24236	21.90
237	MANCHESTER....................	NH	NORTHEAST	NEW ENGLAND	83417	12.7	4192	17360	23.90
238	NASHUA........................	NH	NORTHEAST	NEW ENGLAND	61002	8.5	4682	19296	23.90
239	BAYONNE.......................	NJ	NORTHEAST	MIDDLE ATLANTIC	73574	11.0	5025	22965	26.73
240	BLOOMFIELD....................	NJ	NORTHEAST	MIDDLE ATLANTIC	52162	12.4	5688	24036	26.73
241	CAMDEN........................	NJ	NORTHEAST	MIDDLE ATLANTIC	89214	10.5	3207	8414	26.73
242	CLIFTON.......................	NJ	NORTHEAST	MIDDLE ATLANTIC	79467	11.8	5826	27147	26.73
243	EAST ORANGE...................	NJ	NORTHEAST	MIDDLE ATLANTIC	73420	14.3	4940	19761	26.73
244	ELIZABETH.....................	NJ	NORTHEAST	MIDDLE ATLANTIC	104405	11.9	4778	20530	26.73
245	IRVINGTON.....................	NJ	NORTHEAST	MIDDLE ATLANTIC	58196	18.0	4986	19281	26.73
246	JERSEY CITY...................	NJ	NORTHEAST	MIDDLE ATLANTIC	243756	11.3	4298	16127	26.73
247	NEWARK........................	NJ	NORTHEAST	MIDDLE ATLANTIC	339568	8.0	3348	17231	26.73
248	PATERSON......................	NJ	NORTHEAST	MIDDLE ATLANTIC	136098	11.3	3699	19579	26.73
249	TRENTON.......................	NJ	NORTHEAST	MIDDLE ATLANTIC	101365	12.3	3831	9379	26.73
250	UNION CITY....................	NJ	NORTHEAST	MIDDLE ATLANTIC	52648	11.8	4149	17278	26.73
251	VINELAND......................	NJ	NORTHEAST	MIDDLE ATLANTIC	53637	9.7	4202	16166	19.50
252	ALBUQUERQUE...................	NM	WEST	MOUNTAIN	279401	6.5	4544	16261	17.42
253	ALBANY........................	NY	NORTHEAST	MIDDLE ATLANTIC	110311	14.9	4748	20929	17.46
254	BINGHAMTON....................	NY	NORTHEAST	MIDDLE ATLANTIC	60666	15.6	4207	17291	17.74
255	BUFFALO.......................	NY	NORTHEAST	MIDDLE ATLANTIC	407160	13.3	3928	12984	17.46
256	MOUNT VERNON..................	NY	NORTHEAST	MIDDLE ATLANTIC	67687	12.5	5138	31266	36.17
257	NEW ROCHELLE..................	NY	NORTHEAST	MIDDLE ATLANTIC	71841	12.0	6236	43882	36.17

OBS	CITYGOVT	ROBBERY	JANTEMP	JULYTEMP	SUNSHINE	POPGRP	OVR65GRP	INCOMGRP	HOUSGRP	ELECGRP	ROBGRP	JANGRP	JULYGRP	SUNGRP
232	1	105	20.5	69.3	61	1	2	2	2	1	2	1	1	2
233	3	47	22.2	77.3	64	3	2	2	2	2	1	1	2	2
234	3	326	22.6	77.2	63	3	2	2	1	2	4	1	2	2
235	1	921	44.2	89.6	85	3	1	2	2	1	4	2	2	3
236	1	245	31.9	69.3	72	2	2	2	2	3	3	1	1	3
237	3	82	22.2	70.0	52	2	3	1	2	3	1	1	1	1
238	3	25	22.8	70.1	59	1	2	2	2	3	1	1	1	2
239	3	60	31.4	76.4	60	1	2	2	2	3	1	1	2	2
240	3	90	31.4	76.4	60	1	3	2	2	3	1	1	2	2
241	3	1134	32.3	76.8	59	2	2	1	1	3	4	2	2	2
242	1	88	30.3	75.9	59	2	2	2	3	3	1	1	2	2
243	3	850	31.4	76.4	59	1	3	2	2	3	4	1	2	2
244	3	519	31.6	75.5	60	3	2	2	2	3	4	1	2	2
245	3	326	31.4	76.4	59	1	3	2	2	3	4	1	2	2
246	3	757	31.0	74.8	60	3	2	1	2	3	4	1	1	2
247	3	1258	31.4	76.4	60	3	1	1	2	3	4	1	2	2
248	3	766	30.3	75.9	60	3	2	1	2	3	4	1	2	2
249	3	767	32.1	75.9	58	3	3	1	1	3	4	2	2	2
250	2	165	31.0	74.8	59	1	2	2	2	3	2	1	1	2
251	3	123	32.7	76.1	59	1	2	2	2	2	2	2	2	2
252	3	293	35.2	78.7	72	3	1	2	2	2	3	2	2	3
253	1	91	21.5	72.0	50	3	3	2	2	2	1	1	1	1
254	3	45	22.0	69.1	50	1	3	1	2	2	1	1	1	1
255	3	575	23.7	70.1	50	3	3	1	1	2	4	1	1	1
256	3	165	32.2	76.6	60	1	3	2	3	3	2	2	2	2
257	1	125	32.2	76.6	60	1	2	2	3	3	2	2	2	2

CENSUS DATA: OUTPUT FROM PRINT PROCEDURE   23

OBS	CITY	ST	REGION	DIVISION	POP1975	OVER65	INCOME	HOUSING	ELECTRIC
258	NEW YORK.....................	NY	NORTHEAST	MIDDLE ATLANTIC	7481613	12.1	4939	25864	36.64
259	NIAGARA FALLS.................	NY	NORTHEAST	MIDDLE ATLANTIC	80773	10.8	3928	14759	17.46
260	ROCHESTER....................	NY	NORTHEAST	MIDDLE ATLANTIC	267173	13.7	4335	15142	18.03
261	SCHENECTADY..................	NY	NORTHEAST	MIDDLE ATLANTIC	74995	14.9	4493	15115	17.46
262	SYRACUSE.....................	NY	NORTHEAST	MIDDLE ATLANTIC	182543	13.0	4123	16735	17.46
263	TROY.........................	NY	NORTHEAST	MIDDLE ATLANTIC	60312	13.9	3695	15187	17.46
264	UTICA........................	NY	NORTHEAST	MIDDLE ATLANTIC	82443	15.0	3631	16734	17.46
265	YONKERS......................	NY	NORTHEAST	MIDDLE ATLANTIC	192509	11.8	5677	35185	36.17
266	ASHEVILLE....................	NC	SOUTH	SOUTH ATLANTIC	59591	14.6	4411	13860	17.37
267	CHARLOTTE....................	NC	SOUTH	SOUTH ATLANTIC	281417	7.2	4926	16511	17.57
268	DURHAM.......................	NC	SOUTH	SOUTH ATLANTIC	101224	9.2	4421	14692	17.57
269	FAYETTEVILLE.................	NC	SOUTH	SOUTH ATLANTIC	65915	6.5	4166	16997	15.55
270	GREENSBORO...................	NC	SOUTH	SOUTH ATLANTIC	155848	7.3	5016	16779	17.57
271	HIGH POINT...................	NC	SOUTH	SOUTH ATLANTIC	61330	9.5	4394	13436	17.17
272	RALEIGH......................	NC	SOUTH	SOUTH ATLANTIC	134231	7.4	4904	19673	17.37
273	WILMINGTON...................	NC	SOUTH	SOUTH ATLANTIC	53818	10.1	4074	11794	17.37
274	WINSTON-SALEM................	NC	SOUTH	SOUTH ATLANTIC	141018	8.8	4847	15940	17.57
275	FARGO CITY...................	ND	NORTH CENTRAL	WEST NORTH CENTRAL	56058	9.5	5676	19673	20.34
276	AKRON........................	OH	NORTH CENTRAL	EAST NORTH CENTRAL	251747	11.5	4614	15072	16.49
277	CANTON.......................	OH	NORTH CENTRAL	EAST NORTH CENTRAL	101852	13.1	4337	12714	16.02
278	CINCINNATI...................	OH	NORTH CENTRAL	EAST NORTH CENTRAL	412564	13.0	4517	16618	14.23
279	CLEVELAND....................	OH	NORTH CENTRAL	EAST NORTH CENTRAL	638793	10.6	3925	16899	19.92
280	CLEVELAND HGHTS..............	OH	NORTH CENTRAL	EAST NORTH CENTRAL	51141	15.1	6289	23152	19.92
281	COLUMBUS %PART<..............	OH	NORTH CENTRAL	EAST NORTH CENTRAL	535610	8.5	4333	17248	19.94
282	DAYTON.......................	OH	NORTH CENTRAL	EAST NORTH CENTRAL	205986	10.7	4091	15478	17.62
283	ELYRIA.......................	OH	NORTH CENTRAL	EAST NORTH CENTRAL	52474	8.0	4471	17636	16.62

OBS	CITYGOVT	ROBBERY	JANTEMP	JULYTEMP	SUNSHINE	POPGRP	OVR65GRP	INCOMGRP	HOUSGRP	ELECGRP	ROBGRP	JANGRP	JULYGRP	SUNGRP
258	3	1112	32.2	76.6	60	3	3	2	3	3	4	2	2	2
259	1	297	23.7	71.3	50	2	2	1	1	2	3	1	1	1
260	1	435	24.0	71.2	50	3	3	1	2	2	4	1	1	1
261	1	261	21.8	72.9	50	1	3	1	2	2	3	1	1	1
262	3	315	23.6	71.5	50	3	3	1	2	2	4	1	1	1
263	1	162	21.5	72.0	50	1	3	1	2	2	2	1	1	1
264	3	99	19.5	69.3	50	2	3	1	2	2	1	1	1	1
265	1	275	32.2	76.6	60	3	2	2	3	3	3	2	2	2
266	1	136	37.9	73.5	62	1	3	1	1	2	2	2	1	2
267	1	292	42.1	78.5	62	3	2	2	2	2	3	2	2	2
268	1	223	40.5	77.5	63	3	2	1	1	2	3	2	2	2
269	1	684	43.0	79.6	65	1	1	1	2	2	4	2	2	2
270	1	141	38.7	77.2	62	3	2	2	2	2	2	2	2	2
271	1	155	40.9	77.4	62	1	2	1	1	2	2	2	2	2
272	1	165	40.5	77.5	63	3	2	2	2	2	2	2	2	2
273	1	286	46.4	80.4	65	1	2	1	1	2	3	2	2	2
274	1	179	38.7	77.2	62	3	2	2	2	2	2	2	2	2
275	2	46	5.9	70.7	55	1	2	2	2	3	1	1	1	1
276	3	342	26.3	71.7	50	3	2	1	2	2	4	1	1	1
277	1	522	26.3	71.7	50	3	3	1	1	2	4	1	1	1
278	1	423	31.1	75.6	56	3	3	1	2	1	4	1	2	2
279	3	1111	26.9	71.4	50	3	2	1	2	2	4	1	1	1
280	1	252	26.9	71.4	50	1	3	2	2	2	3	1	1	1
281	3	448	28.4	73.6	53	3	2	1	2	2	4	1	1	1
282	1	1165	28.1	71.3	57	3	2	1	2	2	4	1	1	2
283	3	242	26.9	71.4	50	1	2	1	2	2	3	1	1	1

CENSUS DATA: OUTPUT FROM PRINT PROCEDURE   24

OBS	CITY	ST	REGION	DIVISION	POP1975	OVER65	INCOME	HOUSING	ELECTRIC
284	EUCLID.......................	OH	NORTH CENTRAL	EAST NORTH CENTRAL	63307	9.2	5799	22925	19.92
285	HAMILTON.....................	OH	NORTH CENTRAL	EAST NORTH CENTRAL	66469	10.4	4354	15535	18.06
286	KETTERING....................	OH	NORTH CENTRAL	EAST NORTH CENTRAL	69949	6.6	5977	22967	16.76
287	LAKEWOOD.....................	OH	NORTH CENTRAL	EAST NORTH CENTRAL	65395	14.7	5863	21840	19.92
288	LIMA.........................	OH	NORTH CENTRAL	EAST NORTH CENTRAL	51372	11.2	4184	13248	16.02
289	LORAIN CITY..................	OH	NORTH CENTRAL	EAST NORTH CENTRAL	84907	7.7	4545	17017	16.62
290	MANSFIELD....................	OH	NORTH CENTRAL	EAST NORTH CENTRAL	56916	11.1	4283	14554	16.62
291	PARMA........................	OH	NORTH CENTRAL	EAST NORTH CENTRAL	98883	7.5	5257	24079	19.92
292	SPRINGFIELD..................	OH	NORTH CENTRAL	EAST NORTH CENTRAL	77317	12.1	4012	14061	16.62
293	TOLEDO.......................	OH	NORTH CENTRAL	EAST NORTH CENTRAL	367650	11.1	4571	16209	20.54
294	WARREN.......................	OH	NORTH CENTRAL	EAST NORTH CENTRAL	60486	10.0	4677	16505	16.62
295	YOUNGSTOWN...................	OH	NORTH CENTRAL	EAST NORTH CENTRAL	132203	12.7	4181	12806	16.49
296	LAWTON.......................	OK	SOUTH	WEST SOUTH CENTRAL	76421	5.2	3819	13939	16.74
297	MIDWEST CITY.................	OK	SOUTH	WEST SOUTH CENTRAL	50105	4.6	4508	12833	11.24
298	NORMAN.......................	OK	SOUTH	WEST SOUTH CENTRAL	59948	7.2	4047	15563	11.24
299	OKLAHOMA CITY................	OK	SOUTH	WEST SOUTH CENTRAL	365916	9.8	4731	13155	11.24
300	TULSA........................	OK	SOUTH	WEST SOUTH CENTRAL	331726	9.1	5173	14499	16.74
301	EUGENE.......................	OR	WEST	PACIFIC	92451	9.0	4677	18143	8.80
302	PORTLAND.....................	OR	WEST	PACIFIC	356732	14.9	5192	14423	11.36
303	SALEM........................	OR	WEST	PACIFIC	78168	13.0	4427	15696	10.90
304	ALLENTOWN....................	PA	NORTHEAST	MIDDLE ATLANTIC	106624	13.8	4735	12672	19.32
305	ALTOONA......................	PA	NORTHEAST	MIDDLE ATLANTIC	59692	15.0	3758	7718	19.41
306	BETHLEHEM....................	PA	NORTHEAST	MIDDLE ATLANTIC	73827	11.0	5042	14399	19.32
307	ERIE.........................	PA	NORTHEAST	MIDDLE ATLANTIC	127895	11.1	4043	13482	19.41
308	HARRISBURG...................	PA	NORTHEAST	MIDDLE ATLANTIC	58274	14.7	4071	9459	19.32
309	LANCASTER....................	PA	NORTHEAST	MIDDLE ATLANTIC	56669	13.4	3751	11705	19.32

(continued on next page)

(continued from previous page)

OBS	CITYGOVT	ROBBERY	JANTEMP	JULYTEMP	SUNSHINE	POPGRP	OVR65GRP	INCOMGRP	HOUSGRP	ELECGRP	ROBGRP	JANGRP	JULYGRP	SUNGRP
284	3	103	26.9	71.4	50	1	2	2	2	2	2	1	1	1
285	1	223	31.5	75.3	57	1	2	1	2	2	3	1	2	2
286	1	96	28.1	71.3	57	1	1	2	2	2	1	1	1	2
287	3	61	26.9	71.4	50	1	3	?	?	?	1	1	1	1
288	3	224	27.3	73.4	55	1	2	1	1	2	3	1	1	1
289	3	210	26.9	71.4	50	2	2	1	2	2	3	1	1	1
290	3	292	28.0	73.5	52	1	2	1	1	?	3	1	1	1
291	3	44	26.9	71.4	50	?	?	?	?	?	1	1	1	1
292	1	307	28.4	73.6	54	2	3	1	1	2	4	1	1	1
293	3	440	24.8	72.3	50	3	2	1	2	3	4	1	1	1
294	3	260	27.5	71.8	50	1	2	1	?	2	3	1	1	1
295	3	392	25.7	70.7	50	3	3	1	1	2	4	1	1	1
296	3	279	39.7	83.3	70	2	1	1	1	2	3	2	2	2
297	1	68	36.8	81.5	70	1	1	1	1	1	1	2	2	2
298	1	62	38.9	82.4	70	1	2	1	2	1	1	2	2	2
299	1	271	36.8	81.5	70	3	2	2	1	1	3	2	2	2
300	2	175	36.6	82.1	65	3	2	2	1	2	2	2	2	2
301	1	120	39.4	66.9	50	2	2	1	2	1	2	2	1	1
302	2	517	38.1	67.1	48	3	3	2	1	1	4	2	1	1
303	1	104	38.8	66.6	55	2	3	1	2	1	2	2	1	1
304	3	128	27.8	74.1	52	3	3	2	1	2	2	1	1	1
305	2	70	29.0	72.7	50	1	3	1	1	2	1	1	1	1
306	3	122	27.8	74.1	52	1	2	2	1	2	2	1	1	1
307	3	217	25.1	68.7	50	3	2	1	1	2	3	1	1	1
308	3	1016	30.1	76.1	52	1	3	1	1	2	4	1	2	1
309	3	120	30.5	74.3	55	1	3	1	1	2	2	1	1	1

CENSUS DATA: OUTPUT FROM PRINT PROCEDURE   25

OBS	CITY	ST	REGION	DIVISION	POP1975	OVR65	INCOME	HOUSING	ELECTRIC
310	PHILADELPHIA..................	PA	NORTHEAST	MIDDLE ATLANTIC	1815808	11.7	4330	10703	20.00
311	PITTSBURGH....................	PA	NORTHEAST	MIDDLE ATLANTIC	458651	13.5	4426	12795	20.80
312	READING......................	PA	NORTHEAST	MIDDLE ATLANTIC	81592	15.9	4091	8546	19.14
313	SCRANTON.....................	PA	NORTHEAST	MIDDLE ATLANTIC	95884	14.7	4018	11578	19.32
314	WILKES-BARRE.................	PA	NORTHEAST	MIDDLE ATLANTIC	57040	14.9	3702	9421	19.32
315	CRANSTON.....................	RI	NORTHEAST	NEW ENGLAND	74381	12.9	5026	18710	20.83
316	PAWTUCKET....................	RI	NORTHEAST	NEW ENGLAND	72024	14.1	4328	16690	21.51
317	PROVIDENCE...................	RI	NORTHEAST	NEW ENGLAND	167724	14.8	4337	17098	20.83
318	WARWICK......................	RI	NORTHEAST	NEW ENGLAND	85875	9.4	4991	17390	20.83
319	CHARLESTON...................	SC	SOUTH	SOUTH ATLANTIC	57470	9.7	4191	20439	20.23
320	COLUMBIA.....................	SC	SOUTH	SOUTH ATLANTIC	111616	7.3	4076	17227	20.23
321	GREENVILLE...................	SC	SOUTH	SOUTH ATLANTIC	58518	10.1	4565	16017	16.75
322	SIOUX FALLS %PART<...........	SD	NORTH CENTRAL	WEST NORTH CENTRAL	73925	10.2	4853	15920	20.49
323	CHATTANOOGA..................	TN	SOUTH	EAST SOUTH CENTRAL	161978	12.6	4081	11050	15.17
324	KNOXVILLE....................	TN	SOUTH	EAST SOUTH CENTRAL	183383	11.1	4044	12124	14.60
325	MEMPHIS......................	TN	SOUTH	EAST SOUTH CENTRAL	661319	8.5	4383	14064	14.60
326	NASHVILLE-DAVIDSON...........	TN	SOUTH	EAST SOUTH CENTRAL	446941	8.8	4891	15881	14.42
327	ABILENE......................	TX	SOUTH	WEST SOUTH CENTRAL	96459	8.6	3918	10851	16.28
328	AMARILLO.....................	TX	SOUTH	WEST SOUTH CENTRAL	138743	8.5	4733	12004	16.23
329	ARLINGTON....................	TX	SOUTH	WEST SOUTH CENTRAL	110543	4.0	5018	17359	11.54
330	AUSTIN.......................	TX	SOUTH	WEST SOUTH CENTRAL	301147	7.1	4379	16246	25.44
331	BEAUMONT.....................	TX	SOUTH	WEST SOUTH CENTRAL	113696	9.3	4569	11948	13.11
332	BROWNSVILLE..................	TX	SOUTH	WEST SOUTH CENTRAL	72157	7.8	2196	8268	23.23
333	CORPUS CHRISTI...............	TX	SOUTH	WEST SOUTH CENTRAL	214838	6.2	3941	12297	19.80
334	DALLAS.......................	TX	SOUTH	WEST SOUTH CENTRAL	812797	7.9	5285	16668	13.41
335	EL PASO......................	TX	SOUTH	WEST SOUTH CENTRAL	385691	6.0	3479	13826	13.38

OBS	CITYGOVT	ROBBERY	JANTEMP	JULYTEMP	SUNSHINE	POPGRP	OVR65GRP	INCOMGRP	HOUSGRP	ELECGRP	ROBGRP	JANGRP	JULYGRP	SUNGRP
310	3	573	32.3	76.8	58	3	2	1	1	2	4	2	2	2
311	3	598	30.6	74.6	50	3	3	1	1	3	4	1	1	1
312	2	273	31.9	76.5	55	2	3	1	1	2	3	1	2	1
313	3	75	26.8	72.5	50	2	3	1	1	2	1	1	1	1
314	3	39	26.0	72.2	50	1	3	1	1	2	1	1	1	1
315	3	48	28.4	72.1	60	1	3	2	2	3	1	1	1	2
316	3	50	28.4	72.1	60	1	3	1	2	3	1	1	1	2
317	3	300	28.4	72.1	60	3	3	1	2	3	3	1	1	2
318	3	62	28.4	72.1	60	2	2	2	2	3	1	1	1	2
319	3	583	48.6	80.2	65	1	2	1	2	2	4	2	2	2
320	1	346	45.4	81.2	65	3	2	1	2	3	4	2	2	2
321	1	509	42.3	78.3	62	1	2	1	2	2	4	2	2	2
322	2	35	14.2	73.3	62	1	2	2	2	2	1	1	2	2
323	2	225	40.2	78.8	55	3	3	1	1	2	3	2	2	1
324	3	263	40.6	78.2	52	3	2	1	1	2	3	2	2	2
325	3	451	40.5	81.6	63	3	2	1	1	1	4	2	2	2
326	3	450	38.3	79.6	58	3	2	2	2	1	4	2	2	2
327	1	88	43.7	83.9	71	2	2	1	1	2	1	2	2	3
328	1	110	36.0	78.7	75	3	2	2	1	2	2	2	2	3
329	1	102	44.8	84.8	68	3	2	2	2	1	2	2	2	2
330	1	176	49.7	84.6	65	3	2	1	2	3	2	2	2	2
331	1	258	52.0	83.0	60	3	2	1	1	1	3	2	2	2
332	1	15	60.3	84.4	62	1	2	1	1	3	1	2	2	2
333	1	177	56.3	84.8	62	3	1	1	1	2	2	2	2	2
334	1	417	45.4	85.7	68	3	2	2	2	1	4	2	2	2
335	3	218	43.9	82.3	80	3	1	1	1	1	3	2	2	2

CENSUS DATA: OUTPUT FROM PRINT PROCEDURE   26

OBS	CITY	ST	REGION	DIVISION	POP1975	OVER65	INCOME	HOUSING	ELECTRIC
336	FORT WORTH %PART<.............	TX	SOUTH	WEST SOUTH CENTRAL	358364	9.6	4527	11413	11.54
337	GALVESTON......................	TX	SOUTH	WEST SOUTH CENTRAL	60125	11.7	4252	12885	16.95
338	GARLAND.......................	TX	SOUTH	WEST SOUTH CENTRAL	111322	3.0	4816	17324	19.16
339	GRAND PRAIRIE.................	TX	SOUTH	WEST SOUTH CENTRAL	56842	4.2	4542	14374	11.54
340	HOUSTON.......................	TX	SOUTH	WEST SOUTH CENTRAL	1326809	6.5	5110	14541	16.95
341	IRVING........................	TX	SOUTH	WEST SOUTH CENTRAL	103703	3.0	5112	18264	13.88
342	LAREDO........................	TX	SOUTH	WEST SOUTH CENTRAL	76998	8.1	2279	7822	20.05
343	LONGVIEW......................	TX	SOUTH	WEST SOUTH CENTRAL	52034	9.1	4289	13672	12.86
344	LUBBOCK.......................	TX	SOUTH	WEST SOUTH CENTRAL	163525	6.2	4328	13606	16.63
345	MESQUITE......................	TX	SOUTH	WEST SOUTH CENTRAL	61933	2.5	4424	15131	15.74
346	MIDLAND.......................	TX	SOUTH	WEST SOUTH CENTRAL	62950	5.2	5211	14037	11.54
347	ODESSA........................	TX	SOUTH	WEST SOUTH CENTRAL	84476	4.8	4341	11064	11.54
348	PASADENA......................	TX	SOUTH	WEST SOUTH CENTRAL	94670	3.4	4944	13692	16.95
349	PORT ARTHUR...................	TX	SOUTH	WEST SOUTH CENTRAL	53557	10.6	3856	9555	13.11
350	RICHARDSON....................	TX	SOUTH	WEST SOUTH CENTRAL	59190	2.3	6423	24814	15.74
351	SAN ANGELO....................	TX	SOUTH	WEST SOUTH CENTRAL	66099	10.6	4031	10114	16.28
352	SAN ANTONIO...................	TX	SOUTH	WEST SOUTH CENTRAL	773248	8.4	3601	11671	20.08
353	TYLER.........................	TX	SOUTH	WEST SOUTH CENTRAL	61434	10.6	4621	13135	13.88
354	WACO..........................	TX	SOUTH	WEST SOUTH CENTRAL	97607	12.8	3838	9628	15.74
355	WICHITA FALLS.................	TX	SOUTH	WEST SOUTH CENTRAL	95008	9.5	4257	10556	11.54
356	OGDEN.........................	UT	WEST	MOUNTAIN	68978	10.6	4354	15261	13.97
357	PROVO.........................	UT	WEST	MOUNTAIN	55593	5.5	3226	18456	8.30
358	SALT LAKE CITY................	UT	WEST	MOUNTAIN	169917	13.3	4933	16170	13.97
359	ALEXANDRIA....................	VA	SOUTH	SOUTH ATLANTIC	105220	6.7	7258	27161	21.30
360	CHESAPEAKE....................	VA	SOUTH	SOUTH ATLANTIC	104459	5.6	3968	15985	21.30
361	HAMPTON.......................	VA	SOUTH	SOUTH ATLANTIC	125013	5.0	4420	16852	21.30

OBS	CITYGOVT	ROBBERY	JANTEMP	JULYTEMP	SUNSHINE	POPGRP	OVR65GRP	INCOMGRP	HOUSGRP	ELECGRP	ROBGRP	JANGRP	JULYGRP	SUNGRP
336	1	337	44.8	84.8	68	3	2	1	1	4	2	2	2	2
337	1	552	53.9	83.2	62	1	2	1	1	2	4	2	2	2
338	1	49	45.4	85.7	77	3	1	2	2	2	1	2	2	3
339	1	113	44.8	84.8	68	1	1	1	1	1	2	2	2	2
340	3	484	52.1	83.3	62	3	1	2	1	2	4	2	2	2
341	1	100	45.4	85.7	68	3	1	2	2	1	1	2	2	2
342	3	48	56.5	87.9	70	2	2	1	1	3	1	2	2	2
343	1	67	46.2	83.5	68	1	2	1	1	1	1	2	2	2
344	1	125	39.1	79.7	72	3	1	1	1	2	2	2	2	3
345	1	79	45.4	85.7	65	1	1	1	2	2	1	2	2	2
346	1	73	43.6	82.3	75	1	1	2	1	1	1	2	2	3
347	1	62	43.6	82.3	70	2	1	1	1	1	1	2	2	2
348	3	158	52.1	83.3	70	2	1	2	1	2	2	2	2	2
349	1	265	52.0	83.0	60	1	2	1	1	1	3	2	2	2
350	1	24	45.4	85.7	68	1	1	2	2	2	1	2	2	2
351	1	83	46.4	84.7	70	1	2	1	1	2	1	2	2	2
352	1	224	50.7	84.7	64	3	2	1	1	3	3	2	2	2
353	1	125	46.2	83.5	70	1	2	1	1	1	2	2	2	2
354	1	161	47.0	85.6	75	2	3	1	1	2	2	2	2	3
355	1	161	41.5	85.8	70	2	2	1	1	1	2	2	2	2
356	1	149	27.8	76.9	60	1	2	1	2	1	2	1	2	2
357	2	18	28.8	76.0	65	1	1	1	2	1	1	1	2	2
358	2	343	28.0	76.7	60	3	3	2	2	1	4	1	2	2
359	1	444	35.6	78.7	55	3	1	2	3	3	4	2	2	1
360	1	139	40.0	78.6	60	3	1	1	2	3	2	2	2	2
361	1	173	40.0	78.6	60	3	1	1	2	3	2	2	2	2

CENSUS DATA: OUTPUT FROM PRINT PROCEDURE   27

OBS	CITY	ST	REGION	DIVISION	POP1975	OVER65	INCOME	HOUSING	ELECTRIC
362	LYNCHBURG.....................	VA	SOUTH	SOUTH ATLANTIC	63066	12.1	5487	13586	16.83
363	NEWPORT NEWS..................	VA	SOUTH	SOUTH ATLANTIC	138760	5.3	4657	18967	21.30
364	NORFOLK.......................	VA	SOUTH	SOUTH ATLANTIC	286694	6.8	4233	15935	21.30
365	PORTSMOUTH....................	VA	SOUTH	SOUTH ATLANTIC	108674	8.1	4300	13850	21.30
366	RICHMOND......................	VA	SOUTH	SOUTH ATLANTIC	232652	11.3	4952	15342	21.30
367	ROANOKE.......................	VA	SOUTH	SOUTH ATLANTIC	100585	13.6	5448	13161	16.83
368	VIRGINIA BEACH................	VA	SOUTH	SOUTH ATLANTIC	213954	3.5	4794	21353	21.30
369	BELLEVUE......................	WA	WEST	PACIFIC	65365	3.0	6424	30063	10.64
370	SEATTLE.......................	WA	WEST	PACIFIC	487091	13.1	5800	19644	5.42
371	SPOKANE.......................	WA	WEST	PACIFIC	173698	14.0	4499	12809	8.36
372	TACOMA........................	WA	WEST	PACIFIC	151267	12.2	4607	15040	8.05
373	CHARLESTON....................	WV	SOUTH	SOUTH ATLANTIC	67348	12.6	5088	19131	18.60
374	HUNTINGTON....................	WV	SOUTH	SOUTH ATLANTIC	68811	14.0	4254	15766	18.60
375	APPLETON......................	WI	NORTH CENTRAL	EAST NORTH CENTRAL	59182	9.6	4855	18170	15.83
376	GREEN BAY.....................	WI	NORTH CENTRAL	EAST NORTH CENTRAL	91189	9.5	4338	15887	19.94
377	KENOSHA.......................	WI	NORTH CENTRAL	EAST NORTH CENTRAL	80727	10.1	4776	16774	17.47
378	MADISON.......................	WI	NORTH CENTRAL	EAST NORTH CENTRAL	168196	7.2	4885	21999	15.63
379	MILWAUKEE.....................	WI	NORTH CENTRAL	EAST NORTH CENTRAL	665796	11.0	4680	18075	17.47
380	OSHKOSH.......................	WI	NORTH CENTRAL	EAST NORTH CENTRAL	50107	11.3	4199	14955	19.94
381	RACINE........................	WI	NORTH CENTRAL	EAST NORTH CENTRAL	94744	10.4	4823	16894	17.47
382	WAUWATOSA.....................	WI	NORTH CENTRAL	EAST NORTH CENTRAL	56514	14.5	6260	26631	17.47
383	WEST ALLIS....................	WI	NORTH CENTRAL	EAST NORTH CENTRAL	69084	10.6	5319	18990	17.47

(continued on next page)

(continued from previous page)

OBS	CITYGOVT	ROBBERY	JANTEMP	JULYTEMP	SUNSHINE	POPGRP	OVR65GRP	INCOMGRP	HOUSGRP	ELECGRP	ROBGRP	JANGRP	JULYGRP	SUNGRP
362	1	117	36.6	75.8	60	1	3	2	1	2	2	2	2	2
363	1	264	40.5	78.3	60	3	1	1	2	3	3	2	2	2
364	1	413	40.5	78.3	60	3	1	1	2	3	4	2	2	2
365	1	502	40.5	78.3	60	3	2	1	1	3	4	2	2	2
366	1	591	37.5	77.9	60	3	2	2	2	3	4	2	2	2
367	1	239	36.4	75.2	60	3	3	2	1	2	3	2	2	2
368	1	91	40.0	78.6	60	3	1	2	2	3	1	2	2	2
369	1	41	38.2	64.5	50	1	1	2	3	1	1	2	1	1
370	3	432	38.2	64.5	50	3	3	2	2	1	4	2	1	1
371	1	139	25.4	69.7	60	3	3	1	1	1	2	1	1	2
372	1	266	38.2	64.5	50	3	3	1	2	1	3	2	1	1
373	3	266	34.5	75.0	50	1	3	2	2	2	3	2	1	1
374	1	222	34.3	75.3	50	1	3	1	2	2	3	2	2	1
375	3	22	16.9	71.4	55	1	2	2	2	2	1	1	1	1
376	3	24	15.4	69.2	52	2	2	1	2	2	1	1	1	1
377	3	253	22.3	71.8	52	2	2	2	2	2	3	1	1	1
378	3	96	16.8	70.1	55	2	2	2	2	2	1	1	1	1
379	3	296	19.4	69.9	52	3	2	2	2	2	3	1	1	1
380	1	30	17.0	71.3	54	1	2	1	1	2	1	1	1	1
381	3	324	22.3	71.8	52	2	2	2	2	2	4	1	1	1
382	3	85	19.4	69.9	54	1	3	2	3	2	1	1	1	1
383	3	52	19.4	69.9	52	1	2	2	2	2	1	1	1	1

Descriptive statistics with FREQ, SUMMARY, and TABULATE   The observations in data set CITIES are now ready to input to FREQ, SUMMARY, and TABULATE procedures. Since the SUMMARY procedure does not produce any printed output, the PRINT procedure is used to print the output data set from SUMMARY.

Comparing the output from the UNIVARIATE, FREQ, SUMMARY, and TABULATE procedures, the list of descriptive statistics available with each procedure is similar, but the procedures differ in other important respects. See the descriptions of these procedures later in the manual for more detailed information.

```
PROC FREQ DATA=CITIES;
  TABLES DIVISION JANGRP JULYGRP POPGRP REGION INCOMGRP
  ROBGRP SUNGRP OVR65GRP HOUSGRP ELECGRP;
  TABLES POPGRP*CITYGOVT;
  TABLES REGION*OVR65GRP / NOCOL NOPERCENT;
  TABLES JANGRP*JULYGRP*ELECGRP / LIST;
  TABLES (POPGRP INCOMGRP)*ROBGRP / NOCOL NOPERCENT
    EXPECTED DEVIATION CELLCHI2 CHISQ;
  TABLES CITYGOVT*ROBGRP / ALL NOCOL NOPERCENT;
  FORMAT POPGRP PC. OVR65GRP OC. INCOMGRP IC. HOUSGRP HC.
    ELECGRP EC. CITYGOVT CC. ROBGRP RC. JANGRP JAN.
    JULYGRP JUL. SUNGRP SC.;
  TITLE CENSUS DATA: OUTPUT FROM FREQ PROCEDURE;

PROC SUMMARY DATA=CITIES;
  CLASS POPGRP REGION;
  VAR OVER65 INCOME HOUSING ELECTRIC ROBBERY;
  OUTPUT OUT=CITYDATA
    N=NOVER65 NINCOME NHOUS NELEC NROB
    MEAN=
    STD(INCOME HOUSING ELECTRIC)=
      INCOMSTD HOUSESTD ELECSTD;
  FORMAT POPGRP PC.;

PROC PRINT DATA=CITYDATA;
  TITLE CENSUS DATA: RESULTS FROM SUMMARY PROCEDURE;
```

```
PROC TABULATE DATA=CITIES;
   TITLE CENSUS DATA: OUTPUT FROM TABULATE PROCEDURE;
   FORMAT POPGRP PC.;
   VAR INCOME;
   CLASS POPGRP REGION;
   TABLE POPGRP*REGION, INCOME*(N*F=4.0 MEAN STD);
```

CENSUS DATA: OUTPUT FROM FREQ PROCEDURE   28

DIVISION	FREQUENCY	CUM FREQ	PERCENT	CUM PERCENT
EAST NORTH CENTR	79	79	20.627	20.627
EAST SOUTH CENTR	13	92	3.394	24.021
MIDDLE ATLANTIC	37	129	9.661	33.681
MOUNTAIN	23	152	6.005	39.687
NEW ENGLAND	33	185	8.616	48.303
PACIFIC	80	265	20.888	69.191
SOUTH ATLANTIC	47	312	12.272	81.462
WEST NORTH CENTR	27	339	7.050	88.512
WEST SOUTH CENTR	44	383	11.488	100.000

MEAN JANUARY TEMPERATURE (DEGREES F)

JANGRP	FREQUENCY	CUM FREQ	PERCENT	CUM PERCENT
UNDER 32 DEGREES	179	179	46.736	46.736
32 DEGREES OR HI	204	383	53.264	100.000

MEAN JULY TEMPERATURE (DEGREES F)

JULYGRP	FREQUENCY	CUM FREQ	PERCENT	CUM PERCENT
UNDER 75 DEGREES	213	213	55.614	55.614
75 DEGREES OR HI	170	383	44.386	100.000

1975 POPULATION ESTIMATE

POPGRP	FREQUENCY	CUM FREQ	PERCENT	CUM PERCENT
50,001-75,000	137	137	35.770	35.770
75,001-100,000	84	221	21.932	57.702
OVER 100,000	162	383	42.298	100.000

REGION	FREQUENCY	CUM FREQ	PERCENT	CUM PERCENT
NORTH CENTRAL	106	106	27.676	27.676
NORTHEAST	70	176	18.277	45.953
SOUTH	104	280	27.154	73.107
WEST	103	383	26.893	100.000

PER CAPITA MONEY INCOME (1974)

INCOMGRP	FREQUENCY	CUM FREQ	PERCENT	CUM PERCENT
UNDER $4677	193	193	50.392	50.392
$4677 OR MORE	190	383	49.608	100.000

ROBBERY RATE/100,000 POP (1975)

ROBGRP	FREQUENCY	CUM FREQ	PERCENT	CUM PERCENT
100 OR LESS	84	84	21.932	21.932
101-200	108	192	28.198	50.131
201-300	79	271	20.627	70.757
OVER 300	112	383	29.243	100.000

CENSUS DATA: OUTPUT FROM FREQ PROCEDURE   29

POSSIBLE SUNSHINE ANNUAL % (DAYS)

SUNGRP	FREQUENCY	CUM FREQ	PERCENT	CUM PERCENT
UNDER 55%	109	109	28.460	28.460
55-70%	205	314	53.525	81.984
OVER 70%	69	383	18.016	100.000

% PERSONS 65 & OVER (1970)

OVR65GRP	FREQUENCY	CUM FREQ	PERCENT	CUM PERCENT
UNDER 7%	92	92	24.021	24.021
7-12%	194	286	50.653	74.674
OVER 12%	97	383	25.326	100.000

(continued on next page)

(continued from previous page)

```
                  MEDIAN SINGLE-FAMILY OWNER-OCCUP (1970)
        HOUSGRP   FREQUENCY  CUM FREQ    PERCENT  CUM PERCENT

        LOW          108        108      28.198      28.198
        MEDIUM       221        329      57.702      85.901
        HIGH          54        383      14.099     100.000


                  TYPICAL RESID. ELECTRIC BILL/MO. (1976)
        ELECGRP   FREQUENCY  CUM FREQ    PERCENT  CUM PERCENT

        LOW           88         88      22.977      22.977
        MEDIUM       167        255      43.603      66.580
        HIGH         128        383      33.420     100.000
```

```
                  CENSUS DATA: OUTPUT FROM FREQ PROCEDURE                    30

                        TABLE OF POPGRP BY CITYGOVT

        POPGRP   1975 POPULATION ESTIMATE   CITYGOVT  FORM OF CITY GOVERNMENT

          FREQUENCY  |
           PERCENT   |
           ROW PCT   |
           COL PCT   |         |COUNCIL |COMMISSI|MAYOR CO|
                     |    .    |MANAGER |ON      |UNCIL   |  TOTAL
        -------------+---------+--------+--------+--------+
        50,001-75,000|    0 |     84 |      7 |     46 |    137
                     |    . |  21.99 |   1.83 |  12.04 |  35.86
                     |    . |  61.31 |   5.11 |  33.58 |
                     |    . |  39.81 |  33.33 |  30.67 |
        -------------+------+--------+--------+--------+
        75,001-100,000|   0 |     50 |      3 |     31 |     84
                     |    . |  13.09 |   0.79 |   8.12 |  21.99
                     |    . |  59.52 |   3.57 |  36.90 |
                     |    . |  23.70 |  14.29 |  20.67 |
        -------------+------+--------+--------+--------+
        OVER 100,000 |    1 |     77 |     11 |     73 |    161
                     |    . |  20.16 |   2.88 |  19.11 |  42.15
                     |    . |  47.83 |   6.83 |  45.34 |
                     |    . |  36.49 |  52.38 |  48.67 |
        -------------+------+--------+--------+--------+
        TOTAL             .      211       21      150      382
                                55.24     5.50    39.27   100.00
```

```
                  CENSUS DATA: OUTPUT FROM FREQ PROCEDURE                    31

                        TABLE OF REGION BY OVR65GRP

        REGION      OVR65GRP   % PERSONS 65 & OVER (1970)

          FREQUENCY |
           ROW PCT  |UNDER 7%|7-12%   |OVER 12%|  TOTAL
        ------------+--------+--------+--------+
        NORTH CENTRAL|    21 |     64 |     21 |    106
                     |  19.81|  60.38 |  19.81 |
        ------------+--------+--------+--------+
        NORTHEAST    |     0 |     29 |     41 |     70
                     |  0.00 |  41.43 |  58.57 |
        ------------+--------+--------+--------+
        SOUTH        |    29 |     56 |     19 |    104
                     |  27.88|  53.85 |  18.27 |
        ------------+--------+--------+--------+
        WEST         |    42 |     45 |     16 |    103
                     |  40.78|  43.69 |  15.53 |
        ------------+--------+--------+--------+
        TOTAL             92      194       97      383
```

```
                  CENSUS DATA: OUTPUT FROM FREQ PROCEDURE                    32

        JANGRP           JULYGRP          ELECGRP  FREQUENCY  CUM FREQ  PERCENT  CUM PERCENT
        UNDER 32 DEGREES UNDER 75 DEGREES LOW         24         24      6.266      6.266
        UNDER 32 DEGREES UNDER 75 DEGREES MEDIUM      74         98     19.321     25.587
        UNDER 32 DEGREES UNDER 75 DEGREES HIGH        40        138     10.444     36.031
        UNDER 32 DEGREES 75 DEGREES OR HI LOW          8        146      2.089     38.120
        UNDER 32 DEGREES 75 DEGREES OR HI MEDIUM      22        168      5.744     43.864
        UNDER 32 DEGREES 75 DEGREES OR HI HIGH        11        179      2.872     46.736
        32 DEGREES OR HI UNDER 75 DEGREES LOW         22        201      5.744     52.480
        32 DEGREES OR HI UNDER 75 DEGREES MEDIUM      14        215      3.655     56.136
        32 DEGREES OR HI UNDER 75 DEGREES HIGH        39        254     10.183     66.319
        32 DEGREES OR HI 75 DEGREES OR HI LOW         34        288      8.877     75.196
        32 DEGREES OR HI 75 DEGREES OR HI MEDIUM      57        345     14.883     90.078
        32 DEGREES OR HI 75 DEGREES OR HI HIGH        38        383      9.922    100.000
```

```
              CENSUS DATA: OUTPUT FROM FREQ PROCEDURE                    33

                  TABLE OF POPGRP BY ROBGRP

POPGRP    1975 POPULATION ESTIMATE    ROBGRP    ROBBERY RATE/100,000 POP (1975)

FREQUENCY     |
EXPECTED      |
DEVIATION     |
CELL CHI2     |
ROW PCT       |100 OR L|101-200 |201-300 |OVER 300|
              |ESS     |        |        |        |  TOTAL
--------------+--------+--------+--------+--------+
50,001-75,000 |     49 |     44 |     26 |     18 |   137
              |   30.0 |   38.6 |   28.3 |   40.1 |
              |   19.0 |    5.4 |   -2.3 |  -22.1 |
              |   12.0 |    0.7 |    0.2 |   12.1 |
              |  35.77 |  32.12 |  18.98 |  13.14 |
--------------+--------+--------+--------+--------+
75,001-100,000|     22 |     30 |     18 |     14 |    84
              |   18.4 |   23.7 |   17.3 |   24.6 |
              |    3.6 |    6.3 |    0.7 |  -10.6 |
              |    0.7 |    1.7 |    0.0 |    4.5 |
              |  26.19 |  35.71 |  21.43 |  16.67 |
--------------+--------+--------+--------+--------+
OVER 100,000  |     13 |     34 |     35 |     80 |   162
              |   35.5 |   45.7 |   33.4 |   47.4 |
              |  -22.5 |  -11.7 |    1.6 |   32.6 |
              |   14.3 |    3.0 |    0.1 |   22.5 |
              |   8.02 |  20.99 |  21.60 |  49.38 |
--------------+--------+--------+--------+--------+
TOTAL              84      108       79      112     383

                  STATISTICS FOR 2-WAY TABLES

CHI-SQUARE                         71.797    DF=   6   PROB=0.0001
PHI                                 0.433
CONTINGENCY COEFFICIENT             0.397
CRAMER'S V                          0.306
LIKELIHOOD RATIO CHISQUARE         74.714    DF=   6   PROB=0.0001
```

```
              CENSUS DATA: OUTPUT FROM FREQ PROCEDURE                    34

                  TABLE OF INCOMGRP BY ROBGRP

INCOMGRP  PER CAPITA MONEY INCOME (1974)   ROBGRP   ROBBERY RATE/100,000 POP (1975)

FREQUENCY     |
EXPECTED      |
DEVIATION     |
CELL CHI2     |
ROW PCT       |100 OR L|101-200 |201-300 |OVER 300|
              |ESS     |        |        |        |  TOTAL
--------------+--------+--------+--------+--------+
UNDER $4677   |     34 |     47 |     45 |     67 |   193
              |   42.3 |   54.4 |   39.8 |   56.4 |
              |   -8.3 |   -7.4 |    5.2 |   10.6 |
              |    1.6 |    1.0 |    0.7 |    2.0 |
              |  17.62 |  24.35 |  23.32 |  34.72 |
--------------+--------+--------+--------+--------+
$4677 OR MORE |     50 |     61 |     34 |     45 |   190
              |   41.7 |   53.6 |   39.2 |   55.6 |
              |    8.3 |    7.4 |   -5.2 |  -10.6 |
              |    1.7 |    1.0 |    0.7 |    2.0 |
              |  26.32 |  32.11 |  17.89 |  23.68 |
--------------+--------+--------+--------+--------+
TOTAL              84      108       79      112     383

                  STATISTICS FOR 2-WAY TABLES

CHI-SQUARE                         10.693    DF=   3   PROB=0.0135
PHI                                 0.167
CONTINGENCY COEFFICIENT             0.165
CRAMER'S V                          0.167
LIKELIHOOD RATIO CHISQUARE         10.749    DF=   3   PROB=0.0132
```

PROC Step Applications   285

TABLE OF CITYGOVT BY ROBGRP

CITYGOVT   FORM OF CITY GOVERNMENT   ROBGRP   ROBBERY RATE/100,000 POP (1975)

FREQUENCY ROW PCT	100 OR LESS	101-200	201-300	OVER 300	TOTAL
.	0 .	1 .	0 .	0 .	.
COUNCIL MANAGER	47 22.27	63 29.86	49 23.22	52 24.64	211
COMMISSION	6 28.57	7 33.33	3 14.29	5 23.81	21
MAYOR COUNCIL	31 20.67	37 24.67	27 18.00	55 36.67	150
TOTAL	84	107	79	112	382

STATISTICS FOR 2-WAY TABLES

```
CHI-SQUARE                       7.757   DF=   6   PROB=0.2565
PHI                              0.142
CONTINGENCY COEFFICIENT          0.141
CRAMER'S V                       0.101
LIKELIHOOD RATIO CHISQUARE       7.681   DF=   6   PROB=0.2624

GAMMA                            0.116   ASE1=  0.072
KENDALL'S TAU-B                  0.074
STUART'S TAU-C                   0.070   ASE1=  0.044

SOMER'S D C|R                    0.086   ASE1=  0.054
SOMER'S D R|C                    0.062   ASE1=  0.039

PRODUCT MOMENT CORRELATION       0.085
SPEARMAN CORRELATION             0.083

LAMBDA ASYMMETRIC C|R            0.048
LAMBDA ASYMMETRIC R|C            0.018
LAMBDA SYMMETRIC                 0.036

UNCERTAINTY COEFFICIENT C|R      0.007
UNCERTAINTY COEFFICIENT R|C      0.012
UNCERTAINTY COEFFICIENT SYM      0.009
```

ASE1 IS THE ASYMPTOTIC STANDARD ERROR.
R|C MEANS ROW VAR DEPENDENT ON COLUMN VAR.

OBS	POPGRP	REGION	TYPE	_FREQ_	NOVER65	NINCOME	NHOUS	NELLC
1	.		0	383	383	383	383	383
2	.	NORTH CENTRAL	1	106	106	106	106	106
3	.	NORTHEAST	1	70	70	70	70	70
4	.	SOUTH	1	104	104	104	104	104
5	.	WEST	1	103	103	103	103	103
6	50,001-75,000		2	137	137	137	137	137
7	75,001-100,000		2	84	84	84	84	84
8	OVER 100,000		2	162	162	162	162	162
9	50,001-75,000	NORTH CENTRAL	3	38	38	38	38	38
10	50,001-75,000	NORTHEAST	3	29	29	29	29	29
11	50,001-75,000	SOUTH	3	33	33	33	33	33
12	50,001-75,000	WEST	3	37	37	37	37	37
13	75,001-100,000	NORTH CENTRAL	3	29	29	29	29	29
14	75,001-100,000	NORTHEAST	3	14	14	14	14	14
15	75,001-100,000	SOUTH	3	12	12	12	12	12
16	75,001-100,000	WEST	3	29	29	29	29	29
17	OVER 100,000	NORTH CENTRAL	3	39	39	39	39	39
18	OVER 100,000	NORTHEAST	3	27	27	27	27	27
19	OVER 100,000	SOUTH	3	59	59	59	59	59
20	OVER 100,000	WEST	3	37	37	37	37	37

(continued on next page)

(continued from previous page)

OBS	NROB	OVER65	INCOME	HOUSING	ELECTRIC	ROBBERY	INCOMSTD	HOUSESTD	ELECSTD
1	383	9.8042	4795.70	18825.5	18.2115	281.183	858.81	6291.61	4.26653
2	106	9.6311	4960.05	18567.5	16.8752	280.057	860.72	5722.81	2.12504
3	70	12.4800	4510.31	19042.2	22.8900	307.551	727.60	7092.60	4.59811
4	104	9.6269	4500.93	15127.1	17.0462	276.452	765.83	4050.20	3.36547
5	103	8.3427	5118.14	22678.1	17.5839	269.194	878.44	5907.86	4.37326
6	137	9.8672	4830.37	19394.4	18.3340	191.891	951.54	6639.31	4.36218
7	84	9.3226	4880.42	19714.8	18.1894	228.202	1017.79	6828.74	3.85495
8	162	10.0006	4722.44	17883.3	18.1194	384.167	664.02	5573.48	4.40839
9	38	9.4605	5124.00	20164.6	17.2655	180.947	1013.08	6530.92	1.81988
10	29	12.6379	4574.14	19172.7	22.8810	171.862	599.37	6974.04	4.95995
11	33	9.9515	4367.73	14393.0	16.4073	212.758	758.38	3150.85	3.18440
12	37	8.0378	5142.27	23237.7	17.5859	200.216	1065.33	6103.97	4.30066
13	29	8.9862	5115.69	19287.0	16.5179	223.483	1008.90	6156.94	2.15519
14	14	12.1857	4588.00	18652.7	22.1050	209.214	1049.83	7964.61	3.11776
15	12	11.1250	4241.67	14647.7	16.9342	182.667	1120.23	8203.29	3.73625
16	29	7.5310	5050.62	22752.2	18.4900	260.931	862.08	4808.36	4.25216
17	39	10.2769	4684.56	16476.3	16.7605	418.692	417.71	3687.57	2.35949
18	27	12.4630	4401.48	19103.9	23.3067	504.296	668.50	7021.45	4.92376
19	59	9.1407	4628.17	15635.2	17.4264	331.153	667.63	3205.40	3.38968
20	37	9.2838	5146.92	22060.5	16.8716	344.649	684.30	6552.25	4.52185

```
                CENSUS DATA: OUTPUT FROM TABULATE PROCEDURE                       38
        --------------------------------------------------------------
        |               |PER CAPITA MONEY INCOME (1974)|
        |               |-----------------------------|
        |               | N  |   MEAN    |    STD      |
        |---------------+----+-----------+-------------|
        |1975   |REGION |    |           |             |
        |POPUL- |       |    |           |             |
        |ATION  |       |    |           |             |
        |ESTIM- |       |    |           |             |
        |ATE    |       |    |           |             |
        |-------+-------|    |           |             |
        |50,001 |NORTH  |    |           |             |
        |75,000 |CENTR- |    |           |             |
        |       |AL     | 38 |  5124.00  |  1013.08    |
        |       |-------+----+-----------+-------------|
        |       |NORTH- |    |           |             |
        |       |EAST   | 29 |  4574.14  |   599.37    |
        |       |-------+----+-----------+-------------|
        |       |SOUTH  | 33 |  4367.73  |   758.38    |
        |       |-------+----+-----------+-------------|
        |       |WEST   | 37 |  5142.27  |  1065.33    |
        |-------+-------+----+-----------+-------------|
        |75,001 |NORTH  |    |           |             |
        |100,0- |CENTR- |    |           |             |
        |00     |AL     | 29 |  5115.69  |  1008.90    |
        |       |-------+----+-----------+-------------|
        |       |NORTH- |    |           |             |
        |       |EAST   | 14 |  4588.00  |  1049.83    |
        |       |-------+----+-----------+-------------|
        |       |SOUTH  | 12 |  4241.67  |  1120.23    |
        |       |-------+----+-----------+-------------|
        |       |WEST   | 29 |  5050.62  |   862.08    |
        |-------+-------+----+-----------+-------------|
        |OVER   |NORTH  |    |           |             |
        |100,0- |CENTR- |    |           |             |
        |00     |AL     | 39 |  4684.56  |   417.71    |
        |       |-------+----+-----------+-------------|
        |       |NORTH- |    |           |             |
        |       |EAST   | 27 |  4401.48  |   668.50    |
        |       |-------+----+-----------+-------------|
        |       |SOUTH  | 59 |  4628.17  |   667.63    |
        |       |-------+----+-----------+-------------|
        |       |WEST   | 37 |  5146.92  |   684.30    |
        --------------------------------------------------------------
```

Sales Data: Example 2

This example illustrates some advanced INPUT features and displays sales for three products using the SUMMARY, PRINT, and CHART procedures.

Using FORMAT The input data contain sales for each product recorded monthly. In the first step in the example, the FORMAT procedure is used to expand the monthly codes 1-12 into abbreviations.

```
PROC FORMAT;
   VALUE MMM 1=JAN 2=FEB 3=MAR 4=APR 5=MAY 6=JUN
      7=JUL 8=AUG 9=SEP 10=OCT 11=NOV 12=DEC;
```

Data set SALES   The statements below create a SAS data set SALES.

The INPUT statement reads in a hierarchical file containing three different types of records. This hierarchical arrangement reduces the number of keystrokes required during data entry as well as the size of the file. The types of input records are:

- product records with a PRODUCT number
- date records with a DATE value
- sales records with a variable number of CUSTOMER codes and UNIT values.

Each record starts with a record TYPE coded P, D, or S read with the trailing @ format modifier. This "held" input method allows SAS to read further fields from the same INPUT statement in different forms depending on the record's TYPE. P and D input records are retained with a RETAIN statement. For S records, each pair of CUSTOMER and UNIT is output. The data are coded so that a CUSTOMER value of $$ signifies the end of the record. The trailing @ format modifier is discussed in the INPUT statement description in Chapter 3, "Statements Used in the DATA Step." (The technique for hierarchical data is discussed in greater detail in the *SAS Applications Guide* (1980), pp. 63–66.)

```
DATA SALES;
   LENGTH PRODUCT $8 CUSTOMER $8 ;
   RETAIN PRODUCT MONTH YEAR DATE;
   FORMAT DATE DATE. MONTH MMM.;
   INPUT TYPE $ @;  DROP TYPE;
   IF TYPE = 'P' THEN INPUT PRODUCT @;
   ELSE IF TYPE = 'D' THEN DO;
      INPUT DATE :MONYY5.@;
      MONTH=MONTH(DATE);
      YEAR=YEAR(DATE);
      END;
   ELSE IF TYPE = 'S' THEN DO WHILE(1);
      INPUT CUSTOMER $ @;
      IF CUSTOMER='$$' THEN RETURN;
      INPUT UNITS @;
      OUTPUT;
      END;
   CARDS;
P 8401
D DEC81
S GR 1 JP 11 JP 19 OT 1 OR 8 JP 20 GU 5 $$
D NOV81
S GR 1 GR 1 JP 20 GR 1 JP 20 GR 1 $$
D OCT81
S GE 15 OR 11 JP 20 TU 4 GR 1 GR 2 JP 20 GR 1 GR 1 JP 20 GR 1 $$
D SEP81
S JP 20 GR 1 TU 3 GE 15 TU 3 GR 1 JP 28 GU 5 JP 2 OR 15 GR 1 GE 15 $$
D AUG81
S JP 30 TU 3 GR 1 OR 15 GU 3 JP 20 GE 15 GR 2 JP 20 GR 1 $$
D JUL81
S JP 20 GE 15 OR 15 GR 1 GU 5 JP 15 JP 15 TU 3 OR 11 JP 20 GU 5 GE 15  OR 11 $$
D JUN81
```

```
S GE 11 JP 20 OR 10 TU 3 GR 1 GU 10 GU 5 GR 2 OT 1 JP 20 OR 5 GR 1
  GE 10 OR 10 JP 3 GU 4 JP 17 GR 1 $$
D MAY81
S TU 5 OR 2 GU 5 OR 9 JP 20 GR 1 OR 10 OT 1 GR 1 GR 1 JP 12 JP 8 OR 10
  GR 2 $$
D APR81
S GR 2 GU 5 OR 10 GR 1 GR 1 JP 20 OR 10 JP 10 GR 2 GU 5 GR 1 OR 5 GR 1
  GR 1 GR 2 TU 5 OR 10 $$
D MAR81
S JP 15 GR 1 GR 1 GR 1 GR 2 OR 11 JP 12 GU 5 JP 3 TU 5 OT 1 OR 5 JP 15
  OR 10 $$
D FEB81
S JP 5 JP 10 GU 5 JP 10 OR 10 JP 10 OR 10 $$
D JAN81
S JP 10 OR 10 JP 15 OR 10 GU 5 OR 8 TU 5 $$
D DEC80
S JP 10 JP 10 OR 10 JP 10 OR 10 GU 5 $$
D NOV80
S TU 3 JP 10 OR 5 OT 1 JP 1 JP 9 $$
D OCT80
S JP 10 OT 1 JP 5 OR 10 JP 10 OR 9 TU 3 TU 1 $$
D SEP80
S JP 10 OR 10 JP 10 OR 10 JP 10 OR 5 GU 5 OR 2 JP 10 $$
D AUG80
S JP 10 OR 10 JP 10 OR 9 OR 1 TU 6 $$
D JUL80
S GU 5 JP 10 OR 10 JP 5 TU 5 OR 10 JP 8 JP 7 $$
D JUN80
S TU 5 JP 9 GU 5 JP 1 OR 10 JP 10 OR 10 $$
D MAY80
S JP 10 TU 4 TU 4 OR 10 JP 10 OR 10 JP 10 GU 5 $$
D APR80
S OR 10 JP 10 OT 1 OT 1 OR 10 GU 6 JP 10 OR 7 OR 3 JP 10 $$
D MAR80
S OR 11 JP 10 JP 10 OR 5 JP 10 GU 4 JP 10 $$
D FEB80
S JP 10 OR 9 OR 5 JP 10 JP 5 $$
D JAN80
S OR 11 JP 10 JP 10 OR 5 JP 10 GU 4 JP 10 $$
D DEC79
S OR 5 TU 10 JP 5 OR 5 JP 10 $$
D NOV79
S JP 5 OR 5 GU 5 JP 5 JP 1 JP 1 JP 5 $$
D OCT79
S OR 11 TU 10 JP 5 GU 4 JP 5 JP 5 OR 10 JP 5 OR 10 JP 10 $$
D SEP79
S OT 1 OR 10 GU 5 JP 10 OR 12 JP 10 JP 10 OR 10 $$
D AUG79
S GU 4 OR 12 JP 10 JP 10 JP 5 GU 4 OR 10 JP 5 JP 5 $$
D JUL79
S OR 10 JP 5 OT 2 JP 5 GU 4 JP 5 OR 10 JP 3 $$
P 9054
D DEC81
S OT 2 AM 4 $$
D NOV81
S DR 1 DR 4 $$
D OCT81
S CH 3 GR 1 OT 1 CH 3 OT 1 LU 1 $$
D SEP81
S CH 3 OT 1 OT 1 CH 3 DR 5 OT 1 CA 1 $$
D AUG81
S OT 4 OR 1 $$
D JUL81
S DR 3 OR 2 CH 3 OR 3 OT 1 CA 2 OT 1 CA 2 OT 1 OT 1 $$
D JUN81
```

```
S AM 4 DR 4 OT 3 OR 2 CH 3 OT 1 OT 1 DR 3 OR 2 AM 4 DR 3 $$
D MAY81
S DR 1 GA 2 CA 2 OR 1 DR 4 OR 3 $$
D APR81
S AM 4 OT 1 GA 1 DR 1 CH 3 GA 1 DR 2 OT 1 AM 4 OR 2 $$
D MAR81
S AM 4 CA 2 DR 2 DR 2 GA 2 AM 4 OR 2 DR 1 OR 1 AM 1 CH 3 AM 3 $$
D FEB81
S AM 4 DR 2 CA 2 CH 3 AM 3 CA 2 GA 2 $$
D JAN81
S AM 4 DR 2 DR 2 CA 2 DR 2 DR 1 $$
D DEC80
S GA 2 AM 4 CA 2 AM 4 CH 2 AM 4 GA 3 $$
D NOV80
S GA 1 GA 2 AM 4 DR 1 $$
D OCT80
S AM 1 AM 3 GA 2 CH 2 OR 2 DR 2 AM 4 DR 2 OR 1 $$
D SEP80
S AM 4 DR 1 CH 1 DR 1 AM 4 GA 2 DR 1 $$
D AUG80
S GA 2 AM 2 CH 1 AM 2 CH 2 CH 3 DR 2 AM 2 AM 2 $$
D JUL80
S GA 2 AM 4 DR 1 GA 2 AM 4 GA 1 AM 1 AM 3 CH 10 $$
D JUN80
S DR 1 AM 2 GA 1 DR 2 AM 2 CA 3 CA 2 $$
D MAY80
S GA 2 CH 10 OT 1 CA 3 CH 10 CA 3 $$
D APR80
S CH 10 DR 2 CH 10 OT 1 AM 4 DR 2 CA 3 CH 10 OT 1 CA 3 $$
D MAR80
S AM 4 DR 1 CA 4 CH 10 DR 2 GA 2 CH 10 CA 4 OT 1 $$
D FEB80
S CA 4 CH 10 AM 3 CA 4 CA 4 DR 2 CH 8 OT 1 OT 10 DR 1 CH 6 $$
D JAN80
S AM 2 CA 3 CH 6 GA 1 CH 4 OT 1 CA 3 OT 5 CH 4 OT 5 OT 1 CH 6 DR 2 CA 4 $$
D DEC79
S OT 2 AM 1 CH 4 CA 4 $$
D NOV79
S CH 4 CA 4 DR 1 OT 5 CA 4 OT 2 DR 2 $$
D OCT79
S OT 4 CA 3 CA 5 DR 1 CH 4 CA 5 $$
D SEP79
S OT 5 DR 1 CA 2 CH 2 CA 3 OT 4 CA 2 DR 1 CA 3 $$
D AUG79
S DR 1 OT 4 CA 2 CA 5 DR 1 CA 5 CA 4 $$
D JUL79
S OT 4 CH 4 OT 1 CA 3 CA 5 DR 1 CH 3 CH 3 CH 4 $$
D JUN79
S AM 1 CH 6 DR 1 CA 3 CH 6 CA 2 DR 1 $$
D MAY79
S CH 4 OT 4 CA 3 CH 6 DR 1 $$
D APR79
S OT 1 CH 6 DR 1 OT 4 CA 5 CH 4 DR 1 CH 4 $$
D MAR79
S OT 4 GA 1 CH 4 CH 4 DR 1 OT 4 CH 4 $$
D FEB79
S DR 1 OT 2 OT 4 GA 1 CH 4 $$
D JAN79
S OT 4 CA 3 OT 4 $$
P 4005
D DEC81
S I 6 B 13 AM 7 DT 12 O 2 OT 3 $$
D NOV81
S OT 5 DT 29 DH 2 I 7 B 14 AM 7 $$
D OCT81
```

```
S B 23 DT 31 I 6 AM 7 OT 7 DH 2 O 5 $$
D SEP81
S B 24 DT 26 I 5 O 10 AM 8 OT 6 DH 3 $$
D AUG81
S B 31 DT 20 OT 17 I 5 DH 3 O 5 AM 6 $$
D JUL81
S B 24 DT 22 I 5 DH 4 OT 12 O 10 AM 7 $$
D JUN81
S B 20 DT 6 I 4 O 10 OT 6 AM 7 DH 3 $$
D MAY81
S B 30 DT 20 I 5 O 5 AM 8 DH 2 OT 11 $$
D APR81
S B 22 DT 12 O 15 I 4 AM 7 DH 3 OT 7 $$
D MAR81
S B 29 DT 15 O 20 I 4 DH 5 AM 8 OT 5 $$
D FEB81
S B 23 DT 8 O 10 I 3 AM 6 OT 5 DH 2 $$
D JAN81
S B 25 DT 15 O 10 AM 7 DH 6 OT 4 $$
D DEC80
S B 20 DT 7 O 5 AM 7 DH 1 OT 2 $$
D NOV80
S B 16 DT 15 O 10 AM 7 DH 5 OT 3 $$
D OCT80
S B 15 DT 20 AM 6 O 10 DH 3 OT 4 $$
D SEP80
S B 11 DT 8 AM 7 O 15 DH 3 OT 4 $$
D AUG80
S B 16 DT 0 AM 7 O 5 DH 2 OT 2 $$
D JUL80
S B 15 DT 0 AM 7 O 15 DH 3 OT 2 $$
D JUN80
S B 19 DT 0 AM 8 O 5 DH 7 OT 3 $$
D MAY80
S B 20 DT 4 AM 8 O 5 DH 3 OT 3 $$
D APR80
S B 22 DT 13 AM 8 O 10 DH 3 OT 3 $$
D MAR80
S B 20 DT 12 AM 9 O 15 DH 2 OT 5 $$
D FEB80
S B 21 DT 7 AM 7 O 10 DH 2 OT 2 $$
D JAN80
S B 19 DT 0 AM 8 DH 3 OT 7 $$
D DEC79
S B 10 DT 4 AM 7 DH 3 OT 5 $$
D NOV79
S B 19 DT 12 AM 6 DH 2 OT 2 $$
D OCT79
S B 24 DT 17 AM 6 DH 0 OT 1 $$
D SEP79
S B 15 DT 10 AM 4 DH 2 OT 3 $$
D AUG79
S B 16 DT 12 AM 8 DH 4 OT 2 $$
D JUL79
S B 17 DT 8 AM 6 DH 2 OT 3 $$
D JUN79
S B 18 DT 11 AM 2 DH 2 OT 2 $$
D MAY79
S B 11 DT 19 AM 8 DH 3 OT 8 $$
D APR79
S B 14 DT 14 AM 8 DH 0 OT 15 $$
D MAR79
S B 12 DT 14 AM 6 DH 2 OT 26 $$
D FEB79
S B 15 DT 11 AM 3 DH 0 OT 28 $$
```

D JAN79
S B 15 DT 8 AM 4 DH 3 OT 26 $$
  ;

Data set SALES2 The next DATA step shows how a SET statement can be used
with a KEEP (or DROP) statement to subset the variables in an existing SAS data set.
These statements:

    DATA SALES2;
      SET SALES;
      KEEP PRODUCT DATE YEAR UNITS;

create data set SALES2, which contains only the variables PRODUCT, DATE, YEAR,
and UNIT from data set SALES.

Using SUMMARY and PRINT Below are the statements that ask PROC
SUMMARY to create an output data set containing summary statistics for two
CLASS variables, PRODUCT and DATE. Since SUMMARY produces no printed out-
put, the PRINT procedure is used to display the contents of the SUMMARY data
set.

    PROC SUMMARY DATA=SALES;
      CLASS PRODUCT DATE;
      VAR UNITS;
      ID YEAR;
      OUTPUT OUT=B SUM=SALES;
    PROC PRINT DATA=B;

```
                              SAS                                        1

  OBS   YEAR   PRODUCT      DATE     _TYPE_    _FREQ_    SALES

    1   1981                  .         0        742     4781
    2   1979              01JAN79       1          8       67
    3   1979              01FEB79       1         10       69
    4   1979              01MAR79       1         12       82
    5   1979              01APR79       1         13       77
    6   1979              01MAY79       1         10       67
    7   1979              01JUN79       1         12       55
    8   1979              01JUL79       1         22      108
    9   1979              01AUG79       1         21      129
   10   1979              01SEP79       1         22      125
   11   1979              01OCT79       1         21      145
   12   1979              01NOV79       1         19       90
   13   1979              01DEC79       1         14       75
   14   1980              01JAN80       1         26      144
   15   1980              01FEB80       1         22      141
   16   1980              01MAR80       1         22      161
   17   1980              01APR80       1         26      173
   18   1980              01MAY80       1         20      135
   19   1980              01JUN80       1         20      105
   20   1980              01JUL80       1         23      130
   21   1980              01AUG80       1         21       96
   22   1980              01SEP80       1         22      134
   23   1980              01OCT80       1         23      126
   24   1980              01NOV80       1         16       93
   25   1980              01DEC80       1         19      118
   26   1981              01JAN81       1         19      143
   27   1981              01FEB81       1         21      135
   28   1981              01MAR81       1         33      200
   29   1981              01APR81       1         34      181
   30   1981              01MAY81       1         27      181
   31   1981              01JUN81       1         36      220
   32   1981              01JUL81       1         30      254
   33   1981              01AUG81       1         19      202
   34   1981              01SEP81       1         26      206
   35   1981              01OCT81       1         24      187
   36   1981              01NOV81       1         14      113
   37   1981              01DEC81       1         15      114
   38   1981    4005                    2        212     1967
   39   1981    8401                    2        270     2062
   40   1981    9054                    2        260      752
```

(continued on next page)

(continued from previous page)

41	1979	4005	01JAN79	3	5	56
42	1979	4005	01FEB79	3	5	57
43	1979	4005	01MAR79	3	5	60
44	1979	4005	01APR79	3	5	51
45	1979	4005	01MAY79	3	5	49
46	1979	4005	01JUN79	3	5	35
47	1979	4005	01JUL79	3	5	36
48	1979	4005	01AUG79	3	5	42
49	1979	4005	01SEP79	3	5	34
50	1979	4005	01OCT79	3	5	48
51	1979	4005	01NOV79	3	5	41
52	1979	4005	01DEC79	3	5	29
53	1980	4005	01JAN80	3	5	37
54	1980	4005	01FEB80	3	6	49
55	1980	4005	01MAR80	3	6	63
56	1980	4005	01APR80	3	6	59

SAS

2

OBS	YEAR	PRODUCT	DATE	_TYPE_	_FREQ_	SALES
57	1980	4005	01MAY80	3	6	43
58	1980	4005	01JUN80	3	6	42
59	1980	4005	01JUL80	3	6	42
60	1980	4005	01AUG80	3	6	32
61	1980	4005	01SEP80	3	6	48
62	1980	4005	01OCT80	3	6	58
63	1980	4005	01NOV80	3	6	56
64	1980	4005	01DEC80	3	6	42
65	1981	4005	01JAN81	3	6	67
66	1981	4005	01FEB81	3	7	57
67	1981	4005	01MAR81	3	7	86
68	1981	4005	01APR81	3	7	70
69	1981	4005	01MAY81	3	7	81
70	1981	4005	01JUN81	3	7	56
71	1981	4005	01JUL81	3	7	84
72	1981	4005	01AUG81	3	7	87
73	1981	4005	01SEP81	3	7	82
74	1981	4005	01OCT81	3	7	81
75	1981	4005	01NOV81	3	6	64
76	1981	4005	01DEC81	3	6	43
77	1979	8401	01JUL79	3	8	44
78	1979	8401	01AUG79	3	9	65
79	1979	8401	01SEP79	3	8	68
80	1979	8401	01OCT79	3	10	75
81	1979	8401	01NOV79	3	7	27
82	1979	8401	01DEC79	3	5	35
83	1980	8401	01JAN80	3	7	60
84	1980	8401	01FEB80	3	5	39
85	1980	8401	01MAR80	3	7	60
86	1980	8401	01APR80	3	10	68
87	1980	8401	01MAY80	3	8	63
88	1980	8401	01JUN80	3	7	50
89	1980	8401	01JUL80	3	8	60
90	1980	8401	01AUG80	3	6	46
91	1980	8401	01SEP80	3	9	72
92	1980	8401	01OCT80	3	8	49
93	1980	8401	01NOV80	3	6	29
94	1980	8401	01DEC80	3	6	55
95	1981	8401	01JAN81	3	7	63
96	1981	8401	01FEB81	3	7	60
97	1981	8401	01MAR81	3	14	87
98	1981	8401	01APR81	3	17	91
99	1981	8401	01MAY81	3	14	87
100	1981	8401	01JUN81	3	18	134
101	1981	8401	01JUL81	3	13	151
102	1981	8401	01AUG81	3	10	110
103	1981	8401	01SEP81	3	12	109
104	1981	8401	01OCT81	3	11	96
105	1981	8401	01NOV81	3	6	44
106	1981	8401	01DEC81	3	7	65
107	1979	9054	01JAN79	3	3	11
108	1979	9054	01FEB79	3	5	12
109	1979	9054	01MAR79	3	7	22
110	1979	9054	01APR79	3	8	26
111	1979	9054	01MAY79	3	5	18
112	1979	9054	01JUN79	3	7	20

			SAS			3
OBS	YEAR	PRODUCT	DATE	_TYPE_	_FREQ_	SALES
113	1979	9054	01JUL79	3	9	28
114	1979	9054	01AUG79	3	7	22
115	1979	9054	01SEP79	3	9	23
116	1979	9054	01OCT79	3	6	22
117	1979	9054	01NOV79	3	7	22
118	1979	9054	01DEC79	3	4	11
119	1980	9054	01JAN80	3	14	47
120	1980	9054	01FEB80	3	11	53
121	1980	9054	01MAR80	3	9	38
122	1980	9054	01APR80	3	10	46
123	1980	9054	01MAY80	3	6	29
124	1980	9054	01JUN80	3	7	13
125	1980	9054	01JUL80	3	9	28
126	1980	9054	01AUG80	3	9	18
127	1980	9054	01SEP80	3	7	14
128	1980	9054	01OCT80	3	9	19
129	1980	9054	01NOV80	3	4	8
130	1980	9054	01DEC80	3	7	21
131	1981	9054	01JAN81	3	6	13
132	1981	9054	01FEB81	3	7	18
133	1981	9054	01MAR81	3	12	27
134	1981	9054	01APR81	3	10	20
135	1981	9054	01MAY81	3	6	13
136	1981	9054	01JUN81	3	11	30
137	1981	9054	01JUL81	3	10	19
138	1981	9054	01AUG81	3	2	5
139	1981	9054	01SEP81	3	7	15
140	1981	9054	01OCT81	3	6	10
141	1981	9054	01NOV81	3	2	5
142	1981	9054	01DEC81	3	2	6

Data set C   The purpose of the next DATA step is to reshape SUMMARY's output data set B for display with the CHART procedure. This example of the SET statement subsets the observations in data set B with a subsetting IF statement. The statements are:

```
DATA C;
  SET B;
  IF __TYPE__ = 3;
```

Using CHART   The statements below display the __TYPE__ = 3 observations from the SUMMARY data set, now in data set C, with PROC CHART:

```
PROC CHART;
  HBAR DATE / SUMVAR = SALES GROUP = PRODUCT;
  VBAR YEAR / DISCRETE SUBGROUP = PRODUCT;
  BLOCK PRODUCT / GROUP = YEAR;
  PIE PRODUCT / FREQ = SALES;
```

See the CHART procedure for a complete discussion of HBAR, VBAR, BLOCK, and PIE CHARTs.

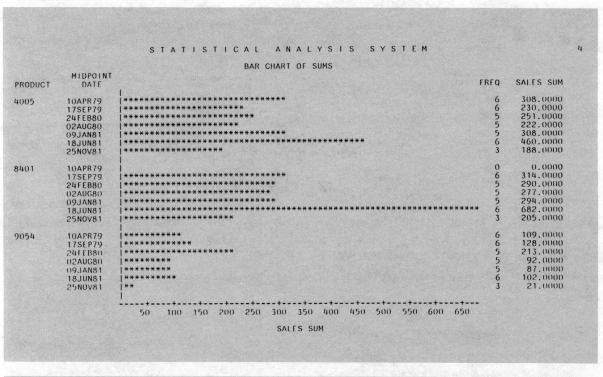

```
                    S T A T I S T I C A L   A N A L Y S I S   S Y S T E M                                    4
                                        BAR CHART OF SUMS
              MIDPOINT
PRODUCT        DATE                                                                           FREQ    SALES SUM
                          |
4005          10APR79     |*****************************                                        6     308.0000
              17SEP79     |*********************                                                6     230.0000
              24FEB80     |***********************                                              5     251.0000
              02AUG80     |********************                                                 5     222.0000
              09JAN81     |****************************                                         5     308.0000
              18JUN81     |*******************************************                          6     460.0000
              25NOV81     |*****************                                                    3     188.0000
                          |
8401          10APR79     |                                                                    0       0.0000
              17SEP79     |*****************************                                        6     314.0000
              24FEB80     |**************************                                           5     290.0000
              02AUG80     |*************************                                            5     277.0000
              09JAN81     |**************************                                           5     294.0000
              18JUN81     |**************************************************************       6     682.0000
              25NOV81     |*******************                                                  3     205.0000
                          |
9054          10APR79     |**********                                                           6     109.0000
              17SEP79     |************                                                         6     128.0000
              24FEB80     |*******************                                                  5     213.0000
              02AUG80     |********                                                             5      92.0000
              09JAN81     |********                                                             5      87.0000
              18JUN81     |*********                                                            6     102.0000
              25NOV81     |**                                                                   3      21.0000
                          |
                          -----+----+----+----+----+----+----+----+----+----+----+----+----+---
                              50   100  150  200  250  300  350  400  450  500  550  600  650

                                               SALES SUM
```

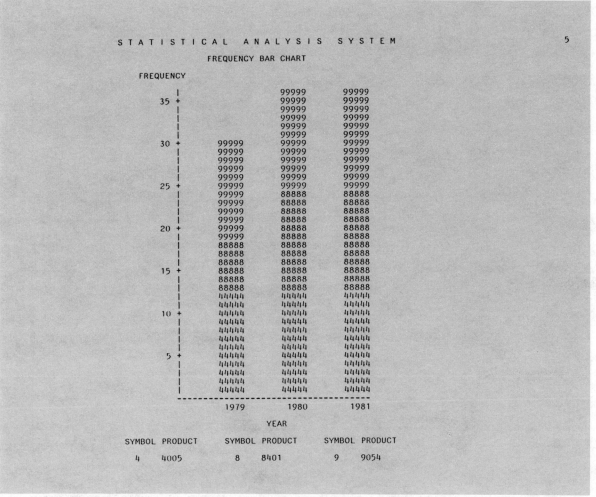

```
                    S T A T I S T I C A L   A N A L Y S I S   S Y S T E M                                    5
                                      FREQUENCY BAR CHART
         FREQUENCY
                 |                            99999          99999
            35 + |                            99999          99999
                 |                            99999          99999
                 |                            99999          99999
                 |                            99999          99999
                 |                            99999          99999
            30 + |             99999          99999          99999
                 |             99999          99999          99999
                 |             99999          99999          99999
                 |             99999          99999          99999
                 |             99999          99999          99999
            25 + |             99999          99999          99999
                 |             99999          88888          88888
                 |             99999          88888          88888
                 |             99999          88888          88888
                 |             99999          88888          88888
            20 + |             99999          88888          88888
                 |             99999          88888          88888
                 |             88888          88888          88888
                 |             88888          88888          88888
                 |             88888          88888          88888
            15 + |             88888          88888          88888
                 |             88888          88888          88888
                 |             88888          88888          88888
                 |             44444          44444          44444
                 |             44444          44444          44444
            10 + |             44444          44444          44444
                 |             44444          44444          44444
                 |             44444          44444          44444
                 |             44444          44444          44444
                 |             44444          44444          44444
             5 + |             44444          44444          44444
                 |             44444          44444          44444
                 |             44444          44444          44444
                 |             44444          44444          44444
                 |             44444          44444          44444
                 ------------------------------------------------------
                                 1979           1980           1981

                                               YEAR

              SYMBOL  PRODUCT       SYMBOL  PRODUCT       SYMBOL  PRODUCT

                4      4005            8      8401           9      9054
```

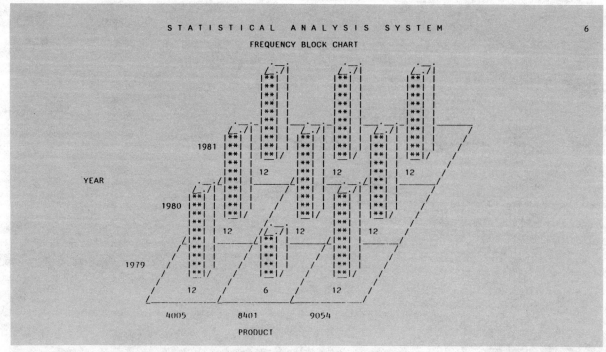

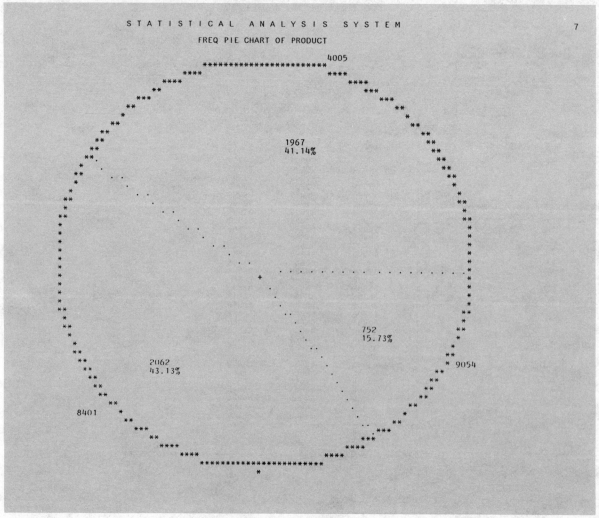

REFERENCE

U.S. Bureau of the Census (1977), *County and City Data Book, 1977* (Machine-readable data file) Washington, D.C.: U.S. Government Printing Office.

FEATURES FOR BOTH DATA AND PROC STEPS

Introduction to the SAS System

SAS Statements Used Anywhere

SAS Data Sets

SAS Informats and Formats

Missing Values

SAS Macro Language

SAS Log and Procedure Output

Introduction to the SAS System

INTRODUCTION

To provide insight into SAS's structure for the advanced programmer, this chapter describes the current internal organization of SAS as implemented for IBM System/360- and System/370-compatible machines. In its general charter to be a complete tool for managing and analyzing data, the design goals described below were adopted to make SAS easy to use. You do not need to learn any of the material in this section in order to use SAS. Future versions of SAS may look completely different internally, yet perform the same from a user's point of view.

DESIGN GOALS

The following goals shaped the development of SAS:

- SAS should be immediately usable, even by those who do not have extensive computer experience. Basics should be teachable in a few minutes. SAS should enable end-users to do their own computer processing if they choose to do so, rather than relying on computer specialists.
- SAS should be a complete tool for the researcher; SAS should manage the data as well as analyze them. Users should not have to learn one system to maintain and process data and another system to analyze them.
- Data management should be separate from analysis. Data processing functions need the flexibility of a programming language. Data analysis, however, can be packaged into the terms of the analysis. Thus in the DATA step you specify a program for how to process data. In a PROC step you simply request what you want done. Since all the data preparation is done in the DATA step, packaging the data in a uniform way, the procedure is freed from considering the form of the data.

- A special-purpose analysis that is not encompassed within any procedure that SAS provides may be programmed in either the DATA step or PROC MATRIX or by combining existing PROCs and DATA step programming.
- SAS should maintain a uniform and concise syntax. Procedures have similar control languages. The DATA step language is reasonably small. All control language is specified in a free-format syntax.
- SAS should require a minimum of instructions. The user should not have to specify anything the system can figure out for itself. For example, most SAS DATA steps do not need declarations or attribute statements for variables or files. Where the user can make a choice, reasonable default choices are made by the system if the user does not specify.
- User errors should be diagnosed clearly and immediately.
- SAS should not be limited in the number or size of data sets, nor in the number or size of the analyses.
- Results from one step should be available as input for the next step.
- Procedures should be as general and widely applicable as possible and have a variety of options for specifying the format, nature, and extent of their output.
- Procedures should be able to run repeatedly on breakdowns of the data according to a grouping variable. The BY-group facility handles this.
- Data should be handled in a simple, standardized, easy-to-use form. The rectangular self-describing data model serves most data processing needs well. Variables have few attributes, and they usually can be determined from context. Once the data are in the form of a SAS data set, the data are described inside the file.
- Missing values should be handled naturally and consistently.
- SAS should operate interactively in the same form as in batch.
- SAS should be extendable by users and shall be extended by SAS Institute.

In addition to the general goals described above, more specific design goals were related to the implementation of SAS.

- The core of the system should be compact and reentrant so that it can be installed in a read-only, shareable system area.
- A minimum of operating system control language should be used.
- The system should be able to run most jobs in under 192K of memory.
- SAS should be able to group many data sets in a library-like file. In this way, data are managed more simply, and fewer operating system limitations are encountered. Space can be managed intelligently, unlike OS partitioned data sets, which need to be periodically compressed to recover unused space.
- The SAS supervisor should provide the facilities and supporting interfaces so that the statistical and reporting procedures can be written in higher-level languages so they may be better written and maintained.
- Procedures should be separate modules so that there are no limits to their number, and so they can be developed and maintained as individual units.

SYSTEM OVERVIEW

SAS is a library of modules tied together by a central supervisory program. The supervisor and its service routines provide a common way of handling basic system functions.

The supervisor brings in other modules as needed from the program library. There are two classes of modules that may be called in, depending on whether SAS is running a DATA step or a PROC step. Within each DATA or PROC step, there are separate modules that are brought in: first "parsing" modules are called to examine the control language and compile it into a control information file; next the "execution" module is loaded and called to actually perform the step.

Supervisor

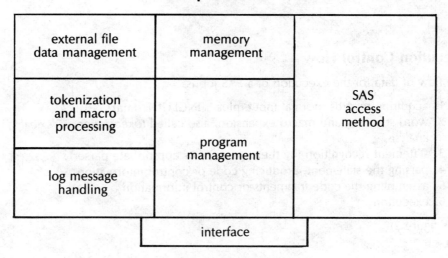

Library

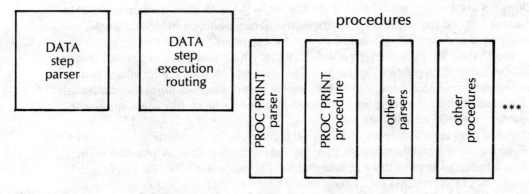

Fig. 1

Implementation

The supervisor and DATA step are written exclusively in reentrant System/360-370 assembler language. This provides SAS with the opportunity to be compact and efficient, especially for data-processing jobs. Most procedures are written in PL/I, although assembler, FORTRAN, and COBOL procedures are also supported.

The Supervisor

The supervisor handles the following:

- program management, that is, initiating and terminating steps
- memory management
- access method services for SAS data libraries
- data management services for external files
- control language and macro processing
- log message handling
- global statements such as OPTIONS.

Execution Control Flow

The flow of data for the execution of a SAS job is:

1. acquiring records (normal input, plus %INCLUDE data)
2. word scanning and macro expansion, also called *tokenization* or *lexical analysis*
3. statement recognition (by the supervisor or appropriate parser)
4. parsing the statement, producing code or control information
5. assembling the code fragments or control information
6. execution.

(See figure 2)

SAS Data Library Access Method

Under OS and VSE, SAS uses channel program-level access to manage data on direct-access storage devices in the form of SAS data libraries. Although SAS data libraries are marked with the attribute DSORG=DA, SAS does not use the BDAM access method (basic direct access method). (Preformatting a BDAM data set is too inefficient and, once formatted, it cannot be extended.)

A SAS data library starts with a directory file, which may have additional pieces (subextents) scattered later in the file. The directory records the locations and attributes of the SAS data sets and other logical files in the data library. Each logical file described by the directory is mapped into one or more physical "subextent" pieces in the OS or VSE data set.

A SAS data set is written to a SAS logical file in two pieces: the descriptor records describe the file and its variables, then the data records follow. A SAS data set may be extended to any length by aquiring additional "subextents" in the physical data set or blocks in the CMS file system. Empty space may appear in OS and VSE data libraries as files are deleted or replaced. SAS always uses the lowest unreserved space available to form new "subextents" to store data. In this way, the data set does not need to be "compressed" periodically. (See figure 3)

Control Flow: compiling

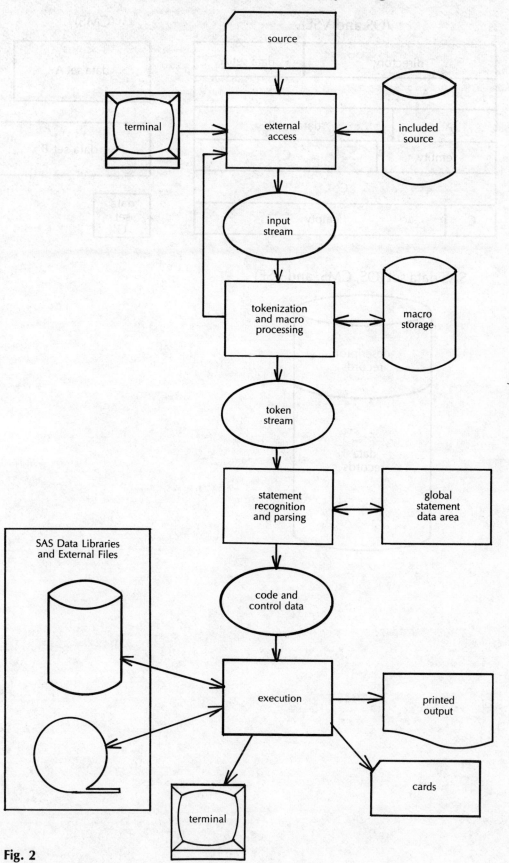

Fig. 2

SAS Data Library

(OS and VSE)   (CMS)

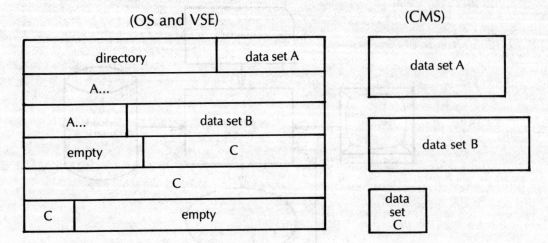

SAS data set (OS, CMS, and VSE)

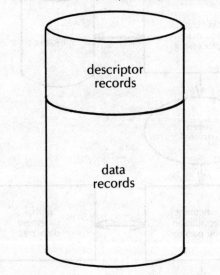

Fig. 3

The DATA Step

The DATA step, like all steps, is handled in two phases: compilation, then execution. The compilation phase includes these components:

- symbol table manager and list processor
- arithmetic statement and external file I/O compiler
- SAS data set access compiler and definition routines
- machine code generation
- object code assembler.

The compile phase produces an object file of control information, which is available for the execution phase. The execution phase consists of:

- object code relocating linking loader
- compiled program execution monitor
- arithmetic statement and external file transient support routines
- SAS data set access transient support routines
- library functions, formats, and similar items.

The execution phase loads and relocates the compiled object file, link edits any required transient support routine and library function references into the loaded program, and directs the execution of the resulting machine language program.

The PROC Step

The supervisor looks in the program libraries available to the SAS job for a module with the name of the procedure. Usually this module is a "parsing" module, a small program built from assembler macros to recognize control language and construct an internal control information object file. Then the "parsing" module is deleted, and the real procedure module is brought in and run.

In addition to the procedure "parsing" module, all of the services required for the DATA step compilation are available. Indeed, several SAS procedures dynamically generate machine language subroutines for efficient data handling.

During execution, the procedure requests various services from the supervisor through an interface routine that accomplishes the jump across the modules. The services are grouped into those which:

- obtain control information from the parser internal control information object file
- read and write observations in SAS data sets
- allocate/free memory
- perform other services, such as printing titles.

The entry points that are used for these services are all documented in the *SAS Programmer's Guide*. Users can write their own FORTRAN or PL/I procedures for use with SAS, following the directions and examples in that book. It is also possible to write COBOL procedures.

SAS FEATURES FOR BOTH DATA AND PROC STEPS

The remainder of this section of the manual describes SAS features that are applicable to both DATA and PROC steps. Topics discussed include SAS data sets, SAS informats and formats, missing values, the macro language, the SAS log, and output from procedures.

The following statements can be used anywhere in a SAS program, either outside of or within either DATA or PROC steps. The statements are divided into four groups: information and system control, listing/printout control, external services, and source language processing. The statements used with the SAS macro language can be used anywhere. These are documented in Chapter 15, "SAS Macro Language."

Information and system control

HELP	allows you to access additional information about SAS and your SAS installation.
OPTIONS	allows you to change SAS system options.
RUN	causes the previously entered SAS step to begin execution.
TITLE	specifies title lines to be written with SAS output.

Listing/printout control

CLEAR	used interactively under TSO or CMS, optionally pauses and then causes the terminal screen to be cleared and execution to proceed.
COMMENT	allows you to write comments with your SAS statements to document the program.
PAGE	causes SAS to skip to the top of the next page of the SAS log.
%PUT	prints text on the SAS log.
SKIP	causes SAS to skip a number of lines on the SAS log.

External services

CMS	causes CMS commands to be executed during a SAS session.
TSO	causes TSO commands or CLISTs to be executed during a SAS session.
X	is used to issue a TSO or CMS command from within a SAS job.

Source language processing

ENDSAS	causes SAS to terminate execution immediately.
%INCLUDE	includes SAS source lines from external files in a SAS program.
%LIST	lists previously entered SAS statements.
MACRO	allows you to name and store a segment of a SAS program and call it later with a macro name.
%RUN	ends source statements included by a %INCLUDE statement.

SAS Statements Used Anywhere

The SAS statements that can appear anywhere in a SAS job are described alphabetically in this chapter.

    CLEAR Statement
    CMS Statement
    Comment Statement
    ENDSAS Statement
    HELP Statement
    %INCLUDE Statement
    %LIST Statement
    MACRO Statement
    OPTIONS Statement
    PAGE Statement
    %PUT Statement
    RUN Statement
    %RUN Statement
    SKIP Statement
    TITLE Statement
    TSO Statement
    X Statement

CLEAR Statement

The CLEAR statement is used when SAS is executing interactively under TSO or CMS; otherwise it is ignored. The CLEAR statement causes the screen of the terminal to be cleared and SAS execution to proceed. The form of the CLEAR statement is:

CLEAR [PAUSE];

where

> **PAUSE** tells SAS to wait for you to press ENTER on your terminal before proceeding. The screen is cleared **after** you respond, so that you may review SAS output up to that point.

Unless you are executing SAS under TSO or CMS on a full-screen terminal (for example, an IBM 3275, 3276, 3277, 3278, or 3279), the system option DEVICE= must be set to the type of terminal that you are using (see the OPTIONS statement later in this chapter).

Note: the following terminal device names are supported by the CLEAR statement (the names follow SAS/GRAPH conventions):

HP2647	TEK4012	TEK4024	TEK4052
HP2648	TEK4013	TEK4025	TEK4053
RAM6200	TEK4014	TEK4027	TEK4054
TEK4010	TEK4016		

Additional terminals may be supported at your installation. Check with your installation personnel to see if they have customized SAS to support your display terminal.

CMS Statement

The CMS statement is used to invoke a CMS or CP command during a SAS job. The statement may appear in a DATA or PROC step, or between steps in the job. The form of the CMS statement is:

>   **CMS** *CMScommand*;

or

>   **CMS CP** *CPcommand*;

where

>>   *CMScommand*   is any CMS command.
>>   *CPcommand*   is any CP command.

The command is invoked immediately when the CMS statement is executed. Any CMS or CP command may be issued from the CMS statement as long as the statement does not destroy your environment.
Enter the command

>   CMS;

to enter the CMS subset. The system prompts you for CMS commands. When you want to return to SAS, issue the CMS command

>   RETURN   .

The CMS statement is treated as a comment when it appears in a job running under some other operating system.
See the *SAS CMS Companion* for more information.

COMMENT Statement

The COMMENT statement may be used anywhere in your SAS job to document the purpose of the job, to explain any unusual segments of the program, or to describe the steps in a complex program or calculation. The form of the COMMENT statement is:

    COMMENT *message*;

or

   * *message*;

where

        message   explains or documents the job. The message can be any length, although it cannot contain semicolons.

Any number of COMMENT statements may be used in a job. The COMMENT statement **must** end in a semicolon. Macro variables and macro calls are not expanded in SAS comments.

Both of these statements are comments:

```
*THIS CODE FINDS THE NUMBER IN THE BY GROUP;
COMMENT PRINT MAXIMUM EARNED THIS YEAR;
```

Drawing a box around comments is a useful way to document your SAS job:

```
* -------------------------------------------------------------------------------- *
|                              This is a box-style                                 |
|                                   comment                                        |
* -------------------------------------------------------------------------------- *  ;
```

Comments of the form

```
/* message */
```

can also be used, and can appear within SAS statements anywhere a single blank can appear.

For example, the statement

```
PROC SORT /* SORT THE DATA SET */;
```

is a valid SAS statement. Comments within a TITLE statement are replaced with blanks when the title is printed. (Do not begin comments of this form in column 1. When the /* appears in columns 1 and 2, it is treated as JCL.)

ENDSAS Statement

The ENDSAS statement causes SAS to terminate execution immediately.
The form of the ENDSAS statement is:

ENDSAS;

HELP Statement

If the SAS HELP facility was selected by your installation at the time SAS was installed, then you can use the HELP statement to obtain additional information about SAS procedures, statements, formats and informats, functions and call routines, and the status of SAS products installed at your computing installation.
 The form of the HELP statement is:

   HELP [*keyword*] [*/options*];

where

keyword	specifies the name of a SAS procedure, statement, or other feature about which you want to obtain additional information. For a complete list of possible keywords, enter the statement

   HELP;

These special keywords can also be specified:

SASNEWS	gives the status of the current SAS release at your installation. This information is provided initially for each major SAS release by SAS Institute and may be updated locally for each maintenance release.
SITEINFO	provides information on your computing installation. This information is maintained by your installation personnel, and normally includes the name of your SAS Installation Representative and the individual you should contact to report problems or to obtain assistance.
NEWS	gives news supplied and maintained by your installation personnel.
PROCS	briefly describes each SAS procedure for which HELP is available.
FORMATS	lists SAS formats and informats and their attributes.
FUNCTIONS	lists SAS functions and call routines and gives a brief description of each.
STMTS	lists other SAS statements.

The option below may be specified on the HELP statement following a slash (/).

FS/NOFS	If you are executing SAS interactively on a full screen terminal and the SAS system option FS is in effect or has been specified, then the information is presented in full-screen format and you can use all of the facilities of FSLIST to examine the text.
	Specify FS if you have SAS/FSP installed but the SAS system option NOFS is in effect and you want to review the help information in full screen browse mode.
	Specify NOFS if you have SAS/FSP installed and the SAS system option FS is in effect but you do **not** want to review the help information in full screen browse mode.

If no keyword or option is specified in the HELP statement, SAS prints a brief description of how to use the HELP statement and provides a listing of keywords that may be specified.

%INCLUDE Statement

The %INCLUDE (or %INC) statement is used to include SAS source lines from external files. Any input from sequential data sets or members of a partitioned data set may be included. (The %INCLUDE statement is not supported under VSE.)
   The form of the %INCLUDE statement is:

   %INCLUDE *source ... / options* **;**

or

   %INC *source ... / options* **;**

where

source	specifies the SAS source lines to be input.
options	specifies one or more options effective only for the execution or duration of the %INCLUDE statement (unless an OPTIONS statement in the included source overrides an option in the %INCLUDE statement).

Source values that may be specified are:

DDname	includes input from an external sequential file described in the job control by *DDname*.
DDname (member,...member)	includes input from one or more members of a partitioned data set.
n	includes the nth spooled line.
n:m	includes the nth through m^{th} spooled line.
*	includes input source from the terminal. This feature is useful for embedding statements into fixed code contained in an external file, or for embedding one or more lines between lines included from the spooled file or external file. Indicate the end of the source with the %RUN statement, described in this chapter.

For example, suppose a file with DDname IN1 contains the SAS statements below:

```
DATA;
  INFILE NEW;
  INPUT X Y Z;
  %INCLUDE *;
PROC PRINT;
RUN;
```

When you issue the statement

```
%INCLUDE IN1;
```

and the %INCLUDE * is encountered, the system waits for you to enter statements. You enter

```
MONTH='JANUARY';
TITLE DATA FOR MONTH OF JANUARY;
%RUN;
```

The %RUN returns execution to the statements in IN1 where processing continues. These options may appear in the %INCLUDE statement:

> SOURCE2   lists the source from included files on the SAS log, regardless of how the SOURCE2/NOSOURCE2 system option is specified. (See the OPTIONS statement description for more information about the SOURCE2/NOSOURCE2 system option.)
>
> JCLEXCL   ignores any lines in the included source that begin with two slash marks or a slash and an asterisk in columns 1 and 2.
>
> S2=*length*   specifies the length of the record to be used for input.

A %INCLUDE statement must begin at a statement boundary. That is, it must be the first statement in a SAS job or immediately follow a semicolon ending another statement. A %INCLUDE statement may be a statement in a file that is %INCLUDEd. There is no limit to the level of nesting of %INCLUDE statements.

Below are two examples using the %INCLUDE statement:

Example 1: Including Parmcards

Although a %INCLUDE statement may not immediately follow a PARMCARDS or CARDS statement, it is possible to %INCLUDE parmcards using the following approach. Suppose a file described with DDname DD1 contains the SAS statement

```
PARMCARDS;
```

and the file DD2 contains the parmcards you want to include with an invocation of your own procedure. Then these statements let you input the parmcards:

```
PROC MYPROC;
%INCLUDE DD1 DD2;
RUN;
```

Example 2: Variable in a TITLE Statement

You can include a variable in a SAS TITLE statement using the %INCLUDE statement. The statements below create a title that includes a variable named TODAY containing the current date. The TITLE statement is written to an output file using PUT statements. (The file with DDname NEW has been described in the control language for the job.) In the PROC step, the %INCLUDE statement reads the file containing the TITLE statement.

```
DATA_NULL_;
  TODAY = TODAY( );
  FILE NEW;
  PUT 'TITLE DAILY REPORT'
  'FOR' TODAY DATE. ';  ';
RUN;
PROC PRINT DATA = ANYDATA;
  %INCLUDE NEW;
```

Note that you can use màcro variables to include a variable in a TITLE statement. See Chapter 15, "SAS Macro Language," for details.

%LIST Statement

The %LIST statement can be used anywhere in a SAS job (except after a CARDS or PARMCARDS statement) to list spooled lines. Spooled lines are the SAS source statements in your job that SAS saves when the system option SPOOL is in effect.

The form of the %LIST statement is:

> **%LIST** [[n]:m];

where

> n   gives the first spooled line you want listed. If only one line is to be listed, specify only the n value.
>
> m   gives the last spooled line in a range that you want listed. If only one line is to be listed, no *m* value is needed.

If neither n nor m is specified, all spooled lines are listed.

MACRO Statement

The MACRO statement allows you to name and store a segment of a SAS program, then substitute that name for the program segment wherever the segment is to appear later in the job. The segment can be part of a SAS statement, a complete statement, or several statements. The stored segment is called a macro.

The MACRO statement, a feature of earlier versions of SAS, should not be confused with the %MACRO statement, used to define macros in the new macro language. Although this MACRO statement is still supported, the new SAS macro language provides much more power and flexibility. While the MACRO statement allows only text substitution, the macro language allows text substitution, parameters, and conditional execution of macros (including macro programming statements and macro functions). See Chapter 15, "SAS Macro Language," for more information.

The form of the MACRO statement is

MACRO *name text***%**

The MACRO statement ends with a % sign, not a semicolon. These terms may be used with a macro statement:

name   names the macro. The name specified must be a valid SAS name.

text   specifies the macro text, which may include part of a SAS statement, a complete SAS statement, or several SAS statements. To include a percent sign (%) as part of a macro without signaling the end of the macro, code two percent signs (%%):

> MACRO PCT IF X=10 THEN A=
>   'EQUALS 10%%';   %

There is no limit to the length of a macro, and a macro definition may appear anywhere in a SAS program. However, before a macro name can be used, it must be defined. If you create two macros with the same name in a single job, the second macro replaces the first.

Statements within a macro are not executed, nor is syntax checked, until the macro name appears in the program (the macro call). Data lines or lines following a PARMCARDS statement may not be included in a macro. There is no limit on the number of levels of macro nesting allowed.

Macro names in titles   Once a macro has been defined, SAS expands the macro anywhere its name appears in the job. You can take advantage of this expansion to change many TITLE statements in a job by changing only one macro definition. For example, say that you want the current month to appear in the title of the reports produced in a program. You might use statements like these:

MACRO THISMNTH APRIL%
TITLE REPORT FOR THISMNTH;

When the word THISMNTH appears in the job, SAS substitutes the word APRIL. See Chapter 15, "SAS Macro Language," for a more efficient way to change the text in a TITLE statement.

If you use a macro name in a TITLE statement and do not want it expanded, enclose the title in single quotes. For example, say you had defined a macro named MONTH but wanted to use the word MONTH, not the expanded macro named MONTH, in a title:

TITLE 'FIGURES FOR THE MONTH';

Printing macro expansions   SAS does not normally print the statements included in a macro on the SAS log when the macro name appears in the job. You can list expanded macros by changing the system option NOMACROGEN to MACROGEN; include this statement at the beginning of your SAS statements:

OPTIONS MACROGEN;

Macro libraries   You can simulate a macro library facility using the %INCLUDE statement (see a description in this chapter) or by putting your macros in a sequential data set which is concatenated to the front of the SYSIN file. (Under VSE data sets cannot be concatenated. The macros must be included at the front of the input stream.)

Macro statements   The following statements are valid only for macros created using the MACRO statement. All of the statements are preceded by a % sign and are executed immediately.

%ACTIVATE Statement

The %ACTIVATE (or %ACT) statement can be used anywhere in a SAS job (except after a CARDS or PARMCARDS statement) to list the names of one or more macros for which you want recognition restored. Only macros defined by a MACRO statement may be specified.

The form of the %ACTIVATE statement is:

%ACTIVATE *macronames*;

or

%ACT *macronames*;

where

       macronames   gives the names of one or more macros that you want
                      recognized.

The %ACTIVATE statement is used to restore recognition of a macro whose name appears in a previous %DEACTIVATE statement.

%DEACTIVATE Statement

The %DEACTIVATE (or %DEACT) statement can be used anywhere in a SAS job (except after a CARDS or PARMCARDS statement) to list the names of one or more macros for which you want recognition temporarily suspended. Only macros defined by a MACRO statement may be specified.

The form of the %DEACTIVATE statement is:

%DEACTIVATE *macronames;*

or

%DEACT *macronames;*

where

macronames   gives the names of one or more macros that you want temporarily unrecognized. Deactivated macro names still appear in the macro directory and, when listed with %MLIST, are flagged with an asterisk. The macro can be reactivated by a %ACTIVATE statement.

%DELETE Statement

The %DELETE (or %DEL) statement can be used anywhere in a SAS job (except after a CARDS or PARMCARDS statement) to remove macros from the macro directory. (Only macros defined by a MACRO statement may be specified.)

The form of the %DELETE statement is:

%DELETE *macronames;*

or

%DEL *macronames;*

where

macronames   gives the names of one or more macros that you want deleted.

%MLIST Statement

The %MLIST (or %LISTM) statement can be used anywhere in a SAS job (except after a CARDS or PARMCARDS statement) to specify the name of a macro that you want listed.

The form of the %MLIST statement is:

%MLIST *macroname;*

or

%LISTM *macroname;*

where

macroname   gives the name of the macro you want listed. If no
macroname is given, the names of all currently defined
macros are listed.

Example

Suppose you want to run the DISCRIM procedure several times with different class
variables but the same PROC DISCRIM statement. You can define the macro
DISCMAC:

```
MACRO DISCMAC
  PROC DISCRIM POOL=TEST LIST;
  CLASS CLASSMAC;
  VAR X Y Z;   %
```

The CLASS statement calls a macro CLASSMAC, which can be redefined each time
DISCMAC is invoked. If the class variables are AGE, SEX, and RACE, you can run
DISCRIM for each variable using these statements:

```
MACRO CLASSMAC AGE %
DISCMAC
MACRO CLASSMAC SEX %
DISCMAC
MACRO CLASSMAC RACE %
DISCMAC
```

See Chapter 15, ''SAS Macro Language,'' for a description of macro variables in the
new macro facility, which could be used in this application.

OPTIONS Statement

The OPTIONS statement is used to change one or more system options from the default value set by your installation. (For a list of the default values set by your installation, see a description of the OPTIONS procedure.)

The form of the OPTIONS statement is:

OPTIONS *option*...;
where

option   specifies one or more system options you want to change. The list of available system options is described below.

The changes made by an OPTIONS statement are in effect for the duration of the SAS job, or until they are changed by another OPTIONS statement.

For example, suppose you want to suppress the date normally printed on the SAS output pages and to left-align the output on the page. You can use this OPTIONS statement:

OPTIONS NODATE NOCENTER;

System options may also be changed when you invoke SAS by specifying options in your JCL EXEC statement or your SAS command. See the system appendix for your operating system for details.

An OPTIONS statement can be entered at any place in the SAS input stream. However, an OPTIONS statement entered within a DATA step or PROC step is effective for the *execution* of the entire DATA or PROC step. An OPTIONS statement entered *after* the statements of a DATA or PROC step is effective for that step, unless you precede the OPTIONS statement with a RUN statement.

Frequently Used Options

The following list gives a brief description of system options most frequently needed by SAS users. These options are described more fully in the main options list, below.

Initialization options

INITSTMT=	specifies statements to be executed before statements from SYSIN file
NEWS	prints installation-maintained news information at beginning of job
SYSIN=	specifies DDname for primary SAS input stream data set

SAS input stream format options

CAPS	translates lower-case SAS input into uppercase
CHARCODE	substitutes characters for terminals which lack underscore (__), vertical bar (|), or logical not sign (⌐)
DQUOTE	allows character literals bounded by either single quotes (') or double quotes ('')

S=   specifies length of statements on each line of source statements and data on lines following a CARDS statement

Options for data sets

GEN=   specifies number of generations of history information about SAS data sets to save

OBS=   specifies last observation to be processed from existing SAS data sets

REPLACE   replaces permanently allocated SAS data sets with others of the same name

Other options

BAUD=   specifies communications line data transmission rate

DEVICE=   specifies the terminal device you are using

PAGES=   gives maximum pages printed as output from SAS jobs

PARM=   specifies PARM string passed to procedures

TIME=   gives maximum time in seconds allowed for SAS jobs

CMS SAS interface options

CPSP   issues CP SPOOL commands for virtual printer

ERASE   erases SAS WORK data sets at beginning and end of SAS session

NULLEOF   allows a null line to signal end of SAS source file in interactive mode

SIODISK *mode letter*   forces all temporary files to a particular minidisk

TXTLIB   searches text libraries included in a CMS GLOBAL TXTLIB specification before invoking SAS

VIOBUF   gives number of 8K buffers of memory allocated for SAS WORK data library

Output formatting options

CENTER   centers printed output of SAS procedures

DATE   prints date at top of page

LABEL   specifies that variable labels are to be available to SAS procedures

LINESIZE=   gives printer line width for log and procedure output

MISSING=   specifies character SAS prints for missing values of numeric variables

NUMBER   prints page numbers on SAS output

OVP   overprints on SAS output

PAGESIZE=   gives number of lines printed per page of SAS output

TLINESIZE=   gives linesize for printing SAS output at a terminal

Sorting options

SORTMSG   specifies that PROC SORT default is to be MESSAGE

SORTWKNO=   gives minimum number of sort work areas allocated

Macro options

MACROGEN	prints text generated by macros
SYMBOLGEN	prints text generated by expansion of macro variables

Source list options

SOURCE	lists SAS source statements on SAS log
SOURCE2	lists secondary source statements from files included by %INCLUDE on SAS log

SAS System Options

Most options supported by SAS are listed below. Other options are defined but are not listed here, because they are intended for use only by installation personnel to tailor SAS to the installation's operating system environment or to restrict the availability of certain SAS facilities.

When two or more options are listed, separated by a slash, the first one is the default value. Many default values are different under CMS and VSE. The default values for most of these options can be changed by your installation. For options which require an equal sign and a value, the default value is shown.

A few of the options in the list below may only be specified in the JCL EXEC statement or SAS command when you invoke SAS; these options are identified by the phrase "only at SAS invocation." Your installation can restrict the ability to specify some of the options listed below. If you specify a restricted option, SAS issues an error message.

BATCH/ INTERACTIVE	specifies whether the interactive defaults for options are to be taken if SAS is being executed under an interactive system such as CMS, ICCF, or TSO. This option can be specified only on the JCL EXEC statement or SAS command at SAS invocation. If SAS is being executed under an interactive system, the default value for this option is INTERACTIVE. The noninteractive (batch) defaults for all options (for example, CENTER, CHKPT, NOCMS, DATE, D=LOCAL or BATCH, NOTSO, NUMBER, OPLIST, OVP, PS=60, and NOSPOOL) are implied if the BATCH option is specified and SAS is being executed under TSO, CMS, or ICCF. INTERACTIVE is ignored if SAS is not being executed under TSO, CMS, or ICCF.
BAUD=1200	specifies the communications line data transmission rate. BAUD should be set to the baud rate (typically 300 or 1200) that most asynchronous ASCII display or graphics terminals at your installation use. This option is used by SAS/GRAPH, SAS/FSP, and the CLEAR statement.
BLDLTABLE/ NOBLDLTABLE BLDL/NOBLDL	specifies whether the dynamic BLDL table facility is to be active. The program management component of the SAS supervisor optionally maintains a BLDL table of loaded modules that allows faster execution and a reduction of I/O activity on STEPLIB and TASKLIB, including SAS.LIBRARY. If SAS.LIBRARY or any STEPLIB data set is to be modified (for example, compressed)

during the execution of a SAS job, NOBLDLTABLE should be specified. This option is ignored under CMS and VSE. Under VSE, a table of directory entries for loaded modules is always maintained.

BLKSIZE=0   specifies the default block size for SAS data sets. For FBA disks under VSE, BLKSIZE is a logical block size. A value of 0 indicates that the value given by the BLKSIZE(*devicetype*) option, below, is to be used. Except under CMS, if the storage device in use has a smaller maximum block size than the default specified here, the maximum value for the storage device is used. The actual block size used for a data set may exceed the BLKSIZE= option value if the length of an observation is greater than the specified value. Depending on the computer system, large block sizes can sometimes increase the efficiency of SAS jobs. The BLKSIZE value can be 0 or range from 1024 to 32760.

Note that the BLKSIZE= options indicate the block size to be used for individual SAS data sets. Under OS, the SAS data library BLKSIZE value recorded in the data set label (if there is one) is **always** the maximum value permitted for the device. This is to allow for the possibility of differing block sizes among the SAS data sets in the SAS data library. Under CMS, the SAS data set's BLKSIZE is the corresponding CMS file's (logical) record length.

BLKSIZE   specifies the default block size for SAS data sets by
(*devicetype*)=*value*   *devicetype*. Any valid generic device type may be specified for *devicetype*, as well as DISK or DASD, TAPE, CMS, FBA, and OTHER. DISK, DASD and TAPE set all of the corresponding values; CMS specifies the BLKSIZE to use for SAS data sets stored on CMS minidisks; FBA specifies the logical block size to use for SAS data sets on FBA devices in the VSE environment; OTHER is used when SAS is unable to determine the exact device type.

The following may be specified for *value*:

value   **meaning**

number

specifies the block size that SAS is to use for the device.

OPT

specifies that SAS is to choose an optimum block size for the device.

MAX or FULL

specifies that SAS is to use the maximum permitted block size for the device.

HALF, THIRD, FOURTH, or FIFTH

specify that SAS is to use the largest value which results in obtaining two, three, four, and five, respectively, blocks per track (if a disk device) or the maximum permitted block size divided by two, three, four, and five, respectively (if not a disk device).

The following example tells SAS to choose optimum BLKSIZE values for all disk devices except 3380s, for which third track blocking is requested, and to use the maximum permitted block size on all tape devices:

```
OPTIONS BLKSIZE(DISK) = OPT
    BLKSIZE(3380) = THIRD
    BLKSIZE(TAPE) = MAX ;
```

BUFNO = 2   gives the number of buffers to use for each SAS data set. Only values of 1 or 2 are permitted. Under CMS, specify BUFNO = 1 (BUFNO = 2 provides no benefit).

C60/C48/C96   controls whether SAS output is printed using the 60-character set, the 48-character set, or the 96-character set. The C60 character set is the same as the PL/I character set. The C96 character set is the same as the C60 character set with the addition of the lowercase letters. C96 is the default under CMS. If all printers on which SAS output will be printed and all terminals on which SAS output will be displayed have lowercase alphabetic graphics installed, or if lowercase alphabetic characters are always translated by system software or folded by hardware to their uppercase equivalents, then specify C96. Otherwise, specify C60. (At present, the only use of the C96 option within SAS is by the LIST and HELP statements.)

NOCAPS/CAPS   determines whether lowercase SAS input (including CARDS and PARMCARDS) is translated to uppercase. When NOCAPS is in effect, **all** input to SAS is translated to uppercase **except** data following CARDS and PARMCARDS statements, text contained within single quotes (and double quotes if the DQUOTE option is in effect), titles, footnotes, element values in VALUE statements in PROC FORMAT, and variable and data set labels. If the CAPS option is specified, the above exceptions are also translated to uppercase.

CARDS = MAX or n   gives the maximum number of cards a SAS job may
C = MAX or n   punch to the standard SAS punch file (FILE PUNCH). If CARDS = MAX or C = MAX is specified, SAS does not limit the number of cards punched. When this option is used in the OPTIONS statement, the value given cannot exceed the value given or defaulted at the invocation of SAS. In all cases, local computer installation limits also apply to SAS jobs.

NOCASORT/CASORT   specifies that the CA-SORT™ program product is used as the system sort utility. CA-SORT is a trademark of Computer Associates International, Inc.

CENTER/NOCENTER   controls whether the printed output of SAS procedures is centered. Using NOCENTER when working interactively can save printing time at terminals. The default is CENTER when executing under batch and NOCENTER when executing interactively.

NOCHARCODE/ CHARCODE	for users with no underscore character (__) , vertical bar (|) , or logical not sign (¬) on their interactive terminals, allows substitution of the characters ?- for the underscore; the characters ?/ for the vertical bar; and the characters ?= for the logical not sign.
NOCHKPT/CHKPT	checkpoints certain SAS options and status at the end of every SAS step. Checkpointing is useful when using SAS interactively under TSO if you want to restart your SAS session after an attention or abend. However, checkpointing increases the cost of a session. Under TSO, CHKPT is the default. The default under CMS and ICCF is NOCHKPT.
NOCLIST/CLIST	controls whether SAS obtains its input from the terminal directly via TGET (NOCLIST) or via the PUTGET service routine (CLIST) when SAS is being run interactively under TSO. When CLIST is specified it is possible to write TSO CLISTs in which SAS statements follow the TSO command that invokes SAS. This option is ignored under CMS and VSE.
NOCMDMSG/ CMDMSG	specifies whether the text of error messages from CMS commands issued from SAS should be written to the terminal. CMDMSG is useful for debugging. This option is used under CMS only.
NOCMS/CMS	under CMS, controls the format of the SAS log and whether SAS notes the memory and CPU time used for each step. CMS is the default when SAS is being executed interactively, and NOCMS is the default for noninteractive (batch) execution of SAS. If the CMS option is in effect, the resource utilization notes are suppressed; if the NOCMS option is in effect, the notes are printed. NOCMS is implied if the BATCH option is specified; CMS is implied if the INTERACTIVE option is specified, and SAS is being executed interactively under CMS.
CPSP/NOCPSP	determines whether or not the CMS SAS interface issues CP SPOOL commands for the virtual printer. NOCPSP is intended for running SAS on a CMS batch machine where spooling commands issued by SAS may interfere with those issued by CMS batch facilities. If the CPSP and PPrint options are specified, the CMS SAS interface issues

CP SPOOL PRINTER CONT

when SAS is invoked, and

CP SPOOL PRINTER NOCONT CLOSE

	before returning to CMS at the end of the SAS session. This option is used under CMS only.
DATE/NODATE	controls whether the current date is printed at the top of each page of the SAS log, the standard SAS print file, and any FILE with the PRINT attribute. If NODATE is specified, the date will be omitted from the first title

line of each page. The default is NODATE when executing SAS interactively.

DEFAULT=*name*
D=*name* gives the name of a set of default system options and parameters set by your SAS installation representative. D=LOCAL (D=BATCH under CMS) is the standard DEFAULT value when executing SAS under batch (noninteractively) and either D=TSO, D=CMS, or D=ICCF (as appropriate) when executing SAS interactively.

DEVADDR= specifies a list of TCAM QNAMES, VTAM node names, VM device addresses, or VSE logical unit numbers. This option is used by the IBM3287 device driver in SAS/GRAPH.

DEVICE= specifies a terminal device name designation. This option is used by SAS/GRAPH, SAS/FSP, and the CLEAR statement. Note: under CMS, you **must** specify DEVICE=IBM3279 to use any extended attributes of an IBM 3279 display terminal such as blinking, hilighting, reverse video, and seven colors.

DISK=DISK gives the generic or esoteric name defined at OS system generation for direct access devices. This option is ignored by CMS and VSE.

DQUOTE/
NODQUOTE specifies whether character literals may be bounded by double quotes (''). If the DQUOTE option is specified, character literals of the form ''ABCDE'' are accepted and may contain unpaired single quotes ('). For example, ''DON'T'' is an accepted character literal if DQUOTE is specified. However, double quotes that are part of the character value must be paired. This may affect existing TITLE, FOOTNOTE, NOTE, LABEL, and VALUE statements and data set label specifications. If the NODQUOTE option is in effect, character literals must be surrounded by single quotes, and single quotes that are part of the character value must be paired (as in 'DON''T').

Macro variable references and macro calls within a string enclosed in single quotes (') **are not** expanded. However, if the DQUOTE option is in effect, macro variable references and macro calls within a string enclosed in double quotes ('') **are** expanded.

DSNFERR/
NODSNFERR controls whether SAS treats a SAS data set not found in a data library as an error. If DSNFERR is specified and you attempt to reference a SAS data set that does not exist, SAS issues an error message as in prior releases. If NODSNFERR is specified, this error is ignored and the data set reference is treated as if you specified __NULL__.

DSRESV/NODSRESV controls whether certain SAS utility procedures (for example, PDS, PDSCOPY, and RELEASE) issue the RESERVE macro instruction when accessing OS partitioned data sets on shared disk volumes. If DSRESV is specified, the device is reserved, thus locking out other processors sharing the volume upon which the

PDS resides. If NODSRESV is specified, then the OS defined resources are enqueued instead. This option is ignored under CMS and VSE.

NODUMP/DUMP   controls whether a SAS memory dump is produced at abnormal termination of SAS. This option may only be specified at SAS invocation. (Note: under VSE, dumping is controlled by the // OPTION [NO|PART]DUMP JCL statement.) This option is ignored under CMS and VSE.

The DUMP option invokes a special error handler for SAS procedures, so that error diagnostics, system control blocks, and all low subpools of memory are dumped to the SAS log file. If a SASDUMP DD statement is included, that file is used in place of the SAS log. Error diagnostics include the abend code, PSW's, program registers at abend, and a save area trace including the module name and assembler-type offset. When you rerun a SAS job that has abended to report a problem to SAS Institute, use the DUMP option; under VSE, however, use the DUMPSYS option, below, instead.

NODUMPM/
DUMPM
NODUMPSHORT/
DUMPSHORT   controls whether a short SAS dump is produced at abend. This option may only be specified at SAS invocation. This dump is for diagnostic use only and is a standard SAS dump with no storage subpools. This option is ignored under CMS and VSE.

NODUMPP/DUMPP
NODUMPLONG/
DUMPLONG   controls whether a SAS long dump that includes program storage is produced at abend. This option may only be specified at SAS invocation. This option is for diagnostic use only, and is ignored under CMS and VSE.

NODUMPSYS/
DUMPSYS   controls whether SAS attempts to disable any interception of program checks and abnormal termination while SAS is executing. Specify DUMPSYS if neither SAS nor any procedure is to be allowed to intercept program checks and abnormal terminations (abends). This option is for diagnostic use where the DUMP option is ineffective or unusable, and should be specified under VSE when rerunning a failing job to obtain a memory dump. This option is valid under OS, CMS, and VSE.

NODYNALLOC/
DYNALLOC   controls whether SAS (NODYNALLOC) or the system sort utility (DYNALLOC) is to dynamically allocate sort work areas. If the DYNALLOC option is specified, the DYNALLOC=(SORTDEV,SORTWKNO) parameter is passed to the system sort utility by PROC SORT. This option is valid only under MVS. It is ignored under CMS and VSE.

ERASE/NOERASE   specifies whether or not the SAS WORK data sets are erased at the beginning and end of the SAS session. If NOERASE is not specified, the CMS SAS interface issues a CMS ERASE for all files with filetype WORK on the disk to be used for the current SAS WORK data library.

Although NOERASE prevents the WORK data sets from being deleted, it has no effect on initialization of the WORK data library by SAS. SAS normally initializes the WORK data library at the start of each session—effectively wiping out any pre-existing information. Initialization of the WORK data library can be suppressed by specifying the SAS system option NOWORKINIT on the SAS command. Consult the chapter "SAS Data Sets" for a complete discussion. This option is used under CMS only.

NOERRORABEND/
ERRORABEND

When ERRORABEND is in effect, most errors (including syntax errors) that would cause SAS to issue an error message, set OBS=0, and go into "syntax check mode" cause SAS to abnormally terminate (abend). The ERRORABEND option is recommended for debugged, production SAS programs that presumably should not encounter any errors at all, so that any errors that do occur are immediately brought to your attention by the abnormal termination of SAS.

ERRORS=20

specifies the maximum number of observations for which complete error messages are printed. The errors referred to are those caused by incorrect data (nonnumeric characters in numeric fields, and so on) rather than by syntax errors such as misspellings.

NOFILCLR/FILCLR

specifies whether SAS issues the command 'FILEDEF * CLEAR' during SAS termination. NOFILCLR specifies that only FILEDEFs issued by SAS will be cleared. FILCLR will clear all FILEDEFs except those issued with the PERM option. This option is used under CMS only.

FILEBLKSIZE
(*devicetype*)=*value*

specifies, by *devicetype*, the default maximum block size for external files used by certain SAS procedures (for example, PROC SOURCE) and DATA step FILEs.

Any valid generic device type may be specified for *devicetype*, as well as DISK or DASD, TAPE, CMS, FBA, SYSOUT, and OTHER. DISK, DASD and TAPE set all of the corresponding values; CMS specifies the block size to use for external files stored on CMS minidisks; FBA specifies the logical block size to use for external files on FBA devices in the VSE environment; SYSOUT specifies the block size to use for external files whose operating system control language includes a "print" specification, or any FILE with the PRINT attribute; OTHER is used when SAS is unable to determine the exact device type.

The actual block size that will be used will be consistent with the record format and logical record length of the file, if that information is known or specified. For compatibility with previous releases of SAS, the default value of this option for all device types is 6400, except SYSOUT, which is 141, and CMS, which is 32760.

The following may be specified for *value*:

value	meaning
number	specifies the block size that SAS is to use for the device.
OPT	specifies that SAS is to choose an optimum block size for the device.
MAX or FULL	specifies that SAS is to use the maximum permitted block size for the device.
HALF, THIRD, FOURTH, or FIFTH	specify that SAS is to use the largest value which results in obtaining two, three, four, and five, respectively, blocks per track (if a disk device) or the maximum permitted block size divided by two, three, four, and five, respectively (if not a disk device).

The following example requests SAS to use a maximum block size of 6400 for all external files on all disk and tape devices, except for 3350s where a value of 6160 is to be used:

```
OPTIONS FILEBLKSIZE(DISK) = 6400
   FILEBLKSIZE(TAPE) = 6400
   FILEBLKSIZE(3350) = 6160 ;
```

FILSZ/NOFILSZ   specifies whether the OS or CMS system sort utility supports the FILSZ parameter. This option is ignored under VSE. Specify the FILSZ option if the IBM ICEMAN (SM01), SYNCSORT™ or CA-SORT™ program product sort utility (or equivalent) is installed, and supports specification of the FILSZ parameter to increase the efficiency of the sort. Specify NOFILSZ if the sort utility does not support specification of the FILSZ parameter. Specify NOFILSZ if you specify SORTPGM = SM023 under CMS. This option is ignored if you specify SORTPGM = SAS.

FIRSTOBS = 1   specifies the number of the first observation that SAS is to process. Normally SAS begins with the first observation in each SAS data set. For example, specifying FIRSTOBS = 50 causes SAS to begin processing with the 50th observation of existing SAS data sets.

Note that this option applies to every SAS data set used in a job. Thus, in this example:

```
OPTIONS FIRSTOBS=11;
DATA A;
  SET OLD; /* 100 OBSERVATIONS */
DATA B;
  SET A;
DATA C;
  SET B;
```

data set OLD has 100 observations, data set A has 90, B has 80, and C has 70. To avoid decreasing the number of observations in successive data sets, set FIRSTOBS=1 at an appropriate point in your SAS statements.

The data set option FIRSTOBS= takes precedence over the FIRSTOBS= system option. (See Chapter 12, "SAS Data Sets," for a discussion of the FIRSTOBS= data set option.)

FMTERR/NOFMTERR   controls whether SAS indicates an error if it cannot find a format associated with a variable. When NOFMTERR is in effect, SAS processes the variable using a default format (usually w. or $\$w$.). When FMTERR is specified, missing formats are considered errors.

FORMCHAR (*printdevice*)= (*formatting characters*)   specifies the output *formatting characters* to be used for *printdevice*. Formatting characters are used for constructing tabular output outlines and dividers. This option is effective only in conjunction with the PRINTDEVICE= option, below.

The value given for *formatting characters* is any string or list of strings of characters no greater than 64 bytes long; if fewer than 64 bytes are specified, the value is padded with blanks on the right. In the initial release of SAS82, the first 11 characters define the two bar characters, vertical and horizontal, and the nine corner characters: upper left, upper middle, upper right, middle left, middle middle (cross), middle right, lower left, lower middle, and lower right. The remaining 53 bytes are reserved for future use.

The standard value is FORMCHAR(STANDARD)= ('|----|+|---'). Any character or hexadecimal string may be substituted to customize the table appearance. Specifying FORMCHAR(STANDARD) = (' ') (all blanks) will produce tables with no outlines or dividers. If standard printers at your installation do not include the vertical bar (|), we suggest that you substitute the capital letter I. If you are routing your printed output to an IBM 6670 using an extended font (typestyle 27 or 225) with input character set 216, we recommend:

```
FORMCHAR(IBM6670)=
  ('FABFACCCBCEB8FECABCBBB'X)
```

If you are using a printer with the standard "text" graphics (for example, a TN print train on an IBM

1403, 3211, or 3203; or a text character set on an IBM 3800), we recommend:

FORMCHAR(TEXT) = ('4FBFACBFBC4F8F4FABBFBB'X)

See the CALENDAR procedure for an illustration of these characters.

FS/NOFS   specifies whether certain SAS facilities and procedures are to operate in full-screen mode if you are executing SAS interactively on a full screen terminal. The SAS HELP facility and certain procedures have this capability in the initial release of SAS82; more are planned in later releases of SAS.

FSP/NOFSP   specifies that SAS full-screen terminal support and the facilities of SAS/FSP are to be available. This option must be specified at SAS invocation. If you specify NOFSP, SAS execution requires slightly less memory, and you cannot run any SAS/FSP procedures or use the SAS HELP facility in full-screen mode. It is not necessary for you to have the SAS/FSP product installed in order to specify this option. This option applies to OS, CMS, and VSE.

GCLASS = 'G'   specifies the SYSOUT class to be used by the IBM3287 device driver for its spooled output. Any valid SYSOUT class (A–Z,0–9,$,*) may be specified. This option may be restricted by your installation.

GCOPIES = ([d][,m])   specifies the *current* (d) and *maximum* (m) number of copies of each spooled output file produced by the SAS/GRAPH IBM3287 device driver that are to be printed. The *current* value specified can be from 0–255, but cannot exceed the *maximum* value specified. The *maximum* value specified can be from 1–255, but cannot exceed a limit which can be set by each installation. If a *current* value of 0 is specified, then the desired number of copies may be indicated by the COPIES= parameter of an appropriate JCL DD statement or job entry subsystem control statement, or the installation dynamic allocation exit. Under CMS, a value of 0 is interpreted to be 1. If GCOPIES= is not specified, the default values are 1 for current and 20 for maximum. This option may be restricted by your installation.

GDEST = 'LOCAL'   specifies the destination to which OS/MVS SAS/GRAPH IBM3287 device driver spooled output files are to be sent. Any valid 8-character DEST recognized by the installation may be specified. This option may be restricted by your installation.

GEN = 5   specifies the number of generations of history records to save on each SAS data set. The CONTENTS procedure is used to print the saved generations of historical information about each data set. The GEN value can range from 0 to 1000.

GFORMS = ''   specifies the SYSOUT forms code to be used by the IBM3287 device drive for its spooled output. Any

	forms code specification of up to four characters recognized by the installation may be specified. This option may be restricted by your installation.
GRAPHICS/ NOGRAPHICS GRAPH/NOGRAPH	specifies that the facilities of SAS/GRAPH are to be available. If you specify NOGRAPHICS and you have SAS/GRAPH installed, SAS execution requires slightly less memory and you cannot run any graphics procedures. If NOGRAPHICS is made the default, GRAPHICS must be specified at SAS invocation (not on an OPTIONS statement) in order to use any graphics procedures. GRAPHICS is the default if SAS/GRAPH is installed; the option has no effect if SAS/GRAPH is not installed.
GWRITER= 'SASWTR'	specifies the SYSOUT writer name to be used for spooled output from the OS/MVS SAS/GRAPH IBM3287 device driver. This option may be restricted by your installation.
NOICCF/ICCF	under ICCF, controls the format of the SAS log and whether SAS notes the memory and CPU time used for each step. ICCF is the default when SAS is being executed interactively, and NOICCF is the default for noninteractive (batch) execution of SAS. If the ICCF option is in effect, the resource utilization notes are suppressed; if the NOICCF option is in effect, the notes are printed. NOICCF is implied if the BATCH option is specified; ICCF is implied if the INTERACTIVE option is specified, and SAS is being executed interactively under ICCF.
IMS/NOIMS	specifies that the facilities of SAS/IMS-DL/I are to be available. If the SAS/IMS-DL/I product is installed and you specify NOIMS, no IMS or DL/I data bases may be accessed. The option is ignored if the SAS/IMS-DL/I product is not installed.
INCLUDE/ NOINCLUDE	specifies that the %INCLUDE facility is available. This option must be specified at SAS invocation, and is invalid under VSE. If you specify NOINCLUDE, SAS execution requires slightly less memory and you cannot use %INCLUDE to include SAS statements from external files (but you may still include statements from the internal file of saved statements provided the SPOOL option, below, is in effect).
INITSTMT=''	specifies a statement or SAS statements to be executed prior to any SAS statements from the SYSIN file (see the SYSIN= option, below).
INTERACTIVE /BATCH	specifies whether the interactive defaults for options are to be taken if SAS is being executed under an interactive system such as CMS, ICCF, or TSO. This option can be specified only on the JCL EXEC statement or SAS command at SAS invocation. If SAS is being executed under an interactive system, the default value for this option is INTERACTIVE. The noninteractive (batch) defaults for all options (for example, CENTER, CHKPT, NOCMS, DATE, D=LOCAL or BATCH,

NOTSO, NUMBER, OPLIST, OVP, PS=60, and NOSPOOL) are implied if the BATCH option is specified and SAS is being executed under TSO, CMS, or ICCF. INTERACTIVE is ignored if SAS is not being executed under TSO, CMS, or ICCF.

INVALIDDATA=.   specifies the SAS missing value that SAS is to assign to a variable when invalid data are encountered with an input format (such as in an INPUT statement or the INPUT function). The value specified can be a letter (A–Z), period (.), or underscore (__).

LABEL/NOLABEL   controls whether variable labels are available to SAS procedures. When the NOLABEL option is in effect, variable labels are not available.

__LAST__=
__NULL__   specifies the __LAST__ data set name. After a SAS data set has been created in a SAS job, the value of __LAST__ becomes the name of the most recently created SAS data set.

LDISK
LD   writes the SAS log to a disk file with filetype SASLOG. The filename of the SASLOG file is determined by the NAME option on the SAS command. If the NAME is not specified, the SASLOG file assumes the filename of the first SAS source file listed on the SAS command. If NAME is not specified and no SAS source file is specified on the SAS command, the default filename SAS is used. This option is used under CMS and only at SAS invocation.

LEAVE=n
LEAVE=nK   Leave n or nK bytes of memory unallocated. If SAS abnormally terminates with indication of insufficient memory or, under VSE, a console message indicates that a VSE system component has insufficient memory, the value of LEAVE should be increased. The default value is 0 for OS, 8K for VSE, and 64K for CMS. A value specified without a K will not be multiplied by 1024; LEAVE=2048 and LEAVE=2K are equivalent.

LINESIZE=132
LS=132   specifies the printer line width for the SAS log and the standard SAS print file used by the DATA step and procedures. LINESIZE values can range from 64 to 132. LINESIZE= controls line width for files not directed to the terminal. Under CMS, when executing in non-interactive (batch) mode, LINESIZE is used; however, when executing SAS interactively, TLS is used for output lines written to the terminal and LINESIZE is used for output lines directed to disk or printer. Under VSE, the line width for procedure output is limited to 120.

LOG=FT11F001   specifies the SAS log file DDname. This option is reset when you specify the UNITS= option, below.

LPRINT
LP   sends the SAS log to the virtual printer. This option is used under CMS and only at SAS invocation.

LTYPE
LT   types the SAS log at the terminal. This option is used under CMS and only at SAS invocation.

NOMACRO/MACRO   specifies whether the SAS macro language, as well as the SYMGET and SYMPUT functions, is to be available. This option can only be specified at SAS invocation. If you specify NOMACRO, SAS execution requires slightly less memory, and you cannot use any facilities from the new macro language.

NOMACROGEN/
MACROGEN
specifies whether statements generated by macros (either from the SAS macro language or the MACRO statement) are to be printed.

NOMCOMPILE/
MCOMPILE
specifies whether the compiler for the SAS macro language is to be loaded by default. The macro language compiler will be loaded at any time that a macro definition is encountered in the SAS program. If you frequently define (or redefine) macros, then specifying MCOMPILE could reduce overhead.

NOMEMERR/
MEMERR
controls whether a diagnostic program check abnormal termination occurs whenever SAS would ordinarily give a memory-exceeded message. If MEMERR is in effect, the abend occurs. This option is for diagnostic use only.

MERROR/
NOMERROR
controls whether the SAS macro language produces a warning message if a percent sign followed by a SAS name is present that the macro processor cannot match with an appropriate macro keyword. This situation occurs if you misspell a macro keyword (including a macro call), if you call a macro before you define it, or if percent signs in your job are attached to words that could be macro keywords. Specify NOMERROR if your job contains percent signs in words that could be confused with macro keywords.

MISSING='.'
specifies the character to be printed for missing values of numeric variables.

MLEAVE=6144
specifies the amount of memory given by MSIZE, below, to leave unallocated for use by the macro language processor. The value specified for MLEAVE must be at least 2K less than the value specified for MSIZE.

NOMLOGIC/
MLOGIC
specifies whether or not the macro language processor is to trace its execution. If MLOGIC is specified, trace information is printed on the SAS log. This option is for diagnostic use only.

MODECHARS='?>*'
specifies characters that SAS uses for prompting at a terminal in various submodes when SAS is executing interactively. The first character is used in primary input mode, that is, when entering SAS statements. The second character is used when SAS is reading data following a CARDS statement, and by PROC EDITOR and any other interactive procedure to indicate interactive submode. The third character is used when a %INCLUDE statement is executed.

MSIZE=12228
specifies the amount of memory available to the macro language processor. The value specified for MSIZE must be at least 2K more than the value specified for MLEAVE.

MSYMSIZE = 1024   specifies the initial size of each macro language processor symbol table.

MWORK = 2048   specifies the size of the work area available to the macro language processor.

NAME *filename*
NA *filename*   specifies the filename to be assigned to the disk files for printed procedure output (filetype LISTING), the SAS log (filetype SASLOG), and lines entered at the terminal in interactive mode (filetype SAS). This option is used under CMS and only at SAS invocation.

NDSVOLS = ' '   specifies the volume serial which, when SAS determines that a SAS data library has been allocated to or defined in the control language, results in SAS treating the SAS data set reference as if you had specified __NULL__ and no SAS data set processing occurs. This option is useful for production SAS job streams that need to, for example, initialize catalog generation data groups.

NONEWS/NEWS   controls whether the text identified by the SASNEWS= option (see below) in the SAS HELP library is to be printed on the SAS log or displayed on the terminal at the beginning of each SAS execution. If NEWS is in effect, the installation-maintained news information is printed at the beginning of every SAS job or at the start of every SAS execution under TSO, CMS, or ICCF.

NOTES/NONOTES   controls whether notes are printed in the SAS log. (These messages usually begin with ''NOTE:''.) If the NONOTES option is specified, no informatory messages are printed in the SAS log. NOTES must be specified on SAS jobs which are sent to SAS Institute for problem determination and resolution; SAS Institute cannot help with program or system problems if notes are not printed.

NOTLog/TLog
NOTL/TL   determines whether or not the SAS statements entered at the terminal are written to a disk file. NOTLog is the default setting; TLog is only recognized when SAS is invoked in interactive mode. When TLog is specified, lines entered in response to SAS prompting are routed to a file with filetype SAS. The filename is determined by the NAme option on the SAS command; filename SAS is the default if no NAme is specified. This option is used under CMS only.

NONULL/NULLEOF   determines whether or not to allow a null line to signal end of the SAS source file in interactive mode. A line beginning with '/*' always signals the end of the SAS source, whether or not NULLEOF is specified. This option is used under CMS only.

NONUMBER/
NUMBER   controls whether the page number appears on the first title line of each SAS print output page. When executing SAS interactively, the default is NONUMBER.

OBS = MAX
OBS = *n*   specifies the **last** observation that SAS is to process from existing SAS data sets. Normally, all the observa-

tions in a data set are used by SAS. For purposes of testing, only observations up to the nth observation of each SAS data set may be selected by specifying the OBS= parameter.

For example, specifying

OPTIONS OBS=50;

as the first statement of a SAS job causes SAS to read only through the 50th observation when reading a SAS data set. Analysis of SAS data sets in PROC steps would also be limited to only up to the 50th observation in each data set.

You can check the syntax of SAS statements in a job by specifying

OPTIONS OBS=0 NOREPLACE;

as the first statement in a job. However, since SAS actually executes each DATA and PROC step in the job (using no observations), SAS can take certain actions even when the OBS=0 and NOREPLACE options are in effect. For example, SAS executes procedures that process the directories of SAS data sets (such as CONTENTS, DELETE, and DATASETS). SAS also executes PROC RELEASE. External files are also opened and closed; thus, if you are writing to an external file with a PUT statement, an end-of-file mark is written and any existing data in the file is deleted.

You can use the FIRSTOBS= and OBS= options together to process a set of observations from the middle of data sets. For example, to process only observations 1000 through 1100, specify

OPTIONS FIRSTOBS=1000 OBS=1100;

The OBS= data set option takes precedence over the OBS= system option. See Chapter 12, "SAS Data Sets," for a discussion of the OBS= data set option.

OFFLINE=0.000   gives the offline storage cost. The cost of storing an off-line data set is computed from this option; this cost is printed by the SAS procedure CONTENTS. The OFFLINE value is in units of dollars per track per day. Using OFFLINE=0 suppresses this feature. This option is ignored under CMS.

ONLINE=0.000   gives the online cost for disk storage. The cost of storing an online data set is computed from this option and is printed by the SAS procedure CONTENTS. The ONLINE value is in units of dollars per track per day. Using ONLINE=0 suppresses this feature. This option is ignored under CMS.

OPLIST/NOOPLIST   specifies whether options given at the invocation of SAS are listed at the beginning of the SAS log. The default is OPLIST in batch and NOOPLIST in TSO, CMS, and ICCF.

OVP/NOOVP — controls whether SAS printed output lines can be over-printed. For example, when SAS encounters an error in a SAS statement, it prints underscores beneath the word in error if OVP is in effect. If NOOVP is in effect, SAS prints dashes on the next line below the error. The default is NOOVP when SAS is being executed interactively.

PAGES=MAX
PAGES=n
P=MAX
P=n — specifies the maximum number of pages of printed output a SAS job may print. If PAGES=MAX is specified, SAS does not limit the number of pages printed. NOTE: when used in the OPTIONS statement, the value of this option cannot exceed the value given or defaulted at SAS invocation. In all cases, local computer installation limits also apply to SAS jobs.

PAGESIZE=60
PS=60 — specifies the number of lines that may be printed per page of SAS output. If SAS is running in an interactive environment, the PAGESIZE= option defaults to the terminal screen size (if this information is available from the operating system). The value specified can be from 20–500.

PARM='' — specifies a PARM string passed to both SAS and external procedures. When a PARM string is specified with this parameter, the string is passed to the next external procedure executed under control of the SAS supervisor, for example, via **PROC** *program*;. Because the string is also passed to all SAS procedures, which generally do not support its specification, it should be reset to a null string (for example OPTIONS PARM='';) after the external procedure is executed and before the next SAS procedure is invoked. For example:

```
PROC program CC=4;
OPTIONS PARM='parm to external procedure';
RUN;
OPTIONS PARM='' /* RESET FOR SAS PROCS */ ;
more SAS statements
```

PARMCARDS=
FT15F001 — specifies the DDname for the PARMCARDS data set. This option is reset when the UNITS= option, below, is specified.

PDISK
PD — writes the printed procedure output to a disk file with filetype LISTING. The filename of the LISTING file is determined by the NAME option on the SAS command. If the NAME is not specified, the LISTING file assumes the filename of the first SAS source file on the SAS command. If NAME is not specified and no SAS source file is specified on the SAS command, the default filename SAS is used. This option is used under CMS and only at SAS invocation.

PLIF *filename* — names the PL/I(F) run-time subroutine library on your system. The PLIF library must be specified to execute SAS procedures compiled with the PL/I(F) compiler. This option should be specified at the installation of SAS. This option is used under CMS and only at SAS invocation.

PLIO *filename* names the PL/I optimizing compiler run-time subroutine library on your system. The PLIO library must be specified to execute SAS procedures compiled with the PL/I optimizing compiler. This option should be specified at the installation of SAS. This option is used under CMS and only at SAS invocation.

PPRINT
PP sends the printed procedure output to the virtual printer. This option is used under CMS and only at SAS invocation.

PRINTDEVICE=
STANDARD
PRINTDEV=
STANDARD specifies the device description or name of the intended ultimate destination of SAS printed output. This option is used to determine, for example, which set of FORMCHAR(*printdevice*) formatting characters to use. The following names are currently standardized:

name characteristics assumed
STANDARD
    none
TEXT
    text (TN print train) graphics
IBM6670
    model 2 with extended fonts
IBM3800
    text plus grey scale graphics

PROCSIZE=MAX specifies the maximum number of bytes a procedure can allocate in a single request to the SAS procedure interface routine. This option is intended for use in special environments where more than one copy of SAS is executing in a region or partition. This option is specifically **not** applicable to ICCF, CMS, or TSO.

PROMPTCHARS=
'110A010D01000000'X
(OS)
PROMPTCHARS=
'110A000D01000000'X
(CMS) specifies the terminal prompt characters to be used by SAS/GRAPH procedures. The value specified must be exactly eight hexadecimal bytes and must be consistent with the DEVICE= option. This option is not applicable under VSE.

PSEG=SHARED
PSEG=NONSHARED
PSEG=OFF determines the use of SAS procedures in a CMS saved segment. If a CMS installation has installed SAS procedures in a saved segment, the memory requirements for procedure steps can be significantly reduced. This option is used under CMS only.

Note that saved segments are installed for certain sizes of virtual machines. If you increase your virtual machine size above the segment's load point, the saved segment is not used. Check with your CMS installation for appropriate virtual machine sizes to use with CMS SAS saved procedure segments.

SHARED specifies that the saved procedure segment is to be used and reentrant portions are to be shared among CMS SAS users.

NONSHARED specifies that the saved procedure segment is to be used but no portions are to be shared with other users. Use NONSHARED and only at SAS invocation as a temporary bypass if some of the shared portions turn out not to be reentrant.

OFF specifies that SAS procedures be executed from the modules on the CMS SAS disk; the saved procedure segment is not to be used.

SHARED is the default. However, if SAS cannot use the saved procedure segment, either because it has not been installed at your installation or because of the virtual machine size, the status of the PSEG option is set to NOT__USED. If a SAS procedure step has not yet been executed in the SAS session, the status of the PSEG option is not yet established. In this case SAS sets the status of PSEG to a null string ' '.

PTYPE types the printed procedure output at the terminal.
PT   This option is used under CMS and only at SAS invocation.

REPLACE/   controls the replacement of permanently allocated
NOREPLACE   SAS data sets. If NOREPLACE is specified, a SAS data set in a permanently allocated SAS data library cannot be replaced with one of the same name. This protects previously existing SAS data sets in a SAS data library from being inadvertently replaced.

The REPLACE= data set option takes precedence over the REPLACE/NOREPLACE system option. See Chapter 12, "SAS Data Sets," for a discussion of the REPLACE= data set option.

S=   specifies the length of statements on each line of source statements and data on lines following a CARDS statement. S=0 means SAS determines whether or not the input is sequence numbered by looking at the sequence field of the first card. If the sequence field of the first card is all numeric then SAS assumes the entire file is sequence numbered. If S>0 then SAS uses that value of S as the length of the data to be scanned and does not look for sequence numbers. S<0 is not allowed. Currently, primary input to SAS must be fixed length records of 80 characters; if sequence numbers are present they should be in columns 73–80 (refer to the SEQ= option, below, for more information on sequence numbers).

S2=S   specifies the length of secondary source statements. S2=S means that text included by a %INCLUDE statement uses the current S= value. S2=number behaves exactly like S=number but controls only input through %INCLUDE. Text included via %INCLUDE may be either fixed or varying length; fixed length records are either sequenced in the last eight columns or unsequenced, while varying length records are either sequenced in the first eight columns or unsequenced. For varying length records, S2 is the starting column of the data, rather than the ending column as for fixed length records.

S370/NOS370   specifies that the machine upon which SAS is executing supports the IBM System/370 instruction set (for example, a 303X, 43XX, or 308X processor). Specify NOS370 only if you are executing SAS on an IBM System/360 and the OS/360 program check first level interrupt handler (FLIH) has been modified to simulate in software the execution of the System/370 nonprivileged instructions.

SASHELP=SASHELP   specifies the DDname of the HELP library. The HELP library is referred to by the HELP statement and when the NEWS option has been specified at SAS invocation.

SASLIB *filename*   directs the CMS SAS interface to issue a CMS FILEDEF to associate the file

    filename TXTLIB A

with ddname SASLIB and adds that file to the list of libraries searched during a SAS session.

    The SASLIB file is automatically searched for formats defined with the FORMAT procedure. To store formats produced by PROC FORMAT in the SASLIB file, specify DDNAME=SASLIB on the procedure. See "SAS under CMS" for a complete discussion. This option is used under CMS and only at SAS invocation.

SASNEWS=SASNEWSB   specifies the member of the HELP library to be printed
SASNEWS=SASNEWST   on the SAS log when the NEWS option has been specified at SAS invocation for batch (B) and TSO (T).

SEQ=8   specifies the length of the numeric portion of the sequence field. SEQ=8 means that all eight characters in the sequence field are numeric. SAS always assumes an eight-character sequence field; however, some editors place some alphabetic information in the first several characters, such as the file name. The SEQ= value specifies the number of digits that are right-justified in the eight-character field. Thus, if the sequence fields look like AAA00010 specify SEQ=5. In this case, SAS looks at only the last five characters of the eight-character sequence field, and, if numeric, assumes that the whole eight-character field is a sequence field.

SERIES/A   specifies which series of discontiguous saved segments should be used. This option is used under CMS and only at SAS invocation.

SERROR/NOSERROR   controls whether a warning message is produced when SAS encounters a macro variable (also called a symbolic variable) reference for which it cannot find the variable referred to. This situation occurs if you misspell the name in a macro variable reference, if you refer to the variable before you define it, or if your job contains ampersands (&) followed by SAS names without an intervening blank. Specify NOSERROR if ampersands in your job could be interpreted as macro variable references (for example, if you use the amper-

	sand as a symbol for the logical operator AND with no intervening blanks as in X=Y&Z;).
SIODISK *modeletter*	forces all temporary files allocated by the CMS SAS interface to a particular CMS minidisk. If the SIODISK option is not specified, SAS allocates temporary files on the write-disk with the most available free space when SAS is invoked. This option is used only at SAS invocation.
SKIP=0	specifies the number of lines to skip at the top of each page of SAS output before printing the first title line. The location of the first line also depends on the carriage control tape or forms control buffer used on the printer. Most installations define this so that the first line of a new page (top of form) begins 3 or 4 lines down the form. In this case, specify SKIP=0. The SKIP value can range from 0 to 20. The SKIP value does not affect the maximum number of lines that are printed on each page.
NOSNP/SNP	SNP specifies that internal SAS system information is dumped in hexadecimal as a diagnostic trace of SAS activity. This option is for diagnostic use only and may only be specified at the invocation of SAS.
NOSNPPROG/ SNPPROG	SNPPROG specifies that the compiled SAS code is to be dumped on the SAS log. If you specify SNPPROG, then SNP (see above) is assumed. This option is for diagnostic use only and may only be specified at SAS invocation.
SORT=1	specifies the minimum size in cylinders of the temporary data sets that PROC SORT dynamically allocates under MVS for sort work areas. The SORT= option is ignored if the DYNALLOC option is specified. This option is ignored under CMS, VSE, and non-MVS OS systems.
SORTDEV=SYSDA	specifies the device (unit) name used under MVS to dynamically allocate the sort work data sets. The value specified must be a generic or esoteric name defined at MVS system generation for real, non-VIO, direct access devices. This option is ignored under CMS, VSE, and non-MVS OS systems.
SORTLIB= 'SYS1.SORTLIB'	specifies for MVS the data set name to be dynamically allocated by PROC SORT to DDname SORTLIB. For CMS it specifies the CMS sort utility library to be GLOBALed. The SORTLIB= option is ignored under OS/360, OS/VS2(SVS), OS/VS1, and VSE. SYNCSORT (OS) does not require a sort library. In this case, and in those cases where you do not wish SAS to dynamically allocate SORTLIB, specify SORTLIB=' '. This option may be restricted by your installation.
NOSORTLIST/ SORTLIST	controls whether the LIST parameter is passed to the system sort utility. If the SORTLIST option is specified, SAS passes the LIST parameter to the system sort utility. If NOSORTLIST is specified, SAS does not pass the LIST parameter to the system sort utility.

NOSORTMSG/ SORTMSG	specifies whether or not the MSG=AP option is to be passed to the system sort utility. If you specify SORTMSG, then it is equivalent to specifying the MESSAGE option on each PROC SORT statement.
SORTMSG=SYSOUT	specifies the DDname to be dynamically allocated on MVS systems by PROC SORT for the system sort utility message print file. This option is ignored except under MVS. Under TSO, this file is allocated to the terminal. This option may be restricted by your installation.
SORTPGM=SORT SORTPGM=SAS SORTPGM=SM023 SORTPGM= 'epname'	specifies the name of the system sort utility to be invoked by SAS. If SORTPGM=SAS is specified, then a SAS-supplied sort utility is invoked which is suitable for sorting data sets with a small number of observations and variables. Under CMS, if SORTPGM=SM023 is specified, then the IBM OS/360 SM-023 sort utility which has been modified to run under CMS is invoked. This option may be restricted by your installation.
SORTSIZE= MAX SORTSIZE=SIZE SORTSIZE=n SORTSIZE=nK	specifies the SIZE parameter to be passed to the system sort utility.

Under CMS and OS, when SORTSIZE=SIZE is specified, the sort executes with the amount of free space in the region or partition less 16K. When SORTSIZE=n or nK is specified, n*1024 (bytes of memory) is passed to the sort. When SORTSIZE=MAX is specified, the characters 'MAX' are passed to the sort. This causes the system sort to "size" itself. Not all sort programs support this feature. When SORTSIZE=0 is specified, a value of zero is passed to the sort. The sort then uses a value assigned by the installation at the time of sort generation/installation.

Under VSE, this option has a different meaning and would not normally be used. Refer to the PROC SORT chapter for more information about the use of the SORTSIZE options in a VSE environment.

SORTWKDD='SASS'	specifies under MVS the prefix of the sort work area DDnames to be dynamically allocated by either SAS (NODYNALLOC) or the system sort utility (DYNALLOC). For example, if SORTWKDD='XYPG' is specified, DDnames XYPGWK01, XYPGWK02, and so forth, are dynamically allocated. This option is ignored except under MVS. This option may be restricted by your installation.
SORTWKNO=3	specifies the minimum number of sort work areas to be allocated. This option is ignored under CMS. Under OS, the value specified can be a period (.) or a number from 0–6. A period indicates that a default value appropriate for the sort utility in use is to be used. Under VSE, the value specified can be from 0–9, and specifies the number of SORTWK files to be used. Refer to the PROC SORT chapter for more information on the use of the SORTWKNO options. Under MVS, if

DYNALLOC is specified this option is passed to the system sort utility. This option may be restricted by your installation.

Under MVS, a specification of 0 causes no sort work areas to be allocated and the sort to proceed without them. The system sort utility in use must support "in-core" sorting without sort work areas.

If you are not running under MVS, then a specification of 0 permits the sort attempt to proceed even if there are no sort work areas allocated. The system sort utility in use must support "in-core" sorting without sort work areas.

SOURCE/ NOSOURCE	controls whether a listing of input SAS source statements is printed on the SAS log.
SOURCE2/ NOSOURCE2	controls whether secondary source statements from files included by %INCLUDE are listed on the SAS log. This option is ignored under VSE.
NOSPOOL/SPOOL	controls whether SAS statements are spooled to a utility data set in the WORK data library. While the SPOOL option is in effect, SAS statements are saved for later use by a %INCLUDE statement. While the NOSPOOL option is in effect the SAS statements are not saved. Switching from NOSPOOL to SPOOL erases any previously saved statements; however, previously saved statements may be included while NOSPOOL is in effect. SPOOL is the default under interactive CMS, ICCF, and TSO; NOSPOOL is the default under VSE and OS batch, and non-interactive CMS.
SSEG SHARED SSEG NONSHARED SSEG OFF	determines the use of a CMS saved segment for portions of the SAS supervisor and associated library routines. If your CMS installation has installed a CMS SAS saved supervisor segment, memory requirements for SAS DATA and PROC steps are reduced.

Note that saved segments are installed for certain sizes of virtual machines. If you increase your virtual machine size above the segment's load point, the saved segment is not used. Check with your CMS installation for appropriate virtual machine sizes to use with CMS SAS saved supervisor segments.

SHARED specifies that the saved supervisor segment is to be used and reentrant portions are to be shared among CMS SAS users.

NONSHARED specifies that the saved supervisor segment is to be used but no portions are to be shared with other users. Use NONSHARED only as a temporary bypass if some of the shared portions turn out not to be reentrant.

OFF specifies that SAS be executed from the modules on the CMS SAS disk; the saved supervisor segment is not to be used.

SHARED is the default. However, if SAS cannot use the saved supervisor segment, either because it has not been installed at your installation or because of the virtual machine size, the status of the SSEG option is set to NOT__USED. This option is used under CMS and only at SAS invocation.

STIMER/NOSTIMER
specifies whether or not operating system task timing facilities are available for use by the SAS supervisor. If NOSTIMER is specified, then SAS may not be able to report the amount of CPU time used by each SAS step under all operating systems. NOSTIMER is assumed under ICCF.

SVCHND/ NOSVCHND
determines if SAS supervisor call handling is turned off when executing a CMS statement. This option is used under CMS only.

NOSYMBOLGEN/ SYMBOLGEN
controls whether the text produced by expanding macro variable (also called symbolic variable) references is printed on the SAS log.

NOSYNCSORT/ SYNCSORT
specifies that the SYNCSORT program product is used as the system sort utility. SYNCSORT is a trademark of Syncsort Incorporated.

SYSIN = SYSIN (OS and CMS) SYSIN = SYSIPT (VSE)
specifies the DDname for the primary SAS input stream data set. The DDname for the SAS input stream is normally SYSIN. It may be changed to another DDname with this option, which must be specified at SAS invocation. When SAS is executing in an interactive environment such as CMS, TSO, or ICCF, and this option is **not** explicitly specified at SAS invocation, then SAS does not use this file to read the primary SAS input stream, but rather requests input directly from the terminal. (If the CLIST option is specified in a TSO environment, SAS requests input from the statements in the CLIST following the SAS command or any other stacked input statements, or any other input source identified to TSO, including the terminal.)

SYSIN/NOSYSIN
specifies whether or not SAS is to read the primary SAS input stream from the SYSIN= DDname. NOSYSIN specifies that the SYSIN= file is not to be used. In this case, you must use either the INITSTMT= option or the CLIST option (both described above) to provide a primary input stream to SAS. This option can only be specified at SAS invocation.

SYSPARM = ''
specifies a character string that can be passed to SAS programs. The character string specified can be accessed in a SAS DATA step by the SYSPARM( ) function (see Chapter 5, "SAS Functions"), or at any time during the job by using the automatic macro variable reference &SYSPARM (see Chapter 15, "The SAS Macro Language"). The maximum length for SYSPARM is 200 characters. NOTE: under OS, if the SYSPARM= option is specified in the JCL EXEC statement OPTIONS= parameter (that is, an EXEC statement that is invoking a cataloged procedure), then four single quotes are required around the option value; under VSE, only two single quotes are required, because the VSE JCL EXEC statement PARM= parameter can only

be specified directly:

OS: // EXEC SAS,OPTIONS = 'SYSPARM =
''''value'''' *more options*'

VSE: // EXEC SASVSE,PARM = 'SYSPARM =
''value'' *more options*'

TAPE = TAPE — gives the esoteric or generic name defined at OS system generation for tape devices. This option is ignored under CMS and VSE.

TAPECLOSE =
REREAD
TAPECLOSE = LEAVE
TAPECLOSE =
REWIND
TAPECLOSE = DISP
— specifies the default CLOSE disposition (volume positioning) to be performed when a SAS data library on tape is closed. The default value for this option is REREAD, except for tape data libraries accessed by PROC COPY. The default value for tape data libraries accessed by PROC COPY is LEAVE and may not be overridden. The FILECLOSE = data set option takes precedence over the TAPECLOSE = system option. See Chapter 12, "SAS Data Sets," for a discussion of the FILECLOSE = data set option. This option is ignored under VSE.

Specify TAPECLOSE = REREAD if you are accessing one or more tape data libraries several times in a SAS job. SAS leaves the tape volume positioned at the beginning of the tape data library. REREAD overrides a FREE = CLOSE specification in the job control.

Specify TAPECLOSE = REWIND if you are not repeatedly accessing one or more tape data libraries in a SAS job. SAS rewinds the tape volume to the beginning. A FREE = CLOSE specification in the job control overrides the REWIND specification.

Specify TAPECLOSE = LEAVE if you are not repeatedly accessing the same tape data libraries in a SAS job, but, once used, you are creating or accessing one or more tape data libraries in a subsequent file on the same tape volume. SAS leaves the tape positioned at the end of the data library. LEAVE overrides a FREE = CLOSE specification in the job control.

If you specify TAPECLOSE = DISP, then the tape volume is positioned as determined by the operating system, according to specifications in the job control.

TIME = MAX or *n*
T = MAX or *n*
— gives the maximum execution time (elapsed time under VSE) in seconds allowed for a SAS job. The value must be an integer and cannot exceed that specified or defaulted at the time of SAS invocation. SAS terminates abnormally when the execution time for the SAS job exceeds the specified value. If TIME = MAX, SAS does not limit the time used. In all cases, local computer installation limits also apply to SAS jobs. This option is ignored under CMS.

TLINESIZE = 0
TLS = 0
— specifies the linesize for printing SAS output at a terminal. If TLINESIZE = 0 when executing SAS interactively, the default linesize of the user's terminal is used to print SAS output at the terminal. The TLINESIZE option

may be used to set the terminal linesize to a value ranging from 64 to 132. The LINESIZE= option sets the linesize for all files that are not directed to a terminal.

TMSG=NOTES
TMSG=NOTE
TMSG=ERRORS
TMSG=ERRO
TMSG=OFF

determines what informatory messages appear at the terminal when the entire SAS log is not directed to the terminal. The default terminal message level is ERRORS. This option is used under CMS only.

NOTES specifies that all notes and errors appear.

ERRORS specifies that only error messages appear.

OFF suppresses the appearance of any informatory messages.

TRANTAB=
GTABVTCAM (OS)
TRANTAB=
GTABCMS (CMS)

specifies the terminal I/O translation table to be used by SAS/GRAPH.

NOTSO/TSO

under TSO, controls the format of the SAS log and whether SAS notes the memory and CPU time used for each step. TSO is the default when SAS is being executed interactively, and NOTSO is the default for noninteractive (batch) execution of SAS. If the TSO option is in effect, the resource utilization notes are suppressed; if the NOTSO option is in effect, the notes are printed. NOTSO is implied if the BATCH option is specified; TSO is implied if the INTERACTIVE option is specified, and SAS is being executed interactively under TSO.

TXTLIB/NOTXTLIB

determines whether or not text libraries included in a CMS GLOBAL TXTLIB specification before invoking SAS are searched during a SAS session.

If TXTLIB is specified, the text libraries included in a CMS GLOBAL TXTLIB specification before invoking SAS are added to the end of the list of libraries searched during a SAS session.

With either setting of this option, the list of global text libraries is returned to its pre-SAS status at the end of the SAS session. This option is used under CMS and only at SAS invocation.

UNITS=11 12 13 14
15 16 17 18 19 20

controls units (DDname) assignment. Do **not** use this option under CMS. SAS output files use DDnames of the form FT*nn*F001, where *nn* is a unit number: for example, FT11F001. Under VSE, unit numbers are treated as VSE logical unit numbers. Thus, unit 11 means SYS011. Internally, SAS unit numbers are defined as:

1 = Log file: source statements, notes, errors
2 = Print file: output of procedures
3 = Punch file
4 = Plot output file
5 = PARMCARDS file
6–10 Not currently used

To eliminate possible conflicts with FORTRAN and other programs, these unit numbers are usually defined with the UNITS= option to the values below:

    11 = Log file
    12 = Print file
    13 = Punch file
    14 = Plot file
    15 = PARMCARDS file
    16–20 Undefined

The SAS cataloged procedures and CLISTs reference these unit numbers. The keyword UNITS must be followed by a list of up to ten numbers, separated by blanks. The first number given becomes the unit number for log output; the second for procedure output; and so on.

Specifying the UNITS= option causes the PARMCARDS= and LOG= options to be reset. If both UNITS= and LOG= or PARMCARDS= are to be specified, UNITS= should precede the LOG= or PARMCARDS= specification.

USER=USER specifies the DDname for the USER data set. If the control language acompanying the SAS job defines the DDname USER, SAS uses USER (USER010 under VSE) as default DDname for SAS data sets that specify only a one-level name. The DDname for the USER data set may be changed to another DDname with this option. If the DDname USER (USER010 under VSE) is not defined in the control language acompanying your SAS job, then USER=WORK (WORK000 under VSE) is the default.

USERPARM='' specifies up to 200 bytes of data to be made available to SAS installation exits.

VIOBUF n specifies the number of 8K buffers of memory allocated for the SAS WORK data library. By storing the most active portions of the WORK data library in memory, disk activity is reduced. This option is used under CMS and only at SAS invocation.

The default number of buffers in the virtual I/O area is a function of your virtual machine size; up to 40 pages of virtual storage (160K) can be allocated for a virtual I/O work area. Since only SAS internal WORK data sets are maintained in the virtual I/O WORK area, there is little benefit in extending its size beyond the default. To force the entire WORK data library to be written to disk, specify VIOBUF 0.

WORK=WORK gives the DDname for the WORK data set. The DDname for the SAS work data set is normally WORK (WORK000 under VSE). It may be changed to another DDname with this option, which can only be specified at SAS invocation.

NOWORKINIT/
WORKINIT controls whether the WORK data set is initialized at the start of the SAS job. The default for CMS (both batch and interactive) is WORKINIT.

NOZEROMEM/   controls whether all memory is set to binary 0s. This
ZEROMEM   option is for diagnostic use only and should be used
             only when requested by a SAS consultant. This option
             is used under CMS only.

PAGE Statement

The PAGE statement is used to skip to a new page on the log.
    The form of the PAGE statement is:

PAGE;

The PAGE statement is not printed on the log.

%PUT Statement

The %PUT statement can be used anywhere in a SAS job (except after a CARDS or PARMCARDS statement) to send a message to the SAS log.
    The form of the %PUT statement is:

   %PUT *message*;

where

   message   is any message you want printed on the log.

RUN Statement

The RUN statement is used to cause the previously entered SAS step to be executed immediately. The statement is often used in interactive jobs entered at a terminal where, without a RUN statement, a SAS step is executed only after the first statement in the next DATA or PROC step is entered.

The form of the RUN statement is:

RUN;

%RUN Statement

The %RUN statement can be used anywhere in a SAS job (except after a CARDS or PARMCARDS statement) to end source statements following a %INCLUDE * statement.

See the %INCLUDE statement description for more information.

The form of the %RUN statement is:

%RUN;

SKIP Statement

You can use the SKIP statement to skip lines on the SAS log.
    The form of the SKIP statement is:

SKIP *n*;

where

    n   is the number of lines that you want to skip on the
        log. If the number specified is greater than the number
        of lines remaining on the page, SAS treats the SKIP
        statement like a PAGE statement and skips to the top
        of the next page. If n is omitted, SAS skips one line on
        the log.

The SKIP statement is not printed on the log.

TITLE Statement

The TITLE statement is used to specify up to ten title lines to be printed on the SAS print file and other SAS output.

The form of the TITLE statement is:

TITLE*n title*****;**

where

n immediately follows the word TITLE, with no intervening blank, to specify the number of the title line. For example, the statement

TITLE3 THIS IS THE THIRD TITLE LINE;

specifies a title for the third line from the top of the page. For the first title line, either TITLE or TITLE1 may be specified.

title gives a title of up to 132 characters that you want printed. If a title longer than the current linesize is specified, it is truncated to the linesize length. If the title contains a semicolon, enclose the entire title in single quotes. If the title itself contains a single quote, write it as two single quotes; SAS translates them to one quote when it prints the title. Any title may be enclosed in single quotes, and future releases of SAS may require it.

Once you specify a title for a line, it is used for all subsequent output until you cancel the title or define another title for that line. If you want a title associated with a given PROC step, include the title:

- after a RUN statement for the previous step, if one is present

or

- anywhere after the PROC statement and before the next DATA, PROC, or RUN statement.

For example,

```
PROC PRINT;
TITLE TITLE FOR FIRST PROC;
PROC MEANS;
```

In this example, the title is printed on the output for both the PRINT and the MEANS procedures.

These statements

```
PROC PRINT;
RUN;
TITLE TITLE FOR SECOND PROC;
PROC MEANS;
RUN;
```

print the title only on the PROC MEANS output.

These statements

PROC PRINT;
PROC MEANS;
TITLE TITLE FOR SECOND PROC;

also print the title only on the output pages from MEANS.

You can include a macro name or a macro variable in a TITLE statement, and the macro will be expanded, or the value of the macro variable substituted in the title. If you do not want the macro name or macro variable name expanded, enclose the title in single quotes.

Changing titles   To change from one title to another, use a new TITLE statement in the step whose output you want to have the new title. The new TITLE statement cancels the old title for that line.

A new TITLE statement also cancels any earlier TITLE statements with larger n values. For example, if you defined TITLE and TITLE3 statements in one step of a SAS job, defining a new TITLE (or TITLE1) in a later step cancels the earlier TITLE and TITLE3 statements.

Note that when some title lines are not specified, the title lines omitted are assumed to be blank. For example, if TITLE1 and TITLE3 statements appear, a blank line appears between the two titles on the SAS output.

Suppressing titles   If you use the single word

TITLE;

you get a blank line as the title rather than the default SAS title or any title defined earlier. To suppress the nth and later titles, use

TITLEn;

TSO Statement

The TSO statement is used to execute TSO commands during a SAS session.
The form of the TSO statement is:

TSO *TSOcommand*;

where

> *TSOcommand*   is any TSO command or CLIST except the TEST,
> LOGON, or LOGOFF commands, or any command
> which must be given control in an authorized state.
> CLIST attention exits defined by the ATTN command
> may not be specified.

You may specify any TSO command up to 200 characters in length; SAS executes
the statement as soon as it is encountered. The TSO statement **must** end in a
semicolon. For example, the TSO statement

TSO ALLOC FI(IN) DA('USERID.MY.SASDATA');

allocates the data set named USERID.MY.SASDATA without exiting from SAS.
If you enter the statement

TSO;

SAS enters TSO submode and prompts you for TSO commands. Commands
entered in TSO submode are not processed as SAS statements and can be any
length. The subcommand

RETURN

issued from TSO submode, returns you to SAS. Any characters following the
RETURN subcommand are ignored. You can also return to SAS from TSO submode
by entering the subcommand

END

directly from the terminal. END commands appearing within a CLIST terminate
command procedures without ending TSO submode.
Here is an example:

1? *SAS statements*
...
11? tso;
TSO SUBMODE, ENTER "RETURN" OR "END" TO RETURN TO SAS
TSO
submit misc(compress)
JOB COMPRESS(JOB01931) SUBMITTED
TSO
status compress
JOB COMPRESS(JOB01931) ON OUTPUT QUEUE
TSO
return
12? proc print; run;

The TSO statement is ignored if it appears in a job that is not run under TSO.

X Statement

The X statement is used to issue a TSO or CMS command from within a SAS job. If you are running under TSO, the X statement becomes a TSO statement; under CMS, the X statement becomes a CMS statement; in other environments, the statement is treated as a comment. The X statement is a useful abbreviation for the TSO or CMS statement.

The form of the X statement is:

    X *command*;

where

        command   specifies a CMS or TSO command to be issued.

See the CMS and TSO statement descriptions for more information.

When the same SAS program is run under both TSO and CMS, then both TSO and CMS statements should be used. The TSO statement is ignored when the job is run in CMS; the CMS statement is ignored in the TSO environment.

SAS Data Sets

INTRODUCTION

To analyze data with SAS procedures you must first have the data in a SAS data set. This chapter describes SAS data sets and SAS data libraries, and discusses ways to store and manage them.

SAS data sets are created by SAS in the DATA step and by SAS procedures. See Chapter 2, "Introduction to the DATA Step," and Chapter 3, "Statements Used in the DATA Step," for details on creating SAS data sets. Also consult procedure documentation about the types of data sets created by different procedures and for the syntax required to create them. The **Special SAS Data Sets** section in this chapter describes some of the data sets that can be created with SAS procedures.

THE SAS DATA SET: DEFINITION

A *SAS data set* is a computer file of data packaged in a convenient way for SAS to use. SAS data sets contain observations for which variable values (data) have been recorded, descriptor information on the variables, and the history of the data set. SAS data sets can be permanent, stored for repeated use, or temporary, used in only one job or session.

SAS data sets differ from other computer files in the way they store data and because they automatically maintain descriptive information about the data set. The data are arranged in a rectangular table with the rows of the table representing the observations and the columns representing the variables. The descriptor information is at the beginning of each SAS data set, and includes the names and certain attributes of the variables in the data set. The descriptor information stored for each variable is:

- name (from one to eight characters in length)
- type (character or numeric)
- length (the number of bytes used to store a variable)
- position (the location of the variable within an observation)
- informat name (for reading the variable values)
- format name (for printing the values)
- label (a variable descriptor consisting of from one to 40 characters).

The descriptor section of a SAS data set also contains history information: the date and time of the data set's creation, the name of the job that created it, and the SAS statements used to create it. You can specify how many generations of this history information are stored for a data set with the SAS system option GEN = (see Chapter 10, "Introduction to Systems").

A SAS data set can contain any number of observations, but an observation cannot contain more than approximately 32,000 bytes of information (in other words, no more than about 4000 variables with lengths of eight bytes). The exact upper limit varies and depends upon:

- the number of automatic variables that SAS creates for your use
- the maximum size of the program data vector
- the maximum size of a block or VSE FBA control interval on the device (whether disk or tape) on which the SAS data library is being stored.

(See Chapter 2, "Introduction to the DATA Step," for information about the program data vector, and see Chapter 1, "Introduction to the SAS Language," for a complete discussion of variable lengths.)

Whether you intend to store a data set permanently or temporarily, you must have your data in a SAS data set. SAS relies on the information in the descriptor section to process variable values correctly, and most SAS procedures only handle data that are in a SAS data set.

THE SAS DATA LIBRARY: DEFINITION

A *SAS data library* is a specially formatted file that may contain any number of SAS data sets. Like SAS data sets, SAS data libraries can be temporary or permanent. There is a default temporary SAS data library called the WORK library. The WORK library is used to keep temporary SAS data sets available for the duration of a job or session. (It is possible to create your own temporary SAS data library for this purpose, but this is rarely done.) When you want to store a SAS data set permanently so that it is also available for later SAS jobs, you can store the data set in a permanent SAS data library that you create on disk or tape. Storing SAS data sets in permanent libraries reduces maintenance chores and processing time, and keeps you free to concentrate on the contents of your data sets rather than on the mechanics of creating, storing, documenting, and retrieving them.

Any SAS data library under TSO, OS batch, and VSE contains a directory that keeps track of the data sets in the data library. SAS automatically creates this directory and updates it whenever a new data set is added to or deleted from the data library.

While SAS data sets are created by SAS in DATA or PROC steps, SAS data libraries are created and named through the control language of the operating system you are using. Creating SAS data libraries is discussed later in this chapter.

In SAS statements, SAS data libraries are not referred to by their library names, but by a name that refers to the library, the *DDname*. (CMS is an exception to this general rule, because the SAS library name and DDname are the same word in CMS.) DDnames are discussed in the next section.

PERMANENT AND TEMPORARY SAS DATA SETS: SAS DATA SET NAMES

Every SAS data set, whether temporary or permanent, belongs to a SAS data library. The name you use for a SAS data set determines where the data set is stored (that is, in which SAS data library it is stored), and therefore, whether the data set is temporary or permanent. If you store a SAS data set in a temporary library, the data set is temporary. If you store a data set in a permanent library, it is a permanent data set.

A SAS data set is named in a DATA statement or by a specification in a PROC step at the time it is created. A data set's complete name consists of two words, each from one to eight characters long, separated by a period; for example, TREE.OAK. The first word (first-level name) is a reference to the SAS data library to which the data set belongs (TREE), and the second word (second-level name) identifies the specific data set (OAK). The second-level name is necessary because a SAS data library can contain many SAS data sets. (Note: the first-level name is limited to seven characters under VSE.)

As mentioned above, the first level of a data set name is a reference to the SAS data library to which the data set will belong. The first-level name of a SAS data set corresponds to the following elements of job control under different systems:

OS: the *DDname* of the DD statement that references the SAS data library to which the data set will belong

TSO: the *filename* of the ALLOCATE command that references the SAS data library to which the data set will belong

CMS: the *DDname* of the FILEDEF command that references the SAS data library to which the data set will belong (the FILEDEF command is optional when the library is on the A disk.)

VSE: the *filename* of the DLBL statement that references the SAS data library to which the data set will belong.

For ease of reference, we use DDname to refer to both DDnames and filenames.

When naming a new data set, you do not always need to specify a two-level name; in some cases SAS automatically names the data set for you. These are the three most common ways of naming data sets (exceptions are noted later in this chapter):

1. You specify both names to create a permanent data set. For example:

    DATA FOOD.PRICES;

2. You can specify one name to create a temporary data set. For example:

    DATA PRICES;

3. You can also omit a name entirely to create a temporary SAS data set. For example:

    DATA;

Naming Permanent SAS Data Sets

If you want to create a permanent data set you must:

- store the data set in a permanent SAS data library,
- specify a two-level name in the DATA or PROC step (except when USER= is in effect; see below),
- use control language at the beginning of your SAS job or session that references the SAS data library to which the data set will belong. Under OS, use a DD statement; under VSE, use a DLBL statement; under CMS, use a FILEDEF command; and under TSO, use an ALLOCATE command.

Here is a data set naming example. You want to create a permanent data set called PRICES (second-level name), so you know you must store it in a permanent SAS data library. You choose the SAS library referenced by the DDname FOOD, and use this DATA statement:

```
DATA FOOD.PRICES;
```

The USER= Option   There is an exception to the rule that you must always specify both names of a permanent data set. You can use the SAS system option USER= to specify a default DDname (first-level name), and as long as you are creating a data set to be stored in that library, you need only specify the second-level name.

USER= is specified in an OPTIONS statement or when you invoke SAS; give the DDname after USER= . For example, if you wanted to specify FOOD as the default DDname, the OPTIONS statement could be written:

```
OPTIONS USER = FOOD;
```

For the duration of the job, or until another default DDname is specified, you can specify just one name for any data set that you want to store in the FOOD library. For example:

```
DATA JUNK;
```

creates a permanent data set called FOOD.JUNK. The USER= option is also effective in data set retrieval (for example, in a SET statement).

The default DDname can be changed at any time with an OPTIONS statement.

Miscellaneous Notes on DDnames   The exact form of the DDname and the job control language to reference a SAS data library depend on the system you are using: OS, TSO, CMS, or VSE. If you are unfamiliar with the control language for the system you are using, consult your installation's technical personnel for information. Also see the appendix for your operating system at the end of this manual. For a complete discussion of SAS under CMS, see *SAS CMS Companion*; for a complete discussion of SAS under VSE, see the *SAS VSE Companion*. SAS data library names are also dependent on the operating system and your installation's local naming conventions. Consult the appropriate documentation to learn about data library naming conventions.

Under OS, TSO, and VSE you can change the DDname, and therefore the SAS data set's first-level name, from job to job. As long as you remember to refer to your data sets by the correct name, that is, using the current DDname as the first-level name, this is perfectly acceptable. For example, if a permanent data set called WAGES is created in a job where the DDname is EMPLOY, any reference to the data set in a SAS statement in that job must be EMPLOY.WAGES:

```
DATA TAX;
  SET EMPLOY.WAGES;
```

If the WAGES data set is used in a later job that uses the DDname LABOR to refer to the same data library, any reference to the WAGES data set must be LABOR.WAGES:

```
DATA BENEFITS;
  SET LABOR.WAGES;
```

There are DDnames that are used by the operating system and SAS for special purposes. You should not use them except as they are intended to be used. The reserved DDnames include: DFHLIB, DFSRESLB, DFSURCDS, DFSURWF1,

DFSVSAMP, FT*nn*F001 (where *nn* is a UNIT number), IEFRDER, IEFRDER2, IMS, IMSACB, IMSMON, IMSUDUMP, JOBCAT, JOBLIB, LIBRARY, MACLIB, PLIDUMP, PL1DUMP, PROCLIB, SASDUMP, SASLIB, SASSWK*nn*, SORTLIB, SORTWK*nn*, STEPCAT, STEPLIB, SYSABEND, SYSHELP, SYSIN, SYSLIB, SYSMDUMP, SYSOUT, SYSPRINT, SYSUADS, SYSUDUMP, SYS*nnnnn*, TASKLIB, USER, WORK, and $ORTPARM; and under VSE, WORK000, USER010, and SYSIPT.

Naming Temporary SAS Data Sets

Specifying one name   If you want to create a temporary data set (one that exists only for the duration of the job or session), you usually specify one name in the DATA or PROC statement (exceptions to this are noted below). The name you specify becomes the second-level name of the data set and SAS automatically uses WORK for the first-level name. WORK is the DDname of the default temporary SAS data library. (Under VSE, WORK000 is the DDname of the default SAS library; however, for convenience we shall refer to it as the WORK library.)

The WORK library is necessary to the operation of SAS. It stores any temporary data sets you create, and much that is internally generated in SAS as well. For example, the WORK library contains the compiled program, current TITLE and FOOTNOTE lines, any macros that have been defined, and so on.

At most installations, the WORK library is erased and initialized at the beginning of a SAS job. When you use SAS under an interactive system, the WORK library is not erased between SAS job steps in one interactive session so it can be reused. This allows you to retain macros and temporary data sets between job steps. For example, in a TSO or CMS session you can execute SAS DATA and PROC steps, leave SAS and work on something else, and then return to SAS with your WORK library intact. The EXECs or CLISTs necessary to do this are installation-dependent, so you should consult the appropriate sources to learn how to return to the WORK library between job steps in an interactive environment.

Usually, specifying one name in a DATA or PROC statement creates a data set that is in the WORK data library and is temporary; however, there are exceptions to this general rule:

- If the USER= system option is in effect and you give a one-level name to a new data set, the USER= DDname is used as the first-level name instead of WORK and the data set is permanent. (See **The USER= Option**, above.)
- It is possible to create your own temporary SAS data libraries to use for temporary data sets instead of the WORK library. It is not common practice to do so. If you do create another temporary library, you must specify a two-level name for any temporary data sets when they are created or used. Use the DDname that references the library as the first-level name. If you fail to specify a two-level name, the data sets are assigned the DDname WORK, or the USER= DDname, if one exists. Discussion of data set names throughout this book and *SAS User's Guide: Statistics, 1982 Edition* assumes that temporary data sets are stored in the WORK library.
- The WORK data library can be made into a permanent data library by using the appropriate job control. If this is done, SAS still assigns WORK as a first-level name to data sets given one name in DATA or PROC statements, but they are permanent data sets because the WORK library is permanent. It is **not** recommended that you change the WORK library to a permanent library.

Omitting the data set name If you do not specify any name in the DATA statement, SAS still creates a data set. It is named automatically by SAS. The first-level name is WORK or the USER= DDname, if one exists, as it is when you specify only one name in the DATA statement. The data set is temporary if WORK is the first-level name, and permanent if the USER= option is in effect. The second-level name is DATA*n*, where *n* is 1 for the first such data set, 2 for the second, 3 for the third, and so on through the job. Assuming that the USER= option is not in effect, the first time SAS executes the statement:

```
DATA;
```

it creates a data set named WORK.DATA1.
The statement:

```
DATA;
```

is equivalent to the statement:

```
DATA __DATA__;
```

where __DATA__ is a special SAS variable indicating that the data set is to be named according to the DATA *n* convention.
Note: if you are creating more than one data set in a job it is easier to keep track of them if you specify names rather than letting SAS name them according to the DATA*n* convention.
You should avoid explicitly naming data sets DATA1, DATA2, DATA3, and so on. SAS keeps track of its variable __DATA__, and when it encounters a DATA or PROC statement that does not specify a data set name, SAS uses the current __DATA__ value. If you have named a data set DATA*n*, it could be written over later in the job if SAS uses that name. For example:

```
DATA DATA1;
   SET GRADES;
   IF AVG=A;
DATA;
   SET SCORES;
   IF MATH>90;
```

The DATA1 data set containing a subset of the GRADES data set is overwritten in the second DATA step. The new version contains a subset of data from the SCORES data set. This happens because SAS automatically names the second data set DATA1, according to the DATA*n* naming convention.

Specifying __NULL__ If you want to execute a DATA step but do not want to create a data set, you can specify __NULL__ in the DATA statement:

```
DATA __NULL__;
```

For example, if you are writing a report based on the values in a SAS data set, you probably do not want to create another SAS data set containing the same information. Using __NULL__ means that SAS goes through the DATA step just as if it were creating a new data set, but does not write any observations. This can be a more efficient use of computer time.

RETRIEVING AND USING SAS DATA SETS

As you have seen, all SAS data sets have two names, even if you do not specify two names when you create a data set. When SAS refers to an existing data set, it uses both names. If you specify the name PRICES, SAS calls the data set WORK.PRICES (for example, when it refers to the data set in notes on the SAS log). However, you do not always have to use both names to refer to an existing data set. The following section discusses what to call your data sets when you retrieve and use them.

Temporary SAS Data Sets

When you refer to a temporary data set in program statements or procedures, you need use only the second-level name (unless USER= is in effect). For example, if you want to use the data set WORK.PRICES in a SET statement, you could say:

    SET PRICES;

You do not need to say:

    SET WORK.PRICES;

although it is correct.

Unless the USER= system option is in effect, whenever SAS sees a one-word data set name, it assumes that the data set is temporary and that it is in the data library identified by the name WORK.

Permanent SAS Data Sets

To use a SAS data set stored on disk or tape in a later SAS job, include job control language describing the SAS data library containing the data set (unless you are using CMS and the library is on the A disk). Then specify the two-level data set name in the PROC statement or in a SET, MERGE, or UPDATE statement (except when USER= is in effect). For example, if you use the DATA statement:

    DATA FOOD.PRICES;

to create a permanent SAS data set, and you want to refer to the data set in a SET statement later, you would use the statement:

    SET FOOD.PRICES;

If you use the statement:

    SET PRICES;

SAS assumes that the data set belongs to the default SAS data library for temporary data sets (the WORK library) and would not be able to find the data set.

Do **not** use an INFILE statement to retrieve a SAS data set; INFILE statements are for input data lines in non-SAS files only, not for SAS data sets.

For details on the precise job control language to use see the various system appendices in this volume. If you use CMS you should also refer to the *SAS CMS Companion*; and under VSE, see the *SAS VSE Companion*. In general, if you are not familiar with the job control language for your operating system, consult the technical staff at your computer installation.

The __LAST__ Data Set

Another system option that simplifies using permanent SAS data sets is the __LAST__= option. SAS procedures analyze the data set specified in the PROC statement. If no data set is specified, the last SAS data set created in that job or session is used. The special SAS variable __LAST__ keeps track of the most recently created data set, temporary or permanent. You can use the __LAST__= system option to designate a permanent SAS data set from a previous job or session as the __LAST__ data set for the current job or session. See Chapter 10 for more information on the __LAST__ = system option.

Advantages of Permanent SAS Data Sets

There are many advantages to storing your data in a permanent SAS data set rather than leaving them in an external file:

- SAS automatically documents the data set, and you can keep track of its contents easily. You always know which variables the data set contains, the date it was created, and other information that often gets lost for un-documented files or card decks.
- You leave reading of the data to SAS; you need not be concerned about format and you do not need to execute INPUT statements each time a data set is used.
- No data conversion is necessary, since data are stored in the form in which SAS uses them, saving computer time.

SAS DATA SETS AND SAS DATA LIBRARIES: MANAGING AND STORING

Allocating SAS Data Libraries

When you create a SAS data library (on a disk or tape) you must tell the computer where you want to store it; what its name is; and for OS, TSO, and VSE how much space the library needs.

The host operating system manages all disk and tape storage. For SAS to create a SAS data library, the physical space must be made available to SAS (allocated) from the host operating system. You create (allocate space for) a new SAS data library with job control language, either prior to or accompanying the SAS job or session that creates the first SAS data set in the library.

File names and job control language for file allocation are system-dependent so you should consult your installation's technical staff, the appropriate job control language manuals, and the appendix for your operating system at the end of this manual for complete information on data library allocation.

Storing SAS Data Libraries on Disk or Tape

You can choose to store SAS data libraries on either disk or tape. Some considerations that may affect your decision are given here:

- Data stored on on-line disk are always available, and your SAS jobs do not have to wait for a tape or off-line disk to be mounted.
- Under TSO and CMS, only on-line disk data sets are accessible at most computer centers.
- Tape storage of SAS data sets is less flexible, since the data set you want to use cannot be accessed directly. Replacing a data set on tape means deleting all data sets after it on the tape.

- On-line disk space is usually more expensive than off-line disk space and tapes.
- Tapes are able to accommodate large data sets for which disk storage may be impractical.
- SAS data sets in tape format are transportable across operating systems. They can be processed by OS/VS, VSE, and CMS versions of SAS.

Other considerations specific to your installation may affect your choice of disk or tape. Check with the staff of your computer installation if you are not familiar with using disk and tape.

SAS data libraries on tape   When you store SAS data sets on tape, keep these points in mind:

- At any point in a SAS job, you can access only one of the SAS data sets on a tape. For example, you cannot read two SAS data sets on the same tape in a single DATA step. However, you can access two or more SAS data sets on different tapes at the same time (if there are enough tape drives available to your job). You can also access a data set on a tape during one DATA or PROC step in the job, then access another data set on the tape during a later DATA or PROC step.
- When you add a new SAS data set to a SAS data library on tape, it is written at the end of the data library.
- When you replace a SAS data set on tape with another data set that has the same name, the original data set is overwritten and any other data sets after it on the tape are erased. This is true even if PROTECT passwords have been assigned to the other data sets on the tape. (This is a limitation of tapes rather than SAS.)
- If you delete a SAS data set on tape with PROC DELETE or PROC DATASETS, that data set as well as any other data sets after it on the tape are deleted.
- **Never** use the DCB parameters RECFM, LRECL, BLKSIZE, BFTEK, or BUFNO for tape data sets. If you want to override the default BLKSIZE or BUFNO, use data set options (described below); for example,

      DATA M.SURVEY(BLKSIZE = 32000);

- You do not need a SPACE specification for SAS data libraries on tape.

Tape-format data libraries on disk   SAS data libraries can be stored on disk in tape format under OS, CMS, and TSO, but not under VSE. The sequential nature of the tape format has limitations, but tape-format data libraries can be processed by both the OS and CMS versions of SAS in a shared-disk system. Under VSE you can process tape-format data libraries that have been copied from disk to tape under OS or CMS. This feature is useful when direct-access data sets are not handled by local utility programs, when SAS data sets need to be interchanged between processors and/or operating systems, or when transmitting SAS data sets from one node to another in a network.

Under both OS and CMS, store the SAS data library in tape-format by beginning the DDname with the characters TAPE.

How Much Space?

For disk storage under OS, TSO, and VSE, you specify the amount of space the SAS data library needs when you allocate the library. Often, the space allocation has to be estimated because you do not know what data sets you will store in the library.

Sometimes you do know the data sets to be stored, and in these cases you can use the formula below to calculate how much space to allocate for your SAS data library.

This formula can be used to estimate the space required for a SAS data set. Sum the SIZE values for each data set in the library to calculate the space needed for the library. Remember that each SAS data library requires at least one extra track to hold directory information.

$$\text{SIZE} = \text{CEIL}(\text{NOBS}/\text{FLOOR}(\text{TRACKLEN}/(\text{LEN}+4))) +$$
$$\text{CEIL}((\text{GEN}*(3000+\text{SRC}*86)+\text{NVAR}*78)/\text{TRACKLEN})$$

where:

SIZE is the number of tracks needed

NOBS is the number of observations

TRACKLEN is the length of a track on the disk device being used

LEN is the length of the data in an observation. If the data set contains all numeric variables, LEN = 8*NVAR, where NVAR is the number of variables. When the data set contains character variables or variables of length other than 8, sum the lengths of all variables to compute LEN.

GEN is the number of generations of data set history and descriptor information stored with the data set

SRC is the number of source statements in the SAS DATA step that creates the data set.

Note: CEIL is a SAS function that returns the smallest integer greater than or equal to an argument, and FLOOR is a SAS function that returns the largest integer less than or equal to an argument.

Note: a track corresponds to a control interval on FBA disks.

If you have already run a DATA step for a data set, you can get the number of observations per track from the note that SAS prints on the log. Divide the total number of observations by this number and add the number of tracks required for descriptor, header, and history records to get the number of tracks required to hold the data set. (A liberal estimate of the space required to store data set history and descriptor information, other than source statements and variable descriptor records, is 3000 bytes.)

Data set too large   If a SAS data set uses much more space than your calculations indicate it should, consider changing the value of the SAS system option GEN = .

The GEN = value refers to the generations of history information that are stored with SAS data sets. This information contains the statements used to create the data set, plus the statements used to create earlier generations of the data set. These statements provide a valuable record of the data set's history and are especially important when several people are working on a project and all must understand what the others have done with a data set. However, sometimes the space required to store the data set's history becomes excessive. In that case, you can use the statement:

OPTIONS GEN = 2;

to store only the immediate source statements and those from the preceding generation. To prevent SAS from storing any statements with the data set, use:

OPTIONS GEN = 0;

Space considerations when replacing SAS data sets   If you are creating a SAS data set that has the same name as an existing data set in your SAS data library, the library must have enough free space to hold a copy of the SAS data set being replaced. The original data set is deleted only **after** the new data set has been written completely with no errors.

MANAGING SAS DATA LIBRARIES

Methods for managing SAS data libraries are available in SAS. Each of these is described briefly below; for more information, refer to the appropriate procedure description or system option.

Replacing SAS Data Sets

If you are creating a SAS data set that has the same name as an existing data set in your SAS data library, the original data set is deleted by default when the new data set has been written completely with no errors. However, if the system or the SAS job abends before the new data set is finished, the original data set is preserved.

You can allow or disallow replacement of a permanent data set with the REPLACE/NOREPLACE system option. REPLACE is the default value; if you do not want data sets to be automatically replaced, specify NOREPLACE as a system option. In addition, you can override the system option specification with the REPLACE= data set option. For example, the NOREPLACE system option is in effect in the SAS job shown below, but it is temporarily overridden for the FOOD.MEAT data set.

```
OPTIONS NOREPLACE;
DATA FOOD.MILK;
  SET FOOD.DAIRY;
  IF PRODUCT=MILK;
DATA FOOD.MEAT(REPLACE=YES);
  SET FOOD.MEAT;
  IF DATE>'1MAR82'D;
```

Documenting the Contents of SAS Data Libraries

PROC CONTENTS gives you complete documentation on the contents of the SAS data library and the data sets it contains. Variable names and labels, the number of observations, when the data sets were created, and other information can be displayed by PROC CONTENTS. See Chapter 32, "The CONTENTS Procedure," for complete information.

Copying SAS Data Libraries

PROC COPY can be used to copy SAS data libraries from disk to disk, disk to tape, tape to disk, and tape to tape. It is especially designed for backups.

Except under CMS, SAS data libraries should only be moved using the COPY procedure. Data sets may become unreadable if you use other non-SAS utility procedures to copy them. See "The COPY Procedure" for a complete description. Under CMS, the CMS COPYFILE, MOVEFILE, and TAPE DUMP comments can also be used to copy SAS data libraries.

Renaming and Deleting SAS Data Sets

You can use PROC DATASETS to rename disk-format SAS data sets, delete SAS data sets, and systematically rename a group of functionally-related data sets. DATASETS also allows you to rename and relabel variables. See the discussion of the DATASETS procedure for more information.

Deleting SAS Data Sets

PROC DELETE can also be used to delete SAS data sets. See the discussion of the DELETE procedure for more information.

Releasing Unused Space

PROC RELEASE can be used to release unused space at the end of a SAS data library under OS and TSO. "The RELEASE Procedure" gives a complete discussion.

DATA SET OPTIONS

Data set options are those that appear after data set names. They specify actions that are applicable only to the processing of the data set with which they appear and let you perform such operations as:

- giving a descriptive label to a data set
- protecting a data set from unauthorized use or deletion
- specifying variables to be included or dropped in later processing
- selecting only the first or last *n* observations for processing.

Data set options are specified in parentheses after the data set name in DATA step or PROC statements, for example:

    DATA NEW (PROTECT = RUMPLE);

The PROTECT= option here assigns the password RUMPLE to the data set called NEW, to protect it against unauthorized alteration or deletion.

To specify two or more options, leave at least one space between them in the parenthesized list. For example:

    DATA NEW(PROTECT = RUMPLE READ = STILT);

Some options are valid only when a data set is created: that is, they can only appear with a data set name in a DATA statement or with a data set name after an OUT= option in a PROC statement. Others are valid only when a data set is used for processing and can appear only when the data set name appears in a PROC statement, or in a SET, MERGE, or UPDATE statement. Some options can be used in both situations.

The data set options are listed below. The accompanying explanation gives the circumstances under which the option can appear.

BLKSIZE = *blocksize*   specifies the blocksize used to write the data set. If the blocksize specified is too small to contain one observation, SAS uses a value large enough to contain one observation. If the value is not four plus a multiple of the LRECL, SAS uses:

$$(FLOOR(BLKSIZE/LRECL)*LRECL) + 4$$

where LRECL equals the observation length plus four. BLKSIZE= can only be specified when a data set is created.

BUFNO=*n*   specifies the number of I/O buffers used when accessing SAS data sets. The value specified may be either 1 or 2. See Chapter 2, "Introduction to the DATA Step," for a discussion of input buffers.

DROP=*variables*   causes the specified variables to be omitted from the data set that is being created or during the processing of the data set. If the DROP= option appears in a DATA statement and only one data set is being created, DROP= functions exactly as the DROP program statement does. If the DATA statement specifies several data sets, the DROP= option can be used to control which variables appear in which data sets. For example, consider the following statements:

```
DATA HISCHOOL
  (DROP=COLLNAME COLLCODE) COLLEGE;
  INPUT YRS__EDUC HSNAME $ COLLNAME $
    COLLCODE;
  IF YRS__EDUC<=12 THEN OUTPUT HISCHOOL;
  IF YRS__EDUC>12 THEN OUTPUT COLLEGE;
```

The data set COLLEGE contains all the variables in the INPUT statement; the data set HISCHOOL includes all those variables except COLLNAME and COLLCODE.

The DROP= option is useful with the OUT= option on a PROC statement. For example, you may want to plot residuals produced with the OUTPUT statement of PROC GLM against the dependent variable. The procedure normally includes all variables from the original data set in the output data set. The following statements produce an output data set containing only the residuals and the dependent variable values and ask PROC PLOT to plot those values against each other:

```
PROC GLM DATA=EXP;
  MODEL Y=X1-X5;
  OUTPUT OUT=RESID(DROP=X1-X5)
    RESIDUAL=RESID Y;
PROC PLOT;
  PLOT Y*RESID Y;
```

The DROP= option can also appear when a data set is being processed. The listed variables are not available to SAS during the processing. This could be useful if, for example, you want to update only some of the variables of a data set. Variables that are not to be updated could be excluded from the update operation with a DROP= option:

```
DATA NEW;
    UPDATE OLD (DROP=PAYCODE) UPS;
    BY SSN;
```

FILECLOSE=*position*   specifies the volume positioning to be performed
when a SAS data library on tape is closed. The values
that may be specified are REREAD, REWIND, LEAVE,
DISP, and FREE. This option is accepted by all
operating systems but is only effective for OS and TSO;
furthermore the FREE specification is only effective
under MVS. The FILECLOSE= option overrides the
SAS system option TAPECLOSE=.

Specify FILECLOSE=REREAD if you intend to use
that tape data library again in the same SAS job. SAS
leaves the tape volume positioned at the beginning of
the data library. REREAD overrides a FREE=CLOSE
specification in the job control.

Specify FILECLOSE=REWIND if you do not want to
use the tape volume again in the same job, or if you
want to use the first data library (file) on the tape
volume. SAS rewinds the tape volume to the beginning. A FREE=CLOSE specification in the job control
overrides the REWIND specification.

Specify FILECLOSE=LEAVE if you are not using the
tape data library again in that job, but you are creating
or accessing a subsequent tape file on the same tape
volume. SAS leaves the tape positioned at the end of
the data library. LEAVE overrides a FREE=CLOSE
specification in the job control.

FILECLOSE=DISP causes the volume to be positioned as determined by the operating system, according to specifications in the job control.

FILECLOSE=FREE causes the data library to be
dynamically deallocated under MVS operating systems
so that thereafter it is not possible to access it. FREE is
equivalent to the job control specification
FREE=CLOSE. If you try to access the data library, SAS
issues an error message that the DDname is not
defined. The FREE specification is useful for freeing the
data library allocation during a long job, so that other
jobs and users can allocate the library, tape volume,
tape drive, or unit.

FILEDISP=NEW   specifies the initial disposition (status) of the tape-
FILEDISP=OLD   format data library in which the SAS data set is written.
This option is used only when a data set is created.
Under OS a specification of FILEDISP=NEW overrides
a DISP=OLD specification in the DD statement.
Under TSO, specifying FILEDISP=NEW overrides an
OLD specification on the ALLOCATE statement. Under
CMS and VSE, where it is not possible to specify NEW
for tape-format libraries, a FILEDISP=NEW specifica-
tion causes SAS to behave as though you could specify
it.

When the initial disposition (status) of a tape-format
SAS data library is NEW, SAS assumes that the data

library is empty and does not look for previously written SAS data sets. For as long as the data library is allocated (which could span several SAS sessions) SAS knows that the data library is not empty, even if you subsequently specify FILEDISP=NEW.

FILEDISP=OLD specifies that the tape-format data library is not initially empty. Specifying FILEDISP=OLD under OS does not override a DD statement specification of DISP=NEW, nor does it override a specification of NEW in a TSO ALLOCATE statement.

FIRSTOBS=n causes processing to begin with the nth observation. The n value must be a positive integer. For example, the statement:

PROC PRINT DATA=STUDY (FIRSTOBS=20);

results in printing observations beginning with number 20.

GEN=n specifies the number of generations of historical information that SAS keeps for a data set. This information can be printed with the CONTENTS procedure. If GEN=2 is specified, for example, SAS keeps information on the creation of the current data set and on the previous generation of SAS data sets from which the current one was built. The GEN value can range from 0 to 1000.

IN=*variable*   names a new variable in a SET, MERGE, or UPDATE statement that contains values indicating the data set from which an observation comes. The variable's value is 1 if values in the current observation were taken from that data set, and is 0 otherwise. The IN= option is specified in parentheses after a data set name in the SET, MERGE, or UPDATE statement; for example:

MERGE FOOD.DAIRY(IN=INDAIRY)FOOD.VEGIE;

Values of IN= variables are available to program statements during the DATA step, but the variables are not included in the data set being created.

KEEP=*variables*   causes only the listed variables to be retained for processing or output to the SAS data set. If KEEP= appears when a data set is created, only the listed variables appear in the new data set. KEEP= is useful when several data sets are created with one DATA statement: it can specify which variables are to be included in which data sets.

If the KEEP= option is used when a data set is processed, only the variables listed are available to SAS during processing. The variables not listed are still in the data set, however.

LABEL=*label*   specifies a label for the data set that is stored with the data set and printed whenever the CONTENTS procedure is used to print the data set's contents. The label consists of up to 40 characters. If the label characters include right parentheses, semicolons, or equal signs, enclose the label with single quotes (or double quotes if the DQUOTE option is in effect). As usual, if the label characters include single quotes, write them as two single quotes and enclose the entire label in single quotes. For example:

```
DATA W2(LABEL=1976 W2 INFO, HOURLY);
DATA NEW(LABEL='DAVE''S LIST');
DATA SALES(LABEL='SALES FOR MAY(NE)');
```

The LABEL= option is used only when a data set is created.

OBS=*n*   specifies the last observation of the data set that will be processed. The *n* value must be a positive integer.

PROTECT=*password*   specifies a password that protects a data set from alteration and deletion. The PROTECT= option can only be used to assign a password when a data set is created or in the DATASETS procedure. If the PROTECT= option is in effect, another data set of the same name cannot be created unless the password is given with the PROTECT= option, nor can the data set be deleted or modified without the option.

For example, suppose an instructor creates and stores a SAS data set with appropriate job control and these SAS statements:

```
DATA HOMEWORK(PROTECT=ST361);
  INPUT X Y S;
```

The data set HOMEWORK can be used in PROC statements and in SET, MERGE , and UPDATE statements (that is, it can be read). It cannot be used in DATA statements or with any procedure that writes or updates a data set with the same name (for example, PROC EDITOR, PROC SORT, PROC RANK, or PROC APPEND) unless PROTECT=ST361 appears also (that is, it cannot be altered or deleted).

READ=*password*   specifies a password that protects the data set from being read unless that same password is given. The password must be a valid SAS name.

For example, if the statement:

```
DATA TEST.SALARY(READ=EXEC);
```

is executed, the data set SALARY can only be used if READ=EXEC is specified. The statement:

```
PROC MEANS DATA=TEST.SALARY;
```

would therefore fail, but the statement:

PROC MEANS DATA=TEST.SALARY(READ=EXEC);

would be executed.

The READ= option can only be used to assign a password when the data set is created or with PROC DATASETS. For example, if you did not assign TEST.SALARY a password when it was created, you could use these statements to assign one:

PROC DATASETS DDNAME=TEST;
  MODIFY SALARY (READ=EXEC);

A data set protected with a READ= password but not a PROTECT= password is not fully protected from alteration and deletion.

RENAME=
(oldname=
newname...)

changes the name of a variable. If RENAME= is specified when a data set is created, the new name is permanent. If RENAME= is specified at any other time, the new name exists only for the duration of the procedure. For example, the statements:

DATA NEW (RENAME=(X=X1976));
  SET OLD;

create the data set NEW. NEW contains the same variable values as data set OLD; however, the variable named X in data set OLD is named X1976 in data set NEW.

Several variables can be renamed with one RENAME option, for example:

DATA NEW (RENAME=(X=1976 Y=YNEW));

If RENAME= is used and either DROP= or KEEP= is also used, DROP= and KEEP= are applied before RENAME=. Thus, use the oldname in the KEEP= or DROP= option.

You cannot use an abbreviated variable list (for example, X1-X10) with the RENAME= option.

REPLACE=YES
REPLACE=NO

is used to override the REPLACE/NOREPLACE system option allowing replacement of permanent data sets.

TYPE=DATA
TYPE=CORR
TYPE=COV
TYPE=SSCP
TYPE=EST
TYPE=FACTOR
TYPE=DISCAL

specifies a special data set type for input data. The TYPE= option's primary use is in the CANCORR, CANDISC, PRINCOMP, VARCLUS, DISCRIM, FACTOR, SCORE, and REG procedures, which accept data in specially structured SAS data sets. These special data sets are usually created by earlier runs of one of these procedures. The TYPE= option need not be used if the special data set was created by a SAS procedure. It would be used, for example, if correlation values had been produced by a non-SAS program. In this case, the values would have to be put into a SAS data set with the proper format. Here is an example of the TYPE= option's use in such a case:

PROC FACTOR DATA=OLD(TYPE=CORR);

The TYPE=DATA data set is an ordinary SAS data set. Each of the other types of SAS data sets is described below, in **Special SAS Data Sets**.

SPECIAL SAS DATA SETS

In addition to the standard SAS data sets that are typically created with a DATA statement, several specially structured data sets are available in SAS. These data sets contain special variables and observations and are usually created by SAS procedures. You can also use a DATA statement and program statements to create a special SAS data set in the proper format, and in that case you would use the TYPE= data set option to indicate its type to SAS.

TYPE=CORR Data Sets

A TYPE=CORR data set contains a correlation matrix along with the variable means, standard deviations, the number of observations in the original data set from which the correlation matrix was computed, and possibly other statistics (depending on which procedure created the data set).

Using PROC CORR with an output data set specification automatically produces a TYPE=CORR data set. You can also create a TYPE=CORR data set from input data that contain a correlation matrix (see the example below). In this case, TYPE=CORR must be specified as a data set option.

TYPE=CORR data sets can be used as input for PROC FACTOR, PROC REG, and other procedures.

Variables in a TYPE=CORR data set When a BY statement is used with PROC CORR, the BY variable(s) appears first in the data set. Next come two special character variables, each eight characters long. The first is named __TYPE__, and its values identify the type of each observation in the TYPE=CORR data set (MEAN, STD, N, CORR). The second special variable is named __NAME__, and its values identify the variable with which a given row of the correlation matrix is associated. The variables from the original data set that were analyzed by PROC CORR come next.

Observations in a TYPE=CORR data set For the first observation, which contains the variable mean, the __TYPE__ variable's value is 'MEAN'; for the second observation, containing standard deviations, __TYPE__'s value is 'STD'; for the third observation, containing the number of observations, __TYPE__'s value is 'N'. The __NAME__ variable's value is blank for these first three observations.

The first three observations are produced when PROC CORR creates the TYPE=CORR data set. However, if you create the TYPE=CORR data set, the data set need not contain these three observations. Any procedure that uses the data set uses 0 for all the variable means, 1 for all the standard deviations, and 100 for the number of observations, with the exception of CANCORR, CANDISC, FACTOR, PRINCOMP, and VARCLUS, which use 10,000 for the number of observations.

Following the first three observations are the observations containing the correlation matrix; one for each row of the matrix. __TYPE__'s value for each of these observations is 'CORR'. __NAME__'s value for each observation is the variable name associated with that observation (row).

Example: a TYPE = CORR data set   Here is a TYPE = CORR data set containing a 2-variable correlation matrix:

OBS	_TYPE_	_NAME	X	Y
1	MEAN		12.2	-4.5
2	STD		3.2	1.1
3	N		5.0	5.0
4	CORR	X	1.0	0.7
5	CORR	Y	0.7	1.0

12.2 and − 4.5 are the means of X and Y; 3.2 and 1.1 are the standard deviations of X and Y; 5 is the number of observations containing X and Y; and .7 is the correlation between X and Y.

Example: using BY variables   Here is another example that shows a TYPE = CORR data set created with PROC CORR and a BY statement:

```
PROC CORR DATA = MEASURE OUTP = CORMAT;
  BY SEX;
  VAR A B C;
PROC PRINT;
```

OBS	SEX	_TYPE_	_NAME_	A	B	C
1	F	MEAN		14.7	29.6	9.6
2	F	STD		1.2	3.1	0.7
3	F	N		23.0	22.0	23.0
4	F	CORR	A	1.0	0.8	0.3
5	F	CORR	B	0.8	1.0	0.6
6	F	CORR	C	0.3	0.6	1.0
7	M	MEAN		12.3	33.4	7.6
8	M	STD		1.1	2.9	0.9
9	M	N		31.0	33.0	32.0
10	M	CORR	A	1.0	0.4	0.8
11	M	CORR	B	0.4	1.0	0.3
12	M	CORR	C	0.8	0.3	1.0

Example: creating a TYPE = CORR data set in a DATA step   The input data containing the correlation matrix in this example are on cards. Since the matrix contains correlations for three variables, there are three cards and each card has three values. These values were punched onto the cards by another program, using an output format of F10.7 for each value. The SAS program below puts these values into a TYPE = CORR data set.

```
DATA CORRMATR(TYPE = CORR);
  INPUT (A B C) (10.7);
  __TYPE__ = 'CORR';
  LENGTH __NAME__ $ 8.;
  IF__N__ = 1 THEN __NAME__ = 'A';
  IF__N__ = 2 THEN __NAME__ = 'B';
  IF__N__ = 3 THEN __NAME__ = 'C';
  CARDS;
1.0000000 0.6198688 0.5297345
0.6198688 1.0000000 0.4292545
0.5297345 0.4292545 1.0000000
PROC PRINT;
```

OBS	A	B	C	_TYPE_	_NAME_
1	1.00000	0.61987	0.52973	CORR	A
2	0.61987	1.00000	0.42925	CORR	B
3	0.52973	0.42925	1.00000	CORR	C

TYPE = COV Data Sets

A TYPE=COV data set is similar to a TYPE=CORR data set, except that it has __TYPE__ = 'COV' observations rather than __TYPE__ = 'CORR' observations, and it contains a covariance matrix rather than a correlation matrix. COV data sets are created by PROC PRINCOMP if the COV option is specified. PROC CORR produces COV data sets if the COV and NOCORR options are specified, and the OUT= data set is assigned TYPE=COV with the TYPE= data set option. For example:

    PROC CORR COV NOCORR OUT=CVMTRX(TYPE=COV);

TYPE=COV data sets are used by these procedures: CANCORR, CANDISC, FACTOR, PRINCOMP, and VARCLUS.

TYPE = SSCP Data Sets

TYPE=SSCP data sets are used to store the uncorrected sums of squares and crossproducts for variables. TYPE=SSCP data sets are produced automatically by PROC REG when OUTSSCP= is specified in the PROC REG statement. You can also create TYPE=SSCP data sets in a DATA step, and in this case TYPE=SSCP must be specified as a data set option.

Variables in a TYPE = SSCP data set   If a BY statement is used with PROC REG, the BY variable(s) is first in the TYPE=SSCP data set. The next variable is a special character variable, __NAME__, eight characters long, whose values are the variable names in the original data set from which the SSCP matrix was computed. The next variable is INTERCEP, whose values are the variable sums. Finally come the variables from the original data set that appear in the VAR statement or a MODEL statement.

Observations in a TYPE = SSCP data set   For the first observation in the TYPE=SSCP data set, the __NAME__ variable's value is 'INTERCEP'. The value of the INTERCEP variable for this first observation is the number of observations in the original data set. The values of the remaining variables for the INTERCEP observation are the sums of the variables. For the second and following observations in the TYPE=SSCP data set, the __NAME__ variable's value is the name of the corresponding variable in the original data set. The INTERCEP variable's values contain the variable sums. The other variables' values are the sums of the products for the variables.

Example: using REG with a BY statement   In this example, REG was used with a BY STATE statement. The variables were X and Y.

OBS	STATE	_NAME_	INTERCEP	X	Y
1	NC	INTERCEP	7.0	350.6	126.6
2	NC	X	350.6	17722.8	6416.9
3	NC	Y	126.6	6416.9	2334.5
4	VA	INTERCEP	8.0	413.1	114.3
5	VA	X	413.1	21484.9	6058.8
6	VA	Y	114.3	6058.8	1811.1

For STATE='NC', 7 is the number of observations; 350.6 and 126.6 are the sums of X and Y, respectively; 17722.8 and 2334.5 are the sums of X2 and Y2; and 6416.9 is the sum of the crossproducts of X and Y. If a WEIGHT statement is used with PROC REG (for weighted least squares analyses), then the sum of the weights replaces the number of observations in the TYPE=SSCP data set, and all sums of products are weighted.

TYPE=FACTOR Data Sets

TYPE=FACTOR data sets, created automatically by PROC FACTOR when an output data set is specified, contain information about factor analyses. PROC FACTOR and PROC SCORE use TYPE=FACTOR data sets as input.

Variables in a TYPE=FACTOR data set   The variables in a TYPE=FACTOR data set correspond to those in a TYPE=CORR data set: BY variables, if any; __TYPE__; __NAME__; and the names of the variables used by PROC FACTOR.

Observations in a TYPE=FACTOR data set   Each observation in the output data set contains some type of statistic as indicated by the __TYPE__ variable. The __NAME__ variable is blank except where otherwise indicated. The values of the __TYPE__ variable are as follows:

__TYPE__	Contents
MEAN	means.
STD	standard deviations.
N	sample size.
CORR	correlations. The __NAME__ variable contains the name of the variable corresponding to each row of the correlation matrix.
IMAGE	image coefficients. The __NAME__ variable contains the name of the variable corresponding to each row of the image coefficient matrix.
IMAGECOV	image covariance matrix. The __NAME__ variable contains the name of the variable corresponding to each row of the image covariance matrix.
COMMUNAL	final communality estimates.
PRIOR	prior communality estimates, or estimates from the last iteration for iterative methods.
WEIGHT	variable weights.
EIGENVAL	eigenvalues.
UNROTATE	unrotated factor pattern. The __NAME__ variable contains the name of the factor.

RESIDUAL	residual correlations. The __NAME__ variable contains the name of the variable corresponding to each row of the residual correlation matrix.
TRANSFOR	transformation matrix from rotation. The __NAME__ variable contains the name of the factor.
FCORR	inter-factor correlations. The __NAME__ variable contains the name of the factor.
PATTERN	factor pattern. The __NAME__ variable contains the name of the factor.
RCORR	reference axis correlations. The __NAME__ variable contains the name of the factor.
REFERENC	reference structure. The __NAME__ variable contains the name of the factor.
STRUCTUR	factor structure. The __NAME__ variable contains the name of the factor.
SCORE	scoring coefficients. The __NAME__ variable contains the name of the factor.

For an example of a TYPE=FACTOR data set, see the description of PROC FACTOR in *SAS User's Guide: Statistics, 1982 Edition*.

TYPE = EST Data Sets

TYPE=EST data sets, produced by PROC REG when the OUTEST= option is specified, store the coefficients of linear models.

Variables in a TYPE = EST data set   If a BY statement is used with PROC REG, the BY variables appear first in the TYPE=EST data set. Next comes the character variable __TYPE__, eight characters long, which indicates the source of the coefficients (identity, OLS, 2SLS). The variable __MODEL__ is next, and it contains the label that is associated with the MODEL statement in PROC REG. Next is the variable __SIGMA__, which contains the standard deviation for the dependent variable. The regression coefficients of the variables in the model appear next in the order they first appear in a MODEL statement. The last variable in the data set is INTERCEP, which contains the equation constant.

Observations in a TYPE = EST data set   The TYPE=EST has one observation for each dependent variable on the left-hand side of a MODEL STATEMENT specified with PROC REG.

Example: creating a TYPE = EST data set

```
PROC REG OUTEST=B;
  L1: MODEL Y=XW;
  L2: MODEL W=Z;
PROC PRINT;
```

OBS	_TYPE_	_MODEL_	_SIGMA_	Y	X	W	Z	INTERCEP
1	OLS	L1	0.567	-1	0.234	0.045	.	4.3338
2	OLS	L2	0.400	.	.	-1.000	0.309	2.9877

TYPE = DISCAL Data Sets

The TYPE= DISCAL data set contains calibration information developed by PROC DISCRIM. TYPE=DISCAL data sets can be used by PROC DISCRIM to classify observations in other data sets.

Variables in a TYPE = DISCAL data set   The first variable in a TYPE= DISCAL data set is the __TYPE__ variable; its values identify the type of each observation in the data set. The second variable is the variable specified in the CLASS statement of PROC DISCRIM. __LNDET__ is the third variable; it contains the log determinant of the covariance matrix. The next variable is __PRIOR__, the prior probability of classification membership. The remaining variables are those specified in the VAR statement of PROC DISCRIM.

Observations in a TYPE = DISCAL data set   The first observation has one of four values for __TYPE__: PLEQ, PLPR, NOEQ, or NOPR. These values indicate whether the analysis is based on the pooled (PL) or within-group (NO) covariance matrix, and whether the prior probabilities are equal (EQ) or proportional (PR). The next observation contains the means for all variables listed in the VAR statement (__TYPE__ ='MEAN'). If POOL=YES, all __TYPE__ ='MEAN' observations are printed before the remaining observation types. The next observation contains the standard deviation (__TYPE__ ='STD'). There is one __TYPE__ ='STD' observation if POOL=YES; if POOL=NO there are as many STD observations as levels of the CLASS variable. The remaining observations are __TYPE__ ='RINV'; one for each row of each correlation inverse matrix. There is one matrix if POOL=YES. If POOL=NO, there is a matrix for each level of the CLASS variable.

Example: a DISCAL data set with POOL= NO   This is an example of a TYPE= DISCAL data set produced by PROC DISCRIM with POOL= NO.

REMOTE SENSING DATA ON FIVE CROPS
CLASSIFICATION OF CROP DATA

OBS	_TYPE_	CROP	_LNDET_	_PRIOR_	X1	X2	X3	X4
1	NOEQ		5.0000	.	.	.	.	.
2	MEAN	CLOVER	23.6462	0.2	46.364	32.636	34.182	36.636
3	STD	CLOVER	23.6462	0.2	25.905	17.078	20.517	20.568
4	RINV	CLOVER	23.6462	0.2	1.294	-0.002	-0.557	-0.450
5	RINV	CLOVER	23.6462	0.2	-0.002	1.346	-0.653	0.091
6	RINV	CLOVER	23.6462	0.2	-0.557	-0.653	1.633	0.435
7	RINV	CLOVER	23.6462	0.2	-0.450	0.091	0.435	1.238
8	MEAN	CORN	11.1347	0.2	15.286	22.714	27.429	33.143
9	STD	CORN	11.1347	0.2	1.799	6.448	5.623	18.632
10	RINV	CORN	11.1347	0.2	3.768	1.063	1.815	5.153
11	RINV	CORN	11.1347	0.2	1.063	2.055	0.372	2.486
12	RINV	CORN	11.1347	0.2	1.815	0.372	4.146	5.115
13	RINV	CORN	11.1347	0.2	5.153	2.486	5.115	10.915
14	MEAN	COTTON	13.2357	0.2	34.500	32.667	35.000	39.167
15	STD	COTTON	13.2357	0.2	9.566	8.664	19.890	20.478
16	RINV	COTTON	13.2357	0.2	49.877	1.466	-53.645	-14.704
17	RINV	COTTON	13.2357	0.2	1.466	36.516	-39.363	-16.900
18	RINV	COTTON	13.2357	0.2	-53.645	-39.363	97.963	33.239
19	RINV	COTTON	13.2357	0.2	-14.704	-16.900	33.239	12.888
20	MEAN	SOYBEANS	12.4526	0.2	21.000	27.000	23.500	29.667
21	STD	SOYBEANS	12.4526	0.2	5.060	10.714	5.128	11.843
22	RINV	SOYBEANS	12.4526	0.2	10.861	-2.052	-6.386	5.558
23	RINV	SOYBEANS	12.4526	0.2	-2.052	4.287	-1.082	1.377
24	RINV	SOYBEANS	12.4526	0.2	-6.386	-1.082	6.097	-4.675
25	RINV	SOYBEANS	12.4526	0.2	5.558	1.377	-4.675	5.355
26	MEAN	SUGARBEETS	17.7629	0.2	31.000	32.167	20.000	40.500
27	STD	SUGARBEETS	17.7629	0.2	11.967	13.152	10.257	16.489
28	RINV	SUGARBEETS	17.7629	0.2	2.020	-0.454	-2.003	-2.569
29	RINV	SUGARBEETS	17.7629	0.2	-0.454	3.091	4.098	3.572
30	RINV	SUGARBEETS	17.7629	0.2	-2.003	4.098	8.702	7.895
31	RINV	SUGARBEETS	17.7629	0.2	-2.569	3.572	7.895	8.534

Example: a DISCAL data set with POOL=YES This example shows a TYPE=DISCAL data set produced by PROC DISCRIM using the same original data set, but with POOL=YES.

REMOTE SENSING DATA ON FIVE CROPS
CLASSIFICATION OF CROP DATA

OBS	_TYPE_	CROP	_LNDET_	_PRIOR_	X1	X2	X3	X4
1	PLEQ		5	.	.	.	.	.
2	MEAN	CLOVER	.	0.2	46.3636	32.6364	34.1818	36.6364
3	MEAN	CORN	.	0.2	15.2857	22.7143	27.4286	33.1429
4	MEAN	COTTON	.	0.2	34.5000	32.6667	35.0000	39.1667
5	MEAN	SOYBEANS	.	0.2	21.0000	27.0000	23.5000	29.6667
6	MEAN	SUGARBEETS	.	0.2	31.0000	32.1667	20.0000	40.5000
7	STD		.	.	16.0960	12.6748	15.0642	18.3787
8	RINV		.	.	1.2881	-0.0463	-0.5969	-0.4027
9	RINV		.	.	-0.0463	1.2270	-0.4620	0.1129
10	RINV		.	.	-0.5969	-0.4620	1.6007	0.5365
11	RINV		.	.	-0.4027	0.1129	0.5365	1.2672

386

SAS Informats and Formats

INTRODUCTION

In SAS there are several ways that you can give SAS directions for reading and writing data values.

A set of directions for reading a value is an **informat**. For example, the BZ. informat directs SAS to read trailing blanks in a numeric field as zeros, instead of ignoring the trailing blanks. SAS provides informats for you to use in reading numeric and character data; date, time, and datetime values; and column-binary data.

A set of directions for writing or printing a value is a **format**. For example, the WORDS. format tells SAS to print a numeric value in words. SAS provides many formats for you to use with numeric and character data and with date, time, and datetime values. In addition, you can define your own formats using the FORMAT procedure.

This table illustrates the techniques available for using SAS informats and formats in particular situations.

	TECHNIQUES	ASSOCIATE INFORMATS/ FORMATS WITH VARIABLES USING...	USE INFORMAT/ FORMAT DIRECTLY IN...
READING VALUES	SAS informats (including date, time, datetime, and column-binary informats)	INFORMAT statement	INPUT statement INPUT function
WRITING VALUES	SAS formats (including date, time, and datetime formats) Formats you define with PROC FORMAT	FORMAT statement	PUT statement PUT function

SAS informats and formats have the form

informatw.d
formatw.d

where *informat* or *format* is the name of the informat or format, *w* is a width value (the number of columns in the input or output field), and *d* is an optional decimal scaling factor. If you omit the *w* and *d* values from the informat or format, SAS uses a default *w* value. However, you **must** use a period after the informat or format name.

USING SAS INFORMATS

The simplest way to read values with a SAS informat is to follow the name of the variable or variables in the INPUT statement with an informat. For example, the statements

```
DATA A;
   INPUT @15 (COLOR STYLE) (3.) @21 PRICE 5.2;
```

use the *w.* and *w.d* informats, respectively.

You can also associate an informat with a variable in an INFORMAT statement like this one:

```
DATA B;
   INFORMAT BIRTHDAT INTERVW DATE.;
   INPUT @63 BIRTHDAT INTERVW;
```

SAS uses the INFORMAT statement to determine the variable's type (for example, numeric, character, or date), but uses it to determine a length for the variable only in the case of character variables. See Chapter 3, ''Statements Used in the DATA Step,'' for more information on the INFORMAT statement.

Note: if you use an informat to describe a field and the contents of that field are not valid for the informat (for example, alphabetic characters in a numeric field), SAS prints an error message on the SAS log describing the problem and sets the resulting value to missing. See **Illegal characters in input data** in Chapter 14, "Missing Values," for information about this problem.

SAS Numeric Informats

Informat	Description	Width Range	Decimal Range	Default Width
w.	standard numeric	1–32		1
w.d			no limit	
BZw.d	blanks are zeros	1–32	no limit	1
COMMAw.d	commas in numbers	1–32	no limit	1
Ew.d	scientific notation	1–32	no limit	12
HEXw.	numeric hexadecimal	1–16		8
IBw.d	integer binary	1–8	0–10	4
PDw.d	packed decimal	1–16	0–10	1
PIBw.d	positive integer binary	1–8	0–10	1
PKw.d	unsigned packed decimal	1–16	0–10	1
RBw.d	real binary (floating point)	2–8	0–10	4
ZDw.d	zoned decimal	1–32	0–10	1
ZDBw.d	zoned decimal with blanks legal	1–32	0–10	1

SAS Character Informats

Informat	Description	Width Range	Decimal Range	Default Width
$w.	standard character	1–200		1 or length of variable
$CHARw.	characters with blanks	1–200		1 or length of variable
$CHARZBw.	characters with binary zeros as blanks	1–200		1 or length of variable
$HEXw.	character hexadecimal	1–200		2
$PHEXw.	packed hexadecimal as character data	1–100		2
$VARYINGw.	varying-length values	1–200		8 or length of variable

Additional informats are described in **Using SAS Date, Time, and Datetime Informats and Formats** later in this chapter.

Informat Descriptions: Numeric

w.d informat: standard numeric data

> range: 1–32
> default: 1

If your numeric data values are stored in a standard form (one digit per byte) you can use the standard SAS numeric informat *w.d* to read them, where

> *w* is a number giving the length, in columns, of the field containing the value
>
> *d* is an optional number giving the number of digits to the right of the decimal point in the value.

The *w.d* informat can be used to read numeric values located anywhere in the field; a value may be preceded or followed by blanks. A minus sign precedes negative values, with no blank between the sign and the value Values read with the *w.d* informat may include decimal points; values in scientific E-notation may be read with either the *w.d* informat or the *Ew.d* informat, described below.

Include a *d* value in the *w.d* informat only when you want SAS to insert a decimal point in numeric values that appear without decimal points on the input lines. When a *d* value appears in the informat, the data value is read and if no decimal point appears in the data value, it is divided by 10^d. (However, a decimal point already in the data value remains in its original position.)

Note that with the *w.d* informat, trailing blanks are not the same as trailing zeros. (If you want trailing blanks to be read as zeros, use the BZ. informat, below.)

example 1   The following DATA step shows several representations of the number 23, all of which can be read with the numeric informat 6.:

```
DATA A;
  INPUT @1 X 6.;
  CARDS;
23        left-aligned
    23    right-aligned
   23     in the middle
   23.0   with decimal point
2.3E1     in scientific notation
  -23     negative value
```

example 2   The data lines below show four representations of the number 23, each of which can be read with the informat 6.2:

```
DATA A;
  INPUT @1 X 6.2;
  CARDS;
    2300      right-aligned
2300          left-aligned
   -2300      negative value
    23.       explicit decimal point
```

Using column input is equivalent to using a pointer direction and a *w.d* informat. For example, the statement

> INPUT X 1–6 2;

is equivalent to

> INPUT @1 X 6.2;

BZw.d informat: blanks are zeros

range: 1–32
default: 1

Sometimes data are entered with trailing zeros not punched. For example, say that the value 340 is entered in columns 2–4; however, instead of zero in column 4, a blank appears. When FORTRAN is used to read this value, it translates the blank to zero; however, the *w.* and *w.d* SAS informats read the value as 34.

To read the value as 340, use the BZ. (**B**lanks are **Z**eros) informat. The BZ. informat is identical to the standard *w.d* informat except that it treats all blanks except leading blanks as zeros.

example 1 X's value is 340 but is entered as 34 followed by a blank.

hex: F3 F4 40
informat: BZ3.

INPUT @10 X BZ3.;

example 2 Y's value is –200 but is entered as '–2 '.

hex: 60 F2 40 40
informat: BZ4.

INPUT @ 5 Y BZ4.;

COMMAw.d informat: embedded characters

The COMMA informat removes embedded commas, blanks, dollar signs, percent signs, and parentheses from input data. Parentheses at the start of a field are converted to minus signs. The resulting field, possibly shorter than the input field, passes to the standard numeric informat.

Ew.d informat: scientific notation

range: 1–32
default: 12

You can read values of numeric variables in scientific notation using the *Ew.* informat; however, the *E.* informat is normally not needed since the standard *w.d* numeric informat can read numbers in scientific notation.

example X's value is 1.257E3, and it is stored in columns 10–16 of a data line.

informat: E7.

INPUT @10 X E7.;

HEXw. informat: numeric hexadecimal

range: 1–16
default: 8

The HEXw. informat converts a hexadecimal display to fixed point binary Each two columns of hex digits results in one byte of corresponding fixed point binary.

When HEX16. is used, the floating-point representation of the number is used, rather than the fixed-point representation.

example Columns 21–25 contain the value 1003A which represents the hexadecimal, fixed-point representation of the decimal number 65594.

```
hex:      F1 F0 F0 F3 C1
informat: HEX5.

   INPUT @21 X HEX5.;
```

IBw.d informat: integer binary

```
range:    1–8
default:  4
```

The IB informat brings in numbers that have been stored as binary integers, that is, as fixed point binary. For integer binary data, the high-order bit represents the value's sign: 0 for positive values, 1 for negative. Two's complement notation is used to represent negative values. If the d value is used in the informat, the number is divided by the 10^d. It is usually impossible to key in binary data directly from a terminal, though many programs write data in binary. The notation for integer binary in several programming languages is

```
SAS         IB2.            IB4.
PL/I        FIXED BIN(15)   FIXED BIN(31)
FORTRAN     INTEGER*2       INTEGER*4
COBOL       COMP PIC 9(4)   COMP PIC 9(8)
assembler   H               F
```

example 1   The value 128 is stored as a 4-byte integer binary number in columns 20–23 of a data line.

```
hex:         00 00 00 80
informat: IB4.

   INPUT @20 X IB4.;
```

example 2   The value –255 is stored in columns 20–23 of the data line:

```
hex:         FF FF FF 01
informat: IB4.

   INPUT @10 X IB4.;
```

PDw.d informat: packed decimal

```
range:    1–16
default:  1
```

For data stored in packed decimal form, each byte contains two digits. The value's sign is carried in the last half of the last byte: a C or F if the value is positive, a D if it is negative. Although it is usually impossible to key in packed decimal data directly from a terminal, many programs write data in packed decimal. The notation for packed decimal in several programming languages follows:

```
SAS         PD4.
PL/I        FIXED DEC(7,0)
COBOL       COMP-3 PIC S9(7)
assembler   PL4
```

example 1   The value 128 is stored in packed decimal form in columns 4–7 of a data line.

```
hex:         00 00 12 8C
informat: PD4.

   INPUT @4 X PD4.;
```

example 2   You have a date value stored in packed decimal form and you want to create a SAS date variable from it:

```
DATA NEW;
   INPUT MNTH PD4.;
   DATE=INPUT(PUT(MNTH,6.),MMDDYY6.);
```

The PUT function converts the packed decimal value to standard numeric—the way it looks when printed. Then the INPUT function uses the MMDDYY informat to read that value as a SAS date value.

PIBw.d informat: positive integer binary

range: 1–8
default: 1

Positive integer binary values are the same as integer binary (see the IB. informat, above), except that all values are treated as positive. Thus, the high-order bit is part of the value rather than the value's sign.

If a *d* value appears in the PIB. informat, the data value is divided by 10^d.

If you are planning to test the bits of a byte, read the value with the PIB1. informat. Another way is to read it with the $1. informat.

When you want the decimal equivalent of one of the 256 EBCDIC characters, read the character with the PIB. informat. For example, the hex code for the letter A is C1, and its decimal equivalent is 193. The statements

```
DATA X;
   INPUT CHAR PIB1.;
   PUT CHAR;
   CARDS;
A
;
```

produce the line

```
193
```

example   The value 12 is stored as a 1-byte positive integer binary value in column 43 of a data line.

hex: 0C
informat: PIB1.

```
INPUT @43 X PIB1.;
```

PKw.d informat: unsigned packed decimal

range: 1–16
default: 1

The PK. informat is like the PD. informat described above, except that all values are positive, and the last half of the last byte contains a digit rather than the value's sign. W represents the number of bytes, not the number of digits.

example   The value 128 is stored in packed decimal form in columns 5–7 of a data line.

hex: 00 01 28
informat: PK3.

```
INPUT @5 X PK3.;
```

RBw.d informat: real binary (floating point)

range: 2–8
default: 4

Floating point representation is commonly used to store numeric data fo scientific calculations. (SAS stores all numeric values in floating point.) A floating point value consists of two parts: a mantissa giving the value, and an exponent giving the value's magnitude. It is usually impossible to key in floating point binary data directly from a terminal, though many programs write data in floating point binary. This table compares the names of floating point notation in several languages:

	4 bytes	8 bytes
SAS	RB4.	RB8.
PL/I	FLOAT BIN(21)	FLOAT BIN(53)
FORTRAN	REAL*4	REAL*8
COBOL	COMP-1	COMP-2
assembler	E	D

example The value 128 as an 8-byte floating point value is stored in columns 10–17 of a data line.

hex: 41 80 00 00 00 00 00 00
informat: RB8.

    INPUT @10 X RB8.;

ZDw.d informat: zoned decimal

range: 1–32
default: 1

Zoned decimal is similar to standard numeric informat in that every digit requires one byte. However, the value's sign is carried in the last byte along with the last digit: if the value is positive, the next-to-last hex digit is A, C, E, or F; if the value is negative, the next-to-last hex digit is B or D. Positive values may be entered in zoned decimal form on a terminal. Some keying devices allow negative values to be entered by overstriking the last digit with a minus sign. Use this table to compare the zoned decimal informat with notation in several languages:

SAS	ZD3.
PL/I	PICTURE'99T'
COBOL	DISPLAY PIC S 999
assembler	ZL3

example The value 128 is stored in zoned decimal form in columns 4-7 of a data line.

hex: F0 F1 F2 C8
informat: ZD4.

    INPUT @4 X ZD4.;

ZDBw.d informat: zoned decimal with blanks

range: 1–32
default: 1

The ZDB. informat reads zoned decimal data produced in IBM 1410, 1401, and 1620 form, in which zeros were left blank rather than punched. The *w* value is the number of columns of the field containing a value, and the optional *d* value gives the number of decimal places for the value. The *d* value may be larger than the *w* value.

example The value 102 is stored in columns 10–12 on a data line in zoned decimal form, with blanks representing zeros.

    hex: F1 40 C2
    informat: ZDB3.

    INPUT@10 X ZDB3.;

Character Informats

$w. informat: standard character data

    range: 1–200
    default: 1 if the length of the variable is not yet defined; otherwise, the
              length of the variable

To read character data, use the SAS informat $*w*. The *w* value gives the number of columns in the field containing the character value. The $*w*. informat trims leading blanks before storing values: that is, it automatically left-aligns when reading values.

example Columns 10–12 of the input data line contain the value 'ABC'.

    hex: C1 C2 C3
    informat: $3.

The statement

    INPUT @10 NAME $3.;

reads the value as

    'ABC'   .

This statement is equivalent to

    INPUT NAME $ 10–12;

example 2 Columns 21–25 of an input data line contain the value " XYZ".

    hex: 40 40 E7 E8 E9
    informat: $5.

    INPUT @21 NAME $5.;

reads the value as

    'XYZ '   .

$CHARw. informat: leading and trailing blanks

    range: 1–200
    default: 1 if the length of the variable is not yet defined; otherwise, the
              length of the variable

The $CHARw. informat is identical to the $*w*. informat above, except that $CHAR. does not trim leading blanks. This table compares the SAS informat $CHAR8. with notation in other languages.

SAS	$CHAR8.
PL/I	CHAR(8)
FORTRAN	A8
COBOL	PIC X(8)
assembler	CL8

example   The value ' ABC' with one leading blank appears in columns 7–10 of the data line.

    hex: 40 C1 C2 C3
    informat: $CHAR4.

The statement

    INPUT @7 NAME $CHAR4.;

reads this value as

    ' ABC'   .

$CHARZBw. informat: binary zeros as blanks

    range: 1–200
    default: 1 if the length of the variable is not yet defined; otherwise, the
             length of the variable

The $CHARZB. informat is identical to the $CHARw. informat, except that $CHARZB. reads the specified input area and changes any byte of binary zero (X'00') to a blank character (X'40'). Binary zeros instead of blanks are occasionally found in various account code and programmer name fields of OS/360 and OS/VS SMF records and accounting data.

example   The value 'SMITH, JOHN   ' appears at offset +42 in a data record with trailing binary zeros instead of blanks.

    hex: E2 D4 C9 E3 C8 6B 40 D1 D6 C8 D5 00 00 00 00 00 00 00 00 00
    informat: $CHARZB20.

    INPUT @43 NAME $CHARZB20.;

$HEXw. informat: character hexadecimal

    range: 1–200
    default: 2

The $HEX. informat is like the HEX. informat in that you can use it to read values in which each hex digit occupies one byte. Use the $HEX. informat when you want to encode binary information into a character variable, but your input data are limited to printable characters.

example   Columns 21–24 contain the value C1C2.

    hex: C3 F1 C3 F2
    informat: $HEX4.

    INPUT @21 NAME $HEX4.;

In the SAS data set, the character variable NAME has a length of 2, even though the *w.* value in the informat was 4, since SAS stores the 4 hex digits C1C2 in 2 bytes. If the value is printed in standard SAS character format, it appears as 'AB'.

$PHEXw. informat: packed hexadecimal as character data

range   1–100
default   2

The $PHEX. informat converts packed hexadecimal data to character data. Packed hexadecimal data are like packed decimal data, except that all hex digits are valid and the value of the low-order nibble (which would indicate the sign in the case of packed decimal data) is ignored. Unlike the packed decimal informat, however, the $PHEX. informat returns a character value, and the value of the sign nibble is treated as if it were X'F', regardless of its actual value. Packed hexadecimal can be found in SMF record type 74 (RMF Device Activity) field SMF74ADD.

example   The two bytes at offset + 4 in a record contain a value consisting of hexadecimal '1E0F'.

hex: 1E 0F
informat: $PHEX2.

```
INPUT @5 DEVADDR $PHEX2.;
```

In the SAS data set, the character variable DEVADDR has a length of 3, even though the *w.* value in the informat was 2, since SAS requires 3 bytes to store the character representation (X'F1C5F0') of the 3 hexadecimal digits 1E0. If the value is printed using the standard SA character format, it appears as '1E0'. In general, the length of the character variable whose length is implicitly defined by the use of the $PHEXw. informat is 2w–1.

$VARYINGw. informat: varying-length values

range   1–200
default   8 or length of variable

Use the $VARYINGw. informat when the length of a character value differs from record to record. Typically, the length of the character value in the current record is given in a numeric field in the record (or implicitly by the fact that the character variable occupies the entire varying portion of a variable-length record). The informat name $VARYING. is usually followed by a numeric value *w* which gives the maximum length of the character variable.

When you use the $VARYINGw. informat, SAS first obtains the value of a numeric variable containing the length of the character value in the current observation. It can obtain the value in several ways, such as by reading a field described in the same INPUT statement as the character variable, by reading a field in another INPUT statement, or by calculating a value. SAS then uses that value to specify the number of columns it will read to obtain the value of the character variable in that observation. When SAS stores the value of the character variable, it adds trailing blanks as necessary to make the length equal to the maximum value of the variable (specified in *w*).

You must include a length variable when you use the $VARYINGw. informat. If the length variable has a value of 0 or less (including missing values) for a given observation, SAS uses a length of 1 for the character variable. If the value of the length variable is greater than 0 but less than or equal to the value given in *w*, SAS reads as many columns as the value of the length variable specifies, then adds trailing blanks as necessary to make the value equal to the maximum length of the variable. If the value of the length variable is greater than the value given in *w*, SAS uses the value of *w* for the length of the character variable. The length variable cannot be an array name.

SAS always associates a value *w* with the $VARYING. informat. If you do not specify a value for *w*, SAS assigns a length to the character variable and uses that length as the value of *w*. SAS assigns a length to the character variable using the same rules that it does for assigning lengths to character variables in other situations: if you have given the variable a length earlier (for example, with a LENGTH statement) it uses that length; if you have not given the variable a specific length, it uses a length of 8.

The pointer's value after reading a data value with the $VARYINGw. informat is the first column after the value.

example   DSNAME is a character variable whose length may vary from 1 to 44 characters.

In the input lines, a variable LENVAR contains DSNAME's length, in bytes, for the current line. The INPUT statement first reads the LENVAR variable and then uses it after the $VARYING44. informat to give the current length of the DSNAME value, up to a maximum of 44 characters:

```
DATA TEST;
   INPUT LENVAR PIB1. DSNAME $VARYING44. LENVAR;
```

USING SAS FORMATS

The simplest way to use a format with a variable is to give the name of the variable in a PUT statement followed by the name of the format. The following example uses the DOLLAR. format to write numeric values as dollar amounts:

```
DATA MONEY;
   AMOUNT=1145.32;
   PUT AMOUNT DOLLAR10.2;
```

produces the line

```
$1,145.32
```

In DOLLAR10.2, the *w* value of 10 and the *d* value of 2 mean that you want SAS to use a maximum of 10 columns to write the value, with two of these columns used for the decimal part of the value, one for the decimal point, and seven reserved for the minus sign (if the value is negative), dollar sign, comma, and dollar part of the value.

You can also associate a format with a variable in a FORMAT statement.

If you want to permanently associate a format with a variable so that later PROC and DATA steps use the format, you **must** specify the variable and format in a FORMAT statement in a DATA step. For example,

```
DATA WHOLEYR;
  INPUT SALES1-SALES12;
  SALESYR = SUM(OF SALES1-SALES12);
  FORMAT SALES1 SALES7 SALESYR DOLLAR10.;
PROC PRINT;
  VAR SALES1 SALES7 SALESYR;
```

The PRINT procedure prints the variables SALES1, SALES7, and SALESYR preceded by dollar signs and with commas separating each three columns of figures.

If you want to associate a format with a variable only for the duration of a procedure, use a FORMAT statement in the PROC step. For example, the statements

```
PROC PRINT DATA = PRODUCTS;
  FORMAT PRICE DOLLAR8.2;
  VAR STYLE COLOR PRICE;
```

cause SAS to print the values of PRICE with dollar signs, commas, and two decimal places.

If a variable appears in more than one FORMAT statement, SAS uses the format given in the last FORMAT statement. To delete a variable's format, use the variable name in a FORMAT statement with no format. You can also change or delete formats with PROC DATASETS. See Chapter 35, "DATASETS," for more information.

If the value of a variable does not fit into the width of the format you are using, SAS tries to squeeze the value into the space available. Character formats truncate values on the right. Numeric formats sometimes revert to the BEST. format. If representing the value is impossible, SAS prints asterisks.

All the instructions for using SAS formats apply also to formats you create using PROC FORMAT.

You can store formats that you create using PROC FORMAT to use in later jobs. To store formats, first create a permanent library (a partitioned data set if you are using OS, a TXTLIB library if you are using SAS under CMS). Use the DDNAME= option in PROC FORMAT to cause the procedure to write the formats to that library. Then include a line identifying the library in the job control language of later jobs where you want to use those formats. (See Chapter 37, "FORMAT," for instructions on storing formats under OS, and the *SAS CMS Companion* for instructions if you use SAS under CMS.)

Note: storing formats is an important consideration when you are associating formats with variables for permanent SAS sets, especially when other SAS users will work with those data sets. When the system option NOFMTERR is in effect, a variable associated with a format SAS cannot find is processed with a default format (usually w. or $w.). When the FMTERR option is in effect, SAS produces an error message if it cannot find the format. Although the NOFMTERR option allows SAS to work with the variable, you lose the information supplied by the format. To avoid having information in formats you have created become unavailable, always give directions for accessing the format library with directions for accessing the data set. Or, if you ship a tape containing a SAS data set with user-created formats to a SAS user at another installation, be sure that one file on the tape contains the format library. (Under OS you can copy the format library to a tape with PROC PDSCOPY.)

SAS Numeric Formats

Format	Description	Width Range	Decimal Range	Default Width	Alignment
w.	standard numeric	1–32		1	right
w.d			d<w		
BESTw.	SAS chooses best notation	1–32		12	right
COMMAw.d	commas in numbers	2–32	0 or 2	6	right
DOLLARw.d	dollar sign, commas	2–32	0 or 2	6	right
Ew.	scientific notation	7–32		12	right
FRACTw.	fractions	4–32		10	right
HEXw.	numeric hexadecimal	1–16		8	left
IBw.d	integer binary	1–8	0–10	4	left
PDw.d	packed decimal	1–16	0–10	1	left
PIBw.d	positive integer binary	1–8	0–10	1	left
RBw.d	real binary (floating point)	2–8	0–10	4	left
ROMANw.	Roman numerals	2–32		6	left
SSNw.	social security numbers	11		11	
WORDFw.	numbers as words with fractions as numbers	5–200		10	left
WORDSw.	numbers as words with fractions as words	5–200		10	left
Zw.d	print leading zeros	1–32		1	right
ZDw.d	zoned decimal	1–32	0–10	1	left

SAS Character Formats

Format	Description	Width Range	Default Width	Alignment
$w.	standard character	1–200	1 or length of variable	left
$CHARw.	characters with blanks	1–200	1 or length of variable	left
$HEXw.	character hexadecimal	1–200	2	left
$VARYINGw.	varying-length character values	1–200	8 or length of variable	left

Additional formats are described in **Using SAS Date, Time, and Datetime Informats and Formats** later in this chapter.

Format Descriptions: Numeric

w.d. format: standard numeric data

range: 1–32
default: 1

You can use the *w.d.* format to write values in a field *w* positions wide, with *d* positions to the right of the decimal point. If *d* is 0 or if it is omitted, the value includes no decimal point.

Numbers written using the *w.d.* format are rounded to the nearest number that can be represented in the output field. If the number is too large to fit, the BEST. format, described below, is used instead. Negative numbers are printed with a leading minus sign.

In choosing a *w* value, allow enough space to write the value, the decimal point, and a minus sign if necessary.

example The statements

    DATA;
      X = 23.45;
      PUT X 6.3;

produce the line

    23.450

Using column output is equivalent to using a pointer direction and a *w.d.* format. For example, the statement

      PUT X 1-8 2;

is equivalent to

      PUT @1 X 8.2;

BESTw. format: SAS chooses best notation

range: 1–32
default: 12
alignment: right

SAS frequently uses the BEST. format as a default format when no format is specified. Given the number of columns that are available to write the value, SAS chooses the notation that gives the most information about the value.

example 1 X's value is 1257000, and you want to write it in the 6 columns 10–15. Since 7 columns are needed to represent the value exactly, SAS squeezes the value into E-notation to get it into 6 columns: the statement

      PUT @10 X BEST6.;

prints the value

    1.26E6

example 2 X's value is 1257000, and you want to write it in columns 10–12. SAS does the best it can to get the value into 3 columns: the statement

      PUT @10 X BEST3.;

prints the value

    1E6

Although part of the value is lost, the value is still printed. If you give SAS only 2 columns to print the data value (three columns for a negative value), it gives up trying to represent the value and instead prints asterisks.

COMMAw.d format: commas

    range: 2–32
    default: 6
    alignment: right

The COMMA. format is like the DOLLAR. format, below, except that it does not print a dollar sign in front of the value. You might use DOLLAR. to print a total, and use COMMA. to print the detail lines. The d value, if specified, must be either 0 or 2.

example   SALES' value is 23451.23, and you want to print it in columns 24–33 of the output lines.

    PUT @24 SALES COMMA10.2;

prints the value

    23,451.23

DOLLARw.d format: dollar sign, commas, and decimal point

    range: 2–32
    default: 6
    alignment: right

You can print numeric values as dollar amounts with the DOLLAR. format. A dollar sign precedes the value, commas separate every three digits, and if the format includes a decimal value, two decimal digits representing cents are printed following a decimal point.

The d value, if specified, must be either 0 or 2. If the value is too large for the field, the BEST. format is used instead.

example   NETPAY'S value is 1254.71, and you want to print it in columns 53–62 of the output line.

    PUT @53 NETPAY DOLLAR 10.2;

prints the value

    $1,254.71

Ew. format: scientific notation

    range: 7–32
    default: 12
    alignment: right

You can write values of numeric variables in scientific notation using the E. format.

example   X's value is 1257, and you want to write it in columns 10–19 of a data line in scientific notation.

    format: E10.

    PUT @10 X E10.;

prints the value

    1.257E+03

Column 10 will be blank, since that is where a minus sign would go.

FRACTw. format: fractions

range: 4–32
default: 10
alignment: right

The FRACT. format prints values as fractions. For example, it is common in matrix operations to divide the number 1 by 3 to produce the value .33333333. If you prefer to see this value printed as 1/3, you can use the FRACT. format. FRACT. prints fractions in reduced form, that is, 1/2 instead of 50/100.

example 1 X's value is .6666666667, and you want to print it in columns 13–15 of the output lines.

    PUT @13 X FRACT4.;

prints the value

    2/3

example 2 Y's value is .2784. You want the FRACT. format to print it.

    PUT Y FRACT.;

The PUT statement prints the value

    174/625

HEXw. format: numeric hexadecimal

range: 1–16
default: 8
alignment: left

The HEXw. format converts between a number's fixed-point binary representation and its hexadecimal display. Each byte requires two columns to represent the corresponding hex digits.

When HEX16. is used, the floating-point representation of the number is used, rather than the fixed-point representation.

example X's value is 100, and you want to print the hex equivalent 64 in columns 2 and 3 of the data line:

    PUT @2 X HEX2.;

prints the value

    64

IBw.d format: integer binary

range: 1–8
default: 4
alignment: left

Integer binary, or fixed point, is used to store integers. The value is stored as the hexadecimal equivalent of the decimal value. If the *d* value is used in the format, the number is divided by 10^d. The following table compares integer binary notation in several languages:

SAS	IB2.	IB4.
PL/I	FIXED BIN(15)	FIXED BIN(31)
FORTRAN	INTEGER*2	INTEGER*4
COBOL	COMP PIC 9(4)	COMP PIC 9(8)
assembler	H	F

example You want to write the numeric variable X's value of 128 in columns 20–23 of the data line:

    PUT @20 X IB4.;

PDw.d format: packed decimal

    range: 1–16
    default: 1
    alignment: left

For data stored in packed decimal form, each byte except the last contains two digits. The *w* value represents the number of bytes, not the number of digits. The value's sign is carried in the last half of the last byte: a C or F if the value is positive, a D if it is negative. This table compares the SAS format PD4. with notation in some other languages:

SAS	PD4.
PL/I	FIXED DEC(7,0)
COBOL	COMP-3 PIC S9(7)
assembler	PL4

example X's value is 128, and you want to store it in packed decimal format in columns 4–7 of a data line.

    PUT @4 X PD4.;

PIBw.d format: positive integer binary

    range: 1–8
    default: 1
    alignment: left

Positive integer binary values are the same as integer binary (see the IB. format, above), except that all values are treated as positive. Thus, the high-order bit is part of the value rather than the value's sign.

If a *d* value appears in the PIB. format, the data value is divided by 10^d.

example X's value is 12, and you want to write it as a 1-byte positive integer binary value in column 43 of a data line:

    PUT @43 X PIB1.;

RBw.d format: real binary (floating point)

    range: 2–8
    default: 4
    alignment: left

Floating point representation is commonly used to store numeric data for scientific calculations. (SAS stores all numeric values in floating point.) A floating point value consists of two parts: a mantissa giving the value, and an exponent giving the value's magnitude.

Real binary is the most efficient format for representing numeric values, since SAS already represents numbers this way and no conversion is needed. This table compares the names of floating point notation in several languages:

	4 bytes	8 bytes
SAS	RB4.	RB8.
PL/I	FLOAT BIN(21)	FLOAT BIN(53)
FORTRAN	REAL*4	REAL*8
COBOL	COMP-1	COMP-2
assembler	E	D

example The numeric variable X's value is 128, and you want to write it in columns 10–17 of a data line:

PUT @10 X RB8.;

ROMANw. format: Roman numerals

range: 2–32
default: 6
alignment: left

The ROMAN. format prints numeric values as Roman numerals. Noninteger values are truncated to integers before printing.

example   X's value is 1982, and you want to print it in columns 25–35 of the output line.

PUT @25 X ROMAN10.;

prints the value

MCMLXXXII

SSNw. format: social security numbers

range: 11
default: 11

The SSN. format prints 9-digit numeric values as U.S. social security numbers, with dashes between the third and fourth digits and between the fifth and sixth digits. If the value is missing, SAS prints nine single periods with dashes between the third and fourth period and between the fifth and sixth periods. If the value contains fewer than nine digits, SAS aligns the value on the right and pads the value with zeros on the left.

example: ID's value is 263878439, and you want to print it in columns 21–31 of the output line:

PUT @21 ID SSN11.;

prints the value

263-87-8439

WORDFw. format

range: 5–200
default: 10
alignment: left

The WORDF. format writes out numeric values in words. It is identical to the WORDSw. format except that fractions appear as numbers instead of words. All fractions appear as hundredths. For example, 8.2 is printed as "EIGHT AND 20/100." Negative numbers are preceded by the word "MINUS."

Numbers greater than 99,999,999 print as "LARGE__NUMBER." When words do not fit into the specified field, they are truncated on the right and the last character prints as an asterisk.

example   PRICE'S value is 29.95, and you want to print it in columns 40–69 of the output line.

    PUT @40 PRICE WORDF30.;

prints the value

    TWENTY-NINE AND 95/100

WORDSw. format

    range: 5–200
    default: 10
    alignment: left

The WORDS. format writes out numeric values in words. For example, you might want to print checks with the amount written out below the payee line.

Negative numbers are preceded by the word "MINUS." If the number is not an integer, hundredths are described; for example, 5.3 is printed as "FIVE AND THIRTY HUNDREDTHS."

Numbers greater than 99,999,999 print as "LARGE__NUMBER." When words do not fit into the specified field, they are truncated on the right and the last character prints as an asterisk.

example   NETPAY'S value is 354, and you want to print it in columns 20–69 of the output line.

    PUT @20 NETPAY WORDS50.;

prints the value

    THREE HUNDRED FIFTY-FOUR

Zw.d format: print leading zeros

    range: 1–32
    default: 1
    alignment: right

The Z. format fills in zeros rather than blanks to the left of the data value.

example   SEQNUM'S value is 1350, and you want to print it in columns 73–80 of the output line, with zeros in the columns before the value.

    PUT @73 SEQNUM Z8.;

prints the value

    00001350

ZDw.d format: zoned decimal

    range: 1–32
    default: 1
    alignment: left

Zoned decimal is similar to standard numeric format in that every digit requires one byte. However, the value's sign is carried in the last byte along with the last digit: if the value is positive, the next-to-last hex digit is C; if the value is negative, the next-to-last hex digit is D. Use this table to compare the zoned decimal format with notation in several languages:

SAS	ZD3.
PL/I	PICTURE '99T'
COBOL	DISPLAY PIC S 999
assembler	ZL3

example X's value is 102, and you want to write it in ZD. format in columns 4–7 of data line:

    PUT @4 X ZD4.;

Character Formats

To write a character variable, you must use a character format. Character formats all begin with a dollar sign ($).

$w. format: standard character data

    range: 1–200
    default: 1 if length of variable not yet defined; otherwise, the length of the
                variable
    alignment: left

To write character data, use the SAS format $w. In this format the *w* value gives the number of columns SAS will use to write the character value.

example NAME's value is 'ABC', and you want to write it in columns 10–12 of the output line.

    PUT @10 NAME $3.;

or

    PUT NAME $ 10–12;

or

    PUT NAME 10–12;

You may omit the dollar sign when you are using a PUT statement, since SAS knows that NAME is a character variable.

$CHARw. format: leading blanks

    range: 1–200
    default: 1 if length of variable not yet defined; otherwise, the length of the
                variable
    alignment: left

The $CHARw. format is identical to the $w. format above, except that $CHAR. does not trim leading blanks. This table compares the $CHARw. format to notation in some other languages.

SAS	$CHAR8.
PL/I	CHAR(8)
FORTRAN	A8
COBOL	PIC X(8)
assembler	CL8

example   NAME's value is ' ABC', with one leading blank, and you want to write it in columns 7–10 of an output line.

    PUT @7 NAME $CHAR4.;

$HEXw. format: character hexadecimal

    range: 1–200
    default: 2
    alignment: left

The $HEX. format is like the HEX. format, above, in that it is used to convert a character value to its corresponding hexadecimal display where each byte requires two columns. Use $HEX. when the variable whose representation in hexadecimal you want displayed is a SAS character variable.

example   The character variable NAME's value is 'AB', and you want to print its hex equivalent, C1C2, in columns 21–24. Note that 4 columns will be required for the output value.

    PUT @21 NAME $HEX4.;

$VARYINGw. format: varying-length values

    range: 1–200
    default: 8 or length of variable
    alignment: left

The $VARYINGw. format can be used when the length of a character value differs from record to record. Typically, the length of the character value in the current record is given in a numeric field in the record (or implicitly, by the fact that the character variable occupies the entire varying portion of a variable-length record). The format name $VARYING. is usually followed by a numeric value *w* which gives the maximum length of the character variable.

When you use the $VARYINGw. format, SAS first determines the value of the length variable, then uses that value to determine how many of the columns the character variable is stored in (specified in *w*) to print. SAS does not print the value of the length variable.

You **must** include a length variable when you use the $VARYINGw. format. If the length variable has a value of 0 or less (including missing values) for a given observation, SAS uses a length of 1 for the character variable. If the value of the length variable is greater than 0 but less than or equal to the value given in *w*, SAS prints as many fields as the value of the length that variable specifies. If the value of the length variable is greater than the value given in *w*, SAS uses the value of *w* for the length of the character variable. The length variable cannot be an array name.

SAS always associates a value *w* with the $VARYING. format. If you do not specify a value for *w*, SAS assigns a length to the character variable and uses that length as the value of *w*. SAS assigns a length to the character variable using the same rules that it does for assigning lengths to character variables in other situations: if you have given the variable a length earlier (for example, with a LENGTH statement) it uses that length; if you have not given the variable a specific length, it uses a length of 8.

The pointer's value after printing a data value with the $VARYINGw. format is the first column after the value.

example   CITY is a variable in your data set whose length ranges from 1 to 30 characters, although it is stored with a length of 30. LEN is another variable in the data set giving the actual length of CITY for the current observation. You want to write the CITY value beginning in column 10; the pointer's value after writing the value should be the first column after the actual CITY value.

> PUT @10 CITY $VARYING30. LEN;

Again, note that LEN in this statement functions not as a variable name, but as part of the $VARYING30. format.

USING SAS DATE, TIME, AND DATETIME INFORMATS AND FORMATS

You can read, work with, and write values that represent dates and times in SAS. SAS represents each of these values as a number associated with an implicit time unit. These units are:

- A date in SAS is represented by the number of days between January 1, 1960 and that date.
- A time in SAS is represented in seconds.
- A date and time is represented by the number of seconds between midnight, January 1, 1960, and the date and time.

For example, consider the date July 4, 1982. Say that this date appears on an input data line as 7-4-82. To read the value as a SAS date value, you use the date informat MMDDYY8., which reads 7-4-82 and converts it to the number of days between January 1, 1960 and July 4, 1982: 8220 days.

> DATA DAYS;
>   INPUT BIRTHDAY MMDDYY8.;
>   CARDS;
> 7-4-82

After execution of the INPUT statement, BIRTHDAY's value is 8220, and if you print the value with the statement

> PUT BIRTHDAY;

SAS prints 8220.

In order to print 8220 as a date, you must assign a format to the variable BIRTHDAY. There are several formats available that print the date; one is DATE., which prints the date as the day of the month, followed by the first three letters of the month, and then the year. So the statement

> PUT BIRTHDAY DATE7.;

prints the line

> 04JUL82

You can associate a format with the value for the duration of the job with a FORMAT statement in the DATA step. For example, the statement

    FORMAT BIRTHDAY DATE7.;

causes the BIRTHDAY value to print as 04JUL82 for the remainder of the job.

This representation of dates and times has several advantages: date, time, and datetime values sort correctly; finding intervals between two dates or two times involves only a simple subtraction; and the standards are not internationally ambiguous.

SAS dates are valid back to A.D. 1582 and ahead to A.D. 20,000, and leap year, century, and fourth-century adjustments are handled properly. However, leap seconds are ignored, and SAS does not adjust for daylight saving time.

If the width of your informat is not sufficient to read all the columns containing the date, time, or datetime value in your data lines, you will get unexpected results. (Remember that blanks or special characters between the day, month, year, or time add columns to the length of the value.) For example, if you use the informat DATE8. to read these values:

    01/JAN/82
    3/MAR/1955

SAS assigns date values corresponding to 01JAN08 and 03MAR19, respectively. If the width is such that the last column SAS reads is a special character, SAS produces an invalid data message.

If the width of a date, time, or datetime format is not sufficient to write all the information about the value, SAS truncates the value on the right. In some formats SAS abbreviates the name of the month, the name of the weekday, or both, in order to print as much information as possible. If the format specifies more columns than SAS needs, SAS aligns the value on the right.

If you give a two-digit value for a year, SAS assumes that the year is in the 1900's.

Duration vs. Date

When you are working with date and datetime values, it's important to keep in mind the units associated with the values, and to consider these units when you manipulate the values.

For example, say you want to calculate the ages of employees from their birth dates. You read the birth dates with a date informat (say DATE7.), and you use the function TODAY to assign today's date to a variable. To find the employees' ages, you subtract BIRTHDAY from TODAY:

    DATA EMPLAGE;
      INPUT ID BIRTHDAY DATE7.;
      TODAY = TODAY( );
      AGE = TODAY-BIRTHDAY;

What exactly is the value of AGE? It is the number of days between the employees' birthdays and today, and represents a duration in days rather than in years.

Here is an example. Say an employee's birthday is December 1, 1959. The internal representation of that date is –31. Today's date is January 15, 1983; the internal representation of that date is 8415. Subtracting –31 from 8415 gives us 8446, which is the number of days between today and December 1, 1959. This number is **not** a SAS date value since it represents a duration not based on January

1, 1960. To print the value in a form that makes sense (such as the number of years since the employee's birthday), you must calculate how many years are in 8446 days:

AGEYEARS = AGE/365.25;

SAS Date, Time, and Datetime Informat Descriptions

Informat	Description	Width Range	Default Width
DATEw.	dates of form ddMMMyy	7–32	7
DATETIMEw.d	date-time values	13–40	16
DDMMYYw.	date values	6–32	6
MMDDYYw.	date values	6–32	6
MONYYw.	month and year	5–32	5
MSECw.	TIME MIC values	8	8
PDTIMEw.	packed-decimal time from SMF/RMF records	4	4
RMFDURw.	RMF time interval measurements	4	4
RMFSTAMPw.	time-date field from RMF records	8	8
SMFSTAMPw.	time-date field from SMF records	8	8
TIMEw.d	time values	5–32	8
TODSTAMPw.	8-byte time-of-day stamp	8	8
TUw.	timer units	4	4
YYMMDDw.	date values	6–32	6
YYQw.	year and quarter	4–32	4

Date, Time, and Datetime Informat Descriptions

DATEw. informat: ddMMMyy

range: 7–32
default: 7

The DATE. informat reads SAS date values in the form ddMMMyy, where dd is the day of the month, 01–31; MMM is the first three letters of the month name; and yy or yyyy is the year. Blanks and other special characters may appear before and after the date, and also between the day, month, and year values.

example The statements

```
DATA DATES;
  INPUT DAY1 DATE10.;
  CARDS;
1JAN1982
01 JAN 82
1 JAN 82
1-JAN-1982
;
```

read each of these values as SAS date values corresponding to 01JAN82.

DATETIMEw. informat: date and time

    range: 13–40
    default: 16

Datetime values are those that include both a date and a time, written as the date first and then the time. The date must be in the SAS date form ddMMMyy, followed by a blank or special character, and the time must be in the time form hh:mm, with an optional part ss.ss representing seconds and decimal fractions of seconds. The value of hh ranges from 00 to 23. You must give both a value for date and a value for time.

example These fields are read with the DATETIMEw. informat as SAS datetime values corresponding to 10:03:17.2 a.m., December 23, 1976:

    23DEC76:10:03:17.2
    23DEC1976/10 03 17.2

DDMMYYw. informat: day-month-year

    range: 6–32
    default: 6

You can use the DDMMYY. informat to read a SAS date value in ddmmyy form, where dd is the day of the month, mm the month, and yy the year. Blanks may appear before and after the date. The month, day, and year fields may be separated by blanks or special characters; however, if any of these fields are separated by blanks or special characters, all of them must be separated by blanks or special characters.

example If you use the informat DDMMYY8., all of the values in the example below read as values corresponding to 15OCT82:

    151082
    15/10/82
    15 10 82

MMDDYYw. informat: month-day-year

    range: 6–32
    default: 6

The MMDDYY. informat reads a SAS date value in mmddyy form, where mm is the month, dd the day of the month, yy the year. Blanks may appear before and after the date. The month, day, and year fields may be separated by blanks or special characters; however, if any of these fields are separated by blanks or special characters, all of them must be separated by blanks or special characters.

example All of the values in the example below read as SAS date values corresponding to 01JAN81 if you use the informat MMDDYY8.:

    010181
    1/1/81
    01 1 81

MONYYw. informat: month and year

    range: 5–32
    default: 5

The MONYYw. informat reads SAS date values in the form MMMyy, where MMM is the first three letters of the month name and yy or yyyy is the year.

A value read with the MONYYw. informat results in a SAS date value corresponding to the first day of the specified month. The value must be in the form MMMyy or MMMyyyy; the MMM and yy or yyyy values may not be separated by blanks.

example The statement

    INPUT MONTH MONYY5.;

reads the field JUN81 and produces a SAS date value corresponding to

    01JUN81

MSECw. informat: TIME MIC values

    range: 8
    default: 8

The MSEC. informat reads a TIME MIC value (bit 51 equals one microsecond) as a SAS time value. This informat is also useful for reading the difference between two TIME MIC or STCK values or two TODSTAMP. values, whereas TODSTAMP. provides the datetime informat for a stored TOD clock or TIME STCK value.

example A value produced by an OS TIME macro instruction with the MIC operand (00 00 EA 04 4E 65 A0 00 in hexadecimal) is stored in a record at offset +8. The statements

    DATA TIME;
      INFILE TRACE;
      INPUT @1 +8 TIMEMIC MSEC8.;
      FORMAT TIMEMIC TIME11.;
      PUT 'THE TIME IS ' TIMEMIC=;

read this field and write on the SAS log

    THE TIME IS TIMEMIC=17:26:58

PDTIMEw. informat: packed decimal time of SMF and RMF records

    range: 4
    default: 4

The PDTIME. informat reads the packed decimal time (in the form 0hhmmssF) of SMF and RMF records as a SAS time value. If SAS encounters a field of all zeros, it treats the field as a missing value.

RMFDURw. informat: RMF time interval measurements

    range: 4
    default: 4

The RMFDUR. informat reads the duration of RMF measurement intervals in RMF records as SAS time values. The data have the form mmsstttF in packed decimal, where mm is minutes, ss is seconds, ttt is thousandths of seconds, and F is the sign. If the field does not contain packed decimal data, SAS treats the value as missing.

RMFSTAMPw. informat: time and date fields of RMF records

    range: 8
    default: 8

The RMFSTAMP informat reads the time and date fields of RMF records as SAS datetime values. The first four bytes are 0hhmmssF in packed decimal; the second four bytes contain 00yydddF in packed decimal.

example

```
DATA A;
  INPUT @2 TYPE PIB1. @3 DATTIM RMFSTAMP8.;
```

SMFSTAMPw. informat: time-date field of SMF records

    range: 8
    default: 8

The SMFSTAMP. informat reads the time-date field of SMF records as a SAS datetime value. The first four bytes of this field are the time in hundredths of seconds, in integer binary (full-word fixed point), and the next four bytes are the Julian date in packed decimal.

example

```
DATA A;
  INPUT @2 TYPE PIB1.
  @3 DATTIM SMFSTAMP8.;
```

TIMEw.d informat: hours, minutes, and seconds

    range: 5–32
    default: 8

The TIME. informat reads SAS time values in the form hh:mm:ss.ss, where hh is the hour, mm the minute, and ss.ss an optional fractional part representing seconds and hundredths of seconds. If you do not give a value for seconds, SAS assumes a value of 0 seconds.

example   These SAS statements read a value of the variable BEGIN:

```
DATA TIMEDATA;
  INPUT BEGIN TIME8.;
  CARDS;
14:22:25
;
```

TODSTAMP. informat: 8-byte time-of-day stamp

    range: 8
    default: 8

The TODSTAMP informat converts an 8-byte, time-of-day clock value into a SAS datetime value. The time-of-day clock value is returned by the OS TIME macro with the STCK operand, as well as the STCK System/370 instruction. If the 8 bytes of input contain all zeros, then a regular SAS missing value is returned. The time-of-day clock value is described in *IBM System/370 Principles of Operation* (IBM SRL form number GA22-7000).

example   These SAS statements read a TOD clock value (93 B2 00 C1 9E 7A 20 00 in hexadecimal) stored at offset +49 in a record.

```
INPUT @50 TIMESTCK TODSTAMP8.;
FORMAT TIMESTCK DATETIME17.;
PUT 'THE TIME IS ' TIMESTCK=;
```

The SAS log contains the result of the PUT statement:

THE TIME IS TIMESTCK=03MAY82:17:26:58

TUw. informat: timer units

range: 4
default: 4

The TU. informat reads IBM OS/360 and OS/VS (software) timer units as a SAS time value. A time value in (software) timer units is returned by the OS TIME macro with the TU operand. Since there are exactly 38,400 (software) timer units per second, the low-order bit represents approximately 26.041667 microseconds.

example   A value produced by an OS TIME macro instruction with the TU operand (8F C7 A9 BC in hexadecimal) is stored in a record at offset +208. The statements

INPUT @1 +208 TIMETU TU4.;
FORMAT TIMETU TIME11.;
PUT 'THE TIME IS ' TIMETU=;

read this field and write on the SAS log

THE TIME IS TIMETU=17:26:58

YYMMDDw. informat: year-month-day

range: 6–32
default: 6

The YYMMDD. informat may be used to read a SAS date value in yymmdd form, where yy is the year, mm the month, dd the day of the month. (The YYMMDD. informat is FIPS standard 4.) Blanks may appear before and after the date, and the month, day, and year fields may be separated by blanks or special characters; however, if any of these fields are separated by blanks or special characters, all of them must be separated by blanks or special characters. The YYMMDD. informat accepts a four-digit year value.

example 1   All of the data values in the example below read as SAS date values corresponding to 1JAN76:

DATA NEWYEAR;
 INPUT BEG YYMMDD8.;
 CARDS;
760101
76 1 1
76-01-01
76/1/1
19760101
;

example 2   The first value below reads as a SAS date value corresponding to 01JAN1952; the second reads as a value corresponding to 16OCT1884.

DATA A;
 INPUT DATE YYMMDD10.;
 CARDS;
19520101
1884/10/16
;

YYQw. informat: quarters of year

range: 4–32
default: 4

The YYQw. informat reads SAS date values in the form yyQq, where yy or yyyy is the year, Q is the letter Q, and q is the quarter of the year (1, 2, 3, or 4).

A value read with the YYQw. informat results in a SAS date value corresponding to the first day of the specified quarter. For input, the value must be in the form yyQq or yyyyQq; the year value, the letter Q, and the quarter value may not be separated with blanks.

example   The statement

    INPUT ENTERED YYQ5.;

reads the value 82Q2 and results in a SAS date value for ENTERED corresponding to

    1MAR1982

SAS Date, Time, and Datetime Format Descriptions

Format	Description	Width Range	Default Width
DATEw.	dates of form ddMMMyy	5–9	7
DATETIMEw.d	date-time values	7–40	16
DDMMYYw.	date values	2–8	8
HHMMw.d	hour and minutes	2–20	5
HOURw.d	hour	2–20	2
MMDDYYw.	date values	2–8	8
MMSSw.d	minutes and seconds	2–20	5
MONYYw.	month and year	5–7	5
TIMEw.d	time values	2–20	8
TODw.	time-of-day	2–20	8
WEEKDATEw.	date values	3–37	29
WORDDATEw.	date values	3–32	18
YYMMDDw.	date values	2–8	8
YYQw.	year and quarter	4–6	4

DATEw. format: ddMMMyy

range: 5–9
default: 7

The DATE. format writes SAS date values in the form ddMMMyy, where dd is the day of the month, 01–31; MMM is the first three letters of the month name; and yy or yyyy is the year.

example

format	value printed
DATE5.	12SEP
DATE6.	12SEP
DATE7.	12SEP79
DATE8.	12SEP79
DATE9.	12SEP1979

DATETIMEw.d format: date and time

>range: 7–40
>default: 16

Datetime values are those that include both a date and a time, written as the date first and then the time. The DATETIME. format prints datetime values as DDMMMYY:hh:mm:ss.s. When the field width is 18, the *d* value may be 1. When the field width is greater than 18, the *d* value may be 2.

example The statement

    PUT EVENT DATETIME18.;

prints the value

    23DEC81:10:03:17.2

format	value printed
DATETIME7.	12SEP79
DATETIME8.	12SEP79
DATETIME9.	12SEP79
DATETIME10.	12SEP79:03
DATETIME11.	12SEP79:03
DATETIME12.	12SEP79:03
DATETIME13.	12SEP79:03:19
DATETIME14.	12SEP79:03:19
DATETIME15.	12SEP79:03:19
DATETIME16.	12SEP79:03:19:43
DATETIME17.	12SEP79:03:19:43
DATETIME18.	12SEP79:03:19:43
DATETIME18.1	12SEP79:03:19:43:2
DATETIME19.2	12SEP79:03:19:43.22
DATETIME20.2	12SEP79:03:19:43.22
DATETIME21.2	12SEP1979:03:19:43.22
DATETIME22.2	12SEP1979:03:19:43.22

DDMMYYw. format: day-month-year

>range: 2–8
>default: 8

You can use the DDMMYY. format to write a SAS date value in ddmmyy form, where dd is the day of the month, mm the month, and yy the year.

When the field width is from 2 to 5, as much of the month and day values as possible is shown. When the width is 7, the date is printed with a two-digit year without slashes, and the value is right-aligned in the output field.

example The DDMMYY6. format writes the date as ddmmyy: for example, 251282. The DDMMYY8. format writes the date as dd/mm/yy: for example, 25/12/82.

HHMMw.d format: hours and minutes

>range: 2–20
>default: 5

The HHMM. format prints the hours and minutes of a SAS time value, and is similar to the TIME. format except that seconds are not shown. If the optional *d* value is given, decimal fractions of minutes are shown. SAS rounds minutes and hours based on the value of the seconds in the SAS time value.

example 1   The statements

```
DATA NEW;
   TIME = '12:34:56'T;
   PUT TIME HHMM.;
```

print

    12:35

example 2   The statements

```
DATA NEW;
   TIME = '12:59:56'T;
   PUT TIME HHMM.;
```

print

    13:00

HOURw.d format: hours and decimal fractions of hours

    range: 2–20
    default: 2

The HOUR. format writes only the hour part of a SAS time value. If the optional *d* value is given, decimal fractions of the hour are shown. SAS rounds hours based on the value of the minutes in the SAS time value.

example   The statements

```
DATA __NULL__;
   TIME = '11:30:00'T;
   PUT TIME HOUR4.1;
```

print

    11.5

MMDDYYw. format: month-day-year

    range: 2–8
    default: 8

The MMDDYY. format writes a SAS date value in mmddyy form, where mm is the month, dd the day of the month, yy the year.

example   The MMDDYY6. format writes the date as mmddyy: for example, 122582. The MMDDYY8. format writes the date as mm/dd/yy: for example, 12/25/82.

format	value printed
MMDDYY2.	09
MMDDYY3.	09
MMDDYY4.	0912
MMDDYY5.	09/12
MMDDYY6.	091279
MMDDYY7.	091279
MMDDYY8.	09/12/79

MMSSw.d format: minutes and seconds

range: 2–20
default: 5

The MMSS. format prints a SAS time value as the number of minutes and seconds since midnight. If the optional *d* value is used, decimal fractions of seconds are shown.

example   The statements

```
DATA __NULL__;
  TIME='1:15:30'T;
  PUT TIME MMSS.;
```

write on the SAS log

```
75:30
```

MONYYw. format: month and year

range: 5–7
default: 5

The MONYYw. format writes SAS date values in the form MMMyy, where MMM is the first three letters of the month name and yy or yyyy is the year.

example   The statement

```
PUT ACQUIRED MONYY7.;
```

writes the line

```
JUN1981
```

TIMEw.d format: hours, minutes, and seconds

range: 2–20
default: 8

The TIME. format writes SAS time values in the form hh:mm:ss.ss, where hh is the hour, mm the minute, and ss the seconds, with an optional fractional part representing hundredths of seconds.

example   The statement

```
PUT BEGIN TIME.;
```

prints a value of BEGIN as

```
16:24:43
```

TODw. format: time portion of datetime values

range: 2–20
default: 8

The TOD. format prints a SAS time value as a duration from midnight of the day in a datetime value so that you can print the time portion of datetime values.

example   Say you read the datetime value 29APR82:3:24:00 into the variable BDTIME. This value is stored internally as the number of seconds between 1JAN60:00:00 and 29APR82:3:24:00. To print just the time part of the value (from midnight, 29APR82), use the TOD. format.

    PUT BDTIME TOD7.;

prints the line

    3:24:00

WEEKDATEw. format: day of week and date

    range: 3–37
    default: 29

The WEEKDATE. format writes a date value in the form day-of-week, month name, dd, yyyy. If the value of *w* is too small for writing the complete name of the day of the week and the month, SAS will abbreviate them as needed.

example   The statement

    PUT BEG WEEKDATE.;

writes the line

    MONDAY, NOVEMBER 27, 1979

format	value printed
WEEKDATE3.	WED
WEEKDATE9.	WEDNESDAY
WEEKDATE15.	WED, SEP 12, 79
WEEKDATE17.	WED, SEP 12, 1979
WEEKDATE23.	WEDNESDAY, SEP 12, 1979
WEEKDATE29.	WEDNESDAY, SEPTEMBER 12, 1979

WORDDATEw. format: date with name of month written as word

    range: 3–32
    default: 18

The WORDDATE. format writes a date value in the form month name, dd, yyyy.

example   The statement

    PUT TERM WORDDATE.;

writes the value of TERM as

    SEPTEMBER 30, 1980

format	value printed
WORDDATE3.	SEP
WORDDATE9.	SEPTEMBER
WORDDATE12.	SEP 12, 1979
WORDDATE18.	SEPTEMBER 12, 1979
WORDDATE20.	SEPTEMBER 12, 1979

YYMMDDw. format: year-month-day

    range: 2–8
    default: 8

You can use the YYMMDD. format to write a SAS date value in yymmdd form, where yy is the year, mm the month, dd the day of the month.

example   The statement

PUT DAY YYMMDD2.;

writes January 1, 1983 as 83. The statement

PUT DAY YYMMDD.;

writes March 18, 1982 as 82-03-18.

format	value printed
YYMMDD2.	79
YYMMDD3.	79
YYMMDD4.	7909
YYMMDD5.	79-09
YYMMDD6.	790912
YYMMDD7.	790912
YYMMDD8.	79-09-12

YYQw.: quarters of year

range: 4–6
default: 4

The YYQw. format writes SAS date values in the form yyQq or yyyyQq where yy or yyyy is the year, Q is the letter Q, and q is the quarter of the year (1, 2, 3, or 4).

example   The statement

PUT ACQUIRED YYQ4.;

prints any value of ACQUIRED between 1SEP82 and 31DEC82 as

82Q4

USING SAS COLUMN-BINARY (MULTIPUNCH) INFORMATS

When punched cards are used to store information, the maximum number of data items that can be stored on a card is usually 80: one item of information in each of the 80 columns of the card.

However, it is possible to store more than 80 items on a card by taking advantage of the fact that each of the 80 columns contains 12 positions where punches may occur. If the possible values of the item to be stored have a narrow range, only a few of these 12 positions may be needed to store the item.

For example, consider a variable SEX whose values are 1 for females, 2 for males. Only one position of the 12 available in a column is really needed to store a SEX value. If the position is blank, the value is assumed to be 1; if a punch occurs in the position, the value is assumed to be 2. Or perhaps two positions might be used: if the punch occurs in the first, the value is 1; if the punch occurs in the second, the value is 2.

Consider another variable RACE whose values are 1, 2, 3, or 4. Four positions are needed to store the value.

Both a SEX and a RACE value could thus be stored in a single column: the SEX value in rows 1 and 2, and the RACE value in rows 3–6. Six rows would be unused.

Data that have been stored using this compressed form are called column-binary data, or multipunched data. The advantage of using this approach to store data is that more information can be stored than would be possible using one column per information item. However, the difficulties frequently encountered in getting at the data after they have been stored usually outweigh the advantages, and so storing data in a column-binary form is now out of fashion.

Since many multipunched decks and card-image data sets remain in existence, SAS provides informats to read column-binary data.

Because each card column of column-binary data is expanded to two bytes before reading the fields, the LRECL = 160 parameter should appear in the INFILE statement for the input file. For example, if the column-binary data were in a disk data set described by the IN DD statement, the statement

INFILE IN LRECL = 160;

would appear before the INPUT statement.

This expansion does **not** affect the column pointer's value: column addressing with the @ is done as usual, since the formats automatically compute the true location on the doubled record. If a value is in column 23, use the pointer direction @23 to move the pointer there.

The rows in a card column are numbered, from the top:

```
12
11
(0 or 10)
1
2
3
4
5
6
7
8
9
```

When column-binary data are transmitted using EBCDIC, the 12 punch bits are divided into two sets of six bits; the six bits are mapped into the end of each 8-bit byte.

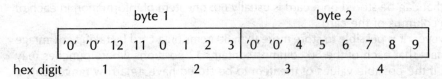

Column-binary (multipunch) informat descriptions

PUNCH.d informat: rows

Using the PUNCH.d informat to read a value of a numeric variable results in a value of 1 if row d of the current column is punched; a value of 0 if row d is not punched. The d item may have the values 1 to 9, 10, 11, or 12. After the variable has been read with the PUNCH.d informat, the pointer is **not** advanced to the next column.

The example below uses the PUNCH.d informat to read rows 3, 4, 5 in the first column of the card, and rows 11 and 0 from the second column of the card.

```
DATA PUNCH;
  INFILE IN LRECL=160;
  INPUT X3 PUNCH.3 X4 PUNCH.4 X5 PUNCH.5 @2 X11 PUNCH.11
    X0 PUNCH.10;
```

The values of the variables X3, X4, X5, X11, and X0 will be either zeros or ones, depending on whether the corresponding rows were punched on the input card.

ROWw.d informat: columns

The ROW. informat is used to read a column-binary field down a column of a card. The *w* item, which may range from 0 to 12, defines the row where the field begins; the *d* value gives its length in rows. If the *d* value is omitted, it is assumed to be 1. The maximum *d* value is 25. The value assigned the variable being read, which must be a numeric variable, is the relative position of the punch in the field.

For example, suppose that the field to be read begins at row 2 in column 10 and continues through row 5, for a length of 4 rows. The INPUT statement to read this field would be

```
INPUT @10 X ROW2.4;
```

If the punch occurs in row 2, X's value is 1, since the punch is in the first row of the field. If the punch occurs in row 4, X's value is 3.

No more than one punch should occur in the specified field. If more than one punch does occur, the variable is assigned a missing value and the automatic variable __ERROR__ is set to 1. If no punches occur in the field, the variable is also assigned a missing value.

Here is another example. Consider this INPUT statement:

```
INPUT @25 AGE ROW3.3 RACE ROW6.4;
```

Two variables have been coded into column 25 of the card. The AGE field begins in row 3 and continues through row 5; the RACE field begins in row 6 and continues through row 9. The values of the AGE and RACE variables:

RACE: missing if none of the rows 6–9 are punched
        missing, __ERROR__ = 1 if more than one punch in rows 6–9
        1 if row 6 is punched
        2 if row 7 is punched
        3 if row 8 is punched
        4 if row 9 is punched

AGE: missing if none of the rows 3–5 are punched
        missing, __ERROR__ = 1 if more than one punch in rows 3–5
        1 if row 3 is punched
        2 if row 4 is punched
        3 if row 5 is punched

Fields read with the ROW. informat may extend to the next column; the scan continues with row 12 of the new column and proceeds down the column. After a field has been read with the ROW. informat, the pointer is set to the row after the last one scanned.

For example, consider this INPUT statement:

```
INPUT @34 X ROW3.3 Y ROW6.4 Z ROW12.15 @37 W $CB1.;
```

X is read from rows 3–5 of column 34; Y is read from rows 6–9 of column 34. Z is read from rows 12–9 of column 35 and rows 12–0 of column 36. W is read from column 37. However, if the @37 pointer direction had not appeared, W would have been read from column 36. Use the @ pointer direction often to insure the correct position of the pointer.

$CBw. informat: standard character values

Use the $CB. informat to read standard character data from column-binary files. The column binary code is first translated to standard EBCDIC characters. If the punch combinations are not valid EBCDIC punch codes, blanks are returned and the automatic variable __ERROR__ is set to 1.

CBw.d informat: standard numeric values

Use the CB. informat to read standard numeric values from column-binary files. The column binary code is first translated to EBCDIC before the number is read from the field. As with the $CB. informat, an invalid punch code results in a missing value and an __ERROR__ value of 1.

Alternative methods   Sometimes it may be more convenient to read the 160 bytes of information as if they made up two 80-byte records. In this case, treat information in columns 41–80 of the record as if it were in columns 1–40 of a second record.

For example, these two groups of statements have the same effect:

```
DATA NEW;
INFILE COLBIN LRECL=160;
INPUT @62 X CB2.;
```

```
DATA NEW;
INFILE COLBIN LRECL=80;
INPUT #2 @22 X CB2.;
```

Missing Values

Most collections of data include missing values. For example, if a respondent in a survey fails to answer a given question, an analyst may classify that data item as missing. Sales figures for various products may include a missing value for last year's sales of a product introduced this year. In addition, errors in entering data can produce unidentifiable values.

Values like these can be recognized as missing at the time SAS reads them. Other missing values can be produced during the DATA step: you can use program statements to assign missing values to variables, and SAS can automatically generate missing values for variables when certain conditions arise.

Missing Values in Input Data Lines

Blanks for missing values You can represent missing values on data lines for numeric and character variables with either blanks or single periods. If you are not using list input, the easiest way to indicate a missing value is simply to leave blank the columns that the value would occupy if it were not missing. When SAS reads the data line, it sets the value to missing.

For example, say your data values are pre- and post-test scores for students. If Susan is absent the day of the post-test, you simply leave Susan's POSTTEST field blank on the input lines:

```
DATA TESTSCOR;
 INPUT NAME $ 1-6 PRETEST 8-9 POSTTEST 11-12;
 CARDS;
ANN 92 96
SUSAN 84
BILL 81 95
more data lines
;
```

Periods for missing values You can also use a single period (.) to represent a missing value. When SAS sees a single period in the columns corresponding to a variable value, it sets the value to missing. (To read a single period as the value of a character variable without having SAS consider the value missing, use the $CHAR. informat.)

If you are using list input, you **must** use periods rather than blanks to represent missing values. With list input, SAS begins reading the next data value at the next non-blank column, so you must use the period to prevent SAS from reading the value of the following variable in place of the value which is missing. (See the description of the INPUT statement in Chapter 3, "Statements Used in the DATA Step," for more information about list input.)

For example, say you are using list input to read the test scores in the example above. Use a single period to represent Susan's POSTTEST value:

```
DATA TESTSCOR;
  INPUT NAME $ PRETEST POSTTEST;
  CARDS;
ANN 92 96
SUSAN 84 .
BILL 81 95
more data lines
;
```

Other ways to represent missing values You can also use 9s, 99s, or other values clearly out of the expected range to represent missing values. Although SAS does not automatically read values like these as missing values, you can use program statements to convert them to missing.

For example, say you are reading values of the variable SCORE. The values range from 0 to 7; a value of 9 indicates a missing value. You can use this SAS statement to convert all values of 9 in SCORE to a SAS missing value:

```
IF SCORE=9 THEN SCORE=.;
```

Special missing values At times you may want to differentiate among missing values. For example, in a survey one missing value might mean that the respondent refused to answer a given question, while another missing value might mean that the respondent gave an invalid answer.

For numeric variables only, you can designate up to 27 special missing values, the uppercase letters A through Z and the special character underscore (__), when you want to differentiate among missing values. In the survey example you could use the letter R to indicate that the person refused to respond to a question and the letter X to indicate that the response is invalid.

MISSING statement When your data lines contain special missing values, you **must** include a MISSING statement in your DATA step. (See a description of the MISSING statement in Chapter 11.) For example, in the survey above, you might create a data set like this one:

```
DATA SURVEY;
  MISSING R X;
  INPUT ID ANSWER1;
  CARDS;
1001 2
1002 R
1003 1
1004 X
1005 2
more data lines
;
```

in which the MISSING statement indicates that values of R and X in the input data lines are to be considered special missing values rather than invalid numeric data values.

Illegal characters in input data In addition to blanks or periods and special missing values, you may find that numeric values in your data lines contain illegal characters such as letters or underscores not identified in a MISSING statement, other special characters, or embedded blanks. When SAS encounters these values it prints a warning message and sets each invalid data value to missing (.).

You can use the system option INVALIDDATA to cause SAS to assign a special missing value instead of (.). For example, suppose that you want any invalid data value set to the special missing value A. Use this statement as the first in your SAS program:

  OPTIONS INVALIDDATA=A;

The INVALIDDATA option does not affect blanks, periods, or values that are specified in a MISSING statement.

Working With Missing Values

Missing initial values   At the beginning of each execution of the DATA step, SAS sets the value of each variable you create in the DATA step to missing (except for RETAINED variables); SAS then replaces the missing values as it encounters values you assign to the variables. (See the discussion of the program data vector in Chapter 2, "Introduction to the DATA Step," for more information.) Thus, if you use program statements to create new variables, their values in each observation are missing until you assign the values in an assignment statement.

For example, consider these statements:

```
DATA NEW;
  INPUT X;
  IF X=1 THEN Y=2;
CARDS;
4
1
3
1
;
```

When X equals 1, Y's value is set to 2. But since there are no assignment statements that set Y's value when X is not equal to 1, Y remains missing for those observations where X does not equal 1.

Magnitudes of missing values   Within SAS, a missing value for a numeric variable is smaller than all numbers: if you sort your data set by a numeric variable, observations with missing values for that variable appear first in the sorted data set. For numeric variables, you can compare missing values with numbers and with each other as shown in this table. From smallest to largest, the order of magnitude for SAS missing values for numeric variables is:

—
.
A
B
↓
Z
numbers

Missing values of character variables are smaller than any printable character value. However, some usually unprintable characters (for example, machine carriage-control characters, real or binary numeric data that have been read in error as character data) have values less than the blank. Thus, when you sort a data set by a character variable, observations with missing (blank) values of the sorting variable may not appear first in the sorted data set, but they always appear before observations in which values of the sorting variable contain only printable characters.

Specifying missing constants   When your input data lines contain special missing values, enter the values without periods in front of them. However, when you use a special missing value in an expression or in an assignment statement, put a period before the letter or underscore so that SAS will identify it as a missing value instead of a variable name.

For example, suppose that you are checking the ages that people report for themselves in a survey by subtracting their date of birth from the date of the interview and comparing that with their answer to the question on age. If the subtraction gives a different age than they report, you assign a value of .D (for discrepancy) to AGE:

```
DATA SURVEY;
  INPUT SURVDATE BIRTHDAT AGE;
  IF (SURVDATE-BIRTHDAT)¬=AGE THEN AGE=.D;
  CARDS;
;
```

When SAS prints a special missing value, it prints only the letter or underscore.

Missing values in comparison operations   To check for missing values in your data, you can use statements like the following:

```
IF XXX=. THEN DO;
```

for numeric variables, or

```
IF XXX=' ' THEN DO;
```

where ' ' is a blank literal for character variables. In each case, SAS checks to see if XXX's value in the current observation is equal to the missing value specified. If it is, SAS executes the DO group.

Note that, for numeric variables, the first statement checks only for missing values represented by a period (.); it does not check for special missing values such as A or __. If your data contain special missing values, you can check for all missing values of a variable with the following statement:

```
IF XXX<=.Z THEN DO;
```

Since Z is the largest missing value, if any missing values for XXX are present, SAS executes the DO group. To produce a data set containing no observations that have missing values for XXX, use

```
IF XXX>.Z;
```

You can set values to missing within your DATA step with program statements. For example, the statement

    IF AGE<0 THEN AGE=.;

sets the value of AGE to missing (.) if AGE has a value less than 0. Note that if you already have special missing values for AGE, you are resetting them to (.). To avoid resetting them use:

    IF .Z<AGE<0 THEN AGE=.;

Missing values in logical operations   Missing values and zero have a value of "false" when you use them with logical operators such as AND or OR. All other values have a value of "true." (See Chapter 4, "SAS Expressions," for more information on logical operators.)

Printing missing values   SAS prints a period (.) for a missing value of a numeric variable; however, if you have special missing values for numeric variables, it prints the letter or the underscore. For character variables, SAS prints a series of blanks equal to the length of the variable.

You can ask SAS to substitute another character for numeric missing values if you do not want a period (.) printed; however, SAS continues to store the number as (.). Use the system option MISSING to define the character you want: for example, to print a blank instead of (.) for numeric missing values, use this statement at the beginning of your SAS job:

    OPTIONS MISSING=' ';

The MISSING option does not affect special missing values: for example, the value .A will appear as A in printed output even if you specify another value with the MISSING option. To change special missing values you must use program statements.

Missing Values Generated by SAS

In addition to the missing values that are present in your data and that you assign in program statements, SAS can assign missing values to protect you from problems arising in three common computing situations: using missing values in calculations, performing illegal operations, and converting character values to numeric ones when the character variable contains non-numeric information.

Missing values used in arithmetic calculations   If you use a missing value in an arithmetic calculation, SAS sets the result of that calculation to missing. Then, if you use that result in another calculation, the next result is also missing. This action of SAS is called **propagation of missing values**. Propagation of missing values is important because SAS continues working at the same time that it lets you know, via warning messages, which arithmetic expressions have missing values and at what point it created them.

If you do not want missing values to propagate in your arithmetic expressions, you can use the functions described in Chapter 5 to omit missing values from the computations. For example, consider the DATA step below.

```
DATA TEST;
  X = .;
  Y = 5;
  A = X + Y;
  B = SUM(X,Y);
```

X's value is missing; Y's value is 5. Adding X and Y together in an expression produces a missing result, so A's value is missing. However, using the SUM function to add X and Y produces the value 5, since the SUM function ignores missing values.

Illegal operations   If you try to perform an illegal operation (for example, dividing by zero or taking the logarithm of zero), SAS prints a warning message and assigns a missing value to the result.

Illegal character-to-numeric conversions   SAS automatically converts character values to numeric values if a character variable is used in an arithmetic expression. If a character value contains non-numeric information and SAS tries to convert it to a numeric value, SAS prints an error message and sets the result of the expression to missing. (For more information about character-to-numeric conversion of data values, see the INPUT statement description in Chapter 4, "SAS Expressions.")

Usage Note: Summary

When you are reading data, use the MISSING statement in a DATA step to indicate that numeric fields in your data contain the characters specified in the MISSING statement and that SAS is to read those characters as special missing values. SAS interprets all invalid characters not identified in a MISSING statement as (.). Use the INVALIDDATA option to cause SAS to read all invalid characters in numeric fields (except blanks, periods, and characters identified in a MISSING statement) as the special missing value you choose rather than as (.). When you are printing data, use the MISSING option to print missing values of numeric variables as the character you specify rather than as (.). The MISSING option does not affect character variables or special missing values of numeric variables.

SAS Macro Language

THE MACRO PROCESSOR

What is it?   The macro processor can be used to construct and edit SAS statement text. This processing is done before the text is recognized by SAS as a part of DATA or PROC steps. The macro processor is controlled by a special macro language that uses the percent sign (%) and ampersand (&) to denote macro actions. The macro processor simplifies repetitive data entry tasks and provides a way to store and retrieve SAS jobs that must be tailored to changing details. A macro is stored text combining SAS code and macro code that is referred to by name. The macro facility makes it possible to define macros that accept parameters, retain macro variables across SAS steps, and conditionally create SAS statements. The SAS macro facility allows you to package long and detailed programs and invoke them with a simple command. You can design a custom language which is translated by your macros to SAS code.

How does it work?   When you invoke SAS, your SAS job is first seen by the macro processor. If your job does not contain any macro operations, then the code is passed directly to SAS DATA and PROC step processors. If % actions are present, the macro processor executes them. The result of executing macro program statements is to produce SAS code, which is then passed to SAS to be executed.

THE MACRO LANGUAGE

The following SAS statements define a macro named ANALYZE:

```
%MACRO ANALYZE;
  PROC PRINT  DATA=A;
  PROC MEANS  DATA=A;
%MEND;
```

The statements below show a DATA step and the macro call %ANALYZE:

```
DATA A;
  INPUT X;
  CARDS;
data lines
;
%ANALYZE
```

The text that makes up the macro ANALYZE is now substituted for the %ANALYZE macro call:

```
DATA A;
  INPUT X;
  CARDS;
data lines
;
PROC PRINT DATA=A;
PROC MEANS DATA=A;
```

The simplest macro definition uses the form:

```
%MACRO macroname;
  macrotext
  %MEND;
```

The macro text includes:

1. constant text
2. macro variable references
3. macro function references
4. macro program statements.

Constant text   Constant text in the macro language is treated as character strings. The text can include SAS variable names, SAS data set names, or all or parts of SAS statements.

Macro variables   The values of macro variables (sometimes called *symbolic variables*) are character strings that may become parts of SAS code when processed. These values can change at any time in the SAS job. One way to define and assign a value to a macro variable is with a macro program statement of the form:

```
%LET macrovariable = text ;
```

Another way to define macro variables is by using a parameter list. The macro variable names appear in parentheses after the macro name in the %MACRO statement:

```
%MACRO macroname(parameters);
  macrotext
  %MEND;
```

Values are supplied to macro variables in the parameter list when you invoke the macro:

```
%macroname(values)
```

Rules for naming macro variables are the same as the rules for SAS names: length of one to eight characters; begin with a letter or underscore; letters, numbers, and underscores follow.

The value of a macro variable can range from 0 to 1024 or more bytes in length. (Check with your computing center staff for the maximum length at your installation.) A string of length 0 is called a *null string*. A macro variable that has not been assigned a value has a value of null; or you can assign a null value:

```
%LET NAME=;
```

To refer to the value of the variable, specify the name prefixed by an ampersand (&). A macro variable may be referenced inside or outside a macro. The macro processor replaces the macro variable reference with the value of the macro variable. Continuing the previous example, you can give the value A to the macro variable NAME, and then reference the variable within a SAS macro:

```
%LET  NAME=A;
%MACRO ANALYZE;
  PROC PRINT  DATA=&NAME;
  PROC MEANS  DATA=&NAME;
  %MEND;
```

When you invoke the macro ANALYZE with the statement %ANALYZE as before, the value of &NAME is A:

```
DATA A;
  INPUT X;
  CARDS;
data lines
;
PROC PRINT DATA=A;
PROC MEANS DATA=A;
```

You can also reference NAME in a TITLE statement outside a macro:

```
TITLE ANALYSIS OF DATA SET &NAME;
```

which becomes

```
TITLE ANALYSIS OF DATA SET A;
```

In each case the value of the macro variable NAME is substituted for &NAME in the text. See **Resolving Macro Variable References** below.

Macro variables are either local or global in scope. A variable is local to a macro when its value is available only to that macro or any macro nested within it. A global variable is available to statements either inside or outside of a macro. The area to which a macro variable is available is called its referencing environment. (See **Communication Among Macros** later for details.)

SAS also provides a list of automatic macro variables with names beginning with the letters SYS. These automatic macro variables are described later in this chapter.

Macro functions   The macro functions are similar to the SAS functions of the same names. For example, macro functions allow you to evaluate arithmetic expressions involving macro variables, to determine a macro expression's length, and to scan a macro expression for "words." The macro functions include:

%EVAL(*expression*)	evaluate arithmetic and logical expressions
%INDEX(*argument1,argument2*)	find the first occurrence of a string
%LENGTH(*argument*)	find the length of an argument
%SCAN(*argument,n[,delimiters]*)	scan for "words"
%STR(*argument*)	express strings containing special characters
%SUBSTR(*argument,position[,n]*)	substring a character string
%UPCASE(*argument*)	translate lowercase characters to uppercase

Each macro function is fully described later in this chapter.

Macro program statements   The macro processor is controlled by macro program statements, which are preceded by a percent sign (%). Macro program statements are executed by the macro processor and produce SAS statements or parts of SAS statements. Macro program statements include:

%MACRO *name*[(*parameters*)];	defines a macro
%CMS *command*;	invokes a CMS or CP command

%*comment;	documents the macro
%DO;-%END;	DO group
%DO %UNTIL(expression);-%END;	repetitive DO group
%DO %WHILE(expression);-%END;	repetitive DO group
%DO macrovariable=start %TO stop [%BY increment];-%END;	iterative DO group
%GLOBAL macrovariables;	declares global variables
%GO TO label; or %GOTO label;	skips to label
%IF expression %THEN statement; [%ELSE statement;]	conditional execution
%LET macrovariable=value;	creates macro variable
%LOCAL macrovariables;	declares local variables
%TSO command;	invokes TSO command
%MEND [name];	ends a macro definition

The macro program statements are described later in this chapter under **Specifications**.

Calling the macro   Once you have defined a macro, you call (invoke) it with the command

    %macroname

No semicolon is necessary. When the macro is called, SAS executes the statements generated by the macro of that name.

Macro expressions   Some macro functions and program statements use macro expressions—a sequence of macro variable names, constant text, and/or macro function names linked together by operators and, where appropriate, by parentheses. A macro call may also be viewed as an expression. Here are some examples of macro expressions:

    &X<5
    &N/2*2=&N
    &START+&STOP>%LENGTH(&TARGET)
    %MACCLL(%SUBSTR(&NAME,1,1)=%STR(%'))

Macro expressions may appear as conditions in %DO-%WHILE and %DO-%UNTIL statements, %IF-%THEN statements, and with %EVAL functions. When the expression is an arithmetic or logical expression with a numerically valued result, it is evaluated by the macro processor as a number rather than a character string. That is, a numeric expression is evaluated as if the %EVAL function were used.

Keep in mind that macro text may include parts of SAS statements. Thus, when you call the macro, the text supplied by the macro processor must fit in the context of the remaining SAS statements. For example, the macro

    %MACRO IN(IN1,CUTOFF,OUT1);
      SET &IN1;
      IF AGE<&CUTOFF THEN &OUT1;
      %MEND;

should only be called after a DATA statement. For example,

```
DATA OLDER;
  %IN(STORE.DATA,12,DELETE)
```

generates this complete DATA step for SAS to execute:

```
DATA OLDER;
  SET STORE.DATA;
  IF AGE<12 THEN DELETE;
```

SPECIFICATIONS

Macro program statements

```
%MACRO name[(parameter list)];
  %MEND [name];
  %CMS command;
  %*comment;
  %DO;-%END;
  %DO %UNTIL(expression);-%END;
  %DO %WHILE(expression);-%END;
  %DO macrovariable=start %TO stop[%BY increment];-%END;
  %GLOBAL macrovariables;
  %GO TO label;
  %GOTO label;
  %IF expression %THEN statement;
    [%ELSE statement;]
  %label:
  %LET macrovariable=value;
  %LOCAL macrovariables;
  %TSO command;
```

Macro functions

```
%EVAL(expression)
%INDEX(argument1,argument2)
%LENGTH(argument)
%SCAN(argument,n[,delimiters])
%SUBSTR(argument,position[,n])
%STR(argument)
%UPCASE(argument)
```

DATA step functions used with the macro language

```
SYMGET(argument)
SYMPUT(argument1,argument2)
```

Automatic macro variables

```
SYSDATE
SYSDAY
SYSDEVIC
SYSDSN
SYSINDEX
SYSENV
SYSPARM
```

SYSRC
SYSSCP
SYSTIME
SYSVER

Macro Program Statements

%MACRO Statement

%MACRO name[(parameters)];

These terms may appear on the %MACRO statement:

· name	names the macro. Name must be a valid SAS name.
parameter list	optionally specifies a list of macro variables for which values are supplied in the macro call (or in the macro itself). The variables are local variables. The macro variables specified in this list are referenced in the macro. Separate macro variables in the list by commas.

The parameters in the list may be positional or keyword. Positional parameters appear without an equal sign; their order is important. Values for positional parameters are given in the same order in the macro call as they appear in the %MACRO statement. Positional parameters have null values when the macro is defined. If you want a positional parameter to retain its null value, hold its position with a comma in the list when you call the macro (unless it is the last in the list).

Keyword parameters are listed with an equal sign; a default value may also be given. Keyword parameters may be given in any order. If both positional and keyword parameters appear in a macro definition, positional parameters must come first.

The %MACRO statement begins the definition of a macro, assigns the macro a name, and optionally includes a parameter list of macro variables. The %MACRO statement can appear anywhere in the SAS job; however, the macro must be defined before it can be called. Macro definitions may be nested. If two macros are defined with the same name, the second one replaces the first.

Here is an example:

```
%MACRO BUILD(NEW,IN=INDD);
  DATA &NEW;
    INFILE &IN;
  INPUT A B C;
  PROC PRINT;
    RUN;
  %MEND BUILD;
```

The call

```
%BUILD(APRIL82,IN=INA)
```

yields

```
DATA APRIL82;
  INFILE INA;
  INPUT A B C;
PROC PRINT;
  RUN;
```

Macro BUILD creates a SAS data set from input data in an external file, and then prints the data. The macro variable NEW contains the name of the SAS data set; IN contains the DDname of the external file of raw data. The default value for IN is defined to be INDD in the macro definition. In the macro call, IN is given the value INA.

In the macro BUILD above, NEW is a positional parameter; its value is given first in the macro call. IN is a keyword parameter.

Macro CREATE has two positional parameters, NEW and OLD:

```
%MACRO CREATE(NEW,OLD);
  DATA &NEW;
    SET &OLD;
    IF PROFIT>0;
  %MEND CREATE;
```

To call CREATE, supply values for NEW and OLD in the same order they were defined:

```
%CREATE(REVENUE,YEAR82)
```

The statements SAS sees are:

```
DATA REVENUE;
  SET YEAR82;
  IF PROFIT>0;
```

Here is an example of holding the place of a positional parameter with a comma:

```
%CREATE(,YEAR81)
```

SAS sees these statements:

```
DATA ;
  SET YEAR81;
  IF PROFIT>0;
```

Macro CHOOSE, below, has two keyword parameters. The macro variable P is given the default value PRINT; T by default has a null value:

```
%MACRO CHOOSE(P=PRINT,T=);
  PROC &P;
  TITLE &T;
  %MEND CHOOSE;
```

Select the PROC step you want when you call the macro:

```
%CHOOSE(T=PRINTOUT OF DATA)
```

to execute these statements:

```
PROC PRINT;
  TITLE PRINTOUT OF DATA;
```

or

```
%CHOOSE
```

to execute

```
PROC PRINT;
  TITLE;
```

The order for keyword variables is not important. This macro call:

```
%CHOOSE(T=AVERAGE VALUES,P=MEANS)
```

yields

```
PROC MEANS;
  TITLE AVERAGE VALUES;
```

Consider the following macro:

```
%MACRO  PUTLAB(A,B,C,D);
  LABEL GOVERN1=&A
        GOVERN2=&B
        GOVERN3=&C
        GOVERN4=&D
        ;
  %MEND PUTLAB;
```

The call

```
%PUTLAB (NATIONAL,,,CITY)
```

supplies values only for macro variables A and D and yields

```
LABEL GOVERN1=NATIONAL
      GOVERN2=
      GOVERN3=
      GOVERN4=CITY
      ;
```

The call with no values supplied

```
%PUTLAB
```

yields

```
LABEL GOVERN1=
      GOVERN2=
      GOVERN3=
      GOVERN4=
      ;
```

%MEND Statement

%MEND [*macroname*];

where

> *macroname*   optionally names the macro being closed. Repeating
> the name of the macro for clarity is useful when you
> create macros nested within other macros.

The %MEND statement ends a macro definition.

%CMS Statement

%CMS *command*;

where

> *command*   may be any CMS or CP command or any sequence of
> macro operations that generates a CMS or CP
> command.

The %CMS statement works in the macro language as the CMS statement does in
SAS. It allows you to execute CMS or CP commands immediately and places the
return code for the action into the automatic macro variable SYSRC. Thus, you can
test for the successful completion of the command. You can use the %CMS statement inside or outside a macro. For example:

    %CMS FILEDEF IN DISK MYFILE DATA NEW;

If you are not running under CMS, the %CMS command is ignored.

%*comment Statement

%*any comment;

Use the macro comment statement when you want to place comments in the
macro. No text is produced from the comments as it is from the SAS statement

    *comment;

which the macro language treats as text. Macro comment statements can only
appear inside a macro. Note that macro variable references are not resolved if they
appear in a SAS comment statement.
   For example, the following macro produces code to check for errors in the data:

```
%MACRO  VERIFY(IN);
  %*                                          ;
  %*USE THIS MACRO ONLY ON PROJECT EA-84.;
  %*                                          ;
  DATA CHECK;
    INFILE &IN;
    INPUT X Y Z;
    IF  X<0 OR Y<0 OR Z<0 THEN LIST;
    *CHECKS FIRST VARIABLES IN FILE &IN;
  %MEND  VERIFY;
```

When you call macro VERIFY with the statement

%VERIFY(INA)

SAS sees these statements:

```
DATA CHECK;
  INFILE INA;
  INPUT X Y Z;
  IF X<0 OR Y<0 OR Z<0 THEN LIST;
  *CHECKS FIRST VARIABLES IN FILE &IN;
```

Notice that in the SAS comment statement, the macro variable reference &IN is unresolved.

%DO–%END Statements

```
%DO;
  text and macro program statements
%END;
```

The %DO–%END statements work in the macro language as the DO–END statements work in SAS. Text and program statements following the %DO are processed until a matching %END appears.

%DO %UNTIL–%END and %DO %WHILE–%END Statements

```
%DO %UNTIL(expression);
  text and macro program statements
%END;

%DO %WHILE(expression);
  text and macro program statements
%END;
```

Expression may be any valid macro expression. The macro processor evaluates the expression, substituting macro variable values or the result of a macro call. For example:

```
%DO %WHILE(&A + &B<&C);
%DO %WHILE(%BUILD);
%DO %UNTIL(&HOLD = NO);
```

are acceptable statements.

The %DO %UNTIL and %DO %WHILE statements work as the DO WHILE and DO UNTIL statements do in SAS.

Iterative %DO Statement

%DO macrovariable = start %TO stop [%BY increment];

The iterative %DO statement works as the iterative DO does in the SAS DATA step except that in the %DO, the index variable is a macro variable. Thus the start, stop, and increment values may be any valid expressions; lists are not allowed.

This example shows the use of the iterative %DO statement:

```
%MACRO HEADING;
  TITLE;
    %DO X=2 %TO 10 %BY 2;
      TITLE&X THIS TITLE APPEARS ON LINE &X;
      %END;
  %MEND HEADING;
```

The call

```
%HEADING
```

produces these SAS statements:

```
TITLE;
TITLE2 THIS TITLE APPEARS ON LINE 2;
TITLE4 THIS TITLE APPEARS ON LINE 4;
TITLE6 THIS TITLE APPEARS ON LINE 6;
TITLE8 THIS TITLE APPEARS ON LINE 8;
TITLE10 THIS TITLE APPEARS ON LINE 10;
```

The following macro includes an iterative %DO with a beginning value that is a character string, an ending value that is a macro variable reference, and an increment that is a macro call.

```
%MACRO INTERVAL;
  %*MACRO INTERVAL SELECTS AN INTERVAL FOR MACRO VARLIST;
    %IF &BASE<=5 %THEN 1;
    %ELSE %IF &BASE<=10 %THEN 2;
    %ELSE 5;
    %MEND INTERVAL;
%MACRO VARLIST(BASE);
  %DO X=1 %TO &BASE %BY %INTERVAL;
    VAR&X
    %END;
  %MEND VARLIST;
```

Suppose you want to print a subset of the 100 variables (named VAR1–VAR100) in HUGE. Use these statements:

```
PROC PRINT DATA=HUGE;
  VAR %VARLIST(100);
```

These statements are produced:

```
PROC PRINT DATA=HUGE;
  VAR VAR1 VAR6 VAR11 VAR16 VAR21 ... VAR91 VAR96;
```

Every fifth variable in HUGE appears in the list of variables. (The %IF–%THEN statements are described below.)

If the macro variable used as the index has the same name as another macro variable available to the local environment, the %DO statement changes the value of the previously defined macro variable. An unnoticed conflict in macro variable names can thus lead to unexpected results. This example:

```
%LET I=INDUSTRIAL PRODUCTION;
TITLE REPORT ON &I AT VARIOUS TIMES;
%MACRO CREATE;
  %DO I=1 %TO 5;
    DATA DATA&I;
      INFILE IN&I;
      INPUT PRODUCT COST DATE;
    RUN;
    %END;
  %MEND CREATE;
%CREATE
TITLE REPORT ON LATEST &I;
PROC PRINT DATA=DATA5;
```

produces the SAS statements:

```
TITLE REPORT ON INDUSTRIAL PRODUCTION AT VARIOUS TIMES;
DATA DATA1;
    INFILE IN1;
    INPUT PRODUCT COST DATE;
  RUN;
DATA DATA2;
    INFILE IN2;
    INPUT PRODUCT COST DATE;
  RUN;
DATA DATA3;
    INFILE IN3;
    INPUT PRODUCT COST DATE;
  RUN;
DATA DATA4;
    INFILE IN4;
    INPUT PRODUCT COST DATE;
  RUN;
DATA DATA5;
    INFILE IN5;
    INPUT PRODUCT COST DATE;
  RUN;
TITLE REPORT ON LATEST 6;
PROC PRINT DATA=DATA5;
```

In the second TITLE statement the current value of the macro variable I is substituted. Thus the title, "REPORT ON LATEST 6," **not** "REPORT ON LATEST INDUSTRIAL PRODUCTION," is printed. (See the DO statement in Chapter 3, "Statements Used in the DATA Step," for a discussion of the value of an index variable after the last execution of a loop.)

To avoid this result either change the name of the index variable or use a %LOCAL statement to make a local macro variable I for CREATE. (See a description of the %LOCAL statement, below.)

%GLOBAL Statement

%GLOBAL *macrovariables*;

The %GLOBAL statement is used to make macro variables available to all referencing environments of a job, except where replaced by local macro variables of the same names. (See **Communication Among Macros** for a discussion of referencing environments.) The %GLOBAL statement can appear anywhere in a SAS job; it is an executable statement.

One %GLOBAL statement can contain many macro variables. This %GLOBAL statement creates three global macro variables:

```
%GLOBAL DATAVAR KEEP1 KEEP2;
```

Only macro variables specified in a %GLOBAL statement or those defined outside all macros are considered global. Once a macro variable has been defined as local, it may not be made global with a %GLOBAL statement. Macro variables created with a %GLOBAL statement have null values until you assign them other values.

If you have already created a global macro variable and assigned it another value, including that variable in a %GLOBAL statement does not remove the value. For example, you may want to keep track of global macro variables in a job by recording them all in a %GLOBAL statement at some point. If you want to create a global macro variable within a macro, specify it in a %GLOBAL statement before you create the variable, as in this example:

```
%MACRO VARIABLE(TYPE);
   %GLOBAL LIST;
   %IF &TYPE=1 %THEN %LET LIST=HEIGHT WEIGHT;
   %ELSE %IF &TYPE=2 %THEN %LET LIST=NAME SEX AGE;
   %MEND VARIABLE;
```

Macro VARIABLE produces a global macro variable whose value represents one of two lists of variables. Each PROC step uses a different value of the macro variable LIST as a variable list for the VAR statement, as shown:

```
%VARIABLE(2)
PROC PRINT;
   VAR &LIST;
%VARIABLE(1)
PROC MEANS;
   VAR &LIST;
```

SAS sees these statements:

```
PROC PRINT;
   VAR NAME SEX AGE;
PROC MEANS;
   VAR HEIGHT WEIGHT;
```

If the %GLOBAL statement were not included in macro VARIABLE, the value of LIST assigned within the macro would not be available to the rest of the job. An error message reporting that &LIST is not a valid name for a SAS variable would be printed.

%GOTO or %GO TO Statement

```
%GOTO label;
%GO TO label;
```

where

> *label*   is the label of a statement to which you want execu-
> tion to branch. Labels are named using the SAS rules

for names. When you label a statement in the macro language, put a % sign in front of the label. However, do not put a % sign in front of the label in a %GOTO or %GO TO statement unless you intend to call a macro of that name. (You can use a macro to produce a label or one of several labels. See **%label:** later in this chapter.)

The %GOTO or %GO TO statements cause the macro processor to branch to the label specified in the %GOTO or %GO TO statement. The statements work the same way as the GOTO and GO TO statements in the DATA step.

%IF-%THEN-%ELSE Statements

%IF *expression* %THEN *statement*;
%ELSE *statement*;

where

    expression   is any valid macro expression. The macro processor evaluates the expression, substituting macro variable values or the result of a macro call. If the expression is true (has a nonzero value) the %THEN is processed. If the expression is false (zero) the %ELSE, if one is present, is processed.

    statement   is any macro program statement, constant text, expression, or macro call. If *statement* includes constant text containing semicolons, enclose the semicolons in the %STR function, described below.

The %IF-%THEN and %ELSE statements work like the corresponding statements IF-THEN and ELSE in the SAS DATA step. However, you cannot use %IF without %THEN; thus, you cannot use %IF to create subsets as you do in the DATA step.
  For example:

```
%MACRO FISCAL;
  %IF &SYSDATE=1JUL82 %THEN %DO;
    PROC MEANS DATA=TOTAL;
    PROC CHART DATA=TOTAL;
      HBAR REVENUE/TYPE=MEAN;
    %END;
  %ELSE %DO;
    PROC MEANS DATA=MONTHLY;
    PROC PRINT DATA=MONTHLY;
    %END;
  %MEND;
```

If the value of the automatic macro variable SYSDATE is 1JUL82, the expression is true, and macro FISCAL processes the statements following the %THEN. If the value of SYSDATE is not 1JUL82, the statements following the %ELSE are generated.

%label:

  %label: *statement*;

where

>   *label*   is any valid SAS name.

Labels in the macro language are the same as labels in SAS, and the rules for naming labels in the macro language are also the same.

When you label a statement in the macro language, put a % sign in front of the label. When you use the label in a %GOTO statement, do not use a % sign. A % sign in front of a label name in a %GOTO statement tells the macro processor to call a macro of that name. If the macro processor cannot find the macro called, an error message is issued.

This example illustrates the use of labels in the macro language.

```
%GLOBAL SWITCH;
%MACRO INFO(LONG,HIST);
  %IF &SWITCH=1 %THEN %GOTO SKIP;

  %MACRO CHOOSE;
    %*THIS MACRO CHOOSES A LABEL FOR MACRO INFO;
    %IF &HIST=HIST %THEN LABEL1;
    %ELSE LABEL2;
    %MEND CHOOSE;

  %LET SWITCH=1;
%SKIP:
  %IF &LONG=LONG %THEN %GOTO %CHOOSE;
  %ELSE %GOTO LABEL3;
  %LABEL1: PROC CONTENTS HISTORY;
  %LABEL2: PROC FREQ;
             TABLES __NUMERIC__;
  %GOTO LABEL4;
  %LABEL3: PROC PRINT DATA=__LAST__(OBS=10);
  %LABEL4: RUN;
  %MEND INFO;
```

The call

```
%INFO(LONG,HIST)
```

yields

```
PROC CONTENTS HISTORY;
PROC FREQ;
  TABLES __NUMERIC__;
RUN;
```

The call

```
%INFO(LONG)
```

yields

```
PROC FREQ;
  TABLES __NUMERIC__;
RUN;
```

Any other call, such as

```
%INFO(SHORT)
%INFO
%INFO(,HIST)
```

yields

```
PROC PRINT DATA=__LAST__(OBS=10);
RUN;
```

Macro INFO illustrates several features.

1. The macro variable SWITCH causes the inner macro CHOOSE to be compiled only once.
2. The macro call %CHOOSE appears in the %GOTO statement and generates the appropriate label based on the parameter values specified in the call of macro INFO.
3. The values of macro variables LONG and HIST are the same characters as the variable names.
4. The special SAS data set name __LAST__(defined as the most recent SAS data set created) is used so that the data set option OBS= may be specified without knowing the name of the data set.

%LET Statement

%LET *macrovariable name=value*;

Use the %LET statement either inside or outside a macro to create a macro variable and assign it a value or to change the value of an existing macro variable. A %LET statement can define only one macro variable.

This example uses %LET to create a macro variable named STATE with a value of NC:

```
%LET STATE=NC;
```

Macro LISTING references STATE:

```
%MACRO LISTING;
  PROC PRINT DATA=&STATE;
  TITLE LISTING OF &STATE RESIDENTS;
%MEND;
```

Values can be supplied with a %LET statement before calling the macro:

```
%LET STATE=NC;
%LISTING
%LET STATE=SC;
%LISTING
```

%LOCAL Statement

%LOCAL *macrovariables*;

The %LOCAL statement is used to specify macro variables that are to be local to the macro. The statement is useful for ensuring that values of macro variables that may have been specified earlier are not inadvertently used in the current macro.

One %LOCAL statement can contain many macro variables. The %LOCAL statement may only be specified inside the definition of a macro; the statement is executed as soon as the macro language encounters it.

Variables created with a %LOCAL statement have null values until you assign them another value. However, if a previously defined local macro variable is included in a %LOCAL statement, the macro variable retains its previously assigned value.

You can use the %LOCAL statement to avoid possible conflicts between the macro variable names used elsewhere outside of the current macro.

```
%MACRO PRINTIT;
  %LOCAL COUNT;
  %LET COUNT=1;
  %DO %UNTIL (&COUNT>10);
    PROC PRINT DATA=DATA&COUNT;
    %LET COUNT=%EVAL(&COUNT+1);
    %END;
  %MEND PRINTIT;
```

COUNT is defined as a local macro variable for macro PRINTIT. Thus, if COUNT is defined as a macro variable outside macro PRINTIT, the previously defined value does not influence the value of COUNT in macro PRINTIT. The %EVAL function is used to increment COUNT's value. See a description of the %EVAL function in the section **Macro Functions**, below. When you call the macro:

```
%PRINTIT
```

SAS sees these statements:

```
PROC PRINT DATA=DATA1;
PROC PRINT DATA=DATA2;
PROC PRINT DATA=DATA3;
PROC PRINT DATA=DATA4;
PROC PRINT DATA=DATA5;
PROC PRINT DATA=DATA6;
PROC PRINT DATA=DATA7;
PROC PRINT DATA=DATA8;
PROC PRINT DATA=DATA9;
PROC PRINT DATA=DATA10;
```

For details on how the macro processor resolves strings like DATA&COUNT and others containing macro variables, see **Resolving Macro Variable References** in the **SPECIAL TOPICS** section below.

A %LOCAL statement can be executed conditionally. For example:

```
%LET TIME=YEAR;
TITLE CUMULATIVE REPORT FOR &TIME;
%MACRO SUBSETS(MONTH);
  %*REMEMBER TIME IS A GLOBAL MACRO VARIABLE
    BECAUSE IT WAS CREATED OUTSIDE THE MACRO;
  %IF &MONTH¬=DEC %THEN %DO;
    %LOCAL TIME;
    %*NOW YOU HAVE CREATED A LOCAL MACRO VARIABLE
      NAMED TIME;
    %LET TIME=&MONTH;
    TITLE2 COVERING JANUARY--&TIME;
    %END;
  %ELSE TITLE2 REPORT FOR &TIME;
  %MEND SUBSETS;
```

When the macro SUBSETS is called, if the value supplied for MONTH is anything other than DEC, a local variable TIME is created. The month value given is assigned to macro variable TIME and used in the TITLE2 statement. If the call %SUBSET(DEC) is given, the value YEAR is used in the TITLE2 statement. Thus, the call %SUBSETS(OCTOBER) produces these statements:

    TITLE CUMULATIVE REPORT FOR YEAR;
    TITLE2 COVERING JANUARY--OCTOBER;

and the call %SUBSETS(DEC) produces

    TITLE CUMULATIVE REPORT FOR YEAR;
    TITLE2 REPORT FOR YEAR;

%TSO Statement

    %TSO command;

where

    command is a TSO command.

The %TSO statement works as the TSO statement does in SAS, and can be used inside or outside a macro. You can issue any TSO command with the %TSO statement except the TEST, LOGON, or LOGOFF commands, or any command which must be given control in an authorized state. The %TSO statement places the return code for the action into the automatic macro variable SYSRC. Thus, you can test for the successful completion of the command. For example:

    %MACRO SASDATA;
      %TSO ALLOC FI(IN) DA('USERID.MY.SASDATA') OLD;
      %IF &SYSRC⌐=0 %THEN
        %TSO ALLOC FI(IN) DA('USERID.MY.SASDATA') SHR;
      %MEND SASDATA;

Macro Functions

%EVAL: evaluation of arithmetic and logical expressions

    %EVAL(expression)

The %EVAL function evaluates arithmetic and logical expressions in the macro language. The function may be used both inside and outside of macros. Note that all statements in the macro language which evaluate expressions contain an implied %EVAL that evaluates the condition and returns a value of 1 if the condition is true and 0 if it is false.

Suppose for example that the statement

    %LET X=2;

appears in a SAS job. Then the statement

    %LET Y=%EVAL(&X+1);

assigns Y a value of 3. The %EVAL function allows the value of macro variable X to have numeric properties in order to perform the evaluation. In the following example:

```
%LET  X=100;
%LET  Y=80;
%MACRO OUTDATA;
  %IF &X>&Y %THEN %DO;
    OUTPUT;
    RETURN;
    %END;
  %ELSE %STR(DELETE;);
  %MEND OUTDATA;
```

the condition of the %IF statement contains a logical expression, &X>&Y, which is evaluated as though the %EVAL function appeared. (The %STR function is used to enclose a string containing a semicolon. It is described below.)

The use of %EVAL resembles the use of expressions in SAS in most ways; however, three characteristics of %EVAL are different from the way SAS handles expressions.

- %EVAL only performs integer arithmetic. If you attempt to use %EVAL to perform a calculation on noninteger values, the macro processor issues an error message. Thus, although the values of PI and R in this example are acceptable to the macro language:

```
%LET  PI=3.14;
%LET  R=5;
```

you cannot use the statement

```
%LET  C=%EVAL(2*&PI*&R);
```

to calculate a value for C.
- the %EVAL function does not allow the use of SAS operators for concatenation (||), minimum (><), or maximum (<>).
- the mathematical symbol for ''greater than or equal'' must be >=, since the symbols '>=' and '=>' are not equivalent in the macro language. The same restrictions apply to the mathematical symbol for ''less than or equal,'' which must appear as '<='.

A list of the operators available to the %EVAL function, their symbols, and their mnemonic forms follows. The order in which operations are performed in the macro language is the same as in SAS. As in SAS, operations within parentheses are performed first.

OPERATOR	MNEMONIC	NAME	PRECEDENCE
**		exponentiation	1
¬	NOT	logical not	2
*		multiplication	3
/		division	3
+		addition	4
−		subtraction	4
<	LT	less than	5
<=	LE	less than or equal	5
=	EQ	equal	5
¬=	NE	not equal	5
>	GT	greater than	5
>=	GE	greater than or equal	5
&	AND	logical and	6
		OR	logical or	7

Using %EVAL in counting applications If the value of a condition is numeric, you can increment the value of the condition with a %LET statement that uses the %EVAL function, as in this example:

```
%MACRO GENIT;
  DATA GENERATE;
  %LET A=1;
  %DO %WHILE(&A<=10);
    B=&A*UNIFORM(0);
    OUTPUT;
    %LET A=%EVAL(&A+1);
    %END;
  %MEND GENIT;
```

Thus, the call %GENIT produces these statements:

```
DATA GENERATE;
  B=1*UNIFORM(0);
  OUTPUT;
  B=2*UNIFORM(0);
  OUTPUT;
  B=3*UNIFORM(0);
  OUTPUT;
  B=4*UNIFORM(0);
  OUTPUT;
  B=5*UNIFORM(0);
  OUTPUT;
  B=6*UNIFORM(0);
  OUTPUT;
  B=7*UNIFORM(0);
  OUTPUT;
  B=8*UNIFORM(0);
  OUTPUT;
  B=9*UNIFORM(0);
  OUTPUT;
  B=10*UNIFORM(0);
  OUTPUT;
```

Suppose you want to increment a value in constant text by a fraction. Since %EVAL accepts only integers, you must use a two-stage process as in this example.

```
%MACRO LINES;
  %DO X=1 %TO 2;
    %DO Y=0 %TO 9;
      %LET X2=&X..&Y;
      &X2
      %IF &X=2 %THEN %GO TO LABEL1;
      %END;
    %LABEL1: %END;
  %MEND;
```

Macro LINES creates X2 by concatenating the value of X, the value of Y, and a decimal point so that X2 can take on values such as 1.0, 1.1, and 1.2. (See **Resolving Macro Variable References** for the use of two decimal points in the value of

X2.) Notice that allowing the Y-loop to execute ten times when X is 2 produces values from 2.0 to 2.9. The %IF statement in the Y-loop is executed the first time that X = 2 (when Y = 0), thus the last value that X2 receives is 2.0. This example uses macro LINES in a PROC PLOT statement:

```
PROC PLOT;
  PLOT Y*X/VREF= %LINES
    HREF= %LINES;
```

SAS sees the statements

```
PROC PLOT;
  PLOT Y*X/VREF=1.0 1.1 1.2 1.3 1.4 1.5 1.6 1.7 1.8 1.9 2.0
    HREF=1.0 1.1 1.2 1.3 1.4 1.5 1.6 1.7 1.8 1.9 2.0;
```

Using %EVAL in comparisons Although %EVAL does not perform mathematical operations on noninteger values, you can use noninteger values in comparisons. For example:

```
%MACRO TEST(X,Y);
  %IF &Y>&X %THEN %DO;
    ...statements...
  %END;
  %MEND TEST;

%TEST(5.62,8)
```

When you call the macro %TEST with the values 5.62 and 8, the condition &Y>&X is true and the macro processor executes the statements after the %THEN. The macro language compares character strings character by character beginning at the left until it reaches the end of the strings or until it reaches a pair of characters for which the comparison is false (see the SORT procedure description for the comparison sequence used).

If one string contains fewer characters than the other, the shorter string is padded with trailing blanks to make the lengths equal. If a character string is compared with an integer, the integer remains a character string to make the comparison, instead of being assigned numeric properties as it is for the evaluation of mathematical expressions.

%INDEX: the first occurrence of a character string

%INDEX(argument1,argument2)

Argument1 and *argument2* can be character strings, macro variable references, expressions, or macro calls. The %INDEX function searches *argument1* for the first occurrence of the string identified in *argument2*. If the string is not found, the function returns a 0. The %INDEX function may be used inside and outside a macro definition. This example uses %INDEX to calculate the value of B:

```
%LET A=A VERY LONG VALUE;
%LET B= %INDEX(&A,V);
```

The value of macro variable B is 3, since the character V appears in the value of A at position 3. When B is referenced as in

```
%IF &B<10 %THEN %DO;
```

the value 3 is substituted for B. You can use %INDEX much as you do the DATA step INDEX function. This example shows %INDEX as part of an expression within a macro:

```
%LET  NAME = SAVE.DATA;
%MACRO  CHECK;
  %IF  %INDEX(&NAME,SAVE) ¬= 1  %THEN  %LET  NAME = SAVE.DATA;
  SET  &NAME;
  %MEND  CHECK;
```

Macro CHECK is used to see if the character string SAVE is the first part of the value of macro variable NAME. If not, the %LET statement sets the value of name to SAVE.DATA; then the SET statement is issued.

%LENGTH: length of an argument

%LENGTH(*argument*)

Argument can be a macro variable value, another macro function, or a macro call. The %LENGTH function returns the length of *argument*; if *argument* has a null value, %LENGTH returns a value of 0. If you use a macro call as the argument of %LENGTH, %LENGTH returns the length of the result of the macro, not the length of the macro definition. The %LENGTH statement works both inside and outside macros. The following example illustrates the use of %LENGTH.

```
%MACRO  LONG(C);
  DATA  NEW;
    INFILE  IN;
  %IF  %LENGTH(&C) <= 200  %THEN  %DO;
    CORRECT = SYMGET('C');
    LABEL  CORRECT = 'FROM SYMGET("C")';
    %END;
  %ELSE  %DO;
    CORRECT = ' ';
    LABEL  CORRECT = TRUNCATION  PROBLEM;
    %END;
  RUN;
  %MEND  LONG;

%LET  LIST = ...a long value...;

%LONG(&LIST)
```

In this example, you assign the value of macro variable C to the DATA step variable CORRECT if that value can be supplied without truncation (see a description of the DATA step function SYMGET, below). If the value of C is too long to be passed without truncation (that is, greater than a length of 200), you assign a missing value to CORRECT.

%SCAN: scans for ''words''

%SCAN(argument,n[,delimiters])

Argument, *n*, and *delimiters* may be character strings, macro variable references, or macro calls. In addition, *n* may be an expression; an implied %EVAL gives *n* numeric properties. %SCAN returns the nth ''word'' of *argument*, where ''words'' are strings of characters separated by one or more delimiters. If you do not specify delimiters, %SCAN uses the same list of delimiters as the DATA step SCAN function. If the number of words in *argument* is less than *n*, the result of the function is a null string. %SCAN works both inside and outside macros. For example:

```
%LET  A=A//-VALUE.WITH$DELIMITERS;
%LET  B=%SCAN(&A,3);
```

assigns B a value of WITH, the third ''word'' in the value of macro variable A. However, the statements

```
%LET  C=EFGHAIJK/LMNOAPQ.RSTAUVW XYZ;
%LET  D=%SCAN(&C,3,A);
```

assign D a value of PQ.RST, the third ''word'' in C (delimited by the letter A).

%STR: the macro language quoting mechanism

%STR(*argument*)

Argument can be any character string.

Just as you use single quotes in SAS to surround a character string that contains special characters, the %STR function is used in the macro language to ''surround'' a character string containing characters special to the macro language.

For example, you may want to use a %LET statement to create a macro variable whose value represents a complete SAS statement or several SAS statements. Since the %LET statement itself ends in a semicolon, the first semicolon in the value must not signal the end of the %LET statement. A semicolon enclosed by the %STR function is treated by the macro processor as part of the character string. For example,

```
%LET SORT1=PROC SORT %STR(;) BY DESCENDING DURATION %STR(;);
```

The macro processor treats the two semicolons enclosed in the %STR function like the other characters in the value of SORT1; the semicolon not enclosed in %STR ends the %LET statement. Note that the entire value of SORT1 is a character string to the macro language and can be enclosed in the %STR function for clarity:

```
%LET SORT1=PROC %STR(SORT;) BY DESCENDING %STR(DURATION;);
```

```
%LET SORT1=%STR(PROC SORT; BY DESCENDING DURATION;);
```

You cannot use %STR to avoid invoking the meaning of the ampersand (&), percent sign (%), or macro functions. For example:

```
%LET A=THIS VALUE;
%LET B=%STR(&A);
```

assigns B a value of THIS VALUE just as if you had specified

```
%LET A=THIS VALUE;
%LET B=&A;
```

You can use %STR to prevent the macro processor from evaluating a macro expression in a %IF, %DO %WHILE, or %DO %UNTIL statement as if a %EVAL function were present. For example:

```
%MACRO  SHOW;
  %LET  X= 1;
  %LET  Y= 2;
  %IF  &X+&Y=&Y+&X  %THEN  %DO;
    %*THIS EXPRESSION IS TRUE;
    %*TREATED AS IF %EVAL FUNCTION WERE SPECIFIED;
    %END;
  %IF  %STR(&X+&Y)=%STR(&Y+&X)  %THEN  %DO;
    %*THIS EXPRESSION IS NOT TRUE;
    %*%STR PREVENTS NUMERIC EVALUATION;
    %END;
  %MEND  SHOW;
```

Since the expression in the first %IF statement is evaluated using the rules of the %EVAL function, the expression is true for any numbers. The expression 3=3 is evaluated. The expression in the second %IF statement is true only if the values of X and Y contain the same characters in the same order, since the use of %STR on each side of the expression causes the expression to read "the character string on the left equals the character string on the right." In this case, the expression 1+2=2+1 is evaluated.

If an expression contains a character string with a word that is also an arithmetic or logical operator, you should enclose the character string in the %STR function so that the expression is not evaluated as if a %EVAL function were present.

If the argument of %STR contains a single parenthesis, a single quote, or a double quote (quotation marks), put a % sign in front of the symbol. For example,

```
%LET  FIRST=%STR(DATA __NULL__; X=3; Y=2; Z=%(X+);
%LET  SECOND=%STR(Y%)/2; PUT X= Y= Z=; RUN;);
%LET  THIRD=&FIRST&SECOND;
```

The first %LET statement defines macro variable FIRST, and assigns it the value DATA __NULL__;X=3; Y=2; Z=(X+. In FIRST, the left parenthesis immediately after %STR and the right parenthesis immediately before the final semicolon enclose the argument of %STR; the % sign in front of the left parenthesis following Z= causes this parenthesis to be treated like the other characters in the string. (If you do not use a % sign in front of the parenthesis, the macro processor tries to find a matching parenthesis and produces an error message if it cannot.) Macro variable SECOND is assigned the value

```
Y)/2; PUT  X=  Y=  Z=; RUN;
```

by the second %LET statement. The value of THIRD thus becomes

```
DATA __NULL__;  X=3;  Y=2;  Z=(X+Y)/2; PUT  X=  Y=  Z=; RUN;
```

Since both single quotes and double quotes are used in pairs in the DATA step, the macro processor must produce them in pairs. There is a difference between the use of single quotes (') and double quotes (") within %STR in the macro language; the difference occurs when SAS reads the text produced by the processor. SAS processes single and double quotes based on the system option DQUOTE/NODQUOTE. See the OPTIONS statement description in Chapter 11 "SAS Statements Used Anywhere" for a discussion of the DQUOTE/NODQUOTE option.

%SUBSTR: substring

%SUBSTR(*argument,position*[,*n*])

Argument, *position*, and *n* can be character strings, macro variable references, expressions, macro functions, or macro calls. %SUBSTR produces a substring of *argument* beginning at *position* for a length of *n* characters. If you do not supply a value for *n*, %SUBSTR produces a string containing the characters from *position* to the end of *argument*. %SUBSTR works both inside and outside macros. For example:

```
%LET FIRST = THIS VALUE;
%LET SECOND = %SUBSTR(&FIRST,6,5);
```

SECOND has a value of VALUE, the result of selecting a character string from the value of FIRST, beginning at position 6 for a length of 5.

```
%LET THIRD = %SUBSTR(&FIRST,%INDEX(&FIRST,H),2);
```

THIRD has a value of HI, the result of selecting a character string from the value of FIRST, beginning at the first occurrence of H and having a length of 2.

```
%LET FOURTH = %SUBSTR(&FIRST,%INDEX(&FIRST,H));
```

FOURTH has a value of HIS VALUE, the result of selecting a character string from the value of FIRST beginning at the first occurrence of H and continuing to the end of the value of FIRST.

%UPCASE: translate lower case characters to upper case

%UPCASE(*argument*)

Argument can be any character string.

The %UPCASE function translates lowercase characters in *argument* into uppercase. For example,

```
%MACRO SHORT(MONTH);
  %IF &MONTH = DEC %THEN %STR(PROC PRINT DATA = ENDYR;);
  %ELSE %STR(PROC CONTENTS;);
%MEND SHORT;
```

If you invoke the macro with the call

```
%SHORT(dec)
```

the expression in the %IF statement is not true. However, if you use the %UPCASE function as in this example:

```
%MACRO SHORT(MONTH);
  %IF %UPCASE(&MONTH) = DEC %THEN %STR(PROC PRINT
    DATA = ENDYR;);
  %ELSE %STR(PROC CONTENTS;);
%MEND SHORT;
```

both calls %SHORT(dec) and %SHORT(DEC) make the expression in the %IF statement true.

DATA Step Functions Used with the Macro Language

SYMGET: return the value of a macro variable

SYMGET(*argument*)

Argument can be the name of a DATA step character variable or a character string representing the name of a macro variable.

The SYMGET function can be used in a DATA step to create a variable whose values are macro variable values. The value returned is the value of a macro variable identified by *argument*. If *argument* is a DATA step variable, the value of the DATA step variable must be the name of a macro variable. For example:

```
%LET  A1 = BEGIN;
%LET  A2 = END;
%LET  A3 = CONTINUE;
DATA  ONE;
   INPUT  CODE $;
   KEY = SYMGET(CODE);
   CARDS;
A1
A1
A2
A3
A1
A2
;
PROC  PRINT;
```

In DATA step ONE, SAS reads a character variable CODE with values of A1, A2, or A3. (Note that each value of CODE must conform to the rules for a SAS name and that each is a macro variable name.) Each time the DATA step is executed, the SYMGET function causes the value read for CODE to be replaced by its macro variable value (specified here by %LET statements). This value becomes the value of KEY. The result of the PRINT procedure is:

OBS	CODE	KEY
1	A1	BEGIN
2	A1	BEGIN
3	A2	END
4	A3	CONTINUE
5	A1	BEGIN
6	A2	END

If the value of CODE for an observation does not conform to the rules for a SAS name, or if SAS cannot find a macro variable of that name, SAS prints a warning message and sets the resulting value to missing. If *argument* is a character string representing the name of a macro variable, enclose the string in quotes:

```
%LET  G = GOOD;
DATA  TEST2;
   SET  TEST1;
   X = SYMGET('G');
```

In each observation of data set TEST2, X has the value GOOD.

The SYMGET function produces a character value, and a variable you create in an assignment statement using SYMGET is a character variable (unless you have previously established the variable as numeric, for example with a LENGTH statement). If the value of the macro variable is more than 200 characters (the maximum length of a DATA step character variable), SAS truncates the value of the macro variable on the right. If the macro variable has a value which represents a number, as in this example:

```
%LET START = 3;
```

the value of SYMGET('START') is character. However, SAS has several methods for changing character values to numeric ones.

You can use SYMGET('START') in calculations, since SAS automatically converts a character value used in a calculation to a numeric value. The following example illustrates several uses of SYMGET.

```
%LET START = 3;

DATA NEW;
  SET OLD;
  A = SYMGET('START');
  LENGTH B 8;
  B = SYMGET('START');
  C = SYMGET('START')/4;
  D = B/4;
```

A is a character variable with a value of '3' and a length of 200 (the 3 is padded with trailing blanks to make 200 characters). B is a numeric variable with a length of 8, since B is defined by the LENGTH statement as numeric. SAS automatically converts the character value of SYMGET('START') to a numeric value when it assigns the value to B. To create C, the SYMGET function is used in a calculation, and for D the same calculation uses the variable created from SYMGET('START') instead of the function itself.

SYMPUT: assign a value to a macro variable

```
CALL SYMPUT(argument1,argument2);
```

Argument1 and *argument2* can be character strings or DATA step variables; *argument1* should identify the name of a macro variable. SYMPUT assigns the value identified by *argument2* to a macro variable identified by *argument1*. If you have not already created the macro variable identified in the value of *argument1*, the SYMPUT function creates it in the current referencing environment (as though a %LET statement were present). You must use the DATA step statement CALL with SYMPUT (see Chapter 3, "Statements Used with the DATA Step," for a discussion of the CALL statement).

If *argument1* and *argument2* are DATA step variables, the function assigns the value of *argument2* in an observation to a macro variable whose name is the value of *argument1* in that observation. Notice that *argument1* must be a character variable; however, *argument2* may be either character or numeric. For example:

```
DATA NEW;
  INPUT CODE $ COUNTRY $;
  CALL SYMPUT(CODE,COUNTRY);
  CARDS;
X1  USA
X2  CANADA
X3  MEXICO
;
PROC  PRINT;
```

Data set NEW:

OBS	CODE	COUNTRY
1	X1	USA
2	X2	CANADA
3	X3	MEXICO

In this example, SYMPUT creates three macro variables: X1, X2, and X3. The value of X1 is USA; the value of X2 is CANADA; and the value of X3 is MEXICO. The result is the same as if you had specified

```
%LET  X1 = USA;
%LET  X2 = CANADA;
%LET  X3 = MEXICO;
```

You can assign a literal value to the macro variables in *argument1* by enclosing *argument2* in single quotes, as in

```
CALL SYMPUT(argument1,'argument2');
```

SAS assigns the value *argument2* to the macro variable identified in *argument1* for each observation. For example, the statements

```
DATA  NEW;
  INPUT  CODE $;
  CALL SYMPUT(CODE,'FROM DATA STEP VARIABLE CODE');
  CARDS;
X1
X2
X3
;
```

create three macro variables: X1, X2, and X3, each with the value FROM DATA STEP VARIABLE CODE.

If *argument1* is the name of a macro variable instead of a DATA step variable, enclose *argument1* in single quotes, as in

```
CALL SYMPUT('argument1',argument2);
```

In this case, the value identified in *argument2* is assigned to the macro variable named *argument1*. For example, the statements

```
DATA NEW;
  INPUT ID $ X1-X10;
  N+1;
  CALL SYMPUT('NOBS', N);
  CARDS;
 data lines
;
PROC PRINT;
  TITLE LISTING OF ALL &NOBS OBSERVATIONS;
```

create MACRO variable NOBS, whose value at the end of the DATA step is the number of observations in the data set. The macro variable NOBS can then be referenced as in the TITLE statement.

The macro below can be used to check for input data errors.

```
%MACRO CHECK(VARLIST);
  %LET ERROR=NO;
  DATA NEW ERROR;
    INFILE IN;
    INPUT &VARLIST;
    IF __ERROR__=1 THEN DO;
      CALL SYMPUT('ERROR','YES');
      OUTPUT ERROR;
      END;
    OUTPUT NEW;
    RUN;
  %IF &ERROR=YES %THEN %DO;
  PROC PRINT DATA=ERROR;
    VAR &VARLIST;
  %END;
  %MEND;
```

If SAS finds an error in your data and sets the automatic variable __ERROR__ to 1, the value of macro variable ERROR is given the value YES. The observation in error is written to SAS data set ERROR. When the DATA step is complete, if an error was found and ERROR's value was YES, SAS prints the data set ERROR.

Automatic Macro Variables

The macro language includes some automatic macro variables which can be referenced anywhere in your SAS job by preceding their name with an ampersand (&). All variables begin with SYS and are global. You use them exactly as you do other macro variables that you create. Caution: avoid giving your own macro variable names beginning with the letters SYS in order to avoid conflicts with current or future SAS-defined macro variables.

SYSDATE	gives the date (in DATE6. or DATE7. format) on which the SAS job started execution, for example, 2JUN82.
SYSDAY	gives the day of the week the SAS job started execution. SYSDAY appears as a word, for example, MONDAY.
SYSDEVIC	gives the name of the current graphics device, the value of the SAS system option DEVICE=.
SYSDSN	gives the name of the last SAS data set created.

SYSINDEX   gives the number of macros that have started execution so far in the current SAS job.

SYSENV   returns FORE (as in foreground) if you are working interactively and BACK (as in background) if you are not.

SYSPARM   returns the same string as that returned by the DATA step function SYSPARM( ).

SYSRC   gives the last return code set by the macro language. SYSRC is determined by the macros and the macro language service routines.

SYSSCP   returns one of three responses: OS, CMS, or DOS, depending on which operating system you are using.

SYSTIME   gives the time the SAS job started execution, as in 15:25.

SYSVER   gives the version of SAS you are using, as in 82.0.

SPECIAL TOPICS

Resolving Macro Variable References

The macro processor resolves a macro variable reference such as

&CLASS

by substituting the value of the macro variable CLASS for the reference. All characters after the ampersand are processed as part of the macro variable name until a character is encountered which cannot be part of the name. Consider the following macro:

```
%MACRO STUDENT(CLASS,IN);
   TITLE STUDENTS IN &CLASS CLASS;
   DATA &CLASS;
     INFILE &IN;
     INPUT NAME $ HEIGHT WEIGHT;
PROC SORT;
   BY NAME;
PROC PRINT;
%MEND STUDENT;
```

In macro STUDENT the blank after the second S in CLASS in the TITLE statement signals the end of the macro variable name, since a blank cannot be part of a macro variable name. In the statement DATA &CLASS, the semicolon after the second S in CLASS cannot be part of a macro variable name.

Any special character except an underscore signals the end of a macro variable name. Another ampersand in a character string tells the macro language that it has reached the end of a variable name. Thus, you can concatenate macro variables to modify existing variable names. For example,

```
%LET AAA=CARO;
%LET BBB=LINA;
%LET CCC=&AAA&BBB;
```

The resulting value of CCC is

CAROLINA .

If a character string contains a reference to a macro variable whose value is a null string, that macro variable reference is replaced with **no** characters. Thus:

```
%LET AAA=CARO;
%LET BBB=;
%LET CCC=&AAA&BBB;
```

assigns CCC a value of

    CARO   .

If a character string contains an ampersand followed by characters which can be a macro variable name, and the macro processor cannot find that name, it leaves the reference unresolved in the string it produces. This example:

```
%LET AAA=CARO;

&AAA&BBB
```

produces the string

    CARO&BBB   .

This situation occurs if you refer to a macro variable in a job before you define it; in that case the macro processor cannot find the value of the variable and leaves the reference unresolved. In the following example:

```
%LET AAA=CARO;
&AAA&BBB
%LET BBB=LINA;
```

the variable BBB has not been created at the time the macro processor reads the string &AAA&BBB; the macro processor therefore produces

    CARO&BBB   .

The value substituted for a macro variable may actually be another macro variable (nested macro variables). If there are nested macro variables, the macro processor can scan the line more than once until all macro variables are resolved. For example,

```
%LET XXX=&BBB;
%LET AAA=CARO;
%LET BBB=LINA;
%LET CCC=&AAA&XXX;
```

The macro variable BBB has not been defined when the variable XXX is defined. Thus, the value of CCC is first resolved to produce:

    CARO&BBB   .

Then this string is resolved to produce

    CAROLINA   .

The macro processor rescans portions of text which result from previous resolutions, and does not rescan portions which were not changed in the preceding scan. In this example, CARO&BBB can be rescanned because it was changed from &AAA&XXX. To enable the macro processor to rescan a macro variable reference, use two ampersands instead of one in the reference. Two ampersands resolve into one in the initial scan, and in the second scan, the single ampersand followed by the macro variable name is a reference the macro processor can resolve. See Example 4 under **Examples** for an illustration of the use of double ampersands.

Suppose you want to add a literal to the end of a macro variable value. The macro processor stops building the variable name when it encounters a period. Add the character string after the period. For example, suppose you want all data set names in a job to begin with the first three letters of the current month. Then

%LET NAME=JUL;

You can end the name with any values you want as in

DATA &NAME.82;

which resolves to

DATA JUL82;

No delimiter is needed when the character string precedes the macro variable value as in

DATA __31&NAME.82;

which resolves to

DATA __31JUL82;

Suppose you want to create SAS statements referring to a series of variables SCORE1–SCORE50. Create a macro variable S with a value of SCORE:

%LET S=SCORE;

Then, to reference the 50 variables in an ARRAY statement, use

ARRAY &S &S.1–&S.50;

This resolves to

ARRAY SCORE SCORE1–SCORE50;

If you want a fully resolved character string to contain a period immediately following the value of a macro variable, put two periods in the string to produce one period in the text. For example, suppose you want to produce a two-level data set name. The first level name is stored as macro variable NAME1:

%LET NAME1=OUT;

You can reference NAME1 and name the data set as in

DATA &NAME1..JUL82;

The first period signals the end of the variable reference &NAME1; the second period remains a character when the macro processor resolves the references in the string. Thus, the fully resolved character string is

DATA OUT.JUL82;

Or with two macro variable references:

DATA &NAME1..&NAME2;

You can also refer to symbolic variable values indirectly. For example:

%LET COW=DAIRY;
%LET ANIMAL=COW;

The value of ANIMAL is a character string that is the the name of another macro variable, COW. You can refer to the value of COW from ANIMAL by placing three ampersands in front of the macro variable name ANIMAL:

TITLE REPORT OF N.C. ASSOCIATION OF &&&ANIMAL PRODUCERS;

The macro processor always resolves two ampersands into one; the third ampersand and symbolic variable name constitute a symbolic variable reference. Thus the macro processor produces an intermediate step of &COW, recognizes &COW as a macro variable reference, and produces the result:

TITLE REPORT OF N.C. ASSOCIATION OF DAIRY PRODUCERS;

Communication Among Macros

This section discusses the ways you can make the information in a macro available to another macro. For a discussion of how you can transfer information from a macro to the execution of a DATA step, see **DATA Step Functions Used with the Macro Language**, above.

Referencing environments   Whether a macro variable can communicate between macros or between macros and SAS depends on its referencing environment or the area in which the macro variable is available for use. The largest possible referencing environment is the global environment, that is, the entire SAS job. A macro is a local environment, and, if you nest macros within other macros, each level of nest is another level of local referencing environment. Consider this example:

```
%LET  A=1;
TITLE EXAMPLE  WITH  A=&A;
TITLE2 A  GLOBAL  AND  A  LOCAL  REFERENCING  ENVIRONMENT;
%MACRO OUT;
  %IF  &A=1  %THEN  %DO;
    %LET  B=1;
    %DO  %WHILE(&B<=20);
      DATA  DATA&B;
        INFILE  IN;
        INPUT  X  Y  Z;
        YEAR=YR&B;
      %LET  B=%EVAL(&B+2);
      %END;
    %END;
  %ELSE  %DO;
    %LET  B=100;
    DATA  DATA&B;
      SET;
    %END;
  %MEND OUT;
%OUT
```

Macro variable A is defined outside any macros, that is, in the global environment. (Notice that A is referenced within macro OUT.) Macro variable B is defined in the local environment of macro OUT. A job can also contain nested referencing environments or unrelated local referencing environments.

A macro variable is available in the environment in which it is defined and in all environments nested within that environment ("farther in"). You can block the availability of a macro variable in an environment by creating a local macro variable of the same name at that level. The new variable blocks the availability of the original variable in that environment, and is available in the environment in which you created it and in all environments more deeply nested.

Performance Considerations

The most important performance consideration to remember in using the macro processor is that you are creating SAS statements and your computer costs reflect the cost of executing those statements, exactly as though you had entered all the statements yourself. For example:

```
%MACRO CREATE;
  %DO I=1 %TO 50;
    DATA  DATA&I;
    INFILE  IN&I;
    INPUT  X  Y  Z;
    RUN;
    PROC PRINT  DATA=DATA&I;
    RUN;
  %END;
%MEND CREATE;
```

With macro CREATE you enter only a few statements. However, the SAS statements produced create and print **fifty** data sets, which can reflect a considerable use of computer resources.

To perform text substitution, such as placing the name of a particular month in the title of a report, put the information into the value of a macro variable instead of into a macro. If you want conditional substitution (changing the text substituted depending on various factors), or if the text to be substituted is longer than the maximum length of a macro variable value at your installation (see your computing center staff for information), enclose the text in a macro. In general, macro variables are faster than macros, both to create and to execute.

Macro variables are also more efficient than macros used in earlier versions of SAS. The simplest way to transform one of these earlier macros into a macro variable is to use a %LET statement with the name of the macro as the name of the variable and the body of the macro as the value of the variable. Be sure to insert %STR( ) wherever a semicolon occurs that would incorrectly end the value of the macro variable. Consider this macro from a SAS79 job:

```
MACRO PR PROC PRINT;  BY DEPT;%
```

If you specify

```
%LET PR = %STR(PROC PRINT;  BY DEPT;);
```

then you can refer to the value of the macro variable in your job by putting an ampersand in front of the variable name. These two jobs perform the same function:

```
TITLE EXAMPLE USING OLD MACRO;
MACRO PR PROC PRINT; BY DEPT;%
DATA NEW;
  INPUT X Y Z;
PR

TITLE EXAMPLE USING MACRO VARIABLES FROM MACRO LANGUAGE;
%LET PR = %STR(PROC PRINT;  BY DEPT;);
DATA NEW;
  INPUT X Y Z;
&PR
```

However, the second one is much more efficient.

If you use the system option NOMACRO at the beginning of your job, then the macro processor will be unavailable for use in your job. (See the OPTIONS statement in Chapter 11 for a discussion of the NOMACRO option.) Using NOMACRO removes the availability of the macro language from SAS, including macro variables and the SYMPUT and SYMGET DATA step functions. Macro variables, SYMPUT, and SYMGET do not invoke the entire macro language, so you may want to have the macro language available for these purposes even when you have no macros in your job.

Finally, when deciding whether to use a macro in a certain situation, or whether to use a macro variable or a macro, consider the overhead cost of using macros. When you create a macro, the macro language must compile and store it; when you use a macro, SAS must retrieve and execute it. The cost of these actions varies directly with the number of macros you use; however, the execution of a macro is less expensive than its definition.

EXAMPLES

To see the SAS statements generated by the examples below, insert the statement OPTIONS MPRINT; at the beginning of your job.

Example 1

This macro generates SAS statements to recode the variable identified in the macro variable OLD into the variable identified in NEW. This macro has advantages over other methods in that you can recode variables by any interval, whereas most other simplified methods of recoding depend on grouping values by 10 or multiples of 10. See also macro FORMAT for an example of more complex grouping.

```
%MACRO CODEIT(START=,STOP=,COUNT=,OLD=,NEW=);
  IF &START<=
  %DO X=&START+&COUNT %TO &STOP %BY &COUNT;
    &OLD<&X THEN &NEW=&START;
    %LET START=&X;
    ELSE IF &START<=
  %END;
  &OLD THEN &NEW=&START;
  %MEND CODEIT;
```

Suppose you have a survey of persons age 30–59 whose ages in years are recorded in variable AGEYR. You want to create a new variable AGE3 in which persons are assigned to a three-year age group: 30–32, 33–35,36–38, and so on. This DATA step using macro CODEIT does that:

```
DATA AGES;
  INFILE IN;
  INPUT AGEYR;
%CODEIT(START=30,STOP=59,COUNT=3,OLD=AGEYR,NEW=AGE3)
```

The call given above produces these SAS statements:

```
IF 30<=AGEYR<33 THEN AGE3=30;
ELSE IF 33<=AGEYR<36 THEN AGE3=33;
ELSE IF 36<=AGEYR<39 THEN AGE3=36;
ELSE IF 39<=AGEYR<42 THEN AGE3=39;
ELSE IF 42<=AGEYR<45 THEN AGE3=42;
ELSE IF 45<=AGEYR<48 THEN AGE3=45;
ELSE IF 48<=AGEYR<51 THEN AGE3=48;
ELSE IF 51<=AGEYR<54 THEN AGE3=51;
ELSE IF 54<=AGEYR<57 THEN AGE3=54;
ELSE IF 57<=AGEYR THEN AGE3=57;
```

Macro CODEIT produces SAS statements using this logic:

1. In the first section of constant text the macro variable reference &START is replaced by the value of START and the first part of a SAS statement is produced:

   IF 30<=

2. The %DO loop begins execution. The first value of X is determined by adding the interval COUNT to the value of START. In this case, the first

value of X is 33. Notice that &START still has the value that begins the lowest grouping. The macro variables in the constant text are replaced by their values and the next piece of constant text is produced:

AGEYR<33 THEN AGE3=30;

This complete SAS statement has now been produced:

IF 30<AGEYR<33 THEN AGE3=30;

The %LET statement changes the value of START to the current value of X (33). This action means that, after the value of X is incremented for the next execution of the %DO loop, START will contain the former value of X. The next portion of constant text is produced:

ELSE IF 33<=

At this point the first execution of the %DO loop is complete. The value of X is now incremented by the value of COUNT and the second execution of the loop begins. The first section of text produced is

AGEYR<36 THEN AGE3=33;

which completes the SAS statement begun in the previous execution of the loop. The second complete SAS statement produced is thus

ELSE IF 33<=AGEYR<36 THEN AGE3=33;

The %LET statement changes the value of START to the current value of X (36) and the next portion of constant text is produced:

ELSE IF 36<=

3. At the end of the last execution of the %DO loop, this partial SAS statement has been produced:

ELSE IF 57<=

The value of X is now incremented to 60 and the %DO loop is no longer executed. Then the last section of constant text is produced:

AGEYR THEN AGE3=57;

The final SAS statement is therefore

ELSE IF 57<=AGEYR THEN AGE3=57;

Example 2

This macro invokes PROC FORMAT and generates VALUE statements for PROC FORMAT of the form shown in this example. This macro also allows for an irregular interval in the lowest grouping. The DQUOTE option must be in effect to use this macro.

```
%MACRO FORMAT(VAL=VAL,LOW=,START=,STOP=,COUNT=);
  PROC FORMAT;
   VALUE &VAL
%DO X=&START %TO &STOP %BY &COUNT;
  &LOW-&X="&LOW-&X"
  %LET LOW=%EVAL(&X+1);
  %END;
    ;
%MEND FORMAT;
```

Suppose you have a survey of persons age 18–75. You want to use PROC FORMAT to print their ages in 5-year groups beginning with age 21 (21–25, 26–30, and so on) and you want persons age 18–20 to have a separate group. Use this call of macro FORMAT:

```
%FORMAT(LOW=18,START=20,STOP=75,COUNT=5)
```

Macro FORMAT produces these statements:

```
PROC FORMAT;
VALUE VAL  18-20="18-20"
           21-25="21-25"
           26-30="26-30"
           31-35="31-35"
               . . .
           71-75="71-75"
                  ;
```

This is the logic macro FORMAT uses:

1. First the PROC FORMAT statement and the beginning of the VALUE statement are produced, with the value of macro variable VAL substituted for the reference &VAL:

   ```
   PROC FORMAT;
    VALUE VAL
   ```

   Notice that macro variable VAL was given a default value of VAL when the macro was created. Since another value is not given in the call, the default value is used.

2. The %DO loop is executed for the first time. Values for LOW and X are substituted and the text is produced:

   ```
   18-20="18-20"
   ```

   Since special characters in VALUE statements must be enclosed in quotes, the value label "18–20" (which contains a hyphen) must be enclosed in quotes. Double quotes (quotation marks) are used here because the DQUOTE option allows macro variable references within double quotes to be resolved. (If single quotes (apostrophes) were used, the value label would be produced as '&LOW–&X'.)

   The value of LOW is now changed to 1 more than the current value of X (20). In this case, 18 is changed to 21 by the %EVAL function. The first execution of the %DO loop has ended; the value of X is now incremented by the value of COUNT and the second execution of the loop begins.

   The second execution of the loop produces this text:

   ```
   21-25="21-25"
   ```

   The value of LOW is now incremented to 26. At the end of the loop, the value of X is incremented to 30 and the third execution of the loop produces the text

   ```
   26-30="26-30"
   ```

3. After the last execution of the loop, the final value label has been produced:

   ```
   71-75="71-75"
   ```

Macro FORMAT now produces a single semicolon to end the VALUE statement.

Notice that the initial value of LOW (18) does not affect the production of value labels in a regular pattern because all values of LOW after the initial one are generated from values of X, which always changes in a regular pattern.

Example 3

This macro allows you to see the results of PROC GSLIDE with several different character heights for the two title lines. It also uses two automatic macro variables. GSLIDE is a SAS/GRAPH procedure.

```
%MACRO HIGH(HEIGHT,LIMIT);
  %DO %WHILE(&HEIGHT<=&LIMIT);
    PROC GSLIDE;
    TITLE1;
    TITLE2 .H=&HEIGHT .F=COMPLEX &SYSDAY;
    TITLE4 .H=&HEIGHT .F=COMPLEX &SYSDATE;
    RUN;
    %LET HEIGHT=%EVAL(&HEIGHT+1);
    %END;
  %MEND HIGH;
%HIGH(1,5)
```

For example, suppose you call macro HIGH on Tuesday, July 26, 1983. The %DO loop is executed five times, and the first execution produces these SAS statements:

```
PROC GSLIDE;
TITLE1;
TITLE2 .H=1 .F=COMPLEX TUESDAY;
TITLE4 .H=1 .F=COMPLEX 26JUL83;
RUN;
```

The GSLIDE procedure displays the lines TUESDAY and 26JUL83 using the COMPLEX font in characters 1 line high. Each execution of the %DO loop increases the value of HEIGHT by 1. The final set of statements produced is:

```
PROC GSLIDE;
TITLE1;
TITLE2 .H=5 .F=COMPLEX TUESDAY;
TITLE4 .H=5 .F=COMPLEX 26JUL83;
RUN;
```

When the value of HEIGHT is incremented to 6, the expression in the %DO %WHILE statement is no longer true and the %DO loop ceases to be executed.

Example 4

This macro computes the factorial (N!) of the value of macro parameter N. It illustrates recursive execution of a macro, that is, a macro calling itself.

```
%MACRO  FACTORL(N);
  %IF  &N=0  %THEN  1;
  %ELSE  %IF  &N=1  %THEN  1;
  %ELSE  %EVAL(&N*%FACTORL(%EVAL(&N-1)));
  %MEND  FACTORL;
```

Suppose you call macro FACTORL with a value of 5 for N: %FACTORL(5). Macro FACTORL executes as follows:

1. The first %IF statement is checked and skipped, since the value of N is not 0.
2. The first %ELSE statement is also checked and skipped, since the value of N is not 1.
3. The second %ELSE statement is executed, since this statement covers all remaining cases.

   a. The value of N (5 in this case) is substituted into the argument of %EVAL, and the %EVAL function evaluates the value of N times the result of macro FACTORL called with a parameter value of &N-1 (4 in this case). Note that the expression %EVAL(&N-1) is the value supplied for macro parameter N in this call of FACTORL. At this point, the product of the evaluation is

   5*%FACTORL(4)

   b. Since the result of %FACTORL(4) is not known, the evaluation is not complete. The call %FACTORL(4) yields

   4*%FACTORL(3)

   c. The result of %FACTORL(3) is

   3*%FACTORL(2)

   d. The result of %FACTORL(2) is

   2*%FACTORL(1)

   e. The evaluation of %FACTORL(1) yields the number 1 (from the first %ELSE statement). The terms to be evaluated are all known after this call of FACTORL, and the argument of the %EVAL function is

   5*4*3*2*1

   The %EVAL function thus returns a value of 120 for %FACTORL(5).

Notice that macro FACTORL does not produce a complete SAS statement. One way to use it is to assign its result to a macro variable:

%LET NUMBER=%FACTORL(5);

The value of NUMBER is the result of macro FACTORL, or 120.

Example 5

This example creates a plot of AGE*SALARY for each BY group in data set EMPLOY with a reference line drawn on the horizontal axis of each plot at the mean salary for that group. This example is designed for use on large data sets and is efficient in that the data set is read only three times: once for PROC SORT, once for PROC MEANS, and once for the PROC PLOT (although the PLOT procedure is invoked twice).

```
DATA EMPLOY;
  INPUT SEX $ AGE SALARY;
  CARDS;
F 21 17000
F 18 10500
M 19 10900
M 33 31000
F 32 27000
M 23 21000
M 24 21000
PROC SORT;
  BY SEX;
PROC MEANS;
  VAR SALARY;
  OUTPUT OUT = MEAN N = TOTAL MEAN = MSAL;
  BY SEX;
PROC PRINT;
  RUN;
TITLE AGE * SALARY;
DATA FORPLOTS;
  SET MEAN END = EOF;
  LENGTH NCNT $3;
  RETAIN FIRSTOBS 1;
  OBS + TOTAL;
  CNT + 1;
  NCNT = LEFT(CNT);
  CALL SYMPUT('FIRST'||NCNT,FIRSTOBS);
  CALL SYMPUT('LAST'||NCNT,OBS);
  CALL SYMPUT('REF'||NCNT,MSAL);
  FIRSTOBS + OBS;
  IF EOF THEN CALL SYMPUT('TOTAL',CNT);
  RUN;
%MACRO PLOTIT;
  %DO I = 1 %TO &TOTAL;
    PROC PLOT DATA = EMPLOY(FIRSTOBS = &&FIRST&I OBS = &&LAST&I);
      PLOT AGE*SALARY/HREF = &&REF&I;
    TITLE2 GROUP &I;
    %END;
  %MEND;
%PLOTIT
  RUN;
```

DATA step EMPLOY creates the data set to be analyzed. The SORT procedure sorts EMPLOY by SEX, and the MEANS procedure calculates the number of observations in each BY group (TOTAL) and the mean salary for each BY group (MSAL). The output of the MEANS procedure is contained in the data set MEAN, which has 1 observation for each BY group.

The next DATA step uses information from data set MEAN to create several macro variables that macro PLOTIT can use. In the first execution of the DATA step FORPLOTS, the value of OBS is the number of observations in the first BY group of EMPLOY, since TOTAL is the number of observations in each BY group. During the last execution of the DATA step, CNT contains the number of BY groups in the original data set EMPLOY (since MEAN contains 1 observation for each BY group).

NCNT is a left-justified character variable created from CNT. It is created so that the CALL SYMPUT statements following it can create the name of a macro variable by concatenating the first part of the name with the character value of NCNT. In the first execution of the DATA step:

1. The first CALL SYMPUT produces a macro variable FIRST1 with a value of 1, since FIRSTOBS was initialized to 1 with the RETAIN statement.
2. The second CALL SYMPUT statement produces a macro variable LAST1 with a value of the number of observations in the first BY group (OBS).
3. The third CALL SYMPUT statement produces a macro variable REF1 with a value of the mean salary for persons in BY group 1.

After the three macro variables are created, FIRSTOBS is increased by the number of observations in the first BY group (OBS). Thus, FIRSTOBS now contains the number of the observation in EMPLOY that begins the second BY group.

In the second (and last) execution of DATA step FORPLOTS:

4. OBS is equal to the total number of observations in EMPLOY.
5. CNT and NCNT are both 2.
6. The macro variable FIRST2 has a value representing the number of the first observation in the second BY group.
7. The value of macro variable LAST2 is the number of the last observation in the second BY group, that is, the last observation in data set EMPLOY.
8. REF2 contains the mean salary for persons in BY group 2.
9. FIRSTOBS is equal to the number of the first observation in the (nonexistent) third BY group.
10. Since EOF has a value of 1 (true) during the second execution of FORPLOTS, the IF statement creates a macro variable named TOTAL whose value represents the number of BY groups in EMPLOY (that is, CNT).

The %DO loop in macro PLOTIT is executed as many times as the value of macro variable TOTAL indicates, that is, once for each BY group. For each plot, the observations to read from EMPLOY are selected automatically. The first time the %DO loop is executed the FIRSTOBS= option has a value of 1, since that is the value of macro variable FIRST1. Note that the macro variable reference &&FIRST&I begins with a double ampersand. In the first scan of &&FIRST&I the double ampersand is resolved to a single ampersand, the characters FIRST are left unchanged, and &I is resolved to 1. Since results of resolutions are always rescanned, the string &FIRST1 is rescanned and resolved into 1. If a single ampersand had been used at the beginning of the string as in &FIRST&1, the characters &FIRST would have been produced without resolution (because there is no macro variable FIRST in this job) and &I would have been resolved into 1. The macro variable reference &FIRST1 would have been left unresolved because the characters &FIRST would not be rescanned. The OBS= option has the number of the last observation to read from EMPLOY for that BY group, since that is the information contained in macro variable LAST1. A line is drawn at the mean salary of group 1 (the value of REF1). The second (and last) time the %DO loop is executed, the PROC PLOT statement has a FIRSTOBS= value equal to the first observation in the second BY group, and an OBS= value equal to the number of the last observation in the file. A line appears on the plot at the mean salary for BY group 2 (given in macro variable REF2).

Thus, this job creates seven macro variables: FIRST1, LAST1, REF1, FIRST2, LAST2, REF2, and TOTAL. The SAS statements generated by macro PLOTIT are:

```
PROC PLOT DATA=EMPLOY(FIRSTOBS=1 OBS=3);
   PLOT AGE*SALARY/HREF=18166;
TITLE2 GROUP1;
PROC PLOT DATA=EMPLOY(FIRSTOBS=4 OBS=7);
   PLOT AGE*SALARY/HREF=2075;
TITLE2 GROUP2;
```

Example 6

This example uses the SYMPUT and SYMGET functions to transfer information from a data set created by PROC SUMMARY into a data set containing information about employees' salaries. The resulting data set contains each employee's name, department, salary, the employee's salary as a percentage of his department's total salary expenditure and of store's total salary expenditure, and the mean salary for his department.

```
DATA DUSTY;
   INPUT DEPT $ NAME $ SALARY;
   CARDS;
BEDDING WATLEE 18000
BEDDING PARKER 9000
BEDDING JOINER 8000
BEDDING IVES 16000
BEDDING GEORGE 8000
CARPET KARO 20000
CARPET RAY 12000
CARPET MCNAIR 10000
CARPET JONES 9000
CARPET THOMAS 12000
GIFTS JOHNSON 8000
GIFTS RANKIN 7000
GIFTS MATTHEW 19000
KITCHEN BANKS 14000
KITCHEN WHITE 8000
KITCHEN MARKS 9000
KITCHEN CANNON 15000
TV SMITH 8000
TV JONES 9000
TV ROGERS 15000
TV MORSE 16000
PROC SUMMARY;
   CLASS DEPT;
   VAR SALARY;
   OUTPUT OUT=STATS N=N__SAL MEAN=M__SAL SUM=S__SAL;
PROC PRINT;
TITLE SUMMARY OF SALARY INFORMATION;
TITLE2 FOR DUSTY DEPARTMENT STORE;
DATA __NULL__;
   SET STATS;
   IF __N__=1 THEN DO;
     CALL SYMPUT ('S__TOT',S__SAL);
     CALL SYMPUT ('M__TOT',M__SAL);
     END;
```

```
     ELSE  DO;
       CALL  SYMPUT('M'||DEPT,M__SAL);
       CALL  SYMPUT('S'||DEPT,S__SAL);
       CALL  SYMPUT('N'||DEPT,N__SAL);
       END;
  DATA  NEW;
    SET  DUSTY;
    PCTDEPT = (SALARY / SYMGET('S'||DEPT)) * 100;
    PCTTOT = (SALARY / SYMGET('S__TOT')) * 100;
    DEPTMEAN = SYMGET('M'||DEPT);
    NUM = SYMGET('N'||DEPT);

  PROC  PRINT  SPLIT = *;
    LABEL  PCTDEPT = PERCENT OF *DEPARTMENT
      PCTTOT = PERCENT OF * TOTAL
      DEPTMEAN = MEAN SALARY OF *DEPARTMENT
      NUM = NUMBER OF EMPLOYEES*   IN DEPARTMENT;
  TITLE  SALARY  PROFILES  FOR  EMPLOYEES;
  TITLE2  OF  DUSTY  DEPARTMENT  STORE;
    RUN;
```

DUSTY is a SAS data set containing each employee's department, name, and salary. The SUMMARY procedure analyzes data set DUSTY to produce an output data STATS containing the number of observations, mean salary, and sum of salaries for each department and for the store as a whole as well as the special variables __TYPE__ and __FREQ__.

The next DATA step creates macro variables for variables in STATS. Since the first observation in STATS contains information about all observations in DUSTY (__TYPE__ = 0), the first execution of the DATA step places the sum of salaries for all employees (S__SAL) into the value of macro variable S__TOT. The mean salary for all employees (M__SAL) is placed into the value of macro variable M__TOT.

In the second execution of DATA __NULL__, a macro variable is created by concatenating the letter M and the name of the department, in this case BEDDING. MBEDDING contains the mean salary (M__SAL) for employees of the bedding department. Likewise, macro variable SBEDDING contains the sum of the salaries of employees in that department, and NBEDDING contains the number of employees in that department. Subsequent executions of the DATA step produce analogous macro variables for other departments in Dusty Department Store. In all, the DATA step produces 17 macro variables: three for each of the five departments, plus two for the store as a whole.

DATA set NEW contains each employee's salary as a percentage of the departmental salary expenditure (PCTDEPT) and as a percentage of the store's total salary expenditure (PCTTOT). It also contains the mean salary of that employee's department (DEPTMEAN) and the number of employees in the department (NUM) for each observation. To form PCTDEPT, the appropriate macro variable is selected by concatenating the letter S with the name of the department. DEPTMEAN and NUM are constructed in the same way. PCTTOT is created by dividing the employee's salary by the total of salaries in the store (returned by SYMGET (S__TOT)).

Finally, the PRINT procedure lists the resulting information for each employee: department, name, salary, salary as a percentage of the department's total salaries, salary as a percent of the store's total salaries, mean salary of the employee's department, and number of employees in the department.

SAS Log and Procedure Output

SAS produces printed output in the form of the SAS log, a description of the SAS job or terminal session, and in the printed results of SAS procedures. This chapter discusses these forms of SAS printed output and how you can tailor them to meet your specific needs. The last section describes SAS errors and error messages.

SAS LOG

The SAS log includes information about the processing of the SAS job: what statements were executed; what data sets were created and how many variables and observations they contain; how much time and memory each step in the job required; and, for batch jobs, the page number for locating the printed results of each procedure that was executed. The log is also used by some of the SAS procedures that perform SAS or OS utility functions, like DATASETS, SOURCE, and TAPECOPY. Messages are written on the log by certain ERROR and PUT statements.

The log is necessary and important documentation that gives a journal of the processing and can help you solve problems that arise during the job. For interactive jobs, the log is typed or displayed at your terminal as you enter statements along with the results from each SAS step. For OS batch jobs, the SAS statements are normally printed on the log before the results of SAS procedures or printed reports from DATA steps. In CMS batch, the log is usually created as a separate disk file; if the log and procedure output are both sent directly to a printer, then a spooled print file is created with log and procedure output interspersed. For VSE batch jobs, the log is output as a separate VSE/POWER spooled print file.

Structure of the SAS Log

Each line in your SAS job containing SAS statements is printed and numbered on the log: for example, the small number 1 printed to the left of the OPTIONS statement in the example below means that it was the first line in the job.

Interspersed with your SAS statements are messages from SAS. These messages sometimes begin with the word NOTE, the word ERROR, or an error number. They sometimes refer to a SAS statement by its line number on the log.

Below is the SAS log from a simple SAS job run under OS batch. The raw data input to the DATA step are stored on a file described in the control language by DDname IN1. The numbered items appear on the log from a SAS job run under any operating system.

```
1  S A S   L O G    SAS/OS 82.0   VS2/MVS JOB JOBNAME  STEP SAS PROC    9:47 WEDNESDAY, JULY 28, 1982
    NOTE: THE JOB JOBNAME HAS BEEN RUN UNDER RELEASE 82.0 OF SAS AT SAS INSTITUTE INC. (00000000)

    NOTE:  CPUID  VERSION = 04  SERIAL = 020091  MODEL = 0158 .
           CPUID  VERSION = 03  SERIAL = 024001  MODEL = 0158 .

    NOTE: NO OPTIONS SPECIFIED.
    1            OPTIONS LS=80;
    2            DATA ONE;
    3               INFILE IN1;
    4               INPUT ID $ X Y;

    NOTE: INFILE IN1(OUTPUTIN) IS:
          DSNAME=SAS.USERS.GUIDE(OUTPUTIN),
          UNIT=DISK,VOL=SER=SAS333,DISP=SHR,
          DCB=(BLKSIZE=6160,LRECL=80,RECFM=FB)

    NOTE: 4 LINES WERE READ FROM INFILE IN1(OUTPUTIN).
    NOTE: DATA SET WORK.ONE HAS 4 OBSERVATIONS AND 3 VARIABLES. 680 OBS/TRK.
    NOTE: THE DATA STATEMENT USED 0.94 SECONDS AND 304K.

    5            PROC PRINT;

    NOTE: THE PROCEDURE PRINT USED 0.94 SECONDS AND 344K AND PRINTED PAGE 1.
    NOTE: SAS USED 344K MEMORY.

    NOTE: SAS INSTITUTE INC.
          SAS CIRCLE
          BOX 8000
          CARY, N.C. 27511-8000
```

1. date and time the job was run
2. name of the job taken from the JOB statement in the job control language of your batch job
3. release of SAS used to run this job
4. name of the installation where the job was run
5. SAS site number (this reference number is used in our files to identify the installation given in (4))
6. CPU serial number for your installation
7. SAS options specified when you invoke SAS. (This line is printed when the OPLIST system option is in effect. See the chapter on SAS system options for more information.)
8. SAS statements for each DATA or PROC step in the job
9. for each external file of raw data read or written in a DATA step, information about the file, including the number of lines read or written
10. for each SAS data set created, its name, the number of observations and variables, and (except under CMS) the number of observations that can be stored in one track of disk space
11. computer time and memory used by the step; for a step that produces printed output, the pages printed
12. maximum amount of memory actually used by the steps in the job

13. the name and address of SAS Institute. When you see this note, you know that your job ran to completion. If you cannot find the note, check the first part of your printout—the messages from the computer's operating system—to see if the job needed more time or ran into a system problem.

Writing on the Log

You can tell SAS to write on the log in three ways: the LIST statement automatically prints the current data line on the log; PUT statements can be directed to the log; ERROR statements can be directed to the log. Below is the log of a SAS job which uses a LIST statement and a PUT statement directed to the log. (Note that in this DATA step FILE LOG is assumed since no FILE statement is present.)

```
1  S A S  L O G   SAS/OS 82.0   VS2/MVS JOB JOBNAME  STEP SAS PROC      9:47 WEDNESDAY, JULY 28, 1982

NOTE: THE JOB JOBNAME HAS BEEN RUN UNDER RELEASE 82.0 OF SAS AT SAS INSTITUTE INC. (00000000).

NOTE:  CPUID  VERSION = 04  SERIAL = 020091  MODEL = 0158 .
       CPUID  VERSION = 03  SERIAL = 024001  MODEL = 0158 .

NOTE: NO OPTIONS SPECIFIED.

1            OPTIONS LS=80;
2            DATA ONE;
3              INPUT ID $ X Y;
4              LIST;
5              IF X=Y THEN PUT 'X AND Y ARE EQUAL ' X=;
6            CARDS;


RULE:    1234567 101234567 201234567 301234567 401234567 501234567 601234567 70

7            a01 1.2 3
8            a21 2.4 4
X AND Y ARE EQUAL X=2
9            a02 2   2
10           b01 3   0
X AND Y ARE EQUAL X=3
11           b21 3   3
12           b02 1   .
13           c01 .   5
NOTE: DATA SET WORK.ONE HAS 7 OBSERVATIONS AND 3 VARIABLES. 680 OBS/TRK.
NOTE: THE DATA STATEMENT USED 0.98 SECONDS AND 288K.

14           PROC PRINT;

NOTE: THE PROCEDURE PRINT USED 1.03 SECONDS AND 312K
      AND PRINTED PAGE 1.
NOTE: SAS USED 312K MEMORY.

NOTE: SAS INSTITUTE INC.
      SAS CIRCLE
      BOX 8000
      CARY, N.C. 27511-8000
```

When SAS encounters a LIST statement, it flags the current data line and prints it on the SAS log before returning to the beginning of DATA step for a new execution. On the other hand, the PUT statement causes SAS to print immediately. Thus, for observations with X and Y equal, the PUT statement prints before the LIST statement writes the data line.

Suppressing All or Part of the Log

When you have large SAS programs that you run on a regular basis without changes, you may want to suppress the listing of your SAS statements on the log. You can use the system option NOSOURCE in the control language when you invoke SAS or in an OPTIONS statement at the beginning of your job to suppress these lines.

Sometimes you may want to suppress the notes that SAS prints on the log. You can use the system option NONOTES to prevent SAS from printing any of the messages beginning with NOTE. **Do not** use this option until your program is error-free, or if you are planning to telephone SAS Institute's consulting staff about an error in your program. The notes that SAS prints are required for debugging.

When data errors occur in your SAS job, SAS prints error messages for up to *n* errors where *n* is the value of the system option ERRORS=. Normally, the default value for ERRORS= is 20, and SAS prints messages for up to twenty data errors. You can set the value of ERRORS= to another number to specify the maximum number of error messages you want printed on your log. If ERRORS=0, no error messages are printed. (Note that the ? or ?? format modifiers in the INPUT statement also affect the printing of error messages. See the description of the INPUT statement for more information.)

For more information about these and other system options, see the OPTIONS statement in Chapter 11, "SAS Statements Used Anywhere."

Skipping Lines and Pages

You can use the SKIP and PAGE statements to control the appearance of the SAS log. See the SKIP and PAGE statements in Chapter 11, "Statements Used Anywhere," for more information.

PRINTED RESULTS OF SAS PROCEDURES

The pages after the SAS log contain the results of PROC steps as well as reports printed by DATA steps using the PUT and FILE statements routed to a print file. These results and reports appear in the same order as the corresponding PROC and DATA steps appeared in the job, and notes on the log tell which output pages were produced by which PROC or DATA step. Under CMS, SAS procedure output is usually written to a separate disk file. You can print log and procedure output using a CMS PRINT command. Under VSE, SAS procedure output is routed to a separate VSE/POWER spooled print file.

Several examples of reports written in DATA steps with PUT and FILE statements are shown in the **Report Writing** section of Chapter 6, "Data Step Applications." This chapter discusses the output produced by SAS procedures.

Each SAS procedure produces a different form of output. Consult the procedure descriptions in this manual and the *SAS User's Guide: Statistics, 1982 Edition* for examples of output from SAS procedures. You can tailor SAS printouts using certain SAS statements and system options.

Titles

SAS prints the title

    S A S

at the top of each page of output unless you specify your own titles with one or more TITLE statements. See the TITLE statement in Chapter 11, "SAS Statements Used Anywhere," for more information.

Printing Values

You have some control over the way SAS prints values in procedure output. For example, by default SAS prints a single dot (.) as a missing value for a numeric variable. To have SAS print some other character for a missing value, use the SAS system option MISSING= in the control language when you invoke SAS or in an OPTIONS statement. For example, if you specify

OPTIONS MISSING='B';

when the value of a numeric variable is missing, the letter B is printed instead of a single period.

You can use a FORMAT statement to associate formats with variables. This format is then used to print the values of variables. The SAS formats available are described in Chapter 13, "SAS Informats and Formats."

You can define your own formats using the FORMAT procedure. This procedure gives you a great deal of flexibility in printing the results of procedures. The formats you define can be permanently stored for later use under OS or CMS.

See the FORMAT statement descriptions in Chapter 3, "Statements Used in the DATA Step," and Chapter 8, "Statements Used in the PROC Step," and the FORMAT procedure description for more information.

Printing Variable Names

For most SAS procedures, if a LABEL statement has been specified in the DATA step used to create the data set being analyzed or in the current PROC step, the LABEL rather than the variable name is printed. The LABEL may be up to 40 characters long, thus giving a more descriptive name to the variable.

See Chapter 3, "Statements Used in the DATA Step," and Chapter 8, "Statements Used in the PROC Step," for more information about LABEL statements.

Page and Line Sizes

The default number of lines per page (pagesize) and characters per line (linesize) is determined by the values of the SAS system options PAGESIZE (or PS) and LINESIZE (or LS). You can reset these options to your own values with the OPTIONS statement or in the control language when you invoke SAS.

For example, say you are planning to photo-reduce your output to fit on an 8 ½" x 11" page. Instead of the default values of 60 lines per page and 132 (120 for VSE) characters per line, you will be able to fit 76 lines per page but only 100 characters per line. If you use the OPTIONS statement below in your SAS job, output printed with the OPTIONS statement in effect uses 76 lines per page and 100 characters per line.

OPTIONS PAGESIZE=76 LINESIZE=100;

The values you use for LINESIZE and PAGESIZE can affect the output SAS produced by some SAS procedures. For example, the default set of descriptive statistics printed by the MEANS procedure is dependent on the linesize in effect at the time. The appearance of the output from procedures changes slightly for different linesizes. When running SAS interactively at a terminal, the system option TLS (terminal linesize) controls the width of the line (except for ICCF under VSE where the LINESIZE from table 10 is used.) SAS provides a default TLS value appropriate for your terminal, but you can reset the TLS value using the OPTIONS statement.

Page Number

SAS numbers the output pages in batch jobs in the top right-hand corner, beginning with page 1.

If you do not want page numbers printed on your output, use the SAS system option NONUMBER. For example, you could specify this OPTIONS statement:

OPTIONS NONUMBER;

as the first statement in your SAS job to suppress page numbering.

Date and Time

The date and time that the job was run appear on the printout. These values become important when you are running a program several times.

If you do not want the time and date values to appear, you can use the system option NODATE. For example, this OPTIONS statement

OPTIONS NODATE;

causes SAS to leave off the current date and time from each page of output.

Centering Output

SAS normally centers titles and procedure output on the pages in batch jobs. If you want the output left-aligned rather than centered, you can use the system option NOCENTER:

OPTIONS NOCENTER;

See the OPTIONS statement in Chapter 11, "SAS Statements Used Anywhere," for more information about SAS systems options including NOCENTER, LINESIZE, PAGESIZE, NONUMBER, and NODATE.

ERRORS

There are three kinds of errors that SAS can detect: syntax errors, programming errors, and data errors. SAS finds syntax errors as it compiles each SAS step, before the statements are executed. Programming errors and data errors are discovered when your SAS job is being executed.

Syntax Errors

If you misspell a SAS keyword, forget a semicolon, or make similar mistakes, SAS prints the word ERROR followed by an error number. A message explaining the error is printed at the end of the DATA or PROC step.

Some errors are explained fully by the message that SAS prints. For example, in the job below, the INFILE statement in the DATA step references a DDname that has not been previously defined in the control language for the job. In the PROC PRINT step, the VAR statement specifies the name of a variable that is not in the data set being analyzed.

```
1  S A S  L O G   SAS/OS 82.0   VS2/MVS JOB JOBNAME  STEP SAS PROC     9:47 WEDNESDAY, JULY 28, 1982

NOTE: THE JOB JOBNAME HAS BEEN RUN UNDER RELEASE 82.0 OF SAS AT SAS INSTITUTE INC. (00000000).

NOTE:   CPUID  VERSION = 04  SERIAL = 020091  MODEL = 0158 .
        CPUID  VERSION = 03  SERIAL = 024001  MODEL = 0158 .

NOTE: NO OPTIONS SPECIFIED.

1           OPTIONS LS=80;
2           DATA ONE;
3              INFILE IN2;
ERROR:            526
4           INPUT ID $ X Y;


526:  DDNAME IS NOT DEFINED.

NOTE: SAS STOPPED PROCESSING THIS STEP BECAUSE OF ERRORS.
NOTE: SAS SET OPTION OBS=0 AND WILL CONTINUE TO CHECK STATEMENTS.
      THIS MAY CAUSE NOTE: NO OBSERVATIONS IN DATA SET.
NOTE: DATA SET WORK.ONE HAS 0 OBSERVATIONS AND 3 VARIABLES. 680 OBS/TRK.
NOTE: THE DATA STATEMENT USED 0.67 SECONDS AND 292K.

5           PROC PRINT;
6              VAR X Y Z;
ERROR:                155

155:   THE VARIABLE NAME IS NOT ON THE DATA SET.

NOTE: SAS STOPPED PROCESSING THIS STEP BECAUSE OF ERRORS.
NOTE: THE PROCEDURE PRINT USED 0.52 SECONDS AND 300K.
NOTE: SAS USED 300K MEMORY.

ERROR: ERRORS ON PAGES 1.

NOTE: SAS INSTITUTE INC.
      SAS CIRCLE
      BOX 8000
      CARY, N.C. 27511-8000
```

The error number is printed so that the first digit of the number is below the first character of the word in error. The number 526 at the end of the step explains the error.

Other error messages are not as clear as in the example above. For example, because SAS statements are free format and can begin and end anywhere, when you fail to end a SAS statement with a semicolon, SAS does not always detect the error. Here is an example:

```
DATA A;
  INPUT X Y
  Z=X + Y;
  LIST;
  CARDS;
1 2
2 3
4 5
6 7
;
PROC PRINT;
```

The log from the program above shows that the missing semicolon in the INPUT statement is not detected as an error by SAS.

```
1  S A S  L O G   SAS/OS 82.0   VS2/MVS JOB JOBNAME  STEP SAS PROC     9:47 WEDNESDAY, JULY 28, 1982

NOTE: THE JOB JOBNAME HAS BEEN RUN UNDER RELEASE 82.0 OF SAS AT SAS INSTITUTE INC. (00000000).

NOTE:   CPUID  VERSION = 04  SERIAL = 020091  MODEL = 0158 .
        CPUID  VERSION = 03  SERIAL = 024001  MODEL = 0158 .
```

(continued on next page)

```
(continued from previous page)
    NOTE: NO OPTIONS SPECIFIED.

    1              OPTIONS LS=80;
    2              DATA A;
    3                INPUT X Y
    4                Z=X + Y;
    5                LIST;
    6                CARDS;

    RULE:    1234567 101234567 201234567 301234567 401234567 501234567 601234567 70

    8          2 3
    10         6 7
    NOTE: SAS WENT TO A NEW LINE WHEN INPUT STATEMENT
          REACHED PAST THE END OF A LINE.
    NOTE: DATA SET WORK.A HAS 2 OBSERVATIONS AND 3 VARIABLES. 680 OBS/TRK.
    NOTE: THE DATA STATEMENT USED 1.57 SECONDS AND 288K.

    11         ;
    12           PROC PRINT;

    NOTE: THE PROCEDURE PRINT USED 1.04 SECONDS AND 312K
          AND PRINTED PAGE 1.
    NOTE: SAS USED 312K MEMORY.

    NOTE: SAS INSTITUTE INC.
          SAS CIRCLE
          BOX 8000
          CARY, N.C. 27511-8000
```

The assignment statement is considered part of the INPUT statement: Z= is treated as named input, X tells SAS to read a value for X (this value replaces the first X value read), and +Y is a valid pointer control telling SAS to skip the next Y columns.
  The message

  NOTE: SAS WENT TO A NEW LINE WHEN INPUT STATEMENT REACHED
    PAST THE END OF A LINE.

is often an indication that your data lines are not being read as you expect. When the LIST statement is executed, the current record is the second in each group of two lines. The PRINT procedure prints the data set created:

```
                    SAS        15:50 MONDAY, JULY 19, 1982              1

              OBS    X    Y    Z

               1     2    2    .
               2     6    5    .
```

  Below is a DATA step where a semicolon was left off the DATA statement. Again, SAS did not detect the error.

```
DATA A
  INPUT X Y;
  Z= X + Y;
  LIST;
  CARDS;
1 2
3 4
5 6
7 8
;
PROC PRINT;
```

```
1  S A S  L O G   SAS/OS 82.0   VS2/MVS JOB JOBNAME  STEP SAS PROC     9:47 WEDNESDAY, JULY 28, 1982

NOTE: THE JOB JOBNAME HAS BEEN RUN UNDER RELEASE 82.0 OF SAS AT SAS INSTITUTE INC. (00000000).

NOTE:  CPUID  VERSION = 04  SERIAL = 020091  MODEL = 0158 .
       CPUID  VERSION = 03  SERIAL = 024001  MODEL = 0158 .

NOTE: NO OPTIONS SPECIFIED.

1            OPTIONS LS=80;
2            DATA A
3              INPUT X Y;
4              Z=X + Y;
5              LIST;
6              CARDS;

NOTE: THE VARIABLE X IS UNINITIALIZED.
NOTE: THE VARIABLE Y IS UNINITIALIZED.
NOTE: MISSING VALUES WERE GENERATED AS A RESULT OF PERFORMING
      AN OPERATION ON MISSING VALUES.
      EACH PLACE IS GIVEN BY: (NUMBER OF TIMES) AT (LINE):(COLUMN).

      1 AT 4:5

NOTE: DATA SET WORK.A HAS 1 OBSERVATIONS AND 3 VARIABLES. 680 OBS/TRK.
NOTE: DATA SET WORK.INPUT HAS 1 OBSERVATIONS AND 3 VARIABLES. 680 OBS/TRK.
NOTE: DATA SET WORK.X HAS 1 OBSERVATIONS AND 3 VARIABLES. 680 OBS/TRK.
NOTE: DATA SET WORK.Y HAS 1 OBSERVATIONS AND 3 VARIABLES. 680 OBS/TRK.
NOTE: THE DATA STATEMENT USED 1.10 SECONDS AND 328K.

11           ;
12           PROC PRINT;

NOTE: THE PROCEDURE PRINT USED 1.03 SECONDS AND 312K
      AND PRINTED PAGE 1.
NOTE: SAS USED 328K MEMORY.

NOTE: SAS INSTITUTE INC.
      SAS CIRCLE
      BOX 8000
      CARY, N.C. 27511-8000
```

The INPUT statement was assumed to be part of the DATA statement. Thus, SAS was prepared to build four data sets: A, INPUT, X, and Y. One observation was written to each data set when the DATA step was executed.

The messages on the SAS log indicate that four data sets were created—WORK.A, WORK.INPUT, WORK.X, AND WORK.Y—each with one observation. This is your clue that an error occurred. Since no INPUT statement was executed, X and Y were assumed to be missing in the assignment statement and the LIST statement had no record to write. The resulting PROC PRINT:

```
                  SAS       16:07 MONDAY, JULY 19, 1982                    1
          OBS   Z   X   Y
           1    .   .   .
```

When SAS finds a syntax error, it does not run the step in which the error occurred. To warn you, it prints:

NOTE: SAS STOPPED PROCESSING THIS STEP BECAUSE OF ERRORS.

Syntax Check Mode

In the step in which the syntax error occurred, if you were executing PROC DATASETS or an external procedure or creating a SAS data set, then SAS prints:

NOTE: SAS SET OPTION OBS=0 AND WILL CONTINUE TO CHECK
      STATEMENTS. THIS MAY CAUSE NOTE: NO OBSERVATIONS IN DATA SET.

In an effort to continue processing, SAS executes later steps in the job with OBS=0
if

- a SAS data set is created in the step
- no SAS data sets are used as input to the step.

If either of these conditions holds, the step is executed. However, permanent SAS
data sets are not replaced.

When OBS=0, SAS reads zero observations from data sets or external files. Thus,
any data set created in the step may contain zero observations. When a SAS procedure tries to analyze one of these data sets, it prints the message

NOTE: NO OBSERVATIONS IN DATA SET.

and stops.

Programming Errors

The class of execution time errors that cause your SAS job to fail is called programming errors. For example, if your program processes an array and SAS encounters a
value of the array's index variable that is out of range, SAS prints an error message
and stops.

Below is an example. The DATA step defines an array with index variable I. The
value of I is read with an INPUT statement before the array is processed in a programming statement. A miscoded I value results in an error message:

```
DATA A;
  ARRAY ALL(I) X1–X10;
  INPUT I MEASURE;
    IF MEASURE>0 THEN ALL=MEASURE;
    CARDS;
1 1.5
. 3
2 4.5
;
PROC PRINT;
```

```
1 S A S   L O G   SAS/OS 82.0   VS2/MVS JOB JOBNAME  STEP SAS PROC    9:47 WEDNESDAY, JULY 28, 1982

NOTE: THE JOB JOBNAME HAS BEEN RUN UNDER RELEASE 82.0 OF SAS AT SAS INSTITUTE INC. (00000000).

NOTE:  CPUID  VERSION = 04  SERIAL = 020091  MODEL = 0158 .
       CPUID  VERSION = 03  SERIAL = 024001  MODEL = 0158 .

NOTE: NO OPTIONS SPECIFIED.

1          DATA A;
2            ARRAY ALL (I) X1–X10;
3            INPUT I MEASURE;
4              IF MEASURE>0 THEN ALL=MEASURE;
5              CARDS;

ERROR: ARRAY SUBSCRIPT OUT OF RANGE AT LINE 4 COLUMN 22.

RULE:      1234567 101234567 201234567 301234567 401234567 501234567 601234567 701234567 80

7          .  3
I=. X1=. X2=. X3=. X4=. X5=. X6=. X7=. X8=. X9=. X10=. MEASURE=3 _ERROR_=1 _N_=2
NOTE: SAS SET OPTION OBS=0 AND WILL CONTINUE TO CHECK STATEMENTS.
      THIS MAY CAUSE NOTE: NO OBSERVATIONS IN DATA SET.
NOTE: DATA SET WORK.A HAS 1 OBSERVATIONS AND 12 VARIABLES. 190 OBS/TRK.
NOTE: THE DATA STATEMENT USED 0.92 SECONDS AND 288K.

9          ;
10           PROC PRINT;
```

(continued on next page)

```
(continued from previous page)

NOTE: THE PROCEDURE PRINT USED 0.45 SECONDS AND 312K.
NOTE: SAS USED 312K MEMORY.

ERROR: ERRORS ON PAGES 1.

NOTE: SAS INSTITUTE INC.
      SAS CIRCLE
      BOX 8000
      CARY, N.C. 27511-8000
```

Data Errors and Other Warning Messages

Like programming errors, data errors are detected during the execution of the job. However, unlike programming errors, data errors do not cause execution to stop. SAS warns you of the data errors on the SAS log.

The DATA step below reads seven data lines:

```
OPTIONS LS=80;
DATA ONE;
  INPUT ID $ X Y;
  Z=X/Y;
  LG=LOG(X);
  CARDS;
a01 1.2  3
a21 2.4  4
a02 0    2
b01 3    0
b21 A    3
b02 1    .
c01 .    5
PROC PRINT;
```

The SAS log produced when the job is run in batch contains several warning messages; however, the job ran to completion. Notice that data lines following a CARDS statement are numbered along with the SAS statements.

```
1  S A S   L O G   SAS/OS 82.0   VS2/MVS JOB JOBNAME  STEP SAS PROC      9:47 WEDNESDAY, JULY 28, 1982
NOTE: THE JOB JOBNAME HAS BEEN RUN UNDER RELEASE 82.0 OF SAS AT SAS INSTITUTE INC. (00000000).

NOTE: CPUID VERSION = 04  SERIAL = 020091  MODEL = 0158.
      CPUID VERSION = 03  SERIAL = 024001  MODEL = 0158.

NOTE: NO OPTIONS SPECIFIED.

1          OPTIONS LS=80;
2          DATA ONE;
3            INPUT ID $ X Y;
4            Z=X/Y;
5            LG=LOG(X);
6            CARDS;

NOTE: ILLEGAL ARGUMENT TO FUNCTION AT LINE 5 COLUMN 6.

RULE:     1234567 101234567 201234567 301234567 401234567 501234567 601234567 70
9         a02 0   2
ID=a02 X=0 Y=2 Z=0 LG=. _ERROR_=1 _N_=3

NOTE: DIVISION BY ZERO AT LINE 4 COLUMN 6.
10        b01 3   0
ID=b01 X=3 Y=0 Z=. LG=1.098612 _ERROR_=1 _N_=4
```

(continued on next page)

```
(continued from previous page)
   NOTE: INVALID DATA FOR X IN LINE 11 5-5.     3:14
   11        b21 A    3
   ID=b21 X=. Y=3 Z=. LG=. _ERROR_=1 _N_=5

   NOTE: MATHEMATICAL OPERATIONS COULD NOT BE PERFORMED AT THE
         FOLLOWING PLACES. THE RESULT OF THESE OPERATIONS HAVE
         BEEN SET TO MISSING VALUES.
         EACH PLACE IS GIVEN BY: (NUMBER OF TIMES) AT (LINE):(COLUMN).
         1 AT 4:5   1 AT 5:6

   NOTE: MISSING VALUES WERE GENERATED AS A RESULT OF PERFORMING
         AN OPERATION ON MISSING VALUES.
         EACH PLACE IS GIVEN BY: (NUMBER OF TIMES) AT (LINE):(COLUMN).
         3 AT 4:5   2 AT 5:6

   NOTE: DATA SET WORK.ONE HAS 7 OBSERVATIONS AND 5 VARIABLES. 433 OBS/TRK.

   NOTE: THE DATA STATEMENT USED 0.46 SECONDS AND 52K.

   14          PROC PRINT;

   NOTE: THE PROCEDURE PRINT USED 0.60 SECONDS AND 112K
         AND PRINTED PAGE 1.


   NOTE: SAS USED 112K MEMORY.

   NOTE: SAS INSTITUTE INC.
         SAS CIRCLE
         BOX 8000
         CARY, N.C. 27511-8000
```

The first data error occurs when X is 0. Zero is an illegal argument to the LOG function. The error causes SAS to print:

1. the warning message, in this case:

   NOTE: ILLEGAL ARGUMENT TO FUNCTION AT LINE 5 COLUMN 6.

2. for the first error, the RULE, which gives the column numbers referred to in this and later messages
3. the current record in the input buffer (usually the line in error)
4. the current values of all the variables.

For each subsequent error that occurs while SAS is executing the DATA step, SAS prints the warning message, the line in error, and the current values of the variables.

5. At the end of the step, SAS prints a summary of the operations that could not be performed because of invalid arguments or divisors. The number of times a missing value was the result of an operation is also given. The operations which resulted in missing values are summarized in the form:

   (NUMBER OF TIMES) AT (LINE):(COLUMN)

For example, the SAS log above summarizes the number of times that missing values were generated as a result of performing operations on missing values:

   3 AT 4:5 2 AT 5:6

This note tells you that missing values resulted 3 times at line 4, column 5 of the SAS log—the location of the variable X in the assignment statement

   Z = X/Y;

and 2 times at line 5, column 6 of the SAS log in the statement

LG = LOG(X);

where the LOG function appears.

DESCRIPTIVE STATISTICS

Introduction to SAS Descriptive Procedures

CORR

FREQ

MEANS

SUMMARY

TABULATE

UNIVARIATE

Introduction to SAS Descriptive Procedures

The following SAS descriptive procedures read through SAS data sets collecting univariate descriptive summary statistics, such as means, sums, standard deviations, and frequency counts. Two of the procedures also include bivariate measures.

MEANS   computes and prints means and other descriptive statistics

UNIVARIATE   computes univariate statistics including quantiles

SUMMARY   outputs descriptive statistics across classifications

FREQ   prints tables of frequency counts, crosstabulations, and bivariate measures of association for categorical variables

TABULATE   prints general tables of descriptive statistics

CORR   computes bivariate correlations and other measures of association for continuous variables.

Another descriptive procedure documented in the reporting section is:

CHART   draws bar charts and other charts of counts, means, or sums.

Comparison of Procedures

There are two basic kinds of variables—categorical and continuous. These two ways of treating values lead to two fundamental SAS descriptive procedures, PROC FREQ and PROC MEANS. The FREQ procedure collects frequency counts for categorical variables. The MEANS procedure accumulates means, standard deviations, and other statistics for continuous variables.

If you need a series of means for sub-groups of observations, you can use MEANS with a BY statement to control the classification. However, BY-group processing requires sorting the data set, which can be expensive for large data sets. Two other procedures, SUMMARY and TABULATE, can produce means across a classification without sorting. PROC SUMMARY is used to reduce a large amount of data to statistics placed on a SAS data set. PROC TABULATE is specialized for presenting descriptive statistics in hierarchical crosstabulations for either continuous or categorical variables.

Quantile statistics are much more expensive to compute than moment statistics like the mean and standard deviation. MEANS, SUMMARY, and TABULATE are unable to compute medians and other quantiles. You can use the UNIVARIATE procedure when you need selected quantiles and other distributional details. If you want a complete ranking of the data for computing other quantile statistics, then use PROC RANK.

In addition to these procedures, graphical procedures, such as CHART, can also effectively present descriptive statistics.

In addition to univariate statistics, bivariate statistics are available to measure the association between pairs of variables. For categorical variables, the FREQ procedure produces crosstabulations with chi-square and other bivariate test statistics. For continuous variables, the CORR procedure computes correlations and several other measures of association.

Keywords for Univariate Descriptive Statistics

A standardized set of keywords is used to refer to the univariate descriptive statistics in SAS procedures. These keywords are used in SAS statements to request statistics for printing or storing on an output data set.

Define the following:

x_i = the ith nonmissing observation on the variable
z_i = $(x_i - MEAN)/STD$ standardized variables.

Then define the keyword statistics:

N	number of nonmissing observations
NMISS	number of missing observations
MIN	minimum value
MAX	maximum value
RANGE	MAX–MIN, the range from minimum to maximum
SUM	Σx_i, the total
MEAN	SUM/N, the arithmetic mean
USS	Σx_i^2, uncorrected sum of squares
CSS	USS–MEAN^{2}N, sum of squares corrected for the mean
VAR	CSS/(N–1), the sample variance
STD	sqrt(VAR), the sample standard deviation
STDERR	STD/sqrtN, standard error of the mean
CV	(STD/MEAN)×100, coefficient of variation
SKEWNESS	$\Sigma z_i^3 \times N/(N-1)(N-2)$, measures sidedness
KURTOSIS	$\Sigma z_i^4 \times N(N+1)/(N-1)(N-2)(N-3) - 3(N-1)^2/(N-2)(N-3)$, measures tail heaviness
T	MEAN/STDERR, Student's t for H0: mean=0
PRT	$1 - 2 \times PROBT(T,N-1)$, probability of (abs(T), N–1), the absolute t under the null hypothesis..

Data Requirements for Univariate Statistics

Statistics are reported as missing if they cannot be computed. N and NMISS do not require any nonmissing observations. SUM, MEAN, MAX, MIN, RANGE, USS, and CSS require only one nonmissing observation. The requirements for other statistics are:

- VAR, STD, STDERR, CV, T, and PRT require at least 2 observations.
- SKEWNESS requires at least 3 observations.
- KURTOSIS requires at least 4 observations.
- SKEWNESS, KURTOSIS, T, and PRT require STD>0.
- CV requires MEAN≠0.

Statistics and Procedures Checklist

This table shows which procedures compute each statistic.

```
                statistic                    s k            q
                                             k u            u
                                       s     e r         m a
                                  r    t     w t         e n
                             m    a    d     n o         d t m
                             e s m m n u c v s e        e s p i i o
                             a u i a g s s a t r        c s r a l d
      procedure             n m n x e s s r d v        s s t n e e
      ──────────
      MEANS                 X X X X X X X X X X X X X
      UNIVARIATE            X X X X X X X X X X X X X X X X X X X
      SUMMARY               X X X X X X X X X X        X X
      TABULATE              X X X X X X X X X X X       X X
      CHART                 X X
```

BACKGROUND: UNIVARIATE CONTINUOUS DATA

Descriptive statistics for a sample can provide information about the distribution of a population: its location, variability, and shape. For example, data on students in a class for whom you have measures of height and weight (the sample) can be used to infer the height and weight distribution of all students in the school (the population).

Measures of Location

Measures of location include the mean, the mode, and the median.

Mean　The mean of a variable is its expected value (called the *first moment*):

$$\text{mean}(x) = \mu = E(x) \ .$$

　The sample mean of a variable is the arithmetic average of all values of that variable in the sample, that is, the sum of all values x_i divided by the total number of values, n. The sample mean, (denoted $\bar{x}$) estimates the true mean:

$$\text{MEAN} = \bar{x} = \Sigma x_i / n \ .$$

Mode　The mode is the value at which the density of the distribution is at a maximum. Some distributions have more than one mode. The sample mode is the value that occurs most often in the sample. For a distribution with multiple modes, the common convention is to select the lowest mode for reporting. If the distribution is continuous, then all values occur once and the sample mode has little use.

Median　The median is the value above and below which half the density falls. The sample median is the middle value when the measurements are arranged in ascending or descending order. For an even number of observations, the midpoint between the two middle values is usually reported as the median.

Measures of Variability

Another group of statistics important for studying a variable's distribution measures the *variability*, or spread, of values.

Range   The simplest statistic in this category is the range, the difference between the highest and the lowest value, telling you nothing about the distribution of values between the maximum and minimum.

Variance   A statistic that gives more information about the distribution is the variance. The variance is the expected value of the squared difference of the values from their mean:

$$var(x) = \sigma^2 = E(x - E(x))^2 \ .$$

The sample variance is computed by first subtracting the sample mean from each value, squaring these differences, adding them up, and dividing the sum by the number of values minus 1. This sample variance, denoted s^2, is an unbiased estimate of the population variance σ^2:

$$VAR(x) = s^2 = \Sigma(x_i - \overline{x})^2/(n-1) \ .$$

It is clear from this formula that when all the values lie close to the mean, the variance is small; when values are more scattered, the variance is large.

Standard Deviation   The square root of the variance is the standard deviation, which is denoted σ. An estimate of the standard deviation is given by the sample standard deviation, which is the square root of the sample variance:

$$STD(x) = s = \sqrt{(s^2)} \ .$$

This statistic s (keyword STD) is expressed in the same units as the observations themselves, rather than in the units squared.

Distributions and Tests

Normal distribution   If your data have a normal distribution, you only need the mean and standard deviation to completely characterize the distribution of values. If your data are normally distributed, approximately two-thirds of the values in a sample fall within one standard deviation of the mean. Approximately 95% of the values fall within two standard deviations of the mean.

Distribution of the sample mean   If many samples of size n are drawn from a population with mean μ and standard deviation σ, then these sample means together form a new distribution. The mean of the sample of means is still μ, but the standard deviation of the distribution of means is smaller than the standard deviation of the population. The standard deviation of the sample of means, the *standard error of the mean* (keyword STDERR), is calculated by

$$\sigma/n \ .$$

It is estimated in a sample by

$$s/n \ .$$

Testing hypotheses about the mean   You can test the hypothesis that the mean in the population is some value by using the Student's t statistic. The test statistic for the null hypothesis that the mean is some value μ_0 is constructed:

$$t = (\bar{x} - \mu_0)/(s/n) \quad,$$

which is the difference between the sample mean and the hypothesized mean divided by the standard error of the mean. This statistic has a Student's t distribution under the null hypothesis. Many SAS procedures print out the t statistic for the hypothesis that the mean is zero (keyword T, labeled T FOR H0:MEAN=0) and a two-tailed significance probability (keyword PRT, labeled PROB>|T|).

Coefficient of variation   The coefficient of variation is a unitless measure of variation in the population. It is calculated by dividing the standard deviation by the mean and expressing the result as a percentage. The coefficient of variation is meaningful only for variables that are measured on at least a ratio scale.

Quantiles   Percentiles are useful for studying the variability in large samples. For a set of measurements arranged in order of magnitude, the pth percentile is the value that has $p\%$ of the measurements below it and $(100-p)\%$ above it. The median is the 50th percentile. Since it may not be possible to divide your data so that you get exactly the desired percentile, a more precise definition is used (see the UNIVARIATE procedure).

The upper quartile of a distribution is the value below which 75% of the measurements fall (the 75th percentile). Twenty- five percent of the measurements fall below the lower quartile value. The interquartile range is the difference between the upper and lower quartiles. Selected percentiles and quartiles are calculated by the UNIVARIATE procedure. The RANK procedure can calculate any quantile statistic.

Measures of Shape

Skewness   Sometimes a distribution is not symmetric; values are distributed differently below the mean than above the mean. For example, a few very large values may exert a disproportionate influence on the calculation of the mean compared to a larger number of values in the distribution close to the mean. A histogram of such data may look like this:

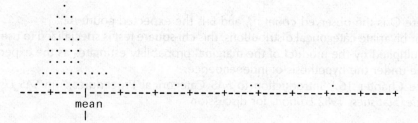

This distribution is said to be "skewed." Since the tail of values occurs in the values larger than the mean, the distribution is positively skewed, or skewed to the right. If the tail occurs in the smallest values, the distribution is negatively skewed, or skewed to the left. The statistic that measures skewness is calculated:

$$[n/(n-1)(n-2)] \sum_{i=1}^{n} (x_i - \bar{x})^3/s^3 \quad.$$

Kurtosis   Another characteristic of a distribution, kurtosis is a measure of the extent of the heaviness of the tails of a distribution. The measure of kurtosis for a normally distributed population is zero. A heavy tailed distribution (like the double exponential) has positive kurtosis. Flat distributions with short tails (like the UNIFORM) have negative kurtosis. When almost all of the data values appear very close to the mean, the kurtosis is negative. SAS uses the formula below to measure kurtosis:

$$\text{Kurtosis} = [n(n+1)/(n-1)(n-2)(n-3)]\sum_{i=1}^{n}(x_i-\bar{x})^4/s^4 - 3(n-1)(n-1)/(n-2)(n-3) \ .$$

These statistics for higher moments (skewness and kurtosis) are often avoided, since they are relatively unstable. Trust them only if you have a very large sample, or if the distribution is known to be well behaved. Procedures that calculate measures of the skewness and kurtosis of a distribution are UNIVARIATE and MEANS.

BACKGROUND: CATEGORICAL DATA

Count Data   The basic statistics for categorical data are frequency counts and percentages. If a categorical variable can be considered a random response parameterized by the probabilities for each level occurring, then the frequency counts have a multinomial distribution. To estimate the response probabilities π_i, divide each count n_i by the total n

$$p_i = n_i/n \ .$$

Distribution   Though the counts n_i and the portions $p_i=n_i/n$ have a discrete distribution, a continuous normal approximation is used to approximate it in order to form test statistics. As n gets large, the distribution of $p_i=n_i/n$ approaches a normal distribution with mean π_i and variance $\pi_i(1-\pi_i)/n$ (Rao, 1965, p. 316–347).

Tests   This normal approximation is used in the construction of test statistics. The most popular of these is a chi-square goodness-of-fit test for frequency counts (Pearson, 1900). This test is computed:

$$\chi^2 = \Sigma(n_i-n\pi_i)^2/n\pi_i = \Sigma(O-E)^2/E$$

where O is the observed count n_i, and E is the expected count $n\pi_i$.

For bivariate categorical distributions, this chi-square test is specialized to use the n multiplied by the product of the marginal probability estimates as the expected value under the hypothesis of independence.

See Chapter 16, "Introduction to SAS Categorical Procedures," in *SAS User's Guide: Statistics, 1982 Edition,* for discussion.

BACKGROUND: BIVARIATE MEASURES

Bivariate statistics measure how two variables relate to each other. Bivariate measures for continuous variables are available in PROC CORR. These include correlations, rank correlations, and measures of concordance. Bivariate measures for categorical variables are available in PROC FREQ. These include chi-square tests of independence, and various measures of association. These measures are discussed in detail in the CORR and FREQ procedure descriptions.

REFERENCES

Pearson, K. (1900), *Phil. Mag. Ser. (5)*, 50, 157–172.
Rao, C.R. (1965), *Linear Statistical Inference and Its Application*, John Wiley & Sons.

500

The CORR Procedure

ABSTRACT

The CORR procedure computes correlation coefficients between variables, including Pearson product-moment and weighted product-moment correlations. Two nonparametric measures of association (Spearman's rank-order correlation and Kendall's tau-b) can also be produced. CORR also computes some univariate descriptive statistics.

INTRODUCTION

Correlation measures the closeness of a linear relationship between two variables. If one variable x can be expressed exactly as a linear function of another variable y, then the correlation is 1 or –1, depending on whether the two variables are directly related or inversely related. A correlation of 0 between two variables means that each variable has no linear predictive ability for the other. If the values are normally distributed, then a correlation of 0 means that the variables are independent.

The true product-moment correlation (Pearson), denoted ϱ_{xy}, is defined:

$$\varrho_{xy} = \text{cov}(x,y)/\sqrt{\text{var}(x)\text{var}(y)}$$
$$= E((x - Ex)(y - Ey))/\sqrt{(E(x - Ex)^2 E(y - Ey)^2)}.$$

The sample correlation estimates the true correlation. It is computed:

$$r_{xy} = \Sigma(x - \bar{x})(y - \bar{y})/\sqrt{(\Sigma(x - \bar{x})^2 \Sigma(y - \bar{y})^2)}$$

where $\bar{x}$ and $\bar{y}$ are the sample means of x and y.

The full name of this statistic is the *Pearson product-moment correlation*.

For example, Figure 1 is a scatterplot of the variables x and y, whose correlation is close to zero, $r = .02$.

When variables are highly correlated, their points tend to fall on or near a line of fit. x and z have a correlation r of .81, as in Figure 2.

If the variables are negatively correlated, the line of fit has a negative slope; in other words, the variables are related inversely such that high values of one variable tend to occur with low values of the other. This is the case in Figure 3 with z and y, which have a correlation r of –.57.

Correlations among a set of variables are statistics that contain sufficient information for computing regressions, partial correlations, canonical correlations, factor patterns, principal component coefficients, and many other statistics.

In addition to correlations, several other statistics have been proposed to measure association between two continuous variables. Spearman's rank order correlation coefficient is a nonparametric measure that is calculated as the correlation of the ranks of the data. Kendall's tau-b is a measure calculated from concordances and discordances. Concordance is measured by determining for pairs of observations whether values of two variables vary together (in concord) or differently (in discord).

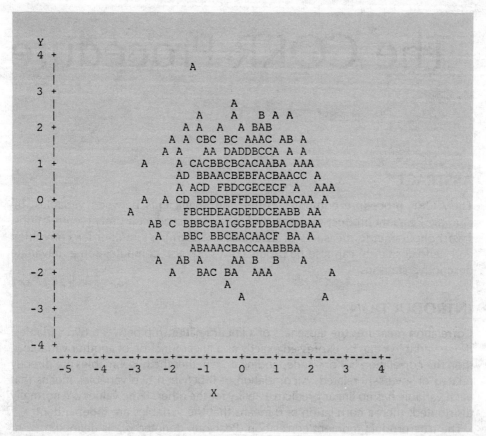

Fig. 1

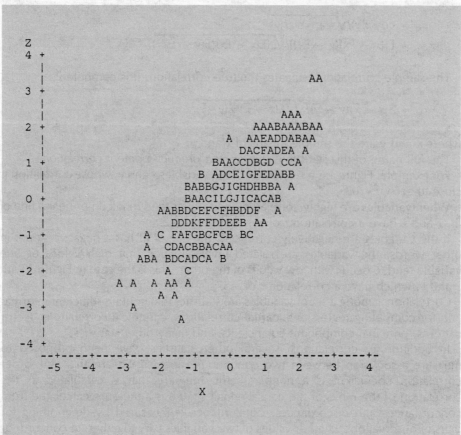

Fig. 2

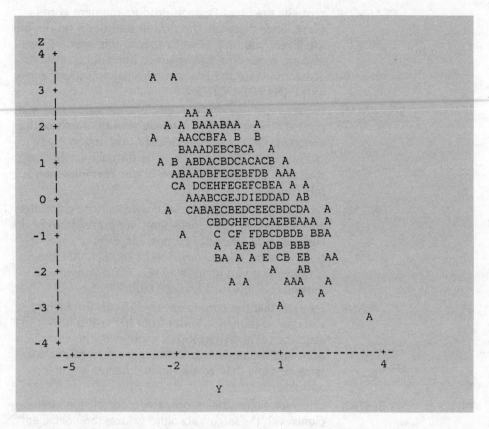

Fig. 3

SPECIFICATIONS

The following statements can be used in the CORR procedure:

PROC CORR *options;*
   VAR *variables;*
   WITH *variables;*
   WEIGHT *variable;*
   FREQ *variable;*
   BY *variables;*

The PROC CORR statement invokes the procedure. VAR and WITH statements are used to specify variables for the analysis. WEIGHT, FREQ, and BY statements are optional.

There is no fixed order for statements following the PROC CORR statement.

PROC CORR Statement

The PROC CORR statement has the form:

PROC CORR *options;*

The options that may appear in the PROC CORR statement are given below. If no options are specified, CORR calculates Pearson product-moment correlations and significance probabilities, printing them in a rectangular table along with univariate statistics.

DATA=*SASdataset*   gives the name of the SAS data set to be used by PROC CORR. If it is omitted, the most recently created SAS data set is used.

PEARSON requests the usual Pearson product-moment correlations. Since these are the default statistics if no options are given, you only need to specify this option if you also are requesting Spearman or Kendall correlations. The formula for the Pearson correlation is given above in the **INTRODUCTION**.

SPEARMAN requests that Spearman coefficients be calculated and printed. These are the correlations of the ranks of the variables. Do not use the SPEARMAN option if you include a WEIGHT statement. The formula for the Spearman rank correlation is given under **Formulas** later in this chapter.

KENDALL requests that Kendall's tau-b coefficients be calculated and printed. Kendall coefficients are correlations of the signs of comparisons of all possible pairs of observations in terms of concordances. The KENDALL option is not valid if you include a WEIGHT statement. See **Formulas** below for Kendall's tau-b.

RANK requests that the correlation coefficients for each variable be printed in order from highest to lowest in absolute value. When RANK is omitted, the correlations and the other two statistics are printed in a rectangular table defined by variable names at the top and side.

BEST=n prints for each variable only the n correlation coefficients with the largest absolute values; the coefficients are printed in descending order.

NOSIMPLE suppresses printing the simple descriptive statistics for each variable.

NOPRINT suppresses printing the correlations. This option is used when the only purpose of using CORR is to create an output data set containing correlations.

NOPROB suppresses the printing of significance probabilities associated with the correlations.

NOMISS specifies that an observation with a missing value for any variable previously used in the analysis be dropped from all calculations. Otherwise, CORR includes observations that have nonmissing values for pairs. Specifying NOMISS may be much faster and cheaper.

SSCP requests that the sums of squares and crossproducts (SSCP) be printed. If both SSCP and OUTP= (below) are specified, the output data set contains the SSCP matrix as well as the correlation matrix. For the SSCP observations, the __TYPE__ variable's value is SSCP.
    The SSCP option is only meaningful with the PEARSON option; do not use with SPEARMAN or KENDALL.

COV requests that covariances be printed. If COV and OUTP= (below) are both specified, the output data set contains the covariance matrix as well as the correlation matrix. For the observations containing the covariance matrix, the __TYPE__ variable's value is

COV. The COV option is only meaningful with the PEARSON option; do not use with SPEARMAN or KENDALL.

NOCORR specifies that correlations not be output to the output data set. If NOCORR is specified, the data set does not contain correlations, but PROC CORR still makes the data set TYPE=CORR. You can change the data set type to COV or SSCP by using the TYPE= data set option:

PROC CORR NOCORR COV OUT=B(TYPE=COV);

OUTP=*SASdataset* requests that CORR create a new SAS data set containing Pearson correlations. The new data set is TYPE=CORR and includes means, standard deviations, simple statistics, and correlation coefficients. The example at the end of this chapter lists a TYPE=CORR data set. If you want to create a permanent SAS data set, you must specify a two-level name (see Chapter 12, ''SAS Data Sets,'' in *SAS User's Guide: Basics, 1982 Edition*, for more information on permanent SAS data sets. Also see **Output Data Sets** at the end of this chapter for a complete description of the data set's structure.

OUTS=*SASdataset* requests that CORR create a new SAS data set containing Spearman correlations. OUTS= is similar in other respects to OUTP=.

OUTK=*SASdataset* requests that CORR create a new SAS data set containing Kendall correlations. OUTK= is similar in other respects to OUTP= and OUTS=.

VAR Statement

VAR *variables*;

The names of the variables to be correlated are listed in the VAR statement. If you omit the VAR statement, CORR calculates correlations between all the numeric variables in the input data set.

For example, the statements

PROC CORR;
  VAR A B C;

produce correlation coefficients between three pairs of variables: A and B, A and C, B and C.

WITH Statement

WITH *variables*;

If you want correlations for specific combinations of variables, list the variables in the VAR statement that you want on the top of the printed correlation matrix and list in the WITH statement variables you want on the side of the correlation matrix.

For example, the statements

```
PROC CORR;
  VAR A B;
  WITH X Y Z;
```

produce correlations for these combinations:

A and X   B and X
A and Y   B and Y
A and Z   B and Z .

WEIGHT Statement

WEIGHT *variable*;

If you want to compute weighted product-moment correlation coefficients, give the name of the weighting variable in a WEIGHT statement. A WEIGHT statement should only be used with Pearson correlations; Spearman and Kendall options are not valid with a WEIGHT statement.

FREQ Statement

FREQ *variable*;

If one variable in your input data set represents the frequency of occurrence for values of another variable in the observation, include the variable's name in a FREQ statement. CORR then treats the data set as if each observation appeared n times, where n is the value of the FREQ variable for the observation. The total number of observations is considered equal to the sum of the FREQ variable when CORR calculates significance probabilities. WEIGHT and FREQ statements have similar effects except in calculating degrees of freedom.

BY Statement

BY *variables*;

A BY statement may be used with PROC CORR to obtain separate analyses on observations in groups defined by the BY variables. When a BY statement appears, the procedure expects the input data set to be sorted in order of the BY variables. If your input data set is not sorted in ascending order, use the SORT procedure with a similar BY statement to sort the data, or, if appropriate, use the BY statement options NOTSORTED or DESCENDING. For more information, see the discussion of the BY statement in Chapter 8, "Statements Used in the PROC Step," in *SAS User's Guide: Basics, 1982 Edition*.

DETAILS

Missing Values

The default method of handling missing values is to use all the nonmissing pairs of values for each pair of variables. This means that some correlations are computed using more observations than others.

An alternative method is available with the NOMISS option, which uses an observation only if none of the variables is missing.

There are two strong reasons for specifying NOMISS and avoiding the pairwise default method. First, this method is much more efficient computationally. Second, if the correlations are used as input to regression or other statistical procedures, a pairwise-missing correlation matrix leads to several statistical difficulties. Pairwise correlation matrices may not be positive definite. The pattern of missing values may bias the results.

Output Data Sets

Output data sets are requested by the OUTP=, OUTS=, and OUTK= specifications on the PROC CORR statement. OUTS= and OUTK= produce SAS data sets with Spearman and Kendall correlations, respectively, and these are valid only if the SPEARMAN or KENDALL options are given. The data sets are marked with the special data set name TYPE=CORR. This type of data set is recognized by many SAS procedures, including REG and FACTOR.

The variables on the data set are:

- BY variables
- __TYPE__, identifying the type of observation
- __NAME__, identifying variable names
- the variables listed on the VAR statement.

The observations, as identified by __TYPE__, are:

- MEAN, the mean of each variable
- STD, the standard deviation of each variable
- N, the number of nonmissing observations for each variable.

The following kinds of observations are further identified by the combination of the variables __TYPE__ and __NAME__.

- SSCP, the crossproducts (if the SSCP option is given)
- COV, the covariances (if the COV option is given)
- CORR, a sequence of observations containing correlations.

Formulas

The formula for the Spearman correlation is

$$\varrho = \frac{\Sigma(r_i - \bar{r})(s_i - \bar{s})}{\sqrt{(\Sigma(r_i - \bar{r})^2 \Sigma(s_i - \bar{s})^2)}}$$

where r_i is the rank of the ith x value, s_i is the rank of the ith y value, and $\bar{r}$ and $\bar{s}$ are the means of the r_i and s_i values, respectively. Averaged ranks are used in the case of ties.

The formula for Kendall's tau-b is

$$\tau = \frac{\Sigma_{i<j} \text{sgn}(x_i - x_j) \, \text{sgn}(y_i - y_j)}{\sqrt{((n(n-1)/2 - \Sigma t_i(t_i-1))(n(n-1)/2 - \Sigma u_i(u_i-1)))}}$$

where the t_i (the u_i) are the number of tied x (respectively y) values in the ith group of tied x (respectively y) values, n is the number of observations, and sgn(z) = 1 if z>0, 0 if z=0, and -1 if z<0.

Computational Method

For the Spearman or Kendall correlations the data are first truncated to single precision (approximately seven decimal digits) and then ranked. The Spearman correlation is then computed on the ranks using the formula for the Pearson correlation. Averaged ranks are used in case of ties. The Kendall correlation is computed using a method similar to Knight (1966). Briefly, the method proceeds in this way: observations are ranked in order according to values of the first variable; the observations are then re-ranked according to values of the second variable; and the number of interchanges of the first variable that occur is noted and used to compute Kendall's tau-b.

Probability values for the Pearson and Spearman correlations are obtained by treating $(n-2)^{1/2}p/(1-p^2)^{1/2}$ as coming from a t distribution with $n-2$ degrees of freedom, where p is the appropriate correlation. The probability values for the Kendall correlations are obtained by treating $s/(\text{var}(s))^{1/2}$ as coming from a normal distribution where

$$s = \Sigma_{i<j}\text{sgn}(x_i-x_j)\text{sgn}(y_i-y_j)$$

and where x_i are the values of the first variable, y_i are the values of the second variable. The variance of s is computed as (Noether, 1967):

$$((2n+5)(n-1)n - \Sigma_i t_i(t_i-1)(2t_i+5) - \Sigma_i u_i(u_i-1)(2u_i+5))/18$$
$$+ (\Sigma_i t_i(t_i-1)(t_i-2))(\Sigma u_i(u_i-1)(u_i-2))/(9n(n-1)(n-2))$$
$$+ (\Sigma t_i(t_i-1))(\Sigma u_i(u_i-1)) /(2n(n-1))$$

where the sums are over tied groups of values, t_i is the number of tied x values, and u_i is the number of tied y values.

Computer Resources

Let K denote the number of correlations to be computed. Then if n, the number of observations, is large, the cputime required varies linearly in n and linearly in K when only Pearson correlations are requested. If Spearman correlations are requested, the cputime varies as $n\log n$ times the number of variables involved. If Kendall correlations are requested, the cputime scales as $n\log n$ times K.

If n is small and K is large, the cputime scales as K for all of the types of correlations.

Resources for Spearman or Kendall options   For the most time-efficient processing, the amount of temporary storage needed in bytes is

    8*V*W*C + N*(28+8*NV)

where

    V is the number of variables in the VAR list (or the number of
        numeric variables if the VAR list is omitted),
    W is the number of variables in the WITH list (or is equal to V if there
        is no WITH list),
    C is the number of types of correlations desired,
    N is the number of observations, and
    NV is V if there is no WITH list and V+W if there is a WITH list.

The minimum temporary storage needed to process the data is

8*V*W*C + 44*N.

Resources for Pearson correlations alone If only Pearson correlations are requested, the resource use is somewhat different. For time-efficient processing, memory for temporary storage should be at least M, where

M = K*8 if the NOMISS option is specified
  = K*60+V*8 otherwise

where

K = V*W if a WITH list is used
K = $V^2/2$ if not.

If M bytes are not available, CORR must pass through the data several times to collect all the statistics. If this happens, CORR prints a note suggesting a larger memory region.
  Cputime varies with D*N*K, where D is much smaller if NOMISS is given than if not given. Without NOMISS, processing is much faster if most of the observations have no missing values.

Printed Output

For each variable, CORR prints:

1. the VARIABLE name
2. N, the number of observations having non-missing values of the variable
3. the MEAN
4. STD DEV, the standard deviation
5. the MEDIAN, if the SPEARMAN or KENDALL option is specified
6. the MINIMUM value
7. the MAXIMUM value
8. the SUM, if only Pearson product-moment correlations are calculated (not shown).

For each pair of variables, CORR prints:

9. the SPEARMAN, KENDALL, and PEARSON correlation coefficients that were requested
10. N, the number of observations used to calculate the coefficient; if a FREQ statement is used, this number is the sum of the frequency variable
11. PROB>|R|, the significance probability of the correlation; this probability is approximate for Spearman and Kendall correlations.

Among its optional features, CORR can:

12. print only the correlations requested with no simple statistics (the NOSIMPLE option)
13. produce the correlations for specific combinations of variables (the WITH statement)
14. produce a specially structured SAS data set containing a correlation matrix, which can be used as input to the FACTOR and SYSREG procedures, among others.

EXAMPLE

In this example PROC CORR is called three times: (1) to obtain all three kinds of measures of association; (2) to show a rectangular correlation matrix; and (3) to show an output data set with covariances as well as correlations.

```
*--- DATA COURTESY A.C. LINNERUD, N.C. STATE UNIV.;
DATA SKINFOLD;
   INPUT CHEST ABDOMEN ARM @@;
   CARDS;
09.0 12.0 3.0 20.0 20.0 7.5 10.0 23.0 6.0 12.0  6.0 5.0
08.5 15.0 3.0 12.0 17.0 4.0 11.0 13.0 6.0 05.0 14.0 3.0
13.0 19.0 3.0 22.0 20.0 6.0 10.5 12.0 3.5 17.0 15.0 4.5
10.0  7.0 4.0 17.0 28.0 5.5 15.0 15.5 3.0 16.0 11.0 3.0
07.0 13.0 2.5 16.0 18.0 3.0 09.0 12.5 5.0 17.5 18.0 3.0
15.5 28.5 5.0 21.0 27.5 6.0 23.0 24.0 6.5 11.5 15.0 3.0
22.5 20.0 4.5 13.0 14.0 4.0 14.0 21.0 2.5 04.0  3.0 2.0
05.5  8.5 3.0 21.0 13.0 9.0 16.0 11.0 3.0 17.5 15.0 4.5
25.0 35.0 6.5 21.0  6.0 3.5 16.5 17.0 4.0 09.5 11.5 2.5
15.0 19.0 4.0 13.5  6.5 3.5 16.0 15.0 3.0 26.0 38.0 4.0
12.5 20.0 3.0 05.0  7.5 3.5 12.0 15.0 3.5 15.0 13.0 4.5
17.0 19.5 5.0 16.0 20.0 5.5 09.0  4.0 2.0 19.0 12.0 3.0
16.0 17.5 6.0 14.5 14.5 4.0
;

PROC CORR PEARSON SPEARMAN KENDALL;
   VAR CHEST ABDOMEN ARM;
   TITLE SPEARMAN''S RHO, KENDALL''S TAU-B & PEARSON''S CORRELATIONS;

PROC CORR DATA=SKINFOLD NOSIMPLE;
   VAR ABDOMEN ARM;
   WITH CHEST;
   TITLE RECTANGULAR CORRELATION MATRIX;

PROC CORR DATA=SKINFOLD COV OUTP=CORROUT;
   VAR CHEST ABDOMEN ARM;
   TITLE COVARIANCES AND CORRELATIONS;
PROC PRINT DATA=CORROUT;
   TITLE2 OUTPUT DATASET FROM PROC CORR;
```

① VARIABLE	② N	③ MEAN	④ STD DEV	⑤ MEDIAN	⑥ MINIMUM	⑦ MAXIMUM
SPEARMAN'S RHO, KENDALL'S TAU-B & PEARSON'S CORRELATIONS						1
CHEST	50	14.41000000	5.25637611	15.00000000	4.00000000	26.00000000
ABDOMEN	50	16.01000000	7.19090270	15.00000000	3.00000000	38.00000000
ARM	50	4.15000000	1.48547388	4.00000000	2.00000000	9.00000000

(continued on next page)

(continued from previous page)

PEARSON CORRELATION COEFFICIENTS / PROB > |R| UNDER H0:RHO=0 / N = 50 ⑩

	CHEST	ABDOMEN	ARM
CHEST	1.00000	0.61986	0.52973
	0.0000	0.0001	0.0001
ABDOMEN	0.61986	1.00000	0.42925
	0.0001	0.0000	0.0019
ARM	0.52973	0.42925	1.00000
	0.0001	0.0019	0.0000

⑨ ⑪

SPEARMAN CORRELATION COEFFICIENTS / PROB > |R| UNDER H0:RHO=0 / N = 50

	CHEST	ABDOMEN	ARM
CHEST	1.00000	0.54825	0.51761
	0.0000	0.0001	0.0001
ABDOMEN	0.54825	1.00000	0.45687
	0.0001	0.0000	0.0009
ARM	0.51761	0.45687	1.00000
	0.0001	0.0009	0.0000

SPEARMAN'S RHO, KENDALL'S TAU-B & PEARSON'S CORRELATIONS   2

KENDALL TAU B CORRELATION COEFFICIENTS / PROB > |R| UNDER H0:RHO=0 / N = 50

	CHEST	ABDOMEN	ARM
CHEST	1.00000	0.41246	0.38974
	0.0000	0.0000	0.0002
ABDOMEN	0.41246	1.00000	0.33048
	0.0000	0.0000	0.0015
ARM	0.38974	0.33048	1.00000
	0.0002	0.0015	0.0000

⑫ RECTANGULAR CORRELATION MATRIX   3

CORRELATION COEFFICIENTS / PROB > |R| UNDER H0:RHO=0 / N = 50

	ABDOMEN	ARM
CHEST	0.61986	0.52973 ⑬
	0.0001	0.0001

COVARIANCES AND CORRELATIONS   4

COVARIANCE MATRIX

	CHEST	ABDOMEN	ARM
CHEST	27.6295	23.4295	4.13622
ABDOMEN	23.4295	51.7091	4.5852
ARM	4.13622	4.5852	2.20663

COVARIANCES AND CORRELATIONS   5

VARIABLE	N	MEAN	STD DEV	SUM	MINIMUM	MAXIMUM
CHEST	50	14.41000000	5.25637611	720.50000000	4.00000000	26.00000000
ABDOMEN	50	16.01000000	7.19090270	800.50000000	3.00000000	38.00000000
ARM	50	4.15000000	1.48547388	207.50000000	2.00000000	9.00000000

CORRELATION COEFFICIENTS / PROB > |R| UNDER H0:RHO=0 / N = 50

	CHEST	ABDOMEN	ARM
CHEST	1.00000	0.61986	0.52973
	0.0000	0.0001	0.0001
ABDOMEN	0.61986	1.00000	0.42925
	0.0001	0.0000	0.0019
ARM	0.52973	0.42925	1.00000
	0.0001	0.0019	0.0000

(14) COVARIANCES AND CORRELATIONS   6
      OUTPUT DATASET FROM PROC CORR

OBS	_TYPE_	_NAME_	CHEST	ABDOMEN	ARM
1	COV	CHEST	27.6295	23.4295	4.1362
2	COV	ABDOMEN	23.4295	51.7091	4.5852
3	COV	ARM	4.1362	4.5852	2.2066
4	MEAN		14.4100	16.0100	4.1500
5	STD		5.2564	7.1909	1.4855
6	N		50.0000	50.0000	50.0000
7	CORR	CHEST	1.0000	0.6199	0.5297
8	CORR	ABDOMEN	0.6199	1.0000	0.4292
9	CORR	ARM	0.5297	0.4292	1.0000

REFERENCES

Noether, G.E. (1967), *Elements of Nonparametric Statistics*, New York: John Wiley & Sons.

Knight, W.E. (1966), "A Computer Method for Calculating Kendall's Tau with Ungrouped Data," *Journal of the American Statistical Association*, 61, 436–439.

The FREQ Procedure

ABSTRACT

The FREQ procedure produces one-way to *n*-way frequency and crosstabulation tables.

INTRODUCTION

Frequency tables show the distribution of variable values; for example, a variable A has six possible values. The frequency table for A shows how many observations in the data set have the first value of A, how many have the second value, and so on.

Crosstabulation tables show combined frequency distributions for two or more variables. For example, a crosstabulation table for the variables SEX and EMPLOY shows the number of observations for working females, the number for non-working females, the number for working males, and the number for non-working males.

Other features of FREQ:

- a variable in the data set may be used as a weighting variable
- for two-way tables, FREQ computes several measures of association
- results can be output to a SAS data set.

One-Way Frequencies

If you want a one-way frequency table, simply name the variable in a TABLES statement. For example, the statements

```
PROC FREQ;
   TABLES A;
```

produce a one-way frequency table giving the values of A and the number of observations corresponding to each A value.

Two-Way Crosstabulation Tables

If you want a crosstabulation table, give the two variables for the table, separating the names with an asterisk (*). Values of the first variable form the rows of the table, values of the second variable form the columns. For example, the statements

```
PROC FREQ;
   TABLES A*B;
```

produce a crosstabulation table with values of A down the side and values of B across the top.

N-Way Crosstabulation Tables

If you want a three-way (or *n*-way) crosstabulation table, join the three (or *n*) variables with asterisks. Values of the last variable form the columns, values of the next-to-last variable form the rows. A separate table is produced for each level (or combination of levels) of the other variables. For example, the statements

```
PROC FREQ;
  TABLES A*B*C;
```

produce *n* tables, where *n* is the number of different values for the variable A. Each table has the values of B down the side and the values of C across the top. There is no limit to the number of dimensions that a crosstabulation table may have.

Note: multi-way tables can generate a great deal of printed output. For example, if the variables A, B, C, D, and E each have ten levels, requesting five-way tables of A*B*C*D*E generates 1000 pages of output.

PROC FREQ Contrasted with Other SAS Procedures

Many other procedures in SAS can collect frequency counts. PROC FREQ is distinguished by its ability to compute chi-square tests and measures of association for two-way tables. Other procedures to consider for counting are: TABULATE for more general table layouts, SUMMARY for output data sets, CHART for bar charts and other graphical representations, and FUNCAT for statistical analysis of categorical models.

SPECIFICATIONS

The statements available in PROC FREQ are:

PROC FREQ *options*;
  TABLES *requests / options*;
  WEIGHT *variable*;
  BY *variables*;

PROC FREQ Statement

PROC FREQ *options*;

The options that may be used in the PROC FREQ statement are:

DATA=*SASdataset*	specifies the data set to be used by PROC FREQ. If the DATA= option is omitted, FREQ uses the most recently created data set.
ORDER=FREQ ORDER=DATA ORDER=INTERNAL ORDER=FORMATTED	requests the order in which you want the levels to be reported. If ORDER=FREQ, levels are ordered by descending frequency count so that levels with the most observations come first. If ORDER=DATA, levels are put in the order in which they first occur in the input data. If ORDER=INTERNAL, then the levels are ordered by the internal value. If ORDER=FORMATTED, levels are ordered by the external formatted value. If you omit ORDER= or give an unrecognized value, PROC FREQ orders by the internal value.
FORMCHAR=*'string'*	defines the characters used to construct boxes in tables. See the CALENDAR procedure for discussion.

TABLES Statement

TABLES *requests / options*;

For each frequency or crosstabulation table that you want, put a table request in the TABLES statement.

requests   are composed of one or more variable names joined by asterisks. A one-way frequency is generated by each variable name. Two-way crosstabulations are generated by two variables joined with an asterisk. Any number of variables may be joined for a multi-way table. A grouping syntax is also available to make the specifications of many tables easier. Several variables may be put in parentheses and joined to other effects. For example,

TABLES A*(B C);	is equivalent to	TABLES A*B A*C;
TABLES (A B)*(C D);	is equivalent to	TABLES A*C A*D B*C B*D;
TABLES (A B C)*D;	is equivalent to	TABLES A*D B*D C*D;
TABLES A--C;	is equivalent to	TABLES A B C;
TABLES (A--C)*D;	is equivalent to	TABLES A*D B*D C*D;
TABLES A--C*D;	is illegal.	

Any number of requests may be given on one TABLES statement, and any number of TABLES statements may be included in one execution of PROC FREQ.

When no options are included, FREQ produces crosstabulation tables that include cell frequencies, cell percentages of the total frequency, cell percentages of row frequencies, and cell percentages of column frequencies. The options below may be used in the TABLES statement after a slash (/):

EXPECTED   requests that the expected cell frequency under the hypothesis of independence (or homogeneity) be printed.

DEVIATION   requests that FREQ print the deviation of the cell frequency from the expected value.

CELLCHI2   requests that FREQ print the cell's contribution to the total χ^2 statistic. This is computed as *(frequency-expected)**2/expected* and is approximately distributed χ^2 with 1 df.

CHISQ   requests a chi-square (χ^2) test of homogeneity or independence for each two-way table requested in a TABLES statement. For 2 by 2 tables, Fisher's Exact Test is performed. The formula for χ^2 is given in Chapter 17, "Introduction to Descriptive Statistics."

ALL   requests the basic set of measures of association popularized by Goodman and Kruskal for two-way tables, including some of the standard errors, the contingency coefficient, Cramer's V, gamma, Kendall's tau-b, Stuart's tau-c, Somer's D, and lambda asymmetric and symmetric, in addition to Pearson and Spearman correlations. Of course, not all statistics are appropriate for the data in a given table, (See **ALL Option: Measures of Association** below.)

NOFREQ   suppresses printing the cell frequencies for a crosstabulation.

NOPERCENT	suppresses printing the cell percentages for a crosstabulation.
NOROW	suppresses printing the row percentages in cells of a crosstabulation.
NOCOL	suppresses printing the column percentages in cells of a crosstabulation.
CUMCOL	requests cumulative column percentages be printed in the cells.
LIST	prints two-way to *n*-way tables in a list format rather than as crosstabulation tables. Expected cell frequencies are not printed when LIST is specified, even if EXPECTED is specified.
NOCUM	suppresses the cumulative frequencies, percentages, and cumulative percentage columns for one-way frequencies and frequencies in list format when the LIST option is included.
MISSING	asks FREQ to consider missing values like other values in calculations of percents and other statistics.
SPARSE	causes the procedure to write out or print information about all possible combinations of levels of the variables in the table request, even when some combinations of levels do not occur in the data. This option affects printouts under the LIST option and output data sets.
NOPRINT	suppresses all printed output except that controlled by CHISQ and ALL.
OUT=*SASdataset*	sets up an output SAS data set containing variable values and frequency counts. If more than one table request appears in the TABLES statement, the contents of the data set correspond to the last table request in the TABLES statement. For details on the output data set created by PROC FREQ, see **Output Data Set** below. If you want to create a permanent SAS data set, you must specify a two-level name. See Chapter 12, "SAS Data Sets," for more information on permanent SAS data sets.

WEIGHT Statement

WEIGHT *variable*;

Normally, each observation contributes a value of 1 to the frequency counts. However, when a WEIGHT statement appears, each observation contributes the weighting variable's value for that observation. The values do not have to be integers: FREQ uses floating point arithmetic to accumulate the counts or weights. Values are summed and then rounded to integers before printing in crosstabulations; output from the LIST option and the OUT= data set contain decimals.

Only one WEIGHT statement may be used, and that statement applies to counts collected for all tables.

For example, suppose a data set contains variables RACE, SEX, and HRSWORK. The statements

```
PROC FREQ;
  TABLES RACE*SEX;
```

produce a table showing how many black females, black males, white females, and white males are present. The statements

```
PROC FREQ;
  TABLES RACE*SEX;
  WEIGHT HRSWORK;
```

produce a table showing the number of hours worked by black females, by black males, and so on.

BY Statement

> BY *variables*;

A BY statement may be used with PROC FREQ to obtain separate analyses on observations in groups defined by the BY variables. When a BY statement appears, the procedure expects the input data set to be sorted in order of the BY variables. If your input data set is not sorted in ascending order, use the SORT procedure with a similar BY statement to sort the data, or, if appropriate, use the BY statement options NOTSORTED or DESCENDING. For more information, see the discussion of the BY statement in Chapter 8, "Statements Used in the PROC Step."

DETAILS

Missing Values

When a variable has missing values, the missing value frequencies appear in the tables. However, the frequency statistics do not include missing values.

When the MISSING option is specified in the TABLES statement, the statistics for table, row, and column frequencies do include missing values.

Limitations

Any number of TABLES statements may be included after the PROC FREQ statement. Since FREQ builds all the tables requested in all TABLES statements in one pass of the data, efficiency is not sacrificed by multiple TABLES statements.

A TABLES statement may contain any number of table requests, and each request may include any number of variables.

FREQ stores each combination of values in memory. When FREQ is compiling and developing multi-way tables or when some variables have many levels, you may run out of main storage. If increasing the region size is impractical, use PROC SORT to sort the data set by one or more of the variables and then use PROC FREQ with a BY statement that includes the sorted variables.

The FREQ procedure handles both internal and formatted values up to length 16 on both the printout and the output data set. Longer data values are truncated to 16 characters.

Frequency values greater than 9,999,999 are not printed.

For very large, sparse tables or for frequencies above ten million, you should use the SUMMARY procedure instead of FREQ. You may also consider the UNIVARIATE, CHART, and TABULATE procedures for counting applications.

Output Data Set

The new data set produced by PROC FREQ contains one observation for each combination of the variable values in the table request. Each observation contains these variables plus two new variables, COUNT and PERCENT, which give respectively the frequency and cell percentage for the combination of variable values.

For example, consider the statements

```
PROC FREQ;
  TABLES A A*B / OUT=D;
```

The output data set D corresponds to the rightmost table request, A*B. If A has two values (1 and 2) and B has three values (1, 2, and 3), the output data set D can have up to six observations, one for each combination of the A and B values that occurs. In observation 1, A=1 and B=1; in observation 2, A=1 and B=2; and so on. The data set also contains the variables COUNT and PERCENT. COUNT's value in each observation is the number of times that each combination of A and B values appears in the input data set; PERCENT's value is the percent of the total number of observations having that A and B combination.

When FREQ collects different class values into the same formatted level, it saves the smallest internal value to output on the output data set.

Computer Resources

PROC FREQ needs to store all the levels in memory, requiring 56 bytes for each level. If FREQ runs out of memory, it quits collecting levels on the variable with the most levels and returns the memory so that counting can continue. The procedure then reports on the tables that do not contain the disabled variables.

For a small number of levels, FREQ is able to collect all statistics in memory. If there are a large number of combinations of levels, FREQ uses a utility file to help collect counts.

Grouping With Formats

When you use PROC FREQ, remember that FREQ groups the variables depending on their formatted values. If you assign a format to a variable with a FORMAT statement, the variable's values are formatted for printing before FREQ divides the observations into groups for the frequency counts.

For example, say a variable X has the values 1.3, 1.7, and 2.0 among others. Each of these values appears as a level in the frequency table. If you want each value rounded to a single digit, you include the statement

```
FORMAT X 1.;
```

after the PROC FREQ statement. The frequency table levels are then 1 and 2.

Formatted character variables are treated in the same way: the formatted values are used to divide the observations into groups. For character variables, formatted or not, only the first 16 characters are used to determine the groups.

You can also use the FORMAT statement to assign formats created by PROC FORMAT to variables. Formats created by PROC FORMAT can serve two uses: they can define the levels, and they can label the levels. You can use the same data with different formats to collect counts on different partitions of the class values. For an example, see Chapter 9, "PROC Step Applications."

In frequency tables, values of both character and numeric variables appear in ascending order by the original (unformatted) values unless you specify otherwise with the ORDER= option.

ALL Option: Measures of Association

The statistics printed by the ALL option in the TABLES statement are useful for indicating the strength of relationship between two categorical variables.

Gamma, Kendall's tau-b, Stuart's tau-c, and Somer's D are rank-order measures based on whether pairs of observations show concordance or discordance.

A pair of observations, i and j on variables X and Y shows concordance if the signs of their differences are the same, that is, when

$$(X_i > Y_i \text{ and } X_j > Y_j) \text{ or}$$
$$(X_i < Y_i \text{ and } X_j < Y_j).$$

A pair of observations shows discordance when the signs of their differences are different, that is, when

$$(X_i > Y_i \text{ and } X_j < Y_j) \text{ or}$$
$$(X_i < Y_i \text{ and } X_j > Y_j).$$

Pairs of observations may also be tied only on X, the independent variable, or tied only on Y, the dependent variable. These statistics differ in how ties are handled and adjustments for table size, which are determined by the number of levels of the variables.

Let the rows of a two-way table be labeled by the values X_i, $i = 1,2,...,r$ and the columns by Y_j, $j = 1,2,...,c$. Let the frequency in a cell in the ith row and the jth column be denoted n_{ij}.

Then define the following:

$$n_{+j} = \Sigma_i n_{ij} \text{ column totals}$$
$$n_{i+} = \Sigma_j n_{ij} \text{ row totals}$$
$$n = \Sigma_{ij} n_{ij} \text{ grand total}$$
$$N = n(n-1)/2 \text{ number of possible pairs}$$
$$= N_C + N_D + N_X + N_Y - N_{XY}$$

N_C the number of concordant pairs

N_D the number of discordant pairs

N_X the number of pairs of observations tied on X

N_Y the number of pairs of observations tied on Y

N_{XY} the number of pairs of observations tied on both X and Y

$$r_i = \max_j(n_{ij}) \text{ row maximums}$$
$$r = \max_j(n_{+j}) \text{ maximum column total}$$
$$c_j = \max_j(n_{ij}) \text{ column maximums}$$
$$c = \max_i(n_{i+}) \text{ maximum row total}$$
$$U(X) = -\Sigma_{i=1}^{R} n_{i+}/n \ln(n_{i+}/n)$$
$$U(Y) = -\Sigma_{j=1}^{R} n_{+j}/n \ln(n_{+j}/n)$$
$$U(XY) = -\Sigma_{ij}^{R} n_{ij}/n \ln(n_{ij}/n)$$

Gamma is based only on the number of concordant and discordant pairs ignoring tied observations. The formula for gamma using the definitions above is:

$$\text{gamma} = (N_C - N_D)/(N_C + N_D) \quad .$$

Kendall's tau-b is similar to gamma except that tau-b uses a different correction for ties. The formula for the Kendall coefficient is:

$$\text{tau-b} = (N_C - N_D)/(\sqrt{(N - N_X)(N - N_Y)})\ .$$

Stuart's tau-c makes an adjustment for table size. The formula is

$$\text{tau-c} = ((N_C - N_D)\min(R,C))/(n^2(\min(R,C) - 1)).$$

Somer's D is used for directional hypotheses and penalizes for pairs tied only on Y (where Y is assumed to cause or predict X) and tied only on X. The formulas for C|R (the column variable given the row variable) and for R|C (the row variable given the column variable) are:

$$D_{C|R} = (N_C - N_D)/(N - N_X)$$

$$D_{R|C} = (N_C - N_D)/(N - N_Y)\ .$$

Lambda is interpreted as the probable improvement in predicting the dependent variable from knowing the independent variable. The two asymmetric lambdas are averaged to obtain the non-directional lambda. The formulas for the three types of lambdas are:

$$\text{lambda } C|R = (\Sigma_i r_i - r)/(n - r)$$

$$\text{lambda } R|C = (\Sigma_j c_j - c)/(n - c)$$

$$\text{lambda symmetric} = (\Sigma_i r_i + \Sigma_j c_j - r - c)/(2n - r - c)\ .$$

The uncertainty coefficient, an entropy measure, is the reduction in uncertainty in predicting one variable that results from knowing the value of the other variable. The directional and non-directional formulas for the uncertainty coefficient are:

$$\text{uncertainty } C|R = (U(X) + U(Y) - U(XY))/U(Y)$$

$$\text{uncertainty } R|C = (U(X) + U(Y) - U(XY))/U(X)$$

$$\text{uncertainty symmetric} = (U(X) + U(Y) - U(XY))/(U(X) + U(Y)/2.$$

These measures of association make different assumptions about the level of measurement of the data, the number of levels of the variables, and tied rankings. For more information to guide you in choosing one of these statistics for a specific set of data, see Hayes (1963) and Garson (1971). For an advanced treatment, refer to Goodman and Kruskal (1979) and Bishop, Fienberg, and Holland (1975).

Printed Output

For a one-way table showing the frequency distribution of a single variable, FREQ prints these items:

1. the name of the variable and its values
2. FREQUENCY counts giving the number of observations containing the value
3. cumulative frequencies, labeled CUM FREQ, giving the sum of the frequency counts of that value and all other values listed above it in the table (the total number of non-missing observations is the last cumulative frequency)

4. percentages, labeled PERCENT, giving the percent of the total number of observations represented by that value

5. cumulative percentages, labeled CUM PERCENT, giving the percent of the total number of values represented by that value and all others listed above it in the table.

Two-way tables may be printed as either crosstabulation tables (the default) or as lists (when the LIST option is specified). Each cell of a crosstabulation table contains these items:

6. FREQUENCY counts, giving the number of times the indicated values of the two variables both appear in an observation

7. PERCENT, the percentage of the total frequency count represented by that cell

8. ROW PCT or the row percentage, the percent of the total frequency count for that row represented by the cell

9. COL PCT or column percent, the percent of the total frequency count for that column represented by the cell

10. if the EXPECTED option is specified, the expected cell frequency under the hypothesis of independence

11. if the DEVIATION option is specified, the deviation of the cell frequency from the expected value

12. if the CELLCHI2 option is specified, the cell's contribution to the total chi-square statistic

13. if the CHISQ option is specified, the CHI-SQUARE statistic (χ^2), its DF or degrees of freedom, and its significance probability, PROB

14. if the ALL option is specified, these statistics are computed: chi-square, phi, contingency coefficient, Cramer's V, likelihood ratio chi-square, gamma, Kendall's tau-b, Stuart's tau-c, Somer's D, Pearson's product-moment correlation, Spearman's rank correlation, lambda asymmetric and symmetric, and the uncertainty coefficient asymmetric and symmetric.

EXAMPLE

Data for the following example are selected characteristics of U.S. cities with population over 50,000, from the *County and City Data Book, 1977*. The first TABLES statement requests univariate frequencies on all the variables. The second TABLES statement requests a two-way frequency table. Other TABLES statements illustrate different request forms and options of PROC FREQ. The FORMAT statement associates a format that has been previously defined using PROC FORMAT with each variable.

Another example in Chapter 9, "PROC Step Applications," shows the DATA step that reads these census data into a SAS data set, the use of PROC UNIVARIATE to determine cutoff points for categories, and PROC FORMAT to define the formats for the variables.

These statements produce the output shown below:

```
DATA CITIES;    (see Chapter 9 for complete DATA step)
more SAS statements
;
PROC FREQ DATA=CITIES
  FORMCHAR='FABFACCCBCEB8FECABCBBB'X;
  TABLES DIVISION JANGRP JULYGRP POPGRP REGION INCOMGRP
    ROBGRP SUNGRP OVR65GRP HOUSGRP ELECGRP;
  TABLES POPGRP*CITYGOVT;
```

```
TABLES REGION*OVR65GRP / NOCOL NOPERCENT;
TABLES JANGRP*JULYGRP*ELECGRP / LIST;
TABLES (POPGRP INCOMGRP)*ROBGRP / NOCOL NOPERCENT
  EXPECTED DEVIATION CELLCHI2 CHISQ;
TABLES CITYGOVT*ROBGRP / ALL NOCOL NOPERCENT;
FORMAT POPGRP PC. OVR65GRP OC. INCOMGRP IC. HOUSGRP HC.
  ELECGRP EC. CITYGOVT CC. ROBGRP RC. JANGRP JAN.
  JULYGRP JUL. SUNGRP SC.;
```

```
    ①       CENSUS DATA: RESULTS FROM FREQ PROCEDURE      ⑤                    1

DIVISION        ② FREQUENCY   CUM FREQ      PERCENT   CUM PERCENT

EAST NORTH CENTR     79    ③    79    ④  20.627        20.627
EAST SOUTH CENTR     13          92        3.394        24.021
MIDDLE ATLANTIC      37         129        9.661        33.681
MOUNTAIN             23         152        6.005        39.687
NEW ENGLAND          33         185        8.616        48.303
PACIFIC              80         265       20.888        69.191
SOUTH ATLANTIC       47         312       12.272        81.462
WEST NORTH CENTR     27         339        7.050        88.512
WEST SOUTH CENTR     44         383       11.488       100.000


                  MEAN JANUARY TEMPERATURE (DEGREES F)
JANGRP            FREQUENCY   CUM FREQ      PERCENT   CUM PERCENT

UNDER 32 DEGREES    179         179       46.736        46.736
32 DEGREES OR HI    204         383       53.264       100.000


                   MEAN JULY TEMPERATURE (DEGREES F)
JULYGRP          FREQUENCY   CUM FREQ      PERCENT   CUM PERCENT

UNDER 75 DEGREES    213         213       55.614        55.614
75 DEGREES OR HI    170         383       44.386       100.000


                      1975 POPULATION ESTIMATE
POPGRP           FREQUENCY   CUM FREQ      PERCENT   CUM PERCENT

50,001-75,000       137         137       35.770        35.770
75,001-100,000       84         221       21.932        57.702
OVER 100,000        162         383       42.298       100.000

REGION           FREQUENCY   CUM FREQ      PERCENT   CUM PERCENT

NORTH CENTRAL       106         106       27.676        27.676
NORTHEAST            70         176       18.277        45.953
SOUTH               104         280       27.154        73.107
WEST                103         383       26.893       100.000


                   PER CAPITA MONEY INCOME (1974)
INCOMGRP         FREQUENCY   CUM FREQ      PERCENT   CUM PERCENT

UNDER $4677         193         193       50.392        50.392
$4677 OR MORE       190         383       49.608       100.000


                  ROBBERY RATE/100,000 POP (1975)
ROBGRP           FREQUENCY   CUM FREQ      PERCENT   CUM PERCENT

100 OR LESS          84          84       21.932        21.932
101-200             108         192       28.198        50.131
201-300              79         271       20.627        70.757
OVER 300            112         383       29.243       100.000
```

CENSUS DATA: RESULTS FROM FREQ PROCEDURE   2

POSSIBLE SUNSHINE ANNUAL % (DAYS)

SUNGRP	FREQUENCY	CUM FREQ	PERCENT	CUM PERCENT
UNDER 55%	109	109	28.460	28.460
55-70%	205	314	53.525	81.984
OVER 70%	69	383	18.016	100.000

% PERSONS 65 & OVER (1970)

OVR65GRP	FREQUENCY	CUM FREQ	PERCENT	CUM PERCENT
UNDER 7%	92	92	24.021	24.021
7-12%	194	286	50.653	74.674
OVER 12%	97	383	25.326	100.000

MEDIAN SINGLE-FAMILY OWNER-OCCUP (1970)

HOUSGRP	FREQUENCY	CUM FREQ	PERCENT	CUM PERCENT
LOW	108	108	28.198	28.198
MEDIUM	221	329	57.702	85.901
HIGH	54	383	14.099	100.000

TYPICAL RESID. ELECTRIC BILL/MO. (1976)

ELECGRP	FREQUENCY	CUM FREQ	PERCENT	CUM PERCENT
LOW	88	88	22.977	22.977
MEDIUM	167	255	43.603	66.580
HIGH	128	383	33.420	100.000

CENSUS DATA: RESULTS FROM FREQ PROCEDURE   3

TABLE OF POPGRP BY CITYGOVT

POPGRP   1975 POPULATION ESTIMATE   CITYGOVT   FORM OF CITY GOVERNMENT

(6) FREQUENCY
(7) PERCENT
(8) ROW PCT
(9) COL PCT

	COUNCIL MANAGER	COMMISSION	MAYOR COUNCIL	TOTAL
50,001-75,000	(6) 84	7	46	137
	(7) 21.99	1.83	12.04	35.86
	(8) 61.31	5.11	33.58	
	(9) 39.81	33.33	30.67	
75,001-100,000	50	3	31	84
	13.09	0.79	8.12	21.99
	59.52	3.57	36.90	
	23.70	14.29	20.67	
OVER 100,000	77	11	73	161
	20.16	2.88	19.11	42.15
	47.83	6.83	45.34	
	36.49	52.38	48.67	
TOTAL	211	21	150	382
	55.24	5.50	39.27	100.00

CENSUS DATA: RESULTS FROM FREQ PROCEDURE   4

TABLE OF REGION BY OVR65GRP

REGION   OVR65GRP   % PERSONS 65 & OVER (1970)

FREQUENCY ROW PCT	UNDER 7%	7-12%	OVER 12%	TOTAL
NORTH CENTRAL	21 / 19.81	64 / 60.38	21 / 19.81	106
NORTHEAST	0 / 0.00	29 / 41.43	41 / 58.57	70
SOUTH	29 / 27.88	56 / 53.85	19 / 18.27	104
WEST	42 / 40.78	45 / 43.69	16 / 15.53	103
TOTAL	92	194	97	383

```
              CENSUS DATA: RESULTS FROM FREQ PROCEDURE                        5

JANGRP              JULYGRP            ELECGRP    FREQUENCY   CUM FREQ    PERCENT    CUM PERCENT

UNDER 32 DEGREES    UNDER 75 DEGREES   LOW            24         24       6.266        6.266
UNDER 32 DEGREES    UNDER 75 DEGREES   MEDIUM         74         98      19.321       25.587
UNDER 32 DEGREES    UNDER 75 DEGREES   HIGH           40        138      10.444       36.031
UNDER 32 DEGREES    75 DEGREES OR HI   LOW             8        146       2.089       38.120
UNDER 32 DEGREES    75 DEGREES OR HI   MEDIUM         22        168       5.744       43.864
UNDER 32 DEGREES    75 DEGREES OR HI   HIGH           11        179       2.872       46.736
32 DEGREES OR HI    UNDER 75 DEGREES   LOW            22        201       5.744       52.480
32 DEGREES OR HI    UNDER 75 DEGREES   MEDIUM         14        215       3.655       56.136
32 DEGREES OR HI    UNDER 75 DEGREES   HIGH           39        254      10.183       66.319
32 DEGREES OR HI    75 DEGREES OR HI   LOW            34        288       8.877       75.196
32 DEGREES OR HI    75 DEGREES OR HI   MEDIUM         57        345      14.883       90.078
32 DEGREES OR HI    75 DEGREES OR HI   HIGH           38        383       9.922      100.000
```

```
              CENSUS DATA: RESULTS FROM FREQ PROCEDURE                        6

                        TABLE OF POPGRP BY ROBGRP

POPGRP    1975 POPULATION ESTIMATE   ROBGRP    ROBBERY RATE/100,000 POP (1975)

FREQUENCY
EXPECTED
DEVIATION
CELL CHI2
ROW PCT        100 OR L  101-200   201-300   OVER 300
               ESS                                          TOTAL

50,001-75,000       49        44        26        18         137
                  30.0      38.6      28.3      40.1
                  19.0       5.4      -2.3     -22.1
                  12.0       0.7       0.2      12.1
                  35.77     32.12     18.98     13.14

75,001-100,000      22        30        18        14          84
                  18.4      23.7      17.3      24.6
                   3.6       6.3       0.7     -10.6
                   0.7       1.7       0.0       4.5
                  26.19     35.71     21.43     16.67

OVER 100,000        13        34        35        80         162
                  35.5      45.7      33.4      47.4
                 -22.5     -11.7       1.6      32.6
                  14.3       3.0       0.1      22.5
                   8.02     20.99     21.60     49.38

TOTAL               84       108        79       112         383

                    STATISTICS FOR 2-WAY TABLES

CHI-SQUARE                     71.797    DF=  6   PROB=0.0001
PHI                             0.433
CONTINGENCY COEFFICIENT         0.397
CRAMER'S V                      0.306
LIKELIHOOD RATIO CHISQUARE     74.714    DF=  6   PROB=0.0001
```

```
              CENSUS DATA: RESULTS FROM FREQ PROCEDURE                        7

                       TABLE OF INCOMGRP BY ROBGRP

INCOMGRP   PER CAPITA MONEY INCOME (1974)   ROBGRP    ROBBERY RATE/100,000 POP (1975)

FREQUENCY
EXPECTED
DEVIATION
CELL CHI2
ROW PCT        100 OR L  101-200   201-300   OVER 300
               ESS                                          TOTAL

UNDER $4677         34        47        45        67         193
                  42.3      54.4      39.8      56.4
                  -8.3      -7.4       5.2      10.6
                   1.6       1.0       0.7       2.0
                  17.62     24.35     23.32     34.72

$4677 OR MORE       50        61        34        45         190
                  41.7      53.6      39.2      55.6
                   8.3       7.4      -5.2     -10.6
                   1.7       1.0       0.7       2.0
                  26.32     32.11     17.89     23.68

TOTAL               84       108        79       112         383

                    STATISTICS FOR 2-WAY TABLES

CHI-SQUARE                     10.693    DF=  3   PROB=0.0135
PHI                             0.167
CONTINGENCY COEFFICIENT         0.165
CRAMER'S V                      0.167
LIKELIHOOD RATIO CHISQUARE     10.749    DF=  3   PROB=0.0132
```

⑭ CENSUS DATA: RESULTS FROM FREQ PROCEDURE   8

TABLE OF CITYGOVT BY ROBGRP

CITYGOVT   FORM OF CITY GOVERNMENT   ROBGRP   ROBBERY RATE/100,000 POP (1975)

FREQUENCY ROW PCT	100 OR LESS	101-200	201-300	OVER 300	TOTAL
.	0 .	1 .	0 .	0 .	.
COUNCIL MANAGER	47 22.27	63 29.86	49 23.22	52 24.64	211
COMMISSION	6 28.57	7 33.33	3 14.29	5 23.81	21
MAYOR COUNCIL	31 20.67	37 24.67	27 18.00	55 36.67	150
TOTAL	84	107	79	112	382

CENSUS DATA: RESULTS FROM FREQ PROCEDURE   9

STATISTICS FOR 2-WAY TABLES

CHI-SQUARE	7.757	DF=	6	PROB=0.2565
PHI	0.142			
CONTINGENCY COEFFICIENT	0.141			
CRAMER'S V	0.101			
LIKELIHOOD RATIO CHISQUARE	7.681	DF=	6	PROB=0.2624
GAMMA	0.116	ASE1=	0.072	
KENDALL'S TAU-B	0.074			
STUART'S TAU-C	0.070	ASE1=	0.044	
SOMER'S D C|R	0.086	ASE1=	0.054	
SOMER'S D R|C	0.062	ASE1=	0.039	
PRODUCT MOMENT CORRELATION	0.085			
SPEARMAN CORRELATION	0.083			
LAMBDA ASYMMETRIC C|R	0.048			
LAMBDA ASYMMETRIC R|C	0.018			
LAMBDA SYMMETRIC	0.036			
UNCERTAINTY COEFFICIENT C|R	0.007			
UNCERTAINTY COEFFICIENT R|C	0.012			
UNCERTAINTY COEFFICIENT SYM	0.009			

ASE1 IS THE ASYMPTOTIC STANDARD ERROR.
R\|C MEANS ROW VAR DEPENDENT ON COLUMN VAR.

REFERENCES

Bishop, Y., Fienberg, S.E., and Holland, P.W. (1975), *Discrete Multivariate Analysis: Theory and Practice*, Cambridge: The MIT Press, Chapter 11.

Blalock, Hubert M., Jr. (1960), *Social Statistics*, New York: McGraw-Hill Book Company.

Brown, Morton B. and Benedetti, Jacqueline K. (1976), "Asymptotic Standard Errors and Their Sampling Behavior for Measures of Association and Correlation in the Two-way Contingency Table," Technical Report No. 23, Health Sciences Computing Facility, University of California, Los Angeles.

Garson, G. David (1971), *Handbook of Political Science Methods*, Boston, Mass.: Holbrook Press, Inc.

Goodman, L.A. and Kruskal, W.H. (1954, 1959, 1963, 1972), "Measures of Association for Cross-Classification I, II, III, and IV," *Journal of the American Statistical Association*, 49, 732-764 58, 310-364 67, 415-421.

Goodman, L.A. and Kruskal, W.H. (1979), *Measures of Association for Cross Classification*, New York: Springer-Verlag. (Reprints of JASA articles above)

Hayes, William L. (1963), *Psychological Statistics*, New York: Holt, Rinehart and Winston.

U.S. Bureau of the Census (1978), *County and City Data Book, 1977: A Statistical Abstract Supplement*, Washington, D.C.: U.S. Government Printing Office.

The MEANS Procedure

ABSTRACT

The MEANS procedure produces simple univariate descriptive statistics for numeric variables.

INTRODUCTION

PROC MEANS can compute statistics for an entire SAS data set or separately for groups of observations in the data set. A BY statement causes MEANS to calculate descriptive statistics separately for groups of observations, where a group is composed of observations having the same values of the variables in a BY statement. MEANS can also create one or more new SAS data sets containing the statistics calculated. If you want descriptive statistics in a data set and do not require printed output, use the SUMMARY procedure.

Other SAS procedures also compute univariate statistics. While MEANS is the easiest-to-use descriptive procedure, other procedures provide more features. See UNIVARIATE, SUMMARY, CHART, and TABULATE.

Note: In this discussion names of statistics refer to the sample estimates of the true parameters. Thus, the term *mean* refers to the sample mean, *variance* refers to the sample variance, and so forth.

SPECIFICATIONS

The procedure is controlled by the statements:

> **PROC MEANS** *options*;
>   **VAR** *variables*;
>   **BY** *variables*;
>   **FREQ** *variable*;
>   **ID** *variables*;
>   **OUTPUT OUT**=*SASdataset keyword*=*names* ... ;

There is no limit to the number of OUTPUT statements that may accompany a PROC MEANS statement.

PROC MEANS Statement

   PROC MEANS *options*;

The options below may appear in the PROC MEANS statement.

   DATA=*SASdataset*   names the SAS data set to be analyzed by PROC

MEANS. If DATA= is omitted, the most recently created SAS data set is used.

NOPRINT   tells MEANS not to print any of the descriptive statistics. Use NOPRINT when the only purpose of using the procedure is to create a new SAS data set.

MAXDEC=n   specifies the maximum number of decimal places (0 to 8) for MEANS to use in printing results. Since the maximum field width for a result is 15, which includes two blank columns to separate values, MEANS may have to print fewer decimal places than the MAXDEC= value.

The statistics below may be requested with the MEANS procedure by giving the keyword names of the statistics in the PROC MEANS statement. These keywords are also used in the OUTPUT statement described below. The statistics are defined in Chapter 17, "Introduction to Descriptive Statistics."

N	the number of observations on which calculations are based
NMISS	the number of missing values
MEAN	the mean
STD	the standard deviation
MIN	the smallest value
MAX	the largest value
RANGE	the range
SUM	the sum
VAR	the variance
USS	the uncorrected sum of squares
CSS	the corrected sum of squares
STDERR	the standard error of the mean
CV	the coefficient of variation (percent)
SKEWNESS	the measure of skewness
KURTOSIS	the measure of kurtosis
T	the Student's t value for testing the hypothesis that the population mean is 0
PRT	the probability of a greater absolute value of Student's t.

VAR Statement

VAR *variables*;

Statistics are calculated for each numeric variable listed in the VAR statement. If a VAR statement is not used, all numeric variables on the input data set except for those listed in either a BY or ID statement are analyzed. The results are printed in the order of the variables on the VAR statement.

BY Statement

BY *variables*;

A BY statement may be used with PROC MEANS to obtain separate analyses on observations in groups defined by the BY variables. When a BY statement appears, the procedure expects the input data set to be sorted in order of the BY variables. If your input data set is not sorted in ascending order, use the SORT procedure with a similar BY statement to sort the data, or, if appropriate, use the BY statement options NOTSORTED or DESCENDING. For more information, see the discussion of the BY statement in Chapter 8, "Statements Used in the PROC Step."

FREQ Statement

FREQ *variable*;

When a FREQ statement appears with PROC MEANS, each observation in the input data set is assumed to represent *n* observations in the calculation of statistics, where *n* is the value of the FREQ variable. If the value of the FREQ variable is less than 1, the observation is not used in the calculations. If the value is not an integer, only the integer portion is used.

ID Statement

ID *variables*;

An ID statement can be used with PROC MEANS to include additional variables in the output data set. The value of any variable listed in an ID statement in the first observation of each BY group is included in the new data set.

OUTPUT Statement

OUTPUT OUT = *SASdataset keyword* = *names* ... ;

The OUTPUT statement requests PROC MEANS to output statistics to a new SAS data set. The options name the data set and the variables to be included.

OUT = *SASdataset*   names the output SAS data set. If OUT = is not given, MEANS names the new data set according to the DATA*n* convention as if OUT = __DATA__ were specified. If you want to create a permanent SAS data set, you must specify a two-level name (see Chapter 12, "SAS Data Sets," for more information on permanent SAS data sets).

keyword = *names*   specifies the statistics you want in the new data set and names the variables containing these statistics. Any of the statistics available in the PROC MEANS statement may be output by using the keyword for that statistic:

      N NMISS MEAN STD MIN MAX
      RANGE SUM VAR USS CSS STDERR
      CV SKEWNESS KURTOSIS T PRT

The list of variable names after the equal sign names statistics for respective variables in the VAR statement. This list may be shorter than the VAR list.

For example, consider these statements:

```
PROC MEANS;
   VAR X1 X2;
   BY GROUP;
   OUTPUT OUT = STATS MEAN = MA MB STD = SA;
```

If the BY variable, GROUP, has two values A and B, the data set STATS contains two observations. Each of these observations contains the variables GROUP, MA, MB, and SA. MA and MB are the means of X1 and X2 respectively. SA is the standard deviation of X1. No standard deviation of X2 is output. The statistics are printed, since NOPRINT is not specified.

There is no limit to the number of OUTPUT statements that can accompany a PROC MEANS statement. Each OUTPUT statement creates one SAS data set.

DETAILS

Missing Values

PROC MEANS excludes missing values before calculating statistics. Each variable is treated individually: a missing value in one variable does not affect the calculations for other variables. Missing values for a BY variable form a separate BY group and are treated in the same way as BY groups with nonmissing values.

Output Data Set

The number of observations in the new data set corresponds to the number of BY groups for which statistics are calculated. If no BY statement is used, the output data set contains one observation. BY variables and ID variables as well as the computed statistics are included in the new data set.

Printed Output

When no statistics are specifically requested on the PROC MEANS statement, MEANS prints these statistics for each variable in the VAR statement:

1. the name of the variable
2. N, the number of nonmissing values for the variable
3. the MEAN or average of the variable
4. the STANDARD DEVIATION of the variable
5. the MINIMUM VALUE of the variable
6. the MAXIMUM VALUE of the variable.

If there is space available on the output (depending on the computer terminal used and LINESIZE specified), MEANS also prints these statistics:

7. STD ERROR OF MEAN, the standard error of the mean
8. the SUM of all the values for a variable
9. the VARIANCE of each variable
10. C.V., or the coefficient of variation expressed as a percentage.

If statistics are specifically requested on the PROC statement, only those statistics are printed. In addition to the statistics above, upon request MEANS can print these statistics:

11. N MISSING, the number of missing values for each variable
12. the RANGE of each variable
13. the UNCORRECTED SS, the raw sum of squares (not adjusted for the mean)
14. the CORRECTED SS, the sum of squares adjusted for the mean
15. SKEWNESS
16. KURTOSIS
17. T, the Student's t value for testing the hypothesis that the population mean is 0

18. PR > |T|, the probability of a greater absolute value for Student's *t* under the hypothesis that the mean is zero.

If a statistic cannot be computed because of insufficient or inappropriate data, the statistic is reported as missing. See Chapter 17, "Introduction to Descriptive Statistics."

If a BY statement is included, a line is drawn to separate the statistics for each BY group.

EXAMPLES

Univariate Statistics: Example 1

The following example requests univariate statistics for two variables, RATING and EXCESS. The first PROC MEANS statement asks for statistics on all numeric variables (including DAY) for all observations.

The second PROC MEANS statement asks for the statistics that must be specifically requested. In this small sample, statistics like skewness and kurtosis are not reliable.

The third PROC MEANS statement requests statistics for each combination of values of the variables PLACE and DAY. MAXDEC=3 requests that only three decimal places be used to print the results. MEANS creates an output data set that includes the means and standard errors of the means for the two variables. The PRINT procedure is used to print the new data set.

```
DATA A;
  INPUT RATING EXCESS PLACE $ DAY @@;
  CARDS;
04 54 S 1  07 70 N 1  10 69 N 2  04 52 S 1
07 70 S 2  08 74 N 1  04 60 S 1  07 62 S 2
07 80 N 1  06 61 S 2  06 77 N 2  08 75 N 2
;
PROC MEANS;
  TITLE OUTPUT FROM MEANS PROCEDURE;
PROC MEANS DATA=A MAXDEC=3 NMISS RANGE USS CSS
  SKEWNESS KURTOSIS T PRT;
  VAR RATING EXCESS;
  TITLE REQUESTED STATISTICS;
PROC SORT;
  BY PLACE DAY;
PROC MEANS MAXDEC=3;
  BY PLACE DAY;
  VAR RATING EXCESS;
  OUTPUT OUT=NEW MEAN=RMEAN EMEAN STDERR=RSE ESE;
  TITLE STATISTICS BY PLACE AND DAY;
PROC PRINT;
  TITLE NEW DATA SET;
```

(1) VARIABLE	(2) N	(3) MEAN	(4) STANDARD DEVIATION	(5) (6) MINIMUM VALUE	MAXIMUM VALUE	OUTPUT FROM MEANS PROCEDURE (7) STD ERROR OF MEAN	(8) SUM	(9) VARIANCE	(10)₁ C.V.
RATING	12	6.50000000	1.83402191	4.00000000	10.00000000	0.52943652	78.0000000	3.36363636	28.216
EXCESS	12	67.00000000	9.08545291	52.00000000	80.00000000	2.62274434	804.0000000	82.54545455	13.560
DAY	12	1.50000000	0.52223297	1.00000000	2.00000000	0.15075567	18.0000000	0.27272727	34.816

VARIABLE	(11) N MISSING	(12) RANGE	(13) UNCORRECTED SS	(14) CORRECTED SS	REQUESTED STATISTICS (15) SKEWNESS	(16) KURTOSIS	(17) T	(18)₂ PR>|T|
RATING	0	6.000	544.000	37.000	0.053	-0.165	12.28	0.0001
EXCESS	0	28.000	54776.000	908.000	-0.312	-1.056	25.55	0.0001

STATISTICS BY PLACE AND DAY   3

VARIABLE	N	MEAN	STANDARD DEVIATION	MINIMUM VALUE	MAXIMUM VALUE	STD ERROR OF MEAN	SUM	VARIANCE	C.V.
--- PLACE=N   DAY=1 ---
RATING	3	7.333	0.577	7.000	8.000	0.333	22.000	0.333	7.873
EXCESS	3	74.667	5.033	70.000	80.000	2.906	224.000	25.333	6.741
--- PLACE=N   DAY=2 ---
RATING	3	8.000	2.000	6.000	10.000	1.155	24.000	4.000	25.000
EXCESS	3	73.667	4.163	69.000	77.000	2.404	221.000	17.333	5.652
--- PLACE=S   DAY=1 ---
RATING	3	4.000	0.000	4.000	4.000	0.000	12.000	0.000	0.000
EXCESS	3	55.333	4.163	52.000	60.000	2.404	166.000	17.333	7.524
--- PLACE=S   DAY=2 ---
RATING	3	6.667	0.577	6.000	7.000	0.333	20.000	0.333	8.660
EXCESS	3	64.333	4.933	61.000	70.000	2.848	193.000	24.333	7.668

NEW DATA SET   4

OBS	PLACE	DAY	RMEAN	EMEAN	RSE	ESE
1	N	1	7.33333	74.6667	0.33333	2.90593
2	N	2	8.00000	73.6667	1.15470	2.40370
3	S	1	4.00000	55.3333	0.00000	2.40370
4	S	2	6.66667	64.3333	0.33333	2.84800

T Test for Paired Comparisons: Example 2

See the description of the TTEST procedure in the *SAS User's Guide: Statistics, 1982 Edition* for an example of using PROC MEANS to compute a *t* for paired comparisons.

The SUMMARY Procedure

ABSTRACT

The SUMMARY procedure computes descriptive statistics on numeric variables in a SAS data set and outputs the results to a new SAS data set.

INTRODUCTION

The SUMMARY procedure creates a SAS data set containing summary statistics. Each observation in the new data set contains the statistics for a different subgroup of the observations in the input data set. These subgroups represent all possible combinations of the levels of the variables in the CLASS statement.

Similarly, PROC MEANS also computes descriptive statistics with these important differences. MEANS produces subgroup statistics only when a BY statement is used, and the input data must be sorted by the BY variables. For more than one grouping variable, several executions of MEANS are needed to produce the information that SUMMARY outputs in one execution.

SUMMARY does not produce any printed output. Its output data set is typically printed with PROC PRINT or is input to a DATA step that extracts the desired information.

SPECIFICATIONS

The SUMMARY procedure is controlled by these statements:

> **PROC SUMMARY** options;
>   **CLASS** variables;
>   **VAR** variables;
>   **BY** variables;
>   **FREQ** variable;
>   **ID** variables;
>   **OUTPUT OUT**=SASdataset statistics;

An OUTPUT statement and a VAR statement must be specified. The VAR statement must precede the OUTPUT statements. Any number of OUTPUT statements are permitted.

PROC SUMMARY Statement

PROC SUMMARY options;

The options below may appear in the PROC SUMMARY statement:

DATA=*SASdataset*   names the data set to be used by SUMMARY. If DATA= is omitted, the most recently created SAS data set is used.

MISSING   requests that SUMMARY treat missing values as valid subgroup values for the CLASS variables.

NWAY   specifies that statistics for only the observation with the highest __TYPE__ value (highest level of interaction among CLASS variables) are to be output.

IDMIN   specifies that the value of the ID variable should be its minimum rather than its maximum value for the corresponding observations of the input data set.

CLASS Statement

CLASS *variables*;

In the CLASS or CLASSES statement you can name the variables to be used to form subgroups. The CLASS statement must be present to produce subgroup statistics. Without a CLASS statement SUMMARY produces only one observation per BY group.

VAR Statement

VAR *variables*;

In the VAR statement, give the numeric variables for which you want summary statistics. The VAR statement must precede the OUTPUT statement.

BY Statement

BY *variables*;

A BY statement may be used with PROC SUMMARY to obtain separate analyses on observations in groups defined by the BY variables. When a BY statement appears, the procedure expects the input data set to be sorted in order of the BY variables. If your input data set is not sorted in ascending order, use the SORT procedure with a similar BY statement to sort the data, or, if appropriate, use the BY statement options NOTSORTED or DESCENDING. For more information, see the discussion of the BY statement in Chapter 8, "Statements Used in the PROC Step." The BY statement is not often used in PROC SUMMARY, since the CLASS statement serves a similar but more general role without the need to sort.

FREQ Statement

FREQ *variable*;

Sometimes some or all of the observations in the input data set actually represent more than one original observation. If one variable is the count of the number of original observations that each observation in the input data set represents, specify its name in the FREQ statement. SUMMARY then uses the FREQ variable's values rather than observation counts in calculating statistics. FREQ values are always integers or are truncated to integers.

ID Statement

> ID *variables*;

The ID statement includes additional variables in the output data set. If your ID statement names only one variable, the value of the ID variable for a given observation in the output data set is the maximum value it has in the corresponding observations of the input data set, unless IDMIN is specified on the PROC statement. When your ID statement includes two or more variables, the maximum value is chosen as though the values of the ID variables were concatenated into one value for each observation. Thus the maximum value comes from only one of the corresponding observations in the input data set.

OUTPUT Statement

> OUTPUT OUT = *SASdataset statistics*;

OUT =	names the output SAS data set. If OUT = is not specified, SUMMARY names the new data set as though OUT = __DATA__ were specified. If you want to create a permanent SAS data set, you must specify a two-level name (see Chapter 12, "SAS Data Sets," for more information on permanent SAS data sets).
statistics	specifies the statistics you want in the new data set and names the variables containing these statistics. Output requests have four forms:

> *keyword = names*
> *keyword(variables) = names*
> *keyword =*
> *keyword(variables) =*

Below is a list of the keywords that may be specified in the output requests and corresponding statistics:

N	number of observations in the subgroup with non-missing values
NMISS	number of observations in the subgroup having missing values for the variable
MEAN	mean
STD	standard deviation
MIN	minimum value
MAX	maximum value
RANGE	range
SUM	sum
VAR	variance
USS	uncorrected sum of squares
CSS	corrected sum of squares
CV	coefficient of variation
STDERR	standard error of the mean
T	Student's t value for testing the hypothesis that the population mean is 0
PRT	probability of a greater absolute value for the Student's t value above.

Formulas for these statistics are presented in Chapter 17, "Introduction to Descriptive Statistics." To request statistics, give any number of keywords in the OUTPUT statement. The form of the output request determines the name of the new variable containing the statistic. Four choices are described below.

Form 1: *keyword = names;*

If you want the statistic's values to have names different from the original variables, follow the equal sign with a list of new variable names. These names will then be used for the statistic's values in the new data set.

The first variable name following the equal sign is given to the corresponding statistic for the first variable in the VAR statement; the second name is given to the statistic for the second variable in the VAR statement; and so on, as in PROC MEANS.

For example, say that you want to calculate means for the variables PRE and POST. In the output data set named RESULTS, the variable containing the PRE mean is PREMEAN; the variable containing the POST mean is POSTMEAN.

```
PROC SUMMARY;
  CLASS TEACHER;
  VAR PRE POST;
  OUTPUT OUT = RESULTS MEAN = PREMEAN POSTMEAN;
```

Form 2: *keyword(variables) = names;*

You can calculate a statistic for only certain variables in the VAR statement and give those statistics new names in the output data set. Give the variables for which you want statistics in parentheses after the keyword name and then follow the equal sign with the names you want those statistics to have.

For example, say you want to compute standard deviations for only the POST variable, but want means for both variables:

```
PROC SUMMARY;
  CLASS TEACHER;
  VAR PRE POST;
  OUTPUT OUT = RESULTS MEAN = PREMEAN POSTMEAN
    STD(POST) = STDPOST;
```

Form 3: *keyword = ;*

The statistic in the new data set will have the same name as the corresponding variable in the input data set if you simply follow the keyword with an equal sign.

For example, say you want the output data set to contain means for the variables PRE and POST, and the variables containing the means are also to be called PRE and POST:

```
PROC SUMMARY;
  CLASS TEACHER;
  VAR PRE POST;
  OUTPUT OUT = RESULTS MEAN = ;
```

Do not use this form or the next one for more than one keyword in the OUTPUT statement. If you do, two or more variables in the output data set will have the same name. Although PROC SUMMARY will not identify this as an error, other SAS procedures will not be able to access these variables later.

Form 4: *keyword(variables) = ;*

You can compute the statistic for a subset of the variables in the VAR statement by giving the names of the variables for which you want the statistic in parentheses after the keyword name. When no new variable names follow the equal sign, the statistics will have the same names as the original variables. Do not use this method for more than one statistic.

For example, say that you want the output data set to contain the mean for the variable PRE, but standard deviations for both PRE and POST. The mean will have the name PRE, but the standard deviations will have new names.

```
PROC SUMMARY;
  VAR PRE POST;
  OUTPUT OUT = RESULTS MEAN(PRE) =  STD = STDPRE STDPOST;
```

DETAILS

Missing Values

If any CLASS variable has a missing value for an observation, that observation is not used in SUMMARY unless the MISSING option is specified on the PROC SUMMARY statement.

Limitation

The maximum number of combinations of CLASS levels is 32767 or $2^{15} - 1$.

Output Data Set

SUMMARY produces an output data set and no printed output. The output data set's contents are described below.

Variables

Variables in the output data set are:

- the variables in the BY statement if a BY statement is used
- the ID variables, if an ID statement is used
- the variables in the CLASS statement. When formats combine several internal values into one formatted value, the lowest internal value is output
- a variable created by SUMMARY named __TYPE__ whose values contain information about the CLASS variables which define each subgroup
- a variable created by SUMMARY named __FREQ__ which gives the number of observations (both missing and non-missing) for the current subgroup
- the variables containing the subgroup statistics requested by the keywords in the OUTPUT statement.

For example, consider the data set created by SUMMARY with these statements:

```
PROC SUMMARY;
  CLASS TMT;
  VAR X Y;
  OUTPUT OUT = STATS MEAN = MX MY N = NX NY;
```

The data set STATS contains these variables:

```
TMT __TYPE__ __ FREQ__ MX MY NX NY
```

Computer Resources

The SUMMARY procedure is designed to collect descriptive statistics in a very efficient manner. The following guidelines for calculating the memory required by PROC SUMMARY are accurate in most cases. The amounts given are the minimum requirements; if SUMMARY has more memory available, it will usually be more efficient. If CLASS variables are specified, SUMMARY always uses the utility (WORK) file.

SUMMARY requires 175K for program space in addition to the maximum of the following three calculations divided by 1024:

- The sum of

    $$NLEVELS * (VLEN + FLEN + 8)$$

    for each class variable where

    NLEVELS   is the number of levels (values) for the CLASS variable
    VLEN   is the internal length for the CLASS variable
    FLEN   is the external (formatted) length for the CLASS variable

- The sum of

    $$NLEVELS * (VLEN + 2)$$

    for each class variable plus

    $$NINT * (10 + (NC * 4))$$

    where

    NLEVELS   are as defined above
    and VLEN
    NINT   is the number of CLASS interactions found on the input data set
    NC   is the number of CLASS variables

- $(2**NC) * (NC * 2 + 28) + NINT * 6$

    where

    NINT and NC   are defined above

Notes: NINT can be much less than the potential number of CLASS interactions if the data are sparse. The 175K of program space includes a large allowance for input and output variable space, and so on. If there is an unusually large number of these variables, however, the 175K should be increased.

Observations

The number of observations in the output data set produced by PROC SUMMARY depends on the number of distinct values or levels (for example, a, b, c) of the CLASS variables (A, B, C).

Observations in the data set produced by SUMMARY are identified by a variable named __TYPE__. Values of __TYPE__ indicate which subgroup (defined by values of the CLASS variables) produced the summary statistics in that observation in the output data set.

Table 1 shows how values of __TYPE__ are determined for one CLASS variable (A), two CLASS variables (A and B), and three CLASS variables (A, B, C). The same logic can be extended to analyses by PROC SUMMARY with more than three CLASS variables. The table assumes that all combinations of class levels occur in the data.

For a CLASS statement with one class variable,

    CLASS A;

the output data set contains one observation for totals (__TYPE__ = 0) and an observation for each level of A (__TYPE__ = 1).

Table 1
Observations in SUMMARY's Output Data Set

C	B	A	__TYPE__	Subgroup Defined By	Number of Observations of this __TYPE__ in the Data Set	Total Number of Observations in the Data Set
0	0	0	0	Total	1	
0	0	1	1	A	a	1+a
0	1	0	2	B	b	
0	1	1	3	A*B	a*b	1+a+b+a*b
1	0	0	4	C	c	
1	0	1	5	A*C	a*c	1+a+b+a*b
1	1	0	6	B*C	b*c	+c+a*c
1	1	1	7	A*B*C	a*b*c	+b*c+a*b*c
Binary equivalent of __TYPE__ value				A, B, C = CLASS variables	a, b, c = number of levels of A, B, C respectively	

three CLASS variables · *two CLASS variables* · *one CLASS variable* (column labels)

one CLASS variable · *two CLASS variables* · *three CLASS variables* (right side labels for total observations)

For a CLASS statement with two class variables,

   CLASS B A;

an observation for each level of B (__TYPE__ = 2) and an observation for each level of A*B (__TYPE__ = 3) are added.

For a CLASS statement with three class variables,

   CLASS C B A;

observations for levels of C (__TYPE__ = 4), levels of A*C (__TYPE__ = 5), B*C (__TYPE__ = 6), and A*B*C (__TYPE__ = 7) are added.

You can extend the table to an N-way analysis by adding columns to the table on the left. A value of one is entered in a column if that CLASS variable is involved in defining the subgroup, a zero otherwise. Note that the ones and zeros in the CLASS variable columns form binary numbers across the row for each subgroup.

The decimal equivalent of one of these binary numbers for a subgroup is the __TYPE__ value for that subgroup. There are 2^n different values of __TYPE__ produced by SUMMARY for a given analysis, where n is the number of CLASS variables. The number of observations of each __TYPE__ in the data set depends on the number of levels of the CLASS variables as shown in the table above.

For example, consider the case where the CLASS statement contains two variables, SEX and RACE. The variable SEX has the two values F and M; the variable RACE has the two values B and W. The observations in the output data set are determined as in Table 2.

Table 2
Example: Two CLASS Variables

Sex	Race	__TYPE__	Subgroup Defined By	Number of Observations of this __TYPE__ in the Data Set	Total Number of Observations in the Data Set
0	0	0	Total	1	
0	1	1	Race	2	
1	0	2	Sex	2	
1	1	3	Race*Sex	4	9

These statements

```
PROC SUMMARY;
  CLASS SEX RACE;
  VAR AGE;
  OUTPUT OUT=STATS MEAN=AGEMEAN;
```

produce the data set in Table 2.

The __TYPE__=0 observation contains the overall means for the data set. The SEX and RACE values for this output observation are missing. The value of __FREQ__ is 10, because 10 observations were used to form this group.

The __TYPE__=1 observations contain the group means for the rightmost variable in the CLASS statement, in this case RACE. The first of these contains the mean for the 4 observations having a value of B for RACE; the second contains the mean for the 6 observations having the value of W for RACE.

The __TYPE__=2 observations contain the means for the two groups of observations defined by the SEX values.

The __TYPE__=3 observations contain the means for the subgroups defined by the combinations of the RACE and SEX values. For example, the first observation in this set contains the mean for the two observations having a SEX value of F and a RACE value of B.

Usage Note: SAS Bit-Testing Feature

The __TYPE__ variable is a good candidate for use with the SAS bit-testing feature. For example, say that you want to print a report using just the observations with the B and C combinations:

```
PROC SUMMARY;
  CLASS A B C;
  VAR X Y Z;
  OUTPUT OUT=STATS MEAN= ;
DATA __NULL__;
  SET STATS;
  IF __TYPE__='011'B;
  .
  .
  .
  more SAS statements
```

The IF statement could also be written

IF __TYPE__ = 3;

EXAMPLES

Sales Data: Example 1

Below are the statements that ask SUMMARY to create an output data set containing summary statistics for two class variables, PRODUCT and DATE. PROC PRINT prints the summary file.

```
DATA SALES;
 more SAS statements
 ;
PROC SUMMARY DATA = SALES;
  CLASS PRODUCT DATE;
  VAR UNITS;
  ID = YEAR;
  OUTPUT OUT = B SUM = SALES;
PROC PRINT DATA = B;
```

1

OBS	YEAR	PRODUCT	DATE	_TYPE_	_FREQ_	SALES
1	1981		.	0	742	4781
2	1979		01JAN79	1	8	67
3	1979		01FEB79	1	10	69
4	1979		01MAR79	1	12	82
5	1979		01APR79	1	13	77
6	1979		01MAY79	1	10	67
7	1979		01JUN79	1	12	55
8	1979		01JUL79	1	22	108
9	1979		01AUG79	1	21	129
10	1979		01SEP79	1	22	125
11	1979		01OCT79	1	21	145
12	1979		01NOV79	1	19	90
13	1979		01DEC79	1	14	75
14	1980		01JAN80	1	26	144
15	1980		01FEB80	1	22	141
16	1980		01MAR80	1	22	161
17	1980		01APR80	1	26	173
18	1980		01MAY80	1	20	135
19	1980		01JUN80	1	20	105
20	1980		01JUL80	1	23	130
21	1980		01AUG80	1	21	96
22	1980		01SEP80	1	22	134
23	1980		01OCT80	1	23	126
24	1980		01NOV80	1	16	93
25	1980		01DEC80	1	19	118
26	1981		01JAN81	1	19	143
27	1981		01FEB81	1	21	135
28	1981		01MAR81	1	33	200
29	1981		01APR81	1	34	181
30	1981		01MAY81	1	27	181
31	1981		01JUN81	1	36	220
32	1981		01JUL81	1	30	254
33	1981		01AUG81	1	19	202
34	1981		01SEP81	1	26	206
35	1981		01OCT81	1	24	187
36	1981		01NOV81	1	14	113
37	1981		01DEC81	1	15	114
38	1981	4005	.	2	212	1967
39	1981	8401	.	2	270	2062
40	1981	9054	.	2	260	752
41	1979	4005	01JAN79	3	5	56
42	1979	4005	01FEB79	3	5	57
43	1979	4005	01MAR79	3	5	60
44	1979	4005	01APR79	3	5	51
45	1979	4005	01MAY79	3	5	49
46	1979	4005	01JUN79	3	5	35
47	1979	4005	01JUL79	3	5	36
48	1979	4005	01AUG79	3	5	42
49	1979	4005	01SEP79	3	5	34
50	1979	4005	01OCT79	3	5	48
51	1979	4005	01NOV79	3	5	41
52	1979	4005	01DEC79	3	5	29
53	1980	4005	01JAN80	3	5	37
54	1980	4005	01FEB80	3	6	49
55	1980	4005	01MAR80	3	6	63
56	1980	4005	01APR80	3	6	59

2

OBS	YEAR	PRODUCT	DATE	_TYPE_	_FREQ_	SALES
57	1980	4005	01MAY80	3	6	43
58	1980	4005	01JUN80	3	6	42
59	1980	4005	01JUL80	3	6	42
60	1980	4005	01AUG80	3	6	32
61	1980	4005	01SEP80	3	6	48
62	1980	4005	01OCT80	3	6	58
63	1980	4005	01NOV80	3	6	56
64	1980	4005	01DEC80	3	6	42
65	1981	4005	01JAN81	3	6	67
66	1981	4005	01FEB81	3	7	57
67	1981	4005	01MAR81	3	7	86
68	1981	4005	01APR81	3	7	70
69	1981	4005	01MAY81	3	7	81
70	1981	4005	01JUN81	3	7	56
71	1981	4005	01JUL81	3	7	84
72	1981	4005	01AUG81	3	7	87
73	1981	4005	01SEP81	3	7	82
74	1981	4005	01OCT81	3	7	81
75	1981	4005	01NOV81	3	6	64
76	1981	4005	01DEC81	3	6	43
77	1979	8401	01JUL79	3	8	44
78	1979	8401	01AUG79	3	9	65
79	1979	8401	01SEP79	3	8	68
80	1979	8401	01OCT79	3	10	75
81	1979	8401	01NOV79	3	7	27
82	1979	8401	01DEC79	3	5	35
83	1980	8401	01JAN80	3	7	60
84	1980	8401	01FEB80	3	5	39
85	1980	8401	01MAR80	3	7	60
86	1980	8401	01APR80	3	10	68
87	1980	8401	01MAY80	3	8	63
88	1980	8401	01JUN80	3	7	50
89	1980	8401	01JUL80	3	8	60
90	1980	8401	01AUG80	3	6	46
91	1980	8401	01SEP80	3	9	72
92	1980	8401	01OCT80	3	8	49
93	1980	8401	01NOV80	3	6	29
94	1980	8401	01DEC80	3	6	55
95	1981	8401	01JAN81	3	7	63
96	1981	8401	01FEB81	3	7	60
97	1981	8401	01MAR81	3	14	87
98	1981	8401	01APR81	3	17	91
99	1981	8401	01MAY81	3	14	87
100	1981	8401	01JUN81	3	18	134
101	1981	8401	01JUL81	3	13	151
102	1981	8401	01AUG81	3	10	110
103	1981	8401	01SEP81	3	12	109
104	1981	8401	01OCT81	3	11	96
105	1981	8401	01NOV81	3	6	44
106	1981	8401	01DEC81	3	7	65
107	1979	9054	01JAN79	3	3	11
108	1979	9054	01FEB79	3	5	12
109	1979	9054	01MAR79	3	7	22
110	1979	9054	01APR79	3	8	26
111	1979	9054	01MAY79	3	5	18
112	1979	9054	01JUN79	3	7	20

3

OBS	YEAR	PRODUCT	DATE	_TYPE_	_FREQ_	SALES
113	1979	9054	01JUL79	3	9	28
114	1979	9054	01AUG79	3	7	22
115	1979	9054	01SEP79	3	9	23
116	1979	9054	01OCT79	3	6	22
117	1979	9054	01NOV79	3	7	22
118	1979	9054	01DEC79	3	4	11
119	1980	9054	01JAN80	3	14	47
120	1980	9054	01FEB80	3	11	53
121	1980	9054	01MAR80	3	9	38
122	1980	9054	01APR80	3	10	46
123	1980	9054	01MAY80	3	6	29
124	1980	9054	01JUN80	3	7	13
125	1980	9054	01JUL80	3	9	28
126	1980	9054	01AUG80	3	9	18
127	1980	9054	01SEP80	3	7	14
128	1980	9054	01OCT80	3	9	19
129	1980	9054	01NOV80	3	4	8
130	1980	9054	01DEC80	3	7	21
131	1981	9054	01JAN81	3	6	13
132	1981	9054	01FEB81	3	7	18
133	1981	9054	01MAR81	3	12	27
134	1981	9054	01APR81	3	10	20
135	1981	9054	01MAY81	3	6	13
136	1981	9054	01JUN81	3	11	30
137	1981	9054	01JUL81	3	10	19
138	1981	9054	01AUG81	3	2	5
139	1981	9054	01SEP81	3	7	15
140	1981	9054	01OCT81	3	6	10
141	1981	9054	01NOV81	3	2	5
142	1981	9054	01DEC81	3	2	6

Census Data: Example 2

Data for the following example are selected characteristics of U.S. cities with populations over 50,000 according to the *County and City Data Book, 1977*. The class variables are POPGRP with three levels and REGION with four levels. The OUTPUT statement specifies statistics for the dependent variables with several different kinds of output requests.

Another example in Chapter 9, "PROC Step Applications," shows the DATA step that read these census data into a SAS data set. PROC UNIVARIATE is used to determine cutoff points for the POPGRP variable. The FREQ and TABULATE procedures are used for other approaches to these same data.

```
DATA CITIES;      (see Chapter 9 for complete DATA step)
   more SAS statements
   ;
PROC SUMMARY DATA=CITIES;
   CLASS POPGRP REGION;
   VAR OVER65 INCOME HOUSING ELECTRIC ROBBERY;
   OUTPUT OUT=CITYDATA   N=NOVER65 NINCOME NHOUS NELEC NROB
                     MEAN=      STD(INCOME HOUSING ELECTRIC)
                           =INCOMSTD HOUSESTD ELECSTD;
   FORMAT POPGRP PC.;
PROC PRINT DATA=CITYDATA;
   TITLE CENSUS DATA: RESULTS FROM SUMMARY PROCEDURE;
```

CENSUS DATA: RESULTS FROM SUMMARY PROCEDURE 37

OBS	POPGRP	REGION	_TYPE_	_FREQ_	NOVER65	NINCOME	NHOUS	NELEC
1	.		0	383	383	383	383	383
2	.	NORTH CENTRAL	1	106	106	106	106	106
3	.	NORTHEAST	1	70	70	70	70	70
4	.	SOUTH	1	104	104	104	104	104
5	.	WEST	1	103	103	103	103	103
6	50,001-75,000		2	137	137	137	137	137
7	75,001-100,000		2	84	84	84	84	84
8	OVER 100,000		2	162	162	162	162	162
9	50,001-75,000	NORTH CENTRAL	3	38	38	38	38	38
10	50,001-75,000	NORTHEAST	3	29	29	29	29	29
11	50,001-75,000	SOUTH	3	33	33	33	33	33
12	50,001-75,000	WEST	3	37	37	37	37	37
13	75,001-100,000	NORTH CENTRAL	3	29	29	29	29	29
14	75,001-100,000	NORTHEAST	3	14	14	14	14	14
15	75,001-100,000	SOUTH	3	12	12	12	12	12
16	75,001-100,000	WEST	3	29	29	29	29	29
17	OVER 100,000	NORTH CENTRAL	3	39	39	39	39	39
18	OVER 100,000	NORTHEAST	3	27	27	27	27	27
19	OVER 100,000	SOUTH	3	59	59	59	59	59
20	OVER 100,000	WEST	3	37	37	37	37	37

OBS	NROB	OVER65	INCOME	HOUSING	ELECTRIC	ROBBERY	INCOMSTD	HOUSESTD	ELECSTD
1	383	9.8042	4795.70	18825.5	18.2115	281.183	858.81	6291.61	4.26653
2	106	9.6311	4960.05	18567.5	16.8752	280.057	860.72	5722.81	2.12504
3	70	12.4800	4510.31	19042.2	22.8900	307.557	727.60	7092.60	4.59811
4	104	9.6269	4500.93	15127.1	17.0462	276.452	765.83	4050.20	3.36547
5	103	8.3427	5118.14	22678.1	17.5839	269.194	878.44	5907.86	4.37326
6	137	9.8672	4830.37	19394.4	18.3340	191.891	951.54	6639.31	4.36218
7	84	9.3226	4880.42	19714.8	18.1894	228.202	1017.79	6828.74	3.85495
8	162	10.0006	4722.44	17883.3	18.1194	384.167	664.02	5573.48	4.40839
9	38	9.4605	5124.00	20164.6	17.2655	180.947	1013.08	6530.92	1.81988
10	29	12.6379	4574.14	19172.7	22.8810	171.862	599.37	6974.04	4.95995
11	33	9.9515	4367.73	14393.0	16.4073	212.758	758.38	3150.85	3.18440
12	37	8.0378	5142.27	23237.7	17.5859	200.216	1065.33	6103.97	4.30066
13	29	8.9862	5115.69	19287.0	16.5179	223.483	1008.90	6156.94	2.15519
14	14	12.1857	4588.00	18652.7	22.1050	209.214	1049.83	7964.61	3.11776
15	12	11.1250	4241.67	14647.7	16.9342	182.667	1120.23	8203.29	3.73625
16	29	7.5310	5050.62	22752.2	18.4900	260.931	862.08	4808.36	4.25216
17	39	10.2769	4684.56	16476.3	16.7605	418.692	417.71	3687.57	2.35949
18	27	12.4630	4401.48	19103.9	23.3067	504.296	668.50	7021.45	4.92376
19	59	9.1407	4628.17	15635.2	17.4264	331.153	667.63	3205.40	3.38968
20	37	9.2838	5146.92	22060.5	16.8716	344.649	684.30	6552.25	4.52185

The TABULATE Procedure

ABSTRACT

TABULATE constructs tables of descriptive statistics from compositions of classification variables, analysis variables, and statistic names. Tables may have up to three dimensions: row, column and page.

INTRODUCTION

TABULATE displays descriptive statistics in hierarchical tables. Each table cell contains a descriptive statistic calculated on all values of an analysis variable from observations sharing the same set of class variable values. The statistics that TABULATE computes are many of the same statistics computed by other descriptive procedures such as MEANS, FREQ, and SUMMARY. TABULATE provides

- a concise and powerful control language
- a greater degree of complexity in classification hierarchies
- flexible mechanisms for titling and formatting.

Introductory Example

Sample data set Tables in the following examples contain demographic information extracted from a data set which contains at least the following variables:

Variable	Description
REGION	Code for region of the country
CITYSIZE	Code for relative population size (S=small, M=medium, L=large)
POP	Urban population

Each observation contains data for one city.

Specify tables with TABLE statements. (Most applications also use CLASS and VAR statements in addition to the PROC TABULATE statement.) The first example contains a single column with population figures for each region:

TABLE REGION, POP;

	POP
	SUM
REGION	
NC	4650000
NE	6666000
SO	6864000
WE	8376000

The next table is a cross-tabulation of population values for REGION by CITYSIZE. These values can also be obtained by using PROC FREQ with a WEIGHT statement.

TABLE REGION, CITYSIZE*POP*SUM;

	CITYSIZE		
	L	M	S
	POP	POP	POP
	SUM	SUM	SUM
REGION			
NC	3750000	750000	150000
NE	5022000	1422000	222000
SO	4488000	2088000	288000
WE	5592000	2592000	192000

The same values can be displayed in one column as follows.

TABLE REGION*CITYSIZE, POP*SUM;

		POP
		SUM
REGION	CITYSIZE	
NC	L	3750000
	M	750000
	S	150000
NE	L	5022000
	M	1422000
	S	222000
SO	L	4488000
	M	2088000
	S	288000
WE	L	5592000
	M	2592000
	S	192000

Requesting MEAN as well as SUM produces two columns.

    TABLE REGION*CITYSIZE, POP*(SUM MEAN);

		POP	
		SUM	MEAN
REGION	CITYSIZE		
NC	L	3750000	625000
	M	750000	125000
	S	150000	25000
NE	L	5022000	837000
	M	1422000	237000
	S	222000	37000
SO	L	4488000	748000
	M	2088000	348000
	S	288000	48000
WE	L	5592000	932000
	M	2592000	432000
	S	192000	32000

Fundamentals

The fundamental topics to understand before using TABULATE are

- types of variables—classification and analysis
- the components that define the contents of an individual table cell—class variables, analysis variables, statistics keywords, and format items
- expressions—nesting, concatenation, grouping
- table dimensions—pages, rows, columns.

Types of variables TABULATE operates on two types of variables: classification (or class) variables and analysis variables. Class variables typically have a few discrete values called *levels* that define the classification. In the sample data set referred to above, REGION and CITYSIZE are potential class variables. Analysis variables have values on which statistics are calculated. In the sample data set, POP can be used as an analysis variable.

Components of a table cell A table is an organized collection of cells. Four items define the contents of each cell.

1. Classification levels (from class variables)
2. An analysis variable
3. A statistic
4. A format specification

For example, a cell may be associated with the statistic SUM for the analysis variable POP for two layers of classification: the level 'S' (small) for the class variable CITYSIZE and the level 'SO' for the class variable REGION. The cell value is formatted using the w.d specification 12.0. See SPECIFICATIONS for a discussion of the TABLE statement and a list of the statistic keywords. See DETAILS for a discussion of format specifications.

Expressions   Each dimension of a table is defined by an expression involving the four items discussed above. The expression is written using two basic operations and grouping.

- Nesting (the '*' operator) compounds items into a hierarchy.
- Concatenation (adjacent items) joins items one after another.
- Grouping (parentheses) is used to control the binding of the other two operations.

The nesting operation arranges all levels of its second operand within each level of its first operand. For two class variables A and B, with A having two levels and B having three levels, "B nested within A" is written **A*B** and produces

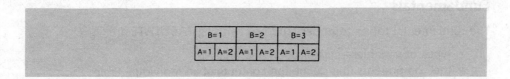

Using the same data levels, A nested within B is written **B*A**, and produces the following hierarchy:

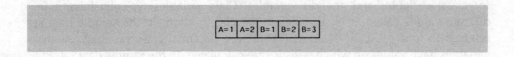

The concatenation operation causes all levels of its second operand to follow all levels of its first operand. For the same class variables and levels used above, B concatenated with A, (written **A B**) produces

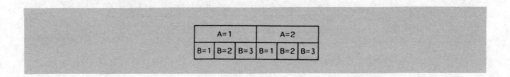

Compound expressions, which involve several operations, can be written. For example, **A B*C** (where the class variable C has two levels) produces

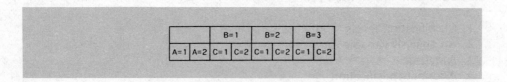

In compound expressions, the nesting operator (*) takes precedence over concatenation. Parentheses may be used to alter the binding produced by this operator precedence. For example, the operations in the expression above can be distributed differently by **(A B)*C**, which produces

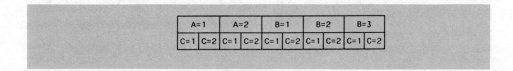

Table dimensions TABULATE produces tables that can contain up to three dimensions:

- page (or wafer)
- row (or stub, side)
- column (or banner, top)

Each dimension is specified by an expression and dimension expressions are separated by a comma. If all the dimensions are included the first expression defines the page dimension, the second the row dimension, and the third the column dimension. The column dimension is the set of columns in the table; the row dimension is the set of rows; and the page dimension is the set of row by column tables that make up the logical pages. If only one dimension is present that dimension is column; if two dimensions are present, rows and columns are used. In order to specify a page dimension, you must specify rows and columns also.

Concatenation and nesting can be expressed in any of the three dimensions. For example, concatenation in the column dimension causes all values of the left name or nesting to be followed horizontally by all values of the name or nesting to its right. Thus, the concatenation **A B** produces

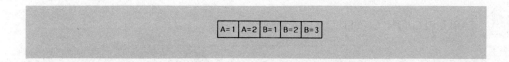

Nesting in the column dimension is expressed vertically. Therefore, **A B*C** produces

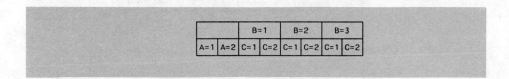

Concatenation in the row dimension causes all values of the left name or nesting to be followed vertically by all values of the name or nesting to its right. In the row dimension, nesting is expressed horizontally. For example:

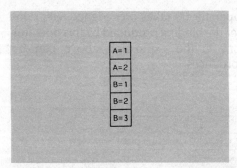

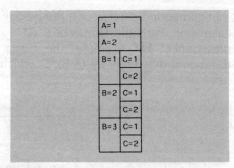

In the page dimension, a nesting specifies the set of class values, statistics and variable information for each logical page. When any classification value, analysis variable, statistic, or class variable in the page dimension changes, TABULATE begins a new logical page. Therefore, nesting is expressed verbally in the page titles and concatenation is expressed by beginning a new logical page. Pages for the left name or nesting are followed by pages for the name or nesting to its right.

Dimensions are crossed (for example, row * column) by nesting dimensions with each other, column within row and row within page, in the definition of individual table cell values. TABULATE expands the dimension expressions into a series of nestings with no concatenations. (See **Expanding TABLE Statement Nestings**, under **DETAILS**.) Each of these expanded nestings fully defines the values that will appear in associated cells of the table. Each cell corresponds to one statistic calculated on all values of an analysis variable from observations sharing the same set of nested class variable values. As this statement implies, an analysis variable may not be nested with another analysis variable and a statistic may not be nested with another statistic. These invalid nestings would result in two analysis variables or two statistics defining the same table cell.

In the above examples the analysis variable and statistic both appear in the column dimension. The set of analysis variables and the set of statistics may appear together in any dimension or they may appear in any combination of different dimensions. However, all statistics must appear in the same dimension; likewise, all analysis variables must appear in the same dimension. The following example shows the analysis variable in the column dimension and the statistics in the row dimension.

TABLE REGION*CITYSIZE*(SUM MEAN), POP;

REGION	CITYSIZE		POP
NC	L	SUM	3750000
		MEAN	625000
	M	SUM	750000
		MEAN	125000
	S	SUM	150000
		MEAN	25000
⋮	⋮	⋮	⋮
WE	L	SUM	5592000
		MEAN	932000
	M	SUM	2592000
		MEAN	432000
	S	SUM	192000
		MEAN	32000

Now four additional variables are added to the example: PRODUCT and SALETYPE are CLASS variables; QUANTITY and AMOUNT (price) are analysis variables.

The desired report contains a one-page table for each product. The table provides an analysis of wholesale and retail sales by REGION and by CITYSIZE.

TABLE PRODUCT, REGION CITYSIZE, SALETYPE*(QUANTITY AMOUNT);

When an analysis variable but no statistic is specified, the default statistic is SUM. If neither an analysis variable nor a statistic is specified, the default statistic is N, the frequency of occurrence of each set of nested class values.

In this table the page dimension is PRODUCT; the row dimension is REGION CITYSIZE, a concatenation; the column dimension is SALETYPE*(QUANTITY AMOUNT). The pages for the first two products follow.

PRODUCT A100

	SALETYPE			
	R		W	
	QUANTITY	AMOUNT	QUANTITY	AMOUNT
	SUM	SUM	SUM	SUM
REGION				
NC	1250	31250	1250	25000
NE	1600	40000	1600	32000
SO	1880	47000	1880	37600
WE	1840	46000	1840	36800
CITYSIZE				
L	3190	79750	3190	63800
M	2440	61000	2440	48800
S	940	23500	940	18800

PRODUCT A200

	SALETYPE			
	R		W	
	QUANTITY	AMOUNT	QUANTITY	AMOUNT
	SUM	SUM	SUM	SUM
REGION				
NC	1295	32375	1295	25900
NE	1645	41125	1645	32900
SO	1925	48925	1925	38500
WE	1885	47125	1885	37700
CITYSIZE				
L	3250	81250	3250	65000
M	2500	63500	2500	50000
S	1000	24800	1000	20000

Important Features

The universal classifier ALL   The universal class variable, ALL, represents a special class that has only one value. ALL is useful for including statistics on totals and subtotals within a classification group in a table. See **DETAILS** for more information.

Percentages   Percentages are calculated on two types of statistics. PCTN is the percentage that the number of observations in a subgroup (N) is of the number of observations in a containing group. PCTSUM is the percentage that the sum of analysis variable values in a subgroup is of the sum of analysis variable values in a containing group. The two keywords PCTN and PCTSUM are used as if they were statistics keywords. It is not necessary to request N or SUM in order to request PCTN or PCTSUM. Each percentage is calculated on a denominator defined by nestings of classification variables. Denominator definitions follow the percent keyword in <> brackets. If percent keywords are labeled in the TABLE statement (see below), the label specification follows the bracketed denominator definition list. For example:

```
TABLE (REGION*CITYSIZE ALL),
  (QUANTITY AMOUNT)*
    (SUM*F=8 PCTSUM<REGION*CITYSIZE ALL>='PERCENT'*F=8.2);
```

REGION	CITYS-IZE	QUANTITY SUM	QUANTITY PERCENT	AMOUNT SUM	AMOUNT PERCENT
NC	L	4544	11.38	102240	11.37
	M	2132	5.34	47920	5.33
	S	944	2.36	21240	2.36
NE	L	4842	12.13	108945	12.12
	M	3650	9.14	82125	9.14
	S	1246	3.12	28035	3.12
SO	L	4606	11.54	103635	11.53
	M	4298	10.77	97705	10.87
	S	2508	6.28	56230	6.25
WE	L	5310	13.30	119475	13.29
	M	4720	11.82	106200	11.81
	S	1122	2.81	25245	2.81
ALL		39922	100.00	898995	100.00

Titling and formatting   There are four sources of text for page, row, and column titles:

- formatted class values
- literals attached to variable or keyword names in the TABLE statement
- variable names or labels (for both class and analysis variables)
- keyword names or labels (for statistics and ALL).

See **DETAILS** for the use of each of these sources.

SPECIFICATIONS

The TABULATE procedure is controlled by the following statements:

PROC TABULATE *options;*
  CLASS *variables;*
  VAR *variables;*
  FREQ *variable;*
  WEIGHT *variable;*
  FORMAT *variables format.;*
  LABEL *variable = label;*
  BY *variables;*
  TABLE [*dimension __expression,*] [*dimension __expression,*]
    dimension __expression/options;
  KEYLABEL *keyword = text;*

The PROC TABULATE statement is always accompanied by one or more TABLE statements specifying the tables to be produced. Classification variables used in TABLE statements must be specified in the CLASS statement. Analysis variables used in TABLE statements must appear in the VAR statement. A variable that appears in both a CLASS statement and a VAR statement is used as a CLASS variable only. The WEIGHT, FREQ, and BY statements are optionally specified once for the entire procedure step.

The TABLE and KEYLABEL statements must follow any other statements (including LABEL, FORMAT, and TITLE statements) used with the TABULATE procedure.

PROC TABULATE Statement

PROC TABULATE *options;*

The options below may appear on the PROC TABULATE statement:

DATA = *SASdataset* specifies the SAS data set to be used by TABULATE. If not specified, TABULATE uses the most recently created SAS data set.

MISSING requests that missing values be considered as valid levels for the classification variables. Special missing values are considered as different level values. Unless MISSING is specified, TABULATE does not include observations with a missing value for one or more classification variables in the analysis.

FORMAT = *w.d* specifies a default format for the formatting of each table cell where *w* is the field width and *d* is the number of digits to the right of the decimal (*d* may be omitted). If no value is specified, the default value is 12.2. The default format is always overridden by any formats specified in a TABLE statement. This option is especially useful for decreasing the number of print positions required to print a table.

ORDER = FREQ
ORDER = DATA
ORDER = INTERNAL
ORDER = FORMATTED

specifies the order in which the class variable values are displayed in each table. If ORDER = FREQ, the class values are ordered by descending frequency count so that class values occurring in the most observations will come first. If ORDER = DATA, class values are kept in the order they were encountered in the data set. If ORDER=INTERNAL, the class values are ordered by the internal representation of the values. If ORDER=FORMATTED, the class values are ordered by the formatted (external representation) of the value. If you omit ORDER= or give an unrecognized value, TABULATE orders by the internal value.

FORMCHAR='*string*' defines the characters to be used for constructing the table outlines and dividers. The value is a string 11 characters long defining the two bar characters, vertical and horizontal, and the nine corner characters: upper left, upper middle, upper right, middle left, middle middle (cross), middle right, lower left, lower middle, and lower right. The default value is FORMCHAR='|----|+|---'. Any character or hexadecimal string may be substituted to customize the table appearance. Specifying FORMCHAR='   ' (11 blanks) will produce tables with no outlines or dividers. If you have your printout routed to an IBM 6670 using an extended font (typestyle 27 or 225) with input character set 216, we recommend:

FORMCHAR='FABFACCCBCEB8FECABCBBB'X.

If you are printing on a printer with a TN (text) print train, we recommend:

FORMCHAR='4FBFACBFBC4F8F4FABBFBB'X.

See the CALENDAR procedure for an illustration of these characters.

CLASS Statement

CLASS *variables;*

The CLASS (or CLASSES) statement is used to identify variables in the input data set as classification variables. Any classification variable used in a TABLE statement must be included in this list. The variables may have either numeric or character values. Normally each class variable has a small number of discrete values or unique levels. Continuous values for a numeric variable can be grouped into discrete levels using PROC FORMAT.

VAR Statement

VAR *variables;*

The VAR (or VARIABLES) statement is used to identify numeric variables in the input data set as analysis variables. All analysis variables used in TABLE statements must be included in this list.

FREQ and WEIGHT Statements

FREQ *variable;*
WEIGHT *variable;*

Both the FREQ and WEIGHT statements specify a numeric variable on the input SAS data set whose values are used to weight each observation. Only one variable may be used in each statement; both statements may be used.

If the FREQ statement is used, each observation in the input data set is assumed to represent *n* observations, where *n* is the value of the FREQ variable. If the value is not an integer, the value is truncated to the integer portion. If the FREQ variable has a value less than 1, the observation is skipped.

If the WEIGHT statement is used, TABULATE uses the value of the WEIGHT variable to calculate a weighted mean and weighted variance. An observation with a WEIGHT value less than or equal to zero is skipped. Note that the WEIGHT variable value need not be an integer and does not affect the degrees of freedom.

BY Statement

BY *variables*;

A BY statement may be used with PROC TABULATE to obtain separate analyses on observations in groups defined by the BY variables. When a BY statement appears, the procedure expects the input data set to be sorted in order of the BY variables. If your input data set is not sorted in ascending order, use the SORT procedure with a similar BY statement to sort the data, or, if appropriate, use the BY statement options NOTSORTED or DESCENDING. For more information, see the discussion of the BY statement in Chapter 8, "Statements Used in the PROC Step."

Note that the page dimension expression of a TABLE statement can have a similar effect. The page dimension should be used in most cases where a new page is desired for a given level of a class variable or combination of variables.

FORMAT and LABEL Statements

The FORMAT and LABEL statements are especially useful with PROC TABULATE. You can use PROC FORMAT to specify discrete levels for a classification variable. The format specified is also used in any page, row, or column titles where the class variable appears. Any label text specified in a LABEL statement for a classification or analysis variable is used in any page, row, or column titles where that variable appears.

TABLE Statement

The form of the TABLE statement is:

TABLE [*expression*,] [*expression*,] *expression* [/*options*];

where *expression* is of the form:

(*expression*expression*	(Nesting)
or *expression expression*	(Concatenation)
or (*expression*)	(Grouping)
or *classvariable*[=*labeltext*]	
or *analysisvariable*[=*labeltext*]	
or *statistic*[=*labeltext*])	
[* *formatspecification*],	

statistic is of the form:

statistic keyword
or (PCTN or PCTSUM)<*denominatornesting*...>,

denominatornesting is of the form:

  classvariable[**classvariable*...],

and *formatspecification* is of the form:

  (F or FORMAT) = (*w.d* or *w*) .

A TABLE statement consists of one to three dimension expressions separated by commas and followed by an option list. If all three are specified, the leftmost expression defines pages, the middle expression defines rows, and the rightmost expression defines columns. If two expressions are specified, the left defines rows and the right defines columns. If a single expression is specified, it defines columns. An expression is an alternation of operands and operators. The operators are:

  *   for nesting
  space for concatenation

If both nesting and concatenation are used in an expression the nesting operator takes precedence. Parentheses may be used to group expressions and alter the order of operator evaluation.
  The operands are:

  expressions in parentheses
  class variables (from the CLASS statement) or "ALL"
  analysis variables (from the VAR statement)
  statistics
  format specifications.

Analysis variable names and statistic names may appear in the same dimension or in any combination of different dimensions. However, all analysis variables must appear together in one dimension and all statistic names must appear together in one dimension. An analysis variable cannot be nested with another analysis variable and a statistic cannot be nested with another statistic. If a variable name (classification or analysis) and a statistic name are the same, specify the statistic name in single quotes. The ALL keyword may also be specified in this manner in case of a name conflict. (See **DETAILS** below for a discussion of the keyword ALL.) The following are examples of valid expressions using analysis variable X and class variables A, B, C, and D:

A	class variable
MEAN	statistic
X	analysis variable
A*B	class nesting
A*B*C	multiple class nesting
A*MEAN*X	mean for X within A
A B	class concatenation
A B*C	concatenation of A and B*C
(A B)*C	nesting of C within A B (equivalent to A*C B*C)
(A B)*(C D)*E	nesting of E within C D which is nested within A B (equivalent to A*C*E A*D*E B*C*E B*D*E) .

If any analysis variables are specified, one or more of the following statistics may be requested:

N	number of observations with nonmissing analysis variable values in the subgroup determined by the

	combination of class variable values
NMISS	number of observations in the subgroup having missing values for the analysis variable
MEAN	mean
STD	standard deviation
MIN	minimum value
MAX	maximum value
RANGE	range of values
SUM	sum
USS	uncorrected sum of squares
CSS	sum of squares corrected for the mean
STDERR	standard error of the mean
CV	coefficient of variation
T	Student's t value for testing the hypothesis that the population mean is 0
PRT	probability of a greater absolute value for the Student's t value
VAR	variance
SUMWGT	sum of weight variable values
PCTN	the percentage that the number of observations in a subgroup is of the number of observations in the group. If no denominator is given, the total number of observations in the data set or BY-group is used.
PCTSUM	the percentage that the sum of analysis variable values in a subgroup is of the sum of analysis variable values in the group. If no denominator is given, the sum for the data set or BY-group is used.

If no analysis variables are specified in the TABLE statement, either N or PCTN may be requested as a statistic. If analysis variables are specified, but no statistic, the statistic is assumed to be SUM. If neither an analysis variable nor a statistic appears in the TABLE statement, each table cell will be the frequency count for a particular combination of the class variables specified.

Format items have the form FORMAT=$w.d$ or F=$w.d$ where w is the field width and d is the number of digits to the right of the decimal place. Zero positions after the decimal may be specified as F=$w.$ or F=$w.0$.

A TABLE statement may define only one table. Multiple TABLE statements may appear after the PROC TABULATE statement, each defining a separate table.

The options that may appear on the TABLE statement are described below:

PRINTMISS	specifies that rows containing only missing values are to be printed. Unless PRINTMISS is specified, these rows are not printed. Although rows that contain only missing values may be suppressed, all columns must print. If nonmissing values are sparse and only nonmissing table cells are of interest, you can organize the table so that entire rows are missing rather than entire columns whenever possible. If an entire logical page contains only missing values, that page will not print regardless of the PRINTMISS option specification.
MISSTEXT = 'text'	supplies up to 20 characters of text to be printed in table cells containing missing values.
FUZZ = nnn	supplies a numeric value against which analysis

variable values and table cell values are compared to eliminate trivial values (absolute values less than FUZZ) from computation and printing. A number whose absolute value is less than FUZZ is treated as zero for computations and printing. The default FUZZ value is 1E–70.

RTSPACE=*n* supplies an integer value that specifies the number of
RTS=*n* print positions allotted to row titles. The print positions include those for the left and right boundaries of row titles. (The right row title boundary is also the left boundary of table cells.) The default value is one-fourth of the LINESIZE value.

KEYLABEL Statement

KEYLABEL *keyword*=*text;*

keyword is one of the valid statistic names discussed above or the universal class variable ALL, and

text is up to 40 characters of labeling information. If *text* includes blanks or special characters, *text* must be enclosed in quotes.

The replacement text will be used in any label where the specified keyword is used, unless another label is specified in the TABLE statement. The KEYLABEL statement is useful for relabeling a keyword name once rather than for each occurrence in one or more TABLE statements. Only one keyword label may be specified for each keyword in a particular PROC TABULATE step; if multiple labels are requested for the same keyword, the last one specified is used. An example of a KEYLABEL statement is:

```
KEYLABEL ALL='TOTAL $'
   MEAN=AVERAGE
   PCTSUM='PERCENT OF SUM';
```

DETAILS

Input Data Set

Classification variables may have either alphabetic or numeric values. PROC FORMAT may be used to reduce many input values for a classification variable to a few class levels and to give more descriptive titles to raw level values. Analysis variables must be numeric.

Missing Values

A missing value in a classification variable causes the observation to be ignored unless MISSING is specified on the PROC statement. The MISSING option causes a missing value to be treated as another classification level; special missing values form other distinct levels. A missing analysis variable increments the statistic NMISS, the number of observations in the sub-group having a missing value in the analysis variable. The missing value does not affect any other calculations.

Expanding TABLE Statement Nestings

To understand how TABULATE expands the dimension expressions, first imagine that the commas separating dimension expressions are nesting operators (*). (The commas merely indicate which portion of the titling should appear in which dimension.) In order to eliminate concatenations, nest each element of a concatenation within all sub-nestings that precede it and above all sub-nestings that follow it. For convenience, begin at the left and repeat for each succeeding concatenation until none are left.

Example: TABLE A,(B C*D),(E F);

Replace commas:	A*(B C*D)*(E F)
Expand (B C*D):	A*B*(E F)
	A*C*D*(E F)
Expand (E F):	A*B*E
	A*B*F
	A*C*D*E
	A*C*D*F

Thus, the TABLE statement for the second example in the chapter expands to

REGION*CITYSIZE*POP*SUM

and the TABLE statement for the third example expands to

REGION*CITYSIZE*POP*SUM
REGION*CITYSIZE*POP*MEAN.

The Universal Class Variable ALL

The universal class variable represents a special class that has only one value. That value represents all of the observations that share a common level of the next higher classification variable. Thus, this subset of observations is the entire subset defined by the class values nested above ALL in the expanded nesting. Recall the hierarchy discussed earlier:

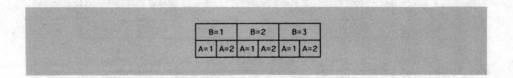

If B and A are CLASS variables then the expression that specifies the hierarchy is B*A. To summarize all values of A within each value of B, use the expression B*(A ALL). The new hierarchy follows:

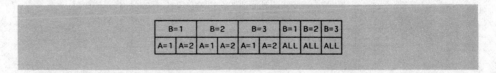

The additional nodes at the bottom level represent the unions of all A values that share a common B value.

ALL may be specified more than once in an expression. For example, (ALL B)*(ALL A) produces the following hierarchy:

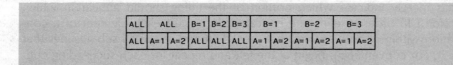

Consider the marketing research example we have been developing. You can use ALL to produce sales summaries in several dimensions. There are two sets of columns, one for wholesale and one for retail sales. (SALETYPE ALL)*(QUANTITY AMOUNT) produces a third set of columns that summarize the previous two. There are also two sets of rows, one for REGION and one for CITYSIZE. Each of these sets individually accounts for all sales of a given product. If totalled, each set should yield the same total sales value for each product (unless one of the class variables has missing values). REGION ALL CITYSIZE ALL produces two summary rows, one for REGION and one for CITYSIZE. There is an individual logical page for each product code. The concatenation, ALL PRODUCT, in the page dimension produces a summary page which incorporates sales for all products. The entire TABLE statement is:

```
TABLE ALL PRODUCT, REGION ALL CITYSIZE ALL,
    (SALETYPE ALL)*(QUANTITY*F=6 AMOUNT*F=10.2);
```

ALL

	SALETYPE					
	R		W		ALL	
	QUANT-ITY	AMOUNT	QUANT-ITY	AMOUNT	QUANT-ITY	AMOUNT
	SUM	SUM	SUM	SUM	SUM	SUM
REGION						
NC	3810	95200.00	3810	76200.00	7620	171400.00
NE	4869	121725.00	4869	97380.00	9738	219105.00
SO	5706	143450.00	5706	114120.00	11412	257570.00
WE	5576	139400.00	5576	111520.00	11152	250920.00
ALL	19961	499775.00	19961	399220.00	39922	898995.00
CITYSIZE						
L	9651	241275.00	9651	193020.00	19302	434295.00
M	7400	185950.00	7400	148000.00	14800	333950.00
S	2910	72550.00	2910	58200.00	5820	130750.00
ALL	19961	499775.00	19961	399220.00	39922	898995.00

PRODUCT A100

	SALETYPE				ALL	
	R		W			
	QUANT-ITY	AMOUNT	QUANT-ITY	AMOUNT	QUANT-ITY	AMOUNT
	SUM	SUM	SUM	SUM	SUM	SUM
REGION						
NC	1250	31250.00	1250	25000.00	2500	56250.00
NE	1600	40000.00	1600	32000.00	3200	72000.00
SO	1880	47000.00	1880	37600.00	3760	84600.00
WE	1840	46000.00	1840	36800.00	3680	82800.00
ALL	6570	164250.00	6570	131400.00	13140	295650.00
CITYSIZE						
L	3190	79750.00	3190	63800.00	6380	143550.00
M	2440	61000.00	2440	48800.00	4880	109800.00
S	940	23500.00	940	18800.00	1880	42300.00
ALL	6570	164250.00	6570	131400.00	13140	295650.00

PRODUCT A200

	SALETYPE				ALL	
	R		W			
	QUANT-ITY	AMOUNT	QUANT-ITY	AMOUNT	QUANT-ITY	AMOUNT
	SUM	SUM	SUM	SUM	SUM	SUM
REGION						
NC	1295	32375.00	1295	25900.00	2590	58275.00
NE	1645	41125.00	1645	32900.00	3290	74025.00
SO	1925	48925.00	1925	38500.00	3850	87425.00
WE	1885	47125.00	1885	37700.00	3770	84825.00
ALL	6750	169550.00	6750	135000.00	13500	304550.00
CITYSIZE						
L	3250	81250.00	3250	65000.00	6500	146250.00
M	2500	63500.00	2500	50000.00	5000	113500.00
S	1000	24800.00	1000	20000.00	2000	44800.00
ALL	6750	169550.00	6750	135000.00	13500	304550.00

PRODUCT A300

	SALETYPE				ALL	
	R		W			
	QUANT-ITY	AMOUNT	QUANT-ITY	AMOUNT	QUANT-ITY	AMOUNT
	SUM	SUM	SUM	SUM	SUM	SUM
REGION						
NC	1265	31575.00	1265	25300.00	2530	56875.00
NE	1624	40600.00	1624	32480.00	3248	73080.00
SO	1901	47525.00	1901	38020.00	3802	85545.00
WE	1851	46275.00	1851	37020.00	3702	83295.00
ALL	6641	165975.00	6641	132820.00	13282	298795.00
CITYSIZE						
L	3211	80275.00	3211	64220.00	6422	144495.00
M	2460	61450.00	2460	49200.00	4920	110650.00
S	970	24250.00	970	19400.00	1940	43650.00
ALL	6641	165975.00	6641	132820.00	13282	298795.00

Denominator Definitions for Percents

The general form of a percent specification is

   (PCTN or PCTSUM) <*denominatordefinitions*> [=*label*].

Each denominator definition is a nesting of class variables. Multiple definitions may appear within the enclosing brackets and the definitions may be in any order. Denominator values are the totals of N or SUM cells within each specified nesting. In order to obtain percentages of nesting totals within a table dimension, specify denominator definitions that include all classes in the portion of the expanded nesting for the appropriate dimension. For example, to request percentages of column totals for row nestings, specify denominator definitions that contain all row dimension classes. The examples below illustrate percentages of row and column totals.

Percentages of row totals   If all classes in the column dimension and only classes in the column dimension appear in the denominator definition, TABULATE calculates percentages of row totals for each column dimension nesting. If there is only one column nesting, the percentages are of row totals. For example:

   TABLE A*F=8,B*(N PCTN<B>)/RTS=8;

	B			
	1		2	
	N	PCTN	N	PCTN
A				
1	10	25	30	75
2	20	33	40	67

The denominator value for PCTN in row 1 is 40, the total of N values in row 1. The denominator value for PCTN in row 2 is 60, the total of N values in row 2.

Percentages of column totals   If all classes in the row dimension and only classes in the row dimension appear in the denominator definition, TABULATE calculates percentages of column totals for each row dimension nesting. If there is only one row nesting, the percentages are of column totals. For example:

TABLE A*F=8,B*(N PCTN<A>)/RTS=8;

		B		
		1		2
	N	PCTN	N	PCTN
A				
1	10	33	30	43
2	20	67	40	57

The denominator value for PCTN in column 2 is 30, the total of N values in column 1. The denominator value for PCTN in column 4 is 70, the total of N values in column 3.

Percentages of other totals   If all classes in the page dimension and only classes in the page dimension appear in the denominator definition, TABULATE calculates percentages of row and column totals for each page dimension nesting.

Denominator definitions may contain class variables from more than one dimension. The percentages calculated are of sub-table totals. For example:

TABLE A*F=8,B*(N PCTN<A*B>);

		B		
		1		2
	N	PCTN	N	PCTN
A				
1	10	10	30	30
2	20	20	40	40

The denominator value for all PCTN cells in this table is 100, the total of the N values in the sub-table of the denominator definition.

If no denominator definition list follows the percent keyword, the percentages are calculated on data set totals (or BY-group totals if a BY statement is used).

Relation to TABLE statement nestings   Specifying a denominator definition causes all N or SUM values within each interaction of non-denominator class variable levels to be accumulated into denominator totals. For example, if A and B are class variables each with values 1 and 2, the statement

TABLE A,B*(N PCTN<A>);

produces the following class level interactions for the nesting A*B: A=1*B=1, A=1*B=2, A=2*B=1, A=2*B=2. TABULATE generates special internal nestings which substitute the universal classification variable ALL for each class in the denominator definition: ALL*B. The new interactions are ALL*B=1 and ALL*B=2. The effect of collecting N values for these internal interactions is to include the values associated with table interactions A=1*B=1 and A=2*B=1 in a single total associated with internal interaction ALL*B=1 and values associated with table interactions A=1*B=2 and A=2*B=2 in a single total associated with internal interaction ALL*B=2. Each percent cell is calculated by dividing its associated N or SUM cell value by the appropriate denominator and multiplying by 100.

Denominator values may be included in the table by incorporating the internal nestings into the TABLE statement. For row, column, and page percentages, concatenate ALL in the appropriate dimension and include ALL as a denominator definition.

The following example illustrates the use of ALL with column percentages. The denominator value is 460, the total of SUM values in column 1.

TABLE A*B ALL,X*(SUM PCTSUM<A*B ALL>)/RTS=16;

A	B	X SUM	X PCTSUM
1	1	160	35
	2	80	17
2	1	100	22
	2	120	26
ALL		460	100

TABLE statement nestings may be abbreviated by embedding concatenations within nestings. For example, A*B*(C D) abbreviates the longer expression (A*B*C A*B*D). However, no embedded concatenations are allowed in denominator definitions. Nevertheless, all concatenations that contain a percent keyword must be represented among the denominator definitions for that keyword. In the above example, if the denominators are B*C and B*D, then both nestings must appear in the denominator list, as in

TABLE A*B,(C D)*(N PCTN<B*C B*D>);

If the denominator is A*B, the nesting needs to be specified only once since it is fully contained in both concatenations. For example:

TABLE A*B,(C D)*(N PCTN<A*B>);

Titling and Formatting

There are four sources of text for page, row, and column titles:

- formatted class values,
- literals attached to variable or keyword names in the TABLE statement,
- variable names or labels (for both class and analysis variables),
- keyword names or labels (for statistics and ALL).

Formatted class values can be supplied directly from the input data set or variables can be associated with formats created by the FORMAT procedure. Variable names and keywords will be used as titles unless some text has been designated for use in place of the name. Literals may be included in the TABLE statement following the name to which they apply (for example, ALL='REGIONAL TOTAL'). If there are no embedded blanks or special characters the quotes may be omitted. Literals attached to percent keywords must follow the bracketed denominator definition list. Multiple instances of the same name may be attached to different literals. (See ALL in the following example.)

If a LABEL or KEYLABEL statement has been used for a variable or keyword and no literal has been attached to the name in the TABLE statement, then the label text is used in the table titles. Some instances of a name may be attached to a literal in the TABLE statement while others are associated with a label. The appropriate text is used in each case. The syntax of the KEYLABEL statement is identical with that of the LABEL statement.

TABULATE automatically splits title text to fit the space allotted. If a blank or space appears in the title, the split will occur at the blank or hyphen. If there is not a blank or hyphen, TABULATE inserts a hyphen at the last position of the current line and continues the title on the next line. If a word in a title is known to be too long to fit in the allotted space, you can force a split by inserting a hyphen into the label or formatted value. For example, if SEPTEMBER is the title of a column 7 or 8 positions wide, you can force a break between M and B by formatting the value as 'SEPTEM-BER'.

Table cell values are formatted using $w.d$ format items (FORMAT=$w.d$ or F=$w.d$). Format items appear in the TABLE statement as though they were class or variable names. Format items may appear in any dimension. If two or more format items become nested with each other in the expanded nesting, the format with the least scope (in other words, the format closer to the column dimension, or closer to the end of the statement) overrides the other formats.

Formats that appear in the page dimension apply to all rows and columns in the associated pages. Formats that appear in the row dimension apply to all columns in the associated rows. Formats that appear in the column dimension apply to all rows in the associated columns. More than one format may apply to rows on the same logical page. Each column width for the logical page is the width of the widest row element in that column. The d portion of the format is applied to each row as specified. The default format is F=12.2. The following example reworks the marketing research tables from above.

```
PROC FORMAT;
   VALUE $REGFMT NC='NORTH CENTRAL'
                 NE=NORTHEAST
                 SO=SOUTH
                 WE=WEST;
   VALUE $SIZEFMT S='UNDER 50000'
                  M='50000 TO 500000'
                  L='OVER 500000';
   VALUE $SALEFMT W=WHOLESALE
                  R=RETAIL;
```

```
PROC TABULATE;
  CLASS PRODUCT REGION CITYSIZE SALETYPE;
  VAR QUANTITY AMOUNT;
  FORMAT REGION $REGFMT.;
  FORMAT CITYSIZE $SIZEFMT.;
  FORMAT SALETYPE $SALEFMT.;
  LABEL PRODUCT='PRODUCT CODE'
        REGION='REGION OF COUNTRY'
        CITYSIZE='CITY SIZE'
        SALETYPE='TYPE OF SALE'
        AMOUNT='$ AMOUNT';
  TABLE (ALL PRODUCT)*F=8, REGION ALL='REGIONAL TOTAL',
        (SALETYPE ALL)*(QUANTITY AMOUNT);
  KEYLABEL SUM='OF SALES'
           ALL=TOTAL;
```

TOTAL

REGION OF COUNTRY	RETAIL QUANTITY OF SALES	RETAIL $ AMOUNT OF SALES	WHOLESALE QUANTITY OF SALES	WHOLESALE $ AMOUNT OF SALES	TOTAL QUANTITY OF SALES	TOTAL $ AMOUNT OF SALES
NORTH CENTRAL	3810	95200	3810	76200	7620	171400
NORTHEAST	4869	121725	4869	97380	9738	219105
SOUTH	5706	143450	5706	114120	11412	257570
WEST	5576	139400	5576	111520	11152	250920
REGIONAL TOTAL	19961	499775	19961	399220	39922	898995

PRODUCT CODE A100

REGION OF COUNTRY	RETAIL QUANTITY OF SALES	RETAIL $ AMOUNT OF SALES	WHOLESALE QUANTITY OF SALES	WHOLESALE $ AMOUNT OF SALES	TOTAL QUANTITY OF SALES	TOTAL $ AMOUNT OF SALES
NORTH CENTRAL	1250	31250	1250	25000	2500	56250
NORTHEAST	1600	40000	1600	32000	3200	72000
SOUTH	1880	47000	1880	37600	3760	84600
WEST	1840	46000	1840	36800	3680	82800
REGIONAL TOTAL	6570	164250	6570	131400	13140	295650

```
PRODUCT CODE A200
-----------------------------------------------------------------------
|          |                      TYPE OF SALE                         |
|          |-----------------------------------------------------------|
|          |     RETAIL      |    WHOLESALE     |       TOTAL           |
|          |-----------------+------------------+----------------------|
|          |QUANTITY|$ AMOUNT|QUANTITY|$ AMOUNT |QUANTITY |$ AMOUNT     |
|          |--------+--------+--------+---------+---------+-------------|
|          |OF SALES|OF SALES|OF SALES|OF SALES |OF SALES |OF SALES     |
|----------+--------+--------+--------+---------+---------+-------------|
|REGION OF |        |        |        |         |         |             |
|COUNTRY   |        |        |        |         |         |             |
|----------|        |        |        |         |         |             |
|NORTH     |        |        |        |         |         |             |
|CENTRAL   |   1295 |  32375 |   1295 |   25900 |    2590 |    58275    |
|----------+--------+--------+--------+---------+---------+-------------|
|NORTHEAST |   1645 |  41125 |   1645 |   32900 |    3290 |    74025    |
|----------+--------+--------+--------+---------+---------+-------------|
|SOUTH     |   1925 |  48925 |   1925 |   38500 |    3850 |    87425    |
|----------+--------+--------+--------+---------+---------+-------------|
|WEST      |   1885 |  47125 |   1885 |   37700 |    3770 |    84825    |
|----------+--------+--------+--------+---------+---------+-------------|
|REGIONAL  |        |        |        |         |         |             |
|TOTAL     |   6750 | 169550 |   6750 |  135000 |   13500 |   304550    |
-----------------------------------------------------------------------
```

```
PRODUCT CODE A300
-----------------------------------------------------------------------
|          |                      TYPE OF SALE                         |
|          |-----------------------------------------------------------|
|          |     RETAIL      |    WHOLESALE     |       TOTAL           |
|          |-----------------+------------------+----------------------|
|          |QUANTITY|$ AMOUNT|QUANTITY|$ AMOUNT |QUANTITY |$ AMOUNT     |
|          |--------+--------+--------+---------+---------+-------------|
|          |OF SALES|OF SALES|OF SALES|OF SALES |OF SALES |OF SALES     |
|----------+--------+--------+--------+---------+---------+-------------|
|REGION OF |        |        |        |         |         |             |
|COUNTRY   |        |        |        |         |         |             |
|----------|        |        |        |         |         |             |
|NORTH     |        |        |        |         |         |             |
|CENTRAL   |   1265 |  31575 |   1265 |   25300 |    2530 |    56875    |
|----------+--------+--------+--------+---------+---------+-------------|
|NORTHEAST |   1624 |  40600 |   1624 |   32480 |    3248 |    73080    |
|----------+--------+--------+--------+---------+---------+-------------|
|SOUTH     |   1901 |  47525 |   1901 |   38020 |    3802 |    85545    |
|----------+--------+--------+--------+---------+---------+-------------|
|WEST      |   1851 |  46275 |   1851 |   37020 |    3702 |    83295    |
|----------+--------+--------+--------+---------+---------+-------------|
|REGIONAL  |        |        |        |         |         |             |
|TOTAL     |   6641 | 165975 |   6641 |  132820 |   13282 |   298795    |
-----------------------------------------------------------------------
```

   A logical page can contain more rows and columns than can be printed on one physical page. If so, TABULATE automatically divides the logical page into subsets and prints all rows for a given set of columns before moving to the next set of columns. The single logical page depicted below would be divided as indicated:

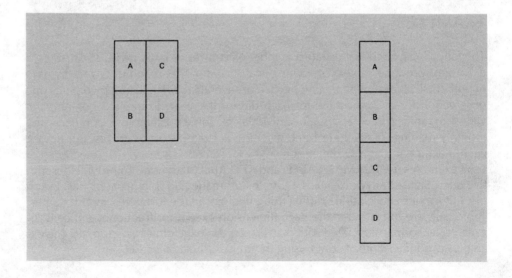

TABULATE never places multiple logical pages on one physical page.

Limitations

All cell values for a logical page must fit in memory at one time. Increasing the memory available to SAS will increase the number of table cells per logical page that can be handled.

All columns comprising a base pattern for the column hierarchy must fit on a physical page. A base pattern is a group of columns which form a constant width. For example, A*(X*F = 5 Y*F = 7) can produce the following columns:

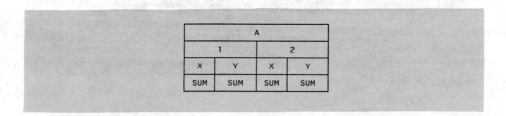

At the level of X and Y column widths may vary. However, the columns spanned by A = 1 form a base pattern whose width is the same for all values of A. This base width is used as a constant in constructing column titles for A and for any classes nested above A. If statistics and/or analysis variables are in the column dimension, one level of the lowest class variable spans a base pattern. The number of columns in the pattern is either the number of variables times the number of statistics, the number of analysis variables, or the number of statistics. If neither analysis variables nor statistics are in the column dimension, one level of the next to the lowest classification variable spans the pattern and the number of columns in the pattern is the number of levels of the lowest classification variable.

Historical Note

TABULATE was inspired in part by the pioneer software package TPL (Table Producing Language) developed at the Bureau of Labor Statistics.

EXAMPLES

The following examples illustrate a number of features of TABULATE. The first three examples produce tables containing statistics on the readings given by two hypothetical laboratory machines in each of several labs. The data set contains one observation for each machine for each day of the year. Example 1 contains the values organized into reports on individual machines. Example 2 compares the monthly readings of machine 1 and machine 2. Example 3 juxtaposes statistics for each machine in the row dimension.

All examples use FORMAT, LABEL, and KEYLABEL statements to provide descriptive titles. Statistic keyword labels illustrate automatic title splitting at blanks. Example 3 illustrates explicit title splitting using hyphens in the formatted month names. Table cells are formatted in the page dimension except for frequency (N) cells. In each case a format associated with N overrides the page dimension format. The examples produce summary rows using the universal classifier ALL.

Individual Reports of Machine Readings: Example 1

```
PROC FORMAT;
    VALUE MONFMT 1=JANUARY
                 2=FEBRUARY
                 3=MARCH
                 4=APRIL
                 5=MAY
                 6=JUNE
                 7=JULY
                 8=AUGUST
                 9=SEPTEMBER
                 10=OCTOBER
                 11=NOVEMBER
                 12=DECEMBER;
    VALUE MFMT 1='MACHINE 1'
               2='MACHINE 2';
PROC TABULATE FORMCHAR='FABFACCCBCEB8FECABCBBB'X;
    CLASS LAB__ID M__ID MONTHNUM;
    VAR READING;
    FORMAT MONTHNUM MONFMT.;
    FORMAT M__ID MFMT.;
    LABEL LAB__ID=LABORATORY
          M__ID='MACHINE LAB REPORT'
          MONTHNUM=MONTH;
    KEYLABEL ALL=SUMMARY
             N=FREQUENCY
             STD='STANDARD DEVIATION';
    TABLE LAB__ID*F=9.3, MONTHNUM ALL, M__ID*READING*
       (N*F=9 MEAN RANGE STD);
```

LABORATORY 1

MONTH	MACHINE LAB REPORT			
	MACHINE 1			
	READING			
	FREQUENCY	MEAN	RANGE	STANDARD DEVIATION
JANUARY	31	0.500	1.895	0.466
FEBRUARY	28	0.587	1.937	0.497
MARCH	31	0.403	1.727	0.388
APRIL	30	0.511	2.099	0.437
MAY	31	0.361	1.979	0.499
JUNE	30	0.364	1.639	0.441
JULY	31	0.474	1.734	0.510
AUGUST	31	0.466	2.094	0.550
SEPTEMBER	30	0.548	1.798	0.410
OCTOBER	31	0.581	2.189	0.523
NOVEMBER	30	0.432	2.068	0.496
DECEMBER	31	0.526	2.042	0.501
SUMMARY	365	0.479	2.532	0.478

Comparative Reports of Machine Readings by Columns: Example 2

This example reports the same data as Example 1, but in a different format.

```
TABLE LAB__ID*F=9.3, READING*(N*F=9 MEAN RANGE STD),
      MONTHNUM*M__ID/RTS=22;
```

LABORATORY 1

		MONTH			
		JANUARY		FEBRUARY	
		MACHINE LAB REPORT		MACHINE LAB REPORT	
		MACHINE 1	MACHINE 2	MACHINE 1	MACHINE 2
READING	FREQUENCY	31	31	28	28
READING	MEAN	0.500	0.606	0.587	0.565
READING	RANGE	1.895	1.817	1.937	2.078
READING	STANDARD DEVIATION	0.466	0.477	0.497	0.571

LABORATORY 1

		MONTH			
		MARCH		APRIL	
		MACHINE LAB REPORT		MACHINE LAB REPORT	
		MACHINE 1	MACHINE 2	MACHINE 1	MACHINE 2
READING	FREQUENCY	31	31	30	30
READING	MEAN	0.403	0.560	0.511	0.515
READING	RANGE	1.727	2.110	2.099	1.840
READING	STANDARD DEVIATION	0.388	0.565	0.437	0.535

Comparative Reports of Machine Readings by Rows: Example 3

This example uses the same machine data as the previous examples, but formats it a third way.

```
PROC FORMAT;
   VALUE MONFMT 1='JANU-ARY'
                2='FEBRU-ARY'
                3=MARCH
                4=APRIL
                5=MAY
                6=JUNE
                7=JULY
                8=AUGUST
                9='SEPTEM-BER'
               10='OCTO-BER'
               11='NOVEM-BER'
               12='DECEM-BER';
   VALUE MFMT 1='1'
              2='2';
```

```
PROC TABULATE FORMCHAR='FABFACCCBCEB8FECABCBBB'X;
  CLASS LAB__ID M__ID MONTHNUM;
  VAR READING;
  FORMAT MONTHNUM MONFMT.;
  FORMAT M__ID MFMT.;
  LABEL LAB__ID=LABORATORY
        M__ID=MACHINE
        MONTHNUM=MONTH;
  KEYLABEL ALL=SUMMARY
           N='NUMBER OF READINGS'
           STD='STANDARD DEVIATION';
  TABLE LAB__ID*F=7.3, (M__ID ALL )*(N*F=7 MEAN RANGE STD),
     (MONTHNUM ALL)*READING/RTS=22;
```

LABORATORY 1

		\multicolumn{7}{c}{MONTH}
		JANU-ARY	FEBRU-ARY	MARCH	APRIL	MAY	JUNE	JULY
		READING	READING	READING	READING	READING	READING	READING
MACHINE								
1	NUMBER OF READINGS	31	28	31	30	31	30	31
2	NUMBER OF READINGS	31	28	31	30	31	30	31
MACHINE								
1	MEAN	0.500	0.587	0.403	0.511	0.361	0.364	0.474
2	MEAN	0.606	0.565	0.560	0.515	0.548	0.472	0.606
MACHINE								
1	RANGE	1.895	1.937	1.727	2.099	1.979	1.639	1.734
2	RANGE	1.817	2.078	2.110	1.840	2.006	1.368	2.140
MACHINE								
1	STANDARD DEVIATION	0.466	0.497	0.388	0.437	0.499	0.441	0.510
2	STANDARD DEVIATION	0.477	0.571	0.565	0.535	0.496	0.408	0.569
SUMMARY	NUMBER OF READINGS	62	56	62	60	62	60	62
SUMMARY	MEAN	0.553	0.576	0.481	0.513	0.455	0.418	0.540
SUMMARY	RANGE	2.017	2.400	2.110	2.242	2.271	1.682	2.194
SUMMARY	STANDARD DEVIATION	0.470	0.531	0.487	0.484	0.502	0.425	0.540

Demographic Data Application: Example 4

Data for the following table are selected characteristics of U.S. cities with populations over 50,000 according to *County and City Data Book, 1977.* The class variables are POPGRP with three levels and REGION with four levels. The TABLE statement requests a table of POPGRP by REGION containing the number of observations, means, and standard deviation for the variable INCOMES, which is specified in the VAR statement.

Another example in Chapter 9, "PROC Step Applications," shows the DATA step that reads these census data into a SAS data set. PROC UNIVARIATE is used to determine cutoff points for the POPGRP variable. The FREQ, SUMMARY, and UNIVARIATE procedures are used for other approaches to these data.

```
PROC TABULATE DATA=CITIES FORMCHAR='FABFACCCBCEB8FECABCBBB'X;
   TITLE CENSUS DATA: OUTPUT FROM TABULATE PROCEDURE;
   FORMAT POPGRP PC.;
   VAR INCOME;
   CLASS POPGRP REGION;
   TABLE POPGRP*REGION, INCOME*(N*F=4.0 MEAN STD) / RTSPACE=22;
```

CENSUS DATA: OUTPUT FROM TABULATE PROCEDURE

		PER CAPITA MONEY INCOME (1974)		
		N	MEAN	STD
1975 POPULATI-ON ESTIMATE	REGION			
50,001-75,000	NORTH CENTRAL	38	5124.00	1013.08
	NORTHEAST	29	4574.14	599.37
	SOUTH	33	4367.73	758.38
	WEST	37	5142.27	1065.33
75,001-100,000	NORTH CENTRAL	29	5115.69	1008.90
	NORTHEAST	14	4588.00	1049.83
	SOUTH	12	4241.67	1120.23
	WEST	29	5050.62	862.08
OVER 100,000	NORTH CENTRAL	39	4684.56	417.71
	NORTHEAST	27	4401.48	668.50
	SOUTH	59	4628.17	667.63
	WEST	37	5146.92	684.30

A Marketing Research Application: Example 5

The following marketing research example analyzes advertisement recognition. Each observation contains the sex, income, and yes/no responses of a participant in the study. A "yes" response is coded as 1, a "no" response as 0. The DATA step sets the variable NORESP to 1 if all participant responses are missing; otherwise, it sets NORESP to missing. "No" responses are recoded to missing. The first table accumulates the count of non-missing response values for each ad variable (AD1–AD7) and cross-tabulates response frequencies with participant age, sex, and income. The second table cross-tabulates income with ad recognition frequencies and calculates row percentages.

Ideas for this example were contributed by The Guttman Group, Inc.

```
DATA;
   ARRAY ADS AD1-AD7;
   INPUT AGE SEX $ INCOME AD1-AD7;
   NORESP=1;
   DO OVER ADS;
     IF ADS¬=. THEN NORESP=.;
     IF ADS=0 THEN ADS=.;
     END;
CARDS;
50 M 30000 1 1 0 1 0 . 0
.
.
.
;
PROC FORMAT;
   VALUE AGEFMT 0-29='UNDER 30'
                30-49='30-49'
                50-70='50-70'
                OTHER='OVER 70';
   VALUE INCFMT 0-9999='UNDER 10,000'
                10000-15000='10,000-15,000'
                15001-50000='OVER 15000'
                .='NO ANSWER';
   VALUE $SEXFMT 'M'=MALE
                 'F'=FEMALE;
PROC TABULATE F=10 MISSING FORMCHAR='  ';
   TITLE 'AD RECOGNITION STUDY';
   CLASS SEX AGE INCOME;
   VAR AD1 AD2 AD3 AD4 AD5 AD6 AD7 NORESP;
   FORMAT AGE AGEFMT.;
   FORMAT INCOME INCFMT.;
   FORMAT SEX $SEXFMT.;
   LABEL AD1='MAN IN CLOWN SUIT'
         AD2='MAN IN ONE RED SHOE'
         AD3='CLOCK FACE'
         AD4='SILHOUETTE'
         AD5='SAW SOMETHING IN MAGAZINE'
         AD6='SAW SOMETHING ON TV'
         AD7='SAW SOMETHING IN NEWSPAPER'
         NORESP = 'NO RESPONSE';
   TABLE ALL='----    TOTAL    ----'                /*ROW DIMENSION*/
         AD1 AD2 AD3 AD4 AD5 AD6 AD7 NORESP,
         (ALL                           /*COLUMN DIMENSION*/
         SEX='+---S E X---+'
         AGE='+----------A G E----------+'
         INCOME='+-------I N C O M E-------+')
         *N='------'*F=6/RTS=30;
   TABLE ALL*(N PCTN) INCOME*PCTN,
         ALL AD1 AD2 AD3 AD4 AD5 AD6 AD7/RTS=18;
   KEYLABEL N=COUNT
            ALL=TOTAL
            PCTN=PERCENT;
```

AD RECOGNITION STUDY

	TOTAL	+---S E X---+ FEMALE	MALE	+----------A G E----------+ UNDER 30	30-49	50-70	OVER 70	+-------I N C O M E-------+ NO ANSWER	UNDER 10,000	10,000 15,000	OVER 15000
---- TOTAL ----	100	53	47	34	26	15	25	11	21	11	57
MAN IN CLOWN SUIT	34	18	16	18	5	5	6	3	7	4	20
MAN IN ONE RED SHOE	62	25	37	21	16	10	15	6	15	6	35
CLOCK FACE	31	15	16	9	5	5	12	2	8	2	19
SILHOUETTE	27	11	16	7	6	5	9	3	5	3	16
SAW SOMETHING IN MAGAZINE	44	28	16	17	14	3	10	7	7	6	24
SAW SOMETHING ON TV	28	14	14	7	8	4	9	3	7	1	17
SAW SOMETHING IN NEWSPAPER	19	13	6	6	5	3	5	2	6	3	8
NO RESPONSE	2	2	0	2	0	0	0	0	1	1	0

AD RECOGNITION STUDY

		TOTAL	MAN IN CLOWN SUIT	MAN IN ONE RED SHOE	CLOCK FACE	SILHOUETTE	SAW SOMETHING IN MAGAZINE	SAW SOMETHING ON TV	SAW SOMETHING IN NEWSPAPER
TOTAL	COUNT	100	34	62	31	27	44	28	19
	PERCENT	100	100	100	100	100	100	100	100
INCOME									
NO ANSWER	PERCENT	11	9	10	6	11	16	11	11
UNDER 10,000	PERCENT	21	21	24	26	19	16	25	32
10,000- 15,000	PERCENT	11	12	10	6	11	14	4	16
OVER 15000	PERCENT	57	59	56	61	59	55	61	42

The UNIVARIATE Procedure

ABSTRACT

The UNIVARIATE procedure produces simple descriptive statistics (including quantiles) for numeric variables.

INTRODUCTION

UNIVARIATE differs from other SAS procedures that produce descriptive statistics because it provides greater detail on the distribution of a variable. Features in UNIVARIATE include:

- detail on the extreme values of a variable
- quantiles, such as the median
- several plots to picture the distribution
- frequency tables
- a test that the data are normally distributed

If a BY statement is used with PROC UNIVARIATE, descriptive statistics are calculated separately for groups of observations. UNIVARIATE can also create one or more data sets containing calculated statistics.

SPECIFICATIONS

The following statements control the UNIVARIATE procedure:

PROC UNIVARIATE *options;*
   VAR *variables;*
   BY *variables;*
   FREQ *variable;*
   WEIGHT *variable;*
   ID *variables;*
   OUTPUT OUT =*SASdataset keyword* =*names ...;*

Several OUTPUT statements are permitted, but only one each of the other statements. The statements after the PROC statement can be in any order.

PROC UNIVARIATE Statement

   PROC UNIVARIATE *options;*

The options that may appear in the PROC UNIVARIATE statement are listed below.

DATA=*SASdataset*   names the SAS data set to be used by UNIVARIATE. If it is omitted, the most recently created SAS data set is used.

NOPRINT   suppresses all printed output. NOPRINT can be used when the only purpose for executing the procedure is to create new data sets.

PLOT   causes UNIVARIATE to produce a stem-and-leaf plot (or a horizontal bar chart), a box plot, and a normal probability plot.

FREQ   requests a frequency table consisting of the variable values, frequencies, percentages, and cumulative percentages.

NORMAL   causes UNIVARIATE to compute a test statistic for the hypothesis that the input data come from a normal distribution. The probability of a more extreme value of the test statistic is also printed.

DEF=*value*   specifies which of the four definitions given below in the section **Computational Method** is to be used to calculate percentiles. The DEF value may be 1, 2, 3, 4, or 5. If DEF= is omitted, definition 4 is used.

VAR Statement

VAR *variables*;

Univariate descriptive measures are calculated for all numeric variables listed in the VAR statement. If no VAR statement appears, all numeric variables in the data set are analyzed. A VAR statement must be included when an OUTPUT statement (below) is used.

BY Statement

BY *variables*;

A BY statement may be used with PROC UNIVARIATE to obtain separate analyses on observations in groups defined by the BY variables. When a BY statement appears, the procedure expects the input data set to be sorted in order of the BY variables. If your input data set is not sorted in ascending order, use the SORT procedure with a similar BY statement to sort the data, or, if appropriate, use the BY statement options NOTSORTED or DESCENDING. For more information, see the discussion of the BY statement in Chapter 8, "Statements Used in the PROC Step."

FREQ Statement

FREQ *variable*;

When a FREQ statement appears, each observation in the data set being analyzed is assumed to represent *n* observations, where *n* is the value of the FREQ variable. If the FREQ variable has a value that is less than one, the observation is not used in the analysis. If the value is not an integer, only the integer portion is used.

The statistics calculated using a FREQ statement are identical to an analysis produced using a data set that contains *n* observations in place of each observation in the input data set.

WEIGHT Statement

WEIGHT *variable*;

When a WEIGHT statement is specified, UNIVARIATE uses the value of the WEIGHT variable, w_i, to calculate a weighted mean $\bar{x}_w$ and a weighted variance s^2_w as

$$\bar{x}_w = \Sigma_i w_i x_i / \Sigma_i w_i$$

and

$$s^2_w = \Sigma_i w_i (x_i - \bar{x}_w)^2 / (n - 1)$$

where x_i is the variable value and n is the number of values.

If the value of the WEIGHT variable is less than zero, then a value of zero for the weight is assumed.

The value of the WEIGHT statement is used only to calculate the first two sample moments and related statistics. Hence, if a WEIGHT statement is used, measures of skewness and kurtosis are not calculated and are reported as missing values. The WEIGHT variable has no effect on the calculation of quantiles or extremes.

ID Statement

ID *variables*;

When an ID statement is used, the values of the first variable specified are used to identify observations in the printout listing of the five largest and five smallest values. In addition, if one or more OUTPUT statements are used, the values of the ID variables are placed in each output data set. The values of the ID variables used in the output data set are taken either from the first observation in the data set analyzed by UNIVARIATE or from the first observation in the current BY group, if a BY statement is used.

OUTPUT Statement

OUTPUT OUT=*SASdataset keyword*=*names*;

The OUTPUT statement requests PROC UNIVARIATE to output statistics to a new SAS data set. The options name the new data set and specify the variables to be included.

OUT=*SASdataset*   names the output data set. If you want to create a permanent SAS data set, you must specify a two-level name (see Chapter 12, "SAS Data Sets," for more information on permanent data sets).

keyword=*names*   specifies the statistics you want in the new data set and names the new variables that will contain the statistics. Write the keyword for the desired statistic, an equal sign, and the variable or variables to contain the statistic.

In the output data set, the first variable listed after a keyword in the OUTPUT statement contains that statistic for the first variable listed in the VAR statement; the second variable contains the statistic for the second variable in the VAR statement, and so on.

The list of variables following the equal sign may be shorter than the list of variables in the VAR statement.

The keywords represent the statistics as follows:

N	the number of observations on which the calculations were based
NMISS	the number of missing values
NOBS	the number of observations
MEAN	the mean
SUM	the sum
STD	the standard deviation
VAR	the variance
SKEWNESS	skewness
KURTOSIS	kurtosis
SUMWGT	the sum of the weights
MAX	the largest value
MIN	the smallest value
RANGE	the range
Q3	the upper quartile or the seventy-fifth percentile
MEDIAN	the median or the fiftieth percentile
Q1	the lower quartile or the twenty-fifth percentile
QRANGE	the difference between the upper and lower quartiles, that is, Q3-Q1
P1	the first percentile
P5	the fifth percentile
P10	the tenth percentile
P90	the ninetieth percentile
P95	the ninety-fifth percentile
P99	the ninety-ninth percentile
MODE	the most frequent value. If the mode is not unique, the smallest mode is used

The number of observations in the new data set corresponds to the number of groups for which statistics are calculated. The variables in the BY statement and ID statement as well as the computed statistics are included in the new data set.

For example, consider these statements:

```
PROC UNIVARIATE;
  VAR GRADE1 GRADE2;
  BY SEX;
  OUTPUT OUT=NEW MEAN=AVE1 AVE2 VAR=VAR1;
```

If the BY variable SEX has two values, F and M, the data set NEW contains two observations. Each of these observations contains the variables SEX, AVE1, AVE2, and VAR1.

Any number of OUTPUT statements may be used with each execution of PROC UNIVARIATE.

DETAILS

Missing Values

If a variable for which statistics are to be calculated has a missing value, that value is ignored in the calculation of statistics and the missing values are tabulated separately. A missing value for one such variable does not affect the treatment of other variables in the same observation.

If the WEIGHT variable has a missing value, the weight is taken to be zero. However, the observation is still used to calculate quantiles and extremes. If the FREQ variable has a missing value, the observation is not used at all.

If a variable in a BY or ID statement has a missing value, the procedure treats it as it would treat any other value of a BY or ID variable.

Output Data Set

If an OUTPUT statement is used, the corresponding output data set contains an observation for each unique set of values of the variables on the BY statement, or a single observation if there is no BY statement. The variables in each observation consist of the variables on the BY statement, the variables on the ID statement, and a selection of the statistics from the list above as selected on the OUTPUT statement.

The values of the variables listed on the BY statement are taken as those of the corresponding BY group, the values of the ID variables will be taken from the first observation of each BY group and the values of the statistics will be computed from the values of the variables within each BY group, or across all the data if there is no BY statement.

Computational Method

The sample mean, the sample standard deviation, the minimum, and the maximum are computed using the original data. All other statistics are computed after the data have been truncated to seven significant digits (single precision).

Standard algorithms (Fisher, 1973) are used to compute the moment statistics. Using the DEF= option, you can specify one of five methods for computing quantile statistics.

Let n be the number of non-missing values for a variable and let X_1, X_2, ..., X_n represent the ordered values of the variable. For the tth percentile, where $p = t/100$, let

$$np = j + g$$

where j is the integer part and g is the fractional part of np.

The tth percentile, y, say, is defined as:

Definition 1: weighted average at x_{np}

$$y = (1-g)x_j + gx_{j+1}$$

where x_o is taken to be x_1

Definition 2: observation numbered closest to np

$$y = x_i$$

where i is the integer part of $np + \frac{1}{2}$

Definition 3: empirical distribution function

$$y = x_j \text{ if } g = 0$$

$$y = x_{j+1} \text{ if } g > 0$$

Definition 4: weighted average aimed at $x_{p[n+1]}$

$$y = (1-g)x_j + gx_{j+1}$$

where $(n+1)p = j + g$

where x_{n+1} is taken to be x_n

Definition 5:   empirical distribution function with averaging

$$y = (x_j + x_{j+1})/2 \text{ if } g = 0$$

$$y = x_{j+1} \text{ if } g > 0$$

where $np = j + g$.

Computer Resources

The data are stored internally in single precision. For most efficient processing, an amount of temporary storage of $16\Sigma_i n_i$ bytes is required where n_i is the number of unique values for the ith variable. The minimum amount of temporary storage required is 16 MAX (n_i) in bytes. Additional storage is required for buffers for each output data set and for the input data set.

Test of Normality

When the NORMAL option is specified on the PROC UNIVARIATE statement, the procedure produces a test statistic for the null hypothesis that the input data values are a random sample from a normal distribution.

If the sample size is less than 51, the Shapiro-Wilk statistic, W, is computed. The W statistic is the ratio of the best estimator of the variance (based on the square of a linear combination of the order statistics) to the usual corrected sum-of-squares estimator of the variance. W must be greater than 0 and less than or equal to 1, with small values of W leading to rejection of the null hypothesis. The computed value of W is used to linearly interpolate within the range of sjmulated critical values given in Shapiro and Wilk (1965).

If the sample size is greater than 50, the data are tested against a normal distribution with mean and variance equal to the sample mean and variance. The usual Kolomogorov D statistic is computed and printed. The probability of a larger test statistic is obtained by forming the value

$$\sqrt{n - .01 + .85/\sqrt{n}}D$$

where n is the number of non-missing values. This value is used to linearly interpolate within the range of simulated critical values given in Stephens (1974).

Plots

When the PLOT option is specified on the PROC statement, UNIVARIATE generates three data plots.

The first plot is a stem-and-leaf plot (Tukey, 1977) if no more than 48 observations fall into a single interval. Otherwise, the procedure plots a horizontal bar chart.

The second plot is a box plot or schematic plot. The bottom and top edges of the box are located at the sample 25th and 75th percentiles. The center horizontal line is drawn at the sample median and the central plus sign (+) is at the sample mean. It is possible for all of these statistics to fall on the same printer line. The central vertical lines, called "whiskers," extend from the box as far as the data extend, to a distance of at most 1.5 interquartile ranges. (An interquartile range is the distance between the 25th and the 75th sample percentiles.) Any value more extreme than this is marked with a 0 if it is within 3 interquartile ranges of the box, or with an * if it is still more extreme. For more explanation about this plot see Tukey (1977).

The third plot, a normal probability plot, is a quantile-quantile plot of the data. The empirical quantiles are plotted against the quantiles of a standard normal distribution. Asterisks (*) mark the data values. The vertical coordinate is the data value and the horizontal coordinate is

$$\Phi^{-1}((r_i - 3/8)/ (n + 1/4))$$

where r_i is the rank of the data value, Φ^{-1} is the inverse of the standard normal distribution function, and n is the number of non-missing data values. The plus signs (+) provide a reference straight line that is drawn using the sample mean and standard deviation. If the data are from a normal distribution, they should tend to fall along the reference line.

Printed Output

For each variable, UNIVARIATE prints:

1. VARIABLE=, the name of the variable
2. the variable label
3. N, the number of observations on which the calculations are based
4. SUM WGTS, the sum of the weights of these observations
5. the MEAN
6. the SUM
7. STD DEV, the standard deviation
8. the VARIANCE
9. the measure of SKEWNESS
10. the measure of KURTOSIS
11. USS, the uncorrected sum of squares
12. CSS, the corrected sum of squares
13. CV, the coefficient of variation
14. STD MEAN, the standard error of the mean
15. T: MEAN=0, the Student's t value for testing the hypothesis that the population mean is 0
16. PROB>|T|, the probability of a greater absolute value for this t value
17. SGN RANK, the centered signed rank statistic for testing the hypothesis that the population mean is 0
18. PROB>|S|, an approximation to the probability of a greater absolute value for this statistic
19. NUM⌐=0, the number of nonzero observations
20. MAX, the largest value
21. Q3, Q1, and MED, the upper and lower quartiles, and the median
22. MIN, the smallest value
23. the RANGE
24. Q3-Q1, the difference between the upper and lower quartiles
25. the MODE
26. the first, fifth, tenth, ninetieth, ninety-fifth, and ninety-ninth percentiles (1%, 5%, 10%, 90%, 95%, 99%)
27. the five largest, HIGHEST, and five smallest, LOWEST, values.

If missing values occur for a variable, the following are printed:

28. the MISSING VALUE
29. COUNT, the number of occurrences
30. %COUNT/NOBS, the count as a percentage of the total number of observations
31. %COUNT/NMV, the count as a percentage of the total number of missing values (not shown).

UNIVARIATE can also print:

32. W:NORMAL...D:NORMAL, test statistics
33. associated probabilities, PROB<W or PROB>D, for testing the hypothesis that the data come from a normal distribution.
34. STEM LEAF, a stem-and-leaf plot (if any value's count is greater than 48,

a horizontal bar chart is printed instead)
35. BOX PLOT, a box plot
36. a NORMAL PROBABILITY PLOT
37. VALUE, a frequency table of variable values
38. COUNT, frequencies
39. CELL, percentages
40. CUM, cumulative percentages.

State Data: Example 1

In the following example, descriptive statistics are produced for the 1970 population of each of the 50 states (plus two fictional states to illustrate missing values). The ID statement makes it possible to identify the states with extreme populations.

```
DATA STATEPOP;
  INPUT STATE $ POP@@;
  LABEL POP=1970 CENSUS POPULATION IN MILLIONS;
  CARDS;
ALA 3.44      ALASKA 0.30    ARIZ 1.77     ARK 1.92      CALIF 19.95
COLO 2.21     CONN 3.03      DEL 0.55      FLA 6.79      GA 4.59
HAW 0.77      IDAHO 0.71     ILL 11.01     IND 5.19      IOWA 2.83
KAN 2.25      KY 3.22        LA 3.64       ME 0.99       MD 3.92
MASS 5.69     MICH 8.88      MINN 3.81     MISS 2.22     MO 4.68
MONT 0.69     NEB 1.48       NEV 0.49      NH 0.74       NJ 7.17
NM 1.02       NY 18.24       NC 5.08       ND 0.62       OHIO 10.65
OKLA 2.56     ORE 2.09       PA 11.79      RI 0.95       SC 2.59
SD 0.67       TENN 3.92      TEXAS 11.2    UTAH 1.06     VT 0.44
VA 4.65       WASH 3.41      W.VA 1.74     WIS 4.42      WYO 0.33
YY .          ZZ .
PROC UNIVARIATE FREQ PLOT NORMAL;
  VAR POP;
  ID STATE;
```

```
                                        UNIVARIATE                                                    1

①                        ②
VARIABLE=POP                 1970 CENSUS POPULATION IN MILLIONS

           MOMENTS                           QUANTILES(DEF=4)                              EXTREMES
                                          ⑳                                                   ㉗
③N            50④SUM WGTS        50 100%  MAX    19.95   99%        19.95   LOWEST    ID      HIGHEST    ID
 MEAN⑤       4.0472  SUM⑥     202.36  75%  Q3      4.78   95%       14.6925    0.3(ALASKA )    11.01(ILL   )
⑦STD DEV   4.32932⑧VARIANCE  18.743⑳50% MED      2.71  ㉖90%       10.974     0.33(WYO   )    11.2(TEXAS )
 SKEWNESS⑨ 2.05522  KURTOSIS⑩ 4.54561  25% Q1      0.98   10%        0.557     0.44(VT    )    11.79(PA    )
⑪USS        1737.4⑫CSS        918.407 ㉒0% MIN      0.3    5%        0.3905    0.49(NEV   )    18.24(NY    )
 CV ⑬      106.971⑭ STD MEAN⑭ 0.612258                   1%        0.3       0.55(DEL   )    19.95(CALIF )
⑮T:MEAN=0  6.61028⑯PROB>|T|    0.0001㉓RANGE     19.65
 SGN RANK⑰  637.5  PROB>|S|⑱  0.0001  Q3-Q1㉔     3.8
⑲NUM ¬= 0       50                    ㉕MODE      3.92
 W:NORMAL  0.763045 PROB<W      <0.01
   ㉜                  ㉝

                                          ㉘ MISSING VALUE              .
                                              COUNT ㉙        2
                                          ㉚ % COUNT/NOBS    3.85
```

(continued on next page)

(continued from previous page)

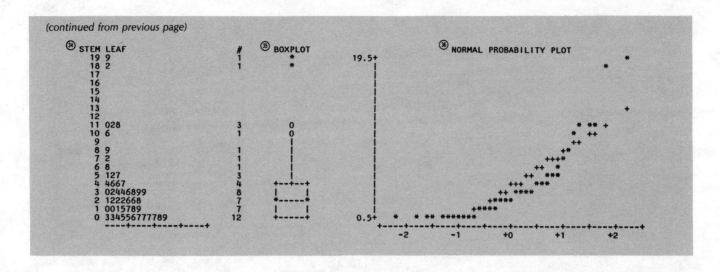

VARIABLE=POP   1970 CENSUS POPULATION IN MILLIONS

FREQUENCY TABLE

VALUE	COUNT	PERCENTS CELL	CUM	VALUE	COUNT	PERCENTS CELL	CUM	VALUE	COUNT	PERCENTS CELL	CUM
0.3	1	2.0	2.0	1.77	1	2.0	36.0	4.59	1	2.0	72.0
0.33	1	2.0	4.0	1.92	1	2.0	38.0	4.65	1	2.0	74.0
0.44	1	2.0	6.0	2.09	1	2.0	40.0	4.68	1	2.0	76.0
0.49	1	2.0	8.0	2.21	1	2.0	42.0	5.08	1	2.0	78.0
0.55	1	2.0	10.0	2.22	1	2.0	44.0	5.19	1	2.0	80.0
0.62	1	2.0	12.0	2.25	1	2.0	46.0	5.69	1	2.0	82.0
0.67	1	2.0	14.0	2.56	1	2.0	48.0	6.79	1	2.0	84.0
0.69	1	2.0	16.0	2.59	1	2.0	50.0	7.17	1	2.0	86.0
0.71	1	2.0	18.0	2.83	1	2.0	52.0	8.88	1	2.0	88.0
0.74	1	2.0	20.0	3.03	1	2.0	54.0	10.65	1	2.0	90.0
0.77	1	2.0	22.0	3.22	1	2.0	56.0	11.01	1	2.0	92.0
0.95	1	2.0	24.0	3.41	1	2.0	58.0	11.2	1	2.0	94.0
0.99	1	2.0	26.0	3.44	1	2.0	60.0	11.79	1	2.0	96.0
1.02	1	2.0	28.0	3.64	1	2.0	62.0	18.24	1	2.0	98.0
1.06	1	2.0	30.0	3.81	1	2.0	64.0	19.95	1	2.0	100.0
1.48	1	2.0	32.0	3.92	2	4.0	68.0				
1.74	1	2.0	34.0	4.42	1	2.0	70.0				

Census Data: Example 2

See Chapter 9, "PROC Step Applications," for another example using PROC UNIVARIATE to analyze selected characteristics of U.S. cities with populations over 50,000 according to *County and City Data Book, 1977*. The approaches of the FREQ, SUMMARY, and TABULATE procedures to these same data are compared.

REFERENCES

Fisher, R.A. (1973), *Statistical Methods for Research Workers*, 14th Edition, New York: Hafner Publishing Company.

Shapiro, S.S. and Wilk, M.B. (1965), "An Analysis of Variance Test for Normality (complete samples)," *Biometrika*, 52, 591-611.

Stephens, M.A. (1974), "EDF Statistics for Goodness of Fit and Some Comparisons," *Journal of the American Statistical Association*, 69, 730-737.

Tukey, J.W. (1977), *Exploratory Data Analysis*, Reading, Massachusetts: Addison-Wesley.

REPORTING

Introduction to SAS Reporting Procedures

CALENDAR

CHART

FORMS

PLOT

PRINT

Introduction to SAS Reporting Procedures

Reporting procedures produce a display of information. The display can be a listing of data, an organized display of data, or a graphical display such as a bar chart or a scatter plot. Most descriptive and statistical procedures also produce reports to display results, but the procedures in this section are specialized for reporting.

PRINT   prints values from a SAS data set

FORMS   prints mailing list labels or other data laid out in repetitive forms

CHART   charts frequencies and other statistics with bar charts and other pictorial representations

PLOT   plots variables in a scatter diagram

CALENDAR   prints data in the form of a summary or schedule calendar.

In addition to these procedures, several reporting methods are covered outside this chapter.

PUT statements   are used to program custom reports. (See Chapter 6, "Data Step Applications".)

COMPUTAB   is a row-by-column financial reporting procedure available with the SAS/ETS product.

GCHART and GPLOT   produce graphical reports like CHART and PLOT on graphics devices. These are available with the SAS/GRAPH product.

The PRINT Procedure

The PRINT procedure is an easy procedure for listing the data in a SAS data set. The simplest invocation

```
PROC PRINT;
```

prints the most recently created SAS data set. Each variable in the data set forms a column of the report; each observation of the data set forms a row of the report. If you want variables to form rows and observations to form columns, use PROC TRANSPOSE to change variables into observations and vice versa before you print the data set. PROC PRINT is able to:

- use FORMAT statements to associate variables with formats
- use TITLE statements to define up to ten title lines
- use LINESIZE= and PAGESIZE= system options to control size
- print any subset of the variables
- use an ID variable to identify observations

- divide the report into sections when there are too many variables to fit across the page
- separate groups of observations according to BY groups
- print totals and other statistics for all observations and BY groups
- print variable labels as column headings.

You tell PROC PRINT what to do, not how to do it. While other reporting methods in SAS can require a lot of programming, no programming is required with PROC PRINT.

But the PRINT procedure may be too limited for some applications. It cannot select subsets of the observations to print, and almost all computations must be done ahead of time in DATA steps.

The following example creates a SAS data set and then prints it twice using PROC PRINT, once in a very simple manner and again using formats, totals, variable labels, and an ID variable.

```
DATA A;
  INPUT YEAR SALES COST;
  PROFIT=SALES-COST;
  CARDS;
1977 12132 11021
1978 19823 12928
1979 16982 14002
1980 18432 14590
;
PROC PRINT DATA=A;
  TITLE SIMPLE PROC PRINT REPORT;
PROC PRINT DATA=A SPLIT=*;
  LABEL SALES=SALES FOR * YEAR
    COST=TOTAL COST
    PROFIT=PROFIT BEFORE * TAXES;
  FORMAT SALES COST PROFIT DOLLAR10.2;
  ID YEAR;
  SUM SALES COST PROFIT;
  TITLE PROC PRINT WITH TOTALS, FORMATS, LABELS, AND ID VARIABLE;
```

```
                   SIMPLE PROC PRINT REPORT                            1

        OBS    YEAR    SALES    COST      PROFIT

         1     1977    12132    11021     1111
         2     1978    19823    12928     6895
         3     1979    16982    14002     2980
         4     1980    18432    14590     3842
```

```
PROC PRINT WITH TOTALS, FORMATS, LABELS, AND ID VARIABLE               2

  YEAR    SALES FOR      TOTAL COST      PROFIT BEFORE
            YEAR                            TAXES

  1977    $12,132.00    $11,021.00       $1,111.00
  1978    $19,823.00    $12,928.00       $6,895.00
  1979    $16,982.00    $14,002.00       $2,980.00
  1980    $18,432.00    $14,590.00       $3,842.00
          ==========    ==========       ==========
          $67,369.00    $52,541.00      $14,828.00
```

The FORMS Procedure

The FORMS procedure is designed to print mailing labels and other types of repetitive forms. This example adds labeling variables to the data in order to identify the fields on the form units. The forms are laid out three units across the page.

```
DATA B;
   SET A;
   TYEAR ='YEAR  =';
   TSALES='SALES = ';
   TCOST ='COST  = ';
PROC FORMS W=20 D=1 NA=3 NB =5 DATA=B;
   FORMAT SALES COST COMMA10.2;
   LINE 1 TYEAR YEAR;
   LINE 2 TSALES SALES;
   LINE 3 TCOST COST;
```

```
                                        SAS                                                    1

YEAR  =        1977    YEAR  =        1978    YEAR  =        1979
SALES =   12,132.00    SALES =   19,823.00    SALES =   16,982.00
COST  =   11,021.00    COST  =   12,928.00    COST  =   14,002.00

YEAR  =        1980
SALES =   18,432.00
COST  =   14,590.00
```

The CHART Procedure

The CHART procedure draws a variety of charts: horizontal and vertical bar charts, block charts, pie charts, and star charts. The procedure can chart counts, percentages, means, and sums. This example is a block chart of the PROFIT variable from the PRINT example.

```
PROC CHART DATA=A;
   TITLE PROC CHART REPORT ON PROFIT;
   BLOCK YEAR / SUMVAR=PROFIT DISCRETE SYMBOL='XOA';
```

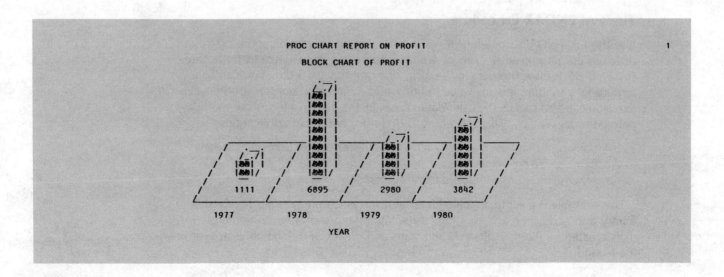

The PLOT Procedure

The PLOT procedure draws scatter plots. The following example plots three variables against YEAR. The three variables appear on the same plot, identified by different plotting characters.

```
PROC PLOT DATA=A;
  TITLE PROC PLOT REPORT: P=PROFIT S=SALES C=COST;
  PLOT PROFIT*YEAR='P'
    SALES*YEAR='S'
    COST*YEAR='C' /OVERLAY VPOS=20 HPOS=32;
```

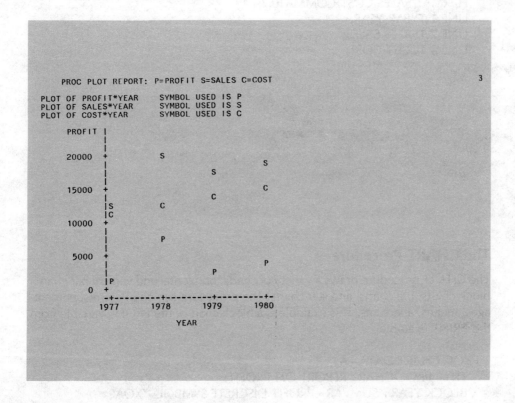

The CALENDAR Procedure

Use the CALENDAR procedure if you have either daily data on some activity or data representing events, each of which is identified by a date. In both cases, CALENDAR displays the data in the form of a monthly calendar. You can specify formats for variables, missing value options, and customized borders for the calendar. You can also specify the calendar to cover all the days in a month or weekdays only (Monday–Friday). This procedure is useful for two main applications:

- daily reporting, such as daily tallies of sales or usage. Sums and means can also be collected.
- scheduling, to make calendars of events.

This example is a summary calendar that displays telephone calls received by a library during daytime and evening hours. Variables are printed using picture formats created by PROC FORMAT, and sums and means of the variables appear in the legend.

```
DATA TEL;
  INPUT DATE :DATE. DAY NIGHT @@;
  CARDS;
  1OCT82 33 48   2OCT82 29 10   3OCT82 18 35   4OCT82 18 23
  5OCT82 36 45   6OCT82 25 44   7OCT82 28 40   8OCT82 29 49
  9OCT82 31 17  10OCT82 20 .   11OCT82 19 29  12OCT82 30 11
 13OCT82 28 49  14OCT82 27 46  15OCT82 20 36  16OCT82 27 48
 17OCT82 20 39  18OCT82 27 46  19OCT82 20 36  20OCT82 27 48
 21OCT82 33 48  22OCT82 29 10  23OCT82 18 35  24OCT82 18 23
 25OCT82 36 45  26OCT82 25 44  27OCT82 28 40  28OCT82 29 49
 29OCT82 31 17  30OCT82 20 .   31OCT82 19 29
;
PROC FORMAT;
  PICTURE DDD OTHER='000 DAY';
  PICTURE NNN OTHER='000 NIGHT';
PROC CALENDAR HEADER=SMALL LEGEND;
  ID DATE;
  VAR DAY NIGHT;
  SUM DAY NIGHT;
  MEAN DAY NIGHT;
  LABEL DAY=DAYTIME CALLS NIGHT=NIGHT CALLS;
  FORMAT DAY DDD. NIGHT NNN. ;
  TITLE TELEPHONE CALLS RECEIVED AT CITY LIBRARY;
```

```
                 TELEPHONE CALLS RECEIVED AT CITY LIBRARY                    5
                             OCTOBER   1982

 -----------------------------------------------------------------------------
| SUNDAY    | MONDAY    | TUESDAY   | WEDNESDAY | THURSDAY  | FRIDAY    | SATURDAY  |
|-----------|-----------|-----------|-----------|-----------|-----------|-----------|
|           |           |           |           |           |    1      |    2      |
|           |           |           |           |           |           |           |
|           |           |           |           |           | 33 DAY    | 29 DAY    |
|           |           |           |           |           | 48 NIGHT  | 10 NIGHT  |
|-----------|-----------|-----------|-----------|-----------|-----------|-----------|
|    3      |    4      |    5      |    6      |    7      |    8      |    9      |
| 18 DAY    | 18 DAY    | 36 DAY    | 25 DAY    | 28 DAY    | 29 DAY    | 31 DAY    |
| 35 NIGHT  | 23 NIGHT  | 45 NIGHT  | 44 NIGHT  | 40 NIGHT  | 49 NIGHT  | 17 NIGHT  |
|-----------|-----------|-----------|-----------|-----------|-----------|-----------|
|   10      |   11      |   12      |   13      |   14      |   15      |   16      |
| 20 DAY    | 19 DAY    | 30 DAY    | 28 DAY    | 27 DAY    | 20 DAY    | 27 DAY    |
|      .    | 29 NIGHT  | 11 NIGHT  | 49 NIGHT  | 46 NIGHT  | 36 NIGHT  | 48 NIGHT  |
|-----------|-----------|-----------|-----------|-----------|-----------|-----------|
|   17      |   18      |   19      |   20      |   21      |   22      |   23      |
| 20 DAY    | 27 DAY    | 20 DAY    | 27 DAY    | 33 DAY    | 29 DAY    | 18 DAY    |
| 39 NIGHT  | 46 NIGHT  | 36 NIGHT  | 48 NIGHT  | 48 NIGHT  | 10 NIGHT  | 35 NIGHT  |
|-----------|-----------|-----------|-----------|-----------|-----------|-----------|
|   24      |   25      |   26      |   27      |   28      |   29      |   30      |
| 18 DAY    | 36 DAY    | 25 DAY    | 28 DAY    | 29 DAY    | 31 DAY    | 20 DAY    |
| 23 NIGHT  | 45 NIGHT  | 44 NIGHT  | 40 NIGHT  | 49 NIGHT  | 17 NIGHT  |      .    |
|-----------|-----------|-----------|-----------|-----------|-----------|-----------|
|   31      |           |           |           |           |           |           |
| 19 DAY    |           |           |           |           |           |           |
| 29 NIGHT  |           |           |           |           |           |           |
 -----------------------------------------------------------------------------

         ------------------------------------------------
        | LEGEND          |  SUM     |  MEAN    |
        | DAYTIME CALLS   |    798   |  25.7419 |
        | NIGHT CALLS     |   1039   |  35.8276 |
         ------------------------------------------------
```

Reports Written with PUT Statements

The PUT statement is a program statement used in a DATA step. Reports written with PUT statements use program statements to create the form of the report. You specify the column positions and program with every calculation.

Using PUT statements for report writing is documented in detail in Chapter 6. (See also the PUT Statement in Chapter 3.) Here is an example of a report produced with PUT statements.

You want to print the observations as columns and the variables as rows in the report. This is most conveniently done with the N=PS feature (see the FILE statement in Chapter 3) and by computing column positions with program statements. The variable C indexes column positions corresponding to observations from the data and a column for the total.

```
DATA __NULL__;
  FILE PRINT N=PS;
  TITLE PUT STATEMENT REPORT;
  *---BRING IN THREE OBSERVATIONS PER PAGE---;
  DO C=25 TO 61 BY 12;  *--C WILL BE THE PRINTING COLUMN--;
    SET A END=EOF;        *---BRING IN AN OBSERVATION HERE--;
    *---COMPUTE GROSS PROFIT AND ACCUMULATE TOTALS---;
    TOTSALES+SALES;  TOTCGS+COST;  TOTPROF+PROFIT;
    *---PRINT OUT A COLUMN FOR THIS MONTH---;
    PUT #5
        'YEAR'                  @C YEAR    10.
     // 'GROSS REVENUE'         @C SALES   10.2
      / 'COST OF GOODS SOLD'    @C COST    10.2
      /                         @C 10*'='
      / 'GROSS PROFIT'          @C PROFIT  10.2;
    *---AT END OF DATA---;
    IF EOF THEN DO;
      C=C+12;
      *---COMPUTE MARGIN AND PRINT TOTALS---;
      PCTMARG=100*TOTPROF/TOTCGS;
      PUT #5
          @C '    TOTAL'
       // @C TOTSALES    10.2
        / @C TOTCGS      10.2
        / @C 10*'='
        / @C TOTPROF     10.2
       // 'PROFIT MARGIN PERCENT OF COST' @C PCTMARG 10.2;
    END;
  END;
```

```
                                        PUT STATEMENT REPORT                                      1


YEAR                      1977         1978         1979         1980        TOTAL

GROSS REVENUE         12132.00     19823.00     16982.00     18432.00     67369.00
COST OF GOODS SOLD    11021.00     12928.00     14002.00     14590.00     52541.00
                     ==========   ==========   ==========   ==========   ==========
GROSS PROFIT           1111.00      6895.00      2980.00      3842.00     14828.00

PROFIT MARGIN PERCENT OF COST                                               28.22
```

The CALENDAR Procedure

ABSTRACT

The CALENDAR procedure displays data from a SAS data set in a month-by-month calendar format.

INTRODUCTION

PROC CALENDAR produces either of two calendar formats: summary or schedule. A summary calendar provides information about the same variables over time. For example, the summary calendar below displays the number of meals served daily in a hospital cafeteria during the month of December, 1982.

```
                    MEALS SERVED IN COMMUNITY HOSPITAL CAFETERIA
                                  DECEMBER  1982
-----------------------------------------------------------------------------------------
|  SUNDAY    |   MONDAY   |  TUESDAY   | WEDNESDAY  |  THURSDAY  |   FRIDAY   |  SATURDAY  |
|------------|------------|------------|------------|------------|------------|------------|
|            |            |            |     1      |     2      |     3      |     4      |
|            |            |            | 334 BRKFST | 289 BRKFST | 184 BRKFST | 179 BRKFST |
|            |            |            | 484 LUNCH  | 501 LUNCH  | 352 LUNCH  | 228 LUNCH  |
|            |            |            | 368 DINNER | 380 DINNER | 292 DINNER | 212 DINNER |
|------------|------------|------------|------------|------------|------------|------------|
|     5      |     6      |     7      |     8      |     9      |    10      |    11      |
| 360 BRKFST | 245 BRKFST | 280 BRKFST | 294 BRKFST | 309 BRKFST | 199 BRKFST | 186 BRKFST |
| 450 LUNCH  | 440 LUNCH  | 399 LUNCH  | 489 LUNCH  | 569 LUNCH  |      .     | 294 LUNCH  |
| 332 DINNER | 386 DINNER | 312 DINNER | 316 DINNER | 449 DINNER | 202 DINNER | 260 DINNER |
|------------|------------|------------|------------|------------|------------|------------|
|    12      |    13      |    14      |    15      |    16      |    17      |    18      |
| 301 BRKFST | 276 BRKFST-| 272 BRKFST | 204 BRKFST | 266 BRKFST | 195 BRKFST | 164 BRKFST |
| 511 LUNCH  | 488 LUNCH  | 460 LUNCH  | 356 LUNCH  | 480 LUNCH  | 388 LUNCH  | 280 LUNCH  |
| 403 DINNER | 365 DINNER | 421 DINNER | 345 DINNER | 470 DINNER | 311 DINNER | 234 DINNER |
|------------|------------|------------|------------|------------|------------|------------|
|    19      |    20      |    21      |    22      |    23      |    24      |    25      |
| 210 BRKFST | 311 BRKFST | 402 BRKFST | 420 BRKFST | 339 BRKFST | 201 BRKFST |            |
| 394 LUNCH  | 595 LUNCH  | 654 LUNCH  | 530 LUNCH  | 590 LUNCH  | 400 LUNCH  |            |
| 256 DINNER | 541 DINNER | 580 DINNER | 501 DINNER | 489 DINNER | 266 DINNER |            |
|------------|------------|------------|------------|------------|------------|------------|
|    26      |    27      |    28      |    29      |    30      |    31      |            |
| 412 BRKFST | 292 BRKFST | 309 BRKFST | 330 BRKFST | 321 BRKFST | 220 BRKFST |            |
| 663 LUNCH  | 559 LUNCH  |      .     | 771 LUNCH  | 605 LUNCH  | 415 LUNCH  |            |
| 581 DINNER | 503 DINNER | 552 DINNER | 495 DINNER | 550 DINNER |      .     |            |
-----------------------------------------------------------------------------------------

             -------------------------------------------------------
             |      LEGEND         |     SUM     |     MEAN         |
             |---------------------|-------------|-----------------|
             | BREAKFASTS SERVED   |    8304     |    276.8        |
             | LUNCHES SERVED      |   13345     |    476.607      |
             | DINNERS SERVED      |   11372     |    392.138      |
             -------------------------------------------------------
```

In a summary calendar, each day is represented by one observation, and each kind of information is a variable. Each piece of information for a given day is the value of a variable for that day. Variables displayed may be numeric or character and may use formats. Sums and means for any of the numeric variables displayed may be collected; these are printed after the body of the calendar.

A schedule calendar displays the duration of an event by a continuous line through each day for the event. The example below is a planning calendar for the month of August, 1983.

```
            SUMMER PLANNING CALENDAR: BRIAN Q. WYDGET, PRESIDENT
                          BETTER PRODUCTS INC.

|----------------------------------------------------------------------------------------------------------------------|
|                                                                                                                      |
|                                             AUGUST   1983                                                            |
|                                                                                                                      |
|----------------------------------------------------------------------------------------------------------------------|
|     SUNDAY    |     MONDAY    |    TUESDAY    |   WEDNESDAY   |   THURSDAY    |     FRIDAY    |   SATURDAY    |
|----------------+---------------+---------------+---------------+---------------+---------------+----------------|
|               |       1       |       2       |       3       |       4       |       5       |       6       |
|               |               |               |               |               | +VIP BANQUET/BQW+|            |
|               +================================================BAND CAMP/JULIE/MONTICELLO================================>|
|               +====MGRS. MEETING/DISTRICT_6=====+|                +|==========TRADE SHOW/KNOX/LOS ANGELES===========+|
|               +DIST. MTG./ALL/+|          +INTERVIEW/TIMES+|+PLANNG COUNCIL/+|+=====SALES_DRIVE/DISTRICT_6======>|
|----------------+---------------+---------------+---------------+---------------+---------------+----------------|
|       7       |       8       |       9       |      10       |      11       |      12       |      13       |
|               |               |               |               |               | +SEMINAR/SPERBER+|           |
|               |               |               |               |+PLANNG COUNCIL/+|+====TENNIS CLINIC/BORG/CHICAGO====+|
|<============================================SALES_DRIVE/DISTRICT_6========================================>|
|<============================================BAND CAMP/JULIE/MONTICELLO====================================>|
|----------------+---------------+---------------+---------------+---------------+---------------+----------------|
|      14       |      15       |      16       |      17       |      18       |      19       |      20       |
|               |               | +==DENTIST/BQW==+|             |+PLANNG COUNCIL/+|            |               |
|               +=================SHORT COURSE/CANNON================+|                             |               |
|               +=============================VISIT/FRED=============================+|            |               |
|+SEMINAR/SPERBER+|+====================VACATION/VIVIAN/HOUSTON==========================|         |               |
|+CO. PICNIC/ALL/+|+====MGRS. MEETING/DISTRICT_7=====+|        |+NEWSLETR DEADLN+|+SEMINAR/SPERBER+|          |
|<============SALES_DRIVE/DISTRICT_6============+|+=========TOY SHOW/MARKS==========+|+=====SALES_DRIVE/DISTRICT_7======>|
|----------------+---------------+---------------+---------------+---------------+---------------+----------------|
|      21       |      22       |      23       |      24       |      25       |      26       |      27       |
|               |               |               |               | +==========GOLF TOURNAMENT/BQW/PEBL BCH===========>|
|+=================================================VACATION/PEARL/TORONTO===========================================>|
|+SEMINAR/SPERBER+|          |               |+=BIRTHDAY/MARY=+|+PLANNG COUNCIL/+|+======INVENTORS SHOW/MELVIN=====>|
|<================================================SALES_DRIVE/DISTRICT_7=============================================>|
|----------------+---------------+---------------+---------------+---------------+---------------+----------------|
|      28       |      29       |      30       |      31       |               |               |               |
|<INVENTORS SHOW/+|            |               |               |               |               |               |
|<GOLF TOURNAMENT+|            |               |               |               |               |               |
|<VACATION/PEARL/+|+==SCHOOL OPEN==+|         |               |               |               |               |
|<============SALES_DRIVE/DISTRICT_7=============+|            |               |               |               |
|----------------------------------------------------------------------------------------------------------------------|
```

Note that the line for an event begins and ends with a cross (+). If an event continues from one week to another, an arrow appears at the point of continuation. In a schedule calendar, each event is one observation, and a single day can display several events (observations) on successive lines. One event (observation) can also appear in several days, weeks, or months.

PROC CALENDAR determines the amount of data that may be displayed with either calendar type from the number of lines available on the page (PAGESIZE= system option) and the line width (LINESIZE= system option). See the OPTIONS statement in Chapter 11 for more information on these options.

SPECIFICATIONS

The CALENDAR procedure is invoked by using the following statements:

PROC CALENDAR *options*;
  BY *variables*;
  ID *variables*;
  VAR *variables*;
  SUM *variables*;
  MEAN *variables*;
  DURATION *variables*;

PROC CALENDAR Statement

PROC CALENDAR *options*;

The following options may appear on the PROC CALENDAR statement and may be used with either a summary or a schedule calendar:

DATA=*SASdataset*	gives the name of the SAS data set to be used by the CALENDAR procedure. If DATA= is omitted, the most recently created SAS data set is used.
SCHEDULE	specifies that a schedule calendar is to be printed. A summary calendar is the default.
FILL	specifies that all months between the first and last observation dates inclusive are to be displayed even if no data are present for a particular month. By default, CALENDAR leaves out months with no data.
WEEKDAYS	specifies that CALENDAR should display and use in calculations only weekdays (excluding Saturday and Sunday). The default is to display and use all days.
MISSING	specifies for a summary calendar that when a day has no associated observation, the values of the VAR variables for that day are to be printed using the format specified for missing values. If MISSING is not given, the day contains only the date. For a schedule calendar, MISSING specifies that missing values for VAR variables appear in the label of an observation. If MISSING is not specified, missing values of VAR variables are ignored in labeling the observation.
DATETIME	specifies that the ID variable contains SAS datetime values rather than SAS date values. PROC CALENDAR then uses only the date portion of the datetime value. Use this option if the ID variable is associated with the DATETIME., SMFSTAMP., or RMFSTAMP. informat. By default, CALENDAR assumes that the ID variable is a SAS date variable.
HEADER=LARGE HEADER=SMALL	specifies the type of heading for CALENDAR to use in formatting the month name. HEADER=LARGE prints the month name 7 lines high with an additional blank line above and below the month name. The year is also printed if space is available (as determined by the LINESIZE= option). HEADER=SMALL prints the month and year on a single line like a regular printed title. By default, CALENDAR prints the month and year in a box 4 lines high.

FORMCHAR=*'string'*   defines a string 11 characters long identifying the characters to be used for constructing the calendar outlines and dividers. See **Using the FORMCHAR= Option**, below.

The following options may be used for a summary calendar (they are ignored if the SCHEDULE option is specified):

LEGEND   requests that CALENDAR print a legend block containing the label or name of each variable displayed on the calendar. The legend appears at the bottom of the page for each month or on a following page if there is insufficient room on the calendar page.

MEANTYPE=NOBS
MEANTYPE=NDAYS   gives the type of mean to be calculated for each month. MEANTYPE=NOBS specifies that the mean is to be calculated for the number of observations on the input data set for each month. MEANTYPE=NDAYS specifies that the mean is to be calculated for the number of days displayed in the month (the number of days displayed depends on the WEEKDAYS option). The default MEANTYPE is NOBS.

BY Statement

BY *variables*;

A BY statement may be used with PROC CALENDAR to obtain separate calendars for observations in groups defined by the BY variables. When a BY statement appears, the procedure expects the input data set to be sorted in order of the BY variables, in addition to the ID variable. If your input data set is not sorted in ascending order, use the SORT procedure with a similar BY statement to sort the data, or, if appropriate, use the BY statement options NOTSORTED or DESCENDING. For more information, see the discussion of the BY statement in Chapter 8, "Statements Used in the PROC Step."

ID Statement

ID *variable*;

For a summary calendar, the ID statement specifies the SAS date variable to be used as the date of each observation. The ID statement is required. The input data set must be sorted by this variable (within any BY variables). For a summary calendar there should be only one observation per day in the input data set; if multiple observations for the same day appear, only the last is used. Observations with missing values for the ID variable are ignored.

For a schedule calendar, the ID statement specifies the variable used as the beginning date for the observation (event). Several observations may have the same ID value.

VAR Statement

VAR *variables*;

For a summary calendar, the VAR statement specifies the variables in the input data set to be displayed on the calendar for each day. Variables may be either character or numeric. If no VAR statement is used, all variables on the data set (excluding BY and ID variables) are displayed. Note that the number of lines available per page determines the actual number of variables that a summary calendar displays.

For a schedule calendar, the values of the VAR variables label each observation and are printed in the middle of the line for a given event (observation). VAR variables may be character or numeric. The number of VAR variable values that can be printed for a given observation depends on the number of days that observation occupies, that is, the length of the observation's line.

SUM Statement

    SUM *variables*;

The SUM statement specifies for a summary calendar the variables to be totaled for each month. If a variable specified in the SUM list is not in the VAR list, SAS adds that variable to the VAR list.

The SUM statement is valid only for a summary calendar; if the SCHEDULE option is specified, the SUM list is ignored.

MEAN Statement

    MEAN *variables*;

The MEAN statement specifies for a summary calendar the variables for which a mean value is to be calculated for each month. If a variable specified in the MEAN list is not in the VAR list, SAS adds that variable to the VAR list.

The MEAN statement is valid only for a summary calendar; if the SCHEDULE option is specified, the MEAN list is ignored.

DURATION Statement

    DURATION *variable*;

The DURATION (or DUR) statement specifies for a schedule calendar the variable containing the duration of each event in days. Duration is measured inclusively from the first day of an event (given in the ID variable). For example, the line for an event (observation) with an ID value of 1JUL82 and a DUR value of 3 appears in July 1, July 2, and July 3 of a schedule calendar. Any noninteger portion of the DURATION variable value is truncated, and any observation with a missing value or a value less than or equal to 0 is skipped. Note that if you use the WEEKDAYS option, CALENDAR assumes that DUR refers to the number of weekdays. Thus, an event with an ID value of 1JUL82 and a DUR value of 31 extends into August if the WEEKDAYS option is used.

The DURATION statement is valid only for a schedule calendar; if the SCHEDULE option is not specified, the statement is ignored.

DETAILS

Input Data Set

For a summary calendar the input data set should consist of one observation per day. The data set must be sorted by the ID variable. If multiple observations for one day are encountered, only the last is used. You may use PROC SUMMARY or a DATA step to collapse the data by day.

For a schedule calendar the input data set should contain one observation per event.

Missing Values

The following table shows how CALENDAR handles missing values of various types.

SUMMARY	
TYPE OF MISSING DATA	ACTION
No observation for a day	MISSING option specified: variables represented by missing values MISSING option not specified: day in calendar contains only date
Missing value for ID variable	Observation ignored
Missing value for VAR variable	Value represented by a missing value for that day; treatment of other VAR variables for that day not affected
Missing value for SUM variable	Value ignored in calculating sum
Missing value for MEAN variable	Value included in calculating mean unless ID variable missing

SCHEDULE	
TYPE OF MISSING DATA	ACTION
Missing ID or DUR variable	Observation is ignored
Missing value for VAR variable	MISSING option specified: variables represented by missing values: blanks if a character variable, a period if a numeric variable MISSING option not specified: missing value ignored in labeling event lines

Limitations

Since PROC CALENDAR attempts to fit the calendar within a single page, the page dimensions determine the number of variables and observations that may be displayed. You should select the values for the system options PAGESIZE= and LINESIZE= (TLINESIZE= under TSO or CMS) carefully.

Using the FORMCHAR= Option

The FORMCHAR= option defines the characters used to construct the boxes in tables produced by FREQ, TABULATE, and CALENDAR. The value is a string 11 characters long defining the vertical and horizontal bars and nine corner characters. Both CALENDAR and TABULATE can use all the characters shown in the table below. Although you must also specify 11 characters for the FREQ procedure, FREQ uses only the vertical and horizontal bars (first and second characters in the string) and the middle-middle or cross (seventh character). FREQ ignores the other characters since it does not print lines around the outside of its tables.

The default value of the FORMCHAR= option is '|----|+|---'. If you do not want boxes produced, use blanks by specifying:

FORMCHAR='   ' (11 blanks).

If you use an IBM 6670 printer with an extended font (typestyle 27 or 225) with input character set 216, we recommend:

FORMCHAR='FABFACCCBCEB8FECABCBBB'X .

If you use an IBM 1403, 3211, or 3203-5 printer, or equivalent, with a TN (text) print train, we recommend:

FORMCHAR='4FBFACBFBC4F8F4FABBFBB'X .

The following table shows the characters produced by the default value and by the two suggested values. You may substitute any character or hexadecimal string for those given here to customize the appearance of the calendar.

	Default	TN(text) print train	IBM 6670 printer with extended font
Vertical bar	| 4F	| 4F	| FA
Horizontal bar	– 60	– BF	– BF
Upper left	– 60	⌐ AC	⌐ AC
Upper middle	– 60	– BF	⊤ CC
Upper right	– 60	¬ BC	¬ BC
Middle left	| 4F	| 4F	⊢ EB
Middle middle	+ 4E	+ 8F	+ 8F
Middle right	| 4F	| 4F	⊣ EC
Lower left	– 60	L AB	L AB
Lower middle	– 60	– BF	⊥ CB
Lower right	– 60	⌐ BB	⌐ BB

Printed Output

The printed output for a summary calendar consists of the following: (1) any titles specified, (2) the month name and year heading, (3) day of the week heading, (4) data for each day listed week by week, and (5) a combination legend, sums, and means block if these are requested. The legend/summary block appears on a following page if it does not fit on the same page as the calendar.

The printed output for a schedule calendar consists of items (1) through (3) above and a week-by-week listing of the events on each day. Each event is represented by a continuous line through the days on which it occurs. The values of the variables specified in the VAR list are used to label this line. An arrow at the right end of an event line indicates that the event continues into the next week. An arrow at the left end of an event line indicates that the event continues from the previous day or week.

EXAMPLES

Summary Calendar: Example 1

The summary calendar displays computer usage at the Dusty National Bank for the month of March, 1983. Note that the calendar records only use from Monday through Friday of each week (the WEEKDAYS option). The mean is calculated on the number of days displayed in the month (MEANTYPE=NDAYS). Values for March 4 (for which there is no observation) are printed using the format for missing values (the MISSING option). This example was produced on an IBM 6670 printer with an extended font (typestyle 225) using the value of the FORMCHAR= option suggested for that printer.

```
OPTIONS LINESIZE=80 NODATE NONUMBER;
DATA CAL;
  INPUT OPDATE: DATE. JOBS ACT CPU;
  LIST;
  CARDS;
1MAR83 873 22.1 7.6
2MAR83 881 23.8 11.7
3MAR83 940 24.0 7.7
5MAR83 877 23.5 9.1
6MAR83 194 5.3 1.5
7MAR83 154 17.4 7.1
8MAR83 807 24 10.5
9MAR83 829 23.4 10.5
10MAR83 915 24 10.6
11MAR83 582 19.2 6.2
12MAR83 647 17.1 4.3
13MAR83 388 21 6.9
14MAR83 194 22.5 10.9
15MAR83 806 23.5 7.5
16MAR83 848 23.6 10.5
17MAR83 906 23 10.1
18MAR83 505 14.9 5.8
19MAR83 4 0.1 0
21MAR83 3 0.1 0
22MAR83 729 24 4.9
23MAR83 652 21.3 12.2
24MAR83 809 23.8 12.3
25MAR83 15 3.5 1.6
```

```
26MAR83 103 23.4 18.7
27MAR83 168 15.8 10.7
28MAR83 108 15.3 6
29MAR83 896 21.5 5.8
30MAR83 760 18.7 8
31MAR83 200 10 5
;
PROC FORMAT;
  PICTURE JFMT . ='    0 JOBS' (NOEDIT)
    OTHER=' 999 JOBS';
  PICTURE AFMT . ='    0 ACT ' (NOEDIT)
    OTHER='99. 9 ACT ';
  PICTURE CFMT . ='    0 CPU ' (NOEDIT)
    OTHER='99. 9 CPU ';
PROC CALENDAR WEEKDAYS HEADER=SMALL MEANTYPE=NDAYS
    MISSING FORMCHAR='FABFACCCBCEB8FECABCBBB'X;
ID OPDATE;
VAR JOBS ACT CPU;
SUM JOBS ACT CPU;
MEAN JOBS ACT CPU;
FORMAT JOBS JFMT.
        ACT AFMT.
        CPU CFMT. ;
LABEL JOBS=JOBS RUN DURING THE MONTH
      ACT=ACTIVE HOURS
      CPU=CPU HOURS;
TITLE1 'SYSTEM PERFORMANCE SUMMARY';
TITLE2 'DUSTY NATIONAL BANK COMPUTER CENTER';
```

```
                  SYSTEM PERFORMANCE SUMMARY
               DUSTY NATIONAL BANK COMPUTER CENTER
                          MARCH  1983

  +----------+----------+-----------+----------+----------+
  |  MONDAY  | TUESDAY  | WEDNESDAY | THURSDAY |  FRIDAY  |
  +----------+----------+-----------+----------+----------+
  |          |    1     |     2     |    3     |    4     |
  |          |          |           |          |          |
  |          | 873 JOBS | 881 JOBS  | 940 JOBS |   0 JOBS |
  |          | 22.1 ACT | 23.8 ACT  | 24.0 ACT |   0 ACT  |
  |          |  7.6 CPU | 11.7 CPU  |  7.7 CPU |   0 CPU  |
  +----------+----------+-----------+----------+----------+
  |    7     |    8     |     9     |    10    |    11    |
  |          |          |           |          |          |
  | 154 JOBS | 807 JOBS | 829 JOBS  | 915 JOBS | 582 JOBS |
  | 17.4 ACT | 24.0 ACT | 23.4 ACT  | 24.0 ACT | 19.2 ACT |
  |  7.1 CPU | 10.5 CPU | 10.5 CPU  | 10.6 CPU |  6.2 CPU |
  +----------+----------+-----------+----------+----------+
  |    14    |    15    |    16     |    17    |    18    |
  |          |          |           |          |          |
  | 194 JOBS | 806 JOBS | 848 JOBS  | 906 JOBS | 505 JOBS |
  | 22.5 ACT | 23.5 ACT | 23.6 ACT  | 23.0 ACT | 14.9 ACT |
  | 10.9 CPU |  7.5 CPU | 10.5 CPU  | 10.1 CPU |  5.8 CPU |
  +----------+----------+-----------+----------+----------+
  |    21    |    22    |    23     |    24    |    25    |
  |          |          |           |          |          |
  |  03 JOBS | 729 JOBS | 652 JOBS  | 809 JOBS |  15 JOBS |
  |  0.1 ACT | 24.0 ACT | 21.3 ACT  | 23.8 ACT |  3.5 ACT |
  |  0.0 CPU |  4.9 CPU | 12.2 CPU  | 12.3 CPU |  1.6 CPU |
  +----------+----------+-----------+----------+----------+
  |    28    |    29    |    30     |    31    |          |
  |          |          |           |          |          |
  | 108 JOBS | 896 JOBS | 760 JOBS  | 200 JOBS |          |
  | 15.3 ACT | 21.5 ACT | 18.7 ACT  | 10.0 ACT |          |
  |  6.0 CPU |  5.8 CPU |  8.0 CPU  |  5.0 CPU |          |
  +----------+----------+-----------+----------+----------+


  +-------------------------------+--------+----------+
  |                               |  SUM   |   MEAN   |
  | JOBS RUN DURING THE MONTH     | 13412  |  583.13  |
  | ACTIVE HOURS                  | 423.6  |  18.4174 |
  | CPU HOURS                     | 172.5  |      7.5 |
  +-------------------------------+--------+----------+
```

Schedule Calendars: Example 2

The following SAS statements produced the schedule calendar shown in the **Introduction**. Notice that the observation with the HAPPEN value of 'BANK MTG' for August 16 is not printed for lack of space. Since the MISSING option is not specified, the missing value for WHO in the 'SCHOOL OPEN' observation on August 29 is ignored in labeling that event.

```
DATA PLAN;
  INPUT DATE:DATE. HAPPEN $ 9-36 WHO $ 38-48
        LONG 50-51 WHERE $ 53-70;
  CARDS;
1AUG83   DIST. MTG.                ALL           1  CARY
1AUG83   MGRS. MEETING             DISTRICT__6   2
1AUG83   BAND CAMP                 JULIE        13  MONTICELLO
4AUG83   PLANNG COUNCIL            GROUP I       1
4AUG83   TRADE SHOW                KNOX          3  LOS ANGELES
12AUG83  TENNIS CLINIC             BORG          2  CHICAGO
16AUG83  DENTIST                   BQW           1
18AUG83  NEWSLETR DEADLN           ALL           1
5AUG83   SALES__DRIVE              DISTRICT__6  12
11AUG83  PLANNG COUNCIL            GROUP II      1
15AUG83  MGRS. MEETING             DISTRICT__7   2
15AUG83  VACATION                  VIVIAN        5  HOUSTON
15AUG83  VISIT                     FRED          5
19AUG83  SALES__DRIVE              DISTRICT__7  12
25AUG83  PLANNG COUNCIL            GROUP IV      1
5AUG83   VIP BANQUET               BQW           1
15AUG83  SHORT COURSE              CANNON        3
3AUG83   INTERVIEW                 TIMES         1
29AUG83  SCHOOL OPEN                             1
16AUG83  BANK MTG.                 1ST NATL      1
24AUG83  BIRTHDAY                  MARY          1
17AUG83  TOY SHOW                  MARKS         2
26AUG83  INVENTORS SHOW            MELVIN        3
14AUG83  CO. PICNIC                ALL           1  PARK
19AUG83  SEMINAR                   SPERBER       1
21AUG83  SEMINAR                   SPERBER       1
21AUG83  VACATION                  PEARL         8  TORONTO
25AUG83  GOLF TOURNAMENT           BQW           4  PEBL BCH
12AUG83  SEMINAR                   SPERBER       1
14AUG83  SEMINAR                   SPERBER       1
18AUG83  PLANNG COUNCIL            GROUP III     1
PROC SORT;
  BY DATE;
PROC CALENDAR SCHEDULE;
  ID DATE;
  VAR HAPPEN WHO WHERE;
  DUR LONG;
  TITLE SUMMER PLANNING CALENDAR: BRIAN Q. WYDGET, PRESIDENT;
  TITLE2 BETTER PRODUCTS INC. ;
```

The CHART Procedure

ABSTRACT

The CHART procedure produces vertical and horizontal bar charts (also called *histograms*), block charts, pie charts, and star charts. These charts are useful for showing pictorially a variable's values or the relationships between two or more variables.

INTRODUCTION

Method

The way a chart produced by PROC CHART looks is determined by three factors: (1) the method chosen to present the chart, (2) the summary measures that are shown for the variable whose values are charted, and (3) features of the procedure that specify how the values are grouped.

You request each chart presentation method in PROC CHART by a different statement:

- vertical bar chart (VBAR statement)
- horizontal bar chart (HBAR statement)
- block chart (BLOCK statement)
- pie chart (PIE statement)
- star chart (STAR statement).

In each case, the variable listed (the chart variable) determines the values that label the bars or sections. Options are used to control the kind of statistics presented and any grouping that is done. For example, you use TYPE= to choose a measure to compute and display:

- frequency counts (TYPE=FREQ)
- percentages (TYPE=PCT)
- cumulative frequencies (TYPE=CFREQ)
- cumulative percentages (TYPE=CPCT)
- totals (TYPE=SUM)
- averages (TYPE=MEAN).

Among the characteristics that determine how values are grouped are:

- the type of variable charted, numeric or character
- the DISCRETE option for categorical grouping variables
- the GROUP= option for side-by-side grouping
- the SUBGROUP= option for sub-grouping
- the MIDPOINTS= option to locate interval midpoints for continuous variables.

CHART produces charts for both numeric and character variables. Character variables and formats cannot exceed a length of 16. For continuous numeric variables, CHART automatically selects display intervals, although you may explicitly define interval midpoints. If a value falls exactly halfway between two midpoints, the procedure puts the value in the higher interval. For character variables and discrete numeric variables, which contain several distinct values rather than a continuous range, the data values themselves define the intervals.

Introductory Examples

To give you an idea of CHART's capabilities, the kinds of charts that you can produce are described below. If you have a specific chart in mind, glance through the examples for a similar one. Many other charts can be produced by combining the options.

Frequency bar charts   When you want to divide your data into groups based on the values of a variable, frequency bar charts are useful. For example, say you have a data set containing information about employees. You want a bar chart comparing the number of male employees and the number of female employees. This chart is a frequency chart, since it shows the number of employees (observations) of each sex:

```
PROC CHART;
  VBAR SEX;
```

(See Figure 1)

At the bottom of the chart are the two values of SEX, F and M. The vertical axis represents the number of observations in the data set containing the value; 75 of the employees are females and 97 are males.

If you prefer a horizontal bar chart, use the HBAR statement instead of the VBAR statement. You can use the keyword HBAR in any of the examples below instead of VBAR:

```
PROC CHART;
  HBAR SEX;
```

(See Figure 2)

Percentage bar charts   These charts are handy for showing what percentage of the observations falls into different groups. For example, say you want to show the percentage of employees of each sex. The TYPE=PERCENT option produces the percentage bar chart:

```
PROC CHART;
  VBAR SEX / TYPE=PERCENT;
```

(See Figure 3)

Cumulative frequency charts   Sometimes you want a cumulative frequency chart where each bar represents the frequency of a given value plus the frequencies of all the values to its left in the chart. For example, using the data set containing

CHART   605

employee information, you might want to show how many employees have not attended college. The TYPE=CFREQ option produces the cumulative frequency chart:

    PROC CHART;
        VBAR EDUC / TYPE=CFREQ;

(See Figure 4)

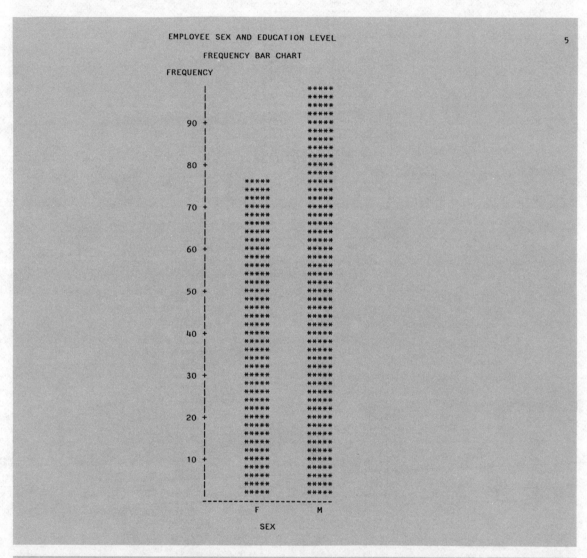

Fig. 1

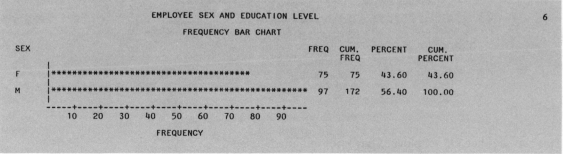

Fig. 2

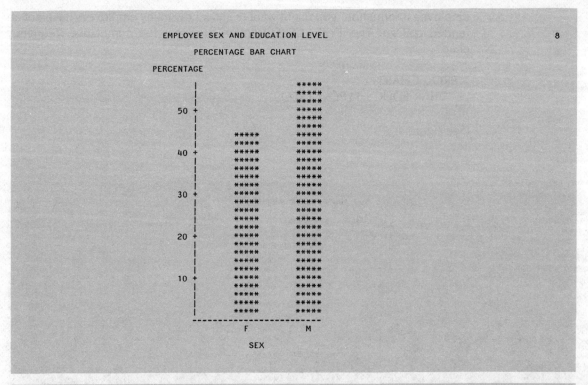

Fig. 3

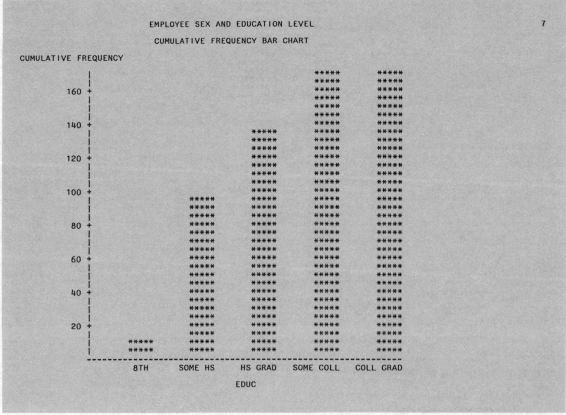

Fig. 4

You can see that 135 employees have not attended college.

CHART   607

Cumulative percentage charts   The bars of a cumulative percentage chart represent the percentage of the observations having a given value plus the percentages of all the values appearing to the left in the chart.

For example, say you want to represent the educational attainments of the employees in terms of percentages rather than frequencies. The TYPE=CPERCENT option produces the cumulative percentage chart:

```
PROC CHART;
   VBAR EDUC / TYPE=CPERCENT;
```

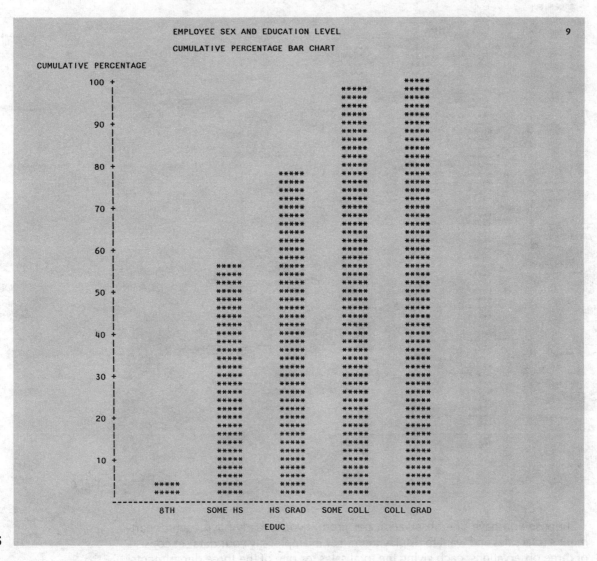

Fig. 5

Bar charts of group totals   These charts are like the frequency and percentage charts described above, but the vertical axis represents the group totals for another variable in the data set instead of frequencies or percentages. This variable is usually a continuous variable, such as SALES.

Your data set consists of twelve observations for each department.

Each observation contains DEPT, the chart variable, identifying the department and a variable SALES giving the department's sales for that month. Suppose you want to see the total sales for the year for each department. You use the option SUMVAR= to specify SALES as the sum variable, since you want each department's monthly sales summed for the chart.

```
PROC CHART;
  VBAR DEPT / SUMVAR=SALES;
```

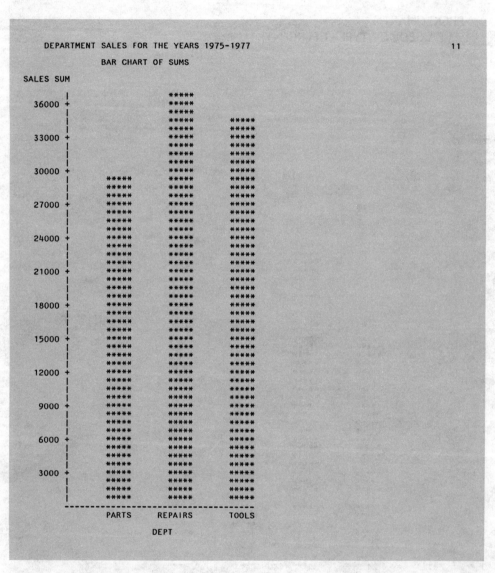

Fig. 6

Suppose you have one observation per group—you already have each department's total sales and want to display them. For example, say your data set consists of three observations, each giving the total sales for one of the three departments. You can use exactly the same statements as above:

```
PROC CHART;
  VBAR DEPT / SUMVAR=SALES;
```

Even though CHART does not need to sum the SALES values, they do represent a sum, and thus SUMVAR=SALES is the correct option to use. The results are like the chart above, but marked as VALUE rather than SUM. You can use this technique

CHART 609

to present any value that has been entered as the value of a variable, such as a mean, standard deviation, or percentage.

Bar charts for group means   Bar charts of group means are like the bar chart of group totals described above. However, the vertical axis represents the means of another variable rather than the sums. For example, to show each department's average monthly sales, you use these statements:

```
PROC CHART;
   VBAR DEPT / TYPE=MEAN SUMVAR=SALES;
```

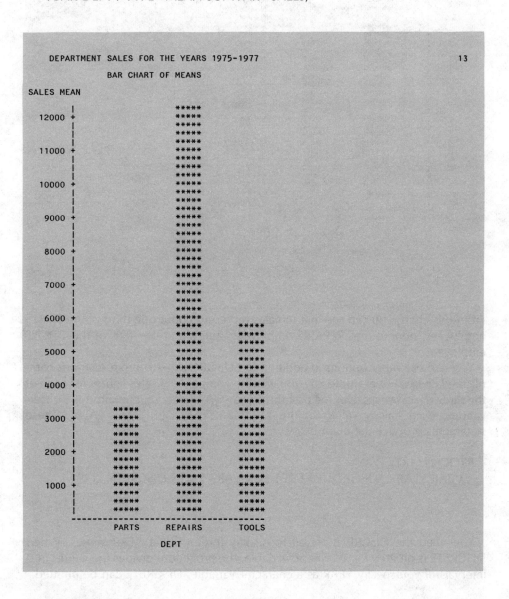

Fig. 7

Subdividing the bars   You can show the distribution of a second variable by using the first character of each of the values to print the bars. For example, say you want to compare the number of males and females in each of the three departments. You can ask CHART to subdivide the bars using F and M with these statements:

```
PROC CHART;
   VBAR DEPT / SUBGROUP=SEX;
```

```
DEPARTMENT SALES FOR THE YEARS 1975-1977                          14
                    FREQUENCY BAR CHART

FREQUENCY
        |         MMMMM
        |         MMMMM
        |         MMMMM                        MMMMM
   160 +         MMMMM                        MMMMM
        |         MMMMM                        MMMMM
        |         MMMMM                        MMMMM
        |         MMMMM                        MMMMM
   140 +         MMMMM                        MMMMM
        |         MMMMM                        MMMMM
        |         MMMMM                        MMMMM
        |         MMMMM                        MMMMM
   120 +         MMMMM                        MMMMM
        |         MMMMM                        MMMMM
        |         MMMMM                        MMMMM
        |         MMMMM                        MMMMM
   100 +         MMMMM        MMMMM           MMMMM
        |         MMMMM        MMMMM           MMMMM
        |         MMMMM        MMMMM           MMMMM
        |         MMMMM        MMMMM           MMMMM
    80 +         MMMMM        MMMMM           MMMMM
        |         MMMMM        MMMMM           MMMMM
        |         MMMMM        MMMMM           MMMMM
        |         MMMMM        MMMMM           MMMMM
    60 +         MMMMM        MMMMM           MMMMM
        |         MMMMM        MMMMM           MMMMM
        |         FFFFF        MMMMM           MMMMM
        |         FFFFF        MMMMM           MMMMM
    40 +         FFFFF        MMMMM           MMMMM
        |         FFFFF        MMMMM           FFFFF
        |         FFFFF        MMMMM           FFFFF
        |         FFFFF        MMMMM           FFFFF
    20 +         FFFFF        MMMMM           FFFFF
        |         FFFFF        MMMMM           FFFFF
        |         FFFFF        MMMMM           FFFFF
        |         FFFFF        FFFFF           FFFFF
        ----------------------------------------------
                  PARTS        REPAIRS         TOOLS
                             DEPT

             SYMBOL SEX      SYMBOL SEX

               F    F          M    M
```

Fig. 8

From this chart, you can see that females represent about one-third of the PARTS employees, none of the REPAIRS employees, and about one-fifth of the TOOLS employees.

You can use other options in addition to SUBGROUP= to produce more complicated charts. For example, say you want to compare the sales figures for each of the three departments over the past three years. Your data set contains nine observations, each having values of the variables YEAR, DEPT, and SALES. These statements produce the chart below:

```
PROC CHART;
    VBAR YEAR / SUBGROUP=DEPT SUMVAR=SALES DISCRETE;
```

(See Figure 9)

You need the DISCRETE option to display three distinct YEAR values. When DISCRETE is omitted for a numeric variable, the procedure divides the values into intervals. If you specify YEAR as a character variable, DISCRETE can be omitted.

Side-by-side charts   Another way of comparing quantities is with side-by-side charts. You can show the information—total sales for the three departments over the past three years—with these statements:

```
PROC CHART;
    VBAR DEPT / SUMVAR=SALES GROUP=YEAR;
```

(See Figure 10)

CHART 611

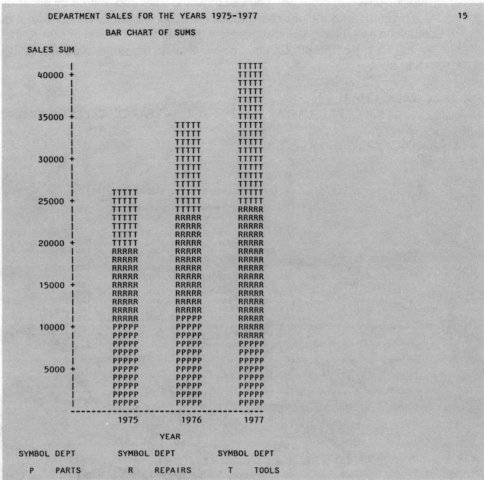

Fig. 9
Fig. 10

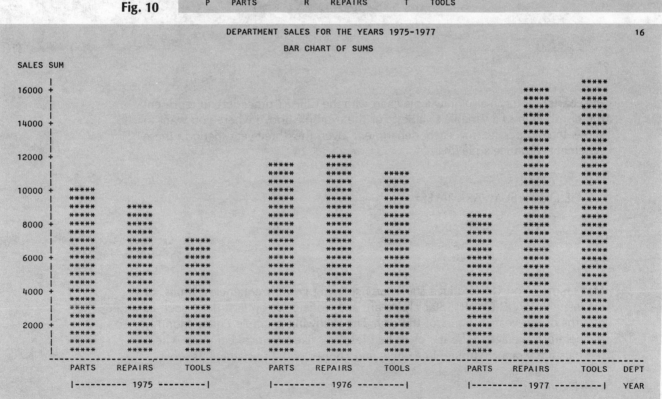

Block charts   Another way you can show the sales information by department for each year is with a block chart. Block charts look like city blocks with a building drawn in each block. You can represent the frequency, mean, or sum by the height of the building. The BLOCK chart below displays the same total sales as the VBAR chart above:

```
PROC CHART;
   BLOCK DEPT / SUMVAR = SALES GROUP = YEAR DISCRETE SYMBOL = 'XOA';
```

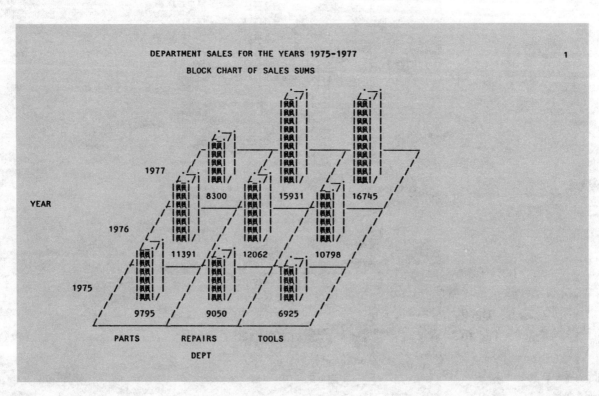

Fig. 11

Pie charts   You can also draw a pie chart with the CHART procedure to represent the distribution of a variable's values. For the example above where you want to show the total sales for each department over the three-year period, these statements produce a pie chart:

```
PROC CHART;
   PIE DEPT / SUMVAR = SALES;
```

(See Figure 12)

Star charts   You can produce star charts showing group frequencies, totals, or means with PROC CHART. Star charts are appropriate for cyclical data, such as months of the year or hours of the day. The following example charts monthly temperature averages. (The star chart that results is like a vertical bar chart where the bars are wrapped around in a circle and connected.) The statements are:

(See Figure 13)

CHART 613

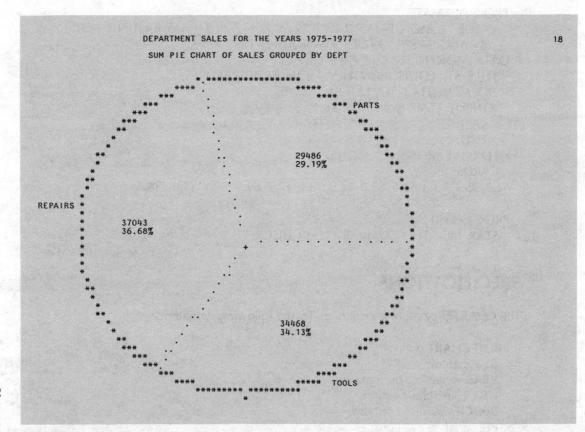

Fig. 12

Fig. 13

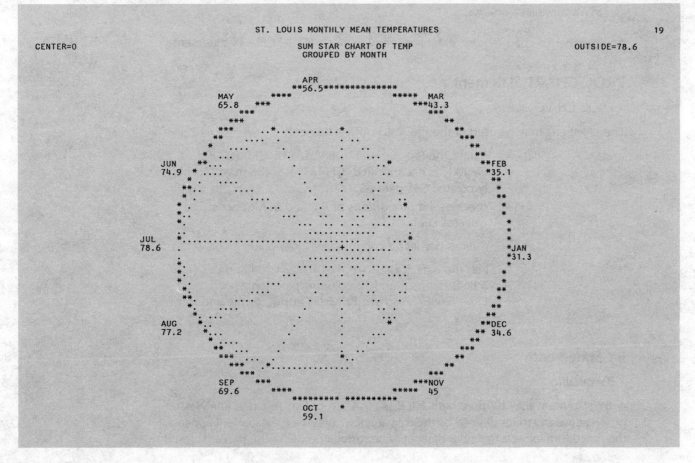

```
PROC FORMAT;
  VALUE  __MON 1=JAN 2=FEB 3=MAR 4=APR 5=MAY 6=JUN 7=JUL
    8=AUG 9=SEP 10=OCT 11=NOV 12=DEC;
DATA MONTHLY;
  TITLE ST. LOUIS MONTHLY MEAN TEMPERATURES;
  DO MONTH=1 TO 12;
    INPUT TEMP @@;
    OUTPUT;
    END;
  FORMAT MONTH __MON.;
  CARDS;
31.3 35.1 43.3 56.5 65.8 74.9 78.6 77.2 69.6 59.1 45.0  34.6
;
PROC CHART;
  STAR MONTH / SUMVAR=TEMP DISCRETE;
```

SPECIFICATIONS

The CHART procedure is controlled by the following statements:

PROC CHART *options*;
  BY *variables*;
  VBAR *variables / options*;
  HBAR *variables / options*;
  BLOCK *variables / options*;
  PIE *variables / options*;
  STAR *variables / options*;

Any number of chart request statements may follow a PROC CHART statement.

PROC CHART Statement

PROC CHART *options*;

These options may be used in the PROC CHART statement.

DATA=*SASdataset* names the SAS data set to be used by CHART. If
DATA= is not specified, CHART uses the most recently created SAS data set.

LPI= specifies the proportions of PIE and STAR charts. The value of LPI is

  (lines per inch / columns per inch) * 10

  and the default is LPI=6. For an IBM 3800 printer with 8 lines per inch and 12 columns per inch, specify LPI=6.6667. Also see **Printed Output** for pie and star charts.

BY Statement

BY *variables*;

A BY statement may be used with PROC CHART to obtain separate analyses on observations in groups defined by the BY variables. When a BY statement appears, the procedure expects the input data set to be sorted in order of the BY variables. If

CHART 615

your input data set is not sorted in ascending order, use the SORT procedure with a similar BY statement to sort the data, or, if appropriate, use the BY statement options NOTSORTED or DESCENDING. For more information, see the discussion of the BY statement in Chapter 8, "Statements Used in the PROC Step."

VBAR Statement

   VBAR *variables* / *options*;

In the VBAR statement, list the variables for which you want vertical bar charts. (The options with VBAR are described later.) If you list X as one of the chart variables, then a vertical bar chart is produced with the values of X underneath the bars.

   Each chart takes one page. Along the vertical axis, CHART describes the chart frequency, cumulative frequency, percentage, cumulative percentage, sum, or mean. At the bottom of each bar, CHART prints a value. For character variables or discrete numeric variables, this value is the actual value represented by the bar. For continuous numeric variables, the value gives the midpoint of the interval represented by the bar.

   CHART can automatically scale the vertical axis, determine the bar width, and choose spacing between the bars. However, the options and parameters described below allow you to choose bar intervals and the number of bars, include missing values in the chart, produce side-by-side charts, and subdivide the bars.

   The number of lines in the body of the VBAR chart is limited to 66, regardless of the system PAGESIZE option in effect. If the number of characters per line (LINESIZE) does not allow at least one blank space between bars, an error message is printed and CHART produces an HBAR chart instead of a VBAR chart, unless the NOSPACE option is included.

HBAR Statement

   HBAR *variables* / *options*;

The HBAR statement requests a horizontal bar chart for each variable listed. For example, the statements

   PROC CHART;
     HBAR A X1 X2;

produce three horizontal bar charts. Each chart occupies one or more pages, depending on the number of levels; each bar is one line. (The options available in the HBAR statement are discussed later.)

BLOCK Statement

   BLOCK *variables* / *options*;

In the BLOCK statement, list the variables for which you want block charts. Since each block chart must fit on one output page, there are some restrictions on the number of levels of the BLOCK and GROUP variables. (BLOCK statement options are described later.)

   The table below shows the maximum number of levels of GROUP and BLOCK variables for selected LINESIZEs that may be represented in a block chart using a 66-line page:

maximum number of levels

groups	LS=132	LS=120	LS=105	LS=90	LS=76	LS=64
0,1	9	8	7	6	5	4
2	8	8	7	6	5	4
3	8	7	6	5	4	3
4	7	7	6	5	4	3
5,6	7	6	5	4	3	2

If the value of any GROUP level is longer than 3 characters, the maximum number of BLOCK levels that can be produced may be reduced by one. BLOCK level values are truncated to 12 characters. If these limits are exceeded, data are represented as an HBAR chart.

PIE Statement

PIE *variables* / *options*;

The PIE statement requests a pie chart for each variable listed. For example, the statements

    PROC CHART;
      PIE A X1 X2;

produce three one-page pie charts. (Options available for PIE charts are discussed later.)

PROC CHART determines the number of slices for the pie in the same way that it determines the number of bars for VBAR charts. Any slices of the pie accounting for less than 3 print positions are lumped together into a slice called OTHER.

The pie's size is determined only by the LINESIZE and PAGESIZE system parameters. The pie looks elliptical if your printer doesn't print 6 lines per inch and 10 columns per inch. If your printer prints 8 lines per inch and 10 columns per inch, specify LPI=8 in the PROC CHART statement:

    PROC CHART LPI=8;

If a PIE chart is requested for a variable with over 50 levels, an HBAR chart is produced instead.

STAR Statement

STAR *variables* / *options*;

The STAR statement requests a star chart for each variable listed. (Options on the STAR statement are discussed later.) For example, the statements

    PROC CHART;
      STAR Z;

produce a one-page star chart for the variable Z.

The number of points in the star is determined in the same way as the number of bars for VBAR charts.

If all the data to be charted with STAR are positive, the center of the star represents zero and the outside circle represents the maximum value. If negative values occur in the data, the center represents the minimum. See the AXIS= option below for more about how to specify maximum and minimum values. If a STAR

CHART   617

chart is requested for a variable with over 24 levels, an HBAR chart is produced instead.

Note: if you want different variables to form the rays of the star, use an OUTPUT statement in a DATA step to create new observations having one variable with values equal to the variables you want represented by the rays; create another variable whose values are the original variable names.

Options for VBAR, HBAR, BLOCK, PIE, and STAR Statements

If any of the options below are used, a slash (/) precedes the option keywords. The slash is not necessary if no options are specified.

These options may be used with all the types of charts in the CHART procedure: vertical bar, horizontal bar, block, pie, or star charts.

MISSING makes missing values considered valid levels for the chart variable.

DISCRETE is used when the numeric chart variable specified is discrete rather than continuous. If DISCRETE is omitted, PROC CHART assumes that all numeric variables are continuous. If MIDPOINTS= or LEVELS= options are not specified, the procedure automatically chooses the intervals for the chart.

TYPE=FREQ
TYPE=PCT
TYPE=CFREQ
TYPE=CPCT
TYPE=SUM
TYPE=MEAN

specifies what the bars or sections in the chart represent. If the TYPE= option is omitted, the default TYPE is FREQ. When SUMVAR= is specified, the default TYPE is SUM.

TYPE=FREQ makes each bar or section represent the frequency with which a value or range occurs for the chart variable in the data.

TYPE=PERCENT or PCT makes each bar or section represent the percentage of observations of the chart variable having a given value or falling into a given range.

TYPE=CFREQ makes each bar or section represent cumulative frequency, which is the frequency for the group plus all the frequencies shown to its left.

TYPE=CPERCENT or CPCT makes each bar represent the cumulative percentage of observations of the chart variable, which is the percentage of the group plus the percentages of the bars shown to its left.

TYPE=SUM makes each bar or section represent the sum of the SUMVAR= variable for observations having the bar's value. For example, the statement

VBAR DEPT / SUMVAR=SALES;

produces a chart with one bar or section for each DEPT value. The bar height for a given DEPT corresponds to the total of the SALES values for observations having that DEPT value.

TYPE=MEAN makes each bar or section represent the mean of the SUMVAR= variable for observations having the bar's value.

SUMVAR=*variable*   names the variable to collect summaries for means, sums, or frequencies. The SUMVAR= option is useful for producing bar charts showing total expenditures for each department, or means at each level of an experiment. For example, the statement

    VBAR LOCATION / TYPE=MEAN SUMVAR=YIELD;

produces a chart showing the mean yield for each location. Another example

    VBAR DEPT / SUMVAR=EXPEND;

charts total expenditures by department. If SUMVAR is specified but TYPE= is not MEAN or SUM, then TYPE=SUM overrides whatever TYPE= is specified.

MIDPOINTS=*values*   defines the range of values for the chart variable each bar or section represents by specifying the range midpoints. For example, the statement

    VBAR X / MIDPOINTS=10 20 30 40 50;

produces a chart with five bars: the first bar represents the range of data values with a midpoint of 10; the second bar represents the range of data values with a midpoint of 20; and so on. When the variables given in the VBAR statement are numeric, the midpoints must be given in ascending or descending order, although they need not be uniformly distributed. For example, the statement

    VBAR X / MIDPOINTS=10 100 1000 10000;

produces a chart of X with logarithmic intervals. Numeric MIDPOINTS lists of the form

    MIDPOINTS=10 TO 100 BY 5

are also acceptable.

For character variables, MIDPOINTS may be specified in any order. This is useful in ordering the bars or in specifying a subset of the possible values. For example, you can give a list of the form

    MIDPOINTS='JAN' 'FEB' 'MAR'

Without the MIDPOINTS= option, the values are displayed in sorted order.

FREQ=*variable*   is used when a variable in the data set represents a count (or weight) for each observation. Normally, each observation contributes a value of 1 to the frequency counts. When FREQ appears, each observation contributes the FREQ variable's value. If the FREQ variable's values are not integers, they are truncated to integers. If the values are missing or negative, the contribution is zero. If SUMVAR= is specified, the sums are multiplied by the FREQ value.

AXIS=*value*   specifies the maximum value to use in constructing the FREQ, PCT, CFREQ, CPCT, SUM, or MEAN axis. If the VBAR or HBAR chart is of TYPE=SUM or

CHART 619

TYPE=MEAN and if any of the sums or means are less than zero, then a negative minimum value may also be specified on the AXIS= option. Otherwise a minimum value of zero is always assumed. Counts or percentages outside the maximum (or minimum) override the AXIS= specification. If AXIS= is specified and a BY statement also appears, uniform axes are produced over BY groups. When AXIS= appears on the STAR statement, the first value specified is the center (minimum) of the star and the second value is the outside circle (maximum). If only one AXIS value is specified on the STAR statement, CHART assumes this value as the maximum and zero as the minimum. For example, the statements

```
PROC CHART;
    STAR A / SUMVAR=XTYPE=SUM AXIS=100 200;
```

produce a star chart for the sums of X classified by A and scaled from 100 at the center to 200 at the outside circle.

More Options for VBAR, HBAR, and BLOCK Statements

GROUP=*variable* produces side-by-side charts, with each chart representing the observations having a given value of the GROUP= variable. The GROUP variable may be character or numeric and is assumed to be discrete. For example, the statement

```
VBAR SEX / GROUP=DEPT;
```

produces a frequency bar chart for males and females in each department. Missing values for a GROUP variable are treated as valid levels when a chart is produced.

SUBGROUP= requests that each bar be subdivided into characters
variable that show the SUBGROUP variable's contribution to the bar. For example, the statement

```
VBAR DEPT / SUBGROUP=SEX;
```

produces a chart with one bar for each department. The portion of each bar filled in with the character M represents those observations that have a SEX value of M.

The first character of the value is used to fill in the portion of the bar corresponding to the value, unless more than one value begins with the same first character. In that case, the letters A, B, C, and so on are used. The characters used in the chart and the values they represent are given in a table at the bottom of the chart.

Missing values for a SUBGROUP= variable are treated as valid levels when a chart is produced.

CHART calculates the height of the bar for each subgroup individually and then rounds each bar's percentage of the total bar up or down. Thus, the total height of the bar may be higher or lower than the same bar without SUBGROUP=.

With both TYPE=MEAN and the SUBGROUP= option, CHART first calculates the mean for each bar and then subdivides the bar into the percentages contributed by each subgroup.

LEVELS=*n*   can be used to specify the number of bars representing each chart variable when the variables given in the VBAR statement are continuous.

SYMBOL=*'char'*   defines the symbol to be used in the body of standard HBAR and VBAR charts with no subgrouping. The default SYMBOL value is the asterisk '*'.

If overprinting is available on your printer, you can specify 2 or 3 characters with SYMBOL= that will be printed over each other for the symbol. For example, specifying SYMBOL='XOA' means that the three characters X, O, and A will be printed on top of each other to make up the symbol.

For IBM 3800 printers that can print shaded characters, you can specify the symbol as a hex constant. The hex characters are enclosed in quotes, followed by the letter X:

VBAR DEPT / SYMBOL='A5'X;

NOSYMBOL   suppresses the subgrouping symbol table printed below the chart for VBAR and HBAR charts.

NOZEROS   specifies that any bar with zero value be suppressed.

G100   used in conjunction with the GROUP= option, forces the bars and statistics to add to 100% for each group.

Options for VBAR and HBAR Statements

ASCENDING   prints the bars and any associated statistics in ascending order of size within groups.

DESCENDING   prints the bars and any associated statistics in descending order of size within groups.

REF=*value*   requests that a single reference line be drawn on the response axis. For TYPE=FREQ or TYPE=CFREQ, this REF= value should be a frequency; for TYPE=PCT or TYPE=CPCT, the REF= value should be a percent between 1 and 100. For TYPE=SUM or TYPE =MEAN, the REF= value should be a sum or mean.

More HBAR Options

These options are used only on the HBAR statement:

NOSTAT   specifies that no statistics be printed with a horizontal bar chart.

FREQ   specifies for a horizontal bar chart that the frequency of each bar be printed to the side of the chart.

CFREQ   specifies that the cumulative frequency be printed.

CHART 621

PERCENT	specifies that the percentages of observations having a given value for the chart variable be printed.
CPERCENT	specifies that the cumulative percentages be printed.
SUM	specifies that the total number of observations that each bar represents be printed.
MEAN	specifies that the mean of the observations represented by each bar be printed.

   For charts produced with any TYPE= specification without a SUMVAR= variable, CHART can print FREQ, CFREQ, PERCENT, and CPERCENT.

   For TYPE=MEAN with a SUMVAR= variable, CHART can print FREQ and MEAN. For a TYPE=SUM specification, CHART can print FREQ and SUM.

Another VBAR Option

This option is used only on the VBAR statement:

NOSPACE	specifies that if the LINESIZE does not allow room for spaces between the bars, CHART can print a VBAR chart without spaces between bars. If space is still insufficient, an HBAR chart is printed instead.

DETAILS

Missing Values

   The way that PROC CHART handles missing values depends on whether or not the MISSING option is specified. See the section, **Options for VBAR, HBAR, BLOCK, PIE, and STAR Statements**, above.

EXAMPLES

Data for CHART Examples

Employee sex and education level data   The statements below produced the data used in the CHART procedure for the charts on employee sex and education.

   These statements include a DATA step to enter the values and the FORMAT procedure to define a format for the EDUC variable (for more information, see the chapter on PROC FORMAT):

```
PROC FORMAT;
  VALUE __E 1=8TH 2=SOME HS 3=HS GRAD 4=SOME COLL
    5=COLL GRAD;
DATA WSEXED;
  TITLE EMPLOYEE SEX AND EDUCATION LEVEL;
  INPUT SEX $ EDUC @@;
  FORMAT EDUC __E.;
  CARDS;
M 1 M 2 M 2 M 1 M 4 M 5 M 3 F 2 F 2 M 1 F 4
more data lines
;
```

Department sales for the years 1975-1977   These statements produced the data
for the charts on departmental sales:

```
DATA SALES;
  TITLE DEPARTMENT SALES FOR THE YEARS 1975-1977;
  INPUT DEPT :$7. SEX :$1. WT P75 P76 P77;
  YEAR=1975;  SALES=P75;  OUTPUT;
  YEAR=1976;  SALES=P76;  OUTPUT;
  YEAR=1977;  SALES=P77;  OUTPUT;
  CARDS;
PARTS     F   17    3500  2500   800
PARTS     M   21    3651  5391  4500
PARTS     M   21    2644  3500  3000
TOOLS     F   12    5672  6100  7400
TOOLS     M   45    1253  4698  9345
REPAIRS   F    2    9050 12062 15931
more data lines
;
```

Sales Statistics from PROC SUMMARY

The statements below produce charts from summary statistics for three variables:
PRODUCT with three levels, YEAR with three levels, and DATE. An example in
Chapter 9, "PROC Step Applications," shows the DATA step that reads these data
into a SAS data set (named A) and the PROC SUMMARY step that produces data set
B containing the summary statistics.

PROC CHART displays charts of a subset of the summary statistics contained in
data set C.

The first chart is a horizontal bar chart showing SALES for each PRODUCT by
DATE. You need the DISCRETE option to display each value of DATE rather than
the midpoints of the DATE values. The next chart is a block chart showing number
of products by year. The pie chart of PRODUCT uses SALES as a weighting variable
specified with the FREQ= option. The final vertical bar chart by YEAR shows
number of products as the SUBGROUP= variable. You must specify DISCRETE so
that the chart does not show YEAR with continuous values.

```
DATA C;
  SET B;
  IF __TYPE__=3;
PROC CHART;
  HBAR DATE / SUMVAR=SALES GROUP=PRODUCT DISCRETE;
  BLOCK PRODUCT / GROUP=YEAR;
  PIE PRODUCT / FREQ=SALES;
  VBAR YEAR / DISCRETE SUBGROUP=PRODUCT;
```

See Chapter 9 for the complete example and output from the CHART procedure.

The FORMS Procedure

ABSTRACT

The FORMS procedure can produce labels for envelopes, mailing labels, external tape labels, file cards, and any other printer forms that have a regular pattern.

INTRODUCTION

For each observation in the input SAS data set, FORMS prints data in a rectangular block called a **form unit**. For example, a mailing label is a form unit.

The results can be routed to a specified external file or printed on the SAS print file. For external files, carriage controls can be used or suppressed.

Form layout The size and spacing of the forms is controlled by options as illustrated in the following diagram. The keyword options for the PROC FORMS statement are shown with their abbreviations in upper case.

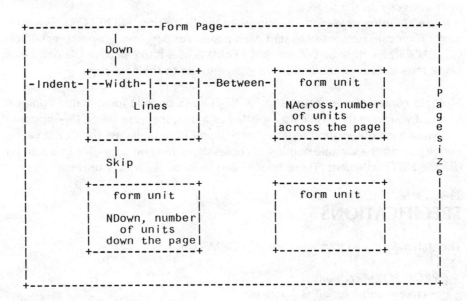

The values specified in LINE statements are formatted into a form unit that is WIDTH columns wide, and LINES lines long. Values that do not fit into WIDTH columns are truncated. NACROSS form units are printed across the page, with BETWEEN columns between adjacent form units. The forms are indented INDENT spaces from the left margin. SKIP blank lines are printed between form units down the page.

PROC FORMS has two modes of operation: continuous mode and page mode. Page-mode operation is used if NDOWN= or PAGESIZE= options are specified, or if the SAS print file is used rather than a DDNAME= file.

Continuous-mode operation For continuous-mode operation, the procedure first skips DOWN spaces, then alternately prints LINES print lines and SKIP blank lines until all the data are printed. No carriage control characters are used to skip to the top of the form. Continuous-mode operation is suitable for most forms unless the distance between form units changes between pages.

Page-mode operation First, PROC FORMS goes to the start of a new page and then prints DOWN blank lines (see **Carriage control** below). Then NDOWN sets of form units are printed down the page. If the NDOWN option is not specified, it will be set to the maximum allowed by the PAGESIZE= specified or assumed.

If the SAS print file is used (which occurs if DDNAME= is not specified), all the page calculations are done with respect to the lines remaining on the page after the title lines are printed.

Carriage control When you route the forms to an external file specified by the DDNAME= option, you must choose whether to use carriage control characters or not. A carriage control is an extra character prefixed to each record that controls the printer for line spacing and top-of-form ejection. If you want PROC FORMS to use carriage controls, you must specify the CC option in the PROC FORMS statement, and an appropriate specification for the record format of the print file. In OS batch jobs, specify the print file attributes:

DCB = (RECFM = VBA,LRECL = 137,BLKSIZE = 141)

If you do not use carriage controls, PROC FORMS prints blank lines to align form units correctly on the page.

If you are using page-mode printing with the CC option, PROC FORMS uses the top-of-form carriage control to start each page. For page-mode operation without CC, PAGESIZE= must be correct, since FORMS uses it to calculate the number of blank lines to print at the bottom of a page to get to the next page.

Multiple copies Three features in PROC FORMS provide for multiple copies of forms. If you want the whole list repeated as a unit, then use the SETS= option. If you want each observation repeated in adjacent form units, use the COPIES= option. If you want a variable number of copies depending on a variable in a data set, use the FREQ statement. These options can be used separately or together.

SPECIFICATIONS

The statements used to control PROC FORMS are:

PROC FORMS *options;*
LINE *number variables / options;*
FREQ *variable;*
BY *variables;*

PROC FORMS Statement

PROC FORMS *options;*

The options listed below may appear in the PROC FORMS statement:

DATA=*SASdataset*   names the input data set for PROC FORMS. If DATA= is omitted, the most recently created data set is used.

DDNAME=*DDname* DD=*DDname*	specifies an external file where PROC FORMS writes the forms. If not specified, PROC FORMS uses the SAS print file. Under OS batch, the DDname corresponds to a JCL DD statement. Under TSO this corresponds to an ALLOCATE filename. Under CMS this corresponds to a FILEDEF DDNAME. Consult the section **Using External Files** for details.

Options to control form placement

WIDTH=*number* W=*number*	specifies the number of print positions across the form unit. The minimum is 1, the maximum is 255, and the default is 40.
LINES=*number* L=*number*	specifies the number of lines on a form unit. The minimum is 1, the maximum is 255, and the default is the maximum LINE statement number.
DOWN=*number* D=*number*	specifies the number of lines to skip on a page before printing the first line. The minimum is 0, the maximum is 200, and the default is 0.
SKIP=*number* S=*number*	specifies the number of lines to skip between form units. The minimum is 0, the maximum is 200, and the default is 1.
NACROSS=*number* NA=*number*	specifies the number of form units across the page. The minimum is 1, the maximum is 200, and the default is 1.
BETWEEN=*number* B=*number*	specifies the number of print positions between form units. The minimum is 0, the maximum is 200, and the default is 1.
INDENT=*number* I=*number*	specifies the number of positions to indent the first form unit across the page. The minimum is 0, the maximum is 200, and the default is 0.

Page layout options

NDOWN=*number* ND=*number*	specifies the number of form units printed down the page. This option triggers page-mode operation. The default is:

$$FLOOR((PAGESIZE-DOWN+SKIP)/(LINES+SKIP))$$

PAGESIZE=*number* P=*number*	specifies the number of lines on a form page. This information is only needed for page-mode operation if CC is not specified. The minimum is DOWN+LINES, the maximum is 255, and the default is 66 if DDNAME= is specified; otherwise it is inferred from SAS print file characteristics and titling information. This option triggers page-mode operation.

Other options

CC	requests that the procedure add carriage control characters to the beginning of each print line. This option is only relevant if the DDNAME= option is specified.
COPIES=*number* C=*number*	specifies that *number* copies be produced for each observation in the input data set. The copies are produced together rather than in separate sets (as in the SETS option).

SETS=*number*   specifies that *number* multiple copies of the entire list be printed. For page-mode operation, FORMS skips to a new page to start each set. This option is different from COPIES=, which prints the multiples in adjacent positions.

ALIGN=*number*   controls the number of XXXX form units printed so that the printer can be aligned. The default is 8 if DDNAME= is specified; 0 otherwise.

LINE Statement

LINE *linenumber variables / options;*

LINE statements come directly after the PROC FORMS statement and specify the information to be printed on each line of the form unit.

The *linenumber* value gives the number of the line, and must be an integer from 1 to the value of the LINES= option specified on the PROC FORMS statement. A LINE statement need not be given for a blank line.

Values of the *variables* specified in the LINE statement are printed on the specified line of the form unit. Up to 100 variables may be given. One blank space is inserted between each value. If the length of the values is longer than the WIDTH= specified on the PROC FORMS statement, the field is truncated to the WIDTH specified. The PACK option can squeeze out extra blanks to get more fields onto a small form unit. However, if you must squeeze fields onto a form unit, it is better to use a FORMAT statement to truncate each field individually, rather than risk losing an entire field. For example,

FORMAT CITY $20. STATE $2.;

reduces the defined width of variables CITY and STATE to 20 and 2 columns, respectively.

The options below may appear in LINE statements. If any appear, they must be preceded by a slash (/). If none are given, the slash is not needed.

INDENT=*number*   specifies that the line is to be indented by the *number*.
I=*number*   This indent is done within the form unit (in contrast to the INDENT= option for the PROC FORMS statement).

PACK   removes extra blanks from the line so that all the
P   values are separated by one space. For example, if a variable NAME has a length of 20 and the value of NAME is 'SMITH', the PACK option removes the extra 15 blanks.

LASTNAME   looks for commas in a character variable containing a
L   name and rotates the words after the comma if it finds one. For example, a variable NAME might have the value 'SMITH, JAMES P.'. If the LASTNAME option is given, the value is printed 'JAMES P. SMITH'.

REMOVE   deletes the entire line if the values of the variables are
R   all blanks or missing values.

FREQ Statement

FREQ *variable;*

When a FREQ statement is included, the value of the frequency variable determines the number of form units printed for each observation.

The variable given in the FREQ statement must be numeric. If the value is not an integer, the integer portion of the value determines the number of form units printed. If the value is less than 1 or is missing, one form unit is printed for each observation.

The actual number of copies produced in adjacent form units is the product of the FREQ variable multiplied by the value of the COPIES= option. For example, if the FREQ variable is 3 and the COPIES value is 2, then 6 copies are printed.

BY Statement

> BY *variables;*

A BY statement may be used with PROC FORMS to force new pages to be started (in page-mode operation) when the BY values change. When a BY statement appears, the procedure expects the input data set to be sorted in order of the BY variables. If your input data set is not sorted in ascending order, use the SORT procedure with a similar BY statement to sort the data, or, if appropriate, use the BY statement options NOTSORTED or DESCENDING. For more information, see the discussion of the BY statement in Chapter 8, "Statements Used in the PROC Step."

DETAILS

Missing Values

PROC FORMS prints missing values as blanks.

Using External Files

The DDNAME= option directs PROC FORMS to route the output to an external file.

You must also provide for the file or SYSOUT file with suitable control statements. You may need to request special forms to be mounted in your printer. For example, suppose PROC FORMS is to print mailing labels, which have a special-forms number at your installation of 6666. The following JCL and SAS statements put the FORMS output on special form 6666:

```
// EXEC SAS
//LABELS DD SYSOUT=(A,,6666)
   .
   . SAS Statements
   .
   PROC FORMS DDNAME=LABELS...;
```

Your installation's rules determine how special forms are handled. Check with your computer center staff for specific details.

At many installations, the operating system automatically skips to a new page after printing a given number of lines. Check with your computer center staff to disable this skip for continuous forms like labels. One convention used in JES2 is:

```
/*JOBPARM LINECNT=0
```

Compatibility Features

PROC FORMS is similar to the former FORMS procedure in the supplemental library. The following option names are still supported to insure compatibility:

NSKIP and NS for SKIP, NBETWEEN and NB for BETWEEN, NCOPIES and N for COPIES.

The options BURST, TRUNCATE, NOALIGN, and EIGHTLPI are still allowed, but ignored. New options serve their needs better. The CODE= option is still supported. The DOWN option works slightly differently.

EXAMPLE

The job below prints a listing of a set of names and addresses.

```
DATA MAILLIST;
   INPUT NAME &$20. STREET &$20. CITY &&$15. STATE :$2. ZIP :$5.;
   CARDS;
JOHN SMITH            202 MAIN ST.          ANYTOWN      IN   22432
JOE WILLIAMS          101 BROADWAY          GOTHAM       NY   32334
ALICE GORDON          55 HAZEL WAY          ATLANTA      GA   68549
GEORGE HAYES          2132 GOODVIEW         MUNCIE       IN   54345
PENELOPE PETERS       543 PEANUT CIRCLE     COLUMBIA     MD   53455
HARRISON HARRISON     898 7TH ST            BIG ROCK     AK   98733
BILL SMITH            123 STATE             ROCKFORD     IL   81522
WILL RED              544 HILLSIDE AV       ROCQUEFORT   KY   98783
ANN ANDERSON          5456 PLEASANT BLVD    SEATTLE      WA   49747
ARISTOTLE JOHNSON     234 PEACE             PHOENIX      AZ   77898
GARRY MILLER          7 GRAY DRIVE          ST. LOUIS    MO   26578
WINSTON MARTIN        34 RED ROAD           NEWTON       MA   34678
ALISON TOWSON         44 MARS HILL DR.      REDWOOD      CA   23432
MATHEW MACKEM         78 HIGHVIEW CT.       VIRGIL       VA   87373
;
PROC SORT;
   BY ZIP;
PROC FORMS WIDTH=25 LINES=3 DOWN=2 SKIP=2 NACROSS=4
   BETWEEN=1;
   LINE 1 NAME;
   LINE 2 STREET;
   LINE 3 CITY STATE ZIP/PACK;
```

```
                                      SAS                                      1

JOHN SMITH           ALISON TOWSON        GARRY MILLER         JOE WILLIAMS
202 MAIN ST.         44 MARS HILL DR.     7 GRAY DRIVE         101 BROADWAY
ANYTOWN IN 22432     REDWOOD CA 23432     ST. LOUIS MO 26578   GOTHAM NY 32334


WINSTON MARTIN       ANN ANDERSON         PENELOPE PETERS      GEORGE HAYES
34 RED ROAD          5456 PLEASANT BLVD   543 PEANUT CIRCLE    2132 GOODVIEW
NEWTON MA 34678      SEATTLE WA 49747     COLUMBIA MD 53455    MUNCIE IN 54345


ALICE GORDON         ARISTOTLE JOHNSON    BILL SMITH           MATHEW MACKEM
55 HAZEL WAY         234 PEACE            123 STATE            78 HIGHVIEW CT.
ATLANTA GA 68549     PHOENIX AZ 77898     ROCKFORD IL 81522    VIRGIL VA 87373


HARRISON HARRISON    WILL RED
898 7TH ST           544 HILLSIDE AV
BIG ROCK AK 98733    ROCQUEFORT KY 98783
```

The PLOT Procedure

ABSTRACT

The PLOT procedure graphs one variable against another, producing a printer plot. The coordinates of each point on the plot correspond to the two variables' values in one or more observations of the input data set.

INTRODUCTION

PLOT takes the values that occur for each observation in an input SAS data set on two variables, say X and Y, and then represents the intersection of these values as points on the plot. All you need to do to produce a plot is to tell the procedure which variables to plot. For example, these statements

```
PROC PLOT;
  PLOT Y*X;
```

produce the simple plot shown below.

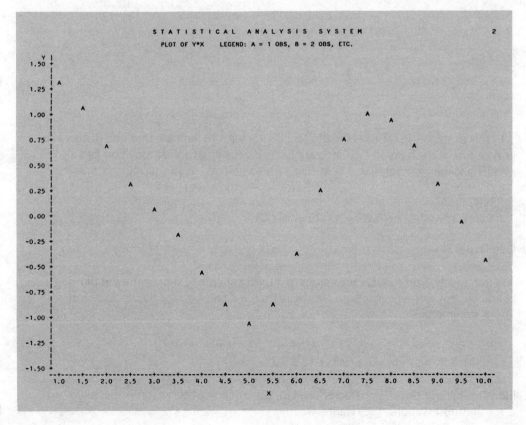

Fig. 1

Note that PLOT automatically scales the values of X and Y on the plot. Or you can specify the tickmarks, the lines on the axis marking specific values that you want. For example,

```
PROC PLOT;
    PLOT Y*X / HAXIS=0 TO 12 BY 2;
```

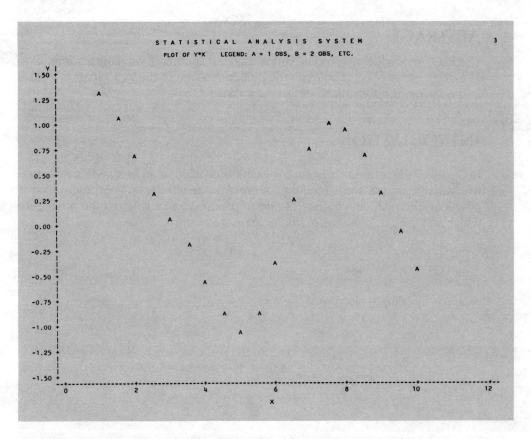

Fig. 2

In this example, PLOT uses the plotting character A to indicate that one observation occurs at each point, B to indicate two observations, and so on. You can also specify another symbol, like a plus sign (+), to be used as the plotting character.

```
PROC PLOT;
    PLOT Y*X='+' / HAXIS = 0 TO 12 BY 2;
```

(See Figure 3)

Alternatively, you can use the values of a third variable to determine the plotting character. For example, suppose another variable Z takes on the values 1, 2, and 3. These statements

```
PROC PLOT;
    PLOT Y*X=Z / HAXIS = 0 TO 12 BY 2;
```

indicate that the plotting character used for a particular observation is the value of Z for that observation. (See Figure 4)

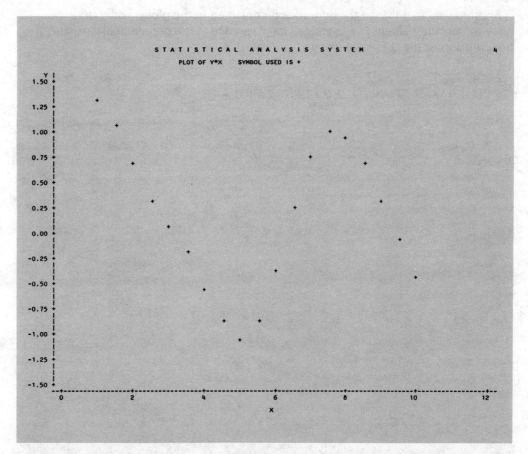

Fig. 3

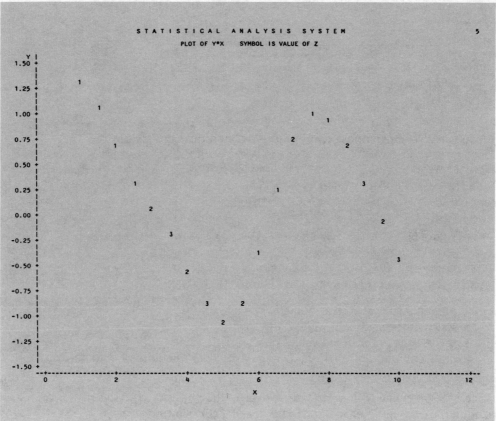

Fig. 4

Another way to enhance the information contained in the plot is with reference lines at specific values. For example, for reference lines perpendicular to the horizontal axis, use these statements:

```
PROC PLOT;
  PLOT Y*X=Z / HAXIS = 0 TO 12 BY 2 HREF=4 8;
```

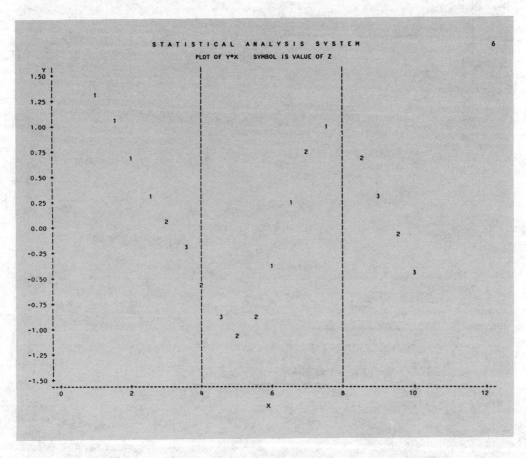

Fig. 5

You can also superimpose two or more plots on the same axes.

```
PROC PLOT;
  PLOT Y*X=Z A*B / OVERLAY;
```

(See Figure 6)

You can also use PLOT to:

- plot character as well as numeric variables
- specify the length and width of the plot
- reverse the order of the values on the vertical axis
- draw contour plots with shading intensity determined by a third variable in the data set.

The SAS statements that generated the data for the plots shown in this section are listed at the end of the chapter in **Examples of PLOT Output**.

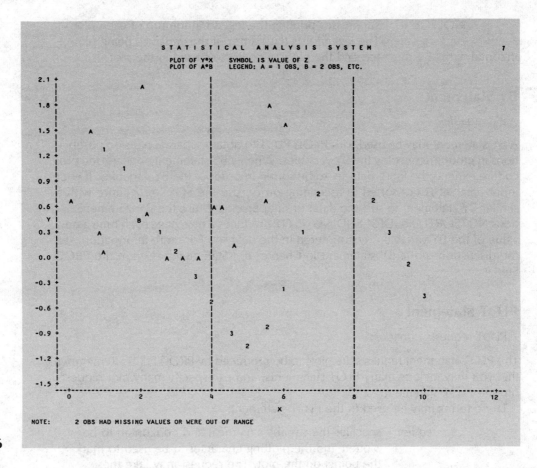

Fig. 6

SPECIFICATIONS

The PLOT procedure is controlled by these statements:

> **PROC PLOT** *options*;
>   **BY** *variables*;
>   **PLOT** *requests* / *options*;

A PLOT statement must be present to tell the procedure which variables to plot. Any number of PLOT statements may be specified each time the procedure is invoked, and any number of plots may be requested on one PLOT statement.

PROC PLOT Statement

PROC PLOT *options*;

The options below may appear in the PROC PLOT statement.

DATA=*SASdataset*   names the input SAS data set to be used by PROC PLOT. When the DATA= option is omitted, PLOT uses the most recently created SAS data set.

UNIFORM   requests uniform axis scaling across BY groups when a BY statement is used. The same scaling allows you to compare the plots for different levels of the BY variables directly.

NOLEGEND   suppresses printing the legend at the top of each plot. The legend lists the names of the variables being plotted and the plotting characters used in the plot.

BY Statement

BY *variables*;

A BY statement may be used with PROC PLOT to obtain separate plots on observations in groups defined by the BY variables. When a BY statement appears, the procedure expects the input data set to be sorted in order of the BY variables. If your input data set is not sorted in ascending order, use the SORT procedure with a similar BY statement to sort the data, or, if appropriate, use the BY statement options NOTSORTED or DESCENDING. PLOT produces a new page each time a new value of the BY variable is encountered in the data set. For more information, see the discussion of the BY statement in Chapter 8, "Statements Used in the PROC Step."

PLOT Statement

PLOT *requests* / *options*;

The PLOT statement requests the plots to be produced by PROC PLOT. Remember that you may include many PLOT statements, and can specify many plot requests on one PLOT statement.

These terms may be used in the PLOT statement:

request   specifies the variables (vertical and horizontal) to be plotted and the plotting character to be used to mark the points on the plot. The request may take these forms:

> *vertical**horizontal
> *vertical**horizontal = '*character*'
> *vertical**horizontal = *variable*

vertical*horizontal   names the variable to be shown on the vertical axis and the variable to be shown on the horizontal axis. For example, the statements

> PROC PLOT;
>   PLOT Y*X;

request a plot of Y by X. Y appears on the vertical axis, X on the horizontal.

This form of the plot request uses the default method of choosing a plotting symbol to mark plot points. When a point on the plot represents the values of one observation in the data set, PLOT puts the character A at that point. When a point represents the values of two observations, a B appears. When a point represents values of three observations, a C appears, and so on through the alphabet. The letter Z is used for the occurrence of 26 or more observations at the same printing position.

vertical*horizontal=
'character'
names the variables to be shown on the vertical and horizontal axes and also specifies a character constant to mark each point on the plot. A single character is used to represent values from one or more observations.

For example, the statements

```
PROC PLOT;
  PLOT Y*X='+';
```

request a plot of Y by X with each point on the plot represented by a plus sign (+).

vertical*horizontal=
variable
names the variables to be plotted on the vertical and horizontal axes and also specifies a variable whose values are to mark each point on the plot. The variable may be either numeric or character. The first (left-most) nonblank character in the formatted value of the variable is used as the plotting symbol. When more than one observation maps to the same plotting position, the value from the first observation marks the point. For example,

```
PROC PLOT;
  PLOT HEIGHT*WEIGHT=SEX;
```

SEX is a character variable with values of FEMALE and MALE: the values F and M mark each observation on the plot.

Note: the plotting symbol is the first nonblank character of each value even if more than one value starts with the same letter.

To request two or more plots, write one request after another:

```
PROC PLOT;
  PLOT A*B R*S;
```

If you want to plot all the combinations of one set of variables with another, you can use a grouping specification. Enclose each set of variables in parentheses, joining them with an asterisk (*). For example, the following PLOT statements are equivalent:

```
PLOT (Y X)*(A B);
```

```
PLOT Y*A Y*B X*A X*B;
```

You can also abbreviate a variable list to request a number of plots:

```
PLOT Y*(A--Z);
```

The options below may appear in the PLOT statement. A slash (/) separates these options from the plot requests. No slash is needed if no options are specified.

Scale of axes

VAXIS=*values*   specifies the tickmark values to be equally spaced along the vertical axis. When the variable is numeric, VAXIS values must be given in either ascending or descending order.

The statements

```
PROC PLOT;
   PLOT Y*X / VAXIS = 10 TO 100 BY 5;
```

ask for a plot of Y by X, with tickmarks at 10, 15, 20 and on up to 100 on the vertical axis.

Numeric values need not be uniformly distributed; a specification of the form

```
VAXIS= 10  100  1000  10000
```

is valid and produces a logarithmic plot.

For character variables, the values may be given in any order.

HAXIS=*values*   specifies tickmark values for the horizontal axis. The HAXIS option follows the same rules as the VAXIS option above.

VZERO   requests that tickmarks on the vertical axis begin in the first position with a zero. The VZERO request is ignored if the vertical variable has negative values or if an optional VAXIS= specification does not begin with zero.

HZERO   requests that tickmarks on the horizontal axis begin in the first position with a value of zero. The HZERO request is ignored if the horizontal variable has negative values or if an optional HAXIS= specification does not begin with zero.

VREVERSE   asks that the order of the values on the vertical axis be reversed. (No option is available to reverse the horizontal axis.)

Reference lines

VREF=*values*   requests that a horizontal line be drawn on the plot at the specified values on the vertical axis.

VREFCHAR='c'   gives the character to define the horizontal lines requested by the VREF option. If you do not specify a character with VREFCHAR=, the hyphen (-) is used.

HREF=*values*   requests that a vertical line be drawn on the plot at the specified values on the horizontal axis. For example, the statements

```
PROC PLOT;
   PLOT Y*X / HREF=5;
```

request a plot of Y by X with a vertical line at 5 on the horizontal axis.

HREFCHAR='c' specifies the character to define the vertical lines requested by the HREF= option. If you do not use HREFCHAR=, the vertical bar (|) is used.

Plot size Plots normally occupy one page each. You can use the options below to change the length and width of the plot. You can also use the system options LINESIZE and PAGESIZE to change plot sizes. (See the OPTIONS statement in Chapter 10.)

VPOS=n specifies the number of vertical print positions on the vertical axis. The maximum VPOS must be at least 8 less than the page size; the exact number depends on the titles used, whether plots are overlaid, and whether CONTOUR is specified.

HPOS=n specifies the number of print positions on the horizontal axis. At least 3 additional positions are needed to print vertical axis information; the exact number depends on the number of characters in the vertical variable's values.

VSPACE=n specifies the number of print lines to be used between tickmarks on the vertical axis.

HSPACE=n specifies the number of print positions to be used between tickmarks on the horizontal axis.

Overlaying plots

OVERLAY requests PLOT to combine the plots specified in the PLOT statement on one page. The variables in the first plot label the axes. Unless HAXIS or VAXIS is given, the axes are automatically scaled to best fit all the variables, and the variable labels (if any) associated with the first pair of variables are printed next to the axes. When the SAS system option OVP is in effect and overprinting is allowed, the plots are superimposed; otherwise, when NOOVP is in effect, points appearing in more than one plot are represented by the value from the first plot. Using the OVP system option and the OVERLAY option is the only case where the PLOT procedure overprints.

Contour plots

CONTOUR=value requests plotting symbols with varying degrees of shading where value is the number of levels for dividing the range of the response variable. The plot request must be of the form vertical*horizontal= variable where variable is a numeric variable in the data set. The intensity of shading is determined by the values of this variable. CONTOUR's value can range from 1 to 10. For example, the statements

```
PROC PLOT;
  PLOT A*B=Z / CONTOUR=10;
```

request a plot whose points vary in darkness depending on the value of Z. Since the CONTOUR value is 10, ten darkness levels are used.

Overprinting is used to produce the shading if it is allowed. Otherwise, single characters varying in darkness are used. The CONTOUR option is most effective when the plot is dense.

S1 = *value*
S2 = *value*
... specify plotting symbols to use for each contour value in ascending order. When PLOT produces contour plots, it automatically chooses the symbols to use for each level of intensity. It is possible to override these symbols and specify your own symbols for intensity levels using the S options. Up to three characters may be specified in quotes. If overprinting is not allowed, only the first character is used. For example, to specify three levels of shading for the Z variable, these statements might be used:

```
PROC PLOT;
  PLOT X*Y=Z / CONTOUR=3
    S1='A' S2='+' S3='X0A';
```

The symbols may be specified as hex constants.

```
PROC PLOT;
  PLOT X*Y=Z / CONTOUR=3
    S1='7A'X S2='7F'X S3='A6'X;
```

This feature was designed especially for IBM 3800 printers where the hex constants can represent grey-scale fill characters.

DETAILS

Missing Values

If values on either of the plotting variables are missing, PROC PLOT does not include the observation in the plot.

Generating Data with Program Statements

When you generate data to be plotted, a good rule is to generate fewer observations than the number of positions on the horizontal axis. PLOT then uses the increment of the horizontal variable as the interval between tickmarks.

Since PLOT prints one character for each observation, using SAS program statements to generate the data set for PLOT can enhance the effectiveness of continuous plots (see **Example 3**) and contour plots (see **Example 5**).

For example, suppose that you want to generate data in order to plot the equation

$$y = 2.54 + 3.83*x$$

for x ranging from 0 to 100 with these statements:

```
OPTIONS LINESIZE=80;
DATA GENERATE;
  DO X=0 TO 100 BY 2;
    Y=2.54+3.83*X;
    OUTPUT;
    END;
PROC PLOT;
  PLOT Y*X;
```

If the plot is printed with a LINESIZE of 80, about 75 positions are available on the horizontal axis for the X values. Thus 2 is a good increment: 51 observations are generated, which is less than 75.

However, if the plot is printed with a LINESIZE of 132, an increment of 2 produces a plot with a space between each plotting character. For a smoother line, a better increment is 1, since 101 observations are generated.

Printed Output

Each plot uses one full page unless the plot's size is changed by the VPOS and HPOS options or the system options PAGESIZE and LINESIZE. Titles, legends, and variable labels are printed at the top of each page. Each axis is labeled with the variable name or the variable label, if one is specified. (See the LABEL statement in Chapter 8, "Statements Used in the PROC Step.")

EXAMPLES

Plotting Observed Data: Example 1

The example below plots the two variables RATED and ACTUAL against each other. PLOT uses an increment of 5 for tickmarks on the vertical axis; tickmarks on the horizontal axis have an increment of 4. Since two observations have a RATED value of 118 and an ACTUAL value of 121, PLOT uses a B to represent the point corresponding to RATED=118 and ACTUAL=121. Other points are represented by As.

```
DATA SPEED;
  INPUT RATED ACTUAL;
  LABEL RATED=RATED SPEED   ACTUAL=ACTUAL SPEED;
  CARDS;
 75  85
110 112
 75  81
105 108
112 115
 75  77
 90  89
 70  73
118 121
103 100
118 121
;
PROC PLOT;
  PLOT RATED*ACTUAL;
  TITLE RATED SPEED VS. ACTUAL SPEED;
```

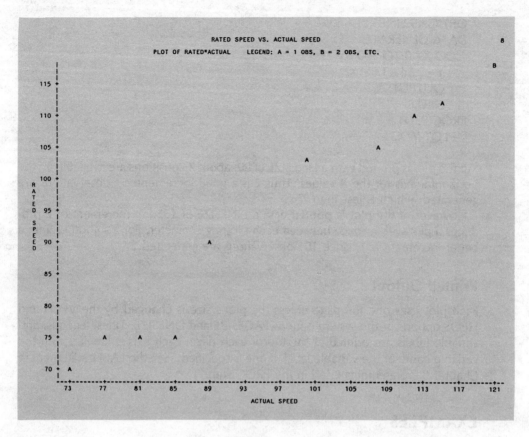

Fig. 7

Using a Plot Character and Defining Tickmarks: Example 2

This example uses variables from an analysis of covariance: RESPONSE is the
response variable, and NUISANCE is a presumed covariate. To keep track of which
observations are associated with different values of the variable TREAT, values of
TREAT are used for the plotting characters.

You can use the VAXIS= option to define tickmarks for the vertical axis, beginning with 125 and going up to 185 by 5s.

```
DATA COVAR;
  INPUT TREAT $ RESPONSE NUISANCE;
  CARDS;
P    125   3.1
P    135   9.0
P    144   14.9
P    153   20.2
Q    136   2.0
Q    152   8.5
Q    160   12.6
Q    165   17.1
R    154   3.2
R    164   10.5
R    173   15.4
R    183   20.7
PROC PLOT;
   PLOT RESPONSE*NUISANCE=TREAT / VAXIS=125 TO 185 BY 5;
   TITLE RESPONSE VS. NUISANCE;
   TITLE2 THREE TREATMENTS;
```

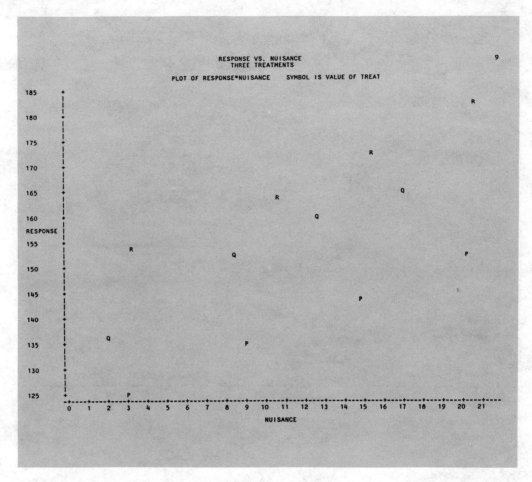

Fig. 8

Plotting the Graph of an Equation: Example 3

In the example below, program statements in the DATA step are used to create observations to plot the equation

$$Y = X \sin(2X)$$

for values of X ranging from 0 to 5.

No INPUT statement is used: all the X and Y values are generated by the program statements, and the OUTPUT statement creates the observations. In the PLOT statement, an asterisk (*) is specified as the plotting character.

```
DATA PROGRAM;
  DO X=0 TO 5 BY .05;
    Y=X*SIN(2*X);
    OUTPUT;
    END;
PROC PLOT;
  PLOT Y*X='*';
  TITLE Y=X*SIN(2*X);
```

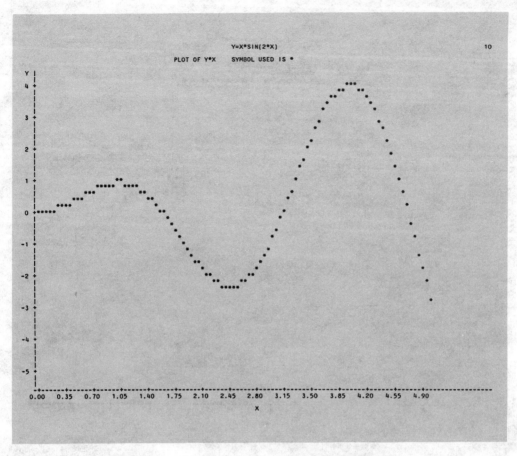

Fig. 9

Plotting Predicted vs. Actual Values: Example 4

It is often useful to plot the graph of an equation and the observed data for which
the equation was developed.

In regression analysis you often want to plot the regression equation as well as
the actual values. You can use the OUTPUT statement with PROC REG to produce
a data set containing both observed and predicted values, and then use PROC
PLOT to overlay plots of these values. Here is an example:

```
DATA HTWT;
  INPUT HEIGHT WEIGHT @@;
  CARDS;
69.0 112.5 56.5 84.0 65.3 98.0 62.8 102.5 63.5 102.5
57.3 83.0 59.8 84.5 62.5 112.5 62.5 84.0 59.0 99.5
51.3 50.5 64.3 90.0 56.3 77.0 66.5 112.0 72.0 150.0
64.8 128.0 67.0 133.0 57.5 85.0 66.5 112.0
;
PROC REG;
  MODEL HEIGHT=WEIGHT;
  OUTPUT OUT=BOTH P=PREDHT;
PROC PLOT DATA=BOTH;
  PLOT HEIGHT*WEIGHT PREDHT*WEIGHT='*' / OVERLAY;
  TITLE PREDICTED VS. ACTUAL;
```

Actual values are indicated with As, predicted values with *s.

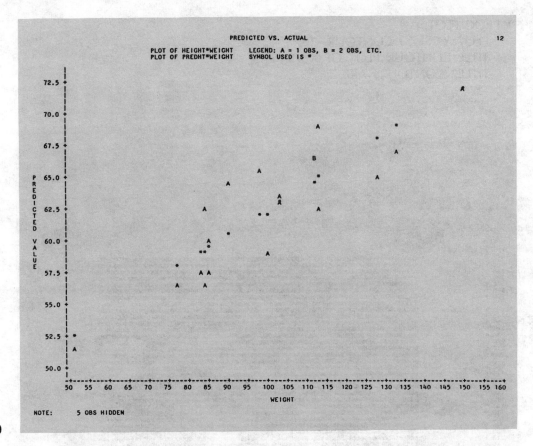

Fig. 10

Contour Plotting: Example 5

It's possible to represent the values of three variables using a two-dimensional plot by setting one of the variables as the CONTOUR variable. When the value of that variable is high, it is represented by a dark point on the plot; when the value is low, it is represented by a light point.

In the example below, the three variables represented in the plot are X, Y, and Z. X and Y appear on the axes, and Z is the contour variable. You can see from the plot where high values of Z occur: if this were a three-dimensional plot, the dark areas would be a hilltop. Program statements are used to generate the observations for the plot, and the equation

$$Z = 45.2 + .09X - .0005X^2 + .1Y - .0005Y^2 + .0004XY$$

describes the contour surface. Data set CONTOURS contains observations with values of X ranging from 0 to 400 by 5 and for values of Y ranging from 0 to 350 by 10.

The shadings associated with the values of Z appear at the bottom of the plot.

```
DATA CONTOURS;
  FORMAT Z 5.1;
  DO X=0 TO 400 BY 5;
    DO Y=0 TO 350 BY 10;
      Z=46.2+.09*X-.0005*X**2+.1*Y-.0005*Y**2+.0004*X*Y;
      OUTPUT;
      END;
  END;
```

```
PROC PLOT;
  PLOT Y*X=Z / CONTOUR=10;
  TITLE CONTOUR PLOT OF X VS. Y;
  TITLE2 CONTOURS ARE Z;
```

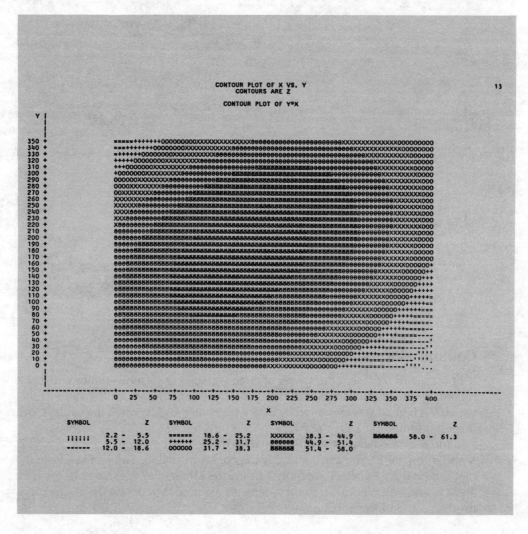

Fig. 11

Labeling an Axis with Date Values: Example 6

When you plot a variable against a date variable, you can label the tickmarks on an axis with date values by using SAS date constants after the VAXIS= or HAXIS= option. (See Chapter 4, "SAS Expressions," for a description of date, time, and datetime constants.) To cause the constants to be printed in an understandable form, specify a format for the date variable. This example uses date constants to label the tickmarks on the horizontal axis with the first day of each month. Note that in order to have room on the axis for observations in the month of December, you must specify a tickmark for January of the following year.

```
DATA SAMPLE;
  INPUT DATE:DATE7. CALLS;
  LABEL DATE=DATE
        CALLS=NUMBER OF CALLS;
  CARDS;
1APR82 134
2MAR82 289
3JUN82 184
4JAN82 179
5APR82 360
6MAY82 245
7JUL82 280
8AUG82 494
9SEP82 309
11APR82 384
21MAR82 201
13JUN82 152
14JAN82 128
15APR82 350
15DEC82 150
16MAY82 240
17JUL82 499
18AUG82 248
19SEP82 356
10OCT82 222
11NOV82 294
2DEC82 511
22DEC82 413
13FEB82 488
14MAR82 460
15APR82 356
16JUN82 480
17JUL82 388
17NOV82 328
18AUG82 280
19SEP82 394
23NOV82 590
24FEB82 201
25MAR82 183
26APR82 412
27MAY82 292
28JUN82 309
29JUL82 330
30AUG82 321
;
PROC PLOT;
  PLOT CALLS*DATE/HAXIS= '1JAN82'D '1FEB82'D '1MAR82'D
    '1APR82'D '1MAY82'D '1JUN82'D '1JUL82'D '1AUG82'D '1SEP82'D
    '1OCT82'D '1NOV82'D '1DEC82'D '1JAN83'D;
  FORMAT DATE DATE7.;
  TITLE 'CALLS TO CITY EMERGENCY SERVICES NUMBER';
  TITLE2 'SAMPLE OF DAYS FOR 1982';
```

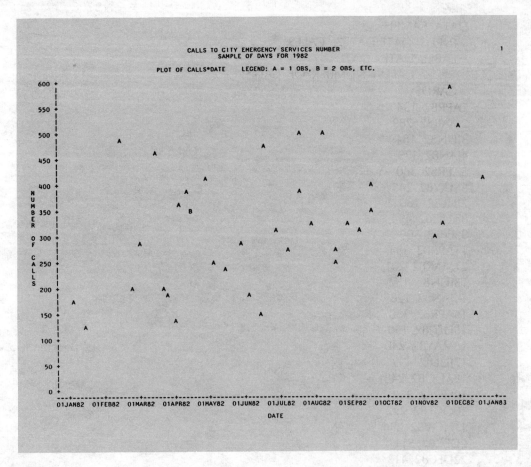

Fig. 12

Examples of PLOT Output

The data for the examples in the earlier section of this chapter were generated with the following SAS statements.

```
DATA GENERATE;
   DO X= 1 TO 10 BY .1;
      Y = SIN(X) + SIN(2*X)/(X + 1);
      Z = SIN(X) + SIN(2*X)/(X + 1);
      A = CEIL(UNIFORM(13131)*3);
      B = 3*(1–MOD(Y,X));
      OUTPUT;
      END;
```

The PRINT Procedure

ABSTRACT

The PRINT procedure prints the observations in a SAS data set, using all or some of the variables. Totals and subtotals for numeric variables can also be printed.

INTRODUCTION

PROC PRINT is a procedure that lists data as a table of observations by variables. You can produce customized reports using procedure options and statements: for example, with a BY statement, PROC PRINT separates observations into groups defined by the BY variables. Numeric variable totals are printed if a SUM statement is used. As many as ten TITLE statements can be specified, and you can control the size of a report with the SAS system options LINESIZE= and PAGESIZE=.

SPECIFICATIONS

The following statements and options can be used with PROC PRINT:

> **PROC PRINT** *options*;
>   **VAR** *variable* ...;
>   **ID** *variable* ...;
>   **BY** *variable* ...;
>   **PAGEBY** *variable*;
>   **SUM** *variable* ...;
>   **SUMBY** *variable*;

PROC PRINT Statement

> PROC PRINT *options*;

The options below can be specified in the PROC PRINT statement:

DATA=*SASdataset*   names the SAS data set to be used by PROC PRINT. If DATA= is omitted, the most recently created data set is used.

N   requests that the number of observations be printed at the end of the data set. If a BY statement is used, the number of observations in each BY group is printed at the end of the BY group.

UNIFORM   requests that the values of a variable be printed in the same columns of each page in the output. Without the UNIFORM option, the PRINT procedure fits as many variables and observations on a page as possible. This can result in a different number of variables being printed on each page.

DOUBLE   causes the printed output to be double-spaced.

ROUND   rounds values to the number of decimal places specified for a variable in a FORMAT statement, or if no format is specified, to two decimal places. The only variables whose values are rounded are those being summed (see the SUM and SUMBY statements, below). Values are rounded before printing, and the rounded values are accumulated for printing of totals.

LABEL   uses variables' labels as column headings. Labels can be specified in LABEL statements in the DATA step that creates the data set, or in the PROC PRINT step. See Chapter 8, "Statements Used in the PROC Step," for a description of the LABEL statement. If LABEL is not specified, or if there is no label for a variable, the variable name is used. If the LABEL option is specified, and there is at least one variable with a label, column headings are not printed vertically; therefore, the number of output pages may be greater than if printed without the use of the LABEL option. PROC PRINT splits labels if necessary, in order to conserve space. Labels are printed for BY variables but are not printed in SUM lines (see the example output at the end of this chapter).

SPLIT=*splitchar*   splits labels used as column headings where the *splitchar* appears. It is not necessary to use both the LABEL and SPLIT= options, since SPLIT= implies that labels are to be used.

Here is an example. With these statements:

```
PROC PRINT DATA=CLASS SPLIT=*;
   LABEL X=THIS IS*A LABEL;
```

the label for X prints like this:

```
THIS IS
A LABEL
```

The split character is not printed, and blanks are significant. Up to three lines of labels are allowed; that is, no more than two split characters can be used. To print a column with no heading, use the split character as the variable's label. For example, these statements:

```
DATA TEST;
   INPUT X $ @@;
   LABEL X=*;
   CARDS;
AAA BBB CCC DDD
;
PROC PRINT DATA=TEST LABEL SPLIT=*;
```

produce this output:

```
OBS
  1    AAA
  2    BBB
  3    CCC
  4    DDD
```

Labels of BY variables are not split, even if SPLIT= is specified. The split character is printed as part of the label.

VAR Statement

VAR *variable* ...;

The VAR statement names the variables to be printed. The variables are printed in the order in which they appear in the VAR statement. If no VAR statement is used, all variables in the data set are printed.

ID Statement

ID *variable* ...;

The formatted values of the *variable* in the ID statement are used instead of observation numbers to identify observations in the output. More than one variable can be specified. When an observation is too long to print on one line, the values of the ID variables are printed at the beginning of every line containing data values for the observation. The ID variables may be up to one-half the width of the page as determined by the current value of the LINESIZE= option (TLINESIZE= under TSO and CMS), which usually has a default value of 132.

BY Statement

BY *variable* ...;

A BY statement may be used with PROC PRINT to obtain separate analyses on observations in groups defined by the BY variables. When a BY statement appears, the procedure expects the input data set to be sorted in order of the BY variables. If your input data set is not sorted in ascending order, use the SORT procedure with a similar BY statement to sort the data, or, if appropriate, use the BY statement options NOTSORTED or DESCENDING. For more information, see the discussion of the BY statement in Chapter 8, ''Statements Used in the PROC Step.''

The LABEL and SPLIT= options have no effect on BY variables since the BY variable values are printed in a dashed line above the remaining printed output for the BY group.

PAGEBY Statement

PAGEBY *variable*;

The PAGEBY statement causes PROC PRINT to begin printing a new page when the specified BY *variable* changes value, or when any BY variable listed before it in the

BY statement changes value. For example:

```
PROC PRINT;
  BY X Y Z;
  PAGEBY Y;
```

causes SAS to print a new page when X or Y changes value, but not when Z changes value.

A BY statement is required with the PAGEBY statement. (The PAGEBY statement serves the same purpose as the PAGE and PAGE= options described for earlier releases of SAS.)

SUM Statement

SUM *variable* ...;

The SUM statement specifies variables whose values are to be totaled. You can specify a variable in the SUM statement that is not listed on the VAR statement, and the procedure adds the variable to the VAR list. PRINT ignores requests for totals on BY and ID variables.

When a BY statement is used and only one BY variable is specified, the SUM variable is totaled for each BY group (subtotaled) containing more than one observation. Consider this example:

```
DATA A;
  INPUT X Y Z @@;
  CARDS;
1 1 1 1 2 2 1 1 2 1 2 3 1 1 3 3 1 3 3 2 3 4 1
PROC PRINT;
  BY X;
  SUM Z;
```

Data set A is created and then printed with the Z variable values subtotaled according to variable X BY groups. Since the observations are already sorted by the X and Y values it is not necessary to use PROC SORT. Subtotals are printed for each BY group since they all contain more than one observation.

```
------------------------------------ X=1 ---------------------------------------2

             OBS      Y      Z

              1       1      1
              2       1      2
              -              -
              X              3

------------------------------------ X=2 ----------------------------------------

             OBS      Y      Z

              3       1      1
              4       1      2
              -              -
              X              3

------------------------------------ X=3 ----------------------------------------

             OBS      Y      Z

              5       1      1
              6       3      1
              7       3      2
              8       4      1
              -              --
              X               5
                             ==
                             11
```

When a BY statement is used and multiple BY variables are specified, subtotals are printed for a BY variable only when it changes value and there is more than one observation with that value. (Any BY variables listed after a given BY variable change value when that BY variable changes value. This is shown in the example output below; when X changes value, Y changes value also.) For example, if the data set A (above) is printed with X and Y as BY variables:

```
PROC PRINT;
   BY X Y;
   SUM Z;
```

the output looks like this:

```
                                                                                    3
-------------------------------------- X=1    Y=1 ----------------------------------

                                       OBS    Z

                                        1     1
                                        2     2
                                        -     -
                                        Y     3
                                        X     3


-------------------------------------- X=2    Y=1 ---------------------------------

                                       OBS    Z

                                        3     1
                                        4     2
                                        -     -
                                        Y     3
                                        X     3


-------------------------------------- X=3    Y=1 ---------------------------------

                                       OBS    Z

                                        5     1


-------------------------------------- X=3    Y=3 ---------------------------------

                                       OBS    Z

                                        6     1
                                        7     2
                                        -     -
                                        Y     3


-------------------------------------- X=3    Y=4 ---------------------------------

                                       OBS    Z

                                        8     1
                                        -     --
                                        X     5
                                              ==
                                              11
```

SUMBY Statement

    SUMBY *variable*;

The SUMBY statement is used to print totals when the specified BY *variable* changes value, or when any BY variable listed before it in the BY statement changes value. A BY statement is required with the SUMBY statement.

The variables that are totaled are those that appear in the SUM statement. If there is no SUM statement, SAS totals all numeric variables in the data set except those listed in a BY statement.

These statements:

```
PROC PRINT;
   SUM A B C;
   BY X Y Z;
   SUMBY Y;
```

total the variables A, B, and C when either X or Y changes value, but not when Z changes value.

The effect of the SUMBY statement is to limit the printing of subtotals for BY groups; without it, subtotals are printed when any BY variable changes value and there is more than one observation with the value.

DETAILS

Usage Notes

Formats If you provide formats for the numeric variables (for example, with FORMAT statements), decimal points are not shifted each time a value is printed (that is, they align in the column). Numeric values not associated with a specific format are given a maximum width of 12 columns. (The FORMAT statement is described in Chapter 8, "Statements Used in the PROC Step.")

Page format PROC PRINT formats one page at a time, and by default, attempts to use as few pages as possible. First, it attempts to print observations on a single line. Column headings may be rotated (printed vertically rather than horizontally) to accomplish this, unless the SPLIT= or LABEL options are specified. If it cannot fit the observations on single lines, the observations are split into two or more sections on the page, and the observation number or ID variable(s) is printed at the beginning of each line.

UNIFORM option The maximum number of observations that fit on a page is based on data widths, so the columns used to print certain variables can vary from page to page. The UNIFORM option prevents this, but requires more pages to print a data set.

The data width of an unformatted character variable is its length, or the pagesize minus the length of the ID variable, whichever is less. The width of an unformatted numeric variable is 12.

Printed Output

The printed output for PROC PRINT includes:

1. OBS, the number of each observation in the data set, appears in the left-most column of the output. (OBS is not a variable in the data set; it is only used by the procedure to identify observations when the ID statement is not used.) If an ID variable is used, ID values rather than observation numbers are printed, and the column is headed with the name of the ID variable.
2. the names or labels of all variables that are printed
3. the current value(s) of the BY variable, if any, above each section
4. totals for the specified variables.

EXAMPLES

Printing Reports: Example 1

A company's sales and expense reports for four regions of the United States are printed in three different ways in this example. The data set is first created and a simple listing of the data is printed.

```
DATA BRANCH;
   INPUT REGION $ STATE $ MONTH MONYY5.
     HEADCNT EXPENSES REVENUE;
   FORMAT MONTH MONYY5.;
   CARDS;
EASTERN      VA     FEB78        10      7800      15500
SOUTHERN     FL     MAR78         9      9800      13500
SOUTHERN     GA     JAN78         5      2000       8000
NORTHERN     MA     MAR78         3      1500       1000
SOUTHERN     FL     FEB78        10      8500      11000
NORTHERN     NY     MAR78         5      6000       5000
EASTERN      VA     MAR78        11      8200      16600
PLAINS       NM     MAR78         2      1350        500
SOUTHERN     FL     JAN78        10      8000      10000
NORTHERN     NY     FEB78         4      3000       4000
SOUTHERN     GA     FEB78         7      1200       6000
PROC PRINT;
```

```
                                                                    4
   OBS    REGION      STATE    MONTH    HEADCNT    EXPENSES    REVENUE

    1     EASTERN      VA      FEB78      10         7800       15500
    2     SOUTHERN     FL      MAR78       9         9800       13500
    3     SOUTHERN     GA      JAN78       5         2000        8000
    4     NORTHERN     MA      MAR78       3         1500        1000
    5     SOUTHERN     FL      FEB78      10         8500       11000
    6     NORTHERN     NY      MAR78       5         6000        5000
    7     EASTERN      VA      MAR78      11         8200       16600
    8     PLAINS       NM      MAR78       2         1350         500
    9     SOUTHERN     FL      JAN78      10         8000       10000
   10     NORTHERN     NY      FEB78       4         3000        4000
   11     SOUTHERN     GA      FEB78       7         1200        6000
```

Now sort the data set and use PRINT to create a report showing revenue and expense totals.

```
PROC SORT;
   BY REGION STATE MONTH;
PROC PRINT SPLIT=*;
   LABEL REGION=SALES REGION
     HEADCNT=SALES*PERSONNEL;
   BY REGION STATE;
   SUM REVENUE EXPENSES;
```

```
                                                                    5
------------------------- SALES REGION=EASTERN    STATE=VA -------------------

   OBS    MONTH     SALES       EXPENSES     REVENUE
                    PERSONNEL

    1     FEB78        10          7800       15500
    2     MAR78        11          8200       16600
          ------                 ------      ------
   STATE                          16000       32100
   REGION                         16000       32100

------------------------- SALES REGION=NORTHERN   STATE=MA -------------------

   OBS    MONTH     SALES       EXPENSES     REVENUE
                    PERSONNEL

    3     MAR78         3          1500        1000
```

(continued on next page)

(continued from previous page)

```
------------------------ SALES REGION=NORTHERN   STATE=NY ------------------------

        OBS      MONTH     SALES       EXPENSES      REVENUE
                           PERSONNEL

          4      FEB78         4         3000         4000
          5      MAR78         5         6000         5000
        ------                           -----        -----
        STATE                            9000         9000
        REGION                          10500        10000


------------------------ SALES REGION=PLAINS     STATE=NM ------------------------

        OBS      MONTH     SALES       EXPENSES      REVENUE
                           PERSONNEL

          6      MAR78         2         1350          500


------------------------ SALES REGION=SOUTHERN   STATE=FL ------------------------

        OBS      MONTH     SALES       EXPENSES      REVENUE
                           PERSONNEL

          7      JAN78        10         8000        10000
          8      FEB78        10         8500        11000
          9      MAR78         9         9800        13500
        ------                           -----        -----
        STATE                           26300        34500
```

```
                                                                                6
------------------------ SALES REGION=SOUTHERN   STATE=GA ------------------------

        OBS      MONTH     SALES       EXPENSES      REVENUE
                           PERSONNEL

         10      JAN78         5         2000         8000
         11      FEB78         7         1200         6000
        ------                           -----        -----
        STATE                            3200        14000
        REGION                          29500        48500
                                        =====        =====
                                        57350        91100
```

A different type of summary report is printed when the same variables are specified in both ID and BY statements.

```
PROC PRINT SPLIT=*;
   LABEL REGION=SALES REGION
      HEADCNT=SALES*PERSONNEL;
   BY REGION STATE;
   ID REGION STATE;  /* PUT EACH BY VARIABLE IN ID */
   SUM REVENUE EXPENSES;
   VAR REVENUE EXPENSES HEADCNT MONTH;
   FORMAT HEADCNT 3. REVENUE EXPENSES COMMA8.;
   TITLE BRANCH HEAD COUNT, SALES AND EXPENSES;
```

```
                                                                                7
                  BRANCH HEAD COUNT, SALES AND EXPENSES

   SALES REGION    STATE     REVENUE     EXPENSES    SALES        MONTH
                                                     PERSONNEL

   EASTERN         VA        15,500       7,800         10        FEB78
                             16,600       8,200         11        MAR78
   --------        --------  --------    --------
   EASTERN         VA        32,100      16,000
   EASTERN                   32,100      16,000
```

(continued on next page)

(continued from previous page)

NORTHERN	MA	1,000	1,500	3	MAR78
NORTHERN	NY	4,000	3,000	4	FEB78
		5,000	6,000	5	MAR78
--------	--------	--------	--------		
NORTHERN	NY	9,000	9,000		
NORTHERN		10,000	10,500		
PLAINS	NM	500	1,350	2	MAR78
SOUTHERN	FL	10,000	8,000	10	JAN78
		11,000	8,500	10	FEB78
		13,500	9,800	9	MAR78
--------	--------	--------	--------		
SOUTHERN	FL	34,500	26,300		
SOUTHERN	GA	8,000	2,000	5	JAN78
		6,000	1,200	7	FEB78
--------	--------	--------	--------		
SOUTHERN	GA	14,000	3,200		
SOUTHERN		48,500	29,500		
		========	========		
		91,100	57,350		

Vertical Column Headings: Example 2

This example shows how rotation of column headings occurs to help keep the output on a smaller number of pages.

```
DATA SMALL;
  DO I=1 TO 5;
    ARRAY X X1-X50;
    DO OVER X;
      X=MOD(__I__,5);
      END;
    OUTPUT;
    END;
PROC PRINT;
  TITLE PRINT WILL ROTATE TITLES IF IT HELPS;
```

```
                          PRINT WILL ROTATE TITLES IF IT HELPS                                    8
O             X X X X X X X X X X X X X X X X X X X X X X X X X X X X X X X X X X X X X X X X X X X X X X
B    X X X X X X X X X 1 1 1 1 1 1 1 1 1 1 2 2 2 2 2 2 2 2 2 2 3 3 3 3 3 3 3 3 3 3 4 4 4 4 4 4 4 4 4 4 5
S I 1 2 3 4 5 6 7 8 9 0 1 2 3 4 5 6 7 8 9 0 1 2 3 4 5 6 7 8 9 0 1 2 3 4 5 6 7 8 9 0 1 2 3 4 5 6 7 8 9 0

1 1 1 2 3 4 0 1 2 3 4 0 1 2 3 4 0 1 2 3 4 0 1 2 3 4 0 1 2 3 4 0 1 2 3 4 0 1 2 3 4 0 1 2 3 4 0 1 2 3 4 0
2 2 1 2 3 4 0 1 2 3 4 0 1 2 3 4 0 1 2 3 4 0 1 2 3 4 0 1 2 3 4 0 1 2 3 4 0 1 2 3 4 0 1 2 3 4 0 1 2 3 4 0
3 3 1 2 3 4 0 1 2 3 4 0 1 2 3 4 0 1 2 3 4 0 1 2 3 4 0 1 2 3 4 0 1 2 3 4 0 1 2 3 4 0 1 2 3 4 0 1 2 3 4 0
4 4 1 2 3 4 0 1 2 3 4 0 1 2 3 4 0 1 2 3 4 0 1 2 3 4 0 1 2 3 4 0 1 2 3 4 0 1 2 3 4 0 1 2 3 4 0 1 2 3 4 0
5 5 1 2 3 4 0 1 2 3 4 0 1 2 3 4 0 1 2 3 4 0 1 2 3 4 0 1 2 3 4 0 1 2 3 4 0 1 2 3 4 0 1 2 3 4 0 1 2 3 4 0
```

SAS UTILITIES

Introduction to SAS Utility Procedures

APPEND

BMDP

BROWSE

CONTENTS

CONVERT

COPY

DATASETS

DELETE

EDITOR

FORMAT

OPTIONS

PRINTTO

SORT

TRANSPOSE

Introduction to SAS Utility Procedures

Utility procedures are those that do some kind of intermediate processing rather than an analysis or a report. Utility applications include interfacing, data processing, editing, transforming data, and so on. Utility procedures are usually small procedures with little control language or printed output. The name of each utility procedure indicates its purpose. If you are unable to find a utility procedure to do exactly what you want, then you can probably do it in a DATA step instead.

APPEND	appends data from one SAS data set to the end of another SAS data set
BMDP	interfaces with a BMDP program
BROWSE	enables you to read but not to modify a SAS data set
CONTENTS	describes the contents of a SAS data set or SAS data library
CONVERT	converts files from other systems to SAS data sets
COPY	copies SAS data sets and libraries
DATASETS	deletes and changes names of SAS data sets
DELETE	deletes SAS data sets from the disk or tape data library on which they are stored
EDITOR	edits values directly in SAS data sets
FORMAT	defines output formats for value labeling
OPTIONS	lists current values of all SAS system options
PRINTTO	allows you to define the destination of SAS procedure
SORT	sorts a SAS data set according to one or more variables
TRANSPOSE	turns a SAS data set on its side, changing variables into observations and observations into variables.

In addition to these SAS utilities, there are a number of operating-system-dependent utility procedures described elsewhere.

The APPEND Procedure

ABSTRACT

The APPEND procedure adds the observations from one SAS data set to the end of another SAS data set. The SAS data sets must be in disk format.

INTRODUCTION

Refer to Chapter 2, "Introduction to the DATA Step," and Chapter 12, "SAS Data Sets," to familiarize yourself with SAS data sets and related terminology.

Often you need to add new observations to a SAS data set. If you use a DATA step to do this through concatenation, SAS must process all the observations in both data sets to create a new one. The APPEND procedure bypasses the processing of data in the original data set, and adds new observations directly to the end of the original data set.

SPECIFICATIONS

PROC APPEND BASE= *options*;

The only statement used with the APPEND procedure is the PROC statement.

PROC APPEND Statement

PROC APPEND BASE= *options*;

BASE=*SASdataset*   names the data set to which you want to add observations. If APPEND cannot find an existing data set with this name, it creates a new data set. In other words, you can use PROC APPEND to create a data set by specifying a new data set name in BASE=. BASE= must be specified.

The APPEND procedure may be used with these options:

DATA=*SASdataset*   names the SAS data set containing observations you want APPEND to add to the end of another SAS data set (named by BASE=). If DATA= is omitted, the most recently created data set is used.

FORCE   causes truncation of values if variables in the DATA= data set have longer lengths than the corresponding variables in the BASE= data set. FORCE also causes variables in the DATA= data set to be dropped if there are not corresponding variables in the BASE= data set. If DATA= variables are too long or do not

match BASE= variables and FORCE is not specified,
SAS prints a message on the log and stops processing.

DETAILS

Usage Notes

If all variables in the BASE= data set have the same length and relative position as
the variables in the DATA= data set, and if all variables are in both data sets, the
procedure executes faster. You can use PROC CONTENTS with the POSITION option for each data set to see if the variable lengths and positions are identical.

If the BASE= data set is large and the DATA= data set is small, APPEND runs
much faster than a DATA step that uses the SET statement to concatenate two data
sets. The procedure is very useful if observations are frequently added to a SAS data
set; for example, in production programs that are constantly appending data to a
journal-type data set.

Note: APPEND operates in UPDATE mode when it adds observations. If the
system crashes during an APPEND procedure execution, or some other kind of in-
terruption occurs, it is possible that none of the observations will be added to the
data set.

Output Data Set

All observations from the DATA= data set are added to the BASE= data set. If the
BASE= data set does not exist, APPEND creates a new SAS data set consisting of
the observations in the DATA= data set.

If there are variables in the BASE= data set that are not in the DATA= data set,
those variables have missing values in the new observations.

No printed output is produced.

EXAMPLES

Appending an Update File: Example 1

An update file called ADD contains information on average temperatures in cities
around the country. It is appended to a master file, EXP.MASTER. PROC PRINT lists
the master file before and after the execution of PROC APPEND.

```
DATA ADD;
  INPUT CITY $15. MONTH $15. TEMP;
  CARDS;
HONOLULU      AUGUST         80.7
HONOLULU      JANUARY        72.3
BOSTON        JULY           73.3
BOSTON        JANUARY        29.2
DULUTH        JULY           65.6
DULUTH        JANUARY         8.5
PROC PRINT DATA=EXP.MASTER;
  TITLE MASTER BEFORE ADD DATA APPENDED;
PROC APPEND BASE=EXP.MASTER DATA=ADD;
PROC PRINT DATA=EXP.MASTER;
  TITLE MASTER AFTER ADD DATA APPENDED;
```

```
            MASTER BEFORE ADD DATA APPENDED                        1

      OBS    CITY           MONTH       TEMP

       1     RALEIGH        JULY        77.5
       2     RALEIGH        JANUARY     40.5
       3     MIAMI          AUGUST      82.9
       4     MIAMI          JANUARY     67.2
       5     LOS_ANGELES    AUGUST      69.5
       6     LOS_ANGELES    JANUARY     54.5
       7     JUNEAU         JULY        55.7
       8     JUNEAU         JANUARY     23.5
       9     PHOENIX        JULY        91.2
      10     PHOENIX        JANUARY     51.2
      11     BISMARCK       JANUARY      8.2
      12     BISMARCK       JULY        70.8
      13     CHICAGO        AUGUST      71.1
      14     CHICAGO        JANUARY     22.9
      15     WICHITA        JULY        80.7
      16     WICHITA        JANUARY     31.3
```

```
            MASTER AFTER ADD DATA APPENDED                         2

      OBS    CITY           MONTH       TEMP

       1     RALEIGH        JULY        77.5
       2     RALEIGH        JANUARY     40.5
       3     MIAMI          AUGUST      82.9
       4     MIAMI          JANUARY     67.2
       5     LOS_ANGELES    AUGUST      69.5
       6     LOS_ANGELES    JANUARY     54.5
       7     JUNEAU         JULY        55.7
       8     JUNEAU         JANUARY     23.5
       9     PHOENIX        JULY        91.2
      10     PHOENIX        JANUARY     51.2
      11     BISMARCK       JANUARY      8.2
      12     BISMARCK       JULY        70.8
      13     CHICAGO        AUGUST      71.1
      14     CHICAGO        JANUARY     22.9
      15     WICHITA        JULY        80.7
      16     WICHITA        JANUARY     31.3
      17     HONOLULU       AUGUST      80.7
      18     HONOLULU       JANUARY     72.3
      19     BOSTON         JULY        73.3
      20     BOSTON         JANUARY     29.2
      21     DULUTH         JULY        65.6
      22     DULUTH         JANUARY      8.5
```

Appending a Data Set to Itself: Example 2

In this example, a data set is created and then appended to itself:

```
DATA TEMP;
  DO I=1 TO 10;
    OUTPUT;
    END;
PROC APPEND BASE=TEMP;
PROC PRINT DATA=TEMP;
```

```
STATISTICAL ANALYSIS SYSTEM                                    1

                      OBS      I

                        1      1
                        2      2
                        3      3
                        4      4
                        5      5
                        6      6
                        7      7
                        8      8
                        9      9
                       10     10
                       11      1
                       12      2
                       13      3
                       14      4
                       15      5
                       16      6
                       17      7
                       18      8
                       19      9
                       20     10
```

The BMDP Procedure

ABSTRACT

The BMDP procedure calls any BMDP program to analyze data in a SAS data set.

INTRODUCTION

BMDP is a library of statistical analysis programs developed at the UCLA Health Sciences Computing Facility, and available from:

> BMDP Statistical Software Inc.
> PO Box 24A26
> Los Angeles, CA 90024
> (213) 825-5940

The BMDP procedure in SAS is an interface that allows you to call a BMDP program from SAS to analyze data from a SAS data set, or to convert a SAS data set to a BMDP save file.

PROC BMDP handles most versions of the P-series BMDP programs up to and including BMDP (1981).

It does not handle the older BMD non-P programs. If you have a version of BMDP prior to the 1977 version or if you are using CMS, you must specify the UNIT= option in the PROC BMDP statement so that the interface can convert the data to a BMDP save file. For versions after 1977, the interface provides data to the BMDP program directly from a SAS data set. Note: PROC BMDP cannot be executed under DOS/VSE.

To use PROC BMDP, first specify the name of the BMDP program that you want to use in the PROC BMDP statement; follow this statement with the PARMCARDS statement and your BMDP control cards. The results of the BMDP program are printed after the SAS log and any SAS procedure output that your job produces.

You can use PROC BMDP any number of times in a SAS job to request BMDP programs. You can create a BMDP save file in a BMDP program, and use the SAS procedure CONVERT to convert the save file to a SAS data set. Then the data can be further analyzed with other SAS procedures.

When you use PROC BMDP under OS, the EXEC job control statement must request the cataloged procedure SASBMDP rather than the usual cataloged procedure SAS. If SASBMDP is not available on your computer, or if it has a different name, ask your computing center staff for help in setting it up. Directions are given in the SAS installation instructions which are available to your installation's SAS representative. Under CMS, the SASBMDP EXEC should be used. Ask your computer center staff about its availability.

SPECIFICATIONS

The PROC BMDP statement invokes the interface procedure and specifies which BMDP program to call. The VAR and BY statements can follow, but are optional. The BMDP control statements follow the PARMCARDS statement.

> **PROC BMDP** *options*;
>   **VAR** *variables*;
>   **BY** *variables*;
>   **PARMCARDS;**
>   *BMDP control statements*
>   ;

If you are using CMS, see **PROC BMDP Under CMS** in Appendix 1, "SAS Under CMS."

PROC BMDP Statement

PROC BMDP *options*;

The options below may appear in the PROC BMDP statement. You must include the UNIT= option if you are using a version of BMDP released before 1977 or if you are executing SAS under CMS.

DATA=*SASdataset*   specifies the SAS data set that the BMDP program is to process. If DATA= is omitted, PROC BMDP uses the most recently created SAS data set.

PROG=BMDP*nn*   specifies the BMDP program that you want to run. For example, if you want to run BMDP3S, the PROC BMDP statement might look like this:

>   PROC BMDP PROG=BMDP3S;

Note: if you only want to convert a SAS data set to a BMDP save file and do not want to run a BMDP program, omit the PROG= option, and include the UNIT= option, described below.

UNIT=*n*   specifies the FORTRAN logical unit number for the BMDP save file that PROC BMDP creates. If you are using a version of BMDP released before 1977, or executing SAS under CMS, or creating a BMDP save file (see the PROC= option above), you must include the UNIT= option. The SASBMDP cataloged procedure under OS, or SASBMDP EXEC under CMS, automatically sets up UNIT=3 for you to use; FT03F001 is the corresponding DDname in the procedure or EXEC. FT04F001 is the DDname for output save files. You should not specify FT01F001 or FT02F001 because BMDP reserves them for other uses. If you use any other unit you must add the appropriate job control language to your job:

>   OS:
>   //FT*nn*F001 DD UNIT=SYSDA,
>   // SPACE=(3520,(100,20)),
>   // DCB=(RECFM=VBS,BLKSIZE=3520,
>   // LRECL=3616)

CMS:
FILEDEF *nn* DSK filename filetype mode
(RECFM VBS LRECL 3616 BLKSIZE 3520)

TSO:
ATTR ATR1 RECFM(V B S) LRECL(3616)
BLKSIZE(3520)
ALLOC F(FT*nn*F001) SPACE(3520 100)
BLOCKS USING(ATR1)

where *nn* is the unit you use.

CODE=*savefile*   assigns a name to the BMDP save file created by
PROC BMDP when you convert a SAS data set to a
BMDP save file. The *savefile* corresponds to the CODE
sentence in the BMDP INPUT paragraph. For example,
if you use the statement:

PROC BMDP PROG=BMDP3S CODE=JUDGES;

the BMDP INPUT paragraph must contain the
sentence:

CODE='JUDGES'

CODE= is usually omitted in the PROC statement.
When CODE= is omitted, the name of the SAS data
set is used for the BMDP save file name.

Whether or not you use the CODE= option in the
PROC BMDP statement, if you want to convert a SAS
data set to a BMDP save file you must include the
CODE sentence in your BMDP INPUT paragraph to
specify a name for save file. If you want to use the
name of the SAS data set, specify that name in the
BMDP INPUT paragraph. If you are using a different
name, it must match the name supplied in the
CODE= option.

CONTENT=DATA   lets BMDP know if your SAS data set is a standard SAS
CONTENT=CORR   data set (CONTENT=DATA) or if it contains a correla-
CONTENT=MEAN   tion matrix (CORR), variable means (MEAN), or fre-
CONTENT=FREQ   quency counts (FREQ). You need not specify the
CONTENT= option for specially structured SAS data
sets created by other SAS procedures, since if you
omit the CONTENT= option, the data set's TYPE value
is used.

Note: BMDP may use a structure for special data
sets (for example, a correlation matrix) that is different
from the SAS structure. You must be sure that the input SAS data set is in the form that BMDP expects.

LABEL=*variable*   specifies a variable whose values are to be used as
case labels for BMDP. Only the first four characters of
the values are used. The variable name must also be
included in the VAR statement if you use one.

LABEL2=*variable*   specifies a variable whose values are to be used as second case labels for BMDP; as with LABEL, only the first
four characters are used. The variable name must also
be given in the VAR statement if you use one.

NOMISS   specifies that you want the BMDP program or save file to include only observations with no missing values.

WRKSPCE=*nn*   controls the allocation of a workspace in BMDP. The
PARM=*nn*   WRKSPCE= or PARM= value is passed as a parameter to BMDP programs and corresponds to the WRKSPCE= feature in BMDP OS cataloged procedures. The default is PARM=30.

VAR Statement

VAR *variables*;

The VAR statement specifies the variables to be used for the BMDP program. If no VAR statement appears, all the numeric variables in the SAS data set are used.

BY Statement

BY *variables*;

A BY statement may be used with PROC BMDP to obtain separate analyses on observations in groups defined by the BY variables. When a BY statement appears, the procedure expects the input data set to be sorted in order of the BY variables. If your input data set is not sorted in ascending order, use the SORT procedure with a similar BY statement to sort the data, or, if appropriate, use the BY statement options NOTSORTED or DESCENDING. For more information, see the discussion of the BY statement in Chapter 8, "Statements Used in the PROC Step."

When a BY statement is used, the LABEL IS field of the BMDP file contains the BY information so that you can identify BY groups.

PARMCARDS Statement

PARMCARDS;
BMDP control statements
;

The PARMCARDS statement signals that the BMDP control statements follow.

Put your BMDP control cards after the PARMCARDS statement. These are similar for all BMDP programs; see *BMDP Statistical Software 1981* for information on their form and function.

The BMDP INPUT paragraph must include UNIT and CODE sentences. Their values must match the UNIT= and CODE= values given in the PROC BMDP statement; if the PROC BMDP statement does not specify a UNIT= value, use 3 as the UNIT value in the BMDP statements. Use the SAS data set name as the CODE value unless you have specified a different name with the CODE= option in the PROC statement. Omit the VARIABLES paragraph from the BMDP statements, since it is not needed when the program uses a save file for input.

DETAILS

Missing Values

Before PROC BMDP sends data to BMDP, it converts SAS missing values to the BMDP missing value of 16^{32}. If the NOMISS option is used in the PROC BMDP statement, observations with missing values are omitted from the data set sent to the BMDP program.

Invoking BMDP Programs that Need FORTRAN Routines

Some BMDP programs, such as the ones for nonlinear regression, need to invoke the FORTRAN compiler and linkage editor before the BMDP program is executed. If you want to use SAS to invoke BMDP you must perform all the necessary compile and link edit work before SAS is invoked. A cataloged procedure under OS or an EXEC under CMS can be set up for this.

EXAMPLE

The example below creates a SAS data set called TEMP. PROC CONTENTS shows the description information for TEMP. PROC BMDP requests that the BMDP program BMDP1D be called to analyze the data set. Note the BMDP program statements include UNIT = 3 and CODE = 'TEMP' and that the results are stored in a BMDP save file BOUT.

After invoking PROC BMDP, PROC CONVERT converts the BMDP save file BOUT to a SAS data set called FROMBMDP. PROC CONTENTS and PROC PRINT are then used to show the new SAS data set.

```
* EXAMPLE OF USE OF PROC BMDP *;
DATA TEMP;
  INPUT A B C;
  CARDS;
1 2 3
4 5 6
7 8 9
PROC CONTENTS;
  TITLE CONTENTS OF SAS DATA SET TO BE RUN THROUGH BMDP1D;
  * RUN THE BMDP1D PROGRAM ON THE TEMP DATA SET, AND
    CREATE AN OUTPUT BMDP SAVE FILE THAT WILL BE CONVERTED
    INTO A SAS DATA SET FOR FURTHER PROCESSING. NOTE THAT THE
    WORD 'NEW' MUST BE IN THE SAVE PARAGRAPH. UNIT = NN
    SHOULD REFER TO THE FTNNF001 DDNAME DEFINED IN YOUR FILE
    DEFINITION STATEMENTS. *;
PROC BMDP PROG = BMDP1D DATA = TEMP;
  PARMCARDS;
  /PROB TITLE = 'SHOW SAS/BMDP INTERFACE'.
  /INPUT UNIT = 3. CODE = 'TEMP'.
  /SAVE CODE = 'BOUT'. NEW. UNIT = 4.
  /END
  /FINISH
  ;
  * CONVERT THE BMDP SAVE FILE 'BOUT' TO A SAS DATA SET NAMED
    FROMBMDP. 'BOUT' IS ON UNIT 4, I.E., FT04F001. *;
PROC CONVERT BMDP = FT04F001 OUT = FROMBMDP;
PROC CONTENTS;
  TITLE SAS DATA SET CONVERTED FROM BMDP SAVE FILE;
PROC PRINT;
```

CONTENTS OF SAS DATA SET TO BE RUN THROUGH BMDP1D   1

CONTENTS OF SAS DATA SET WORK.TEMP

TRACKS USED=2 SUBEXTENTS=1 OBSERVATIONS=3 CREATED BY JOB PRINT AT 14:01 FRIDAY, APRIL 23, 1982

BY SAS RELEASE 79.6 DSNAME=SYS82113.T140109.RA000.PRINT.R0000001 BLKSIZE=19044 LRECL=28 OBSERVATIONS PER TRACK=680

GENERATED BY DATA

ALPHABETIC LIST OF VARIABLES

```
#  VARIABLE  TYPE LENGTH POSITION  FORMAT        INFORMAT  LABEL

1  A         NUM     8       4
2  B         NUM     8      12
3  C         NUM     8      20
```

```
+----------------------------- SOURCE STATEMENTS -----------------------------+
|DATA TEMP;                                                                   |
|    INPUT A B C;                                                             |
|    CARDS;                                                                   |
+----------------------------------------------------------------------------+
```

SAS DATA SET CONVERTED FROM BMDP SAVE FILE   2

CONTENTS OF SAS DATA SET WORK.FROMBMDP

TRACKS USED=2 SUBEXTENTS=1 OBSERVATIONS=3 CREATED BY JOB PRINT AT 14:01 FRIDAY, APRIL 23, 1982

BY SAS RELEASE 79.6 DSNAME=SYS82113.T140109.RA000.PRINT.R0000001 BLKSIZE=19069 LRECL=20 TYPE=DATA

LABEL=   APRIL 23, 1982   14:01:40 OBSERVATIONS PER TRACK=953 GENERATED BY PROC CONVERT

ALPHABETIC LIST OF VARIABLES

```
#  VARIABLE  TYPE LENGTH POSITION  FORMAT        INFORMAT  LABEL

1  A         NUM     4       4
2  B         NUM     4       8
3  C         NUM     4      12
4  USE       NUM     4      16
```

SAS DATA SET CONVERTED FROM BMDP SAVE FILE   3

```
OBS    A    B    C    USE

1      1    2    3     1
2      4    5    6     1
3      7    8    9     1
```

PAGE   1

BMDP1D - SIMPLE DATA DESCRIPTION AND DATA MANAGEMENT
DEPARTMENT OF BIOMATHEMATICS
UNIVERSITY OF CALIFORNIA, LOS ANGELES, CA 90024
(213) 825-5940   TWX UCLA LSA
PROGRAM REVISED JUNE 1981
MANUAL REVISED -- 1981
COPYRIGHT (C) 1981 REGENTS OF UNIVERSITY OF CALIFORNIA
    APRIL 23, 1982 AT 14:01:40

TO SEE REMARKS AND A SUMMARY OF NEW FEATURES FOR
THIS PROGRAM, STATE NEWS. IN THE PRINT PARAGRAPH.

PROGRAM CONTROL INFORMATION

/PROB TITLE='SHOW SAS/BMDP INTERFACE'.
/INPUT UNIT=3. CODE='TEMP'.
/SAVE CODE='BOUT'. NEW. UNIT=4.
/END

(continued on next page)

BMDP output

(continued from previous page)

```
PROBLEM TITLE IS
SHOW SAS/BMDP INTERFACE

NUMBER OF VARIABLES TO READ IN. . . . . . . .        3
NUMBER OF VARIABLES ADDED BY TRANSFORMATIONS. .       0
TOTAL NUMBER OF VARIABLES . . . . . . . . . . .       3
NUMBER OF CASES TO READ IN. . . . . . . . . . .  TO END
CASE LABELING VARIABLES . . . . . . . . . . .
MISSING VALUES CHECKED BEFORE OR AFTER TRANS. . NEITHER
BLANKS ARE. . . . . . . . . . . . . . . . . . . MISSING
INPUT UNIT NUMBER . . . . . . . . . . . . . .         3
REWIND INPUT UNIT PRIOR TO READING. . DATA. . .     YES
NUMBER OF WORDS OF DYNAMIC STORAGE. . . . . . .   23038

INPUT BMDP FILE
CODE. . . IS      TEMP
CONTENT . IS      DATA
LABEL . . IS
STATISTICAL ANALYSIS SYSTEM
VARIABLES
      1 A            2 B            3 C

VARIABLES TO BE USED
      1 A            2 B            3 C
-------------------------------------------
BMDP FILE IS BEING WRITTEN ON UNIT        4
CODE. . . IS      BOUT
CONTENT . IS      DATA
LABEL . . IS
     APRIL 23, 1982      14:01:40
```

BMDP
output

```
PAGE   2      SHOW SAS/BMDP INTERFACE

VARIABLES ARE
      1 A            2 B            3 C

BMDP    FILE ON UNIT  4 HAS BEEN COMPLETED.
----------------------------------------------
NUMBER OF CASES WRITTEN TO FILE        3

NUMBER OF CASES READ. . . . . . . . . . . . .        3


PAGE   3      SHOW SAS/BMDP INTERFACE
```

VARIABLE NO. NAME	TOTAL FREQUENCY	MEAN	STANDARD DEVIATION	ST.ERR OF MEAN	COEFF. OF VARIATION	SMALLEST VALUE	Z-SCORE	LARGEST VALUE	Z-SCORE	RANGE
1 A	3	4.000	3.000	1.7320	0.75000	1.000	-1.00	7.000	1.00	6.000
2 B	3	5.000	3.000	1.7320	0.60000	2.000	-1.00	8.000	1.00	6.000
3 C	3	6.000	3.000	1.7320	0.50000	3.000	-1.00	9.000	1.00	6.000

```
NUMBER OF INTEGER WORDS OF STORAGE USED IN PRECEDING      PROBLEM     180
CPU TIME USED       0.903 SECONDS


PAGE   4

BMDP1D - SIMPLE DATA DESCRIPTION AND DATA MANAGEMENT
     APRIL 23, 1982  AT 14:01:48

PROGRAM CONTROL INFORMATION

/FINISH

NO MORE CONTROL LANGUAGE.

PROGRAM TERMINATED
```

BMDP
output

REFERENCE

Dixon, W.D., Brown, M.B., Engleman, L., Frane, J.W., Hill, M.A., Jennrich, R.I., and Toporek, J.D., editors (1981), *BMDP Statistical Software 1981*, Los Angeles: University of California Press.

[1] The BMDP interface was developed with the cooperation of Jerry Toporek of BMDP Statistical Software and James Frane, now at Genetech Inc.

The BROWSE Procedure

ABSTRACT

The BROWSE procedure enables you to read a SAS data set. BROWSE is primarily an interactive procedure, but it can be used in batch mode.

INTRODUCTION

The BROWSE procedure is the same as the EDITOR procedure except that certain commands used to modify the data set in PROC EDITOR are not allowed: REPLACE, ADD, DELETE, and DUP. Since you are not altering the data set, you can read a SAS data set to which you have only read access. This means that under OS, you access the SAS data library as DISP=SHR; under CMS, you access the SAS data library from a disk in read-only mode.

SPECIFICATIONS

These are the statements and commands that can be used with BROWSE:

> **PROC BROWSE** *options*;
>   **FORMAT** *variable format. ...*;
>   **INFORMAT** *variable format. ...*;
>   **RUN**;
>   **FIND** *options range variable1 operator1 value1 ...*;
>   **LOCATE** *options range value ...*;
>   **SEARCH** *options range string ...*;
>   **NAME** *variable*;
>   **STRING** *variable ...*;
>   **VERIFY** *option*;
>   **END**;
>   **LIST** *range variable ...*;
>   **HELP** *command*;
>   **TOP**;
>   **BOTTOM**;
>   **UP** *n*;
>   **DOWN** *n*;

Refer to PROC EDITOR for details on using BROWSE. Everything described in EDITOR applies to BROWSE, except documentation on the change commands: REPLACE, DELETE, DUP, and ADD.

The CONTENTS Procedure

ABSTRACT

The CONTENTS procedure prints descriptions of the contents of one or more SAS data sets.

INTRODUCTION

Refer to chapters on the DATA step and PROC step, and especially to Chapter 12, "SAS Data Sets," to familiarize yourself with the basic features of SAS data sets and SAS data libraries and other terminology (for example, DDname) used in this procedure description.

The printout from PROC CONTENTS includes information about the physical characteristics of a SAS data set (except under CMS): where and how it is stored, its size, and when it was created. Also listed are the variables in the data set, and their types, lengths, formats, and labels.

CONTENTS is particularly useful for documenting SAS data sets that have been stored on disk or tape. It is a good idea to run PROC CONTENTS as soon as you store a data set. But if you should forget what the data set contains, you can always use CONTENTS to remind yourself of the data set's contents.

For SAS data sets stored on tape, CONTENTS shows the file sequence number and the actual tape recording density (BPI). For standard-labeled tapes, the actual creation date is given.

SPECIFICATIONS

The PROC statement is the only statement associated with the CONTENTS procedure.

PROC CONTENTS *options*;

PROC CONTENTS Statement

PROC CONTENTS *options*;

The options below may appear in the PROC CONTENTS statement:

DATA=*SASdataset*   names the SAS data set to be described by CONTENTS. If you want information about all the SAS data sets in a SAS data library and the data library directory, use the keyword __ALL__ as the second-level name of the SAS data set.

To print the contents of a data set called STUDY.HTWT use the statement:

PROC CONTENTS DATA=STUDY.HTWT;

To print a description of all the SAS data sets in the SAS data library referenced by the DDname STUDY, use the statement:

PROC CONTENTS DATA=STUDY._ALL_;

The STUDY data library directory is also printed if the library is stored on disk.

DIRECTORY   prints the SAS data library description and the list of SAS data sets contained in that SAS data library. This option is useful when you are printing the contents of just one data set in a data library, but also want to see the directory. (When _ALL_ is specified in the DATA= option of the PROC statement, the directory is automatically printed.)

Since tape-format SAS data libraries have no directory, the DIRECTORY option has no meaning for tape-format data libraries.

HISTORY   prints the history of a SAS data set. The history includes the SAS statements and descriptions of other data sets (if any) used to create a data set. In the history, the current SAS data set is called data set #1. If data set #1 was created from other SAS data sets (by a SET, MERGE, or UPDATE statement), those data sets are called #2, #3, and so on, of generation 1. This process continues until all the history information of all the generations stored is printed. The number of generations stored depends on the value of the SAS system option GEN.

NODS   suppresses printing of the contents of individual data sets when _ALL_ is specified in the DATA= option. Only the SAS data library directory is printed.

Tape-format SAS data sets have no directory. Specifying NODS for a tape-format data set is equivalent to specifying the SHORT option (see below).

NOSOURCE   suppresses printing of the SAS statements used to create a SAS data set.

SHORT   prints only the list of variable names in the SAS data set.

MAP   prints a map showing the tracks occupied by the directory and by each SAS data set in the SAS data library. MAP is only effective when _ALL_ is specified as the second-level name in the DATA= option of the PROC statement.

The MAP option is ignored under CMS.

POSITION   prints the variable names in the order of their position in the data set, as well as alphabetical order.

DETAILS

Printed Output

The printed output for CONTENTS differs somewhat between systems. Differences are noted.

Under OS and TSO, CONTENTS prints these PHYSICAL CHARACTERISTICS of the SAS data library:

1. DSNAME, the physical data set or file where the library is stored by the operating system; the UNIT value for the device on which the library is stored; VOL=SER, the volume serial of the device; DISP, disposition of the library; the DEVICE type; MAX BLKSIZE, the maximum length of a standard physical block on the device; CREATED, the date that the SAS data library was created; TRACKS ALLOCATED, the number of tracks and EXTENTS currently allocated; and the COST of storing the data library on- and off-line (cost information may or may not appear, depending on your installation).

Under VSE, the PHYSICAL CHARACTERISTICS printed are:

2. FILENAME, the filename (DDname) referencing the JCL statement defining the data set; VOL=, the volume of the device; STARTING TRACK (STARTING BLOCK for FBA disks), the track on which the data set starts; NUMBER OF TRACKS (NUMBER OF BLOCKS for FBA disks) allocated to the data set; the DEVICE type; MAX BLKSIZE, the maximum length of a logical block on the device; TRACKS ALLOCATED (BLOCKS ALLOCATED for FBA disks), the number of tracks and extents currently allocated; for FBA disks, ONE TRACK=ONE CONTROL INTERVAL= n BLOCKS, where n indicates the number of blocks defined for a control interval in the JCL; and the cost of storing the data library on- and off-line (cost information may or may not appear, depending on your installation). Note that for FBA disks, a track corresponds to a control interval.

When the DIRECTORY option is specified or __ALL__ is specified in the DATA= option, a SAS DATA SET DIRECTORY is printed that includes:

3. the NAME of each SAS data set contained in the SAS data library; # OBS, the number of observations; the number of TRACKS used (except under CMS); and the number of SUBEXTENTS that the data set occupies (except under CMS).
4. TOTAL TRACKS USED, the sum of the TRACKS each SAS data set uses; HIGH TRACK USED, the highest-numbered track used; and under VSE, PERCENT OF FILE USED.

CONTENTS also prints a description of the SAS data sets in the library, as requested. Under OS, TSO, and VSE the information printed is:

5. the number of TRACKS USED for the SAS data set; the number of SUBEXTENTS (a subextent is space allocated to the data set on contiguous tracks) that the data set occupies; the number of OBSERVATIONS in the data set; CREATED BY JOB, the jobname of the job that created the data set; the date and time of creation; the release of SAS that created the data set; under OS and TSO, DSNAME, the name of the SAS data library containing the data set; BLKSIZE, the size of the blocks (for FBA disks, the logical blocksize) written on the tape or disk device that contain observations for this individual SAS data set;

LRECL, the logical record (observation) length of this individual SAS data set; the data set LABEL, if one exists; OBSERVATIONS PER TRACK, the number of observations that will fit on one track; and how the data were generated, that is, by a DATA step or by a PROC step.

Under CMS, the data set descriptions include:

6. the number of OBSERVATIONS in the data set; CREATED BY, the userid that created the data set; the date and time of creation; the release of SAS that created the data set; LRECL, the logical record (observation) length of this individual SAS data set; the data set LABEL, if one exists; and how the data were generated, that is, by a DATA step or by a PROC step.

The ALPHABETIC LIST OF VARIABLES in the SAS data set includes:

7. #, the position of the variable in the data set; the VARIABLE name; the TYPE of the variable (character or numeric); the LENGTH; the starting POSITION of the variable in the observation; the FORMAT and INFORMAT; and the variable's LABEL.

Also printed (unless NOSOURCE is specified) are:

8. SOURCE STATEMENTS, SAS statements that generated the data set.

Except under CMS, when the MAP option is specified CONTENTS prints:

9. SUBEXTENT MAP, a map of the SAS data library, showing the starting and ending tracks for each subextent of each SAS data set.

EXAMPLES

PROC CONTENTS Under OS or TSO: Example 1

The first PROC CONTENTS statement in this example shows how the procedure, under OS or TSO, prints the contents of all SAS data sets in a SAS library. The NOSOURCE option suppresses the printing of source statements, and the MAP option prints a map of all allocated subextents in the data library. The second CONTENTS statement prints one data set's description and the data library directory.

```
PROC CONTENTS DATA=MISC.__ALL__ NOSOURCE MAP;
PROC CONTENTS DATA=MISC.ECONOMIC DIRECTORY;
```

```
                                        SAS                                              1
                               CONTENTS PROCEDURE
  ┌─┐                   PHYSICAL CHARACTERISTICS OF OS DATA SET
  │1│
  └─┘
DSNAME=xxxxxx.yyy.zzzz  UNIT=DISK    VOL=SER=SAS333  DISP=SHR  DEVICE=3350 DISK  MAX BLKSIZE=19069 BYTES
CREATED MONDAY, NOVEMBER 9, 1981        19 TRACKS ALLOCATED IN 2 EXTENTS  COST IF DATA STORED ONLINE= $0.2280/DAY
COST IF DATA STORED OFFLINE= $0.0760/DAY
```

(continued on next page)

(continued from previous page)

③ SAS DATA SET DIRECTORY

NAME	# OBS	TRACKS	SUBEXTENTS
CARS	82	2	1
COFFEE	13	2	2
ECONOMIC	69	2	1
MASTER	22	2	2
REPAIR	114	2	2
STATS	114	2	1

④ TOTAL TRACKS USED: 13
HIGH TRACK USED: 13

SUBEXTENT MAP

(STARTING TRACK,ENDING TRACK)

⑨

#DIRE	(0,0)	
CARS	(6,7)	
COFFEE	(3,3)	(5,5)
ECONOMIC	(8,9)	
MASTER	(1,1)	(10,10)
REPAIR	(2,2)	(4,4)
STATS	(11,12)	

SAS   2

CONTENTS OF SAS DATA SET MISC.CARS

⑤ TRACKS USED=2 SUBEXTENTS=1 OBSERVATIONS=82 CREATED BY JOB RUN AT 10:11 TUESDAY, JUNE 8, 1982

BY SAS RELEASE 82.0 DSNAME=xxxxxx.yyy.zzzz BLKSIZE=19004 LRECL=125 LABEL= CARS RATED ON TEN SCALES

OBSERVATIONS PER TRACK=152 GENERATED BY DATA

⑦ ALPHABETIC LIST OF VARIABLES

#	VARIABLE	TYPE	LENGTH	POSITION	FORMAT	INFORMAT	LABEL
5	ACCEL	NUM	8	50			ACCELERATION
6	BRAKING	NUM	8	58			
12	CARGO	NUM	8	106			CARGO SPACE
10	COMFORT	NUM	8	90			
7	HANDLING	NUM	8	66			
14	IMPORT	CHAR	3	122			
1	MAKE	CHAR	10	4			
2	MODEL	CHAR	20	14			
3	MPG	NUM	8	34			
13	ORIGIN	CHAR	8	114			
11	QUIET	NUM	8	98			
4	RELIABLE	NUM	8	42			RELIABILITY
8	RIDE	NUM	8	74			
9	VISIBLE	NUM	8	82			VISIBILITY

SAS   3

CONTENTS OF SAS DATA SET MISC.COFFEE

TRACKS USED=2 SUBEXTENTS=2 OBSERVATIONS=13 CREATED BY JOB RUN AT 10:11 TUESDAY, JUNE 8, 1982

BY SAS RELEASE 82.0 DSNAME=xxxxxx.yyy.zzzz BLKSIZE=18964 LRECL=120 DF=94 TYPE=CORR OBSERVATIONS PER TRACK=158

GENERATED BY DATA

ALPHABETIC LIST OF VARIABLES

#	VARIABLE	TYPE	LENGTH	POSITION	FORMAT	INFORMAT	LABEL
1	_NAME_	CHAR	8	4			
15	_TYPE_	CHAR	4	116			
7	ALIVE	NUM	8	52	4.2		
10	BREWED	NUM	8	76	4.2		
6	COMFORT	NUM	8	44	4.2		
9	DEEP	NUM	8	68	4.2		
5	EXPENSIV	NUM	8	36	4.2		
14	FRESH	NUM	8	108	4.2		
11	HEARTY	NUM	8	84	4.2		
4	MELLOW	NUM	8	28	4.2		
2	PLEASANT	NUM	8	12	4.2		
12	PURE	NUM	8	92	4.2		
8	REAL	NUM	8	60	4.2		
13	ROASTED	NUM	8	100	4.2		
3	SPARKLIN	NUM	8	20	4.2		

```
                                          SAS                                                      4
                            CONTENTS OF SAS DATA SET MISC.ECONOMIC

TRACKS USED=2  SUBEXTENTS=1  OBSERVATIONS=69  CREATED BY JOB RUN  AT 10:11 TUESDAY, JUNE 8, 1982

BY SAS RELEASE 82.0  DSNAME=xxxxxx.yyy.zzzz  BLKSIZE=19012  LRECL=64  OBSERVATIONS PER TRACK=297  GENERATED BY DATA
                            ALPHABETIC LIST OF VARIABLES

        #  VARIABLE  TYPE LENGTH POSITION  FORMAT       INFORMAT  LABEL

        2  AGRICULT  NUM      8      24
        4  CONSTRUC  NUM      8      40
        1  COUNTRY   CHAR    20       4
        3  INDUSTRY  NUM      8      32
        5  TRADE     NUM      8      48
        6  TRANSCOM  NUM      8      56
```

```
                                          SAS                                                      5
                            CONTENTS OF SAS DATA SET MISC.MASTER

TRACKS USED=2  SUBEXTENTS=2  OBSERVATIONS=22  CREATED BY JOB PRINT  AT 14:43 THURSDAY, JUNE 24, 1982

BY SAS RELEASE 82.0  DSNAME=xxxxxx.yyy.zzzz  BLKSIZE=19030  LRECL=42  OBSERVATIONS PER TRACK=453  GENERATED BY DATA
                            ALPHABETIC LIST OF VARIABLES

        #  VARIABLE  TYPE LENGTH POSITION  FORMAT       INFORMAT  LABEL

        1  CITY      CHAR    15       4
        2  MONTH     CHAR    15      19
        3  TEMP      NUM      8      34
```

```
                                          SAS                                                      6
                            CONTENTS OF SAS DATA SET MISC.REPAIR

TRACKS USED=2  SUBEXTENTS=2  OBSERVATIONS=114  CREATED BY JOB RUN  AT 16:10 WEDNESDAY, JUNE 30, 1982

BY SAS RELEASE 82.0  DSNAME=XXXXXX.YYY.ZZZZ  BLKSIZE=19004  LRECL=152  OBSERVATIONS PER TRACK=125

GENERATED BY PROC SORT
                            ALPHABETIC LIST OF VARIABLES

        #  VARIABLE  TYPE LENGTH POSITION  FORMAT       INFORMAT  LABEL

        3  AC        NUM      8      24
        8  BRAKES    NUM      8      64
       11  COOLING   NUM      8      88
        9  DRIVELIN  NUM      8      72
       10  ELECTRIC  NUM      8      80
       13  EXHAUST   NUM      8     104
       14  FUEL      NUM      8     112
        6  HARDWARE  NUM      8      48
       15  IGNITION  NUM      8     120
        7  INTEGRIT  NUM      8      56
        1  MAKE      CHAR     8       4
       12  MECHANIC  NUM      8      96
        2  MODEL     CHAR    12      12
        4  PAINT     NUM      8      32
        5  RUST      NUM      8      40
       16  STEERING  NUM      8     128
       17  SUSPENSN  NUM      8     136
       18  TRANSMIS  NUM      8     144
```

```
                                       SAS                                              7
                        CONTENTS OF SAS DATA SET MISC.STATS

TRACKS USED=2  SUBEXTENTS=1  OBSERVATIONS=114  CREATED BY JOB PRINT  AT 11:39 TUESDAY, JULY 20, 1982

BY SAS RELEASE 82.0  DSNAME=XXXXXX.YYY.ZZZZ  BLKSIZE=19004  LRECL=152  OBSERVATIONS PER TRACK=125

GENERATED BY PROC SORT

                              ALPHABETIC LIST OF VARIABLES

        #  VARIABLE  TYPE LENGTH POSITION  FORMAT        INFORMAT  LABEL

        1  MAKE      CHAR    8       4
        2  MODEL     CHAR   12      12
        3  V1        NUM     8      24
        4  V2        NUM     8      32
        5  V3        NUM     8      40
        6  V4        NUM     8      48
        7  V5        NUM     8      56
        8  V6        NUM     8      64
        9  V7        NUM     8      72
       10  V8        NUM     8      80
       11  V9        NUM     8      88
       12  V10       NUM     8      96
       13  V11       NUM     8     104
       14  V12       NUM     8     112
       15  V13       NUM     8     120
       16  V14       NUM     8     128
       17  V15       NUM     8     136
       18  V16       NUM     8     144
```

```
                                       SAS                                              8
                              CONTENTS PROCEDURE
                    PHYSICAL CHARACTERISTICS OF OS DATA SET

DSNAME=XXXXXX.YYY.ZZZZ  UNIT=DISK     VOL=SER=SAS333  DISP=SHR  DEVICE=3350 DISK  MAX BLKSIZE=19069 BYTES

CREATED MONDAY, NOVEMBER 9, 1981        19 TRACKS ALLOCATED IN 2 EXTENTS  COST IF DATA STORED ONLINE= $0.2280/DAY

COST IF DATA STORED OFFLINE= $0.0760/DAY

                              SAS DATA SET DIRECTORY

              NAME        # OBS     TRACKS   SUBEXTENTS

              CARS          82         2          1
              COFFEE        13         2          2
              ECONOMIC      69         2          1
              MASTER        22         2          2
              REPAIR       114         2          2
              STATS        114         2          1

              TOTAL TRACKS USED:        13
              HIGH TRACK USED:          13
```

```
                                       SAS                                              9
                      CONTENTS OF SAS DATA SET MISC.ECONOMIC

TRACKS USED=2  SUBEXTENTS=1  OBSERVATIONS=69  CREATED BY JOB RUN  AT 10:11 TUESDAY, JUNE 8, 1982

BY SAS RELEASE 82.0  DSNAME=XXXXXX.YYY.ZZZZ  BLKSIZE=19012  LRECL=64  OBSERVATIONS PER TRACK=297  GENERATED BY DATA

                              ALPHABETIC LIST OF VARIABLES

        #  VARIABLE  TYPE LENGTH POSITION  FORMAT        INFORMAT  LABEL

        2  AGRICULT  NUM     8      24
        4  CONSTRUC  NUM     8      40
        1  COUNTRY   CHAR   20       4
        3  INDUSTRY  NUM     8      32
        5  TRADE     NUM     8      48
        6  TRANSCOM  NUM     8      56

    (8) +----------------------------- SOURCE STATEMENTS -----------------------------+
        |DATA MISC.ECONOMIC;                                                          |
        |   TITLE PERCENT DISTRIBUTION OF GROSS DOMESTIC PRODUCT;                     |
        |   INPUT COUNTRY $1-20 AGRICULT INDUSTRY CONSTRUC TRADE TRANSCOM;            |
        |   CARDS;                                                                    |
        +-----------------------------------------------------------------------------+
```

PROC CONTENTS Under VSE: Example 2

The first PROC CONTENTS statement in this example shows how the procedure, under VSE, prints the contents of all SAS data sets in a SAS library. The NOSOURCE option suppresses the printing of source statements, and the MAP option prints a map of all allocated subextents in the data library. The second CONTENTS statement prints one data set's description and the data library directory. Note that the data library is on an FBA disk.

```
PROC CONTENTS DATA=UFBA009.__ALL__ NOSOURCE MAP;
PROC CONTENTS DATA=UFBA009.FORECAST DIRECTORY;
```

The output shown for this VSE example does not include the data set description pages, since they are the same as the output for OS and TSO. However, the data library directory produced by the first CONTENTS statement is shown.

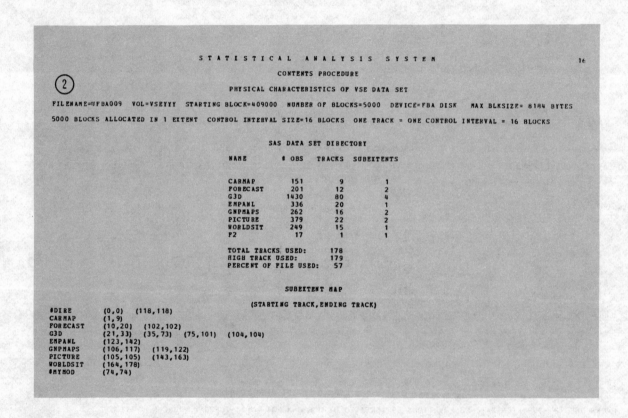

PROC CONTENTS Under CMS: Example 3

The first PROC CONTENTS statement in this example shows how the procedure, under CMS, prints the contents of all SAS data sets in a SAS library. The NOSOURCE option suppresses the printing of source statements. The second CONTENTS statement prints one data set's description and the data library directory.

```
PROC CONTENTS DATA=TRAIN.__ALL__ NOSOURCE;
PROC CONTENTS DATA=TRAIN.MARKLIN DIRECTORY;
```

```
                  S T A T I S T I C A L   A N A L Y S I S   S Y S T E M                    1
                                                          11:48 FRIDAY, JULY 16, 1982

                              CONTENTS PROCEDURE

                             SAS DATA SET DIRECTORY

                    NAME        # OBS


                    MARKLIN       144
                    SCREEN         65
```

```
                  S T A T I S T I C A L   A N A L Y S I S   S Y S T E M                    2
                                                          11:48 FRIDAY, JULY 16, 1982

                          CONTENTS OF SAS DATA SET TRAIN.MARKLIN

OBSERVATIONS=144  CREATED BY  TEDDY  AT 10:52 FRIDAY, JULY 16, 1982        BY SAS RELEASE 79.6   LRECL=74

GENERATED BY DATA

                                    ALPHABETIC LIST OF VARIABLES

     #   VARIABLE   TYPE LENGTH POSITION  FORMAT        INFORMAT  LABEL

     7   ACQDATE    NUM     8      66     DATE7.        DATE      Acquisition Date
     2   CATALOGN   CHAR    4      14
     1   CATEGORY   CHAR   10       4
     3   DESCRIPT   CHAR   30      18
     6   PRICEPD    NUM     8      58     DOLLAR8.2               Price Paid
     4   QUANTITY   NUM     2      48
     5   RETAIL     NUM     8      50     DOLLAR8.2               1980 Retail Price
```

⑥

```
                  S T A T I S T I C A L   A N A L Y S I S   S Y S T E M                    3
                                                          11:48 FRIDAY, JULY 16, 1982

                          CONTENTS OF SAS DATA SET TRAIN.SCREEN

OBSERVATIONS=65  CREATED BY  TEDDY  AT 10:52 FRIDAY, JULY 16, 1982         BY SAS RELEASE 79.6   LRECL=92

GENERATED BY DATA

                                    ALPHABETIC LIST OF VARIABLES

     #   VARIABLE   TYPE LENGTH POSITION  FORMAT        INFORMAT  LABEL

     2   TEXT#      CHAR   80      12
     1   TYPE#      NUM     8       4
```

```
                  S T A T I S T I C A L   A N A L Y S I S   S Y S T E M                    4
                                                          11:48 FRIDAY, JULY 16, 1982

                              CONTENTS PROCEDURE

                             SAS DATA SET DIRECTORY

                    NAME        # OBS


                    MARKLIN       144
                    SCREEN         65
```

```
                    S T A T I S T I C A L   A N A L Y S I S   S Y S T E M                    5
                                                              11:48 FRIDAY, JULY 16, 1982

                           CONTENTS OF SAS DATA SET TRAIN.MARKLIN

OBSERVATIONS=144  CREATED BY  TEDDY  AT 10:52 FRIDAY, JULY 16, 1982        BY SAS RELEASE 79.6  LRECL=74

GENERATED BY DATA

                               ALPHABETIC LIST OF VARIABLES

      #  VARIABLE  TYPE LENGTH POSITION  FORMAT      INFORMAT  LABEL

      7  ACQDATE   NUM      8      66    DATE7.      DATE      Acquisition Date
      2  CATALOGN  CHAR     4      14
      1  CATEGORY  CHAR    10       4
      3  DESCRIPT  CHAR    30      18
      6  PRICEPD   NUM      8      58    DOLLAR8.2             Price Paid
      4  QUANTITY  NUM      2      48
      5  RETAIL    NUM      8      50    DOLLAR8.2             1980 Retail Price


            +------------------------------ SOURCE STATEMENTS ------------------------------+
            |data train.marklin; set sastrain.marklin;                                      |
            |  keep catalogn category descript pricepd quantity retail acqdate;             |
            |  acqdate = mdy(month,1,year);                                                 |
            |  format acqdate  date7.;                                                      |
            |  informat acqdate  date7.;                                                    |
            |  label acqdate='Acquisition Date';                                            |
            +-------------------------------------------------------------------------------+
```

The CONVERT Procedure

ABSTRACT

The CONVERT procedure converts BMDP, DATA-TEXT, OSIRIS, SAS72, and SPSS system files to SAS data sets.

INTRODUCTION

CONVERT produces one output data set, but no printed output. The new data set contains the same information as the input system file; exceptions are noted below under **Output Data Sets.**

The procedure converts system files from these packages: BMDP save files through and including BMDP 81; SPSS save files up to release 7; DATA-TEXT files up to version 3.4; OSIRIS files through OSIRIS IV (hierarchical file structures are not supported); and SAS72. (SAS72 was the precursor to the current SAS product. It is no longer supported as a product, but SAS72 files may still exist that need to be converted to the current structure of SAS data sets).

Since these packages are maintained by other companies, changes may be made that make the system files incompatible with the current version of CONVERT. SAS Institute cannot be responsible for upgrading CONVERT to support changes to the aforementioned packages, although attempts will be made to do so as necessary with each new version of SAS.

Information associated with each package is given in the **Usage Notes** section at the end of the procedure description.

SPECIFICATIONS

PROC CONVERT *options;*

Usually only the PROC CONVERT statement is used, although data set attributes can be controlled by DROP, KEEP, and RENAME options in the OUT= option, and by LABEL and FORMAT statements.

PROC CONVERT Statement

PROC CONVERT *options;*

The options below may appear in the PROC CONVERT statement. Only one of the five options specifying a system file (BMDP, DATATEXT, OSIRIS, SAS72, or SPSS) may be given.

In the descriptions below, the word "DDname" refers to a file name available to the job or session. In OS it refers to the JCL DD statement describing the system file. This statement usually appears after the EXEC SAS statement, and has the form

//BMDPFILE DD DSN=bmdp.save.file,DISP=SHR

The DDname is the word immediately after the two slashes //. In this case, BMDPFILE is the DDname.

If you are using TSO, DDname refers to the FILENAME of the system file. This file must be allocated with a TSO command of the form

ALLOC FI(BMDPFILE) DA(bmdp.save.file) SHR

which corresponds to the JCL DD statement above. BMDPFILE is again the DDname to use for the PROC CONVERT specification.

If you are using CMS, only BMDP and SPSS system files can be converted, since DATATEXT, OSIRIS, and SAS72 systems are not supported under CMS. Use a FILEDEF statement to refer to the system file. For example:

FILEDEF BMDPFILE DISK BMDP SAVEFILE A

Each option is described below.

BMDP=*DDname* specifies the *DDname* of a data set containing a BMDP save file. The first save file in the data set is converted. If you have more than one save file in the data set, you can use two additional options in parentheses after the *DDname*. The CODE= option lets you specify the CODE of the save file you want, and the CONTENT= option lets you give the save file's content. For example, if a file CODE=JUDGES had a CONTENT of DATA, you could use this statement:

PROC CONVERT BMDP=SAVE(CODE=JUDGES
  CONTENT=DATA);

DATATEXT=*DDname* specifies a *DDname* for a data set containing a DATA-TEXT file. This option is available under OS only.

OSIRIS=*DDname* gives a *DDname* for a data set containing an OSIRIS file. This data set may contain no more than 1024 variables. You must also include the DICT option, described below, when you use the OSIRIS= option. This option is available under OS only.

DICT=*DDname2* gives the *DDname* of a data set containing the dictionary file for the OSIRIS data set. DICT= must be specified if you use the OSIRIS= option. This option is available under OS only.

SAS72=*DDname* specifies a *DDname* for a data set containing a SAS72 file. If the SAS72 data set is a member of a partitioned data set, the DD statement must include the member name of the SAS72 data set. This option is available under OS only.

SPSS=*DDname* gives a *DDname* for a data set containing an SCSS file. CONVERT processes only SPSS system files; it does not handle SCSS masterfiles. To convert an SCSS masterfile to a SAS data set, you must first convert the masterfile to an SCSS save file, then use PROC CONVERT with the SPSS option. Alphabetic SPSS values are converted to SAS character values properly only if a PRINT FORMATS (A) statement was used when the SPSS file was created.

FIRSTOBS=*n*   gives the number of the observation where the conversion is to begin. This allows you to skip over observations at the beginning of the BMDP, DATA-TEXT, OSIRIS, SAS72, or SPSS system file.

OBS=*n*   specifies the number of the last observation to be converted. This allows you to exclude observations at the end of the file.

OUT=*SASdataset*   names the SAS data set created to hold the converted data. IF OUT= is omitted, SAS still creates a data set, and automatically names it DATA*n*, just as if you omitted a data set name in a DATA statement. If it is the first such data set in a job or session, SAS names it DATA1; the second is DATA2, and so on. If OUT= is omitted or if you do not specify a two-level name in the OUT= option, the data set converted to SAS is not permanently saved. See Chapter 12, "SAS Data Sets," for more information.

DETAILS

Missing Values

If a numeric variable in the input data set has no value or a system missing value, CONVERT assigns it a missing value.

Caution

Since some variable name translation may occur as indicated in the appropriate section, be sure that the translated names will be unique.

Output Data Sets

BMDP output   Variable names from the BMDP save file are used in the SAS data set, except that non-trailing blanks and all special characters are converted to underscores in the SAS variable names. The subscript in BMDP variable names such as x(1) becomes part of the SAS variable name, with the parentheses omitted: X1. Alphabetic BMDP variables become SAS character variables of length 4. Long category records from BMDP may not be accepted. The current maximum record length is 12000. The BMDP CATEGORY information is copied into the SAS data set history section.

Data-Text output   Unsubscripted DATA-TEXT variable names are used without change; the subscript in subscripted variable names becomes part of the name. If necessary, the name is truncated on the right so that the name and subscript are eight characters or less; for example, LOCATION(10) becomes LOCATI10. Variable labels are copied without change, as are numeric variables. DATA-TEXT value labels are not copied. The DATA-TEXT codebook is copied to the SAS data set history section. A maximum of 1000 variables can be converted into a SAS data set.

OSIRIS output   For single-response variables, the V1-V9999 name becomes the SAS variable name. For multiple-response variables, the suffix R*n* is added to the variable name, where *n* is the response: for example, V25R1 would be the first response of the multiple-response V25. If the variable after V1000 has 100 or more responses, responses above 99 are eliminated. Numeric variables that OSIRIS stores in character, fixed-point binary, or floating-point binary mode become SAS numeric variables. Alphabetic variables become SAS character variables; any alphabetic variable of length greater than 200 is truncated to 200. The OSIRIS variable description becomes a SAS variable label, and OSIRIS print format information becomes a SAS format. The OSIRIS codebook is copied to the SAS data set history section.

SAS72 output   CONVERT copies variable names, variables, and missing values from a SAS72 data set without change.

SPSS output   SPSS variable names and variable labels become variable names and labels without change. SPSS alphabetic variables become SAS character variables of length 4. SPSS blank values are converted to SAS missing values. SPSS print formats become SAS formats, and the SPSS default precision of no decimal places becomes part of the variables' formats. The SPSS codebook is copied to the SAS data set history section. SPSS value labels are not copied.

Usage Notes

BMDP:
  BMDP Statistical Software
  Department of Biomathematics, UCLA
  Los Angeles, California 90024
  213/825-5940

SPSS:
  SPSS
  Suite 3300
  444 North Michigan Avenue
  Chicago, Illinois 60611
  312/329-2400

DATA-TEXT:
  Pro-Systems/Amcor
  6561 Gillis Drive
  San Jose, California 95120
  408/866-1170

OSIRIS:
  Institute for Social Research
  Box 1248
  Ann Arbor, Michigan 48106
  313/764-4417

EXAMPLE: BMDP Save File Conversion

In the example below, a BMDP save file called WERNER (on the data set pointed to by the DDname BMDPSAVE) is converted to a SAS data set. The BMDP job that creates the BMDP save file is shown first: the unit number for the BMDP save file is 8, FT08F001 is the corresponding DDname. The variables are input to BMDP in free format.

```
PAGE    1

BMDP1D - SIMPLE DATA DESCRIPTION AND DATA MANAGEMENT
DEPARTMENT OF BIOMATHEMATICS
UNIVERSITY OF CALIFORNIA, LOS ANGELES, CA 90024
(213) 825-5940           TWX  UCLA LSA
PROGRAM REVISED JUNE 1981
MANUAL REVISED -- 1981
COPYRIGHT (C) 1981 REGENTS OF UNIVERSITY OF CALIFORNIA
   APRIL 14, 1982  AT 14:19:34

TO SEE REMARKS AND A SUMMARY OF NEW FEATURES FOR
THIS PROGRAM, STATE NEWS. IN THE PRINT PARAGRAPH.

PROGRAM CONTROL INFORMATION

/BMDP1D                                                                    00000010
/COMMENT   THIS EXAMPLE IS FROM THE BMDP1D EXAMPLE PROVIDED IN
           THE BMDP INSTALLATION PACKAGE. THE INPUT DATA HAVE BEEN
           SHORTENED, HOWEVER.
/PROBLEM   TITLE IS 'WERNER BLOOD CHEMISTRY DATA'.
           LENGTH IS 4000.
/INPUT     VARIABLES ARE 9.
           CASES ARE 188.
           FORMAT IS FREE. RECLEN=40.
           SORTS ARE HEIGHT,WEIGHT.
           ORDERS ARE ASCENDING,DESCENDING.
/VARIABLE  NAMES ARE ID,AGE,HEIGHT,WEIGHT,BRTHPILL,CHOLSTRL,
              ALBUMIN,CALCIUM,URICACID.
           MAXIMUM IS (6)400.
           MINIMUM IS (6)150.
           BLANKS ARE MISSING.
           LABEL IS ID.
           GROUPING IS AGE.
/GROUP     CODES(BRTHPILL) ARE 1,2.
           NAMES(BRTHPILL) ARE NOPILL,PILL.
           CUTPOINTS(AGE) ARE 25,35,45.
           NAMES(AGE) ARE '25ORLESS','26 TO 35','36 TO 45','OVER 45'.
/PRINT     MISSING.
           MINIMUM.
           MAXIMUM.
           NEWS.
           DEBUG IS TEST.
/SAVE      UNIT IS 4.
           NEW.
           CODE IS WERNER.
           KEEPERS ARE ID,AGE,CHOLSTRL,WEIGHT.
/END
```

*BMDP
output*

```
PAGE    2    WERNER BLOOD CHEMISTRY DATA

PROBLEM TITLE IS
WERNER BLOOD CHEMISTRY DATA

NUMBER OF VARIABLES TO READ IN. . . . . . . . .      9
NUMBER OF VARIABLES ADDED BY TRANSFORMATIONS. .      0
TOTAL NUMBER OF VARIABLES . . . . . . . . . . .      9
NUMBER OF CASES TO READ IN. . . . . . . . . . .    188
CASE LABELING VARIABLES . . . . . . . . . . .ID
MISSING VALUES CHECKED BEFORE OR AFTER TRANS. .  BEFORE
BLANKS ARE. . . . . . . . . . . . . . . . . . MISSING
INPUT UNIT NUMBER . . . . . . . . . . . . . .      5
REWIND INPUT UNIT PRIOR TO READING. . DATA. . .     NO
NUMBER OF WORDS OF DYNAMIC STORAGE. . . . . . .   4000

VARIABLES TO BE USED
      2 AGE        3 HEIGHT       4 WEIGHT      5 BRTHPILL     6 CHOLSTRL
      7 ALBUMIN    8 CALCIUM      9 URICACID

INPUT FORMAT IS
FREE

MAXIMUM LENGTH DATA RECORD IS    40 CHARACTERS.

IN THIS VERSION OF BMDP1D

DUPLICATE GROUP NAMES NOW PERMITTED FOR GROUPING VARIABLES.

  PRINT CASES CONTAINING MISSING VALUES.

  PRINT CASES CONTAINING VALUES GREATER THAN THE STATED MAXIMA.
```

(continued on next page)

*BMDP
output*

(continued from previous page)

```
    PRINT CASES CONTAINING VALUES LESS THAN THE STATED MINIMA.

    PRINT SUMMARY STATISTICS OVER ALL CASES AND
    BROKEN DOWN BY INDIVIDUAL CATEGORY ON AGE

********************************************

    PROCESSING REQUEST TO SORT INPUT FILE

    SORTING ON

      HEIGHT        ASCENDING
      WEIGHT        DESCENDING

    ALL AVAILABLE STORAGE USED FOR INTERNAL SORT AREA
    INTERNAL SORT CAPACITY    336 CASES

NUMBER OF CASES READ. . . . . . . . . . . . .      12

    INPUT FILE HAS BEEN SORTED

************************************************
```

BMDP output

```
PAGE   3      WERNER BLOOD CHEMISTRY DATA

----------------------------------------------
BMDP FILE IS BEING WRITTEN ON UNIT        4
CODE. . . IS     WERNER
CONTENT . IS     DATA
LABEL . . IS
    APRIL 14, 1982       14:19:34
VARIABLES ARE
    1 ID            2 AGE          3 CHOLSTRL    4 WEIGHT
```

BMDP output

```
PAGE   4      WERNER BLOOD CHEMISTRY DATA

 C A S E           2           3           4           5           6           7           8           9
 NO. LABEL        AGE       HEIGHT      WEIGHT     BRTHPILL    CHOLSTRL     ALBUMIN     CALCIUM     URICACID
-----  -----    ----------  ----------  ----------  ----------  ----------  ----------  ----------  ----------
    4 1946         22          64         160          2        TOO BIG        35        MISSING        72
   12 1797         25          68         150          2        TOOSMALL       38          96           30

BMDP   FILE ON UNIT  4 HAS BEEN COMPLETED.
----------------------------------------------
NUMBER OF CASES WRITTEN TO FILE        12
```

```
                                                        INTERVAL RANGE
    VARIABLE      MINIMUM  MAXIMUM  MISSING CATEGORY CATEGORY   GREATER LESS THAN
    NO. NAME       LIMIT    LIMIT    CODE     CODE     NAME      THAN    OR = TO

     2 AGE
                                                    25ORLESS              25.0000
                                                    26 TO 35    25.0000  35.0000
                                                    36 TO 45    35.0000  45.0000
                                                    OVER 45     45.0000

     5 BRTHPILL
                                           1.00000 NOPILL
                                           2.00000 PILL

     6 CHOLSTRL  150.000  400.000
```

BMDP output

PAGE 5 WERNER BLOOD CHEMISTRY DATA

VARIABLE NO. NAME	GROUPING VARIABLE LEVEL		TOTAL FREQUENCY	MEAN	STANDARD DEVIATION	ST.ERR OF MEAN	COEFF. OF VARIATION	SMALLEST VALUE	Z-SCORE	LARGEST VALUE	Z-SCORE	RANGE
2 AGE	AGE	25ORLESS 26 TO 35 36 TO 45 OVER 45	12 12 0 0 0	21.333 21.333	1.969 1.969	0.5685 0.5685	0.09232 0.09232	19.000 19.000	-1.18 -1.18	25.000 25.000	1.86 1.86	6.000 6.000
3 HEIGHT	AGE	25ORLESS 26 TO 35 36 TO 45 OVER 45	12 12 0 0 0	64.417 64.417	2.234 2.234	0.6450 0.6450	0.03469 0.03469	60.000 60.000	-1.98 -1.98	68.000 68.000	1.60 1.60	8.000 8.000
4 WEIGHT	AGE	25ORLESS 26 TO 35 36 TO 45 OVER 45	12 12 0 0 0	128.000 128.000	17.310 17.310	4.9970 4.9970	0.13523 0.13523	100.000 100.000	-1.62 -1.62	160.000 160.000	1.85 1.85	60.000 60.000
5 BRTHPILL	AGE	25ORLESS 26 TO 35 36 TO 45 OVER 45	12 12 0 0 0	1.500 1.500	0.522 0.522	0.1508 0.1508	0.34816 0.34816	1.000 1.000	-0.96 -0.96	2.000 2.000	0.96 0.96	1.000 1.000
6 CHOLSTRL	AGE	25ORLESS 26 TO 35 36 TO 45 OVER 45	10 10 0 0 0	221.700 221.700	33.163 33.163	10.4871 10.4871	0.14959 0.14959	158.000 158.000	-1.92 -1.92	260.000 260.000	1.15 1.15	102.000 102.000
7 ALBUMIN	AGE	25ORLESS 26 TO 35 36 TO 45 OVER 45	12 12 0 0 0	40.083 40.083	3.848 3.848	1.1110 1.1110	0.09601 0.09601	34.000 34.000	-1.58 -1.58	47.000 47.000	1.80 1.80	13.000 13.000
8 CALCIUM	AGE	25ORLESS 26 TO 35 36 TO 45 OVER 45	11 11 0 0 0	100.091 100.091	4.614 4.614	1.3912 1.3912	0.04610 0.04610	93.000 93.000	-1.54 -1.54	106.000 106.000	1.28 1.28	13.000 13.000
9 URICACID	AGE	25ORLESS 26 TO 35 36 TO 45 OVER 45	12 12 0 0 0	50.083 50.083	15.240 15.240	4.3995 4.3995	0.30430 0.30430	30.000 30.000	-1.32 -1.32	83.000 83.000	2.16 2.16	53.000 53.000

BMDP output

PAGE 6 WERNER BLOOD CHEMISTRY DATA

VARIABLE NO. NAME	CATEGORY NAME	CATEGORY FREQUENCY	TOTAL FREQUENCY	NO. OF VALUES MISSING OR OUTSIDE THE RANGE
2 AGE			12	0
	25ORLESS	12		
	26 TO 35	0		
	36 TO 45	0		
	OVER 45	0		
5 BRTHPILL			12	0
	NOPILL	6		
	PILL	6		

NUMBER OF INTEGER WORDS OF STORAGE USED IN PRECEDING PROBLEM 712
CPU TIME USED 4.769 SECONDS

BMDP output

The SAS job begins by executing PROC CONVERT; a SAS data set called SASBMDP is created from the BMDP save file called WERNER. PROC CONTENTS shows the descriptor information, and PROC PRINT shows the SAS data set variable values.

```
PROC CONVERT BMDP=BMDPSAVE OUT=SASBMDP;
PROC CONTENTS;
    TITLE CONTENTS OF THE CONVERTED BMDP SAVE FILE;
PROC PRINT;
    TITLE PRINTED LISTING OF THE CONVERTED BMDP SAVE FILE;
```

```
1                      S T A T I S T I C A L   A N A L Y S I S   S Y S T E M

NOTE: THE JOB CONVERT HAS BEEN RUN UNDER RELEASE 79.6 OF SAS AT SAS INSTITUTE INC. (F) (00000).

NOTE: NO OPTIONS SPECIFIED.


1            /* PROC CONVERT EXAMPLE. BMDPSAVE POINTS TO A BMDP SAVE FILE
2               CREATED BY THE BMDP1D PROGRAM. */
3
4            OPTIONS LS=120 NODATE;
5            PROC CONVERT BMDP=BMDPSAVE OUT=SASBMDP;

NOTE: BMDP FILE CODE=WERNER CONTENT=DATA
NOTE:   LABEL='     APRIL 14, 1982        14:19:34          '.
NOTE: DATA SET WORK.SASBMDP HAS 12 OBSERVATIONS AND 5 VARIABLES. 794 OBS/TRK.
NOTE: THE PROCEDURE CONVERT USED 0.62 SECONDS AND 512K.

6            PROC CONTENTS;
7                TITLE CONTENTS OF THE CONVERTED BMDP SAVE FILE;

NOTE: THE PROCEDURE CONTENTS USED 0.36 SECONDS AND 184K AND PRINTED PAGE 1.

8            PROC PRINT;
9                TITLE PRINTED LISTING OF THE CONVERTED BMDP SAVE FILE;

NOTE: THE PROCEDURE PRINT USED 0.55 SECONDS AND 184K AND PRINTED PAGE 2.


NOTE: SAS INSTITUTE INC.
      SAS CIRCLE
      BOX 8000
      CARY, N.C. 27511-8000
```

```
                        CONTENTS OF THE CONVERTED BMDP SAVE FILE

                        CONTENTS OF SAS DATA SET WORK.SASBMDP

TRACKS USED=2  SUBEXTENTS=1  OBSERVATIONS=12  CREATED BY JOB CONVERT  AT 14:19 WEDNESDAY, APRIL 14, 1982

BY SAS RELEASE 79.6   DSNAME=SYS82104.T141927.RA000.CONVERT.R0000005   BLKSIZE=19060   LRECL=24   TYPE=DATA

LABEL=     APRIL 14, 1982       14:19:34  OBSERVATIONS PER TRACK=794  GENERATED BY PROC CONVERT

                        ALPHABETIC LIST OF VARIABLES

    #   VARIABLE   TYPE  LENGTH  POSITION   FORMAT        INFORMAT   LABEL

    2   AGE        NUM      4         8
    3   CHOLSTRL   NUM      4        12
    1   ID         CHAR     4         4
    5   USE        NUM      4        20
    4   WEIGHT     NUM      4        16
```

```
PRINTED LISTING OF THE CONVERTED BMDP SAVE FILE                    2

OBS    ID    AGE   CHOLSTRL   WEIGHT   USE

  1   1649   21      246       107      1
  2   1610   25      243       128      1
  3   1375   21      208       100      1
  4   1946   22       .        160      1
  5    561   19      158       125      1
  6   2936   21      260       120      1
  7    225   20      210       118      1
  8   3108   21      245       135      1
  9   2420   20      192       119      1
 10   2381   22      200       144      1
 11   2519   19      255       130      1
 12   1797   25       .        150      1
```

The COPY Procedure

ABSTRACT

The COPY procedure copies SAS data libraries or individual SAS data sets. The procedure can copy from disk to disk, from disk to tape, from tape to tape, or from tape to disk. COPY is especially useful for backing up SAS data sets from disk to tape.

INTRODUCTION

Refer to chapters on the DATA step and PROC step, and especially to Chapter 12, "SAS Data Sets," to familiarize yourself with the basic features of SAS data sets, SAS data libraries, and terminology (for example, DDname) used in this procedure description.

The COPY procedure works as though a series of DATA and SET statements were used to copy data sets. For example:

```
DATA TREE.OAK;
  SET BOTANY.OAK;
DATA TREE.HICKORY;
  SET BOTANY.HICKORY;
```

You can copy all the SAS data sets within a library, or you can select or exclude certain data sets. Data set labels and read (READ=) and write (PROTECT=) passwords are also copied.

You can limit the number of observations copied by using the system options FIRSTOBS= and OBS= in an OPTIONS statement preceding the PROC COPY statement.

Note: these system options apply to all data sets copied.

SPECIFICATIONS

    PROC COPY IN=*DDname* **OUT**=*DDname*;
      SELECT *SASdataset* ...;
      EXCLUDE *SASdataset* ...;

PROC COPY Statement

    PROC COPY IN=*DDname* OUT=*DDname*;

The following specifications must appear in the PROC COPY statement:

INDD=*DDname*	specifies the *DDname* referencing the library of SAS
IN=*DDname*	data sets to be copied. IN= must be specified.
OUTDD=*DDname*	specifies the *DDname* referencing the library that is to
OUT=*DDname*	contain the data sets copied by PROC COPY. OUT=
	must be specified.

SELECT Statement

SELECT *SASdataset* ... ;

If you want to copy only selected SAS data sets from the library, give their second-level names in a SELECT statement. It is not necessary to use the first-level SAS name (the DDname of the library) because it is already specified in the PROC statement.

When a specification in the SELECT statement is followed by a colon (:), all data sets whose names begin with the characters preceding the colon are included in the copy operation. For example, say you want to copy five data sets from a library that contains ten data sets. The data sets you want to copy are called TEST1, TEST2, TEST3, TEST4, and TEST5. The remaining data sets are called A, B, C, D, and E. You can use these statements to copy the data sets you want:

```
PROC COPY IN=MASTER OUT=COPY;
   SELECT T:;
```

EXCLUDE Statement

EXCLUDE *SASdataset* ... ;

If you do not want to copy certain SAS data sets in the library, specify the second-level names in an EXCLUDE statement. When a specification in the EXCLUDE statement is followed by a colon (:), all the data sets whose names begin with the characters preceding the colon are excluded from the copy operation. If you want to copy the A, B, C, D, and E data sets from the example above, you can use these statements:

```
PROC COPY IN=MASTER OUT=NEW;
   EXCLUDE T:;
```

Note: You cannot use both a SELECT statement and an EXCLUDE statement.

DETAILS

Cautions

The output SAS data library on disk or tape may already contain SAS data sets. If you copy a SAS data set with the same name as a SAS data set already in the output library and the output library is on disk, the new copy replaces the existing data set in the library. When you copy SAS data sets to tape (or to tape-format data libraries on disk) you run the risk of creating duplicate data sets and/or inadvertently deleting data sets. Duplicate data sets are created if:

1. you copy multiple data sets to tape, and
2. the tape already has SAS data sets on it, and
3. one of the data sets being copied has the same name as a data set already on the tape, and
4. the data set with the duplicate name is not the first data set copied.

Data sets are deleted if the first SAS data set you copy to a tape has the same name as a SAS data set already on the tape and other data sets follow the original SAS data set on the tape. The data set being copied is written over the old data set with that name, and any data sets that follow on the tape are deleted.

Both of these problems arise because of the way tapes are processed. PROC COPY copies data sets either in the order they are specified in a SELECT statement, or in the order they appear in the library directory if no SELECT statement is used. When you copy data sets to tape, SAS takes the first data set to be copied and scans the tape to see if a data set with that name already exists on the tape. If one does, SAS writes the new data set over the old data set, deleting any data sets after it on the tape.

Whether or not the first data set copied is written over an old data set, the tape remains positioned at the end of the first data set copied. After copying the first data set, SAS does not scan the tape for duplicate data set names because the tape would have to be repositioned for each data set being copied. If a data set copied subsequently has the same name as a data set already on the tape (that is, a data set that precedes the first data set copied), there will be two data sets with the same name, and only the first one would be accessible normally.

Here is an example of duplication and deletion. You have a tape that contains a SAS data library, with data sets called WAGE, LABOR, BENEFITS, DEDUCT, CLAIMS, and HOURS, in that order. You are copying a disk SAS data library with the data sets CLAIMS, LABOR, and HEALTH (in that order) to the tape. PROC COPY scans the tape for a data set called CLAIMS, and when it finds the tape CLAIMS data set, COPY writes the disk CLAIMS data set over it. The HOURS data set is erased automatically. The tape remains positioned at the end of the new version of the CLAIMS data set, and COPY goes to the next disk data set, LABOR, and copies it. Now there are two data sets called LABOR on the tape, and only the old one (the first one on the tape) is accessible. Finally, the HEALTH data set is copied.

If you want to copy SAS data sets to tape (or to tape-format data libraries on disk), be sure that you know the contents of both the input and output data library before copying, and the position of the data sets in the library. PROC CONTENTS can be used for this purpose.

Output Data Set

COPY produces output data sets on tape or disk that are copies of the input data sets. No printed output is produced. A message appears on the SAS log when each data set is successfully copied.

EXAMPLES

Copying a SAS Data Library: Example 1

This example copies all data sets in the SAS data library referenced by the DDname MISC to a library referenced by the DDname NEW.

```
PROC COPY IN=MISC OUT=NEW;
```

Copying Selected SAS Data Sets: Example 2

In this example, selected data sets in the library referenced by the DDname MISC are copied to a library referenced by the DDname NEW. Only data sets whose names begin with C are copied.

```
PROC COPY IN=MISC OUT=NEW;
   SELECT C:;
```

The DATASETS Procedure

ABSTRACT

The DATASETS procedure lists, deletes, and alters SAS data sets in a SAS data library. DATASETS also renames data sets, exchanges data set names, and automatically renames related data sets as they are aged. Variable names, labels, informats, and formats can be altered or removed with this procedure.

INTRODUCTION

See Chapter 12, "SAS Data Sets," to familiarize yourself with SAS data sets, SAS data libraries, and related terminology.

The DATASETS procedure performs a number of basic data library management functions. The procedure processes one SAS library at a time. You can list and delete SAS data sets; change data set attributes; and change variable informats, formats, labels, or names. The SAS data library directory is updated at the end of a PROC DATASETS step if no errors are found, or if the FORCE option (see below) has been specified.

SPECIFICATIONS

PROC DATASETS uses the following statements. The FORMAT, INFORMAT, LABEL, and RENAME statements must be used in conjunction with a MODIFY statement.

```
PROC DATASETS DDNAME=DDname options;
    DELETE SASdataset ...;
    SAVE SASdataset ...;
    CHANGE oldname=newname ...;
    EXCHANGE name=anothername ...;
    AGE currentname name2 name3 ... lastname;
    MODIFY SASdataset (options);
    FORMAT variable ... format. variable ... format. ...;
    INFORMAT variable ... informat. variable ... informat. ...;
    LABEL variable=newlabel ...;
    RENAME variable=newname ...;
```

PROC DATASETS Statement

PROC DATASETS DDNAME=DDname options;

DDNAME=*DDname*   specifies the *DDname* that references the SAS data
library to be processed. If DDNAME= is not specified,
the current default data library (either WORK or
USER—see Chapter 12, "SAS Data Sets") is the default.

The options below may appear in the PROC DATASETS statement.

NOLIST   suppresses printing of the listing of SAS data sets in the
SAS data library.

KILL   deletes **all** data sets in the SAS data library except
those having PROTECT= passwords.

NOWARN   prevents SAS from printing the warning message that a
data set in a DELETE or SAVE statement or the last
data set in an AGE statement is not in the referenced
SAS data library.

FORCE   updates the directory of the SAS data library even if errors are encountered in some of the PROC DATASETS
statements.
Note: if the NOREPLACE system option has been
specified, the FORCE option is ignored, and the directory is not updated.

DELETE Statement

DELETE *SASdataset* ...;

If you want to delete SAS data sets from the SAS data library, specify their names in
the DELETE statement. For example, say you want to delete the SAS data sets ONE
and TWO from the SAS data library referenced by the DDname SASDB:

PROC DATASETS DDNAME=SASDB;
  DELETE ONE TWO;

You can use an abbreviated data set list where appropriate. For example:

DELETE RDU1-RDU5;

If a data set has a write-password, the password must appear in the PROTECT=
data set option after the data set name in the DELETE statement. For example:

DELETE RDU1(PROTECT=RUN) RDU2(PROTECT=WAY);

Caution: use of the DELETE statement with SAS data sets on tape deletes not only
the data set(s) specified, but any data sets following those specified. This occurs
even if data set names and protect passwords are not specified. See Chapter 12,
"SAS Data Sets," for more information about tape data sets.

SAVE Statement

SAVE *SASdataset* ...;

If you want to delete some, but not all, of the data sets in a SAS data library, specify
the names of the data sets you want to keep in a SAVE statement. SAS deletes any
data set not listed in the SAVE statement that is not protected. Note: password-
protected data sets cannot be deleted using the SAVE statement, because there is

no place to specify the password. However, protected data sets can be saved without specifying their passwords.

Abbreviated data set lists (for example, STUDY1-STUDY10) can be used with the SAVE statement where appropriate.

CHANGE Statement

CHANGE *oldname=newname* ...;

If you want to rename a SAS data set, use the CHANGE statement. Specify the old data set name on the left side of the equal sign, the new data set name on the right. For example, the statements:

PROC DATASETS DDNAME=OIL;
  CHANGE PERSIA=IRAN;

change the name of the SAS data set PERSIA to IRAN.

More than one data set name can be changed with one CHANGE statement.

EXCHANGE Statement

EXCHANGE *name=anothername* ...;

Use the EXCHANGE statement to exchange the names of two SAS data sets in the SAS data library. For example, if your data library contains the SAS data sets A and Z, the statements:

PROC DATASETS DDNAME=MYLIB;
  EXCHANGE A=Z;

would change the name of the SAS data set originally called A to Z, and vice versa.

More than one pair of data set names can be changed with one EXCHANGE statement.

AGE Statement

AGE *currentname name2 name3 ... lastname;*

If you have a group of related data sets in your SAS data library to which data sets are periodically added, you can use the AGE statement to rename the data sets in the group. Then programs can access the current data set using one name that does not change.

When an AGE statement is used, the name of the first SAS data set is changed to the second name; the name of the second data set is changed to the third name, and so on until the name of the next-to-last data set is changed to the last name. The last data set is then deleted.

For example, say that each day you run a SAS program that creates the data set TODAY. You keep that data set together with the previous seven data sets in a SAS data library. Each time you want to create a new data set, the oldest data set must be deleted and the remaining data sets renamed, leaving the TODAY name available for the new data set. You can delete and rename the data sets using PROC DATASETS with the AGE statement:

PROC DATASETS DDNAME=DAILY;
  AGE TODAY DAY1-DAY7;

After PROC DATASETS is executed, the data set originally named TODAY is re-named DAY1; the data set originally named DAY1 is renamed DAY2; and so on. The data set originally named DAY6 is renamed DAY7, and the data set originally named DAY7 is deleted. Since there is now no data set named TODAY, the name TODAY is available for the new data set.

Abbreviated data set lists (such as DAY1-DAY7) can be used with the AGE statement.

If the PROTECT= data set option was specified when the data set to be deleted with an AGE statement was created, it must also appear in the AGE statement after that data set name. For example:

    AGE TODAY DAY1-DAY7(PROTECT=LMN);

The AGE statement is not executed unless the first data set given in the AGE statement is contained in the SAS data library. If any other data sets listed are not present, SAS prints a note on the log and renames all the data sets that are present.

MODIFY Statement

    MODIFY SASdataset (options);

Use the MODIFY statement and options when you want to change an individual data set's attributes such as a label, passwords, or the data set type. The MODIFY statement is also used with other SAS statements to specify a data set when you want to change variable names, labels, informats, or formats. The data set named in the MODIFY statement must be a member of the SAS data library specified in the DATASETS statement. Only one MODIFY statement is allowed for each data set in the data library.

The MODIFY statement updates descriptor records in place, so no extra space is needed for the data set. History records are not updated, and the number of generations does not increase.

Note: a SAS data set may have a read password (READ=) and a write password (PROTECT=) at the same time. Some procedures, such as PROC DELETE, require the write password, but not the read password. The MODIFY statement requires **both** passwords if they exist.

Any number of the following options can be specified with the MODIFY statement; all options must be enclosed in parentheses.

LABEL=newlabel
LABEL=
specifies a newlabel or removes a label for the data set named in the MODIFY statement. If a new label is specified, it must consist of 40 characters or less, and if right parentheses, semicolons, or equal signs are used, the label must be enclosed in single quotes. If nothing is specified after LABEL=, the old label is removed but not replaced. For example:

    PROC DATASETS DDNAME=TEST;
      MODIFY EXP1 (LABEL=);
      MODIFY EXP2 (LABEL=TESTS ON THREE YEAR
        OLDS);

The label of the data set TEST.EXP1 is removed by the first MODIFY statement and the label of TEST.EXP2 is changed in the second MODIFY statement.

PROTECT=
write password
PROTECT= *old/new*

specifies or changes or removes the *write password* for the data set named in the MODIFY statement. Passwords are usually assigned to data sets when they are created by using the PROTECT= data set option. If a write password exists for a data set, it must be specified with the PROTECT= option or PROC DATASETS does not access the data set. To change a data set's write password, specify the *old* password after PROTECT=, followed by a slash and the *new* password. To remove a password, just give the old password and a slash; the password is removed and not replaced. For example:

```
PROC DATASETS DDNAME=TEST;
  MODIFY EXP1 (PROTECT=RED/);
  MODIFY EXP2 (PROTECT=GREEN/BLUE);
```

The write password for TEST.EXP1 is removed by the first MODIFY statement and the password for TEST.EXP2 is changed to BLUE by the second MODIFY statement.

PROTECT= can also be used in the MODIFY statement to specify a password for a previously unprotected data set. Simply specify the password as you would an existing password. For example, if EXP7 is unprotected, specifying:

```
MODIFY EXP7 (PROTECT=SAFE);
```

assigns the write password SAFE to the data set.

READ=
read password
READ= *old/new*

specifies or changes or removes the *read password* for the data set named in the MODIFY statement. Passwords are usually assigned to a data set when it is created by using the READ= data set option. If a read password exists for a data set, it must be specified with the READ= option or PROC DATASETS does not access the data set. To change a read password, specify the *old* password after READ=, followed by a slash and a *new* password. To remove a password, give the old password and a slash. The password is removed but not replaced. For example:

```
PROC DATASETS DDNAME=TEST;
  MODIFY EXP1 (READ=NCS/DU);
  MODIFY EXP2 (READ=APPLE/);
```

The first MODIFY statement changes the read password for TEST.EXP1 to DU and the second MODIFY statement removes the read password for TEST.EXP2.

READ= can also be used in the MODIFY statement to assign a password to a previously unprotected data set. Simply specify the password as you would an existing password. For example, if EXP7 has no read protection, you can assign a password with this MODIFY statement:

MODIFY EXP7 (READ=SECURE);

TYPE=   assigns a type to a special SAS data set or changes a
datasettype   special SAS data set type designation. Specially structured data sets are created by some SAS procedures
(for example, PROC CORR and PROC FACTOR); they
can also be created in a DATA step. See Chapter 12,
"SAS Data Sets," for a discussion of special SAS data
sets.
You must be sure that the specified value of TYPE=
corresponds to the actual data set type. The data set
type specified by TYPE= is not validated by SAS (except to check if it is a length of eight characters or
less). SAS does not verify that the data set's structure is
appropriate for the type you have designated, or even
that the type specified is actually a special SAS data set
type.

The variable labels, names, informats, and formats in a data set can be altered by using the following statements in conjunction with the MODIFY statement.

FORMAT Statement

FORMAT *variable ... format. variable ... format. ...;*

Variable formats can be changed or removed with the FORMAT statement. To change a format, specify the name of the variable and then the new format. When the variable name is given but there is no accompanying format, the old format is removed, but not replaced. Multiple variables can be used, and abbreviated variable lists, such as X1-X5, can be used where appropriate. You can change as many formats as you want with one FORMAT statement. Here is an example:

PROC DATASETS DDNAME=STUDY;
  MODIFY GROUP1 (PROTECT=CCCDDD);
  FORMAT X1-X3 4.1 TIME HHMM2.2 AGE;

The data set GROUP1 is a member of the SAS data library STUDY. The password CCCDDD must be given to access the data set. Variables X1, X2, and X3 are assigned the 4.1 format; the variable TIME is assigned the HHMM*w.d* format and the format of the AGE variable is removed.

Note that you must list any variables whose formats are to be removed last in the FORMAT statement; otherwise they are assigned the first format that follows. For example, if you write the FORMAT statement from the example above like this:

FORMAT X1-X3 4.1 AGE TIME HHMM2.2;

the AGE variable would have its format changed to HHMM2.2, rather than re-moved.

INFORMAT Statement

INFORMAT *variable ... informat. variable ... informat.;*

Informats can be changed or removed using the INFORMAT statement. To change an informat, specify the name of the variable and then the new informat. When a variable name is specified but no accompanying informat, the old informat is removed.

Multiple variables and abbreviated variable lists can be used. For example, in the data set GROUP1 the variables A, B, and X1-X3 are assigned new informats, and the variable C has its informat removed, with these statements:

```
PROC DATASETS DDNAME=STUDY;
  MODIFY GROUP1 (PROTECT=CCCDDD);
  INFORMAT A B 2. X1-X3 4.1 C;
```

Note that you must list any variables whose informats are to be removed last in the INFORMAT statement; otherwise they are assigned the first informat that follows. For example, if you write the INFORMAT statement from the example above like this:

```
INFORMAT A B C 2. X1-X3 4.1;
```

the variable C has its informat changed to 2., rather than removed.

LABEL Statement

LABEL *variable=newlabel* ...;

The LABEL statement changes or removes variable labels. You can use as many variables as you want in the LABEL statement, as long as each variable name is followed by an equal sign. To specify a new label, follow the equal sign with a new label. To remove a label do not specify anything after the equal sign. If the new label includes a right parenthesis, equal sign, or semicolon, it must be enclosed in single quotes. If a single quote appears in the label, it must be written as two single quotes in the LABEL statement. The new label can be up to 40 characters long.

These statements:

```
PROC DATASETS DDNAME=STUDY;
  MODIFY GROUP1 (PROTECT=CCCDDD);
  LABEL X1='Score 1=' X2='Score 2=' A=;
```

change the labels for variables X1 and X2 and remove the label for variable A.

RENAME Statement

RENAME *variable=newname* ...;

Variables can be assigned new names using the RENAME statement. The new name must be a valid SAS name. Any number of variables can be renamed in one statement. Abbreviated variable lists are not allowed. For example:

```
RENAME DAY2=TIME2;
```

DETAILS

Printed Output

DATASETS prints a list of the SAS data sets in the SAS data library before and after the directory is updated, unless the NOLIST option is specified in the PROC DATASETS statement. The listing is printed on the SAS log following the statements used in the DATASETS step.

EXAMPLE

In the example below, PROC CONTENTS produces information on a SAS data library referenced by the DDname MISC. PROC DATASETS is invoked to delete a data set, change a data set's name, and modify characteristics of two of the data sets. The output from DATASETS appears on the SAS log following the statements in the DATASETS step. Finally, PROC CONTENTS is executed to show the changes in the data sets that were made by PROC DATASETS.

```
PROC CONTENTS DATA=MISC._ALL_ NOSOURCE;
PROC DATASETS DDNAME=MISC;
  DELETE GEORGIA;
  CHANGE GDPSTATS=ECONOMIC;
  MODIFY CARS(LABEL=CARS RATED ON TEN SCALES);
    RENAME NOISE=QUIET;
    LABEL ACCEL=ACCELERATION
      VISIBLE=VISIBILITY
      CARGO=CARGO SPACE;
  MODIFY COFFEE(TYPE=CORR);
      FORMAT PLEASANT SPARKLIN MELLOW EXPENSIV COMFORT
      ALIVE REAL DEEP BREWED HEARTY PURE ROASTED FRESH 4.2;
PROC CONTENTS DATA=MISC._ALL_ NOSOURCE;
```

```
1       S A S   L O G   SAS/OS 82.0      VS2/MVS JOB PRINT    STEP SAS       PROC

NOTE: THE JOB PRINT HAS BEEN RUN UNDER RELEASE 82.0 OF SAS AT SAS INSTITUTE INC.      (00000000).

NOTE: CPUID   VERSION = 04   SERIAL = 020091   MODEL = 0158 .
      CPUID   VERSION = 03   SERIAL = 024001   MODEL = 0158 .

NOTE: NO OPTIONS SPECIFIED.

1              PROC CONTENTS DATA=MISC._ALL_ NOSOURCE;

NOTE: THE PROCEDURE CONTENTS USED 0.94 SECONDS AND 260K AND PRINTED PAGES 1 TO 5.

2              PROC DATASETS DDNAME=MISC;
3                  DELETE GEORGIA;
4                  CHANGE GDPSTATS=ECONOMIC;
5                  MODIFY CARS(LABEL=CARS RATED ON TEN SCALES);
6                      RENAME NOISE=QUIET;
7                      LABEL ACCEL=ACCELERATION
8                      VISIBLE= VISIBILITY
9                      CARGO=CARGO SPACE;
10                 MODIFY COFFEE(TYPE=CORR);
11                     FORMAT PLEASANT SPARKLIN MELLOW EXPENSIV COMFORT
12                          ALIVE REAL DEEP BREWED HEARTY PURE ROASTED FRESH 4.2;
```

(continued on next page)

(continued from previous page)

```
DSNAME=XXXXXX.YYY.ZZZZ

LIST OF DATA SETS BEFORE UPDATE OF DIRECTORY.

NAME            OBS TRACKS PROT
CARS            82      2
COFFEE          13      2
GDPSTATS        68      2
GEORGIA          5      2

LIST OF DATA SETS AFTER UPDATE OF DIRECTORY.

NAME            OBS TRACKS PROT
CARS            82      2
COFFEE          13      2
ECONOMIC        68      2

       7 TRACKS USED
      10 TRACKS ALLOCATED
      10 HIGH TRACK USED
       0 TRACKS THAT CAN BE RELEASED FROM OS DATA SET
       1 EXTENTS

NOTE: THE PROCEDURE DATASETS USED 0.83 SECONDS AND 284K.

13              PROC CONTENTS DATA=MISC._ALL_ NOSOURCE;

NOTE: THE PROCEDURE CONTENTS USED 0.92 SECONDS AND 260K AND PRINTED PAGES 6 TO 9.
NOTE: SAS USED 336K MEMORY.

NOTE: SAS INSTITUTE INC.
      SAS CIRCLE
      PO BOX 8000
      CARY, N.C. 27511-8000
```

```
                               SAS                                      1

                         CONTENTS PROCEDURE

                PHYSICAL CHARACTERISTICS OF OS DATA SET

DSNAME=xxxxxx.yyy.zzzz  UNIT=DISK    VOL=SER=SAS333  DISP=OLD  DEVICE=3350 DISK  MAX BLKSIZE=19069 BYTES

CREATED MONDAY, NOVEMBER 9, 1981       19 TRACKS ALLOCATED IN 1 EXTENT   COST IF DATA STORED ONLINE= $0.1200/DAY

COST IF DATA STORED OFFLINE= $0.0400/DAY


                         SAS DATA SET DIRECTORY

          NAME        # OBS    TRACKS   SUBEXTENTS


          CARS          82        2         1
          COFFEE        13        2         2
          GEORGIA        5        2         1
          GDPSTATS      69        2         1

          TOTAL TRACKS USED:      9
          HIGH TRACK USED:       10
```

```
                               SAS                                      2

                    CONTENTS OF SAS DATA SET MISC.CARS

TRACKS USED=2  SUBEXTENTS=1  OBSERVATIONS=82  CREATED BY JOB RUN  AT 10:11 TUESDAY, JUNE 8, 1982

BY SAS RELEASE 82.0  DSNAME=xxxxxx.yyy.zzzz  BLKSIZE=19004  LRECL=125  LABEL= STATISTICS ON CARS FOR CONSUMERS

OBSERVATIONS PER TRACK=152  GENERATED BY DATA

                           ALPHABETIC LIST OF VARIABLES

     #   VARIABLE  TYPE LENGTH POSITION FORMAT        INFORMAT LABEL

     5   ACCEL     NUM     8      50
     6   BRAKING   NUM     8      58
    12   CARGO     NUM     8     106
    10   COMFORT   NUM     8      90
     7   HANDLING  NUM     8      66
    14   IMPORT    CHAR    3     122
     1   MAKE      CHAR   10       4
     2   MODEL     CHAR   20      14
     3   MPG       NUM     8      34
    13   ORIGIN    CHAR    8     114
    11   NOISE     NUM     8      98
     4   RELIABLE  NUM     8      42                           RELIABILITY
     8   RIDE      NUM     8      74
     9   VISIBLE   NUM     8      82
```

SAS   3

CONTENTS OF SAS DATA SET MISC.COFFEE

TRACKS USED=2 SUBEXTENTS=2 OBSERVATIONS=13 CREATED BY JOB RUN AT 10:11 TUESDAY, JUNE 8, 1982

BY SAS RELEASE 82.0 DSNAME=xxxxxx.yyy.zzzz BLKSIZE=18964 LRECL=120 DF=94 TYPE=DATA OBSERVATIONS PER TRACK=158

GENERATED BY DATA

ALPHABETIC LIST OF VARIABLES

#	VARIABLE	TYPE	LENGTH	POSITION	FORMAT	INFORMAT	LABEL
1	_NAME_	CHAR	8	4			
15	_TYPE_	CHAR	4	116			
7	ALIVE	NUM	8	52			
10	BREWED	NUM	8	76			
6	COMFORT	NUM	8	44			
9	DEEP	NUM	8	68			
5	EXPENSIV	NUM	8	36			
14	FRESH	NUM	8	108			
11	HEARTY	NUM	8	84			
4	MELLOW	NUM	8	28			
2	PLEASANT	NUM	8	12			
12	PURE	NUM	8	92			
8	REAL	NUM	8	60			
13	ROASTED	NUM	8	100			
3	SPARKLIN	NUM	8	20			

SAS   4

CONTENTS OF SAS DATA SET MISC.GEORGIA

TRACKS USED=2 SUBEXTENTS=1 OBSERVATIONS=5 CREATED BY JOB RUN AT   10:11 TUESDAY, JUNE 8, 1982

BY SAS RELEASE 82.0 DSNAME=XXXXXX.YYY.ZZZZ BLKSIZE=19056 LRECL=44 OBSERVATIONS PER TRACK=433 GENERATED BY DATA

ALPHABETIC LIST OF VARIABLES

#	VARIABLE	TYPE	LENGTH	POSITION	FORMAT	INFORMAT	LABEL
3	AGTOT	NUM	8	20			
1	COUNTY	NUM	8	4			
4	INDTOT	NUM	8	28			
2	SIZE	NUM	8	12			
5	UNDEV	NUM	8	36			

SAS

CONTENTS OF SAS DATA SET MISC.GDPSTATS

TRACKS USED=2 SUBEXTENTS=1 OBSERVATIONS=68 CREATED BY JOB RUN AT 10:11 TUESDAY, JUNE 8, 1982

BY SAS RELEASE 82.0 DSNAME=xxxxxx.yyy.zzzz BLKSIZE=19012 LRECL=64 OBSERVATIONS PER TRACK=297 GENERATED BY DATA

ALPHABETIC LIST OF VARIABLES

#	VARIABLE	TYPE	LENGTH	POSITION	FORMAT	INFORMAT	LABEL
2	AGRICULT	NUM	8	24			
4	CONSTRUC	NUM	8	40			
1	COUNTRY	CHAR	20	4			
3	INDUSTRY	NUM	8	32			
5	TRADE	NUM	8	48			
6	TRANSCOM	NUM	8	56			

SAS   6

CONTENTS PROCEDURE

PHYSICAL CHARACTERISTICS OF OS DATA SET

DSNAME=XXXXXX.YYY.ZZZZ UNIT=DISK   VOL=SER=SAS333 DISP=OLD DEVICE=3350 DISK MAX BLKSIZE=19069 BYTES

CREATED MONDAY, NOVEMBER 9, 1981   10 TRACKS ALLOCATED IN 1 EXTENT COST IF DATA STORED ONLINE= $0.1200/DAY

COST IF DATA STORED OFFLINE= $0.0400/DAY

(continued on next page)

(continued from previous page)

```
                        SAS DATA SET DIRECTORY

            NAME        # OBS    TRACKS   SUBEXTENTS


            CARS          82       2          1
            COFFEE        13       2          2
            ECONOMIC      69       2          1

            TOTAL TRACKS USED:      7
            HIGH TRACK USED:       10
```

```
                                  SAS                                      7

                    CONTENTS OF SAS DATA SET MISC.CARS

TRACKS USED=2  SUBEXTENTS=1  OBSERVATIONS=82  CREATED BY JOB RUN  AT 10:11 TUESDAY, JUNE 8, 1982

BY SAS RELEASE 82.0  DSNAME=xxxxxx.yyy.zzzz  BLKSIZE=19004  LRECL=125  LABEL= CARS RATED ON TEN SCALES

OBSERVATIONS PER TRACK=152  GENERATED BY DATA

                          ALPHABETIC LIST OF VARIABLES

      #   VARIABLE  TYPE LENGTH POSITION  FORMAT       INFORMAT  LABEL

      5   ACCEL     NUM      8      50                           ACCELERATION
      6   BRAKING   NUM      8      58
     12   CARGO     NUM      8     106                           CARGO SPACE
     10   COMFORT   NUM      8      90
      7   HANDLING  NUM      8      66
     14   IMPORT    CHAR     3     122
      1   MAKE      CHAR    10       4
      2   MODEL     CHAR    20      14
      3   MPG       NUM      8      34
     13   ORIGIN    CHAR     8     114
     11   QUIET     NUM      8      98
      4   RELIABLE  NUM      8      42                           RELIABILITY
      8   RIDE      NUM      8      74
      9   VISIBLE   NUM      8      82                           VISIBILITY
```

```
                                  SAS                                      8

                   CONTENTS OF SAS DATA SET MISC.COFFEE

TRACKS USED=2  SUBEXTENTS=2  OBSERVATIONS=13  CREATED BY JOB RUN  AT 10:11 TUESDAY, JUNE 8, 1982

BY SAS RELEASE 82.0  DSNAME=xxxxxx.yyy.zzzz  BLKSIZE=18964  LRECL=120  DF=94  TYPE=CORR  OBSERVATIONS PER TRACK=158

GENERATED BY DATA

                          ALPHABETIC LIST OF VARIABLES

      #   VARIABLE  TYPE LENGTH POSITION  FORMAT       INFORMAT  LABEL

      1   _NAME_    CHAR     8       4
     15   _TYPE_    CHAR     4     116
      7   ALIVE     NUM      8      52     4.2
     10   BREWED    NUM      8      76     4.2
      6   COMFORT   NUM      8      44     4.2
      9   DEEP      NUM      8      68     4.2
      5   EXPENSIV  NUM      8      36     4.2
     14   FRESH     NUM      8     108     4.2
     11   HEARTY    NUM      8      84     4.2
      4   MELLOW    NUM      8      28     4.2
      2   PLEASANT  NUM      8      12     4.2
     12   PURE      NUM      8      92     4.2
      8   REAL      NUM      8      60     4.2
     13   ROASTED   NUM      8     100     4.2
      3   SPARKLIN  NUM      8      20     4.2
```

```
                                           SAS                                                    9

                          CONTENTS OF SAS DATA SET MISC.ECONOMIC

TRACKS USED=2  SUBEXTENTS=1  OBSERVATIONS=68  CREATED BY JOB RUN  AT 10:11 TUESDAY, JUNE 8, 1982

BY SAS RELEASE 82.0  DSNAME=xxxxxx.yyy.zzzz  BLKSIZE=19012  LRECL=64  OBSERVATIONS PER TRACK=297  GENERATED BY DATA

                                    ALPHABETIC LIST OF VARIABLES

           #   VARIABLE   TYPE LENGTH POSITION  FORMAT          INFORMAT  LABEL

           2   AGRICULT   NUM      8       24
           4   CONSTRUC   NUM      8       40
           1   COUNTRY    CHAR    20        4
           3   INDUSTRY   NUM      8       32
           5   TRADE      NUM      8       48
           6   TRANSCOM   NUM      8       56
```

The DELETE Procedure

ABSTRACT

The DELETE procedure deletes SAS data sets from the disk or tape data library on which they are stored.

INTRODUCTION

Refer to chapters on the DATA step and PROC step, and especially to Chapter 12, "SAS Data Sets," to familiarize yourself with the basic features of SAS data sets and SAS data libraries and other terminology (for example, DDname) used in this procedure description. Note: you can also delete SAS data sets with the DELETE statement in PROC DATASETS.

DELETE can be used to delete permanent or temporary SAS data sets. The space freed is then available for new SAS data sets.

If the DELETE procedure is applied to a permanent data set it deletes the data set **only** if no errors have been made in the SAS statements before the PROC DELETE statement (except when SAS is being executed interactively under TSO or CMS).

Be careful when using PROC DELETE with tape SAS data sets. Deleting a tape data set automatically deletes any data sets after it on the tape, even if they are protected by passwords. Chapter 12, "SAS Data Sets," contains further information on tape data sets.

SPECIFICATIONS

The PROC statement is the only statement used.

PROC DELETE *option*;

PROC DELETE Statement

PROC DELETE *option*;

The following option may be specified in the PROC statement:

DATA=*SASdataset* ...   specifies the data set to be deleted. More than one data set can be specified. For example:

> PROC DELETE DATA=MY.STUDY MY.GRADES;

To delete all SAS data sets in a SAS data library, use __ALL__ as the second-level name in the DATA= option. For example:

> PROC DELETE DATA=MY.__ALL__;

If the DATA= option is omitted, the most recently created SAS data set (the __LAST__ data set) is deleted.

DETAILS

Printed Output

PROC DELETE produces no printed output.

EXAMPLE

The job below deletes two SAS data sets, CARS and COFFEE, from the SAS data library referenced by the DDname STATS. PROC CONTENTS is executed before and after PROC DELETE to show the change in the data library.

```
PROC CONTENTS DATA=STATS.__ALL__ NODS;
PROC DELETE DATA=STATS.CARS STATS.COFFEE;
PROC CONTENTS DATA=STATS.__ALL__ NODS;
```

```
                                    SAS                                                    1

                           CONTENTS PROCEDURE

                       PHYSICAL CHARACTERISTICS OF OS DATA SET

DSNAME=xxxxxx.yyyy.zzzz  UNIT=DISK     VOL=SER=SAS333  DISP=OLD  DEVICE=3350 DISK  MAX BLKSIZE=19069 BYTES

CREATED MONDAY, JUNE 21, 1982          30 TRACKS ALLOCATED IN 1 EXTENT  COST IF DATA STORED ONLINE= $0.3600/DAY

COST IF DATA STORED OFFLINE= $0.1200/DAY


                              SAS DATA SET DIRECTORY

                     NAME      # OBS    TRACKS   SUBEXTENTS


                     CARS        82       2          1
                     COFFEE      13       2          2
                     ECONOMIC    69       2          2
                     MASTER      82       2          2

                     TOTAL TRACKS USED:      9
                     HIGH TRACK USED:       12
```

```
                                    SAS                                          2

                            CONTENTS PROCEDURE

                   PHYSICAL CHARACTERISTICS OF OS DATA SET

DSNAME=xxxxxx.yyyy.zzzz  UNIT=DISK    VOL=SER=SAS333  DISP=OLD  DEVICE=3350 DISK  MAX BLKSIZE=19069 BYTES

CREATED MONDAY, JUNE 21, 1982        30 TRACKS ALLOCATED IN 1 EXTENT  COST IF DATA STORED ONLINE= $0.3600/DAY

COST IF DATA STORED OFFLINE= $0.1200/DAY

                            SAS DATA SET DIRECTORY

             NAME        # OBS    TRACKS   SUBEXTENTS

             ECONOMIC     69        2         2
             MASTER       82        2         2

             TOTAL TRACKS USED:     5
             HIGH TRACK USED:       9
```

The EDITOR Procedure

ABSTRACT

The EDITOR procedure is used to examine and make changes to a SAS data set without using a SAS DATA step. PROC EDITOR is primarily an interactive procedure.

INTRODUCTION

When a data set is edited in a DATA step, you must create a copy to make changes. The EDITOR procedure allows you to edit a SAS data set directly with search, list, addition, deletion, and replacement commands. Since PROC EDITOR is interactive, you get a response to each command as it is executed. (It is possible to execute PROC EDITOR as a batch job, however.)

Note: use of PROC EDITOR is restricted to disk-format SAS data sets.

Interactive Capability

In interactive mode most SAS procedures and DATA steps are executed by entering all statements pertaining to the step and then a RUN statement. PROC EDITOR is slightly different. To use it, you enter the PROC statement, INFORMAT and FORMAT statements if they are appropriate, and a RUN statement. Then PROC EDITOR prompts you for further commands with the message:

ENTER COMMANDS OR 'HELP;'
NOTE ENHANCEMENTS: LOCATE, SEARCH, FIND.

When you use PROC EDITOR, keep in mind that EDITOR operates directly on the input data set. This means that as commands are executed, changes are made to the data set, and it is not possible to start again with the original data set. If you make mistakes when changing a data set, you cannot return to the original. Begin by making a backup copy of any data set that would be difficult to recreate if errors are made.

EDITOR vs. BROWSE

The EDITOR procedure and the BROWSE procedure are very similar but they differ in two ways: (1) The BROWSE procedure can operate on a data set using read access (DISP = SHR under OS and TSO). The EDITOR procedure must have write access (DISP = OLD under OS and TSO) to the SAS data set. (2) No change commands (REPLACE, ADD, DELETE, DUP) are allowed with the BROWSE procedure; that is, you cannot edit a SAS data set with PROC BROWSE.

Introductory Example

In the following example, PROC EDITOR is used to edit the SAS data set SAVE.HTWT. Commands are entered in lowercase in response to line number prompts from SAS. SAS responses are in uppercase. (Note that under ICCF the line number prompts do not appear. Instead, ICCF prompts you for further commands by displaying the message ''*enter data?''.) First, invoke the EDITOR procedure with the PROC statement and a RUN command.

1? proc editor data = save.htwt;run;

SAS responds:

ENTER COMMANDS OR 'HELP;'
NOTE ENHANCEMENTS: LOCATE, SEARCH, FIND.

Ask SAS to list some observations using the LIST command (SAS responds after each command):

2> list 1;
  1 NAME=ALFRED SEX=M AGE=14 HEIGHT=69 WEIGHT=112.5 ;

3> list 1000;
THERE ARE ONLY 19 OBSERVATIONS IN THE DATA SET.
RE-ENTER COMMAND

4> list 19;
  19 NAME=WILLIAM SEX=M AGE=15 HEIGHT=66.5 WEIGHT=112 ;

Next search for suspiciously high WEIGHT values using the FIND command:

5> find all 1,last weight>140;

SAS responds with observations having WEIGHT values greater than 140:

FOUND AT OBS=10
FOUND AT OBS=15
END OF SEARCH. OBS=19

List the NAME and WEIGHT values for observation 10, then replace the WEIGHT value with 99.5, and list observation 10 again:

6> list 10 name weight;
  10 NAME=JOHN WEIGHT=995 ;

7> rep weight=99.5; list;
  10 NAME=JOHN SEX=M AGE=12 HEIGHT=59 WEIGHT=99.5 ;

Then, list NAME and WEIGHT values for observation 15:

8> list 15 name weight;
  15 NAME=PHILIP WEIGHT=150 ;

End the session with the END command:

9> end;
EXIT FROM SAS EDITOR.

10?

SPECIFICATIONS

The EDITOR procedure operates in two stages. The first stage involves the PROC, FORMAT, INFORMAT, and RUN statements. The PROC statement and associated FORMAT and INFORMAT statements are examined as a unit before the RUN statement is executed. After the RUN statement is executed, PROC EDITOR is in interactive mode.

The interactive mode is the second stage of the procedure and involves commands that are executed immediately after they are entered.

Below are the statements and commands used with PROC EDITOR.

PROC EDITOR *options;*
  FORMAT *variable format. ...;*
  INFORMAT *variable format. ...;*
  RUN;
  FIND *options range variable1 operator1 value1 ...;*
  LOCATE *options range value ...;*
  SEARCH *options range string ...;*
  NAME *variable;*
  STRING *variable ...;*
  VERIFY *option;*
  END;
  LIST *range variable ...;*
  HELP *command;*
  REPLACE *options range*
    variable1 = value1 variable2 = value2 ...;
  ADD *variable1 = value1 variable2 = value2 ...;*
  DELETE *range;*
  DUP *range;*
  TOP;
  BOTTOM;
  UP *n;*
  DOWN *n;*

PROC EDITOR Statement

PROC EDITOR *options;*

The following options can be specified on the EDITOR statement.

DATA=*SASdataset*   names the SAS data set to be edited. If DATA= is omitted the most recently created data set is used.

FUZZ=*value*   specifies the "fuzz" value to be used in the FIND command. See the **FIND command** for further explanation.

FORMAT Statement

FORMAT *variable format. ...;*

Use the FORMAT statement to assign output formats to variables for the duration of your PROC EDITOR session. (See Chapter 8, "Statements Used in the PROC Step," for a complete discussion of the FORMAT statement.) The maximum widths allowed by PROC EDITOR are 16 for numeric variables and 64 for character variables. The width restrictions on output formats are important for the PROC EDITOR commands that display values; that is, the REPLACE command with the VERIFY command in effect, and the LIST command. (REPLACE and LIST are discussed later in this chapter.)

If formats were assigned to variables when the data set was created, it is not necessary to repeat the FORMAT statement for the EDITOR procedure.

Date, time, and datetime variables must be assigned a corresponding date, time, or datetime format if you want them to be printed in a readable form.

The FORMAT statement, if used, must be entered after the PROC statement and before the RUN statement.

INFORMAT Statement

INFORMAT *variable format. ...*;

The INFORMAT statement assigns informats to variables for the duration of your PROC EDITOR session. (See Chapter 3, "Statements Used in the DATA Step," for a complete discussion of the INFORMAT statement.) If informats were assigned to variables when the data set was created, it is not necessary to repeat the INFORMAT statement for the EDITOR procedure.

The maximum widths allowed for informats are 32 for numeric variables and 200 for character variables (the standard limits for informats). However, it is important to note that PROC EDITOR uses only up to 64 characters of an informatted character value. If an informatted character value is 70 characters long, any searching or changing command in PROC EDITOR uses only the first 64 characters. The commands affected by this PROC EDITOR width restriction are: FIND, LOCATE, SEARCH, REPLACE, and ADD.

Note: when values are specified in any EDITOR command, they are read with the informat associated with the variable in the data set. For example, if the DATE7. informat had originally been used to read the values of a variable named STARTWK, only date values informatted DDMMMYY (for example, 01JUN77) should be specified for STARTWK in EDITOR commands.

Character and datetime constants can be used in PROC EDITOR commands, but only if there is no informat assigned to the variable. (Chapter 4, "SAS Expressions," discusses constants.)

The INFORMAT statement must be entered after the PROC EDITOR statement and before the RUN statement.

RUN Statement

RUN;

A RUN statement must **always** be entered after the PROC EDITOR statement and before any editing statements, both in batch mode and interactive mode. After the RUN statement has been entered, SAS responds with:

ENTER COMMANDS OR 'HELP;'
NOTE ENHANCEMENTS: LOCATE, SEARCH, FIND.

PROC EDITOR Commands

There are five types of EDITOR commands: searching commands, specification commands, display commands, change commands, and positioning commands. The commands in each category are:

searching	FIND, LOCATE, SEARCH
specification	NAME, STRING, VERIFY, END
display	LIST, HELP
change	REPLACE, ADD, DELETE, DUP
positioning	TOP, BOTTOM, UP, DOWN

There are options and other specifications with most of the EDITOR commands.

With many EDITOR commands it is possible to specify a **range** of observations to search, display, or change. The range specification follows the command keyword and is usually given by two numbers separated by a comma. If only one number is given, only that observation is searched. If no number is given, only the current observation is searched. (There is an exception to this explained in **Repeating FIND, LOCATE, or SEARCH Commands**, below.) The keyword LAST can be used instead of the second number to indicate the last observation number. Here are some examples of ranges:

1,5   from observation 1 through observation 5
3,LAST   from observation 3 through the last observation
6   observation 6 only

Each EDITOR command is explained below, within the appropriate category.

Searching Commands

The searching commands are those that search the SAS data set for an occurrence of a set of values specified in the command. The general form of the searching commands is:

COMMAND options range values;

where *options* can be VERIFY and/or ALL, *range* specifies the range of observations to search, and *values* is the list of values to search for. The *options* are discussed below. The value list is explained with each command since it operates differently with each command.

The following options can be used with searching commands:

VERIFY   causes the NOGO switch to be set on if a search is
VER   not successful. The switch prevents any further
         changes to the SAS data set (using REPLACE or
         DELETE) until a VERIFY RESET; command is given. This
         feature is especially useful in a batch job since you
         cannot respond to EDITOR when it tells you that the
         values cannot be found.

ALL   specifies a search for all matches within the given
         range. If ALL is not given, searching stops after the first
         match is found, and that observation becomes the cur-
         rent observation. When ALL is used, all observations in
         the designated range are searched, and the last obser-
         vation becomes the current observation.

FIND command

FIND *options range variable1 operator1 value1 variable2 operator2 value2 ...*;

where *operator* can be =, ¬=, >, >=, <, or <=.

The FIND command searches a given range of observations for occurrences of specified variable/value relationships. For example:

FIND 1,5 X=2 Y<6 Z¬=7;

searches observations 1 through 5 for the first observation in which X is equal to 2, Y is less than 6, and Z is not equal to 7.

The same variable can appear more than once in a value list. This FIND command:

FIND ALL 1,LAST X>=5 X<=10;

searches for all observations in the data set which have X values between 5 and 10.

If none of the observations searched meets the specified conditions, the message:

NOT FOUND. OBS=n

is issued, where *n* is the number of observations in the data set.

If a character variable is specified in the FIND command and the value contains special characters (for example, blanks, underscores, or semicolons), the value must be enclosed in single quotes.

There are times when searches involve comparisons between values that are very close but not exact matches due to rounding that occurs when creating the data set. The FUZZ= option can be specified when entering PROC EDITOR to indicate how closely the searching value must match the variable value in order for it to be considered matched. The default fuzz value is 1E-12. Fuzzing is performed only if the = operator is used, and only on numeric variables. The type of fuzzing used is called "relative fuzzing." The conditional formula is:

$$|x-y|/(|x|+|y|)<fuzz$$

If this condition is met, a match is found. For example, suppose the value of a variable Z in an observation is equal to 1234567890123, and FUZZ=1E-12 (the default). The command:

FIND ID=1234567890124;

finds a match, since:

$$|1234567890123-1234567890124|/(1234567890123+1234567890124)$$

is less than 1E-12.

For very large numbers, use small FUZZ values. In the example above, if FUZZ=1E-15 the two values do not match.

See **Repeating FIND, LOCATE, or SEARCH Commands** (below) for an explanation of repeating a FIND command.

LOCATE command

LOCATE *options range value*;
LOC *options range value*;

The LOCATE command searches for the occurrence of a single value in a range of observations. Before a LOCATE command can be issued, a NAME command must be given:

NAME *variable*;

The NAME command, described below under **Specification Commands** gives the name of the variable that the LOCATE command evaluates. For example:

```
NAME X;
LOCATE 1,10 2.35;
```

searches the variable X in observations 1 through 10 for an occurrence of the value 2.35.

The type of the value (numeric or character) specified in the LOCATE command should match the type of the variable given in the NAME command. That is, do not specify a character string as the value if the NAME variable is numeric, or a numeric value if the NAME variable is character.

If a character value specified in the LOCATE command contains special characters (for example, blanks, underscores, or semicolons), the value string must be enclosed in single quotes.

Below are some examples of LOCATE commands:

```
LOCATE 1,LAST ABC;
LOCATE 6,20 'X Y Z';
LOCATE 15,LAST 10;
```

The value given in the last example, 10, could be used for either a character or a numeric variable. If character, the procedure searches for the characters 10; if numeric, the procedure searches for the number 10.

The LOCATE command can be used to search for leading characters only. You indicate this type of search by adding a colon (:) after the LOCATE keyword. For example, in a SAS data set containing data on individuals there are names of the form 'PUBLIC, JOHN Q.'. You are looking for anyone named SMITH, but you don't care about the first name. You enter:

```
LOCATE: 1,LAST SMITH;
```

to look at the first five characters of each NAME value to see if they are SMITH. Note that EDITOR would also find matches with names such as SMITHFIELD. To access only those whose last name is exactly SMITH, enter:

```
LOCATE: 1,LAST 'SMITH,';
```

and names such as SMITHFIELD are not considered matches.

See **Repeating FIND, LOCATE or SEARCH Commands** (below) for a discussion of repeating the LOCATE command.

SEARCH command

SEARCH *options range string1 string2 ...*;
S *options range string1 string2 ...*;

The SEARCH command searches for occurrences of *strings* within a group of character variables. Before a SEARCH command is invoked, a STRING command must be given.

STRING *charactervariable ...*;

The STRING command, described below under **Specification Commands**, names the variables used by the SEARCH command. If you enter:

```
STRING NAME SPOUSE;
SEARCH 1,LAST SMITH 'SMITH-JONES';
```

the variables NAME and SPOUSE are searched on all observations for the strings SMITH and SMITH-JONES.

A string can be found anywhere within a value, not just at the beginning.

The string list for a SEARCH command consists of one to ten strings and cannot exceed 200 characters in total length. Only character variables can be searched by the SEARCH command. Single quotes are not necessary unless special characters appear in the string.

Any string in the list can apply to more than one of the specified variables, so the string is processed by each variable's informat before a comparison is made.

There are two types of searching: "any" and "all." "Any" is indicated by a "@" after the word SEARCH. "All" is the default. In an "any" search, only one of the strings must be found in the variables specified in the STRING command. In an "all" search, all strings specified in the list must be found somewhere in the variables specified by the STRING command. Suppose, for example, that the variable NAME has the value PUBLIC, JOHN Q. and SPOUSE has the value PUBLIC, MARY J. Consider these commands:

```
STRING NAME SPOUSE;
SEARCH 'JOHN' 'MARY';
```

For this SEARCH command the string JOHN has to be found somewhere in either NAME or SPOUSE. It is found in NAME. In addition, MARY must be found in NAME or SPOUSE. It is found in SPOUSE. Therefore, the SEARCH is successful.

```
STRING NAME SPOUSE;
SEARCH 'JOHN' 'JANE';
```

In this example, JOHN is found, but JANE is not. Since SEARCH "all" is requested (by default) and no match is found, the SEARCH is not successful.

```
STRING NAME SPOUSE;
SEARCH@ 'JOHN' 'JANE';
```

For the third example, SEARCH "any" is requested. JOHN is found, so the search is successful.

```
STRING NAME SPOUSE;
SEARCH@ 'JANE';
```

In the final example, JANE is not found. Since no strings were found, the SEARCH "any" request is not successful.

See **Repeating FIND, LOCATE, or SEARCH Commands** for a description of repeating the SEARCH command.

Specification Commands

The specification commands are those that do not (for the most part) display information and do not operate on the SAS data set. These commands are NAME, STRING, VERIFY, and END.

NAME command

NAME *variable*;

The NAME command precedes the LOCATE command. It indicates a single variable that LOCATE searches for matches. The specified variable can be numeric or character. If no variable name is given, the command displays the name of the current NAME variable. Only one variable name can be specified.

The NAME command can be reissued as often as necessary. It does not have to be reissued between uses of the LOCATE or any other searching command. For example, if you are looking for occurrences of two particular values of the variable SIZE, you can enter:

    NAME SIZE;
    LOCATE 1,LAST XXL;

and after the computer responds, enter:

    LOCATE 1,LAST MED;

SAS again searches the variable SIZE on all observations for the value MED.

STRING command

    STRING variable ...;
    STR variable ...;

The STRING command precedes the SEARCH command. It gives a list of character variables that SEARCH searches for matches.

All variables listed **must** be character variables. If no variable name is given, the command displays the names of all the current STRING variables.

The STRING command can be reissued as often as necessary. It does not have to be reissued between uses of any of the searching commands. For example, if you want to find two particular character strings in the variable PLACE, you could use the statements:

    STRING PLACE;
    SEARCH ALL 1,LAST BURGH;

and after SAS responds, enter:

    SEARCH ALL 1,LAST BERG;

SAS again searches the variable PLACE in all observations for the string BERG.

VERIFY command

    VERIFY option;
    VER option;
    V option;

The VERIFY command allows you to selectively monitor the action taken by change commands, by displaying or not displaying changes according to the option that is specified. The option can be either ON, OFF, or RESET.

If VERIFY ON is specified, all changes made to the data set through the use of the change commands are displayed. VERIFY OFF turns off this facility. VERIFY OFF is the default when you invoke the EDITOR procedure. VERIFY RESET indicates that the NOGO switch is to be turned off. The NOGO switch is set on if a searching command with the VERIFY option does not find a match (see **Searching Commands**), and prevents EDITOR from executing REPLACE and DELETE commands.

Note: do not confuse the VERIFY command with the VERIFY option used with searching commands.

END command

```
END;
E;
QUIT;
Q;
```

The END command exits from the EDITOR procedure. It has no operands. A PROC, DATA, or RUN statement, or an end-of-file occurrence also causes the EDITOR procedure to exit.

Display Commands

The display commands are those that display information. The two display commands are LIST and HELP. They are explained below.

LIST command

```
LIST range variable ...;
L range variable ...;
```

The LIST command lists the values of one or more specified variables in a range of observations.

If *range* is not specified, only the current observation is listed. If no *variable* is specified, all variables are listed.

If more than one variable is given, the variables indicated are listed in the order specified. Suppose variables A, B, and C have the values 1, 2, and 3, respectively, and that the current observation is 1. The command:

```
LIST;
```

displays:

```
1 A=1 B=2 C=3 ;
```

```
LIST C A;
```

displays:

```
1 C=3 A=1 ;
```

```
LIST 1 B;
```

displays:

```
1 B=2 ;
```

LIST always gives the observation number and ends the list with a semicolon. If formats have been specified for the variables, the formatted values are listed. (Remember the format width restrictions for PROC EDITOR discussed in **Format Statement**.)

See the description of the REPLACE command to learn how the LIST command is used in conjunction with the REPLACE command.

HELP command

HELP *command*;
H *command*;

Since EDITOR is primarily used interactively, a HELP facility exists that allows you to get help from the procedure. *Command* is the name of the command with which you need help. The command:

HELP OTHER;

requests other information, not necessarily related to a single command. The command HELP with no operands describes all available commands.

Change Commands

The change commands make modifications to the existing SAS data set. These commands are REPLACE, ADD, DELETE, and DUP. Each is explained below.

If the NOGO switch is set on by a searching command that did not find a match, the REPLACE and DELETE commands do not perform the change. The NOGO switch is reset (turned off) by the VERIFY command (see above).

REPLACE command

REPLACE *options range variable1 = value1 variable2 = value2* ...;
REP *options range variable1 = value1   variable2 = value2* ...;
R *options range variable1 = value1   variable2 = value2* ...;

The REPLACE command changes one or more values of specified variables in a range of observations.

For example, this statement:

REPLACE 1,5 YEAR = 1982 COST = 2000;

causes the value of YEAR to be changed to 1982 and the value of COST to be changed to 2000 for observations 1 through 5.

If the VERIFY ON command has been given, the variables to be changed are displayed before and after changing. If formats have been specified for the variables, the formatted values are displayed. (Remember the PROC EDITOR format width restrictions discussed in **Format Statement**.)

The REPLACE command can also be invoked without the REPLACE keyword, by entering the range followed by the value list. Therefore:

REPLACE 2 I = 2;
2 I = 2;

are identical commands. This feature is especially useful if you have buffered terminals and a system that handles full-screen command entry. With such a system, the LIST command can be performed on a range of observations, and after the response is displayed the cursor can be positioned over the values to be changed to edit them. You do not have to insert the REPLACE command word or the semicolon (the LIST command automatically includes a semicolon when displaying each observation). Each changed line can be invoked as a REPLACE command to make the change.

For example, you can enter:

LIST 3 AGE;

and the computer responds:

3 AGE = 18 ;

You want to change the AGE value to 19, so you position the cursor on the character 8, change it to 9, and press ENTER. EDITOR treats the line as if it had the keyword REPLACE in front of it and changes the value of AGE on observation 3 to 19.

ADD command

ADD *variable1 = value1 variable2 = value2 ...;*
A *variable1 = value1 variable2 = value2 ...;*

The ADD command adds a new observation to the end of a data set. This statement:

ADD X = 3.5 Y = 2.0 Z = 0.7;

adds one observation to the data set.

The ADD command does not use a range specification, because it only adds one observation at a time. To add several observations with the same value, enter the ADD command once, then enter the DUP command as many times as necessary to add the observation.

DELETE command

DELETE range;
DEL range;
D range;

The DELETE command sets all the variables in a specified range of observations to missing. All numeric variables are set to "." and all character variables are set to blank. The DELETE command does not entirely delete the observation in the way the DATA step's DELETE statement does. In order to fully delete the observation, you have to process the data set with a subsequent DATA step.

DUP command

DUP range;

The DUP command is used to duplicate observations in a specified range in the SAS data set. For example, the statement:

DUP 1,3;

duplicates observations 1 through 3 and adds the copies to the end of the SAS data set.

As another example, suppose you want an observation duplicated 20 times. The observation to be copied is observation 50. Enter:

DUP 50;   copy the observation
L;   determine the observation number (say, 100)
DUP 100;   make a second copy

DUP 100,LAST;	copy both copies for 4 copies
DUP 100,LAST;	copy all copies for 8 copies
DUP 100,LAST;	copy all copies for 16 copies
DUP 100,103;	make four copies for a total of 20

Positioning Commands

PROC EDITOR uses an observation pointer that points to the current observation. At the beginning of an EDITOR session the pointer moves to the first observation. When an observation number is specified in an EDITOR command the pointer is moved to that observation. For example, specifying:

    LIST 14;

moves the pointer to observation 14 and lists the values in observation 14. When a range of observations is specified, the pointer is moved to the first observation in the range and the command executed for the observation; next the pointer is moved to the second observation in the range, and so on.

The pointer remains at the observation for which a command has just been executed until it is repositioned by one of the positioning commands or by a range specification in another EDITOR command. (Using a range specification in a command has the effect of repeating the command for each observation in the range.)

You can use the positioning commands to reposition the pointer at any time in an EDITOR session.

TOP command

    TOP;

The TOP command moves the pointer to the first observation.

BOTTOM command

    BOTTOM;

The BOTTOM command moves the pointer to the last observation.

UP command

    UP n;

The UP command moves the pointer up n observations. If the pointer is at observation 23, specifying:

    UP 3;

moves the pointer to observation 20.

DOWN command

    DOWN n;

The DOWN command moves the pointer down n observations. If the pointer is at observation 90, specifying:

```
DOWN 10;
```

moves the pointer to observation 100.

DETAILS

Repeating FIND, LOCATE, or SEARCH Commands

With searching commands it is often convenient to find an occurrence based on a value list, look more closely at the observation, then continue the search for occurrences in other observations. If the value list is long, it is inconvenient to reenter it and to calculate the range of observations; therefore, a repeat facility is available under EDITOR.

To repeat a FIND, LOCATE, or SEARCH command, reenter the command **without** the value list, and the previous value list is used. A range can be specified, but if no range is specified, the default range is *m,n* where *m* equals the current observation plus one, and *n* is the same as the last observation of the previously indicated range. For example:

```
FIND 1,10 X = 1;     (found at observation 3)
FIND;                (interpreted as FIND 4,10 X = 1; found at 6)
FIND 20,LAST;        (interpreted as FIND 20,LAST X = 1; found at 30)
FIND;                (interpreted as FIND 31,LAST X = 1;)
```

To use the repeat facility, the new searching command must be the same as the previous searching command. That is, you cannot enter a LOCATE command with a value list, then enter a FIND command without a value list.

Using PROC EDITOR in Batch Mode

Although the EDITOR procedure is designed for interactive use, it can be used in batch mode to make changes to existing SAS data sets.

To use PROC EDITOR in batch, you need the SAS statements:

```
PROC EDITOR DATA=SASdataset;
RUN;
```

where *SASdataset* is the name of the SAS data set to be edited.

Follow the PROC EDITOR and RUN statements with the EDITOR commands needed to make the desired changes in the data set.

PROC EDITOR's responses to the commands are printed on the SAS log. Each response appears **before** the listing of the associated command.

In batch mode, the VERIFY option should always be used with the FIND command to guard against inadvertently changing or deleting the wrong values or observations.

For example, suppose you want to find the observation where the value for NAME was JOHN DOE, and then change the value of the variable CITY in that observation to CHICAGO. In a batch environment, you would use these statements:

```
PROC EDITOR DATA=MY.NAMEFILE;
  RUN;
  FIND VER 1,LAST NAME='JOHN DOE';
  REP CITY=CHICAGO;
```

The VER option in the FIND command protects against changing the CITY value in the last observation of the data set if no observation with a NAME value of JOHN DOE is found. (Recall that when a searching command does not find an observation with the specified value, it stops at the last observation in the range specified.)

When a search fails in batch mode, the NOGO switch is set on, which means that EDITOR stops executing REPLACE and DELETE commands. To reset the NOGO switch so that EDITOR begins executing these commands again, use the statement:

VERIFY RESET;

To further protect against mistakes, EDITOR stops executing REPLACE, DELETE, and ADD commands if a syntax error is encountered in the EDITOR commands.

Output Data Set

The output from PROC EDITOR is the edited version of the SAS data set used for input. There is no printed output.

EXAMPLES

Editing a SAS Data Set: Example 1

The example session below shows the data set ECONOMIC before editing, a PROC EDITOR interactive session, and the edited data set. If you use VSE/SAS remember that ICCF prompts you with a message, "*enter data?" rather than line numbers.

1? proc print data=economic; run;

OBS	COUNTRY	AGRICULT	INDUSTRY	CONSTRUC	TRADE	TRANSCOM
1	AFGHANISTAN	49	17	8	12	3
2	BANGLADESH	54	8	5	9	6
3	BOLIVIA	18	25	4	19	8
4	BURMA	47	10	1	29	3
5	CHILE	10	27	2	29	4
6	ECUADOR	20	29	6	13	5
7	EGYPT	24	23	4	11	7
8	ETHIOPIA	44	11	4	9	5
9	GHANA	51	14	5	13	4
10	GUATEMALA	28	14	2	32	4
11	HAITI	41	15	4	10	2
12	INDIA	36	18	5	11	5
13	IRAN	9	48	9	5	3
14	IRAQ	7	63	2	5	4
15	KENYA	34	13	4	10	4
16	MEXICO	9	30	6	31	3
17	NEPAL	67	10	1	5	3
18	NIGERIA	26	38	6	11	3
19	PAKISTAN	31	16	5	13	6
20	PERU	13	36	4	15	7
21	RHODESIA	15	29	3	11	6
22	SUDAN	39	11	4	16	6
23	TURKEY	27	21	5	13	8
24	UGANDA	53	10	2	9	3

25	VENEZUELA	6	39	17	10	11
26	VIETNAM	29	7	1	18	4
27	YEMEN ARAB					
	REP.	35	6	8	22	3
28	YUGOSLAVIA	17	40	10	21	8
29	ZAIRE	19	22	6	16	4
30	ZAMBIA	13	35	9	12	5

```
2? proc editor data=exp.economic;
3? run;
ENTER COMMANDS OR 'HELP;'
NOTE ENHANCEMENTS: LOCATE, SEARCH, FIND


4> verify on;
5> find 1,last country=rhodesia;
FOUND AT OBS=21


6> replace 21 country=zimbabwe;
21 COUNTRY=RHODESIA ;
21 COUNTRY=ZIMBABWE ;


7> add country=kampuchea agricult=60 industry=10 construc=18
   trade=10 transcom=2;
   31 COUNTRY=KAMPUCHEA AGRICULT=60 INDUSTRY=10
     CONSTRUC=18 TRADE=10 TRANSCOM=2 ;


8> name agricult;
9> locate all 1,last 50;
NOT FOUND. OBS=31


10> find all 1,last agricult>60;
FOUND AT OBS=17
END OF SEARCH. OBS=31


11> delete 28;
   28 COUNTRY=YUGOSLAVIA AGRICULT=17
     INDUSTRY=40 CONSTRUC=10 TRADE=21 TRANSCOM=8 ;
   28 COUNTRY= AGRICULT=. INDUSTRY=. CONSTRUCT=.
     TRADE=. TRANSCOM=. ;


12> end;
EXIT FROM SAS EDITOR.


13? proc print; run;
```

OBS	COUNTRY	AGRICULT	INDUSTRY	CONSTRUC	TRADE	TRANSCOM
1	AFGHANISTAN	49	17	8	12	3
2	BANGLADESH	54	8	5	9	6
3	BOLIVIA	18	25	4	19	8
4	BURMA	47	10	1	29	3
5	CHILE	10	27	2	29	4
6	ECUADOR	20	29	6	13	5
7	EGYPT	24	23	4	11	7
8	ETHIOPIA	44	11	4	9	5

9	GHANA	51	14	5	13	4
10	GUATEMALA	28	14	2	32	4
11	HAITI	41	15	4	10	2
12	INDIA	36	18	5	11	5
13	IRAN	9	48	9	5	3
14	IRAQ	7	63	2	5	4
15	KENYA	34	13	4	10	4
16	MEXICO	9	30	6	31	3
17	NEPAL	67	10	1	5	3
18	NIGERIA	26	38	6	11	3
19	PAKISTAN	31	16	5	13	6
20	PERU	13	36	4	15	7
21	ZIMBABWE	15	29	3	11	6
22	SUDAN	39	11	4	16	6
23	TURKEY	27	21	5	13	8
24	UGANDA	53	10	2	9	3
25	VENEZUELA	6	39	17	10	11
26	VIETNAM	29	7	1	18	4
27	YEMEN ARAB					
	REP.	35	6	8	22	3
28		.	.	.	.	.
29	ZAIRE	19	22	6	16	4
30	ZAMBIA	13	35	9	12	5
31	KAMPUCHEA	60	10	18	10	2

Using a Macro with PROC EDITOR: Example 2

The following example shows how you can use the SAS macro language within PROC EDITOR (see Chapter 15, ''SAS Macro Language''). There is a data set that contains the variables AGE, BENEFIT, SEX, and DEDUCT. You want to find all observations in which AGE>=65, BENEFIT=2, and DEDUCT <100, and change the BENEFIT value to 3 and the DEDUCT value to 100. A macro issues a REPLACE command to change the BENEFIT and DEDUCT values, and then issues a FIND command. Notice that the macro does not have to repeat the entire FIND command; instead, it takes advantage of the ''repeat find'' facility, repeating the initial FIND command in line 7.

```
1? proc print data=ssdata;run;
```

OBS	AGE	BENEFIT	SEX	DEDUCT
1	59	2	1	95
2	66	2	1	50
3	72	3	2	100
4	58	1	2	75
5	68	2	1	80
6	48	2	1	95
7	65	2	1	50
8	72	3	2	100
9	58	1	2	75
10	68	2	1	80
11	55	1	1	20

```
2? proc editor data=ssdata;run;
ENTER COMMANDS OR 'HELP;'
NOTE ENHANCEMENTS: LOCATE, SEARCH, FIND.
```

```
3> %macro doit;
4> replace benefit = 3 deduct = 100;
5> find;
6> %mend doit;
7> find 1,last age>= 65 benefit = 2 deduct<100;
FOUND AT OBS = 2

8> %doit;
FOUND AT OBS = 5

9> %doit;
FOUND AT OBS = 7

10> %doit;
FOUND AT OBS = 10

11> %doit;
NOT FOUND. OBS = 11

12> end;
EXIT FROM SAS EDITOR.

13? proc print data = ssdata; run;
```

OBS	AGE	BENEFIT	SEX	DEDUCT
1	59	2	1	95
2	66	3	1	100
3	72	3	2	100
4	58	1	2	75
5	68	3	1	100
6	48	2	1	95
7	65	3	1	100
8	72	3	2	100
9	58	1	2	75
10	68	3	1	100
11	55	1	1	20

734

The FORMAT Procedure

ABSTRACT

The FORMAT procedure is used to define new formats for value labeling or numeric editing. The new formats can later be associated with variables in a DATA step or within the execution of a procedure by using a FORMAT statement or can be used directly in PUT statements. See Chapter 13, "SAS Informats and Formats," for general information on how informats and formats are used in SAS. Also see the FORMAT statement in Chapter 11.

INTRODUCTION

The FORMAT procedure allows you to define formats according to your specifications.

PROC FORMAT produces two kinds of formats:

- Value-labeling formats associate labels with values. The VALUE statement is used to generate these formats. For example, you might store SEX as a numeric code, 1 or 2, but wish to print it according to the specification:

    VALUE SEX 1 = MALE 2 = FEMALE;

    Value-labeling formats can be used for either numeric or character variables.

- Picture formats print numbers according to a pattern. The PICTURE specification controls such features as leading zeros, comma and decimal punctuation, fill characters, prefixes, and the method of representing negative values. For example, you might want to define a format for phone numbers according to the specification:

    PICTURE PHONENUM LOW-HIGH = '000/000-0000';

Background

PROC FORMAT examines your format specification, compiles an executable module to implement the format, and stores the module in a library. Although you may want formats only for the duration of a job or session, you can store formats for reuse if you are using SAS under OS batch or TSO by setting up a partitioned data set (PDS), using PROC FORMAT to define and store the formats in the PDS, and referencing the PDS when you use SAS so that SAS can find the formats. Under CMS you can set up a TXTLIB to store the formats created by PROC FORMAT or you can use the TEXT option to store the formats as individual text files. (You cannot store formats permanently when using SAS under VSE.)

Formats, whether standard SAS formats or those that you create with PROC FORMAT, are used in PUT statements and in various procedures. In procedures, formats associated with variables cause the procedure to print the value of the variable in a certain way, and in some cases to classify values according to formatted values rather than internal values. For example, to have the PRINT procedure print values according to a format, specify the variables followed by the format in a FORMAT statement:

```
PROC PRINT;
  VAR PHONE;
  FORMAT PHONE PHONENUM.;
```

When you use the name of a format, whether it is a standard SAS format or a format you create with PROC FORMAT, you **must** put a period after the name of the format. Formats you create can also have width and decimal specifications like SAS-provided formats (for example, DOLLAR10.2). If your format contains a width and decimal specification, you do not need an additional period after the format name; the decimal point is sufficient, as in SAS-provided formats. In picture formats the decimal specification is ignored.

Be careful not to confuse the function of PROC FORMAT, which is a procedure that you use to create your own formats, with that of a FORMAT statement. A FORMAT statement associates an existing format (whether a SAS standard format or one you create with PROC FORMAT) with a variable or variables. A FORMAT statement can be used in either a DATA or a PROC step. If the FORMAT statement is used in the DATA step, the format is associated permanently with the variable. If it is used in the PROC step, it is used only for that step.

Note: remember that permanently associating a format with a variable is not the same as storing the format permanently. Serious complications occur if a format that has been associated with a variable in a permanent data set is not saved. (Since you cannot store formats when using SAS under VSE, you should avoid associating formats you create with variables that will be stored in permanent data sets if you are using SAS under VSE.) The data set directory marks the variable as having a format, but when the variable is referenced in later jobs, SAS is not able to find that format because it has not been saved. If the system option FMTERR is in effect, SAS issues an error message stating that the format is not found. If the system option NOFMTERR is in effect, SAS processes the variable using a default format; however, you lose the information contained in the format. Be sure to store permanently all formats associated with variables that are in permanent SAS data sets. See the section **Creating Temporary and Permanent Formats** for more information.

Here is an example that uses PROC FORMAT to define picture formats and then uses the formats with a PUT statement and PROC PRINT.

```
PROC FORMAT;
  PICTURE PHONENUM OTHER='000/000-0000';
  PICTURE SSNUM OTHER='999-99-9999';
DATA A;
  INPUT PHONE SS;
  PUT PHONE PHONENUM.;
  FORMAT SS SSNUM.;
  CARDS;
9194678000 333221111
9198344381 555667777
;
PROC PRINT;
  FORMAT PHONE PHONENUM.;
```

The results of the PUT statement are printed on the log:

919/467-8000
919/834-4381

The values of PHONE appear on the log in the pattern specified by PHONENUM. but the format PHONENUM. is not permanently associated with PHONE the way SSNUM. is associated with SS. To associate PHONENUM. with PHONE permanently, the FORMAT statement in the DATA step would be:


```
FORMAT SS SSNUM. PHONE PHONENUM.;
```


The FORMAT statement in the PROC PRINT step causes the procedure to use the format PHONENUM. in printing the values of PHONE.

SSNUM is permanently associated with SS because the format was associated with the variable in the DATA step. The PRINT procedure prints both the SS and PHONE values using the picture formats created for them by PROC FORMAT. The output from PROC PRINT looks like this:

OBS	PHONE	SS
1	919/467-8000	333-22-1111
2	919/834-4381	555-66-7777

Value-labeling formats are especially useful when data are coded into uninformative values on a data set. For example, say you are analyzing the results of a questionnaire. One variable in your data set is PARTY, which represents the political party of the respondent. PARTY'S values are 1 for DEMOCRAT, 2 for REPUBLICAN, 3 for INDEPENDENT, and 4 for OTHER. Every time SAS prints the values of the variable PARTY, you want the name of the party used rather than the corresponding number. So you use PROC FORMAT to give SAS the directions for printing. These SAS statements read the political questionnaire data, define a format called P., associate the P. format with the PARTY variable, and then produce a crosstabulation table of AGE by PARTY:

```
DATA POLIT;
  INPUT NAME $ ID AGE PARTY;
  CARDS;
JOHN 191 18 1
JOYCE 218 19 2
HARRY 923 21 4
JAMES 432 20 3
;
PROC FORMAT;
  VALUE P 1 = DEMOCRAT
          2 = REPUBLICAN
          3 = INDEPENDENT
          4 = OTHER;
PROC PRINT;
  TITLE WITHOUT FORMAT;
PROC PRINT;
  TITLE WITH FORMAT;
  FORMAT PARTY P.;
PROC FREQ;
  TABLES PARTY*AGE;
  FORMAT PARTY P.;
```

For another example of the FORMAT procedure, see Chapter 9, "PROC Step Applications."

SPECIFICATIONS

The FORMAT procedure is controlled by the following statements:

> **PROC FORMAT** *options*;
> **VALUE** *name (options)*
>   *range = label*
>   ...;
> **PICTURE** *name (options)*
>   *range = picture (options)*
>   ...;

Each new VALUE or PICTURE statement defines a format. You can specify as many formats as you want in a PROC FORMAT step, with one format per VALUE or PICTURE statement.

PROC FORMAT Statement

> PROC FORMAT *options*;

The following options may be used in the PROC FORMAT statement:

PRINT   requests a listing of the values and labels for a value-labeling format as the format is being created. This option does not apply to PICTURE formats.

DDNAME = *name*   specifies the DDname of a library in which to store the format. If not given, the formats are stored on LIBRARY, which refers to a temporary data set. If you want to store formats permanently for later use, set up a library and refer to it with this option (see **Creating Temporary and Permanent Formats** below). The DDNAME= option is ignored when using SAS under VSE, since formats cannot be stored permanently under that system.

TEXT   causes PROC FORMAT to write the format in a TEXT file on the user's A disk when using SAS under CMS. The filename is the name specified on the VALUE statement. If a TEXT file with that name already exists, a warning is issued and the file is not replaced. This option is valid only when using SAS under CMS.

VALUE Statement

    VALUE *name (options)*
      range1 = label1
      range2 = label2
      ... ;

These items may be specified in the VALUE statement:

name   names the format being created. (You **must** give a name in the VALUE statement.) The name must be a valid SAS name up to eight characters long, not ending in a number. If the format is for character variables, the first character must be a dollar sign ($), while the remaining seven characters must follow the rules for a valid SAS name. The name may not duplicate a name already used in SAS as the name of a procedure, a SAS-provided format, a function, or, under VSE, the name of any SAS system module; otherwise, a warning message is issued (a fatal error under VSE). Refer to the format later by using the name followed by a decimal point. (A decimal point is not used after the name in the VALUE statement.)

options   are specified inside parentheses after the format name. Omit the parenthetical field if no options are needed. The valid options (MAX=, MIN=, DEFAULT=, and FUZZ=) are described in detail below.

ranges   specifies a range of values, a list of values, or a list of ranges. You **must** specify one or more ranges in the VALUE statement. The syntax is:

value	*(single values)*
value-value	*(a range of values)*
range,range	*(list of ranges or values)*

The values in either character or numeric ranges or value lists should not overlap.

When formatting a number, the format looks for the range containing the number to obtain the appropriate label. For example:

```
VALUE ABC  1=A  2=B  3=C ;
VALUE AGEFMT  0-12=CHILD
              13-19=TEEN
              20-HIGH=ADULT;
VALUE SEXFMT  1=FEMALE
              2=MALE
              0,3-9=MISCODED;
```

The first example uses single values; the second uses ranges; the third uses both single values and ranges.

Formats for numeric variables may include the keywords LOW and HIGH in a range specification. (The LOW keyword does not include missing values.) In the AGEFMT. example above, the range 20–HIGH refers to all values from 20 through the largest value of the variable.

The keyword OTHER may be used on the left side of the equal sign to mean all values not given in any other range or value specification for the format. In the SEXFMT. example above, the specification OTHER=MISCODED can be substituted for 0,3–9=MISCODED to mean that all values other than 1 and 2 are to be printed as the word MISCODED. In that case, the value SEXFMT. in the example above looks like this:

```
VALUE SEXFMT  1=FEMALE
              2=MALE
              OTHER=MISCODED;
```

Character values must be enclosed in single quotes if they include any special characters:

```
VALUE $HOTEL
  S=SHERATON
  'T&C'=TOWN AND COUNTRY;
```

labels The labels that are assigned to the values can contain up to 40 characters. (However, some procedures use only the first 8 or 16 characters of a label.) If any of these special characters [= – ' ; , ( )] appear in the label, the label must be enclosed in single quotes. Here is an example:

```
VALUE INC     1=UNDER $5000
              2='$5000-9999'
              3='$10000-19999'
              4=OVER $20000;
```

Since a dash appears in the second and third labels, they are enclosed in single quotes. It is good policy to enclose all labels in quotes.

If a single quote is actually part of the label, write it as two separate single quotes:

VALUE SECT   1 = 'SMITH''S CLASS'
              2 = 'DOE''S CLASS';

If a VALUE statement includes some, but not all, of a variable's values, the values included in the VALUE statement are printed with that format, while other values are printed with a default format. For example, these statements

```
PROC FORMAT;
  VALUE TEMP 98.6 = NORMAL;
DATA A;
  INPUT T;
  PUT T TEMP6.1;
  CARDS;
98.4
98.6
101.2
```

produce these lines

```
   98.4
NORMAL
  101.2
```

Note: any numeric value using a default format is right-aligned in a field width equal to that given in the PUT statement. If no field width is given, the default width of the format is used. Character values using a default format are left-aligned.

PICTURE Statement

    PICTURE   *name (options)*
               range1 = picture1 (options)
               range2 = picture2 (options)
               ... ;

The elements of the PICTURE statement are listed below.

name   names the new format. The name must be a valid SAS name up to eight characters long, not ending in a number. The name may not duplicate a name already used in SAS; if it does, SAS issues a warning message (under VSE, a fatal error). Refer to the format later with the name followed by a period.

options   can be specified inside parentheses after the format name. If no options are needed, no parenthetical field is used. The valid options are: MAX=, MIN=, DEFAULT=, and FUZZ=. They are described in detail below.

ranges   specifies a range of values, a list of values, or a list of ranges. The syntax is:

            value   (single values)
            value-value   (a range of values)
            range,range   (list of ranges or values)

When formatting a number, the format looks for the range containing the number to obtain the appropriate picture. For example:

```
PICTURE FM LOW -- 0 = '99999-'
               0-HIGH = '99999+';
```

LOW and HIGH are keywords representing the largest negative and positive numbers, respectively. Minus zero (–0) denotes the negative number closest to zero. A special range OTHER can be used to collect numbers not included in any other range. Missing values appear as '.'.

pictures specifies how a number is to be formatted. The picture is a sequence of characters in single quotes. The maximum length for a picture is 24 characters.

Pictures are specified with two types of characters: digit selectors and message characters. Digit selectors are characters that define positions for numeric values. You may use as digit selectors either 0, or the numbers 1 through 9. If the picture is specified with zeros and the number to be formatted contains leading zeros, the leading zeros are not formatted into the field. To print leading zeros, you may use any digit 1 through 9 to define the positions. All digits, even leading zeros, are formatted. Message characters are non-numeric characters that are printed just as they appear in the picture. They are inserted into the picture after the numeric digits are formatted.

For example, this PICTURE statement:

```
PICTURE DAY 01-31='00';
```

causes the value 02 to be printed like this:

```
2
```

This PICTURE statement:

```
PICTURE DAY 01-31='99'
   OTHER='99-ILLEGAL DAY VALUE';
```

prints the values 02 and 67 as:

```
02
67-ILLEGAL DAY VALUE
```

In this PICTURE statement, the characters '99' are digit selectors, and the characters '-ILLEGAL DAY VALUE' are message characters.

options specify fill characters, prefix characters, and multipliers, described below. If no options are needed, no parenthetical field is given.

PICTURE Options

These options can be specified for each picture in a picture format.

FILL=' ' specifies a fill character. This character replaces the leading characters of the picture until a significant digit is encountered. The default is FILL=' ' (blank). Using FILL='*' helps to protect a number from alteration because there are no leading blanks.

PREFIX=' ' is a one- or two-character prefix that is placed in front of the first significant character of the value; the default is no prefix. The prefix occupies positions within the picture, not additional positions. Thus, if the picture is not wide enough to contain both the value and the prefix, the prefix is truncated or omitted. The PREFIX= option is often used for leading dollar signs and minus signs. For example, the picture

>   PICTURE PAY OTHER='00,000,000.00'
>   (FILL='*' PREFIX='$');

prints the value 25500 as

>   ***$25,500.00

MULTIPLIER=n
MULT=n specifies a number by which to multiply a value before it is formatted. The main use of the MULT= option is to allow data values containing decimal points to be edited correctly, since decimal points in picture formats are part of the editing pattern, not part of the data value. If you do not specify a value for MULT=, the procedure uses a default value of 10^n, where n is the number of digits after the first decimal point in the picture. For example, suppose your data contain a value 123.456 and you want to print it using a picture of '999.999'. FORMAT multiplies 123.456 by 10^3 to obtain a value of 123456; it then edits this value into the picture to produce 123.456. You can also specify values for MULT= other than the default to have a value edited in a particular pattern. For example, to have 1600000 print as $1.6M use this PREFIX= and MULTIPLIER= specification:

>   PICTURE MILLION LOW-HIGH='00.0M'
>   (PREFIX='$' MULT=.00001);

NOEDIT forces the format to treat the picture as a value label rather than as a picture specification. This means that numbers are message characters rather than digit selectors; that is, the numbers in the picture are printed as they appear. For example, the statements:

```
PROC FORMAT;
   PICTURE MILES 1–99='000000'
      100–HIGH='>100 MILES' (NOEDIT);
DATA TEMP;
   INPUT NAME $ DISTANCE 3.;
   CARDS;
JOHN 300
MARY 600
DAVID 27
ANN 2
;
PROC PRINT;
   FORMAT DISTANCE MILES.;
```

produce this output:

OBS	NAME	DISTANCE
1	JOHN	>100 MILES
2	MARY	>100 MILES
3	DAVID	27
4	ANN	2

Format Options (for VALUE or PICTURE)

When a format is stored, it is stored with width attribute information that is used to check its use. On rare occasions you may wish to specify the following attributes of the format:

MIN=*n*   specifies the minimum width allowed by the format. If MIN= is not given, the length of the longest picture or value label is the minimum width.

MAX=*n*   specifies the maximum width allowed by the format. This can be larger than the picture or value label, since picture formats can pad with fill characters on the left. The maximum MAX= width allowed is 40. If MAX= is not specified, the default is 40.

DEFAULT=*n*   specifies the default width if the format is used without a width specification. The default value for DEFAULT is the length of the longest picture or value.

FUZZ=*n*   specifies a fuzz factor. If a number does not match a value or fall in a range exactly, but comes within the fuzz value, it is considered a match. For example:

```
PROC FORMAT;
   VALUE ABC (FUZZ=.5) 1=A 2=B 3=C;
```

FUZZ=.5 means that if a variable value falls within .5 of a value specified in the VALUE statement, the corresponding label is used to print the variable value. So using the ABC. format to print a value of 1.2 produces an A; printing a value of 1.7 produces a B; and printing a value of 2.8 produces a C. When the fuzz value is .5 and the fractional part of the value is also .5, the value is rounded up to the next integer. Thus, using the ABC. format above to print a value of 1.5 produces a B.

Only VALUE formats use FUZZ=; PICTURE formats do not.

DETAILS

Character Data Limitations

The VALUE statement of PROC FORMAT only processes character values of 16 characters or less. If character values are longer than 16, the procedure truncates the value and processes the first 16 characters. If more than one character value in a VALUE statement has the same first 16 characters, SAS issues an error message indicating that the value has already been given. Format labels can be up to 40 characters long.

PICTURE Logic

To understand how SAS formats a value using a picture format, look at the PICTURE examples. Here is the logic used by a picture format to format a value:

- Look up a picture according to which range contains the number to be formatted. If no range contains the number, use the OTHER specification. If there is no OTHER specification, use the standard SAS numeric format.
- If the picture has no digit selectors or has the NOEDIT option, then output the label and ignore the rest of the steps.
- Multiply the number by the multiplier.
- Take the absolute value.
- Truncate the value to an integer. If the number is within 10^{-8} of a higher integer, it is rounded up.
- Convert the number to a string of digits, the "source string."
- Point to the digit corresponding to the high-order (left-most) digit selector in the picture. If the number is too large to fit into the picture, the high-order digits are ignored. There is no error condition for this "overflow," although you can use special error ranges to control it.
- Turn the significance switch off.

Now the format starts scanning the picture and source strings.

- If the picture character is a non-numeric (message) character and if the significance switch is off, the fill character is placed in the result. If the significance switch is on, the message character is placed in the result.
- If the picture character is a numeric digit (digit selector), a digit is retrieved from the source string. If the picture character is nonzero or if the source string digit is nonzero, then the significance switch is turned on. If the significance switch is on, the source digit is placed in the result. If the picture character and the source string digit are zero, the fill character is placed in the result.

Now the number is edited. Prefix characters are placed before the first non-fill character in the result. If the format width is larger than the picture length, the result is padded on the left with one fill character and the rest blanks. If the format width is smaller than the picture, the result is truncated on the left.

Creating Temporary and Permanent Formats Under OS Batch

To create temporary formats under OS batch, use a PROC FORMAT statement without a DDNAME= option. For example,

```
PROC FORMAT;
  VALUE GRADE 0–69= F 70–74= D 75–84= C  85–94= B 95–100= A;
```

To store formats permanently under OS batch, create a permanent partitioned data set (PDS) for your format library using JCL. Use SASLIB as the DDname for the partitioned data set. In your PROC FORMAT statement, specify DDNAME= SASLIB.

This example shows a job that creates a format library in OS batch and stores two formats in it:

```
// EXEC SAS
//SASLIB DD DSN= acct.me.store,UNIT= SYSDA,VOL= SER= volume,
// SPACE= (TRK,(4,2,2)),DISP= (NEW,CATLG)
PROC FORMAT DDNAME= SASLIB;
  PICTURE PHONE OTHER= '000/000-0000';
  VALUE P  1= DEMOCRAT
           2= REPUBLICAN
           3= INDEPENDENT
           4= OTHER;
```

To use the stored formats in other jobs, include a DD statement in your JCL referring to the partitioned data set; the DDname of this statement **must** be SASLIB, as in this example:

```
// EXEC SAS
//SASLIB DD DSN= acct.me.store,DISP= SHR
DATA POLIT;
  INPUT NAME $ ID AGE PARTY PHONENUM;
  FORMAT PARTY P. PHONENUM PHONE.;
  CARDS;
JOHN 191 18 1 3142345
JOYCE 218 19 2 9872987
HARRY 923 21 4 2343323
JAMES 432 20 3 2344432
;
PROC PRINT;
```

To store additional formats in an existing PDS, use the DDNAME= SASLIB option in PROC FORMAT as in the example above; the only change is that the SASLIB DD statement now refers to an existing data set into which the formats are written, for example:

```
// EXEC SAS
//SASLIB DD DSN= acct.me.store,DISP= (OLD,KEEP)
PROC FORMAT DDNAME= SASLIB;
  PICTURE STUDNTID OTHER= '000-000-000';
```

Creating Temporary and Permanent Formats Under TSO

Two methods of creating and storing formats with PROC FORMAT are available to TSO users. If the TSO command facility is available at your installation, you may use either method. (If the TSO statement works, the TSO command facility is available. See Chapter 11, "SAS Statements Used Anywhere," for a description of the TSO statement.) If the TSO facility is not available, you may use the only method described below under **TSO command facility not available**.

TSO command facility available   To create temporary formats, simply use a PROC FORMAT statement without the DDNAME= option. You do not need to allocate any files.

You can create permanent formats in two ways.

1. You can allocate a file SASLIB:

        ALLOC FI(SASLIB) DA(data set name)
          SPACE(primary) TRACKS
          VOL(volser) DIR(directory)

with the appropriate information (see your computing center staff for information). Use this PROC FORMAT statement:

    PROC FORMAT DDNAME=SASLIB;

to create formats to be stored permanently. You can create some permanent formats and some temporary formats in the same SAS session by using a PROC FORMAT statement with DDNAME=SASLIB for the permanent formats and a PROC FORMAT statement without that option to create the temporary formats.

2. Another method is to allocate a file LIBRARY as follows:

        ALLOC FI(LIBRARY) DA(data set name)
          SPACE(primary) TRACKS
          VOL(volser) DIR(directory)

with the appropriate information (see your installation staff for information). In this case use a PROC FORMAT statement without the DDNAME= option; however, all formats you create in the SAS session are permanent.

To use the stored formats in another SAS session, allocate the file as either:

    ALLOC FI(SASLIB) DA(data set name) SHR
    ALLOC FI(LIBRARY) DA(data set name) SHR

depending on which file you used when you created them. To use the stored formats in a batch job, use a SASLIB DD statement as described above.

TSO command facility not available   To create temporary formats with PROC FORMAT, first allocate a SASLIB file as follows:

    ALLOC FI(SASLIB) SPACE(primary secondary) TRACKS DIR(directory)

In most cases, a value of 20 for the primary and secondary allocations and 10 for the directory is sufficient. This file is not permanent because it does not contain a data set name.

Use the option DDNAME=SASLIB in your PROC FORMAT statement.

    PROC FORMAT DDNAME=SASLIB;

SAS stores your formats in a temporary file and retrieves them for use in your SAS session.

To create permanent formats, first allocate a file as follows:

```
ALLOC FI(SASLIB) DA(data set name)
   SPACE(primary secondary) TRACKS
   VOL(volser) DIR(directory)
```

Specify the data set name, primary and secondary allocations, volume serial, and directory space as appropriate (see your computing center staff for information). This file is permanent because it contains a data set name.

To store formats, use the DDNAME = SASLIB option in the PROC FORMAT statement:

```
PROC FORMAT DDNAME = SASLIB;
```

To use stored formats in another SAS session, allocate the file SASLIB with the appropriate data set name as follows:

```
ALLOC FI(SASLIB) DA(data set name) SHR
```

You can also use these formats in OS batch jobs by specifying the SASLIB DD statement in your control language as described above.

Creating Temporary and Permanent Formats Under CMS

To create temporary formats for use in the same job simply use a PROC FORMAT statement, for example:

```
PROC FORMAT;
   VALUE GROUP 1-10='1-10' 11-20='11-20';
```

The CMS/SAS interface automatically sets up a temporary format library $SASLIB TXTLIB on your A disk. When SAS terminates, it erases $SASLIB TXTLIB.

You can create permanent formats in two ways.

One way is to use the SASLIB option with the SAS command:

```
SAS (SASLIB filename)
```

as in

```
SAS (SASLIB SAVEFMTS)
```

SAS automatically issues two CMS commands (FILEDEF and GLOBAL) that create the library SAVEFMTS TXTLIB in which to store the formats and tell CMS where it may search for the formats. (The two commands together are equivalent to creating a partitioned data set with a DDname of SASLIB under OS.)

To store formats in the TXTLIB file SAVEFMTS, specify the DDNAME = SASLIB in the PROC FORMAT statement.

```
PROC FORMAT DDNAME = SASLIB;
   VALUE GROUP 1-10='1-10' 11-20='11-20';
```

To use formats stored in a TXTLIB file in later jobs, specify the filename of the TXTLIB file with the SASLIB option on the SAS command:

SAS (SASLIB SAVEFMTS)

SAS/CMS is now able to search SAVEFMTS for formats in your SAS session.

You can also issue the CMS FILEDEF and GLOBAL commands yourself instead of having SAS issue them. See Appendix 1, "CMS Appendix," and the *SAS CMS Companion* for more information.

Another method is to use the TEXT option on the PROC FORMAT statement, as in:

PROC FORMAT TEXT;

In this case, the SAS/CMS interface produces a separate TEXT file for each format. These TEXT files are not automatically erased, and you may add them to a permanent TXTLIB at any time with the CMS TXTLIB command. (You do not have to add them to the TXTLIB in order to use them.) Using the TEXT option may avoid problems arising, for example, from local modifications of TXTLIB.

Creating Temporary Formats Under VSE

To create temporary formats under VSE use a PROC FORMAT statement without a DDNAME= option. For example:

```
PROC FORMAT;
   VALUE AGE  1-19='<20'
              20-39='20-39'
              40-64='40-64'
              65-HIGH='65+';
```

You cannot store formats permanently when using SAS under VSE.

Printing the Contents of Format Libraries

The PRINT option on the PROC FORMAT statement can be used to print the contents of a format as it is being added to the library. However, the FORMAT procedure has no facility for printing formats once the formats have been created. The SAS supplemental procedure FMTLIB can both print and output the contents of a format library. See the *SAS Supplemental Library User's Guide* for documentation.

EXAMPLES

VALUE Examples

The following three format definitions are useful for transforming state codes or abbreviations into the state names. The $ZIPST. format corresponds to the ZIPNAME function; $STATE to STNAME; and STATE to FIPNAME. You can, of course, use a format in a PROC step without accessing a DATA step, whereas you must use a DATA step to use the state functions. In addition, you can use these formats with the PUT function in the DATA step to create variables. For example, in this DATA step:

```
DATA NEW;
  INPUT ZIP $ ABBREV $ CENSUSBU;
  STATE1 = PUT(ZIP,$ZIPST.);
  STATE2 = PUT(ABBREV,$STATE.);
  STATE3 = PUT(CENSUSBU, STATE.);
  CARDS;
27511 NC 37
  ;
```

STATE1, STATE2, and STATE3 all have a value of NORTH CAROLINA. See Chapter 6, "DATA Step Applications," for more information on creating variables with the PUT function. Also see Chapter 9, "PROC Step Applications," for more examples using PROC FORMAT.

Since these formats have potential for wide use, they may be generated and stored by your installation on the SAS load library to be available for general use.

```
PROC FORMAT PRINT;
  *——$ZIPST: CONVERTS CHARACTER ZIP CODES TO STATE NAMES——;
  VALUE $ZIPST
    00600-00999 = PUERTO RICO
    01000-02799 = MASSACHUSETTS
    02800-02999 = RHODE ISLAND
    03000-03899 = NEW HAMPSHIRE
    03900-04999 = MAINE
    05000-05999 = VERMONT
    06000-06999 = CONNECTICUT
    07000-08999 = NEW JERSEY
    09000-14999 = NEW YORK
    15000-19699 = PENNSYLVANIA
    19700-19999 = DELAWARE
    20000-20599 = DISTRICT OF COLUMBIA
    20600-21999 = MARYLAND
    22000-24699 = VIRGINIA
    24700-26899 = WEST VIRGINIA
    27000-28999 = NORTH CAROLINA
    29000-29999 = SOUTH CAROLINA
    30000-31999 = GEORGIA
    32000-33999 = FLORIDA
    35000-36999 = ALABAMA
    37000-38599 = TENNESSEE
    38600-39799 = MISSISSIPPI
    40000-42799 = KENTUCKY
    43000-45899 = OHIO
    46000-47999 = INDIANA
    48000-49999 = MICHIGAN
    50000-52899 = IOWA
    53000-54999 = WISCONSIN
    55000-56799 = MINNESOTA
    57000-57799 = SOUTH DAKOTA
    58000-58899 = NORTH DAKOTA
    59000-59999 = MONTANA
    60000-62999 = ILLINOIS
    63000-65899 = MISSOURI
    66000-67999 = KANSAS
```

68000-69399 = NEBRASKA
70000-71499 = LOUISIANA
71600-72999 = ARKANSAS
73000-74999 = OKLAHOMA
75000-79999 = TEXAS
80000-81699 = COLORADO
82000-83199 = WYOMING
83200-83899 = IDAHO
84000-84799 = UTAH
85000-86599 = ARIZONA
87000-88499 = NEW MEXICO
89000-89899 = NEVADA
90000-96699 = CALIFORNIA
96700-96899 = HAWAII
96900-96999 = GUAM
97000-97999 = OREGON
98000-99499 = WASHINGTON
99500-99999 = ALASKA ;

```
FORMAT: $ZIPST

LOW VALUE          HIGH VALUE          LABEL
----------         ----------          -----

00600              00999               PUERTO RICO
01000              02799               MASSACHUSETTS
02800              02999               RHODE ISLAND
03000              03899               NEW HAMPSHIRE
03900              04999               MAINE
05000              05999               VERMONT
06000              06999               CONNECTICUT
07000              08999               NEW JERSEY
09000              14999               NEW YORK
15000              19699               PENNSYLVANIA
19700              19999               DELAWARE
20000              20599               DISTRICT OF COLUMBIA
20600              21999               MARYLAND
22000              24699               VIRGINIA
24700              26899               WEST VIRGINIA
27000              28999               NORTH CAROLINA
29000              29999               SOUTH CAROLINA
30000              31999               GEORGIA
32000              33999               FLORIDA
35000              36999               ALABAMA
37000              38599               TENNESSEE
38600              39799               MISSISSIPPI
40000              42799               KENTUCKY
43000              45899               OHIO
46000              47999               INDIANA
48000              49999               MICHIGAN
50000              52899               IOWA
53000              54999               WISCONSIN
55000              56799               MINNESOTA
57000              57799               SOUTH DAKOTA
58000              58899               NORTH DAKOTA
59000              59999               MONTANA
60000              62999               ILLINOIS
63000              65899               MISSOURI
66000              67999               KANSAS
68000              69399               NEBRASKA
70000              71499               LOUISIANA
71600              72999               ARKANSAS
73000              74999               OKLAHOMA
75000              79999               TEXAS
80000              81699               COLORADO
82000              83199               WYOMING
83200              83899               IDAHO
84000              84799               UTAH
85000              86599               ARIZONA
87000              88499               NEW MEXICO
89000              89899               NEVADA
90000              96699               CALIFORNIA
96700              96899               HAWAII
96900              96999               GUAM
97000              97999               OREGON
98000              99499               WASHINGTON
99500              99999               ALASKA
```

```
*——$STATE: CONVERTS STATE ABBREV. TO STATE NAMES——;
  VALUE $STATE AL=ALABAMA AR=ARKANSAS  AZ=ARIZONA
CA=CALIFORNIA IL=ILLINOIS WI=WISCONSIN 99=FOREIGN
GA=GEORGIA NJ=NEW JERSEY ID=IDAHO VA=VIRGINIA
SC=SOUTH CAROLINA FL=FLORIDA IN=INDIANA IA=IOWA MO=MISSOURI
MD=MARYLAND DC=DISTRICT OF COLUMBIA MN=MINNESOTA
LA=LOUISIANA NY=NEW YORK  OH=OHIO NB=NEBRASKA
PA=PENNSYLVANIA TX=TEXAS NC=NORTH  CAROLINA OK=OKLAHOMA
WV=WEST VIRGINIA TN=TENNESSEE  DE=DELAWARE KS=KANSAS
KY=KENTUCKY MI=MISSISSIPPI NM=NEW MEXICO ND=NORTH  DAKOTA
MI=MICHIGAN MA=MASSACHUSETTS CO=COLORADO RI=RHODE ISLAND
SD=SOUTH DAKOTA UT=UTAH WA=WASHINGTON;
```

```
FORMAT: $STATE

LOW VALUE       HIGH VALUE        LABEL
----------      ----------        -----
AL              AL                ALABAMA
AR              AR                ARKANSAS
AZ              AZ                ARIZONA
CA              CA                CALIFORNIA
CO              CO                COLORADO
DC              DC                DISTRICT OF COLUMBIA
DE              DE                DELAWARE
FL              FL                FLORIDA
GA              GA                GEORGIA
IA              IA                IOWA
ID              ID                IDAHO
IL              IL                ILLINOIS
IN              IN                INDIANA
KS              KS                KANSAS
KY              KY                KENTUCKY
LA              LA                LOUISIANA
MA              MA                MASSACHUSETTS
MD              MD                MARYLAND
MI              MI                MICHIGAN
MN              MN                MINNESOTA
MO              MO                MISSOURI
MS              MS                MISSISSIPPI
NB              NB                NEBRASKA
NC              NC                NORTH CAROLINA
ND              ND                NORTH DAKOTA
NJ              NJ                NEW JERSEY
NM              NM                NEW MEXICO
NY              NY                NEW YORK
OH              OH                OHIO
OK              OK                OKLAHOMA
PA              PA                PENNSYLVANIA
RI              RI                RHODE ISLAND
SC              SC                SOUTH CAROLINA
SD              SD                SOUTH DAKOTA
TN              TN                TENNESSEE
TX              TX                TEXAS
UT              UT                UTAH
VA              VA                VIRGINIA
WA              WA                WASHINGTON
WI              WI                WISCONSIN
WV              WV                WEST VIRGINIA
99              99                FOREIGN
```

```
*——STATE: OFFICIAL CENSUS BUREAU CODES FOR STATE——;
VALUE STATE
  01=ALABAMA
  02=ALASKA
  04=ARIZONA
  05=ARKANSAS
  06=CALIFORNIA
  08=COLORADO
  09=CONNECTICUT
  10=DELAWARE
  11='D.C.'
  12=FLORIDA
```

```
13 = GEORGIA
15 = HAWAII
16 = IDAHO
17 = ILLINOIS
18 = INDIANA
19 = IOWA
20 = KANSAS
21 = KENTUCKY
22 = LOUISIANA
23 = MAINE
24 = MARYLAND
25 = MASSACHUSETTS
26 = MICHIGAN
27 = MINNESOTA
28 = MISSISSIPPI
29 = MISSOURI
30 = MONTANA
31 = NEBRASKA
32 = NEVADA
33 = NEW HAMPSHIRE
34 = NEW JERSEY
35 = NEW MEXICO
36 = NEW YORK
37 = NORTH CAROLINA
38 = NORTH DAKOTA
39 = OHIO
40 = OKLAHOMA
41 = OREGON
42 = PENNSYLVANIA
44 = RHODE ISLAND
45 = SOUTH CAROLINA
46 = SOUTH DAKOTA
47 = TENNESSEE
48 = TEXAS
49 = UTAH
50 = VERMONT
51 = VIRGINIA
53 = WASHINGTON
54 = WEST VIRGINIA
55 = WISCONSIN
56 = WYOMING;
```

```
FORMAT: STATE

LOW VALUE          HIGH VALUE         LABEL
----------         ----------         -----
         1                  1         ALABAMA
         2                  2         ALASKA
         4                  4         ARIZONA
         5                  5         ARKANSAS
         6                  6         CALIFORNIA
         8                  8         COLORADO
         9                  9         CONNECTICUT
        10                 10         DELAWARE
        11                 11         D.C.
        12                 12         FLORIDA
        13                 13         GEORGIA
        15                 15         HAWAII
        16                 16         IDAHO
        17                 17         ILLINOIS
        18                 18         INDIANA
```

(continued on next page)

(continued from previous page)

```
        19        19      IOWA
        20        20      KANSAS
        21        21      KENTUCKY
        22        22      LOUISIANA
        23        23      MAINE
        24        24      MARYLAND
        25        25      MASSACHUSETTS
        26        26      MICHIGAN
        27        27      MINNESOTA
        28        28      MISSISSIPPI
        29        29      MISSOURI
        30        30      MONTANA
        31        31      NEBRASKA
        32        32      NEVADA
        33        33      NEW HAMPSHIRE
        34        34      NEW JERSEY
        35        35      NEW MEXICO
        36        36      NEW YORK
        37        37      NORTH CAROLINA
        38        38      NORTH DAKOTA
        39        39      OHIO
        40        40      OKLAHOMA
        41        41      OREGON
        42        42      PENNSYLVANIA
        44        44      RHODE ISLAND
        45        45      SOUTH CAROLINA
        46        46      SOUTH DAKOTA
        47        47      TENNESSEE
        48        48      TEXAS
        49        49      UTAH
        50        50      VERMONT
        51        51      VIRGINIA
        53        53      WASHINGTON
        54        54      WEST VIRGINIA
        55        55      WISCONSIN
        56        56      WYOMING

NOTE: THE PROCEDURE FORMAT USED 1.42 SECONDS AND 272K.
```

PICTURE Examples

The ten formats in this example show the various features of picture formats. Note especially the specifications of the PROT format that establish error ranges so that numbers that do not fit the picture are flagged with an error message. The last value in the example shows that most of the formats produce a misleading value for an overflowed field.

```
PROC FORMAT;
  PICTURE ACCT     LOW--0 = '000,009.99)' (PREFIX='(')
                   0-HIGH = '000,009.99 ' ;
  PICTURE PROT     LOW--1E5= '-OVERFLOW'
                   -99999.99--0= '000,009.99' (PREFIX='-' FILL='*')
                   0-999999.99= '000,009.99' (FILL='*')
                   1E6-HIGH='OVERFLOW';
  PICTURE DOL      LOW--0 = '000,009.99' (PREFIX='$-')
                   0-HIGH = '000,009.99' (PREFIX='$');
  PICTURE RSIGN    LOW--0 = '000,009.99-'
                   0-HIGH = '000,009.00+';
  PICTURE CREDIT   LOW--0 = '00,009.99DR'
                   0-HIGH = '00,009.99CR';
  PICTURE EUROPE   LOW--0 = '00.009,00' (PREFIX='-' MULT =100)
                   0-HIGH = '00.009,00' (MULT=100);
  PICTURE BLANK    LOW--0 = '000 009.99' (PREFIX='-')
                   0-HIGH = '000 009.99';
  PICTURE THOUS    0-HIGH = '00,009K' (MULT=.001);
  PICTURE PHONE    LOW-HIGH = '000/000-0000';
  PICTURE SSNUM    LOW-HIGH = '999-99-9999';
PROC PDS DDNAME= LIBRARY;
  *-THIS LISTS THE FORMATS IN THE LIBRARY;
```

```
DSNAME=SYS82201.T162730.RA000.FMTEX.LIBRARY,VOL=SER=(NONE)

MEMBERS

ACCT BLANK CREDIT DOL EUROPE PHONE PROT RSIGN SSNUM THOUS


     150  TRACKS ALLOCATED
       2  TRACKS USED
     148  TRACKS UNUSED
       1  EXTENTS
      20  DIRECTORY BLOCKS ALLOCATED
       2  DIRECTORY BLOCKS USED

   NOTE: THE PROCEDURE PDS USED 0.56 SECONDS AND 272K.
```

```
DATA A;
  INPUT X PHONE SSN;
  ACCT=X;  PROT=X;  DOL=X;  RSIGN=X;  CREDIT=X;  EUROPE=X;
    BLANK=X;  THOU=X;
  FORMAT ACCT ACCT. PROT PROT. DOL DOL. RSIGN RSIGN.
    CREDIT CREDIT. EUROPE EUROPE. BLANK BLANK. THOU THOU.
    PHONE PHONE. SSN SSNUM. X 12.2;
  CARDS;
        12345      9194678000      123456789
            0        4678000        987654321
       -12345            .               .
      -187.65      9194678000      111111111
       187.65            .               .
          .23            .               .
       101.23            .               .
       1.1E6            .               .
PROC PRINT; ID X;
    VAR ACCT PROT DOL RSIGN CREDIT EUROPE BLANK THOU PHONE SSN;
```

```
                                       SAS

          X          ACCT           PROT           DOL          RSIGN         CREDIT

   12345.00      12,345.00     *12,345.00     $12,345.00     12,345.00+     12,345.00CR
       0.00           0.00     ******0.00          $0.00          0.00+          0.00CR
  -12345.00     (12,345.00)    -12,345.00     -12,345.00     12,345.00-     12,345.00DR
     -187.65        (187.65)   ***-187.65       $-187.65        187.65-        187.65DR
      187.65         187.65    ****187.65        $187.65        187.65+        187.65CR
        0.23           0.23    ******0.23          $0.23          0.23+          0.23CR
      101.23         101.23    ****101.23        $101.23        101.23+        101.23CR
  1100000.00     100,000.00     OVERFLOW      100,000.00     100,000.00+        0.00CR

          X         EUROPE          BLANK          THOU          PHONE            SSN

   12345.00      12.345,00      12 345.00           12K     919/467-8000    123-45-6789
       0.00           0,00           0.00            0K         467-8000     987-65-4321
  -12345.00      12.345,00     -12 345.00        -12345             .              .
     -187.65        -187,65        -187.65       -187.65     919/467-8000    111-11-1111
      187.65         187,65         187.65            0K            .              .
        0.23           0,23           0.23            0K            .              .
      101.23         101,23         101.23            0K            .              .
  1100000.00           0,00     100 000.00         1,100K           .              .
```

The OPTIONS
Procedure

ABSTRACT

The OPTIONS procedure lists the current values of all SAS system options. While the OPTIONS statement (described in Chapter 11, "SAS Statements Used Anywhere") sets SAS system options specifications during a SAS job, the OPTIONS procedure simply reports the setting of the SAS system options currently in effect.

INTRODUCTION

The SAS system options are used to control certain SAS data library and SAS data set attributes, SAS output features, the efficiency of program execution, and so on. You usually do not need to specify SAS system options, but can rely on their default values instead. (The default values of SAS system options are set by your installation rather than by SAS.) When you do want to use system options, consult the description of the OPTIONS statement and all SAS system options in Chapter 11, "SAS Statements Used Anywhere."

The listing of SAS system options printed by PROC OPTIONS gives default settings and/or settings you have specified for options in an OPTIONS statement or in the job control language invoking SAS.

SPECIFICATIONS

The only statement used is the PROC statement:

   PROC OPTIONS *options*;

PROC OPTIONS Statement

   PROC OPTIONS *options*;

The following options are available in the PROC OPTIONS statement:

SHORT	requests an abbreviated listing of the system options. If SHORT is not specified, the listing of each option begins on a separate line and includes an explanation.
CMS	lists the SAS system options specific to CMS SAS by using the CMS option.
DLI IMS	lists the SAS system options specific to SAS/IMS-DL/I.

Additional options are defined for use during SAS installation and for use when other SAS products are installed. They are documented in their respective installation instructions and product user's guides.

DETAILS

Printed Output

PROC OPTIONS prints a list headed SYSTEM PARAMETERS AND OPTIONS on the SAS log. The output is in two columns if SHORT is not specified, with option names and values in the left column and explanations in the right column. If SHORT is specified, the option names and their values are listed in paragraph format.

EXAMPLE

This example shows the default output from PROC OPTIONS.

    PROC OPTIONS;

```
2      S A S   L O G   SAS/OS 82.0      VS2/MVS JOB OPTIONSX STEP SAS      PROC EXAMPLE1
6           PROC OPTIONS;


SYSTEM PARAMETERS AND OPTIONS

BAUD=1200              COMMUNICATIONS LINE BIT RATE
BLDLTABLE              USE BLDL TABLE FOR PROGRAM MANAGEMENT?
BLKSIZE=23476          DEFAULT BLKSIZE
BUFNO=2                DEFAULT NUMBER OF BUFFERS
BYERR                  NULL BY LIST/STMT ON _NULL_ INPUT DATA SETS AN ERROR?
NOCAPS                 TRANSLATE QUOTED STRINGS AND TITLES TO UPPER CASE?
CARDS=MAX              CARDS PUNCHED LIMIT
NOCASORT               SYSTEM SORT IS CASORT?
C96                    EITHER C48, C60 OR C96 FOR 48, 60 OR 96 CHARACTER SET
CENTER                 CENTERING?
NOCHARCODE             CHARACTER CODES ?-,?=,?/ FOR _,¬,|
NOCHKPT                CHECKPOINT AT END OF EVERY STEP?
NOCLIST                SAS STATEMENTS FROM TSO COMMAND PROCEDURES?
DATE                   DATE PRINTED IN TITLE?
DEVADDR=(IBM3287A .    PRINTER1) DEVICE ADDRESS, QNAME OR NODE NAME
DEVICE=IBM3279         TERMINAL DEVICE NAME
DISK=DISK              NAME FOR DISK UNIT
DQUOTE                 ALLOW DOUBLE-QUOTED (QUOTATION MARKS:"") LITERALS?
DSNFERR                TREAT DATA SET NOT FOUND AS AN ERROR? NO = SET TO _NULL_
DSRESV                 OS DATA SETS RESERVED OR ENQUEUED?
NODUMP                 SAS ERROR HANDLER INVOKED?
NODYNALLOC             SORT UTILITY TO DYNAMICALLY ALLOCATE SORT WORK AREAS?
NOERRORABEND           ABEND ON ERROR CONDITIONS?
ERRORS=20              MAXIMUM NUMBER OF OBSERVATIONS WITH ERROR MESSAGES
NOFILSZ                SORT UTILITY SUPPORT FILSZ PARAMETER?
FMTERR                 TREAT MISSING FORMAT OR INFORMAT AS AN ERROR?
FIRSTOBS=1             DEFAULT FIRST OBSERVATION TO BE PROCESSED
FS                     PROCEDURES TO OPERATE IN FULL SCREEN MODE?
FSP                    SAS/FSP ENABLED?
GCLASS='G'             SAS/GRAPH IBM3287 SYSOUT CLASS
GDEST='LOCAL'          SAS/GRAPH IBM3287 SYSOUT DESTINATION
GEN=5                  DEFAULT NUMBER OF GENERATIONS OF HISTORY KEPT
GFORMS=''              SAS/GRAPH IBM3287 SYSOUT FORMS CODE
GRAPHICS               SAS/GRAPH SUPERVISOR REQUIRED?
GWRITER='SASWTR'       SAS/GRAPH IBM3287 SYSOUT WRITER NAME
IMS                    SAS/IMS-DL/I ENABLED?
INCLUDE                PROCESS %INCLUDE STATEMENT(S)?
INITSTMT=''            INITIAL SAS STATEMENT(S) EXECUTED BEFORE SYSIN
INVALIDDATA=.          MISSING VALUE FOR INVALID DATA
LABEL                  PRINT VARIABLE LABELS?
_LAST_=_NULL_          LAST DATA SET CREATED
LEAVE=0                UNALLOCATED MEMORY PARAMETER
LOG=FT11F001           DDNAME FOR LOG
LOWERCASE              LOWER CASE LETTERS ON PRINTER?
LS=132                 LINE SIZE FOR PRINT
MACRO                  PERFORM MACRO PROCESSING?
NOMACROGEN             LIST MACRO TEXT GENERATED?
NOMCOMPILE             MACRO COMPILER LOADED BY DEFAULT?
MERROR                 UNDEFINED MACROS COSIDERED AN ERROR?
MISSING='.'            PRINTED SYSTEM MISSING VALUE
MLEAVE=4096            UNALLOCATED MACRO MEMORY PARAMETER?
NOMLOGIC               MACRO LOGIC TRACE OPTION?
```

```
3      S A S   L O G    SAS/OS 82.0      VS2/MVS JOB OPTIONSX STEP SAS      PROC EXAMPLE1

MODECHARS='?>*'         PROMPT MODE CHARACTERS
MSIZE=12288            AMOUNT OF MEMORY RESERVED FOR MACRO FACILITY
MSYMSIZE=1024          INITIAL MACRO SYMBOL TABLE SIZE
MWORK=2048             MACRO WORK AREA SIZE
NDSVOLS=               VOL SER UPON WHICH NO SAS DATA LIBRARY PROCESSING IS TO OCCUR (_NULL_ IS ASSUMED).
NONEWS                 CURRENT NEWS PRINTED ON LOG?
NOTES                  SAS NOTES ARE TO BE PRINTED.
NUMBER                 PAGES NUMBERED?
OBS=MAX                DEFAULT LAST OBSERVATION TO BE PROCESSED
OFFLINE=0.0040         COST OF OFFLINE DISK STORAGE PER TRACK PER DAY
ONLINE=0.0120          COST OF ONLINE DISK STORAGE PER TRACK PER DAY
OPLIST                 LIST EXEC OPTIONS ON LOG?
OVP                    NOOVP IF NO OVERPRINTING ALLOWED, OVP OTHERWISE
PAGES=MAX              PAGES PRINTED LIMIT
PARM=''                PARM FOR EXTERNAL PROGRAMS
PARMCARDS=FT15F001     DDNAME FOR PARMCARDS
PROCSIZE=16776192      MAXIMUM PROCEDURE MEMORY ALLOCATION
PROMPTCHARS='000A000D01000100'X  TERMINAL PROMPT CHARACTERS
PS=60                  PAGE SIZE FOR PRINT
REPLACE                ALLOW REPLACE OF PERMANENTLY ALLOCATED SAS DATA SETS?
S=0                    SOURCE STATEMENT LENGTH
S2=S                   %INCLUDE STATEMENT LENGTH
S370                   IS MACHINE A SYSTEM 370, 303X, 43XX, OR 308X?
SASHELP=SASHELP        DDNAME OF NEWS/HELP STATEMENT LIBRARY
SASNEWS=SASNEWSB       MEMBER OF HELP LIBRARY TO PRINT WHEN NEWS OPTION SPECIFIED
SEQ=8                  NUMBER OF NUMERIC DIGITS IN SEQUENCE NUMBERS
SERROR                 ARE UNDEFINED SYMBOLIC REFERENCES AN ERROR?
SKIP=0                 NUMBER OF LINES TO SKIP BEFORE TITLE
NOSNP                  SNAP MACROS ENABLED?
NOSNPPROG              SNAP PROGRAM DATA SET?
SORT=1                 MINIMUM SIZE OF SORT WORK AREAS IN CYLINDERS
SORTDEV=DISK           DEVICE NAME USED TO DYNAMICALLY ALLOCATE SORT WORK AREAS
SORTLIB='SYS1.SORTLIB'
                       SORT LIBRARY DSNAME
NOSORTLIST             PASS LIST OPTION TO SORT?
NOSORTMSG              PASS MSG OPTION TO SYSTEM SORT UTILITY?
SORTMSG=SYSOUT         DDNAME OF SORT UTILITY MESSAGE FILE
SORTPGM='SORT'         ENTRY POINT NAME OF SYSTEM SORT
SORTSIZE=MAX           SIZE PARAMETER FOR THE SYSTEM SORT
SORTWKDD='SASS'        PREFIX OF DYNAMICALLY ALLOCATED SORT WORK AREA DDNAMES
SORTWKNO=3             DEFAULT NUMBER OF SORT WORK AREAS TO ALLOCATE
SOURCE                 LIST SAS SOURCE STATEMENTS?
SOURCE2                LIST INCLUDED SAS SOURCE STATEMENTS?
NOSPOOL                SPOOL TERMINAL INPUT?
STIMER                 SAS ALLOWED TO USE SCP TASK TIMING FACILITIES?
SYSIN=SYSIN            DDNAME FOR SYSIN
SYSINFL               READ STATEMENTS FROM SYSIN FILE?
NOSYMBOLGEN            PRINT SYMBOLIC REPLACEMENT TEXT?
NOSYNCSORT            SYSTEM SORT IS SYNCSORT?
SYSPARM=''            VALUE TO BE RETURNED BY SYSPARM( ) FUNCTION
TAPE=TAPE             TAPE UNIT NAME
TAPECLOSE=DISP        CLOSE DISPOSITION(VOLUME POSITIONING) FOR TAPE DATA LIBRARIES
TIME=MAX              TIME LIMIT IN SECONDS
TLS=0                 LINE SIZE FOR TERMINAL
TRANTAB=GTABVTAM      TERMINAL TRANSLATE TABLE
UNITS=11 12 13 14 15 16 17 18 19 20   SAS DD ASSIGNMENTS
USER=WORK             DDNAME FOR USER
USERPARM=''           PARM TEXT AVAILABLE TO USER EXITS
```

```
4      S A S   L O G    SAS/OS 82.0      VS2/MVS JOB OPTIONSX STEP SAS      PROC EXAMPLE1

VNFERR                TREAT VARIABLE NOT FOUND ON _NULL_ DATA SET AS ERROR?
WORK=WORK             DDNAME FOR WORK
WORKINIT              INITIALIZE WORK FILE?
```

DEVICE TYPE	2301	2302	2303	2305-1	2305-2	2311	2314
BLKSIZE	4096	4984	4892	14136	14660	3625	7294
FILEBLKSIZE	4080	4960	4880	6800	7200	3600	3520

DEVICE TYPE	2321	3330	3330-1	3340	3350	3375	3380
BLKSIZE	2000	13030	13030	8368	19069	17600	23476
FILEBLKSIZE	2000	6400	6400	4080	6160	6800	9040

DEVICE TYPE	2400	3400	SYSOUT	CMS	OTHER
BLKSIZE	20480	32760	0	24548	
FILEBLKSIZE	6400	8000	132	0	

```
NOTE: THE PROCEDURE OPTIONS USED 0.48 SECONDS AND 284K.
NOTE: SAS USED 284K MEMORY.

NOTE: SAS INSTITUTE INC.
      SAS CIRCLE
      PO BOX 8000
      CARY, N.C. 27511-8000
```

The PRINTTO Procedure

ABSTRACT

PROC PRINTTO allows you to define the destination of SAS procedure output. The procedure cannot be used under VSE.

INTRODUCTION

Refer to Chapter 16, "SAS Log and Procedure Output," for a complete discussion of SAS procedure output, and to the various system appendices for information on output specific to different operating systems.

Normally, SAS procedure output is routed to the *standard SAS print file*, which is the file referenced by the DDname FT*nn*F001, where *nn* is the second number of the SAS system option UNITS=. (See Chapter 11, "SAS Statements Used Anywhere," for a description of UNIT= and all system options.) The standard print file is usually a printer under OS batch, your terminal under interactive systems, and a disk file under non-interactive CMS. At most installations you do not have to use job control statements or commands defining the standard SAS print file, because the installation has defined a catalog procedure (under OS), a CLIST (under TSO), or an EXEC (under CMS) that automatically issues the necessary statements or commands.

With PROC PRINTTO you can direct output anywhere you want it to go, as well as:

- write SAS output on tape for COM (computer output to microfiche)
- selectively suppress SAS output by routing output to a DUMMY file
- print several copies of SAS output
- use SAS output as input data in the same job using SAS programming statements.

SPECIFICATIONS

The PROC PRINTTO statement is the only statement used.

   PROC PRINTTO *options*;

PROC PRINTTO Statement

   PROC PRINTTO *options*;

The options below may appear in the PROC PRINTTO statement.

UNIT=*nn*   defines the unit number of the FORTRAN-style DDname that references the output file in the job control accompanying your job or session. For example, UNIT=20 specifies that the output is written to the file with the DDname FT20F001. The UNIT= option must appear when procedure output is to be sent to a file other than the standard SAS print file, or when it is to be suppressed.

You should not use any unit number that is also defined in the SAS system option UNITS=, unless you know that it is not being used by SAS already, or will not be used by a SAS procedure. Normally, SAS and current SAS procedures use only the first five unit numbers defined by UNITS= (usually 11, 12, 13, 14, and 15).

To begin sending procedure output back to the standard SAS print file after a different output file has been defined, use a PROC PRINTTO statement without the UNIT= option.

NEW   tells SAS that this is the first execution of PROC PRINTTO with a given UNIT number in this job. For example, say that output is currently routed to the printer. To start routing output to FT18F001, use the statement:

PROC PRINTTO UNIT=18 NEW;

If the statement:

PROC PRINTTO;

appears later in the job, output is routed to the printer again. Then, to send more output to FT18F001, use the statement:

PROC PRINTTO UNIT=18;

Subsequent output is written in the file after the earlier output.

If you want subsequent output to be written **over** (replace) earlier output, repeat the NEW specification with the PROC PRINTTO statement when you redefine the unit as the output destination.

DETAILS

Output

PRINTTO does not produce an output data set or printed output.

Usage Notes

- If you are not familiar with the job control statements or commands needed to define output files, consult the appropriate documentation about your operating system. Under CMS, also refer to the *SAS CMS Companion*.

- PRINTTO is useful when you want to route output from different steps of a SAS job to different files. If the NUMBER system option is in effect the output from an entire job is page numbered in one sequence; that is, SAS does not set the page number back to 1 when output is routed to a new file.

- DCB attributes for output files can be defined in the job control, or the default values can be used. The default values are RECFM=VBA, LRECL=137, and BLKSIZE=6391 under OS and TSO, BLKSIZE=141 under CMS. If you specify RECFM attributes on the DD statement, an A must be included: for example, RECFM=VBA or RECFM=FBA. This is because the files that are created contain carriage control characters.

EXAMPLES

Writing FREQ Output to Tape: Example 1

In this example, the DDname FT20F001 references a tape file. The first PRINTTO statement changes the output unit from the standard SAS print file (in this case, the printer) to the tape file; output from PROC FREQ is routed to the tape file. The second PRINTTO statement causes output for PROC CORR to be sent to the standard SAS print file again. Notice that the page number on the PROC CORR output is 121, not 1. This is because only one sequence of page numbers is used by SAS in the job, beginning with the PROC FREQ output.

```
DATA NUMBERS;
  INPUT X Y Z;
  CARDS;
14.2 25.2  96.8
10.8 51.6  96.8
 9.5 34.2 138.2
 8.8 27.6  83.2
11.5 49.4 287.0
 6.3 42.0 170.7
 4.2 16.8 129.5
 6.0 24.9 157.0
10.2 39.6 187.9
11.7 31.1 140.5
 7.2 25.5 128.0
 5.5 19.4  39.6
 9.9 21.8 211.3
 7.4 26.5 123.2
 2.3 10.6  41.2
 6.6 22.0 100.7
10.1 19.1  81.1
15.5 30.9 142.9
 2.4 13.5  38.7
 8.0 34.8 292.1
PROC PRINTTO NEW UNIT=20;
PROC FREQ;
  TABLES X*Y*Z;
PROC PRINTTO;
PROC CORR;
```

121

VARIABLE	N	MEAN	STD DEV	SUM	MINIMUM	MAXIMUM
X	20	8.40500000	3.51934130	168.10000000	2.30000000	15.50000000
Y	20	28.32500000	11.09347248	566.50000000	10.60000000	51.60000000
Z	20	134.32000000	70.83407298	2686.40000000	38.70000000	292.10000000

CORRELATION COEFFICIENTS / PROB > |R| UNDER HO:RHO=0 / N = 20

	X	Y	Z
X	1.00000 0.0000	0.53435 0.0152	0.35346 0.1263
Y	0.53435 0.0152	1.00000 0.0000	0.59041 0.0061
Z	0.35346 0.1263	0.59041 0.0061	1.00000 0.0000

Printing Several Copies of Procedure Output: Example 2

This example prints four copies of output from PROCs FREQ and MEANS. The output is written to a disk file, referenced by the DDname FT22F001, which is then read back in and printed four times by using a macro called PR.

```
DATA RATES;
  INPUT RATE1-RATE3;
  CARDS;
16 27 27
18 20 25
15 15 31
15 32 32
12 15 16
20 23 23
24 24 25
21 25 23
27 45 24
12 13 15
22 32 31
31 32 33
29 24 26
34 32 28
26 25 23
53 48 75
PROC PRINTTO UNIT=22 NEW;
PROC FREQ;
PROC MEANS;
PROC PRINTTO;
%MACRO PR;
```

```
      DATA __NULL__;
        FILE PRINT NOPRINT;
        INFILE FT22F001;
        INPUT;
        PUT __INFILE__;
      %MEND PR;
      %PR
      %PR
      %PR
      %PR
```

1

RATE1	FREQUENCY	CUM FREQ	PERCENT	CUM PERCENT
12	2	2	12.500	12.500
15	2	4	12.500	25.000
16	1	5	6.250	31.250
18	1	6	6.250	37.500
20	1	7	6.250	43.750
21	1	8	6.250	50.000
22	1	9	6.250	56.250
24	1	10	6.250	62.500
26	1	11	6.250	68.750
27	1	12	6.250	75.000
29	1	13	6.250	81.250
31	1	14	6.250	87.500
34	1	15	6.250	93.750
53	1	16	6.250	100.000

RATE2	FREQUENCY	CUM FREQ	PERCENT	CUM PERCENT
13	1	1	6.250	6.250
15	2	3	12.500	18.750
20	1	4	6.250	25.000
23	1	5	6.250	31.250
24	2	7	12.500	43.750
25	2	9	12.500	56.250
27	1	10	6.250	62.500
32	4	14	25.000	87.500
45	1	15	6.250	93.750
48	1	16	6.250	100.000

RATE3	FREQUENCY	CUM FREQ	PERCENT	CUM PERCENT
15	1	1	6.250	6.250
16	1	2	6.250	12.500
23	3	5	18.750	31.250
24	1	6	6.250	37.500
25	2	8	12.500	50.000
26	1	9	6.250	56.250
27	1	10	6.250	62.500
28	1	11	6.250	68.750
31	2	13	12.500	81.250
32	1	14	6.250	87.500
33	1	15	6.250	93.750
75	1	16	6.250	100.000

2

VARIABLE	N	MEAN	STANDARD DEVIATION	MINIMUM VALUE	MAXIMUM VALUE	STD ERROR OF MEAN	SUM	VARIANCE	C.V.
RATE1	16	23.43750000	10.33420695	12.00000000	53.00000000	2.58355174	375.0000000	106.7958333	44.093
RATE2	16	27.00000000	9.79795897	13.00000000	48.00000000	2.44948974	432.0000000	96.0000000	36.289
RATE3	16	28.56250000	13.39138405	15.00000000	75.00000000	3.34784601	457.0000000	179.3291667	46.884

1

RATE1	FREQUENCY	CUM FREQ	PERCENT	CUM PERCENT
12	2	2	12.500	12.500
15	2	4	12.500	25.000
16	1	5	6.250	31.250
18	1	6	6.250	37.500
20	1	7	6.250	43.750
21	1	8	6.250	50.000
22	1	9	6.250	56.250
24	1	10	6.250	62.500
26	1	11	6.250	68.750
27	1	12	6.250	75.000
29	1	13	6.250	81.250
31	1	14	6.250	87.500
34	1	15	6.250	93.750
53	1	16	6.250	100.000

RATE2	FREQUENCY	CUM FREQ	PERCENT	CUM PERCENT
13	1	1	6.250	6.250
15	2	3	12.500	18.750
20	1	4	6.250	25.000
23	1	5	6.250	31.250
24	2	7	12.500	43.750
25	2	9	12.500	56.250
27	1	10	6.250	62.500
32	4	14	25.000	87.500
45	1	15	6.250	93.750
48	1	16	6.250	100.000

RATE3	FREQUENCY	CUM FREQ	PERCENT	CUM PERCENT
15	1	1	6.250	6.250
16	1	2	6.250	12.500
23	3	5	18.750	31.250
24	1	6	6.250	37.500
25	2	8	12.500	50.000
26	1	9	6.250	56.250
27	1	10	6.250	62.500
28	1	11	6.250	68.750
31	2	13	12.500	81.250
32	1	14	6.250	87.500
33	1	15	6.250	93.750
75	1	16	6.250	100.000

2

VARIABLE	N	MEAN	STANDARD DEVIATION	MINIMUM VALUE	MAXIMUM VALUE	STD ERROR OF MEAN	SUM	VARIANCE	C.V.
RATE1	16	23.43750000	10.33420695	12.00000000	53.00000000	2.58355174	375.0000000	106.7958333	44.093
RATE2	16	27.00000000	9.79795897	13.00000000	48.00000000	2.44948974	432.0000000	96.0000000	36.289
RATE3	16	28.56250000	13.39138405	15.00000000	75.00000000	3.34784601	457.0000000	179.3291667	46.884

1

RATE1	FREQUENCY	CUM FREQ	PERCENT	CUM PERCENT
12	2	2	12.500	12.500
15	2	4	12.500	25.000
16	1	5	6.250	31.250
18	1	6	6.250	37.500
20	1	7	6.250	43.750
21	1	8	6.250	50.000
22	1	9	6.250	56.250
24	1	10	6.250	62.500
26	1	11	6.250	68.750
27	1	12	6.250	75.000
29	1	13	6.250	81.250
31	1	14	6.250	87.500
34	1	15	6.250	93.750
53	1	16	6.250	100.000

(continued on next page)

(continued from previous page)

RATE2	FREQUENCY	CUM FREQ	PERCENT	CUM PERCENT
13	1	1	6.250	6.250
15	2	3	12.500	18.750
20	1	4	6.250	25.000
23	1	5	6.250	31.250
24	2	7	12.500	43.750
25	2	9	12.500	56.250
27	1	10	6.250	62.500
32	4	14	25.000	87.500
45	1	15	6.250	93.750
48	1	16	6.250	100.000

RATE3	FREQUENCY	CUM FREQ	PERCENT	CUM PERCENT
15	1	1	6.250	6.250
16	1	2	6.250	12.500
23	3	5	18.750	31.250
24	1	6	6.250	37.500
25	2	8	12.500	50.000
26	1	9	6.250	56.250
27	1	10	6.250	62.500
28	1	11	6.250	68.750
31	2	13	12.500	81.250
32	1	14	6.250	87.500
33	1	15	6.250	93.750
75	1	16	6.250	100.000

2

VARIABLE	N	MEAN	STANDARD DEVIATION	MINIMUM VALUE	MAXIMUM VALUE	STD ERROR OF MEAN	SUM	VARIANCE	C.V.
RATE1	16	23.43750000	10.33420695	12.00000000	53.00000000	2.58355174	375.0000000	106.7958333	44.093
RATE2	16	27.00000000	9.79795897	13.00000000	48.00000000	2.44948974	432.0000000	96.0000000	36.289
RATE3	16	28.56250000	13.39138405	15.00000000	75.00000000	3.34784601	457.0000000	179.3291667	46.884

1

RATE1	FREQUENCY	CUM FREQ	PERCENT	CUM PERCENT
12	2	2	12.500	12.500
15	2	4	12.500	25.000
16	1	5	6.250	31.250
18	1	6	6.250	37.500
20	1	7	6.250	43.750
21	1	8	6.250	50.000
22	1	9	6.250	56.250
24	1	10	6.250	62.500
26	1	11	6.250	68.750
27	1	12	6.250	75.000
29	1	13	6.250	81.250
31	1	14	6.250	87.500
34	1	15	6.250	93.750
53	1	16	6.250	100.000

RATE2	FREQUENCY	CUM FREQ	PERCENT	CUM PERCENT
13	1	1	6.250	6.250
15	2	3	12.500	18.750
20	1	4	6.250	25.000
23	1	5	6.250	31.250
24	2	7	12.500	43.750
25	2	9	12.500	56.250
27	1	10	6.250	62.500
32	4	14	25.000	87.500
45	1	15	6.250	93.750
48	1	16	6.250	100.000

RATE3	FREQUENCY	CUM FREQ	PERCENT	CUM PERCENT
15	1	1	6.250	6.250
16	1	2	6.250	12.500
23	3	5	18.750	31.250
24	1	6	6.250	37.500
25	2	8	12.500	50.000
26	1	9	6.250	56.250
27	1	10	6.250	62.500
28	1	11	6.250	68.750
31	2	13	12.500	81.250
32	1	14	6.250	87.500
33	1	15	6.250	93.750
75	1	16	6.250	100.000

VARIABLE	N	MEAN	STANDARD DEVIATION	MINIMUM VALUE	MAXIMUM VALUE	STD ERROR OF MEAN	SUM	VARIANCE	C.V.
RATE1	16	23.43750000	10.33420695	12.00000000	53.00000000	2.58355174	375.0000000	106.7958333	44.093
RATE2	16	27.00000000	9.79795897	13.00000000	48.00000000	2.44948974	432.0000000	96.0000000	36.289
RATE3	16	28.56250000	13.39138405	15.00000000	75.00000000	3.34784601	457.0000000	179.3291667	46.884

Putting Statistics From GLM into a SAS Data Set: Example 3

In this example, GLM output is written to a temporary disk file with the DDname FT20F001. The output is then read back in and each line printed; this output looks the same as if the PROC PRINTTO statement had not appeared. Next, the temporary file is read again, and this time, error mean square values are read and put into a SAS data set. PROC PRINT is used to print the new data set, and PROC MEANS is used to find the mean of the ERRORMS values.

```
DATA EXAMPLE;
  INPUT Y1-Y3 X1-X3;
  CARDS;
  57.2  96.0 83.0  50.0 22.0 81.9
  22.5   0.0  0.0  55.0    0 63.6
  15.2  62.0 16.0  62.0 67.0 29.8
  17.8  17.0  0.0   0.0  0.0 55.3
   3.6 100.0 17.0  17.0 28.0 78.0
 188.0  17.0  0.0   0.0  0.0 62.0
  46.9  17.0  0.0 100.0  0.0 12.0
  63.8  33.0  0.0  84.0  0.0 18.3
   2.5 100.0 17.0  82.8 67.0  4.6
 250.0   0.0  0.0  12.0  0.0  8.8
 250.0  17.0  0.0   0.0  0.0 21.3
  67.4  78.0  0.0  33.0 12.0 16.7
  49.3  23.0 48.0   0.0 54.0 33.5
 155.0   0.0 12.3  83.0  0.0 22.8
 250.0   2.0  0.0   0.0  0.0  9.5
 250.0  65.0 99.8  32.6  0.0 19.1
 192.0   0.7 16.0  77.0 22.0 12.8
 250.0   4.0  0.0   0.0 11.0 19.3
 250.0  33.0 57.4  23.5 11.0 18.0
 250.0  61.0 17.0   0.7  0.0  1.9
 250.0  17.0  9.0  59.0  6.0  4.9
 250.0  44.0  0.0  29.5 11.0  6.0
 250.0   0.0 24.0   0.4  0.0 13.0
 123.0  19.0  0.0  33.0 33.0  5.0
 250.0  33.0 17.0   0.8  0.0  2.0
 350.0  31.0 17.0 100.0 54.0  9.8
 250.0  17.0 90.0   4.9  0.0 17.0
 540.0  99.0 78.0  46.2  0.0 21.0
 250.0  17.0 55.0   5.2 67.3 54.0
 250.0   0.0 89.0   0.0  0.0 12.0
PROC PRINTTO UNIT=20 NEW;
PROC GLM;
  MODEL Y1-Y3=X1-X3;
```

```
PROC PRINTTO;
DATA EMS;
   FILE PRINT NOPRINT;
   INFILE FT20F001;
   INPUT @2 NAME $ @;
   PUT __INFILE__;
   IF NAME='ERROR' THEN DO;
      INPUT @2 NAME $12. DUM1 DUM2 ERRORMS;
      KEEP ERRORMS;
      OUTPUT;
   END;
PROC PRINT;
PROC MEANS;
```

1

GENERAL LINEAR MODELS PROCEDURE

DEPENDENT VARIABLE: Y1

SOURCE	DF	SUM OF SQUARES	MEAN SQUARE	F VALUE	PR > F	R-SQUARE	C.V.
MODEL	3	126089.40702688	42029.80234229	3.39	0.0328	0.281363	61.8967
ERROR	26	322047.95163978	12386.45967845			ROOT MSE	Y1 MEAN
CORRECTED TOTAL	29	448137.35866667				111.29447281	179.80666667

SOURCE	DF	TYPE I SS	F VALUE	PR > F	DF	TYPE III SS	F VALUE	PR > F
X1	1	21242.08290601	1.71	0.2018	1	21302.15024071	1.72	0.2012
X2	1	25738.72420078	2.08	0.1614	1	12090.33501164	0.98	0.3323
X3	1	79108.59992010	6.39	0.0179	1	79108.59992010	6.39	0.0179

PARAMETER	ESTIMATE	T FOR H0: PARAMETER=0	PR > |T|	STD ERROR OF ESTIMATE
INTERCEPT	278.83736593	7.32	0.0001	38.11127089
X1	-0.82798292	-1.31	0.2012	0.63136900
X2	-0.92577857	-0.99	0.3323	0.93704738
X3	-2.34245584	-2.53	0.0179	0.92690059

2

GENERAL LINEAR MODELS PROCEDURE

DEPENDENT VARIABLE: Y2

SOURCE	DF	SUM OF SQUARES	MEAN SQUARE	F VALUE	PR > F	R-SQUARE	C.V.
MODEL	3	4786.31777135	1595.43925712	1.50	0.2384	0.147385	97.6369
ERROR	26	27688.59589532	1064.94599597			ROOT MSE	Y2 MEAN
CORRECTED TOTAL	29	32474.91366667				32.63351032	33.42333333

SOURCE	DF	TYPE I SS	F VALUE	PR > F	DF	TYPE III SS	F VALUE	PR > F
X1	1	1171.18658150	1.10	0.3040	1	719.49088009	0.68	0.4186
X2	1	2296.77406784	2.16	0.1539	1	1681.60067002	1.58	0.2201
X3	1	1318.35712201	1.24	0.2760	1	1318.35712201	1.24	0.2760

PARAMETER	ESTIMATE	T FOR H0: PARAMETER=0	PR > |T|	STD ERROR OF ESTIMATE
INTERCEPT	15.64104937	1.40	0.1734	11.17489953
X1	0.15216764	0.82	0.4186	0.18512857
X2	0.34526248	1.26	0.2201	0.27475889
X3	0.30239604	1.11	0.2760	0.27178367

3

GENERAL LINEAR MODELS PROCEDURE

DEPENDENT VARIABLE: Y3

SOURCE	DF	SUM OF SQUARES	MEAN SQUARE	F VALUE	PR > F	R-SQUARE	C.V.
MODEL	3	1239.83264718	413.27754906	0.36	0.7813	0.040043	133.0275
ERROR	26	29723.04901948	1143.19419306			ROOT MSE	Y3 MEAN
CORRECTED TOTAL	29	30962.88166667				33.81115486	25.41666667

SOURCE	DF	TYPE I SS	F VALUE	PR > F	DF	TYPE III SS	F VALUE	PR > F
X1	1	707.99336799	0.62	0.4384	1	680.41593391	0.60	0.4474
X2	1	214.66351794	0.19	0.6683	1	129.70942315	0.11	0.7389
X3	1	317.17576125	0.28	0.6028	1	317.17576125	0.28	0.6028

PARAMETER	ESTIMATE	T FOR H0: PARAMETER=0	PR > |T|	STD ERROR OF ESTIMATE
INTERCEPT	25.19209083	2.18	0.0388	11.57816781
X1	-0.14797791	-0.77	0.4474	0.19180930
X2	0.09589009	0.34	0.7389	0.28467410
X3	0.14832336	0.53	0.6028	0.28159152

4

OBS	ERRORMS
1	12386.5
2	1064.9
3	1143.2

5

VARIABLE	N	MEAN	STANDARD DEVIATION	MINIMUM VALUE	MAXIMUM VALUE	STD ERROR OF MEAN	SUM	VARIANCE	C.V.
ERRORMS	3	4864.866622	6514.008157	1064.945996	12386.45968	3760.864363	14594.59987	42432302.27	133.899

The SORT Procedure

ABSTRACT

The SORT procedure sorts observations in a SAS data set by one or more variables, storing the resulting sorted observations in a new SAS data set, or replacing the original.

INTRODUCTION

See Chapter 11, "SAS Statements Used Anywhere," for complete descriptions of SAS system options mentioned in this chapter.

SORT is used most often when you want to sort a data set so that other SAS procedures can process it in subsets using BY statements. Data sets must also be sorted before they can be match-merged or updated.

PROC SORT calls a system sort utility to sort data sets. There are many sort utilities provided by different vendors. PROC SORT operates slightly differently, depending on the operating system and the sort being used. For many PROC SORT applications the sort utility used makes no difference. However, if you need to know more about the sort utility or utilities at your installation, or where to find documentation on the sort(s), check with your installation's technical staff.

SORT rearranges the data set's observations according to the values of the variables in the BY statement, which **must** accompany the PROC SORT statement (see below). Suppose you want to sort a data set by an ID value that occurs in every observation. SORT rearranges the data set so that the observation with the lowest ID value is first, the observation with the second lowest ID value is second, and so on. Optionally, SORT arranges observations in descending order.

When you want to sort by two or more variables, SORT first arranges the data set in the order of the first BY variable. Then SORT arranges the observations having the lowest value of the first variable (if several observations have the same value) in the order of the second variable. This continues for every BY variable specified. For example, if you sort a data set containing state and city information by state and then by city, SORT first arranges the data so that Alabama's observations are first, then Alaska's, and so on. Next, SORT arranges Alabama's observations by the city value, so that Birmingham's observations are followed by Dothan's, and so on.

SORT uses the EBCDIC collating sequence (standard for IBM 360/370) when it compares character values. From smallest to largest values, this sequence is:

```
blank ¢ . < ( + | & ! $ * ) ; ¬ - / | , % _ > ? ` : # @ ' = "
abcdefghijklmnopqr~stuvwxyz{ABCDEFGHI}J
KLMNOPQR\STUVWXYZ0123456789
```

For numeric variables, the smallest-to-largest comparison sequence is:

special missing value .___
SAS system missing value .
special missing value .A to .Z
negative numeric values
zero
positive numeric values

SPECIFICATIONS

The statements used with PROC SORT are:

PROC SORT *options*;
   BY *option variable option variable ...*;

PROC SORT Statement

PROC SORT *options*;

The options below may appear in the PROC SORT statement. If the SAS data set that you want to sort is on tape, you **must** include the OUT= option.
Note: not all sort utilities support all of the PROC SORT statement options. Consult your installation SAS representative about the options that are pertinent to your system's sort, and valid values to specify for those options.

DATA=*SASdataset*	names the SAS data set that you want to sort. If DATA= is omitted, the most recently created SAS data set is used.
OUT=*SASdataset*	specifies a name for the output data set. If OUT= is omitted, the DATA= data set is sorted and the sorted version replaces the original data set. If you want the OUT= data set to be permanent, specify a two-level name (see Chapter 12, "SAS Data Sets").
EQUALS NOEQUALS	specifies the order of the observations in the output data set. EQUALS specifies that observations with identical BY variable values are to retain the same relative positions in the output data set as in the input data set. NOEQUALS specifies that this restriction is not necessary.
NODUPLICATES NODUP	checks for and eliminates duplicate records. Duplicate records frequently occur when the data you are sorting were derived from log or journal files that were accidentally dumped more than once. This option causes PROC SORT to compare all variable values for each observation to the previous one written to the output data set. If an exact match is found, the record is not written to the output data set. A message is produced on the SAS log, indicating the number of duplicate records dropped.

The next four options are used to specify a different collating sequence:

NATIONAL	specifies that character variables are to be sorted using an alternate collating sequence as defined by your installation to reflect a country's National Symbol Use

Differences (see the examples under DANISH option). Your installation must have customized PROC SORT at the time SAS was installed to reflect national use differences.

REVERSE specifies that character variables are to be sorted using an alternate collating sequence that is reversed from the normal EBCDIC collating sequence.

This option is similar to the BY statement DESCENDING option; however, DESCENDING can be used with both character and numeric variables.

DANISH specifies that character variables are to be sorted using
NORWEGIAN the alternate collating sequence matching the Danish and Norwegian National Use Differences standard.

In the Danish and Norwegian National Use Differences alternate collating sequence, the following standard graphics are redefined:

	UPPER CASE				LOWER CASE		
HEX	Standard Graphic	Alternate Collating Sequence	National Use Graphic	HEX	Standard Graphic	Alternate Collating Sequence	National Use Graphic
7B	#	EA	Æ	C0	{	AA	æ
7C	@	EB	Ø	6A	¦	AB	ø
5B	$	EC	Å	D0	}	AC	å

Thus, the Danish/Norwegian collating sequence is (in part):

a,b,c,...,x,y,z,æ,ø,å,A,B,C,...,X,Y,Z,Æ,Ø,Å

FINNISH specifies that character variables be sorted using an
SWEDISH alternate collating sequence matching the Finnish and Swedish National Use Differences standard.

In the Finnish and Swedish National Use Differences alternate collating sequence, the following standard graphics are redefined:

	UPPER CASE				LOWER CASE		
HEX	Standard Graphic	Alternate Collating Sequence	National Use Graphic	HEX	Standard Graphic	Alternate Collating Sequence	National Use Graphic
5B	$	EA	Å	D0	}	AA	å
7B	#	EB	Ä	C0	{	AB	ä
7C	@	EC	Ö	6A	¦	AC	ö

Thus, the Finnish/Swedish collating sequence is (in part):

a,b,c,...,x,y,z,å,ä,ö,A,B,C,...,X,Y,Z,Å,Ä,Ö

The following options are rarely needed:

MESSAGE
M

prints a summary of the system sort's actions. This option is the default action if the SAS system option SORTMSG is in effect. MESSAGE is useful if you run PROC SORT and the SAS log prints a message that the sort did not work properly. Explanations of the messages can be found in the IBM or vendor reference manual that describes your system sort utility.

LIST
L

provides additional information about the system sort. Note: not all sort utilities support the specification of the LIST option; they may require that it be specified at the time the sort utility is generated or installed. This option is the default action if the SAS system option SORTLIST is in effect.

For VSE, LIST has the same effect as the MESSAGE option.

LEAVE=n

specifies the number of bytes to leave unallocated in the region. Occasionally the SORT procedure runs out of main storage, abending with the system completion code 80A (under OS and TSO) or an error message indicating that there was insufficient virtual storage (under CMS). If this happens to you, rerun the job increasing the LEAVE= value by 30000, and it will usually work properly. The default LEAVE= value for SORT is 16000 (under OS), and 64000 (under CMS), unless SORTSIZE=MAX is specified.

The LEAVE= option is ignored under VSE. Under VSE, the sort utility is executed in the program area and does not allocate storage elsewhere.

TECHNIQUE=xxxx
T=xxxx

specifies a four-character sort technique to be passed to the system sort utility. SAS does not check the validity of the specified value in any way, so you must be sure that it is correct.

This option is ignored under VSE.

SORTWKNO=
number

specifies the *number* of sort work areas to be allocated by PROC SORT. This option is ignored under CMS.

Under OS/MVS the option specifies the minimum number of sort work areas if the SAS system option NODYNALLOC is in effect. The number specified can be from 0 to 6 under MVS; a specification of 0 causes no sort work areas to be allocated and the sort to proceed without them. The system sort utility in use must support "in-core" sorting without sort work areas. If you are not running under MVS, a specification of 0 permits the sort attempt to proceed even if there are no sort work areas allocated in the job control; if any other value (1 to 6) is specified, SAS checks that sort work areas have been allocated in the job control.

Under OS/MVS, if the SAS system option DYNALLOC is specified, the SORTWKNO= specification is passed to the system sort utility.

Under OS, this option is ignored if a SORTWK01 DD

statement is used. The default for this option is given by the SAS system option SORTWKNO=.

Under VSE, the SORTWKNO= value specified can be from 0 to 9. If a number other than 0 is specified, there must be DLBL and EXTENT statements for each file, with DLBL names SORTWK1 to SORTWK*n*, either in the JCL or in partition standard labels. If 0 is specified, the sort utility does an in-core sort.

If SORTWKNO= is not specified under VSE, the value of the SAS system option SORTWKNO= is used. If the system option is not specified either, the installation default value for SORTWKNO= is used. If there is no installation default, PROC SORT checks for a DLBL statement for SORTWK1. If one is present, PROC SORT sets SORTWKNO= to 1; otherwise it is set to 0 and an in-core sort is done.

DIAG passes the DIAG parameter to the sort utility. For those sort utilities that support this option, additional diagnostic information is produced in the event of a sort failure. (Note that VSE always supplies this information.)

SORTSIZE=
parameter
SIZE=*parameter*
specifies the maximum virtual storage that can be used by the system sort utility. If not specified, the default is given by the SAS system option SORTSIZE=. Note that VSE and OS work differently with regard to this option. Be sure to refer to "SAS Under VSE" for details on space requirements with PROC SORT under VSE.

When SORTSIZE=SIZE is specified, the sort executes with the amount of free space in the program area/region/partition/machine minus the LEAVE= option value.

When SORTSIZE=*nnnnn* is specified, *nnnnn* bytes of memory are passed to the sort utility.

When SORTSIZE=*n*K is specified, *n*K bytes of memory are passed to the sort utility.

When SORTSIZE=MAX is specified, the parameter 'MAX' is passed to the sort utility. This causes the sort utility to "size" itself. Note that not all sort utilities support the MAX specification.

When SORTSIZE=0 is specified, a value of zero is passed to the sort utility. In this case, most sort utility programs use a value assigned by the installation at the time of the sort utility's generation/installation.

The SORTSIZE= specifications of SIZE, MAX, and 0 are invalid under VSE.

BY Statement

BY *option variable option variable ...;*

Any number of variables can be specified in the BY statement. A BY statement **must** be used with PROC SORT.

As described above, SORT first arranges the observations in the order of the first variable in the BY statement, then it sorts observations with a given value of the first variable by the second variable, and so on.

The following option can be specified in the BY statement:

DESCENDING   sorts variables in descending order. Use the keyword
DESCENDING before the name of each variable in the
BY statement whose values are to be in descending
order. For example, these statements:

PROC SORT DATA = RANDOM;
  BY DESCENDING SIZE AGE;

sort the RANDOM data set first by descending order of
SIZE values, then by ascending order of AGE values.
To sort by descending AGE values, the DESCENDING
keyword would have to precede the AGE variable
name.
  The DESCENDING option has the same effect as the
PROC SORT statement REVERSE option, except that
DESCENDING can be used for both numeric and
character variables. If both are specified, however,
character variables are sorted in reverse descending
sequence, which is identical to ascending order.

The BY statement is also discussed in Chapter 8, "SAS Statements Used in the
PROC Step."

Output Data Set

If an OUT= option appears in the PROC SORT statement, a new data set is created
containing the sorted observations. Otherwise, the original data set is sorted and
the sorted observations replace the original values, **after** the procedure is executed
without errors. As always when a data set is replaced, there must be space in the
data library for a second copy of the old data set when PROC SORT is invoked.

Usage Notes

Multiple sorts   When you know that you need to sort a data set for several purposes, you can sometimes plan ahead and reduce the number of sorts needed. For
example, suppose you want to run a procedure for the same data set twice, once
with the BY statement:

BY STATE;

and again with the BY statement:

BY STATE CITY;

You can sort the data set once and use it for both these runs if you use the
statements:

PROC SORT;
  BY STATE CITY;

It does not matter for the BY STATE; run that the data set is sorted by both state and
city. If the first statement above were BY CITY;, you would need to sort the data
twice.

Sorting Large Data Sets Occasionally a data set is too large for the sort to handle. When this happens, if your installation uses an IBM or equivalent system sort, SORT prints a message explaining the situation.

Under OS, you can increase the sort's capacity by adding a SORT parameter to the EXEC statement in your JCL:

// EXEC SAS,SORT = s

The s value to use depends on what kind of disk drive the system sort uses for its work files at your installation; consult your computing center staff to find out what disk is used.

The formula for calculating the s value is:

$s = n*v/d$

where

> n number of observations in the data set
> v number of variables in the data set
> d depends on the sort work device type; see the table below.

SORT WORK DEVICE TYPE	d
2311	3,500
2314/2319	35,000
3330/3330V/3330-1	57,000
3340/3344	24,000
3350	135,000
3375	97,000
3380	164,000

These formulas are based on the assumption that all the variables are numeric. If your data set includes long character variables, the SORT value must be larger. For safety, you should use an s value 20–50% larger than the values given by the formulas.

For example, suppose you want to sort a data set consisting of 5000 observations and 200 variables. Your installation uses 3330-type disks for the sort work space. You calculate the SORT value as:

> $s = n*v/57000$
> $= 5000*200/57000$
> $= 17.5$
> $= 18$

Adding 50% to 18 gives an s value of 27, so the SORT EXEC specification is SORT = 27.

For very large sorts, it may be necessary to use tape SORTWKnn areas.

Under VSE, to increase the sort's capacity you must either increase the size of the SORTWK1 file or allocate additional sort work files. You may need to consult with your computing center staff to accomplish this. If you increase the size of the SORTWK1 file by allocating more than one extent to it, you must specify (or default to) SORTWKNO = 1 when you invoke PROC SORT. If you allocate additional sort/work files, these must have DLBL names SORTWK2, SORTWK3 ... SORTWK9. You must also use the SORTWKNO = option to tell the sort utiltity how many sort files are available. If, for example, you allocated a SORTWK2 and a SORTWK3 file, but specified SORTWKNO = 2, only SORTWK1 and SORTWK2 would be used.

To increase the sort's capacity under CMS, you must take the specific action required by the particular sort utility that you are using. If you have specified the SAS system option SORTPGM=SAS, you must define and format a larger temporary disk. If you are using SYNCSORT, you must contact your computing center staff to increase the sort work area allocation made internally by SYNCSORT. For other sort utilities, contact your computing center staff.

EXAMPLE

The example below sorts the data in a SAS data set called AUTO.STATS, which contains performance measures on cars. The data set is sorted first by the variable MAKE, and then by the variable MODEL. PROC PRINT prints the data set by MAKE.

```
PROC SORT DATA=AUTO.STATS;
  BY MAKE MODEL;
PROC PRINT;
  BY MAKE;
```

SAS   1

-- MAKE=AMC --

OBS	MODEL	V1	V2	V3	V4	V5	V6	V7	V8	V9	V10	V11	V12	V13	V14	V15	V16
1	GREMLIN 6	3	3	3	3	2	3	3	4	3	4	3	4	3	3	2	3
2	HORNET 6	3	3	2	3	3	3	3	3	3	3	3	3	3	2	3	3
3	MATADOR 8	4	3	2	4	3	4	3	3	3	3	3	3	3	3	2	3
4	PACER 6	3	3	3	3	3	3	3	3	3	3	3	3	3	3	2	3

-- MAKE=AUDI --

OBS	MODEL	V1	V2	V3	V4	V5	V6	V7	V8	V9	V10	V11	V12	V13	V14	V15	V16
5	AUDI 100	1	4	4	4	3	2	3	1	1	3	2	3	1	3	4	3
6	FOX	1	4	4	3	3	2	3	1	3	3	3	3	3	3	4	3

-- MAKE=BMW --

OBS	MODEL	V1	V2	V3	V4	V5	V6	V7	V8	V9	V10	V11	V12	V13	V14	V15	V16
7	BMW 2002	1	4	4	4	4	3	3	4	3	3	3	3	3	3	3	2
8	BMW 530I	4	4	4	4	5	1	3	3	1	3	3	3	3	3	4	3

-- MAKE=BUICK --

OBS	MODEL	V1	V2	V3	V4	V5	V6	V7	V8	V9	V10	V11	V12	V13	V14	V15	V16
9	CENTURY 6	4	3	3	4	3	3	3	4	3	3	3	2	3	3	3	3
10	CENTURY 8	3	3	3	3	3	3	3	3	3	3	3	3	3	3	3	3
11	ELECTRA 225	3	3	3	4	3	4	3	3	3	3	3	4	4	3	3	3
12	LESABRE 6	3	3	3	4	4	4	3	3	3	3	3	2	3	3	3	3
13	LESABRE 8	4	3	3	3	4	3	3	3	3	3	3	4	3	3	3	3
14	RIVIERA	3	3	3	3	4	3	3	3	3	3	3	4	4	3	3	4
15	SKYHAWK 6	3	2	3	3	3	3	3	3	3	3	3	2	2	3	2	3
16	SKYLARK 6	4	3	2	3	3	3	3	3	3	3	3	2	3	3	3	3
17	SKYLARK 8	3	3	2	3	3	3	3	3	3	3	3	3	4	3	3	3

-- MAKE=CADILLAC --

OBS	MODEL	V1	V2	V3	V4	V5	V6	V7	V8	V9	V10	V11	V12	V13	V14	V15	V16
18	ELDORADO	3	3	3	3	3	3	3	1	3	3	3	2	3	3	3	2
19	OTHER CAD	4	3	3	3	3	3	3	2	3	3	3	3	3	3	3	3
20	SEVILLE	3	3	3	3	4	3	3	2	3	3	3	3	3	3	3	4

--- MAKE=CHEV ---

OBS	MODEL	V1	V2	V3	V4	V5	V6	V7	V8	V9	V10	V11	V12	V13	V14	V15	V16
21	CAMARO 8	3	2	3	3	1	3	3	3	3	3	3	3	3	3	3	3
22	CHEVETTE	3	3	3	4	4	3	3	3	3	3	4	3	3	3	3	3
23	CORVETTE	1	1	3	1	1	2	2	1	2	3	1	3	4	2	3	3
24	IMPALA 6	4	3	3	4	4	4	3	3	3	3	3	4	3	3	3	3
25	IMPALA 8	4	3	3	4	4	3	3	3	3	3	3	4	3	3	3	3
26	MALIBU 6	4	3	2	3	3	3	3	3	4	3	3	2	3	3	4	3
27	MALIBU 8	4	3	3	3	3	3	3	3	3	3	3	3	3	3	3	3
28	MONTE CARLO	4	2	2	3	3	3	3	3	3	3	3	3	3	3	3	3
29	MONZA 4	3	2	3	3	3	3	3	2	2	3	3	2	2	3	3	3
30	NOVA 6	3	3	3	3	3	3	3	3	3	3	3	2	3	3	3	3
31	NOVA 8	3	3	3	2	3	3	3	3	3	3	3	3	3	3	3	3
32	VEGA	4	3	3	3	3	3	3	3	3	2	3	2	2	3	3	3

--- MAKE=CHRYS ---

OBS	MODEL	V1	V2	V3	V4	V5	V6	V7	V8	V9	V10	V11	V12	V13	V14	V15	V16
33	CORDOBA	3	3	3	3	3	2	3	2	3	2	3	2	2	3	2	3
34	LEBARON 8	3	3	3	2	2	2	2	2	3	2	3	2	2	3	2	3
35	NEWPORT	4	3	3	3	3	3	3	3	3	2	3	2	2	3	2	3

--- MAKE=DATSUN ---

OBS	MODEL	V1	V2	V3	V4	V5	V6	V7	V8	V9	V10	V11	V12	V13	V14	V15	V16
36	B-210	3	4	4	4	5	3	3	4	3	4	3	4	3	3	4	3
37	F-10 COUPE	3	4	4	4	3	3	3	4	3	3	3	4	3	3	3	1
38	F-10 WAGON	3	4	3	3	4	2	3	4	3	4	3	4	3	3	4	3
39	200-SX	2	4	3	4	3	4	3	3	1	3	3	3	4	3	3	4
40	280Z	3	4	3	4	4	3	3	4	3	3	3	3	4	3	4	4
41	510	2	4	4	4	3	3	3	4	2	3	3	3	3	3	3	4
42	810	3	4	4	5	4	3	3	3	3	3	3	3	3	3	3	3

--- MAKE=DODGE ---

OBS	MODEL	V1	V2	V3	V4	V5	V6	V7	V8	V9	V10	V11	V12	V13	V14	V15	V16
43	ASPEN 6	3	3	2	2	2	1	3	3	3	3	3	1	3	3	2	3
44	ASPEN 8	3	3	2	2	2	1	3	2	3	3	3	1	2	2	2	3
45	CHARGER	3	2	2	3	2	2	3	2	3	3	3	1	2	3	2	3
46	COLT	2	4	3	4	4	3	3	3	3	3	3	3	3	3	3	3
47	DIPLOMAT 8	3	3	3	2	3	1	3	2	3	3	3	2	2	3	2	3
48	MONACO 8	3	3	2	1	2	3	3	2	3	2	3	1	2	2	1	3

--- MAKE=FIAT ---

OBS	MODEL	V1	V2	V3	V4	V5	V6	V7	V8	V9	V10	V11	V12	V13	V14	V15	V16
49	FIAT 128	3	3	4	3	3	1	3	1	2	3	3	3	2	3	3	3
50	FIAT 131	3	3	3	2	3	2	3	1	3	3	3	3	3	3	4	3

--- MAKE=FORD ---

OBS	MODEL	V1	V2	V3	V4	V5	V6	V7	V8	V9	V10	V11	V12	V13	V14	V15	V16
51	GRANADA 6	3	2	2	3	3	3	3	3	3	3	3	3	3	1	3	3
52	GRANADA 8	4	3	3	3	3	3	3	3	3	3	3	3	3	2	3	3
53	LTD	4	3	3	3	3	3	3	3	3	3	3	3	3	3	3	3
54	LTD II	3	3	3	3	3	3	3	3	3	3	3	3	3	3	3	3
55	MAVERICK 6	3	3	3	3	3	2	3	4	3	3	3	3	3	2	2	3
56	MUSTANG 4	3	3	3	3	3	4	3	4	3	3	3	3	3	3	3	3
57	MUSTANG 6	3	2	3	4	4	3	3	3	3	3	3	3	3	3	2	3
58	PINTO 4	3	3	3	3	2	3	3	4	3	3	3	3	3	3	3	3
59	PINTO 6	3	3	4	3	3	3	3	4	3	3	3	3	3	3	3	3
60	THUNDERBIRD	4	3	3	4	3	3	3	3	3	3	3	3	3	3	3	3

--- MAKE=HONDA ---

OBS	MODEL	V1	V2	V3	V4	V5	V6	V7	V8	V9	V10	V11	V12	V13	V14	V15	V16
61	ACCORD	3	4	4	4	4	3	3	4	3	3	3	4	4	3	3	3
62	CIVIC	3	4	4	4	5	3	3	4	3	3	3	4	3	3	4	4
63	CIVIC CVCC	1	4	4	4	5	3	3	4	3	2	3	4	3	3	4	3

(continued on next page)

(continued from previous page)

```
------------------------------------------------- MAKE=LINCOLN -------------------------------------------------
```

OBS	MODEL	V1	V2	V3	V4	V5	V6	V7	V8	V9	V10	V11	V12	V13	V14	V15	V16
64	CONT MARK IV	3	3	4	4	4	3	3	3	4	4	3	4	3	3	4	4
65	CONTINENTAL	4	3	4	4	4	3	3	3	3	3	3	4	3	3	4	4

```
------------------------------------------------- MAKE=MAZDA -------------------------------------------------
```

OBS	MODEL	V1	V2	V3	V4	V5	V6	V7	V8	V9	V10	V11	V12	V13	V14	V15	V16
66	GLC	3	4	3	4	4	3	3	4	4	4	3	2	3	3	4	3
67	MAZDA RX-4	3	4	4	4	4	4	3	3	3	3	3	3	3	3	4	4

```
------------------------------------------------- MAKE=MERCEDES -------------------------------------------------
```

OBS	MODEL	V1	V2	V3	V4	V5	V6	V7	V8	V9	V10	V11	V12	V13	V14	V15	V16
68	BENZ 220D	4	5	4	4	5	3	4	4	3	3	3	5	3	3	4	3
69	BENZ 300D	3	4	4	5	4	4	3	4	4	3	3	5	3	3	4	4
70	BENZ 6	3	4	5	4	5	3	3	4	3	4	3	4	3	3	3	3
71	BENZ 8	3	5	4	4	5	2	3	4	3	3	3	4	4	3	3	4

```
------------------------------------------------- MAKE=MERCURY -------------------------------------------------
```

OBS	MODEL	V1	V2	V3	V4	V5	V6	V7	V8	V9	V10	V11	V12	V13	V14	V15	V16
72	BOBCAT 4	3	2	3	3	1	3	3	4	3	3	3	3	2	3	3	4
73	COMET 6	3	3	3	3	3	2	3	3	3	2	3	3	3	3	2	3
74	COUGAR	3	3	3	3	3	3	3	3	3	3	3	3	3	3	3	3
75	MARQUIS	3	4	4	4	3	3	3	4	3	3	3	3	3	3	3	4
76	MONARCH 6	3	2	2	2	2	3	3	3	3	2	3	3	3	1	3	3
77	MONARCH 8	4	3	3	3	3	3	3	3	3	3	3	3	3	2	3	3

```
------------------------------------------------- MAKE=MGB -------------------------------------------------
```

OBS	MODEL	V1	V2	V3	V4	V5	V6	V7	V8	V9	V10	V11	V12	V13	V14	V15	V16
78	MGB	3	3	1	1	2	3	3	1	1	2	1	2	1	3	3	3

```
------------------------------------------------- MAKE=OLDS -------------------------------------------------
```

OBS	MODEL	V1	V2	V3	V4	V5	V6	V7	V8	V9	V10	V11	V12	V13	V14	V15	V16
79	CUTLASS 6	4	3	3	3	3	3	3	3	4	3	3	2	3	3	4	3
80	CUTLASS 8	4	3	3	3	3	3	3	3	3	4	3	4	3	3	3	3
81	OMEGA 8	3	2	3	2	3	3	4	3	3	3	3	3	3	3	2	3
82	TORONADO	3	3	2	3	3	4	3	2	3	3	4	3	3	4	3	3
83	88 8	3	3	3	3	4	4	3	3	3	3	4	3	3	3	3	3
84	98	3	3	3	3	4	4	3	2	3	3	4	3	3	3	3	3

```
------------------------------------------------- MAKE=OPEL -------------------------------------------------
```

OBS	MODEL	V1	V2	V3	V4	V5	V6	V7	V8	V9	V10	V11	V12	V13	V14	V15	V16
85	ISUZU	3	4	3	4	4	3	3	3	3	3	4	3	3	4	4	

```
------------------------------------------------- MAKE=PEUGEOT -------------------------------------------------
```

OBS	MODEL	V1	V2	V3	V4	V5	V6	V7	V8	V9	V10	V11	V12	V13	V14	V15	V16
86	PEUGEOT 504	1	4	4	3	3	4	3	3	2	3	2	4	3	3	4	3

```
------------------------------------------------- MAKE=PLYMOUTH -------------------------------------------------
```

OBS	MODEL	V1	V2	V3	V4	V5	V6	V7	V8	V9	V10	V11	V12	V13	V14	V15	V16
87	ARROW	1	4	3	4	4	3	3	4	3	3	3	2	3	3	3	4
88	FURY 8	4	3	2	2	1	2	3	2	3	3	3	1	2	2	1	3
89	GRAN FURY 8	4	3	2	2	3	4	3	3	3	3	3	3	3	3	2	3
90	VOLARE 6	4	3	2	2	2	1	3	3	3	3	3	1	3	3	2	3
91	VOLARE 8	3	3	2	2	2	1	3	3	3	3	3	1	2	3	1	3

```
                                                    SAS                                                          5
-------------------------------------------------- MAKE=PONTIAC -------------------------------------------------

    OBS     MODEL        V1   V2   V3   V4   V5   V6   V7   V8   V9   V10  V11  V12  V13  V14  V15  V16

    92    ASTER           2    4    3    2    2    3    3    2    3    2    1    3    3    3    2    2
    93    CATALINA 8       4    3    3    3    4    3    3    3    3    3    3    4    3    3    3    3
    94    FIREBIRD 8       3    2    3    3    1    3    2    3    3    3    3    3    3    3    3    2
    95    GRAND PRIX 8     4    2    3    3    3    3    3    3    3    3    3    4    3    3    3    3
    96    LEMANS 6         3    2    2    3    3    3    3    4    2    3    3    3    3    3    3    3
    97    LEMANS 8         4    2    2    3    3    3    3    3    3    3    3    3    3    3    3    3
    98    SUNBIRD 4        3    3    3    2    2    3    3    3    2    2    1    3    3    3    2    2
    99    SUNBIRD 6        3    3    3    3    3    3    3    3    3    3    3    3    3    3    2    3
   100    VENTURA 6        3    3    2    2    3    3    3    3    3    3    3    1    3    3    3    3
   101    VENTURA 8        3    2    2    2    2    3    3    3    3    3    3    3    3    3    3    3

-------------------------------------------------- MAKE=SAAB ---------------------------------------------------

    OBS     MODEL        V1    V2    V3    V4    V5    V6    V7    V8    V9   V10   V11   V12   V13   V14   V15   V16

   102    SAAB 99        2     4     4     3     4     1     3     3     1     3     3     3     3     3     4     4

-------------------------------------------------- MAKE=SUBARU -------------------------------------------------

    OBS     MODEL        V1    V2    V3    V4    V5    V6    V7    V8    V9   V10   V11   V12   V13   V14   V15   V16

   103    SUBARU         2     4     3     4     4     3     3     4     3     3     3     3     3     3     4     3

-------------------------------------------------- MAKE=TOYOTA -------------------------------------------------

    OBS     MODEL        V1    V2    V3    V4    V5    V6    V7    V8    V9   V10   V11   V12   V13   V14   V15   V16

   104    CELICA         4     4     4     4     4     3     3     4     3     4     3     5     4     3     3     4
   105    COROLLA        4     4     4     5     5     3     3     4     3     4     3     4     4     3     4     4
   106    CORONA         4     4     4     4     4     3     3     4     3     4     3     5     4     3     4     4

-------------------------------------------------- MAKE=TRIUMPH ------------------------------------------------

    OBS     MODEL        V1    V2    V3    V4    V5    V6    V7    V8    V9   V10   V11   V12   V13   V14   V15   V16

   107    TR7            1     1     2     1     2     2     3     1     1     2     3     3     2     3     2     1

-------------------------------------------------- MAKE=VOLVO --------------------------------------------------

    OBS     MODEL        V1    V2    V3    V4    V5    V6    V7    V8    V9   V10   V11   V12   V13   V14   V15   V16

   108    VOLVO 240      3     4     4     4     4     3     3     4     3     3     3     4     3     3     3     4
   109    VOLVO 260      3     4     4     3     5     2     3     3     3     3     3     3     3     3     3     3
```

```
                                                    SAS                                                          6
-------------------------------------------------- MAKE=VW -----------------------------------------------------

    OBS     MODEL        V1    V2    V3    V4    V5    V6    V7    V8    V9   V10   V11   V12   V13   V14   V15   V16

   110    BEETLE         3     3     3     3     3     3     3     3     3     3     3     2     3     3     3     3
   111    DASHER         1     4     4     3     3     2     3     2     2     3     3     3     3     3     4     3
   112    RABBIT         1     4     4     3     4     3     3     1     3     3     3     3     3     3     4     3
   113    RABBIT D       3     4     4     3     4     3     3     3     3     3     3     3     3     3     3     2
   114    SCIROCCO       1     4     4     4     4     3     3     1     2     3     3     3     3     3     4     4
```

REFERENCE

International Business Machines Corporation (1970), *IBM System/360 Operating System Sort/Merge*, Order Number GC28-6543.

The TRANSPOSE Procedure

ABSTRACT

The TRANSPOSE procedure transposes a SAS data set, changing observations into variables and vice versa.

INTRODUCTION

The TRANSPOSE procedure reads a SAS data set and creates a new data set as its only output. The rows of the original data matrix become columns, and columns become rows. Variables in the new data set correspond to observations in the old data set, and observations in the new data set correspond to variables in the old data set.

TRANSPOSE may be used with a BY statement to rearrange complex data sets in a variety of ways.

SPECIFICATIONS

The statements used with PROC TRANSPOSE are:

> **PROC TRANSPOSE** *options*;
> **VAR** *variables*;
> **ID** *variable*;
> **IDLABEL** *variable*;
> **COPY** *variables*;
> **BY** *variables*;

PROC TRANSPOSE Statement

> PROC TRANSPOSE *options*;

These options may appear in the PROC TRANSPOSE statement:

DATA=*SASdataset*	names the SAS data set to be transposed. If DATA= is omitted, the most recently created SAS data set is used.
PREFIX=*name*	specifies a prefix to be used in constucting new variable names. For example, if PREFIX=VAR, the new variable names will be VAR1, VAR2,..., VARn.
OUT=*SASdataset*	specifies the name of the SAS dataset that is created. If you want to create a permanent SAS data set, you

must specify a two-level name (see Chapter 12, "SAS Data Sets," for more information on permanent SAS data sets). If OUT= is omitted, SAS still creates an output data set, and automatically names it according to the DATA*n* convention, just as if you omitted a data set name in a DATA statement. If OUT= is omitted, the data set is not permanently saved.

VAR Statement

VAR *variables*;

The VAR statement lists the variables to be transposed. Both numeric and character variables may be included. If no VAR statement is used, only the numeric variables in the old data set are transposed. Variables that are not transposed are omitted from the new data set unless listed in the COPY statement.

ID Statement

ID *variable*;

The formatted values of the variable in the ID statement are used for the output variable names. For example, consider these statements:

```
DATA;
  INPUT A B C D $;
  CARDS;
1 2 3 X
4 5 6 Y
7 8 9 Z
PROC TRANSPOSE;
  VAR A B C;
  ID D;
PROC PRINT;
```

The transposed data set looks like this:

OBS	__NAME__	X	Y	Z
1	A	1	4	7
2	B	2	5	8
3	C	3	6	9

Each ID variable value should occur only once in the old data set, or, if a BY statement is used, only once within a BY group. Duplicate values cause TRANSPOSE to issue an error message and stop.

If the ID variable is character but the formatted value is not a valid SAS name, then the illegal characters are replaced by underscores. If the ID variable is numeric, an underscore is prefixed to its formatted value, and the characters "+", "–", and "." are replaced by "P","N", or "D", respectively.

If an ID statement is used, observations with missing ID values are omitted from the new data set.

IDLABEL Statement

IDLABEL *variable*;
IDL *variable*;

If the ID statement is used, the IDLABEL statement names a character or numeric variable that provides labels for the output variables.

COPY Statement

COPY *variables*;

All variables in the COPY statement are copied directly from the input data set to the output data set without being transposed. The output data set is padded with missing values if necessary. For example, this is the data set BEFORE:

OBS	A	B	C
1	1	2	3
2	4	5	6
3	7	8	9
4	11	22	33

It is transposed with this PROC step:

```
PROC TRANSPOSE DATA=BEFORE OUT=AFTER;
  COPY C;
```

The resulting data set (AFTER) looks like this:

OBS	C	__NAME__	COL1	COL2	COL3	COL4
1	3	A	1	4	7	11
2	6	B	2	5	8	22
3	9		.	.	.	.
4	33		.	.	.	.

If the variables __NAME__ or __LABEL__ appear in the COPY statement, PROC TRANSPOSE does not create new variables by the same name.

BY Statement

BY *variables*;

A BY statement may be used with PROC TRANSPOSE to transpose each group of observations defined by the BY variables. When a BY statement appears, the procedure expects the input data set to be sorted in order of the BY variables. If your input data set is not sorted in ascending order, use the SORT procedure with a similar BY statement to sort the data, or, if appropriate, use the BY statement options NOTSORTED or DESCENDING. For more information, see the discussion of the BY statement in Chapter 8, "Statements Used in the PROC Step" and **Using a BY Statement** below. BY variables are not transposed.

DETAILS

Output Data Set

Contents The new data set has a character variable __NAME__ that contains the variable names from the old data set. If the old data set has variable labels, they are placed in a character variable __LABEL__ in the new data set. All output variables except __NAME__ and __LABEL__ are the same type and length. If all input variables are numeric, then the output variables are numeric. If **any** input variable is character, then **all** output variables are character. The character values of transposed numeric variables in the output data set are the formatted values of the input numeric variables. The length of the output variables is equal to the length of the longest input variable.

Variable names   There are four ways that the variables in the new data set may be named:

1. by an ID statement specifying the name of a variable in the old data set. The formatted values of this variable are used as names for the output variables.
2. by the PREFIX= option on the PROC TRANSPOSE statement. For example, if you request PREFIX=VAR, the new variable names will be VAR1, VAR2,..., VARn.
3. by an input variable __NAME__. If you do not use an ID statement or the PREFIX= option, TRANSPOSE looks for an input variable called __NAME__ to get the output variable names. The variable __NAME__ may be the result of a previous execution of PROC TRANSPOSE. If so, the variable names are identical to the variable names in the original (untransposed) data set.
4. by default. If you do not use an ID statement or the PREFIX= option, and there is no input variable called __NAME__, TRANSPOSE assigns the names COL1, COL2,..., COLn to the variables in the output data set.

Using a BY Statement

If a BY statement is used with PROC TRANSPOSE, there is one observation corresponding to each variable of the old data set in each BY group in the new data set. The method of naming the output variables determines what output variables appear in the new data set.

If the PREFIX= option is used, the number of output variables is the maximum number of observations in any BY group of the old data set. If a BY group in the old data set has fewer than the maximum number of observations, then the BY group in the new data set has missing values for the variables with no corresponding input observations. The following example shows the use of a BY statement and the PREFIX= option with a data set called GROWTH.

```
PROC TRANSPOSE DATA=GROWTH OUT=TRAN PREFIX=VAR;
  BY SEX;
PROC PRINT DATA=GROWTH;
PROC PRINT DATA=TRAN;
```

The GROWTH data set looks like this:

OBS	SEX	AGE	HEIGHT	WEIGHT
1	F	12	55	80
2	F	13	55	95
3	F	11	50	65
4	M	12	60	100
5	M	14	65	120

The TRAN data set looks like this:

OBS	SEX	__NAME__	VAR1	VAR2	VAR3
1	F	AGE	12	13	11
2	F	HEIGHT	55	55	50
3	F	WEIGHT	80	95	65
4	M	AGE	12	14	.
5	M	HEIGHT	60	65	.
6	M	WEIGHT	100	120	.

If an ID statement is used and the output names are taken from an input variable, there is one output variable for each distinct value of the naming variable. The output variables are ordered according to the first appearance of their names in the old data set. If a value of the naming variable does not appear in a BY group, the corresponding output variable has missing values in that BY group. For example, when the GROWTH data set is transposed with an ID statement in the program:

```
PROC TRANSPOSE DATA=GROWTH OUT=TRAN2;
  ID WEIGHT;
  BY SEX;
```

the output data set looks like this:

OBS	SEX	__NAME__	__80	__95	__65	__100	__120
1	F	AGE	12	13	11	.	.
2	F	HEIGHT	55	55	50	.	.
3	M	AGE	.	.	.	12	14
4	M	HEIGHT	.	.	.	60	65

EXAMPLES

Simple Transpose Example: Example 1

This example shows that transposing a data set twice can produce a data set similar to the original data set, except for the new variable __NAME__.

```
DATA A;
  TITLE SIMPLE TRANSPOSE EXAMPLE;
  INPUT A B C;
CARDS;
1 2 3
4 5 6
7 8 9
10 11 12
PROC PRINT;
  TITLE2 DATA SET A;
PROC TRANSPOSE DATA=A OUT=B;
PROC PRINT;
  TITLE2 DATA SET B;
PROC TRANSPOSE DATA=B OUT=C;
PROC PRINT;
  TITLE2 DATA SET C;
```

```
                         SIMPLE TRANSPOSE EXAMPLE                          1
                              DATA SET A

                         OBS     A     B     C

                          1      1     2     3
                          2      4     5     6
                          3      7     8     9
                          4     10    11    12
```

```
                         SIMPLE TRANSPOSE EXAMPLE                          2
                              DATA SET B

        OBS    _NAME_    COL1    COL2    COL3    COL4

         1       A        1       4       7       10
         2       B        2       5       8       11
         3       C        3       6       9       12
```

```
                         SIMPLE TRANSPOSE EXAMPLE                          3
                              DATA SET C

             OBS    _NAME_     A     B     C

              1      COL1      1     2     3
              2      COL2      4     5     6
              3      COL3      7     8     9
              4      COL4     10    11    12
```

BY Groups and ID Variables: Example 2

This example shows how TRANSPOSE can rearrange a more complicated data set.

```
DATA A1;
  TITLE TRANSPOSE EXAMPLE WITH BY GROUPS AND AN ID VARIABLE;
  TITLE2 REARRANGING A SUBJECT BY DRUG
       BY EXERCISE FACTORIAL DESIGN;
  INPUT SUBJECT $ DRUG $ EXERCISE $ RESPONSE;
  CARDS;
SMITH      ASPIRIN    LIGHT      5
SMITH      ASPIRIN    MEDIUM     8
SMITH      ASPIRIN    HEAVY      9
SMITH      PLACEBO    LIGHT      4
SMITH      PLACEBO    HEAVY      7
JONES      ASPIRIN    LIGHT      6
JONES      ASPIRIN    MEDIUM     7
JONES      ASPIRIN    HEAVY      9
JONES      PLACEBO    LIGHT      3
JONES      PLACEBO    MEDIUM     4
JONES      PLACEBO    HEAVY      6
PROC SORT;
  BY SUBJECT DRUG;
```

```
PROC PRINT;
  BY SUBJECT;
  TITLE3 DATA SET A1;
PROC TRANSPOSE OUT=A2(DROP=__NAME__);
  BY SUBJECT DRUG;
  ID EXERCISE;
  VAR RESPONSE;
PROC PRINT;
  BY SUBJECT;
  TITLE3 DATA SET A2;
PROC TRANSPOSE OUT=A3(RENAME=(__NAME__=EXERCISE));
  BY SUBJECT;
  ID DRUG;
  VAR LIGHT MEDIUM HEAVY;
PROC PRINT;
  BY SUBJECT;
  TITLE3 DATA SET A3;
PROC TRANSPOSE
    OUT=A4(RENAME=(__NAME__=DRUG COL1=RESPONSE));
  BY SUBJECT EXERCISE NOTSORTED;
PROC PRINT;
  BY SUBJECT;
  TITLE3 DATA SET A4;
```

```
                    TRANSPOSE EXAMPLE WITH BY GROUPS AND AN ID VARIABLE                          1
                REARRANGING A SUBJECT BY DRUG BY EXERCISE FACTORIAL DESIGN
                                    DATA SET A1
------------------------------------- SUBJECT=JONES -------------------------------------

              OBS        DRUG        EXERCISE      RESPONSE

               1        ASPIRIN       LIGHT           6
               2        ASPIRIN       MEDIUM          7
               3        ASPIRIN       HEAVY           9
               4        PLACEBO       LIGHT           3
               5        PLACEBO       MEDIUM          4
               6        PLACEBO       HEAVY           6

------------------------------------- SUBJECT=SMITH -------------------------------------

              OBS        DRUG        EXERCISE      RESPONSE

               7        ASPIRIN       LIGHT           5
               8        ASPIRIN       MEDIUM          8
               9        ASPIRIN       HEAVY           9
              10        PLACEBO       LIGHT           4
              11        PLACEBO       HEAVY           7
```

```
                    TRANSPOSE EXAMPLE WITH BY GROUPS AND AN ID VARIABLE                          2
                REARRANGING A SUBJECT BY DRUG BY EXERCISE FACTORIAL DESIGN
                                    DATA SET A2
------------------------------------- SUBJECT=JONES -------------------------------------

              OBS        DRUG        LIGHT     MEDIUM     HEAVY

               1        ASPIRIN        6         7          9
               2        PLACEBO        3         4          6

------------------------------------- SUBJECT=SMITH -------------------------------------

              OBS        DRUG        LIGHT     MEDIUM     HEAVY

               3        ASPIRIN        5         8          9
               4        PLACEBO        4         .          7
```

```
                TRANSPOSE EXAMPLE WITH BY GROUPS AND AN ID VARIABLE                    3
              REARRANGING A SUBJECT BY DRUG BY EXERCISE FACTORIAL DESIGN
                                  DATA SET A3
-------------------------------- SUBJECT=JONES --------------------------------

              OBS    EXERCISE    ASPIRIN    PLACEBO

               1      LIGHT         6          3
               2      MEDIUM        7          4
               3      HEAVY         9          6


-------------------------------- SUBJECT=SMITH --------------------------------

              OBS    EXERCISE    ASPIRIN    PLACEBO

               4      LIGHT         5          4
               5      MEDIUM        8          .
               6      HEAVY         9          7
```

```
                TRANSPOSE EXAMPLE WITH BY GROUPS AND AN ID VARIABLE                    4
              REARRANGING A SUBJECT BY DRUG BY EXERCISE FACTORIAL DESIGN
                                  DATA SET A4
-------------------------------- SUBJECT=JONES --------------------------------

              OBS    EXERCISE    DRUG       RESPONSE

               1      LIGHT     ASPIRIN        6
               2      LIGHT     PLACEBO        3
               3      MEDIUM    ASPIRIN        7
               4      MEDIUM    PLACEBO        4
               5      HEAVY     ASPIRIN        9
               6      HEAVY     PLACEBO        6


-------------------------------- SUBJECT=SMITH --------------------------------

              OBS    EXERCISE    DRUG       RESPONSE

               7      LIGHT     ASPIRIN        5
               8      LIGHT     PLACEBO        4
               9      MEDIUM    ASPIRIN        8
              10      MEDIUM    PLACEBO        .
              11      HEAVY     ASPIRIN        9
              12      HEAVY     PLACEBO        7
```

SYSTEM-DEPENDENT UTILITIES

Introduction to SAS System-Dependent Utilities

PDS

PDSCOPY

RELEASE

SOURCE

TAPECOPY

TAPELABEL

Introduction to SAS System-Dependent Utilities

The SAS system-dependent utilities perform some kind of processing (other than analysis or report writing) and are not supported by all of the operating systems that SAS runs under. Several of the system-dependent utilities handle OS data sets (PDS, PDSCOPY, RELEASE, and SOURCE); two utilities (TAPECOPY and TAPELABEL) deal with tape volumes under OS batch, TSO, and CMS; and PROC PRINTTO can be used under OS batch, TSO, and CMS to route SAS procedure output to destinations other than the standard SAS print file.

PDS	lists, deletes, and renames members of OS partitioned data sets.
PDSCOPY	copies OS partitioned data sets containing load modules.
PRINTTO	defines the destination of SAS procedure output under OS batch,TSO, and CMS.
RELEASE	releases unused space at the end of an OS disk data set.
SOURCE	prints or unloads the contents of OS partitioned data sets containing card-image records.
TAPECOPY	copies files from one or more tape volumes to one output tape under OS batch, TSO, and CMS.
TAPELABEL	lists the label information on a standard-labeled tape under OS batch, TSO, and CMS.

The PDS Procedure

ABSTRACT

The PDS procedure can list, delete, and rename the members of an OS partitioned data set.

INTRODUCTION

Partitioned data sets are libraries containing files (called members) on OS and OS/VS operating systems. These libraries are used to store program source code, macros, catalogued procedures, load modules, and other data. Partitioned data sets are not the same as SAS data libraries. PROC PDS operates on the directory of a partitioned data set to list, delete, and rename members and aliases.

SPECIFICATIONS

PROC PDS DDNAME=*DDname options;*
  DELETE *member ...;*
  CHANGE *oldname=newname oldname=newname ...;*
  EXCHANGE *name=anothername ...;*

PROC PDS Statement

PROC PDS DDNAME=*DDname options;*

DDNAME=*DDname*   specifies the *DDname* of the JCL DD statement defining the partitioned data set to be processed. The DDNAME= specification must appear.

The options below may appear in the PROC PDS statement:

NOLIST   suppresses the listing of the member names and aliases in the directory of the partitioned data set.

KILL   deletes all the members of the partitioned data set specified by DDNAME=.

DELETE Statement

DELETE *member ...;*

If you want to delete a member or members from the PDS, specify their names in a DELETE statement. When a specification in the DELETE statement is followed by a colon (:), all members whose names begin with the characters preceding the colon are deleted. For example, when this statement is executed:

DELETE PRGM:;

PROC PDS deletes all members whose names begin with the characters PRGM.

CHANGE Statement

CHANGE *oldname* = *newname* *oldname* = *newname* ...;

If you want to rename a member or members of the partitioned data set, use the CHANGE statement. Specify the old name on the left side of the equal sign, the new name on the right. For example, the statements:

PROC PDS DDNAME=LIB;
  CHANGE TESTPGM=PRODPGM;

change the name of member TESTPGM to PRODPGM.

If there are multiple members whose names begin with the same sequence of characters, and you want to change all of the names so they begin with a different sequence, use the colon (:) notation after the *oldname* and *newname*. Here is an example:

CHANGE EXAM:=TEST:;

All of the members that had names beginning with the characters EXAM now have names beginning with the characters TEST.

It is not necessary for the lengths of the sequence of characters specified with colon notation to match. For example:

CHANGE AM:=MORN:;

EXCHANGE Statement

EXCHANGE *name* = *anothername* *name* = *anothername* ...;

Use the EXCHANGE statement to interchange the names of members of the partitioned data set. For example, after these statements are executed:

PROC PDS DDNAME=MYLIB;
  EXCHANGE A=Z;

the member of MYLIB originally called A is now Z and the member originally called Z is now A.

If there are multiple members whose names begin with the same sequence of characters, and you want to exchange that sequence with the sequence from another group of data sets, use the colon (:) notation after *name* and *anothername*. For example, when this statement is executed:

EXCHANGE ABC:=DEFG:;

all data sets that originally began with ABC now begin with DEFG. All of the data sets that began with DEFG now begin with ABC.

It is not necessary for the lengths of the sequence of characters specified with colon notation to match.

DETAILS

Output Data Set

PDS updates the directory of the partitioned data set when members are deleted or renamed.

Usage Note

Unlike other SAS procedures that deal with partitioned data sets (for example, PDSCOPY and SOURCE), PROC PDS does not make any distinction between a member name and an alias, other than to report which names in the PDS directory are aliases for which members. If an alias is renamed, it is still an alias. PROC PDS allows you to delete a member that has aliases in the PDS directory, but then other procedures (PROC PDSCOPY, for example) cannot process the aliases.

Printed Output

Unless NOLIST is specified PROC PDS prints an updated listing of the members in the partitioned data set. The list on the SAS log reflects member name changes and deletions.

EXAMPLE

The example below lists the contents of the partitioned data set XXXXXX.YYYYYYY.ZZZZ, and then prints a second listing showing member changes and deletions specified by the second PROC step.

```
//jobname JOB account,user
// EXEC SAS
//LIB DD DSN=XXXXXX.YYYYYYY.ZZZZ,DISP=SHR
PROC PDS DDNAME=LIB;
PROC PDS DDNAME=LIB;
  DELETE IMS: ERA MARQ;
  CHANGE TEXT=CONJOB;
```

```
1      S A S   L O G    SAS/OS 82.0      VS2/MVS JOB PDS      STEP SAS  PROC
NOTE: THE JOB PDS HAS BEEN RUN UNDER RELEASE 82.0 OF SAS AT SAS INSTITUTE INC.       (00000000).
NOTE: CPUID   VERSION = 04   SERIAL = 020091   MODEL = 0158 .
      CPUID   VERSION = 03   SERIAL = 024001   MODEL = 0158 .
NOTE: NO OPTIONS SPECIFIED.
1         PROC PDS DDNAME=LIB;

      DSNAME=XXXXXX.YYYYYYY.ZZZZ,VOL=SER=QQQ333

      MEMBERS

      A107 CAA COST CREDITS ERA FSP7 IMS IMSAN IMSI IMSX MARQ NEWAN RUN
      SASJOB TA107 TEXT UP


         60 TRACKS ALLOCATED
         57 TRACKS USED
          5 TRACKS UNUSED
          1 EXTENTS
         15 DIRECTORY BLOCKS ALLOCATED
          4 DIRECTORY BLOCKS USED
```

(continued on next page)

```
(continued from previous page)
NOTE: THE PROCEDURE PDS USED 0.72 SECONDS AND 316K.

2          PROC PDS DDNAME=LIB;
3             DELETE IMS: ERA MARQ;
4             CHANGE TEXT=CONJOB;


       DSNAME XXXXXX.YYYYYYY.ZZZZ,VOL-SER QQQ333

       MEMBERS

       A107 CAA CONJOB COST CREDITS FSP7 NEWAN RUN SASJOB TA107 UP


          60 TRACKS ALLOCATED
          57 TRACKS USED
           5 TRACKS UNUSED
           1 EXTENTS
          15 DIRECTORY BLOCKS ALLOCATED
           3 DIRECTORY BLOCKS USED

NOTE: THE PROCEDURE PDS USED 0.94 SECONDS AND 316K.
NOTE: SAS USED 316K MEMORY.

NOTE: SAS INSTITUTE INC.
      SAS CIRCLE
      PO BOX 8000
      CARY, N.C. 27511-8000
```

The PDSCOPY Procedure

ABSTRACT

The PDSCOPY procedure copies OS partitioned data sets containing load modules from disk to disk, disk to tape, tape to tape, or tape to disk.

INTRODUCTION

PDSCOPY can be used to copy an entire library, or you can specify that only certain·modules be copied. PDSCOPY is useful for backing up load module libraries to tape. If PDSCOPY is used to copy a library to tape, it must be used if you want to copy that library to another tape or disk. When libraries are moved between disks with different optimal blocksizes, PDSCOPY can be used to reblock the libraries. PDSCOPY handles overlay programs and alias names.

Modules that are copied with PDSCOPY are 13% to 18% smaller after copying, because PDSCOPY uses space left on a partially filled track to store records. The linkage editor constructs records that do not fit on a partially used track.

No attempt is made to copy scatter-loaded modules.

SPECIFICATIONS

> **PROC PDSCOPY INDD=** *DDname* **OUTDD=** *DDname options;*
>   **SELECT** *modulename ...;*
>   **EXCLUDE** *modulename ...;*

PROC PDSCOPY Statement

PROC PDSCOPY INDD=*DDname* OUTDD=*DDname options;*

INDD=*DDname*	specifies the *DDname* of the load module library to be copied. INDD= must be specified.
OUTDD=*DDname*	specifies the *DDname* of the output partitioned data set. OUTDD= must be specified.

The options that may appear in the PROC PDSCOPY statement are listed below.

BLKSIZE=*b*	specifies the blocksize to be used for reblocking the copied load modules on the output device. If BLKSIZE= is omitted, there are two rules for establishing the default value. Rule 1 is: the default is

the maximum permissible blocksize for the output device or 32742, whichever is smaller (For 3375 and 3380 disk devices smaller values are used, by default, that result in greater space usage.) Rule 2 is: if the DCBS option is specified (see below), and the output data set is a partitioned data set on disk, the default value is the value established by Rule 1 or the partitioned data set's DSCB BLKSIZE, whichever is smaller. For tape (sequential) format output, the specified blocksize cannot be less than the maximum input device blocksize plus 18, nor greater than 32760.

DCBS   specifies that the DCB characteristics of the output partitioned data set on disk are to be preserved, thereby establishing the maximum permissable value of the BLKSIZE= parameter (or its default).

If DCBS is not specified, PDSCOPY normally causes the output disk partitioned data set's DSCB BLKSIZE to be changed to the maximum permissible blocksize for the device.

NOREPLACE   copies only members in the INDD= library that are
NOR   not found in the OUTDD= library; that is, members with the same name are not replaced.

NE   specifies that the output library should not contain records used in the link editing process. Although programs in the output library are executable, they cannot be reprocessed by the linkage editor, nor can they be modified by the IMASPZAP program. Using the NE option can reduce disk space required for the output library by an additional 10 to 20%.

NOALIAS   prevents automatic copying of all aliases of each
NOA   module selected for copying. Any aliases that you want to be copied must be specifically selected. Note that if you select only an alias of a module, the module (that is, the main module name) is still automatically copied, along with the selected aliases.

INTAPE   specifies that the INDD= library is in tape (sequential) format. INTAPE is assumed if the device allocated to the input data set is a tape drive.

OUTTAPE   specifies that the OUTDD= library is to be in tape (sequential) format. OUTTAPE is the default if the device allocated to the output data set is a tape drive.

DC   specifies that load modules marked "downward compatible" are eligible for processing. After copying by PDSCOPY, downward compatible load modules are not marked "DC" in their directory entry, because PDSCOPY does not produce downward compatible load modules or preserve their attributes. If you do not specify the DC option and you attempt to copy load modules marked DC, PDSCOPY issues an error message.

SELECT Statement

> SELECT *modulename* ...;

Use the SELECT statement to specify the names of modules to be copied if you do not want to copy the entire library.

   If you follow a specification in the SELECT statement with a colon (:), all modules beginning with the characters preceding the colon are included in the copy operation. For example:

> SELECT FCS:;

All data sets whose names begin with the characters FCS are copied.

EXCLUDE Statement

> EXCLUDE *modulename* ...;

Use the EXCLUDE statement if you want to exclude certain modules from the copying operation. The EXCLUDE statement is useful if you want to copy more files than you want to exclude. All modules not listed in the EXCLUDE statement are copied.

   If you follow a specification in the EXCLUDE statement with a colon (:), all modules beginning with the characters preceding the colon are excluded from the copying.

   Note: You cannot use both the SELECT statement and the EXCLUDE statement in one PROC PDSCOPY step.

DETAILS

Output Data Set

PDSCOPY produces an output partitioned data set on disk or tape that contains copies of the requested members of the input partitioned data set.

Usage Note

If a module specified in a SELECT statement does not exist, PDSCOPY issues a warning message and continues processing.

Printed Output

PDSCOPY prints:

1. INPUT and OUTPUT, the data set names and volume serials of the input and output libraries
2. MODULE, a list of the modules copied
3. the modules' ALIASes, if any
4. whether the copied modules REPLACED others of the same name.

If the output device is a disk, PDSCOPY prints:

5. TRACKS, the sizes of the modules, in tenths of tracks
6. the SIZE, in decimal bytes, of the modules copied.

EXAMPLE

The example below copies all modules that begin with the letters OZ and AS, from the partitioned data set SYS1.VDR.LINKLIB to the partitioned data set OLD. PROGRAMS.SAVE.

```
// EXEC SAS
//OLD DD DSN=SYS1.VDR.LINKLIB,DISP=SHR
//NEW DD DSN=OLD.PROGRAMS.SAVE,DISP=OLD
PROC PDSCOPY INDD=OLD OUTDD=NEW;
   SELECT OZ: AS:;
```

```
1       SAS  LOG    SAS/OS 82.0       VS2/MVS JOB PDSCOPYX STEP SASTEST   PROC EXAMPLE

NOTE: THE JOB PDSCOPYX HAS BEEN RUN UNDER RELEASE 82.0 OF SAS AT SAS INSTITUTE INC. (SYSTEMS) (00000000).

NOTE: CPUID     VERSION = 04   SERIAL = 020091   MODEL = 0158 .
      CPUID     VERSION = 03   SERIAL = 024001   MODEL = 0158 .

NOTE: NO OPTIONS SPECIFIED.

1          PROC PDSCOPY INDD=OLD OUTDD=NEW;
2             SELECT OZ: AS:;

   INPUT   DSNAME=SYS1.VDR.LINKLIB,VOL=SER=SYS111

   OUTPUT  DSNAME=OLD.PROGRAMS.SAVE,VOL=SER=SCR111

      MODULE      TRACKS      SIZE

      AS1510       2.1       34272
      AS1520       1.6       23832
      AS1530       1.8       24952
      AS1540       1.2       19448
      AS1550       1.4       22800
      AS1560       1.0       16560
      AS1570        .6        8672
      AS1580       2.2       36752
      BLGOZB        .5        6216  REPLACED
      BLGOZC       2.2       40040  REPLACED
      BLGOZD       1.9       32656  REPLACED
      BLGOZJ       1.4       23040  REPLACED
      BLGOZM        .3        2912  REPLACED
      IKJEUP00      .7       10616
      OZSGENER      .1         920  REPLACED

         USED       25.8
         UNUSED      4.2
         TOTAL      30.0
         EXTENTS       1

      ALIAS       MODULE

      ASM         IKJEUP00
      COPY        AS1520
      FORM        AS1550
      FORMAT      AS1550
      IKJEBEME    AS1540
      L           AS1510
      LIST        AS1510
      LISTJES     AS1580
      LJ          AS1580
      M           AS1530
      MERGE       AS1530
      OZB         BLGOZB      REPLACED
      OZC         BLGOZC      REPLACED
      OZD         BLGOZD      REPLACED
      OZJ         BLGOZJ      REPLACED
      OZM         BLGOZM      REPLACED
      TSOSORT     AS1560

NOTE: THE PROCEDURE PDSCOPY USED 3.26 SECONDS AND 260K.


2       SAS  LOG    SAS/OS 82.0       VS2/MVS JOB PDSCOPYX STEP SASTEST   PROC EXAMPLE

NOTE: SAS USED 260K MEMORY.

NOTE: SAS INSTITUTE INC.
      SAS CIRCLE
      BOX 8000
      CARY, N.C. 27511-8000
```

The RELEASE Procedure

ABSTRACT

The RELEASE procedure releases unused space at the end of an OS disk data set.

INTRODUCTION

The RELEASE procedure has several advantages over the SPACE = (,,RLSE) specification on a JCL DD statement, or the RELEASE operand of the TSO ALLOCATE command, which are also used to request release of unused space. One advantage is that you, rather than the operating system, control when the space is released. This advantage is especially applicable to TSO users. If you release space with the RELEASE specification under TSO, the release of unused space takes place every time the data set is closed. Since you may execute commands or programs that cause the data set to be closed many times during a single TSO session, the limit of 16 extents can be exceeded easily. You can avoid this problem by using PROC RELEASE instead. Another advantage is that you can reduce the file's space to a specified number of tracks by using the TOTAL= option.

There is no danger of erasing all or part of a data set, because RELEASE frees unused space only. The space released by PROC RELEASE is returned to the pool of available space on the disk volume and therefore is still available for allocation to the data set, provided that the data set has a secondary allocation quantity specified and the space is not subsequently allocated to another data set.

There are four ways to tell PROC RELEASE how much unused space is to be released from a data set. The options are described in **Specifications**.

1. Use the TOTAL= option to specify the total number of tracks in the data set after unused space is released. The procedure releases the amount of space that is the difference between the size of the data set and the size you specify in the TOTAL= option.
2. Specify the exact amount of unused space to be released from the data set with the RELEASE= option.
3. Specify the amount of unused space to remain in the data set after releasing unused space with the UNUSED= option. The procedure releases the amount of space that is the difference between the size of the data set and the sum of the used space in the data set plus the unused space that is to remain.
4. Use the EXTENTS option to request that only secondary extents that are completely unused be released. After the procedure releases unused space from the data set, the size of the data set is the sum of the size of the primary extent plus the size of all secondary extents that have any portion of them used.

PROC RELEASE can be used with any sequential, partitioned, or direct OS data set, not just one containing SAS data sets. PROC RELEASE cannot be used with ISAM or VSAM data sets.

SPECIFICATIONS

The PROC statement is the only statement used.

PROC RELEASE DDNAME=*DDname options*;

PROC RELEASE Statement

PROC RELEASE DDNAME=*DDname options*;

DDNAME=*DDname*   specifies the *DDname* referring to the data set for which space is to be released. DDNAME= must be specified.

The options below may appear in the PROC RELEASE statement. You cannot specify more than one of these four options: TOTAL=, UNUSED=, RELEASE=, or EXTENTS.

TOTAL=*number*
TRACKS=*number*   specifies the total *number* of tracks that the data set should contain after PROC RELEASE has been run. If the value you specify is smaller than the amount of used space in the data set, SAS releases only the unused space at the end of the data set.
For example, the statement:

PROC RELEASE DDNAME=SURVEY TOTAL=10;

asks SAS to release all but ten tracks of the data set referenced by the DDname SURVEY.

UNUSED=   specifies the number of tracks of unused space that the data set should contain after PROC RELEASE has been run. If the value you specify is greater than the amount of unused space in the data set, SAS does not release any space at the end of the data set.

RELEASE=   specifies the number of tracks of unused space that are to be released. If the value you specify is greater than the amount of unused space in the data set SAS releases all of the unused space at the end of the data set.

EXTENTS
EXTENT
EX   requests that only the space allocated to completely unused secondary extents be released.

By default, all unused space at the end of the data set is released if none of these options (TOTAL=, UNUSED=, RELEASE=, or EXTENTS) is specified.

BOUNDARY=*type*
TYPE=*type*   specifies whether space is to be released from the data set by tracks or by cylinders.
BOUNDARY=CYL (or CYLS, CYLINDER, or CYLINDERS) specifies that space is to be released in

multiples of cylinders. This specification is only effective if the data set is currently allocated in multiples of cylinders.

BOUNDARY = TRK (or TRKS, TRACK, or TRACKS) specifies that space need not be released on cylinder boundaries.

BOUNDARY = JCL (or DD for OS batch, ALLOC for TSO) specifies that space is to be released in units of either tracks or cylinders, depending upon the space allocation specification in the job control. For example:

```
//DD2 DD DISP = OLD,DSN = MY.DATA,
// SPACE = (CYL,2)
```

in combination with BOUNDARY = DD is equivalent to specifying BOUNDARY = CYL.

BOUNDARY = DSCB (or DATASET) specifies that space is to be released in the same units (tracks or cylinders) in which it is currently allocated. BOUNDARY = DSCB is the default value for this option.

DETAILS

Usage Notes

RELEASE issues an error message if it is asked to release the space of the current SAS WORK data set, any SAS data library that is currently open or in use by SAS, either of the SAS macro libraries, the temporary LIBRARY data set that stores PROC FORMAT output for the duration of the job step, or any other data set that SAS can determine to be currently open or in use.

When PROC RELEASE is invoked on OS/VS systems, the operating system's disk space management function (DADSM) must be able to obtain exclusive control of the data set. If it cannot, no space is released from the data set. No indication of this is passed to SAS; therefore, SAS does not issue an error message. If the messages on the SAS log indicate that no space was released from the data set, you should check to see if the data set is allocated to another job or user.

Printed Output

PROC RELEASE prints a message on the SAS log giving the number of tracks allocated to the data set before and after execution of RELEASE, the number of tracks used, and the number of extents used.

EXAMPLE

The example below releases the unused secondary extents for an OS data set referenced by the DDname LIB.

```
// EXEC SAS
//LIB DD DISP = SHR,DSN = XXXXXX.YYYYYYY.ZZZZ
PROC RELEASE DDNAME = LIB EXTENTS;
```

```
1       S A S   L O G     SAS/OS 82.0      VS2/MVS JOB PRINT    STEP SAS   PROC            16:43 THURSDAY, JULY 22, 1982

NOTE: THE JOB PRINT HAS BEEN RUN UNDER RELEASE 82.0 OF SAS AT SAS INSTITUTE INC. (SYSTEMS) (00000000).

NOTE: CPUID    VERSION = 04   SERIAL = 020091   MODEL = 0158 .
      CPUID    VERSION = 03   SERIAL = 024001   MODEL = 0158 .

NOTE: NO OPTIONS SPECIFIED.


1          PROC RELEASE DDNAME=LIB EXTENTS;

NOTE: 60 TRACKS ALLOCATED, 57 USED, 3 EXTENTS, BEFORE RELEASE.
NOTE: 60 TRACKS ALLOCATED, 57 USED, 1 EXTENTS, AFTER RELEASE.

NOTE: THE PROCEDURE RELEASE USED 0.78 SECONDS AND 268K.
NOTE: SAS USED 300K MEMORY.

NOTE: SAS INSTITUTE INC.
      SAS CIRCLE
      PO BOX 8000
      CARY, N.C. 27511-8000
```

REFERENCES

International Business Machines Corporation (1979), *OS/VS2 MVS JCL*, Order
   Number GC28-0692.
International Business Machines Corporation (1979), *OS/VS1 JCL Reference*,
   Order Number GC24-5099.

The SOURCE Procedure

ABSTRACT

The SOURCE procedure prints or unloads the contents of OS partitioned data sets (PDSs) containing card-image (80-byte) records. Examples of such data sets include JCL procedure libraries, macro libraries, and source statement libraries. PROC SOURCE also provides some general PDS directory processing facilities, not limited to card-image record PDSs.

INTRODUCTION

Consult the books listed in the **REFERENCES** section of this chapter for more information on OS partitioned data sets and PDS directories.
   SOURCE capabilities include:

- printing the contents of an entire library on the SAS log
- constructing an unloaded form of the library suitable for reloading by IEBUPDTE or other source library maintenance utilities, including the ability to recognize and properly handle aliases
- creating a sequential, easily-processed, unloaded version of the directory records of any partitioned data set, not just a card-image source library PDS
- processing only the directory of any PDS, while ignoring the data in the members, to produce control statements or data records for processing by other programs, PDS utilities, and SAS programs.

SOURCE has several advantages over the IBM utility IEBPTPCH:

- SOURCE does not necessarily skip to a new page for each member
- members can be printed in alphabetical order
- the number of records in each member is printed
- an unloaded, portable version of the library can be produced.

SPECIFICATIONS

The following statements are used with PROC SOURCE:

> **PROC SOURCE** *options*;
>   **SELECT** *member* ...;
>   **EXCLUDE** *member* ...;
>   **FIRST** *'card image text'* ...;
>   **LAST** *'card image text'* ...;
>   **BEFORE** *'card image text' options* ...;
>   **AFTER** *'card image text' options* ...;

PROC SOURCE Statement

PROC SOURCE *options;*

The options below may appear in the PROC SOURCE statement.

INDD=*DDname* specifies the *DDname* of the JCL DD statement describing the input partitioned data set. If INDD= is not specified, the default DDname SOURCE is used.

INBLK=*blocksize* specifies the *blocksize* to be used to read the input PDS library. This option can be used to override the data set's (DSCB) BLKSIZE when it has been incorrectly altered or destroyed, and thus permits the contents of the PDS library to be retrieved correctly. The INBLK= specification overrides any JCL DD statement specification of BLKSIZE=.

PRINT prints the entire library. The PRINT option is ignored when NODATA is specified.

PAGE begins the listing of each member on a new page.

NOPRINT suppresses printing of the list of member names and record counts. (These listings are produced even when the PRINT option is **not** specified.) The NOPRINT option is ignored when PRINT is specified.

NOSUMMARY suppresses the printing of the module summary records. Even when PRINT is **not** specified, PROC SOURCE prints all records starting with the first one which has "NAME:", "ENTRY:", or "AUTHOR:" beginning in column 5 and stopping with the first record with "END" in column 5. The NOSUMMARY option is ignored when NODATA, NOPRINT, or PRINT is specified.

NODATA prevents data records from members of the input partitioned data set from being read and output to the OUTDD= file. FIRST, LAST, BEFORE, and AFTER control cards are generated, and a listing of the member names and aliases is produced. Since no records are read, the count of records in each member is not indicated.

You should specify NODATA if the PDS library is not a source library PDS (80-byte, card-image, fixed blocked records). NODATA is particularly useful when you want to process only the PDS directory. Since the FIRST, LAST, BEFORE, and AFTER actions are taken, it is possible to generate control statements for other PDS utilities using only the facilities of PROC SOURCE.

OUTDD=*DDname* specifies the *DDname* of the JCL DD statement describing the output sequential data set to which PROC SOURCE will write the unloaded (sequential) form of the input library and/or any records generated as a result of FIRST, LAST, BEFORE and AFTER statements. Each member in the unloaded data set is preceded by a record of the form:

./   ADD NAME=*member*,SSI=*xxxxxxxx*

and, if the member has one or more aliases, is followed by a record of the form:

./ ALIAS NAME=*alias*

for each alias present so that the data set can be reloaded by the IBM utility IEBUPDTE.

An advantage of having an unloaded data set is that one or several members can be retrieved without reloading the entire library. For an example of how to do this, refer to the RELOAD member in the SAS sample library.

OUTBLK=*blocksize* specifies the default *blocksize* of the OUTDD= data set. If neither the OUTDD= JCL DD statement nor the data set label/DSCB specify a BLKSIZE value, this value is used. If OUTBLK= is not specified, the value of the SAS system option, FILEBLKSIZE(*device*), that is appropriate for the output device is used as the default value.

NULL indicates that null members (source library members with no records, just an immediate end-of-file) should be processed. Such members occasionally appear in source libraries, but are not normally unloaded because IEBUPDTE and most other source library maintenance utilities do not create null members. If the source library maintenance utility you are using can properly recognize and create a null member, specify this option and provide the appropriate BEFORE (and possibly, AFTER) statements.

NOTSORTED causes PROC SOURCE to process the PDS library members in the order in which they appear in SELECT statements or in the order in which they remain after EXCLUDE statements. Normally, PROC SOURCE processes (that is, unloads, prints, and so on) the members of the PDS library in alphabetical order by member name.

NOALIAS treats any aliases as main member names. Normally, unless overridden by BEFORE or AFTER statements, aliases are associated with the main member name and ./ ALIAS cards generated after each main member is unloaded, so that IEBUPDTE would reconstruct a source library identical to the input source library. Specification of this option causes all aliases to be treated as main member names and no ./ ALIAS cards or alias BEFORE or AFTER cards are generated.

MAXIOERROR= *number* specifies the maximum *number* of I/O errors allowed before processing is terminated. Normally, PROC SOURCE detects, issues a warning message about, and then ignores I/O errors that occur while reading the PDS library members. After the number of errors specified by MAXIOERROR= have occurred, however, PROC SOURCE gives up and assumes that the PDS is not readable. The default MAXIOERROR= value is 50.

DIRDD=*DDname* specifies the *DDname* of the JCL DD statement

describing the output data set to which PROC
SOURCE will write a sequential, unloaded form of the
directory of the PDS library. Each directory record is
written into one 80-byte record, left-aligned, and padded on the right with blanks.

SELECT Statement

SELECT *member* ...;

If you want to process only certain members, give their names in a SELECT statement. Any number of SELECT statements can be used.

If a specification is followed by a colon (:), all members beginning with the
characters preceding the colon are selected.

You can include a range of names in the SELECT statement by joining two names
with a hyphen. These two modules, along with any others that fall between them
alphabetically, are processed. For example, if a PDS contains members called
BROWN, GREEN, GRAY, RED, and YELLOW, and you want to process the first
four members, use this SELECT statement:

SELECT BROWN–RED;

You can use both colon notation and a range specification. For example:

SELECT BR:-GR: RED;

is equivalent to the previous SELECT statement.

EXCLUDE Statement

EXCLUDE member ...;

If you do not want to process certain modules, give their names in an EXCLUDE
statement. Any number of EXCLUDE statements can be used.

If a specification is followed by a colon (:), all members with names beginning
with the characters preceding the colon are excluded from processing.

You can include a range of names in the EXCLUDE statement by joining two
names with a hyphen. These two modules, along with any others that fall between
them alphabetically, are not processed (see the example in the SELECT statement
description).

You can use both the colon notation and a range specification in the EXCLUDE
statement (see the example above).

Both EXCLUDE and SELECT statements may be used in an execution of PROC
SOURCE. It is convenient to use SELECT and EXCLUDE statements together when
you want to SELECT many members using colon or range specifications but
EXCLUDE a few of the members selected. For example, if there are 200 members
called SMC1-SMC200, and you want to copy all of them except SMC30-SMC34, use
these statements:

SELECT SMC:;
EXCLUDE SMC30–SMC34;

When both EXCLUDE and SELECT statements are used, the EXCLUDE statements
should specify only modules that are specified by the SELECT statements; excluding
unselected modules, however, has no effect other than generating warning
messages.

FIRST Statement

FIRST   *'card image text'* ...;

Any number of FIRST statements may be used, and any number of strings of text can be specified in one FIRST statement. The *card image text* specified is reproduced, left-aligned, on a record that precedes all members in the unloaded data set. One record is generated for each string of card image text in each FIRST statement, in the order of occurrence of the FIRST statements.

LAST Statement

LAST   *'card image text'* ...;

Any number of LAST statements may be used and any number of strings of text can be specified in one LAST statement. The *card image text* specified is reproduced, left-aligned, on a record that follows all members in the unloaded data set. One record is generated for each LAST card image text specification in each statement, and in the order of occurrence of the LAST statements.

BEFORE Statement

BEFORE   *'card image text'* options ...;

Use as many BEFORE statements as you want. You can specify multiple *card image text* strings and *options* in each BEFORE statement. Each *card image text* specified is reproduced, left-aligned, on a record that precedes each member in the unloaded data set: once for the main member name, or if ALIAS is specified, once for each alias instead.

By default, ./ ADD IEBUPDTE control statements are generated before each member in the unloaded data set. If any BEFORE or AFTER statements are used, this default action is cancelled. In effect, the default action is as if this statement is specified:

BEFORE './   ADD NAME=' 21;

The options that may appear in the BEFORE statement are listed following the AFTER statement description.

AFTER Statement

AFTER   *'card image text'* options ...;

Use as many AFTER statements as you want. You can specify multiple *card image text* strings and *options* in each AFTER statement. The card image text specified is reproduced, left-aligned, on a record that follows each member in the unloaded data set; once for the main member name, or if ALIAS is specified, once for each alias instead.

By default, ./ ALIAS statements are generated for each alias after each member in the unloaded data set. If any AFTER or BEFORE statements are used, this default action is cancelled. In effect, the default action is as if this statement is specified:

AFTER './   ALIAS NAME=' 21 ALIAS;

The options below may appear in both BEFORE and AFTER statements.

column number   specifies a *column number* (1–73) that begins an eight-column field to contain the main member or alias name in the record created by the BEFORE or AFTER statement. The name is left-aligned and padded on the right with blanks.

ALIAS specifies that a record containing the *card image text* is to be produced only for each alias defined (with the alias being placed into the record at the specified column, if any).

RIGHT right-aligns the member name or alias in the eight-column field and pads it with blanks on the left.

NOBLANK all text on the record that is to the right of the field where the member name or alias is placed is moved to the left, adjacent to the member name or alias, leaving no blanks between the end of the member name or alias and any following text.

DETAILS

Printed Output

SOURCE prints:

1. the entire library, if the PRINT option is specified
2. a listing of the member names in the library (unless you specify NOPRINT)
3. the number of records for each member (unless you specify NOPRINT or NODATA)
4. a summary of the attributes and contents of the PDS library.

Even when PRINT is not specified, some records may still be printed. The signal "NAME:" or "ENTRY:" or "AUTHOR:" beginning in column 5 of a record in the library starts the printing; the signal "END" beginning in column 5 stops it. If you do not want this subset of records printed, specify the NOSUMMARY option.

EXAMPLES

The output for Examples 1, 2, and 5 has been shortened to avoid showing the lengthy contents of the libraries used in the examples.

Printing Selected Members: Example 1

The job below begins printing with the member named FORTHC and prints through the member named FORTHCL.

```
//jobname JOB account,user
// EXEC SAS
//SOURCE DD DSN=SYS1.IBM.PROCLIB,DISP=SHR
PROC SOURCE PRINT;
  SELECT FORTHC-FORTHCL;
```

```
1      S A S   L O G     SAS/OS 82.0        VS2/MVS JOB SOURCEX   STEP SAS      PROC EXAMPLE1

NOTE: THE JOB SOURCEX HAS BEEN RUN UNDER RELEASE 82.0 OF SAS AT SAS INSTITUTE INC.        (00000000).

1              PROC SOURCE PRINT;
2                  SELECT FORTHC-FORTHCL;
```

```
2      S A S   L O G     SAS/OS 82.0        VS2/MVS JOB SOURCEX   STEP SAS      PROC EXAMPLE1

   FORTHC
               //FORT     EXEC  PGM=IEKAA00                                        00010000
               //SYSPRINT DD   SYSOUT=S                                            00020001
               //SYSPUNCH DD   SYSOUT=B                                            00030000
               //SYSLIN   DD   DSNAME=&LOADSET,UNIT=VIODA,DISP=(MOD,PASS),        *00040002
               //              SPACE=(400,(200,50),RLSE),DCB=BLKSIZE=3120          00050001
       5-RECORDS
```

```
               //FORT     EXEC  PGM=IEKAA00                                        00010000
               //SYSPRINT DD   SYSOUT=S                                            00020001
               //SYSPUNCH DD   SYSOUT=B                                            00030000
               //SYSLIN   DD   DSNAME=&LOADSET,UNIT=VIODA,DISP=(MOD,PASS),        *00040002
               //              SPACE=(400,(200,50),RLSE),DCB=BLKSIZE=3120          00050001
               //LKED EXEC PGM=IEWL,PARM=(MAP,LET,LIST),COND=(4,LT,FORT)           00060000
               //SYSLIB   DD   DSNAME=SYS1.FORTLIB,DISP=SHR                        00070000
               //SYSPRINT DD   SYSOUT=S                                            00080001
               //SYSLMOD   DD   DSNAME=&GOSET(MAIN),UNIT=VIODA,DISP=(,PASS),      *00090002
               //              SPACE=(3072,(30,10,1),RLSE)                         00100000
               //SYSLIN   DD   DSNAME=&LOADSET,DISP=(OLD,DELETE)                   00110000
               //        DD   DDNAME=SYSIN                                         00120000
               //SYSUT1 DD DSNAME=&SYSUT1,UNIT=VIODA,SPACE=(1024,(200,20)),SEP=SYSLMOD 00130002
     13-RECORDS
- - - - - - - - - - - - - - - - - - - - - - - - - - - - - -

               SOURCE LIBRARY DATA SET: INDD=SOURCE,BLKSIZE=3200,
               DSNAME=SYS1.IBM.PROCLIB,VOL=SER=SYS111

       75     MEMBERS DEFINED IN SOURCE LIBRARY.

        0     ALIASES DEFINED IN SOURCE LIBRARY.

       35     DIRECTORY BLOCKS ALLOCATED.

       12     DIRECTORY BLOCKS USED.

        3     MEMBERS SELECTED.

       18     RECORDS READ FROM SOURCE LIBRARY.
```

```
4      S A S   L O G     SAS/OS 82.0        VS2/MVS JOB SOURCEX   STEP SAS      PROC EXAMPLE1

NOTE: THE PROCEDURE SOURCE USED 0.65 SECONDS AND 280K.
NOTE: SAS USED 280K MEMORY.

NOTE: SAS INSTITUTE INC.
      SAS CIRCLE
      PO BOX 8000
      CARY, N.C. 27511-8000
```

Printing an Entire Library: Example 2

The job below prints the entire contents of a source library.

```
//jobname JOB account,user
// EXEC SAS
//MYLIB DD DSN=MY.SOURCE.LIBRARY,DISP=SHR
PROC SOURCE INDD=MYLIB PRINT;
```

```
1      S A S   L O G     SAS/OS 82.0        VS2/MVS JOB SOURCEX   STEP SAS      PROC EXAMPLE2

NOTE: THE JOB SOURCEX HAS BEEN RUN UNDER RELEASE 82.0 OF SAS AT SAS INSTITUTE INC.        (00000000).

1              PROC SOURCE INDD=MYLIB PRINT;
```

```
2      S A S   L O G    SAS/OS 82.0      VS2/MVS JOB SOURCEX  STEP SAS      PROC EXAMPLE2
       $REGS
                 R0        EQU    0                                              00000100
                 R1        EQU    1                                              00000200
                 R2        EQU    2                                              00000300
                 R3        EQU    3                                              00000400
                 R4        EQU    4                                              00000500
                 R5        EQU    5                                              00000600
                 R6        EQU    6                                              00000700
                 R7        EQU    7                                              00000800
                 R8        EQU    8                                              00000900
                 R9        EQU    9                                              00001000
                 R10       EQU    10                                             00001100
                 R11       EQU    11                                             00001200
                 R12       EQU    12                                             00001300
                 R13       EQU    13                                             00001400
                 R14       EQU    14                                             00001500
                 R15       EQU    15                                             00001600
    16-RECORDS

    DATE
                 DATE      TITLE 'DATE CONVERSION SUBROUTINE'               DATE DA001000
                 * FUNCTION:                                               DATE DA002000
                 *       TO CONVERT FROM JULIAN FORM TO GEORGIAN FORM OR    DATE DA003000
                 *       VISA-VERSA OF DATE REPRESENTATION.                 DATE DA004000
                 *                                                          DATE DA005000
                 * INPUT:                                                   DATE DA006000
                 *       REG 0 TYPE PARAMETER                               DATE DA007000
                 *           =0                GEORGIAN TO JULIAN           DATE DA008000
                 *           ¬=0               JULIAN TO GEORGIAN           DATE DA009000
                 *       REG 1 DATE - FORMATS: PACKED DECIMAL               DATE DA010000
                 *           YYMMDD0F          GEORGIAN                     DATE DA011000
                 *           00YYDDDF          JULIAN                       DATE DA012000
```

```
12     S A S   L O G    SAS/OS 82.0      VS2/MVS JOB SOURCEX  STEP SAS      PROC EXAMPLE2
- - - - - - - - - - - - - - - - - - - - - - - - - - - - - - - - - - -
           SOURCE LIBRARY DATA SET: INDD=MYLIB,BLKSIZE=6160,
           DSNAME=MY.SOURCE.LIBRARY,VOL=SER=SCR111

      7    MEMBERS DEFINED IN SOURCE LIBRARY.

      0    ALIASES DEFINED IN SOURCE LIBRARY.

     20    DIRECTORY BLOCKS ALLOCATED.

      1    DIRECTORY BLOCK USED.

      7    MEMBERS SELECTED.

    542    RECORDS READ FROM SOURCE LIBRARY.
```

Unloading a Library to Tape: Example 3

The job below produces a data set on tape containing an unloaded form of the input source library.

```
//jobname JOB account,user
// EXEC SAS
//IN DD DISP=SHR,DSN=SSD.MVS.ASM
//TAPE DD DSN=SSD.MVSBK.ASM,DISP=(NEW,KEEP),UNIT=TAPE
PROC SOURCE NOPRINT INDD=IN OUTDD=TAPE;
```

```
1     S A S   L O G     SAS/OS 82.0      VS2/MVS JOB SOURCEX  STEP SAS       PROC EXAMPLE3
NOTE: THE JOB SOURCEX HAS BEEN RUN UNDER RELEASE 82.0 OF SAS AT SAS INSTITUTE INC.          (00000000).

  1           PROC SOURCE NOPRINT INDD=IN OUTDD=TAPE;

              SOURCE LIBRARY DATA SET: INDD=IN,BLKSIZE=6160,
              DSNAME=SSD.MVS.ASM,VOL=SER=SNO111

  135   MEMBERS DEFINED IN SOURCE LIBRARY.

    0   ALIASES DEFINED IN SOURCE LIBRARY.

   35   DIRECTORY BLOCKS ALLOCATED.

   23   DIRECTORY BLOCKS USED.

  135   MEMBERS SELECTED.

91926   RECORDS READ FROM SOURCE LIBRARY.

92061   RECORDS WRITTEN TO OUTDD=TAPE,
        LABEL=(1,SL),DISP=NEW,DCB=(DEN=4,BLKSIZE=8000),
        DSNAME=SSD.MVSBK.ASM,VOL=SER=S10108
NOTE: THE PROCEDURE SOURCE USED 13.98 SECONDS AND 328K.
NOTE: SAS USED 328K MEMORY.

NOTE: SAS INSTITUTE INC.
      SAS CIRCLE
      PO BOX 8000
      CARY, N.C. 27511-8000
```

Backing Up a Source Library Using LIBRARIAN®: Example 4

The job below produces a data set on disk containing control lines, suitable for processing by LIBRARIAN, a proprietary product of Applied Data Research, Inc. Executing a LIBRARIAN job step with these lines as input would cause each member of the input library (SYS2.PROCLIB in this example) to be copied to the LIBRARIAN data set specified with the MASTER option.

```
//jobname JOB account,user
// EXEC SAS
//PDS DD DISP=SHR,DSN=MY.SOURCE.LIBRARY
//SDS DD UNIT=DISK,DISP=(,PASS), DSN=&&LIBRNIN,(SPACE=(TRK,4,2))
PROC SOURCE INDD=PDS OUTDD=SDS NOALIAS NODATA;
  FIRST '-OPT NOLIST,NOEXEC,NOPC';
  BEFORE '-DLM XXXXXXXX' 6;
  BEFORE '-ADD XXXXXXXX,SEQ=/81,6,10,10/' 6 RIGHT;
```

```
1     S A S   L O G     SAS/OS 82.0      VS2/MVS JOB SOURCEX  STEP SAS       PROC EXAMPLE4
NOTE: THE JOB SOURCEX HAS BEEN RUN UNDER RELEASE 82.0 OF SAS AT SAS INSTITUTE INC.          (00000000).

  1           PROC SOURCE INDD=PDS OUTDD=SDS NOALIAS NODATA ;
  2             FIRST '-OPT NOLIST,NOEXEC,NOPC';
  3             BEFORE '-DLM XXXXXXXX' 6;
  4             BEFORE '-ADD XXXXXXXX,SEQ=/81,6,10,10/' 6 RIGHT;


NOTE: THE NODATA OPTION HAS BEEN SPECIFIED WITH OUTDD=;
      ONLY 'FIRST', 'BEFORE', 'AFTER', AND 'LAST'
      CONTROL CARDS WILL BE WRITTEN TO OUTDD=.
   $REGS
   DATE
   ENTER
   EXIT
   MAFRCD
   MULTIPLY
   TIME

- - - - - - - - - - - - - - - - - - - - - - - - - - - - - - - - -
```

(continued on next page)

```
(continued from previous page)

           SOURCE LIBRARY DATA SET: INDD=PDS,BLKSIZE=6160,
           DSNAME=MY.SOURCE.LIBRARY,VOL=SER=SCR111

   7   MEMBERS DEFINED IN SOURCE LIBRARY.

   0   ALIASES DEFINED IN SOURCE LIBRARY.

  20   DIRECTORY BLOCKS ALLOCATED.

   1   DIRECTORY BLOCK  USED.

   7   MEMBERS SELECTED.

   0   RECORDS READ FROM SOURCE LIBRARY.

  15   RECORDS WRITTEN TO OUTDD=SDS,
       LABEL=(,SL),DISP=NEW,DCB=(BLKSIZE=6160),
       DSNAME=SYS82201.T193836.RA000.SOURCEX.LIBRNIN
NOTE: THE PROCEDURE SOURCE USED 0.60 SECONDS AND 320K.
NOTE: SAS USED 320K MEMORY.

NOTE: SAS INSTITUTE INC.
      SAS CIRCLE
      PO BOX 8000
      CARY, N.C. 27511-8000
```

Generating Control Cards for IEBCOPY: Example 5

The job below produces control statements for IEBCOPY, and then executes
IEBCOPY to copy only those members selected.

```
//jobname JOB account,user
// EXEC SAS
//LPALIB DD DISP=SHR,DSN=SYS1.LPALIB
//CNTRL DD DISP=(,PASS),
// DSN=&&SYSIN,UNIT=DISK,SPACE=(TRK,(3,1))
PROC SOURCE INDD=LPALIB OUTDD=CNTRL NODATA NOPRINT;
  SELECT ISP: ;   EXCLUDE ISPTCM ISPBAD ISPJ-ISPU: ;
  SELECT ADF: GARBAGE:-G: ;
  SELECT IEF:;   EXCLUDE IEFU-IEFV:;
  SELECT IDC: IKJ: ;   EXCLUDE IKJEB: IKJEG: ;
  SELECT NOTTHERE MISS-MISSING: ;
  EXCLUDE BADNAME BADTOO: ;
  FIRST ' COPY INDD=((LPALIB,R)),OUTDD=NEWLPA';
  BEFORE ' SELECT MEMBER=XXXXXXXX ------------' 17;
  BEFORE '        S      M=XXXXXXXX ***ALIAS***' 17 ALIAS;
//COPY EXEC PGM=IEBCOPY
//SYSPRINT DD SYSOUT=A
//SYSUT3 DD UNIT=DISK,SPACE=(CYL,(1,1))
//SYSUT4 DD UNIT=DISK,SPACE=(CYL,(1,1))
//LPALIB DD DISP=SHR,DSN=SYS1.LPALIB
//NEWLPA DD DISP=(,KEEP),
// DSN=NEW.LPALIB,UNIT=DISK,VOL=SER=SCR111,
// SPACE=(CYL,(5,1,300)),DCB=SYS1.LINKLIB
//SYSIN DD DISP=(OLD,DELETE),DSN=&&SYSIN
```

```
1      S A S   L O G    SAS/OS 82.0      VS2/MVS JOB SOURCEX  STEP SAS     PROC EXAMPLE5

NOTE: THE JOB SOURCEX HAS BEEN RUN UNDER RELEASE 82.0 OF SAS AT SAS INSTITUTE INC.        (00000000).

1               PROC SOURCE INDD=LPALIB OUTDD=CNTRL NODATA NOPRINT;
2                 SELECT  ISP: ;   EXCLUDE ISPTCM ISPBAD ISPJ-ISPU: ;
3                 SELECT  ADF: GARBAGE:-G: ;
4                 SELECT  IEF:;    EXCLUDE IEFU-IEFV:;
5                 SELECT  IDC: IKJ: ; EXCLUDE IKJEB: IKJEG: ;
6                 SELECT  NOTTHERE  MISS-MISSING: ;
7                 EXCLUDE BADNAME BADTOO: ;
8                 FIRST ' COPY INDD=((LPALIB,R)),OUTDD=NEWLPA';
9                 BEFORE ' SELECT MEMBER=XXXXXXXX -----------' 17;
10                BEFORE '       S       M=XXXXXXXX ***ALIAS***' 17 ALIAS;

NOTE: THE NODATA OPTION HAS BEEN SPECIFIED WITH OUTDD=.
      ONLY 'FIRST', 'BEFORE', 'AFTER', AND 'LAST'
      CONTROL CARDS WILL BE WRITTEN TO OUTDD=.

NOTE: NO MEMBER FOUND FOR ALIAS (IGG08116);
      IT WILL BE TREATED AS A NON-ALIAS MEMBER.

NOTE: THE FOLLOWING SELECTED MEMBER NAMES OR RANGES WERE NOT FOUND:

      GARBAGE:-G:
      NOTTHERE
      MISS-MISSING:

NOTE: THE FOLLOWING EXCLUDED MEMBER NAMES OR RANGES WERE NOT FOUND:

      ISPBAD
      BADNAME
      BADTOO:

            SOURCE LIBRARY DATA SET: INDD=LPALIB,BLKSIZE=19069,
            DSNAME=SYS1.LPALIB,VOL=SER=MSPRST

  1243    MEMBERS DEFINED IN SOURCE LIBRARY.

   568    ALIASES DEFINED IN SOURCE LIBRARY.

   359    DIRECTORY BLOCKS ALLOCATED.

   318    DIRECTORY BLOCKS USED.

    72    MEMBERS SELECTED.

     0    RECORDS READ FROM SOURCE LIBRARY.

   174    RECORDS WRITTEN TO OUTDD=CNTRL,
            LABEL=(,SL),DISP=NEW,DCB=(BLKSIZE=6160),
            DSNAME=SYS82201.T193836.RA000.SOURCEX.SYSIN
NOTE: THE PROCEDURE SOURCE USED 4.36 SECONDS AND 460K.
NOTE: SAS USED 460K MEMORY.

NOTE: SAS INSTITUTE INC.
      SAS CIRCLE
      PO BOX 8000
      CARY, N.C. 27511-8000
```

```
                    IEBCOPY MESSAGES AND CONTROL STATEMENTS                      PAGE 0001

COPY INDD=((LPALIB,R)),OUTDD=NEWLPA
 SELECT MEMBER=ADFIDF00 -----------
 SELECT MEMBER=ADFMDFLT -----------
 SELECT MEMBER=ADFMDF01 -----------
 SELECT MEMBER=ADFMDF03 -----------
 SELECT MEMBER=AKJLKL01 -----------
        S        M=IKJLKL01 ***ALIAS***
 SELECT MEMBER=IDCAM01 -----------
        S        M=ALTER    ***ALIAS***
        S        M=DEF      ***ALIAS***
        S        M=DEFINE   ***ALIAS***
        S        M=DEL      ***ALIAS***
        S        M=DELETE   ***ALIAS***
        S        M=EXP      ***ALIAS***
        S        M=EXPORT   ***ALIAS***
        S        M=IMP      ***ALIAS***
        S        M=IMPORT   ***ALIAS***
        S        M=LISTC    ***ALIAS***
        S        M=LISTCAT  ***ALIAS***
        S        M=PRINT    ***ALIAS***
        S        M=REPRO    ***ALIAS***
        S        M=VERIFY   ***ALIAS***
        S        M=VFY      ***ALIAS***
 SELECT MEMBER=IDCAM02 -----------
        S        M=BIX      ***ALIAS***
        S        M=BLDINDEX ***ALIAS***
        S        M=CNVTC    ***ALIAS***
        S        M=CNVTCAT  ***ALIAS***
        S        M=DIAG     ***ALIAS***
```

(continued on next page)

(continued from previous page)

```
         S         M=DIAGNOSE  ***ALIAS***
         S         M=EXPORTRA  ***ALIAS***
         S         M=IMPORTRA  ***ALIAS***
         S         M=LISTCRA   ***ALIAS***
         S         M=LISTR     ***ALIAS***
         S         M=MPRA      ***ALIAS***
         S         M=RCAT      ***ALIAS***
         S         M=RESETCAT  ***ALIAS***
         S         M=XPRA      ***ALIAS***
   SELECT MEMBER=IEFAB4E5 -----------
   SELECT MEMBER=IEFACTRT -----------
   SELECT MEMBER=IEFBR14  -----------
   SELECT MEMBER=IEFDB4D0 -----------
         S         M=IKJDAIR   ***ALIAS***
         S         M=IKJEFD00  ***ALIAS***
   SELECT MEMBER=IEFDEVPT -----------
   SELECT MEMBER=IEFEDTTB -----------
   SELECT MEMBER=IEFENFNM -----------
   SELECT MEMBER=IEFIB600 -----------
         S         M=IEFXB603  ***ALIAS***
   SELECT MEMBER=IEFIRECM -----------
   SELECT MEMBER=IEFJDSNA -----------
   SELECT MEMBER=IEFJJTRM -----------
   SELECT MEMBER=IEFJRASP -----------
```

```
              IEBCOPY  MESSAGES  AND  CONTROL  STATEMENTS              PAGE  0002

COPY INDD=(((LPALIB,R)),OUTDD=NEWLPA
   SELECT MEMBER=ADFIDF00 -----------
   SELECT MEMBER=ADFMDFLT -----------
   SELECT MEMBER=ADFMDF01 -----------
   SELECT MEMBER=ADFMDF03 -----------
   SELECT MEMBER=AKJLKL01 -----------
         S         M=IKJLKL01  ***ALIAS***
   SELECT MEMBER=IDCAM01 -----------
         S         M=ALTER     ***ALIAS***
         S         M=DEF       ***ALIAS***
         S         M=DEFINE    ***ALIAS***
         S         M=DEL       ***ALIAS***
         S         M=DELETE    ***ALIAS***
         S         M=EXP       ***ALIAS***
         S         M=EXPORT    ***ALIAS***
         S         M=IMP       ***ALIAS***
         S         M=IMPORT    ***ALIAS***
         S         M=LISTC     ***ALIAS***
         S         M=LISTCAT   ***ALIAS***
         S         M=PRINT     ***ALIAS***
         S         M=REPRO     ***ALIAS***
         S         M=VERIFY    ***ALIAS***
         S         M=VFY       ***ALIAS***
   SELECT MEMBER=IDCAM02 -----------
         S         M=BIX       ***ALIAS***
         S         M=BLDINDEX  ***ALIAS***
         S         M=CNVTC     ***ALIAS***
         S         M=CNVTCAT   ***ALIAS***
         S         M=DIAG      ***ALIAS***
         S         M=DIAGNOSE  ***ALIAS***
         S         M=EXPORTRA  ***ALIAS***
         S         M=IMPORTRA  ***ALIAS***
         S         M=LISTCRA   ***ALIAS***
         S         M=LISTR     ***ALIAS***
         S         M=MPRA      ***ALIAS***
         S         M=RCAT      ***ALIAS***
         S         M=RESETCAT  ***ALIAS***
         S         M=XPRA      ***ALIAS***
   SELECT MEMBER=IEFAB4E5 -----------
   SELECT MEMBER=IEFACTRT -----------
   SELECT MEMBER=IEFBR14  -----------
   SELECT MEMBER=IEFDB4D0 -----------
         S         M=IKJDAIR   ***ALIAS***
         S         M=IKJEFD00  ***ALIAS***
   SELECT MEMBER=IEFDEVPT -----------
   SELECT MEMBER=IEFEDTTB -----------
   SELECT MEMBER=IEFENFNM -----------
   SELECT MEMBER=IEFIB600 -----------
         S         M=IEFXB603  ***ALIAS***
   SELECT MEMBER=IEFIRECM -----------
   SELECT MEMBER=IEFJDSNA -----------
   SELECT MEMBER=IEFJJTRM -----------
   SELECT MEMBER=IEFJRASP -----------
```

```
                    IEBCOPY MESSAGES AND CONTROL STATEMENTS                PAGE 0003

SELECT  MEMBER=IEFJRECM  -----------
    S          M=IEFJRECF  ***ALIAS***
SELECT  MEMBER=IEFJSDTN  -----------
SELECT  MEMBER=IEFJSREQ  -----------
SELECT  MEMBER=IEFJSUBI  -----------
SELECT  MEMBER=IEFNB903  -----------
SELECT  MEMBER=IEFQB550  -----------
    S          M=IEFQB555  ***ALIAS***
    S          M=IEFQB580  ***ALIAS***
    S          M=IEFXB500  ***ALIAS***
SELECT  MEMBER=IEFQB585  -----------
    S          M=IEFQAGST  ***ALIAS***
    S          M=IEFQASGN  ***ALIAS***
    S          M=IEFQASGQ  ***ALIAS***
    S          M=IEFQBVMS  ***ALIAS***
    S          M=IEFQDELE  ***ALIAS***
    S          M=IEFQDELQ  ***ALIAS***
    S          M=IEFQMLK1  ***ALIAS***
    S          M=IEFQMRAW  ***ALIAS***
    S          M=IEFQMSSS  ***ALIAS***
SELECT  MEMBER=IEFRSTRT  -----------
    S          M=IEFSMR    ***ALIAS***
SELECT  MEMBER=IEFSDTTE  -----------
SELECT  MEMBER=IEFSDXXX  -----------
SELECT  MEMBER=IEFSD060  -----------
    S          M=IEFIIC    ***ALIAS***
    S          M=IEFSMFIE  ***ALIAS***
SELECT  MEMBER=IEFSD087  -----------
SELECT  MEMBER=IEFSD094  -----------
SELECT  MEMBER=IEFW21SD  -----------
    S          M=IEFAB4DC  ***ALIAS***
    S          M=IEFAB4EC  ***ALIAS***
    S          M=IEFAB4F4  ***ALIAS***
    S          M=IEFAB4F5  ***ALIAS***
    S          M=IEFAB4SF  ***ALIAS***
    S          M=IEFAB4UV  ***ALIAS***
    S          M=IEFAB445  ***ALIAS***
    S          M=IEFAB49C  ***ALIAS***
    S          M=IEFBB410  ***ALIAS***
    S          M=IEFTB723  ***ALIAS***
    S          M=IGC00091  ***ALIAS***
SELECT  MEMBER=IEFXB602  -----------
    S          M=IEF602    ***ALIAS***
SELECT  MEMBER=IEFXB610  -----------
SELECT  MEMBER=IKJCB831  -----------
    S          M=GENTRANS  ***ALIAS***
SELECT  MEMBER=IKJEFE11  -----------
    S          M=END       ***ALIAS***
    S          M=WHEN      ***ALIAS***
SELECT  MEMBER=IKJEFF02  -----------
SELECT  MEMBER=IKJEFG00  -----------
    S          M=CALL      ***ALIAS***
SELECT  MEMBER=IKJEFLA   -----------
```

```
                    IEBCOPY MESSAGES AND CONTROL STATEMENTS                PAGE 0004

    S          M=IKJEFLC  ***ALIAS***
    S          M=IKJEFLES ***ALIAS***
    S          M=IKJLB1   ***ALIAS***
    S          M=IKJLJ1   ***ALIAS***
    S          M=IKJLK1   ***ALIAS***
    S          M=IKJLM1   ***ALIAS***
SELECT  MEMBER=IKJEFLF   -----------
SELECT  MEMBER=IKJEFT01  -----------
    S          M=IKJEFT0A ***ALIAS***
SELECT  MEMBER=IKJEFT02  -----------
    S          M=IKJEFT0B ***ALIAS***
    S          M=IKJEFT03 ***ALIAS***
SELECT  MEMBER=IKJEFT04  -----------
    S          M=IKJEFT0D ***ALIAS***
    S          M=IKJEFT0E ***ALIAS***
    S          M=IKJEFT05 ***ALIAS***
SELECT  MEMBER=IKJEFT07  -----------
SELECT  MEMBER=IKJEFT09  -----------
SELECT  MEMBER=IKJEHAL1  -----------
    S          M=LISTA    ***ALIAS***
    S          M=LISTALC  ***ALIAS***
SELECT  MEMBER=IKJEHDEF  -----------
    S          M=IKJDFLT  ***ALIAS***
    S          M=IKJEHCIR ***ALIAS***
SELECT  MEMBER=IKJEHDS1  -----------
    S          M=LISID    ***ALIAS***
    S          M=LISTDS   ***ALIAS***
SELECT  MEMBER=IKJEHMEM  -----------
SELECT  MEMBER=IKJEHPRO  -----------
    S          M=PROT     ***ALIAS***
    S          M=PROTECT  ***ALIAS***
SELECT  MEMBER=IKJEHREN  -----------
    S          M=REN      ***ALIAS***
    S          M=RENAME   ***ALIAS***
```

(continued on next page)

(continued from previous page)

```
SELECT MEMBER=IKJEIISIR -----------
SELECT MEMBER=IKJPARS  -----------
SELECT MEMBER=IKJPARS2 -----------
SELECT MEMBER=IKJPTGT  -----------
     S      M=IKJGETL  ***ALIAS***
     S      M=IKJPUTL  ***ALIAS***
     S      M=IKJSTCK  ***ALIAS***
SELECT MEMBER=IKJSCAN  -----------
SELECT MEMBER=ISPBRO   -----------
SELECT MEMBER=ISPCALL  -----------
SELECT MEMBER=ISPDPT   -----------
SELECT MEMBER=ISPEDIT  -----------
SELECT MEMBER=ISPFOR   -----------
SELECT MEMBER=ISPICP   -----------
     S      M=ISPF     ***ALIAS***
     S      M=ISPTASK  ***ALIAS***
     S      M=SPF      ***ALIAS***
SELECT MEMBER=ISP3277  -----------
SELECT MEMBER=ISP3277K -----------
```

```
              IEBCOPY MESSAGES AND CONTROL STATEMENTS              PAGE 0005

                    SELECT MEMBER=ISP3278  -----------
                    SELECT MEMBER=ISP3278C -----------
                    SELECT MEMBER=ISP3278K -----------
                    SELECT MEMBER=SMCOPY   -----------
                         S      M=ADFMCOPY ***ALIAS***
                         S      M=SMC      ***ALIAS***
                    SELECT MEMBER=SMFIND   -----------
                         S      M=ADFMFIND ***ALIAS***
                         S      M=SMF      ***ALIAS***
                    SELECT MEMBER=SMPUT    -----------
                         S      M=ADFMPUT  ***ALIAS***
                         S      M=SMP      ***ALIAS***
                    SELECT MEMBER=STATUS   -----------
                         S      M=IKJEFFCA ***ALIAS***
                         S      M=ST       ***ALIAS***
IEB167I  FOLLOWING MEMBER(S) COPIED  FROM INPUT DATA SET REFERENCED BY LPALIB  -
IEB154I  ADFIDF00 HAS BEEN SUCCESSFULLY COPIED
IEB154I  ADFMCOPY HAS BEEN SUCCESSFULLY COPIED
IEB154I  ADFMDFLT HAS BEEN SUCCESSFULLY COPIED
IEB154I  ADFMDF01 HAS BEEN SUCCESSFULLY COPIED
IEB154I  ADFMDF03 HAS BEEN SUCCESSFULLY COPIED
IEB154I  ADFMFIND HAS BEEN SUCCESSFULLY COPIED
IEB154I  ADFMPUT  HAS BEEN SUCCESSFULLY COPIED
IEB154I  AKJLKL01 HAS BEEN SUCCESSFULLY COPIED
IEB154I  ALTER    HAS BEEN SUCCESSFULLY COPIED
IEB154I  BIX      HAS BEEN SUCCESSFULLY COPIED
IEB154I  BLDINDEX HAS BEEN SUCCESSFULLY COPIED
IEB154I  CALL     HAS BEEN SUCCESSFULLY COPIED
IEB154I  CNVTC    HAS BEEN SUCCESSFULLY COPIED
IEB154I  CNVTCAT  HAS BEEN SUCCESSFULLY COPIED
IEB154I  DEF      HAS BEEN SUCCESSFULLY COPIED
IEB154I  DEFINE   HAS BEEN SUCCESSFULLY COPIED
IEB154I  DEL      HAS BEEN SUCCESSFULLY COPIED
IEB154I  DELETE   HAS BEEN SUCCESSFULLY COPIED
IEB154I  DIAG     HAS BEEN SUCCESSFULLY COPIED
IEB154I  DIAGNOSE HAS BEEN SUCCESSFULLY COPIED
IEB154I  END      HAS BEEN SUCCESSFULLY COPIED
IEB154I  EXP      HAS BEEN SUCCESSFULLY COPIED
IEB154I  EXPORT   HAS BEEN SUCCESSFULLY COPIED
IEB154I  EXPORTRA HAS BEEN SUCCESSFULLY COPIED
IEB154I  GENTRANS HAS BEEN SUCCESSFULLY COPIED
IEB154I  IDCAM01  HAS BEEN SUCCESSFULLY COPIED
IEB154I  IDCAM02  HAS BEEN SUCCESSFULLY COPIED
IEB154I  IEFAB4DC HAS BEEN SUCCESSFULLY COPIED
IEB154I  IEFAB4EC HAS BEEN SUCCESSFULLY COPIED
IEB154I  IEFAB4E5 HAS BEEN SUCCESSFULLY COPIED
IEB154I  IEFAB4F4 HAS BEEN SUCCESSFULLY COPIED
IEB154I  IEFAB4F5 HAS BEEN SUCCESSFULLY COPIED
IEB154I  IEFAB4SF HAS BEEN SUCCESSFULLY COPIED
IEB154I  IEFAB4UV HAS BEEN SUCCESSFULLY COPIED
IEB154I  IEFAB445 HAS BEEN SUCCESSFULLY COPIED
IEB154I  IEFAB49C HAS BEEN SUCCESSFULLY COPIED
IEB154I  IEFACTRT HAS BEEN SUCCESSFULLY COPIED
```

```
IEB1541  RENAME    HAS BEEN SUCCESSFULLY  COPIED
IEB1541  REPRO     HAS BEEN SUCCESSFULLY  COPIED
IEB1541  RESETCAT  HAS BEEN SUCCESSFULLY  COPIED
IEB1541  SMC       HAS BEEN SUCCESSFULLY  COPIED
IEB1541  SMCOPY    HAS BEEN SUCCESSFULLY  COPIED
IEB1541  SMF       HAS BEEN SUCCESSFULLY  COPIED
IEB1541  SMFIND    HAS BEEN SUCCESSFULLY  COPIED
IEB1541  SMP       HAS BEEN SUCCESSFULLY  COPIED
IEB1541  SMPUT     HAS BEEN SUCCESSFULLY  COPIED
IEB1541  SPF       HAS BEEN SUCCESSFULLY  COPIED
IEB1541  ST        HAS BEEN SUCCESSFULLY  COPIED
IEB1541  STATUS    HAS BEEN SUCCESSFULLY  COPIED
IEB1541  VERIFY    HAS BEEN SUCCESSFULLY  COPIED
IEB1541  VFY       HAS BEEN SUCCESSFULLY  COPIED
IEB1541  WHEN      HAS BEEN SUCCESSFULLY  COPIED
IEB1541  XPRA      HAS BEEN SUCCESSFULLY  COPIED
IEB1441  THERE ARE 0000074 UNUSED TRACKS IN OUTPUT DATA SET REFERENCED BY NEWLPA
IEB1491  THERE ARE 0000267  UNUSED DIRECTORY BLOCKS IN OUTPUT DIRECTORY
IEB1471  END OF JOB -00 WAS HIGHEST SEVERITY CODE
```

REFERENCES

International Business Machines Corporation (1980), *OS/VS2 MVS Data Management Services Guide*, Release 3.8, SRL Form Number GC26-3875.

International Business Machines Corporation (1977), *OS/VS2 MVS Utilities*, Release 3.8, SRL Form Number GC26-3902.

International Business Machines Corporation (1979), *OS/VS2 MVS JCL*, Release 3.8, SRL Form Number GC28-0692.

822

The TAPECOPY Procedure

ABSTRACT

The TAPECOPY procedure copies an entire tape volume (tape) or files from one or several tape volumes to one and only one output tape volume. TAPECOPY always begins writing at the beginning of the output tape volume; any files that exist on the output tape prior to the copy operation are destroyed. The procedure works under OS and CMS. For the sake of clarity the procedure is described in separate sections for each system: first for OS, and then for CMS. Examples for TAPECOPY under both systems are at the end of the chapter.

INTRODUCTION TO PROC TAPECOPY UNDER OS

TAPECOPY can copy standard-labeled or non-labeled 9-track tapes. You can specify, within limits, whether the output tape is standard-labeled (SL) or non-labeled (NL). You cannot create an SL tape using an NL input tape because TAPECOPY cannot manufacture tape labels. Nor can you change an output tape volume for which LABEL=(,SL) is specified in a DD statement into a non-labeled tape. TAPECOPY does allow you to write over an existing label on a standard-labeled tape if you specify LABEL=(,BLP) in the DD statement.

The JCL DD statement parameter LABEL=(,BLP) must be authorized specifically by each computing installation. If your installation allows the BLP specification, ANSI-labeled, non-standard-labeled, and standard-user-labeled tapes can be treated as non-labeled tape volumes. If the BLP specification is not authorized at your installation, LABEL=(,BLP) is treated as LABEL=(,NL). PROC TAPECOPY will work as you expect if your tape is in fact non-labeled; otherwise, the operating system does not allow TAPECOPY to use the tape, thus preserving the label.

References to specifying LABEL=(,BLP) throughout this OS description assume that LABEL=(,BLP) is a valid specification at your installation.

SPECIFICATIONS UNDER OS

The following statements are used in PROC TAPECOPY.

> **PROC TAPECOPY** *options*;
> **INVOL** *options*;
> **FILES** *filenumbers*;

PROC TAPECOPY Statement

> PROC TAPECOPY *options*;

The options listed below can appear in the PROC TAPECOPY statement.

NOLIST   suppresses printing of the tape characteristics and a summary of copied files. Whether NOLIST is specified or not, the SAS log contains a brief summary of TAPECOPY's action; this summary is usually enough to verify proper functioning of TAPECOPY if you are familiar with the contents of the input tape(s).

DEN=*density*   specifies the *density* of the output tape. If the DEN= option appears in the PROC TAPECOPY statement, it overrides any DCB=DEN specification in the DD statement for the output tape volume. If you do not specify a density in the PROC TAPECOPY statement or in the DD statement, the operating system writes the tape at its default density, usually the highest density at which the unit allocated to the output tape volume can record.

Valid density values are:

DEN=2 DEN=800 DEN=800BPI
DEN=3 DEN=1600 DEN=1600BPI
DEN=4 DEN=6250 DEN=6250BPI

LABEL=SL   specifies whether the output tape volume is to be
LABEL=NL   standard-labeled (LABEL=SL) or non-labeled
(LABEL=NL).

Be careful not to confuse the LABEL= option on the PROC statement with the DD statement parameter LABEL=(,*specification*). The PROC statement LABEL = option specifies whether the output tape will be standard labeled or non-labeled **after** the copy operation. The output tape volume's DD statement LABEL= parameter specifies what the output tape's label status is **before** the copy operation.

The DD statement for non-labeled output tapes must specify LABEL=(,NL) or LABEL=(,BLP). If the output tape has an existing label (before the copy operation), and the output tape is to be non-labeled (after the copy operation), the DD statement **must** specify LABEL=(,BLP).

The default LABEL= option value is NL when multiple input volumes are used and the DD statements for any of them specify LABEL=(,NL). If there are multiple input tapes and LABEL=(,NL) is **not** specified for any of them, and the first input tape volume is actually standard-labeled, the default LABEL= option value is SL. This holds even if the DD statement specifies LABEL=(,BLP) for the first tape; in this case, PROC TAPECOPY reads the tape volume's first record to determine the actual label type.

COPYVOLSER   specifies that the output tape should have a standard label with the same volume serial as the first input tape.

COPYVOLSER is only effective when:

1. the output tape volume is to be standard-labeled, that is, LABEL=SL, and
2. the output tape DD statement specifies LABEL=(,NL) or LABEL=(,BLP)

When these conditions are not met, TAPECOPY stops processing.

INDD=*DDname*   specifies the *DDname* of the JCL DD statement describing the first input tape volume. The default INDD= value is VOLIN.

OUTDD=*DDname*   specifies the *DDname* of the JCL DD statement describing the output tape. The default OUTDD= value is VOLOUT.

INVOL=   specifies the *volume serial* of the first input tape when
volume serial   deferred mounting is specified in the DD statement for the first input tape. The INVOL= option specification overrides the volume serial, if any, specified in the DD statement for the tape.

You should not specify the INVOL= option unless you are using deferred mounting.

OUTVOL=   specifies the *volume serial* of the output tape when
volume serial   deferred mounting is specified in the DD statement for

the output tape. The OUTVOL= option specification overrides the volume serial, if any, specified on the DD statement for the tape.

   You should not specify the OUTVOL= option unless you are using deferred mounting.

NORER
: requests that the "reduced error recovery for tape devices" feature of the operating system not be specified for each input tape volume. Some tapes of marginal quality can be read successfully by TAPECOPY when NORER is specified, since the error recovery procedures are more exhaustive.

NEWVOLSER=
new volume serial
: specifies a *new volume serial* for the output tape. NEWVOLSER is effective only if the output tape is to be standard-labeled. If the output tape has an existing label, the DD statement for the output tape must specify LABEL=(,BLP); otherwise, TAPECOPY stops processing and does not write over the label.

NOFSNRESEQ
NFR
: specifies that file sequence numbers in the file labels should not be resequenced when a standard-labeled output tape volume is being produced. TAPECOPY normally resequences these numbers and updates the label to reflect the ordinal position of the file on the output tape as it is copied and the actual density at which the output tape is written.

INVOL Statement

INVOL *options;*

The INVOL statement defines an input tape volume from which some or all files are to be copied to the output tape volume. The INVOL statement is not necessary if you are using only one input tape, or for the first of several input tapes (use the INDD= and INVOL= options of the PROC TAPECOPY statement instead). When you are using several input tapes, use an INVOL statement for each tape after the first input tape.

   The options below may be used in the INVOL statement.

INDD=*DDname*
: specifies the *DDname* of the JCL DD statement describing the current input tape. The default INDD= value is the DDname already in effect for the previous input tape volume, as specified in the PROC TAPECOPY statement or in the last INVOL statement.

INVOL=
volume serial
: specifies the *volume serial* of the current input tape. Use the INVOL= option when the JCL DD statement for the input tape specifies deferred mounting (as described above in **PROC TAPECOPY Statement**), or when you are "reusing" a DD statement (and tape drive); that is, the DDname is the same, but you want a different tape volume on the same unit.

NL
: specifies that the input tape is non-labeled; if LABEL=(,SL) or LABEL=(,BLP) has been specified in the DD statement for the input tape and the tape is actually standard-labeled, specifying the NL option causes the tape to be treated as if it were non-labeled.

In this case, any file numbers specified in FILES statements must be physical file numbers, not logical file numbers.

SL   specifies that the input tape is standard-labeled. If you specify LABEL=(,BLP) in the DD statement for the input tape, and specify SL in the INVOL statement, TAPECOPY verifies that the tape is standard-labeled. Do not specify SL unless the tape is actually standard-labeled.

If you do not specify NL or SL in the INVOL statement, the actual input tape label type determines whether TAPECOPY treats the tape as NL or SL, even when LABEL=(,BLP) is specified in the DD statement.

DSNAME=   specifies the *data set name* of the first file of the cur-
'data set name'   rent input tape. You **must** use this option when:
DSN='data set name'

1. the data set name specified in the DD statement is incorrect or missing, and
2. when LABEL=(,SL) is specified (or implied by default) on the input tape volume DD statement.

You typically use this option when:

1. the DD statement for the input tape specifies deferred mounting, or
2. you are "reusing" a DD statement (and tape drive); that is, when the DDname is the same but you want another standard-labeled tape volume on the same unit. LABEL=(,SL) should be specified or defaulted, and the data set name cannot be the same as that on the previous tape used with this DDname.

NORER   requests that the "reduced error recovery for tape devices" feature of the operating system not be specified for the input tape volume. Some tapes of marginal quality can be read successfully by TAPECOPY when this option is specified, since the error recovery procedures are more exhaustive. If NORER is specified in the PROC TAPECOPY statement, then NORER is in effect for all input tape volumes and INVOL statements.

FILES Statement

FILES *filenumbers*;
FILE *filenumbers*;

When you want to copy certain files from an input tape, use the FILES statement to specify the files you want to copy. Use as many FILES statements as you want. Give the physical file numbers for non-labeled tapes, or labeled tapes being treated as non-labeled. Give the logical file numbers for standard-labeled tapes not being treated as non-labeled, even when the output tape volume is to be non-labeled (LABEL=NL).

You can specify a range of files by putting a dash between two file numbers:

```
PROC TAPECOPY;
   FILES 1-7;
```

In a range, the second number must be greater than the first. The keyword EOV may be used as the second file in a range; TAPECOPY copies all files on the input tape until the end of the volume (in most cases, a double tapemark). On a non-labeled tape, you can copy files beyond the double tapemark by specifying the physical file number, counting tapemarks as usual. If another double tapemark exists on the input tape volume, you can then specify EOV in another range.

File numbers in a FILES statement can be specified in any order; you might want to copy file 5 and then file 2 and then file 1.

```
PROC TAPECOPY;
   FILES 5 2;
   FILE 1;
```

If you are using only one input tape, the FILES statement(s) may follow the PROC TAPECOPY statement directly. When several input tape volumes are used, follow each INVOL statement with the FILES statement(s).

DETAILS UNDER OS

Usage Notes

Input tape DD statement requirements   In the DD statement describing an input tape, you need to specify only UNIT, VOL=SER, DISP, and usually either LABEL or DSN. The VOL=SER value gives the volume serial of the first input tape; VOL=SER can be omitted if the UNIT parameter specifies deferred mounting; for example, UNIT=(tape,,DEFER). (If you specify deferred mounting, remember to use the INVOL= option in the PROC statement and/or INVOL statement(s) to specify the volume serial of the input tape.)

For a non-labeled input tape, you must specify LABEL=(,NL) or LABEL=(,BLP) in the DD statement. If you are unsure whether the input tape volume is labeled or non-labeled, specify LABEL=(,BLP) in the input tape DD statement, if your installation allows it.

For a standard-labeled input tape at an installation that does not allow LABEL=(,BLP), specify LABEL=(,SL) and the DSN parameter, giving the DSNAME of the first data set on the tape.

Output tape DD statement requirements   In the DD statement describing the output tape you usually need to specify only the UNIT, VOL=SER, DISP, and possibly LABEL or DSN parameters. The VOL=SER value gives the volume serial of the output tape. VOL=SER can be omitted if the UNIT parameter specifies deferred mounting; for example, UNIT=(tape,,DEFER). (If you specify deferred mounting, use the OUTVOL= option in the PROC statement to specify the volume serial of the output tape.)

You should normally specify DISP=(NEW,KEEP) for the output tape in the DD statement. At some installations it may be necessary to specify DISP=(OLD,KEEP) along with the DSN parameter, giving the DSNAME of the first data set on the tape volume. The LABEL parameter should give the tape's label type before the TAPECOPY procedure is executed, regardless of its label type after the copying operation.

Printed Output

TAPECOPY prints a listing of the input and output tape characteristics and a summary of the files copied on the SAS log.

INTRODUCTION TO PROC TAPECOPY UNDER CMS

TAPECOPY can copy standard-labeled or non-labeled 9-track tapes under CMS. You can specify, within limits, whether the output tape is standard-labeled (SL) or non-labeled (NL). You cannot create an SL tape using an NL input tape because TAPECOPY cannot manufacture tape labels. You can create a non-labeled output tape volume from a labeled input tape. Under CMS, TAPECOPY writes over any existing labels on the output tape.

It is not possible to use tapes (and therefore, TAPECOPY) at all CMS sites. Some CMS sites do not have any CMS tape mount commands, but allow you to mount tapes by contacting the computer operator. If your installation does not support CMS tape mount commands, you can use TAPECOPY, but you cannot specify deferred tape mounting for input tapes. If your installation does have a CMS tape mount command(s), you can specify deferred tape mounting with an option in the procedure's INVOL statement (see below).

Note: TAPECOPY supports deferred mounting of input tapes only.

SPECIFICATIONS UNDER CMS

The following statements are used in PROC TAPECOPY.

> **PROC TAPECOPY** *options*;
>   **INVOL** *options /CMSmount*;
>   **FILES** *filenumbers*;

PROC TAPECOPY Statement

PROC TAPECOPY *options*;

The options listed below can appear in the PROC TAPECOPY statement.

NOLIST   suppresses printing of the tape characteristics and a summary of copied files. Whether NOLIST is specified or not, the SAS log contains a brief summary of TAPECOPY's action; this summary is usually enough to verify proper functioning of TAPECOPY if you are familiar with the contents of the input tape(s).

DEN=*density*   specifies the density of the output tape. If the DEN= option appears in the PROC TAPECOPY statement, it overrides any density specification in the FILEDEF for the output tape volume. If you do not specify a density in the PROC TAPECOPY statement, the tape is written at the highest density possible.

Valid density values are:

DEN=2 DEN=800 DEN=800BPI
DEN=3 DEN=1600 DEN=1600BPI
DEN=4 DEN=6250 DEN=6250BPI

LABEL=SL   specifies whether the output tape volume is to be
LABEL=NL   standard-labeled (LABEL=SL) or non-labeled
LABEL=BLP (LABEL=NL), or that all label processing should be
bypassed (LABEL=BLP). The default LABEL= option
value is BLP. Do not specify SL if you intend to copy
any non-labeled tapes.

   If SL is specified, the output tape will be SL; if NL is
specified the output tape will be NL. When BLP is
specified, all files are treated as physical files and the
distinction between data files and label files is irrele-
vant; therefore, the output tape will have the label
status of the input tape.

COPYVOLSER   specifies that the output tape should have a standard
label with the same volume serial as the first input
tape.

   COPYVOLSER is only effective when the output tape
volume is to be standard-labeled, that is, LABEL=SL.
When this condition is not met, TAPECOPY stops processing.

INDD=*DDname*   specifies the *DDname* of the FILEDEF describing the
first input tape volume. The default INDD= value is
VOLIN.

TAP1   specifies tape drive 181 as the input tape device. There
is no need for an input tape FILEDEF if this option is
used. If INDD= is not specified and there is no
FILEDEF for VOLIN, TAP1 is the default. Do not use
both INDD= and TAP1.

OUTDD=*DDname*   specifies the *DDname* of the FILEDEF describing the
output tape. The default OUTDD= value is VOLOUT.

TAP*n*   specifies tape drive 18*n* as the output tape device,
where *n* is 2, 3, or 4. If TAP*n* is specified, there is no
need for an output tape FILEDEF. If OUTDD= has not
been specified and there is no FILEDEF for VOLOUT,
TAP*n* defaults to TAP2. Do not specify both INDD=
and TAP*n*.

INVOL=   specifies the *volume serial* of the first input tape.
volume serial

NEWVOLSER=   specifies a *new volume serial* for the output tape.
new volume serial   NEWVOLSER is effective only if the output tape is to
be standard-labeled.

DETACH   requests that all tape drives used by TAPECOPY be
detached after the procedure has executed.

NOFSNRESEQ   specifies that file sequence numbers in the file labels
NFR   should not be resequenced when a standard-labeled
output tape volume is being produced. TAPECOPY
normally resequences these numbers and updates the
label to reflect the ordinal position of the file on the
output tape as it is copied and the actual density at
which the output tape is written.

INVOL Statement

INVOL options /CMSmount;

The INVOL statement defines an input tape volume from which some or all files are to be copied to the output tape volume. The INVOL statement is not necessary if you are using only one input tape, or for the first of several input tapes (use the INDD= and INVOL= options of the PROC TAPECOPY statement instead). When you are using several input tapes, use an INVOL statement for each tape after the first input tape.

If you want to use deferred mounting for an input tape you must use an INVOL statement with the /CMSmount option (below). (You cannot use deferred mounting for an output tape.)

The options below may be used in the INVOL statement.

INDD=DDname   specifies the DDname of the FILEDEF describing the current input tape. The default INDD= value is the DDname already in effect for the previous input tape volume, as specified in the PROC TAPECOPY statement or the last INVOL statement.

TAPn   specifies the tape drive to use, where n is 1, 2, 3, or 4. The default value is the TAPn in effect from the PROC statement or previous INVOL statement. Do not use both INDD= and TAPn.

INVOL=   specifies the volume serial of the current input tape.
volume serial

NL   specifies that the input tape is non-labeled; if the input tape is actually standard-labeled, specifying the NL option causes the tape to be treated as if it were non-labeled. In this case, any file numbers specified in FILES statements must be physical file numbers, not logical file numbers.

If you specify LABEL=SL in the PROC statement (for the output tape), do not specify NL on a subsequent INVOL statement. In other words, do not copy labeled and non-labeled tapes onto the same output tape, unless the labeled tapes are to be treated as non-labeled.

SL   specifies that the input tape is standard-labeled. Do not specify SL unless the tape is actually standard-labeled.

BLP   specifies that label processing is to be by-passed. BLP is the default if neither SL or NL is specified.

Be sure that you know the contents of any tape for which you specify BLP on an INVOL statement to avoid copying labeled and non-labeled tapes to the same output tape.

/CMSmount   specifies the tape mount command that your installation uses to mount a tape. Follow the slash with the text of the mount command. This option causes deferred mounting of the input tape; it must be used following the DETACH option.

At installations that do not have any mount commands this option is invalid; therefore, you cannot use deferred mounting.

The mount request is executed via the standard CMS function call (SVC 202). If the return code is not zero (for example, if TAPECOPY cannot find the specified mount command), SAS prints a message on the SAS log and TAPECOPY stops processing. Some mount commands require that the tape drive be detached before the mount is issued (for example, VLIB). If this is a requirement, then DETACH must be specified on the INVOL statement.

DETACH   specifies that the tape drive be detached before issuing a mount command.

FILES Statement

FILES *filenumbers*;
FILE *filenumbers*;

When you want to copy certain files from an input tape, use the FILES statement to specify the files you want to copy. Use as many FILES statements as you want. Depending on the kind of tape (labeled or non-labeled) being copied and the intended label status of the output tape, you need to specify physical or logical file numbers in the FILES statement. The table below shows what kind of file numbers to specify.

Input tape is	LABEL= is	Output tape is	File # is in units of
SL	SL	SL	logical
SL	NL	NL	logical
NL	NL	NL	physical
NL	BLP	NL	physical
SL	BLP	SL	physical

Note: a physical file consists of the information on a tape between two tapemarks. A logical file consists of three physical files; the first containing a header label; the second, data; and the third, a trailer label. "Logical file" implies a standard-labeled tape.

You can specify a range of files by putting a dash between the two files:

PROC TAPECOPY;
    FILES 1–7;

In a range, the second number must be greater than the first. The keyword EOV may be used as the second file in a range; TAPECOPY copies all files on the input tape until the end of the volume (in most cases, a double tapemark). On a non-labeled tape, you can copy files beyond the double tapemark by specifying the physical file number, counting tapemarks as usual. If another double tapemark exists on the input tape volume, you can then specify EOV in another range.

File numbers in a FILES statement can be specified in any order; you might want to copy file 5 and then file 2 and then file 1.

PROC TAPECOPY;
    FILES 5 2;
    FILE 1;

If you are using only one input tape, the FILES statement(s) may follow the PROC TAPECOPY statement directly. When several input tape volumes are used, follow each INVOL statement with the FILES statement(s).

DETAILS UNDER CMS

FILEDEF requirements FILEDEFs for input and output tapes are optional; however, if you use FILEDEFs you need specify only the device on the FILEDEF command, for example, TAP*n*, where *n* is 1, 2, 3, or 4.

Printed Output

TAPECOPY prints a listing of the input and output tape characteristics and a summary of the files copied on the SAS log.

EXAMPLES

SL to SL Under OS: Example 1

The job below copies a standard-labeled tape (volume serial XXXXXX) onto another standard-labeled tape (volume serial YYYYYY).

```
//jobname JOB account,name
//   EXEC SAS
//VOLIN DD UNIT=tape,DISP=OLD,
//    VOL=SER=XXXXXX,LABEL=(,SL),DSN=first.dsname.on.tape
//VOLOUT DD UNIT=tape,DISP=(,KEEP),
//   VOL=SER=YYYYYY,LABEL=(,SL)
PROC TAPECOPY;
```

After TAPECOPY executes, the output tape volume is labeled YYYYYY.

If LABEL=(,BLP) had been specified in the input tape DD statement (VOLIN), then it would not have been necessary to give the DSN= parameter. Since some installations do not permit the BLP label type specification and no volume label checking is performed when it is specified, it is recommended that you specify (or allow to default) LABEL=(,SL).

The specification of LABEL=(,SL) in the output tape DD statement (VOLOUT) causes volume label checking to be performed by the operating system when a tape volume is mounted on the tape drive. The operating system ensures that a tape with volume serial YYYYYY is mounted. However, if the tape with external volume label YYYYYY were, in fact, internally labeled something other than YYYYYY, TAPECOPY would fail. In this case, you would have to specify LABEL=(,BLP) or else give the actual internal volume serial in the output tape DD statement. If the output tape is not labeled internally, you can specify LABEL=(,NL) (as well as LABEL=(,BLP)).

SL to NL Under OS: Example 2

The job below copies a standard-labeled tape with volume serial TAPEIN to a non-labeled tape, FCSTP1. After executing the job, the output tape volume is still a non-labeled tape, presumably with only an external volume label of FCSTP1. It is necessary to specify LABEL=NL in the PROC TAPECOPY statement because TAPECOPY would otherwise default to LABEL=SL since the first (and only) input tape volume is standard-labeled.

```
//jobname JOB account,name
//   EXEC SAS
//VOLIN DD UNIT=tape,DISP=OLD,VOL=SER=TAPEIN,LABEL=(,BLP)
//VOLOUT DD UNIT=tape,DISP=(,KEEP),VOL=SER=FCSTP1,LABEL=(,NL)
PROC TAPECOPY LABEL=NL;
```

NL to NL Under OS: Example 3

The job below copies a non-labeled tape with volume serial QDR123 to a non-labeled, 1600bpi tape, SLXATK.

```
//jobname JOB account,name
//  EXEC SAS
//INTAPE DD UNIT=tape,DISP=OLD,VOL=SER=QDR123,LABEL=(,NL)
//OUTTAPE DD UNIT=2400-3,DISP=(,KEEP),VOL=SER=SLXATK
 PROC TAPECOPY INDD=INTAPE OUTDD=OUTTAPE DEN=1600;
```

Copying Several Files Under OS: Example 4

The job below copies the first seven files from the standard-labeled input tape U02746 and four files from the standard-labeled input tape T13794 to an initially unlabeled output tape with volume serial MINI01. The output tape is standard-labeled and has a volume serial of U02746 after the procedure is executed.

```
//jobname JOB account,name
//  EXEC SAS
//TAPI1 DD DISP=SHR,UNIT=tape,
//   VOL=SER=U02746,LABEL=(,SL),DSN=first.file.dsname
//TAPI2 DD UNIT=(tape,,DEFER)
//OUTDDN DD DISP=(,KEEP),UNIT=tape,VOL=SER=MINI01,LABEL=(,NL)
 PROC TAPECOPY OUTDD=OUTDDN INDD=TAPI1 COPYVOLSER;
   FILES 3 2 1;
   INVOL INDD=TAPI2 INVOL=T13794
     DSN='first.dsname.on.this.tape';
   FILE 3;
   INVOL INDD=TAPI1;
   FILES 5-7 4;
   INVOL INDD=TAPI2;
   FILES 2 4 1;
```

Copying Multiple Files From Multiple Input Tapes Under OS: Example 5

The job below copies several files from several input tape volumes onto one output tape volume.

```
//REARRNGE JOB account,name
//  EXEC SAS
//DEN2IN DD UNIT=(2400-4,,DEFER),LABEL=(,BLP)
//DEN3IN DD UNIT=(2400-3,,DEFER),LABEL=(,SL)
//TAPE1 DD UNIT=TAPE,DISP=SHR,VOL=SER=XR8475,LABEL=(,BLP)
//TAPE2 DD UNIT=TAPE,DISP=OLD,VOL=SER=BKT023,
//   DSN=first.files.dsname
//OUTPUT DD UNIT=(3400-5,,DEFER),DISP=(,KEEP)
```

```
PROC TAPECOPY LABEL=SL DEN=6250 NOLIST
  OUTDD=OUTPUT OUTVOL=HISTPE;
  INVOL INDD=DEN2IN INVOL=PTFTP0;
    FILES 2-4 8-EOV 7 6;
  INVOL INDD=TAPE1;
    FILES 5 7 9-EOV;
  INVOL INDD=TAPE2;
    FILES 4 5 1;
  INVOL INDD=TAPE1;
    FILE 1;
  INVOL INDD=DEN3IN INVOL=S03768 DSN='XRT.BKT120.G0081V00';
    FILES 1-6 22-34;
  INVOL INVOL=SO3760 DSN='T.BKT120.G0023V00';
    FILES 4 5 6 9;
  INVOL INDD=TAPE2;
    FILES 7-EOV;
```

Using Default Values Under CMS: Example 6

In the example below, TAPECOPY defaults to TAP1 for input and TAP2 for output. After TAPECOPY executes, the output tape volume is labeled with the same label as the input tape. All files, including labels, are copied because LABEL=BLP is assumed.

```
PROC TAPECOPY;
```

SL to NL Under CMS: Example 7

The job below copies a standard-labeled tape; after executing TAPECOPY, the output tape volume is a non-labeled tape. It is necessary to specify LABEL=NL in the PROC TAPECOPY statement because TAPECOPY would otherwise default to LABEL=BLP and copy all files (both data and labels).

```
PROC TAPECOPY LABEL=NL NOLIST;
```

Using FILEDEFs with TAPECOPY: Example 8

The job below copies a tape to a 1600bpi tape. BLP is assumed for the label status of both tapes.

```
CMS FILEDEF INTAPE TAP1;
CMS FILEDEF OUTTAPE TAP2;
PROC TAPECOPY INDD=INTAPE OUTDD=OUTTAPE DEN=1600 NOLIST;
```

Copying Multiple Files from Multiple Tapes: Example 9

The job below copies files from four standard-labeled input tapes to one output tape (which becomes standard-labeled). Since there is no LABEL= specification in the PROC statement, it defaults to BLP. An INVOL statement is used for each input tape to specify that the tapes are SL and to provide the deferred tape mount command. Each tape must be standard-labeled, or PROC TAPECOPY will fail.

```
PROC TAPECOPY TAP1 NOLIST TAP2 COPYVOLSER;
  INVOL SL / MOUNT T13794 ON 181 NORING;
  FILE 3;
  INVOL SL /MOUNT TXXXXX ON 181 NORING;
  FILES 4 5-7;
  INVOL SL /MOUNT TYYYYY ON 181 NORING;
  FILES 2 4 1 9-EOV;
```

The TAPELABEL Procedure

ABSTRACT

The TAPELABEL procedure lists the label information of an IBM standard-labeled tape volume under OS batch, TSO, and CMS.

INTRODUCTION

One or more standard-labeled tape volumes can be processed by TAPELABEL. Only one volume per job control statement or command is processed; however, multiple job control statements or commands can be used in one job to process more than one tape volume. At some installations, it may be necessary to specify the data set name of the first file on the tape volume in the job control describing the volumes to be processed.

The procedure prints information from the tape label, including the data set name, DCB information, and data set history.

SPECIFICATIONS

The only statement used with this procedure is the PROC statement.

PROC TAPELABEL *options*;

PROC TAPELABEL Statement

PROC TAPELABEL *options*;

The options below may appear in the PROC TAPELABEL statement:

DDNAME=
(*DDname*...)

specifies a *DDname* referring to the tape volume to be processed. More than one DDname can be specified. If DDNAME= is omitted the default DDname is TAPE for OS and TAP1 for CMS.

PAGE

begins the output for each tape volume on a new page.

TAP*n*

specifies a CMS tape symbolic address, where *n* can be a value of 1, 2, 3, or 4. TAP1 corresponds to virtual address 181, TAP2 to 182, TAP3 to 183, and TAP4 to 184. This option can be used instead of the DDNAME= option to specify a tape volume to be processed. A corresponding FILEDEF command is unnecessary if TAP*n* is used. This option is only effective under CMS.

DETAILS

Printed Output

For each file on a tape volume, TAPELABEL prints:

1. FILE NUMBER, the file sequence number
2. DSNAME, the data set name
3. RECFM, the record format
4. LRECL, the logical record length
5. BLKSIZE, the block size
6. BLOCK COUNT, the number of blocks in the file (from trailer label)
7. EST. FEET, the estimated length of the file in feet
8. CREATED, the file creation date
9. EXPIRES, the file expiration date
10. CREATED BY JOB NAME STEPNAME, the job and step names of the job that created the file
11. TRTCH, the track recording technique
12. DEN, the file recording density code
13. PSWD, the file protection indicator
14. UHL, the number of user header labels
15. UTL, the number of user trailer labels

TAPELABEL also prints the sum of the estimated file lengths.

EXAMPLES

An OS Example: Example 1

The job below lists the label information for all files on tape volumes referenced by the DDnames TAPE1 and TAPE2:

```
//jobname JOB acct,name
//  EXEC SAS
//TAPE1 DD UNIT=TAPE,VOL=SER=SAS796,DISP=OLD,DSN=SAS.INSTRUCT
//TAPE2 DD UNIT=AFF=TAPE1,VOL=SER=SAS793,DISP=OLD,
//  DSN=SAS.INSTALL
PROC TAPELABEL DDNAME=(TAPE1 TAPE2);
```

```
            S T A T I S T I C A L   A N A L Y S I S   S Y S T E M        8:41 THURSDAY, JULY 15, 1982    1
                                    TAPE LIST FOR DDNAME - TAPE1
  CONTENTS OF TAPE VOLUME - SAS796                                                              OWNER - SAS INST
```

①FILE NUMBER	② DSNAME	③ RECFM	④ LRECL	⑤ BLKSIZE	⑥ BLOCK COUNT	⑦ EST. FEET	⑧ CREATED	⑨ EXPIRES	⑩ CREATED BY JOB NAME STEPNAME	⑪ TRTCH	⑫ DEN	⑬ PSWD	⑭ UHL	⑮ UTL
1	SAS.INSTRUCT	VBA	137	32720	7	4.5	31MAR82	0000000	SASINSTR/SAS		4	NO	0	0
2	SAS.CNTL	FB	80	32720	5	3.5	26MAR82	0000000	SAS796 /SAS		4	NO	0	0
3	SAS.OBJECT	FB	80	800	28	2.8	25MAR82	0000000	BLD796 /		4	NO	0	0
4	SAS.LIBRARY	VB	32756	32760	32	16.7	25MAR82	0000000	BLD796 /SAS		4	NO	0	0
5	SAS.LIBRARYO	VB	32756	32760	148	73.1	31MAR82	0000000	TMP796 /SAS		4	NO	0	0
6	SAS.LIBRARYF	VB	32756	32760	177	87.3	31MAR82	0000000	TMP796 /SAS		4	NO	0	0
7	SAS.SLIBRARY	VB	32756	32760	35	18.1	25MAR82	0000000	BLD796 /		4	NO	0	0
8	SAS.SLIBRARYO	VB	32756	32760	19	10.3	25MAR82	0000000	BLD796 /		4	NO	0	0
9	SAS.SLIBRARYF	VB	32756	32760	34	17.6	25MAR82	0000000	BLD796 /		4	NO	0	0
10	SAS.PLFTRAN	VB	32756	32760	3	2.6	25MAR82	0000000	BLD796 /		4	NO	0	0
11	SAS.OUTPUT	VBA	137	32720	7	4.5	25MAR82	0000000	BLD796 /SAS		4	NO	0	0
12	SAS.SAMPLE	FB	80	32720	40	20.5	25MAR82	0000000	BLD796 /		4	NO	0	0
13	SAS.SUBLIB	VB	32756	32760	3	2.6	25MAR82	0000000	BLD796 /		4	NO	0	0
14	SAS.SUBLIBO	VB	32756	32760	7	4.5	25MAR82	0000000	BLD796 /		4	NO	0	0
15	SAS.SUBLIBF	VB	32756	32760	8	5.0	25MAR82	0000000	BLD796 /		4	NO	0	0
16	SAS.MACLIB	FB	80	32720	17	9.4	25MAR82	0000000	BLD796 /SAS		4	NO	0	0
17	SAS.MACLIBP	FB	80	32720	4	3.0	25MAR82	0000000	BLD796 /		4	NO	0	0
18	SAS.SOURCE	FB	80	32720	29	15.2	25MAR82	0000000	BLD796 /SAS		4	NO	0	0
19	SAS.SSOURCE	FB	80	32720	105	52.1	25MAR82	0000000	BLD796 /		4	NO	0	0
20	SAS.MISCLIB	VB	32756	32760	4	3.0	25MAR82	0000000	BLD796 /		4	NO	0	0

						357.3								

```
                                    TAPE LIST FOR DDNAME - TAPE2
  CONTENTS OF TAPE VOLUME - SAS793                                                              OWNER - CUSTOMER
```

FILE NUMBER	DSNAME	RECFM	LRECL	BLKSIZE	BLOCK COUNT	EST. FEET	CREATED	EXPIRES	CREATED BY JOB NAME STEPNAME	TRTCH	DEN	PSWD	UHL	UTL
1	SAS.INSTALL	FB	80	6400	7	3.8	10JAN80	0000000	ARS1TFOR/COPY		3	NO	0	0
2	SAS.INST800	FB	80	6400	7	3.8	10JAN80	0000000	ARS1TFOR/COPY		3	NO	0	0
3	SAS.CLIST	FB	80	800	3	1.4	10JAN80	0000000	ARS1TFOR/COPY		3	NO	0	0
4	SAS.HELP	FB	80	800	4	1.5	10JAN80	0000000	ARS1TFOR/COPY		3	NO	0	0
5	SAS.TEST	FB	80	6400	11	5.3	10JAN80	0000000	ARS1TFOR/COPY		3	NO	0	0
6	SAS.OUTPUT	VBA	137	6160	44	17.4	10JAN80	0000000	ARS1TFOR/COPY		3	NO	0	0
7	SAS.BLIBRARY	FB	80	800	217	21.0	10JAN80	0000000	ARS1TFOR/COPY		3	NO	0	0
8	SAS.MACRO	FB	80	800	300	28.6	10JAN80	0000000	ARS1TFOR/COPY		3	NO	0	0
9	SAS.PL1MACRO	FB	80	800	147	14.6	10JAN80	0000000	ARS1TFOR/COPY		3	NO	0	0
10	SAS.SAMPLE	FB	80	800	1454	134.4	10JAN80	0000000	ARS1TFOR/COPY		3	NO	0	0
11	SAS.LIBRARY	VB	31996	32000	190	327.3	10JAN80	0000000	ARS1TFOR/COPY		3	NO	0	0
12	SAS.LIBRARYO	VB	31996	32000	122	210.5	10JAN80	0000000	ARS1TFOR/COPY		3	NO	0	0
13	SAS.SLIBRARY	VB	31996	32000	43	74.9	10JAN80	0000000	ARS1TFOR/COPY		3	NO	0	0
14	SAS.SLIBRAYO	VB	31996	32000	8	14.8	10JAN80	0000000	ARS1TFOR/COPY		3	NO	0	0
15	SAS.SUBLIB	VB	31996	32000	4	8.0	10JAN80	0000000	ARS1TFOR/COPY		3	NO	0	0
16	SAS.SUBLIBO	VB	31996	32000	1	2.8	10JAN80	0000000	ARS1TFOR/COPY		3	NO	0	0
17	SAS.BLIBIEBC	VS	1044	1044	287	31.1	10JAN80	0000000	ARS1TFOR/COPY		3	NO	0	0
18	SAS.SOURCE	FB	80	6400	1210	464.9	10JAN80	0000000	ARS1TFOR/COPY		3	NO	0	0
19	SAS.SSOURCE	FB	80	6400	360	139.1	10JAN80	0000000	ARS1TFOR/COPY		3	NO	0	0
20	SAS.MERRILL	FB	80	6400	61	24.5	10JAN80	0000000	ARS1TFOR/COPY		3	NO	0	0

						1530.6								

A CMS Example: Example 2

The statements below list the label information for all files on the tape volume currently mounted on virtual address 182:

```
PROC TAPELABEL TAP2;
RUN;
```

```
            S T A T I S T I C A L   A N A L Y S I S   S Y S T E M       16:57 FRIDAY, JULY 16, 1982    1
                                    TAPE LIST FOR DDNAME - 182
  CONTENTS OF TAPE VOLUME - SAS796                                                              OWNER - SAS INST
```

FILE NUMBER	DSNAME	RECFM	LRECL	BLKSIZE	BLOCK COUNT	EST. FEET	CREATED	EXPIRES	CREATED BY JOB NAME STEPNAME	TRTCH	DEN	PSWD	UHL	UTL
1	SAS.INSTRUCT	VBA	137	32720	7	4.5	31MAR82	0000000	SASINSTR/SAS		4	NO	0	0
2	SAS.CNTL	FB	80	32720	5	3.5	26MAR82	0000000	SAS796 /SAS		4	NO	0	0
3	SAS.OBJECT	FB	80	800	28	2.8	25MAR82	0000000	BLD796 /		4	NO	0	0
4	SAS.LIBRARY	VB	32756	32760	32	16.7	25MAR82	0000000	BLD796 /SAS		4	NO	0	0
5	SAS.LIBRARYO	VB	32756	32760	148	73.1	31MAR82	0000000	TMP796 /SAS		4	NO	0	0
6	SAS.LIBRARYF	VB	32756	32760	177	87.3	31MAR82	0000000	TMP796 /SAS		4	NO	0	0
7	SAS.SLIBRARY	VB	32756	32760	35	18.1	25MAR82	0000000	BLD796 /		4	NO	0	0
8	SAS.SLIBRAYO	VB	32756	32760	19	10.3	25MAR82	0000000	BLD796 /		4	NO	0	0
9	SAS.SLIBRAYF	VB	32756	32760	34	17.6	25MAR82	0000000	BLD796 /		4	NO	0	0
10	SAS.PLFTRAN	VB	32756	32760	3	2.6	25MAR82	0000000	BLD796 /		4	NO	0	0
11	SAS.OUTPUT	VBA	137	32720	7	4.5	25MAR82	0000000	BLD796 /SAS		4	NO	0	0
12	SAS.SAMPLE	FB	80	32720	40	20.5	25MAR82	0000000	BLD796 /		4	NO	0	0
13	SAS.SUBLIB	VB	32756	32760	3	2.6	25MAR82	0000000	BLD796 /		4	NO	0	0
14	SAS.SUBLIBO	VB	32756	32760	7	4.5	25MAR82	0000000	BLD796 /		4	NO	0	0
15	SAS.SUBLIBF	VB	32756	32760	8	5.0	25MAR82	0000000	BLD796 /		4	NO	0	0
16	SAS.MACLIB	FB	80	32720	17	9.4	25MAR82	0000000	BLD796 /SAS		4	NO	0	0
17	SAS.MACLIBP	FB	80	32720	4	3.0	25MAR82	0000000	BLD796 /		4	NO	0	0
18	SAS.SOURCE	FB	80	32720	29	15.2	25MAR82	0000000	BLD796 /SAS		4	NO	0	0
19	SAS.SSOURCE	FB	80	32720	105	52.1	25MAR82	0000000	BLD796 /		4	NO	0	0
20	SAS.MISCLIB	VB	32756	32760	4	3.0	25MAR82	0000000	BLD796 /		4	NO	0	0

						357.3								

REFERENCE

International Business Machines Corporation (1973), *OS/VS Tape Labels*, Order Number GC26-3795.

APPENDICES

SAS under CMS

SAS under OS

SAS under TSO

SAS under VSE

SAS under CMS

INTRODUCTION

This appendix describes some features of SAS that are specific to using SAS under CMS. The appendix is not intended to instruct you in the use of CMS, or to give an exhaustive discussion of CMS SAS, but simply to give you an overview. See the *IBM CMS User's Guide* and the *SAS CMS Companion* for more detail.

SAS sessions under CMS at a terminal are either interactive or non-interactive. Both methods invoke SAS with the CMS SAS command (see below), which can be executed directly from CMS or from a CMS EXEC file. You can also submit a SAS job to a CMS batch system. Since CMS batch systems vary, you should check with your installation's support personnel for details on SAS job submission. (Note that what is referred to as non-interactive or batch mode in SAS does not mean the job is running in a CMS batch machine.) You can run interactive or non-interactive SAS jobs in your own virtual machine or invoke SAS in interactive or non-interactive mode from a CMS batch machine.

The SAS Command

SAS *filename* ... *(options*
SAS ?

The SAS command is a CMS command that invokes the SAS system. The following specifications can be made in the SAS command:

> *filename*   specifies the *filename* of a CMS file containing SAS program statements. More than one filename can be given. Each file must have the filetype SAS. If no filename is specified, SAS goes into interactive mode.
>
> ?   displays a brief summary of the SAS command at the terminal.

Some of the SAS command options are listed below. The option name and the minimum abbreviation for the name are shown; however, any shortened form of an option name is acceptable (for example, LTYPE; LTYP; LTY; or LT). For additional options and usage notes, consult the *SAS CMS Companion*.

> LTYPE   types the SAS log at your terminal.
> LT
>
> LPRINT   sends the SAS log to your virtual printer.
> LP
>
> LDISK   writes the SAS log to a disk file with filetype SASLOG.
> LD   The filename of the SASLOG file is determined by the NAME option (see below) if specified, and if not specified, by the first filename specified in the SAS command. If you are in interactive mode and do not use the NAME option, the filename SAS is used.

PTYPE   types the printed procedure output at your terminal.
PT

PPRINT   sends the printed procedure output to your virtual
PP   printer.

PDISK   writes the printed procedure output to a disk file with
PD   filetype LISTING. The filename of the LISTING file is
determined by the NAME option (see below) if
specified, and if not specified, by the first filename
specified in the SAS command. If you are in interactive
mode and do not use the NAME option, the filename
SAS is used.

TMSG *level*   determines what informatory messages are typed at
the terminal when not in interactive mode. If NOTE is
specified for *level*, all notes and error messages are
typed; if ERRO (or ERRORS) is specified, only error
messages are typed; if OFF is specified, no messages
appear. The default message level is ERRO.

NOTLOG/TLOG   determines whether or not SAS statements entered at
NOTL/TL   the terminal are written to a disk file. This option is
only applicable in interactive mode. NOTLOG is the
default setting. When TLOG is specified, lines entered
in response to SAS prompting are routed to a file with
filetype SAS. The filename used is the filename
specified by the NAME option, or SAS if the NAME option has not been specified. The file can be processed
subsequently with a CMS editor, and re-executed using GETSAS, %INCLUDE, or SAS in non-interactive
mode.

NAME *filename*   specifies the *filename* to be assigned to printed pro-
NA *filename*   cedure output (filetype LISTING), the SAS log (filetype
SASLOG), and TLOG output (filetype SAS). If the
NAME option is not specified in non-interactive mode,
the first filename specified in the SAS command is
used. If the NAME option is not specified in interactive
mode, SAS is used for the filename.

SASLIB *filename*   directs the CMS SAS interface to issue a FILEDEF to
associate the file:

     filename TXTLIB A

with the DDname SASLIB, and adds that file to the list
of libraries searched during a SAS session by issuing a
CMS GLOBAL command for the library.

The SASLIB file is automatically searched for formats
defined with the FORMAT procedure. To store formats
produced by PROC FORMAT in the SASLIB file,
specify DDNAME=SASLIB in the PROC statement (see
the FORMAT procedure description). Consult the *SAS
CMS Companion* for more information on format
libraries.

Note: SAS system options can also be specified in the SAS command, to the right of
a left parenthesis as with the options above. Use a blank rather than an equal sign
to separate an option name and the specified value. For example:

SAS *filename* (LPRINT PPRINT LS 78 NOCENTER

Interactive Mode

In interactive mode, you give the SAS command without filenames to enter the SAS environment. SAS then prompts you to enter SAS statements. After you have entered a DATA or PROC step, SAS executes the statements in that step, and output from SAS is displayed at your terminal. The results of one SAS step can help you decide what to do next. The *SAS CMS Companion* gives many examples of the use of SAS in interactive mode.

Non-interactive Mode

To use SAS in non-interactive mode, first use a CMS editor (XEDIT, EDGAR, or EDIT) to create a CMS disk file containing your SAS statements. The filetype of the file must be SAS, but it can have any filename you choose. The CMS file should contain fixed-length records of length 80 (which is the default record length for the CMS editors). To run the program, enter the SAS command:

SAS *filename*

where *filename* specifies the name of the CMS disk file of SAS statements.

You can specify multiple filenames when you invoke SAS in the non-interactive mode. SAS concatenates the files in the order in which they are listed, and executes them as if they were all one file. For example, if you have a file called ALLMAC SAS containing SAS macros, and a program that uses some of the macros in a file called ANALYZE1 SAS, the SAS command to execute both files could be:

SAS ALLMAC ANALYZE1 (NAME REPORT1

The NAME option specifies the filename REPORT1 for the SASLOG and LISTING files. (If the NAME option is not specified, the first filename in the list is used for the output files by default.)

Output

SAS produces two categories of printed output: the log and the procedure output. Output can go to a terminal, a virtual printer, a CMS disk file, or more than one of these destinations. You control the output's destination with options specified in the SAS command; by default, output from an interactive session is routed to the terminal, and output from a non-interactive session is routed to disk files.

The disk files that SAS produces by default in non-interactive mode are formatted for a line printer. The two files have the same filename as the file of SAS statements or the name specified in the NAME option. The file containing the SAS log has filetype SASLOG; it contains a numbered list of all your SAS statements, as well as SAS error messages and notes. (The SASLOG file is created with carriage control characters. To use the CMS PRINT command with this file, you must use the CC option.) The file containing the SAS procedure output has filetype LISTING.

Here is a sample terminal session with SAS executed in non-interactive mode. In the example, the editor EDIT is used to build the file of SAS statements. CMS commands and SAS statements are typed in lowercase, and CMS responses are typed in uppercase.

```
edit test sas
NEW FILE:
EDIT:
input
INPUT:
data htwt;
    input name $ sex $ age height weight;
    cards;
alfred m 14 69 112
alice f 13 56 84
barbara f 14 62 102
henry m 14 63 102
james m 12 57 83
janet f 15 62 112
mary f 15 66 112
philip m 16 72 150
robert m 12 64 128
thomas m 11 57 85
proc print;
proc plot;
    plot height * weight = sex;
                    (null line to return from input to edit mode)
EDIT:
file
R;

listfile *
TEST    SAS        A1
R;
```

The CMS LISTFILE command shows that TEST SAS is on the A disk. Issue the CMS command SAS TEST to invoke SAS and execute the program statements in the file TEST.

```
sas test
R;
```

After the program is executed, another LISTFILE command shows there are two new files on the A disk: one called TEST SASLOG, the other called TEST LISTING. (The output is routed to the A disk by default.)

```
listfile *
TEST LISTING       A1
TEST SAS           A1
TEST SASLOG        A1
R;
```

You may specify more than one destination for a given file, and a copy goes to each place. The SASLOG and LISTING files can also go to different destinations. For example, suppose you want to check the SASLOG for errors, but do not need to keep it, and that you want a printed copy of the procedure output. The command:

SAS TEST (LTYPE PPRINT

types the log at the terminal and sends the procedure LISTING file to your virtual printer.

CMS Commands Used With SAS

Any nondestructive CP or CMS command may be included in a SAS program by prefacing the command with CMS and putting a semicolon after it. You should start a new line for each CP or CMS command (although you can put multiple SAS statements on a line). For example, the statements below access data from another user's minidisk:

```
CMS CP LINK JONES 191 222 RR;
CMS ACCESS 222 H;
CMS FILEDEF PHONLIST DISK PHONE LIST H;
```

Usually, CMS and CP commands in a SAS DATA or PROC step are executed when SAS scans the program before SAS begins execution of that step. SAS does not recognize a CMS or CP command as the start of a new job step, only DATA or PROC statements. If a job step begins with a CMS or CP command, SAS executes that command with the previous job step. To avoid problems this can cause, use a RUN statement to indicate the end of a job step. See the *SAS CMS Companion* for additional information.

SAS Data Sets

See Chapter 12, "SAS Data Sets," for a complete discussion of SAS data sets.

When you want to create a permanent SAS data set you must give the data set a two-level name. SAS data set names are reversed relative to the usual CMS order. The first-level name of the data set corresponds to the CMS filetype (and is also the DDname); the second-level name corresponds to the CMS filename. For example:

```
DATA SMITH.MARY;
```

creates a SAS data set called SMITH.MARY that is stored as a CMS disk file called MARY SMITH.

In addition to specifying a two-level name to create a permanent SAS data set, you must use a FILEDEF command specifying the disk on which the data set will be stored, unless the data set will be stored on the A disk. (It is not necessary to issue a FILEDEF if you want to store the data set on your A disk because SAS issues the FILEDEF automatically.) Be sure to specify the correct filemode. The following example creates a SAS data set that is stored in a SAS data library on a C disk.

```
CMS FILEDEF IOWA DISK DUMMY DUMMY C;
DATA IOWA.CORN;
  INPUT COUNTY CYIELD CACRES;
  CARDS;
data lines
;
```

The filename and filetype specified on a FILEDEF for a SAS library are not actually used (here, both words are DUMMY). Any words could be coded for filename and filetype. SAS supplies the second-level SAS data set name for the filename, and the first-level name (the DDname) for the filetype.

To use an existing SAS data set on a disk other than the A disk, issue the same kind of FILEDEF; use the first-level name of the data set for the DDname, and code any words for the filename and filetype. Be sure to specify the correct letter for the filemode.

External Data Files

When your data are stored in a file that is not a SAS data set, you must tell CMS and SAS where to find the data by using a FILEDEF command and a SAS INFILE statement. The FILEDEF command defines a DDname for the file that is subsequently used in a SAS INFILE statement. For example:

    CMS FILEDEF HWDATA DISK SCHOOL CHILDREN D;
    DATA HTWT.YOUNG;
      INFILE HWDATA;
      INPUT NAME $ SEX $ AGE HEIGHT WEIGHT;

The FILEDEF command associates the DDname HWDATA with the CMS disk file SCHOOL CHILDREN, which is on the D disk. (If SCHOOL CHILDREN were stored on the A disk, the filemode specification would not be necessary.) Notice that for files that are not SAS data sets the DDname does not need to match the filetype name. The INFILE statement specifies the DDname HWDATA, so SAS looks for the input data in the file associated with that DDname: SCHOOL CHILDREN. The SAS DATA statement names a new SAS data set, HTWT.YOUNG, that will be created from the data in the SCHOOL CHILDREN file. Since there is no FILEDEF with the DDname HTWT, the HTWT.YOUNG SAS data set is automatically stored on the A disk.

If you want to store the new SAS data set on the B disk include a FILEDEF for the SAS data library with filemode B:

    CMS FILEDEF HTWT DISK DUMMY DUMMY B;

The FILEDEF command may be issued before SAS is invoked or it may be included in a file of SAS statements.

User-Defined Formats

Temporary formats created by PROC FORMAT for use later in the same job require no special CMS commands. SAS automatically creates a file called $SASLIB TXTLIB to store the formats, and erases this file when the job terminates. The *SAS CMS Companion* explains how you can save formats in a permanent CMS text library for use by later jobs. You can also save formats in individual text files by using the TEXT option on the PROC FORMAT statement. These formats can be used later with no effort on your part since CMS automatically searches for TEXT files. The person who maintains SAS on your system can add formats created with the TEXT option to the SAS format library using the CMS command:

    TXTLIB ADD SASTXTL *formatname*

Using the CMS EXEC Language with SAS

This section shows an application of the CMS EXEC language with SAS. If you are not familiar with the EXEC language and want to learn about it, see the *IBM CMS User's Guide*, the *IBM CMS Command and Macro Reference*, or the *IBM VM/SP EXEC 2 Reference* for more information about the EXEC and EXEC 2 languages. Note that the SAS macro language can also be used for many of the applications for which you might use EXEC or EXEC2.

The EXEC languages are useful for executing SAS programs that are almost but not quite alike. The file AGRI SAS, shown below, is a SAS program that can be modified by an EXEC to produce output for specified states.

```
CMS FILEDEF DATAIN DISK CORN   QQQ ;
DATA CORN;
  INFILE DATAIN;
  INPUT COUNTY CYIELD CACRES;
TITLE SOYBEAN YIELD VS CORN YIELD FOR THE STATE OF   QQQ ;
RUN;
CMS FILEDEF DATAIN DISK SOY   QQQ ;
DATA SOY;
  INFILE DATAIN;
  INPUT COUNTY SYIELD SACRES;
DATA   QQQ .MERGECS;
  MERGE CORN SOY;
  BY COUNTY;
PROC PLOT;
  PLOT SYIELD * CYIELD;
```

In the AGRI SAS file, the string QQQ appears wherever a state name should be inserted.

Below is an EXEC called AGRI EXEC that uses XEDIT to change every occurrence of QQQ in the AGRI SAS file to the specified state name, and then invokes SAS using a second EXEC. (Many CMS installations have a SAS EXEC on a CMS system disk to access the SAS disk and then invoke the SAS system. If one EXEC is invoked from another EXEC, you must use the word EXEC before the nested EXEC's name.)

```
&TRACE
&IF &INDEX=0 &GOTO -MSG
&STACK TOP
&STACK C /  QQQ  / &1 / * *
&STACK FILE CSNEW
XEDIT AGRI SAS
EXEC SAS CSNEW (LT LD
&EXIT
-MSG
&TYPE PLEASE SPECIFY STATE NAME (LIMIT OF 8 CHARACTERS)
&EXIT
```

An EXEC is invoked by typing its name (here, AGRI) followed by a list of arguments. In this case, a state name is the only argument. The log from an execution of AGRI EXEC is shown below. The line beginning with DMSXCG517I is a note from XEDIT.

```
agri indiana

DMSXCG5171 4 OCCURRENCE(S) CHANGED ON 4 LINE(S)

1   S T A T I S T I C A L   A N A L Y S I S   S Y S T E M
NOTE: CMS/SAS RELEASE 79.6 AT SAS INSTITUTE INC(F) (00000).

1         CMS FILEDEF DATAIN DISK CORN INDIANA ;
2         DATA CORN;
3            INFILE DATAIN;
4            INPUT COUNTY CYIELD CACRES;
5         TITLE SOYBEAN YIELD VS CORN YIELD FOR THE STATE OF INDIANA ;

NOTE: INFILE DATAIN IS FILE CORN INDIANA A1
NOTE: 5 LINES WERE READ FROM INFILE DATAIN.
NOTE: DATA SET WORK.CORN HAS 5 OBSERVATIONS AND 3 VARIABLES.


6         RUN;
7         CMS FILEDEF DATAIN DISK SOY INDIANA ;
8         DATA SOY;
9            INFILE DATAIN;
10           INPUT COUNTY SYIELD SACRES;

NOTE: 5 LINES WERE READ FROM INFILE DATAIN.
NOTE: DATA SET WORK.SOY HAS 5 OBSERVATIONS AND 3 VARIABLES.

11        DATA  INDIANA .MERGECS;
12           MERGE CORN SOY;
13           BY COUNTY;

NOTE: DATA SET INDIANA.MERGECS HAS 5 OBSERVATIONS AND 5 VARIABLES.

14        PROC PLOT;
15           PLOT SYIELD * CYIELD;

NOTE: THE PROCEDURE PLOT USED 0.41 SECONDS AND 718K AND PRINTED PAGE 1.
```

CMS GETSAS Command

The GETSAS facility of CMS SAS can be used to insert one or more CMS files of SAS statements (with filetype SAS) in the middle of an interactive SAS session by entering:

   CMS GETSAS filename1 ... ;

when SAS prompts you with a line number. The statements retrieved from the disk files are treated as if they had been entered at the terminal. The GETSAS command can also be used in a non-interactive mode. The GETSAS command functions much like %INCLUDE with a few differences: GETSAS does not require a CMS FILEDEF statement; %INCLUDE does. GETSAS requires fixed-length records of length 80 and a filetype of SAS; %INCLUDE has no restriction on filetype.

   The sample program below (in a file called MERGECS) produces the same output as the example in the section on EXECs, but by different means. A SAS DATA step asks at the terminal for the state name, then uses the PUT statement to create a new SAS disk file. A GETSAS command then includes that file as the next part of the program.

```
options ls=78 ps=24;
cms filedef in term ;
cms filedef out term ( recfm va ;
cms filedef newfile disk csget sas ;
data _null_;
infile in unbuffered;
file out;
   put 'What state do you want to use for the corn-soybean plot?';
   input statenam;
   file newfile;
   put 'CMS FILEDEF DATAIN DISK CORN 'statenam $8.';'/
   'DATA CORN;'/
   '   INFILE DATAIN;'/
   '   INPUT COUNTY CYIELD CACRES;'/
   'TITLE SOYBEAN YIELD VS CORN YIELD FOR THE STATE OF'statenam $8.';'/
   'RUN;'/
   'CMS FILEDEF DATAIN DISK SOY 'statenam $8.';'/
   'DATA SOY;'/
   '   INFILE DATAIN;'/
   '   INPUT COUNTY SYIELD SACRES;'/
   'DATA 'statenam $8.'.MERGECS;'/
   '   MERGE CORN SOY;'/
   '   BY COUNTY;'/
   'PROC PLOT;'/
   '   PLOT SYIELD * CYIELD;';
stop;
run;
cms getsas csget;
run;
```

Execution of the program is shown below.

```
   sas mergecs (pt


            S T A T I S T I C A L   A N A L Y S I S   S Y S T E M

What state do you want to use for the corn-soybean plot?
indiana



            SOYBEAN YIELD VS CORN YIELD FOR THE STATE OF INDIANA

         PLOT OF SYIELD*CYIELD     LEGEND: A = 1 OBS, B = 2 OBS, ETC.

  40  +                                A
      |
      |
      |
  36  +                                                        A
      |
SYIELD|                        A
      |
  32  +              A
      |
      |
      |
  28  +        A
      ----+-------+-------+-------+-------+-------+--------+-------
         90      95     100     105     110     115      120
                              CYIELD
```

Reading Data from Tape

The *SAS CMS Companion* contains sections on reading and writing data on tape (both external files and SAS data sets). There is no standard CMS command for having a tape mounted, so check with your installation's support staff for information about local tape mount command syntax.

CMS installations tend to use mostly non-labeled tapes and the CMS FILEDEF command assumes that no label processing is required. You must specify the SL option on the FILEDEF command to use a labeled tape or use the CMS TAPE command to skip labels and treat the tape as if it were unlabeled. When a standard-labeled tape is used, no DCB information is necessary since SAS gets this information from the label. DCB information for non-labeled tapes is specified in the FILEDEF command; under CMS you cannot give BLKSIZE=, LRECL=, or RECFM= in the INFILE statement. If you do not know the DCB specifications for a non-labeled tape, omit them. SAS assumes BLKSIZE=32767 and RECFM=U. Although the records will not be de-blocked, you will get a readable dump of the tape contents.

CMS allows you to have more than one DCB open at a time for the same tape; therefore, you can have multiple DDnames defined in one job step. For example, here is a SAS program that creates monthly accounting totals from data stored on tape with a separate tape file for each week or partial week. The files are in sequential order on the tape. (The program assumes that the tape has already been mounted and positioned at the start of the file for the first week.)

```
CMS FILEDEF DIN1 TAP1 (RECFM FB LRECL 80 BLKSIZE 3200 ;
CMS FILEDEF DIN2 TAP1 (RECFM FB LRECL 80 BLKSIZE 3200 ;
CMS FILEDEF DIN3 TAP1 (RECFM FB LRECL 80 BLKSIZE 3200 ;
CMS FILEDEF DIN4 TAP1 (RECFM FB LRECL 80 BLKSIZE 3200 ;
CMS FILEDEF DIN5 TAP1 (RECFM FB LRECL 80 BLKSIZE 3200 ;
DATA;
  INFILE DIN1 UNBUFFERED EOF=FILE2;
  GO TO READ;
FILE2: INFILE DIN2 UNBUFFERED EOF=FILE3;
  GO TO READ;
FILE3: INFILE DIN3 UNBUFFERED EOF=FILE4;
  GO TO READ;
FILE4: INFILE DIN4 UNBUFFERED EOF=FILE5;
  GO TO READ;
FILE5: INFILE DIN5 UNBUFFERED;
READ: INPUT COMPID $ 1-8 MACCT $ 13-15 MDY $ 17-22 CLOCKTIM $
    23-28  CPUMSEC 33-40 ;
PROC SORT;
  BY MACCT COMPID ;
PROC MEANS NOPRINT SUM N;
  VAR MSEC;
  BY MACCT COMPID ;
  OUTPUT OUT=W15JAN82.SASCUMT SUM=TCPUMSEC N=NUSE;
```

PROC BMDP Under CMS

SAS has two BMDP interfaces. The older interface is invoked whenever UNIT=3 is specified in the PROC BMDP statement. In most cases, the BMDP procedure can be used without the UNIT= option on the PROC statement. It is preferable to use the procedure without the UNIT= option because it is much more efficient.

However, under certain circumstances, the UNIT= option must be used. One is when an obsolete BMDP program is being invoked (for example, BMDP1F, BMDP2F, and BMDP3F, which have been superseded by BMDP4F). You must also use the UNIT= option when you want to run PROC BMDP using a BMDP program stored as a TEXT file. BMDP Statistical Software distributes CMS programs in the form of TEXT files, but in order for PROC BMDP to run without UNIT=, it must operate on a MODULE file, not a TEXT file. If your BMDP programs are stored as TEXT files, you can:

- request that some or all of the BMDP programs be made into MODULE files, or
- create MODULE files yourself and store them on your mini-disk, or
- use the UNIT= option on the PROC BMDP statement.

For example, to create BMDP1D as a MODULE file, enter the following commands after accessing the disk containing the BMDP TEXT and the disk containing FORTRAN libraries:

```
GLOBAL TXTLIB BMDPFORT BMDPSUB FORTLIB
LOAD BMDP1D
GENMOD BMDP1D
```

PROC BMDP passes control to the BMDP program, which writes printed output to unit 6, wherever it is FILEDEFed. If unit 6 is not FILEDEFed, BMDP writes output to FILE FT06F001. If you use a SAVE paragraph in your PARMCARDS, BMDP writes a BMDP save file to the specified unit. For example, if you issue this FILEDEF:

```
FILEDEF 4 DISK BMDPSAVE FILE (PERM
```

and use this SAVE paragraph:

```
/SAVE UNIT IS 4. NEW. NAME IS XXX.
```

you create a BMDP save file called XXX on unit 4, and the save file is stored in the CMS file BMDPSAVE FILE. (Note that not all BMDP programs can create output save files). If you want to use the output save file in further SAS analysis, use PROC CONVERT:

```
PROC CONVERT BMDP=FT04F001 OUT=FROMBMDP;
```

The SAS data set FROMBMDP is created from the BMDP save file XXX.

Memory requirements   PROC BMDP and the BMDP program it invokes require a large amount of memory. To be sure that you have sufficient memory use the procedure in a 2-meg machine by entering these commands:

```
DEF STOR 2048K   (CP is entered after this command)
IPL CMS          (use to reinvoke CMS)
```

Miscellaneous Notes

1. CMS often uses the characters @, #, and '' as line editing symbols and the semicolon as a tab character. Since SAS also uses some of these characters, especially the semicolon, you need to set things up to avoid conflicts. See the *IBM CMS User's Guide* for more information.

2. SAS can read data (external files or SAS data sets) from any accessed disk, and can write data to any disk which is accessed read/write. When SAS is invoked it looks for the disk accessed in write mode with the most free space and uses that disk for the WORK library. You can force SAS to put the WORK library on a specific disk by using the SIODISK option (see the *SAS CMS Companion*).

3. The CMS PRINT and TYPE commands do not work for SAS data sets. Instead, use PROC PRINT to look at the data, or PROC CONTENTS to look at the descriptor information. You should not edit a SAS data set with a CMS editor. SAS provides PROC EDITOR for inplace editing of a SAS data set in line-oriented mode and PROC FSEDIT (in the SAS Full Screen Product) for full screen editing. You should not erase SAS data sets with the CMS command ERASE; use only PROC DELETE or PROC DATASETS.

REFERENCES

International Business Machines Corporation (1979), *Virtual Machine/System Product: CMS Command and Macro Reference*, File Number SC19-6209.

International Business Machines Corporation (1979), *Virtual Machine Facility/370: CMS Command and Macro Reference*, Order Number GC20-1818.

International Business Machines Corporation (1979), *Virtual Machine/System Product: CMS User's Guide*, File Number SC19-6210.

International Business Machines Corporation (1979), *Virtual Machine Facility/370: CMS User's Guide*, Order Number GC20-1819.

International Business Machines Corporation (1980), *Virtual Machine/System Product: EXEC 2 Reference*, File Number SC24-5219.

International Business Machines Corporation (1979), *Virtual Machine/System Product: System Product Editor User's Guide*, File Number SC24-5220.

SAS Institute Inc (1981), *SAS CMS Companion, 1981 Edition*, Cary, NC: SAS Institute Inc.

SAS under OS Batch

INTRODUCTION

SAS currently runs under the following IBM OS operating systems in batch: OS/360 PCP, MFT-II, and MVT; OS/VS1; and OS/VS2 SVS, MVS, MVS/SE, and MVS/SP Version 1. This appendix describes some features of SAS that are specific to using SAS in batch under OS.

Executing a SAS job

To request execution of an OS batch job, you use Job Control Language (JCL). Each JCL statement begins with two slashes (//) in columns 1 and 2.

JOB statement Each batch job must begin with a JOB statement. JOB statements vary widely among installations and even among facilities within an installation; check with your installation personnel about JOB statement requirements at your computing facility.

EXEC SAS statement The EXEC statement is the JCL statement usually used to invoke SAS. If you are using a batch job monitor to run your SAS jobs, then you may need a $JOB card in place of or in addition to the EXEC statement (at some installations, you need only a different kind of JOB statement). See the **Autobatch SAS** section, below, for more information on running SAS under batch job monitor facilities.

To run a simple SAS job under OS batch with no external files or SAS data libraries, usually the only JCL needed is an EXEC statement, which immediately follows the JOB statement:

```
//jobname JOB account-code,'programmer name'
// EXEC SAS
//SYSIN DD *
SAS program
```

SYSIN DD * statement The SAS statements that comprise your SAS program usually follow in the input stream immediately after a //SYSIN DD * statement. Although the //SYSIN DD * statement is not always needed, some operating systems and installations do require it. Check with your installation personnel to determine whether or not your computing system requires the //SYSIN DD * statement. (Even if it is not required, there is never any harm in using it.) The remaining examples in this appendix assume that it is not required. Be sure to include it before your SAS program if it is required at your installation.

The EXEC JCL statement to run a SAS job has the form:

// **EXEC** *SASname*[,OPTIONS=*'options'*][,SORT=*n*][,ENTRY=*epname*]

where

SASname	is the name at your installation of the SAS cataloged procedure. Usually *SASname* is just **SAS**, but it may be some other name or one that identifies the version or release of SAS. Sometimes there is more than one cataloged procedure that executes SAS at an installation. Check with your installation personnel for the name to use.
options	may be any list of SAS system options you want to change. The list of options must be enclosed in single quotes. For example, you can invoke SAS, change the page size to 42, and ask that the printed output not be centered with this EXEC statement:

// EXEC SAS,OPTIONS='PS=42 NOCENTER'

n	specifies the number of cylinders of sort work space to be allocated to each sort work area data set.
epname	identifies the entry point of SAS that is to be invoked. This parameter is set to the installation default value at the time SAS and the SAS cataloged procedure are installed, usually either SAS or SASLPA. Other entry points are used, however, under special circumstances.

The SAS Cataloged Procedure

Here is a listing of a typical SAS cataloged procedure that is automatically invoked when the EXEC SAS JCL statement is executed:

```
//SAS      PROC OPTIONS=,SORT=4,ENTRY=SASLPA
//*****************************************************************
//*    PRODUCT:  OS SAS   RELEASE 82.0                           *
//*  DOCUMENTATION: SAS USER'S GUIDE: BASICS, 1982 EDITION       *
//*                 SAS USER'S GUIDE: STATISTICS, 1982 EDITION   *
//*  FROM: SAS INSTITUTE INC., PO BOX 8000, CARY, NC 27511-8000  *
//*****************************************************************
//SAS      EXEC PGM=&ENTRY,PARM='&OPTIONS SORT=&SORT',REGION=256K
//LIBRARY  DD  DSN=&LIBRARY,UNIT=SYSDA,SPACE=(CYL,(1,,20)),
//             DISP=(MOD,PASS)
//STEPLIB  DD  DSN=SAS.LIBRARY,DISP=SHR
//         DD  DSN=*.LIBRARY,DISP=(OLD,PASS),VOL=REF=*.LIBRARY
//WORK     DD  UNIT=SYSDA,SPACE=(6160,(450,180),,,ROUND) SAS WORK SPACE
//FT11F001 DD  SYSOUT=A,DCB=(BLKSIZE=141,LRECL=137,RECFM=VBA) LOG
//FT12F001 DD  SYSOUT=A,DCB=(BLKSIZE=141,LRECL=137,RECFM=VBA) PRINT
//FT13F001 DD  SYSOUT=B,DCB=(RECFM=F,BLKSIZE=80)              PUNCH
//FT14F001 DD  DUMMY                                         PLOT
//FT15F001 DD  UNIT=SYSDA,SPACE=(400,(100,300)),             PARMCARDS
//             DCB=(RECFM=FB,LRECL=80,BLKSIZE=400,BUFNO=1)
//*****  SORT UTILITY DATA SET DEFINTIONS (NOT NEEDED FOR OS/VS2 MVS)
//SYSOUT   DD  SYSOUT=A,DCB=BUFNO=1
//SORTLIB  DD  DSNAME=SYS1.SORTLIB,DISP=SHR
//SORTWK01 DD  SPACE=(CYL,(&SORT,,CONTIG),UNIT=SYSDA
//SORTWK02 DD  SPACE=(CYL,(&SORT,,CONTIG),UNIT=SYSDA
//SORTWK03 DD  SPACE=(CYL,(&SORT,,CONTIG),UNIT=SYSDA
//         PEND
```

Invoking the SAS Cataloged Procedure

Here is an example:

```
//MARYSJOB JOB (1234,G704),'MARY JONES'
//STEP1    EXEC SAS,SORT=6,OPTIONS='NODATE NOOVP PAGES=80'
//SAS.WORK  DD SPACE=(CYL,(10,4))
//SAS.RAW   DD DSN=JONESM.SAVE.SASDATA,DISP=SHR
//SAS.SYSIN DD DSN=JONESM.TEST.SAS(PROGRAM3),DISP=SHR
```

Notes

1. The SORT=6 specification in the EXEC statement requests a minimum of 6 cylinders for each sort work area. OPTIONS= asks that several SAS system options be changed for this job.
2. The WORK DD statement asks that the default work area be doubled.
3. The RAW DD statement defines a cataloged SAS data library that is available for use by the SAS program to be executed. Since DISP=SHR is specified in the DD statement, SAS (not the operating system) will not permit the data library to be written into, thus protecting the existing contents of the data library from alteration and prohibiting the accidental replacement or deletion of any SAS data sets.
4. The SYSIN DD statement is supplied in this example because the SAS program to be run is stored in the member named PROGRAM3 of the partitioned data set named JONESM.TEST.SAS, which is also assumed to be cataloged.

Notes on the SAS cataloged procedure

1. The LIBRARY DD statement is used for storing any temporary formats created using PROC FORMAT. The temporary format library cannot have any secondary allocation quantity specified.
2. The WORK DD statement requests approximately 2.8 million bytes of disk storage initially (about five cylinders on a 3350 disk volume, 12 cylinders on 3330); if additional space is needed, an additional 1.1 million bytes are requested (up to 15 times). This amount of DASD space should be enough to run most SAS jobs. If your job processes large amounts of data (for example, 50,000 observations), include a WORK DD statement after the EXEC SAS statement requesting more space. Note: the WORK data library **must** be allocated to a disk device; it cannot be allocated to tape. If you need to allocate the default data library to a tape device, use DDname USER and/or the USER= option instead.
3. FT11F001 is the SAS log file; FT12F001 is the standard SAS print file. These files can be routed to almost any disk or tape data set by substituting the appropriate disk or tape file information in the JCL. For example, to route the SAS print file to a cataloged data set, you could use these statements when you invoke SAS:

```
//  EXEC SAS
//FT12F001 DD DSN=MY.SAS.LISTING,DISP=MOD,
//  DCB=BLKSIZE=6233
```
SAS program

All SAS output and lines printed to FILE PRINT in the SAS program
following this JCL are written to the data set named MY.SAS.LISTING.
DISP=MOD **must** be specified because the standard SAS print file is
opened by each procedure and by FILE PRINT; each time it is used. If
you do not specify DISP=MOD (or if the operating system changes a
DISP=MOD specification to DISP=NEW because the data set indicated
did not previously exist), then the file will contain only the output from
the last procedure, since each procedure's open would be to a
DISP=NEW or DISP=OLD file. For this same reason (the standard SAS
print file is opened multiple times during a single SAS job), it is not
possible to specify a member name in the FT12F001 DD statement in
order to direct the SAS procedure output to a member of a partitioned
data set. If you need to do this, here is an example of how it could be
done:

```
//SAVEPDS3 JOB (1169205,23),'POCAHANTAS'
//LOGPRT EXEC SAS
//FT11F001 DD UNIT=SYSDA,SPACE=(CYL,1),DSN=&&FT11,
//             DISP=(,PASS),
//             DCB=(BLKSIZE=6233,BUFNO=2)
//FT12F001 DD UNIT=SYSDA,SPACE=(CYL,2),DSN=&&FT12,
//             DISP=(,PASS),
//             DCB=(BLKSIZE=19069,BUFNO=3)
PROC OPTIONS;
//*
//PUTPDS EXEC SAS
//FT11 DD DISP=(OLD,DELETE),DSN=&&FT11
//FT12 DD DISP=(OLD,DELETE),DSN=&&FT12
//BIND DD UNIT=SYSDA,SPACE=(CYL,3),
//         DCB=(BLKSIZE=19069,LRECL=137,
//         RECFM=VBA,BUFNO=3)
//LIST DD DISP=OLD,DSN=PCH001.PRINTOUT.LIST(SAVEPDS3)
DATA __NULL__;
  INFILE FT11;
  INPUT;
  FILE BIND NOPRINT;
  PUT __INFILE__;
DATA __NULL__;
  INFILE FT12;
  INPUT;
  FILE BIND MOD NOPRINT;
  PUT __INFILE__;
DATA __NULL__;
  INFILE BIND;
  INPUT;
  FILE LIST NOPRINT;
  PUT __INFILE__;
//
```

Note that any of the DD statements in the cataloged procedure may be
overridden by JCL in your job. However, any overriding JCL statements

must be included after the EXEC SAS statement and must appear in the same order that the DD statements to be overridden appear in the cataloged procedure.

4. Under MVS, SAS is capable of performing dynamic allocation of sort work areas for use by PROC SORT. Cataloged procedures for executing SAS under MVS systems should omit the SYSOUT, SORTLIB, and SORTWK*nn* DD statements; the overhead of allocating all of these data sets for each SAS execution is much greater than dynamically allocating them only when they are actually needed. If SAS dynamically allocates its own sort work areas (the NODYNALLOC option is in effect), the SORT=*n* option tells SAS the minimum size of the sort work files to be dynamically allocated. The SORTWKNO= option tells SAS the number of sort work files to be allocated.

If the operating system you are running SAS under is not MVS, or if the dynamic allocation feature of SAS has not been selected at your installation, you may need to supply your own SORTWK*nn* DD statements. If SORTWK*nn* DD statements are included in the JCL, no dynamic allocation of sort work areas occurs.

SAS Data Libraries Under OS Batch

Under OS operating systems, SAS data sets are stored in SAS data libraries, which are ordinary OS data sets (or files) on disk or tape volumes. There are two kinds of SAS data libraries: disk-format and tape-format. A tape-format data library is also referred to as a sequential-format data library. A disk-format SAS data library **must** reside on disk. However, a tape-format data library can reside on either tape or disk.

SAS data libraries can be cataloged, and they may be protected by the OS password protection mechanism and by other OS data set protection and security systems (for example, RACF). Any operating system-managed data set protection applied to a SAS data library is in effect for all SAS data sets in the data library. There is no provision for interfacing to any OS data set security system to protect individual SAS data sets. SAS provides a simple password protection mechanism to protect individual SAS data sets in a data library; in many cases, SAS password protection is entirely adequate. For more information, refer to Chapter 12, "SAS Data Sets."

Another protection for SAS data libraries is the DD statement DISP= parameter. In order to write into (that is, modify, delete, replace, or add a SAS data set to) a SAS data library, DISP=OLD or DISP=NEW must be specified in the JCL DD statement. This also ensures that the batch job has exclusive control of the data set as a result of the OS data set name enqueue that is performed for all jobs (as well as TSO sessions). Thus, it is not possible to write into a SAS data library unless your job is the only one that has the data library allocated. In order to permit multiple access to a SAS data library, you must specify DISP=SHR in the JCL DD statement (specify SHR in a TSO ALLOCATE command). In this case, multiple jobs and TSO sessions are permitted to allocate the SAS data library, but SAS ensures that **none** are permitted to write into it. If you need exclusive control of a SAS data library, but wish to be protected from inadvertently running a SAS job that writes into it, then you can specify the LABEL=(,,,IN) parameter on the DD statement defining the data library (under TSO, specify INPUT in an ATTRIB command, then reference the attribute list name in the USING parameter of the ALLOCATE command). When LABEL=(,,,IN) is specified along with DISP=OLD, SAS provides the same protection that it does to a data library allocated DISP=SHR.

Temporary data sets may be used for SAS data libraries, and they may be passed from one OS job step to another for processing by a subsequent job step that executes SAS. For example:

```
//DEMOJOB JOB (SD01L,A205),'M SURVEYOR'
//FIRST1 EXEC SAS
//EVAS DD  UNIT=SYSDA,SPACE=(CYL,1),DSN=&&TEMP,DISP=(,PASS)
//FT23F001 DD UNIT=SYSDA,SPACE=(TRK,8),DSN=&&FT23,DISP=(,PASS)
DATA EVAS.SET1;
  INPUT SCHOOL $ STATUS $ STUDENTS FACULTY ENDOWMNT;
  CARDS;
HIGHEDU ACCRED 32000 4234 78760000
PODUNK UNACCRED 230 19 83600
more data
PROC PRINTTO UNIT=23 NEW;
PROC PRINT;
//*
//SEEIT   EXEC PGM=IEBGENER
//SYSPRINT DD DUMMY
//SYSUT2 DD SYSOUT=A
//SYSUT1 DD DISP=(OLD,DELETE),DSN=&&FT23
//SYSIN DD DUMMY
//*
//AGAIN   EXEC SAS
//NEWNAME DD DSN=&&TEMP,DISP=(OLD,DELETE)
DATA;
  SET NEWNAME.SET1;
  IF STATUS =: 'ACCRED';
PROC PRINT;
  ID SCHOOL;
//
```

In the above example, a temporary data set named &&TEMP is created in the first job step, referenced using DDname EVAS, and passed to a subsequent job step that executes SAS where it is referenced using DDname NEWNAME. At the end of the job, the data set &&TEMP is deleted.

Temporary SAS data libraries may also be created on tape:

```
//GIANT JOB QWERTY,'MELVYN',TIME=100
//TAPEXM EXEC SAS
//SAVET DD UNIT=TAPE
DATA SAVET.RUNOUT;
  DO I=1 TO 10000;
    DO J=1 TO 10000;
      K=UNIFORM(0);
      OUTPUT;
    END;
  END;
//
```

Choosing a BLKSIZE for SAS Data Sets

When choosing a BLKSIZE for SAS data sets, several considerations apply:

- A larger BLKSIZE means that fewer I/O operations (EXCPs) are required to read or write the data set (this could reduce job costs).

- But a larger BLKSIZE also means that more memory will be needed for the job (and this could increase job costs).
- Larger BLKSIZEs could result in not having enough memory available in your region or partition to run your SAS job.
- But small BLKSIZEs could result in inefficient utilization of disk space, possibly requiring more than you have available.
- On 3375 and 3380 devices, BLKSIZE values larger than half track (17600 for 3375s, 23476 for 3380s) waste disk space. The maximum BLKSIZE value permitted for these devices is 32760, which is less than the total track capacity. There is never any good reason for BLKSIZE(3375) = FULL or BLKSIZE(3380) = FULL.
- SAS will use the space remaining on a disk track after the header and history records of a SAS data set have been written to store data blocks (observations) **provided** the BLKSIZE(*devicetype*) = option value is **smaller** than the space left on the unfilled disk track. This means that if you are working with small data sets typically, you can better utilize space in a disk-format SAS data library by specifying less than full-track blocking, for example, BLKSIZE(DISK) = HALF (or less: THIRD, FOURTH, or FIFTH). If your SAS data sets typically require more than 26 tracks (the exact break-even point for BLKSIZE(3350) = HALF) of disk space, then specifying half-track blocking or less will actually waste more disk space than it would save (on the average).

Every installation should carefully consider the default settings for the BLKSIZE(*devicetype*) = options based upon the above considerations in both the batch and TSO environments. Performance-oriented (and cost-conscious) users of SAS should evaluate their SAS job streams and use the BLKSIZE(*devicetype*) = system option and the BLKSIZE= data set option to set these values as appropriately as possible. Installations that experience a significant amount of SAS usage under TSO should carefully consider BLKSIZE(DISK) = HALF or THIRD. In fact, a natural application for SAS would be to read the SMF type 14, 15, and 30 records, looking for SAS executions under TSO that access SAS data libraries that are smaller than 1 cylinder in size or required fewer than 50–100 EXCPs. See Chapter 12, "SAS Data Sets," for more information on the BLKSIZE= SAS data set option. PROC CONTENTS lists the **actual** SAS data set block size for all SAS data sets created by SAS releases 79.6 and later, along with LRECL which is correct for all SAS data sets created by SAS releases 76.5 and later.

Disk-Format SAS Data Libraries

Disk-format SAS data libraries have a special structure:

- DSORG (data set organization) = DA (direct access)
- RECFM (record format) = U (undefined)
- BLKSIZE (block size) = the maximum permitted for the disk device
- LRECL (logical record length) = BLKSIZE-4

SAS does not presently support the use of VSAM data sets to store SAS data libraries on OS systems (this is possible under DOS/VSE systems).

The host operating system manages all auxiliary storage (both disk and tape). When you want to create a permanent SAS data library, you must ask the operating system for the physical space necessary to store it. For example, this JCL sets up a new, permanent SAS data library:

```
//ALLOCATE JOB (8210,A105),'SAM, AGAIN'
// EXEC PGM=IEFBR14
//DATALIB DD  DSN=SAM136.DESCRIBE.SASDATA,SPACE=(CYL,(2,2)),
// UNIT=SYSDA,DISP=(NEW,CATLG),VOL=SER=MYPACK
```

After the initial creation of the SAS data library, the JCL necessary to reference the library might be:

```
//ANYNAME DD DSN=SAM136.DESCRIBE.SASDATA,DISP=OLD
```

Note that DDnames in SAS are arbitrary; they tell the SAS supervisor which OS data sets are to be used by SAS during the job. SAS manages the space in the data library. There are some DDnames that are used by the operating system and SAS for special purposes. You should not use them to reference external files or SAS data libraries, except as they are intended to be used. The reserved DDnames include: $ORTPARM, DFHLIB, DFRESLB, DFSURCDS, DFSURWF1, DFSVSAMP, FTnnF001 (where nn is a UNIT number), IEFRDER, IEFRDER2, IMS, IMSACB, IMSMON, IMSUDUMP, JOBCAT, JOBLIB, LIBRARY, MACLIB, PLIDUMP, PL1DUMP, PROCLIB, SASDUMP, SASHELP, SASLIB, SASSWKnn, SASnnnnn, SORTLIB, SORTMSG, SORTWKnn, STEPCAT, STEPLIB, SYSABEND, SYSHELP, SYSIN, SYSLIB, SYSMDUMP, SYSOUT, SYSPRINT, SYSUADS, SYSUDUMP, SYSnnnnn, TASKLIB, USER, and WORK.

If a SAS data set within a data library is deleted, its old space is marked as free space for future use. This allows SAS to use all space within the library, but means that only SAS can read a disk SAS data library.

When SAS creates a new data set, it finds free space to hold the data set. The space SAS finds may not be contiguous within the data library. This means that five observations may be located in one place in the library and five more 10 tracks later. SAS keeps track of where the observations are stored through a directory that tells SAS on which relative track and block an observation is located.

When a non-SAS facility or OS utility program is used to move SAS data libraries, the utility must keep all observations in the same relative location within the data library. If this is not done, when SAS later tries to read the moved library, you may receive an ERROR: 2 I/O ERROR. Although there are utilities and products which will correctly handle SAS data libraries, the COPY procedure is the only recommended way to move or copy SAS data libraries.

Disk-format data libraries are currently limited to a maximum of one disk volume. Do not specify multiple units or more than one volume in a DD statement allocating a disk-format data library. If you have a SAS data set that requires more space than can be contained on the (available) space on one disk volume, you can use a tape-format data library to get around this restriction. The tape-format data library can be on either tape or disk. For more information on tape-format data libraries, refer to Chapter 12, "SAS Data Sets," and the section immediately below.

Tape-Format SAS Data Libraries

Tape-format SAS data libraries have the structure:

- DSORG (data set organization)=PS (sequential)
- RECFM (record format)=U (undefined)
- BLKSIZE (block size)=the maximum permitted for the device (either disk or tape)
- LRECL (logical record length)=BLKSIZE-4.

The BLKSIZE recorded in the file label (tape) or DSCB (disk) is the maximum value permitted by the operating system for the device. This is not related to the block size used to write individual SAS data sets—that is determined by the SAS data set option BLKSIZE= if specified, or, if not, one of the SAS system options BLKSIZE(*device*)= or BLKSIZE=. The purpose of indicating the maximum permitted value in the data set label is to support non-SAS utility programs that may be used to copy the SAS data library. It is necessary to record the maximum value because it is **possible** for any SAS data set in the data library to be written at the actual maximum block size. The specification of the maximum BLKSIZE value, then, supports the **possibility** that one or more individual SAS data sets could be written at the maximum block size.

Tape-format data libraries may be written on either disk or tape devices. If the device allocated to the DDname specified is a tape drive, then a tape- (sequential-) format data library is assumed; if a disk device is allocated, a disk-format data library is assumed. Therefore, if you wish to write a tape-format data library on a disk device, you must use a DDname beginning with "TAPE."

Tape-format data libraries are the common format for interchange and transmission of SAS data sets among the different versions of SAS (OS, CMS, and VSE) and systems (nodes) in a computer network. As of SAS release 79.6, tape-format SAS data libraries may also be moved or copied to a device type different from the one upon which it was originally written.

Tape-format SAS data libraries are not limited to one volume, as OS disk-format SAS data libraries are. Thus you can get extremely large SAS data sets on a data library on tape, which may span as many as 255 volumes. (We are unaware of any that large, however!) Tape-format data libraries may also span volumes when written on disk devices.

Tape-format data libraries may be copied by IEBGENER or any program which will faithfully copy a RECFM=U sequential data set. Although the records in a tape format data library are formatted as RECFM=VB, they **must** be copied as undefined format blocks in order to preserve the relative block structure of the sequential data library.

Tape-format data libraries require special consideration when you placing more than one SAS data set in a single data library (tape file or disk data set). All of these considerations are discussed in Chapter 12, "SAS Data Sets," and need not be repeated here. Refer to that chapter for further information.

External Data Files

When your data are stored in a file that is not a SAS data set, you must tell the OS system where to find the data using a DD statement in the JCL and a SAS INFILE statement. For example,

```
//GETHTWT JOB (4592,X403),'SMITH, JOHN'
// EXEC SAS
//HTWT DD DSN=SMITHJ.HTWT.DATA,DISP=SHR
DATA CLASS;
   INFILE HTWT;
   INPUT NAME $ 1-8 SEX $ 10 AGE 12-13 HEIGHT 15-19
       WEIGHT 21-26;
```

The third JCL statement is a DD statement. The DDname given in this statement is used in the INFILE statement and tells SAS where to find the data. CLASS is a temporary SAS data set stored in the automatically allocated WORK data library.

To write output lines to an external file, you use a DD statement in the JCL and a SAS FILE statement. For example,

```
//SEEHTWT JOB (4592,X403),'SMITH, JOHN'
// EXEC SAS
//HTWT DD DSN=SMITHJ.HTWT.DATA,DISP=SHR
//OUT DD DSN=SMITHJ.TEST.DATA(CLASS),DISP=OLD
DATA __NULL__;
  INFILE HTWT;
  INPUT;
  FILE OUT;
  PUT __INFILE__;
```

The JCL references two external files. DDname HTWT references the file used for input; DDname OUT references the file used for writing the output lines.

In the SAS job, the INPUT statement does not specify any SAS variables. The INPUT statement is used to copy the record into the input buffer; the PUT __INFILE__ statement copies the current record to the output file.

Format Libraries

When you create formats to be associated with variables in a data set, you can store the formats permanently in a format library using the DDNAME= option in the PROC FORMAT statement.

Under OS, formats are stored as load modules in a partitioned data set. Each format is stored separately in the load module library; the member name corresponds to the format name. To store formats, set up a partitioned data set to hold the formats:

```
// EXEC SAS
//ANYNAME DD DSN=MY.SAS.FORMATS,DISP=(NEW,CATLG),
//                SPACE=(TRK,(2,,5)),UNIT=SYSDA,
//                VOL=SER=DISK04
PROC FORMAT DDNAME=ANYNAME;
  VALUE SEXFMT 1=FEMALE
               2=MALE;
```

The DDname given in the DD statement and in the DDNAME= option can be any valid eight-character name as long as both names are the same. See the FORMAT procedure description for details on creating your own formats.

To use the format in a later job, you must make the format library available to SAS so that SAS can find and use the stored formats. There are at least four ways to do this:

1. You can associate the name of the format library with the DDname SASLIB in the JCL:

```
// EXEC SAS
//SASLIB DD DSN=MY.SAS.FORMATS,DISP=SHR
DATA OK;
  INPUT SPECIES $ SEX COUNT;
  CARDS;
data lines
PROC PRINT;
  FORMAT SEX SEXFMT.;
```

When you use this technique, it is possible to store and use formats in the same job. Specify the DDname SASLIB in the PROC FORMAT statement:

```
// EXEC SAS
//SASLIB DD DSN=MY.SAS.FORMATS,DISP=OLD
PROC FORMAT DDNAME=SASLIB;
  VALUE $COLOR R=RED
               B=BLUE
               G=GREEN
               Y=YELLOW ;
DATA OK;
  INPUT SPECIES $ SEX COUNT;
  CARDS;
data lines
PROC PRINT;
  FORMAT SEX SEXFMT. SPECIES $COLOR. ;
```

2. You can associate the name of the format library with the DDname
    LIBRARY in the JCL using the LIBRARY parameter of the SAS cataloged
    procedure:

    ```
    // EXEC SAS,LIBRARY='MY.SAS.FORMATS'
    DATA OK;
      INPUT SPECIES $ SEX COUNT;
      CARDS;
    data lines
    PROC PRINT;
      FORMAT SEX SEXFMT.;
    ```

    When you use this technique, it is possible to store and use formats in
    the same job. Specify the DDname LIBRARY in the PROC FORMAT
    statement (or omit it entirely, since it is the default):

    ```
    // EXEC SAS,LIBRARY='MY.SAS.FORMATS'
    PROC FORMAT;
      VALUE $COLOR R=RED
                   B=BLUE
                   G=GREEN
                   Y=YELLOW ;
    DATA OK;
      INPUT SPECIES $ SEX COUNT;
      CARDS;
    data lines
    PROC PRINT;
      FORMAT SEX SEXFMT. SPECIES $COLOR. ;
    ```

3. You can associate the name of the format library with the DDname
    LIBRARY in the JCL by overriding the LIBRARY DD statement in the SAS
    cataloged procedure:

    ```
    // EXEC SAS
    //LIBRARY DD DSN=MY.SAS.FORMATS,DISP=OLD
    ```

    When you use this technique, it is possible to store and use formats in
    the same job. Specify the DDname LIBRARY in the PROC FORMAT
    statement (or omit it entirely, since it is the default):

```
// EXEC SAS
//LIBRARY DD DSN=MY.SAS.FORMATS,DISP=OLD
PROC FORMAT;
   VALUE $COLOR R=RED
                B=BLUE
                G=GREEN
                Y=YELLOW ;
DATA OK;
   INPUT SPECIES $ SEX COUNT;
   CARDS;
data lines
PROC PRINT;
   FORMAT SEX SEXFMT. SPECIES $COLOR. ;
```

4. You can concatenate the format library to the data sets defined by the STEPLIB DDname in the SAS cataloged procedure:

```
// EXEC SAS
//STEPLIB DD
//       DD
//       DD DSN=MY.SAS.FORMATS,DISP=SHR
```

In order to override the SAS cataloged procedure to add your library to the end of the list of data sets concatenated to DDname STEPLIB, it is necessary to know how many data sets are already defined in the cataloged procedure. In the above example, it is assumed that there are two data sets (DD statements) in the STEPLIB concatenation in the SAS cataloged procedure that is being used. These DD statements (which we do not actually want to override) are "stepped over" with "placeholder" DD statements that specify no operands. The last DD statement (which defines the format library) has nothing in the SAS cataloged procedure to override and is therefore effectively "added" to the STEPLIB concatenation.

When you use this technique, it is **not** possible to store and use formats in the same job unless you repeat the definition of the format library in another DD statement. You **cannot** specify the DDname STEPLIB in the PROC FORMAT statement, because OS does not allow a concatenation of partitioned data sets to be opened for output. Here is an example of concatenating more than one format library to STEPLIB and using PROC FORMAT to store a format in one of those libraries in the same SAS job:

```
// EXEC SAS
//STEPLIB DD
//       DD
//       DD DSN=MY.SAS.FORMATS,DISP=SHR
//       DD DSN=OLD.TESTED.FORMATS,DISP=SHR
//MYFMTS DD DSN=MY.SAS.FORMATS,DISP=OLD
PROC FORMAT DDNAME=MYFMTS;
   VALUE $COLOR R=RED
                B=BLUE
                G=GREEN
                Y=YELLOW ;
DATA OK;
   INPUT SPECIES $ SEX COUNT;
   CARDS;
```

        data lines
        PROC PRINT;
            FORMAT SEX SEXFMT. SPECIES $COLOR. ;

Secondary allocation   If your permanent library has a secondary allocation quantity specified and OS uses it to acquire more space for the library while adding formats to it during a SAS job, SAS may abend with an Sx06-n completion code if you try to access, in the same job, a format stored in one of the secondary extents obtained. For example, suppose you are copying formats from a file into your permanent format library using PROC PDSCOPY. Your format library has a secondary allocation quantity. If the format library needs more space to contain the new formats, and OS uses the secondary allocation to provide more space, later in the same job you will be unable to reference (access) the formats that were stored in the secondary extent.

There is no problem with a format library having a secondary allocation quantity specified if you always create formats in one SAS job and access them in another SAS job.

Autobatch SAS

Under autobatch mode, many SAS jobs can be run sequentially with the system overhead of only one job. Since allocating the devices and loading the SAS supervisor often consumes 60% of the total job time for small SAS jobs, autobatch mode can cut costs substantially. Autobatch mode is particularly useful in educational environments where many small, non-setup jobs are run.

SAS provides an autobatch supervisor that mimics the conventions of the WATFIV compiler. Each new SAS job starts with a $JOB card, for example:

    $JOB *account,name*, PAGES = 50, CARDS = 400, TIME = 4, LINES = 900

    $JOB *account,name*, P = 50, C = 400, T = 4, L = 900

The account code and the programmer name are required parameters. The LINES parameter is converted to pages by using the number of lines per page as a divisor. This page cutoff will be faithful, but since there is no central place where lines are counted, it is not possible to do job cutoff on lines.

The JCL required to execute the batch supervisor is essentially identical to that required to execute a SAS job otherwise in OS batch. The only difference is that ENTRY = SASAUTO must be specified on the EXEC statement, and the first eight characters of the OPTIONS= parameter may be SAS autobatch supervisor parameters. For example:

```
//AUTOBSAS JOB accountcode, 'programmer name'
//FAST EXEC SAS,ENTRY = SASAUTO,OPTIONS = '00T = 30 P = 100 C = 1000'
//SYSIN DD *
$JOB NCS.ES.B4174/BARR,TIME = 12,PAGES = 15
DATA;
    INPUT X1-X3;
    CARDS;
1 2 3
10 20 30
PROC PRINT;
PROC MEANS;
$JOB NCS.ES.C3040/SMITH,TIME = 2
PROC OPTIONS;
//
```

The first character of the OPTIONS= parameter defines whether the SAS log is to be closed after each job in the batch: a value of 1 indicates that the log is to be closed after each job; a value of 0 indicates that the SAS log is to remain open. The second character of the OPTIONS= parameter defines whether an account code field is required on the $JOB cards: a value of 0 indicates that the account code field is required; a value of 1 indicates that the accounting information is not required.

A different set of defaults is usually established by the installation for autobatch executions of SAS. Consult your SAS installation representative for more information, or use PROC OPTIONS to determine how they have been initialized.

If your installation is using:

- HASP-II Version 3.0 or 3.1 for OS/360 MFT or MVT, or
- HASP-II Version 4.0 or 4.1 for OS/VS2 Release 1.6 or 1.7 (SVS), or
- JES2 for OS/VS2 MVS

then you can use the Execution Batch Scheduling (XBATCH) facility of those HASP/JES2 systems to automatically collect the individual SAS autobatch jobs and run all of them under a single invocation of the SAS autobatch supervisor. This technique's advantage is that the HASP/JES2 system automatically schedules the loading and execution of the SAS autobatch supervisor when there are SAS autobatch jobs to be run. Furthermore, each SAS autobatch job is individually named and accounted for, just as if it were a regular job. Each job is still a unique job to HASP/JES2 and it may be submitted from any local or remote terminal, internal reader, or by the TSO SUBMIT command. The job is automatically run under the SAS autobatch supervisor, and then individually and uniquely routed to its submitting location, where it prints as any other spooled job does.

Use of the SAS autobatch supervisor and the XBATCH facility of HASP/JES2 facilitates simple and often elegant solutions to a wide variety of data processing problems. Indeed, at SAS Institute this is precisely the mechanism used (along with PROC TAPECOPY) to produce the product installation tapes distributed to our customers.

If you are submitting jobs to an XBATCH-controlled SAS autobatch supervisor, then your SAS jobs probably require a unique CLASS= parameter specification on the JCL JOB statement, followed by a $JOB card, for example:

```
//TESTJOB JOB 4836,STUDENT,CLASS=S
$JOB 4836/STUDENT,TIME=10,PAGES=20
SAS statements
//
```

Many university installations collect (either manually or automatically) the autobatch SAS jobs to be run. In this case, you probably need only submit a $JOB card or a modified JCL "JOB" statement, for example:

```
//TESTJOB SAS 4836,STUDENT,TIME=10,PAGES=20
SAS statements
//
```

In each of these cases, you are executing SAS, but you do not use a JCL EXEC statement. If you need to alter the default values set for any SAS system options, you must use an OPTIONS statement. Note that an OPTIONS statement is in effect only for each autobatch SAS job; it does not remain in effect from one autobatch job to the next.

SAS System Options Only for OS Batch Jobs

While there are many SAS system options that are applicable only when you are executing SAS under TSO, there are none that are useful only under OS batch.

REFERENCES

International Business Machines Corporation (1980), *OS/VS2 MVS JCL*, SRL Form Number GC28-0692.

Brown, Gary DeWard (1975), *System 370 Job Control Language*, New York: John Wiley & Sons.

870

SAS under TSO

INTRODUCTION

SAS currently runs interactively under TSO under these OS operating systems: MVT, VS2(SVS), and VS2(MVS). This appendix describes some features of SAS that are specific to using SAS under TSO. For additional features which are common to both batch and TSO, refer to the OS batch appendix. SAS also runs under the MVS TSO batch TMP.

TSO commands tell the operating system's Terminal Monitor Program (TMP) how to process an interactive TSO session. For example, using the TSO command "SAS" is analogous to the JCL statement "// EXEC SAS": each invokes a set of actions that allocates files and invokes the SAS system. TSO has a command language of its own; if you are not familiar with it, you will need to check with your local computing installation staff.

Many installations modify TSO. Thus, it is impossible to set down directions and rules here that will apply at every installation. Many installations also regulate the use of disk storage under TSO: some do not allow you to allocate your own OS data sets; some delete user-allocated data sets after a few days; some move them off-line if they have not been accessed for a certain length of time. You are urged to check with the staff of your local computing installation for the information that applies to your use of TSO.

You can use SAS under TSO in several different modes. The same SAS system that is used for batch mode is also used under TSO so there are no new commands or syntax to learn. However, because TSO is an interactive system, there are differences in how you access SAS and in how you enter SAS statements.

Here are some of the ways that SAS and TSO can be used together:

- You can prepare SAS jobs with a TSO editor (such as TSO EDIT or SPF) and then submit the job for batch processing. The results may be printed on a line printer after the job has completed, or, at some installations, may be reviewed at your terminal under TSO before printing.
- You can enter SAS commands interactively. The commands can be executed immediately and the results displayed at the terminal.
- You can use a TSO editor to prepare a SAS job and then call SAS to run the job under TSO. The job is executed immediately, and results may be displayed at the terminal, saved in an OS data set, or printed on a line printer at the end of the session.

Submitting SAS Jobs for Batch Execution

If you use TSO to prepare SAS jobs for submission to batch, two items are relevant:

1. If the SAS system option S=0 is in effect and the first line ("card") of input is line-numbered in columns 73–80, SAS assumes that the input

source statements are located in columns 1 through 72 only, both for SAS statements and for data entered after a CARDS or PARMCARDS statement. Thus, standard TSO line-numbered data sets may be submitted directly as SAS input.

2. If the SAS system option NOCAPS is in effect, SAS does not translate lowercase characters to uppercase. You can, therefore, use upper- and lowercase characters in variable labels, titles, and character data values. If the output is printed on a printer or terminal with upper- and lowercase characters, the labels, titles, or values will be printed as they were entered.

Remember to use the TSO editor ASIS option (CAPS OFF in SPF) when editing a data set containing upper- and lowercase characters so that lowercase characters will not automatically be converted to uppercase.

Below is an example that creates a data set containing a SAS job and submits it for batch execution. Lines in lowercase were entered by the user; lines in uppercase and line numbers were printed by TSO.

```
logon userid/password
IKJ564551 userid LOGON IN PROGRESS AT 06:20:44 ON JULY 27, 1982
READY
edit check.cntl new
INPUT
00010 //check   job (xxx,999),username
00020 //check exec sas
00030 //sysin    dd *
00040 data;
00050 input a b c;
00060 cards;
00070 014 .023 756
00080 18 .0089 620
00100 proc corr;
00110 /*
00120     <--null line
EDIT
save
SAVED
end
READY
submit check
IKJ562501 JOB CHECK(JOB04452) SUBMITTED
READY
```

Entering SAS Commands Interactively

Below is a sample TSO session using SAS. The lines in lowercase were entered by the user; lines in uppercase and line numbers were printed by SAS or TSO. Refer to the sample session while reading the discussion of the steps in using SAS under TSO.

```
logon userid/password
IKJ564551 userid LOGON IN PROGRESS AT 06:20:44 ON JULY 27, 1982
READY
sas

NOTE: SAS RELEASE 82.0 AT SAS INSTITUTE INC. (00000).
NOTE: CPUID   VERSION = 03  SERIAL = 024001  MODEL = 0158 .

  1? data one;
  2? input a b c @@;
  3? cards;
  4> 14 .023 756 11 .046 924 18 .0089 620
  5> ;

NOTE: SAS WENT TO A NEW LINE WHEN INPUT STATEMENT
      REACHED PAST THE END OF A LINE.
NOTE: DATA SET WORK.ONE HAS 3 OBSERVATIONS AND 3 VARIABLES.
```

(continued on next page)

```
(continued from previous page)

    6? proc corr;
    7? run;

VARIABLE      N      MEAN    STD DEV        SUM    MINIMUM   MAXIMUM
A             3   14.3333     3.5119     43.000    11.0000   18.0000
B             3    0.0260     0.0187      0.078     0.0089    0.0460
C             3  766.6667   152.2804   2300.000   620.0000  924.0000

    CORRELATION COEFFICIENTS / PROB > |R| UNDER HO:RHO=0 / N=3


                          A           B           C

          A         1.00000    -0.97592    -0.98979
                    0.0000      0.1400      0.0910
          B        -0.97952     1.00000     0.99704
                    0.1400      0.0000      0.0490
          C        -0.98979     0.99704     1.00000
                    0.0910      0.0490      0.0000

    8? endsas;
```

After logging onto TSO and receiving a READY message, enter the SAS command (see **The SAS Command Procedure** for a detailed description of the SAS command and its options). SAS will respond by printing one or more message lines, skipping a line and prompting with a line number and a question mark.

Enter your SAS statements. Remember that several SAS statements can be put on each line, and that SAS statements can be continued from one line to the next. As each statement is entered, SAS checks it for syntax errors. If an error is found, SAS prints the statement, underlines the error, and prints an error message. SAS also checks data lines processed by an INPUT statement as they are entered for errors such as non-numeric data in numeric fields.

Under TSO, you can enter your statements in either lower- or uppercase. SAS accepts statements with keywords, parameters, and options in lowercase and treats them as though entered in uppercase. Data lines entered after a CARDS or PARMCARDS statement, TITLEs, and labels entered in lowercase remain in lowercase unless the SAS system option CAPS is in effect.

If you make an error in a PROC or DATA step, enter the SAS statement

run;

Then re-enter the PROC or DATA step, making your corrections. If the SPOOL option is in effect, previously entered lines may be automatically re-entered with the %INCLUDE feature. See **NEW TSO FEATURES** below for further information on the %INCLUDE statement.

When you enter data lines to be processed by an INPUT statement, SAS executes the statements in the DATA step as each data line is entered. As always, to signal the end of the data to SAS, the first line after the last data line must contain a semicolon. You can use a single semicolon, the RUN statement, or another DATA or a PROC statement. Note that the END= variable specified on an INFILE statement is not set for the CARDS infile or for any INFILE allocated to the terminal.

SAS prints any diagnostic messages required and, after it has read the last data line, a message noting the number of observations and variables in the data set.

To analyze the data set, enter PROC and accompanying statements. SAS begins executing PROC statements when it encounters a RUN statement or another DATA or PROC statement.

If SAS is printing and you want to interrupt the printing, press the ATTN or BREAK key. SAS responds

SAST013D ENTER "END" TO TERMINATE SAS, OR A NULL LINE TO CONTINUE

Enter "end" to cause SAS to terminate; SAS responds

SAST011I SAS TERMINATED DUE TO ATTENTION

and TSO displays a READY message. Now enter the command

sas go

to continue with the files previously in use.
To exit from SAS, enter the statement

endsas;

or

/*

If you exit from SAS, just as after pressing the ATTN key, you can resume the SAS session (in the same TSO session) and continue with the files you were using by entering the TSO command

sas go

If your input data are on disk, if you want to create and store a SAS data set, or if you want to use the PUT statement to write a disk data set, you can allocate the disk data set before entering SAS or during the SAS session with a TSO statement. For example, if your input data are in an OS data set named *userid*.EMPLOY.DATA, you could enter the command

alloc fi(in) da(employ.data)

before invoking SAS, or the statement

tso alloc fi(in) da(employ.data);

within the SAS job. In either case, an INFILE statement in your SAS program could then be coded

infile in;

Editing Input for Interactive Execution

You can prepare a SAS job with a TSO editor such as EDIT or SPF and then invoke SAS to run the job interactively under TSO. To execute SAS in this way, you must direct SAS to use an OS data set as input rather than reading commands entered at the terminal. Unless you specify otherwise, SAS's output is printed at the terminal immediately. You can work with the data sets created by the job later in the same TSO session.

Below are the steps necessary to run SAS in this manner:

1. Enter your SAS program in an OS data set, using a TSO editor. RUN statements are not necessary, since SAS begins executing each step when it encounters the next one.
2. Invoke SAS, specifying that the input statements should be read from your source data set. For example:

sas input(check.sas)

3. After the results have been printed, you may continue the SAS session in an interactive mode by entering

sas go

SAS Data Libraries Under TSO

Because SAS data libraries **must not** have a data set organization of physical sequential (DSORG=PS), new SAS data libraries may be created under MVS/TSO, but not under MVT/TSO or SVS/TSO. If you want to create a SAS data set for use under MVT/TSO or SVS/TSO, space must first be allocated with a batch job. The OS batch appendix describes how to do this.

In order to create a SAS data library under MVS/TSO, you must ask TSO and the operating system for space in which to store it. For example:

attrib sasdcb dsorg(da) recfm(u)
alloc f(user) da(describe.sasdata) space(2 2) cyl using(sasdcb)

After its initial creation, the data library may be referenced with the following ALLOC command:

alloc f(anyname) da(describe.sasdata)

Note that new SAS data libraries **must not** be allocated by the use of SPF menu 3.2, since SPF will cause the data library to have DSORG=PS.

Aside from the creation of new SAS data libraries under MVT/TSO and SVS/TSO, the organization and access requirements of a SAS data library under TSO are identical to those under a batch environment. Refer to "SAS under OS Batch" for additional information.

Saving Work Data Sets

If you use SAS interactively under TSO, you might want to end a TSO session and yet be able to continue your SAS processing at another time, with all your work data sets intact.

You can resume your processing in this way if you allocate an OS data set with the file name USER before you enter the first SAS command. For example (in MVS/TSO):

attrib sasdcb dsorg(da) recfm(u)
alloc f(user) da(check.sasdata) space(1 1) cyl using(sasdcb)
sas

When a USER DDname has been allocated, SAS automatically adds the first-level name USER (instead of WORK) to the SAS data sets you create. These data sets are stored in the OS data set named *userid*.CHECK.SASDATA.

When you are ready to resume processing, allocate the OS data set again with the file name USER:

allocate fi(user) da(check.sasdata) old
sas

All the data sets that you created in the earlier TSO session are then available to you.

Using PROC FORMAT Under TSO

When you want to define your own formats and store them in a format library, you must first allocate a load module library. For example:

```
READY
alloc da(format.load) new space(2) tracks dir(5)
READY
```

Then specify your format library when you invoke SAS:

```
READY
sas library(format.load)

NOTE: SAS RELEASE 82.0 AT SAS INSTITUTE INC. (00000).
NOTE: CPUID   VERSION = 03  SERIAL = 024001  MODEL = 0158 .

  1? proc format;
  2? value specfmt 1=green 2=blue 3=red;
  3? run;

  4? data;
  5? input species sex count;
  6? cards;
  7> data lines
     data lines
 14? run;

NOTE: DATA SET WORK.DATA1 HAS 7 OBSERVATIONS AND 3 VARIABLES.

 15? proc print;
 16? format species specfmt.;
 17? run;
```

The SAS command procedure will automatically allocate the specified format library to the DDname LIBRARY and make it available for use as a load module library for the SAS session.

Refer to the appendix, "SAS under OS Batch," for the details of using format libraries which are common to batch and TSO.

NEW TSO FEATURES

TSO Command Execution

The TSO statement, function, and CALL routine give you the ability to execute almost any TSO command or CLIST without exiting from SAS. Thus, data sets may be allocated or freed, messages may be sent to other users, and jobs may be submitted without terminating your SAS session. See the TSO function description in Chapter 5, and the TSO statement description in Chapter 11. Note that if the SASLIB mechanism is used to refer to user-written procedures, functions, and so on, the DDname SASLIB must be allocated prior to entering SAS.

%INCLUDE Statement

The %INCLUDE statement allows you to include SAS source from external files or from lines entered previously in the SAS session. Therefore, instead of invoking SAS to process statements only from a data set, you may use a %INCLUDE statement in an interactive session to execute previously coded statements. The results are printed at the terminal and you remain in SAS so that additional SAS steps can be run. The %LIST statement lets you display source lines. Below is an example TSO session which uses the %INCLUDE and %LIST statements to include and list SAS source statements stored in an OS data set:

```
READY
alloc f(update) da(check.sasdata) old
READY
sas options('nodate gen=0 spool')

NOTE: SAS RELEASE 82.0 AT SAS INSTITUTE INC. (00000).
NOTE: CPUID   VERSION = 03   SERIAL = 024001  MODEL = 0158 .

   1? tso alloc f(sas) dsn(check.sas) shr;
   2? %include sas(prog1);
   6? %list 3-5;
   3   DATA ;
   4   INPUT PERSON $ ACCOUNT ID_NUM;
   5   IF 12034<=ID_NUM<=34201 THEN ACCOUNT=ACCOUNT*1.10;
   7? cards;
   8> JOHN 32415 22022
   9> MARY 12050 56032
  10> ;

NOTE: DATA SET WORK.DATA1 HAS 2 OBSERVATIONS AND 3 VARIABLES.

  11? %include sas(update);
  14? %list 12-13;
  12   DATA UPDATE.MARCH;
  13   MERGE UPDATE.MARCH _LAST_;
  15? run;

NOTE: DATA SET UPDATE.MARCH HAS 2 OBSERVATIONS AND 3 VARIABLES.
```

Note that to use the %INCLUDE feature with previously entered lines, the SPOOL option must be in effect, and to use the %INCLUDE feature with external files, the INCLUDE option must be in effect.

System Options Unique To TSO

Some system options, described with the OPTIONS statement in Chapter 11, are of particular interest to TSO users:

NOCAPS/CAPS	translates lowercase SAS input into uppercase.
SPOOL/NOSPOOL	spools SAS statements to a utility data set in the WORK data library.
INCLUDE/ NOINCLUDE	allows the inclusion of SAS statements from external files.
NOCLIST/CLIST	reads SAS statements from a CLIST.
MODECHARS=	specifies terminal prompting characters.
NOCHARCODE/ CHARCODE	substitutes characters for terminals which lack underscore (__),vertical bar (|), or logical not sign (⌐).
NOCENTER/CENTER	centers printed output of SAS procedures.
NONUMBER/ NUMBER	prints page numbers on SAS output.
NODATE/DATE	prints date at top of page.
NOOVP/OVP	overprinting on SAS output.
TLINESIZE=	linesize for printing SAS output at a terminal.
C96/C60	uses lowercase characters in printed SAS output.
FS/NOFS	SAS procedures should operate in full-screen mode.
FSP/NOFSP	SAS/FSP available.
GRAPHICS/ NOGRAPHICS	SAS/GRAPH available.

CHKPT/NOCHKPT	checkpoints SAS options.
SORTWKNO=	number of sort work areas to be allocated.
NOSTIMER/STIMER	task timing facilities available.
DEVICE=	terminal device name.
BAUD=	communications line data transmission rate.
TRANTAB=	SAS/GRAPH terminal I/O translation table.
PROMPTCHARS=	SAS/GRAPH terminal prompt characters.

The SAS Command Procedure

A typical SAS command procedure (CLIST) used to invoke SAS has the form:

```
SAS OPTIONS ('option-string')
    INPUT   ('dsname')
    PRINT   ('size'|'dsname')
    LIBRARY ('size'|'dsname')
    WORK    ('size')
    LOAD    ('dsname')
    LOG     ('size'|'dsname')
    PARMCARD('size')
    UNITS   ('units')
    SASLLIB ('dsname')
    SASHLIB ('dsname')
    ENTRY   ('member')
    GO
    FLUSH/NOFLUSH
    STAE/NOSTAE
    STAI/NOSTAI
    STAX/NOSTAX
    STACK/NOSTACK
    SHARE/NOSHARE
    TRACE
```

where

OPTIONS	specifies the options string to be passed to SAS. If not specified, OPTIONS defaults to a null string.
INPUT	specifies the name of a data set containing SAS statements to be processed. If not specified, INPUT defaults to the terminal.
PRINT	specifies either the size of a temporary data set or the name of a permanent sequential data set to contain SAS output. If not specified, PRINT defaults to the terminal.
LIBRARY	specifies either the size of a temporary data set or the name of a permanent data set to contain formats created by PROC FORMAT. If not specified, LIBRARY defaults to a one-cylinder temporary partitioned data set.
WORK	specifies the size of the WORK temporary data library. If not specified, WORK defaults to a one-cylinder data set with a one-cylinder secondary quantity.
LOAD	specifies the name of a permanent load module library which may contain user-defined procedures, functions, and so on. If not specified, no user procedure load module library is allocated.
LOG	specifies either the size of a temporary data set or the name of a permanent data set to contain the SAS log output. If not specified, LOG defaults to the terminal.

PARMCARD   specifies the size of the temporary data set to be allocated to hold PARMCARDS data lines. If not specified, PARMCARD defaults to a one-cylinder temporary data set.

UNITS   specifies the units in which temporary data sets will be allocated.

SASLLIB   specifies the name of a data set containing SAS system modules.

SASHLIB   specifies the name of a data set containing information to be displayed by the SAS HELP statement.

ENTRY   specifies the entry point name used to invoke SAS.

GO   specifies that a previous SAS session is to be resumed.

FLUSH   specifies that the command processor is to flush the input stack when it cannot successfully invoke SAS. If neither FLUSH nor NOFLUSH is specified, FLUSH is the default.

NOFLUSH   specifies that the command processor is not to flush the input stack when it cannot successfully invoke SAS.

The following options are primarily intended for testing and debugging.

STAE   specifies that the command processor is to intercept an abnormal termination of the main command processor task. If neither STAE nor NOSTAE is specified, STAE is the default.

NOSTAE   specifies that the command processor is not to intercept an abnormal termination of the main command processor task.

STAI   specifies that the command processor is to intercept an abnormal termination of the SAS subtask. If neither STAI nor NOSTAI is specified, STAI is the default.

NOSTAI   specifies that the command processor is not to intercept an abnormal termination of the SAS subtask.

STAX   specifies that the command processor is to intercept an attention and terminate the SAS subtask. If neither STAX nor NOSTAX is specified, STAX is the default.

NOSTAX   specifies that the command processor is not to intercept an attention and terminate the SAS subtask.

STACK   specifies that the command processor is to create a new, local TSO input stack for the SAS subtask. This action is independent of the creation of a new input stack by the TSO statement, function, or CALL routine during the execution of TSO commands.

NOSTACK   specifies that the command processor is not to create a new, local TSO input stack for the SAS subtask. If neither STACK nor NOSTACK is specified, NOSTACK is the default.

SHARE   specifies that the command processor is to share storage subpool 78 with the SAS subtask. This option should be specified if the command processor is running under the TSO TEST processor or if the NOSTAX option is specified. This option should also be specified if SAS may invoke a TSO command processor which expects memory allocated from storage subpool 78 to be retained across multiple invocations (for example, the QED editor command processor and LISP/370).

NOSHARE specifies that the command processor is not to share storage subpool 78 with the SAS subtask. This allows the command processor to clean up any fragmentation of subpool 78 due to the execution of TSO commands and CLISTs by the TSO statement, function, and CALL routine. If neither SHARE nor NOSHARE is specified, NOSHARE is the default.

TRACE specifies that the TSO CLIST processor is to display diagnostic information as the SAS CLIST executes.

Here is a listing of the typical SAS CLIST (for MVS/TSO) that is invoked when the SAS command is entered:

```
PROC 0                                                             +
    OPTIONS ()                     /* options string         */ +
    INPUT   ()                     /* source dsname          */ +
    PRINT   (*)                    /* PRINT dsname/size       */ +
    LIBRARY (1)                    /* FORMAT library dsname/size */ +
    WORK    ('1 1')                /* WORK data library size  */ +
    LOAD    ()                     /* user load library dsname */ +
    LOG     ()                     /* LOG dsname/size         */ +
    PARMCARD(1)                    /* parmcard file size       */ +
    UNITS   (CYL)                  /* allocation units         */ +
    SASLLIB ('''SAS.LIBRARY''')    /* SAS load library dsname  */ +
    SASHLIB ('''SAS.HELP''')       /* SAS help library dsname  */ +
    ENTRY   (SAS)                  /* SAS entry point name     */ +
    GO                             /* continue previous session? */ +
    FLUSH   NOFLUSH                /* flush stack if error?    */ +
    STAE    NOSTAE                 /* trap main task abends?   */ +
    STAI    NOSTAI                 /* trap subtask abends?     */ +
    STAX    NOSTAX                 /* trap attentions?         */ +
    STACK   NOSTACK                /* create new input stack?  */ +
    SHARE   NOSHARE                /* share subpool 78?        */ +
    TRACE                          /* CLIST debugging option   */
    /*
    /* enable CLIST debugging options
    /*
    IF &TRACE NE THEN +
        CONTROL LIST CONLIST SYMLIST
    /*
    /* if SU11 installed then set SU11 to REUSE, else set it to null
    /*
    SET SU11=REUSE
    /*
    /* allocate source data set
    /*
    IF &STR(&INPUT) NE THEN +
        IF &STR(&INPUT) NE &STR(*) THEN DO
            SET OPTIONS=&STR(&OPTIONS SYSIN=SYSIN)
            ALLOC F(SYSIN) DA(&INPUT) SHR &SU11
        END
    /*
    /* allocate log file data set
    /*
    IF &STR(&LOG) NE THEN DO
        SET OPTIONS=&STR(&OPTIONS LOG=FT11F001)
        IF &DATATYPE(&STR(&SUBSTR(1:1,&STR(&LOG)))) EQ CHAR THEN +
            ALLOC F(FT11F001) DA(&LOG) &SU11
        ELSE +
            ALLOC F(FT11F001) &UNITS SP(&LOG) &SU11
    END
    /*
    /* allocate PRINT file data set
    /*
    IF &GO EQ THEN +
        IF &STR(&PRINT) NE THEN DO
            ATTRIB SASDCB RECFM(V B A) LRECL(137) BLKSIZE(141)
            IF &DATATYPE(&STR(&SUBSTR(1:1,&STR(&PRINT)))) EQ CHAR THEN +
                ALLOC F(FT12F001) DA(&PRINT) USING(SASDCB) MOD &SU11
            ELSE +
                ALLOC F(FT12F001) &UNITS SP(&PRINT) USING(SASDCB) &SU11
            FREE ATTR(SASDCB)
        END
```

(continued on next page)

```
(continued from previous page)
    /*
    /* allocate WORK data library
    /*
    IF &GO EQ THEN +
        ALLOC F(WORK) &UNITS SP(&WORK) &SU11
    /*
    /* allocate format library data set
    /*
    IF &GO EQ THEN +
        IF &STR(&LIBRARY) NE THEN +
            IF &DATATYPE(&STR(&SUBSTR(1:1,&STR(&LIBRARY)))) EQ CHAR THEN +
                ALLOC F(LIBRARY) DA(&LIBRARY) OLD &SU11
            ELSE +
                ALLOC F(LIBRARY) &UNITS SP(&LIBRARY) DIR(35) &SU11
    /*
    /* allocate SAS help library
    /*
    IF &SASHLIB NE THEN +
        ALLOC F(SASHELP) DA(&SASHLIB) SHR &SU11
    /*
    /* allocate parmcard file data set
    /*
    IF &GO EQ THEN +
        IF &STR(&PARMCARD) NE THEN +
            ALLOC F(FT15F001) &UNITS SP(&PARMCARD) &SU11
    /*
    /* invoke SAS
    /*
    SASCP TASKLIB(&SASLLIB &LOAD) +
        ENTRY  (&ENTRY)        +
        OPTIONS('&OPTIONS')    +
        &FLUSH &NOFLUSH        +
        &STAE  &NOSTAE         +
        &STAI  &NOSTAI         +
        &STAX  &NOSTAX         +
        &STACK &NOSTACK        +
        &SHARE &NOSHARE
```

Notes

1. To redirect the log output to an OS data set:

   sas log(check.saslog)

2. To read input (SAS source statements) from an OS data set:

   sas input(check.sas)

3. To write the output from SAS procedures into a sequential OS data set named *userid*.CHECK.SASLIST:

   sas print(check.saslist)

4. To invoke the user-written SAS procedure CODEIT from the OS data set named *userid*.CODEIT.LOAD:

   sas load(codeit)
   NOTE: SAS RELEASE 82.0 AT SAS INSTITUTE INC. (00000).
   NOTE: CPUID VERSION=03 SERIAL=024001 MODEL=0158 .
       1? proc codeit;
       2? run;

The SASCP Command Processor

The SASCP command processor is used to invoke SAS and enables the TSO command execution feature. SASCP replaces only the CALL command in older SAS CLISTs, not the entire CLIST itself. The following description of the SASCP command is intended primarily for those who wish to write their own SAS CLIST or who must modify the SAS Institute-supplied CLIST.

The syntax of the SASCP command is:

```
SASCP TASKLIB('dslist')
      ENTRY  ('member')
      OPTIONS('parm')
      FLUSH/NOFLUSH
      STAE/NOSTAE
      STAI/NOSTAI
      STAX/NOSTAX
      STACK/NOSTACK
      SHARE/NOSHARE
```

TASKLIB	specifies a list of one or more data sets containing the SAS library modules and any desired user modules. Data set names not enclosed in quotes are prefixed with the PROFILE-specified prefix (usually the userid) and qualified with '.LOAD' if necessary. The default is 'SAS.LIBRARY'. If the DDname 'LIBRARY' is allocated to a partitioned data set when the SASCP command is issued, that partitioned data set will be automatically included as the **last** TASKLIB data set.
ENTRY	specifies the entry point name used to invoke SAS. The default is 'SAS'.
OPTIONS	specifies the parameter string to be passed to SAS. This parameter is optional.
FLUSH	specifies that the command processor is to flush the input stack when it cannot successfully invoke SAS. If neither FLUSH nor NOFLUSH is specified, FLUSH is the default.
NOFLUSH	specifies that the command processor is not to flush the input stack when it cannot successfully invoke SAS.

The following options are primarily intended for testing and debugging.

STAE	specifies that the command processor is to intercept an abnormal termination of the main command processor task. If neither STAE nor NOSTAE is specified, STAE is the default.
NOSTAE	specifies that the command processor is not to intercept an abnormal termination of the main command processor task.
STAI	specifies that the command processor is to intercept an abnormal termination of the SAS subtask. If neither STAI nor NOSTAI is specified, STAI is the default.
NOSTAI	specifies that the command processor is not to intercept an abnormal termination of the SAS subtask.
STAX	specifies that the command processor is to intercept an attention and terminate the SAS subtask. If neither STAX nor NOSTAX is specified, STAX is the default.
NOSTAX	specifies that the command processor is not to intercept an attention and terminate the SAS subtask.
STACK	specifies that the command processor is to create a new, local TSO input stack for the SAS subtask. This action is independent of the creation of a new input stack by the TSO statement, function, or CALL routine during the execution of TSO commands.

NOSTACK   specifies that the command processor is not to create a new, local TSO input stack for the SAS subtask. If neither STACK nor NOSTACK is specified, NOSTACK is the default.

SHARE   specifies that the command processor is to share storage subpool 78 with the SAS subtask. This option should be specified if the command processor is running under the TSO TEST processor or if the NOSTAX option is specified. This option should also be specified if SAS may invoke a TSO command processor that expects memory allocated from storage subpool 78 to be retained across multiple invocations (for example, the QED editor command processor).

NOSHARE   specifies that the command processor is not to share storage subpool 78 with the SAS subtask. This allows the command processor to clean up any fragmentation of subpool 78 due to the execution of TSO commands and CLISTs by the TSO statement, function, and CALL routine. If neither SHARE nor NOSHARE is specified, NOSHARE is the default.

For example:

sascp tasklib('sas.library' sasproc) options('center')

invokes SAS using the load module libraries SAS.LIBRARY and *userid*.SASPROC.LOAD and specifies that the SAS system option CENTER should be in effect.

MESSAGES

The SAS TSO support modules may issue the following messages:

Messages from the SASCP command processor

SAST001I COMMAND SYSTEM ERROR +
   NOT ENOUGH MAIN STORAGE TO EXECUTE COMMAND
   IKJPARS RETURN CODE rc

The SAS command processor was unable to allocate sufficient memory to begin execution. This message should not normally occur; inform your local technical support staff.

SAST002I DATA SET dsn NOT IN CATALOG
   <message generated by DAIRFAIL>
   DYNAMIC ALLOCATION ERROR,
   IKJDAIR RETURN CODE rc DARC drc CTRC crc

The SAS command processor was unable to locate a data set specified by the TASKLIB operand. This usually indicates a misspelled data set name.

SAST003I MORE THAN 15 TASKLIB DATA SETS SPECIFIED

More than 15 task library data sets have been specified with the TASKLIB operand. Reduce the number of task library data sets.

SAST004I dsn IS NOT A PARTITIONED DATA SET

A task library data set was specified by the TASKLIB operand which is not a partitioned data set. This usually indicates a misspelled data set name.

SAST005I TASKLIB CANNOT BE OPENED

The SAS command processor was unable to open the task library. Probably an invalid load module library has been specified as a task library data set in the TASKLIB operand.

SAST006I SAS ENTRY POINT NAME NOT SPECIFIED

No SAS entry point member name was specified. Specify an entry point name for the SAS system with the ENTRY operand.

SAST007I SAS ENTRY POINT NAME entry NOT FOUND
    BLDL I/O ERROR ON TASKLIB

The SAS entry point member name specified could not be located. This usually indicates a misspelled entry point name. Specify a valid entry point name with the ENTRY operand.

SAST008I OPTIONS FIELD TRUNCATED TO 256 CHARACTERS

The option parameter string to be passed to SAS was too long and was truncated to 256 characters. This is a warning message.

SAST009I COMMAND SYSTEM ERROR +
    NOT ENOUGH MAIN STORAGE TO INVOKE SAS SUBTASK
    ATTACH RETURN CODE rc

The SAS command processor was unable to allocate sufficient memory to invoke SAS. This message should not normally occur; inform your local technical support staff.

SAST010I entry ENDED DUE TO ERROR +
    SYSTEM ABEND CODE sac REASON CODE rc
    USER ABEND CODE uac

SAS ended abnormally with the abend code specified. SAS may terminate with a user abend code of 999 (X'3E7') to indicate an error condition. Other user abend codes may be issued by the ABORT statement. A system abend code should not normally occur; consult your local technical support staff.

SAST011I entry TERMINATED DUE TO ATTENTION

SAS was terminated when the ATTN key was pressed.

SAST012I COMMAND SYSTEM ERROR +
    NOT ENOUGH MAIN STORAGE TO EXECUTE COMMAND
    STAE RETURN CODE rc

The SAS command processor was unable to allocate sufficient memory to invoke SAS. This message should not normally occur; inform your local technical support staff.

SAST013D ENTER ''END'' TO TERMINATE SAS, OR A NULL LINE TO CONTINUE

This is the prompt displayed when the SAS command processor detects that the ATTN key has been pressed. Respond with ''end'' to exit from SAS or with a null line to resume SAS processing.

SAST014I INVALID RESPONSE, MUST BE ''END'' OR A NULL LINE

An invalid response was entered after the previous message. Enter either ''end'' or a null line.

SAST017I INVALID PARAMETER LIST PASSED TO IKJDAIR

An invalid parameter list was passed to the TSO service routine IKJDAIR. This message should not normally occur; inform your local technical support staff.

Messages from the TSO statement/function command executor

SAST101I ERROR IN PUTGET SERVICE ROUTINE

An error occurred while the TSO command executor was attempting to read a line from the terminal or from the TSO input stack using the TSO service routine IKJPTGT. This message should not normally occur; inform your local technical support staff.

SAST102I INVALID COMMAND NAME SYNTAX

An invalid command name was specified on a TSO command or to the TSO function or CALL routine. This usually indicates a mistyped TSO command name.

SAST103I COMMAND cmd NOT SUPPORTED

A TSO command name was specified which the SAS TSO command support feature cannot invoke. Exit from SAS to reenter the command.

SAST104I COMMAND cmd NOT FOUND

The TSO command name specified could not be located. This usually indicates a misspelled command name.

SAST105I cmd ENDED DUE TO ERROR +
SYSTEM ABEND CODE sac REASON CODE rc
USER ABEND CODE uac

A TSO command invoked from a TSO statement or TSO function or CALL routine ended abnormally with the indicated abend code.

SAST106I COMMAND SYSTEM ERROR +
NOT ENOUGH MAIN STORAGE TO EXECUTE COMMAND
ATTACH RETURN CODE rc

The TSO command executor was unable to allocate sufficient memory to execute the requested command. This message should not normally occur; inform your local technical support staff.

SAST107I COMMAND SYSTEM ERROR +
  NOT ENOUGH MAIN STORAGE TO EXECUTE COMMAND
  STAE RETURN CODE rc

The TSO command executor was unable to allocate sufficient memory to execute the requested command. This message should not normally occur; inform your local technical support staff.

SAST108I SEVERE COMMAND SYSTEM ERROR +
  SYSTEM ABEND CODE sac REASON CODE rc
  USER ABEND CODE uac

The TSO command executor encountered severe internal failure. This message should not normally occur; inform your local technical support staff.

SAST109I TSO SUBMODE, ENTER "RETURN" OR "END" TO RETURN TO SAS

This is the prompt displayed when TSO submode is entered.

SAST110I COMMAND cmd TERMINATED DUE TO ATTENTION

A TSO command was terminated when the ATTN key was pressed.

SAST111I SPF COMMAND NOT ALLOWED, SPF ALREADY ACTIVE

The SPF command entered could not be processed because SPF is already active. This message may result when SAS is invoked from SPF menu 6 and an SPF command is specified on a TSO statement. Exit from SAS to return to SPF.

SAST112D ENTER "END" TO TERMINATE COMMAND, OR A NULL LINE TO CONTINUE

This prompt is displayed when the ATTN key is pressed during the execution of a TSO command. Respond with "end" to terminate the command or enter a null line to resume the command.

SAST113I INVALID RESPONSE, MUST BE "END" OR A NULL LINE

An invalid response was entered after the previous message. Enter either "end" or a null line.

SAST114I COMMAND cmd NOT SUPPORTED IN BACKGROUND

The command entered may not be executed under the MVS batch TMP. The command may only be executed from an interactive TSO session.

Messages from the internal CALL command processor

SAST201I COMMAND SYSTEM ERROR +
  NOT ENOUGH MAIN STORAGE TO EXECUTE COMMAND
  IKJPARS RETURN CODE rc

The CALL command was unable to allocate sufficient memory to begin processing. This message should not normally occur; inform your technical support staff.

SAST202I TEMPNAME ASSUMED AS MEMBER NAME

No member name was specified with a CALL command invocation, and the member name TEMPNAME was assumed.

SAST203I PARM FIELD TRUNCATED TO 100 CHARACTERS

The parameter string to be passed by CALL to the problem program was too long and was truncated to 100 characters.

SAST204I DATA SET dsn NOT IN CATALOG
   <message generated by DAIRFAIL>
   DYNAMIC ALLOCATION ERROR,
   IKJDAIR RETURN CODE rc DARC drc CTRC crc

The CALL command processor was unable to locate the specified program data set. This usually indicates a misspelled data set name.

SAST205I MEMBER mem SPECIFIED BUT dsn NOT A PARTITIONED DATA SET

The program library specified in the CALL command is not a valid load module library. This usually indicates a misspelled data set name.

SAST206I DATA SET dsn NOT USABLE +
   CANNOT OPEN DATA SET

The CALL command processor was unable to open the problem program library. This usually indicates an invalid load module library or a misspelled data set name.

SAST207I MEMBER mem NOT IN DATA SET dsn
   BLDL I/O ERROR

The problem program member name specified on the CALL command could not be located. This usually indicates a misspelled program member name.

SAST208I COMMAND SYSTEM ERROR +
   NOT ENOUGH MAIN STORAGE TO EXECUTE COMMAND
   ATTACH RETURN CODE rc

The CALL command processor was unable to allocate sufficient memory to invoke the specified problem program. This message should not normally occur; inform your technical support staff.

SAST209I INVALID PARAMETER LIST PASSED TO IKJDAIR

An invalid parameter list was passed to the TSO service routine IKJDAIR by the CALL command processor. This message should not normally occur; inform your local technical support staff.

Note: all completion codes are displayed in hexadecimal.

REFERENCES

International Business Machines Corporation (1978), *OS/VS2 TSO Command Language Reference*, SRL Form Number GC28-0646.

International Business Machines Corporation (1978), *OS/VS2 TSO Terminal User's Guide*, SRL Form Number GC28-0645.

SAS Under VSE

INTRODUCTION

The purpose of this appendix is to discuss the use of SAS under the DOS/VSE system. It is not our intent to instruct you in the use of VSE or any of its subsidiary programs. For more information on VSE, consult the appropriate IBM manuals: VSE JCL is described in the IBM manual *VSE/Advanced Functions System Control Statements* (SC33-6095), ICCF is described in the IBM manual *VSE/Interactive Computing and Control Facility Terminal User's Guide* (SC33-6068). See the *SAS DOS/VSE Companion* for a complete discussion of SAS under VSE. The staff of your computer installation can provide information on installation defaults.

SAS jobs can be run either in batch or interactively under VSE release 2 or later. (PROC NESTED requires release 3 or later.) Batch jobs are submitted on cards or through an editor/job submission facility such as ICCF; interactive jobs are run using ICCF.

Note that the control language for ICCF is different from batch VSE. The examples in this appendix are for batch VSE.

DETAILS

Naming Conventions

VSE JCL syntax restricts the length of DDnames (called filenames in VSE terminology) to seven characters, so a DDname under VSE cannot exceed seven characters.

The DDname in VSE SAS specifies how the SAS data library is accessed; that is, how the library is opened and whether it is open for input or output. The access mode is specified by the first character of the DDname:

First Character	Access Mode
W	specifies a WORK (temporary) data library. It is always opened for output. The WORK library (DDname WORK000) is automatically accessed by SAS at every execution, so you normally do not need to specify a WORK library. Be sure to see Chapter 12, "SAS Data Sets," for a complete discussion of the WORK SAS library.
O	specifies a new, permanent SAS data library that is being created by the current SAS job. The library is opened for output. If the DDname begins with O, a corresponding EXTENT statement with full extent information must be given in the JCL.
Any except I, O, S, or W	specifies an update library, that is, a library that already exists and is open for input and output.

I or S   specifies an existing library that is read-only.

A third restriction on VSE SAS DDnames is that the logical unit assigned to the data library must be specified by the last one, two, or three characters of the DDname. Here is an example of JCL and a SAS DATA statement incorporating the rules for DDnames:

```
// DLBL ECON2,'MY.LIB.DATA',99/365
// EXTENT SYS002,SCR001,1,0,4444,19
// ASSGN SYS002,3330,VOL=SCR001,SHR
·
·
·
// EXEC SASVSE,SIZE=64K
·
·
·
DATA ECON2.GLOBE;
·
·
·
```

The last character, 2, of the DDname in the DLBL statement corresponds to the logical unit named in the EXTENT statement, SYS002. The DDname corresponds to the first-level name of the new SAS data set, ECON2.GLOBE.

JCL for VSE SAS

The job control needed to execute SAS under VSE consists of JECL to identify the job and spooled print files to VSE/POWER (the VSE spooling subsystem); and JCL that identifies the job, any SAS data libraries and system options you use in the job, and invokes SAS.

The JECL statements (those beginning * $$) are:

JOB   specifies JNM=(job name), CLASS=, and PRI=(priority).

LST   specifies LST= (virtual printer address), FNO= (form number), CLASS= and DISP=. SAS normally uses at least two print files, one for the log and one for procedure output, so at least two LST statements are needed.

Here is an example of JECL statements for a VSE SAS job:

```
* $$ JOB JNM=SASEXMPL,CLASS=3,PRI=4
* $$ LST LST=00E,FNO=STD.,CLASS=B,DISP=H
* $$ LST LST=01E,FNO=STD.,CLASS=A,DISP=H
```

The JCL statements (those beginning with //) normally used are:

JOB   specifies the job name.

DLBL or TLBL   specifies a DDname, a data library, and a retention period for the the library. (Retention period is specified when writing a file.) DLBL is used for a disk data library, and TLBL is used for libraries on tape.

EXTENT   specifies the logical unit for the data library, the volume serial, 1 for a standard data area, 0 for the sequence number, the beginning track or block number, and the number of tracks or blocks needed. (Track or block information is only needed when writing a file.) EXTENT statements are only necessary for libraries on disk.

ASSGN   specifies the logical unit for the data library, the disk volume, VOL= (volume serial), and SHR for disposition of the disk.

EXEC   invokes SAS.

Here is an example of the job control for a SAS job that processes a data set from a library called INFO.STATS. Note that all control language parameters are installation-dependent.

```
* $$ JOB JNM = SASEXMPL,CLASS = 3,PRI = 4
* $$ LST LST = 00E,FNO = STD.,CLASS = B,DISP = H
* $$ LST LST = 01E,FNO = STD.,CLASS = A,DISP = H
// JOB SASEXMPL
// DLBL ECON20,'INFO.STATS'
// EXTENT SYS020,VSEYYY
// ASSGN SYS020,FBA,VOL = VSEYYY,SHR
    .
    .
// EXEC SASVSE,SIZE = 64K
    .
    .
    .
DATA ECON20.EURO;
  SET ECON20.WORLD;
  IF CON = 'EUROPE';
```

Your installation may or may not have a catalog procedure to invoke SAS. If there is not a catalog procedure at your installation, your systems staff can provide you with the JCL necessary to invoke SAS.

Allocating a new library   When you create a new SAS data library, be sure that the DDname of the corresponding DLBL or TLBL statement begins with O. The EXTENT statement for the library should contain full extent information. For example,

```
// DLBL OUT20,'NEW.DATA.LIBRARY',99/365
// EXTENT SYS020,SCR001,1,0,385000,100
// ASSGN SYS020,DISK,VOL = SCR001,SHR
// EXEC PROC = SAS
DATA OUT10.NEW;
  INPUT A B C;
  CARDS;
data lines
```

Specifying a default permanent SAS library   You can specify one SAS data library as a default permanent SAS library for the duration of a job or session. There are two ways to do this: by using USER010 as a DDname and assigning the library to the logical unit SYS010, or by using any DDname and specifying the default library with the USER= system option. (See Chapter 12, "SAS Data Sets," for more information on the USER= system option and default SAS libraries.)

Of course, although there can be only one default SAS library in a job or session, any number of permanent SAS data libraries can be used, as long as you include DLBL, EXTENT, and ASSGN statements for each one.

INFILE and FILE Support

The INFILE statement can read VSAM files or sequential files on disk (any disk device supported by VSE for data files), tape, or from a card reader. The record formats supported are F, FB, V, VB, and U. You must specify RECFM=, BLKSIZE=, and LRECL=, except for VSAM files.

The following INFILE options are not supported under VSE: CCHHR, CLOSE, DEVTYPE, DSCB, EOV, JFCB, UCBNAME, VOLUMES, and VTOC.

To read an unlabeled tape with INFILE you must specify:

```
// UPSI  XXX1
```

in your JCL. When reading an unlabeled tape, the tape must be positioned to the start of the file, following any tapemark, by the JCL statement:

```
// MTC  FSF,SYSnnn,n
```

The FILE statement can write sequential files to a disk (any disk device supported by VSE for data files), tape, or to a printer or punch. The record formats supported are F, FB, V, VB, and U. You may specify RECFM=, BLKSIZE=, and LRECL=, but if you do not, the default values used are RECFM=FB, BLKSIZE=6400 or the device maximum blocksize, whichever is smaller, and LRECL=80.

The following FILE options are not available: CLOSE, DEVTYPE, DSCB, JFCB, MOD, UCBNAME, and VOLUMES.

To write an unlabeled tape, specify:

```
// UPSI  XXXX1
```

in the JCL.

REFERENCES

International Business Machines Corporation (1979), *VSE/Advanced Functions System Control Statements*, SRL Form Number SC33-6095.

International Business Machines Corporation (1980), *VSE/Interactive Computing and Control Facility Terminal User's Guide*, SRL Form Number SC33-6068.

SAS Institute Inc. (1981), *SAS DOS/VSE Companion*, Cary, NC: SAS Institute Inc.

Index

Your Turn

If you have comments about SAS or the *SAS User's Guide: Basics, 1982 Edition*, please let us know by writing your ideas in the space below. If you include your name and address, we will reply to you.

Please return this sheet to Publications Division, SAS Institute Inc., P.O. Box 8000, Cary, NC 27511.